D1463453

The Law and Business Administration in Canada

NINTH EDITION

The Law and Business Administration in Canada

NINTH EDITION

J.E. SMYTH
Late Professor of Commerce
Faculty of Management Studies
University of Toronto

D.A. SOBERMAN
Professor of Law
Faculty of Law
Queen's University

A.J. EASSON
Professor of Law
Faculty of Law
Queen's University

Prentice Hall

TORONTO

Canadian Cataloguing in Publication Data

Smyth, J.E. (James Evril), 1920–1985.
    The law and business administration in Canada
9th ed.
Includes bibliographical references and index.
ISBN 0-13-017668-0
1. Commercial law – Canada   2. Commerical law – Canada – Cases   I. Soberman, D.A.,
1929-   .   II. Easson, A.J   III. Title.

KE919.S69 2001   346.71'07   C00-930016-3
KF889.S69 2001

ISBN 0-13-017668-0

Vice President, Editorial Director: Michael Young
Acquisitions Editor: Mike Ryan
Marketing Manager: James Buchanan
Developmental Editor: Maurice Esses
Production Editor: Jennifer Therriault
Copy Editor: Dawn Hunter
Production Coordinator: Deborah Starks
Page Layout: Bookman Typesetting Co.
Art Director: Mary Opper
Interior Design: Sarah Battersby
Cover Design: Mary Opper
Cover Image: Boden/Ledingham/Masterfile

2 3 4 5 05 04 03 02 01

Printed and bound in U.S.A.

BRIEF TABLE OF CONTENTS

CONTENTS

PREFACE

NEW TO THIS EDITION

The most striking change in the business environment during the past few years — the electronic highway — has influenced the ways in which we communicate with others, whether it be within our own enterprise, with parties who know each other well, or with strangers on other continents. Electronic commerce ("e-commerce") has grown much faster than anyone imagined even three years ago, and with further advances in technology, it will continue to expand in ways we cannot predict. In examining the implications of e-commerce for business law, we must keep in mind two important elements.

First, as striking as the new means of communication are, they do not change basic legal principles ? whether they be the rules of contract and tort, or the rules for creating and managing business organizations and for creating and protecting intellectual property. The challenge is to adapt the rules to the new means of communication, as occurred in the twentieth century in dealing with telephone, telex, and facsimile. Second, the Internet raises questions for both domestic and international law: how to regulate the use of the Internet and determine who is responsible for harm it may cause; how to prevent fraud and make those who abuse the system pay for their wrongs. To discuss the latest developments in this challenging field, we have added the brand new Chapter 34 "Electronic Commerce."

Apart from e-commerce, our legal system continues to evolve quickly. Of course, each area of the law changes at its own pace. We try to accommodate these changes as they occur. In addition, our general perception of the relative weight of different areas of the law changes, as does our judgement about the order in which the different areas should be presented.

We have streamlined the opening of the book by combining the former opening two chapters to form the new Chapter 1 "Law and Society." Furthermore, we have shifted the placement of two former chapters. We believe that the material on "Government Regulation of Business" and on "International Business Transactions" is more easily understood when students have studied as much as possible of the law contained in the rest of the text. Accordingly, these 2 chapters , along with the new chapter on "Electronic Commerce" now form Part 8 "The Modern Legal Environment for Business" at the end of the book.

In addition to clarifying the discussion throughout the book, we have also strengthened the set of special features for this edition. We have added new Checklists where appropriate to facilitate understanding and review. We have replaced or updated most of the Contemporary Issues Boxes. We have revised most of the Review Questions at the ends of the chapters so that students might judge more easily whether they understand the material in the chapter. We have replaced many of the Cases and Problems at the ends of the chapters with new ones. And we have provided new lists of relevant Web sites at the end of each Part Opener.

FEATURES

A careful effort has been made to add and improve features that will facilitate learning and enhance an understanding of business applications.

- An Explanation of Abbreviations, a Table of Statutes, and a Table of Cases are provided near the beginning of the book.

- A list of Weblinks of relevant Internet addresses is provided at the end of each Part Opener.

- The opening section of each chapter summarizes the focus of the material to follow and lists some of the questions that will be considered.

- Case Boxes throughout the book provide examples based on actual cases.
- Illustration Boxes throughout the book provide other realistic examples.

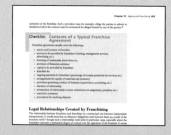

- Checklists in most chapters summarize important points to facilitate understanding and review.

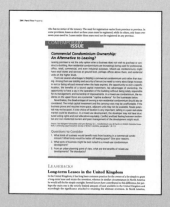

- A Contemporary Issue Box in each chapter highlights a current legal issue in light of changing business practices.

- Key Terms are boldfaced, and concise definitions of them are given in the margins.
- Footnotes at the bottom of the page provide citations and additional explanations.

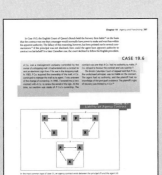

- Diagrams are provided in some chapters to enhance some explanations.

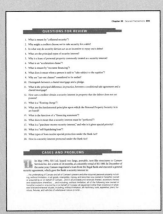

- Questions for Review near the end of each chapter ask students to articulate the important concepts and principles that have been presented.
- Cases and Problems at the end of each chapter ask students to apply the concepts and principles to realistic scenarios and actual cases.

- A Bibliography of selected sources is presented near the back of the book.
- For convenience, a list of the Contemporary Issues Boxes is given on the inside of the front cover, and the Explanation of Abbreviations is restated on the inside of the back cover.

SUPPLEMENTS

The following supplements have been carefully prepared to aid instructors and students in using this edition:

- An Instructor's Resource Manual provides lecture suggestions, a summary of the major changes from the 8th edition, additional information about the cases cited in the text, notes on each of the Contemporary Issues Boxes, and suggested answers to all the Questions for Review and Cases and Problems
- A Test Item File consisting of more than 1500 questions, provides multiple-choice questions, short-answer questions, and essay questions for each chapter. Each question is accompanied by the correct answer, a cross-reference to the appropriate page in the textbook, a level of difficulty (i.e., easy, moderate, or hard), and a description of the general skill tested (i.e., recall or conceptual).
- Pearson Test Manager (for Windows) is a special computerized version of the Test Item File that enables instructors to edit existing questions, add questions, and generate tests. The Pearson Test Manager also combines a powerful database with special tools so that instructors can process and analyze test results. In addition, the Person Test Manager offers the On-Line Testing System, which instructors can use to administer, correct, record, and return computerized exams over a variety of networks.
- A Study Guide provides students with an overview, a set of learning objectives, an outline of the content, and a set of new questions (with answers) on the learning objectives for every chapter in the text.
- A special Companion Web Site (at www.pearsoned.ca/smyth) includes a chapter outline, a set of chapter objectives, a new set of multiple-choice questions (with answers), a new set of short-answer questions (with answers), and hot links to other relevant Web sites for each chapter of the text.

ACKNOWLEDGEMENTS

Over the years, many teachers, colleagues, and students have offered invaluable suggestions for improving our book. Although space does not allow us to name each person individually here, we remain extremely to them for their contributions. For the ninth edition, we would like to thank in particular the following instructors and lawyers for providing formal reviews: John Anderson (Athabasca University), Leonard Glickman (Cassels Brock & Blackwell), Peter J. Holden (Capilano College), and Joe Lucchetti (Sault College of Applied Arts and Technology).

Our special thanks go to research assistant Ryan Mills who carefully checked statutory changes, updated current cases, and provided us with a large amount of recent material — especially in e-commerce — which we have been able to incorporate in this edition.

EXPLANATION OF ABBREVIATIONS

Throughout the text and footnotes, references occur to reported decisions of the courts, to statutes, and to legal periodicals. Listed below are the abbreviations for frequently cited source materials.

Canada

REPORTS

A.J.	Alberta Journal
A.R	Alberta Reports
Alta L.R.	Alberta Law Reports
B.C.J.	British Columbia Journal
B.L.R.	Business Law Reports
C.C.C.	Canadian Criminal Cases
C.C.E.L.	Canadian Cases on Employment Law
C.C.L.I.	Canadian Cases on the Law of Insurance
C.C.L.T.	Canadian Cases on the Law of Torts
C.E.L.R.	Canadian Environmental Law Reports
C.P.R.	Canadian Patent Reports
C.R.	Criminal Reports
C.S.	Cour Supérieure (Québec)
D.L.R.	Dominion Law Reports
D.T.C	Dominion Tax Cases
Ex.C.R.	Exchequer Court Reports
F.C.	Federal Court Reports
F.T.R.	Federal Court Trial Reports
M.J.	Manitoba Journal
M.P.R.	Maritime Provinces Reports
N.B.R.	New Brunswick Reports
N.S.R.	Nova Scotia Reports
O.A.C.	Ontario Appeal Cases
O.A.R.	Ontario Appeal Reports
O.J.	Ontario Journal
O.L.R.	Ontario Law Reports
O.R.	Ontario Reports
O.W.N.	Ontario Weekly Notes
P.P.S.A C.	Personal Property Security Act Cases
S.C.R.	Supreme Court Reports
S.J.	Saskatchewan Journal
Sask.R.	Saskatchewan Reports
W.L.R.	Western Law Reports
W.W.R.	Western Weekly Reports

STATUTES

Revised Statutes of

R.S.A.	Alberta
R.S.B.C.	British Columbia
R.S.C.	Canada
R.S.M.	Manitoba
R.S.N.B.	New Brunswick
R.S.Nfld.	Newfoundland
R.S.N.S.	Nova Scotia
R.S.O.	Ontario
R.S.P.E.I.	Prince Edward Island
R.S.Q.	Québec
R.S.S.	Saskatchewan

(Statutes for individual years are cited as S.A., S.B.C., S.C., S.M., S.N.B., S.Nfld., S.N.S., S.O., S.P.E.I., S.Q., S.S., respectively.)

S.O.R.	Statutory Orders and Regulations

PERIODICALS

C.B.L.J.	Canadian Business Law Journal
Can. Bar Rev.	Canadian Bar Review
Can. B.A.J.	Canadian Bar Association Journal
Osg.H.L.J.	Osgoode Hall Law Journal
UBC L. Rev.	University of British Columbia Law Review
U.T.L.J.	University of Toronto Law Journal

JUDGES

J.	Justice
J.A.	Justice of Appeal
JJ.	Justices
C.J.	Chief Justice
A.G.	Attorney-General

United Kingdom

REPORTS

All E.R.	All England Reports
E.R.	English Reports (Reprint)
I.R.	Irish Reports
L.J. Ex.	Law Journal Exchequer
L.J.P.C.	Law Journal Privy Council
L.T.	Law Times Reports
T.L.R.	Times Law Reports
W.L.R.	Weekly Law Reports

LAW REPORTS SERIES

Law Reports 1865-75

L.R.C.P.	Common Pleas
L.R.Ch.	Chancery
L.R.Eq.	Equity Cases

L.R.Ex.	Exchequer
L.R.H.L.	House of Lords
L.R.Q.B.	Queen's Bench
	Law Reports 1875-80
C.P.D.	Common Pleas Division
Ex.D.	Exchequer Division
	Law Reports 1875-91
App. Cas.	Appeal Cases
Ch.D.	Chancery Division
P.D.	Probate Division
Q.B.D.	Queen's Bench Division
	Law Reports 1891-date
A.C.	Appeal Cases
Ch.	Chancery Division
K.B. or Q.B.	King's (Queen's) Bench Division
P.	Probate Divorce and Admiralty Division
Fam.	Family Division

JUDGES

B.	Baron
C.B.	Chief Baron
C.	Chancellor

L.C.	Lord Chancellor
V.C.	Vice-Chancellor
L.J.	Lord Justice
L.C.J.	Lord Chief Justice
M.R.	Master of the Rolls

United States

A.L.R.	American Law Reports
F.	Federal Reporter
F.R.D.	Federal Rules Decisions
N.E.	Northeastern Reporter
N.W.	Northwestern Reporter
N.Y.	New York Reports
P.	Pacific Reporter
U.C.C.	Uniform Commercial Code

Australia and New Zealand

C.L.R.	Commonwealth Law Reports (Australia)
N.S.W.R.	New South Wales Reports
N.Z.L.R.	New Zealand Law Reports
Qd.R.	Queensland Reports

TABLE OF STATUTES

Note: The page numbers in italics at the end of each entry refer to pages in this book.

TABLE OF CASES

Note: The page numbers in italics at the end of each entry refer to pages in this book.

PART

1

L ike other major disciplines, law cannot be reduced to a simple set of rules and instructions that can be memorized and applied mechanically. Through the press, radio, and television, we are constantly exposed to the complexity and uncertainty of legal disputes. In order to gain an understanding of the legal system, we must learn something about its history and evolution, and about the theories that underlie its principles and rules.

Law provides the framework for virtually all business arrangements. Parties to a contract, investors in a corporation, owners of land and buildings—all desire reliability and predictability in their relations with others. While the legal system provides much of the certainty that business relations require, parties may nevertheless disagree about their respective rights and obligations and end up before the courts. The role of the courts is not only to settle disputes, but also to explain the rules, that is, to give reasons that justify their decisions. In turn, these explanations help others to adjust their relations and to avoid disputes. Thus, while only a very small proportion of business arrangements go before the courts, the courts play a much larger role in society by providing reliable guidelines for business arrangements. Chapter 1 provides an overview of the role of law in society, its special importance in the regulation of business, and the continuing debate about its values.

Law comes from many sources—the legislatures, administrative bodies, and the courts. To the non-lawyer, the structure of the court system is confusing; an overview helps in understanding how disputes get before the courts and are ultimately resolved. Chapter 2 explains how the courts operate and how parties utilize them. We describe the court system in England (where ours originated), Canada, and the United States. We also describe alternative forms of dispute resolution, which often lead to more satisfactory outcomes for both parties than they would achieve by resorting to the courts.

The Law in Its Social Context

PART 1 Weblinks

www.parliament.uk
The House of Lords

duhaime.org/diction.htm
B.C. practitioner Lloyd Duhaime provides a law dictionary online

aix1.uottawa.ca/~geist/cilrp.htm
Canadian Internet Law Resource Page: provides information on a variety of subjects

www.csusm.edu/public/guests/history/docs/ constitution_acts/
Canadian Constitution Acts 1867–1982

canada.gc.ca/howgoc/govorg_e.html
Provides an organizational chart for the Canadian government, including the courts

www.scc-csc.gc.ca/
Supreme Court of Canada

dsp-psd.pwgsc.gc.ca/dsp-psd/Reference/queens-e.html
Queen's University: how a government bill becomes law

dsp-psd.pwgsc.gc.ca/InfoSource/Info_2/HRC-e.html#S
Canadian Human Rights Commission

www.human-rights-coalition.bc.ca/links.htm
Links to most human rights legislation and provincial commissions in Canada

canada.justice.gc.ca/Publications/Info_education/CCS/ index_en.html
Canada's Court System Information online

www.unhchr.ch/
United Nations Web site with links to the Universal Declaration of Human Rights

www.pch.gc.ca/ddp-hrd/english/charter/contents.htm
Department of Canadian Heritage: material on the Canadian Charter of Rights and Freedoms

www.law.indiana.edu/v-lib/
University of Indiana Virtual Law Library: provides links to many law and international legal regimes

LAW AND SOCIETY

What do we mean when we use the word "law"? Since a simple definition is not adequate, we begin by examining the role of law in society, why it is generally accepted and obeyed, and how it applies to the business environment. In this chapter we examine such issues as:

- what is the significance of the law to the business environment?

- how do we distinguish between the "laws of nature" and "laws of human conduct"?

- what is the relationship between the law and business ethics?

- how do courts decide whether the legislation is valid under the Constitution?

- how do they determine what is the effect of that legislation?

- how do they interpret the Charter of Rights and Freedoms to protect our civil liberties?

- in settling disputes how do the courts interpret legislation originating both from Parliament and from provincial legislatures?

- how do they act as arbiters of disputes between private parties?

THE ROLE OF LAW

How Do We Define Law?

A simple definition of law would be misleading because law is so diverse and complex. It is helpful to begin with a brief description of what law does: it provides rules of conduct that are enforceable by government, and also by individuals and groups with the help of government. The law binds all of us; we cannot opt out of the legal system as we may from a club's rules by simply resigning—a club's rules are not law. We shall discuss who makes law and how it is made, later in this chapter and in Chapter 2.

Why do we have—and need—law? First, law is necessary for the protection of persons and property; it prohibits conduct that society believes to be harmful to others. For example, we must not assault another person, or steal that person's property. The law punishes a wrongdoer who is found guilty of such conduct, and usually also gives the victim a right to obtain compensation from the wrongdoer. However, it does much more than forbid harmful conduct: it also prescribes simple but vital rules that allow us to get on with our everyday lives—for example, by requiring all types of vehicles to drive on the right-hand side of the road. There is no moral superiority about driving on the right side rather than on the left, as a number of countries require. But clearly, we must have one rule or the other.

Second, law gives government the powers to act for the benefit of society in general. It authorizes government to provide policing, fire fighting, education, and health care—and to raise taxes to pay for those activities. A government might ignore legal rules when exercising its powers, but that is the sort of conduct we might expect to find in dictatorships; we expect our governments to operate democratically and in accordance with the **rule of law**.

Third, law provides a framework that gives us broader freedom of choice; in particular it enables us to make legally binding agreements enforceable in the courts. Thus we can plan and organize our affairs, and bargain with others for mutual advantages. The essential feature is that we can *rely* on such arrangements because they are enforceable: we can book in advance a flight across the Pacific, accept a long-term employment contract or a lease of business offices, or buy an interest in a partnership or a corporation. The law provides an element of *certainty* in determining contractual and property rights—something that is essential for the efficient carrying on of business.

rule of law
established legal principles that treat all persons equally and that government itself obeys

The Significance of Law for the Business Environment

It is often argued that there are too many laws—that society is over-regulated. Laws are resented because they tell us what to do and what not to do. From this perspective, laws are often perceived as burdensome, adding unnecessarily to the cost of doing business. Excessive regulation is viewed as a restriction on economic freedom, making a country's businesses less competitive than are firms from less regulated countries. That may sometimes be the case, and some regulation may well be excessive and unnecessary. One can legitimately debate whether the law should prohibit the consumption of marijuana or monopolize the domestic sale of alcohol and the exporting of wheat.

There is no doubt, however, that modern society cannot function without laws. Indeed, when business executives are asked what are the key factors that determine whether or not they decide to invest in a particular country, one of the most important is that of legal certainty. To constitute a good environment for business, a country must provide an adequate legal infrastructure in which rights are clearly defined and properly enforced. Over-regulation may be a severe inconvenience—but it is far less of an obstacle to business than is the complete absence of regulation.

Of course, neither law nor business is restricted to a purely national dimension. Increasingly, the world is becoming a single giant marketplace in which firms from different countries compete against and sometimes cooperate with each other. For Canada, more than for most countries, the international dimension of business is especially important; foreign trade and foreign investment result in a wide variety of legal relationships between parties in two or more different countries. Accordingly, the law is a significant element in the international business environment.

LAW AND CONSCIENCE

Why Is Law Generally Accepted and Obeyed?

Assurance of reasonably predictable and orderly relations among human beings is an essential quality of society: we should be able to rely with reasonable certainty on having our normal expectations met and on having a system of rules available and applied fairly to settle serious disputes. Conversely, if individuals felt free to either obey or break the law as they wished, then the legal system would not secure for us the minimum standards that we expect. Accordingly, the vast majority of us instinctively understand the need to "obey the rules."

For this understanding to continue to prevail, the system must appear to be generally just so that the majority is willing to assume that any particular law will produce just results. The assumption should be strong enough that if an unjust result seems to follow, the first step should be a careful re-examination of the process to make sure no mistake has been made along the way, and that it was not the *application* of the law but the law itself that was unjust and needs to be amended.

Can It Ever Be Right to Break the Law?

Even an effective, democratic legal system still leaves us with a number of difficult issues: Is it ever right to break the law? Is "law" the same thing as "justice"? Intelligent, moderate men and women generally agree that there are times when an individual is justified in breaking the law, although they would add that, generally speaking, the law should be obeyed. They would also agree that there are unjust laws, but even these ought to be obeyed because of the chaotic consequences for society if many people failed to obey them. Even while trying to get unjust laws changed by normal, lawful means, we should still comply with them.

ILLUSTRATION 1.1

Mary Brown was at home tending her sick 18-month-old baby. He had a high temperature caused by an undetermined virus. Suddenly she realized that the child had lapsed into a coma. Fearing that he was in a state of convulsion and might die, she rushed the child to her car and drove to the nearest hospital. Within a few moments she was driving 110 km/h in a 50 km/h zone. On arrival at the hospital the child was placed in emergency care, and the doctor commended her for having saved the life of her child. A police officer arrived on the scene and presented her with a summons for dangerous driving.

Mary Brown drove her car far in excess of the speed limit—a speed limit designed to promote safety. She endangered the lives of other users of the streets, but she did so in order to save the life of her own child. She would not argue that the 50 km/h speed limit was unreasonable or unjust, but only that in the circumstances she was justified in breaking the law or, possibly, that the law should not apply to that particular situation. Nonetheless, the law was apparently broken.

Law and justice, then, may not always coincide. But, one may ask, "Is an unjust law really law?" In some rare circumstances, it has been argued that a law is so atrociously unjust that it need not be obeyed by anyone. To put the argument another way, such a "law" is no law at all and should not bind us. If this is so, how can we distinguish an invalid law from a valid law? This question is one of the most perplexing ever raised. To shed a little light on it we shall briefly examine the two oldest contrasting theories of law.

NATURAL LAW

There are two main streams within natural law theory. The first is based on religious belief. When a religion establishes a set of moral and ethical values, it necessarily prescribes rules of conduct based on these values. In ancient societies, the religious leaders were usually the holders of power and translated *their* religious rules into laws. Thus, law originated within religious teachings. Since religious precepts are considered by those who formulate them to be eternal and immutable truths, so too are the fundamental principles of law—natural law—based on them, even though detailed rules and their particular applications may vary as society changes.

The second stream of natural law does not depend on a religious view of the world. Rather, it rests on the assumption that people are rational and by applying their inherent abilities of reason and logic to their perception of the world will arrive at basic principles of justice. This position was taken by some of the ancient Greek philosophers, and although almost forgotten for many centuries, it was reasserted in the 17th century in an extreme form. The Dutch philosopher and lawyer Grotius stated that the truths arrived at by humankind would exist independently of God. Indeed, if God were not in total harmony with these principles, He would not be God.

Despite their differences about how we perceive the underlying principles, both streams lead to the same basic view of law: fundamental, immutable moral principles are expressed in general legal principles, and may be further formulated in detailed rules for a particular society. One of the most eloquent expressions that combines these two views of natural law, based on the teachings of the 17th-century English philosopher John Locke, is found in the Declaration of Independence of the United States: "We hold these *truths to be self-evident:* that all men are created equal, that they are *endowed by their Creator* with certain unalienable rights, that among these are life, liberty and the pursuit of happiness" (italics added).

Paradoxically, natural law can, on the one hand, be a vehicle for reform and revolution or, on the other, give strong support to a highly conservative view of society, upholding the *status quo*. In revolutions, the battle cry is often that the great principles of natural law have been offended by human laws. Yet the same natural law has also been proclaimed in aid of the notion of divine right of kings in order to support a monarchy and to maintain an aristocracy and ranks of privilege, down to the lowliest serf; it has even been used to justify systems of slavery.

As an abstraction, legal philosophy generally tends to be neutral; partisans of different views of society inject their values into the philosophical system to give it the particular political cast of reaction or radicalism desired.

LEGAL POSITIVISM

The 18th-century Scottish thinker David Hume made a significant contribution. Hume first clearly distinguished between the *physical* laws of nature and the **normative** laws of government. A person cannot "break" a physical law, such as the "law of gravity," but he may break a law against stealing and risk the consequences.

normative law
law made by government establishing standards of behaviour and regulating human conduct

Second, Hume made a further crucial distinction among normative rules themselves. He stated that some normative rules were "law" because they created a code of behaviour complete with sanctions for failure to live by that code. In contrast, other normative rules existed without sanctions for their breach. These were moral rules; failure to observe them might create annoyance or indignation in others and a bad conscience in the wrongdoer, but no more than that. Hume's basic distinction, then, was between ascertainable rules that are binding, the law that "is," and rules that people "ought" to observe even in the absence of legal compulsion. His distinction was between the "is" and the "ought," or between *law* and *morals*. What Hume called "law" has since become known as **positive law**. Those who insist upon a clear distinction between the "is" and the "ought" are called **legal positivists**.

positive law
ascertainable rules that are binding—the law that "is"

Legal positivism is concerned with ascertaining the body of law that "is," with describing those criteria or tools that can be used to distinguish positive law from all other rules. How does one define law in a positivist system? The positivist asserts that law must come from a person or group of persons holding power over the general population. Those holding power can impose sanctions on individuals who break the law. John Austin, a 19th-century English legal

legal positivists
those who insist upon a clear distinction between law and morals

philosopher, described law as "the command of a sovereign." He did not view the sovereign as merely a person called "the King." Austin described the sovereign in the England of his time as "the King in Parliament." The "command" of the sovereign was an act of Parliament duly passed by both houses and receiving royal assent from the monarch.

Austin's definition of law is relatively satisfactory when applied to a constitutional monarchy with a *unitary system* of government such as exists in England, but it is more difficult to apply to a **federal country** such as Canada or the United States where the powers are divided between the national government and a number of provinces or states. In the case of both Canada and the United States, Austin's definition faces an added difficulty: lawful authority is allocated by the Constitution, and a document can hardly be personified as a sovereign.

Modern legal thinkers have refined Austin's theory into more sophisticated 20th-century models: in place of a sovereign they recognize a **basic law**, a constitution habitually obeyed by the citizens of a country. This basic law enjoys a sufficient minimum level of acceptance by the general population just as long as they regard it as legitimate and binding. The question of whether that minimum level of acceptance has been met can be very difficult to resolve—as in the midst of a revolution when the old constitution has been denounced by many citizens. How the eventual victor becomes established as the lawful authority remains a practical question that positivist theories do not explain. Usually the question is resolved when a government emerges in apparent effective control and is recognized by a number of major nations.

federal country

where powers are divided between the national government and a number of provinces or states

basic law

a constitution that is habitually obeyed by the citizens of a country and that they regard as legitimate and binding

LAW AND MORALS

Neither legal positivism nor natural law answers the question, "When, if ever, is it right to break the law?" There is an adage that much learning in philosophy does not make a person good. In law, we have a parallel: much learning in legal philosophy does not provide easy answers to difficult moral questions about the law.

CASE 1.1

Three men and a boy were shipwrecked in a small boat 1500 km at sea in the South Atlantic. What little food they had was exhausted within a few days. For the next six days they had no food whatever and subsisted only on rainwater. All three men were married, with young families. Two of the men suggested that if no relief came someone should be sacrificed to save the rest. The third man dissented and the boy was not consulted. A day later, the two men suggested to the third that they should cast lots to determine who should be put to death to save the rest, but the third refused to consent. The proposal was not put to the boy, who at that time was very much weakened and was lying helpless in the bottom of the boat. The three men spoke of their families and suggested that it would be better to kill the boy so that their lives could be saved. The first man proposed that if there was no vessel in sight by the next morning, the boy should be killed. On the following day, the two men offered a prayer for forgiveness, and proceeded to kill the boy with a knife. The three men fed upon the boy's body for four days until they were picked up by a passing ship. The first two men were charged with murder while the third was not charged with any offence.[1]

In Case 1.1, 1500 km at sea in a small boat that could hardly be considered as part of the "national territory" of the home country of the shipwrecked men, is there any ascertainable positive law? (Indeed, should the law of any country apply?) Do these men constitute a miniature community that can make its own laws to suit its needs? If the law of one country is applied to them, should they be acquitted of any crime on the grounds that their dire circumstances justi-

1. Regina v. Dudley and Stephens (1884), 14 Q.B.D. 273.

fied their actions? If the law of a particular country does not apply, are there still immutable principles of justice—of natural law—that ought to be used to judge people's conduct, no matter where they find themselves? And if so, should these principles be applied to override the established positive law of a country?

Case 1.1 shows that legal systems can be confronted with extremely difficult moral questions. No solution is entirely satisfactory, and reasonable people can strongly disagree about the appropriate disposition of a difficult case. Thus, we cannot conclude that law and justice always coincide. There will always be disagreement in ascertaining what the law is in some situations, and even greater disagreement about whether its application has led to a just solution. Nor does legal philosophy help us decide whether it is ever right to break the law. At best, it can make the problem clearer and focus our minds on the central issue.

Law and Business Ethics

We have seen how difficult is the question whether it can ever be right to break the law. We might also ask whether it is always sufficient merely to abide by the law: are there occasions when a higher standard of behaviour is required? In a commercial context, this raises the issue of business ethics. Frequently, businesses are expected to—and do—live up to a higher ethical standard than is imposed on them by law. It is common for their activities to be governed or influenced by "codes of conduct" that require better behaviour.

Codes of conduct take a variety of forms:

(a) *Binding codes*—some activities, particularly of professionals, are regulated by a code of conduct, or a similar set of rules, laid down by a governing body or trade association. Professional codes of conduct are considered further in Chapter 4. Although these rules are not "law," their effect is often similar. A member of a profession or trade association who breaches the code of conduct may face disciplinary proceedings and may even be expelled from that body—a very severe sanction, since often it will deprive the offender of his means of livelihood.

(b) *Voluntary codes*—some industries have established voluntary codes of conduct for their activities. Although "voluntary," they often have a strong persuasive effect. A voluntary code may even be used as a substitute for government regulation: there is an implicit threat that, if an industry—for example, the advertising industry— does not regulate itself satisfactorily, the government will step in and legislate standards. In other cases, voluntary codes are adopted where there is no effective power to legislate. A well-known example is the United Nations Code of Conduct for Transnational Corporations. Multinational enterprises are urged to observe certain minimum standards—for example, on employment of child labour—even though there are no legal restrictions in countries in which they operate.

(c) *Self-imposed codes*—some firms have adopted and published their own codes of conduct, especially in relation to employment conditions and environmental protection. Codes may be a response to public criticism, for example, to criticism of working conditions in overseas factories of manufacturers of clothing and sports goods; sometimes they may be used to impress and attract particular groups of consumers. In other cases they simply reflect the philosophy of the owners or managers of the firm.

Why should a firm commit itself to observing a higher ethical standard than is required by law? The answer may be quite straightforward: a firm behaves ethically because that is how its owners or managers believe it should behave. More often, however, ethical behaviour is a matter of enlightened self-interest. A firm that respects its employees is more likely to have a stable, contented, and productive work force; a firm that operates a liberal "returns" policy is more likely to create consumer loyalty; and a firm that shows concern for the environment and the community in which it is located will benefit from its enhanced public image.

WHO MAKES LAW?

There are a number of sources of law:

(a) The Constitution—as we have already noted, it may derive from a variety of sources, such as a monarchy, and also from general acceptance by a country's citizens of a basic law; a constitution is a "higher" law by which all other laws are governed; all other laws must comply with the constitution in order to be valid and enforceable.

(b) Legislation—also known as statute law or acts, are passed by Parliament and by provincial legislatures in compliance with the Constitution.

  (i) Subordinate legislation—rules passed pursuant to the provisions in a statute by a body designated in the statute, such as the federal or a provincial cabinet, or by a cabinet minister, or by an administrative body such as the Canadian Radio-Television Commission.

  (ii) Administrative rulings—rulings handed down by administrative bodies designated to hear complaints and applications by individuals and groups, pursuant to legislation.

(c) Court decisions—handed down by single judges or a panel of judges after hearing a "case" before the court

As we shall see, the courts play a very special role in our society: whenever the government itself or any private citizen or group tries to gain the benefit or protection of a law against the will of another, the complaining party resorts to the courts. Accordingly, we shall examine the central role of the court in law enforcement.

Checklist: What do Courts do?

- They determine the validity of legislation.
- They interpret legislation.
- They protect civil liberties.
- They resolve disputes between private parties.

THE COURTS AS ARBITER OF THE CONSTITUTION

Legislation and the Courts

How effective is a statute in remedying a problem? After years of study, after the careful drafting of legislation, and after exhaustive debate in the legislature followed by final enactment, we might hope that at last the problem has been solved or at least dealt with as best the present state of our knowledge will permit. But no—frequently the problem has just begun.

If it is to have any effect, a new law must restrict or enlarge someone's activities, or lay down conditions for offering or taking away something of value. When a new law begins to affect people's interests, they may become unhappy about its consequences and complain to an official who administers the law. If the administrator changes the ruling or gives a satisfactory explanation, the complainants, though dissatisfied with the answer, may decide it is not worthwhile to take the matter further. If, however, they decide to press their grievance, then the next stage is a formal complaint before either a court or an administrative board that regularly hears such matters. A serious dispute is often appealed and may go all the way to the Supreme Court of Canada for final disposition. The statute itself may be attacked as unconstitutional. Before its effect is ultimately determined, then, the statute may have travelled a long way from its passage through Parliament.

Federalism

In a federal country such as Canada (and also the United States), the Supreme Court rather than the legislature often has the last word. This is because we have two distinct levels of government—federal and provincial; under the Constitution Act, 1867[2] each level has an independent existence and its own sphere of activity. Thus, our national Parliament cannot alter the structure of provincial governments.[3] The division of legislative power made principally under sections 91 and 92 of the Constitution allocates certain fields of jurisdiction to the federal Parliament and other designated fields (including power over municipalities) to each of the provincial legislatures. Whenever an act—or any provision in an act—passed by Parliament or a provincial legislature is found by the court to be outside the legislature's jurisdiction and therefore beyond its powers (***ultra vires***), that act or provision is void. The Constitution also gives **residual powers** to the federal government, so that all fields not expressly allocated to the provinces are within federal jurisdiction. Examples are new activities developed after 1867, such as air traffic and radio and television broadcasting.

All federations face an inherent difficulty: practical problems refuse to divide themselves into well-defined subjects that fall clearly within either federal or provincial jurisdiction. Many problems overlap both jurisdictions, and often both levels of government seem to have **concurrent powers** to regulate an activity. When both levels have jurisdiction and conflict arises between the statutes, the federal legislation prevails, nullifying the provincial legislation on the basis of the need for uniformity across the nation in areas of federal jurisdiction. For example, the federal government has jurisdiction over radio and television broadcasting, and the provincial governments have jurisdiction to regulate advertising in order to protect consumers. May a province still regulate advertising on television?

ultra vires
beyond the powers and therefore void

residual powers
powers that fall within federal jurisdiction because they are not expressly allocated to the provinces by the Constitution

concurrent powers
overlapping powers of both levels of government to regulate the same activities

CASE 1.2

The Quebec Consumer Protection Act prohibits advertising directed at persons under the age of 13. The provisions of the Act apply to all forms of advertising—newspapers, magazines, television. There already existed extensive federal regulations of television broadcasting. After receiving warnings from the Quebec government about its television advertising for children, Irwin Toys Limited commenced an action for a declaration that the provisions in the provincial act were void because they interfered with the federal government's jurisdiction to regulate television.

The court disagreed; it found that the purpose of the Act was to protect children, "a valid provincial objective" and, while it did have an "incidental" effect on television advertising it was not incompatible with existing federal regulations. "Neither television broadcasters nor advertisers are put into a position of defying one set of standards by complying with the other."[4] Consequently, the court held that the provisions of the Quebec Consumer Protection Act were not void.

2. This Act was formerly known as the British North America Act, but was officially renamed The Constitution Act, 1867 by the Constitution Act, 1982. Both of these acts and all intervening amendments may now be referred to as the Constitution.

3. Such changes may be done only by amending the Constitution, a difficult task that requires approval of the provinces themselves, as discussed under the heading "Constitutional Protection."

4. Irwin Toy Ltd. v. Quebec (Attorney-General), [1989] 1 S.C.R. 927 at 964. This case raised other issues under the Canadian Charter of Rights and Freedoms, noted later in this chapter.

The court's decision was consistent with the principle that it should not easily strike down legislation—that it should defer to the intent of the legislatures—unless the legislation was clearly inconsistent with the constitutional division of powers.

A constitution often does more than allocate jurisdiction between levels of government: it may also prohibit all government interference in certain areas; it may remove them from the legislative power of both levels. (A prohibition of this type may exist in the constitution of a unitary country, but we are here concerned only with federations.) In 1982, the Charter of Rights and Freedoms became part of the Constitution; it places limits on many aspects of government action and will be discussed later in this chapter.

The Two Challenges to the Validity of a Statute

Problems of jurisdiction arose in the United States before Canada was founded. In the early 19th century, the Supreme Court of the United States held that neither the federal nor the state governments could have the last word on interpreting the U.S. Constitution; to give one level the power to interpret the document (doubtless in its own favour) would be to confer supremacy upon it. Instead, the court declared that it must itself be the final arbiter of the Constitution, the umpire between the two levels of government.[5] This position was accepted by the states and by Congress. In Canada, the Supreme Court has come to play the same key role as constitutional umpire.

ILLUSTRATION 1.2

The Canadian Parliament receives a report of a special study of abuses in the stock market that cause investors to lose their savings. In response, it passes a statute prohibiting certain kinds of advertising of securities as misleading, consequently making them criminal in nature. A broker who specializes in these transactions, claiming that his activity is lawful, carries on in defiance of the statute. He is charged with an offence and raises the following arguments in defence: (a) that the law is unconstitutional because it purports to make changes in an area that is exclusively within the jurisdiction of the provinces under the Constitution Act, 1867; and (b) that even if his first argument is wrong, the government as prosecuting authority has placed an unreasonable interpretation upon the statute and has applied it too broadly in charging him with an offence. He argues, in other words, that under any reasonable interpretation of the statute his activity would remain lawful.

We can see from Illustration 1.2 that a legislature faces a double problem in attempting any type of reform. First, it knows that if its entire statute is ruled unconstitutional, it will be void and make *no* change at all in the law. (The broker in the illustration would then be subject to no new regulation whatever.) Indeed, even were the Supreme Court to interpret the statute as not being completely beyond federal powers, it might nonetheless restrict its application to areas within federal jurisdiction and so limit the statute that it would fail to accomplish the desired reform. In effect, the court would then be saying: "If these words were given a broad meaning, they would attempt to regulate activity beyond the powers of the federal Parliament. Clearly, Parliament could not have meant to do such a thing. If, however, we restrict their meaning to 'such and such,' the regulation will be within federal jurisdiction and valid. We will assume that Parliament meant to do only what is possible under the Constitution, and accordingly find that these words have a restricted meaning." (Once again the broker would escape regulation if his activity were outside federal jurisdiction.)

Second, and apart from the constitutional hurdle, courts have sometimes been criticized for interpreting statutes narrowly so as to interfere as little as possible with existing private rights.

---

5. Marbury v. Madison, 5 U.S. Reports, 1 Cranch 137 (1803).

Such an interpretation may in large measure frustrate an intended reform. (Again in this event, the broker might be saved by the narrow interpretation of the statute.)

A constitutional defeat in the courts is more serious than a narrow interpretation. Parliament cannot overcome a decision by the Supreme Court that a statute is unconstitutional unless the Constitution itself is amended—a process that requires a high degree of provincial agreement as well as the consent of Parliament.[6] However, if the problem is simply one of inter-pretation, the government can subsequently introduce an amendment to broaden the applica-tion of the statute. The trouble with relying on the ability to amend legislation is that except for emergencies or extraordinary pressure on government, the wheels of Parliament "grind exceed-ing slow," and a year or several years may pass in the normal course of events before an amend-ment is enacted.

When the Supreme Court nullifies legislation on constitutional grounds it can arouse strong feelings and sometimes vehement attacks, both for and against the judges as individuals and the idea that a court can have so much authority. A variety of cries can be heard: "The Court is a reactionary bastion standing in the way of badly needed reform"; "The Court is nine elderly lawyers, neither elected nor representative of the people, defeating the wishes of a democratically elected legislature"; "The Court has prevented one level of government from running roughshod over the jurisdiction of the other"; "The Court has stopped the government from making an unwarranted intrusion on individual liberties." Judges of the Supreme Court cannot escape making decisions that play a critical role in political, social, and economic change. As a result, the role and the personality of Supreme Court judges in particular, and of judges generally, have become subjects of great interest to legal theorists, sociologists, psychologists, and the media as well as to the practising lawyers who appear before them.

AS PROTECTOR OF CIVIL LIBERTIES

The Various Meanings of "Civil Liberties"

The phrase "civil liberties" is difficult to define because it comprises a number of quite separate ideas related only by a general concern for the well-being of the individual citizen. Two other terms, "civil rights" and "human rights," are often used as synonyms. "Civil liberties" and "civil rights" are the older terms, dating from at least as far back as the 18th century, and referring pri-marily to freedom of the individual in politics and religion. They include freedom of expression (both of speech and of the press), freedom of association and assembly, freedom to practise and preach one's religion, freedom from arbitrary arrest and detention, and the right to a fair trial.[7]

However, the term "civil rights" has a peculiar meaning in Canadian constitutional law. Section 92 of the Constitution designates "property and civil rights" as an area of provincial responsibility. Our courts have generally taken the term to mean something like "private rights"

---

6. A constitution, whether it is of a small social club or a large nation, almost always contains provisions for its own amendment. A "simple majority," that is, any number more than 50 percent (for example, 50.01 percent) may pass an appropriate motion to change any earlier motion or law also passed by a simple majority. But the provi-sions of a constitution are usually "*entrenched*": only a "special majority" may amend them. Typically a special majority is two thirds or three quarters of the ballots cast, but sometimes there are quite complex special majori-ties, giving a specified group the power of veto. Unless *that* group, even if it comprises a very small minority, approves of a proposed amendment, the amendment will be lost.

7. These rights received international recognition after the Second World War. See United Nations documents *Universal Declaration of Human Rights* (1948) and *Covenant on Civil and Political Rights* (1966); *European Convention for the Protection of Human Rights and Fundamental Freedoms*, 213 United Nations Treaty Series 221 (1955); Luini del Russo, A., *International Protection of Human Rights*, Appendices A–E, Washington, D.C.: Lerner Law Book Co. Inc., 1971; Stein, E. and Hay, F., *Law and Institutions in the Atlantic Area*, Ch. VIII. New York: The Bobbs-Merrill Co., 1967.

relating to the ownership of property, contract law, and family relations. Our concern in this chapter is not, of course, limited to this special usage.

Mainly as a result of the horrors of the Second World War—deportation, starvation, and genocide—there arose a greatly heightened awareness of human needs beyond the traditional freedoms mentioned above. Thus, increased awareness of problems of social and economic welfare has often been reflected in legal and constitutional changes such as those discussed in the next section.

Constitutional Protection

Canadian Charter of Rights and Freedoms

The legal base for the protection of human rights in Canada was greatly increased by the Canadian Charter of Rights and Freedoms contained in the Constitution Act, 1982.

First, we should note that the Charter is *entrenched* in the Constitution: it cannot be repealed by an ordinary act of Parliament or of provincial legislatures in each of the areas where formerly they were able to pass and repeal laws at their will. Section 52 (1) states:

> The Constitution of Canada is the supreme law of Canada, and any law that is inconsistent with the provisions of the Constitution is, to the extent of the inconsistency, of no force or effect.

Any change in the Charter can only be by way of amendment as provided for in the Constitution Act, that is, by consent of the Parliament of Canada and the legislatures of at least two-thirds of the provinces containing at least 50 percent of the population of all the provinces. We can see then that the Charter is much more difficult to change than is an ordinary statute.

Second, subject to the important qualifications in the following paragraphs, rights entrenched in the Charter cannot be infringed by ordinary legislation: to the extent that a statute offends a right in the Charter, it will be declared invalid. The legislature cannot interfere with those rights that are founded on the "higher law" of the Constitution. The idea of rights based on a higher law was a major departure from British Parliamentary supremacy, and is more akin to the theory of the United States Constitution.

Although prior to the Charter our courts had not dealt with entrenched human rights, they did have wide experience in deciding whether a piece of legislation is within the competence of the federal Parliament or of provincial legislatures under section 91 or 92 of the Constitution; they struck down legislation when they concluded that it went beyond the powers granted. The Supreme Court of Canada has shown that it is prepared to strike down those provisions in statutes that offend the rights and freedoms guaranteed in the Charter.[8] Indeed, the Supreme Court has gone further: it has "read into" a human rights act (rather than striking down a part of the act) words prohibiting discrimination on the basis of sexual orientation, words that the legislature had not chosen to include as part of the act.[9]

Third, the Charter includes section 33, which permits a legislature to override certain other sections. That is, if a statute states expressly that it "shall operate notwithstanding" those specified sections, a legislature may infringe some of the most important rights guaranteed by the Charter. Section 33 also contains a so-called "sunset" clause: the overriding section of the statute expires five years after it comes into force unless it is re-enacted by the legislature—and subsequently for each further five years. The reasoning behind these provisions seems to be as follows: the declaration of certain rights in our Constitution gives them great moral and political force; govern-

---

8. See, for example: R. v. Big M Drug Mart Ltd. (1985), 18 D.L.R. (4th) 321, striking down the Lord's Day Act of Canada, as a form of compulsory religious practice; and A.G. of Québec v. Québec Association of Protestant School Boards et al. (1984), 10 D.L.R. (4th) 321, nullifying certain sections of Québec's Charter of the French Language, as violating minority language rights under section 23 of the Charter of Rights and Freedoms.

9. Vriend et al. v. The Queen in the Right of Alberta et al. (1998), 156 D.L.R. (4th) 385.

ments will rarely dare to pass legislation expressly overriding the Charter, and very likely for only limited purposes—and they will have to produce strong reasons for continuing the override beyond the first five years. In the first two decades of the Charter, legislatures have operated within these constraints; in general they have not found it politically easy to circumvent the Charter and to use the override section at will.

Fourth, none of the rights set out in the Charter is absolute: section 1 states that they are all subject "to such reasonable limits prescribed by law as can be demonstrably justified in a free and democratic society." The problem of what amounts to "reasonable limits" arises whenever a complainant claims that a right entrenched in the Charter, such as the freedom of expression, has been infringed.

In general, a statute is *presumed to be valid*, that is, to be within the power of a legislature passing it: a person attacking it must show why it is invalid. However, a person need show only that one of his constitutionally guaranteed rights has been infringed by a provision in a statute; the provision would then be *presumed invalid* unless the government could persuade the court that the infringement was "…demonstrably justified…." Thus, the **burden** shifts to the government to establish that the section of a statute that interferes with constitutional rights is justified. It is difficult to predict in a general way how deferential the courts will be to the legislatures. In what circumstances will judges say, "Since the elected majority think this infringement is justified, we will not interfere" rather than "The will of the majority does not justify this interference with individual rights"?

In *R. v. Oakes*[10] the Supreme Court set out a series of tests that the legislation must meet in order to justify itself under section 1. First, the object to be served by the limit must be "of sufficient importance to warrant overriding a constitutionally protected right or freedom." That is, the object must not be trivial but "pressing and substantial." Second, the means chosen must be proportional to the importance of the objective and must impair the Charter right as little as reasonably possible in achieving the objective. Third, on an overview, when the effects of the infringement on rights are compared with the object that has been achieved, that object must on balance justify the infringement. This careful and somewhat labourious process has been undertaken by the courts a number of times, and usually they find that the legislature is justified.

burden
the requirement that, unless a party can establish facts and law to prove its case, it will lose

CASE 1.3

Section 2 states, "Everyone has the following fundamental freedoms:…(b) Freedom of thought, belief, opinion and expression, including freedom of the press and other media of communication." In the *Irwin Toy* case, discussed earlier, the toy manufacturer, among other objections, claimed that the Quebec Consumer Protection Act, prohibiting advertising directed at persons under the age of 13, was unconstitutional because it infringed the manufacturer's section 2(b) freedom.[11] Is such a provision prohibiting advertising an infringement of freedom of expression? If so, is the object the provision serves—protecting children from being incited to buy or to urge another person to buy goods—a pressing and substantial one? The Supreme Court of Canada found that the provision did indeed infringe freedom of expression. However, it went on to hold that the objective was serious and pressing. It further held that the means chosen to restrict such ads (the setting of standards to assure that the ads remained available to adults) were minimal and proportional to the objective, and finally, that on balance the interference was justified.

---

10. [1986] 1 S.C.R. 103. For further interpretation of the test in Oakes, see: R. v. Chaulk, [1990] 3 S.C.R. 1303, and McKinney v. University of Guelph, [1990] 3 S.C.R. 229.

11. Irwin Toy Ltd. v. Quebec (Attorney-General), n. 4, *supra*.

As a consequence of the *Oakes* test, when legislatures draft legislation that might impinge on a right or freedom guaranteed by the Charter, they must do so with great care and seek to minimize its effect on Charter rights.

Fifth, while the Charter clearly applies to governments and governmental activities, it remains uncertain to what extent it applies between private persons. In the private sector, the protection of human rights has been a matter for human rights codes, passed by each of the provinces and by Parliament (to cover those activities that are under federal jurisdiction). These codes are not entrenched and may be amended from time to time by the legislature, or even repealed entirely, although complete repeal is highly unlikely. The Charter itself states that it applies "in respect of all matters within the authority of Parliament...[and]...of the legislature of each province." These words make the Charter applicable to all statutes, to regulations under statute law, to municipal laws, to Crown corporations, and very likely to government-funded institutions such as public schools and community colleges. It may even be argued that the requirements of the Charter should be binding on *all* corporations, whether they are giant enterprises such as Canadian Pacific or incorporated small businesses, since all corporations are creatures of government: a corporation cannot come into existence unless it is registered pursuant to statutory authority. So it could be claimed that incorporation amounts to a form of government action. However, the Supreme Court of Canada has refused to extend Charter requirements to corporations and even to our publicly funded universities because they are considered to be independent of the government.[12] This matter has been left to human rights codes.

The Rights and Freedoms Protected by the Charter

We shall reproduce several of the most important protections given by the Charter, beginning with those rights and freedoms that may be overridden by Parliament or a provincial legislature through use of section 33.

Fundamental Freedoms

2. Everyone has the following fundamental freedoms:
   (a) freedom of conscience and religion;
   (b) freedom of thought, belief, opinion and expression, including freedom of the press and other media of communication;
   (c) freedom of peaceful assembly; and
   (d) freedom of association.

Legal Rights

7. Everyone has the right to life, liberty and security of the person and the right not to be deprived thereof except in accordance with the principles of fundamental justice.

8. Everyone has the right to be secure against unreasonable search or seizure.

9. Everyone has the right not to be arbitrarily detained or imprisoned.

10. Everyone has the right on arrest or detention
    (a) to be informed promptly of the reasons therefor;
    (b) to retain and instruct counsel without delay and to be informed of that right; and
    (c) to have the validity of the detention determined by way of *habeas corpus* and to be released if the detention is not lawful.

---

12. McKinney v. University of Guelph, n. 10; *supra*, at 266, "...the mere fact that an entity is a creature of statute...is in no way sufficient to make its actions subject to the Charter."

Sections 11 to 14 deal in detail with the rights of persons accused of crimes during Criminal proceedings against them.

Equality Rights

15. (1) Every individual is equal before and under the law and has the right to the equal protection and equal benefit of the law without discrimination and, in particular, without discrimination based on race, national or ethnic origin, colour, religion, sex, age or mental or physical disability.

    (2) Subsection (1) does not preclude any law, program or activity that has as its object the amelioration of conditions of disadvantaged individuals or groups including those that are disadvantaged because of race, national or ethnic origin, colour, religion, sex, age or mental or physical disability.

Two aspects of section 15 deserve comment. First, subsection (2) permits "affirmative action" (or "reverse discrimination"), that is, programs aimed at assisting disadvantaged people such as the aged, those who have disabilities, or those who because of racial or ethnic background have lived in impoverished conditions. Without such a provision, it might have been possible for a person not a member of a disadvantaged group to complain that he was not receiving equality of treatment if a disadvantaged person were given an extra benefit such as special funding to obtain higher education or training for a job.

Second, section 28 of the Charter states:

Notwithstanding anything in this Charter, the rights and freedoms referred to in it are guaranteed equally to male and female persons.

This section is not subject to being overridden by Parliament or a legislature; it deals with equality of treatment between the sexes—as does section 15(2)—and it states that equality is guaranteed "notwithstanding anything in the Charter" including, presumably, section 15(2). Does this phrase then mean that affirmative action for the benefit of women offends section 28, so that a man may complain of unequal treatment if a woman is given special benefit?

The following rights and freedoms are also *not* subject to a legislative override:

Democratic Rights

3. Every citizen of Canada has the right to vote in an election of members of the House of Commons or of a legislative assembly and to be qualified for membership therein.

Mobility Rights

6. (1) Every citizen of Canada has the right to enter, remain in and leave Canada.

    (2) Every citizen of Canada and every person who has the status of a permanent resident of Canada has the right

    (a) to move to and take up residence in any province; and

    (b) to pursue the gaining of a livelihood in any province.

    (3) The rights specified in subsection (2) are subject to

    (a) any laws or practices of general application in force in a province other than those that discriminate among persons primarily on the basis of province of present or previous residence; and

    (b) any laws providing for reasonable residency requirements as a qualification for the receipt of publicly provided social services.

    (4) Subsections (2) and (3) do not preclude any law, program or activity that has as its object the amelioration in a province of conditions of individuals in that province who are socially or economically disadvantaged if the rate of employment in that province is below the rate of employment in Canada.

Section 6(4) is an affirmative action provision permitting programs of employment that give preference to local workers in a province with higher-than-average unemployment in Canada.

AS INTERPRETER OF LEGISLATION

The Literal Approach

We know that legislatures may take a long time to seek information and advice before passing legislation. When a court is called on to interpret that legislation, what information and advice, what evidence, will it permit to be brought before it? What will it consider? The traditional English position has been that the meaning of a statute should be apparent on its face, so that it can be understood "on the run." After all, so this argument goes, a person reading a statute should be able to rely on its words alone, without looking further. If one does not understand a particular word or words, a standard dictionary should provide clarification, and if the word happens to be a specialized technical term, a standard technical dictionary or textbook should suffice. But that should be the limit of the necessary outside inquiry.

In theory, that position seems laudable: if it were necessary for a person to read other documents such as a multi-volume report of a royal commission in order to learn what a statute means, that person would be left in a very difficult position, running the risk of misunderstanding the statute taken at its face value. Even if a large law library were available containing the needed material—something few people have—a layperson would not likely have either the time or the expertise to read and understand it.

In practice, the traditional English approach leads to still more difficulties. Many words do not have precise meanings, as mathematical symbols do. Frequently they are ambiguous, capable of different shades of meaning; sometimes they have several distinct meanings. A dictionary does not help solve such dilemmas. Furthermore, a statute rarely breaks entirely new ground; new laws almost always affect existing ones. Most often the express aim of a new statute is to change existing law, and it will not be possible to understand that statute without first knowing what the law was before it was passed. An extreme example occurs when a legislature repeals an existing law.

ILLUSTRATION 1.3

New legislation begins with the following words: "The Widgets Act, Chapter 49 of the Statutes of 1998, is hereby repealed." What is the effect of these words? To understand them one must know what the law was before 1998 when it was changed by the Widgets Act, what change that act made in the law, and how the present repealing act changes the law. It may be less simple than it appears. Suppose that before the Widgets Act was passed the manufacture and sale of widgets was illegal. The 1998 Act set out rules for their legal manufacture and sale. Does the repeal of the Widgets Act make those activities illegal again, or does it make them entirely free from any regulation or prohibition?

It may be foolish for a legislature to pass an act in such ambiguous terms, but statutes similar to the repealing act in Illustration 1.3 occur with disquieting frequency through inadvertence, perhaps as a result of hurrying through a backlog of legislation towards the end of a legislative session. The courts are then left with the problem, and they have had to devise methods of dealing with it. The English courts conceded that it is often necessary to examine the state of the law before a statute was passed in order to determine what change has been made. The result is that a person cannot rely solely on the words of a statute, but if this fact is recognized, is the traditional English position not a myth?

The Liberal Approach

In Canada, the liberal approach—viewing legislation in its larger context by examining its purpose and those who are intended to be affected by it—has long been regarded as important in interpreting statutes. This approach is expressly recognized by the federal Interpretation Act and by similar acts in force in the provinces. Under section 12 of the federal Act:

> Every enactment shall be deemed remedial, and shall be given such fair, large and liberal construction and interpretation as best ensures the attainment of its objects.[13]

The Supreme Court of Canada has followed this view. In a 1994 case, Mr. Justice Gonthier quoted with approval the following statement from E.A. Driedger's text, *The Construction of Statutes*:

> ...the words of an Act are to be read in their entire context and in their grammatical and ordinary sense harmoniously with the scheme of the Act, the object of the Act, and the intention of Parliament.[14]

Gonthier, J. continued:

> The first consideration should therefore be to determine the purpose of the legislation, whether as a whole or as expressed in a particular provision....A legislative provision should be given a strict or liberal interpretation depending on the purpose underlying it, and that purpose must be identified in light of the context of the statute, its objective and the legislative intent: this is the teleological approach.[15]

Legislative History

How far should a court look into the circumstances surrounding the passing of a statute? Should it examine the report of a royal commission or a parliamentary committee that led to the introduction of a bill in Parliament, the statements of the minister whose department was responsible for the bill, and the debates in Parliament itself, in other words, at the **legislative history** of a statute?

legislative history
events in the legislature, including reports and debates, leading to the passing of a statute

For two centuries the position of the courts was that none of these things should be considered because they did not represent the "will" of Parliament as a whole. Instead, the courts should resolve any ambiguities entirely from "objective" evidence: dictionaries, principles of interpretation already developed by the courts, and ascertainment of the state of the law at the time the statute was passed.

In 1976, the Supreme Court of Canada broke with the tradition in the *Reference re Anti-Inflation Act*.[16] An important issue was whether Parliament considered the inflationary situation in the autumn of 1975 to be a national emergency justifying use of the **emergency power** to pass the Anti-Inflation Act and bring wage and price controls into effect. The court referred both to a government *White Paper* (a policy paper published prior to the introduction of new legislation) and to debates in the House of Commons as being necessary for reaching a proper decision. This use of legislative history recognized a long-standing body of opinion in favour of examining all information available to a court in order to help it understand a statute, at least for the purpose of deciding whether it is constitutionally within the power of the legislature to pass it. According to this view, the courts themselves should be able to decide how much weight

emergency power
a power whose use is justified by a national emergency

---

13. Interpretation Act, R.S.C. 1985, c. I-21.

14. E.A. Driedger, *The Construction of Statutes* (2nd ed.) Toronto: Butterworth & Co., 1983, p. 87.

15. Quebec (Communauté urbaine) v. Corp. Notre-Dame de Bon-Secours, [1994] 3 S.C.R. 3 at 17.

16. (1976), 68 D.L.R. (3d) 452.

to give to various aspects of legislative history. In the United States, legislative history is customarily heard by courts and may often be very influential in their decisions.

The Brandeis Brief

brief
written argument presented to the court

In 1907, Louis Brandeis, a noted lawyer who subsequently became a distinguished judge of the United States Supreme Court, prepared an unusual **brief** (a written argument to be presented before the court) for an important constitutional law case.[17] In support of a statute regulating hours of work, he amassed statistical information and expert testimony to persuade the court that the latest knowledge in health and social science should permit it to distinguish an earlier decision that invalidated a similar statute. Rather than argue that the Court was wrong in its first decision, a difficult thing to do successfully, Brandeis argued that it would not be inconsistent for the Court to recognize the new information and distinguish the prior decision made under different circumstances (even if the effect was to overrule the earlier decision): new circumstances demanded a new interpretation of the Constitution. The Court accepted his argument and upheld the statute. This type of argument, known as a **Brandeis Brief**, includes the submission of socio-economic evidence and has become an important part of the U.S. process of constitutional argument.

Brandeis Brief
an argument based on socio-economic evidence establishing important facts that may influence a court's decision

Canadian courts also admit appropriate "Brandeis Brief" evidence, subject to precautions by verifying facts and cross-examining expert witnesses. It may be argued that the state of the economy and social conditions, as well as the results of scientific investigation, are as much "objective" evidence as is the state of the law at the time the statute is being reviewed for its validity.

CASE 1.4

In the 1949 "Margarine Reference,"[18] the Supreme Court of Canada considered expert testimony that earlier beliefs about margarine being a nutritionally inferior product and a possible health hazard were mistaken. As a result, an act of Parliament—passed under the federal power to enact criminal law—prohibiting the manufacture and sale of margarine was held to be unconstitutional; there was no longer any reasonable basis for considering trade in margarine to be criminal activity. The decision permitted the provinces to pass legislation to regulate the production and sale of margarine.

CONTEMPORARY ISSUE

The Role of Judges

Have judges become too "political"? Are they "usurping" the powers of Parliament and the provincial legislatures?

Earlier in this chapter, we discussed the role of our courts in interpreting the Constitution. In Canada since 1867, the courts have been asked to decide, for example, whether a statute enacted by Parliament encroached on powers allocated exclusively to the provinces and, if so, to strike down the offending legislation. The traditional role of the courts in a federation

continued

17. Muller v. Oregon, 208 U.S. 412 (1907).
18. Reference re Validity of Section 5(a) Dairy Industry Act, [1949] S.C.R. 1, [1949] 1 D.L.R. 433.

has been to act as umpire between the two levels of government. However, since the Charter of Rights and Freedoms became part of our Constitution in 1982, increasingly, the courts have been asked to interpret and strike down legislation of both levels as being inconsistent with rights entrenched in the Charter. Two recent cases have added to the controversy about whether our courts have become too "activist".

In *Vriend v. Alberta** in 1998, the Supreme Court of Canada went further than simply striking down a provision in a statute; it in effect ordered the legislature of Alberta to amend its human rights legislation to prohibit discrimination based on a person's sexual orientation. In 1999, our courts upheld the decision of a federal Human Rights Tribunal.* The Tribunal had ordered the federal government to pay several billion dollars in compensation to current federal employees and to former employees—almost entirely women—who were discriminated against because they were not paid fairly for work of equal value usually performed by male counterparts.

Some critics have complained that such court activism is depriving elected legislators of the power to exercise their discretion in legislation and to make policy decisions based on their value judgments and what they believe their constituents want. Others have defended the courts on the basis that our federal and provincial governments made a collective decision in 1981–82, to entrench Charter rights: ever since legislatures must abide by the consequences because the courts have no alternative but to interpret statutes in the light of the Charter. In response, the critics claim that the courts have not shown enough deference to legislatures and to their values as implemented in statutes; instead the courts are imposing their own values.

See: Roger Kerans, "Don't blame the judges." Globe and Mail, March 22, 2000; Raj Anand, "Vriend will affect Charter equality rights and remedies", Lawyers Weekly (June 1988), Vol. 18, No. 7; see also, Craig Bavis, "The latest steps on the winding path to substantive equality", (August, 1999) Alberta Law Review, Vol. 37. p. 683.

*Vriend v. Alberta, [1998] 1 S.C.R. 493.

Questions to Consider

1. When a court determines that a particular provision in a statute is contrary to the Charter of Rights and Freedoms, what alternative does it have apart from striking down the provision?

2. What option may legislatures use to overcome the power of the courts? Why do they not utilize this option frequently?

3. Assuming that a sufficient majority of provincial legislatures along with the federal Parliament could be formed to amend the constitution, what form of amendment would you suggest to limit the powers of the judges?

AS ARBITER OF DISPUTES BETWEEN PRIVATE PARTIES

In this chapter we have considered the role of our courts in arbitrating constitutional issues, in interpreting and applying statutes, and in protecting rights and freedoms. Under a legal system such as ours, derived from the English common law, legislation has historically played only a small part in resolving legal disputes between private parties—individuals, corporations, or other organized groups not connected with the government. Despite the rapid increase in statutory law in recent years, there remain extensive areas of the law unaffected by legislation. In these areas, the courts apply principles that they themselves have developed in the process of rendering decisions in the past, and in novel situations they develop new principles. These activities of the courts are important and complex. We shall discuss the evolution and continuing importance of court decisions based on principles developed by the courts themselves in the next chapter.

QUESTIONS FOR REVIEW

1. Describe the three main roles of law in our society.

2. How is the legal infrastructure of a country significant for business?

3. How do we distinguish between natural law and positive law?

4. Distinguish a normative law from other kinds of laws.

5. Explain Hume's distinction between the "is" and the "ought."

6. How would Austin's definition of law apply in federal countries?

7. Why have business enterprises adopted codes of conduct?

8. What is the special role of the courts in a federal country?

9. What are residual powers? Concurrent powers?

10. What makes a "constitutional defeat" before the courts so serious for a legislature?

11. Describe the liberal approach to interpreting legislation.

12. What is the special meaning of "civil rights" in the context of the Canadian Constitution?

13. Describe the special significance of sections 91 and 92 of the Constitution Act. What problems do these sections encompass?

14. If a citizen claims a provision in a statute to be unconstitutional as being contrary to the Canadian Charter of Rights and Freedoms, must the government then show it is constitutional? Explain.

15. Describe the tests set out in the *Oakes* case to determine whether a provision in an apparent breach of the Charter may nevertheless remain valid.

16. Which activities are governed by the Charter and which are not? Describe the distinction.

17. "We have a parliament to pass laws, a government to administer laws, and a police department to enforce laws. Ironically, these potent instruments for the restriction of liberty are necessary for the enjoyment of liberty." (A.A. Borovoy, *The Fundamentals of Our Fundamental Freedoms*, p. 5, Toronto: The Canadian Civil Liberties Education Trust, 1974.) Comment on the meaning of this quotation.

THE MACHINERY OF JUSTICE

We describe in this chapter the various ways in which law is classified. We consider the sources of law—judge-made, legislation, and administrative rulings. In this chapter we examine such questions as:

- what is the difference between substantive and procedural law? public and private law? civil and common law?

- the theory of precedent—how do we meet the need for certainty as well as for flexibility and change in the law?

- how are the systems of courts organized?

- what are the procedures for using the courts and making out-of-court settlements?

- what alternative methods of resolving disputes are available?

- what is the legal aid system?

- how is the legal profession organized and governed?

WHO MAKES LAW?

We noted in Chapter 1 that making law is the responsibility of government and not of private persons. Thus, a restaurant owner who makes a rule that men will not be admitted to dinner unless they wear neckties and jackets has not made a law. Nor are the rules of a private organization, say, a tennis club, considered law; a tennis club may impose effective sanctions such as fining or expelling a member who breaks an important club rule, but its rules amount to no more than a private arrangement among club members.

On the other hand, law made by government extends down to the local level and includes, for instance, regulations passed by the licence committee of a town council. While the committee's authority can be traced back through municipal by-laws and the town's charter to arrive ultimately at the provincial legislature, as a practical matter the licence committee itself, acting on its own initiative, creates new law. Many lesser public bodies like licence committees are constantly changing existing law and making new law—and the volume generated in this way continues to grow.

SUBSTANTIVE AND PROCEDURAL LAW

Dividing law into broad categories helps us to understand the legal system. The two most basic categories are *substantive* and *procedural* law.

substantive law
the rights and duties that each person has in society

Substantive law consists of the rights and duties that each person has in society. Some examples are the right to own property, to vote, to travel about the country unmolested, to enter into contracts, and to sell or give away property; the duty to avoid injuring others and to perform contractual obligations; and to obey traffic laws, customs regulations, and other laws. These substantive rules are further divided into the fields of *public law* and *private law*, referred to below.

procedural law
law that deals with the protection and enforcement of rights and duties

Procedural law deals with the protection and enforcement of rights and duties. While substantive rules decide which of two parties is at fault in a dispute, the innocent party must use the rules of procedure to obtain a remedy against the wrongdoer. Thus, procedural law provides the *machinery* to enforce rights and duties recognized in substantive law.

PUBLIC AND PRIVATE LAW

public law
law that regulates the conduct of government and the relations between government and private persons

Public law regulates the conduct of government and its relations with private persons (including organizations such as companies, clubs, or unions). Public law divides into several categories, such as constitutional law, criminal law, and administrative law.

private law
the rules governing relations between private persons or groups of persons

Private law comprises the rules governing relations between private persons or groups of persons. These rules provide the fabric and substance of business law. Private law divides into a number of categories, the largest of which are contracts, torts, property, and trusts. In this book we are mostly concerned with contracts since they are the focus of business transactions. We cannot consider contracts in isolation, however, and from time to time in contract problems we encounter the law of torts, property, and, to a lesser extent, trusts. Frequently the term "civil law" is used to mean "private law"; it creates unfortunate ambiguity, especially in a country like Canada, because, as we explain below, the primary meaning of civil law refers to a different legal system.

THE CIVIL LAW AND THE COMMON LAW
Regions of the World Under Each System

Two great systems of law developed in Western Europe, and they have been inherited by most parts of the world colonized by European nations.

The older of the two systems is called the civil law. It covers the whole of continental Europe and to a large extent Scotland, much of Africa, and the whole of South and Central America. In North America it applies in Mexico and to some degree in several of the southern United States, but particularly in Louisiana, which was French territory until early in the 19th century. When the English conquered French Canada, they guaranteed the people of Québec the continued use of French civil law in most areas of private law. To this day most of the private law of the province of Québec is civil law.

The other legal system is called the **common law** and originated in feudal England at the time of the Norman Conquest. It covers the whole of the English-speaking world except Scotland, and is a significant part of the law of many non-English-speaking countries that were part of the British Empire, notably India, Pakistan, Bangladesh, and the former colonies in Africa and the Caribbean. The common law is based on the recorded reasons given by courts for their decisions and adapted by judges in later cases. We describe the common law in the following sections: "The Theory of Precedent" and "The Sources of Law."

The **civil law** has its roots in **Roman law,** in particular in Justinian's Code, drafted in the 6th century A.D., for the famous emperor of the Eastern Roman Empire. The code was inherited by the whole of continental Europe and formed the foundation for most of its legal systems. Napoléon ordered a new French version in 1804, known as the Code Napoléon; it was adopted in or greatly influenced the development of codes in Italy, Spain, Germany, Switzerland, and Belgium. The civil law theory is that a court always refers to the code to settle a dispute. If the code does not seem to cover a new problem then the court is free to reason by analogy to settle the problem from general principles in the code. In theory, a later court need not follow the earlier reasoning in a similar case; the second court may decide that in its view a just result of the law ought to be the reverse of the earlier decision.

common law
the system of law originating in England and covering most of the English-speaking world—based on the recorded reasons given by judges for their decisions

civil law
the system of law derived from Roman law that developed in continental Europe and was greatly influenced by the Code Napoléon of 1804

Roman law
the system of law codified by the Eastern Roman Emperor Justinian in the 6th century

The Need for Consistency and Predictability

Civil law theory could present practical difficulties. In any system of law if judges were continually to follow their own values and personal prejudices and so contradict earlier decisions, the law would become a jungle. No one could learn what the law on a particular point is. It is a requirement of justice, therefore, that *like cases be treated alike*.

ILLUSTRATION 2.1

A contracts to build a house for B but does not carry out the agreement. B sues A and collects money damages for the breach. X makes a similar contract with Y and fails to carry out the contract. Y sues X for damages, but the suit is dismissed by the court.

Either decision, examined entirely separately, might seem reasonable enough: some people might well believe that the builder was justified in backing out; others might favour the owner. But place the two decisions side by side, for example, in adjoining courtrooms on the same day. In these circumstances there would be two very unhappy litigants. A would complain because X in a similar situation escaped without paying any damages; Y would be angry because she obtained nothing while B got substantial damages for breach of a similar contract. A and Y would both feel unjustly treated, and most people would agree with them—the law should be either one way or the other but not consist of two contradictory rules at the same time.

Equal and consistent treatment in like situations is a central concern of justice and hence of law as well. Whether in civil law or in common law countries, judges must be interested in, and influenced by, what other judges have decided in similar cases.

A second major element of law is *predictability*. Suppose, after the contrary decisions we have just discussed, P wishes to make a similar contract with Q. Q asks a lawyer whether the contract is a binding one: if P backs out will he be liable to pay damages to Q for any loss caused by failing to carry out the bargain? Q's lawyer would have to say, "Maybe yes, maybe no; it depends on whether the court prefers the result in the case of A against B or that in X against Y." One can well imagine the state of confusion if this were the normal advice a client were to receive! If people are to be able to find out where they stand and to act with reasonable certainty, *the law itself must be fairly predictable*—another strong reason why like cases ought to be decided alike.

In order to explain how cases are linked, judges develop principles that describe their connection to one another. These principles accumulate into a body of doctrine—a framework of predictable rules that serves as background for the vast majority of legal relations.

As a result, in civil law countries, judges do decide similar cases in the same way most of the time, although they are under no binding rule to do so. Today, in such countries as France and Germany, reports of decisions are regularly published so that lawyers and judges can learn what the courts are deciding and how they are interpreting the Civil Code in modern disputes.

THE THEORY OF PRECEDENT

Certainty Versus Flexibility

stare decisis
to stand by a previous decision

Consistency and predictability became primary goals of the common law judges in England as early as the 13th century. They adopted the custom of following already-decided cases, which is called the theory of precedent. The Latin phrase for the rule is ***stare decisis***—to stand by previous decisions. However, the judges followed previous decisions quite slavishly, even when in changed circumstances the results were nonsensical or manifestly unjust. Such a practice, while it has the merits of certainty and uniformity, can become inflexible and stultifying.

Stare decisis has never been an ironclad rule. Since words are relatively inaccurate vehicles for thought, their vagueness permits judges to draw distinctions between similar problems and so refuse to follow obsolete precedents. In addition, no two sets of facts are identical in every respect—even when the same parties are involved, the time must be different. Judges, when they feel it to be truly necessary, can distinguish the case before them from an earlier precedent by dwelling upon minor differences. In this way they are able to adjust the law rather slowly to changing circumstances and values. Nevertheless, the spirit of the common law system is bound to the theory of precedent: we look to past decisions to glean principles and to apply them to new situations. Accordingly, a large part of the study of law is the study of decided cases.

Despite some flexibility, the theory of precedent hinders the law in accommodating the rapidly increasing rate of change in society. A decision that seemed quite acceptable in, say, 1968, may be entirely out of step with current social standards. A court may only be able to cope with a marked change by directly overruling a prior decision.

Accommodating Change

The danger in overruling decided cases too freely is that doing so would undermine the needed consistency and predictability in law. The approach to this problem has been different in the United States, Britain, and Canada. The Supreme Court of the United States has never considered itself bound to follow its own previous decisions when the result would be manifestly unjust. The House of Lords (the English equivalent of the Supreme Court) reversed its traditional position in 1966 when it announced that it would no longer consider itself bound to follow its own decisions—recognition of the need to depart from older decisions when contemporary standards call for change. The Canadian Supreme Court has not committed itself on this subject, but it seems highly likely that, following the example of the much respected courts of the United States and Britain, it too will accept this needed flexibility.[1]

An understanding of these significant limitations on *stare decisis* is important in proposing answers to the legal problems offered for discussion at the end of Chapters 3 to 34. It is a mistake to assume, when one finds an actual reported case with facts seemingly identical to those in a case under discussion, that the conclusion in a reported case is the most satisfactory one. It

---

1. See statement by Cartwright, J. in R. v. Binus, [1968] 1 C.C.C. 227 at 229: "I do not doubt the power of the court to depart from a previous judgment of its own...." It should be noted, however, that the court did not overrule itself in this case.

is much more useful to consider the case offered for discussion on its legal and social merits and then look at a reported case to see what light it may shed on the problem. Some reported cases have been severely criticized both by learned writers and by other courts in subsequent cases.

Although both civil and common law reach the same conclusions in most areas of the law, there are some important differences. This book deals only with principles of the common law. Much of what is written here does not necessarily apply to the civil law of Québec.

THE SOURCES OF LAW

The Variety of Sources

The earliest source of our law is the body of decisions handed down by the judiciary and permanently recorded in England from Norman times to the present day. A second source consists of the statutes passed by Parliament and by provincial legislatures. The cabinet, in its formal role of adviser to the monarch, can also "legislate" within certain limited areas by issuing orders-in-council.[2] Every province has also passed statutes providing for the creation of municipal governments and their supervision. These statutes give municipalities the power to make law and to raise revenue for the benefit of their citizens. Municipal by-laws and regulations are thus a form of statute law. In addition to judge-made law and statute law, there is a vast area of **subordinate legislation** usually known as administrative law: statutes grant authority to various administrative agencies of government to make rules and regulations in order to carry out the purposes set out in the legislation.

> **subordinate legislation**
> law created by administrative agencies whose authority is granted by statute in order to carry out the purposes of the legislation

Law Made by Judges

The Common Law[3]

Since the common law is based on the theory of precedent, it depends on a flow of reported cases from an organized national system of courts: cases need to be decided by courts with a recognized position within the system in order for their decisions to influence judges in subsequent cases. After the Norman Conquest, William I gave England its first strong, centralized government and thus laid the foundation for a national system of courts.

The earliest decisions were, of course, without the benefit of precedent. Courts were often left entirely to their own resources in reaching a decision. It is not always easy to understand their reasoning, but established local customs clearly played an important role at the outset. Evidence concerning a local custom would be admitted, influence the judge's decision, and then be incorporated in the common law. As the body of precedents increased and as the courts developed into a settled order of importance, prior decisions exerted an ever-increasing influence.

Other Sources of Common Law

Canon law and Roman law also influenced early judicial decisions in England. The Church created canon law when it had its own courts and legal jurisdiction in matters pertaining to itself, to family law, and to wills. The Roman law was important in distinguishing between possession and ownership of personal property. These influences were very strong at a time when practically the only literate people were clerics, and scholars trained on the Continent. In addition, feudal law concerning the ownership of land became part of the common law.

> **canon law**
> law created by the Church, which had its own jurisdiction and courts in matters pertaining to itself, family law, and wills

---

2. An order-in-council is issued by the Privy Council (in effect, the cabinet) in the name of the monarch, either in exercise of the royal prerogative or under authority of a statute.

3. Unfortunately, the term "common law" has three possible meanings: (a) common law as opposed to equity; (b) judge-made law (including equity) as opposed to statute law; and (c) all the law of a common law country as opposed to a civil law country.

Law Merchant
rules and trade practices developed by merchants in medieval trade guilds and administered by their own courts

In the Middle Ages, trade was carried on almost exclusively by merchants who were members of guilds; they used their guilds to resolve disputes among themselves. The rules and acceptable trade practices developed into a body of business customs known as the **Law Merchant**, administered speedily through their own courts. Only guild members came within the jurisdiction of these courts. The Law Merchant was developed and shared by all the trading nations of the medieval world.

The monopoly over trade held by merchant guilds eventually broke down, and persons who were not members increasingly entered commerce. As the ordinary courts of the land were called upon to adjudicate in disputes between non-guild members, they borrowed from the established rules of the Law Merchant. Our present law of negotiable instruments, for example, originated as a part of the Law Merchant.

Equity

writ
an ancient form required in order to take a grievance to court

As the body of reported decisions grew, the common law rules became more precise and increasingly strict. By the late 13th century they had become very formal, with much of their cumbersome procedure rooted in ancient customs and superstitions. An aggrieved party had to find one of the ancient forms, called a **writ**, to suit his particular grievance. If he could not find an appropriate writ, the court would not grant a remedy. As England developed commercially, the old writs did not provide relief for many wrongs suffered by innocent parties, often resulting in great hardship. Aggrieved parties without a remedy began to petition the king, who, in the age of the divine right of the monarchy, looked upon himself as the fountainhead of all law and justice. The king considered the hearing of petitions an important duty to his subjects and often granted relief.

courts of chancery
a system of courts under the king's chancellor and vice-chancellors developed from the hearing of petitions to the king—courts of equity

equity
rules of law developed by the courts of equity

As the number of petitions increased, the king's chancellor (his chief personal adviser, usually a cleric) took over the task of administering them. The flow continued to increase and the chancellor delegated the work to vice-chancellors. Soon another whole system of courts was growing: the courts of the chancellor, or the **courts of chancery** as they became known. These courts were also known as *courts of equity*, and the rules that they developed are called the *principles of equity* or, simply, **equity**. Equity rivals the common law in its contribution to the legal system developed by our judges.

The courts of common law were very narrow in the kinds of remedies they offered; they would award only money damages to a party injured by a breach of contract. Yet sometimes money alone was not adequate compensation.

ILLUSTRATION 2.2

B owned two separate lots of land and agreed to buy the middle lot between them from *S* in order to erect a large building on the three pieces once they were joined. *S* changed his mind and refused to convey the middle lot. If *B* sued for breach of contract in a common law court, he would be awarded only money damages, an inadequate remedy since his project would be frustrated.

specific performance
an order by a court of equity to carry out a binding obligation

contempt of court
a finding by a court that a party has refused to obey it and will be punished

By contrast, the courts of equity were prepared, if they thought fit, to decree **specific performance**, that is, to order the defendant to convey the land. If the defendant refused, he would be jailed for **contempt of court** until he relented and carried out the order. The threat of a medieval jail was highly persuasive!

The approach of the chancery courts was different from that of the common law courts, since the medieval chancellor was a cleric. "Equity was a gloss on common law; it was a set of rules which could be invoked to supplement the deficiencies of common law or to ease the clumsy working of common law actions and remedies."[4] Remedies in equity were discretionary:

---

4. Jackson, *The Machinery of Justice in England* (8th ed.), J.R. Spencer, ed., p. 7. Cambridge: The University Press, 1989.

the relative innocence of the petitioner and the hardship suffered determined whether the individual could hope for equity's special type of intervention. As equity developed, however, the principles upon which relief was given became almost as fixed as the rules of common law.

Merger of the Courts

For centuries, England had two rival sets of courts, but in practice a division of labour developed between them since the advantages of equity were sought in cases where the common law remedies were inadequate. Equity dealt mainly with claims arising out of the administration of estates, the execution of trusts, and the foreclosure of mortgages, and in contracts it dealt with claims for specific performance, *injunction*, and the *rectification* and *rescission* of contracts. We shall examine the contracts remedies in Chapter 15.

In 1865 the British Parliament passed an act merging the two systems of courts into the single system we know today. The Canadian provinces passed similar acts shortly afterwards. For convenience, the division of labour has been preserved in England by having two divisions within the High Court of Justice: a Chancery Division and a Queen's Bench Division.

The amalgamation of the courts of common law and equity did not mean the abandonment of the philosophy of equity. Every judge now is supposed to have two minds, one for equity and one for legal precedent. A judge may exercise the prerogative to apply an "equitable maxim" when it appears warranted in the circumstances. Equity thus provides a conscience for our modern common law; it prevents the law when applied to particular instances from straying too far from reason and fairness.

Statutes

The second main source of our law, statute law, consists of acts of Parliament and of the provincial legislatures and of by-laws passed by municipal governments. A statute overrides all the common law dealing with the same point. Although the volume of statute law continues to grow, the common law still constitutes the bulk of our private law and, in particular, of the law of contracts.

Sometimes legislatures enact statutes to **codify** existing common law in an area rather than to change it, as, for example, in the passing of the Bills of Exchange Act, the Sale of Goods Act, and the Partnership Act. Prior to passing these acts, the related law was to be found in a staggering number of individual cases. The acts did away with the labour and uncertainty of searching through so many cases.

codify
set down and summarize in a statute the common law rules governing a particular area of activity

Courts are often called on to interpret a statute in order to decide whether it applies to the facts of a case, and if it does, to decide also on its consequences. Their decisions then form part of judge-made law and are often referred to in subsequent cases. Judge-made law and statutes are thus closely related. The traditional attitude of the courts towards the common law is quite different from their attitude towards statutes. While the common law is the creation of the courts themselves, statute law, as one writer put it, is "an alien intruder in the house of common law." In deciding a case at common law the courts regularly use principles from earlier decisions, even though the facts may be quite different. On the other hand, the courts are much less likely to apply the provisions of a statute unless the facts of the case are covered specifically by the statute. This attitude of the courts is called the **strict interpretation** of statutes.

strict interpretation
courts apply the provisions of a statute only where the facts of the case are covered specifically by the statute

As we have seen in Chapter 1, the approach of the courts to the interpretation of the words of statutes—such issues as literal versus liberal approach and legislative history—add to the complexity of interpretation.

Administrative Law

Legislation Framework

There are two main classes of legislation. The first and simplest consists of those statutes that change the law: they prohibit an activity formerly permitted or else remove a prohibition, thereby enabling people to carry on a formerly illegal activity. This type of legislation is essentially passive: it provides a framework within which people may legally go about their business; it does not presume to supervise and regulate their activities, but leaves it to an injured party or a law-enforcement official to complain about any activity that has violated a statute of this kind and to initiate court proceedings.

"Active" Government Programs

The second class of legislation authorizes the government itself to carry on a program; to levy taxes and provide revenue for the purpose stated in the statute, such as building a hospital, paying pensions to the elderly, and offering subsidies to encourage a particular kind of economic activity; and to supervise and regulate the related trade or activity. Parliament itself is an inappropriate body to undertake any program requiring continual supervision. Its members from ridings across the country have diverse talents and interests and their primary responsibility is to enact legislation.

From early times in England, Parliament passed legislation to authorize the monarch to levy taxes, pay and equip the armed forces, and construct public works. Projects *authorized* by Parliament were *executed* by the monarch and his officials—hence the term "executive" to describe the agencies of government that carry out Parliament's will. Translated into modern terms, this process means that every government department, agency, and tribunal is established by the legislature in a statute. For example, the Canadian Radio-Television and Telecommunications Commission was established under the Broadcasting Act, which sets out the Commission's purposes and grants it regulatory powers to carry them out.[5]

Subordinate Legislation

In exercising its regulatory powers and acting in its executive capacity, an administrative agency creates new law, which we described earlier as "subordinate legislation." Some subordinate legislation sets down broad criteria, such as regulating the type of guarantee that a licence applicant must supply to carry on a particular activity, and the amount and type of investment required as a precondition. Other subordinate legislation may be detailed and technical (fees for applications, location of transmitters).

Important regulations, normally those setting out broad standards, require the approval of the cabinet in the form of an order-in-council. The agency itself drafts these regulations and the minister responsible for the agency brings them before the cabinet. Lesser regulations may be authorized by the minister, the head of the agency, or even a designated officer of the agency.

As we noted in Chapter 1, the growing complexity of society and government has increased the need for specialized knowledge and control in such areas as environmental protection, energy, transportation, communications, education, and welfare; and the list includes a growing number of business and professional activities that are believed to affect the public interest. Although administrative law is not the main concern in this book, we shall discuss it with respect to labour relations, consumer protection, and the financing and operation of corporations, areas in which government agencies and their regulations play important roles.

THE SYSTEM OF COURTS IN ENGLAND

We have seen that the substance of the law is created by various institutions: the judiciary, legislature, and administrative agencies. A major part of business law continues to be formulated by the judiciary. Accordingly, we should be familiar with the system of courts and their rules of procedure.

---

5. Broadcasting Act, R.S.C. 1985, c. B-9, s. 5.

Two reasons make it useful to begin by studying the English courts. First, much of our own law is derived from English case law, and these cases will be easier to understand if we are familiar with the structure of the courts that decided them. Second, the English system affords a good starting place because England has a single government, and its system of courts is easier to grasp than the more complicated federal structure existing in Canada. The role of the three levels—courts of first instance, appeal courts, final court of appeal—is much the same in England as in Canada.

The Courts of First Instance

Courts of first instance are also sometimes called courts of original jurisdiction because it is in them that actions originate and trials take place. England has many different kinds of courts of original jurisdiction, each having certain types of grievances to decide. Their names differ from those of their Canadian counterparts, and to avoid confusion we shall not list them here, noting only their place in the English system of courts.

The Court of Appeal

The Court of Appeal is the next tier; actions do not originate in this court. A party who is dissatisfied with the decision of a court of first instance may appeal to the Court of Appeal to reconsider the decision. The party who petitions for an appeal is called the **appellant**; the other party, the **respondent**. The appeal is not a trial and no witnesses are called: the court does not listen to questions of fact because they were for the trial judge to decide. The Court of Appeal proceeds on the basis of the written trial record, and lawyers for each side argue only questions of law—the appellant claiming that the trial judge erred in interpreting the law, and the respondent arguing to uphold the decision of the trial judge. The court may do one of four things:

appellant
the party who petitions for an appeal

respondent
the party who defends on an appeal

- agree with the trial judge and *dismiss* the appeal
- agree with the appellant and *reverse* the trial judgment
- *vary* the trial judgment in part
- declare that the trial judge erred in failing to consider certain facts and *send the case back* for a **new trial** in the lower court

new trial
a case sent back by the appeal court for retrial by the lower court

The Court of Appeal usually hears cases in a panel of three judges, but occasionally five judges may hear a very important case.

The House of Lords

Parties dissatisfied with a decision of the Court of Appeal have one more chance before the House of Lords, the ultimate court of appeal and the highest court in the land. It is somewhat surprising to learn that the House of Lords, more widely known as the upper house of the British Parliament, is also the final court of appeal in Britain. Originally, any member of the House of Lords (members of the peerage) could sit with the House when it was convened as a court, but since the mid-19th century only great lawyers and judges who have been elevated to the peerage actually hear and decide appeals. The court usually consists of the Lord Chancellor and up to nine Lords of Appeal in Ordinary, who are full-time salaried judges.

THE SYSTEM OF COURTS IN CANADA

We noted in Chapter 1 that the division of legislative powers between the federal and provincial governments has inevitably led to disputes about which level has jurisdiction over the many problems that overlap the categories in the Constitution. Despite the difficulties inherent in federal constitutions, the division of powers in the Canadian Constitution has not fared badly. Some aspects show great wisdom and have caused little or no trouble. Others appear rather odd at first sight, but can be explained by circumstances at the time of Confederation.

For example, the Constitution gives the provinces jurisdiction over the administration of justice—the organization and operation of police forces and the system of courts. At the same time, the Act gives the federal government jurisdiction over trade and commerce, banking, bankruptcy, and criminal law—matters frequently litigated before the courts—and also the exclusive right to appoint, and the obligation to pay, all county court and superior court judges.[6]

Why this peculiar division in the administration of the legal system? It is due, at least in part, to the fact that at the time of discussions on Confederation in Canada, the United States had just been through a terrible civil war. Many Canadians believed that biased local state legislatures and locally elected judges (sometimes without any legal training) had fanned internal division in the United States by passing discriminatory laws and often by administering laws unfairly against "outsiders" (citizens of other states). The Canadian Constitution sought to avoid the problem of local bias by placing jurisdiction over matters peculiarly susceptible to local influence in the hands of the national government. Our Constitution also requires that only qualified lawyers be appointed to the county and superior court benches. Until retirement, they hold office conditional on good behaviour, and superior court judges can be removed only by "joint address," that is, a vote taken before both the House of Commons and the Senate. These provisions are designed to keep judges as unbiased and immune from local pressures as possible.

There are three tiers of courts: the courts of first instance, the intermediate provincial courts of appeal, and the Supreme Court of Canada. In the late 1980s and the 1990s, the court systems in all provinces went through a reorganization that merged a number of the courts and simplified the court structure. The names and jurisdictions of the courts differ somewhat from province to province, but in general they follow the pattern set out below.

THE PROVINCIAL COURTS

The Courts of First Instance

INFERIOR TRIAL COURTS

Small Claims Court

The court handles disputes for smaller amounts of money. The maximum amounts have been increased in recent years in most provinces and vary considerably from one province to another. Its procedure is quite simple and informal, so that the cost of taking action is small.

Provincial Division

The court decides very little, if any, private law. It hears criminal cases of almost every type except for the most serious offences such as murder, treason, sedition, piracy, sexual assault, and manslaughter. It may hold preliminary hearings in prosecution of these crimes to decide whether there is enough evidence to proceed to trial. No jury trials are held

continued

---

6. The Constitution Act, 1867, ss. 96 and 100. As we note below, in all provinces, these courts have been merged.

before Provincial Division judges. If an accused person elects (as one may) to have a jury trial, the case must be heard in another court.

A division of the court also hears questions of domestic relations but not divorce.

Youth Court

Children and adolescents who the government feels are too young to be dealt with in the ordinary criminal courts and require special care are brought before youth court judges. The organization of youth courts varies from province to province. In some provinces they operate as separate courts. In others, the family division acts as a youth court. Nova Scotia and Ontario have adopted a "two tier" model: 12- to 15-year-olds are dealt with in the family division, while 16- and 17-year-olds are dealt with in the regular adult division although they are subject to punishment as young offenders.

SUPERIOR TRIAL COURTS

Surrogate Court (or Probate Court)

This court supervises the estates of deceased persons. It appoints an administrator to wind up the affairs of anyone who dies *intestate* (without leaving a will), settles disputes over the validity of wills and the division of assets, and approves the accounts of executors and administrators. Four provinces maintain separate probate courts,[7] while the remaining five common law provinces have merged them into the superior court system but with separate divisions.

General Division

The former District and County Courts have been merged in all provinces with the former higher level court, variously known as the High Court of Justice, Court of Queen's Bench, the Superior Court, the Supreme Court, and the Supreme Court Trial Division. It has unlimited jurisdiction in civil and criminal actions. The Court may also serve as a court of appeal from summary convictions made by magistrates or provincial judges for lesser offences.

Divisional Court

The Divisional Court, created in 1972, is peculiar to Ontario. It consists of the Chief Justice of the High Court and such other judges of that court as the Chief Justice designates from time to time. It sits in panels of three judges, more or less continually in Toronto, and at various times throughout the year in several other centres. It hears appeals from various lower provincial courts and from various provincial administrative tribunals.

Intermediate Appellate Court

The Court of Appeal

Each province has one intermediate appellate court, called variously the Appellate Division, the Supreme Court *en banc* (the whole bench), and Queen's Bench Appeals, as well as the Court of Appeal. It performs the same function as the Court of Appeal in England.

continued

---

7. Alberta, New Brunswick, Nova Scotia, and Saskatchewan.

THE FEDERAL COURTS

The Tax Court of Canada

The Tax Court hears appeals of taxpayers against assessments by Revenue Canada. The Court hears only tax appeals and functions with relatively simple procedures. Either the taxpayer or the department may appeal its decisions to the Federal Court of Appeal.

The Federal Court of Canada

The federal government maintains the Federal Court of Canada in two divisions, a Trial Division and an Appeal Division. The Federal Court has exclusive jurisdiction over such matters as patents, copyright and trademarks, disputes concerning ships and navigation, and many sorts of lawsuits against the federal government itself. There remains a large area of concurrent jurisdiction where a plaintiff may sue in either a provincial or the Federal Court. For example, a person injured by the careless operation of a government motor vehicle may sue in a provincial court.

The Supreme Court of Canada

The Supreme Court is the final court of appeal in Canada, the equivalent of the House of Lords in England. It consists of nine judges and hears appeals from both the provincial courts of appeal and the Federal Court of Canada. In addition, it has special jurisdiction under the Supreme Court Act[8] to rule on the constitutionality of federal and provincial statutes when they are referred to the court by the federal cabinet. In private actions the appellant must obtain special leave from the Supreme Court to appeal.[9]

THE SYSTEM OF COURTS IN THE UNITED STATES

Both Canada and the United States have federal systems, but there are major differences between their constitutions. In the United States, the individual states—at least theoretically—have more autonomy, and have the residual power that in Canada rests with the federal government. Although under the Constitution the Canadian government has the power to create a full system of three-tier federal courts throughout Canada, it has felt content to allow the provincial courts to decide cases of first instance (with the exception of the fields reserved exclusively to the Federal and Tax Courts).

On the other hand, the United States has set up a full system of federal courts—including a court of final appeal, the U.S. Supreme Court—that handles a large portion of litigation, although much less than the total handled by the state courts. Criminal law, for example, is a state matter, except in cases involving specific fields of federal jurisdiction, such as national defence, or in cases where an offence is committed in more than one state, such as moving stolen goods across state boundaries. The federal courts have jurisdiction in the following areas: bankruptcy; postal matters; federal banking laws; disputes concerning maritime contracts or wrongs; prosecution of crimes punishable under federal laws of the United States or committed at sea; actions requiring an interpretation of the U.S. Constitution, federal statutes, and treaties; and disputes between citizens of different states.

---

8. R.S.C. 1985, c. S-26, s. 53.

9. *Ibid.*, s. 40.

Most states have a three-tier system of courts, with a final state appellate court; however, some appeals are accepted by the U.S. Supreme Court when the appellant can convince the Supreme Court that a "substantial constitutional issue" is involved.

USING THE COURTS
Who May Sue?

Not everyone has the capacity to start an action. An adult citizen of Canada has the broadest capacity—virtually unlimited access to the courts for any type of action. Generally speaking, non-Canadians may also sue as freely as citizens. But during hostilities any person found to be an enemy alien loses the right to sue. A child is not permitted to bring an action alone but must be represented by an adult person. If a child begins an action, not knowing that an adult representative is required and the error is discovered, the court will "stay" proceedings until a parent or guardian or a "next friend" is appointed. Children are presumed not to have the sound judgment needed to undertake the risks of court proceedings; they must rely on an adult person to act on their behalf. Similarly, an insane person cannot sue without a court-appointed representative.

Generally speaking, corporations (bodies incorporated by conforming to procedures under a statute) may sue and be sued, although foreign corporations may be subject to strict regulation and required to obtain a provincial licence before bringing an action.

In each of the instances referred to above, action is brought by a "person," either for that person's own benefit or for the benefit of another person. For this purpose, a corporation is considered to be a legal "person" or "entity." An incorporated body is referred to as "it" rather than "they"; in other words, it is not thought of as a collectivity but as a single unit. Greater difficulties arise when an action is brought by or against an **unincorporated collectivity**, a group of persons such as a social club, a church, a political party, and perhaps most important, a trade union. In most cases, unincorporated groups are not recognized by the courts and may not sue or be sued. The position of trade unions varies: in some jurisdictions, it is possible to sue and be sued by a trade union, while in others it is not.

unincorporated collectivity
a group of persons that in most cases is not recognized by the courts and that may not sue or be sued

Standing to Sue

Suppose a careless landowner pollutes a stream that runs through a municipal park. If the municipality is reluctant to sue the owner, may an individual resident of the city sue on behalf of herself and all other residents for injury to the park? Suppose a board of censors bans a controversial film. May a resident of the province sue on behalf of himself and other residents who are denied the opportunity to view the film? Do individuals in these circumstances acquire "standing" before the court, and can they establish a right to be vindicated? Generally speaking, courts have been reluctant to permit actions by individuals when their rights are no greater than those of the rest of the public. The courts foresee a risk that especially litigious and cantankerous members of the public may choose to litigate many matters in which they have no direct interest. An ordinary citizen may be a member of several organizations including a trade union, hold shares in a company, vote as a taxpayer in a community, own land adjacent to public waterways, and be a user of a park and a movie fan. One can imagine many other roles in which an individual might be considered a member of a large group. The judiciary has worried that the courts could become clogged by such actions.

On the other hand, with growing awareness of damage to our environment through pollution and failure to practise conservation, with the growing complexity of pharmaceutical products, prepared foods, and mechanical devices sold to the public, the risk of serious injury to large groups of persons has grown. Effective means must be available to the public to protect itself from careless and unscrupulous enterprises, especially if it appears that no governmental body is taking adequate steps to protect the public interest.

Some decisions of the Supreme Court of Canada have recognized the right of a taxpayer to sue when he believes public revenues are being improperly expended, and the right of a movie viewer to bring an action when he believes his right to see a film has been taken away by a provincial censorship body.[10] This area is in a state of flux, and it is likely to be many years before satisfactory rules have been worked out by the legislatures and the courts to achieve a balance between protecting the public interest and minimizing abuse of the judicial process.

Star

Class Actions[11]

Suppose the owner of a car wishes to sue the manufacturer to recover loss caused by a serious defect in the car, and the defect is known to exist in several thousand other cars of the same model. May the owner, indeed ought he to, sue not only on his own behalf, but as representative of a class—that is, on behalf of all the other owners—or must each owner bring his own lawsuit? If he fails in his action, will all other owners necessarily fail, or vice-versa? Courts are reluctant to take away an individual's right to litigate his own claim. On the other hand, it would be unfortunate to clog the courts with hundreds, perhaps thousands, of repetitive claims in which all the salient facts and applicable laws had already been clearly established.

Again, there are no clear rules in this area. A court may first hear argument about whether an individual should represent a group in a **class action** and thus dispose of the matter for all members of the class at once. If the court so decides, then on handing down a judgment it makes the matter *res judicata* and the case cannot be brought before the court again to contest legal liability. In our example of the defective car, if liability has already been established, other owners might then come forward to have the court assess the amount of damage when the parties could not themselves settle on an amount.[12]

Three provinces, Québec with its civil law system, British Columbia, and Ontario, have passed legislation to make it easier to bring class actions.[13] The B.C. and Ontario acts permit either a plaintiff or a defendant to apply to a court to have himself and others in his group declared to be a "class." If the court agrees, it appoints a representative for the class. The acts set out the criteria the court must use in making its decision and create special rules for admitting evidence and awarding damages. There appears to be wide agreement that the legislation is a major improvement, but it will take some time to see the results.

Procedural Law

Most business people will gratefully concede that the intricacies of procedure are properly the responsibility of lawyers. Nevertheless, an overall understanding of what the various steps in legal procedure aim to accomplish should help business administrators to work more effectively with their legal advisers. Moreover, business law students may be needlessly distracted in their study of cases by the occasional reference to procedure if they do not have a general idea of its function.

Rules of procedure remain an important part of the law because a well-defined procedure is necessary to permit the courts to work efficiently. Procedure has now been simplified and the number of steps in legal proceedings greatly reduced. Special procedures are still used to inter-

class action

an action in which an individual represents a group and the judgment decides the matter for all members of the class at once

res judicata

a case that has already been decided by a court and cannot be brought before a court again

---

10. Nova Scotia Board of Censors v. MacNeil (1975), 55 D.L.R. (3d) 632; Minister of Justice of Canada v. Borowski (1981), 130 D.L.R. (3d) 588; Finlay v. Minister of Finance, [1986] 2 S.C.R. 607; Canadian Council of Churches v. Canada, [1992] 1 S.C.R. 236.

11. Branch, W.K. *Class Actions in Canada*, Vancouver: Western Legal Publications, 1996.

12. The difficulties in maintaining a class action in such circumstances are well illustrated by the decision of the Supreme Court of Canada in Naken v. General Motors of Canada Ltd. (1983), 144 D.L.R. (3d) 385. For comment, see Fox, (1984), 6 S.C.L.R. 335.

13. Class Proceedings Act, R.S.B.C. 1996, c. 50; S.O. 1992, c. 6.

pret wills, contracts, and other documents and to bring certain proceedings under statutes. Generally, however, the great bulk of litigation proceeds through the courts in one form, called an action, and in those provinces that follow the English procedure most closely an action is begun by issuing and serving a writ or a statement of claim.[14]

Settlement Out of Court

Advantages

Disagreements, injuries to persons and property, and breaches of a host of laws, all giving rise to legal claims, take place daily in vast numbers, but aggrieved parties litigate only a small proportion of these causes of action. Even when parties start court proceedings the disputes rarely go to trial. (In the City of London, England, fewer than 1 percent of legal proceedings continue to trial.) Do all the remaining aggrieved persons simply abandon their rights? On the contrary, the great majority of serious grievances are resolved by **settlement**.

Settlement is an out-of-court procedure by which one of the parties agrees to pay a sum of money or do certain things in return for a waiver by the other party of all rights arising from the grievance. This process has always been important as it is speedy and definite and avoids the expense of litigation. A party to a settlement also avoids the risk that the court will find against him. Since there are two sides to a story, and since the issues are rarely black and white, there is always some uncertainty in predicting which side the court will favour. Of course, the stronger one party's claim appears to be, the more advantageous a settlement it will demand and usually obtain. Often a person starts legal proceedings to convince her adversary that she will not put up with delays or an inadequate settlement. As a result, many actions are settled soon after they are started.

Why then are the courts and the relatively small body of decisions resulting from an enormous number of disputes so important? There are two main reasons: first, the decided cases supply the principles by which aggrieved parties may gauge the relative merit of their claims, predict the outcome of a possible court action, and strike a value for their claims; second, the court is the last resort, the decisive tribunal when all compromise fails. It settles the issue when the parties themselves cannot.

settlement
an out-of-court procedure by which one of the parties agrees to pay a sum of money or perform an act in return for a waiver by the other party of all rights arising from the grievance

Growing Delay in the Court System

Despite the obvious advantages of settling disputes out of court, the number of cases going to trial has increased steadily over the years, indeed much faster than the growth in population. There are a number of reasons suggested for more frequent resort to the courts, such factors as the higher general level of education and the greater awareness of one's rights, especially since the Charter of Rights and Freedoms became part of our Constitution, the increased complexity of society and of the legal system generally, and the need for many new regulatory schemes. The large increase in the number of cases has led to a backlog causing very long delays in actually getting most cases heard. In the 1950s, cases were generally heard within a few months; rarely did a year pass without a case going to trial. In contrast, currently delays of several years have become the norm. Even trials for relatively small claims that take little time to be heard often wait many months—sometimes more than a year—to be heard.

Delay often creates hardship: a plaintiff who has suffered serious injury may wait many years to be compensated; it may become much more difficult for witnesses to recall evidence; indeed sometimes one of the parties may die before the case is heard. As a result, new rules have been enacted to encourage settlement.[15] The rules penalize parties who do not accept a reasonable

14. Several provinces have now simplified the process by abolishing the writ as a means of starting an action. The process now begins with issue of a statement of claim.
15. Rule 57 (18), B.C. Rules of the Supreme Court; Rule 49, Rules of Civil Procedure, Ont.; Rule 49, Rules of Court, N.S.

offer of settlement. Thus, if a party rejects a reasonable offer to settle from the other party and the court's subsequent judgment shows that the offer was a good one—it orders substantially the same remedy as the offer made—the first party will be ordered to pay the "costs" (as discussed under that heading later in this chapter) incurred by the other party.

Parties have themselves become increasingly aware of the advantages of avoiding court battles and, since the 1970s, often choose to utilize "alternative dispute resolution," discussed under that heading later in this chapter.

Procedure Before Trial

A trial does not follow automatically from a decision to start an action. After a plaintiff decides to sue and has a writ or statement of claim issued by the court, the document is then served on the defendant. In this way, the defendant learns by whom and for what he is being sued, so that he can prepare to defend himself; the plaintiff cannot proceed until the notice has been served. It is axiomatic that as soon as one is served with a writ or statement of claim one should immediately consult a lawyer. It is a long-standing aphorism that "he who acts on his own behalf has a fool for a client." Lawyers have learned that people are so mesmerized by their own cause that they cannot properly evaluate their claims; in personal matters, one lawyer almost always has another lawyer act as representative.

Once a plaintiff has formally commenced an action and served the required documents on the defendant, why should they not go to trial immediately? For one thing, court trials are expensive; the time of the plaintiff and defendant, their **counsel** (lawyers), the judge, and other officers of the court is valuable. It would be wasteful to use time in court to do things that can be done more quickly and cheaply out of court. It is worth some preliminary effort to discover exactly what the disagreement is about; otherwise the parties waste time arguing about some things on which they agree. The procedure followed after an action is started attempts to narrow the trial precisely to those matters on which the parties are at odds. The necessary steps are as follows:

counsel
lawyer

(a) If the action was started by a writ, the defendant gives notice both to the clerk of the court and to the plaintiff that he intends to contest the action by **entering (filing) an appearance**. The plaintiff then delivers a statement of claim. (In the current Ontario procedure an action begins with a statement of claim, thus eliminating the need for the first two documents, a writ and an appearance.) In the statement of claim, the plaintiff sets out in detail the facts that she alleges have given rise to her cause of action, and the damages suffered by her. The defendant replies with a **statement of defence**, admitting those facts not in dispute in the statement of claim and denying all others, and in addition setting out any other facts that the defendant intends to prove in court in support of his defence. The plaintiff may then deliver a reply countering the added facts alleged by the defendant and adding any further facts believed necessary to cope with the defence. Often the defendant may have a claim of his own arising from the same facts. He will then **counterclaim** as well as defend. In turn the plaintiff will defend the counterclaim. Both claims will then be tried together.

entering (filing) an appearance
filing notice of an intention to contest an action

statement of defence
a reply to a statement of claim, admitting facts not in dispute, denying other facts, and setting out facts in support of the defence

counterclaim
a claim by the defendant arising from the same facts as the original action by the plaintiff to be tried along with that action

pleadings
documents filed by each party to an action providing information it intends to prove in court

(b) The documents are assembled to form the main body of **pleadings**. Their purpose is to make clear exactly what each party intends to prove in court so that an adequate counterattack can be prepared if available. The Hollywood element of surprise is contrary to the principle of law that each side should have sufficient notice to put its view of the facts before the court. If a party attempts to introduce surprise evidence, the court may refuse to hear it; or if it admits the evidence, it will usually delay proceedings to give the other side an opportunity to reply and will also penalize the party with loss of costs. Pleadings often reveal an aspect of the claim of which the other side was unaware. For example, the plaintiff may claim to have an important receipt book in her possession. The rules of procedure compel the plaintiff upon demand to surrender it to the defendant for inspection. In some circumstances a party may demand further particulars of a claim so that it can be evaluated more clearly.

(c) Some provinces provide for various forms of **examination for discovery**, processes allowing either party to examine the other in order to narrow the issues further and to decide whether to proceed with a trial.

examination for discovery
processes allowing either party to examine the other in order to narrow the issues

Once both sides have satisfied themselves that the action should go to trial, they ask court officials to place the case on the "docket" for the next sitting of the court.

The Trial

The trial is the culmination of the action. Parties bring their evidence of all facts in dispute before the court. In non-criminal actions the burden is on the plaintiff to prove her case. This she must do by bringing all the evidence of favourable facts before the court. Then she must be prepared to argue that these facts, once established, prove her claim in law. (Of course, counsel for the plaintiff must decide beforehand what facts she must prove in support of the claim.) The defendant, on the other hand, must attempt to establish his own version of the facts or at least to minimize the value of the evidence submitted by the plaintiff. The gap between the versions of the two parties is often astonishing. Sometimes the defendant will argue that even if the facts are as the plaintiff claims, they do not support her claim in law. For example, suppose the defendant had swerved his car off the road at night because of oncoming lights; he might argue that although his conduct was as the plaintiff claimed, it did not constitute negligence but on the contrary had been quite reasonable under the circumstances.

Evidence is brought before the court by the examination of witnesses. Counsel for the plaintiff calls as witnesses those persons whose testimony is favourable to her client. Counsel for the defendant may next cross-examine those witnesses to bring out any aspects of their testimony that he believes to have been neglected and that may serve his client's position. Counsel for the plaintiff may then re-examine the witnesses to clarify any points dealt with in the cross-examination. Counsel for the defendant may also call witnesses of his own.

Certain types of evidence are not **admissible** because they are prejudicial without adding anything to the facts in dispute or because they are **hearsay**; that is, they are words attributed by the witness to a person not before the court. The hearsay rule stems from a prevailing view that the credibility of oral evidence cannot be properly assessed when it is secondhand, and that one who is alleged to have made an assertion should testify in person and be subject to cross-examination and the scrutiny of the court. The rules of admissibility of evidence are intended to winnow bad evidence from good. Unfortunately, in the process they have become technical, more so in the United States than in Canada.

admissible evidence
evidence that is acceptable to the court

hearsay
words attributed by a witness to a person who is not before the court

When the court has heard all the evidence, counsel present the arguments in law favouring their respective clients. In simple cases the judge may give the decision at once or after a short recess, but in complicated and important cases the judge usually **reserves judgment** in order to have time to study his notes of the facts and legal arguments, and to compare the opinions in decided cases and textbooks. When judgment is finally handed down, it is often delivered orally in the court; important cases are invariably given in written form as well and are reprinted in the law reports.

reserve judgment
postpone giving a decision after the hearing ends

Appeals

If either or both parties wish to appeal, they must make up their minds and serve notice within a time limit, usually 30 days or less.

As we have seen, most appeals take the form of a review by an appeal court of evidence forwarded to it from the trial courts. An appeal court also reviews proceedings of the trial court when it is contended that the trial judge erred in instructing the jury or in admitting or excluding certain evidence; in these instances the appeal court may order the case sent back to a new trial, directing the judge to correct the shortcomings of the first trial.

Costs

Who Provides Funds for the Court System?

Quite apart from the time and effort of the parties who are adversaries in the court—their time away from employment and the lost energy—a lawsuit occupies the time of highly trained and expensive judges and court officials, lawyers, and their staffs.

In an important sense, the courts provide a public service, a forum for the peaceful settlement of disputes with the aid of government supervision and enforcement. Redress through the courts is an essential alternative to parties taking matters into their own hands, with the probable risks of violence. Our governments pay the expenses of sustaining the court system, including the salaries of judges, registrars, clerks, and other employees, as well as the maintenance of court buildings. Litigants pay a portion of these overhead **costs** through charges made for specific items such as issuing a writ or registering a judgment against a losing defendant in order to enforce a claim.

costs
funds paid by litigants to cover a portion of the government's expenses in maintaining the court system

Solicitor–Client Fees

Litigants themselves pay the costs of hiring their own lawyers, although, as we shall see, an important development has been the system of **legal aid**, where the government pays for many legal services provided to low-income litigants. A client pays a lawyer a **solicitor–client fee**—payment for time the lawyer spends discussing the case with the client, helping the client decide whether to pursue or defend the action, and agreeing to be retained, that is, to represent the client in negotiations to settle or in a court action. As well, there are usually various expenses associated with a court case, such as time required to prepare for trial, court charges, travel costs when the case is heard or when evidence must be obtained at another location, and the usual array of out-of-pocket costs, all of which must be paid by the litigant. These direct costs of litigation are often substantial, especially if the original hearing is followed by an appeal, and, as we shall discuss below, they play an important part in an individual's decision whether to proceed with a lawsuit.

legal aid
a system where the government pays for many legal services provided to low-income litigants

solicitor–client fee
payment for the time and expenses of a lawyer in preparing a case and representing the client in negotiations to settle or in court

Party and Party Costs

Suppose a person is sued and defends himself successfully, with the court dismissing the action brought by the plaintiff. Should he be left with all the expense of defending an action that, as it turned out, was not supported by the court?

Or suppose a party demands payment for an injury wrongfully inflicted on her, but for which the other party denies any liability; the aggrieved party then sues successfully. Should she have to bear the expense of recovering through court action a sum that the other party ought to have paid without making it necessary to go to court?

Under English and Canadian law there is a principle that at least part of the costs of litigation should be shifted to the losing side by an award known as **party and party costs**.[16] In each province there is a published scale of costs, varying with the level of court in which the case is heard, for the preparation of court documents by the lawyer and for standard payment for each

party and party costs
an award that shifts some of the costs of litigation to the losing side according to a published scale of fees

---

16. See Watson, Bogart, and others, *Civil Litigation*, (4th ed.), Chapter 4. Toronto: Emond Montgomery, 1991.

hour of preparation for presentation of a case and for each appearance or day in court. Accordingly, when a plaintiff wins a case for, say, damages in a traffic accident, the court will award "*x* dollars damages, plus costs," against the defendant; if the defendant successfully defends the action, the court will dismiss the claim "with costs," that is, party and party costs against the plaintiff. If the result of the action is a mixed one—for example, a plaintiff's claim succeeds in part and is rejected in part—the costs may be apportioned, or each party may be left to pay its own costs.

Total Costs of Litigation

A solicitor–client fee is almost always greater than an award of party and party costs. Therefore, even when a client wins a case with an award of costs in her favour, these costs will ordinarily cover only a portion of the fee charged by her lawyer; she will have to pay an amount over and above the costs recovered from the losing side. But she is considerably better off than the losing side with respect to the costs of the litigation; the loser must pay *both* party and party costs to the other side *and* a solicitor–client fee to his own lawyer, as well as, of course, the amount of the judgment.

Occasionally a client may believe that his lawyer has charged too high a fee for representing him in a court action and the two are unable to reach a satisfactory settlement of the bill. If necessary, the client can have the matter referred to an officer of the court to assess the bill, that is, to set a fair fee for the service rendered in the action.

The Economics of Litigation

In quite rare cases, where a plaintiff has proceeded with an action without any reasonable basis for the claim, a court may find that the action is "frivolous and vexatious"—undertaken primarily to harass the defendant—and order the plaintiff to pay costs greater than normal party and party costs in order to compensate the defendant for all expenses, including lawyer's fees.

The subject of costs raises the question of the economics of litigation: is it worthwhile to start an action? First, there is always a risk of losing: a plaintiff who loses is not only denied the remedy she seeks, but also must pay costs to the defendant and a fee to her own lawyer. Even if she seems certain of winning, it would generally be unwise to begin litigating a claim that would occupy the time of the courts and incur heavy expenses in retaining a lawyer in order to collect a paltry sum, or, conversely, to fight such a claim.[17]

Second, even apart from legal costs, often it may not be worth a client's time and effort to fight. For instance, a supplier of perishable goods such as potatoes might be offered payment of a reduced price by a buyer who claims that the potatoes had not arrived in as good condition as promised. The supply firm might decide that it is not worth the trouble to sue for the difference in price of, say, two-hundred dollars; nor for that matter would it wish to alienate the buyer, a good customer. It simply accepts the reduced price in full payment.

On the other hand, if the supply firm has had several similar complaints from customers and is concerned that the carrier has been careless in transporting the potatoes, it may decide to claim against the carrier. If the carrier should deny liability, the supplier would find it necessary to sue the carrier and "join" the buyer in the same suit in order to obtain a ruling from the court about the degree of care that the carrier is bound to show as well as what amounts to satisfactory condition of the potatoes on delivery. In other words, a party may have additional reasons besides the actual recovery of an award of damages for bringing an action for a relatively small sum.

---

17. For a recent discussion about the costs of litigation, see Puri, "Financing of Litigation by Third-Party Investors: A Share of Justice?" (1998), 36 *Osgoode Hall L.J.* 515 (the Introduction).

CONTEMPORARY
ISSUE

The Cost of Justice

It is easy to utter maxims such as "everyone is entitled to their day in court," but it is difficult for many people to finance such a day.

A report by a government task force chaired by Mr. Justice Robert Blair in 1995 estimated "the cost of a 'typical' three-day civil trial [in Ontario]...to be $38 200 plus disbursements to the plaintiff." In 2000 dollars, this sum would be over $40 000.

For many, the decision of whether to bring a matter before the court rests not in whether the plaintiff is morally, or even legally, right or wrong. Rather, it is whether the injury to the plaintiff was significant enough to make it financially worthwhile. Even if the plaintiff believes strongly in his cause—that he is in the right—and has experienced substantial financial loss, the plaintiff must still consider the chance of losing the court battle and having to recoup not only the cost of the injury suffered, but also the cost of a lost trial.

The report says that "the combined legal costs of the parties are on average about three quarters of the judgment obtained and, on a median basis, are perhaps more than the judgment obtained."

Some of the provinces have taken steps to reduce the cost of litigation. For example, Ontario has simplified rules of procedure for claims for $25 000 or less. British Columbia has a simplified procedure for claims under $30 000. Ontario has undertaken mandatory mediation pilot projects, until July 4, 2001, in Toronto and Ottawa-Carleton. Under these pilot projects, certain cases, including estates and trusts cases and randomly selected civil cases, must go to mediation before they can go to trial. The hope is that many cases will be settled in mediation, at less cost to the parties and to the public. The Alberta Provincial Court–Civil Division may refer parties to mediation of its own accord or at a party's request. The British Columbia Superior Court promotes the use of settlement conferences conducted by a judge or a master (a judicial officer who presides over certain types of proceeding).

Sources: "Does Justice Cost More Than It's Worth?" *Law Times*, December 11–17, 1995, pp. 1, 2; Statistics Canada consumer price index; Beth Marlin, "Legal Update: Mandatory Mediation," *Canadian Lawyer*, November/December 1998.

Questions to Consider

1. Even assuming that a trial might be shorter and cost half the amount suggested in the report, how does an individual or a small business cope with a dispute in which the loss is believed to be less than $20 000?

2. Would contingent fee arrangements help small businesses to bring disputes for relatively modest amounts of money before the courts? Are these arrangements of greatest value to plaintiffs with very large claims?

3. Is there an alternative to the "day in court"? Does alternative dispute resolution solve the problem?

Contingent Fees

Origins in the United States

In the United States, most courts do not have a general power to award costs against a losing party. A party, whether winner or loser, is required to pay only his own lawyer's fees. It has been argued that prospective litigants clog American courts with large claims even when the chances of success are poor; a plaintiff who fails does not risk having to pay the defendant's costs. At the same time, the American system of costs "fails to compensate justly the winner whose claim has been vindicated, and it discourages the litigation of small claims."[18]

Under a **contingent fee** arrangement, "the lawyer agrees to act on the basis that if the client is successful the lawyer will take as a fee a certain percentage of the proceeds of the litigation, and in the event that the client is unsuccessful the lawyer will make no charge for the services rendered."[19] From a prospective litigant's point of view—especially in a case where there may be a fairly poor chance of winning but if an award is made it will likely be for a large sum—a contingent fee arrangement may be the only practical way of bringing an action. A lawyer may take several cases and will be content to win one; the single contingent fee will cover his expenses in all the cases and leave him with substantial compensation for his work.

contingent fee

a fee paid for a lawyer's services only if the client is successful—there is no charge if the client is unsuccessful

ILLUSTRATION 2.3

A is injured very seriously while skiing on an open slope. She complains that the accident was caused by an unmarked obstacle. Very likely, a court would find either that she accepted the risks voluntarily, or that she was author of her own misfortune through personal carelessness. Even so, if *A* is in a jurisdiction where a contingent fee agreement was available to her, she might well find it practical to bring an action on the small chance that the court would find the resort owner liable for the injury. She would probably not be able to afford the expense of litigation under the traditional Anglo-Canadian scheme for charging fees.

The Use of Contingent Fees in Canada

There are concerns that contingent fee arrangements

- encourage unnecessary and even frivolous litigation
- expose defendants to the costs of defending themselves against claims that have no merit
- encourage some clients to agree to unconscionably large percentage fees demanded by their lawyers
- drive up the cost of settlements and court awards and thus affect insurance premiums

In Canada there has been growing acceptance of contingent fee systems, subject to supervision by the courts. Only Ontario expressly prohibits their use except in the case of class actions;[20] they are not allowed in Québec, but there appears to be no express prohibition. The remaining eight provinces permit contingent fees, subject to court supervision.[21] Although no statistics are available, it is generally agreed that contingent fees are used infrequently, and the traditional method of charging fees remains the prevailing one. A factor in reducing the demand for a contingent fee system in Canada has probably been the development of legal aid services described later.

18. *Ibid.*, p. 265.

19. *Ibid.*, p. 253.

20. Class Proceedings Act, S.O. 1992, c. 6, s. 33(1). See also: Trebilcock, "The Case for Contingent Fees: The Ontario Legal Profession Rethinks Its Position" (1985), 15 *Can. Bar L.J.* 360–8.

21. "A slice of the settlement: contingency fees across Canada," Vol. 13, No. 9, October 1986, *National*, 12. Ottawa: The Canadian Bar Foundation.

ALTERNATIVE DISPUTE RESOLUTION

The expense and delays involved in resorting to the courts have encouraged a new approach: today, many parties to disputes agree *not* to go to court and instead to use the private procedures of *alternative dispute resolution,* known as **ADR**. The oldest form of ADR is **arbitration**—referring a dispute to an arbitrator who will **adjudicate** the matter; the arbitrator will hear the parties, much as in a court case but with less formality and more promptly, and will deliver a decision with reasons. Normally, the parties agree in advance to be bound by the arbitrator's decision, but under some plans, a party may appeal to the courts.[22] Arbitration is also used in public sector disputes, in such areas as labour relations, worker's compensation and international commerce (as discussed in Chapter 33).

An increasingly important aspect of ADR is **mediation**. In mediation, a neutral third party acceptable to both sides acts as mediator. The mediator has no power to make a binding decision, but assists the parties in reaching a settlement. She hears both parties present their positions, identifies and clarifies the issues, and suggests middle ground that might be acceptable. At some point, the mediator usually meets separately with each side to explore the prospects of agreement and then brings them together again in the hope of reaching settlement. Mediation has a very good record of success, but when it fails, the parties ordinarily resort to arbitration.

The advantages of ADR are:

* *speed*—cases are resolved by mediation or arbitration much more promptly than through the courts

* *cost*—promptness in itself saves money, and in addition, since the parties themselves have chosen this method, they usually cooperate to avoid delays and keep the hearing as short as they can

* *choice of adjudicator or mediator*—unlike the courts, the parties can choose a person who they believe is especially suited to resolve the issue because of her experience and expertise in the area of the dispute

* *confidentiality*—the parties can agree to keep the dispute private to minimize harm to their business through disclosure of confidential information or encouraging others to bring similar complaints

* *preserving ongoing relations*—since ADR is usually less adversarial than litigation, it is less likely to foster antagonism between the parties, and will allow them to continue to work together afterwards[23]

ADR

alternative dispute resolution—using private procedures instead of the courts to resolve disputes

arbitration

a form of ADR where a dispute is referred to an arbitrator who adjudicates the matter and the parties agree to be bound by the arbitrator's decision, although there may be a right to appeal to the courts

adjudicate

hear parties and deliver a decision with reasons

mediation

a form of ADR where a neutral third party who is acceptable to both sides acts as a mediator, assisting the parties to reach a settlement

LEGAL AID

Its Evolution

Legal services, like all other services available in our society, require time and resources and cost money. Some services such as public education and police and fire protection have long been available without fee. Since the 1960s, basic medical and hospital services have also been provided to every resident in each province of Canada. Our view of what basic services ought to be available to everyone has enlarged over the years, especially in times of prosperity. However, there has been a growing concern—indeed controversy—about whether our economy can continue to support all the public services offered in recent decades; a number of services, includ-

---

22. John C. Carson, "Dispute Resolution, Negotiation, Mediation and Arbitration in Ontario" (1993), 10:1 *Business and the Law* 1.

23. For a general overview, see, D. Paul Emond, *Commercial Dispute Resolution: Alternatives to Litigation.* Aurora, Ontario: Canada Law Book, 1989.

ing legal aid, have been cut back and the level of services that will be available in the future is uncertain.

Until the late 1960s, legal services had been available almost exclusively to those who could afford to pay, that is, to business and professional people. Low-income earners could not afford legal services; what services they did receive were usually in the form of charity from lawyers who were willing to provide assistance free of charge to persons in dire circumstances. Ontario began a large-scale, publicly funded legal aid scheme in 1967, and most other provinces followed suit within a few years.

The Two Models

There are two different and, in some senses, competing models of legal aid, both used extensively in Canada. The Ontario model—sometimes known as the **judicare** model—has been adopted by several other provinces as the dominant method of delivering legal services. It has been described as follows:

> The purpose…is to ensure that, generally speaking, no person should be disqualified by lack of financial resources from having a lawyer represent him in either civil or criminal proceedings.…[L]awyers who have agreed to serve "legal aid clients" permit their name to appear on a panel in their county. A person qualifying for legal aid may select as his lawyer any lawyer whose name is on the panel.…The "legal aid lawyer" is guaranteed the payment of his fees and disbursements by the Provincial Government. The lawyer will be paid all of his proper disbursements but only 75 percent of his fees. The fees are calculated according to the tariffs contained in schedules…passed under the authority of The Legal Aid Act. The fees contained in the tariff are designed to represent average fees. The tariffs are strictly enforced by the Legal Accounts Officer who taxes every bill prior to its payment.[24]

judicare
a model of legal aid in which lawyers agree to be paid according to government fee schedules for serving clients who qualify for legal aid

The second model—known as the **community legal services** or **legal clinic** model—is well illustrated by the Saskatchewan scheme, described below:

> [The 1974 Act]…provides that legal services are to be delivered primarily by community law offices employing full-time staff lawyers. Area boards are to be incorporated to provide the services of the plan. Twelve boards have been elected from residents of the area who join the area legal aid society and each board has opened a community law office. Each board is empowered to advise the area staff on the legal need of the area residents, to establish committees to review financial refusals of eligibility, to negotiate area contracts with the provincial director, to establish information and counselling programmes, and to advertise the provision of legal services.[25]

community legal services or legal clinic
a model of legal aid where legal services are delivered by community law offices with full-time staff lawyers and managed by boards elected by residents of the community

Both models had their strident supporters in the first years of experimentation. Judicare and legal clinics were considered mutually incompatible: a province was thought capable of opting for only one or the other. Critics of the judicare model claimed it delivered only a watered-down version of middle-class legal services, and did nothing to alleviate the social problems behind the legal problems of the poor. Critics of the clinical model feared, on the one hand, too much activism by clinics tackling political and social problems to the detriment of individual clients' specific needs for relief, or on the other hand, fear of governmental interference in individual clients' affairs. Each side claimed that the other had higher costs per case and was therefore less justifiable in economic terms. The latter debate still continues, but the earlier contest has much diminished. It is now generally recognized that both systems have some strengths and some weaknesses. Provinces committed to one system—Ontario in particular—experiment extensively with the other. As a result, we now have great diversity and continuing

---

24. Watson and Williams, *Canadian Civil Procedure*, (2nd ed.), pp. 2–70. Toronto: Butterworths, 1977. See also, (4th ed.) (1991), Supplement (1997), pp. 231–70.

25. Zemans, "Legal Aid and Legal Advice in Canada" (1978), 16 *Osgoode Hall L.J.* 633.

experimentation across the country. Alberta, New Brunswick, Newfoundland, and Ontario have predominantly judicare plans; Nova Scotia, Prince Edward Island, and Saskatchewan use community legal centres; while British Columbia, Manitoba, and Québec have mixed schemes utilizing both systems.[26]

Just as in health care, there is bound to be continuing development of delivery systems and changes in criteria for the availability of services. It is interesting to note that while modern legal aid plans had their origin in the United States of the early 1960s, Canada now appears to have gone much further; per capita expenditures on legal aid in Canada are between two and three times those in the United States.[27]

THE LEGAL PROFESSION

solicitor
an "office" lawyer in England who interviews clients, carries on legal aspects of business and family affairs, and prepares cases for trial

barrister
a lawyer in England who accepts cases from solicitors and presents them in court, and also acts as consultant in complex legal issues

brief
a case handed by a solicitor to a barrister

notary
a solicitor in Quebec

advocate
a barrister in Quebec

attorney
a lawyer in the United States, encompassing the roles of both barrister and solicitor

In England the legal profession is divided into two groups, *solicitors* and *barristers*. **Solicitors** are "office" lawyers. They spend most of their time interviewing clients and carrying on the legal aspects of business and family affairs. They look after the drafting of wills, deeds, and contracts, the incorporation of companies, arrangements for adoption of children, and other domestic documents. They also prepare cases for trial, draft pleadings, interview witnesses, and make extensive notes for trial. In addition, they argue cases in some of the lower courts. **Barristers** take **briefs**, that is, cases handed to them by solicitors, and present them in court. They also give opinions with respect to potential litigation and are consulted by solicitors on a wide variety of more complex legal issues such as corporate mergers and tax planning. They are a much smaller group and have their offices mainly in London around the central law courts.

In Canada, from very early times, lawyers became both barristers and solicitors. In the common law provinces, lawyers are qualified to carry out the duties of both professions and often do so, especially in smaller cities and towns. In larger cities, lawyers tend to specialize and to be either "office" lawyers or "litigation" lawyers. Under the civil law of Québec the profession is divided in approximately the same way as in England. Quebec has **notaries** (solicitors) and **advocates** (barristers). In the United States the distinction has broken down completely. A lawyer is not called "barrister and solicitor" as in Canada, but is simply an **attorney**.

The legal profession is organized on a provincial basis in Canada. Each province has its own "bar" (barristers' society), and by provincial statute one must qualify as a member in order to practise law. Membership in one provincial bar does not permit a lawyer to practise in another province. A member in one province must meet the standards and pay the fees of the provincial bar in another province before practising in that province. A member of any provincial bar, however, may appear before the Supreme Court of Canada.

QUESTIONS FOR REVIEW

1. Distinguish the civil law system from common law system.

2. Explain the theory of precedent and its values.

3. Describe the relationship between the courts of common law and equity.

4. What is the purpose of codifying law in a statute?

5. Why has subordinate legislation come to prominence?

---

26. *Ibid.*, p. 666.
27. *Ibid.*, p. 664.

6. How does the operation of an appeal court differ from that of a trial court?

7. Motion pictures and television programs are responsible for a misconception about the way in which trials proceed. Explain.

8. Describe the basic difference between the systems of courts in the United States and in Canada.

9. What are the advantages of a settlement over a court trial?

10. Define appellant; respondent; counterclaim; counsel; bench; writ; settlement; pleadings; party and party costs; *res judicata*.

11. What is a "class action" and when do parties use them?

12. How does a judge decide a case when there is no precedent available in earlier decisions?

13. Explain how a legal rule in one province may differ from that in another province.

14. One of the major purposes of private law is to settle disputes between businesses. How can the settlement of a particular private dispute make a contribution to the business community as a whole?

15. "I was never ruined but twice; once when I won a lawsuit and once when I lost one." How can a successful litigant lose?

16. Explain the nature of a "contingent fee"? How are contingent fees used in Canada?

17. Distinguish between judicare and community legal services.

PART

Torts

Most of this book is devoted to business arrangements entered into between parties on a voluntary basis, but there are important aspects of the law that impose obligations on us without our agreement. For example, government regulation comprises an important area where duties are imposed; it will be discussed in Chapter 32 and in other chapters throughout this book.

In Part 2 we discuss the law of torts. A manufacturer's goods may be defective and injure a consumer; a newspaper may publish a story that libels someone; a driver delivering goods may carelessly injure a pedestrian; an accountant's negligent audit of a business may cause loss to an investor. In these and other situations, the party harmed may successfully claim a remedy against the wrongdoer.

A business may itself suffer injury, for example, by a fire carelessly started on adjoining premises that spreads and damages its property, or because it receives negligent advice from its lawyer. All of these situations raise important issues that are determined under principles of the law of torts.

In Chapter 3 we consider the essential characteristics of tort law that place a duty on everyone to take care and refrain from harming others by their actions. We shall concentrate on the most important tort—negligence—and shall also examine more briefly other torts, such as nuisance and those that contain an element of deliberate conduct, such as defamation and false imprisonment.

Chapter 4 discusses the problems of professional liability. In our complex society there is increasing need for specialized knowledge about highly sophisticated activities. Those without special skills have to rely on "professionals," and those that hold themselves out as being qualified are held to higher standards of care and skill than are members of the general public.

The law of torts is a very broad subject and has an impact upon many aspects of everyday life. The aim of the following two chapters is to concentrate upon those aspects of tort law that most directly affect the carrying on of a business. In particular, a business person needs to be aware of the potential risks, and accompanying legal liability, associated with his activities as well as the remedies available when actions of others harm the interests of the business.

PART 2

Weblinks

The texts of some of the more important torts statutes are available at

www.qp.gov.bc.ca/bcstats/96333_01.htm
The B.C. Negligence Act

www.qp.gov.bc.ca/bcstats/96337_01.htm
The B.C. Occupier's Liability Act

**www.gov.ns.ca/legi/legc/ and
209.195.107.57/en/index.html**
These are the statute indexes for Nova Scotia and for Ontario. From these sites, statutes such as the Negligence Act and the Occupier's Liability Act can be reached.

The following sites may also be helpful

www.hg.org/torts.html
A U.S. site on torts, with links to various national torts regimes

www.law-lib.utoronto.ca/resources/topic/torts.htm
The Bora Laskin Law Library, with links to torts sites

www.wwlia.org/ca-govli.htm
On government liability in Canada

www.wwlia.org/ca-nuis.htm
On the law of nuisance

www.wwlia.org/ca-defam.htm
On the law of defamation

www.wwlia.org/cabcoccu.htm
On occupier's liability

www.wwlia.org/ca-medli.htm
On medical liability

www.ljx.com/litigation/bacpage.htm
A U.S. site on tobacco litigation

In the context of Chapter 4, students may wish to examine the Web sites of various professional bodies—and in particular, their codes of professional conduct. Among the more interesting sites are

www.cica.ca
The Canadian Institute of Chartered Accountants

www.cga-canada.org
The Canadian Association of Certified General Accountants

www.cma.ca
The Canadian Medical Association

www.cdnpharm.ca
The Canadian Pharmaceutical Society

www.realestate.ca
The National Association of Realtors

For other codes of professional conduct, try

strategis.ic.gc.ca/SSG/mi00686e.html
Industry Canada Office of the Ethics Counsellor

csep.iit.edu/codes
Centre for the Study of Ethics in the Professions

www.ethics.ubc.ca/resources/business
Centre for Applied Ethics in British Columbia

www.stuart.iit.edu/ethics/guides.html
University of Illinois, collection of business and financial ethics codes

3 THE LAW OF TORTS

The word *tort* derives from the French, meaning "wrong." A tort is a wrong, that is to say, an injury, done by one person to another, sometimes intentionally but more often unintentionally. The injury may be physical—to the person or property of the victim—or financial.

This chapter examines the circumstances in which the law provides a remedy to the person who suffers the injury and imposes a liability to compensate on the person who causes the injury. In this chapter we examine such questions as:

■ what is the basis for tort liability?

■ what constitutes "negligence"?

■ how does the law of negligence apply to particular situations, such as the liability of manufacturers and of the owners or occupiers of premises?

■ in what other circumstances does the law of torts provide remedies?

■ what remedies are provided?

THE SCOPE OF TORT LAW

tort
a wrongful act done to the person or property of another

The role of the law of **torts** is to *compensate* victims for harm suffered from the activities of others. *Punishment* is left to the criminal law when the particular conduct happens also to amount to a crime. For example, when a drunken driver collides with another vehicle, its owner may sue him in tort for compensation and the state may charge him with the criminal offence of drunken driving.

While there is no entirely satisfactory definition of "tort," it is not difficult to compile a lengthy list of separate "torts," the importance of which increases as society becomes more complex. As a general proposition, one can say that tort law identifies those actions that create a right to compensation.

The basic issue for society, when dealing with such causes of harm as automobile accidents, industrial accidents, and pollution of the environment is to determine who should bear the loss—the victim, the person whose act caused the harm, the group that benefits most directly by a common activity, such as all motor vehicle owners, or an even larger group, such as taxpayers generally. Tort law is one important instrument for apportioning loss, along with such others as insurance and government compensation schemes.[1]

DEVELOPMENT OF THE TORT CONCEPT

In the early stages of development, societies usually have very simple rules of liability for injurious conduct: anyone who causes direct injury to another has to pay compensation. No inquiry is made into the reasons for the injury or whether the conduct of the injurer is justified. Such liability for injury is called **strict liability**. There are records dating from the earliest times of the amount of compensation payable, according to the kind of injury suffered and, sometimes, the importance of the injured party.

strict liability
liability that is imposed regardless of fault

Gradually, the idea developed that a person ought not to be responsible for harm caused to another if he acted without *fault*. For example, suppose *A* were driving his wagon down a road when a sudden clap of thunder caused the horses to bolt. *A* was unable to hold them back and the wagon ran down *B*, a passerby. The old strict law would have held *A* liable for *B*'s injuries. Later, the law was modified to excuse *A* from liability in these circumstances. Both parties were equally innocent, so the loss was left to lie where it had fallen—upon the unfortunate victim, *B*.

The courts also began to consider the way in which the harm had arisen. At first, only direct injuries were recognized by the courts—running down another person or striking a blow. Gradually the courts began to recognize indirect or *consequential* injuries. For example, suppose *A* carelessly dropped a log in the road and did not bother to remove it although it was near sunset. After dark, *B*'s horse tripped over the log and was seriously injured. In early law, *B* would have been without a remedy. Later, however, the courts recognized that *A*'s act was as much responsible for the injury to *B*'s horse as if *A* had struck the horse by throwing the log at it. They allowed *B* to recover damages.[2]

We can see then that early tort law changed in two ways: the law took into account the *fault* of the defendant and it also took into account *causation*—whether the defendant's conduct could be considered the cause of the harm. Both these developments present difficult problems, which we shall examine more closely.

THE BASIS FOR LIABILITY

Fault

Fault, in the context of tort law, refers to blameworthy or culpable conduct—conduct that in the eyes of the law is unjustifiable because it intentionally or carelessly disregards the interests of others. This does not mean that fault is the basis for liability in all of tort law. As we noted at the beginning of this chapter, there is a general problem concerning the distribution of loss caused as a consequence of such activities as the operation of automobiles. For example, statistically we know that each year there will be thousands of victims of car accidents. Should the victim or the victim's family have to bear the financial loss, or should it be borne by the driver or owner of the vehicle responsible for the accident? Should the right to compensation depend on the victim's ability to prove that some other person was at fault?

---

1. For a fuller discussion of the purposes of tort law, see especially Fleming, *The Law of Torts* (8th ed.), Sydney: Law Book Company, 1992. See also Linden, *Canadian Tort Law* (6th ed.), Toronto: Butterworths, 1997.
2. This example was discussed by Fortesque, J. in Reynolds v. Clarke (1726), 93 E.R. 747, and has been cited many times since by both the courts and leading writers as a classic statement of the law.

One justification for basing liability upon fault is a belief in its deterrent effect: people will be more inclined to be careful if they are made to bear the consequences of their carelessness. There is little hard evidence to support this theory, although it may be reasonable to suppose that large, highly publicized awards of damages have had an effect upon the standards and practices of manufacturers, surgeons, and similar persons affected by these awards. But the modern reality is that many of the activities where tort liability arises—driving a car, operating a factory or store, practising medicine—are covered by insurance. Carelessness is more likely to be deterred by the likelihood of criminal penalties (for example, for dangerous driving) and of increased insurance premiums than by the possibility of being sued in tort.

The defects of a compensation system based on fault are well known.[3] Accident victims who are unable to establish fault on the part of some other person go uncompensated and the costs and delays of litigation deter many other claims. These defects have led to suggestions that compensation should be provided in other ways. The most radical proposals would eliminate law suits for all personal injuries and compensate victims through a government scheme. A step in that direction has been taken in Canada with the virtual elimination of fault as a basis for automobile accident claims, through a system of compulsory **"no fault" insurance**.[4] Another example of an alternative to the tort approach is found in the scheme governing **workers' compensation** in Canada.[5] Under this scheme, industrial accidents are seen as the inevitable price of doing business. Employers must contribute to a fund that is in turn used to compensate workers injured in industrial accidents, even when the employer is blameless and the injury is the result of the employee's own carelessness.

"no-fault" insurance
a system of compulsory insurance that eliminates fault as a basis for claims

workers' compensation
a scheme in which employers contribute to a fund used to compensate workers injured in industrial accidents

Strict Liability

As already noted, early tort law took a narrow approach, imposing the burden of compensation upon the person who caused the injury regardless of whether he was at fault. This type of strict liability persists in some areas of modern tort law. For example, a person who collects potentially dangerous things on his land, from which they subsequently escape, is liable for any resulting damage even if he was blameless.[6]

ILLUSTRATION 3.1

A manufacturer stored acid in a large container on his property. The container was accidentally punctured by a visitor's truck; the acid leaked out and damaged a neighbouring farmer's crops. The manufacturer is liable to compensate the farmer. The risk of such damage is a burden the manufacturer must bear as the price for storing chemicals on his land. (The truck driver may also be liable for the damage if he was at fault.)

Social Policy

Whether liability should be based on fault or on other principles is an important question of policy, constantly changing as our social standards change. These social standards force the law to adapt in many ways, ranging from direct legislative intervention, as in workers' compensation statutes, to more subtle influences on judge and jury in determining liability and the amounts of damages awarded.

3. For an interesting study, see Dewees and Trebilcock, "The Efficacy of the Tort System and its Alternatives: a Review of the Empirical Evidence" (1992), 30 *Osgoode Hall L.J.* 57.
4. See "Automobile Insurance" in Chapter 18.
5. See "Workers' Compensation" in Chapter 20.
6. Rylands v. Fletcher (1868), L.R. 3 H.L. 330; Heintzman & Co. Ltd. v. Hashman Construction Ltd. (1972), 32 D.L.R. (3d) 622.

Modern reforms tend to spread the burden of compensation widely, over society as a whole through government schemes, or over identifiable groups such as employers or automobile owners through compulsory insurance schemes. But between comprehensive "no-fault" schemes on the one hand and strict liability on the other, there are many circumstances where liability based on fault is the fairest principle; in most areas of tort law, liability remains firmly on that basis.

Vicarious Liability

One area in which the law has responded to the pressure of social needs is with respect to torts committed by employees in the course of their employment. An employer may be personally at fault for an act committed by an employee. For example, he may instruct an employee to perform a dangerous task for which he knows the employee is not trained. In such a case the employer personally is at fault, and it may be that there is no fault on the part of the employee.[7]

But should an employer be liable when the employee alone is at fault? Nineteenth-century courts evolved a basis for making the employer liable for harm caused by the tortious acts of an employee when the acts arise in the course of employment. Now, the employer is liable even when he has given strict instructions to take proper care or not to do the act that causes the damage, and he may be held liable for criminal, as well as negligent, acts of an employee.[8]

There are two main justifications for this strict approach. First, although an employee is personally liable for the torts he commits while acting for himself or his employer, employees generally have limited assets available to pay compensation for the potential harm they can cause—a train driver may injure hundreds of passengers. Second, there is a strong argument based on fairness: the person who makes the profit should also be liable for the loss. Accordingly, the courts have developed the principle of **vicarious liability**, whereby an employer is liable to compensate persons for harm caused by an employee in the course of employment.

vicarious liability
the liability of an employer to compensate for harm caused by an employee

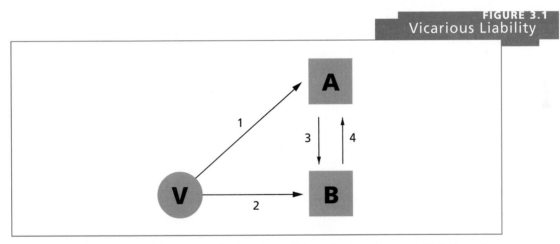

FIGURE 3.1
Vicarious Liability

The victim, *V*, is injured by *A* while *A* is acting in the course of his employment. *V* can sue *A* [1]. *V* can also sue the employer, *B* [2], who will normally have a greater ability to pay. (In practice, *V* is likely to sue *both A* and *B*.) If *V* does sue *A*, it is possible that *A* will have a right to be indemnified by *B* [3]. Or, if *B* has to compensate *V*, *B* may be able to sue *A* [4]. These rights [3 and 4] could arise under the contract of employment.

From a business perspective, an important consequence of the development of vicarious liability has been that employers ordinarily insure themselves against public liability and take into account the cost of the insurance in pricing their products. We shall discuss an employer's liability further in Chapter 20.

---

7. See Edgeworth Construction Ltd. v. N.D. Lee & Associates Ltd. (1993), 107 D.L.R. (4th) 169.
8. British Columbia Ferry Corp. v. Invicta Security Service Corp. (1998), 167 D.L.R. (4th) 193.

NEGLIGENCE

By far the most important tort and the one that best exemplifies the fault theory of liability, is negligence. The concept of **negligence** is quite simple: anyone who carelessly causes injury to another should compensate the victim for that injury. As it has developed in the courts, negligence has become a complex and sophisticated body of law, encompassing a wide variety of situations.

negligence
the careless causing of injury to the person or property of another

Checklist: Elements of a Negligence Action

In establishing the right to recover compensation, a plaintiff must prove three things:

1. The defendant owed the plaintiff a duty of care.
2. The defendant breached that duty.
3. The defendant's conduct caused injury to the plaintiff.

All three of the above requirements may create major difficulties for the plaintiff. The first element requires a policy decision or *value judgment* by the court—is the conduct complained of such that it *ought* to create a duty? The second question is a mixed question of policy and fact—did the defendant's conduct amount to a breach of that duty? The third question is one not only of fact but also of philosophy—what is meant by "cause"?

Duty of Care

duty of care
the duty to take reasonable care to avoid injury to others

In order to establish liability in negligence a plaintiff must establish a **duty of care** owed to her by the defendant. What is the nature of that duty?

The principal criterion is that the alleged wrongdoer, *A*, should have foreseen that his actions might do harm. Another way of putting it, since *A* cannot be expected to anticipate all the possible consequences of his action, is to ask, "Would a normally intelligent and alert person—a reasonable person—have foreseen that *A*'s conduct would likely cause harm?" But the plaintiff must go further: she must establish that the defendant owed a duty of care *to her*. As a general rule, the duty will arise only where the defendant could reasonably have foreseen a risk of harm to the plaintiff or to someone in the plaintiff's position.

CASE 3.1

A courier company contracted with the Province of British Columbia to deliver an envelope to a land registry office in Prince George. Unknown to the courier company, the envelope contained a document relating to land owned by the plaintiff. If delivered on time, the document would have enabled the plaintiff to sell its land. The courier company was unreasonably slow and delivered the document too late; as a result the plaintiff was unable to perform the contract of sale, and it suffered a loss of $77 000.

The Supreme Court of Canada held that the courier company was not liable to the plaintiff. It owed no duty of care to the plaintiff since it could not reasonably have foreseen that the delay would cause a loss to some third person outside its relationship with its client, the Province.[9]

---

9. B.D.C. Ltd. v. Hofstrand Farms Ltd. (1986), 26 D.L.R. (4th) 1.

Two years earlier, in *City of Kamloops v. Nielsen*, the Supreme Court of Canada ruled that, to determine the existence of a duty of care, a court must ask:

> …is there a sufficiently close relationship between the parties (the [defendant] and the person who has suffered the damage) so that, in the reasonable contemplation of the [defendant], carelessness on its part might cause damage to that person? If so, are there any considerations which ought to negative or limit (a) the scope of the duty and (b) the class of persons to whom it is owed or (c) the damages to which a breach of it may give rise?[10]

The courts have sometimes held that a duty of care is owed to persons other than the individual who is directly injured. For example, a negligent driver was held to be liable to a parent who suffered severe nervous shock when she saw her own child, who was standing nearby, run down and killed.[11] In that case the court considered that the type of injury suffered by the parent was foreseeable.

In recent years more and more duties have been imposed by statute, especially upon the operators of businesses—as we shall see further in Chapters 29 and 32. In addition to statutory penalties, breach of these duties may give rise to liability in tort to persons who are injured as a result. The courts have also shown increasing willingness to hold public bodies liable for the negligent performance of their statutory duties. Municipalities have been held liable to homeowners for issuing building permits for defective designs or for not carrying out proper inspections of construction works.[12] A public body may be liable even where the statute imposes no duty but merely confers a discretionary power on it—for example, to maintain a highway—if it is negligent in the exercise of that power.[13] In such cases the courts draw a distinction between "policy" decisions and "operational" implementation of a policy.[14] Governmental agencies must be free to govern and to make true policy decisions without becoming subject to tort liability as a result of those decisions. Thus, the British Columbia government was held not liable when a motorist skidded on an icy road that had not been sanded. The highway department had made a policy decision not to begin regular sanding until mid-November. That decision could not be reviewed according to a private-law standard of reasonableness. The court accepted, however, that the negligent implementation of the policy could give rise to liability.[15]

Standard of Care

The law places a general duty on every person to take *reasonable care* to avoid causing foreseeable injury to other persons and their property. What constitutes a reasonable standard of care? It is often said that the standard demanded is that of the ordinary reasonable person, or "the person on the Yonge Street subway."[16] However, the standard necessarily varies according to the activity in question: the standard expected of a brain surgeon is that of a competent brain surgeon rather than of the person in the subway.

---

10. [1984] 2 S.C.R. 2 at 10 (per Wilson, J.). This test was cited with approval by LaForest, J. in Hercules Managements Ltd. v. Ernst & Young (1997), 146 D.L.R. (4th) 577 (S.C.C.), in a judgment that provides a comprehensive review of the Canadian law on the duty of care. That case is examined further in Chapter 4.

11. Hinz v. Berry, [1970] 1 All E.R. 1074; contrast Schlink v. Blackburn (1993), 18 C.C.L.T. (2d) 173.

12. City of Kamloops v. Neilsen, *supra*, n. 10; Rothfield v. Manolakos (1989), 63 D.L.R. (4th) 449.

13. Just v. British Columbia (1989), 64 D.L.R. (4th) 689.

14. That distinction does not apply where the government body is given express powers to interfere with the rights of individuals: see Lewis v. Prince Edward Island (1998), 157 D.L.R. (4th) 277. In that case the government agency, which was given statutory authority to spray for crop diseases, was not liable for damage to the plaintiff farmer's crops resulting from non-negligent spraying.

15. Brown v. British Columbia (1994), 112 D.L.R. (4th) 1 (S.C.C.); see also Swinamer v. Nova Scotia (1994), 112 D.L.R. (4th) 18. The authority may also be liable for the negligence of an independent contractor hired by it to perform the task: Mochinski v. Trendline Industries Ltd. (1997), 154 D.L.R. (4th) 212 (S.C.C.).

16. Linden, *Canadian Tort Law, supra*, n. 1, at pp. 126–7.

In addition, the court must balance competing interests: on the one hand the court considers the degree of likelihood that harm will result from the activity in question and the potential severity of the harm, and on the other it considers the social utility of the activity and the feasibility of eliminating the risk. It may be permissible not to take every possible precaution where the risk of serious damage or injury is small, but where there is danger of a major catastrophe it would be unreasonable not to take every known precaution.

Increasingly, legislation not only imposes duties but also sets out the appropriate standard of care for particular activities. For example, safety standards for motor vehicles are prescribed by statute and such standards are frequently a good indication of where a court will set the negligence threshold. But it must be remembered that the tort of negligence is based on fault and the fact that a person may be guilty of a breach of a statutory standard does not of itself make him civilly liable to a person injured as a result of the breach—at least if he can show that the offence occurred without fault on his part.[17]

Causation

For an action in negligence to succeed it is necessary for the plaintiff to show not only that a duty of care was owed to her and has been breached, but also that she has been injured as a result of that breach; that is to say, the breach of duty is the *cause* of the injury. Legal cause is a subtle subject about which whole volumes have been written.[18] An extreme view of the theory of causation can link one act to every other act in the world.

ILLUSTRATION 3.2

PQR Inc. were having some renovations done to part of their factory building by *STU (Contractors) Ltd.* One of the *STU* workmen negligently sliced through a cable, causing an electric motor to burn out. The motor was an essential part of the factory's cooling system; without it, the factory could continue in operation for only a few hours. The factory manager, *X*, immediately decided to drive to the nearby town to obtain a replacement motor. On the way, his car was struck by a vehicle carelessly driven by *Y*, and *X* suffered slight injuries and concussion. By the time *PQR* were able to get the motor back to the factory the cooling system had overheated and it had been necessary to close down operations. As a result, four hours of production were lost. Worse, *X*'s injury caused him to miss a meeting with an important client, as a result of which *PQR* lost the opportunity of a lucrative contract.

In Illustration 3.2 it could be argued that the negligence of *STU*'s worker "caused" (1) the shutdown at the factory, (2) the injury to *X*, and (3) the loss of the contract; *but for* his slicing through the cable, none of those consequences would have followed. The same might be argued with respect to *Y*'s careless driving. Yet it would seem unreasonable to hold *STU* liable for items (2) and (3), or to hold *Y* liable for items (1) and (3). Clearly, the "but for" approach to causation does not always provide a satisfactory solution.

For the most part the courts have avoided philosophical discussion and have adopted a common-sense approach. On the one hand it is clear that, no matter how blameworthy a person's conduct may have been, he will not be held liable for damage that he did not cause. In a famous case, a passenger in a small boat accidentally fell overboard into ice-cold water and died. The boat's operator was under a duty to try to rescue him, but although negligent in the

---

17. Sterling Trusts Corp. v. Postma and Little, [1965] S.C.R. 324; R. v. Saskatchewan Wheat Pool, [1983] 1 S.C.R. 205.

18. See, especially, Hart and Honore, *Causation in the Law* (2nd ed.), Oxford: Oxford University Press, 1985.

attempt, was held not liable because even if he had used proper rescue procedures, the passenger would have been dead before he could have been reached.[19]

Again, a person will not be held liable for consequences of his acts that are considered to be too remote. Generally speaking, the closer in time the occurrence of an injury is to a person's careless conduct, the less chance there is of significant intervening acts happening, and the more likely he is to be found the "cause" of the injury.

CASE 3.2

B and his wife were involved in an automobile accident. *B* sustained relatively slight injuries but his wife was severely injured. Two years later, *B* was in another accident and some time after that was diagnosed as suffering from severe depression. In the action arising out of the first accident, *B* claimed damages in respect of the depression.

The claim was rejected. The court held that, if *B*'s depression had resulted from the stress of seeing his wife, day after day, in a severely injured condition, completely unlike her condition before the accident, the damage would have been foreseeable. However, the length of time between the accident and the onset of the depression (more than two years later) cast doubt on the causal relationship.[20]

As both Case 3.2 and Illustration 3.2 demonstrate, an injury may be the result of two or more negligent acts by different defendants. In such a case, which of them should be held liable? Courts in the 19th century devoted much effort to identify the "proximate cause" of injury, and developed the *last opportunity* or *last clear chance* principle. The principle was based on the notion that, where an accident could be said to have been caused by two or more persons, the one who had the last chance to avoid the accident should be held entirely responsible. The principle could result in injustice and has been largely discarded by modern courts. Now, two or more persons who have quite separately contributed to an accident may both be held liable.

CASE 3.3

An innkeeper allowed a customer to drink too much and then turned him out to walk home along a country road, where he was hit by a careless motorist; both the innkeeper and the motorist were held to have contributed to the accident.[21]

In considering the physical closeness or *proximity* of a particular act to a subsequent injury, the courts must eventually decide, as a matter of policy, at what point to cut off the process and decide that the defendant is or is not responsible. The practical necessity of drawing reasonable limits for liability means that a court must break the chain of causation at some point. In choosing that point, the court makes a social judgment.

---

19. Matthews v. MacLaren, [1969] 2 O.R. 137, affirmed sub nom. Horsley v. MacLaren, [1972] S.C.R. 441.

20. Beecham v. Hughes (1988), 52 D.L.R. (4th) 625.

21. Menow v. Honsberger and Jordan House Ltd., [1974] S.C.R. 239. See also Jacobsen v. Nike Canada Ltd. (1996), 133 D.L.R. (4th) 377; Murphy v. Little Memphis Cabaret Inc. (1998), 167 D.L.R. (4th) 190. By contrast, the Supreme Court of Canada held that a restaurant serving alcohol to a party of people, knowing that they had arrived by car, owed a duty to the driver and passengers, but since some members of the party were not drinking it was entitled to assume that a non-drinker would be driving; consequently, it was not responsible for the accident: Mayfield Investments Ltd. v. Stewart (1995), 121 D.L.R. (4th) 222.

Remoteness of Damage

Foreseeability is a major element, as we have seen, both in establishing whether or not a duty of care exists and in determining what is the appropriate standard of care. It reappears yet again when the question of the *extent* of liability for negligence is considered.

Until the 1960s the position seemed to be that, once some sort of damage was reasonably foreseeable as a consequence of a negligent act, the actor was liable for *all* damage resulting directly from that act, however unlikely.[22]

CASE 3.4

Employees of the defendants, who were charterers of a ship called *Wagon Mound*, negligently allowed a large quantity of oil to escape from the ship into Sydney Harbour, Australia. Some of the oil washed up against the plaintiff's dock. Workers on the dock were carrying on welding operations. A spark from a welder ignited some cotton waste floating on the surface of the water and this, in turn, ignited the oil. A severe fire resulted, causing considerable damage to the dock.

The Australian trial judge held the defendants liable. They had been negligent in allowing the oil to escape and it was foreseeable that some damage to the plaintiff's dock might result from the leakage, though the judge found that damage by fire was not foreseeable. Nevertheless, the actual damage was a direct result of the defendants' breach of their duty to the plaintiff.

The defendants appealed and the Privy Council allowed the appeal, holding that liability existed only in respect of the sort of damage that was reasonably foreseeable.[23]

The *Wagon Mound* decision (Case 3.4) seemed to have restricted liability to damage that was reasonably foreseeable. Subsequent decisions in Canada and Britain, however, have largely restored the earlier position by taking a broad view of what is foreseeable.[24] For example, it is a well-established principle that, when one person injures another he "must take his victim as he finds him." He is fully liable even though the victim suffers a far more serious injury than might have been expected, perhaps because the victim had a pre-existing disability, allergy, or an "egg-shell skull." Thus, where a person was injured in a road accident, the fact that his injuries were much more serious than might have been expected because of his pre-existing back condition did not excuse the drivers who caused the accident from full liability.[25]

This principle is not confined to cases of personal injury: when a teenager negligently started his father's snowmobile, which escaped from his control, sped across a schoolyard, and collided with a gas pipe just outside the school, causing gas to escape into the school and explode, he was held liable for all the resulting damage. The damage was considered to be of a general type that might have been foreseen even if the actual extent of the damage was not.[26]

Economic Loss

As we noted at the beginning of this chapter, the object of tort law is to compensate for loss suffered as a consequence of the wrongful act of another and, as we shall see, the remedy given in

22. Re Polemis, [1921] 3 K.B. 560. See also: Cotic v. Gray (1981), 33 O.R. (2d) 356.

23. Overseas Tankship (U.K.) Ltd. v. Morts Dock & Engineering Co. (The Wagon Mound), [1961] A.C. 388.

24. Overseas Tankship (U.K.) Ltd. v. Miller Steamship Co. Pty. Ltd. (The Wagon Mound No. 2), [1966] 2 All E.R. 709; Hughes v. Lord Advocate, [1963] A.C. 837; R. v. Coté (1974), 51 D.L.R. (3d) 244 (S.C.C.).

25. Athey v. Leonati (1996), 140 D.L.R. (4th) 235 (S.C.C.).

26. Hoffer v. School Division of Assiniboine South, [1973] W.W.R. 765 (S.C.C.). The father and the gas company that installed the pipe were also held liable.

cases of negligence is a sum of money by way of **damages**. A plaintiff injured in an automobile collision may be compensated not only for her physical injuries and for the cost of repairing her car, but also for *economic loss*, such as wages lost due to an enforced absence from work and the cost of renting a replacement car. But until relatively recent times the courts were unwilling to compensate for "pure" economic loss; that is, where there was no physical injury or damage to a plaintiff's person or property. That is no longer so.[27]

damages
a sum of money awarded as compensation

Two types of case may be distinguished. In the first type, economic loss is caused without there being any physical damage at all. A classic example is the leading case of *Hedley Byrne v. Heller and Partners*,[28] in which the House of Lords established that financial loss suffered as a result of a negligent misstatement may be recovered. This subject is discussed further in Chapter 4. In the second type of case there is physical damage, but not to the person or property of the plaintiff.

CASE 3.5

B negligently operated a tugboat and it collided with a railway bridge owned by *C*. The bridge was closed for several weeks for repairs. As a result, the railway company, which was the principal user of the bridge, suf-fered a substantial loss of profit because it had to re-route traffic.

The Supreme Court of Canada held that the railway company could recover its loss.[29]

The decision was a narrow one: it turned in part on the close relationship that existed between the owner of the bridge and the railway company. Thus, while it established that there *may* be recovery for pure economic loss in some situations, it left open the question of when the courts will hold that a duty is owed to a plaintiff or when the particular damage is not too remote. In a subsequent decision[30] the Supreme Court of Canada has partly answered those questions.

CASE 3.6

A land developer contracted with the defendant construc-tion company to built an apartment building, which was later sold to the plaintiffs. About 10 years later, a section of cladding fell from the ninth storey. On examination, defects in the construction were found and the plaintiffs had the entire cladding replaced. They successfully sued the defendants for the cost of the repairs.

Although no damage had been suffered, apart from the cladding on the ninth storey, it was foreseeable that without the repairs there was a strong likelihood of physical harm to persons or to property and it was right that the defendants should be liable where a dangerous defect was discovered and the owner of the building took action to mitigate the damage by repairing the defect. In reaching that conclusion, the court recognized the strong underlying policy justifica-tion of providing an incentive to prevent accidents before they happen.

---

27. For a survey, see Mactavish, "Tort Recovery for Economic Loss: Recent Developments" (1992/93), 21 *C.B.L.J.* 395.

28. [1964] A.C. 465.

29. Canadian National Railway Co. v. Norsk Pacific Steamship Co. (1992), 91 D.L.R. (4th) 289.

30. Winnipeg Condominium Corp. No. 36 v. Bird Construction Co., [1995] 1 S.C.R. 85.

Burden of Proof

Like plaintiffs in other actions, a plaintiff in a tort action must prove her case; in certain kinds of cases, however, she is in a peculiarly difficult position. A pedestrian knocked down by a car or a consumer poisoned by a dangerous substance in a jar of food may be unable to ascertain exactly how the defendant driver's or manufacturer's conduct contributed to her injury. For example, the car might suddenly have swerved out of control because of some hidden mechanical defect, or the poisonous substance might have been deliberately inserted into the jar after it had left the manufacturer.

The law takes these difficulties of proof into account. The injured party need only establish that the defendant's car or product physically caused the injury. The burden then shifts to the defendant to exculpate himself. He is presumed to have been in breach of a duty owed to the plaintiff and also to be in possession of any information that might show him to be innocent of any breach. Once the burden has been shifted to him, he will be found liable unless he produces evidence to satisfy the court that on balance he was not in breach of a duty to the plaintiff. This principle is commonly known as ***res ipsa loquitur***, and may be translated as "the facts speak for themselves." It appears to have first emerged in a 19th-century English case[31] in which the plaintiff, standing in a street, was struck by a barrel of flour falling from the upper window of the defendant's warehouse. The not unreasonable conclusion was that, unless the defendant could prove otherwise, the most likely cause was the negligent conduct of the defendant or one of his employees. In a recent case, however, the Supreme Court of Canada described the *res ipsa loquitur* principle as "more confusing than helpful." Rather, the trier of fact should weigh the circumstantial and direct evidence to determine whether the plaintiff had established a *prima facie* case of negligence against the defendant. The court held that there was no presumption of negligence simply because a vehicle leaves the road in a single-vehicle accident.[32]

res ipsa loquitur
the facts speak for themselves

The Plaintiff's Own Conduct

Early in the development of the principles of negligence, the courts recognized that even if the defendant has been negligent, the plaintiff might properly be regarded as the author of her own misfortune. The courts at first took a rather narrow and mechanical approach to the question. If the defendant could establish that the plaintiff contributed in some small measure to her own loss, the plaintiff would fail even if the defendant was mainly at fault. In the 19th century, they attempted to ease the harshness of the **contributory negligence** rule by permitting the plaintiff to recover if, despite the plaintiff's negligence, the defendant nevertheless had the last opportunity or last clear chance to avoid the injury. But that principle could itself be unjust in its application (as we saw when discussing causation), and could not realistically be applied to "instantaneous" events such as most highway accidents.

contributory negligence
negligence of an injured party that contributes to her own loss or injury

The way out of these difficulties was established by statutory reforms pioneered in Canada.[33] These statutes, known as *comparative negligence* or *apportionment of loss* legislation, required courts to apportion damages according to the respective degree of responsibility of the parties. The statutes do not set out in detail the basis for making the apportionment, but leave it to be decided by judges and juries according to their opinion of what is fair in the circumstances. In one recent case, for example, a truck driver parked his vehicle negligently; it was hit by a motorcyclist, who was also driving carelessly. Under the common law the motorcyclist would have been considered entirely to blame for the accident since he had the last clear chance to avoid it.

---

31. Byrne v. Boadle (1863), 159 E.R. 294.

32. Fontaine v. Loewen Estate (1997), 156 D.L.R. (4th) 577.

33. Ontario passed the first statute in the field: Negligence Act, S.O. 1924, c. 32.

However, the Alberta Court of Appeal ruled that the common law principle no longer applies and that liability should be apportioned between the truck driver and the motorcyclist.[34]

By applying an appropriate standard of care to the plaintiff as well as to the defendant, the courts have also been able to give expression to changing standards within our society. For example, courts now commonly find that a person injured in a motor vehicle accident has contributed to some extent to her own injuries by failure to wear a seat belt.[35]

A further problem arises when the victim is wholly blameless in the accident itself but her own *subsequent* conduct contributes to the *extent* of her original injuries—for example, where a plaintiff refuses to undergo safe and simple surgery and thus aggravates her condition. In some cases, the courts have decided that part of the damages were due to the plaintiff's unreasonable conduct and were therefore not recoverable.[36] This result may be justified on the ground that the plaintiff's own conduct has contributed to the seriousness of the injury; alternatively, it may be regarded as an application of the principle that a plaintiff is expected to act reasonably to minimize, or *mitigate*, any damage suffered. This principle is discussed further, in the context of contract law, in Chapter 15.

It is important to note that the defence of contributory negligence is a statutory one and may be raised only in actions based in tort law.[37] Thus, where a farmer whose crops were destroyed sued the manufacturer and supplier of a pesticide, successfully claiming that the instructions for use did not contain an adequate warning of the risks involved, the alleged negligence of the farmer himself was held to be no defence since the action was based on breach of contract.[38]

The Relevance of Insurance

As mentioned earlier in this chapter, the modern reality is that in many tort cases the actual loss will fall on an insurance company. Thus, in the case of automobile collisions, both plaintiff and defendant are ordinarily insured against the loss that occurs. But suppose that *A* decides not to contract for collision insurance on her automobile and it is damaged in an accident caused by the negligence of another driver, *B*. Since *A* is expected to mitigate her loss, should it follow that she has contributed to the loss by failing to take out insurance against the risk? Can *B* successfully defend an action by *A* for negligence on the grounds that *A* might have avoided her loss by taking out adequate insurance coverage? The answer is no. Courts do not admit evidence about the existence or amount of insurance coverage in negligence actions because their decisions must be based strictly on the merits of the dispute being tried and be free from any suspicion that their judgment has been biased by a knowledge of the amount of insurance protection that the plaintiff has voluntarily chosen to purchase. Hence in our example the failure of the plaintiff to have insured her car against damage by collision would not be admitted as evidence and thus would not affect the amount of damages the plaintiff might recover.

Suppose, however, that in our example *A* had contracted for collision insurance. *A* will not be compensated twice—once by her insurance company and again by the defendant. Ordinarily, when an insured party recovers first from her insurance company, her right to pursue the claim

---

34. Wickberg v. Patterson (1997), 145 D.L.R. (4th) 263.

35. A driver of a vehicle may be held negligent for failure to ensure that a child passenger is wearing a seat belt: Galaske v. O'Donnell (1994), 112 D.L.R. (4th) 109 (S.C.C.).

36. See Janiak v. Ippolito (1985), 31 C.C.L.T. 113.

37. It also seems that the defence is not available in strict liability torts, such as conversion; see Boma Manufacturing Ltd. v. Canadian Imperial Bank of Commerce (1996), 140 D.L.R. (4th) 463 (S.C.C.).

38. Caners v. Eli Lilley Canada Inc. (1996), 134 D.L.R. (4th) 730 (Man.C.A.). This aspect of contractual liability is considered in Chapter 16.

subrogation

where one person becomes entitled to the rights and claims of another

against the wrongdoer passes to the insurance company. It "stands in the insured person's shoes"; that is, it becomes **subrogated** to the insured party's rights and may itself sue the defendant and collect. But if *A* recovers her loss, or part of it, by suing *B*, then to that extent she cannot recover from her own insurance company.

Normally, it is simpler for *A* to recover under her insurance policy, leaving the company to decide whether or not to sue *B*. One reason is that under the policy *A* may be entitled to recover the full extent of her loss, even though she may have been partly at fault and, in an action against *B*, the damages might be reduced on account of *A*'s own contributory negligence. Another reason is that *B* might have insufficient assets to pay the claim. If *B* also has insurance, the two insurance companies will usually settle the question of payment between themselves, without resorting to expensive litigation. There may be cases, however, where the amount that the insurance company offers to pay under the policy is less than the sum the plaintiff considers a court would likely order the defendant to pay her.

FIGURE 3.2
Insurance

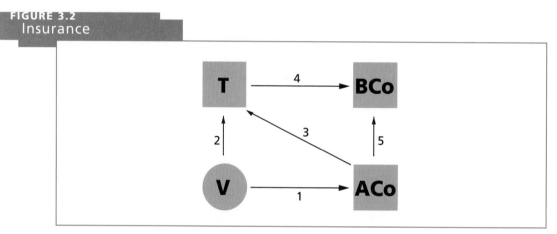

Victim *V* is injured in an automobile accident, caused by the negligence of tortfeasor *T*. *V* is insured by *ACo*, and *T* by *BCo*. *V* may claim under her policy with *ACo* [1], or may sue *T* [2]. If *V* claims under her policy, *ACo* may bring proceedings (in *V*'s name) against *T* [3]. *T* could then claim under his policy with *BCo* [4]. Alternatively, *ACo* might settle with *BCo* [5].

SPECIAL ASPECTS OF NEGLIGENCE

Hazardous Activities

An assumption made in every case of negligence is that the injury sustained by the plaintiff would not have happened if the defendant had exercised reasonable care. However, some activities are inherently dangerous regardless of the care taken—for example, transporting high explosives. A strong argument may be made that in these circumstances, a person carrying on an inherently dangerous activity should be strictly liable for damage, regardless of fault. In other words, a person who undertakes a dangerous activity should charge for his services according to the degree of risk, and should carry adequate insurance to compensate for possible harm done to others. It can be argued that an innocent victim should not suffer a loss caused by a dangerous activity carried on by another person for his own benefit, even when that person has taken proper care. Although some United States courts have reached this conclusion, Canadian courts still apply the principles of negligence. However, they have raised the standard of care proportionally as the danger increases. As a result, in many cases of hazardous activities the defendant finds the standard of care so high that it is virtually impossible for him to show that he has satisfied it. The effect is much the same as if he were strictly liable.

Product Liability

Consider the four cases below. Who should bear the loss in each one?

CASE 3.7

X runs a small refreshment booth at a beach and buys his supplies from Y Bottling Co. Ltd. He sells a dark-green bottle of ginger ale to A who gives it to her friend B. B drinks half the contents and becomes violently ill. The balance is found to contain a decomposed snail. B is hospitalized and is unable to return to work for several weeks.

CASE 3.8

P buys a Q Company sports car from R Dealer. On being driven away from the showroom, the car loses a defective front wheel and collides with a parked vehicle, injuring the occupant, S.

CASE 3.9

M buys from the N Ski Shop a set of thermal underwear manufactured by O Company. The underwear contains a toxic acid and when it comes in contact with perspiration causes M to have a severe skin burn.

CASE 3.10

J buys a bottle of cough medicine, manufactured by the K company, from her local drugstore. To try to get rid of her cold she drinks two stiff whiskies, takes a dose of the medicine, and goes to bed. During the night she has a heart attack. The cough medicine is extremely dangerous if taken with alcohol, but there was no warning to that effect on the bottle or package.

As we shall see in Chapter 16, the retailer in each of our examples may be liable to the buyer for breach of an implied undertaking that a product is not defective. But in Case 3.7, X may well have insufficient assets to compensate B for the loss. In any event, he sold the soft drink to A rather than to B, the injured party. Accordingly, B is not a buyer entitled to the protection of a contractual undertaking of fitness. Similarly, in Case 3.8, the injured person, S, has no contractual relationship with R Dealer. In these circumstances, contractual remedies are not available. If the injured parties are going to be compensated, it must be by imposing liability in tort law or by providing a special statutory remedy. Since the manufacturing companies allowed the defective products to reach the market, public policy would seem to require that they should be liable.

FIGURE 3.3
Product Liability

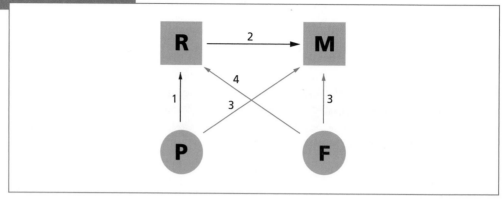

Manufacturer *M* sells a product to retailer *R*, which sells it to purchaser *P*. The product is defective and injures *P* and her friend *F*. *P* can sue *R* in *contract* [1] and *R* can sue *M* for its loss, also in *contract* [2]. *P* and *F* can sue *M* in *tort* [3]. *F* might also be able to sue *R* in *tort*, if *R* should have discovered the defect.

Not until 1932 did the British courts recognize the duty of manufacturers to the ultimate consumers of their products as an obligation in tort law; the House of Lords did so in the famous case of *Donoghue v. Stevenson*,[39] in which the facts were analogous to those in Case 3.7. Case 3.8 is drawn in part from the United States case *MacPherson v. Buick Motor Co.*,[40] decided by the New York Court of Appeals in 1916, a decision that must have influenced the later House of Lords decision.

In the years since *Donoghue v. Stevenson*, its principle has been applied by the courts in a wide variety of circumstances to protect consumers and other members of the public who may be harmed. The increasing complexity and sophistication of manufactured products, and the resultant inability of consumers and even of intermediate distributors to detect dangers in these products, places manufacturers in a position of growing responsibility for the safety of consumers. On the whole, the courts have recognized this development and have widened the application of the duty accordingly.

Simply to hold that manufacturers owe a duty of care to consumers and others who might be injured is only a partial solution to the problem. Normally, an injured party will have no way of proving that the manufacturer did not exercise reasonable care. However, if the product is defective, then it may be reasonable to assume that there has been negligence in some stage of its design, production, or inspection, unless there is evidence of some other reason for the defect. The manufacturer will thus be liable unless it can show that the cause of the defect was not something for which it should be held responsible, or at least that it had taken all reasonable precautions to prevent defective goods from slipping into the distribution system.[41]

In Case 3.9, based on the leading case of *Grant v. Australian Knitting Mills*,[42] the manufacturing company was placed in the following dilemma: if the inspection process permitted such underwear to pass through undetected, the system was inadequate and the company was therefore negligent; if the inspection process was virtually foolproof, as indeed the manufacturer claimed, then one of its employees must surely have been personally at fault, making the man-

39. [1932] A.C. 562.

40. 111 N.E. 1050 (1916).

41. United States courts have gone further. They tend to favour a principle of strict liability, under which the manufacturer impliedly warrants its products to be free of defects regardless of negligence. However, the end result is probably not very different.

42. [1936] A.C. 85.

ufacturer vicariously liable. Accordingly, the present state of our law appears to make manufacturers liable for all product defects of which, given the present state of technology, they can reasonably be expected to be aware. Courts will not accept as a defence the excuse that to eliminate the defect would add to the cost of production; a manufacturer does not have the right to market an inherently dangerous article where a method exists of manufacturing the same article without risk of harm.[43] Thus, manufacturers who choose to reduce costs by omitting necessary safety features, or by using a system of sampling inspection rather than inspecting every item, become responsible for harm that results. In the long run, the savings in production cost may be outweighed by increased insurance premiums for product liability.

Case 3.10 takes us a stage further. Even though a product is not defective in any way, there may be dangers if the product is not properly used; courts have ruled that manufacturers owe a duty to consumers to give proper warning of such dangers.[44]

The duty to warn is a continuing one. If, after a product has been placed on the market, the manufacturer becomes aware of potential dangers in its use, it must issue appropriate warnings to the public. The duty to warn is owed to consumers of the product. Sometimes, however, it may be discharged by issuing the warning to a "learned intermediary." In *Hollis v. Dow Corning Corp.*[45] the Supreme Court of Canada considered that the warning of the dangers of silicone breast implants should have been given to the physicians who would perform the implant operation. Had this been done, a direct warning to the public might not have been necessary.[46]

A plaintiff whose claim is based on a failure to warn must also satisfy the court that, had a proper warning been given, she would not have used the product or would not have used it in the way she did; that is, the failure to warn must have been a cause of the injury.[47]

CONTEMPORARY ISSUE

Tobacco Liability

Contrast the following press reports:

> British Columbia launched a landmark lawsuit against the country's big tobacco companies yesterday, then renewed efforts to get other provinces on board for what promises to be a lengthy struggle. The B.C. action was applauded by the country's health community, but angrily dismissed by the tobacco companies. Imperial Tobacco, RJR-Macdonald Inc. and Rothmans, Benson and Hedges Inc. immediately launched their own court challenge of legislation which accompanied yesterday's court action. That law compels tobacco manufacturers to reveal the contents of their products and orders them to help defray British Columbia's anti-smoking campaign. B.C. says it is seeking billions of dollars—no specific amount was cited—to protect future generations against the hazards of smoking and to recover some of the $400 million it spends annually

continued

---

43. Nicholson v. John Deere Ltd. (1989), 57 D.L.R. (4th) 639.

44. Lambert v. Lastoplex Chemical Co. Ltd., [1972] S.C.R. 569 (inflammable lacquer); Buchan v. Ortho Pharmaceutical (Canada) Ltd. (1984), 28 C.C.L.T. 233 (Ont.) (side effects of contraceptive pills). The duty to warn may be excluded by an express contractual provision; see Bow Valley Husky (Bermuda) Ltd. v. Saint John Shipbuilding Ltd. (1997), 153 D.L.R. (4th) 385 (S.C.C.). For an interesting analysis of the duty to warn see Boivin, "Factual Causation in the Law of Manufacturer—Failure to Warn" (1998–99), 30 *Ottawa Law Rev.* 47.

45. (1995), 129 D.L.R. (4th) 609. See Boivin, *supra*, n. 44.

46. The physician might then be liable if he operated without explaining the risk to the patient; this is discussed in Chapter 4.

47. In Hollis v. Dow Corning Corp. *supra*, n. 45, the Supreme Court of Canada preferred a subjective approach to causation in product liability cases; would the plaintiff have used the product if she had known of the risk? See also Arndt v. Smith (1997), 148 D.L.R. (4th) 48 (S.C.C.).

treating patients with smoking-related illnesses. It alleges cigarette makers failed to warn consumers of the dangers of smoking, targeted children in their advertising and must bear financial responsibility for the cost of treating those made ill by their products....

Source: "B.C. to Battle Tobacco Makers," *Toronto Star*, November 13, 1998.

The Ontario government plans a massive lawsuit against American tobacco manufacturers that sell cigarettes in Canada. Health Minister Elizabeth Witmer announced yesterday that the government expects to sue the major U.S. cigarette producers for as much as $40 billion (U.S.), or $59 billion. The money would be used to pay for smoking-related health-care costs estimated at $1.1 billion a year and to expand anti-smoking programs.

"We're going to sue the tobacco industry for damages, based on the allegations of a criminal conspiracy," Witmer said in unveiling the province's new direction in the battle against smoking. The lawsuit is the first launched in the U.S. by a Canadian province....

The province is essentially going after the manufacturers for the amount of money it has spent since Ontario began tracking smoking-related health-care costs in the early 1970s. The suit has not been launched yet, but it is expected that all major tobacco companies operating in the U.S. will be named since they distribute their products in Canada, either directly, or via Canadian subsidiaries....Witmer said going the U.S. route, as opposed to joining British Columbia in its lawsuit against Canadian tobacco manufacturers, is the best chance for Ontario to see some money. The B.C. suit is stalled because of legal challenges.

"The reality is the law firms that we are presently working with have a track record of success and also this is based on a criminal conspiracy," Witmer said of the decision to retain two American firms that specialize in this type of litigation. Those firms have given the government the estimate of $40 billion (U.S.), which they labelled "conservative."

Source: "Ontario Seeks $59 billion from U.S. Tobacco Giants," *Toronto Star*, April 24, 1999.

Philip Morris Cos. shares fell to a two-year low after an Oregon jury ordered the world's largest tobacco company to pay a record $81 million in damages to a smoker's family, the second big award against the industry this year....The tobacco industry's $206-billion settlement with 46 states last fall was designed to remove its largest litigation concern. Tuesday's Oregon ruling and another $51.5-million judgment against Philip Morris in February raise new concerns that juries no longer agree with the companies' four-decade-long strategy of denying responsibility for the ills of smokers and will continue to give smokers large awards....

A Multnomah County jury in Portland decided on Tuesday that Philip Morris was responsible for the 1997 death of retired school janitor Jesse Williams, who smoked for 42 years and died at age 67. On Feb. 11, a San Francisco jury ordered Philip Morris to pay $51.5-million in punitive damage awards to a long-time smoker. In four decades of litigation, tobacco companies had only lost a handful of lawsuits filed by individuals—and no judgment exceeded $1 million. The trend is raising concerns that the industry could lose more lawsuits....Meantime, the industry's legal challenges are mounting. The number of tobacco-related lawsuits pending against Philip Morris in the United States rose to 660 from 545 a year earlier....

Source: "Tobacco Industry under Legal Fire," *National Post*, April 1, 1999.

Questions to Consider

1. Should individual smokers be compensated for smoking-related illnesses? How can one prove the illness was caused by smoking? Are smokers responsible for their own misfortunes? Are they contributorily negligent?

2. What is the basis for the provincial claims? Why would Ontario choose to sue in the United States rather than in Canada?

(For an interesting review of the issues relating to tobacco liability, see Evans, "Products Liability in Ontario: Is the Tobacco Industry in Trouble?" (1998), 8 *Windsor Review of Legal and Social Issues* 113.)

OCCUPIER'S LIABILITY

Common sense might lead us to assume that an occupier (owner or tenant) of land and buildings would be liable for injuries inflicted upon visitors to the premises according to the ordinary rules of negligence; a visitor should have a claim against the owner or tenant of real property for any harm caused by unreasonable conduct, such as creating or leaving unexpected hazards in places where they might injure an innocent visitor. Unfortunately, this area of the law became bound up with concepts of land law and, as we shall see in Chapter 23, land law developed from often rigid and irrational ancient common law concepts. Distinctions grew up dividing visitors on land and in buildings into several categories, with the obligations of the occupier to take care varying according to the category to which the visitor belongs. The categories in descending order are *invitee*, *licensee*, and *trespasser*. The distinction between invitee and licensee was abolished by statute in England in 1957 and has also disappeared in some Canadian provinces.[48]

At common law, the highest obligation is owed to an **invitee**. An invitee is a person permitted by the occupier to enter for business purposes, where the occupier obtains some material benefit or has the probability of a benefit from the invitee's presence. For example, a customer entering a retail store is an invitee. Courts have disagreed on whether an invitee of a tenant is also an invitee when passing over the landlord's premises in order to reach the tenant's premises.

invitee
a person permitted by an occupier to enter premises for business purposes

CASE 3.11

A had been shopping at *B*'s milk store in a shopping plaza owned by *C*. On his way back to his car he tripped over an uneven paving stone just outside the store, fell, and sustained injuries. He sued both *B* and *C*. On similar facts it has been held that the plaintiff was an invitee of both defendants.[49] The owner of the plaza was negligent in its duty to maintain the sidewalk and the milk store had a duty to provide safe access for its customers.

The duty owed by an occupier to an invitee is to take care to prevent injuries from hazards of which the occupier is aware and also those of which as a reasonable person he *ought* to be aware. Thus, an occupier will be liable for an injury caused to an invitee by a hazard of which he had no knowledge, but would have known about had he taken reasonable care.

The **licensee** category includes all other visitors who enter with the express or implied permission of the occupier. Ordinarily a licensee enters premises for personal benefit rather than for the benefit of the occupier. For example, a social guest is considered to be merely a licensee, even if her host expects ultimately to receive a business advantage as a result of the hospitality he has shown. The duty of an occupier to a licensee is to remove concealed dangers of which he has knowledge; he has no liability for hazards unknown to him, even though a reasonable person in his place ought to have realized that a hazard existed.

licensee
a visitor (other than an invitee) who enters premises with the consent of the occupier

In those provinces that have introduced occupiers' liability legislation, the distinction between invitee and licensee has disappeared and a common duty of care is owed by an occupier to all visitors lawfully on the premises. Essentially, the general principles of negligence now apply.

A **trespasser** is one who enters upon premises unlawfully; she enters without an invitation from or the permission of the occupier and is either unknown to the occupier or, if known to him, would be refused permission. The duty owed in these circumstances is minimal: the occupier must not set out deliberately to harm the trespasser or recklessly disregard the possibility

trespasser
a person who enters premises without the permission of the occupier

48. Occupiers' Liability Act, 1957, 5 and 6 Eliz. 2, c. 31 (U.K.); R.S.A. 1980, c. O-3, s. 5; R.S.B.C. 1996, c. 337, s. 3; R.S.O. 1990, c. O.2, s. 1(a).

49. Snitzer v. Becker Milk Co. (1977), 15 O.R. (2d) 345.

that his acts might injure a trespasser. Thus, he must not set out traps in an open field, or fire a gun in the general area where he knows a trespasser to be. It is sometimes said that even a trespasser is owed a duty of "common humanity."

NUISANCE

Public Nuisance

public nuisance
interference with the lawful use of public amenities

A small group of offences, known as **public nuisances**, includes such misconduct as blocking public roads, interfering with other public amenities such as the use of marketplaces or parks, and emitting dangerous substances in public places. Actions against the wrongdoer may ordinarily be brought only by an organ of government on behalf of the public as a whole. Occasionally, an individual who has shown a special injury that is substantially greater than that sustained by other members of the public in general may successfully maintain an action for compensation against the wrongdoer. These common law public nuisances are of limited significance today.

Private Nuisance

On the other hand, the common law has long recognized an occupier's right to the normal use and enjoyment of her land, free from interference from noxious fumes, from contaminating liquids poured into rivers or percolating through the soil, and from excessive noise. The term "occupier" includes not only the owner of land but tenants as well. Since most members of the public qualify as owners or tenants of their homes, they may legally complain of **private nuisances**. Even a person who acquires land knowing that it is already exposed to a nuisance may have a right to sue the offending party.[50]

private nuisance
interference with an occupier's use and enjoyment of her land

Does the law give an occupier a right to absolute freedom from these various annoyances? The answer must be a relative one weighing competing interests in society. It turns on two main issues: the degree of interference with the occupier's use and enjoyment of the land, and the economic importance of the offending activity. The level of interference that a community as a whole already tolerates, and hence that individual members of it can be expected to tolerate as *reasonable use*, also varies according to local conditions. The standard of reasonable use of adjoining lands in an industrial area such as Hamilton, Ontario, might be quite unreasonable and amount to tortious use in a holiday resort area such as Ingonish, Cape Breton. These are questions that are difficult to resolve in the context of private litigation. Increasingly, they have become the subject of government regulation.

Environmental Protection

A major problem confronting modern society is pollution of the atmosphere and water resources. In common law, the mere discharge of noxious substances into the atmosphere or into water is not itself a breach of duty, either to the community at large or to individuals who may subsequently be harmed by those substances. A person who suffers injury as a result may, of course, be able to establish liability in negligence. But it may be very difficult to establish that the conduct of any one person or industry has caused harm. We can see this difficulty in the buildup of carbon monoxide and other noxious substances in the atmosphere from the opera-

---

50. Belisle v. Canadian Cotton Ltd., [1952] O.W.N. 114.

tion of internal combustion engines in automobiles. Those who breathe the fumes over an extended period of time may suffer serious injury to health, but it is impossible to conclude that any one automobile is responsible for the harm. For these reasons, effective control over pollution can be obtained only through legislation that carefully defines standards limiting the escape of noxious substances and that prescribes heavy penalties for failure to comply with those standards. We shall consider these issues further in Chapters 29 and 32.

OTHER TORTS

One Tort or Many?

Tort law is continually changing and expanding.[51] New activities and technologies are developed, bringing new risks to the public. The law eventually creates standards for carrying on these activities and grants remedies to parties injured by conduct failing to meet those standards. As a result, it is not possible to enumerate a definitive list of torts or a comprehensive description of all conduct for which the law imposes liability. Some writers attempt to rationalize a general principle of tort law: that all conduct that causes unreasonable harm to others is tortious and creates liability. But such a general principle is not very helpful without examining particular torts. For our purposes a discussion of specific areas of tort law is more useful. The torts discussed below by no means constitute an exhaustive list. Some torts are examined in the context of other subjects; we shall discuss them as they arise and need mention them only briefly here.

For example, an outsider who incites a party to break an existing contractual obligation commits a tort known as **inducing breach of contract**. As we see in Chapter 7, any contract pursuing such a result is illegal as being against public policy. The tort of **deceit** takes the form of knowingly making a false statement with a view to inducing another to act upon it to her detriment. We discuss it in Chapters 4 and 9 under the heading of *misrepresentation*. The tort of **conversion** consists in the wrongful exercise of control over goods, inconsistent with the ownership or against the wishes of the party entitled to them. We encounter the tort of conversion in Chapter 16, when examining the liability of a seller who wrongfully disposes of goods that do not belong to him and of a carrier who disobeys instructions and wrongfully delivers goods. We meet it again in Chapter 30 when describing the liability of a buyer of goods under an instalment plan who wrongfully disposes of them before completing his payments.

Trespass

The most ancient and familiar tort is that of **trespass**, the act of entering on the lands of another without consent or lawful right or, after a lawful entry, refusing to leave when ordered to do so by the lawful occupier. In less civilized and less well-policed times trespass was often an incitement to violence. Hence it was originally considered a crime, a breach of the peace. Now, however, an owner is restricted to fencing her lands and to using no more than reasonable force in ejecting a trespasser. She may also bring an action against the trespasser, but she will often get little more than nominal damages unless she can prove that actual harm was done to her property. A brief discussion of this tort arises in Chapter 24 in relation to the rights of landlord and tenant against one another, and again in Chapter 30 as a restraint on an unpaid seller in asserting the right to repossess goods while they are on the land of a defaulting buyer.

inducing breach of contract
intentionally causing one person to breach his contract with another

deceit
knowingly making a false statement with a view to its being acted upon by another person

conversion
dealing with the goods of another in a manner that is inconsistent with the other's ownership

trespass
unlawful entering, or remaining, on the land of another

---

51. For example, some recent cases suggest that there is a tort of "unlawful appropriation of personality." Such cases, however, are more likely to fall within copyright law: see Gould Estate v. Stoddart Publishing Co. (1998), 161 D.L.R. (4th) 321.

Assault and Battery

assault
the threat of violence to a person

battery
unlawful physical contact with a person

One of the earliest torts recognized by English law is that of *trespass to the person*. Initially this tort consisted of direct and violent attack against the victim, a tort easily understood by both the citizen and the courts. The present-day legal terms are **assault** (the threat of violence) and **battery** (the actual physical contact), although the word assault is frequently used by itself in non-legal discussions to include the battery. Assaults are usually committed in the course of a crime; the attacker, if he is caught, may be fined or imprisoned. He may also be liable (in tort) to compensate his victim, though he frequently will have few assets to satisfy a civil judgment, and consequently assault cases are rarely litigated as private actions. There is, however, one important exception. Since the essence of a battery is the unlawful touching of a person without consent, a surgeon who operates on a patient without consent commits a battery. This problem is discussed in the next chapter.

False Imprisonment and Malicious Prosecution

false imprisonment
unlawfully restraining or confining another person

false arrest
causing a person to be arrested without reasonable cause

A more interesting aspect of trespass to the person—and one that has far more importance from a business perspective—is the tort of **false imprisonment**. (**False arrest**, a phrase often used in the same context, ordinarily includes a false imprisonment, but contains the additional feature of holding the victim with the intention that he be turned over to the police authorities for prosecution.) False imprisonment consists of "intentionally and without lawful justification subjecting another to total restraint of movement by either actively causing his confinement or preventing him from exercising his privilege of leaving the place in which he is."[52]

Physical restraint, or even the threat that it will be applied, is not necessary: a reasonable fear that a store detective might shout "Stop, thief!" would be enough restraint to amount to an imprisonment. Accordingly, there is a considerable risk in confronting a member of the public with the charge of a crime without strong evidence. The policy of the law is not to encourage self-help remedies, such as citizen's arrest, except in very clear cases. For example, the store detective who arrests a suspected shoplifter when no shoplifting has in fact occurred has no defence against an action for false imprisonment, even if he believed the suspect had stolen goods.

However, a private citizen who honestly makes a complaint to the police about a suspected crime is not liable for false imprisonment if the person is arrested by the police as a result of the complaint and the complaint turns out to be unfounded. Thus, if a store detective reports a suspected shoplifter to a police officer and the police officer arrests the alleged shoplifter, the store detective is not liable for false imprisonment since he did not attempt to arrest the "shoplifter"; he merely reported his suspicions to a law officer. But if he did not have an honest belief that a crime had been committed he would be guilty of **malicious prosecution**. A charge of malicious prosecution is difficult to prove, because in order to succeed the plaintiff must satisfy the court that the defendant acted from some improper motive, such as a wish to harass the plaintiff. Consequently, it is much less hazardous to report suspicious activity to the police and let them decide whether an arrest is reasonably justified, than to attempt a citizen's arrest and learn too late that no crime has been committed.

malicious prosecution
causing a person to be prosecuted for a crime without an honest belief that the crime had been committed

Defamation

defamation
making an untrue statement that causes injury to the reputation of another person

libel
written defamation

slander
spoken defamation

The tort of **defamation** is better known in each of its two forms, **libel** (written defamation) and **slander** (spoken defamation). Generally speaking, it consists of a statement that causes unjustified injury to the private, professional, or business reputation of another person. In defamation cases, the courts are not concerned with soothing injured feelings or redressing insults. They will not award damages unless the plaintiff can demonstrate that the defendant has made serious alle-

---

52. Fleming, *The Law of Torts, supra*, n. 1, at p. 27.

gations about her character, ability, or business reputation causing genuine and significant injury to the respect and esteem in which she is held by others. Such defamation requires *publication*, that is, communication of the disparaging statement to someone other than the person defamed.

A defence against a charge of defamation is that the alleged defamatory statements are true. The problem for a defendant in this instance is the difficulty of establishing, to the satisfaction of the court, the truth of the statements, which makes it hazardous to make damaging statements in the vague hope of later being able to establish their truth.

The public interest requires that in some circumstances there shall be immunity from defamation suits. Words spoken in parliamentary debate, in proceedings in law courts and inquests, and before royal commissions are subject to **absolute privilege**; the aim is to promote vigorous and candid discussion without the inhibiting effect of defamation laws. As a result, even intentional and malicious falsehoods uttered in Parliament are immune from action in the courts.

absolute privilege
complete immunity from liability for defamation

In a variety of circumstances a person may be asked to disclose information or give an opinion about another. A person may request a letter of reference from a former employer, a teacher, or a bank manager, knowing that the letter may contain some uncomplimentary statements. The person supplying the letter would have difficulty proving everything he has stated. If he were in danger of having to defend his statements in a court of law, he would rarely be willing to give a letter of reference. Obviously, such a situation would not be in the interests of applicants or of those who must rely on such letters to choose among applicants. Consequently, the law extends a **qualified privilege** to anyone giving such information. Provided he gives it in good faith with an honest belief in its accuracy, he can successfully defend an action of defamation even if the statements prove to be untrue. Qualified privilege arises in many other situations. Fair and accurate reports of proceedings in Parliament, courts, administrative tribunals, public inquiries, and meetings enjoy qualified privilege. The common law also tolerates, as a necessary function in a democratic society, statements made as fair comment and criticism in matters of public interest. The basic requisite for a critic is to establish that he had an honest belief in his opinions.[53]

qualified privilege
immunity from liability for defamation provided a statement was made in good faith

Economic Torts

Finally, there is a group of torts sometimes referred to collectively as "economic torts" that, though rarely the subject of litigation, are nevertheless of importance to the business community. These torts fall into two main categories.

First, there are those torts that relate to the carrying on of business. Intentional interference with contractual relations or inducing a breach of contract is a tort whose origins can be traced back to the 14th century when, because of the shortage of labour resulting from the "black death," a statute was passed making it an offence to lure a servant away from his master. In modern times the action has rather limited application: if *A* induces *B* to break his contract with *C*, *C* will normally sue *B* for the breach of contract.[54] **Unlawful interference with trade** is also a tort when, for example, *A* threatens *B* with violence if *B* continues to do business with *C*. Not only will *B* have an action against *A* for assault, but *C* may also sue for the interference with his business. Much of the law in this area has been concerned with the activities of labour unions,[55] and now falls within the sphere of labour relations legislation. A related tort, unfair competition, is considered in Chapter 32.

unlawful interference with trade
attempting by threats to induce one person to discontinue business relations with another

---

53. See, for example, Color Your World Corp. v. Canadian Broadcasting Corp. (1998), 156 D.L.R. (4th) 27.

54. For a recent example of an action brought in tort, see Ernst & Young v. Stuart (1997), 144 D.L.R. (4th) 328. In certain circumstances, the conduct of the parties may be reviewable under the Competition Act, R.S.C. 1985, c. C-34; see Harbord Insurance Services Ltd. v. Insurance Corp. of British Columbia (1993), 9 B.L.R. (2d) 81.

55. See Rookes v. Barnard, [1964] A.C. 1129.

product defamation
making false and damaging statements about the products of another person

passing off
representing one's own goods as those of another

A second category of torts relates to false advertising in relation to another's products.[56] A person commits the tort of injurious falsehood, or **product defamation**, when he intentionally makes false and disparaging statements about the products of another person—for example, a business competitor. Rather than seeking to denigrate the goods of a competitor, a dishonest trader may try to cash in on their established reputation by **passing off** his own goods as those of the competitor, for example, by using a deceptively similar label or form of packaging. Passing off is considered further in Chapter 22.

REMEDIES

Since the purpose of the law of torts is to compensate an injured party, the usual remedy is an award of a sum of money by way of damages. The concept of damages is discussed in greater detail in Chapter 15, but since there are some differences in the principles that govern damages in tort and in contract a few observations will be helpful in this chapter.

punitive or exemplary damages
damages awarded with the intention of punishing a wrongdoer

special damages
damages to compensate for quantifiable injuries

general damages
damages to compensate for injuries that cannot be expressed in monetary terms

restitution
an order to restore property wrongfully taken

injunction
an order restraining a person from doing, or continuing to do, a particular act

mandatory injunction
an order requiring a person to do a particular act

Generally, the purpose of damages is to restore the plaintiff, so far as is possible, to the position she would have been in if the tort had not been committed. The object of awarding damages is not to punish the wrongdoer, though **punitive** or **exemplary damages** may be awarded in rare cases, such as a brutal physical attack, a deliberate libel, or malicious false imprisonment.

Tort damages are often classified in two categories: **special damages** and **general damages**. Special damages refer to items that can be more-or-less accurately quantified—medical bills, the cost of repairing a car, or actual lost wages. General damages include more speculative items, such as future loss of earnings due to disability, and non-pecuniary losses such as awards for the "pain and suffering" of losing a limb or one's sight. Obviously, it is impossible to put a money value on health and happiness, but the courts must attempt to do so. They have thousands of precedents to guide them.

In some cases, remedies other than damages may be available although they are rarely granted. Where a defendant has wrongfully converted the plaintiff's property, the court may order its specific **restitution** to the plaintiff, since to restrict the remedy to damages would in effect allow the defendant to compel a sale of the property. Courts may also grant an **injunction**, that is, order the defendant to refrain from committing further acts of a similar nature, under pain of imprisonment for contempt of court if he disregards the order. For example, an injunction may restrain the defendant from further trespassing on the plaintiff's land. Less frequently, courts grant a **mandatory injunction**, ordering the defendant to rectify a wrong, such as removing a fence blocking the plaintiff's right-of-way to her property.

Injunctions are sometimes granted in cases of nuisance. In such cases the court must carefully balance competing interests. Where a nuisance is so severe as to make the plaintiff's land unusable, to award only damages would be tantamount to expropriation of the land in return for the damage award. But where the interference is less extreme an injunction could restrain what might otherwise be a socially desirable activity and an award of monetary damages would be more appropriate.[57]

Courts are similarly wary of granting injunctions in cases of libel and slander, since such an order would effectively amount to censorship.

---

56. False advertising of one's own products is considered, under the heading "Consumer Protection" in Chapter 32.

57. See K.V.P. Co. Ltd. v. McKie, [1949] 4 D.L.R. 497. The Ontario legislature subsequently dissolved the injunction in that case and legalized the activity, granting the plaintiff compensation instead: K.V.P. Company Limited Act, S.O. 1950, c. 33.

QUESTIONS FOR REVIEW

1. What is the origin of the word "tort," and what does it mean?

2. What is the principal purpose of tort law?

3. What is meant by "strict liability"? Should liability ever be "strict"?

4. Who should bear the loss resulting from an automobile accident? What are the alternatives?

5. What is the main justification for the principle of vicarious liability?

6. What must a plaintiff prove in order to succeed in an action based on negligence?

7. In what circumstances may a public authority be held liable for damage resulting from its failure to carry out a statutory duty imposed on it?

8. How do the courts determine the appropriate standard of care to be expected of a defendant?

9. Is the "but for" test an appropriate way of determining causation?

10. What are the objections to the "last clear chance" principle?

11. What is meant by "economic loss"? What are the two types of economic loss?

12. The Supreme Court of Canada recently expressed the view that the *res ipsa loquitur* principle is "more confusing than helpful." Do you agree?

13. Should an injured party be able to recover damages despite the fact that her own conduct was negligent and contributed to the injury?

14. Is it relevant, in a tort action, that the injured party has taken out insurance against the loss sustained?

15. When is a manufacturer under a duty to warn?

16. Distinguish an invitee, a licensee, and a trespasser.

17. What is the difference between a public and a private nuisance?

18. What constitutes false imprisonment?

19. Distinguish libel and slander. What is meant by "privilege" in the context of defamation?

20. What are "punitive damages"? Should they be awarded in tort actions?

21. What is an injunction?

CASES AND PROBLEMS

1 Western Ferries Inc. entered into a contract with Invincible Security Services Ltd. to provide security for its dockyard buildings. One of Invincible's employees, De Sage, was employed to patrol the premises during the night. For reasons unknown, DeSage deliberately set fire to one of the buildings, causing damage amounting to $65 000.

Western brought an action against Invincible, claiming that Invincible was liable for the actions of their employee, DeSage. Invincible responded that DeSage had come to them with good references and had been properly instructed and trained by them to do the job.

Should Invincible be held liable?

2 Sullivan and his friend Williams were having a quiet drink together one evening in the Tennessee Tavern when they got into an altercation with four young men at the next table, who had obviously had a fair amount to drink and were looking for a fight. There was a brief scuffle when one of the four men attacked Sullivan. The scuffle was broken up by two members of the tavern staff.

The tavern owner had the four men ejected by the back door of the tavern. He then told Sullivan and Williams to leave by the front door. They did so, only to be confronted by the four, who viciously attacked them, causing serious injury to Sullivan.

Sullivan brought an action against the owner of the tavern, alleging that he was partly responsible for causing the injuries.

Should Sullivan succeed?

3 Lawrence, a potato farmer in Prince Edward Island, discovered that part of his crop had become infected with bacterial ring rot. He phoned the office of the provincial Department of Agriculture to ask for advice, and the Department sent an inspector to look at the crop. After a brief examination, the inspector concluded that the infection was serious and that there was a real risk of it spreading. He ordered Lawrence to spray the entire crop with the chemical MH-30, acting under the authority of a provincial statute.

As a result of the spraying Lawrence's yield that year was drastically reduced. He obtained expert opinion that the selected chemical was more powerful than was needed and that it should not have been necessary to spray the entire crop. On the basis of that opinion, he brought an action against the provincial government.

Should the government be held liable?

4 Smiley, a buyer for Carrefour Fashions, entered the store of a rival firm, Boulevard Boutique, in order to find out what were the latest lines they were carrying. He was recognized by Maldini, the manager of Boulevard. A brief argument followed, ending with Maldini calling the store detective, Rocco, and ordering him to "keep an eye" on Smiley while he (Maldini) called the police.

Maldini called the police, informing them that he had a "suspected shoplifter" on the premises. Smiley did not attempt to leave before the police arrived, assuming that Rocco would prevent him if he tried to do so.

Smiley accompanied the police officers to the police station, where they accepted his explanation of why he was in the store and released him.

What claim might Smiley have against Maldini? Does Maldini have any cause of action against Smiley?

5 Peters was driving his truck along a two-lane highway when he saw an overturned truck in the ditch at the side of the road. He stopped his truck immediately and backed up a short distance. His truck was left blocking most of one lane, although he could have pulled over three or four feet more on to the shoulder.

Widman was riding his motorcycle in the same direction. He saw Peters' truck ahead of him, but then his attention was distracted when he saw the overturned truck. He slowed to a speed of about 70 km/h, tried to see if anyone was in the overturned truck, looked back to the road in front of him too late, and ran into Peters' truck. He sustained serious injuries.

Widman brought an action against Peters, alleging that Peters had stopped his vehicle in a dangerous position, thus contributing to the accident.

Should Widman succeed?

6. Prentice, an encyclopedia salesman, telephoned Hall and arranged to visit her at her apartment to show his firm's latest volumes. Entering the apartment building, owned by Newman, Prentice found the staircase lighting out of order. He attempted to climb the stairs in the dark and fell on a loose step, breaking his leg. Hall knew of the faulty light and the loose step but had not thought to warn Prentice. Nor had anyone told Newman of either defect.

What claim does Prentice have against either Hall or Newman?

7. Princess Properties Inc. are the owners of a large office building originally constructed in the 1930s. Renovations were carried out by Fundamental Construction Ltd. in 1975, during which fireproofing material, containing asbestos, was installed. Princess did not know that the material contained asbestos and had relied on Fundamental to select appropriate insulating material.

In the course of further renovations in 1987, the existence of the asbestos material was discovered. Considering the material to be a health hazard, Princess had it removed.

Princess brought an action for the cost of removing the material and for lost rent against

(a) Fundamental Construction Ltd.

(b) the architects, who had specified the use of the material in 1975

(c) the manufacturers of the material

On what basis might Princess have a valid claim against each of these defendants and what are the principal issues that would have to be determined at trial?

PROFESSIONAL LIABILITY

This chapter is primarily concerned with the application of tort law to professionals—persons such as accountants, architects, doctors, engineers, lawyers, and pharmacists. In this chapter we examine such questions as:

- what are the special duties owed by professionals to their clients and to others?

- how do the duties differ when they derive from contract? fiduciary relationship? tort?

- what is the appropriate standard of care expected of professionals?

- how is causation determined when a loss is suffered?

- what is the role of professional organizations in setting standards for professional conduct?

PROFESSIONAL LIABILITY: THE LEGAL DILEMMA

Who are professionals? They are people whose skills have a significant intellectual content and draw on an underlying, developing body of theory affecting the practice of their profession. Members of a profession are usually licensed to offer their services to the public under a system of certification administered by one or more governing bodies of the profession. They have specialized knowledge and skills that their clients rely on and are prepared to pay for.

Professional opinions are not infallible. Their value lies in assisting in clients' decisions and in increasing the likelihood that those decisions will be sound. The purchase of professional services reduces risk. But when a client pays for and relies on professional advice and it turns out to be wrong, the question arises whether the professional is liable for the loss or harm suffered by the client, or even by someone else, who relies on the advice.

As business becomes more complex, professional services have become one of the fastest growing and most important sectors of the economy. While purchasers of professional services have become increasingly aware of their rights and more willing to pursue those rights in the courts, the potential liability for economic harm caused by negligent conduct of professionals has grown considerably.

As in other areas of tort law, the courts face a social problem in determining when liability for professional incompetence or negligence arises. In theory, there is a persuasive argument to be made in favour of widened liability of professionals. In terms of distributive justice,[1] the benefits (or utility) gained by a plaintiff who recovers damages will exceed the losses (or reduced utility) of a professional defendant who has to pay them but who can recoup the loss by increasing fees and by purchasing insurance protection to safeguard against liability. However, if the courts go too far and award damages to compensate everyone who relies on bad advice the increased costs will likely inhibit many activities that are valuable to society as a whole.

In practice, the greater exposure to liability for professional negligence has led to extensive use of liability insurance. Because of uncertainty concerning liability and the risk of heavy damages, insurance premiums have been rising. Professional fees, in turn, increase to cover insurance costs. As fees rise, clients expect more for their money, and when they are disappointed are more likely to sue. The process is something of a vicious circle.

The dilemma facing the courts is well summarized in this passage by Professor Brian Cheffins[2] regarding the potential liability of auditors for incorrect statements in a corporation's financial statement, and quoted with approval by LaForest, J. in the Supreme Court of Canada:

> In addition to providing only limited benefits, imposing widely drawn duties of care on auditors would probably generate substantial costs....One reason [for this] is that auditors would expend more resources trying to protect themselves from liability. For example, insurance premiums would probably rise since insurers would anticipate more frequent claims. Also, auditors would probably incur higher costs since they would try to rely more heavily on exclusion clauses. Hiring lawyers to draft such clauses might be expensive because only the most carefully constructed provisions would be likely to pass judicial scrutiny. Finally, auditors' opportunity costs would increase. Whenever members of an accounting firm have to spend time and effort preparing for litigation, they forego revenue generating accounting activity. More trials would mean that this would occur with greater frequency. The higher costs auditors would face as a result of broad duties of care could have a widespread impact. For example, the supply of accounting services would probably be reduced since some marginal firms would be driven to the wall. Also, because the market for accounting services is protected by barriers to entry imposed by the profession, the surviving firms would pass on at least some of the increased costs to their clients.[3]

THE PROFESSIONAL DUTY OF CARE

The duty of care that is assumed by professionals may be considered under three headings

1. contractual duty
2. fiduciary duty
3. duty in tort

---

1. We have encountered the concept of distributive justice in Chapter 1.
2. B.R. Cheffins, "Auditors' Liability in the House of Lords: A Signal Canadian Courts Should Follow" (1991), 18 *C.B.L.J.* 118, at 125–7.
3. Hercules Managements Ltd. v. Ernst & Young (1997), 146 D.L.R. (4th) 577 at 593.

In the great majority of cases, the professional stands in a contractual relationship with her client. Because of the professional's skill and experience, a special relationship of trust usually exists between professional and client, giving rise to a fiduciary duty. A professional, like anyone else, owes a duty of care under tort law to persons who may foreseeably be injured by her negligence.

Contractual Duty

An agreement to provide professional services to a client contains a promise, whether stated expressly or not, to perform those services with due care. A breach of that promise is a breach of the contract, and the client may then sue for damages. The next part of this book is devoted to the law of contracts, including remedies for breach of contract, and subsequent chapters will discuss liability for breach of a contractual promise, including a promise to perform with due care.

It may come as a surprise to learn that the individual shareholders of a corporation do not have a contractual relationship with the auditor.[4] When shareholders vote to approve the appointment of an auditor at the corporation's annual meeting, they are acting collectively as one of the decision-making organs of the corporation and are making a decision *for the corporation*. The contract by which the auditor is engaged is therefore a contract between the auditor and the corporation as a separate legal entity: the shareholders are not parties to that relationship and any duty owed to them would be a fiduciary one or a duty in tort.[5]

Fiduciary Duty

In addition to possible tort liability, a professional's duty extends beyond the contract in another important way. A principle of equity imposes a **fiduciary duty** of care where a person is in a special relationship of trust, such as usually exists in professional–client relations.[6] This fiduciary duty arises even when the professional donates services free of charge, so that no contract exists.

According to the judgment of Wilson J. in the Supreme Court of Canada, in *Frame v. Smith*,[7] relationships in which a fiduciary obligation have been imposed possess three general characteristics:

1. The fiduciary has scope for the exercise of some discretion or power.

2. The fiduciary can unilaterally exercise that power or discretion so as to affect the beneficiary's legal or practical interests.

3. The beneficiary is peculiarly vulnerable to or at the mercy of the fiduciary holding the discretion or power.

A fiduciary duty arising from a relationship of trust may impose a wider range of duty on a professional than is expressly stated in the contract. For example, a lawyer who entered into a business arrangement with a client of long standing and failed to disclose his own precarious financial situation was held to be in breach of his fiduciary duty to the client.[8] So too was a bank that gave advice to a client regarding a proposed takeover without revealing that the bank, through one of its directors, also had an interest in the takeover and was thus in a position of

fiduciary duty
a duty imposed on a person who stands in a special relation of trust to another

---

4. Roman Corp. v. Peat Marwick Thorne (1992), 8 B.L.R. (2d) 43.

5. See Hercules Managements Ltd. v. Ernst & Young (1997), 146 D.L.R. (4th) 577 (S.C.C.), considered below.

6. Nocton v. Lord Ashburton, [1914] A.C. 932 at 943–58; Hedley, Byrne & Co. Ltd. v. Heller & Partners Ltd., [1964] A.C. 465 at 486. For an example concerning the duty of a bank to its customer, see Hayward v. Bank of Nova Scotia (1985), 32 C.C.L.T. 286.

7. [1987] 2 S.C.R. 99 at 136. See also Air Canada v. M & L Travel Ltd. (1993), 108 D.L.R. (4th) 592; Hodgkinson v. Simms (1994), 117 D.L.R. (4th) 161.

8. Korz v. St. Pierre (1987), 61 O.R. (2d) 609.

conflict of interest.[9] And an accountant may not use information obtained from a client to make an investment without the consent of the client.

Liability for breach of fiduciary duty may also arise although there has been no negligence.

CASE 4.1

Hodgkinson, a stockbroker, was inexperienced in tax planning. He wanted an independent professional to advise him respecting tax planning and tax shelter needs. He retained Simms, an accountant who specialized in these areas. On Simms' advice, Hodgkinson invested in a number of MURBs (multiple unit residential buildings) as tax shelters and lost heavily when the value of the MURBs fell during a decline in the market. Unknown to Hodgkinson, Simms was also acting for the developers in structuring these MURBs and did not disclose that fact to Hodgkinson. The advice was perfectly sound at the time it was given but the client lost heavily when the real estate market subsequently collapsed. The Supreme Court of Canada accepted the client's claim that he would not have undertaken the investment had he known of the adviser's conflict of interest. Simms was held to be in breach of his fiduciary duty to Hodgkinson and consequently liable to compensate Hodgkinson for his loss.[10]

A fiduciary obligation requires complete fidelity and loyalty to the other party to the relationship. We shall examine this requirement again in later chapters when we consider such topics as undue influence, agency, partnership, and the duties of corporate directors.

Duty in Tort

Does a client also have a tort claim for negligence? A complaint, whether in contract or in tort, is based on a breach of the duty of care owed to the client, but until the 1980s the courts appeared to favour the view that a professional's liability should be governed by the duties owed under the contract.[11] They limited a client's right to sue for the tort of negligence to special circumstances where the professional's conduct did not fall within her contractual obligations.[12] Subsequent decisions suggested that a plaintiff might choose to sue either in contract or in tort and this approach has been confirmed by the Supreme Court of Canada. In a case where a solicitor was negligent in arranging a mortgage that was later found to be void, the Court held that the client was entitled to sue in either contract or tort.[13] The common law duty of care is not confined to relationships that arise apart from contract; it exists independently of the duty owed under the contract.

Of greater importance, usually, is the fact that a duty may be owed in tort to persons other than the client who is paying for the services. Many people may rely on a professional opinion given to a single client, as for example:

- in the practice of professional auditing, by the expression of an opinion on the fairness and accuracy of the client firm's financial statement
- in the work of engineers and architects, when they recommend design specifications for structures that, if faulty, may present risks to occupiers and others

---

9. Standard Investments Ltd. v. Canadian Imperial Bank of Commerce (1985), 22 D.L.R. (4th) 410.

10. Hodgkinson v. Simms, *supra*, n. 7. See also Martin v. Goldfarb (1998), 163 D.L.R. (4th) 639.

11. Nunes Diamonds v. Dominion Electric Co. (1972), 26 D.L.R. (3d) 699 at 727–8.

12. See, for example, Beaver Lumber Co. Ltd. v. McLenaghan (1983), 23 C.C.L.T. 12, where a seller of home building materials recommended an incompetent contractor.

13. Central Trust Co. v. Rafuse (1986), 31 D.L.R. (4th) 481; B.G. Checo International Ltd. v. British Columbia Hydro & Power Authority (1993), 14 C.C.L.T. (2d) 233.

- in assessments of creditworthiness prepared by credit analysts or bankers for their customers and which come to the attention of other lenders
- in the estimates of accountants engaged by a corporation to provide it with a valuation of the business or its shares, when the valuation is intended for the use of a third party
- in the preparation of a will by a lawyer whose client intends to leave property to a beneficiary under the will
- in the professional opinion given by one doctor to another on a consulting basis concerning the patient of the second doctor

third-party liability

liability to some other person who stands outside a contractual relationship

Potential **third-party liability** also exists for insurance agents and real estate agents. The contractual duty of a real estate agent is normally owed to the vendor of the property; that of an insurance agent is usually owed to the insurance company with which she arranges insurance.[14] In the course of their work for their principals however, these agents develop close relations with persons to whom they may refer as "clients"—applicants for insurance and prospective purchasers of houses, respectively. While in a strict sense their commissions are paid by their principals, the persons with whom they deal in the course of their work provide them with the opportunity of earning the commissions and frequently rely on their advice.

As we shall see, one of the most difficult questions that the courts have had to answer in recent years is where, precisely, to draw the line in deciding when a professional incurs liability to a non-client for a negligent or inaccurate statement.

The Choice of Action

Before turning to that question, one other issue needs to be addressed. As we have seen, sometimes a professional may be liable in tort but not in contract, or may be liable for breach of fiduciary duty without having been negligent. But there will frequently be cases where the professional is liable in both contract and in tort, and perhaps for breach of fiduciary duty as well. Does it matter whether the client sues for breach of contract, breach of fiduciary duty, or for negligence?

The choice may be important, since the rules governing the time limits for bringing an action might make it advantageous to sue in tort.[15] On the other hand, in a tort action a client's own contributory negligence may be raised as a defence, whereas it seems that this may not be done in an action for breach of contract.[16] However, if the client chooses to sue in tort rather than in contract the defendant may still rely upon any term of the contract that excludes or limits liability.[17]

The form of the action may also affect the amount of damages awarded in some cases. The principles for determining the measure of damages are not exactly the same in contract as in tort.[18] In the case of breach of fiduciary duty, a defendant may be under a **duty to account** for any profit derived from the breach in addition to or as an alternative to damages. However, in

duty to account

the duty of a person who commits a breach of trust to hand over any profits derived from the breach

---

14. By contrast, an insurance *broker* usually acts as agent for the insured: see the discussion in Adams-Eden Furniture Ltd. v. Kansa General Insurance Co. (1996), 141 D.L.R. (4th) 288, and see Chapter 18.

15. The time limit for a tort action is normally calculated from the moment when the breach is *discovered*, rather than when it *occurs*, as is the rule in contract. In Central Trust Co. v. Rafuse, *supra*, n. 13, the invalidity of the mortgage was not discovered until some years after it was executed. This difference in time limits is also important in cases of negligence by an architect or builder, where a defect may only be discovered many years after construction has been completed and it would be too late to sue in contract. See Brook Enterprises v. Wilding (1973), 38 D.L.R. (3d) 472.

16. See Coopers & Lybrand v. H.E. Kane Agencies Ltd. (1985), 32 C.C.L.T. 1; Caners v. Eli Lilley Canada Inc. (1996), 134 D.L.R. (4th) 730. But contrast Cosyns v. Smith (1983), 25 C.C.L.T. 54.

17. Central Trust Co. v. Rafuse, *supra*, n. 13; London Drugs Ltd. v. Kuehne & Nagel International Ltd. (1992), 13 C.C.L.T. (2d) 1. Concurrent liability is not restricted to professionals. In Morrison v. McCoy Bros., [1987] 3 W.L.R. 301, it was held that a negligent truck repairer could be sued in tort as well as in contract.

18. See Chapter 3, under the heading "Remedies," and Chapter 15, under the heading "The Measurement of Damages."

Hodgkinson v. Simms,[19] LaForest, J. (speaking for the majority of the Supreme Court of Canada) held that the proper approach to damages for breach of a fiduciary duty is restitutionary. The appellant is entitled to be placed in as good a position as he would have been in if the breach had not occurred. In *Martin v. Goldfarb*, Finlayson, J.A., delivering the judgment of the Ontario Court of Appeal expressed the view that, regardless of the doctrinal underpinning, plaintiffs should not be able to recover higher damage awards merely because their claim is characterized as breach of fiduciary duty as opposed to breach of contract or tort.[20]

It is also unclear what would be the position of a partner in an Ontario limited liability partnership where an action, based on the negligence of another partner, is brought in contract or is alleged to constitute a breach of fiduciary duty.[21]

FIGURE 4.1
Contractual and Tort Liability

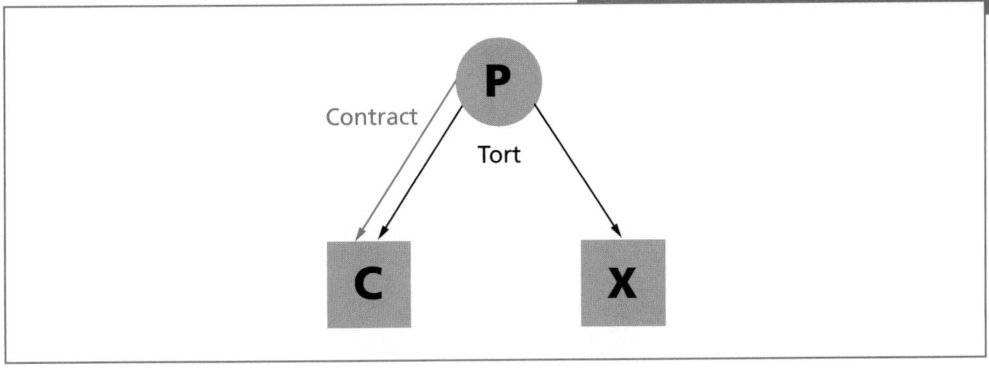

The professional (*P*) owes both a contractual duty and a duty in tort to client (*C*). The only duty owed to a third party (*X*) is a duty in tort. (There may be occasions when a fiduciary duty is owed to *C* or to *X*.)

LIABILITY FOR INACCURATE STATEMENTS

Misrepresentation

If a person makes a false assertion of fact with knowledge of its falsity, or at any rate without an honest belief in its truth and with the intention to mislead some other person, the misrepresentation is fraudulent and amounts to the tort of **deceit**. A victim who relies reasonably on the assertion and suffers a loss may recover from the wrongdoer. The tort of deceit may also be committed when a person deliberately conceals or withholds information.

deceit
the making of a false statement with the intention of misleading another person

CASE 4.2

A bank allowed a customer to invest in a company that owed a substantial debt to the bank. The bank's employees knew that the company was on the verge of insolvency but did not disclose this fact to the customer. The bank was held guilty of fraud and liable to compensate the customer.[22]

---

19. *Supra*, n. 7; see Case 4.1.

20. (1998), 163 D.L.R. (4th) 639 at 652. Despite these recent decisions, some uncertainty remains: see Waddams, "Fiduciary Duties and Equitable Compensation" (1996), 27 *C.B.L.J.* 466.

21. Limited liability partnerships are discussed in Chapter 26.

22. Sugar v. Peat Marwick Ltd. (1988), 55 D.L.R. (4th) 230.

fraudulent misrepresentation
an incorrect statement made knowingly with the intention of causing injury to another

negligent misrepresentation
an incorrect statement made without due care for its accuracy

Whereas deceit or **fraudulent misrepresentation** requires at least some guilty knowledge or willful disregard of the falsity of information provided, **negligent misrepresentation** requires only a breach of the duty of care and skill.

As we saw in Chapter 3, one of the most significant developments in the law of torts has been the extension of liability to include negligent acts causing purely economic loss, as distinguished from those causing injury to persons or property.[23] For a long time the courts drew back from holding persons liable for negligent misrepresentation except when there was a contract with the injured party or when they were subject to a special form of liability arising from their fiduciary duty, as when an accountant audits the accounts of a charitable organization without charging a fee, or when a doctor gives free medical advice. The reluctance of the courts to find persons liable for negligent misrepresentation in the absence of a direct contractual or fiduciary relationship extended especially to professional givers of financial advice and information such as accountants, bankers, trust company officers, and stockbrokers, whose statements often reach large numbers of the public. Concern about the wide scope of potential liability was voiced by an English judge when he observed that "Words are more volatile than deeds, they travel fast and far afield, they are used without being expended."[24]

In a leading case in 1951,[25] the English Court of Appeal held that an accountant who carelessly audited a misleading financial statement, knowing that it would be shown to a prospective investor, was not liable to the investor for the loss caused by reliance on the audited statement. The Court gave as an example a stockbroker who was advising a client about the value of a corporation's shares while they were at lunch, and a stranger at the next table overheard the advice. Would the stockbroker be liable to compensate the stranger for a loss suffered because, relying on the overheard advice, he invested in the corporation? The court feared that this kind of unexpected liability to third persons for advice given to and intended only for a client might make the risk so wide as to limit severely the reasonable freedom of professionals to practise their occupations. Lord Justice Denning, who dissented from the majority opinion in the above case, asserted that such risks were greatly exaggerated: the duty need not be owed to every conceivable person, but should be confined to a particular person or group whom the maker of the statement could reasonably expect to rely on it.

The *Hedley Byrne* Principle

Lord Denning's position was vindicated by the House of Lords 12 years later in the famous case of *Hedley Byrne v. Heller & Partners.*

CASE 4.3

Easipower asked Hedley Byrne, an advertising agency, to handle its account in placing ads in magazines and commercials on radio and TV. Since Hedley Byrne would have to extend credit to Easipower in arranging the advertising, it first decided to ask its own bank to obtain credit information on Easipower, and in particular about whether Easipower would be good for a line of credit up to certain limits. The bank manager made inquiries from Heller & Partners (Easipower's bankers) about Easipower's creditworthiness, without revealing Hedley Byrne's identity. Heller sent the following letter in reply:

continued

---

23. Negligent misstatements causing physical injury have long been actionable. For example, it would be a tort to assure a motorist that the road ahead is safe while carelessly forgetting to say that there is a deep uncovered ditch across the road just over the brow of the next hill.

24. Hedley Byrne v. Heller & Partners, [1964] A.C. 465 at 534, per Lord Pearce.

25. Candler v. Crane, Christmas & Co., [1951] 2 K.B. 164.

CONFIDENTIAL

For your private use and without responsibility on the part of the bank or its officers

Dear Sir:

In reply to your inquiry we advise that Easipower is a respectably constituted company, considered good for its ordinary business obligations. Your figures are larger than we are accustomed to see.

Yours truly,

Heller & Partners.

At no time did Hedley Byrne communicate directly with Heller, but its own bank did inform it of the full contents of the letter, including the disclaimer of responsibility. Hedley Byrne then accepted Easipower as an account and placed extensive advertising for it, running up a balance of many thousands of pounds. Shortly afterwards Easipower became insolvent and was unable to pay Hedley Byrne more than a small portion of the debt. Hedley Byrne sued Heller for the resulting loss, claiming it was caused by Heller's negligent misrepresentation of Easipower's creditworthiness.

The House of Lords found that although Heller neither dealt with nor even knew the identity of Hedley Byrne, Heller should have foreseen that its information would be used by a customer of the other bank. Accordingly, it owed that customer a duty to take reasonable care in expressing an opinion about the financial state of Easipower. On the facts, however, it held that the **disclaimer** of responsibility, clearly stated in the letter, absolved Heller of liability. In effect, the law lords said that Hedley Byrne could not rely on the information because of the disclaimer. Nevertheless, *Hedley Byrne* established the principle of liability to third parties for negligent misrepresentation.

The result seems to be that anyone who makes such a misstatement may be held liable for losses suffered by a wider group than those with whom he has a direct contractual or fiduciary relationship. There is little doubt that the decision widened the ambit of liability of people who give professional advice; the crucial question is "how wide is that ambit"?

disclaimer

an express statement to the effect that the person making it takes no responsibility for a particular action or statement

Limits to the *Hedley Byrne* Principle

If the test of liability for negligent misrepresentation were to turn entirely on who could foreseeably be harmed, banks, public accountants, and other financial analysts might be faced with an almost indeterminate liability. For example, the auditors of a corporation whose financial statements are widely distributed know that the statements will be relied on by many people unknown to them. They could be liable then to anyone who might happen to read the financial statements.[26]

CASE 4.4

Shareholders in two corporations brought an action against a firm of accountants, alleging that audits of the corporations' financial statements had been negligently prepared, and that in consequence, they had incurred investment losses and losses in the value of their shareholdings. Their claim failed.

The Supreme Court of Canada held that (a) there was no contractual relationship between the auditors of a corporation and its shareholders; and (b) the auditors owed them no duty of care in respect of their investments.[27]

---

26. This fear is largely responsible for the enactment in Ontario of legislation allowing for the creation of limited liability partnerships by accounting and other professional firms: see Chapter 26.

27. Hercules Managements Ltd. v. Ernst & Young (1997), 146 D.L.R. (4th) 577.

As to the existence (in Case 4.4) of a duty of care, the court applied a two-part test, expressed as follows:[28]

> First one has to ask whether, as between the alleged wrongdoer and the person who has suffered damage there is a sufficient relationship of proximity or neighbourhood such that, in the reasonable contemplation of the former, carelessness on his part may be likely to cause damage to the latter—in which case a prima facie duty of care arises. Secondly, if the first question is answered affirmatively, it is necessary to consider whether there are any considerations which ought to negative, or to reduce or limit the scope of the duty or the class of person to whom it is owed or the damages to which a breach of it may give rise....[29]

The first branch of the test requires an inquiry into whether there is a sufficiently close relationship between the plaintiff and the defendant that in the reasonable contemplation of the latter, carelessness on its part may cause damage to the former. The court held that a *prima facie* duty of care did exist in the *Hercules* case: the possibility that the shareholders would rely on the audited financial statements of the corporation in conducting their affairs and that they may suffer harm if the reports were negligently prepared must have been reasonably foreseeable to the auditors.

The second branch of the test raises what is essentially a policy issue. On this issue, LaForest, J. said:

> I would agree that deterrence of negligent conduct is an important policy consideration with respect to auditors' liability. Nevertheless, I am of the view that, in the final analysis, it is outweighed by the socially undesirable consequences to which the imposition of indeterminate liability on auditors might lead.[30]

Liability, consequently, should be restricted to the use of the information for the same purpose as that for which it was prepared. As a matter of law, the only purpose for which shareholders receive an auditor's report is to provide them with information in order to be able to oversee the management and affairs of the corporation—not for the purpose of guiding their personal investment decisions. Therefore, no duty of care was owed to them in that regard.

It would seem from this test that eligible plaintiffs must not only be "foreseeable" in a general sense, but also more specifically "foreseen" in relation to a contemplated transaction. So when, in an earlier case, an auditor negligently prepared accounts for a corporation, knowing that they were to be shown to a potential purchaser of the corporation, the Supreme Court of Canada held that he was liable for the loss suffered by the purchaser.[31] But an investor who bought shares in a corporation, having studied its financial statements filed with the Ontario Securities Commission, could not sue the auditor who had been negligent in auditing the statements. Although it was foreseeable that an investor might rely on the statements, such a person was not within the class to whom a duty was owed.[32]

Liability for negligent misrepresentation is not restricted to financial information provided by professionals such as accountants and bankers. A municipality has been held liable for loss

---

28. The test was first enunciated by Lord Wilberforce in the House of Lords in Anns v. Merton London Borough Council, [1978] A.C. 728 at 751–2 (H.L.). It was quoted with approval in the Hercules case, by LaForest, J., at 586. Although the test has been partly rejected in subsequent English decisions it has been followed and applied in a number of other important Canadian decisions; for example Kamloops (City) v. Nielsen (1983), 10 D.L.R. (4th) 641; Winnipeg Condominium Corp. No. 36 v. Bird Construction Co. (1995), 121 D.L.R. (4th) 193. See the discussion of "Duty of Care" in Chapter 3.

29. According to LaForest, J., this test should apply to all negligence cases, not merely those involving negligent misrepresentation.

30. At 593.

31. Haig v. Bamford (1976), 72 D.L.R. (2d) 68.

32. Dixon v. Deacon Morgan McEwan Easson (1989), 64 D.L.R. (4th) 441. The statements showed a profit of $14 million when in reality there had been a loss of $33 million.

suffered by purchasers of land who relied on incorrect information given to them by the zoning department regarding permissible use of the land.[33] An engineering firm that was negligent in preparing drawings and specifications for a provincial construction project was held liable for loss suffered by the construction company that had bid successfully for the contract in reliance on the specifications.[34]

Omissions

The duty to take reasonable care includes the duty not to omit essential steps in providing professional services. It embraces sins of omission as well as sins of commission.

CASE 4.5

Fine's Flowers Ltd. sustained a serious loss from the freezing of flowers and plants in its greenhouse. The freezing conditions were caused by failure of a water pump, which interrupted the supply of water to boilers that heated the greenhouse. Fine's had arranged its insurance with the same agent for many years and its coverage and premium costs were extensive; it relied on the agent to recommend appropriate coverage and paid the necessary premiums without question. An inspector for the insurance company had advised the agent that the insurance policy with Fine's did not cover such matters as the failure of water pumps but the agent did not report this gap in insurance coverage to Fine's. As a result Fine's had no opportunity to arrange the required additional protection.

Since the policy provided no right of recovery from the insurance company, Fine's brought an action against the agent for breach of his duty of care in failing to notify it of the insufficient coverage. The agent defended on the grounds that such a duty of care was so broad and sweeping as almost to make him strictly liable and that it was not part of his duty to know everything about a client's business in order to be in a position to anticipate every conceivable form of loss. The court nevertheless held that on the facts of the case a duty of care did exist, and Fine's succeeded in recovering damages from the agent. The grounds for recovery could equally be classified as negligent omission or breach of a special fiduciary relationship between Fine's Flowers and the insurance agent.[35]

As we noted in Chapter 3, a surgeon who operates on a patient without the patient's consent commits the tort of battery. In this context, "consent" means informed consent: before operating, the surgeon should explain the procedure and the possible risks to the patient. The modern tendency has been to hold a doctor liable in battery only when it can be said that there has been no genuine informed consent at all.[36] However, the courts have recognized a patient's right to full information about the risks inherent in a treatment and the omission of relevant information normally amounts to negligence.[37] The court also considers a second question: would a reasonable person in the position of the plaintiff have decided against the procedure upon a proper disclosure of the risks?[38] If the court is satisfied on the facts that the answer is

---

33. Bell v. City of Sarnia (1987), 37 D.L.R. (4th) 438.

34. Edgeworth Constructions Ltd. v. N.D. Lea & Associates Ltd. (1993), 107 D.L.R. (4th) 169. Interestingly, the individual engineers employed by the firm, who prepared the drawings, were held not to owe a duty to the contractor.

35. Fine Flowers Ltd. v. General Accident Assurance Co. et al. (1974), 49 D.L.R. (3d) 641; affirmed (1977), 81 D.L.R. (3d) 139. See also Martin v. Goldfarb (1998), 163 D.L.R. (4th) 639.

36. See Norberg v. Wynrib (1992), 12 C.C.L.T. (2d) 1.

37. Alternatively, it may be treated as a breach of fiduciary duty: see Seney v. Crooks (1998), 166 D.L.R. (4th) 337.

38. Hopp v. Lepp (1980), 112 D.L.R. (3d) 67; Reibl v. Hughes (1980), 114 D.L.R. (3d) 1. Contrast the "subjective" test applied in product liability cases, in Hollis v. Birch (1995), 27 C.C.L.T. (2d) 1, considered in Chapter 3.

"yes," then it is also saying that the failure to inform was not only a breach of duty but also caused the harm—and the patient will be awarded damages in compensation. But where the court is satisfied that the patient would still have consented to the treatment if the risk had been explained, the physician will not be liable.[39] The question of causation is discussed more fully later in this chapter.

THE STANDARD OF CARE FOR PROFESSIONALS

In Chapter 3 we noted that the standard of care applied in ordinary negligence actions is that of "the person on the Yonge Street subway." That standard is obviously inappropriate when judging the work of an accountant, a lawyer, or a surgeon. A client is often unable to judge whether a professional is performing to an acceptable standard of care while the work proceeds. Substandard professional work may escape detection because ordinarily several unfortunate events must coincide before an actual injury or loss to a client results. But despite suffering no apparent loss, a client may not be receiving the quality of service bargained for. How should one determine what is an appropriate and acceptable standard?

One possible approach is simply to wait and see whether a client incurs any loss from relying on professional advice—a hindsight or *ex post* approach. If the client suffers loss, then the advice must have been unsatisfactory. This approach would tend to turn professionals into insurers of their work and suggests that they would be strictly liable for all consequences of their clients' reliance upon it. Such an approach would make it impossible for many professionals to continue to practise.

The courts are well aware of the dangers of a hindsight approach. As Lord Denning said, in one leading English case :

> …the judge required Mr. Jordan to come up to the very high standard of professional competence that the law requires. That suggests that the law makes no allowance for errors of judgment. This would be a mistake. Else there would be a danger, in all cases of professional men, of their being made liable whenever something happens to go wrong. Whenever I give a judgment, and it is afterwards reversed by the House of Lords, is it to be said that I was negligent? That I did not pay enough attention to a previous binding authority or the like? Every one of us every day gives a judgment which is afterwards found to be wrong. So also with a barrister who advises that there is a good cause of action and it afterwards fails. Is it to be said on that account that he was negligent? Likewise with medical men. If they are found liable whenever they do not effect a cure, or whenever anything untoward happens, it would do a great disservice to the profession itself.[40]

CASE 4.6

Hodgins wished to add an extension with an indoor swimming pool to his house. Through his contractor, he sought the advice of the local hydro-electric commission on heating the addition. An employee of the commission, Runions, provided an estimate of the cost of heating by electricity. In reliance on the estimate, Hodgins specified electric heating for the extension. The estimate proved to be much below the actual costs. Hodgins sued the hydro-electric commission for negligent misrepresentation, on the authority of *Hedley Byrne*. Runions was found not to have been negligent.[41]

---

39. Kitchen v. McMullen (1989), 62 D.L.R. (4th) 481.

40. Whitehouse v. Jordan, [1980] 1 All E.R. 650 at 658.

41. Hodgins v. Hydro-Electric Commission of the Township of Nepean (1975), 60 D.L.R. (3d) 1.

In reaching that conclusion in the *Hodgins* case (Case 4.6) hindsight was explicitly rejected as the appropriate test. In the Ontario Court of Appeal Mr. Justice Evans observed:

> ...the Court is required to consider the information available in 1967 to one in the position of Runions. The question then arises: Did Runions exercise reasonable skill, competence and diligence in the preparation of the cost estimate or did he not? In the opinion of the expert, Runions calculated the heat loss in the same manner as anyone similarly expert in the art would have done in 1967. In the light of that uncontradicted evidence, it would appear that Runions prepared his estimate according to the skill and knowledge available to those engaged in that particular field. If Runions met the standard then he was not negligent and no liability can be imputed to the defendant. That the estimate was incorrect is not questioned, but it is not sufficient that the plaintiff establish merely that Runions' estimate was wrong, he must go further and establish that the incorrect estimate resulted from a lack of skill, competence or diligence on the part of Runions....There was no failure on the part of the defendant to discharge the only duty in law which it owed to the plaintiff, which was to take reasonable care in the preparation of the cost estimate.[42]

The approach taken in the *Hodgins* case is to compare the quality of professional work done or advice given with the standards of the profession prevailing at the time—a forward-looking or *ex ante* approach. This approach tends to assess the adequacy of professional work without reference to the consequences of relying on it. However, complying with normal professional standards is not always an adequate defence. When the case was appealed to the Supreme Court of Canada, Chief Justice Laskin agreed that the action should be dismissed. However, he added:

> In a case like the present, where liability is sought to be based on negligent misrepresentation, I do not think that it is invariably enough to defeat the action that the defendant has used the skill or knowledge known to him or to others in his field of endeavour....In my opinion, the care or skill that must be shown by the defendant must depend, as it does here, on what is the information or advice sought from him and which he has unqualifiedly represented that he can give. He may assume to act in a matter beyond his then professional knowledge or that of others in the field and, if he does, he cannot then so limit the plaintiff's reliance unless he qualifies his information or advice accordingly or unless the plaintiff knows what are the limitations of the defendant's competence when seeking the information or advice.[43]

Consequently, there seem to be two tests. A professional must exercise the same degree of skill and possess the same level of knowledge as is generally expected of members of that profession: that is to say, she must live up to the standards of the profession. The courts will normally consider two types of evidence in determining what those standards are. Many professions publish a code of conduct for their members, or guidelines to be followed in particular types of work. These can usually be taken as laying down an appropriate standard. Frequently, the courts also hear the testimony of practitioners who state what they consider a proper standard. Sometimes, of course, professional opinion is divided—for example, about the best medical treatment in a particular circumstance. In such a case it will normally be sufficient that the defendant has followed a well-recognized practice, even though some other procedure might arguably have been better.[44]

But established standards should not be allowed to become a means for protecting members of a profession from liability:[45] where there is other evidence that can be understood by an ordinary person, that evidence can be taken into account by a court even when it contradicts the

---

42. *Ibid.*, at 4.

43. *Ibid.*, at 5.

44. Belknap v. Meekes (1989), 64 D.L.R. (4th) 452; ter Neuzen v. Korn (1995), 127 D.L.R. (4th) 577.

45. See, for example, the decision of the Supreme Court of Canada in Roberge v. Bolduc, [1991] 1 S.C.R. 374, in which a notary was held to have been negligent in conducting a title search despite having followed the common practice in the profession.

testimony of experts.[46] As Chief Justice Laskin pointed out in the *Hodgins* case, sometimes a professional undertakes a task that is beyond the usual skills of his profession; he cannot then fall back upon the normal professional standard.

The degree of skill and knowledge must consequently be commensurate with the particular task undertaken. The professional who devotes the appropriate amount of skill and care would then meet the required standard, even though the advice should turn out to be wrong. In this approach, foresight includes an element of awareness of the seriousness of harm that may flow from faulty professional advice.

CAUSATION

In the preceding chapter we defined the elements of tort liability, including the conditions that must be met before compensation will be awarded to an injured party. The court must find that: the defendant owed a duty to the injured party; the defendant was guilty of a breach of that duty; and the breach of duty caused the injury. We have discussed the first two of these conditions in this chapter in relation to the liability of a professional and now turn to the special problems of satisfying the requirement of causation.

The essence of causation, in professional–client relationships, is reliance. Did the client rely and act upon the advice of the professional? Would the client not have acted in that way if he had not received that advice?[47]

CASE 4.7

An investment company became interested in acquiring control of an apparently prosperous family business. The company commissioned a report on the prospective acquisition from a well-known firm of investment analysts. The report estimated the family business to be worth more than $4 million and considered it to be a sound investment. Without having read the report, the directors of the investment company decided that they should move quickly; they had heard rumours that there was another prospective purchaser. They purchased all the shares in the family business for $3.5 million. Subsequently, they learned that the major asset of their acquisition was almost worthless and that they had paid several times what the shares were worth.

Despite their negligence, the analysts should not be found liable since their conduct was not in any way a cause of the loss. Case 4.7 is based in part on the decision in *Toromont Industrial Holdings v. Thorne, Gunn, Helliwell & Christenson*.[48] In that case, Mr. Justice Jessup said:

> What loss, if any, flows from the fact that the certificate of the auditors was wrong and that the auditors had been negligent in the audit?...[T]he decision to purchase had already been made. The Toromont board and executive committee were eager to complete the purchase. They made little investigation and were worried about another prospective purchaser lurking in the background. I really do not think I can say that the purchase would not have been completed, or that the loss flowing from the negligence of the defendant is, in this case, the difference between the purchase price and the true value of the shares....[N]o loss has been proved by Toromont flowing from the negligence of the defendant.[49]

46. Anderson v. Chasney, [1949] 4 D.L.R. 71.

47. As we have already noted, a surgeon will not be held liable for failure to fully inform a patient of all known risks if it is clear that the patient would have agreed to the procedure in any event.

48. (1977), 14 O.R. (2d) 87. See also Martin v. Goldfarb (1998), 163 D.L.R. (4th) 639.

49. *Ibid.*, at 94–5. (Some damages were awarded, however, on other grounds.)

Generally speaking, it is up to the plaintiff to establish that the misrepresentation led to the loss. As a matter of policy, legislatures sometimes make it easier for plaintiffs to hold certain classes of defendants liable and relieve plaintiffs of the burden of establishing that they actually relied on a misrepresentation. Securities acts usually give buyers of securities a right to sue those responsible for disclosing corporate information in prospectuses when the information proves false and the buyer appears to have suffered a loss. These acts also give tenderers (sellers) a similar right in relation to information contained in takeover bid circulars. For these types of disclosure, a person who buys or sells shares is deemed to have relied on the misrepresentation.[50] The statutes shift the onus to the misrepresentor, who may then avoid liability by proving that the plaintiff had not relied on the misstatement.

THE ROLE OF PROFESSIONAL ORGANIZATIONS

Origins

Professions are, in some respects, the modern counterpart of medieval guilds. Guilds had their own standards of education and apprenticeship for admission, and their own courts for adjudicating disputes affecting the economic activities of their members. Modern professions are generally more concerned with offering expert opinions than with the practice of crafts requiring manual skills, but the autonomy of professions, that is, their ability to determine and police their own specialized standards of compliance and behaviour, remains a jealously guarded prerogative.

Responsibilities and Powers

Today, most of the major professions—medicine, nursing, dentistry, accounting, law, engineering, and architecture—are governed by professional organizations established under, and to some extent regulated by, provincial statutes. A typical professional organization has a governing council composed mainly of elected representatives of the profession, but it may also have external lay representatives appointed by the government to provide an impartial voice in decision making and to represent the public interest. Professional bodies have a number of special responsibilities:

- to set educational and entrance standards for candidates wishing to become members
- to examine and accredit educational institutions that prepare candidates for membership
- to set and adjust standards of ethical conduct and professional competence
- to hear complaints about and administer discipline to members who fail to live up to the established standards
- to defend the profession against attacks that it considers unfair, and to look after the general welfare of the profession

The governing statute typically gives members of the organization the exclusive right to use a professional designation to identify themselves and often also gives members the exclusive right to practise their profession.[51] Anyone who identifies himself as a member or attempts to practise when not accredited as a member may be—and usually is—prosecuted for committing an offence under the provincial statute.

---

50. See, for example: Securities Act, R.S.O. 1990, c. S.5, ss. 130(1) and 131(1).

51. For example, the exclusive right to practise applies to medicine and law, but not to some areas of accounting.

Two important consequences flow from these powers. First, the right to discipline gives the organizations great power over individual members; expulsion, or suspension for any extended period, may destroy a member's means of livelihood. Second, exclusivity gives these self-governing professions great power over the quality and cost of their services to the public; hence there exists a strong public interest in the affairs of the organizations.

CASE 4.8

Schilling had entrusted some $600 000 to an accountant, Hofman, to invest for him. Hofman absconded with the money. Hofman was a former member of the Association of Certified General Accountants of British Columbia, and having recently been disciplined for other offences, had been forced to resign from the Association, and had been deprived of the right to describe himself as a "CGA." Schilling sued the Association alleging negligence in not preventing Hofman from continuing to practise—as a result of which Hofman had been able to defraud Schilling.

The British Columbia Court of Appeal held that the Association was not liable. There was no private law duty of care that required the Association to bring a criminal prosecution against a former member or to inform potential clients of his resignation.[52]

Codes of Conduct

code of conduct

rules of a professional organization setting out the duties and appropriate standards of behaviour to be observed by its members

Many professional bodies require their members to observe a **code of conduct**. As already noted, such codes may be important as evidence of what constitutes an appropriate standard of professional care, and may thus help to determine the extent of the duty owed by members to their clients. Additionally, codes of conduct may impose *ethical* standards on their members over and above any legal requirements. See the following example of a typical code of conduct.

A CODE OF CONDUCT

Canadian Institute of Management Consultants

CODE OF ETHICS

A. Purpose

The purpose of this Code is to identify those professional obligations which serve to protect the public in general and the client in particular. The Code is also designed to identify clearly the expectations of members with respect to other members and the profession.

B. Definitions

"Council" is the Council or Board of any provincial or regional institute of Certified Management Consultants with membership in the Canadian Association of Management Consultants. "Member" is any individual registered and in good standing with a provincial or regional Institute of Certified Management Consultants in Canada.

continued

---

52. Schilling v. Certified General Accountants Assn. of British Columbia (1996), 135 D.L.R. (4th) 669.

C. Responsibilities To The Public

Legal: A member shall act in accordance with the applicable legislation and laws.

Representation: A member shall make representations on behalf of provincial, regional, or national Institute members only when authorized.

Public Protection: A member shall be liable for suspension or expulsion from membership where that member has behaved in a manner unbecoming to the profession, as judged by Council.

D. Responsibilities To The Profession

Knowledge: A member shall keep informed of the applicable Code of Professional Conduct and the profession's Common Body of Knowledge. A member shall strive to keep abreast of developments in any area of the profession where specific expertise is claimed.

Self Discipline: A member shall recognize that the self disciplinary nature of the profession is a privilege and that the member has a responsibility to merit retention of this privilege. Therefore, a member shall report to Council unbecoming professional conduct by another member.

Responsibilities For Others: A member shall ensure that other management consultants carrying out work on the member's behalf are conversant with, and abide by, the applicable Code of Professional Conduct.

Image: A member shall behave in a manner which maintains the good reputation of the profession and its ability to serve the public interest. A member shall avoid activities which adversely affect the quality of that member's professional advice. A member may not carry on business which clearly detracts from the member's professional status.

E. Responsibilities To Other Members

Review Of A Member's Work: A member who has been requested to review critically the work of another member shall inform that member before undertaking the work.

F. Responsibilities To The Client

Due Care: A member shall act in the best interest of the client, providing professional services with integrity, objectivity, and independence. A member shall not encourage unrealistic client expectations.

Business Development: A member shall not adopt any method of obtaining business which detracts from the professional image of the Institute or its members.

Competence: A member shall accept only those assignments which the member has the knowledge and skills to perform.

Informed Client: A member shall, before accepting an assignment, reach a mutual understanding with the client as to the assignment objectives, scope, workplan, and costs.

Fee Arrangements: A member shall establish fee arrangements with a client in advance of any substantive work and shall inform all relevant parties when such arrangements may impair or may be seen to impair the objectivity or independence of the member. A member shall not enter into fee arrangements which have the potential to compromise the member's integrity or the quality of services rendered.

continued

Conflict: A member shall avoid acting simultaneously for two or more clients in potentially conflicting situations without informing all parties in advance and securing their agreement to the arrangement. A member shall inform a client of any interest which may impair or may be seen to impair professional judgment. A member shall not take advantage of a client relationship by encouraging, unless by way of an advertisement, an employee of that client to consider alternate employment without prior discussion with the client.

Confidentiality: A member shall treat all client information as confidential.

Objectivity: A member shall refrain from serving a client under terms or conditions which impair independence and a member shall reserve the right to withdraw from the assignment if such becomes the case.

Source: Canadian Association of Management Consultants

Discipline

Unfortunately, most professions have an inevitable minority of members who act in an unprofessional, unethical, or illegal manner. The response of governing bodies is uniform: breaches of good faith are severely punished by expulsion or suspension. (There may also be provision for some form of compensation to the injured client by the governing body itself.) These actions are quite apart from any criminal prosecution of the wrongdoer or from private (civil) liability actions discussed in the preceding sections of this chapter.

Perhaps the more pervasive and difficult cases are those arising from alleged breaches of professional standards of skill and care. In what may be considered isolated cases of negligence, governing bodies ordinarily leave the matter to the regular courts, where an aggrieved client may bring an action. However, in repeated cases of violations, or where the conduct of the professional has so grossly offended standards that the competence needed to remain in practice is called into question, the governing body will take disciplinary action in the same manner as it would for unethical conduct. Implicit in the task of maintaining standards is the obligation to take corrective measures to improve performance.

For the conduct of disciplinary proceedings against members, a professional organization usually has a standing discipline committee consisting of experienced members of the profession. In addition, the governing council usually designates one or more other members or a separate committee to act as "prosecutor"; both the prosecutor and the accused member may be represented by lawyers at the disciplinary hearing. Ordinarily, the finding of a discipline committee takes the form of a recommendation to the governing council of the organization, which then acts on the recommendation to expel, suspend, reprimand, or acquit. Disciplinary proceedings of this nature are subject to a general duty to act fairly[53] and are subject to review by the regular courts.

Conflict of Duty Towards Clients and the Courts

A member of a professional body faces a dilemma when required to testify in court proceedings affecting a client or patient. On the one hand, the member is expected to reply to questions under oath when examined and cross-examined in court; on the other hand, the member's testimony may appear to be a breach of confidence in the professional relationship with the client.

---

53. For a recent discussion of this duty see Mondesir v. Manitoba Assn. of Optometrists (1998), 163 D.L.R. (4th) 703. Where the disciplinary body is established by statute, its procedures are also subject to the Charter: see Costco Wholesale Canada Ltd. v. British Columbia (1998), 157 D.L.R. (4th) 725.

A member or student member of a professional organization probably has a duty to ask the court for a ruling before divulging any information obtained in a confidential capacity.[54]

A professional who learns that a client may be engaged in or is contemplating possibly illegal activities may experience a further problem of interpreting her professional duties to the client. Needless to say, the professional must not assist the client (except to advise on possible illegality), and in dissociating herself from the client's activities may have to terminate the relationship. It appears to be generally conceded, however, that a professional would not normally be obliged to reveal confidential knowledge to prosecuting authorities: such information is said to be covered by **privilege**. However, where keeping silent would create a serious threat to public safety, the public interest requires disclosure.[55]

privilege
the right of a professional to refuse to divulge information obtained in confidence from a client

CONTEMPORARY ISSUE

Multi-disciplinary Partnerships

Traditionally, professions have carried on their practice either alone or in partnership with fellow members of the same profession. In the case of some professions—in particular, law— it has in the past been unlawful for a lawyer to practice in partnership with a non-lawyer. That seems about to change. Consider the following recent reports:

Driven by a fear that accounting firms are capturing a substantial part of the judicial market, the Quebec Bar Association last month endorsed the formation of multi-disciplinary partnerships (MDPs), erasing one obstacle to Quebec accounting and law firms forging partnerships. With a growing number of Quebec accounting firms expressing interest in joining forces with law firms to establish a one-stop centre for clients, the Bar felt it had little choice but to accept the recommendation of a 90-page report on the multi-disciplinary partnerships issue. The study points out that "arrangements" between Quebec accountants and lawyers already exist on the sly and are a fait accompli, bypassing the ban that prevents lawyers from sharing fees with other professionals. The study found some "arrangements" really pushed the envelope, with some accounting firms apparently absorbing the costs of maintaining the operations of law firms and in exchange billing and demanding references from the law firms.

"To not forge ahead would compromise the growth and prosperity of law firms and allow accounting firms to capture an even greater share of the judicial market, particularly in taxation, and business and commercial law," says the report, headed by James Robb, a senior partner at Stikeman Elliott.

That has already happened in Europe, where large law firms in France, England and Switzerland have already been acquired or are under the stewardship of international accounting firms. While the Bar acknowledges that it stands much to lose if the worldwide trend keeps pace, it also concedes that MDPs can be financially rewarding for Quebec law firms.

The study estimates that the judicial market in Quebec is worth $1.5 billion, with $1 billion of that generated by services to the business world. But the accounting services market, at an estimated $4.68 billion, is too large for the Quebec legal profession to ignore.

"One must take into account the real needs of the marketplace and be open to change," says the study. "MDPs would allow lawyers to take their place in the market and the judicial market to grow in the consulting sector." Or as Robb told *The Lawyers Weekly*, "We're trying to get our share of the $4 billion market...."

Source: Luis Millan, "Quebec Bar Association solidly endorses MDPs," *The Lawyers' Weekly*, Vol. 19, No. 3 (May 21, 1999).

continued

---

54. See Conkwright v. Conkwright, [1970] 3 O.R. 784.

55. Smith v. Jones (1999), 169 D.L.R. (4th) 385 (S.C.C.). The case concerned conversations between a psychiatrist and an alleged serial rapist.

...Lawyers will be best served by a multi-discipline partnership model where the partnership offers legal services only and is in the control of lawyers, the Law Society of Upper Canada has decided. The final report of the working group on multi-disciplinary partnerships (MDPs) was presented at the law society's September Convocation and recommended rejecting a full MDP. Principal concerns regarding MDPs surrounded privilege, independence, and conflict of interest.

"Fundamentals of the solicitor-and-client relationship, such as the protection of solicitor-and-client privilege and the independence of the Bar, are placed at serious long-term risk by full-blown partnerships between lawyers and heterogeneous groups of other professions, including principally accountants," the report warned.

Source: Elizabeth Raymer, "LSUC committee says MDPs must be lawyer-controlled," *The Lawyers' Weekly*, Vol. 18, No. 21 (October 9, 1998).

Questions to Consider

1. What are the potential advantages of multi-disciplinary partnerships?
2. What are the possible disadvantages?

QUESTIONS FOR REVIEW

1. Why would the principle of distributive justice seem to favour imposing a wide liability on professionals?

2. What is the main effect of increased use of liability insurance?

3. To whom does the auditor of a corporation owe his primary duty?

4. What is the nature of the fiduciary duty owed by a professional? In what way can that duty be wider than a contractual duty?

5. Can a client choose to sue a professional adviser in either contract or tort? What difference might it make?

6. What is the principal basis of a professional's potential liability to persons who are not clients?

7. Why were the courts initially reluctant to impose liability for negligent misstatements?

8. What was the decision reached by the House of Lords in *Hedley Byrne v. Heller & Partners*?

9. What is the test now applied in Canada to determine whether a person is liable for a negligent misstatement?

10. How can a person be liable for an omission?

11. What are the dangers of the "hindsight" approach in determining the appropriate standard of professional care?

12. Does the "person on the Yonge Street subway" approach apply to professionals?

13. What is the essence of causation in most professional–client relationships?

14. What are the main responsibilities imposed or assumed by professional bodies?

15. Should professional bodies be allowed to discipline their members, or should that be left to the courts?

CASES AND PROBLEMS

1 Mitchell was the owner of a thriving restaurant business. He came to know "Simpson," an apparently highly successful businessman who engaged in various speculative investments. In reality, "Simpson" was a former lawyer whose real name was Anderson, and who had been disbarred and had been convicted of a number of offences involving fraud.

Mitchell and Anderson became friendly and Anderson persuaded Mitchell to join him in a number of investments, which at first seemed to be successful. In the course of their business dealings, Mitchell said that he thought it would be sensible for him to retain the services of a lawyer: Anderson recommended him to see a lawyer named Gordon.

Gordon quickly realized that Mitchell's business associate, "Simpson," was actually Anderson, whom he had known before Anderson's conviction. Gordon acted for Mitchell in a number of transactions, but despite his knowledge of Anderson's background, he said nothing about it to Mitchell.

A year or so later, Mitchell discovered that most of the investments that he had undertaken with Anderson (both before and after becoming a client of Gordon) had turned out to be complete failures. Apparently, Anderson had siphoned off most of the value of the properties they had bought.

Mitchell brought an action against Gordon, claiming that Gordon should have told him of Anderson's history and that, if he had done so, Mitchell would have terminated the relationship.

Should Mitchell succeed?

2 Hedgeways Construction Inc. is a company specializing in highway construction. In response to a public invitation from the government of British Columbia to tender for an important road construction project, it submitted what turned out to be the winning bid.

The detailed description of the project in the tender invitation document contained a number of important inaccuracies. As a result, the cost of completing the project was substantially greater than Hedgeways had estimated and it ended up making a loss on the project.

The tender invitation document issued by the province contained a statement to the effect that any representations made therein were "general information" only and were it not guaranteed by the province. The actual specifications and engineering drawings in the document had been prepared by Brown and Green, two qualified engineers employed by the firm Black and Associates Ltd., who had contracted with the province to provide the specifications.

Hedgeways wishes to be compensated for its loss of profits. What claim, if any, does it have against (a) the provincial government; (b) Black and Associates; and (c) Brown and Green?

3 Hopkins' Steel Ltd. was a long-established steel-producing corporation operating in Ontario. A few years ago it decided to change its bank and moved its account to the Canadian Business Bank. Before accepting the account, the bank made various enquiries and, in particular, examined the audited accounts of Hopkins' over the preceding three years. The accounts showed a steady record of profitability, growing from $70 000 in the earliest year to $250 000 in the most recent year. Having concluded its enquiries, the bank agreed to extend a line of credit to Hopkins' and, over the following year or so, made advances to it totalling more than $2 million.

Shortly thereafter, Hopkins' ran into serious trouble and eventually was forced into bankruptcy with debts in excess of $2 million.

The bank brought a claim against Cross, Jones and Sparrow, the accounting firm that had audited the annual accounts of Hopkins' during the years in question. The bank claimed that the accounts for the preceding years, which it had examined before granting the loans, were inaccurate and had been negligently prepared and that Hopkins' was already in serious trouble before the bank took them on as clients.

In each case, the audited accounts contained the following statement:

> We have examined the balance sheet of Hopkins' Steel Limited as at [date] and the statements of earnings, retained earnings and changes in financial position for the year then ended. Our examination was made in accordance with generally accepted auditing standards, and accordingly included such tests and other procedures as we considered necessary in the circumstances.

According to the evidence, during the years in which Cross, Jones and Sparrow provided services to Hopkins', it also from time to time provided further information with respect to Hopkins' to third parties, such as creditors and a bonding insurer for the company, and provided Hopkins' with a number of copies of its financial statements and audit reports.

Does the bank have any claim against the accounting firm?

4 Sauguet broke her wrist and was treated by an orthopaedic surgeon, Chen. Sauguet was an active sportswoman and was anxious to obtain proper treatment so that she might continue her sporting activities, though she did not specifically inform Chen of this. The wrist did not heal properly, and she eventually had to have surgery. The surgery was not fully successful and she was left with a permanent disability that, though relatively minor, prevented her from playing the sports she had enjoyed.

Sauguet brought an action against Chen, alleging negligent treatment. She claimed that Chen had failed to advise of an alternative treatment that was available. The alternative treatment was well known in the profession and, though more intrusive than the treatment that Chen had performed, was possibly more suitable for a patient in Sauguet's position, for whom making a complete recovery was very important. Sauguet claimed that had Chen informed her of the alternative, that was the procedure she would have chosen.

Should Sauguet's claim against Chen succeed?

5 Hansen had practised for a number of years as an investment counsellor, advising clients on how to invest their savings. He had qualified as a Member of the Association of General Investment Counsellors, which entitled him to use the letters "M.A.G.I.C." after his name.

Over the years, the Association (AGIC) had received numerous complaints about Hansen. Many of his suggested investment schemes turned out to be disastrous and there were strong suspicions that he was not only wholly incompetent but that he was also defrauding some of his clients.

Two years ago, after one particularly serious complaint, Hansen was called to attend a meeting of the disciplinary committee of AGIC. The committee informed him that, in view of the long history of complaints against him, it proposed to deprive him of his membership and to inform the Attorney-General's Department of the most recent complaint, about which there was at least a suspicion of fraud.

Hansen, who was a very persuasive talker, eventually convinced the committee not to report him, and to allow him to resign from the Association rather than being dismissed. He signed an undertaking that he would not practise again as an investment consultant and would no longer describe himself as "M.A.G.I.C."

Despite the undertaking, Hansen very soon resumed his practice, in his old office, and continued to use his title. Soon afterwards, he was consulted by Thaler, who said she had heard excellent reports about him from a friend. Hansen quickly talked Thaler into entrusting her life savings to him. It appears that Hansen has disappeared to an island in the South Pacific, taking Thaler's money with him.

Thaler has commenced proceedings against AGIC, claiming that if they had reported Hansen to the proper authorities and had taken steps to see that he abided by his undertaking to them, Hansen would not have been in a position to defraud her.

Should Thaler succeed?

PART

In Chapter 2, we noted that, for business purposes, the largest areas of private law are contracts, torts, property, and trusts. Contracts are the foundation of virtually all business arrangements, whether for employment, for the sale of goods, services, or land, for the formation of a partnership or corporation, or for the settlement of a dispute. An understanding of contract law is essential to an understanding of business arrangements. Chapters 5 to 15 are devoted to a comprehensive overview of contractual arrangements, from their formation, to a discussion of the various things that can go wrong, to their ultimate discharge, either by performance, by mutual agreement among the parties, or by an aggrieved party resorting to the courts for a remedy.

Chapter 5, 6, and 7 discuss the formation of a contract—the various elements needed to make an arrangement legally binding: Chapter 5, the procedures, formal or informal, that the parties to a contract must follow; Chapter 6, the nature of a bargain and the elements required to make a promise binding; Chapter 7, classes of persons who may bind themselves to a contract, and why certain kinds of contracts are not binding. Chapter 8 and 9 consider the things that can "go wrong"—a court may conclude that what seemed like a valid contract does not bind the parties because there is a serious flaw. Chapter 10 discusses the requirement that certain kinds of contracts must be in writing, and the sometimes surprising consequences when such contracts are oral. Chapter 11 describes the process of interpreting terms of a contract when parties disagree about what they mean. Chapter 12 explains how rights under a contract may be acquired by persons who were not originally parties to it. Chapters 13, 14, and 15 discuss respectively, the ways in which contracts come to an end, the consequences of breach by one party, and the remedies available to an aggrieved party.

Contracts

qsilver.queensu.ca/~law120/Contract_Outline.html
Queen's University (prepared by law students): contract law outline with a diagram of contract issues

strategis.ic.gc.ca/SSG/ca01036e.html
Government of Canada contract law site: a general overview

law.uniserve.edu.au/law/pub/edinst/anu/contract/
4CONTRACTFORMATIONOFFERANDACCEP.html
Australian site on offer and acceptance

www.duhaime.org/ca-con1.htm
B.C. practitioner Lloyd Duhaime: general information on contract law for the public

www.law.ualberta.ca/alri/ulc/eindex.htm
Uniform Law Conference of Canada: provides information on common law contract elements and links to e-commerce contract related information and model acts

www.confpriv.qc.ca/doc/csc-scc/en/concept/
Supreme Court of Canada: recent SCC cases on contract law

contractscanada.gc.ca/
Contracts Canada: how to do business with the federal government

www.gov.nb.ca/acts/acts/f-24.htm
New Brunswick Frustrated Contracts Act

www.ufsia.ac.be/~estorme/PECL2en.html
Principles of European Contract Law

FORMATION OF A CONTRACT

Offer and Acceptance

In this chapter we describe the essential qualities of a contract, in particular, why it is enforceable in law and how a contract is formed. In this chapter we examine such questions as:

- why is a contract enforceable in law?

- how is a contract formed?

- the opening stage of forming a contract—what is the nature of an offer and how is it communicated to an offeree?

- how do we determine the terms of a contract?

- why are standard form contracts used? what are their benefits and dangers?

- how does an offer come to an end—by lapse, revocation, rejection, or by "ripening" into a contract through acceptance by the offeree?

- what is the difference between unilateral and bilateral contracts?

- what are the consequences of a failed attempt to form a contract?

THE ROLE OF CONTRACT LAW

As we noted in Chapter 1, the law restrains our conduct in order to protect society but it also expands our freedom of choice: it enables us to bargain with others for mutual advantages. We also noted that many legal rules work as guidelines for voluntary legal relationships such as business partnerships. Law becomes a framework within which parties can decide upon and bargain for their own legal obligations. People make rules for themselves and express their individual preferences. Contract law is the prime example of law in its facilitative role.

On the other hand, there is often great inequality between parties to contracts in terms of bargaining power, expertise, and intelligence, and in some circumstances there is no opportunity whatever to bargain: many unfair contracts are made. Second, the rules of contract law are subject to human frailties; sometimes they lead to unintended or unjust results. In a few instances, it seems beyond the ability of the legal mind to devise a fair solution for a manifestly difficult problem. On the whole, however, contract law responds well—perhaps better than most areas of the law—to the individual's needs and wishes, and it accommodates most relationships with a minimum of conflict.

The Nature of a Contract

Contracts generally begin with a promise, but not all promises become contracts. Although there may be a moral obligation to keep all promises seriously made, it does not follow that there is a legal obligation. Contract law is concerned with legally binding promises. "The most popular description of a contract that can be given is also the most exact one, namely that it is a promise or set of promises which the law will enforce."[1] These words in a leading treatise on the law of contract do not tell us what kinds of promises the law will enforce, that is, whether there is a contract. This question needs to be examined before we discuss how the law "enforces" contracts. Accordingly, in the next 10 chapters we shall examine first, the nature of the promise or promises that may form a contract, and second, the resources available in the law to enforce them.

The Nature of an Offer

A contract does not come into existence until an offer has been made by one party and accepted by the other party. An **offer** is a *tentative* promise made by one party, the **offeror**, subject to a condition or containing a request to the other party, the **offeree**. When the offeree accepts the offer by agreeing to the condition or request, the offer is transformed into a contract. The promise is no longer tentative: the offeror is bound to carry out his promise while the offeree is bound to carry out the condition or request.

A mere *invitation* to do business is not an offer to make a contract. The display of a coat in a shop window does not amount to an offer to sell; a mail-order catalogue does not guarantee that the goods pictured or described will be delivered to all who try to order them. These are simply merchandising or advertising devices to attract customers and to start negotiations for a contract of sale. Perhaps a prospective customer, acting in response to the invitation, will make an offer that the merchant may in turn accept or refuse. Or the merchant may make an offer as soon as the customer shows interest.

Newspaper advertisements to sell goods at a certain price are generally mere invitations to the public to visit the place of business with a view to buying. A business is not expected to sell the goods to everyone who reads its advertisement: its supply is limited, and it cannot accurately predict the number of readers who will be seriously interested. If the advertisement were taken to be an offer and too many people accepted it, the business would be liable for breach of contract to all those who accepted and to whom it could not supply the advertised goods.

On the other hand, this does not mean that advertisements can never be offers; the courts have sometimes held them to be offers when their wording reasonably favoured this intention. An advertisement to sell a fixed number of items at a fixed price to those who accept first, an

offer
a tentative promise made by one party, subject to a condition or containing a request to the other party

offeror
the person making the offer

offeree
the person to whom the offer is made

---

1. Winfield, *Pollock's Principles of Contract* (13th ed.), p. 1. London: Stevens & Sons Limited, 1950.

offer of a reward for information or for the return of a lost object, or a reward to any person using a preventive medicine who still catches an illness, all may be valid offers. This group of advertisements forms a very small proportion of newspaper advertisements—the exception rather than the rule.

CASE 5.1

When self-service supermarkets and drugstores arrived in England, the courts had to decide whether the display of merchandise in itself amounted to an offer—and the act of the customer in taking the merchandise from the shelf amounted to an acceptance—or whether the display was merely an invitation to the customer to make an offer by taking the merchandise to the cashier. The question was important, because an English statute made it unlawful to sell certain medicinal products unless the sale was supervised by a registered pharmacist.[2]

The court held that the statute was not violated because a registered pharmacist was at hand near the cashier and could refuse a customer's offer to purchase any drug. The judge said:

The mere fact that a customer picks up a bottle of medicine from the shelves in this case does not amount to an acceptance of an offer to sell. It is an offer by the customer to buy, and there is no sale effected until the buyer's offer to buy is accepted by the acceptance of the price.[3]

THE COMMUNICATION OF AN OFFER

The form of an offer is not important as long as its sense is understood. The offeror could say, "I offer to sell you my car for $500," or, "I will sell you my car for $500," or even, "I'll take $500 for my car." All are equally good offers, containing a tentative promise is to sell the car if the buyer agrees to pay the stated price.

In most situations, an offeror communicates orally or in writing, but she can also express an offer by conduct without words. Holding up one's hand for a taxi, raising a finger at an auction, and the gestures of floor traders at a stock exchange may also be offers.

An offeree cannot accept an offer until first learning of it. This principle has an unexpected twist. A person may find and return a lost article to its owner and afterwards learn that a reward has been offered for its return. The finder is not entitled to the reward because she did not act *in response to* the offer, and therefore did not accept it.

Crossed offers provide a further example of this rule.

ILLUSTRATION 5.1

A tells B she is interested in selling her car. The next day, A writes to B offering to sell her car for $1500; B has also written a letter crossing A's letter in the mail offering to buy the car for $1500. *There is no contract: B was unaware of A's offer when he wrote and so his* letter could not be an acceptance; similarly, A was unaware of B's offer—A's letter, too, could not be an acceptance. Unless either A or B sends a subsequent acceptance, no contract will be formed.

---

2. Pharmaceutical Society of Great Britain v. Boots Cash Chemists (Southern) Ltd., [1952] 2 All E.R. 456.
3. *Ibid.*, per Lord Goddard, at 458.

Similarly, we cannot be required to pay people who do work for us without our knowledge. We are entitled first to receive an offer to do the work, which we may then accept or reject. A person for whom work has been done without his request, and without his knowledge, may well benefit from it; but as he has not accepted any offer to do the work, he has no contractual obligation to pay for it.

Suppose, however, that goods or services are provided to a person without his request but in circumstances where he has an opportunity to reject them. At common law, if he accepts the services or uses the goods, he is presumed to have accepted the offer and to have promised to pay the price. This rule was found inadequate in dealing with unconscionable selling practices that tempt consumers to bind themselves to pay for goods they did not request. Many provinces have passed legislation to reverse the rule, at least as it relates to goods. For example, section 47 of the British Columbia Consumer Protection Act[4] states:

(2) If …unsolicited goods are received…the recipient has no legal obligation in respect of [them]…unless and until the [recipient]…expressly acknowledges to the sender in writing his or her intention to accept [them].

(3) Unless the acknowledgment…has been given, the sender does not have a cause of action for any loss, misuse, possession, damage or misappropriation in respect of the unsolicited goods.

AN OFFER MADE BY TENDERING A WRITTEN DOCUMENT TO THE OFFEREE

Standard Form Contracts: Their Risks and Benefits

Businesses that deal with the general public often present the terms of their offers in written documents handed to their customers, or they post notices containing terms on their business premises. Sometimes both methods are used together, the delivered document referring to the terms posted in the notice. Common examples are tickets for theatres, railways, and airlines, receipts for dry cleaning, parking, watch repairs, and checked luggage, as well as insurance policies and bills of lading.

Almost without exception, a person receiving any one of these documents is neither asked nor expected to read or approve of its terms. If he were to take time to read it and suggest changes, the agent of the offeror would probably become very annoyed. She would say, "Take it or leave it." Thus, as a practical matter, an offeree cannot change any terms of such a **standard form contract**: there is no real element of bargaining. He must accept the offer as is or not at all. Often, as when travelling by railway or airline, there may be only one practical means of transportation between two points; an offeree does not have the choice of refusing—he *must* accept if he is to make his journey. Consequently an offeror business is strongly tempted to disregard the interests of its offerees, the general public, and give itself every advantage; it rarely resists the temptation.

standard form contract
an offer presented in a printed document or notice, the terms of which cannot be changed by the offeree, but must be accepted as is or rejected

On the other hand, in many situations the standard form contract is essential. Imagine waiting in a queue at a railway ticket office while each would-be passenger bargains separately for each term in his contract!

…Too often, the standard form is presented as an evil. The form is a facet of the efficiency and standardization of modern business; in some situations a form may provide an accumulation of experience and a thorough job of drafting that could not be gathered for one deal alone. But the concentration of economic power, and in particular the rise of the large business

---

4. R.S.B.C. 1996, c. 69.

corporation, has led to many situations in which bargaining power is grossly unequal. Power corrupts. Forms are often used in situations where contract in fact is distorted or denied. They are dictated, not negotiated.[5]

The public has two means of protection from this inequality in bargaining. First, if the business falls within an area regulated by a government board, the terms of such contracts are subject to board approval. When boards operate effectively, the public is usually well protected and unreasonable terms are excluded. Second, in the vast range of unregulated activity the public receives only such protection as the courts can muster from the general law of contract. On the whole, protection by the courts alone is unsatisfactory, but unless we are to sanction government regulation of every niche of business activity, no other means is readily available. What protection can a court offer?

Required Notice of Terms

Courts begin by presuming that an unqualified acceptance of an offer is an acceptance of every term of that offer. Suppose, however, that the offeree does not know that the offer contains a certain term. She purchases a ticket to attend a baseball game. The ticket contains a clause stating that the management reserves the right to remove the ticket-holder at any time without giving reasons. She does not know or suspect that the ticket contains such a term. Is she bound by it? If she satisfies the court that she did not know of it, then the court will ask what steps the management took to bring the term to the attention of its customers generally. If the court decides that the steps were insufficient, the ticket-holder is not bound by the term; and if she has been wrongfully ejected from the baseball park, she will have the same remedy as if the term had not been on the ticket.

On the other hand, if the court finds that the management had done what was reasonably necessary in the circumstances to bring the term to the notice of its customers, then the ticket-holder is bound by the term whether she knew of it or not. "Ticket" cases always turn on their individual facts, and it is difficult to set down any firm guidelines of what is or is not sufficient notice. It will help us to understand the courts' reasoning if we look at some of the leading cases.

CASE 5.2

In *Parker v. South Eastern Railway Co.*,[6] Parker deposited his suitcase in the luggage room of a railway station, paid a fee, and received a ticket on the face of which were the words, "See back." On the reverse side of the ticket it was stated that the railway was not liable for loss in excess of £10. The bag was lost, and Parker sued the railway for his loss, £24. On appeal, the court decided that the issue was whether the railway had done what was reasonably necessary to notify customers of the term. The court ordered a new trial because the trial judge had not asked the jury to decide this question.

The fact that the ticket contained on its face the words, "See back" is important. If a ticket—or other document given to the customer at the time of purchase—contains a short and clear reference to other terms appearing either on the reverse side, or posted on a nearby wall in the form of a notice or sign, it is more likely that "reasonably sufficient notice" of those terms has been given.

A sign in a parking lot disclaiming liability for loss or damage to car or contents may not in itself be reasonably sufficient notice to bind those who park their cars there: we have to ask

---

5. Risk, *Recent Developments in Contracts*, Special Lectures, p. 256. Toronto: Law Society of Upper Canada, 1966.

6. (1877), 2 C.P.D. 416.

whether the ticket or voucher received when a customer parks her car contains a clear reference to the sign and whether, in the circumstances, a customer *ought* to recognize the term stated on the sign as part of the contract she is making with the operator of the lot. A printed ticket or receipt containing the words "subject to the conditions as exhibited on the premises" may be enough to tie the sign to each contract. The sign must, of course, be displayed prominently, but this in itself may not be sufficient; it must be brought home to the customer *at the time of making the contract.* The operator of the parking lot, garage, or other place of storage cannot safely assume that he may exempt himself from liability merely by putting up a sign.[7] Lord Justice Denning has summed up the law on this subject:

> People who rely on a contract to exempt themselves from their common law liability must prove that contract strictly. Not only must the terms of the contract be clearly proved, but also the intention to create legal relations—the intention to be legally bound—must be clearly proved. The best way of proving it is by a written document signed by the party to be bound. Another way is by handing him, before or at the time of the contract, a written notice specifying certain terms and making it clear to him that the contract is in those terms. A prominent public notice which is plain for him to see when he makes the contract would, no doubt, have the same effect, but nothing short of one of these three ways will suffice.[8]

Unusual or Unexpected Terms

An offeree may be willing to accept terms printed on a ticket or displayed on a poster because she assumes, reasonably, that the risk relates closely to the bargain she has made, for instance, a term denying any liability for damage to her car while parked in a parking lot. She would understand that the cost of parking would be higher if the car park operator had to insure against the risk of damage to her vehicle. But she would be surprised to find that the terms also exempted the operator from liability for personal injuries suffered by her as she walked to and from her parked car. Such unexpected terms need to be brought directly to the attention of the offeree; indeed, she might then decide to park elsewhere. In other words, a court may well find that there was adequate notice of usual, expected terms that the offeree chose not to read, but *not* of a surprising and therefore unreasonable term.

Our discussion in this section has been about situations where the offeree receives a ticket, a policy, or some other form of notice of the terms of the contract but where she does not sign a document containing the terms. If the offeree signs a document, a stronger presumption arises that she has accepted all the terms it contains; it becomes much more difficult for her to avoid the consequences. The prospects of persuading a court to disregard onerous terms imposed in a written and signed document have improved somewhat,[9] as we shall see in our discussion of misrepresentation and unconscionability in Chapter 9.

THE LAPSE AND REVOCATION OF AN OFFER

Lapse

An offer may **lapse** in any of the following ways:

(a) when the offeree fails to accept within a time specified in the offer

> **lapse**
> the termination of an offer when the offeree fails to accept it within a specified time, or if no time is specified, then within a reasonable time

---

7. Watkins v. Rymill (1883), 10 Q.B.D. 178. It may be more difficult for the operator of a parking lot to exempt himself from liability when the customer leaves the keys in the car at the request of the parking lot operator, because a bailment for storage and safekeeping is implied. See Chapter 17, *infra*. See also: Brown v. Toronto Auto Parks Ltd., [1954] O.W.N. 86; Samuel Smith & Sons Ltd. v. Silverman (1961), 29 D.L.R. (2d) 98; Hefferon v. Imperial Parking Co. Ltd. (1973), 46 D.L.R. (3d) 642.

8. Olley v. Marlborough Court Ltd., [1949] 1 All E.R. 127, per Denning, L.J., at 134.

9. Tilden Rent-A-Car Co. v. Clendenning (1978), 18 O.R. (2d) 601.

(b) when the offeree fails to accept within a reasonable time, if the offer has not specified any time limit

(c) when either of the parties dies or becomes insane prior to acceptance

When an offer has lapsed, the offeree can no longer accept it even if he is unaware that it has lapsed; it has become void and no longer exists.

It is often difficult to predict what constitutes a "reasonable time." To say "It depends upon the circumstances of each case" may not seem helpful. The Supreme Court of Canada discussed how the subject-matter of the contract may provide a clue for deciding whether a reasonable length of time has elapsed in an offer to buy or sell:

> Farm lands, apart from evidence to the contrary…are not subject to frequent or sudden changes or fluctuations in price and, therefore, in the ordinary course of business a reasonable time for the acceptance of an offer would be longer than that with respect to such commodities as shares of stock upon an established trading market. It would also be longer than in respect to goods of a perishable character. With this in mind the fact, therefore, that it was land would tend to lengthen what would be concluded as a reasonable time which, however, must be determined in relation to the other circumstances.[10]

The "other circumstances" include the manner in which an offer is made and whether its wording indicates urgency. Often when a prospective purchaser makes an offer to buy property, she specifies that the offer must be accepted within 24 hours. The restriction is in her interest because it gives the vendor very little time to use this "firm offer" as a means of approaching other possible purchasers and bidding up the price.

Revocation

Notice of Revocation

An offeror may be able to *revoke* (that is, withdraw) an offer at any time before acceptance, even when it has promised to hold the offer open for a specified time.

ILLUSTRATION 5.2

A Inc. sends a letter by courier on January 15 to *B* offering to sell its warehouse to *B* for $800 000, stating that the offer is open only until January 19 and that it must have heard from *B* by then. *B* receives the letter on January 16, and immediately prepares a letter of acceptance. Before he sends his reply on the morning of January 17, *A* Inc. changes its mind and telephones *B* saying that it withdraws its offer.

The revocation is valid because it has reached *B* before he has accepted. Accordingly, *B* can no longer accept *A*'s offer.

In Illustration 5.2, the offeror clearly revoked the offer before its acceptance: its direct communication of the revocation left no doubt about the offeree's knowledge of it. The legal position of the parties is less certain if the offeree merely hears rumours that the offeror has revoked, or hears that the offeror has made it impossible to carry out the offer because it has sold the property to someone else. The court will consider the offer revoked if it would be unreasonable for the offeree to suppose that the offeror still intended to stand by its offer.[11] Nevertheless, it is

---

10. Barrick v. Clark, [1950] 4 D.L.R. 529, per Estey, J., at 537.
11. See Dickinson v. Dodds (1876), 2 Ch. D. 463. See also Hughes v. Gyratron Developments Ltd., [1988] B.C.J. No. 1598.

always poor business practice to make an offer to sell a particular item to one party and then sell it to another without having directly withdrawn the offer to the first party. Quite apart from damage to goodwill, the offeror runs the risk of the first offeree accepting and of then being in breach when unable to fulfill both contracts.

Options

An offeree may bind an offeror to keep its offer open for a specified time in one of two ways: (1) she may obtain a written offer under seal; (2) she may make a contract called an **option** to keep the offer open. We shall consider the use of a seal in the next chapter. In an option, the offeree makes a contract with the offeror in the following general terms: the offeree agrees to pay a sum of money; in return the offeror agrees (1) to keep the offer open for a specified time (that is, not to revoke the offer); and (2) not to make contracts with other parties that would prevent it from fulfilling its offer (that is, to give the offeree the exclusive right to accept the offer). The exclusive right to such an offer may be very valuable to an offeree, even though she may eventually decide not to accept.

option
a contract to keep an offer open for a specified time in return for a sum of money

ILLUSTRATION 5.3

PreciseComp Inc. purchases a number of options from property owners whose lots would, in the aggregate, provide a suitable location for a new plant. PreciseComp pays $3000 to *A* for the right to buy her farm within three months for $350 000 and also buys similar option agreements from other farmers in the vicinity. In this way PreciseComp can determine at modest cost whether all the necessary property will be available and what the total cost will be. It need not *take up* or **exer-** **cise the options**, that is, accept the offers to sell the farms; it would simply chalk up the price of the relatively small sums paid for the option agreements as the cost of a feasibility study for the projected plant. On the other hand, PreciseComp would be within its rights to require each of the farmers who had sold it these options to sell at the agreed price—provided it accepts the offers contained in the options within the specified time.

In Illustration 5.3, the farmers are in the position of offerors who for an agreed period of time are not free to withdraw their offers without being in breach of contract. The parties are really contemplating two contracts: first, the option agreement itself and, second, the actual sale that will materialize if the option is exercised.

exercise an option
to accept the offer contained in an option

REJECTION AND COUNTER-OFFER BY THE OFFEREE

In business negotiations the parties often make a number of offers and counter-offers, but until an offer by one side is accepted without qualification by the other there is no contract; the parties have no legal obligation to one another. When an offeree receives an offer and, though interested, chooses to vary some of its terms, he has not accepted; rather, he has made a counter-offer of his own and this amounts to rejecting the offer. The initiative in bargaining may shift back and forth until one party finds the last proposal of the other satisfactory and accepts it without qualification. Only then is a contract formed.

The making of a counter-offer necessarily amounts to rejecting the earlier offer and brings it to an end. If the offeror in turn rejects the counter-offer, the original offer does not revive. Only if the offeror agrees to renew it may the offeree accept the original offer. The courts have held, however, that when an offeree merely inquires whether the terms offered are the best he can expect, it does not amount to a rejection.

ILLUSTRATION 5.4

A sent a fax to *B* offering to sell her car for $2000. *B* replied by fax, "I will give you $1900 for the car." Two days later *B* sent a fax again to *A* saying, "I have been reconsidering. I will accept your offer to sell for $2000 after all."

In Illustration 5.4, there is no contract. *B*'s counter-offer of $1900 brought the original offer to sell for $2000 to an end. While *B* has phrased her final statement in the form of an acceptance, she is doing no more than making a fresh offer of her own that *A* may or may not wish to accept. Perhaps someone else has offered *A* $2100 for the car in the meantime. If when *A* made the offer to sell for $2000 *B* had simply inquired whether this was the lowest *A* would go, the offer would have continued to stand. *B* would continue free to accept it within a reasonable period of time, provided *A* did not withdraw her offer first.

THE ELEMENTS OF ACCEPTANCE

Its Positive Nature

Acceptance must be made in some positive form, whether in words or in conduct, with one exception that we note below. If acceptance is by conduct, the conduct must refer unequivocally to the offer made, for example, when an auctioneer asks who will accept a price of, say, $900 for an item and a bidder responds by raising her finger.

On the other hand, one's conduct may happen to comply with the mode of acceptance set out in an offer and yet not amount to an acceptance. Suppose *A* always walks her dog around the park each evening. *B* leaves her a note saying that she will have accepted *B*'s offer to buy her car for $2000 if she walks her dog in the park that evening. She need not abandon her normal conduct to avoid accepting the offer and having the contract foisted on her.

For the same reason, an offeror cannot insist on silence as a mode of acceptance, thus forcing the offeree to act in order to reject the offer.

ILLUSTRATION 5.5

Sanger, a sales representative for Ion Electric Supply Inc. demonstrated a new high-speed Auto-analyzer for Glover, the owner of a car repair service. The price was $2500. Glover thought the device was useful but over-priced: "At $1500 I might consider buying it." Sanger said that he could not reduce the price and removed the machine.

Two weeks later, an Auto-analyzer arrived with a letter from Sanger as follows: "When I reported how impressed you were with our analyzer to the manager, he said it would be worth selling one even at a loss just to break into the market in your city. We know what an excellent reputation you have and it would be a good move to have our product in use in your shop. Our price is reduced, only to you, to $1750. That is below cost. If we don't hear from you in 10 days we shall assume you have accepted this exceptional buy and will expect payment of our invoice."

There will be no contract even if the offeree, Glover, does not reply and simply allows the machine to sit idle; but he may well be bound if he takes the risk of using the machine, even to experiment with it.

Silence can be a sufficient mode of acceptance only if the parties have habitually used this method to communicate assent in previous transactions, or have agreed between themselves in advance that silence is sufficient, as where books are regularly delivered under a contract for membership in a publisher's book club.

CONTEMPORARY ISSUE

The Bottom Line and Business Relationships

Frequently the formation of a contract is the precursor or the culmination of a continuing relationship between the parties forming the contract. How the contract is formed can have a direct impact on the health and success of the underlying business relationship.

In 1995 Rogers Cablesystems introduced seven new specialty channels by negative optioning, which placed the onus on the consumer to reject the new channels or be automatically billed for them. Packaging incentives were also introduced that would take away existing specialty channels unless the new specialty channels were purchased.

Cable customers across Canada inundated local cable companies with complaints of unfair business practice and threats to discontinue service. Colin Watson, president of Rogers Cablesystems, eventually went on TV to apologize to subscribers. Richard E. Rotman, who handled media relations for Showcase, one of the new specialty channels, wrote, "The 'Revolt,' and Rogers Cablesystems' subsequent apology, will now assume a place in the annals of the most notable public relations crises—even though, in hindsight, this was one of the most avoidable ones."

A private member's bill to ban negative option billing was introduced in Parliament. It passed in the House of Commons in September of 1996, but was stalled in the Senate. Similar private member's bills were introduced in 1997 and 1999. As of January 2000, none had gone past first reading. Critics of the legislation asserted that it would threaten funding for cable channels serving minority audiences, such as Anglophones in Quebec and Francophones in the other provinces. If these and other new services had to rely on individual canvassing of each subscriber, they would not get off the ground. According to these critics, such legislation would undermine the public interest and the policy embodied in the *Broadcasting Act*.

Sources: See "Rogers Shows Us a Thing or Two About PR," *Strategy*, February 20, 1995, p. 14; "Public Backlash Jeopardizes New Specialty Channels," *Cablecaster*, February/March, 1995, pp. 4–5; "Public's Attack on Cable Could Harm Specialty Channels," *Broadcaster*, February, 1995, p. 5; *Hansard*, September 26, 1996, statement of Senator Jean-Robert Gauthier.

Questions to Consider

1. Is the bottom line the most important concern in forming a contract? How should the bottom line be balanced with the potential success of a continuing business relationship?
2. How could Rogers Cablesystems have formed contracts with its customers to avoid this public relations nightmare?
3. When should public policy be allowed to affect how private contracts are formed?

Its Communication to the Offeror

Generally speaking, an offeree must communicate acceptance to the offeror. Some types of offers, however, can be accepted without communication because the offeror asks only that the offeree perform an act, implying that the act will constitute acceptance. The offeror may, in other words, dispense with receiving notice of acceptance, and is bound to the terms of the proposition as soon as the offeree has performed whatever was required of him in the offer.

CASE 5.3

Carbolic Smoke Ball Company placed an advertisement in a newspaper promising to pay £100 to anyone who used one of its smoke balls three times daily for two weeks and still contracted influenza. Mrs. Carlill bought a smoke ball and used it following the instructions supplied and contracted influenza. She sued the Smoke Ball Company on its promise to pay £100. As a part of its defence the company pleaded that Mrs. Carlill had never communicated her intention to accept its offer. The court found in favour of Mrs. Carlill.[12] It held that the offer had implied that notice was not necessary. The company had asked only that readers should buy and use the smoke balls. Performance of the conditions set out was a sufficient acceptance without notification to the company.

The *Carlill* case also established that an offer may be made to an indefinite number of people who remain unknown to the offeror even after they have accepted. This result simply follows from the nature of the offer, a newspaper advertisement read by thousands of people. If the offer had been addressed to a particular group of persons, then only a member of that group could have accepted.

The Moment of Acceptance

Business Negotiations: Tenders

If an arrangement is still tentative, that is, it has not yet "ripened into a contract," then either party may withdraw from it. But the moment a contract is formed by acceptance of an offer, each party is bound to its terms. Accordingly, we must be able to analyze business negotiations so that we can identify a specific offer when it is made and the acceptance of that offer if and when it is given.[13]

inviting tenders
seeking offers from suppliers

The common business practice of **inviting tenders** illustrates the need for analyzing the various stages in a business deal to determine the point at which acceptance takes place. The purpose of inviting tenders may be either to obtain firm offers from the tenderers for a fixed quantity of goods and services over a stated period, or it may be to explore the market of available suppliers and ascertain the best terms for proceeding with a project. When the object is to obtain firm offers, the most satisfactory tender will become the basis for a contract between the inviter of the tenders and the successful bidder. This is normal practice when a government or business calls for tenders for the construction of a large project. A recent case suggests that in some circumstances there may be an implied contract that the party inviting the tenders promises—in return for the tenderer taking the trouble to prepare and submit its tender—to consider the tender and not ignore it entirely; if the inviting party fails to consider the tender it will be liable for damages.[14]

In other circumstances, however, no intention to form a contract upon the receipt of tenders is implied; the purpose of inviting tenders is nothing more than to identify a supplier as the appropriate source of work to be done or goods to be supplied, as required for the project. Thus, a municipal corporation may invite tenders by private trucking firms for the removal of snow from city streets during the coming winter. The selection of the successful bidder need not be

---

12. Carlill v. Carbolic Smoke Ball Co., [1892] 2 Q.B. 484. See also, Grant v. Prov. of New Brunswick (1973), 35 D.L.R. (3d) 141, and Dale v. Manitoba (1997), 147 D.L.R. (4th) 605.

13. In an English decision, the House of Lords resisted a tendency in some earlier cases to find that a contract is formed when the parties have substantially agreed on all the material terms, though the explicit acceptance of an offer remains outstanding: Gibson v. Manchester City Council, [1979] 1 W.L.R. 294.

14. See Blackpool and Fylde Aero Club Ltd. v. Blackpool Borough Council, [1990] 1 W.L.R. 1195.

followed up by a contract for a fixed sum, to remove whatever snow may fall—no one knows how severe the winter may be. The successful bidder has made a **standing offer** and the municipality may then make specific requisitions for snow removal as needed over the winter season. Each requisition becomes an acceptance by the municipality of the standing offer of the trucking company; to that extent the trucking company will have a contractual duty to perform for the price specified in its bid. The trucking company remains free to withdraw from the standing agreement if it finds the agreement unsatisfactory, and it will have no liability to do further work after its revocation.[15]

standing offer
an offer that may be accepted as needed from time to time

Whose Offer Has Been Accepted?

Buying an automobile from a car dealer provides a good example of the importance of knowing when, precisely, a contract is formed. Car sales agents employed by a dealer normally have no authority to enter into contracts with customers. The management of the dealership retains the final word on both price and credit terms; the agent's task is to persuade any prospective buyer to submit an offer at a specified price. When the agent takes the offer to the sales manager, the manager may strike out the proposed price and insert a higher one with a request that the prospective buyer initial the change. The manager will have rejected the customer's offer by making a counter-offer. No contract is formed unless and until the customer accepts the counter-offer.

Checklist: The Ways in Which an Offer May Come to an End

Once an offer has been made, it can come to an end in any one of a number of different ways:

- The offer may lapse when the offeree fails to accept within the time stated in the offer, or if no time limit is stated, within a reasonable time.
- The offeror revokes the offer before the offeree has accepted.
- The offeror rejects the offer, or makes a counter-offer (which is in effect a rejection).
- The offeree accepts before any three of the above has occurred (in which case the offer ends and is replaced by a contract between the parties).

TRANSACTIONS BETWEEN PARTIES AT A DISTANCE FROM EACH OTHER

Modes of Acceptance

When the parties are at a distance, an offeree may accept only in the way proposed by the offeror. An offer made by mail may reasonably be taken as inviting acceptance by mail unless the offeror requests another mode of acceptance. Ordinarily, a faster mode may be used: a fax, e-mail, or telephone call in response to a letter can be valid acceptance.

Since contracts made by mail remain common in business, it is important to have a rule that clearly sets out how to determine the time of acceptance. The ordinary rule is that acceptance is complete when a properly addressed and stamped letter of acceptance is dropped in the mail. This rule is as practical and convenient as any alternative; otherwise, during the time

15. See Great Northern Railway v. Witham (1873), L.R. 9 C.P. 16.

required for a letter to reach its destination there would be a period of uncertainty when neither party would know whether a contract exists. The justification for the rule is that an offeror who chooses to use the post office to send an offer is assumed to be willing to have the same means used for acceptance, and to take a chance that the post office will be efficient in delivering it. An offeror who invites acceptance by mail must also be prepared to take the risk that the letter of acceptance may go astray; harsh though this may seem, it follows that the offeror would be bound by a contract without notice of its existence. Professor Waddams has explained the rule as follows:

> ...[T]he usual rationale is that it is the offeror rather than the offeree who could be expected to know that a communication [of acceptance] has gone astray, and to break the silence by enquiry....[T]he offeror has by hypothesis manifested a willingness to be bound and could protect himself either by providing that acceptance must reach him or by enquiring into the silence of the offeree.[16]

An offer may invite acceptance by post even though it was not sent through the mail itself, so long as acceptance by mail constitutes a reasonable response to the offer. It may be reasonable that an offer made orally in the presence of the offeree be accepted by letter; acceptance is complete at the time of mailing.[17] The English courts have held:

> Where the circumstances are such that it must have been within the contemplation of the parties that, according to the ordinary usages of mankind, the post might be used as a means of communicating the acceptance of an offer, the acceptance is complete as soon as it is posted.[18]

The "ordinary usages of mankind" govern the rules of acceptance unless the offeror has stated expressly how acceptance should be communicated, and in general, he has full power over the mode of acceptance. However, if he merely states a *preference* for acceptance by some means other than post as, for example, by telephone or in person, the offeree may still accept by post. But the offeror is not bound unless and until the acceptance reaches him—and it must reach him before the offer has lapsed. When his stated preference is for a mode speedier than mail, there is increased risk that his offer will have lapsed before the letter of acceptance arrives. In these circumstances, the acceptance is not valid when dropped in the mailbox (as it would be if acceptance by mail were reasonably contemplated), but only when received. Even when an offeror invites acceptance by mail he may state that it will be effective *only* if received. Indeed, he may state that acceptance by letter is invalid—it must be made in person. Such stipulations are effective, and unless the offeree complies she cannot bind the offeror.

When instantaneous means of communication such as telephone (or radio) are used, the offeror must receive the acceptance before he is bound. An English court considered what would be the result if the telephone line were to go dead so that the offeror did not hear the offeree's words of acceptance. The court concluded that the acceptance would be ineffective and that the offeror would have no contractual liability.[19] The common sense of this rule is that the offeree would know that the line went dead and that his acceptance might not have been heard. He must then verify that his acceptance was received.

---

16. Waddams, *The Law of Contracts* (4th ed.), pp. 76–7. Toronto: Canada Law Book, 1993; also, Sibtac Corporation Ltd. v. Soo; Lienster Investments Ltd., Third Party (1978), 18 O.R. (2d) 395 at 402.

17. The same principle applies when correspondence is sent by courier service: R. v. Weymouth Sea Products Ltd. (1983), 149 D.L.R. (3d) 637.

18. Henthorn v. Fraser, [1892] 2 Ch. 27, per Lord Herschell, at 33. The law in Canada is probably accurately represented by this case, though there is some confusion caused by a Supreme Court of Canada decision on appeal from the Quebec courts where the post office is referred to as an "agent." See Charlebois v. Baril, [1928] S.C.R. 88. See also Loft v. Physicians' Services Inc. (1966), 56 D.L.R. (2d) 481, where a letter posted in a mailbox but never received was held to be adequate notice to the defendant.

19. Entores, Ltd. v. Miles Far East Corporation, [1955] 2 Q.B. 327, per Denning, L.J., at 332.

It remains unclear which rule applies in the case of fax—can the offeree be certain that her acceptance has been received by the offeror? Suppose the offeror's fax machine has run out of paper? This uncertainty exists also with electronic mail; it is quite common to learn—a day after one has sent an e-mail message—that because of some electronic failure in the system, the message did not get through. More than just a delay, the message may be completely lost—it must be sent again. Despite the rapid increase in electronic transactions, as yet, there are no Canadian decisions on the question of when an acceptance by e-mail becomes effective.[20] When there is no dispute about the actual receipt of messages, transactions by electronic mail are valid. The legal issues that may arise in "e-commerce" generally are discussed more fully in Chapter 34.

Modes of Revocation

Revocation by instantaneous means of communication is subject to the same requirements as acceptance, discussed above.

The usual rule concerning the time of acceptance by post differs from the rule concerning withdrawal of an offer. Revocation by post is effective only when notice is actually received by the offeree, not when it is dropped in the mailbox. As a result, the offeree may accept and a binding contract be formed after revocation of the offer has been mailed but not yet received.

ILLUSTRATION 5.5

Chen, in a letter posted January 15, offered to sell his business to Baker for $70 000. The letter was received by Baker on January 17. On January 19, Baker posted her letter of acceptance, which did not reach Chen until January 21. On January 18, however, Chen had decided to withdraw his offer and posted a letter to Baker revoking it. This letter did not reach Baker until January 20.

Chen's revocation arrived too late. There was a valid contract on January 19 when the acceptance was posted. Chen was bound from the moment the letter was dropped into the mailbox.

What is meant by the requirement that a revocation be "actually received"? Is it "received" when delivered to the place of business or residence of the offeree, or must it reach her in person? The general rule is that, unless the offeror knows or ought to know that the revocation will not reach the offeree at her usual address, delivery at that address establishes the fact and time of revocation, and the offeree is deemed to have notice from that time. This rule applies to other means of communication; if an offeror can establish that his revocation by courier or fax arrived at the offeree's usual address it will be effective. We cannot be certain of an e-mail revocation: is it necessary for the offeree to have turned on her computer and checked her "in" box?

Determining the Jurisdiction Where a Contract Is Made

Parties to a contract are often in different provinces or countries at the time they enter into the arrangement. If a dispute arises it may be important to know where the contract was formed, since the law in the two places may well be different. The place—the **jurisdiction**—where the contract was formed is an important factor in deciding which law applies. The general rule is that a contract is formed at the place where the acceptance becomes effective. That place is determined by the moment in time when the contract is effective. When an offeror invites an acceptance by mail, the contract is formed at the moment *when*—and thus at the place *where*—

jurisdiction
the province, state, or country whose laws apply to a particular situation

---

20. See, Campbell D. ed., *Law of International On-line Business: A Global Perspective.* London: Sweet & Maxwell, 1998, Chapter 5, "Canada," pp. 173–7.

the acceptance is dropped into the mailbox. When an instantaneous means of communication such as fax, e-mail, or telephone is used, the contract is not formed until the offeror receives the acceptance, and that is at the place where he receives it.

UNILATERAL AND BILATERAL CONTRACTS
The Offer of a Promise for an Act

As we have seen in the *Carlill* case, an offer may invite acceptance simply by performing its conditions without communicating acceptance. Indeed, we would not have expected Mrs. Carlill to have telephoned or written to the Smoke Ball Co. to inform it that she intended to accept its offer when she bought the smoke ball!

An offer of a reward is accepted by anyone to whom the offer is made if she performs the conditions stipulated, such as providing information or returning a lost article. When the reward is for providing information, the person who first gave the information is deemed to have accepted and is usually entitled to the reward.[21] However, in a recent case, where a person gave a limited amount of information that ultimately led to a lengthy investigation and conviction for murder (the *Bernardo* case), the provider of the information was awarded only a portion of the reward originally offered.[22]

unilateral contract
a contract in which the offer is accepted by performing an act or series of acts required by the terms of the offer

In the above examples, the offers are of a type that requires *acceptance by performance* of an act. Once the offeree has performed, she need not do anything more. All obligation now rests with the offeror to perform his half of the bargain. These contracts are often called **unilateral contracts**. Some offers require the offeree to perform a series of acts over a long period.

ILLUSTRATION 5.6

Brown offers to pay $4000 to Carson if she will build and deliver a trailer to the offeror in 60 days. Carson may accept only by actually delivering by that date, and until then there is no contract. Consequently, during that 60 days Carson may abandon performance at any time without being in breach. What about Brown—could he simply revoke his offer the day before delivery?

Strictly speaking, the offeror may always revoke before acceptance, and early judges seemed to accept this view. It was apparent that the offeree might suffer considerable hardship, but the answer was, "She knew the risk of revocation was present and accepted the risk." Since, however, parties often do not think about such possibilities, the hardship still occurs. Today, courts try to avoid this unfairness where possible by treating offers "as calling for bilateral rather than unilateral action when the language can be fairly so construed."[23] The advantage of treating an agreement as bilateral is that both parties are bound from the moment the offeree indicates the intention to perform.

subsidiary promise
an implied promise that the offeror will not revoke once the offeror begins performance in good faith and continues to perform

Where the courts find it impossible to construe an offer as bilateral, they may still try to help the offeree by implying a **subsidiary promise** that the offeror will not revoke once the offeree begins performance in good faith and continues to perform. Thus in Illustration 5.6, as soon as Carson starts performance, a subsidiary contract may be formed in which Brown undertakes not to revoke while Carson proceeds reasonably with performance. By this reasoning a court might well hold that revocation would be a breach of the subsidiary contract.[24] Of course, the subsidiary promise is merely implied, and it may be excluded by an express term to the contrary in

21. Lancaster v. Walsh (1838), 150 E.R. 1324.
22. Smirnis v. Sun Publishing Corp. (1997), 3 O.R. (3d) 440.
23. Dawson v. Helicopter Exploration Co. Ltd., [1955] 5 D.L.R 404, per Rand, J., at 410.
24. See Brackenbury v. Hodgkin, 102 A. 106, 116 Me. 399 (1917), and Errington v. Errington, [1952] 1 All E.R. 149.

the offer: if *A* offers to pay *B* $100 for the delivery of a typewriter to her son provided it is delivered at exactly 10 p.m. at a birthday party and provided *A* does not change her mind, *A* may revoke the offer before delivery.

The Offer of a Promise for a Promise

While unilateral contracts are important, most offers require a promise from the offeree rather than performance as the means of acceptance. For example, if *A* Motors offers to sell a truck to *B* Inc. for $22 500 and *B* Inc. replies accepting the offer, a contract is formed though neither party has as yet performed anything. In effect *A* Motors has promised to sell the truck for $22 500 and *B* Inc. in return has promised to buy it for $22 500; the two parties have traded promises. If either party should refuse to perform its promise, then the other would have a right to sue: both parties are bound to perform. This type of contract is called a **bilateral contract**.

The most common business transaction, the credit sale, is an example of the bilateral contract: at the time of the contract, and often for some time thereafter, the goods may be neither delivered by the seller nor paid for by the buyer. Similarly, in a contract of employment the employer promises to pay a wage or salary and the employee promises to work for a future period.

In bilateral contracts each party is both a **promisor** and a **promisee**; each has an obligation to perform and a right to performance by the other. In a court action, the party who sues as the promisee alleges that she has not received the performance to which she is entitled. The promisor may offer one or more defences as a reason or reasons why his conduct should be excused and why he should not be ordered to pay damages for breach of contract.

bilateral contract
a contract where offeror and offeree trade promises and both are bound to perform

promisor
a party who accepts an obligation to perform according to the terms of the contract

promisee
a party who has the right to performance according to the terms of the contract

UNCERTAINTY IN THE WORDING OF AN OFFER

A vague offer may prove to be no offer at all, and the intended acceptance of it cannot then form a contract. If the parties enter into a loosely worded arrangement, a court may find the agreement too ambiguous to be enforced.

CASE 5.4

Phibbs agreed to sell farmland to Choo for a price, "half [of which was] to be cash on possession of clear titles, the balance to be half the crop." Some time later, Phibbs refused to complete the deal and Choo sued him for the land.

The court found the agreement was not sufficiently certain to be enforceable. It was unclear whether the land was to be transferred at once, leaving Phibbs without security for the unpaid balance of the price, or what would be the terms of a mortgage if one were to be given, or whether Phibbs was to wait for full payment before making the transfer. Nor was it clear how the crop-sharing provisions would be applied to a section of the land in which Phibbs owned only a part interest. Choo was not permitted to waive terms, even if for his own benefit, unless he could establish an enforceable agreement in the first place.[25]

Other examples of lack of certainty in the terms of a contract are a promise to give a "fair" share in the profits of a business; a promise to "favourably consider" the renewal of the present contract "if satisfied with you";[26] a promise made by the buyer of a race horse to pay an additional amount on the price "if the horse is lucky."[27]

25. Phibbs v. Choo (1976), 69 D.L.R. (3d) 756.
26. Montreal Gas Co. v. Vasey, [1900] A.C. 595.
27. Cuthing v. Lynn (1831), 109 E.R. 1130.

Apparent uncertainty in the wording of a contract may be resolved by evidence of local customs or trade usage that gives a new precision to the terms. The courts have a policy of giving effect to contracts wherever possible; they hold that (1) anything is certain that is capable of being calculated or ascertained, and (2) where a contract may be construed as either enforceable or unenforceable, they will favour the interpretation that will see the contract enforced. We shall examine these problems in greater detail in Chapter 11, when we discuss the interpretation of contracts.

THE EFFECT OF AN INCOMPLETE AGREEMENT

What are the consequences when parties proceed on the basis of an incomplete agreement?

CASE 5.5

In *Brixham Investments Ltd. v. Hansink*,[28] both parties signed a letter providing for incorporation of the company and for entering into a further agreement. The letter did not set out the share allocation of the parties in the proposed company. When one party decided not to proceed with the project, the other sued for breach.

The Court considered whether the document was binding despite the lack of an agreement about share allocation. It held that, although a court will imply certain terms that arise by necessary inference (for instance, if the letter referred to the parties as "equal partners"), where the document did not deal in any way with this crucial question of share participation, the court will not construct an agreement between the parties. Accordingly, the document did not constitute a binding contract.

In other words, "The law does not recognize a contract to enter into a contract."[29]

A contract for the sale of goods is different from a contract for the sale of land or shares in a proposed corporation. Where the parties have agreed on the quantity, the Sale of Goods Act provides that the price in a contract of sale of goods "may be left to be fixed in manner thereby agreed, or may be determined by the course of dealing between the parties" and that "[W]here the price is not determined in accordance with the foregoing provisions the buyer must pay a reasonable price."[30]

QUESTIONS FOR REVIEW

1. Distinguish an offer from a promise.

2. What is a standard form contract? Describe the different ways in which it may be accepted.

3. Explain the importance of notice of terms in a standard form contract. To what extent does the law protect the interest of the public in standard form contracts?

4. Describe the ways in which an offer may come to an end.

---

28. (1971), 18 D.L.R. (3d) 533.

29. Von Hatzfeldt-Wildenburg v. Alexander, [1912] 1 Ch. 284, per Parker, J., at 289. See also National Bowling and Billiards Ltd. v. Double Diamond Bowling Supply Ltd. and Automatic Pinsetters Ltd. (1961), 27 D.L.R. (2d) 342; Re Pigeon et al. and Titley, Pigeon, Lavoie Ltd. (1973), 30 D.L.R. (3d) 132. For a fuller discussion, see Furmston, *Cheshire and Fifoot's Law of Contract* (13th ed.), pp. 39–43.

30. See, for example: R.S.B.C. 1996, c. 410, s. 12; R.S.O. 1990, c. S.1, s. 9; R.S.N.S. 1989, c. 408, s. 11.

5. What is the legal effect of a counter-offer?

6. "We cannot be obligated by people who do work for us without our knowledge." Why?

7. What elements are required for an acceptance to be effective?

8. What does it mean to "purchase an option"?

9. What does it mean to "invite tenders"? When is a contract normally created?

10. Can acceptance be effective from the moment a letter of acceptance is mailed even when the offer was not itself made through the mails?

11. Explain the different rules that apply to offer and acceptance when, rather than using the postal system, the parties communicate by telephone.

12. Should the same rules apply to the sending of responses by fax or e-mail? Why?

13. Explain the difference between unilateral and bilateral contracts.

14. Did the *Carlill* case concern a unilateral or a bilateral contract?

15. What is the effect of an agreement in which the parties state that certain terms will be discussed and agreed upon at a later date?

16. Give an example of circumstances in which the rule "An offer must be communicated before it can be accepted" would operate.

17. Is it true that an acceptance must be communicated before a contract can be formed?

18. May a person withdraw a bid he makes at an auction sale before the fall of the hammer?

CASES AND PROBLEMS

1. Friday evening after closing, Sackett's Appliances placed an ad in its window, "This weekend only, five Whirlwind Dishwashers, reduced from $1199 to $599! Shop Early!" Martens saw the ad later that evening. She appeared the next morning at 9 a.m. when Sackett's opened its doors and stated to the clerk she would take one of the Whirlwind Dishwashers. The clerk replied that the ad was a mistake; the price should have been $999. Martens demanded to speak with the manager and insisted on Sackett's honouring its offer to sell at $599. The manager said, "I'm sorry madam, but that machine cost us more than $800. We cannot sell it at $599." Martens said Sackett's was in breach of contract and she would see her lawyer about it.

Is Martens right? Explain.

2. Garrett is the manager of Aristo Condos Inc. and is charge of selling vacant units in the Aristo Towers. On October 4, Heilman examined several of the units with Garrett, said that he thought the prices a bit high but would think about it. Several days later, on October 7, Garrett sent Heilman an e-mail stating, "I will sell you any one of the units we examined together (numbers 14, 236, 238, or 307), for $275 000. I am sending you all the details by courier." Garrett then sent by courier to Heilman a formal offer containing all of the necessary terms, including the required down payment and acceptable mortgage financing.

Later that day after he had received the e-mail message but before he had received the letter, Heilman e-mailed Garrett, "I accept your offer with respect to unit 307."

Has a binding contract been formed by Garrett's e-mail? In what circumstances might this question become the basis of a dispute between the parties?

3 Last year, Lambert bought a car on August 15 and insured it with the Reliable Insurance Company, for whom Drake was the local agent. On the following July 29, Drake telephoned Lambert about renewing her policy and learned she was on vacation at her summer cottage. Acting on behalf of Reliable Insurance, Drake wrote to Lambert at her cottage: "As you know, your car insurance policy with us expires on August 15. We will renew this policy on the same terms unless notified to the contrary by you. You may sign the application form and pay after you return to the city."

On her way back from her holidays on August 16, Lambert struck and injured a pedestrian with her car. The pedestrian claimed $100 000 damages from Lambert, and on referring the matter to the Reliable Insurance Company, Lambert was informed that her policy of insurance had expired without renewal on August 15.

Discuss Lambert's legal position.

4 The province and its largest university created a program by which the province would give funding to disadvantaged students. Students were told by the university that they would receive funding over four years and, on that basis, they enrolled in the program. The students dealt only with the university. In the third year of the program, the province restructured it so that students had to obtain their maximum Canada Student Loan before being eligible for funding.

The students sued for a declaration requiring the province to pay them at the original funding level for the full four years on the basis of a binding contract with the province. They claimed that they reasonably believed that they had a contractual arrangement with the province not to alter the terms and conditions of the funding arrangement. The province defended by stating that there was no contract with the students because they had not communicated their acceptance to it, but dealt only with the university; if anyone was bound, it was the university.

Discuss the merits of each party's argument. Who do you think should succeed?

5 Purcell was in failing health and advertised to sell his retail computing equipment business. Quentin was familiar with Purcell's business operations; he sent Purcell a detailed offer to buy for $450 000, paying $75 000 as a cash down payment, with the balance payable in instalments over two years. Purcell promptly sent an e-mail to Quentin stating: "The price and all the other terms seem fair, except that I need substantially more cash by way of down payment—say $125 000. Tell me how high you are willing to go." Quentin replied by e-mail, "There is no way I can increase the cash payment."

Purcell replied the next day, "Okay. I've thought about it, and given the state of my health, I have decided to accept your offer." By then, Quentin had heard that the business had suffered because of Purcell's declining health and he refused to go through with the purchase. He asserted that since Purcell had refused his offer, there was no deal. Is Quentin right? Has Purcell any basis for claiming that there is a binding contract with Quentin?

6 McKight wanted to buy from Chang a lot to build a retail outlet in Waverley several kilometres north of the city of Halifax. McKight lives in Halifax and Chang lives in Waverley.

In May, McKight went to Waverley and offered Chang $135 000. Chang refused the offer. On July 7 McKight went again to see Chang, and this time Chang handed her an offer to sell the property for $155 000 and said he would hold the offer open for 14 days at that price.

Late in the evening of July 8, another person called to see Chang and offered him $165 000 for the property. Chang accepted, subject to a condition for avoiding the contract if he found he could not withdraw from his arrangement with McKight . The next morning at about 10:30 a.m., Chang went to McKight's home and knocked on the door. No one answered and he left a letter stating, "Please take notice that my offer to you of July 7 is withdrawn."

McKight did not see the letter of revocation until she came home for lunch at 12:30 p.m. She was not at home earlier because she had an appointment with her lawyer at 9:30 a.m. She requested her lawyer to write to Chang as follows: "I am instructed by Ms. McKight to accept your offer of July 7, to sell at the price of $155 000. Kindly have the contract prepared and forwarded to me." This letter was handed to a courier at 10 a.m. that morning (July 9) and delivered to Chang at about 2 p.m. When Chang received it, he replied stating that the offer had been withdrawn.

McKight brought an action for breach of contract against Chang. State with reasons what you think the court's decision would be.

7. Daly, a United States citizen, began negotiations with Stevens of Vancouver to investigate and stake mineral claims at the head of the Leduc River in British Columbia. Daly had discovered evidence of deposits there some 20 years earlier.

On January 13, Daly wrote, "A large mining company in Boise is showing an interest. To protect my interest it will be necessary for me to arrive at some definite arrangement soon." Stevens replied on January 17, "Perhaps we can make some arrangement this summer to finance you in staking claims for which I would give you an interest. I would suggest that I should pay for your time and expenses and carry you for a 10 percent interest in the claims." Daly replied on January 22, "Your proposition appeals to me as being a fair one."

Soon after, Daly was called to active duty in the United States Naval Reserve Engineering Corps and was sent to the Marshall Islands. Correspondence continued with some difficulty, but on February 28, Daly wrote, "As I informed you in a previous letter, your offer of a 10 percent interest for relocating and finding these properties is acceptable to me, provided there is a definite agreement to this effect in the near future."

On March 5, Stevens wrote, "I hereby agree that if you will take me in to the showings, and I think they warrant staking, I will stake the claims and give you a 10 percent interest. The claims would be recorded in my name and I will have full discretion in dealing with them—you are to get 10 percent of the vendor interest. I can arrange to get a pilot here." Daly replied on April 12, "If you will inform me when you can obtain a pilot, I will immediately take steps for a temporary release in order to be on hand."

On June 6, Stevens wrote, "I was talking to a prospector who said he had been over your showings at the head of the Leduc River, and in his opinion it would be practically impossible to operate there, as the showings were behind ice fields that, along with the extreme snowfalls, make it very doubtful if an economic operation could be carried on. I now have so much work lined up that I doubt if I would have time to visit your showings and do not think I would be warranted in making the effort to get in there due to the unfavourable conditions. I must advise you, therefore, not to depend on making this trip, and suggest if you are still determined to go in, to make some other arrangements."

Daly did not reply. On his return from the Marshall Islands the following year, he did, however, follow up his interest in the property. He discovered that in July, Stevens had sent prospectors into the area and, as a result of their investigations, had staked claims in his own name and later sold them to a mining development company. Daly brought an action against Stevens claiming damages for breach of contract. Should Daly succeed in his action? Explain.

8. The city of Cameron had grown substantially in the past decade and needed to expand its water purification plant. For this purpose it proposed to buy two hectares of land adjacent to the purification plant from Margot Nurseries, a thriving fruit and vegetable business owning 40 hectares of prime land. As the two hectares were particularly important to Margot she bargained for a substantial price to pay for the relocation of her business's sorting and packaging area.

The city bargained very hard, and threatened to expropriate the land—as it had power to do under the provincial Expropriation Act—if a deal could not be reached. Finally in exasperation, Margot handed the director of the purification plant a detailed written statement of the terms upon which she would sell, the offer to be open for 10 days. She asked for a price of $200 000, with $50 000 paid on acceptance. She would permit the city to begin excavation on the nearest one-quarter hectare, but it must delay moving onto the remainder of the land for 60 days so that she could make the needed relocation. When Margot handed the director the offer she stated that if the city began excavations on the one-quarter hectare that would be acceptance of her offer.

Within a week, city workers began excavating about 20 metres into Margot's land, and two days later she was served with a notice of expropriation under the Expropriation Act, offering her a price of $80 000. Under the Act, if the parties do not reach a settlement, a court will hear evidence about the market value of the land and the costs caused by compulsory displacement to the owner; it then awards a sum in compensation and orders the owner to give up possession.

Margot, claiming that the city had accepted her offer before the expropriation proceedings were started, sued the city for damages for breach of the contract. Discuss the arguments of each side and give your opinion on who should succeed. What general issue of public policy arises when a legislature grants powers of expropriation to municipalities?

FORMATION OF A CONTRACT

Consideration, and Intention to Create Legal Relations

Before an agreement is binding in law, certain essential elements must be present; primarily there must be consideration, although in some instances there may be something else in its place. In this chapter we examine such questions as:

- what is the nature of consideration and what is required for it to be adequate to bind the parties?

- how do we distinguish consideration from a gratuitous promise? from motive for making a promise? from an existing legal duty to perform?

- what is injurious reliance?

- what other means are there by which a promise may become binding?

- why is it essential that parties must intend their promises to be binding, and how may this normal presumption be missing?

THE MEANING OF CONSIDERATION

A bargain—where one party pays a price for the promise obtained from the other party—is central to the idea of a contract. In a unilateral contract the price paid for the offeror's promise is the act done by the offeree. In a bilateral contract, the price paid for each party's promise is the promise of the other. This price is called *consideration*. In short, consideration is "the price for which the promise [or the act] of the other is bought."[1]

A promisor usually bargains for a benefit to himself, such as a promise to pay money, deliver goods, or provide services; but it need not be directly for his own benefit. So long as the promisor bargains for the other party to do something—or to promise to do something—that she otherwise would not do, the promisor will have received consideration.

ILLUSTRATION 6.1

Adams, a creditor of Brown, threatened to sue Brown for an overdue debt. Brown's friend, Cox, then promised to pay Adams Brown's debt if Adams would refrain from suing Brown, and Adams agreed.

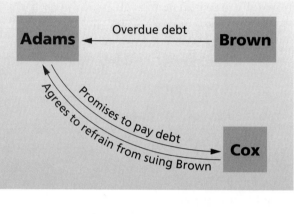

If Cox failed to pay Adams as agreed and Adams sued him for breach of contract, she would succeed. To establish consideration she need only show that she adopted a different course of action, that is, that she refrained from suing Brown, in return for Cox's promise. The "price" she agrees to pay for Cox's promise need not confer a direct benefit on him.

Gratuitous Promises

With some qualifications to be discussed later, consideration is essential to make a contract binding in law. A person may, of course, make a promise to another without bargaining for anything in return. A promise made in the absence of a bargain is called a **gratuitous promise** and, although accepted by the person to whom it is made, does not become a contract and is not enforceable in law. A promise to make a gift and to perform services without remuneration are common examples of gratuitous promises. Such "contracts" are void for lack of consideration, which is another way of saying that they never amounted to a contract.

gratuitous promise
a promise made without bargaining for or accepting anything in return

The law does nothing to prevent performance of a gratuitous promise. It simply asserts that if the promisor does not perform, the promisee has no legal remedy; he cannot seek compensation for his disappointed expectations. As a matter of honour most people do perform their gratuitous promises.

What about charitable donations? Charities seldom find it in their interest to sue those who have made pledges but do not perform. They rely upon their prospective donors' sense of honour to a large extent, but in their budgeting they are wise to discount a small percentage as nonperformers. They understand that people might become reluctant to give pledges if charities were likely to sue them for non-payment.

Occasionally, however, donors have died before honouring large pledges, and charities have sued their estates.[2] A charity claiming payment will be asked what price it paid for the pledge.

---

1. Winfield, *Pollock's Principles of Contract* (13th ed.), p. 133.
2. See, for example: Governors of Dalhousie College v. Boutilier, [1934] 3 D.L.R. 593.

The answer will be none, unless in return for the pledge the charity undertook a new activity and incurred additional expense. A court may find consideration if the charity began a specific project, such as constructing a building, in response to the donor's promise. The court must, however, be able to find an implied request from the promisor—if not an explicit one—that the charity undertake the project as the "price" of the pledge. When a pledge is for general funds, the charity can make it legally binding only if it uses a seal on its pledge cards. We shall discuss the use of a seal in a later section of this chapter.

As long as a gratuitous promise remains unperformed, the promisee has no recourse. But suppose the promise is performed—a gift is actually made. May the donor later change her mind and demand it back on grounds of lack of consideration? Generally speaking, no: once she has voluntarily made the gift, it is no longer her property and she has no control over it, except in the rare case of undue influence, as discussed in Chapter 9.

Though a promisor is not bound by her gratuitous promise, once she begins to perform she has a duty to carry it out with reasonable care. If, through her negligence, she injures the promisee or the promisee's property, she is liable to compensate the promisee according to the principles of the law of torts. A defence that she received no consideration for her promise will not succeed. Thus, a doctor who offers to give free aid to an injured person and negligently aggravates the person's injuries is liable for damages. Similarly, a public accountant who gratuitously undertakes an audit for a charitable organization is liable for damages caused to the organization through her negligence. She is under no obligation to do the audit, but once she begins she must proceed with care.

ADEQUACY OF CONSIDERATION

While the consideration given in return for a promise must have *some* value in the eyes of the law, the court does not inquire whether the promisor made a good bargain. It is not for the court to make a fair bargain for the parties: if a party agreed to a grossly inadequate consideration for his promise, that was up to him. The courts take the view that assessing the adequacy of consideration requires a personal value judgment, and if they were to assume that role they would relinquish their role of impartial arbiter. They might find themselves penalizing the shrewd bargaining of one party and compensating for the stupidity of the other. One party may voluntarily agree to accept a mere trifle with no market value—such as a sugar cube or a broken pencil—in return for a valuable promise made to the other party. The adequacy of the consideration is not for the courts to determine.

However, a court does not always refuse to examine the adequacy of consideration. If, for example, the consideration is grossly inadequate for the promise and if other evidence points to fraud, duress, or undue influence exerted on the promisor, the court may hold that the promise is voidable at the promisor's option. Courts have become increasingly concerned with protecting the interests of consumers from unconscionable conduct.[3]

The question of adequacy of consideration might seem to arise whenever parties to a dispute agree to settle out of court. Suppose that after settling, one party discovers she was mistaken about either the law or the facts: she promised to pay a sum of money to the other party when she really was not bound to pay anything. The threat of the other party to sue was without merit since he would have lost in court. Is his promise *not* to sue, therefore, worthless and hence not really consideration for the promise to pay something in settlement?

---

3. See Chapter 10. See also Chapter 32: unconscionable consideration is now the subject of consumer protection legislation. See, for example: Business Practices Act, R.S.O. 1990, c. B.18, s. 2(b)(ii).

ILLUSTRATION 6.2

In an automobile collision between Juan Alvarez and Sally Brown, Brown's car suffers $3000 damage. The parties have an extended argument by mail about which of them is responsible for the accident. Finally, after many months, Brown threatens to sue Alvarez unless Alvarez agrees to pay 75 percent of Brown's damages, that is, $2250. Alvarez promises to pay the sum in full settlement of all Brown's claims, and she agrees not to sue him. Alvarez then realizes that at the time he made his promise to pay Brown, more than 12 months had passed since the accident had occurred. The provincial

Highway Traffic Act states: "No action shall be brought against a person for the recovery of damages occasioned by a motor vehicle after the expiration of twelve months from the time when the damages were sustained."

Alvarez now refuses to pay Brown $2250. He states that since Brown could not have successfully sued him for damages, her promise not to sue him is no consideration for his promise to pay. It is well established, however, that Brown's promise not to sue Alvarez is good consideration for the settlement, and she will succeed in an action against Alvarez.

Provided the promisee has an honest belief in her right to sue, giving it up is good consideration for the promisor's promise.[4] If this were not the rule, no one could ever be sure that a settlement was binding; subsequent information might upset a settlement made in good faith. Indeed, it could even be argued that until a dispute was actually decided by the courts, neither side could be sure that it had given anything of value as consideration for the promise of the other. Aside from being an intolerable situation for the parties, such a state of affairs would conflict with basic principles of the law: to discourage unnecessary lawsuits and to promote certainty in the law.

MOTIVE CONTRASTED WITH CONSIDERATION: PAST CONSIDERATION

Even though it may be inadequate in a financial sense, consideration is the *price* that makes the promisor's promise binding. On the other hand, the reason for making the promise, the *motive*, is irrelevant, whether it be gratitude, a sense of honour, duty, affection or charity, or even part of an unworthy scheme. Motive cannot change a gratuitous promise into a binding contract, nor can it reduce a binding promise into a merely voluntary obligation.

Ethically, we may believe it is wrong to break *any* promise seriously made and that every promisor has a moral duty to perform. If every promise were legally enforceable simply because the promisor had a moral duty to do as he said he would, we would not need the doctrine of consideration. In civil law legal systems, where **moral cause** may be sufficient to make a promise binding, other difficulties arise in probing internally into a promisor's motive in order to establish moral obligation. While the doctrine of consideration has been attacked as causing unfair decisions in some instances (and undoubtedly it does, as we shall see), it has the virtue of being an external and more objective test of whether a promise should be binding.

moral cause
moral duty of promisor to perform his promise

CASE 6.1

In the classic case of *Eastwood v. Kenyon*,[5] Eastwood, who had been guardian of Mrs. Kenyon while she was a child, had borrowed money in order to finance her education and to maintain the estate of which she was sole heiress.

On coming of age she promised to reimburse him; after her marriage, her husband Kenyon promised Eastwood to pay back the sum, but he failed to do so.

continued

---

4. Haigh v. Brooks (1839), 113 E.R. 119; Famous Foods Ltd. v. Liddle, [1941] 3 D.L.R. 525; Fairgrief v. Ellis, [1935] 2 D.L.R. 806.

5. (1840), 113 E.R. 482.

Eastwood sued Kenyon, claiming that Kenyon had a moral duty to honour his promise, but his action failed. What price had Eastwood paid for Kenyon's promise? The court could find none. Kenyon's promise was not part of a bargain and his motive, a sense of gratitude and a feeling of moral duty, did not bind him in law.

We can see, then, that if one person promises to reward another who has *previously* done an act gratuitously or given something of value, the promise is not binding. That promise is gratuitous—just like the benefit that the promisee had earlier conferred upon the promisor. Another approach is to say that the motive of the promisor was to return the kindness of the promisee, and, of course, motive and consideration are not the same thing. The benefit previously conferred upon the promisor is often called **past consideration**. Since there is no element of bargain, that is, of the benefit being performed *in return for* the promise, the expression is really contradictory, for "past consideration" is no consideration.

past consideration
a gratuitous benefit previously conferred upon a promisor

RELATION BETWEEN EXISTING LEGAL DUTY AND CONSIDERATION

Where *A* has an existing contractual duty to *B*, a later promise by *B* to pay *A* something extra to perform that obligation is not binding. Performance by *A* is not good consideration for the later promise because he was already bound to perform. Indeed, his failure to do so would have been a breach of contract. For example, a promise to members of a crew to increase their pay if they did not desert their ship was held to be unenforceable:[6] the existing contracts of employment between the crew and the employer bound the crew to perform their duties faithfully. On the other hand, a term of such contracts is that the ship be seaworthy. If it proves unseaworthy, the crew are released from their obligation, and then, of course, there will be consideration for the promise to increase their pay if the crew stays with the ship.[7]

The situation arises when one party threatens to default on its obligation to perform and leave the other party to sue for breach. A common example occurs in construction projects.

ILLUSTRATION 6.3

A Inc. has tendered and won the contract to erect an office building for land developer *B*. During construction *A* Inc. runs into unexpected difficulties, and informs *B* that it is thinking of abandoning the project. However, *B*, relying upon completion at the agreed date has already leased out large parts of the building. If *A* Inc. abandons the job, *B* will lose valuable time finding another builder to complete the project and will likely be in breach of leases he has made with prospective tenants.

To avoid these difficulties, *B* offers to pay *A* Inc. an extra $500 000 to enable it to hire extra workers and pay overtime wages in order to complete construction on time. *A* Inc. accepts and completes on the agreed date. However, *B* refuses to pay the additional sum on the grounds that he received no new consideration for his promise: *A* Inc. was already bound by its contract to complete on time.

Some U.S. courts have taken the view that a building firm is at liberty to abandon the job if it chooses, and to pay damages. In this view a fresh promise to proceed, that is, not to abandon the job, is good consideration for an additional sum and the owner is bound to pay it on

---

6. Stilk v. Myrick (1809), 70 E.R. 1168.

7. Turner v. Owen (1862), 6 E.R. 79.

completion. Most courts, including all English and Canadian courts, take the view that this conduct smacks of unfair pressure—a form of economic blackmail—by the party threatening to abandon the contract, and so they hold that there is no consideration for the promise to pay an extra sum.[8] However, a supplier intent on economic blackmail can still exact a legally enforceable promise from its customer to pay an increased price by delivering a "peppercorn" or a paperclip (or any other item of negligible value) to her in return for the promise, or by insisting that the customer make her promise under seal (as discussed later in this chapter).

We can see shortcomings in the doctrine of consideration when parties try to modify an existing contract. The question should not be whether there was new consideration, but rather whether the parties were trying to adjust their legitimate interests in new circumstances without one side extorting a higher price. Not every change in contractual terms amounts to an unfair exploitation of the promisor. For instance, a promisor may believe it is in its best interests to pay the promisee more in order to ease the promisee's hardship and thus obtain better performance. So far the Canadian courts have been reluctant to recognize this reality,[9] although a recent English case allowed a construction company to recover a promised extra sum for completion.[10] The court was satisfied that there was no economic duress; the construction company had not exerted undue pressure and both parties benefited from performance.

A related problem arises when a stranger—a "third party" to a contract—promises to pay a sum to the promisor for his promise to perform already existing obligations to the promisee.

ILLUSTRATION 6.4

As in Illustration 6.3, above, *A* Inc. has made a contract to construct an office building for *B. C,* who has a lease as principal tenant in the building, promises to pay *A* $100 000 if *A* completes the building on time. Is there consideration for *C*'s promise?[11] Since *A* is already under a duty to *B* to construct the building on time, what further price does *A* give for *C*'s promise?

This problem has seldom arisen in the courts, but when it does they seem to agree that *A* can enforce *C*'s promise, and further, that if *A* failed to perform, *A* would be liable to actions by *both B* and *C*.[12] *A* has given new consideration by promising *C* to complete on time and making himself liable to *C* if he fails to do so. Accordingly, we must distinguish between the situation where the later promise is made by the promisee in the original contract, and where it is made by a third party to that contract.

Suppose instead that *A*'s duty to perform is a public duty required by law, as where *A* is a police officer. If *B* promises to pay *A* for services as a police officer, the court is confronted with two problems—the question of public policy *and* of consideration. If police officers have been asked to do something that they are already bound to do or something that will interfere with their regular duties, the court worries that the promise to pay them tends to corrupt public servants and it will likely find the promise unenforceable on grounds of public policy. On the other hand, if the court finds that the officers have been requested to do something beyond their duties and *not* in conflict with them, it will likely find consideration and hold the promise binding, as in *Glasbrook Brothers v. Glamorgan County Council*,[13] where a company agreed to pay for a special police guard during a strike and was held to be bound by its promise.

---

8. See Gilbert Steel Ltd. v. University Construction Ltd. (1976), 67 D.L.R. (3d) 606.

9. See Reiter, "Courts, Consideration and Common Sense" (1977), 27 *U.T.L.J.* pp. 439–512, especially at 459.

10. Williams v. Roffey Brothers & Nicholls (Contractors) Ltd., [1990] 1 All E.R. 512. For a useful commentary, see Dan Halyk, "Consideration, Practical Benefits and Promissory Estoppel" (1991), 55(2) *Sask. L. Rev.* 393.

11. Shadwell v. Shadwell (1860), 142 E.R. 62.

12. Scotson v. Pegg (1861), 158 E.R. 121; Pao On v. Lau Yiu Long, [1979] 3 W.L.R. 435.

13. [1925] A.C. 270.

GRATUITOUS REDUCTION OF A DEBT

The requirement for consideration to make a promise binding can lead to other unsatisfactory results, especially in business transactions.

✳ CASE 6.2

In the leading English case of *Foakes v. Beer*, a debtor owed a large sum of money to his creditor and payment was overdue. The creditor agreed to accept a series of instalments of the principal, and to forgo her right to interest, if the debtor paid promptly and regularly. The debtor paid the full principal as agreed, but the creditor then sued for the interest. She succeeded on the grounds that her promise to accept less than the total sum to which she was entitled, that is, principal plus accrued interest, was a gratuitous promise and thus did not bind her.[14]

This rule is unrealistic. For a number of sensible reasons, a creditor, C, may find it more to its benefit to settle for a reduced amount than to insist on payment in full. For one thing, the compromise may avoid placing a debtor in bankruptcy where, by the time all other creditors' claims have been recognized, C might end up with less money than if it had accepted a reduced sum. Second, the proposed reduction may enable the debtor to persuade friends to lend him enough money to take advantage of it and make a fresh start. Third, the debtor may simply not have the assets to enable him to pay in full, so that a court judgment against him would not in any event realize more than the reduced amount. Finally, C may well need urgently at least part of the sum owed it for other commitments: it may be happier to take the lesser amount at once, instead of later collecting the full account with all the delays inherent in a legal action.

The rule in *Foakes v. Beer* may be avoided in several ways. In the first place, payment *before* the due date is sufficient consideration to make an agreed reduction in the debt binding on the creditor. Thus if the debtor pays $600 one day in advance in settlement of a $1000 debt due the next day, the agreement to accept $600 is binding. As we have seen, the court will not inquire into the adequacy of the consideration; if the creditor chooses to reduce the debt by $400 in order to receive payment one day in advance, it may bind itself to do so.

Second, the rule in *Foakes v. Beer* applies *only* to payments of money. It does not apply to the transfer of goods or to the provision of services. Since an individual may make a contract for a clearly inadequate consideration if he so desires, he may agree to pay $1000 for a trinket, a cheap watch, or a package of cigarettes. Similarly, he may agree to cancel a $1000 debt on receiving any one of these objects. In effect, he is trading the debt for the object, and such an agreement is valid, provided he agrees to it voluntarily. The result of this reasoning creates a paradox: if a person agrees to accept $900 in full settlement of a $1000 debt, he may later sue for the balance successfully; if a person accepts $500 and a string of beads worth 10 cents in full settlement of a $1000 debt, he will fail if he sues for the balance.

Third, the rule in *Foakes v. Beer* applies only to agreements between a creditor and debtor. A third party, who is not bound to pay anything to the creditor, may offer to pay the creditor a lesser sum if it will cancel the debt. A creditor that accepts such an offer is bound by its promise and will fail if it later sues the debtor.[15] The result is the same as if the third person had purchased the debt from the creditor.

---

14. (1884), 9 App. Cas. 605.

15. Hirachand Punamchand v. Temple, [1911] 2 K.B. 330.

ILLUSTRATION 6.5

A Co. Ltd. has an account receivable from *B* for $1000 and sells (assigns) it to *X* for $800. *A* Co. Ltd. no longer has any rights against *B*. It would not matter whether *X* was purchasing the account receivable as a business proposition and intended to hold *B* to her promise for full payment, or whether he wished merely to help her. *X*'s motive is irrelevant. If he deals directly with the creditor, the debt for $1000 can be bought for $800.

The result would have been different, however, if *X* had lent $800 to *B* and *B* had then paid the $800 to *A* Co. Ltd. apparently in full settlement of the account of $1000. So long as *B* deals directly with *A* Co. Ltd., the source of the funds paid by *B* is irrelevant: *A* Co. Ltd. would not be bound by the settlement and could later sue *B* for $200 (apart from the statutory exceptions discussed below.)

Finally, as we shall see shortly, the rule in *Foakes v. Beer* is avoided if the creditor agrees in writing and under seal to reduce the debt.

The rule in *Foakes v. Beer* has been modified by statute in British Columbia, Alberta, Saskatchewan, Manitoba, and Ontario.[16] Under any of these acts, if a creditor agrees to accept part performance (that is, a lesser sum of money) in settlement of a debt, it is bound once it has accepted this part performance. On the other hand, it may be able to go back on its promise to accept a lesser sum of money before the sum is actually paid; the cases are unclear on this point.

INJURIOUS RELIANCE (EQUITABLE ESTOPPEL)

Evolution of the Principle

Suppose a person makes a gratuitous promise to another fully intending to keep it but later finds it inconvenient to perform. Meanwhile the promisee has quite reasonably relied on the promise and has incurred expenses he would otherwise not have made. What happens if the promisor subsequently defaults? According to the strict rules of common law, the answer is "nothing at all." The gratuitous promise remains gratuitous, the promise cannot be enforced, and the promisee suffers the burden of his expenses.

ILLUSTRATION 6.6

A, who has just ordered a new 90-horsepower outboard motor, tells his friend *B* that he will give him his old 35-horsepower motor as soon as the new one arrives. To make use of *A*'s old engine, *B* will have to make expensive modifications to his small boat. Instead, at *A*'s suggestion he buys a new boat for $3000. Subsequently, *A*'s brother reminds him that he had promised the old motor to him, and rather than promote a family quarrel, *A* tells *B* he cannot carry out his promise. *B* has no right in contract law to enforce *A*'s promise.

injurious reliance
loss or harm suffered by a promisee who, to his detriment, relied reasonably on a gratuitous promise

Some parts of the United States adopted a principle that would bind *A* to carry out his promise.[17] Courts in these states assert that since *A* by his conduct *induced B* to rely on his promise and *B* did rely upon it, to his injury, *A* must honour his promise to prevent an injustice. This principle, known as **injurious reliance**, is similar to the tort rules concerning foreseeability of harm in negligence actions. The classic expression of the doctrine is as follows:

---

16. Law and Equity Act, R.S.B.C. 1979, c. 224, s. 40; Judicature Act, R.S.A. 1980, c. J-1, s. 13 (1); Queen's Bench Act, R.S.S. 1978, c. Q-1, s. 45 (7); Mercantile Law Amendment Act, R.S.M. 1987, c. M-120, s. 6; and Mercantile Law Amendment Act, R.S.O. 1990, c. M.10, s. 16. For cases interpreting this section see Rommerill v. Gardener (1962), 35 D.L.R. (2d) 717 and others referred to therein.

17. Ricketts v. Scothorn, 77 N.W. 365 (1898).

A promise which the promisor should reasonably expect to induce action or forbearance of a definite and substantial character on the part of the promisee and which does induce such action or forbearance is binding if injustice can be avoided only by enforcement of the promise.[18]

Thus, although a promisor has not *requested* that, in return for his promise, the promisee act in reliance on it, inducement alone as in the circumstances described above becomes a substitute for the request. (In all common law jurisdictions, if the promisor had requested the act of reliance in return for his promise, there would be an offer, an acceptance, and consideration.) This position, as we are about to discuss, has been gaining more recognition in England and Canada.

Estoppel Based on Fact

When one person asserts as true a certain *statement of fact* and another relies on that statement to his detriment, the maker of the statement will be **estopped** (prevented) from denying the truth of his original statement in a court of law, even if it turns out to have been untrue.

estopped
prevented

ILLUSTRATION 6.7

A purchased a retail shoe business from X in rented premises owned by B. After a few months, A mentions to her landlord, B, that the business does not have an adequate sales area and that she would like to turn a back room into a display and fitting salon. She believes that the room contains a number of pieces of old furniture belonging to B that she would like to get rid of. B says, "That furniture belonged to X and you acquired it when you bought the business. You can do as you like with it." A replies, "I thought it was yours. That's what X told me." "No, it's yours," B answers. The tenant next door to A is present and hears the conversation.

That evening, when B reports the incident to his wife, she becomes furious and reminds B that several antique pieces given to them by her grandmother are stored in the back room of the store. When B arrives at the shoe store the next morning he discovers that the furniture has been taken away to the city dump and compressed by a bulldozer. He then sues A for the value of the antique furniture.

B would fail because A can prove in her defence that B had asserted that the furniture was A's, and the court would estop B from asserting the true state of the facts.

Estoppel applies to an assertion of existing fact; but does it also apply to a promise of future conduct?

ILLUSTRATION 6.8

Suppose that instead of stating the furniture was A's, B had replied, "I wouldn't mind seeing that ugly furniture of ours in the city dump, as long as you don't tell my wife. I promise not to interfere." The following morning, B's wife was shopping in the vicinity and saw the furniture being removed from A's premises. Before she

could stop the workers, several of the best pieces were damaged beyond repair. B reluctantly sued A for the value of the destroyed pieces and the return of the remainder. B would recover the remaining furniture, but would he succeed in getting damages?

To answer this question, we must examine the original meaning of estoppel and its subsequent enlargement. For practical reasons, and generally until recent times, the courts restricted the use of estoppel to assertions of fact. When an assertion of fact is made, its truth or falsity at the time of its assertion is an objective matter that can usually be determined by evidence. The essence of estoppel is *reliance on facts* as they were asserted to be at the time of the statement.

---

18. American Law Institute, *Restatement of Contracts*, Section 90, Washington, 1932.

Only if they were untrue at the time would the maker be estopped. The courts reasoned that the essential element of common law estoppel was missing when a person had made a *promise of future conduct* instead of an assertion of existing facts: a promise of future conduct was exclusively within the sphere of contract law and required consideration. The problem with their reasoning was that a person can act as much to his detriment on the strength of a gratuitous promise as on the strength of an assertion of fact that proves to be incorrect.

Estoppel Based on Reasonable Reliance

Suppose a promisee acts on the strength of a promise when the promisor had no intention of keeping his word. The promisee might argue that she was acting on and relying on an *assertion of fact* by the promisor—that he was making his promise with the present intention of keeping it—which was not the case. Claiming his intention, rather than his promise, to be a fact also presented difficulties. As we have noted, our courts have resisted examining a person's motives; motives cannot be proved by external evidence, except in rare instances when a dishonest promisor gives himself away by his own admission. States of mind are notoriously difficult to ascertain at the best of times. In any event, the harm suffered by the promisee is the same whether the promisor originally intended to keep his promise and later changed his mind, or originally intended to mislead and never meant to keep the promise. While the question of intention is germane to the punishment of a wrongdoer in criminal law, it has little to do with the concern of contract law to seek external standards to determine when a promise is binding as a contractual bargain.

Despite their problems with the idea of estoppel, the courts eventually found themselves unable to ignore the plea of an innocent party who had relied in good faith on a gratuitous promise only to find later that the promisor had changed his mind. In Illustration 6.8 above, *A* relied on *B*'s implied promise that he would not demand the return of his furniture, and *A*'s reliance differs in its effect little, if at all, from his reliance on *B*'s assertion in Illustration 6.7 that the furniture belonged to *A*. On the grounds of fairness, the court would exercise its equitable jurisdiction to estop *B* from claiming that he was not bound by his gratuitous promise as it applied to the furniture already destroyed. This reasoning appears to extend the idea of estoppel to promises. (The argument has been called **promissory estoppel** but the more common phrase is **equitable estoppel** because the court is acting as a court of equity to override a common law rule.) The U.S. term "injurious reliance" and the English term "equitable estoppel" are essentially two sides of the same coin: injurious reliance looks at the situation from the point of view of the promisee, while equitable estoppel views it from the position of the promisor.

The English doctrine of equitable estoppel has not been carried as far as the U.S. doctrine of injurious reliance, at least until the present. It appears to be limited to a *defence* against a claim by the promisor where a legal relationship already exists between the parties. The English courts have not recognized that a gratuitous promisee's claim of equitable estoppel makes the promise to him a binding one. (Hence, in our earlier illustration of the gratuitous promise of an outboard motor, the promisee would not succeed in an English court.)

The doctrine of equitable estoppel originated over a century ago in the leading case of *Hughes v. Metropolitan Railway Co.*[19]

> **promissory estoppel or equitable estoppel**
> the court's exercise of its equitable jurisdiction to estop a promisor from claiming that she was not bound by her gratuitous promise where reliance on that promise caused injury to the promisee

CASE 6.3

Metropolitan Railway, a tenant under a 99-year lease of a large block of buildings, was required to keep the building in good repair. The penalty for failure to honour a notice to repair from the landlord, Hughes, would be forfeiture of possession—the lease would be terminated. Hughes served notice that repairs were needed and the tenant had six months to make them. The tenant then suggested that

continued

19. (1877), 2 App. Cas. 439.

Hughes might be interested in buying back the remaining years of the tenant's 99-year lease. The lease was a valuable one as rents to subtenants had risen greatly over the long years of the master lease. When Hughes expressed interest in the proposal, the two sides began serious negotiations. With Hughes' acquiescence, all repairs were delayed, since they would have increased the tenant's investment in the property and thus the sale price of the lease.

After several months, negotiations broke down and the tenant then proceeded with the repairs. They were not finished within six months of the original notice, but were complete within six months of the termination of negotiations. Hughes sued for forfeiture of the lease, and had he succeeded he would have obtained the remaining years free.

In refusing Hughes' claim, the House of Lords stated that by entering into negotiation Hughes had impliedly agreed to a suspension of the notice during negotiations; he could not later go back on his word and revert to his strict legal rights in the lease. The notice became effective again only on negotiations being broken off, when the tenant could no longer rely on Hughes' implied promise not to pursue his strict rights.

While a gratuitous promise may still be withdrawn, its withdrawal is not allowed to prejudice the promisee in respect of any reliance he has already placed on it. Notice of withdrawal (or an end to circumstances in which the promise is implied) may restore the promisor's rights to any future performance still owed by the promisee. Thus, in the *Hughes* case, the landlord was entitled, *after* the negotiations had broken down, to require repairs to be made within the six-month period provided in the lease.

Although very little use was made of the *Hughes* case for many years, it still illustrates the classic situation in which promissory estoppel arises: (1) some form of legal relationship already exists between the parties; (2) one of the parties promises (perhaps by implication only) to release the other from some or all of the other's legal duties to him; and (3) the other party in reliance on that promise alters his conduct in a way that would make it a real hardship if the promisor could renege on his promise. If the promisor were to ignore his promise and sue to enforce his original rights, the promisee could successfully plead promissory estoppel to defeat the action against him.

The period immediately after the Second World War saw a flurry of cases in England in which Lord Denning sought gradually to develop the use of this doctrine.[20] Canadian courts have followed these developments: the Supreme Court of Canada in *Conwest Exploration Co. v. Letain*[21] pushed the doctrine quite far indeed; it can even be argued that the decision conceded that equitable estoppel might be used as a cause of action.[22] The facts were complicated, but the essential ones for our purposes can be summarized as follows.

CASE 6.4

A held an option to purchase certain mining claims. Before the date of expiry of the option, *B*, the grantor of the option, impliedly agreed to its extension. (As in the *Hughes* case, it appeared to be in his own interest to do so.) As a result, *A* did not hurry to complete the required task under the option before the original expiry date, but he did try to exercise the option shortly afterwards, before *B* had given any notice that he wished to return to his strict legal rights. In an action brought by *A* asking the court to permit him to exercise his option, the court did not allow *B* to revert to the original expiry date, and *A*'s action succeeded.

---

20. See, for example: Central London Property Trust, Ltd. v. High Trees House, Ltd., [1947] K.B. 130.
21. (1964), 41 D.L.R. (2d) 198. See also: Re Tudale Exploration Ltd. and Bruce et al. (1978), 20 O.R. (2d) 593, per Grange J., at 597 and 599.
22. See, for example: Crabb v. Arun District Council, [1976] Ch. 179.

B implicitly promised to extend the period during the original option period, while legal relations existed between the parties. On the one hand, it can be argued that this decision amounts to no more than an application of the *Hughes* case. On the other hand, the opposing view is that once the original option had expired, without an extension having been granted for additional consideration, no subsisting legal relationship between *A* and *B* remained; they were as strangers. Thus, to permit *A* to succeed is to permit him to use equitable estoppel as a cause of action, as in U.S. cases of injurious reliance. It remains to be seen whether in future cases the Canadian courts will favour this second view.

CONTEMPORARY ISSUE

A Promise of a Gift or a Bargain?

In March 1998 it was announced with great fanfare that the Russian hockey star and captain of the Ottawa Senators, Alexei Yashin, had made a charitable pledge of $1 000 000 to the National Arts Centre (NAC). The NAC needed substantial funding and Yashin's pledge was viewed as a major step towards renewal at the NAC. Yashin paid $200 000, the first of five annual instalments, and said that he hoped to see more performers from Russia at the NAC. Yashin's pledge received a great deal of favourable publicity. His public image was enhanced by the perception that he appreciated the arts and wished to bestow a benefit on the city where he played.

However, less than a year later—just before a major fundraising concert at the Corel Centre in January 1999—Yashin withdrew his pledge for the remaining $800 000. In the controversy that followed, it was alleged that there was a "side deal": the NAC would pay Yashin's parents, through a corporation owned by them, up to $85 000 a year to act as translators and organizers for Russian artists who would perform at the NAC. Yashin denied that his parents were to be "paid"; rather, the corporation would simply bill the NAC for "costs incurred." He stated that the NAC was doing too little to bring in Russian artists.

According to a CBC report (Webposted, January 28, 1999), "It's still unclear where the truth lies in this case. It all boils down to one group's word against the other."

Fortunately for the NAC, other benefactors stepped in and made significant contributions when they learned that Yashin had withdrawn his pledge.

Sources: "Yashin Backs Out on NAC Donation," CBC Infoculture, January 20, 1999; Susan Riley, "Yashin's Parents on Payroll in Side Deal, Says NAC," Canadian Press, Webposted on CNEWS, January 21, 1999; "No One Looks Good in the Arts Centre's Latest Fiasco," *Ottawa Citizen*, January 22, 1999; Tim Harper, "Ex-NAC Boss Defends Yashin Deal," *Toronto Star*, January 23, 1999; "NAC Fundraiser in the Works," CBC Infoculture, February 1, 1999.

Questions to Consider

1. Does it make a difference whether Yashin's promise was a charitable one or was part of a larger contract?
2. To what extent, if any, was there injurious reliance by the NAC?
3. Was Yashin implying that the NAC had breached an agreement when he complained it was not doing enough to bring in Russian artists?

THE EFFECT OF A REQUEST FOR GOODS OR SERVICES

When one person requests the services of another and the other performs those services, the law implies a promise to pay. Such a promise is implied between strangers or even between friends, if the services are rendered in a customary business transaction. But a promise to pay is not usually implied when the services are performed between members of a family or close friends; although the services were requested, the circumstances may show that the parties expected them to be given gratuitously because of friendship, kindness, or family duty.

Even though neither party mentions price, the implied promise is for payment of what the services are reasonably worth, that is, for payment **quantum meruit**. Difficult though it may be when the services are not usual professional services with a recognized scale of fees, the court will nonetheless endeavour to find what is reasonable.

quantum meruit
the amount a person merits to be paid for goods or services provided to the person requesting them

After the requested services have been performed, the parties may agree on what they consider to be a reasonable price. If so, neither of them can later change his mind and ask the court to fix a reasonable price. In effect, each party has given up his right to refer the matter to the court by agreeing to a price.

ILLUSTRATION 6.9

A asks computer programmer B for technical assistance. Afterwards, A asks B what her fee is and B suggests a certain sum. A refuses to pay it. In an action for payment for services performed, the court may give judgment in favour of B in the amount she requested or for some other amount that it deems reasonable.

If instead, A had agreed to the figure suggested by B but later changed his mind about paying, the court would not concern itself with what it considered reasonable: it would give judgment in favour of B for the amount earlier agreed upon.

The performance of requested services creates an *existing obligation* to pay a reasonable price for them, and by later agreeing upon a fixed price, the parties have done away with the need for an implied price. Subsequent payment of the fixed price satisfies all obligations owed by the party who requested the services.

We must be careful to distinguish this position from that arising when a promise is made for a past consideration.[23] If, for example, A promises to pay B $100 because B has given her and her family an excellent dinner, A is not bound, since she is under no existing legal obligation at the time she makes her promise. If, however, A promises to pay B $100 because B has catered a dinner for her at her request, A would be bound; in fact, A was already bound to pay B a reasonable price, and she and B have merely agreed later upon what this price should be.

The principle of *quantum meruit* applies to goods supplied on request as well as to services rendered; generally, a court has less difficulty ascertaining the reasonable worth of goods than of services.

THE USE OF A SEAL

In medieval times, when few people could read or write, a serious promise or **covenant** was often recorded by a cleric. He would read the covenant to the **covenantor**, who would then show his consent by impressing his coat of arms into a pool of hot sealing wax poured at the foot of the

covenant
a serious promise

covenantor
one who makes a covenant

---

23. Lampleigh v. Braithwait (1615), 80 E.R. 255.

document under seal

a covenant recorded in a document containing a wax seal, showing that the covenantor adopted the document as his act and deed

deed

a document under seal, which today is usually a small, red, gummed wafer

document. Usually the coat of arms was worn on a signet ring. By impressing his seal in this way, the covenantor adopted the document as *his act and deed*. To this day a **document under seal** is still called a **deed**. Other methods of sealing a document evolved over time, including embossing the coat of arms directly on the paper. Today the usual method is to affix a small, red, gummed wafer to a document, but almost any mark identifiable as a "seal" will do, even the word "seal" simply written in.

A seal must be affixed (or the word "seal" written) on the document *at the time* the party signs it. The word "seal" printed on the document in advance presents difficulties: it may simply indicate the place where the parties are to place a red paper wafer. In *Royal Bank of Canada v. Kiska*[24] the bank used a printed form of guarantee that included the word "seal" and also the words, "Given under seal at…" and "Signed, sealed and delivered in the presence of.…" The bank manager did not affix a red paper wafer, however, until some time after the promisor had signed and without the promisor's instructions to do so. Laskin J. (later Chief Justice of the Supreme Court of Canada) commented:

> The respective words are merely anticipatory of a formality which must be observed and are not a substitute for it. I am not tempted by any suggestion that it would be a modern and liberal view to hold that a person who signs a document that states it is under seal should be bound accordingly although there is no seal on it. I have no regret in declining to follow this path in a case where a bank thrusts a printed form under the nose of a young man for his signature. Formality serves a purpose here and some semblance of it should be preserved.…[25]

A promise made properly under the seal of the promisor does not require consideration to make it binding. Historically, signing under seal was taken as an act of great deliberation. It is still considered so today. The seal says in effect, "I fully intend to be bound by this promise." Its presence means that the court will not, as it otherwise would, insist upon consideration to hold the promisor bound.

Although a seal is an alternative way to make a promise binding, it does not do away with any of the other requirements needed to make a promise enforceable. Other essentials for a binding contract (its legality, for example) remain the same.

Any offer may be made under seal and so rendered irrevocable. When a business firm or public body invites tenders and requires them to be submitted under the seal of the tenderer, the legal effect is much the same as when an option is given: the tenderer cannot withdraw without being liable in damages.[26]

Certain documents, such as a deed of land and a mortgage, may require a seal even if there is consideration. These documents will be explained as they arise in later chapters.

An Intention to Create Legal Relations

Even when an apparently valid offer has been accepted and consideration is present, there is no contract in law unless both sides also intended to create a legally enforceable agreement. Of course, parties do not ordinarily think about the legal effects of their bargains, and the law *presumes* that the necessary intention is present in almost all instances where an agreement appears to be seriously made.

If courts did not presume that the parties to a contract intended to be legally bound, it would be necessary to inquire into their state of mind when they made their agreement and to decide whether they truly had such an intention—an impractical and time-consuming task. The presumed intention is especially strong in dealings between strangers and in commerce generally.

---

24. (1967), 63 D.L.R. (2d) 582.

25. *Ibid.*, at 594.

26. See Sanitary Refuse Collectors Inc. v. City of Ottawa, [1972] 1 O.R. 296 at 308–9.

A defendant may rebut (overcome) the presumption by using the external or objective test of the *reasonable bystander*: if to such a person the outward conduct of the parties lacked a serious intention to make an agreement, then no binding contract results. It is easier to rebut the presumption in arrangements between friends or members of a family, where it is often clear that there was no intention to create legal relations. For example, claiming that a failure to show up for a dinner invitation would give the host a right to sue for breach of contract appears unreasonable to us, even though the host went to considerable trouble and expense. Many domestic arrangements between husband and wife are on the same footing.

The requirement of a serious intention has been important in interpreting the legal effect of advertisements. In *Carlill v. The Carbolic Smoke Ball Company*,[27] discussed in Chapter 5, the company pleaded that its promise to pay a £100 reward was no more than a "mere puff" and was not to be taken seriously. This defence lost any credibility because the advertisement itself stated, "£1,000 is deposited with the Alliance Bank, Regent Street, showing our sincerity in the matter." We shall discuss further the possible legal effects of advertising under the topics of misrepresentation in Chapter 9 and consumer protection in Chapter 32.

Parties may include in their contract an express term that in the event of its breach neither party may sue the other. Such an understanding is usually recognized by the courts and is an effective defence to any action brought under the contract.[28] Terms of this kind occur quite frequently in some types of contracts and particularly now in franchising arrangements, where the franchisee undertakes not to sue the franchisor in the event of disagreement. Since the franchisor often has the greater bargaining power, a franchisee may argue that the franchisor's insistence on such a clause was unconscionable and should be struck down, enabling the franchisee to sue. Unconscionability will be discussed more generally in Chapter 9.

QUESTIONS FOR REVIEW

1. Describe how a promise may become binding although the promisor receives no benefit herself.

2. How might the above situation apply to a promise of a charitable donation?

3. How "valuable" does consideration have to be to make a promise binding? When might a court review the value of consideration?

4. Describe the nature of an out-of-court settlement.

5. Why is gratitude not a sufficient consideration to bind a promisor?

6. In what ways may the common law rules about the need for consideration be unsatisfactory for business purposes in altering an existing contract? How can the defect be remedied?

7. Describe how one important defect in the common law rules has been remedied by statute in five of the provinces.

8. Distinguish between estoppel "based on fact" and estoppel based on a promise.

9. Describe the differing points of view taken in "equitable estoppel" and "injurious reliance."

27. [1892] 2 Q.B. 484.
28. Rose and Frank v. Crompton, [1925] A.C. 445.

10. Explain the significance of "hardship" and how it arises in cases of injurious reliance.

11. What question remains unresolved in the application of the concept of injurious reliance by the Canadian courts?

12. How does *quantum meruit* differ from doing a friend a favour?

13. Explain the nature of a seal.

14. What three essentials of a binding contract have we considered thus far?

15. A firm of public accountants has for years been auditing the accounts of a charitable organization without charge. It now appears that the treasurer of the organization has absconded with a sizeable amount of money and that an application of generally accepted auditing standards would have disclosed the defalcation in time to avoid the loss. Has the charitable organization any recourse against its auditors in these circumstances?

16. Does the use of a seal answer for a failure to satisfy all essentials of a binding contract?

17. A supplier's invoice for goods has the following common term printed on it: "Terms— Net price 30 days; 2 percent discount if paid within 10 days." If the buyer pays the price less 2 percent within 10 days, can the supplier later sue successfully for the sum deducted?

CASES AND PROBLEMS

1 Burowski ran an office supplies business and donated one evening a week of her time helping run a bingo for charity. There she met another donor, Adams, an investment broker. They worked well together for a few months. One evening Burowski said to Adams that she was rather confused about her investment portfolio; she wondered where she might get advice. Adams suggested they have a coffee together after the bingo hall closed. They spent about an hour discussing Burowski's portfolio and Adams made some suggestions about how she might improve her holdings. Burowski suddenly remembered that she was late returning home to her baby sitter and left quickly, thanking Adams as she got up from the table. A week later she received a bill from Adams for $150 for "professional advice."

Discuss whether Adams has contractual grounds for making this claim.

2 During the massive Red River flood of 1997 in Manitoba, the village of Carnostan was saved from being inundated because it is on relatively high land. However, the village was cut off completely because all highways leading to it were flooded; many were washed away and took months to restore. Barney Blake, owner of Barney's Fast Foods, had virtually no customers through a period of six months. At the end of the first month, he told his landlord, Ruth Long, that he would likely have to declare bankruptcy because he could not pay the rent. Ruth said she would reduce the rent from $1000 to $400 to help him out. Barney paid her $400 and with a bank loan managed to do so each month.

In the seventh month when the main road reopened, Barney went to Ruth's office with a big smile and gave her a cheque for $1000. Ruth said, "Where is the $3600 for the other six months?" Barney was surprised; he replied, "I thought you had forgiven me that rent because of the flood." Ruth said, "Of course not, I only delayed payment until the flood ended. You still owe me the money."

Barney disagreed and said he did not owe any arrears of rent and would not pay it. Is Barney or Ruth right? Give reasons.

3. The town of Broomville, along with local arts and athletic groups, decided to erect a new Millennium Centre for sports, music, and theatre. The total estimated cost was $18 000 000. In April, Jane Borkus, president and CEO of the largest local industry, Autotech, promised to match every dollar raised through other donors, up to $9 000 000. Both she and the delighted town mayor, Geoff Johns, made the announcement over the local television station and in a joint statement in the town's newspaper. Borkus said the deadline would be 12 months.

The following January, the campaign was proceeding extremely well: other donors had pledged $5 500 000 and Borkus presented a cheque for $4 000 000 as Autotech's "down payment and pledge of goodwill."

Unfortunately, in March, Autotech lost its major contract to supply car parts to one of the big three auto manufacturers. Anticipating a large loss at year's end, Borkus withdrew the pledge and asked for the return of the down payment.

What arguments may be made on behalf of the town both to keep the money paid and to require Autotech to honour its commitment. What do you think the decision would be?

4. (a) Matsui's bank manager recommended Roberts, a business consultant, to help Matsui appraise a suitable business investment. Matsui wished to buy control of a business and was prepared to pay $200 000 or so if he could find a satisfactory business.

At Matsui's request Roberts devoted most of his time from May to February of the following year investigating three businesses in which Matsui was interested. They did not discuss Roberts' rate of remuneration for performing these services. Finally, after consultation with Matsui, Roberts managed to obtain an option for him to purchase the shares of the A.C. Electrical Co. Ltd., one of the three companies identified by Matsui. When Matsui learned of Roberts' success in obtaining the option, he promised to pay Roberts $50 000 for his services. Roberts said that would be fine.

Matsui later decided not to exercise the option and refused to pay Roberts the $50 000. Roberts brought an action against him for this sum. In defence Matsui asserted that it was expressly agreed that if, as a result of Roberts' services or efforts, Matsui actually made a purchase, he would pay a suitable commission to Roberts but unless he made such a purchase, Roberts would be entitled to nothing. Roberts denied that Matsui's undertaking had been qualified in this manner. Faced with this conflict of evidence, the trial judge stated that he accepted the evidence of the plaintiff in preference to that of the defendant.

What is the main issue? Should Roberts succeed?

(b) Suppose instead that the parties had discussed $50 000 as the appropriate fee *before* the services were rendered and then when Matsui learned of Roberts' success in obtaining the option, he was so elated as to promise him $10 000 more. What issue would arise if Roberts found it necessary to sue Matsui for the $60 000?

5. Harris N. Dealer was sole proprietor of a profitable computer data centre which he sold as a going concern to Alice B. Wheeler for the price of $180 000. The price was paid, $30 000 in cash and the balance in the form of a contract under Wheeler's seal and read in part as follows:

For value received Alice B. Wheeler promises to pay Harris N. Dealer the sum of one hundred and fifty thousand dollars ($150 000) in 10 years from April 1, 1999, together with interest at 8 percent per annum from April 1, 1999, payable monthly on the first day of May 1999 and on the first day of each and every month thereafter until payment of the principal sum on April 1, 2009.

After ten (10) days' default in any interest payment due under this agreement the whole amount payable shall become immediately due.

March 29, 1999. Alice B. Wheeler [SEAL]

Dealer and Wheeler remained on friendly terms throughout the balance of 1999. Wheeler was somewhat dilatory in making her monthly payments of $1000 interest, so that by the end of the year she had made six of the eight monthly payments required by then on dates more than 10 days after they were due; Dealer had acquiesced in the arrangement without complaint, though the parties had never expressly agreed on any change in the due dates and Dealer seemed merely to have been indulgent with his debtor. Unfortunately, however, the parties had a serious personal disagreement early in 2000. On February 5, 2000, the January 1 interest payment then being 35 days overdue, Dealer wrote to Wheeler as follows:

This letter will serve to inform you that, an interest payment due under the terms of the contract dated March 29, 1999 being in default for more than 10 days, the whole amount under the contract is now due.

I hereby demand immediate payment of the principal amount of $150 000 and outstanding interest.

H.N. Dealer

Wheeler immediately paid the outstanding interest but refused to pay the principal sum. Dealer brought an action against her for $150 000.

Develop fully the arguments for both the plaintiff and the defendant. State with reasons, including reference to a relevant case or cases, whether the action should succeed.

6 Krohm and Sterling incorporated Old Colony Silver Mines Ltd. for the purpose of acquiring mining properties and claims owned by them. They received 40 percent of the voting shares of the corporation as consideration for the transfer to the corporation of their mining interests. The remaining 60 percent of the shares were held by others who had bought them from the company for cash.

In the first year of the corporation's operations Krohm and Sterling personally advanced sums totalling $39 500 to it to help defray development costs. They received promissory notes from the corporation and the amounts were included in the corporation's general ledger in an account entitled "Notes Payable." By the end of the year it appeared that the corporation's prospects were good, but that to realize its potential would require additional outside financing.

At the first annual meeting of shareholders, Krohm stated that he and his fellow shareholder Sterling, for whom he was also speaking, had considered the corporation's financial position and concluded that it was imperative that the debt–equity ratio appearing on the balance sheet be improved if the corporation were to succeed in obtaining the additional financing it needed. He therefore asked the meeting to take note of the intention of both Mr. Sterling and himself to forgive the two promissory notes of Old Colony Silver Mines Ltd. in the amounts of $19 750 each. Sterling then spoke briefly to confirm Krohm's statement; the notes, he said, "would never be enforced." At this juncture, another shareholder rose to propose a motion of appreciation to Krohm and Sterling for "this most selfless, altruistic, and loyal gesture." The motion was duly seconded and unanimously approved by the meeting, and recorded by the secretary in the minutes.

The next quarterly financial statements of Old Colony omitted the notes payable to Krohm and Sterling from the corporation's liabilities as presented on its balance sheet, and showed the amount forgiven as an extraordinary item of income in the income statement, after operating profits for the quarter. Krohm and Sterling did not, however, surrender the Old Colony's promissory notes to it for cancellation, nor did they sign any statement acknowledging their expressed intention not to enforce the notes.

The company submitted its quarterly financial statements plus a cash flow projection to its bank in support of an application for a 10-year term loan. The bank evaluated its proposal but was unwilling to lend for so long a term, and the application was rejected.

A few weeks later Old Colony received from another mining corporation an offer of $300 000 for its individual assets. The offer required an undertaking from Old Colony that it would first pay all its debts out of the $300 000 before distributing any liquidating dividend to its shareholders. At a special general meeting of shareholders, Krohm and Sterling opposed the acceptance of this offer on the grounds that the corporation had not exhausted the possibilities for outside financing, but they were voted down. A resolution was then approved instructing Old Colony to accept the offer and proceed to distribute the proceeds of the sale to its creditors and shareholders in the course of winding up the corporation. At this stage Krohm and Sterling insisted that the sum of $39 500 they had previously lent to Old Colony be first paid to them as creditors before any amount should be distributed to shareholders. The majority shareholders then passed a resolution directing the treasurer not to pay these notes, in view of the statement made by Krohm and Sterling at the preceding meeting.

Krohm and Sterling then sued Old Colony Silver Mines Ltd., submitting their promissory notes as evidence of the corporation's indebtedness to them. Outline fully the defence which the corporation could offer, and then comment on its validity.

7 FORMATION OF A CONTRACT

Capacity to Contract and Legality of Object

The Burden of Proving Essential Elements of a Contract

The Meaning of Capacity to Contract

Minors (or Infants)

Other Persons of Diminished Contractual Capacity

Corporations

Labour Unions

Enemy Aliens

Aboriginal Peoples

Bankrupt Debtors

The Role of Legality in the Formation of a Contract

The Difference Between a Void and an Illegal Contract

Contracts Affected by Statute

Contracts Illegal by the Common Law and Public Policy

Agreements in Restraint of Trade

In this chapter we complete our discussion of the essential elements of a contract with two elements usually assumed to be present unless shown otherwise. The first is capacity to contract and the second is the way our legal system makes certain contracts unenforceable. In this chapter we examine such questions as:

- how does capacity depend on the nature of the contract?

- what are "necessaries"?

- what are the effects of other types of contracts?

- what are a minor's obligations upon attaining the age of majority?

- to what extent is the contractual capacity of the following classes of persons treated differently: aboriginal peoples? corporations? labour unions? persons of diminished mental capacity?

- what is the difference between void and illegal contracts?

- what are gaming contracts?

- how are contracts affected in different ways by statute?

- what contracts are illegal by common law and public policy?

THE BURDEN OF PROVING ESSENTIAL ELEMENTS OF A CONTRACT

We have seen that once a plaintiff has shown that there was offer and acceptance and consideration for the promise, the court will ordinarily presume an intention to create legal relations—the elements we discussed in Chapters 5 and 6. At that point, and in the absence of evidence to the contrary, the court will presume that two further elements are present: (1) the defendant had the capacity to make a contract and (2) the contract is "legal." It is up to the defendant to show that she did not have the capacity to enter into the contract or that the contract was not legal, with the result that it would be unenforceable against her. First, we shall examine the question of capacity.

THE MEANING OF CAPACITY TO CONTRACT

When we enter into a contract, we usually assume that the other party has the capacity to make a contract and is bound by it, but this is not always so. As an extreme example, we would hardly expect a six-year-old child to be able to bind herself to pay $100 for a computer game; at that age she would lack the competence—the **capacity**—to enter into legally binding contracts. Thus, while the requirements of Chapters 5 and 6 were met, as a matter of *policy* the law may excuse one party, such as the six-year-old child, from her obligations. Of course, in most cases, a lack of capacity is not so obvious; one party reasonably relies on the capacity of the other to enter into a contract.

legal capacity
competence to bind oneself

In practice, it is remarkable how little litigation arises as a result of minors attempting to repudiate their contracts. An important non-legal sanction is very persuasive: if minors should repudiate on grounds of incapacity, they would all but eliminate their chances of finding others willing to give them credit. Even so, it is important to be aware of the rights and remedies available to both sides in such contracts.

MINORS (OR INFANTS)
Contracts Creating Liability for a Minor

A **minor** or **infant** is a person who has not attained the **age of majority** according to the law of her province. At common law the age was deemed to be 21, but it now varies according to the legislation in each province.[1] The general rule is that a contract made by a minor is unenforceable *against* her but enforceable *by* her against the other side, whether or not the other person is aware that he is dealing with a minor. So a minor may often disregard contractual promises with impunity. When a minor owns considerable assets, her father or mother is ordinarily empowered to look after her affairs or, with supervision of the court, may make contracts concerning her property; if her parents are deceased or are unable to manage her affairs the court will appoint a **guardian** to do so.

minor or infant
a person who has not attained the age of majority according to the law of his or her province

age of majority
the age at which a person is recognized as an adult according to the law of his or her province

guardian
a person appointed to manage the affairs of a minor in the place of his or her parents

necessaries
essential goods and services

While the purpose of these rules is to protect minors, if there were no exceptions that very purpose would be defeated and could cause great hardship: a minor in need of food or clothing—**necessaries**—might be unable to find a merchant willing to sell her these things on credit because she could not bind herself to pay for them. Accordingly, the courts have come to regard contracts for necessaries as exceptions to a minor's immunity from liability.

---

1. It is usually 18 or 19 years. See, for example: Age of Majority Act, R.S.B.C. 1996, c. 5 (19 years); S.N.S. 1989, c. 4 (19 years); R.S.M. 1987, c. A-4 (18 years); Age of Majority and Accountability Act, R.S.O. 1990, c. A.7, s. 6 (18 years).

Necessaries and Beneficial Contracts of Service

A minor is bound to pay for all necessaries, essential goods and services, that she buys. However, she is not bound to pay the contract price as such, but rather a reasonable price on the same basis as *quantum meruit*, discussed in Chapter 6. In the absence of evidence that the minor has been exploited, the court usually regards the contract price as evidence of what a reasonable price should be.

The courts have identified the following as necessaries: food, clothing, lodging, medical attention,[2] legal advice,[3] and also transportation—but transportation includes only the means of getting the minor to and from work, and does not include the purchase price of vehicles even if they are used by the minor in carrying on a business[4] or as a means of going to work.[5]

A minor is also bound by **beneficial contracts of service**: contracts of employment or apprenticeship when they are found to be for his benefit and not exploitative. Participating in a business venture is quite different: the courts are more hesitant to find such an arrangement to be for a minor's benefit, particularly when the minor is in business for himself[6] or in a partnership with others.

beneficial contracts of service

contracts of employment or apprenticeship found to be for a minor's benefit

Contracts Creating No Liability for a Minor

A minor may always repudiate a contract for non-necessaries even where the non-necessaries are clearly beneficial to him. The purchase of a truck for use in his business may well be very useful to a minor; nevertheless, the truck is not a necessary.[7] We can determine the nature of non-necessaries only by reviewing cases that have decided whether a particular subject-matter was a necessary. A fairly large number of things have been held to be necessaries; beyond these things each case must be decided on its own facts, and judges are reluctant to enlarge the class. When a minor is living at home and supported by his parents, his purchases are less likely to be considered as necessaries than when he is on his own. The court assumes that a minor living at home is provided for.

Although there are no decisions on the point, it appears that a minor is not liable for necessaries that he has ordered but not yet received. Accordingly, he can repudiate a contract of sale before delivery of the goods.[8] The point is underlined in the Sale of Goods Act, which defines necessaries for an infant in terms of goods sold *and delivered*.[9]

A minor who repudiates his liability for non-necessary goods will, if the goods are still in his possession, be required to return them to the seller in whatever condition they may be at the time. In *Louden Manufacturing Co. v. Milmine*, Chief Justice Meredith said:

> Upon principle and the authorities cited…it must be that if an infant avails himself of the right he has to avoid a contract which he has entered into and upon the faith of which he has obtained goods, he is bound to restore the goods which he has in possession at the time he so repudiates. If that were not so, a man might buy a farm for a large sum of money, give a mortgage upon it shortly before coming of age, then repudiate the contract, and insist upon holding the property. The authorities are all the other way, and establish that the effect of repudiating the contract is to revest the property in the vendor.[10]

2. Miller v. Smith & Co., [1925] 2 W.W.R. 360 at 377 (Sask. C.A.).

3. Helps v. Clayton (1864), 144 E.R. 222.

4. Mercantile Union Guarantee Corp. v. Ball, [1937] 2 K.B. 498.

5. First Charter Financial Corp. v. Musclow (1974), 49 D.L.R. (3d) 138 (B.C.S.C.).

6. *Supra*, n. 4.

7. *Ibid.*

8. Furmston, Cheshire, *Fifoot and Furmston's Law of Contract* (13th ed.), p. 443.

9. See, for example: R.S.B.C. 1996, c. 410, s. 7, as amended, S.B.C. 1985, c. 10; R.S.O. 1990, c. S.1, s. 3 (1); R.S.N.S. 1989, c. 408, s. 5(1).

10. (1908), 15 O.L.R. 53 at 54; McGaw v. Fisk (1908), 38 N.B.R. 354: Williston, *A Treatise on the Law of Contracts* (4th ed.), Vol. 5, p. 113. R.A. Lord, ed. New York: Lawyers Cooperative Publishing, 1993.

Similarly, when the minor is a seller rather than a buyer in a contract for the sale of goods, he cannot repudiate the contract to recover the goods delivered unless he returns the money paid.[11]

There is nothing to prevent a minor from purchasing non-necessaries if he can find a merchant who is prepared to rely entirely upon his honour for payment, or where he purchases goods for cash, is willing to trust him not to return them for refund.[12]

Ordinarily a seller cannot rely on a statement by a minor that his parents will pay for the purchase.[13] Authority to bind the parents may sometimes be implied from the fact that parents have paid the account for a previous purchase by their child without complaint. Apart from this possibility, a merchant needs express authority from the parents before being able to bind them.

Contracts Indirectly Affecting a Minor

A minor who has benefited from a contract for non-necessaries will not be able to recover money already paid, though he will be able to repudiate his remaining liability.

CASE 7.1

T, a minor, agreed to become tenant of a house and to pay *L*, the landlord, a certain amount for the furniture in it. *T* paid part of the sum, gave a promissory note for the balance, then occupied the house and had the use of the furniture for several months. Later *T* brought an action to have the contract rescinded and to recover from *L* the money he had paid. The court held that *T* could avoid liability on the note, but that he was not entitled to a return of what he had paid.[14]

An adult can recover money lent to a minor only if the minor used the proceeds to purchase necessary goods.[15] If the borrowed money was used to finance a vacation, the lender cannot recover the debt. Minors' contracts that are not binding under the common law may be altered by statute. For example, the Canada Student Loans Act[16] provides that a guaranteed bank loan to a student "is recoverable by the lender from the borrower as though the borrower had been of full age at the time the loan was made."

A minor's freedom from liability is limited to contract; she remains liable for torts such as negligence, assault, defamation, or deceit. If, however, a minor causes a loss while performing the very acts contemplated by a contract, the court will decide the case under the law of contract and not of torts, and the minor will escape liability for the consequences. The other contracting party will not, in other words, be permitted to circumvent the rules protecting minors in contract by suing for damages for a tort where he would otherwise fail if he sued for breach of contract.

---

11. Williston, *supra*, n. 10, Vol. 5, s. 9:16, pp. 113–33. The right to repudiate may be lost when the infant comes of age.

12. Problems may arise for the minor if the goods have been used or damaged. This problem is discussed under the heading of "Rescission" in Chapter 15.

13. Hailsham, *Halsbury's Laws of England* (4th ed. revised), Vol. 5(2) 24, pp. 343–51. London: Butterworth & Co. Ltd., 1993.

14. Valenti v. Canali (1889), 24 Q.B.D. 166.

15. Hailsham, *supra*, n. 13, p. 175.

16. R.S.C. 1985, c. S-23, s. 19.

CASE 7.2

P, a minor, hires a riding horse and promises as a term of the contract to handle the animal with care. In her exuberance *P* injures the horse by riding it too hard.

Q, the owner of the horse, realizes that if he sues *P* for breach of contract he will fail, since the contract is not for a necessary. So instead he sues her for the tort of negligence. *Q* will not succeed by this tactic.[17] He will fail whichever approach he takes.

Suppose, however, that *P* had injured the horse by entering it in equestrian trials, something not at all contemplated in the contract. Since *P*'s act that resulted in loss was outside the scope of the contract, *Q* could sue her for damages for negligence.

The Contractual Liability of Minors Upon Attaining Majority

voidable contract
an obligation that cannot be enforced against a minor, but may under certain conditions become binding when she becomes of age

A minor's liability to pay for necessaries and beneficial contracts of service continues after she attains majority, and in addition, she may *become* liable for obligations that could not be enforced against her while she was a minor. These new obligations become part of a class called **voidable contracts**, of which there are two types.

In the first type the minor acquires "an interest of a permanent, continuous nature." She must repudiate such a contract promptly upon coming of age, or she will be liable on it just as if she had entered into it *after* coming of age. The courts have decided that interests of a permanent or continuous nature occur in contracts for rights in land and in partnership agreements. A partner is not liable for partnership debts contracted while she was under age, but if she does not repudiate the partnership agreement she will be liable for debts incurred by the firm after she attains majority. This class of contracts is quite small but probably includes contracts in which the minor has purchased non-necessary goods, such as a car, that she promised to pay for by instalments over a period during which she becomes of age. In contracts of this type, the minor loses the right to repudiate by not doing so promptly after coming of age, or by accepting the benefits of the contract after that time.

ratify
acknowledge and promise to perform

The second and more common type of voidable contract does not create an interest of a continuous nature and is not binding upon a minor unless she expressly **ratifies** the contract after attaining majority, that is, she acknowledges the contract and promises again to perform. Some provinces require ratification to be in writing and signed by the minor.[18] This type includes a minor's promise to pay for non-necessary goods or for services performed at her request. A promise to pay for necessary goods not delivered by the time she becomes of age also requires ratification.

void
never formed in law

The courts have held some contracts by their very nature to be prejudicial and unfair to minors and, therefore, completely **void** rather than merely voidable. "Ratification" by a minor after she attains majority is ineffective, and her promise to pay is unenforceable. In other words, in these circumstances there is never any contract capable of ratification. Examples are contracts that include forfeiture clauses and penalty clauses.[19]

---

17. Jennings v. Rundall (1799), 101 E.R. 1419.

18. The Statute of Frauds: for example, R.S.O. 1990, c. S.19, s. 7; R.S.N.S. 1989, c. 442, s. 9.

19. Beam v. Beatty (1902), 4 O.L.R. 554; Phillips v. Greater Ottawa Development Co. (1916), 38 O.L.R. 315. See also, Butterfield v. Sibbitt, [1950] 4 D.L.R. 302.

OTHER PERSONS OF DIMINISHED CONTRACTUAL CAPACITY

The law protects a person of unsound mind or incapacitated through drink or drugs in the same way as a minor: he is bound to pay a reasonable price for necessaries; other contracts are voidable at his option but enforceable by him against the other contracting party.

In practice a person who was drunk or insane at the time of making a contract often has a difficult problem of proof. A minor can more easily prove his age than can a person establish that he was so intoxicated or insane as not to know what he was doing.

There is an additional burden of evidence on the party seeking to avoid the contract: he must show not only that he was incapable of a rational decision at the time of the agreement, but also that the other party was aware of his condition. Unfortunately for the person who was so insane or drunk that he did not know what he was doing, his own observations about the other contracting party are unlikely to be reliable, and the necessary evidence must then be adduced from all the surrounding circumstances.

As with voidable contracts generally, the party seeking to avoid must act promptly upon emerging from his state of incapacity. Unless repudiation comes within a reasonable time, the privilege is lost. It is also too late to repudiate if, after regaining sanity or sobriety, the afflicted party accepts the benefits of the contract.

With an aging population, we face a growing problem of diminished contractual capacity among the elderly. In dealing with an aged person it is often difficult to tell whether she is simply physically frail or also suffers from diminished mental capacity that might leave a contract with her open to subsequent attack.

CORPORATIONS

Since a corporation is a "legal fiction"—it is merely a creature of the law[20]—it has no physical existence: it cannot think or act or sign its name as a natural person can. Nevertheless, the law may give corporations the capacity to make any contract or enter into any obligation that a natural person possesses, and business corporations' statutes now give this capacity. However, legislatures have not extended to all corporations the widest possible contractual capacity: public corporations, such as municipalities and Crown corporations, are restricted to the limited power conferred by the statutes creating them. Obligations that they purport to undertake but that are outside the ambit of the statute will, if challenged, be declared by the court to be ***ultra vires*** (beyond their powers) and, therefore, void. The promisee cannot enforce such obligations against the corporation. The legal consequences of *ultra vires* contracts are often complex and difficult.

ultra vires
beyond the powers of

We must wait until we deal with the law relating to principal and agent in Chapter 19 to determine whether the person or persons purporting to act on behalf of a corporation have the power to bind it in contracts. The matter is especially important for a corporation because, not being a natural person, it must make all its contracts through agents. Corporation officers who have the necessary authority usually issue the corporation's signature for important contracts and formal documents, such as share certificates, bonds, debentures, deeds, and mortgages, by impressing the company seal using an embossing device.[21] For ordinary day-to-day business the signature of an authorized officer alone is used.

---

20. As we shall see, our legal system recognizes—or fabricates—legal creatures with some or most of the capacity of a natural person. These creations of the law are referred to variously as a "legal person," "legal entity," "separate legal status," and "corporate persons." For further discussion, see Chapter 27, "The Nature of a Corporation and Its Formation."

21. In most provinces it is no longer necessary for a corporation to have a seal, although it is still common practice to do so.

LABOUR UNIONS

In our legal system, the fact that a group of individuals get together and form an organization, be it a social club, a charity, or a labour union, does not make that group into a legal entity. Only after the group has applied to the appropriate government agency and been recognized as a separate legal person will it be capable of entering into contracts. Despite their significant role in our economy, for the most part the legal status of labour unions remains equivocal, though the law varies significantly from province to province and is changing quite rapidly.[22]

By contrast, the legal status of business corporations as employers is clearly settled. The discrepancy makes uncertain the enforceability of collective agreements between corporations and labour unions. However, most provinces do have statutes[23] that provide for arbitration in the event of a dispute arising out of the collective agreement. If an employer does not implement the decision of the arbitrator, the union may apply to a labour relations board for permission to prosecute and for this purpose is given legal status. If a union rejects the arbitrator's decision and causes an illegal strike, damages have occasionally been awarded against the union; the enforceability of such decisions is currently a matter of debate. In those provinces where an employer may seek permission to prosecute a union for such a strike, the union's liability derives from a statutory provision and not from the contractual capacity of the union in general.

representative action
an action brought by one or more persons on behalf of a group having the same interest

Despite their indefinite status, labour unions may bring actions or defend against them when they so wish. By a legal technique known as a **representative action**, a union may expressly or impliedly authorize one or more persons to represent it in court simply as a group of individuals having a common interest in a particular case. As a result, union officials may bring or defend a representative action on behalf of its members.

ENEMY ALIENS

Ordinarily, an alien has the same rights as a citizen in making contracts and in all other matters of private law. In the event of a declaration of war, however, an enemy alien loses all contractual capacity, apart from any special licence granted by the Crown. For the purposes of contracts, an enemy alien is identified not by citizenship but by the fact that either his residence or business interests are located in enemy territory.

Any evidence that a contract made with an enemy alien is detrimental to the public interest will make the contract void as being against public policy, and the rights and liabilities created by the contract are wholly dissolved. In a few exceptional instances where the public interest is thought not to be affected, a contract may be regarded as being merely suspended for the duration of hostilities.

ABORIGINAL PEOPLES

In Canada, native Indians living on reservations are still considered wards of the Crown. The property comprising the reservation is held by the Crown in trust for the benefit of the Indian band. It is not available as security for the claims of creditors, and any disposition of such property to an outside party is void unless the transaction has been approved by the Minister of Indian Affairs and Northern Development. Aboriginal peoples on reservations may manufac-

---

22. See Chapter 20 under "Legal Status of Trade Unions."
23. See, for example: Labour Relations Code, R.S.B.C. 1996, c. 244, s. 82(2); The Labour Relations Act, S.O. 1995, c. 1, Sched. A. s. 405; The Trade Union Act, R.S.N.S. 1989, c. 475, s. 19(1).

ture and sell chattels to outsiders, although in the prairie provinces, sales of produce must have the approval of a superintendent under the Minister. The legal position of Indians on reservations is set out in detail in the Indian Act.[24] Indians not living on a reservation have the same contractual capacity as that of any other citizen.

BANKRUPT DEBTORS

A bankrupt debtor, until he receives a discharge from the court, is under certain contractual disabilities. We will discuss these disabilities more fully in Chapter 31.

THE ROLE OF LEGALITY IN THE FORMATION OF A CONTRACT

The object of a contract must be **legal**: it must not offend the public good (that is, it must not be contrary to public policy) nor violate any law. We noted at the beginning of this chapter that in the absence of evidence to the contrary, the courts presume that transactions are legal. However, a defendant may introduce evidence to show that this presumption is wrong. If he succeeds, the contract will at least be *void*, which means that in law it was never formed at all. In some circumstances the courts will go further and find that the contract is also *illegal*.

legal
not offensive to the public good and not violating any law

THE DIFFERENCE BETWEEN A VOID AND AN ILLEGAL CONTRACT

No stigma attaches to the parties if their contract is simply void; they have just not succeeded in creating a binding agreement. If they have partly performed their undertakings, the court will do its best, taking all the circumstances into account, to restore them to their respective positions before the contract was attempted. It may order the return of money paid or of property transferred if the party complaining can show cause why it should be returned. Further, each party is released from the performance of any further obligations under the agreement. A court may find that only a *term* of a contract is void and that the remaining parts are valid. If it decides that the void term can be severed without doing injustice to the parties, it will uphold the remainder of the contract.

When a contract is not only void but also illegal, the court will refuse to aid a party who knowingly agreed to an illegal purpose. Not only may he not sue for money promised, but if he has transferred property to the other party, he is not permitted to recover it. When both parties are tainted with knowledge of the illegal object, the fact that a court will assist neither of them leaves the plaintiff without a remedy and thus assists the defendant. The legal maxim is: where both parties are equally in the wrong, the position of the defendant is the stronger. Under the policy towards illegal contracts, a court will not allow a part of the contract that might otherwise be legal to be severed and enforced.

The law is not very helpful in providing standards for deciding when a contract is illegal as well as void. Generally, the more reprehensible its object, the more likely the contract will be regarded as illegal and a plaintiff will be denied any remedy.

---

24. R.S.C. 1985, c. I-5.

CONTRACTS AFFECTED BY STATUTE

Significance of the Wording of a Statute

A statute may merely deprive a particular type of contract of legal effect, or it may go further and express positive disapproval. It achieves the first object by stating that such agreements shall be void. To accomplish the second purpose it may describe the type of agreement as "unlawful" or "illegal." A statute may even declare that performance of the agreement shall be a criminal offence, subject to prescribed penalties of a fine or imprisonment.

Contracts Void by Statute

Agreements Contrary to the Purpose of Legislation

Workers' compensation legislation, for example, states that any provision in an agreement between employer and employee purporting to deprive the employee of the protection of the Act is void.[25] Other statutes declare particular types of transfers of property to be void: ownership does not pass from the transferor and the property may be recovered from the transferee and applied according to the terms of the statute. Thus, the Bankruptcy and Insolvency Act contains a provision that if a person transfers property either by gift or for an obviously inadequate compensation and becomes bankrupt within one year, the transfer is void and the property is available to the trustee in bankruptcy.[26] The trustee may recover the property and apply it to the claims of the bankrupt person's creditors. The same statute provides that a transfer of property by an insolvent person to one of several creditors with a view to giving that creditor a preference over the others is "fraudulent and void" if it occurs within three months preceding bankruptcy.[27]

Promises to Pay a Betting Debt

United Kingdom At common law, debts resulting from bets were not per se considered against public policy and accordingly were not void. Nevertheless, the English courts did not like enforcing wagers that were based simply on prophesying an unknown result, with the winner collecting from the loser. Sometimes they looked at the subject-matter of the bet and would find it to be against public policy, such as "bribing voters"—a wager with voters as to the outcome of an election in their constituency.[28] They even refused a remedy because an "idle wager" wasted the court's time.[29]

   This distaste, as well as a more general concern that gambling was harmful to society, led to early statutes prohibiting certain types of betting, first in 1664, and again in 1710, 1835, and 1845. The Gaming Act of 1845 makes all bets void and unenforceable, but they are not a criminal offence: there is no fine or imprisonment for those who make bets.[30] It simply made it

---

25. See, for example: Workplace Safety and Insurance Act, S.O. 1997, c. 16, s. 16; Workers' Compensation Act, R.S.B.C. 1996, c. 492, s. 13; S.N.S. 1994–95, c. 10.

26. R.S.C. 1985, c. B-3, s. 91 of the Bankruptcy and Insolvency Act, as amended by S.C. 1992, c. 1 and c. 27. Section 3 of the Act also provides, "For the purposes of this Act, a person who has entered into a transaction with another person otherwise than at arm's length shall be deemed to have entered into a reviewable transaction." Under s. 100 a court may give judgment in favour of the trustee against the other party to such a transaction for the difference between the actual consideration given or received by the bankrupt and the fair market value of the property or services concerned. The provisions of the Bankruptcy and Insolvency Act are dealt with in more detail in Chapter 31.

27. Section 95(1).

28. Allen v. Hearn (1875), 1 T.R. 56.

29. Gilbert v. Sykes (1812), 16 East 150 at 162.

30. In Canada, the Criminal Code, R.S.C. 1985, c. C-46, does, however, make certain betting activities illegal. It is a criminal offence to keep a gaming house (s. 201) or to operate a pool (s. 202) or a lottery (s. 206) unless within specified exceptions within the Act.

impossible for a winner to collect through court action. However, an innocent third person who purchases a note or cheque for valuable consideration, say a storekeeper who accepts the instrument from the winner in payment for goods, may be able to enforce payment against the loser who signed the instrument.

Canada   The four western provinces inherited the Gaming Act of 1845 from the United Kingdom since it was law before they became provinces with their own legislatures. Court decisions in Nova Scotia, New Brunswick, and Ontario on betting claims suggest that these three provinces inherited the 1710 Gaming Act, which was received as British law before they had their own legislatures. The three provinces also passed their own gaming acts in the 18th and 19th centuries. Ontario replaced its Gaming Act in 1993 with the Gaming Control Act.[31]

Certain types of betting, such as betting on horse races[32] (and football pools in the United Kingdom) were expressly made legal by statute long ago. The law on betting has never been clear[33] and in recent years has become more complex as various other forms of gambling have been expressly legalized—lotteries, bingo halls, and casinos.

The parties to a **wager**—an agreement between two parties in which each has at the time some probability of winning or losing—must be distinguished from a **stakeholder** who manages a betting arrangement for a fee and redistributes winnings. Organizations that manage lotteries, racetracks, and casinos are stakeholders and therefore not a party to a wagering agreement. They do, however, remain legally accountable for performing their task as stakeholders.[34] For many years, provincial legislation has permitted the placing of bets at authorized race courses, and there has since been legislation to permit the holding of lotteries.[35] A number of contracts commonly regarded as being of a legitimate business nature have a significant element of speculation in them—insurance contracts, stock exchange transactions, and "futures" transactions in commodities. Insurance statutes, in particular, require that contracts of insurance *not* be regarded as wagering contracts if they are to be enforceable.

wager
an agreement between two persons in which each has some probability of winning or losing

stakeholder
a person or organization that manages a betting arrangement for a fee and redistributes winnings

Contracts Exempt From the Betting Prohibition

Insurance Contracts

Contracts of insurance form a large and important class of commercial transactions. In a true insurance contract one does not, of course, *hope* to win the "bet" with the insurance company, but rather that should the feared loss occur, one will receive a measure of compensation. The fear of loss is expressed in the idea of **insurable interest**. For a person to have an insurable interest, he must have a financial benefit from the continued existence of the property or life insured or suffer some financial detriment from its loss or destruction. Provincial insurance acts state that an insurance contract is invalid unless the party making the contract has an insurable interest in the property or life insured.

Insurance statutes describe the circumstances where an insurable interest exists. With respect to life insurance, for policies on one's own life or on certain members of one's family, it is not necessary to show a financial interest—a detriment is presumed to exist in the loss of that life. But for all other persons, a policy holder must show that he has a financial interest in the person

insurable interest
an interest where a person has a financial benefit from the continued existence of the property or life insured or would suffer financial detriment from its loss or destruction

---

31. S.O. 1992, c.24. See, for example, s. 47.1: "No person may use civil proceedings to recover money owing to the person resulting from participating in or betting on a lottery scheme within the meaning of section 207 of the *Criminal Code* (Canada) conducted in Ontario unless the lottery scheme is authorized under subsection 207 (1) of the Code."

32. See, for example: Criminal Code, R.S.C. 1985, c. C-46, s. 204.

33. There is quite a large body of Canadian case law, most of it refusing to enforce debts, although some decisions allowed a creditor to succeed, usually one who has lent money to the debtor but who himself did not participate in the game.

34. Ellesmere v. Wallace, [1929] 2 Ch. 1; Tote Investors Ltd. v. Smoker, [1968] 1 Q.B. 509.

35. Criminal Code, R.S.C. 1985, c. C-46, s. 207, as amended by 1985, c. 52, 1st Supp., s. 3.

whose life is insured, such as a debtor or a business partner. It would add nothing to your peace of mind to learn that a stranger who stood to suffer nothing in the way of personal bereavement or pecuniary loss from your death had purchased life insurance on your life! The acts waive the requirement of an insurable interest only when the person whose life is insured consents in writing to placing the insurance.[36] We discuss insurance contracts more fully in Chapter 18.

Stock Exchange Transactions

Stock exchange transactions are among the more speculative business contracts. While they are no doubt often explained by a difference of opinion between the buyer and the seller about the future price of the shares traded, the essence of the contract is an actual sale of personal property. Bona fide contracts for the purchase and sale of shares are therefore valid and enforceable. If, however, the subject of an agreement is a wager about what the price of a particular security will be at a specified future time, "without a bona fide intention of acquiring, selling or taking delivery" of the shares, such an agreement is an offence under the Criminal Code and accordingly it is illegal.[37]

Contract for the Future Delivery of Goods

Whenever goods are purchased or sold for future delivery at a price agreed upon in advance, one contracting party may gain at the expense of the other because of price changes between the time of the contract and the time of delivery. Again, the speculative element in these contracts is incidental to a larger purpose, and the contracts cannot be impeached on the ground that they amount to wagers. However, the prohibition against wagers on the price of shares, described above, applies equally to goods.

Agreements Illegal by Statute

We have noted that some statutes describe certain types of agreements as illegal. An example is the Competition Act, discussed in a separate section below. A number of other statutes do not deal directly with contracts but impose penalties for certain kinds of conduct. While the most important of these statutes is the Criminal Code, other examples are the Income Tax Act, which imposes penalties for false returns and evasion,[38] and the Customs Act, which exacts penalties for smuggling.[39] Any contract that contemplates such conduct is itself illegal, not because the statute refers directly to contracts, but because the common law holds that when the *object* of a contract is illegal by statute, then the contract itself is illegal.

Provincial statutes and municipal by-laws require the licensing or registration of various classes of business and professional people, ranging from taxicabs and local building trades to moneylenders, trading partnerships, real estate agents, investment advisors and stockbrokers, optometrists, and public accountants.[40] When such a person sues to collect for services provided, the defendant may raise as a defence that the plaintiff has not been properly registered for his trade.

---

36. See, for example: Insurance Act, R.S.B.C. 1996, c. 226, s. 36(2)(b); R.S.O. 1990, c. I.8, s. 178(2)(b); R.S.N.S. 1989, c. 231, s. 180(2)(b).

37. Criminal Code, R.S.C. 1985, c. C-46, ss. 382, 383.

38. S.C. 1970–71–72, c. 63, s. 239, as amended, S.C. 1980–81–82–83, c. 158, s. 58, S.C. 1988, c. 55, s. 182.

39. S.C. 1986, c. C-1, ss. 110–16, 153–61.

40. See, for example, the following Ontario statutes: Business Names Act, R.S.O. 1990, c. B.17, s. 7(1); Real Estate and Business Brokers Act, R.S.O. 1990, c. R.4, s. 3; Securities Act, R.S.O. 1990, c. S.5, s. 25; Drug and Pharmacies Regulation Act, R.S.O. 1990, c. H.4, s. 139; Public Accountancy Act, R.S.O. 1990, c. P.37, s. 14; and others.

CASE 7.3

K, an electrician, sued for work done and materials supplied to *A*, who pleaded in defence that *K* was not licensed as an electrical contractor as required by the local by-law. The court stated that the object of the by-law was to protect the public against mistakes and loss that might arise from work done by unqualified electricians and accordingly held that the contract was unlawful. The court would not assist *K* in his attempt to collect the account.[41]

A later decision asserted that a person in the electrician's position would now be entitled to recover for the materials supplied, though not the fee for the services provided.[42]

We should note that when an action is brought *against* a person who has not been licensed it will not fail on that ground: the defendant cannot use his own misconduct in not complying with a statute as a defence to an action by an innocent person. This result is an application of the general principle that a person (whether as plaintiff or defendant) is not permitted to use evidence of his own wrongdoing for his advantage before the courts.

The courts have also become more flexible and sympathetic towards entirely innocent breaches of a statutory requirement.

CASE 7.4

S, an American citizen was lawfully admitted to Canada and applied for permanent residence status. While waiting for her status to be granted she accepted a position without first obtaining a work permit as required under Immigration Regulations; *S* was unaware of the requirement. She and her employer paid premiums under the Employment Insurance Act. *S* was laid off and applied for benefits but they were denied on the basis that her contract of employment was void for illegality.[43]

The court rejected the "classic common law model of illegality" and stated that the consequences of declaring a contract illegal could often be too extreme. It was preferable to adopt a general principle rather than a rigid rule, and to refuse to give relief only where it would be contrary to public policy to do so. To allow this claim would not offend the policy of making benefits available to a person innocently unemployed. Nor would it encourage illegal immigrants to come to Canada to work illegally. *S* was not an illegal immigrant and she acted in good faith. The Act only imposed sanctions against those who knowingly obtained work without a permit. The court gave *S* the right to collect employment benefits.

---

41. Kocotis v. D'Angelo (1957), 13 D.L.R. (2d) 69. But see Sidmay Ltd. et al. v. Wehttam Investments Ltd. (1967), 61 D.L.R. (2d) 358, affirmed (1968), 69 D.L.R. (2d) 336, for a case in which a mortgagor was required to honour his mortgage obligations even though the mortgagee was a corporation not authorized to lend on mortgages under the Loan and Trust Corporations Act (Ontario).

42. Monticchio v. Torcema Construction Ltd. (1979), 26 O.R. (2d) 305.

43. Re Still and Minister of National Revenue (1997), 154 D.L.R. (4th) 229.

CONTRACTS ILLEGAL BY THE COMMON LAW AND PUBLIC POLICY

The Common Law

Over the years, the common law has condemned certain types of conduct and has granted remedies, usually in the form of damages, to persons aggrieved or harmed by that conduct. Generally the conduct is considered a private wrong or tort, and whenever a contract contemplates the commission of a tort, the contract is illegal.

Among the private wrongs or torts that may be contemplated in an agreement are slander and libel, trespass, deceit (fraud), and, in particular, incitement to break an existing contract with someone else.

CASE 7.5

The Wanderers Hockey Club learned that Johnson had signed a contract to play for the following season with another club managed by Patrick. The Wanderers' manager persuaded Johnson to enter into a second contract with it for the same season by offering him a higher salary. Johnson tore up his contract with Patrick, but as things turned out he failed to perform his new contract with the Wanderers, which then sued him for breach of contract.

The action failed on the grounds that no cause of action can arise out of a wrongdoing; it had been obvious to both parties that the second contract with the Wanderers could not be performed without breaking the earlier contract with Patrick.[44]

An agreement may not have as its primary object the commission of a wrongful act but it nevertheless contains an undertaking by one party to indemnify the other against damages arising from any private wrong committed in the course of performance.

CASE 7.6

W.H. Smith & Son had agreed to print a weekly newspaper, *Vanity Fair*, for Clinton on the terms that it should have a letter of indemnity from Clinton against claims arising out of publication of libellous matter in the paper. In June 1907, the paper published an article containing statements libellous to Parr's Bank. W.H. Smith settled the claim against it by paying Parr's Bank a sum of money; in turn it sought to recover the money from Clinton. The action failed because the court refused to assist in the recovery of money to indemnify a wrongdoer, W.H. Smith, which had printed the libellous paper.[45]

There are important exceptions to this rule for contracts of insurance. For example, an insurance policy that promises to indemnify a motorist for the damages he may have to pay to third parties as a result of his negligent driving is neither void nor illegal; automobile insurance for public liability and property damage is valid. Similar policies of insurance are designed to protect professional people against the consequences of their negligence in the course of practice and such policies are also valid. However, the insurance protects the policy holder from neg-

---

44. Wanderers Hockey Club v. Johnson (1913), 14 D.L.R. 42. See also: Fabbi et al. v. Jones (1972), 28 D.L.R. (3d) 224.
45. Smith v. Clinton (1908), 99 L.T. 840.

ligence *only*, that is, from inadvertent wrongdoing, and *not* from deliberate acts of harm, such as fraud.

In addition, a person or a business may exempt itself from liability for negligence by the terms of a contract. Thus a railway or other carrier may state in its standard form contract for the shipment of goods (bill of lading) that it shall not be liable for damage to goods in excess of a stated amount, whether caused by the negligence of its employees or not. The temptation to include such exemption clauses is great, and as a result these contracts are often subject to government regulation.

Public Policy

Even though a contract does not contemplate the commission of a crime or of any of the recognized private wrongs, it may still be regarded as illegal because it is contrary to public policy. If the court decides that a particular contract is prejudicial to the interests of Canada, its relations with foreign countries, its national defence, its public service, or the administration of justice within the country, the court will declare the contract illegal although its performance is neither a tort nor a crime in itself.

An agreement that has the perversion of justice as its object will be illegal on grounds of public policy. Thus, a promise to pay a witness either for appearing or for not appearing to give evidence in criminal proceedings is illegal.[46]

CASE 7.7

In *Symington v. Vancouver Breweries and Riefel*,[47] the plaintiff, Symington, promised the defendants (who were anxious to see a person named Ball convicted of illegal manufacture of alcohol) to give evidence that would assure Ball's conviction. The defendants promised to pay Syming-ton $1000 for each month of imprisonment in Ball's sentence. Symington gave testimony and Ball was sentenced to 12 months' imprisonment. Symington received only part payment and sued for the balance.

Symington failed on grounds of public policy that the agreement tended to pervert justice. In summarizing his reasons, Mr. Justice Martin said in part:

> There is a peculiar and sinister element in this case that distinguishes it from all the others that have been cited to us, *viz.*, that it provides for remuneration upon a sliding scale corresponding in amount to the amount of the sentence secured by the informer's evidence. This is so direct and inevitable an incentive to perjury and other concomitant nefarious conduct that it cannot be in the public interest to countenance a transaction which is dangerous to such an exceptional degree to the administration of criminal justice.[48]

The arrangements by which a person accused of a crime may be released under bail are intended to be fair and humane.[49] However, they require that the party putting up the bail shall forfeit the bail money should the prisoner abscond. Accordingly, a promise either by the accused or by a third party to indemnify the party putting up bail is illegal.[50]

---

46. Collins v. Blantern (1767), 95 E.R. 847.

47. [1931] 1 D.L.R. 935.

48. *Ibid.*, at 937.

49. See Friedland, *Detention Before Trial*. Toronto: University of Toronto Press, 1965; Criminal Code, R.S.C. 1985, c. C-46, ss. 763–71.

50. Herman v. Jeuchner (1885), 15 Q.B.D. 561; Consolidated Exploration and Finance Co. v. Musgrave, [1900] 1 Ch. 37.

The most common crime committed within the business world is embezzlement, the so-called "white-collar crime." It is often committed by persons without previous criminal records who succumb to temptation or personal misfortune and "borrow" funds without permission. On discovery, the embezzler usually repents and promises to repay every cent if he is not turned over to the police. In many cases, either through sympathy or in the hope of recovering the loss, the victim of the embezzler agrees to the arrangement.

As charitable as the motives of the injured party may be, we must remember that the embezzler has committed a crime for which the law demands conviction, though punishment may turn out to be lenient. While the victim does not think of himself as committing a crime and may well be ignorant of the fact that failure to inform the police is wrong, the agreement tends to pervert justice and is illegal.[51] Thus, in failing to inform the police of the commission of the crime, the victim is also in breach of the criminal law. The most a victim can do is to assure the embezzler that if restitution is made, he will testify to that effect as a mitigating factor in the court's assessment of the crime. The court considers restitution in these cases to be of great weight in arriving at a just punishment. In any event, the victim retains the right to recover the loss from an embezzler by suing for breach of trust or for wrongful conversion in tort.

Agreements that promote unnecessary litigation are also considered to be attempts to obstruct the course of justice. They take up the time of the law courts when more serious matters are awaiting decision. A party may wish to stir up litigation because of its advertising value, on the theory that any kind of publicity is good publicity. In *Dann v. Curzon*,[52] a theatre manager promised to pay a party for intentionally creating a disturbance in a theatre and then suing the manager for assault. The party did create a disturbance and his action for assault was dismissed. When the theatre manager failed to make the promised payment, the party sued him. The second action failed on grounds of public policy.

CONTEMPORARY ISSUE

Confidentiality Clauses and Public Policy

Employment contracts and research contracts often contain clauses that require the employee or the funded researcher to maintain confidentiality about sensitive information. Such information might include the company's financial affairs, its marketing plans, the products it is developing, or the progress of research it is sponsoring. There are good reasons for these clauses. Businesses do not want their competitive position undermined by having information they have paid to develop end up in the hands of their rivals. They do not want the price of their stock or the reputation of their products to be affected by rumours and gossip. Courts award damages and sometimes grant injunctions for breach of confidentiality clauses.

However, what if the clause prevents a person from disclosing information that shows that a company's products place consumers or patients at risk? In that case, public policy concerns arise.

Dr. Nancy Olivieri, a professor of medicine at the University of Toronto and leading researcher at the Hospital for Sick Children, received funding from Apotex, a drug manufacturer, to conduct clinical trials on a new drug. The drug, called L1 or deferiprone, was designed to remove the excess iron that builds up in the bodies of patients who require frequent blood transfusions over long periods.

continued

---

51. See Turner, *Russell on Crime* (12th ed.), pp. 339–41. Turner, ed. London: Stevens & Sons Ltd., 1964; also, U.S. Fidelity and Guarantee Co. v. Cruikshank and Simmons (1919), 49 D.L.R. 674; Keir v. Leeman (1846), 115 E.R. 1315.

52. (1911), 104 L.T. 66.

A few years into the trial, Dr. Olivieri became concerned that the drug was not effective and that dangerously high levels of iron were building up in the livers of some of the patients in the trial. When she reported her concern to the drug company and the hospital research ethics board, the company terminated the trial at the Toronto site. When she made her findings public, Apotex accused her of violating the confidentiality agreement she had signed and threatened to sue her. The company also asserted that her methods were suspect and her findings were unsupported by other researchers. While Dr. Olivieri published her research findings in the highly respected *New England Journal of Medicine*, Apotex did not submit its data for publication.

In her conflicts with the drug company, Dr. Olivieri had strong moral support from a number of her colleagues, many of whom thought the hospital had not properly supported and defended her. Eventually, Dr. Olivieri and the hospital reached a settlement of their differences.

Sources: Susan Jeffrey, "Research Conflict," *The Medical Post*, January 21, 1997; Michael Valpy, "Science Friction," *Elm Street*, December 1998; University of Toronto Faculty Association Press Release, December 17, 1998; Joint Release, The Hospital for Sick Children and Dr. Nancy Olivieri, January 26, 1999; Marina Jimenez, "Olivieri, Foes Take Battle Over Drug to Ottawa," *National Post*, October 5, 1999.

Questions to Consider

1. Should the courts refuse to enforce confidentiality agreements if upholding them would mean that risks to the public are not disclosed? How can the proper balance be established between a company's interest in protecting sensitive information and the public's interest in knowing about risks to health and safety?

2. What sort of legislation, if any, do we need to protect employees and researchers who disclose information about products or activities that pose a risk to consumers or patients?

AGREEMENTS IN RESTRAINT OF TRADE

Perhaps the most common reason for business agreements being challenged on grounds of public policy is that they may be in restraint of trade. The courts have long considered competition a necessary element of our economic life and regard agreements that diminish competition as undesirable. Of the agreements that may be in restraint of trade, some are at worst simply void. Others are illegal because they are prohibited by the Competition Act.

Even if a contract contains a **restrictive covenant** (a term in restraint of trade) that is found to be against public policy, the term may not invalidate the entire contract. The courts may refuse to enforce the offending term while treating the remainder of the contract as valid. The courts initially presume that any term in restraint of trade is against public policy, but the party seeking to enforce the covenant may **rebut** the presumption if it can demonstrate that it is a reasonable arrangement between the parties and does not adversely effect the public interest.

restrictive covenant
a term in restraint of trade

rebut
overcome

In this chapter, we shall examine the consequences of two of the classes of contracts in restraint of trade:

(a) Agreements between the vendor and the purchaser of a business whereby the vendor undertakes not to carry on a similar business in competition with the purchaser.

(b) Agreements between employer and employee in which the employee undertakes that after leaving her present employment she will not compete against the employer, either by setting up her own business or by taking a position with a competing business.

A third class, agreements among manufacturers or merchants to restrict output or fix the selling price of a commodity or service, will be examined in Chapter 32, "Government Regulation of Business."

The courts make an initial presumption that any term in restraint of trade is against public policy and void, but this presumption is not absolute. It may be rebutted by the party seeking to enforce the covenant if it can demonstrate that it is a reasonable arrangement between the parties and does not adversely affect the public interest. In the two types of contracts discussed below the courts put great weight on the interests of the parties themselves.

Agreements Between Vendor and Purchaser of a Business

Often, an important asset of a business is its goodwill, that is, the trade and commercial connections that it has established through years of carrying on business under a particular name and in a particular location. The vendor of a business can only realize this value in a sale if he can make a binding promise to the purchaser that he will do nothing in the future to diminish or destroy the value of what he is selling. He can command a higher price if he is free to covenant with the purchaser that he will not enter into any business that is likely to compete with the business he is selling: there will then be no danger of his attracting old customers away and thus diminishing its value. After the sale, it is important that the law enforce reasonable undertakings of this kind made by the vendor, or else the purchaser, fearing she will be deprived of a valuable part of the asset she has purchased, will refuse to pay the vendor's price.

Accordingly, the law recognizes that both purchaser and vendor of a business may find a mutual advantage in a restrictive covenant and that such a restraint need not be against the public interest. As well, the parties usually deal with each other on a more or less equal footing in striking a bargain with respect to both the price and the protection asked for by the purchaser. The vendor's covenant not to compete with the purchaser as a term of an agreement for the sale of a business, may be enforced if it can be shown that the restrictions placed on the vendor are reasonable in view of the nature of the trade or practice sold.

Whether a particular restriction is so broad that it offends the public interest is for the court to decide. On the one hand, a clause forbidding the vendor ever to enter business again anywhere would, for most types of business, be more than is needed to protect the purchaser and would be considered to deprive the public of the benefits of the vendor's abilities: accordingly, it would be void. On the other hand, a term by which the vendor undertakes for a specified period of time (or perhaps even within his lifetime) not to set up business again within specific geographic limits that reasonably describe the area of competition may well be reasonable in the opinion of a court, and consequently valid. The size of the area and the period of time denied to the vendor vary with the nature of the business.

ILLUSTRATION 7.1

A dentist in Saskatoon sells his practice to a young graduate, promising that he will not practise again anywhere in Canada. The retiring dentist has a change of heart, however, and two years later sets up a practice in the same city. The other dentist brings action to obtain a court injunction restraining him from doing so.

In these circumstances a restrictive clause that denies the seller a right to practise anywhere in Canada is in excess of what is necessary to protect the interests of the purchaser. To argue that a covenant in restraint of trade is not against public policy, it is necessary to show at least that it is reasonable between parties. The scope of this covenant, in view of the nature of a dental practice, is unreasonable, and it is therefore void. The purchaser would fail to obtain the injunction, although if the covenant had been confined to the city of Saskatoon for, say, a period of three years, it would probably have been valid.

With rare exceptions, the courts have refused to take on the task of narrowing to a "reasonable scope" the area within which the seller is not to set up business.[53] The basic objection to narrowing a covenant is that it discriminates in favour of one of the parties: it gives a purchaser who has demanded an unreasonable restriction the benefit of the court's opinion about the allowable maximum area not considered detrimental to the public interest. It would also deter the vendor from taking the risk of opening a new business. If a restrictive clause is held to be too wide, it is highly unlikely that courts will narrow it to a reasonable scope; the clause will be void and a vendor who might otherwise have been bound by a reasonable restriction is free of the restraint. The lesson for the purchaser is that he should demand no more than a reasonable restriction, erring on the conservative side rather than demanding too much.

The case of *Nordenfelt v. Maxim Nordenfelt Guns and Ammunition Co. Ltd.*[54] illustrates how the nature of a business may be important in determining what is a reasonable restriction on its vendor.

CASE 7.8

Nordenfelt had been a manufacturer of guns and ammunition. He transferred his patents and business to Maxim Nordenfelt Guns and Ammunition Co. Ltd. for £287 500 and covenanted that for 25 years he would not engage, except on behalf of this company, either directly or indirectly in the business of a manufacturer of guns or ammunition or in any other business competing or liable to compete in any way with the business of the company. Later, Nordenfelt entered into an agreement with other manufacturers of guns and ammunition, and the plaintiff company brought an action to enforce the covenant.

The House of Lords decided that the clause could be broken into two parts: first, the promise not to engage in the manufacture of guns or ammunition, and second, the promise not to engage in *any other business* competing or liable to compete with the plaintiff company. The court held that the second promise was an unreasonable restriction and declared it void. But it also held it could *sever* the second promise from the first and that the first promise was a reasonable restriction. Accordingly, it granted an injunction to restrain Nordenfelt from working for any other business that manufactured guns and ammunition.

We can see, then, that although the courts will not save unreasonable restrictions by redrafting them or narrowing their effect, they will sever an unreasonable restriction from one that is reasonable—even if the restrictions occur in the same sentence—provided they are two distinct ideas and can be severed without changing the meaning of the reasonable restraint. In enforcing the restraint concerning guns and ammunition, the court pointed out that improved communications and transportation facilities had enabled orders to be directed to and filled from distant sources of supply, and had greatly broadened the market in which competition might be effective in certain lines of business. The decision, though handed down in 1894, recognized that the whole world had become a market in the munitions business. In expressing the opinion of the court, Lord MacNaghten set the law in its present mould:

All interferences with individual liberty of action in trading, and all restraints of trade of themselves, if there is nothing more, are contrary to public policy and therefore void. That is the general rule. But there are exceptions: restraints of trade…may be justified by the special circumstances of a particular case. It is sufficient justification, and indeed it is the only justification, if the restriction is reasonable—reasonable, that is, in reference to the interests of the

53. See Goldsoll v. Goldman, [1915] 1 Ch. 292, and Attwood v. Lamont, [1920] 3 K.B. 571. See also Canadian American Financial Corp. v. King (1989), 60 D.L.R. (4th) 293.

54. [1894] A.C. 535.

public, so framed and so guarded as to afford adequate protection to the party in whose favour it is imposed, while at the same time it is in no way injurious to the public.[55]

Agreements Between Employee and Employer

It is more difficult to convince courts that covenants between employee and employer restricting the future economic freedom of the employee are reasonable and not in restraint of trade.[56] Frequently there is no equality of bargaining power, and an employer is able to impose terms on an employee that the latter must accept if he wants the position. Later he may find that the covenant, if valid, makes it virtually impossible for him to leave his employer in order to accept another position in the vicinity: he would have to sell his house and become established in another city. In protecting employees by striking down unreasonable restraints, the courts at the same time serve a second public interest—they protect the mobility of labour and thereby encourage more efficient allocation of human resources.

We must distinguish agreements that try to govern an employee's means of livelihood *after* he leaves his present employment from those in which the employee undertakes not to compete directly or indirectly *while* he remains in the service of the employer. The law recognizes a full-time employee's primary duty of loyalty to the employer, and an absolute promise not to engage in any other business during the term of the employment is valid, whether that business competes with the employer or not. Similar agreements between partners that are operative during the life of the partnership are also binding.

A plaintiff seeking to enforce a restrictive covenant usually asks the court for the equitable remedy of an injunction to restrain the defendant. A restrictive covenant may be enforced if it can be shown to be reasonable between the parties and not injurious to the public.

The courts more readily accept as reasonable certain restraints placed upon an employee who has access to valuable trade secrets or a knowledge of secret processes in his employment[57] or who has acted as the personal representative of the employer in dealings with the customers of the business.[58] In such circumstances, a promise by the employee not to work for a competing business or to set up a business of his own after leaving his present employment is more likely to be binding upon him, particularly if the employer has evidence that its former employee is acting in a way that is depriving it of its proprietary interest in trade secrets or customer goodwill.

QUESTIONS FOR REVIEW

1. Is a minor bound to pay the agreed contract price for necessaries? Explain.

2. What element is necessary for a contract of employment to bind a minor?

3. What obligation does a minor have when she repudiates a contract for non-necessary goods? Explain the policy reason for the rule.

4. Are minors' contracts for non-necessaries always voidable when the minors attain majority?

---

55. *Ibid*, at 565.

56. Mason v. Provident Clothing & Supply Co. Ltd., [1913] A.C. 724.

57. Reliable Toy Co. and Reliable Plastics Co. Ltd. v. Collins, [1950] 4 D.L.R. 499. For an interesting case that compares covenants both during employment and after termination, see Robinson (William) & Co. Ltd. v. Heuer, [1898] 2 Ch. 451.

58. Fitch v. Dewes, [1921] 2 A.C. 158.

5. What two types of minors' contracts must be distinguished for the purpose of determining the liability of the minors after they become of age?

6. Give examples of persons of diminished contractual capacity. What special problems do such persons face when they want to deny responsibility under a contract?

7. Under what circumstances may a contract voidable at the option of one of the parties cease to be voidable?

8. What is the nature of the legal problem that adds to the uncertainty of an action against a trade union?

9. (a) When Jones was 17 years old, she took her stereo into the Mariposa Service Centre for an extensive repair job, which cost $175. If she does not pay, can the Mariposa Service Centre sue her successfully?

   (b) After Jones becomes of age, she picks up the repaired stereo and does nothing to repudiate her liability to the Mariposa Service Centre. Can the Mariposa Service Centre recover the money now?

   (c) Upon becoming of age, Jones tells the manager of the Mariposa Service Centre in a telephone conversation that she will pay the $175. Can the Mariposa Service Centre recover now?

10. For what types of organization is a representative action important? Explain

11. Why may it be important to a party to a dispute to show that a void contract is not also illegal?

12. How can we tell whether the intention of the legislature is to make a certain type of agreement illegal as well as void?

13. In what way does the Gaming Act inhibit wagering contracts?

14. What quality must an insurance contract possess to prevent it from being a wager and therefore void?

15. What kinds of business contract may have an element of wagering incidental to the main purpose of the transaction?

16. Explain how restrictive covenants play a role in the sale of an active business.

17. What exception is there to the rule that an agreement is illegal if it purports to indemnify a person against the consequences of his own wrongdoing?

18. Distinguish between the two aspects of a restrictive covenant in an employment contract and how they are viewed by the courts.

19. Explain the courts' attitude towards the subsequent use of trade secrets acquired by a former employee.

CASES AND PROBLEMS

1 West was 17 years of age and obtained his driver's licence. He went to Drive-Yourself Ltd., showed his licence, and signed for the hiring of a car. The Drive-Yourself clerk did not notice West's age as being under 18, the minimum age required by the firm to agree to hire. The contract contained clauses requiring the hirer to observe all laws regulating the use of motor vehicles, not to enter the car in any competition, to indemnify the hiring company for any fines imposed in respect of the operation of the automobile, and to return it in good condition.

West then gathered up seven friends and took them for a drive. While attempting to pass another car at 20 km/h above the speed limit, he lost control and wrecked the car against a stump. At the time there were three passengers in the front seat in addition to West, the driver.

Drive-Yourself Ltd. brought an action against West for the value of the wrecked car. What scope, if any, would the plaintiff company have for countering West's defence of infancy? Indicate with reasons whether its action is likely to succeed.

2 For most of a year, Harrison acted as agent for the purpose of obtaining options on property on an island in British Columbia on behalf of the Western Development Company, which planned to develop the island industrially. These plans became known to the property owners on the island, and some of them, believing their holdings to be indispensable to the plan, sought to obtain prices much higher than the market value established there for farm or residential purposes.

Harrison obtained, for a consideration of $1, an option to purchase within one year the property of Mrs. Foy for $200 000. Harrison had negotiated the price with a Miss Foy and a widow, Mrs. Sheridan; he had offered $1000 an hectare, which was the maximum he had been authorized to offer, but the two women had insisted upon $2000 a hectare. He had then reluctantly agreed to take an option at the price demanded, explaining that his principals would not likely take up the option at such an exorbitant price. Miss Foy had next insisted that a further $10 000 be added to the price for the barn; Harrison had agreed to that, too.

It was only when the option agreement was prepared for signing that Harrison learned that he had not been dealing with the registered owner of the property, but with her daughters, both of whom resided there. They told him that Mrs. Foy was a very old lady and was bedridden. Harrison was taken to the bedroom where he explained, carefully and accurately, the terms and effect of the option. Mrs. Foy appeared to understand what he was saying, nodding and smiling and from time to time saying, "Yes." At that point Harrison turned to Miss Foy, who was standing at the foot of the bed, and asked her, "Do you really think your mother understands the difference between an option and an agreement to sell her land?" Miss Foy replied, "Yes, I think she understands." Then Mrs. Sheridan asked Harrison if, before getting her mother to sign, he would wait until they could get the family lawyer to be present. Harrison, exasperated with the way negotiations had been proceeding, replied testily that he was not prepared to put up with any further delay or discussion of terms. He asked Mrs. Foy to sign the option agreement. She did not sign her name but made a cross under the direction of one of her daughters who explained to Harrison that her mother used to be able to sign her name but that her hand was now too unsteady.

Harrison's principals did, in fact, elect to take up the option within the year to obtain property at the agreed price of $200 000; they had taken up the options on the adjoining properties and needed Mrs. Foy's property to complete the land they required. The two daughters denied that the option agreement was "not worth the paper it was written on" because Mrs. Foy was insane at the time of her signing. The principals sued to have the option agreement enforced. It was brought out in evidence that Mrs. Foy was, indeed, insane, a fact of which Harrison denied any knowledge at the time; it was also shown that the fair market value of the property as a farm at the date of the option agreement was about $140 000.

Express an opinion about the likelihood that the action will succeed.

3 During the 1997–98 season Harvey ("Ace") Tilson played hockey for the Medicine Hat Broncos of the Western Junior Hockey League, scoring 30 goals and assisting on another 35 goals. In recent years many players in this league had been offered contracts to play professional hockey upon completion of their junior eligibility. They remain eligible to play in the League until the year in which they reach the age of 21.

In October 1996, Tilson signed a two-year contract with the Medicine Hat Broncos Hockey Club that was to terminate before the start of the hockey season in the early fall of 1998. However, at the beginning of training camp in September 1997, the manager of the Broncos presented Tilson and the other players with a new three-year contract. This contract contained a new set of standardized conditions of employment prescribed by the league and, by agreement among the clubs, was presented to all players in the league on a "take it or leave it" basis; the players understood that if they did not agree to waive their existing contracts and sign the new one they would not be able to play in the league and their professional prospects would be severely harmed. The new contract included the following clauses:

1. This contract supersedes all previous contracts between the Club [Medicine Hat Broncos Hockey Club] and the Player [Harvey J. Tilson].

2. The Club employs the Player as an apprentice hockey player for the term of three years commencing 1998 and agrees, subject to the terms of this contract, to pay the Player a salary of $150.00 per week plus an allowance for room and board of $200.00 per week, these payments to terminate at the last scheduled game of the Club each year.

3. The Player acknowledges that if his hockey skills and abilities develop to the degree that he is tendered and accepts a contract of employment with a professional hockey club, then the Club shall be entitled to compensation for its contribution to his development and, in consideration for such contribution by the Club, the Player agrees to pay the Club a sum equal to 20 percent (20%) of his gross earnings attributable to his employment with such professional hockey club during a period of three (3) years beginning on the date at which he first represents and plays for that professional hockey club.

4. The Player agrees that during the term of this contract he will loyally discharge his obligations to the Club and that he will not play for or be directly or indirectly employed by or interested in any other amateur or professional hockey club. The Player agrees that the Club shall have the right, in addition to any other legal remedies that the Club may enjoy, to prevent him by appropriate injunction proceedings from committing any breach of this undertaking.

5. The Player acknowledges that, if in breach of his obligations under section 4, the Player plays for any other hockey club, the Club will lose his services as a skilled hockey player and will suffer a loss of income from reduced paid attendance at hockey games and broadcasting rights and that a genuine estimate of the amount of this loss would be the salary that the Player can earn as a hockey player for any other amateur or professional club.

The manager of the Broncos advised the players to take their copies of the contract home and discuss them with their parents. He added that a signed copy must be in his hands by the beginning of the following week. Tilson's parents actively encouraged him to sign the contract, and Tilson returned a signed copy to the manager on September 5, 1997.

Tilson played for the Broncos in the 1997–98 season until March 21, 1998. On that day he became 18 years of age, the age of majority in Alberta. On March 22, 1998, in a letter to the club written by his lawyer, Tilson repudiated the contract "without in any way acknowledging the validity thereof." On the same day, in the company of his lawyer, he signed a Pan-American Hockey Conference contract with the Calgary Whippets Hockey Club Ltd. for three seasons commencing September 1 of each of 1998, 1999, and 2000 providing for annual salaries of $70 000, $80 000 and $90 000, respectively.

At the time, the 1997–98 season was almost over, and the Broncos had qualified for the playoffs and were the favourite to win the Junior Cup. Tilson offered to stay with the team at his regular weekly salary and allowance during the 1998 playoffs if the Broncos Club would sign an agreement that Tilson's three-year hockey contract with it would expire when the playoffs ended. The Broncos refused and brought an action against Tilson, seeking an injunction to restrain him from breaking his contract or, in the alternative, damages of $150 000 representing the measure of its loss for being deprived of his services for the next two years.

Explain the legal issues raised in this dispute and offer with reasons an opinion about the probable outcome of the action.

4 Assume the facts of Problem 3 above, with the exception that the Broncos Club did sign the agreement proposed by Tilson in March 1998; that Tilson had played with the team during the 1998 playoffs; and that the Broncos Club had then brought its action against Tilson. What line of reasoning might the Broncos use to support its argument that the March 1998 agreement was not binding on it? Would it be a good argument? Cite any relevant case or cases.

5 Marbett noticed that the ceiling on the upper floor of her house had become damp from water seepage. She mentioned the problem to her neighbour who remarked that Marbett's house was 25 years old and probably needed new roofing; he recommended her to contact Riley, who recently repaired his roof. Marbett phoned Riley and he came promptly to inspect the roof. He said he would replace it for $1800 within a few days. Marbett signed a contract to have the job done.

The day the work was being completed Marbett was told by a friend that Riley did not have the required municipal licence for a roofing contractor. The friend said she believed Marbett did not have to pay Riley for the roofing work because the contract was illegal. Is the friend correct? Give reasons for your opinion.

6 Flanders & Co., a Montréal firm of wine importers, chartered the ship *Bacchus* from its owners, Swan Ltd., to transport a cargo of wine from Madeira to Montréal. The contract of charter party included a term to the effect that the charterer, Flanders & Co., should be liable for an additional $2500 for each additional day at the port of destination if the unloading of the ship were delayed for any reason. Unknown to either party, the wine was a prohibited product under the federal Food and Drugs Act because of a preservative used in its production.

When the ship reached Montréal, customs officers refused permission to unload pending determination of the cargo's compliance with the federal act. The investigation and report from the government laboratory in Ottawa took 10 days; it was determined by customs officials that it would be illegal to import the wine, and the cargo was finally transferred at dockside to another ship for shipment to New York.

When Flanders & Co. refused to pay the additional $25 000 caused by the delay, Swan Ltd. sued for the amount. What defence might Flanders & Co. offer? Would Swan Ltd. succeed?

7 John Gifford and his friend, Karl Holtz, were enthusiastic followers of the commodities market, the market in which such products as wheat, cotton, tobacco, and coffee are bought and sold for future delivery. However, they did not have sufficient capital to engage in the market themselves and so they played a game: they would "buy and sell" futures in various commodities under three-month contracts for delivery and then "settle" their fictional gains and losses on the delivery date. Karl did very well in the game and over a two-year period "earned" over $100 000 at John's expense.

One day John finally said to Karl, "I think I have a real winner here, the price of coffee is going to rise sharply in the next three months. At what price do you want to sell to me?"

Karl disagreed with John's prediction and replied, "I'll sell you $20 000's worth of coffee at today's price. The price is going to drop and you'll lose as usual."

"For once, not only am I right, I'm prepared to back up my words. Are you?" asked John. "Let's make this a real transaction. If the price goes up, you pay me the difference. If it goes down, I pay you."

"Okay, it's your funeral. It's a deal," Karl replied, and they shook hands on it.

Three months later, the price of $20 000's worth of coffee had risen by 30 percent, making John richer by $6000. When John demanded payment, Karl said he didn't have that much in the bank but grudgingly gave John three cheques for $2000 each, one payable immediately and the other two post-dated one month and two months respectively.

John cashed the first cheque at Karl's bank at once. A month later, he used the second cheque to buy a used car from Grace Bukowsky. She has not yet presented it to Karl's bank for payment. John still has the third cheque.

Karl has heard from a friend studying law that the whole transaction might be "illegal." Give him your opinion with reasons.

8

GROUNDS UPON WHICH A CONTRACT MAY BE IMPEACHED

Mistake

The Restricted Meaning of Mistake

Mistakes About the Terms

Mistakes in Assumptions

Mistake and Innocent Third Parties

Mistakes in Performance

In this chapter we discuss what happens when a party realizes that the contract is not the one that was intended. A party may have made any one of several errors. We examine such questions as:

■ what are the legal consequences of a mistake?
>   in recording an agreement?
>   about the meaning of the words?
>   about the existence or qualities of the subject-matter?
>   about unforeseen future events?
>   in performing the contract?

■ what are the legal consequences for innocent third parties in cases of void and voidable contracts and of *non est factum*?

THE RESTRICTED MEANING OF MISTAKE

We may enter into a contract only to regret it afterwards—perhaps it turns out to be quite different from what we intended, or we decide that it was unwise—we made a "mistake" and wish we could be freed from it. However, the prospects for avoiding a contract because one has made a mistake are quite limited.

We must not confuse "legal mistake" with "mistake" in its more general, non-legal meaning: to say, "I made a mistake going for a walk without my overcoat" or "She made a mistake agreeing to work over the weekend," is simply to say that a person, with hindsight, believes it was an error in judgment to have acted in a particular way. Such errors in judgment are not legal justification for avoiding one's obligations under a contract. To excuse performance so easily would undermine certainty in contractual arrangements: parties would be reluctant to rely on their contracts. While, as we shall see, there are circumstances in which the courts will recognize a mistake, such circumstances are very limited. In the words of a United States court:

> Contracts are the deliberate and voluntary obligations of parties capable of contracting and they must be accorded binding force and effect....The owner of property is supposed to know what it is worth and at least know what he is willing to take for his property. The purchaser may likewise exercise his free will and choice as to whether he will purchase property at a given price. After he has received the property, understanding that he is to pay a fixed price for it, he cannot be compelled to pay a different and greater price simply because the vendor was careless and negligent in the transaction of his own business [and had sold it for too little].[1]

ILLUSTRATION 8.1

A leaves a note for B, stating, "I will sell you my car for $5400 cash." B delivers $5400 to A, and obtains possession and a transfer of the registration. A immediately realizes that he had made an error in his note; he had intended to write $6400 rather than $5400. However, B was unaware of the error; she simply thought the price was an attractive one. While in one sense there is a mistake, it is entirely A's doing, and B reasonably relied on it: if a remedy were granted to A, either to increase the price of the car or to require its return, B's reasonable expectations would be defeated. A reasonable bystander reading the note and observing B's acceptance would conclude that there was a contract in the terms of the note as written. Accordingly, A would not have a remedy.

ILLUSTRATION 8.2

L signs a five-year lease to rent a shop on a busy main street. He has misread a street map and believes that a city bus route uses the street and that a bus stop is close to the shop. In fact the bus route runs along a parallel route two blocks to the south. The landlord is completely unaware of the lessee's erroneous belief. Here also, the contract is binding on the lessee despite his innocent and mistaken assumption.

There are two main types of mistake: *mistake about the terms* of a contract and *mistakes in assumptions* about important facts related to a contract although not part of the contract itself.[2] While sometimes courts grant relief on grounds we are about to consider, frequently they refuse to do so. Illustrations 8.1 and 8.2 above are examples respectively of the two types of mistake where relief would be denied because the mistaken parties would be found solely responsible for their own misfortunes. We shall also examine cases where relief has been granted.

MISTAKES ABOUT THE TERMS
Words Used Inadvertently

As Illustration 8.1 shows, one party may inadvertently use the wrong words in stating the terms of a contract. We should ask how those words ought reasonably to have been understood by the other party. If, in the circumstances, it was reasonable for the second party to rely on them and

---

1. Tatum v. Coast Lumber Co. (1909), 101 P. 957 at 960. See also: Scott v. Littledale (1858), 120 E.R. 304.

2. Problems relating to mistake are difficult to classify and analyze. Many different frameworks have been tried and none is entirely satisfactory in explaining the great diversity of problems that can and do arise. We believe that the approach adopted in this chapter, based in part on the work of G.E. Palmer, *Mistake and Unjust Enrichment*, Columbus: Ohio State U. Press, 1962, is the most helpful. Lord Reid's observation is apt: "There was a period when...hard-and-fast dividing lines were sought, but I think that experience has shown that often they do not produce certainty but do produce unreasonable results." (Saunders v. Anglia Building Society, [1971] A.C. 1004 at 1017.)

   For a careful, detailed analysis, see, S.M. Waddams, *The Law of Contracts* (4th ed.). Toronto, Canada Law Book Company, 1999. Chapters 10, 11, and 12.

enter into the contract, then the terms of the contract are binding on the first party. It seems only fair that the consequences of the error should fall on the one who caused the problem.

On the other hand, suppose it is clear to a reasonable bystander that the first party made a mistake in expressing the terms of the contract: the price may be absurdly low or quite unrelated to the range of prices quoted by both sides during negotiations.

CASE 8.1

In *Webster v. Cecil*[3] the parties had been negotiating about the sale to Webster of land owned by Cecil. Initially Cecil had refused Webster's offer of £2000. Later Cecil wrote to Webster mistakenly offering the land for £1250. Immediately after he had mailed his letter, Cecil realized his error and sent a second letter stating that the price should have been £2250, but the second letter arrived after Webster had posted his acceptance. Webster sued to enforce the contract and failed, the court finding that he could not possibly have believed that £1250 was the intended offer price.

The court concluded that no reasonable person could have believed such an offer to have been made intentionally; the attempted acceptance is akin to fraud ("snapping up an offer") and the contract is voidable by the first party. However, it is not always easy to decide whether a party could have relied reasonably on the words used in an offer. Perhaps he should have questioned the offeror to ask whether he really meant them; on the other hand, he could have believed that the offeror simply intended to make the offer so attractive the offeree would find it hard to resist accepting. After all, there may have been a change in the offeror's circumstances.

How does the court exercise its discretion to grant relief? It considers the hardship suffered by either party should it decide against him. In *Paget v. Marshall*,[4] the court adopted an imaginative approach to deal with this dilemma.

CASE 8.2

Paget had offered to lease out the third floor of a warehouse and a large portion of the second floor as well, reserving to herself only that portion of the second floor that was above a store she retained at ground level. Paget's brother explained these conditions to Marshall who found them satisfactory. However, after the lease was drawn up and signed by both parties, Paget discovered that it included the portion of the second floor that she had wished to keep for herself. Paget sued to have the lease corrected to exclude the second floor portion over the store.

In giving judgment, Bacon, V.C., said:

I must in charity and justice to the Defendant believe [him], because I cannot impute to him the intention of taking advantage of any incorrect expression…but…it is plain and palpable that the Plaintiff was mistaken and had no intention of letting…[leasing her own premises]…the Defendant should have an opportunity of choosing whether he will submit…to have the lease rectified…or…choose to throw up the thing entirely, because the object of the Court is, as far as it can, to put the parties into the position in which they would have been if the mistake had not happened.…The Plaintiff does not object, if the agreement is annulled, to pay the Defendant any reasonable expenses to which he may have been put by reason of the Plaintiff's mistake.…[5]

---

3. (1861), 54 E.R. 812.

4. (1884), 28 Ch. D. 255.

5. *Ibid.*, at 266–7.

Perhaps not surprisingly, the defendant elected to keep the lease, as amended by the court, and to return to the plaintiff the portion over the store.[6]

Errors in Recording an Agreement

Sometimes parties may reach agreement—either orally intending later to turn it into written form, or first written informally and later to be put into a more formal contract—but the final written form does not accurately reflect the original agreement: a term may have been left out or important figures may be wrong. The party who stands to benefit from the mistake may insist that the final version represents the bargain and so resist any attempt to revert to the original terms. He may claim that the first agreement was too vague, or that it was subject to any further changes made before finally being *reduced* to writing or to a sealed instrument. Indeed, the defendant so argued, unsuccessfully, in the *Paget* case, above.

A party claiming that the arrangement was improperly recorded may ask the court for **rectification** of the contract. The request will succeed if the following conditions are met:

rectification
correction of a written document to reflect accurately the contract made by the parties

(a) The court is satisfied that there was a complete agreement between the parties, free from ambiguity and not conditional on further adjustments.

(b) The parties did not engage in further negotiations to amend the contract.

(c) The change in the written document appears to be an error in recording, and is most easily explained as such.

CASE 8.3

In *U.S.A. v. Motor Trucks, Ltd.*,[7] the Government of the United States had agreed to pay a large sum of money in compensation for cancellation of war contracts at the end of the First World War. The payments were to reimburse a Canadian manufacturing company for equipment and buildings acquired to carry out the contracts and also in settlement of all contractual obligations of the U.S. Government. In return, the manufacturer agreed to give up all claims under the contract and to transfer certain lands to the U.S. Government. Transfer of the lands was somehow left out of the final formal settlement.

The manufacturer resisted the U.S. Government claim to the land on the grounds that it had originally consented to their inclusion while labouring under an "error as to [its] own] legal rights." The Privy Council rejected the manufacturer's claim that the original settlement was not binding and accordingly ordered the final formal settlement rectified to include the lands. There was no evidence that the parties had engaged in further bargaining before the final formal settlement nor could the omission be explained except on the basis of an error.

It is not easy to establish the conditions necessary for rectification: if the terms were ambiguous in the original agreement or if the parties carried on subsequent negotiations, a court is very reluctant to alter the final agreement. In another leading case, Lord Denning said, "In order to get rectification it is necessary to show that the parties were in complete agreement upon the terms of their contract, but by an error wrote them down wrongly."[8]

---

6. It is interesting to note how the court disposed of the costs in the action. "The Plaintiff is not entitled to costs, because [s]he has made a mistake, and the Defendant ought not to have any costs, because his opposition to the Plaintiff's demand has been unreasonable...," per Bacon, V.C., *ibid.*, at 267.

7. [1924] A.C. 196. For more recent cases, see and compare R. v. Ron Engineering Construction Eastern Ltd. (1981), 119 D.L.R. (3d) 267; Belle River Community Arena Inc. v. W.J.C. Kaufman Co. Ltd. (1978), 87 D.L.R. (3d) 761.

8. Rose v. Pim, [1953] 2 All E.R. 739 at 747; Brisebois v. Chamberland et al. (1991), 77 D.L.R. (4th) 583.

Misunderstandings About the Meanings of Words

Both parties to a contract may have agreed to the words actually used—neither party put them forward inadvertently nor were any of the terms subsequently recorded incorrectly. Nevertheless, the parties may place quite different meanings on those words. In most instances, such disagreements can be treated as questions of interpretation: a court will decide which meaning is the more reasonable in light of the circumstances, including those things each party ought to have known about the subject-matter of the contract and about the intentions of the other party. In some cases it will decide that the meaning given by an offeror to her own words was the more reasonable one. If so, the offeree will be bound by the terms as understood by the offeror. In other cases the court will decide that the offeror was imprudent to use the words as she did and that the offeree interpreted them more reasonably. In that event, the offeror will be bound by the contract as the offeree understands it.

CASE 8.4

In *Lindsey v. Heron*,[9] the seller asked the buyer, "What will you give me for 75 shares of Eastern Cafeterias of Canada?" The buyer said he would make inquiries and then make an offer. Later in the day he replied, "I will give you $10.50 a share for your Eastern Cafeterias." The seller replied, "I accept your offer." The seller delivered the shares for his Eastern Cafeterias of Canada Ltd. and received a cheque in full payment. The buyer then realized that Eastern Cafeterias Ltd. and Eastern Cafeterias of Canada Ltd. were two different companies, and that he had the former company in mind when he made his offer to buy the shares. He stopped payment on his cheque. In defending against an action by the seller, the buyer claimed that his offer to buy "Eastern Cafeterias" was ambiguous, as he could have meant either company. He argued that since he and the seller were talking about different companies in ignorance of the misunderstanding between them, there was never any agreement and no contract was formed.

The court rejected this defence. It held that in the light of the unambiguous statement of the seller when he referred to Eastern Cafeterias of Canada, the offer must be construed as referring to those shares. In giving the decision of the court, Mr. Justice Middleton said:

> I think that, judged by any reasonable standard, the words used by the defendants manifested an intention to offer the named price for the thing which the plaintiff proposed to sell, i.e., stock in the Eastern Cafeterias of Canada Limited. Had the plaintiff spoken of "Eastern Cafeterias," the words used would have been ambiguous, and I should find no contract, for each might have used the ambiguous term in a different sense; but the defendants, by use of these ambiguous terms in response to the plaintiff's request couched in unambiguous language, must be taken to have used it in the same sense.[10]

In rare cases the court is faced by an insoluble set of facts: both parties have been equally reasonable (or unreasonable) in the meaning they attributed to the words, and it would be unjust to hold one party to the other's interpretation. The classic example occurred in the case of *Raffles v. Wichelhaus*.[11]

---

9. (1921), 50 O.L.R. 1.

10. *Ibid.*, at 9.

11. (1864), 159 E.R. 375. See also: Angevaare v. McKay (1960), 25 D.L.R. (2d) 521, and Staiman Steel Ltd. v. Commercial & Home Builders Ltd. (1976), 71 D.L.R. (3d) 17.

CASE 8.5

The contract was for the sale of cotton that was to arrive in England from Bombay on board the ship *Peerless*. By a remarkable coincidence two ships called *Peerless* were sailing from Bombay, one in October, the other in December. The seller believed that he contracted to sell cotton on the later ship; the buyer believed that he contracted to buy cotton on the earlier ship.

A delay of two months in the shipment of a commodity subject to market fluctuations is a major difference in terms. When the cotton arrived on the later ship the buyer refused to accept it or pay for it. The seller sued for breach of contract, and the buyer pleaded mistake in defence. The defence succeeded because the court could not decide which ship *Peerless* was meant. A reasonable person would have been unable to decide that the contract was for cotton on one ship rather than the other.

As suggested by Mr. Justice Middleton in *Lindsey v. Heron*, two parties, both equally careless, may use an ambiguous phrase, and the court will refuse to decide between the two conflicting interpretations. The practical result, then, is that the position of the defendant is the stronger: the party who tries to enforce the contract will fail. In *Falck v. Williams*,[12] a Norwegian ship owner communicated by cable with an Australian ship broker arranging contracts of carriage for the Norwegian's ships. The ship owner sent an ambiguous message in code, and each party interpreted it differently. In rejecting the ship owner's action for breach of contract, Lord MacNaghten said:

> In their Lordships' opinion, there is no conclusive reason pointing one way or the other....It was the duty of the appellant as plaintiff to make out that the construction that he put upon it was the true one. In that he must fail if the message was ambiguous, as their Lordships hold it to be. *If the respondent had been maintaining his construction as plaintiff he would equally have failed*[13] [italics added].

MISTAKES IN ASSUMPTIONS

About the Existence of the Subject-matter of a Contract

The most fundamental of mistakes that radically change the nature of the parties' bargain is a mistake about the very existence of the subject-matter. If at the time the contract was made the subject-matter, such as goods in the hold of a ship at sea, had been destroyed unknown to either party, it is hard to imagine a fair way to enforce the contract: is the buyer required to pay the price for goods that cannot be delivered? Is the seller liable for breach for non-delivery? In *Couturier v. Hastie*,[14] the parties had arranged for the sale of a cargo of corn believed to be en route from Greece to England. Unknown to them, the cargo had become overheated and was in danger of spoiling: the ship put into the port of Tunis where the corn was sold. The seller sued for the price of the cargo but failed; the contract was held to be void.

This rule, as it applies to the sale of goods, has been incorporated in the Sale of Goods Act, which provides that "where there is a contract for the sale of specific goods and the goods without the knowledge of the seller have perished at the time the contract is made, the contract is

---

12. [1900] A.C. 176.

13. *Ibid.* at 181 (italics added).

14. (1852), 155 E.R. 1250, affirmed by the House of Lords (1856), 10 E.R. 1065.

void."[15] Of course, if the seller was aware that the goods had perished, his attempt to sell them would be fraudulent and the buyer could recover damages by suing in tort for deceit.

About the Value of the Subject-matter: Allocation of Risk

Finding a solution that is fair to both parties is much more difficult when the subject-matter of a contract is still in existence but its qualities are radically different from those contemplated by the parties; one party may be paying far too much for what he will receive, or the other may be receiving far too little for parting with something that is much more valuable than he had realized. In either case one party may receive a windfall at the expense of the other. The willingness of a court to grant relief varies according to the reasonable expectations of the parties.

In some types of transactions the parties are expected to know that the subject-matter may quickly rise or fall in value. Indeed, the contract can be thought of as primarily allocating risk. Thus, *A* may be willing to pay $5 per share for 10 000 shares in a corporation she believes is about to make large profits, while *B* is content to accept $5 per share for them in the belief that the price is more likely to drop. If, unknown to either of them, the financial position of the company has already declined or risen sharply before the contract is formed, the court will not grant relief to the party adversely affected: the change of circumstance is one of the risks contemplated in the contract.

It cannot always be so easily inferred that the parties intended to accept a particular risk: the court may conclude it would be unfair to allow the bargain to stand and will grant relief.

CASE 8.6

In *Hyrsky et al. v. Smith*,[16] the plaintiffs purchased a parcel of land for future commercial development. Foolishly, they failed to have a qualified person investigate the title to the property, as is the normal practice, thus taking some risk that the land was subject to "defects," that is, to claims by other parties. More than four years later, when they prepared to develop the property, they discovered that almost half of it had not been owned by the defendant and consequently had not been transferred to them. The remainder was too small to be developed commercially. The plaintiffs sued to have the contract **set aside** or **rescinded**, the purchase price repaid, and the land returned to the defendant.

set aside or rescinded
cancelled or revoked to return the parties as nearly as possible to their original positions

rescission
an order by a court to rescind

The defendant resisted, claiming that the plaintiffs had taken the risk of not investigating title. In response, Lieff, J. said:

> If the mistake as to quantity is so substantial that in essence it changes the quality of the subject-matter, then a proper case for **rescission** may exist.

Later, he stated:

> It is true that under our present-day system of conveyancing, the purchaser has ample opportunity to inquire and to inspect before he is compelled to close the transaction....However that may be and notwithstanding the need for certainty and permanency in the law of...[transferring land], these policy considerations must yield to the desirability of doing equity where there has been...[a substantial error].[17]

---

15. R.S.N.S. 1989, c. 408, s. 9; R.S.O. 1990, c. S.1, s. 7; R.S.B.C. 1996, c. 410, s. 10.

16. (1969), 5 D.L.R. (3d) 385.

17. *Ibid.*, at 392.

Lieff, J. considered requiring the plaintiffs to accept the smaller parcel of land, but he concluded that would be outside any risk that ought to have been assumed by the plaintiffs. Denying any relief to the plaintiffs would leave them with a piece of land too small for their purposes and leave the defendant with a windfall, a much higher price than the land was actually worth. Nor would it make sense for the court to order a reduction in price proportional to the land actually transferred to the plaintiffs; they would still have land they could not use. Accordingly, the court ordered the contract set aside as requested by the plaintiffs. However, it refused to award costs, because "had the plaintiffs searched the title as a prudent purchaser should have done, all of this litigation would never have arisen."[18]

We can see that the above analysis focuses on the reasonable expectations of each of the parties and the consequent fairness of upholding the contract or setting it aside. A 1971 judgment stated:

> ...if the Court finds that there has been honest, even though inadvertent mistake, it will afford relief in any case where it considers that it would be unfair, unjust or unconscionable not to correct it....[19]

There is general approval of this broad approach, attempting to do justice and to minimize the effects of a mistake. Asking whether a party to a contract ought to bear the risk of a change in the subject-matter is the main element in deciding whether it would be unfair to deny a remedy when the change becomes known.

The Challenge of Achieving a Fair Result

Problems resulting from mistakes—situations in which one or both of the parties may have changed their position or forgone other opportunities—may be especially difficult for the courts to resolve.

CASE 8.7

In *Solle v. Butcher*,[20] a landlord had substantially renovated a building containing five flats. A surveyor, who had been the landlord's partner in the business of buying and renovating residential buildings, was himself interested in renting one of the flats. He investigated the rental status of the property and concluded that, because of the renovations, rent controls no longer applied: the flat that formerly was limited to an annual rent of £140 could now be rented for £250 at fair market value.

On that mistaken assumption the parties entered into a seven-year lease. In fact, the property was still subject to rent control, although the landlord might have obtained permission for a rent higher than £140 had he reported the reconstruction of the flat to the rent control authorities and applied for and received consent to increase the rent *before* entering into a lease. The parties had a falling out, and the tenant brought an action to recover his over-payments and for a declaration that only the £140 maximum was owed for the remainder of the lease.

Both parties had believed they were dealing with a flat exempt from rent control while the flat was actually subject to controls—a serious mistake in assumption about the subject-matter of the contract, because rent control made the £250 rent unenforceable. The court found that it would be unfair to hold the landlord to a seven-year lease at a low, uneconomical rent of £140, but also unfair to the tenant to declare the lease void and force him to vacate the flat. Instead, the court gave the tenant a choice: either he could vacate the flat and bring the contract to an end, or he could stay—but then the court would temporarily suspend the lease, enabling the landlord to make an application to the rent control authority to charge the full rent the authority would permit for the remainder of the lease, subject to a maximum of £250 as originally agreed.

18. *Ibid.*, at 393.

19. McMaster University v. Wilchar Construction, [1971] 3 O.R. 801, per Thompson, J., at 810.

20. [1950] 1 K.B. 671.

In Case 8.7, the technicalities involved in avoiding the prohibitions of the rent controls tested the ingenuity of the court in constructing a just solution and it required a particularly imaginative judge in the person of Denning, L.J. A court's willingness to grant relief will be influenced by its ability to fashion a result that seems reasonably fair to both parties. If it cannot see its way clear to a solution, it may simply refuse a remedy and leave the loss to lie where it has fallen.

Unforeseen Future Events

A party to a contract may fail to foresee a crucial change in conditions under which it is to perform. Performance may become physically or legally impossible—as when new government regulations prohibit delivery of a pharmaceutical product to a pharmacy, or performance may have become pointless—as in paying for a seat reserved to watch a play that is cancelled. From the time the contract is formed until the unforeseen event occurs, there exists a valid, binding contract between the parties. However, a court may find that the event frustrated the basic purpose of the contract and declare both parties to be discharged from the moment the event occurred. We shall defer our discussion of discharge by frustration until we deal with discharge of contracts generally, in Chapter 13. We should note, however, that frustrating events differ from mistakes in assumption: mistakes concern the actual state of affairs at the time a contract is formed, while a frustrating event is one that takes place *after* formation and could not be known to either party.

CONTEMPORARY ISSUE

Gas Company's Offer Was a Big Mistake

Direct Energy Marketing Ltd., a large natural gas marketer, bought Alliance Gas Management Ltd. in 1999. To induce Alliance customers to accept new five-year contracts, Direct Energy mailed cheques for $50 to more than 160 000 households. A letter suggested the cheque would provide savings of more than 10 percent for the first year. However, many customers had several years to run on contracts at much lower rates than Direct Energy's 16.99 cents a cubic metre. Cashing the cheque and accepting the offer would cost them money in the long run. Information about the rate and length of existing contracts was on the back of the letter.

According to a newspaper report, some 25 000 people cashed the cheques. Some of them might have been on variable-rate contracts and could have benefited from locking in a fixed rate in a market where natural gas prices had been rising. Others, however, possibly traded in a cheaper contract for a $50 cheque. When the media approached the company, it offered to cancel the five-year contracts for customers who felt they had been misled. Anyone who returned the $50 would be put back to the price they had been paying.

Source: James Daw, "Gas Marketer Will Cancel Contracts," *Toronto Star*, October 28, 1999.

continued

Questions to Consider

1. Is this an example of the legal doctrine of mistake? on the part of the company? on the part of customers who gave up cheap gas contracts? What other arguments might an unhappy customer use to cancel the contract?

2. How could the company have made its five-year contracts attractive while avoiding the appearance of "pulling a fast one"?

MISTAKE AND INNOCENT THIRD PARTIES

How the Problem Arises

Suppose a party to a contract is a rogue who deceives a rather gullible—or at least imprudent—second party; the rogue gains possession of goods or obtains a valuable signed document. Whether the mistake is about assumptions (as where the victim is misled about the identity of the rogue) or about the terms (as where the victim is misled about the terms of a document he signs) does not matter: the rogue has lied and a court would willingly grant the victim relief; the victim would be able to recover the goods or the document. Unfortunately, this would happen only if the victim regained his senses quickly enough to pursue his remedies against the rogue. Usually the rogue profits quickly from his deception and absconds. The contest that remains is between the victim and an innocent third party who has paid the rogue and in return received the goods or document that the rogue extracted from the victim.

Void and Voidable Contracts

Consequences of a Void Contract

To understand the law in this area we must consider the difference between *void* and *voidable* contracts. This distinction was first discussed with regard to infants' contracts, and is important generally in the law of contracts. As we noted, to decide that a contract is **void** is to say that in law it was never formed at all: in this sense calling an agreement a void contract is a contradiction in terms—if it is void it is no contract. Nevertheless, through custom and convenience the term has long been used to describe agreements void from the beginning.

void
never formed in law

The results flowing from a declaration that a contract is void are logical enough and usually fair when only the two original parties are concerned: if *A* sells goods to *B* and the sale is declared void, it follows that ownership never passed from *A* to *B*; if *B* still has the goods, *A* recovers them and repays any part of the purchase price already received.

However, the consequences are more far-reaching if *B* has already resold the goods (which in law he does not own) to *C*, an innocent third party. The second sale is equally void because under common law *B* had no right to the goods. Consequently, the third party, *C*, does not acquire ownership although he has paid fair value for the goods and was unaware of the void sale between *A* and *B*. *C* must restore the goods to *A* and if he cannot, he will be liable to *A* (in the tort of conversion) for damages equal to their value.

The common law recognizes no half measures: either the contract is void or it is not—and if the court decides it is not void, then despite *B*'s deceit, he has acquired title (ownership) to the goods and can transfer title to a third party. *A* will have no rights against the innocent third party; any claim for damages would be against *B*, who has vanished. Unless the third party, *C*, participated in the fraud, the common law rules ignore the relative fault of *A* in carelessly selling on credit to a rogue, and of the third party in risking to buy from that rogue. On the whole, declarations that a contract is void—with the harsh consequences that follow—are more unfair to third persons than to sellers of goods: those who take the risk of selling goods on credit make it easier for rogues in possession of the goods to dupe innocent third persons.

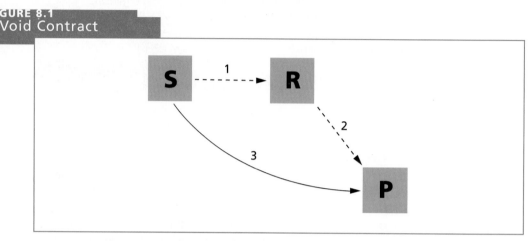

FIGURE 8.1
Void Contract

1. *S* "sells" goods to a rogue, *R*. *R* does not gain title.
2. *R* purports to sell the goods to *P*, the innocent purchaser. *P* does not gain title.
3. *S* may sue and recover the goods from *P*.

Consequences of a Voidable Contract

The principles of equity are more flexible: between the original parties to a contract, equity will often declare a contract to be **voidable** and will order that it be set aside or rescinded, restoring the property to the seller and requiring him to return any benefit he might have received from the rogue (such as a down payment). Thus, while equity recognizes that at common law title has passed to the rogue, it will order him to restore both title and possession to the victim.

voidable
a contract that a court may set aside in an attempt to restore the parties to their original positions

ILLUSTRATION 8.3

A Co., the sole distributor of a certain brand of imported office machines, has received an advance sample of a revolutionary new copier. *B* persuades *A* Co. to sell and deliver the machine to her on the basis that she will test it and if it proves satisfactory will be prepared to buy at least 1000 units for her distribution chain. In fact, *B* has lied: she has no such distribution chain and intends to resell the machine to the highest bidder among several clients who may be interested in dismantling it and copying the innovations as quickly as possible. Fortunately, the next day one of the firms to whom *B* has offered the machine informs *A* Co. about *B*'s scheme. *A* Co. serves *B* with a statement of claim at once, demanding that the contract be set aside for deceit and the machine returned, on repayment of the purchase price by *A*. The court, in exercising its equitable powers, would grant *A* Co. its remedies.

However, equity recognizes that new issues of fairness enter the picture as soon as the rights of an innocent third party are affected. Equity will not deprive an innocent purchaser of goods obtained from the rogue. The seller duped by the rogue is limited to an action for damages against the rogue for the unpaid price of the goods or for the tort of deceit. Unfortunately, the rogue is usually penniless or has absconded and cannot be found. Between the seller and the innocent purchaser, equity does not choose; it lets the loss lie where it had fallen—invariably on the duped seller who has parted with his property on the strength of the rogue's representations.

It is important to note that a third-party purchaser, to receive this protection, must be *innocent* and have paid *value* for the goods. A seller's attempt to recover goods will not be frustrated by someone who buys from the rogue knowing about the rogue's fraud; equity considers such a person as having no greater rights than the rogue himself. Thus, in Illustration 8.3, above, if *B* resold and delivered the copier to one of her "clients," who intended to dismantle the machine and was aware of *B*'s deception, *A* Co. could recover it from that client. If, however, the purchaser innocently bought the machine for its own use, *A* would have no claim against it. But innocence alone is not enough; the third party must have paid a price for the item. Equity will not permit a party who has received the machine as a gift, even without knowledge of the fraud, to retain it against *A* Co.

In summary, we can see that where a contract concerns only the two original parties, it may not matter whether the court declares it void or merely voidable. In either event, the court may order the return of property that has passed between the parties. But if the property has passed to an innocent purchaser, the original owner may recover it only if the original contract is declared void.

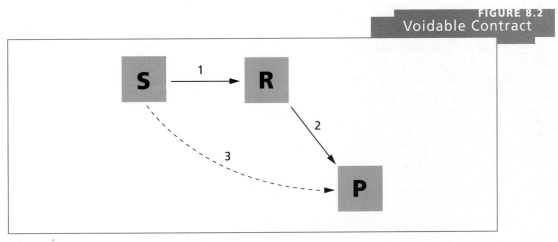

FIGURE 8.2
Voidable Contract

1. *S* "sells" goods to a rogue, *R*. *R*, despite his deceit, obtains title.
2. *R* purports to sell the goods to *P*, the innocent purchaser. *P* obtains title to the goods.
3. *S* cannot recover the goods from *P*.

Mistake About the Identity of a Party to a Contract

The dire consequences of a court finding a contract void are well illustrated by the classic English case of *Cundy v. Lindsay*.[21]

CASE 8.8

Lindsay, a manufacturer in Ireland, was persuaded to send goods on credit to a thief, Alfred Blenkarn. Blenkarn had signed an order for goods with an indistinct signature that appeared to be "Blenkiron & Co.," a reputable firm with offices on the same street but at a different number from that of Blenkarn. Lindsay did not check the street number but simply shipped the goods to Blenkarn, who then sold the goods to Cundy for cash and absconded. Cundy was unaware of the fraud. Lindsay learned the true facts when he attempted to collect payment from Blenkiron & Co.; he then sued Cundy for the goods, claiming that the sale to Blenkarn was void.

The House of Lords accepted this argument. It held that as Lindsay intended to sell to "Blenkiron & Co." and only to them, Blenkarn obtained the goods entirely without Lindsay's consent. The court decided that a mistake by the duped seller about the identity of the other party rendered the contract void. Since there was no contract between Lindsay and Blenkarn, ownership of the goods remained with Lindsay: Cundy was required to return them or pay damages.

21. (1878), 3 App. Cas. 459.

The decision in *Cundy v. Lindsay* offends the general principle that between two innocent parties, both victims of a fraud, the loss should be borne by the more careless of the two. Lindsay had shipped goods on credit without a careful check of the street address of Blenkiron & Co.; as a result of Lindsay's carelessness, Blenkarn gained possession of the goods. But Cundy was blameless. Between the two we should have expected that Lindsay would bear the loss; yet the decision that the contract was void led to a hardship upon Cundy. It is not surprising that the courts attempted to limit the application of this case.

The year after *Cundy*, in *King's Norton Metal Co. v. Edridge*,[22] a thief once again obtained goods on credit, working more cleverly than had Blenkarn.

CASE 8.9

Using an impressive letterhead with the picture of a large factory and the name of a non-existent firm—Hallam & Co.—Wallis sent an order for goods to the plaintiffs, a firm of metal manufacturers. The plaintiffs sent Wallis the goods; he resold them and absconded. The plaintiffs, claiming that their contract with Hallam & Co. was void, sought to recover the goods from the innocent purchaser.

The action failed. The court held that they must have intended to contract with *someone*, and since there was no "Hallam & Co.," it could only be with the writer of the letter, even though he was a very different person from the party they had in mind. Accordingly, although the contract was voidable for fraud, title to the goods had passed to Wallis! The plaintiff could recover the goods from Wallis so long as he still had them, but meanwhile Wallis could pass title to an innocent purchaser.

The decision is technically distinguishable from *Cundy v. Lindsay* because in the *King's Norton* case there was only one party with whom the vendor might have contracted (Wallis, alias Hallam & Co.) and not two separate entities as in *Cundy v. Lindsay* (Blenkarn, and Blenkiron & Co.). Though an innocent purchaser may be excused for failing to see the significance of this distinction, the *King's Norton* case has the virtue of limiting the application of *Cundy v. Lindsay* to fewer situations.

In both cases, the parties dealt by mail at a distance. The same difficulty about identity can occur when the innocent party and the rogue confront each other in person.

CASE 8.10

In 1918, in *Phillips v. Brooks*[23] the English Court of Appeal held that the plaintiff jeweller intended to sell pearls to the man who appeared in his shop, even though the man falsely identified himself as a reputable and wealthy member of the community—whom the jeweller knew by name, but not in person. The contract was voidable and not void.

Consequently, an innocent purchaser from the rogue was protected and able to keep the pearls, despite the jeweller's claim that he intended to deal only with the reputable named person and not the rogue who had appeared in his shop.

22. (1879), 14 T.L.R. 98.
23. [1918–19] All E.R. 246.

The Court reaffirmed this reasoning in *Lewis v. Averay*,[24] where a rogue had obtained a car by paying for it with a bogus cheque while impersonating a well-known English movie actor. It held that since the contract was merely voidable, an innocent purchaser who acquired the car from the rogue was protected.

Canadian courts have followed the English cases. The Supreme Court of Canada held that a car-rental company had "consented" to the rental of a car to a rogue who gave a false identity.[25] Subsequent purchasers are probably better protected when the first transaction takes place face to face than when the transaction takes place by post.

Mistake About the Nature of a Signed Document

Non Est Factum

By signing a document that has been misrepresented to him either innocently or fraudulently, a person may induce an innocent third party to rely on the document. The person who signed may raise the plea known as ***non est factum*** ("it is not my doing"). If the court accepts the plea, it is good even against the third party who believes she has acquired rights under the document. In this respect the effect of a successful plea of *non est factum* is similar to the result in *Cundy v. Lindsay*: an innocent third party may suffer.

non est factum
"it is not my doing"

The plea originated in medieval times when most people could not read or write. A person would bind himself to a written document by making a mark or impressing his family seal, but he had to rely on the honesty of the literate party who presented the document to him. If he were later sued for breach of the terms of the document, he could plead that it was not his deed, because of a serious misrepresentation. In medieval times the result was reasonable. It would still be reasonable today if its application were limited to illiterate and blind persons and those who read and write only in a foreign language—persons who must rely on the honesty of others.

Unfortunately, the plea of *non est factum* was later extended to literate persons who were simply duped into signing documents without reading them. As harsh as the result is from the point of view of innocent third parties who rely on the document without knowledge of the misrepresentation, the signer could nonetheless escape liability. For more than 100 years there was great uncertainty about the rules governing a signer's liability for a mistakenly signed document.

In 1971, in *Saunders v. Anglia Building Society*[26] the House of Lords declared that a careless signer could not avoid liability by pleading *non est factum*. Despite the fact that the plaintiff was a 78-year-old widow who had just broken her glasses, the court found her careless in signing a deed she had been unable to read, and thus she was bound by subsequent dealings in the property transferred in the document. In 1982, in *Marvco Color Research Ltd. v. Harris*[27] the Supreme Court of Canada followed the House of Lords decision in the *Saunders* case. Mr. Justice Estey said:

> This principle of law is based not only upon the principle of placing loss on the person guilty of carelessness, but also upon recognition of the need for certainty and security in commerce [of those persons who rely on signed documents]...the application of the principle...must depend on the circumstances of each case....The magnitude and extent of the carelessness, the circumstances which may have contributed to such carelessness, and all other circumstances must be taken into account...before a court may determine whether estoppel shall arise...so as to prevent the raising of this defence.[28]

---

24. [1971] 3 All E.R. 907.

25. Terry v. Vancouver Motors U-Drive Ltd. and Walter, [1942] 1 W.W.R. 503.

26. [1971] A.C. 1004.

27. [1982] 2 S.C.R. 744.

28. *Ibid.*, at 789–97. See also, Royal Bank of Canada v. Hussain (1997), 37 O.R. (3d) 85.

A person who relies on a document that he did not personally see signed still takes some risk: the signer might be blind, illiterate, or at least unable to read English—or perhaps rarely, might be literate but found by a court not to have been careless.

MISTAKES IN PERFORMANCE

What happens when a party "overperforms" an existing obligation by paying more money than is owed? when it performs in a mistaken belief that an obligation existed, as when an insurance company pays a claim and then discovers that the loss arose from a risk not covered by the policy? when someone simply pays the wrong person?

When the "lucky" recipient knows that the payment does not belong to him, the answer is straightforward: he cannot "snap up" a benefit that belongs to another person—a court will order him to restore it. The question becomes more difficult when the recipient honestly but mistakenly believes that he is entitled to the benefit. A gradually expanding development in this area of **quasi-contract** (so called because the obligations may not arise as a direct result of contractual relations between the parties) has been the concepts of **unjust enrichment** and **restitution**: if, in all the circumstances a court finds that it would be an unjust enrichment to allow the recipient to keep the benefit, it will order restitution by finding a duty implied by law to repay it.

We must be careful not to oversimplify the law in this area by substituting a lay person's intuition about what is "unjust" when a sophisticated analysis of the commercial context is needed. For instance, as we have seen in Chapter 6, if a party accepts a benefit in an honest and not unreasonable belief that it is tendered in settlement of an outstanding dispute, she will not be regarded as having been unjustly enriched even when it later appears that she could not have enforced her claim by court action.

quasi-contract
an obligation that may arise, not as a result of contractual relations, but because one party has received an unfair benefit at the expense of the other

unjust enrichment
an unfair benefit

restitution
repayment or recovery of a loss

QUESTIONS FOR REVIEW

1. Why is the use of mistake to avoid legal obligations strictly limited by the courts?

2. When may a party be granted a remedy for mistakenly using a term in a contract?

3. When parties use a term but intend it to have quite different meanings, how does the court resolve the difference?

4. Describe the nature of risk allocation when the parties make different assumptions. How do the courts deal with the problem? What may a court do when it cannot find a satisfactory solution?

5. What conditions must be satisfied before a court will order rectification? Under what circumstances is a court unlikely to grant such a remedy?

6. Describe the difference between void and voidable contracts. What are the consequences of each for innocent third parties?

7. Jameson appears at Klemper's Jewellery and asks to buy an expensive watch on credit. She identifies herself as Johnson, a wealthy local financier. Klemper agrees and hands over possession of the watch to Jameson. Jameson immediately pawns it at Larry's. Klemper sees the watch in Larry's window the next day. Explain whether he may reclaim it as his own without paying Larry. Are there any further facts that might influence your opinion?

8. Morgan, who is blind, is asked by his cousin Nolan to sign a document indicating that he supports Nolan's nomination as a member of Beaver Club. In fact, the document is a

promise to guarantee a large loan Norris has made from his bank. Is Morgan bound by his guarantee? Describe the nature of the problem.

CASES AND PROBLEMS

1 Brown was the owner of a service station located on a two-lane highway. She learned that a new, four-lane freeway would bypass her service station, and she then put the station up for sale. Seferis purchased the property from Brown for $125 000 and two months later learned that the highway on which it was located would be superseded by the new freeway, to be constructed within the next four years. Seferis then commenced action to have the contract set aside. Should he succeed?

2 Boucher, acting as an agent for an undisclosed principal, secured an option on a farm belonging to Wright. By the terms of the option agreement Wright undertook in return for a payment of $2000 to hold open for six months an offer to sell the farm for $60 000 and not to dispose of it in the meantime.

After Boucher had obtained this and similar options on adjoining property, he disclosed that he was acting for Canada Steel Car Co. Ltd., which would build a large plant in the district. As the company was an important one, the value of the property in the area was generally enhanced. When Canada Steel Car Co. Ltd. tried to exercise its option, Wright refused to convey her property according to the agreed terms. Canada Steel Car Co. Ltd. then brought an action against her for specific performance. In defending the action, Wright claimed that Boucher's failure to disclose the name of the purchaser induced her to sell at too low a price. Discuss the merits of this defence.

3 Quintin's house contained urea formaldehyde foam insulation (UFFI), which was widely criticized as being harmful to health. He had readings taken in the house by the city health department and obtained a certificate showing there was no dangerous level of gas being emitted. Nevertheless, Quintin had the UFFI removed and replaced by an acceptable material, after which there was no trace of toxic gases. He then listed his house for sale and gave his real estate agent instructions not to give any warranty about insulation except to state that no UFFI was present.

After visiting the house Rau decided to make an offer to purchase it. Because he was very concerned to buy only a house that had had no contact with UFFI, his agent prepared an interim agreement containing a warranty that the house did not contain and never had contained the substance. When the agreement was sent to Quintin he changed the wording to state only that the house did not contain UFFI. Rau, unaware of the amendment, signed the agreement.

After further negotiations about the price, both parties signed a second and final agreement. Quintin's agent was upset; she believed Rau was unaware of the change and she wanted to tell Rau that there had once been UFFI in the house—but Quintin said no. Nevertheless the agent informed Rau, who immediately repudiated the transaction and refused to pay his deposit of $20 000.

Quintin sued Rau, who claimed that that his mistake about the changed warranty was a valid defence. Outline the arguments for each of the parties and give your opinion whether the action should succeed.

4 H. Golightly is a professional football player who has played for the Toronto Mercenaries ("Mercs") for the past three football seasons. The Toronto Mercs are a member of the Eastern Conference of the Trans-Canada Football League. Golightly lives in the southern United States during the off-season.

Golightly had an exceptionally good season last year and was in a good bargaining position for negotiating his salary for this season when he met with Rusty Trawler, the general manager of the Mercs last January. The parties discussed salary possibilities for the next two seasons in a tentative way but adjourned their meeting, expecting to come to final terms in early April.

In February, the Trans-Canada Football League had its annual meeting in Vancouver. At that meeting it was decided to increase the number of regular games scheduled to be played in the Eastern Conference from the usual 14 over many previous seasons to 16, commencing with the current season. By contrast, the Western Conference already had a schedule of 16 games for several seasons; this decision brought the Eastern Conference in line with the Western Conference. It received wide publicity in the news media of the various cities with teams in the Eastern Conference.

Last April 3, Golightly telephoned Trawler from Biloxi, Mississippi, and they agreed to meet on April 6 in the offices of O.J. Berman, Q.C., Golightly's solicitor in Toronto. The meeting between Golightly, Trawler, and Berman lasted about three hours. Eventually it was agreed that Golightly should be paid $150 000 for the current season and $225 000 for the following year, plus further amounts for playoffs and bonuses; two separate contracts were signed to cover the two seasons. At the time, neither Golightly nor his lawyer, Berman, had any knowledge that the number of league games in the Eastern Football Conference had been increased from 14 to 16. In fact, the parties did not refer in any way to the number of games in their meeting in Berman's office. Trawler made no mention of the increased schedule. The contracts simply stated,

> The Player agrees that during the term of this contract he will play football and will engage in activities related to football only for the Club and will play for the Club in all its Conference's scheduled and playoff games....

The contract also contained a clause to the effect that the player could be traded to a team in the Western Conference.

It was not until later, when Golightly reported for training, that he learned about the increase in the schedule. He then claimed that he would not have agreed to the salaries of $150 000 and $225 000 respectively had he known about this change; he would have bargained for more. On Berman's advice, he brought an action to have these contracts set aside with a view to their renegotiation.

Express an opinion, with reasons, about whether this action should succeed.

5 The U.S. office-supplies chain Management Depot Inc. planned to establish its main distribution centre for western Canada just outside Calgary. Its property manager at its head office in Chicago, Robert Reiger, entered into preliminary negotiations with Jane Kaleski in Calgary to buy a portion of her farm nearest Highway #77. In discussions between them by telephone, Reiger generally referred to the area of land in acres, the term used in the United States, rather than in hectares (2.2 acres) the term used in Canada. Reiger orally offered Kaleski $10 000 per acre for 45 acres, but Kaleski had insisted on a selling price of $16 000 per acre.

After several weeks of silence, Kaleski became anxious to reach agreement; she needed the cash to finance a new business venture and decided to split the difference. She dictated the price in acres to her secretary—who assumed that her boss meant hectares rather than acres. The secretary prepared a fax to Reiger offering to sell Management Depot, "The 45 hectares of my farm nearest to Highway #77 at $13 000 per hectare." Kaleski did not notice the change to hectares and signed the offer, which was then faxed to Reiger. An hour later, she glanced at the fax on her desk and noticed the error; she immediately phoned Reiger to withdraw the offer. Reiger said it was too late—he had already faxed his acceptance and, indeed, Kaleski found the acceptance in her outer office. She refused to close the deal on the basis of the price "per hectare." Management Depot Inc. sued her for breach of contract. Should it succeed?

6. Last year the Department of Public Works of the City of Saint John called for tenders for the construction of a water and sewage treatment plant according to detailed specifications. The Department issued as part of its required conditions for the submission of tenders a statement entitled "Information for Tenderers," one part of which read:

Tender Deposit

1. A deposit of $150 000 in the form of a certified cheque payable to the Department of Public Works, Saint John, must accompany each tender submitted.
2. Tenders must be submitted on or before 3:00 p.m., July 4, 2000.
3. Tender deposits will be returned to all tenderers other than the successful tenderer immediately following the selection of the successful tender.
4. A tenderer may withdraw or qualify its tender at any time up to the official closing time by submitting to the Department a letter bearing the appropriate signature and seal, as in its tender. The Secretary of the Department will mark thereon the time and date of receipt and will place the letter in the tender box. No telegrams or telephone calls will be considered.
5. The tenderer guarantees that if, following submission of its tender before the Department opens and considers all the tenders submitted, or before it has been notified that its tender has been recommended for acceptance, it withdraws its tender, the Department may retain the tender deposit for its use, and in compensation for the consequential necessity of having to invite and consider other tenders.
6. The tender deposit of the successful tenderer will be returned after the successful tenderer delivers to the Department a performance bond and accepts an offer by the Department to perform the work tendered for, on the terms set out in the tender.

In all, eight tenders with accompanying deposits were delivered to the Department of Public Works before the deadline on July 4. One of the tenders was submitted by Roberts Construction Co. It stated that the company was prepared to undertake the construction of the water and sewage treatment plant, as specified by the Department, for a price of $2 750 000.

Hudson, an employee of Roberts Construction Co., delivered the company's tender to the Department in person on the morning of July 4, and remained for the opening of the tenders at 3:00 p.m. At that time she learned that her employer's tender was the lowest of the bids; in fact, the next lowest was for $3 400 000. From her prior experience, she felt that there must be something radically wrong and at 3:30 p.m. she phoned the general manager of Roberts Construction to report what had happened. On checking his copy of the tender he replied, "We're too low. I see now that we forgot to include two big items of overhead." At 4:10 p.m. on the same day, the general manager dispatched a telex addressed to the Department of Public Works that read:

Today we submitted our tender for the water and sewage treatment plant project and unfortunately, due to the rush of compiling our figures, we neglected to include in our price an amount of $750 000 for indirect labour and depreciation of equipment. Our lump sum tender should therefore be for $3 500 000 instead of for $2 750 000. Due to this unfortunate error we would appreciate being given the opportunity to show to you our estimate indicating the error, and request that we be permitted to withdraw our tender without penalty.

The Department of Public Works insisted that the Roberts Construction Co. had submitted the successful tender and sent the company a formal offer to engage it for the project at a price of $2 750 000. Roberts Construction refused to accept the offer. The Department then refused to return the deposit of $150 000 and Roberts Construction brought an action against it for a judgment ordering the return of the deposit.

Discuss with reasons the probability that this action will succeed.

9 GROUNDS UPON WHICH A CONTRACT MAY BE IMPEACHED

Misrepresentation, Undue Influence, and Duress

Misrepresentation and Torts

Misrepresentation and Contracts

Consequences of
    Misrepresentation in Contracts

Opinion Versus Fact

Signed Documents and
    Misrepresentation by Omission

Contracts Requiring Disclosure

Undue Influence

Duress

Misrepresentations may be made quite apart from a contractual relation, but in this chapter, we are primarily concerned with the consequences of a misrepresentation made by one party to a contract to the other party. In this chapter we shall examine such questions as:

■ why is it important to determine whether a misrepresentation is material?

■ what is the difference between "opinion" and "fact"?

■ what are the implications of signing a document purporting to contain all the terms of a contract when one party claims that one or more important terms have been unintentionally omitted?

■ when should the requirement of utmost good faith be applied?

■ what remedy is available to the innocent party when the other party is found to have exerted undue influence or duress?

MISREPRESENTATION AND TORTS

As we have noted in Chapters 3 and 4, a misrepresentation may amount to a tort when it is made fraudulently[1] or negligently.[2] A victim who relies reasonably on such an assertion and suffers loss may recover from the wrongdoer. However, when a person makes an assertion neither fraudulently nor negligently but nevertheless it proves to be false, no tort has been committed and one who suffers a loss in relying on the statement has no claim in tort against its maker.

ILLUSTRATION 9.1

Andrews asks Barton, a stockbroker acquaintance, whether *X* Corporation is in sound financial condition, and Barton replies that she believes it to be very sound. Andrews then buys $25 000 worth of the shares in *X* Corporation. Unknown to either Andrews or Barton, the company's president had just been charged with embezzling $2 000 000 and the company was insolvent at the time of Barton's assertion. Andrews' newly acquired shares are worthless and he has lost $25 000, but unless Barton should have known of *X* Corporation's difficulties, Andrews will have no claim against her.

A person who innocently makes a misstatement and later learns that it is false is under a duty to inform the other party of the true situation as soon as she can. An innocent misrepresentation becomes fraudulent or negligent if the party responsible fails to correct it when in a position to do so.

MISREPRESENTATION AND CONTRACTS

Misrepresentation most often occurs during preliminary bargaining that precedes formation of a contract. If a misrepresentation is **material**, that is, if it is a statement that could reasonably be expected to influence the decision of a party hearing (or reading) it in favour of entering into a contract, a court may set the contract aside at the request of the innocent party. If the maker of the misrepresentation also acted fraudulently or negligently, the court will grant damages against the wrongdoer as well as order rescission. However, if he made the misrepresentation innocently and without negligence, no damages will be awarded; the aggrieved party's remedy is restricted to the right to rescind.

material
could reasonably be expected to influence the decision of a party to enter into a contract

As we shall see in Chapter 15,[3] the right to rescind is limited by the rules of equity. In particular, if an aggrieved party cannot restore the subject-matter of the contract to the other party—for instance, because the goods have been resold, consumed, or even have substantially deteriorated—the aggrieved party loses the right to rescind. Hence a party who has received less than fair value because of an innocent misrepresentation may be left without any remedy.

An aggrieved party may claim that a misrepresentation became a term of the subsequent contract, and if the court agrees, the party is entitled to a remedy based on breach of contract. At one time, the courts distinguished sharply between pre-contract representations and express terms of a contract.[4] However, in recent years, they have been more willing to consider representations as having been incorporated into a contract and thus part of the contractual obligation of the maker of the statement. If the statement was an important inducement to enter into the contract, if the aggrieved party has suffered a substantial loss—and if there would otherwise

---

1. See section in Chapter 3 on "Deceit."
2. See section in Chapter 4 on "Misrepresentation."
3. Under "Equitable Remedies." Also: Waddams, *The Law of Contracts* (4th ed.), pp. 444–54.
4. For example: Heilbut, Symons & Co. v. Buckleton, [1913] A.C. 30.

be no remedy for an innocent misrepresentation because rescission is unavailable in the circumstances—a court may find that the statement had indeed become a term. If the misrepresentation was made shortly before or at the time of entering into the agreement, it is easier for a court to conclude that it has become a term.[5] So too, courts have occasionally found statements about goods and services in advertisements and sales promotion material, read by a prospective buyer before making a contract, to be incorporated in the contract.[6]

Remedies for breach of contract are separate from, and frequently more extensive than, rescission for misrepresentation.[7] A general rule is that a plaintiff will not be granted a remedy he does not claim. If he sues for damages for fraudulent or negligent misrepresentation but does not also ask for rescission of the contract, he can obtain only damages; if he fails to prove the fraud or negligence, he receives nothing. Since it can be difficult to predict whether a court will find one set of remedies or the other to be appropriate (occasionally it may find both available and give the aggrieved party a choice), a party may seek each remedy in the alternative with the choice left to the court.

CONSEQUENCES OF MISREPRESENTATION IN CONTRACTS

indemnity or compensation

a money award given as a supplement to rescission for loss sustained in performing a contract

When a party who has relied upon an innocent misrepresentation learns the true facts, she must renounce the agreement promptly; if she allows an unreasonable length of time to elapse without repudiating or she takes further benefits under the contract, she will lose her right to rescind. If she has sustained out-of-pocket expenses in the performance of the contract or has paid money to the other party before becoming aware of her right to rescind, she may be entitled to a money award known as an **indemnity** or **compensation** as a supplement to rescission.[8] Such loss must arise directly out of the performance of the contract—the indemnity does not cover nearly as wide a variety of loss as does an award of damages.

CASE 9.1

Appell hired a sales agent to arrange a sale of his business. The agent gave Corbeil, a prospective purchaser, an estimate of the daily gross receipts of the business. When Corbeil asked if there were any records showing the daily turnover, the agent replied that Appell did not have any, but that the former owners of the business did. On meeting with Corbeil, the former owners were unable to produce the records but they confirmed in a general way the information given by the sales agent. Corbeil then purchased the business, delivering his car to Appell at the agreed value of $1000 as a down payment, and began operating the business as of February 2, 1949. When he discovered that its revenue did not approach the amount indicated, he repudiated the purchase by letter dated February 8, 1949. He then sued for recovery of his car and damages for loss of its use, alleging fraud.[9]

5. Dick Bentley Productions Ltd. v. Harold Smith Motors Ltd., [1965] 2 All E.R. 65. See also: Esso Petroleum Co. Ltd. v. Mardon, [1976] 2 All E.R. 5 (C.A.).

6. Goldthorpe v. Logan, [1943] 2 D.L.R. 519; Murray v. Sperry Rand Corp. (1979), 96 D.L.R. (3d) 113.

7. See Chapter 15, sections on "Implications of Breach" and "Damages."

8. Whittington v. Seale-Hayne (1900), 82 L.T. 49.

9. Corbeil v. Appell, [1950] 1 D.L.R. 159. When the court finds that the misrepresentation is not sufficiently serious, it may refuse rescission and limit the innocent party's remedy to damages. See Field v. Zien, [1963] S.C.R. 632; Taggart v. Brancato Construction Ltd. (1998), 16 R.P.R. (3d) 22.

The court held that fraud was not proved by the circumstances but that the contract might still be rescinded for innocent misrepresentation. The purpose of rescission is to restore the parties as nearly as possible to their position before they entered into the contract. Hence Corbeil was entitled to the return of his car and also to *compensation* for depreciation in its value.

In contracts for the sale of land, the right to rescission for innocent misrepresentation is generally lost once title to the property is transferred and the transaction is completed. There are two main reasons for this rule. First, purchasers are expected to "search the title," and to satisfy themselves by inspection of the property that it is as represented in the contract; if they are not satisfied they are expected to exercise a right to rescind *before* the time for completion of the transaction. Second, there is the danger that an outstanding right to rescission would not be apparent to a third party who investigated the ownership of the land and relied on the registered title, for example, to extend credit on the security of the mortgage. When a misrepresentation is not fraudulent, only rarely will a court grant rescission after completion.[10]

OPINION VERSUS FACT

A false assertion is a misrepresentation only if it is made as a statement of fact. Most statements of opinion do not amount to misrepresentation and give no remedy for those who rely on them. The law is lenient towards sellers who rhapsodize about their wares: a bookseller's claim that "this is the best textbook in its field" would leave a disillusioned purchaser without any remedy.

We can see the distinction between an expression of opinion and one of fact by contrasting two statements. If *A* says to *B*, "That property is worth at least $50 000 today," her remarks are just an expression of opinion. But if she says instead, "That property cost me $50 000," she has made a representation of fact.

Unfortunately, it is not always so easy to distinguish between statements of fact and opinion. Suppose a merchant wishing to sell some foreign goods says, "In my opinion these goods can be imported under the lower tariff rate in section ___ of the statute." The buyer later finds that they cannot be imported under that section. The court might hold that the seller merely gave his opinion, but if the court finds that the merchant is an *expert* in marketing these goods, or has purported to be one, it may conclude that he made a misrepresentation. In this context an **expert opinion** is equivalent to a statement of fact.

We normally expect an assertion of fact to be a representation in words, whether oral or written. However, conduct not expressed in words may also constitute an assertion of fact. If a prospective buyer asks to see goods of a certain specification and in response a seller shows him some goods without commenting on them, the seller's conduct alone may be an assertion of fact that the goods meet the buyer's specifications.

expert opinion
an opinion given by a person who purports to have specialized knowledge of a subject

SIGNED DOCUMENTS AND MISREPRESENTATION BY OMISSION

We noted in Chapter 5 that the act of signing a document creates a presumption that the signer accepts all its terms. That presumption may be rebutted when a party (often a consumer) is expected to sign a document hurriedly and without an opportunity to read or understand it and when the other party has good reason to suspect that the signer may not fully comprehend the implications of signing the document. In the words of Professor Waddams (quoted with approval in a 1978 decision of the Ontario Court of Appeal):

---

10. For an exception, see Northern & Central Gas Corp. Ltd. v. Hillcrest Collieries Ltd. (1975), 59 D.L.R. (3d) 533. See also Hyrsky et al. v. Smith (1969), 5 D.L.R. (3d) 385, discussed in Chapter 8 under "Mistakes in Assumptions" at pp. 176–7.

These cases suggest that there is a special onus on the supplier to point out any terms in a printed form that differ from what the consumer might reasonably expect. If he fails to do so, he will be guilty of a 'misrepresentation by omission', and the court will strike down clauses which 'differ from the ordinary understanding of mankind' or (and sometimes this is the same thing) clauses which are 'unreasonable or oppressive'. If this principle is accepted the rule about written documents might be restated as follows: the signer is bound by the terms of the document if, and only if, the other party believes on reasonable grounds that those terms truly express the signer's intention. This principle retains the role of signed documents as a means of protecting reasonable expectations; what it does not allow is that a party should rely on a printed document to contradict what he knows, or ought to know, is the understanding of the other party. Again this principle seems to be particularly applicable in situations involving the distribution of goods and services to consumers, though it is by no means confined to such situations.[11]

Usually, a party who has not signed a document can more easily rebut a presumption that he agreed to all the terms in it, and thus can avoid being bound by them, as discussed in the "ticket" cases in Chapter 5.

CONTRACTS REQUIRING DISCLOSURE
When One Party Has Special Knowledge

The concept of misrepresentation extends to a failure to disclose pertinent information because one of the parties has access to such information not available to the other. When a relationship between parties leads to a special measure of trust by one party in the other, it is unconscionable for the one to withhold information he knows to be material to the other's decision about entering into a contract.[12] The party "in a superior position of knowledge" has a duty to inform the other so that he may have an idea of the risks he would be taking under the proposed contract. Although the courts have gradually widened the ambit of this duty, it would be a serious mistake to suppose that any contract will require the utmost good faith simply because one party knows something the other does not. The facts of each case will determine the court's view.

The requirement of **utmost good faith** almost invariably exists in a continuing business relationship. Partnership depends on mutual trust, and accordingly, partners owe a general duty of utmost good faith to each other in all their transactions. Similarly, directors and officers owe a duty of good faith towards their corporation.

utmost good faith
a duty owed when a special measure of trust is placed in one party by the other

Contracts of Insurance

An important type of contract requiring utmost good faith is the contract of insurance: a party seeking insurance must disclose to the insurance company all pertinent aspects of the risk he is asking it to assume so that it may make an informed judgment about whether to provide the insurance coverage requested and may fix a rate commensurate with the risk. A person who applies for life insurance, for example, must disclose everything about her state of health that will be of value to the insurer in deciding whether to accept or reject her application. The insurer can refuse to pay the insurance money to her estate or beneficiaries if the insured person withheld such information when applying for the insurance. Similarly, an applicant's failure to disclose that she has been refused life insurance by other companies constitutes a breach of good faith and hence a misrepresentation.

11. Waddams, "Contracts Exemption Clauses Unconscionability Consumer Protection" (Comments) (1971), 49 *Can. Bar Rev.* 578 at 590–1; cited in Tilden Rent-A-Car Co. v. Clendenning (1978), 18 O.R. (2d) 601, per Dubin, J.A. at 609. See also Trigg v. MI Movers International Transport Services Ltd. (1991), 4 O.R. (3d) 562.

12. Lloyd's Bank Ltd. v. Bundy, [1974] 3 All E.R. 757 at 765.

The requirement of utmost good faith in applying for fire insurance is governed by statute in each province.[13] In *Sherman v. American Institute Co.*[14] the policy holder, when applying for fire insurance, failed to disclose that he had had a previous fire and that the insurance company affected had then refused to continue the insurance protection. The insured property was damaged by fire again, and when these facts came to light the insurance company refused to pay. It was held that the insured's conduct constituted a fraudulent omission within the terms of the Insurance Act: the insurance company was not required to pay the insurance money.

Public liability insurance—for motor vehicles, for example—presents a special difficulty. Suppose an insured, who failed to disclose important information when applying for insurance, has an accident: on the one hand, this appears to justify his insurer refusing to pay a claim; on the other hand, an innocent third party, say a passenger injured by the negligence of the insured, would be unable to claim from the insurer. If the insured did not have sufficient assets to pay the passenger's claim, the innocent passenger would be the one to suffer the loss as a result of the insured party's non-disclosure *and* his negligence. Accordingly, there may be a strong public interest in requiring insurance to cover harm to third parties to be binding despite a breach of utmost good faith by the insured. The insurer would itself then have to take greater precautions to investigate the safety record of the insured before agreeing to insure. A recent decision of the Supreme Court has left the law in this area uncertain.[15]

Sale of Corporation Securities

A situation in which one party typically has special access to information arises in a subscription for the purchase of shares or bonds in a corporation. The promoters or directors naturally know more about the corporation's affairs and prospects than do the investing public from whom they are soliciting subscriptions. The corporation usually gives the investing public information about a new issue of shares or bonds in a statement called a **prospectus**, or sometimes in other documents such as circulars, letters, or notices published in newspapers.

prospectus
a statement issued to inform the public about a new issue of shares or bonds

All these documents present tempting opportunities for misrepresentation of a corporation's financial position by non-disclosure. Consequently, our various corporations and securities statutes now require disclosure of information in such documents in sufficient detail that directors, by simply omitting pertinent information, are more likely to be liable for violating the statute than for violating the common law.[16] As we shall see in Chapter 29, the securities acts of most provinces require that in many instances prospectuses be approved by the provincial securities commission or another government body before shares can be offered to the public.

Sale of Goods Compared With Sale of Land

Generally a buyer of goods must take them with their defects unless some fact about their quality has been misrepresented. Certain qualifications to this doctrine of **caveat emptor** are discussed in Chapter 16 on the sale of goods. For example, *caveat emptor* applies only to the quality or condition of the goods, not to ownership. Simply by offering goods for sale, a seller implies that he has the right to sell them and to transfer full ownership free from any claims. Failure to disclose an outstanding claim entitles the buyer to rescission. Although the buyer's right to rescind arises from a breach of an implied term rather than from a duty to disclose, the result is the same as if utmost good faith about ownership had been required of the seller.

caveat emptor
let the buyer beware

---

13. See, for example: Insurance Act, R.S.B.C. 1996, c. 226, s. 126; R.S.O. 1990, c. I.8, s. 148; R.S.N.S. 1989, c. 231, Sched. to Part VII, s. 1.

14. [1937] 4 D.L.R. 723.

15. Coronation Insurance Co. v. Taku Air Transport (1991), 85 D.L.R. (4th) 609.

16. See, for example: Securities Act, R.S.O. 1990, c. S.5, s. 1(1) para. 25, 56, 122.

A purchaser of an interest in land has even less protection against undisclosed faults of the property. If the vendor has made no representations, in most cases the purchaser must take it with all its faults.[17] Even if the vendor's ownership is subject to the claims of other persons, he need not disclose these claims. In the absence of representations by the vendor, the law presumes that the vendor offers to sell only the interest he has in the land. The purchaser can protect himself only by making a thorough investigation of title. In a few instances, however, a court may imply a representation if non-disclosure amounts to fraud. For example, *A* purports to sell a piece of land to *B*, when in fact she occupies it only as a tenant and is not the owner. The court would find that *A* impliedly represented herself as owner and would grant rescission to *B*.

UNDUE INFLUENCE

Special Relationships

undue influence

the domination of one party over the mind of another to such a degree as to deprive the latter of the will to make an independent decision

Undue influence is the domination of one party over the mind of another to such a degree as to deprive the latter of the will to make an independent decision. A contract formed as a result of undue influence is voidable at the option of the victim. The victim may avoid the contract only if he acts promptly after he is freed from the domination. If he acquiesces or delays, hoping to gain some advantage, the court will refuse to assist him.

Undue influence is often an issue in disputes not involving contracts: when a gift has been made and the donor wants to recover the gift; perhaps more often when a bequest has been made under a will. Generally speaking, the principles governing undue influence in these circumstances are the same as in contract.

Usually undue influence arises where the parties stand in a special relationship to each other; one party has a special skill or knowledge causing the other to place confidence and trust in him. Typical examples of this relationship are doctor and patient, lawyer and client, minister and parishioner, parent and child.

Dire Circumstances

Sometimes undue influence arises when one party is temporarily in dire straits and will agree to exorbitant and unfair terms because he is desperate for aid.

CASE 9.2

A whaling ship three years at sea sailed into a thick fog near the Bering Strait and ran onto rocks. The coast was barren and the ocean navigable only two months in the year: winter was expected within two or three weeks. Another ship came along, rescued the crew, and bought the cargo of whale oil at a bargain price, to which the captain of the wrecked ship readily agreed. The owners of the wrecked ship later successfully repudiated the contract for the sale of the whale oil.[18]

---

17. In recent years the courts have gradually increased protection to purchasers with regard to serious defects that it would be impossible for them to discover. See, for example, Sevidal v. Chopra (1987), 64 O.R. (2d) 169, where the court held that the vendor had a duty to disclose that radioactive soil had been found on the property after the contract was made but before completion date.

18. Post v. Jones, 60 U.S. 618 (1856).

Burden of Proof

A party alleging undue influence must satisfy the court that the circumstances were such that domination was probable. He may do so relatively easily if a special relationship existed: the law presumes that undue influence was exerted in contracts advantageous to the party in the dominant position, as for example in a contract between a doctor and a patient in which the patient promises to sell the doctor an asset for a small fraction of its value. In the absence of a special relationship, it is more difficult for a party to demonstrate undue influence, but he still may be able to show, for instance, that he was in a desperate state of misfortune at the time of the contract.

Once the alleged victim shows that circumstances likely to lead to undue influence existed, the burden shifts to the dominant party to prove that undue influence was *not* exerted by him. He will often find the task of proving the lack of undue influence almost impossible. The courts are concerned that a dominant position should not be used as a device to exploit the weaker party. Sometimes the advantage taken of weakness on the other side is referred to as *fraud* or **constructive fraud**, but as Lord Selborne has put it:

> Fraud does not here mean deceit or circumvention; it means an unconscientious use of the power arising out of these circumstances and conditions; and when the relative position of the parties is such as **prima facie** to raise this presumption, the transaction cannot stand unless the person claiming the benefit of it is able to repel the presumption by contrary evidence, proving it to have been in point of fact fair, just and reasonable.[19]

constructive fraud
the unconscientious use of power by a dominant party to take advantage of the weakness of the other party

prima facie
at first sight; on the face of it

The most important factors in determining whether there is undue influence are the degree of domination of the stronger party and the extent of the advantage he has received (that is, the unfairness of the bargain). The degree of domination is often difficult to ascertain, because it involves questions of personality; by contrast, unfairness can generally be measured against the market value of the goods or services traded in a contract and is more easily judged.

Arrangements Between Husband and Wife

Undue influence is somewhat more difficult to prove between husband and wife than in the other relationships, because the law presumes that at various times each party may well desire to confer a benefit on the other without exacting a good "price" in return. However, undue influence may arise, especially if one spouse is experienced in business and has persuaded the other, who has had little or no business experience, to pledge her separate assets as security or act as guarantor for his business transactions. Two cases illustrate how undue influence may be found in the husband–wife relationship.

CASE 9.3

A broker to whom a sum of money was owing either suggested to the husband or acquiesced in a misrepresentation made by him to his wife; the husband obtained promissory notes from his wife and made them payable to the broker. The wife later avoided her liability on the notes.[20]

---

19. Aylesford v. Morris (1873), L.R. 8 Ch. 484, at 490.
20. Cox v. Adams (1904), 35 S.C.R. 393.

CASE 9.4

A wife surrendered to a bank all her extensive separate estate in settlement of her husband's debts, in a series of transactions extending over a period of eight years. She was a confirmed invalid who had never had any advice that could be called independent—the only lawyer with whom she had any dealings was the solicitor of the bank and of her husband. She had acted in passive obedience to her husband. The transfers of the wife's property were set aside and recovered for the benefit of her estate.[21]

Importance of Independent Legal Advice

Sometimes a promisor chooses of his own free will to confer a benefit on another by contract, but subsequent events bring a change of heart and he claims undue influence; or the promisor may die, and his executor or heirs may then try to avoid the contract on grounds of undue influence. After the benefit has been promised but before it is actually conferred, the alleged dominant person, relying on the contract, may enter into further obligations. He may, for example, make a contract with a builder to erect a house on a piece of land, relying on an earlier contract in which a friend undertook to sell him the land at a very low price. If a court set aside the contract for the sale of the land because of undue influence the dominant party would have to break the second contract for the construction of the house, and would become liable for payment of damages to the builder.

To avoid such risks whenever undue influence is a possibility, the dominant party would be wise to ask the other party to obtain independent legal advice about his rights and duties before making the agreement. Not only will the suggestion to get advice tend to refute undue influence, but testimony of the independent lawyer, not associated with the transaction, that he explained the nature of the transaction and that the other party freely and with full knowledge made the commitment, will usually be conclusive evidence against the claim.

A lawyer confronted with a situation in which undue influence may exist will almost always send the weaker party to some other completely independent lawyer. The circumstance often arises when a husband brings his wife to sign documents in which she is to guarantee proposed loans for her husband's business. The lawyer will usually suggest several lawyers' names and ask the wife to choose one at random. She will then visit the other lawyer alone with all relevant documents, have them explained carefully, pay the lawyer for his time, and return with a certificate signed by the lawyer stating exactly what took place in his office. Although this procedure seems overly cautious, it is the fair thing to do—and it may save the husband or the creditor untold difficulties if later the possibility of undue influence is raised. Occasionally, after receiving independent legal advice, a wife may well have second thoughts and refuse to sign the documents.

Loan Transactions

A situation of undue influence often arises in contracts of loan. The borrower may be in a financial crisis and desperate for money: he agrees to any exorbitant rate of interest at the time. Later he finds he cannot repay the debt because the interest is so high: it is all he can do to pay the interest regularly. The common law remedies discussed above are available, of course, but many jurisdictions have recognized that loans present a special problem and have passed statutes to provide additional remedies.[22]

---

21. Bank of Montreal v. Stuart, [1911] A.C. 120. See, also, Bertolo v. Bank of Montreal (1986), 57 O.R. (2d) 577.

22. See Unconscionable Transactions Relief Act, R.S.M. 1987, c. U-20, s. 3; R.S.O. 1990, c. U.2, s. 2; Money-Lenders Act, R.S.N.S. 1989, c. 289, ss. 4, 5.

Of particular importance, the Criminal Code[23] makes it an offence to charge a rate of interest in excess of 60 percent per annum on a loan. In practice, criminal prosecutions for this offence are very rare. However, in civil cases, the courts refuse to allow recovery of interest where the "criminal" rate of interest has been exceeded. The loan contract itself is not void: the principal sum remains recoverable, but the illegal interest provision is *severed* from the contract. The courts have not been consistent, however, in the method of severance. One approach has been their "blue pencil" test; for example, in *Mira Design v. Seascape Holdings*[24] a clause that provided for an increase in the principal of the loan after one month was struck out, thus lowering the effective rate of interest below the criminal limit. In other cases the courts have simply held that the principal only is recoverable: the lender may not recover any interest.[25] This is preferable, since the risk of being deprived of any interest acts as a deterrent to lenders who might otherwise attempt to charge an exorbitant rate.

Threat of Prosecution

Undue influence may also arise through fear of prosecution of a near relation.[26] Parents may be prepared to go to great lengths to save their child from prosecution for a relatively minor offence: sometimes they promise money to a person in possession of the necessary evidence if he does not press for prosecution. The matter is very close to the criminal offence of blackmail even though no express threat may have been made; such activities might only come to light if the parent dies and the executor refuses to pay, or the child dies and the possibility of prosecution ceases.

Inequality of Bargaining Power

Courts have gradually become more willing to recognize a category of unconscionable contracts, whether as an application of the law relating to undue influence, as an extension of the concept of utmost good faith, or as a separate basis of complaint under the larger rubric of "constructive fraud." In an English case on this question, Lord Denning said:

> …through all these instances there runs a single thread. They rest on 'inequality of bargaining power'. By virtue of it, the English law gives relief to one who, without independent advice, enters into a contract on terms which are very unfair or transfers property for a consideration which is grossly inadequate, when his bargaining power is grievously impaired by reason of his own needs or desires, or by his own ignorance or infirmity, coupled with undue influences or pressures brought to bear on him by or for the benefit of the other. When I use the word 'undue' I do not mean to suggest that the principle depends on proof of any wrongdoing. The one who stipulates for an unfair advantage may be moved solely by his own self-interest, unconscious of the distress he is bringing to the other.[27]

Although inequality of bargaining power has become an important consideration before the courts, we must emphasize that by no means has it replaced the need for sophisticated legal analysis and careful understanding of the business setting of transactions. Courts insist first on a clear understanding of the problem under consideration; *only then* will they apply, with restraint, the general principle of unconscionability. And for good reason: it is essential that courts do not lightly upset normal habits of reliance on bargains seriously made. The mere fact that with hindsight a contract looks like a "bad deal" does not make it unconscionable.

---

23. R.S.C. 1985, c. C-46, s. 347. See Garland v. Consumer's Gas Co., [1998] 3 S.C.R. 112.

24. [1982] 1 W.W.R. 744 (B.C.S.C.). For an interesting review of this issue see Waldron (1994), 73 *Can. Bar Rev.* 1.

25. See Kebet Holdings Ltd. v. 351173 B.C. Ltd. (1991), 25 R.P.R. (2d) 174 (B.C.S.C.); Milani v. Banks (1997), 145 D.L.R. (4th) 55.

26. Kaufman v. Gerson, [1904] 1 K.B. 591.

27. Lloyds Bank Ltd. v. Bundy, *supra*, n. 12, quoted with approval in McKenzie v. Bank of Montreal (1975), 55 D.L.R. (3d) 641 at 652.

Guarantees and Undue Influence

Frequently, when one party to a contract is making a loan or extending credit to another, the creditor seeks someone to guarantee the debt. The guarantor agrees to pay if the principal debtor defaults on the loan, lease agreement, credit sale, and so on. For example, if a car dealer leases a car to a business, the dealer might seek a personal guarantee from the owner of the business. If one spouse borrows money from a bank, the bank might seek a guarantee from the other spouse.

A guarantee of indebtedness is a contract. Like any contract, it may be ruled invalid if it was obtained by the use of undue influence. In one case, a woman in her early 20s, with a steady job and a modest middle-class income, began dating a slightly younger man. The young man owed $20 000 to a bank on a line of credit. He and his family persuaded the woman to provide a guarantee to the bank. A few weeks later, they persuaded her to guarantee a loan of $46 000 to consolidate the line of credit and other debts. The family said they were about to be thrown out on the street and promised the woman that she would not actually be called upon to pay anything. They would take care of it all. The woman received no benefit from her guarantees and did not have independent legal advice. The boyfriend and his family never paid anything on the loan. The boyfriend declared bankruptcy, and the bank sued the woman for the full amount. Eventually, they settled for $17 000.

Although she chose to settle rather than to test her case fully in a trial, it could be argued that the woman had given her guarantees under undue influence. From a business point of view, she probably was not an appropriate guarantor of so large a loan, given her modest income and lack of assets.

Source: This example is based on an actual case, as described by the lawyer representing the guarantor. For a similar case, in which undue influence was found and the guarantor was not required to pay, see *McKenzie v. Bank of Montreal* (1976), 7 O.R. (2d) 521; affd 12 O.R. (2d) 719 (C.A.).

Questions to Consider

1. What should a creditor seeking a guarantee do to make sure the guarantee will be valid?

2. Does a creditor have duties towards a guarantor? If so, how far should they extend?

3. Does it make good business sense to obtain a guarantee from someone who may not be able to pay the full debt?

DURESS

duress

actual or threatened violence or imprisonment as a means of coercing a party to enter into a contract

Duress consists of actual or threatened violence or imprisonment as a means of coercing a party to enter into a contract. The effect of duress is similar to that of undue influence: the contract is voidable at the option of the victim. The threat of violence need not be directed against the party being coerced—it may be a threat to harm the victim's spouse, parent, or child.

A situation closely resembling duress arises when one party has possession of the goods of another and wrongfully refuses to return them unless the owner promises to give the wrongful possessor some benefit. Suppose *A* had arranged a month's holiday and stored her antique sports car at a garage for $100, paid to the garage owner before leaving. While she was away the garage owner sold his business to *B* without informing him that *A* had prepaid the storage charge. When *A* came to pick up her car *B* demanded a further $100. After paying the $100 under protest, *A* obtained her car. If she wishes to sue *B* for the return of the money, she need not rely on duress; she can more easily prove that there was no right to the payment. There was, in fact, no contract at all with *B*. Since the payment was certainly not a gift, *A* would recover her money. In addition, if *B*'s conduct had deprived *A* of the use of the car even temporarily, she could recover damages for his wrongful possession. Accordingly the remedies available are adequate to protect *A* without using duress as a cause of action.

Historically, duress was a concept recognized by the common law courts and was narrowly construed by them. Today duress is still strictly confined by the courts to the circumstances described above. In contrast, the concept of undue influence was developed by the courts of equity to fill a gap and give remedies in circumstances not covered by the concepts of fraudulent misrepresentation and of duress. As a result, the concept of undue influence is wider ranging and more flexible than the other two concepts and, as Lord Selborne noted, includes circumstances that would not otherwise be called fraud.

QUESTIONS FOR REVIEW

1. What factors might persuade a court to consider an innocent misrepresentation to be a term of the contract?

2. Explain the nature of indemnity as a remedy.

3. In what circumstances will a court find that an "opinion" is a misrepresentation of fact?

4. Felix owns and operates a bookshop. He has just learned from a friend who is a real estate agent that one of the large "super bookstores" has purchased a site and will be establishing a branch in 12 months just across the street from his store. There will be a public announcement in three months. Felix immediately advertises his business for sale and is approached by Gulliver. Felix bargains for a price based on his sales and income over the last three years, but does not mention the almost certain new competition that will arrive across the street. Gulliver makes an offer and Felix accepts it. Before the transaction is completed, Gulliver learns about the new bookstore. What rights, if any, does he have?

5. *D* applies for a car insurance policy from *E* Auto Ins. Co., without disclosing that he has been convicted of driving violations and involved in three collisions in another province. The company issues the policy. *D* subsequently causes a collision in which he injures *F*. The insurance company then learns about *D*'s failure to disclose his bad record and it cancels the policy. What problem does this situation raise for *F*?

6. Under what circumstances does a victim of misrepresentation lose the right to rescind?

7. Describe the implied representation that arises from offering goods for sale.

8. In what circumstances does the burden of proof in claims based on undue influence shift to the party who is alleged to have exerted such an influence?

9. *H*'s business is in financial difficulties and he needs his wife, *W*, to guarantee a loan from a friend *T*. Before *T* accepts *W*'s guarantee what precaution should he take?

10. Suppose *X*, who is in dire financial straits, borrows $10 000 from *Y* at an annual interest rate of 65 percent. *X* defaults on his first payment of interest and *Y* sues. How will the courts respond?

11. What issues arise whenever one party to a contract that is a "bad deal" claims undue influence was exerted on him?

CASES AND PROBLEMS

1 Smart was Hull's lawyer for many years and not only handled legal matters for Hull, but gave him important advice on business matters as well. At one stage, Hull owed Smart about $8500 for professional services and Smart suggested to Hull that the account could be conveniently settled in full if Hull would transfer his new 10-metre sailboat to Smart. Hull hesitated at first, but realizing how indispensable his relationship with Smart had been and how important it was that Smart should continue to respect the confidential nature of his private business affairs, he transferred the sailboat to Smart.

A few months later Hull's daughter, who greatly enjoyed sailing, returned from graduate studies in Europe and persuaded her father to sue for recovery of the sailboat. Explain how the onus of proof will operate in the resulting legal action and indicate the probable outcome.

2 Condor Investments Inc. published the following ad to sell its residential apartment building.

> Newly renovated Condor Suites for sale: 45 high quality one- and two-bedroom residential units in a prime location, $2 300 000.

Dollefson inspected the building and believed it would be a good investment. After negotiating with Condor's manager, the two parties signed a deal for $2 100 000 and Dollefson paid a deposit of $100 000.

In the course of preparing to complete the transaction, his lawyer checked with the city, and she learned that while there were indeed 45 units, the city had issued an occupancy permit for only 41 units; four units at the basement level were occupied without a permit. Dollefson decided that he did not want the property and commenced an action for rescission of the contract on the ground of fraudulent misrepresentation. He asked for the return of his deposit with interest as well as the legal, appraisal, and auditing fees that he had incurred.

What are the main arguments for both sides, and which one should succeed?

3 In response to an advertisement offering a free trial lesson in modern dancing, Galt, a graduate nurse, entered into a contract with the Modern Dancing Studios for 15 two-hour lessons for $350. Before she had taken all the lessons, the dancing instructor, Valentino, told her that she would become a wonderful dancer if she would go on and that if she agreed to more lessons she would "probably get the bronze medal for dancing." On St. Valentine's Day he gave her a rose, and in the course of a lesson whispered in her ear how wonderfully she danced. She eventually signed a second contract to take another 35 hours of dancing lessons for $650. A new instructor was then assigned to her, and all compliments and personal attention ceased. Galt brought action for rescission of the contract and return of the $650.

On what ground might such a contract be avoided? Should the action succeed?

4 Amberton Realty Inc. purchased a small apartment building with four units, each leased as a private dwelling. It renewed the insurance policy of the previous owners with Eagle-eye Insurance Co. Three months later the two ground-floor units became vacant and Amberton leased them to a charitable organization, Help-Our-Youth, which used the space a few hours each day to hold social gatherings. Help-Our-Youth managed the unit with care and the other tenants did not complain. However, after six months a fire started in the hallway and the entire building was destroyed.

Eagle-eye refused to compensate Amberton because the use of the insured premises was changed without its knowledge. Under the terms of the insurance policy, only buildings described in the policy and occupied as a private dwelling were covered at a lower premium. Amberton's manager had not read the terms of the policy, and was not aware of the difference.

Amberton sued Eagle-eye. Give your opinion, with reasons, whether Amberton should succeed.

5. On arriving at Vancouver Airport, Mr. Clemson, a frequent traveller, rented a car from Tilford Car Rentals Ltd., as he had done many times before. The clerk asked him whether he wanted additional collision insurance coverage and, as usual, he said, "Yes." The clerk added a fee of $10 a day for this coverage. She then handed the contract to Clemson and he signed it in her presence. She was aware that he did not read the terms of the contract before signing it.

Clemson's signature appeared immediately below a printed statement that read, "I, the undersigned, have read and received a copy of above and reverse side of this contract." On the back of the contract, in small type and so faint on Mr. Clemson's copy as to be hardly legible, there was a series of conditions, one of which read:

> Notwithstanding the payment of an additional fee for limitation of liability for collision damage to the rented vehicle, customer shall be fully liable for all collision damage if vehicle is used, operated or driven off highways serviced by federal, provincial or municipal governments and for all damages to vehicle by striking overhead objects.

The clerk placed Clemson's copy of the contract in an envelope and gave him the envelope and car keys. He got in the car, placed the contract in the glove compartment, and drove to a nearby shopping plaza to buy a gift. While driving in the plaza parking lot, he collided with another car, causing damage of $2500 to his rented car. The car rental agency claimed that he was personally liable for repairs under the terms of their contract. Clemson refused to pay for the car repairs and Tilford Car Rentals Ltd. sued him for breach of contract.

Outline the nature of the arguments available to Tilford Car Rentals Ltd. and of the defences available to Clemson. Express an opinion, with reasons, about whether the action is likely to succeed.

6. GasCan Ltd. is an integrated oil refining and distributing company that sells its products through a chain of service stations. It owns the land on which the service stations are located and leases them to tenants through its real estate department. As is normal in these arrangements, tenants agree to buy all their gasoline and other products from GasCan.

GasCan wanted to find a tenant for one of its service stations that had become vacant. Barcza expressed an interest in leasing it. The manager of GasCan's real estate department told Barcza that the company's sales division had made a forecast of the estimated annual sales of gasoline at the station: 900 000 litres. Barcza made a rough cash flow projection and signed a five-year lease of the station at a rental of $10 000 a year.

The company's estimate proved to be entirely wrong. The annual volume of the service station proved to be only about 200 000 litres. It appeared that the real estate department of GasCan had consulted with the sales division and that between them they had honestly but foolishly made "a fatal error." A new clerk in the sales division had checked sales made by the former tenant, but had assumed that the figures were in gallons whereas they had already been converted to litres. He converted them a second time, making the figures four and a half times higher than they should have been.

Barcza, who was an experienced and diligent station operator, tried hard to make a success of the business, but there was nothing he could do to raise gasoline sales close to the estimate. Over a three-year period he lost money steadily and finally became insolvent.

What remedies could Barcza seek in an action against GasCan Ltd.? What defences would GasCan raise? Who should succeed? Explain.

7 Virginia McGraw inherited a fruit farm in the Okanagan Valley when her aunt died five years ago. Two years ago, she befriended Val Lawton, a used-car sales agent, and allowed him to operate the fruit farm on the understanding they would live there together when they were married.

Lawton operated the farm at a loss but concealed the mounting debts from McGraw by intercepting her mail. He did his business at the Tower Bank, where he periodically filed statements of largely fictitious assets as a basis for increasing loans. His main assets seem to have been an affable and suave appearance, McGraw's affection for him, and his long friendship with the bank manager.

The bank took possession of McGraw's car when, finally, Lawton defaulted on his bank loan: he had offered her car as collateral security, asserting that it was his. The bank manager soon learned that the car was in fact owned by McGraw but refused to return it to her until Lawton's loan was repaid. McGraw was sympathetic when the matter was explained to her at the bank, and she then applied to her credit union to borrow enough money to repay the bank and recover her car. Three weeks later she returned to the bank with her fiancé and the money required to get her car back. Before handing over the keys to her, the bank manager asked her to sign "this bunch of papers." He advised her that her signature was required "as a matter of formality only." She then signed the papers and was given the car keys.

Six months afterwards, the bank claimed from McGraw a half year's interest on a mortgage on her fruit farm, and she then discovered that the mortgage document had been among the papers she had signed at the bank. The bank proposed to use the mortgage in substitution for other amounts still owed by Lawton.

At this point McGraw broke off her relations with Lawton and on the advice of her lawyer sued the Tower Bank. In her action she asked to have the mortgage set aside and, in addition, claimed $1000 damages in tort as compensation for costs incurred from the wrongful seizure of her car and the loss of its use.

Explain with reasons whether, in your opinion, this action should succeed.

THE REQUIREMENT OF WRITING

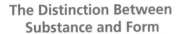

Not only does it make good sense to keep a written record of contracts but there can also be serious legal consequences for failing to do so. The ancient Statute of Frauds, which still applies substantially in all common law provinces, requires that many contracts be in writing to be enforceable. In this chapter we examine such questions as:

- what types of contracts are affected by the Statute?

- what elements need to be in writing in order to comply with the Statute?

- what is the effect of the Statute on contracts that do not comply with the writing requirement?

- what is the doctrine of "part performance"? How have the courts used it to limit the scope of the Statute?

- how does the requirement of writing under the Sale of Goods Act differ from that in the Statute of Frauds?

- what are the writing requirements under consumer protection legislation?

THE DISTINCTION BETWEEN SUBSTANCE AND FORM

The Benefits of a Written Record

Contractual duties, like all other obligations in law, are abstract concepts. Although we speak of the formation of a contract, we mean it in a legal, not in a physical sense. The parties must, of course, have agreed to the terms of their contract. The contract may exist only in their recollection of the spoken words, or it may be recorded in a written document, on a magnetic tape, or stored in a computer. Thus the *substance*—the terms of the contract—may have a variety of physical *forms* or even no form at all, other than in the minds of the parties. The distinction between the substance of the contract and the form in which it is known to the parties is crucial: we must not confuse the two. For the purpose of this chapter the following categories of form are important:

(a) contracts whose terms are entirely oral

(b) contracts some of whose terms are oral and some in writing

(c) contracts whose terms are entirely in writing, whether all in one document or spread through several documents, such as a series of letters

The terms of a contract remain the same whatever form they may take, but from a practical point of view it is almost always advantageous to have them in written form. In good business practice, some record is kept of even the simplest transaction at the time it is made. Of course, the more complicated a contract becomes, the greater will be the benefits of a written record. Human memories are fallible, especially when burdened with many details, and common sense tells us that it is better to trust to written records than to mere memory whenever a contract is complicated or will take effect over a long time. Many disputes may be avoided by keeping accurate records. At this point we must distinguish between the sound business practice of keeping records and their legal significance. Records that are a valuable aid in business may not satisfy the legal requirement of writing, which we are about to discuss. Furthermore, as we shall see, a business record may even assist the other party in enforcing its claim if it should obtain possession of the record.

When a contract is wholly oral the first problem for the court is to determine what exactly the parties agreed to; written evidence will aid a judge in determining what the terms are and in resolving a conflict of testimony between the parties, each with a different recollection of the contract. But written evidence does not resolve all problems. Even when a court has ascertained the exact words of the contract, the words themselves may be open to several interpretations; the court must decide their meaning in the particular contract in dispute. We shall discuss the interpretation of contracts in the next chapter.

The Statute of Frauds

At common law, once the terms are ascertained, a contract is equally effective whether it is in writing or merely oral. However, in 1677 the English Parliament passed a peculiar act known as the Statute of Frauds. It was concerned mainly with settling ownership and the transfer of ownership in land, after the turmoil of the civil war. The statute required written evidence to eliminate perjured testimony in suits concerning land—hence the use of the word "frauds" in the title.[1] The two sections in the Statute that particularly affected contracts made judges unhappy almost immediately. They were poorly drafted and did not accomplish their vague purposes. Unfortunately, the Statute became so much a part of the law that it was re-enacted or adopted virtually unchanged in most common law jurisdictions, including those of Canada and the United States. A notable change in the law occurred in 1954 when England amended the Statute. British Columbia replaced the Statute with the Law and Equity Act,[2] and Manitoba repealed it entirely.[3] In the remaining common law provinces the Statute is in force in its original form.

---

1. See Furmston, *Cheshire, Fifoot and Furmston's Law of Contract* (13th ed.), pp. 209–33. For a recent discussion, see Fridman, "The Necessity for Writing in Contracts Within the Statute of Frauds" (1985), 35 *U.T.L.J.* 43.

2. Law Reform Amendment Act, S.B.C. 1985, c. 10 , s. 8 repealed the Statute of Frauds, and s. 7 revised the requirements for writing by adding a new s. 54 to the Law and Equity Act, R.S.B.C. 1979, c. 224.

3. R.S.M. 1987, c. F-158.

Its Consequences

The effect of the Statute of Frauds is to render certain types of contracts unenforceable unless they are in writing: that is, despite the fact that an oral contract is otherwise valid, if it falls within the Statute, neither party may sue on the contract. We shall discuss the effects of the Statute in more detail later in this chapter.

Parties to oral contracts are often able to avoid their obligations solely because these contracts have been held to come within the scope of the Statute: the contracts might be perfectly valid in every other respect. It has often been said that by defeating the reasonable expectations of parties, the Statute of Frauds promotes more frauds than it prevents. For this reason the courts have striven to limit the application of the Statute wherever possible. The results have not always been logical, but the Statute has certainly been hemmed in by exceptions.

The problem of deciding whether a contract is affected by the Statute of Frauds arises only when an otherwise valid contract has been made. The mere fact that a promise is in writing as required by the Statute does not make the promise binding. There is no contract even to be considered unless all the requirements for the formation of a contract, as discussed in earlier chapters, are fulfilled.

THE TYPES OF CONTRACT AFFECTED BY THE STATUTE OF FRAUDS

The types of contract selected in the 17th century do not make much sense to us today. For example, the first class of contract listed, "A promise by an executor or administrator to answer damages out of his own estate," rarely occurs. An executor or administrator of an estate may find that a debt owed by the deceased is due, but it is not yet convenient for him to pay it out of the estate assets. A creditor is more likely to press him to actually pay the debt from his own resources (later to be reimbursed from the estate) rather than merely give a promise to pay. However, if the executor or administrator should make such a promise, the creditor will be unable to enforce it unless it is in writing.

A Promise to Answer for the Debt or Default or Miscarriage of Another

Distinction Between Guarantee and Indemnity

The courts have attempted to limit the application of the Statute when a promisor would otherwise be bound to perform. Thus, they have narrowed the definition of a promise "to answer for the debt, default or miscarriage of another" by distinguishing between two similar types of promises, a promise of **guarantee** and a promise of **indemnity**. A guarantee is a conditional promise to pay *only if* the debtor defaults: "If he does not pay you, I will." The creditor must look first to the debtor for payment, and only after the debtor has defaulted may the creditor claim payment from the guarantor.

guarantee
a conditional promise to pay only if the debtor defaults

indemnity
a promise by a third party to be primarily liable to pay the debt

In contrast, a person who makes a promise to indemnify a creditor makes herself primarily liable to pay the debt. Accordingly, when the debt falls due the creditor may ignore its claim against the party who benefited from the indemnity and sue the person who gave the promise to indemnify. "Give him the goods and I will see to it that you are paid," would usually be a promise to indemnify.[4] A promise by a purchaser of a business to its employees to pay back-wages owed by the former owner would be a promise to indemnify.

---

4. As Furmston points out in *Cheshire, Fifoot and Furmston's Law of Contract* (13th ed.) at p. 212 it is the intention of the parties and not their language that determines whether the promise is a guarantee or an indemnity.

The courts have applied this part of the Statute of Frauds *only* to guarantees. A guarantee must be made in writing to be enforceable, but a promise to indemnify is outside the Statute and is enforceable without being in writing.

Subsidiary Promises of Guarantee

Even the class of guarantees which falls within the Statute has been narrowed: the courts have excluded those guarantees incidental to a larger contract where the element of guarantee is only one among a number of more important rights and duties created by the contract.

CASE 10.1

Sutton & Co. were stockbrokers and members of the London Stock Exchange with access to its facilities. Grey was not a member, but he had contacts with prospective investors. The parties made an oral agreement by which Grey was to receive half the commission from transactions for his clients completed through Sutton and was to pay half of any bad debts that might develop out of the transactions.

When a loss resulted from one of the transactions and Grey refused to pay his half, Sutton & Co. sued him. Grey pleaded that his promise to pay half the loss was a guarantee and was not enforceable against him because it was not in writing. The court ruled that the whole arrangement between Sutton and Grey had been a much broader one than merely guaranteeing the payment of a debt owing by a particular client, and that the Statute of Frauds should not apply. The agreement was thus enforceable, and Sutton & Co. obtained judgment against Grey for half the loss.[5]

del credere agent
an agent who arranges the sale of the principal's goods and also guarantees payment by the buyer

A further illustration of this approach concerns the liability of a ***del credere* agent**. Not only does he arrange the sale of his principal's goods, but he also guarantees payment by the buyer. If the buyer defaults the agent must pay for the goods. For this additional protection the seller pays the *del credere* agent a higher commission than an ordinary sales agent would receive. The courts have held that the main element of a *del credere* contract is the agency relationship and that the promise of guarantee is merely subsidiary. Accordingly, an oral contract for the services of a *del credere* agent (including his guarantee of customers' debts) does not come under the Statute and is enforceable.

Amendments to the Statute of Frauds

In amending the Statute of Frauds in recent years, England and British Columbia have retained the requirement of writing for contracts of guarantee. In addition, British Columbia has done away with the judge-made distinction between indemnity and guarantee by requiring that both types of promise be in writing.[6]

The Meaning of "Miscarriage"

miscarriage
an injury caused by the tort of another person

In contrast to the restricted meaning given to the words "debt" and "default," the courts have given the word "miscarriage" a wider meaning. They have interpreted a promise to "answer for the **miscarriage** of another" to mean "to pay damages for injury caused by the tort of another person," for example by that person's negligence or fraud. Thus, to be enforceable, the promise, "I will pay you for the injury B caused you if B doesn't settle with you," must be in writing. On the other hand, the promise, "I will pay you for the injury B caused you if you will give up absolutely any rights you have against B," is a promise of indemnity and need not be in writing to be enforceable.[7]

---

5. Sutton & Co. v. Grey, [1894] 1 Q.B. 285; Bassie v. Melnychuk (1993), 14 Alta. L.R. (3d) 31.
6. Law Reform (Enforcement of Contracts) Act, 1954, 2 & 3 Eliz. 2, c. 34, s. 1 (U.K.), and Statute of Frauds, R.S.B.C. 1996, c. 128, s. 48.
7. Kirkham v. Marter (1819), 106 E.R. 490; Read v. Nash (1751), 95 E.R. 632.

An Agreement Made in Consideration of Marriage

This section has always been interpreted as applying not to a promise to marry but to such related matters as arrangements about assets brought into the marriage as common property. The section has been superseded in all provinces by extensive family law reform legislation that recognizes a wide variety of enforceable arrangements in marriage and in cohabitation relations.[8] The legislation requires that these arrangements, since they are expected to apply to relationships over a long time, be in writing to be enforceable.

A Contract Concerning an Interest in Land

Unlike most sections of the Statute, this provision is regarded as necessary to protect interests in property. The special qualities of land, in particular its virtual indestructibility and permanence, make it important to be able to ascertain the various outstanding interests and claims against land. It is essential to have verified written records of transactions affecting interests in land, and these records must be available over many years for inspection by interested persons. To this end we have systems of public records where interested parties may "search" and discover who owns or claims to own the interests in land.

Still, we must distinguish between contracts concerning land to which the Statute applies, and others considered to be too remotely connected with land to be under the Statute. The courts have held that agreements to repair or build a house and to obtain room and board are outside the Statute, while agreements to permit taking water from a well, to lease any land, house, or other building, or even a portion of a building are within the Statute. Thus, an oral agreement to rent an apartment is unenforceable while an oral agreement to repair the apartment is enforceable. We discuss the enforceability of leases again in Chapter 24.

England and British Columbia have retained the requirement of writing for contracts concerning interests in land.[9]

An Agreement Not to Be Performed by Either Party Within One Year

The purpose of this provision seems clear enough: Parliament did not wish to trust to memory the terms of a contract that would be performed over a long period and so chose a one-year limit. Unfortunately, the choice of any definite cut-off date in itself creates difficulties. The injustice of allowing a wholly oral contract extending exactly one year to be enforced while not allowing the enforcement of a similar contract lasting a year plus a day quickly became evident to the judges. Once more they tried to cut down the effect of the Statute by holding that it did not apply to a contract, though it might well extend beyond a year, unless the terms of the contract specified a time for performance clearly longer than a year. The effect of this ruling is to exclude from the Statute contracts for an *indefinite* period.

ILLUSTRATION 10.1

Ajax Co. Ltd. hires Singh as a supervisor for the set up of an electronic data-processing system without setting out a schedule. Although the parties expect the project to take longer than a year, it is not certain to do so. Accordingly the contract is outside the Statute and need not be in writing.

---

8. For example: Family Relations Act, R.S.B.C. 1996, c. 128, s. 61; Family Law Act, R.S.O. 1990, c. F.3, s. 52; Matrimonial Property Act, R.S.N.S. 1989, c. 275, s. 23.

9. Law of Property Act, 1925, 15 & 16 Geo. 5, c. 20, s. 40 (U.K.), and Law and Equity Act, R.S.B.C. 1996, c. 253, as amended by Law Reform Amendment Act, S.B.C. 1985, c. 110, s. 7.

On the other hand, if a contract is by its terms to extend beyond one year, it is governed by the Statute even though it may be brought to an end in less than one year.

ILLUSTRATION 10.2

In an oral contract, the Trojan Co. Ltd. has hired Bergsen as general manager for two years, provided that either party may bring the contract to an end by giving three months' notice to the other. Bergsen has been working for the company for some months when he receives one month's notice of dismissal. He will be unable to enforce the term entitling him to three months' notice.

The courts have also held that the Statute does not apply even though *one* party will necessarily require more than a year to perform provided that the contract also shows an intention that the *other* party will wholly perform within a year.

ILLUSTRATION 10.3

Grigorian agrees to repair promptly a leaking roof on Brown's warehouse for $15 000, with $5000 to be paid on completion of the repairs, plus $10 000 in two annual instalments of $5000 each. Grigorian completes the repairs within five weeks. At the end of the year Brown refuses to pay the first instalment, claiming that their oral agreement is unenforceable because payment could not be wholly performed within one year. Grigorian can enforce the contract. The court again excludes the Statute where it can find the slimmest reason for doing so, in this case because the parties intended that one of them, Grigorian, should complete performance within a year, and did so.

Where the obligations of one party clearly extend beyond one year, the intention that the other should wholly perform within one year must be clear from the terms of the contract or from the surrounding circumstances: it is not enough that the party *might* perform within one year. Hence, an oral promise by *A* to pay *B* a sum of money in three years' time if *B* will tutor *A*'s daughter in accounting until she obtains a professional qualification will not be enforceable, unless it can clearly be shown from the surrounding circumstances that the tutoring was to be done within the succeeding few weeks or months and *not* to continue beyond one year.

The provision of the Statute of Frauds concerning agreements not to be performed within one year illustrates better than any other how far the courts have gone to prevent the Statute from working an injustice. They cannot invariably circumvent the Statute, however, and injustice often results when the plaintiff fails only because the Statute of Frauds bars him. Amending the Statute, as British Columbia has done, would alleviate this problem in other provinces.

Ratification of Infants' Contracts

Contracts requiring ratification by infants upon coming of age (that is, contracts that are not for a permanent interest in property) must in some jurisdictions be ratified in writing to be enforceable.[10] The requirement of writing does not, however, apply to the class of minors' contracts that are valid unless disaffirmed: for these contracts, mere acquiescence is sufficient to bind infants after coming of age.

---

10. See, for example: Statute of Frauds, R.S.O. 1990, c. S.19, s. 7; R.S.N.S. 1989, c. 442, s. 9; also Chapter 8 of this book.

REQUIREMENTS FOR A WRITTEN MEMORANDUM

Suppose that a contract falls clearly within the scope of the Statute of Frauds. What must the memorandum contain to satisfy the Statute and permit a party to maintain an action upon the contract? The Statute requires a "note or memorandum" of the contract "signed by the party to be charged" or the party's authorized agent.[11]

All Essential Terms Must Be Included

The memorandum must contain all the essential terms of the contract, including the identity of the parties. If the contract is for the sale of land, for example, the memorandum must name the parties, adequately describe the subject-matter (the land), and set out the consideration to be given for it.

ILLUSTRATION 10.4

A gives *B* a signed offer to purchase Summerhill. *B* accepts by signing. The offer to purchase simply states the price to be $150 000 and does not say how the money is to be paid. In previous conversations the parties had agreed orally that payment should be $50 000 in cash and $100 000 by way of a five-year mortgage. The memorandum is insufficient: the method of payment is an essential term and it has been omitted.

If *A* and *B* had previously agreed that the whole price should be paid in cash, then the memorandum *would* be sufficient, for by naming the price to be paid, without more, they imply that it should be paid in cash at the time the property is transferred.

The Statute of Frauds makes an exception for contracts of guarantee by stating that the consideration for that type of promise need not appear in the writing.[12]

The memorandum need not be wholly within a single document; several written notes may be taken together to satisfy the requirements of the Statute. No problem arises when one or more of the documents refer directly to the others. The plaintiff will have considerably more trouble if there are no cross-references within the documents. The courts have gone as far as to hear evidence that a signed letter beginning with "Dear Sir" was contained in a particular envelope that bore the name and address of the plaintiff, and in this way to link the two pieces of paper as a sufficient memorandum.[13] The court justified its decision on the grounds that even without oral evidence, it could reasonably assume that the letter was contained in an envelope: it admitted oral evidence merely to identify the envelope. Thus, the court did not have to rely solely on the testimony of the parties—something it rarely if ever will agree to do. In the words of Baron Blackburn:

> If the contents of the signed paper themselves make reference to the others so as to show by internal evidence that the papers refer to each other, they may be all taken together as one memorandum in writing...but if it is necessary, in order to connect them, to give evidence of

---

11. Courts have had to consider whether new forms of transmitting documents such as telex (now obsolete) and facsimile (or fax) satisfy the statutory requirement of being in "writing." In Rolling v. William Investments (1989), 63 D.L.R. (4th) 760, the Ontario Court of Appeal decided that a facsimile transmission of acceptance of an option was a satisfactory acceptance, even though when the parties made the agreement in 1974, they "could not have anticipated delivery of a facsimile of the [accepted]offer by means of a telephone transmission...." The court concluded:

    > Where technological advances have been made which facilitate communications and expedite transmission of documents we see no reason why they should not be utilized. Indeed, they should be encouraged and approved... [The defendant] suffered no prejudice by reason of the procedure followed.

    Subsequent decisions of Canadian courts have assumed that facsimile transmissions are sufficient to satisfy the writing requirement of the Statute of Frauds.

12. See, for example: R.S.O. 1990, c. S.19, s. 6; R.S.N.S. 1989, c. 442, s. 8.

13. Pearce v. Gardner, [1897] 1 Q.B. 688; Harvie and Hawryluk v. Gibbons (1980), 12 Alta. L.R. (2d) 72.

the intention of the parties that they should be connected, shown by circumstances not apparent on the face of the writings, the memorandum is not all in writing, for it consists partly of the contents of the writings and partly of the expression of an intention to unite them and that expression is not in writing.[14]

ILLUSTRATION 10.5

A wrote to *B* on May 4 offering to pay $10 000 for *B's* computer and at the same time stating the terms in detail. *B* wrote back in a signed letter addressed to *A*, "I will accept your offer of May 4." The agreement is enforceable by either party. The two letters may be taken together as providing the necessary written evidence because they relate to each other and contain all the terms.

Signed by the Defendant

The Statute requires that the note or memorandum be signed by the party to be charged—the defendant—and only that person, not the plaintiff. The plaintiff's signature is irrelevant; if the defendant has not signed, the plaintiff's signature on the document does not help and he cannot enforce the contract against the other party.

The courts have been lenient in prescribing what amounts to a sufficient signature; it need not be in the handwriting of the defendant. A printed name will suffice as long as it is intended to validate the whole of the document. A letterhead on an invoice is designed to verify the sale of the goods described below, without a signature and is sufficient; but a letterhead on stationery would probably not be sufficient if the written contents indicated that the letter was to be signed and it was not signed, as when the letter ends with "Yours truly" and no signature.

THE EFFECT OF THE STATUTE ON CONTRACTS WITHIN ITS SCOPE

unenforceable contract
a contract that still exists for other purposes but neither party may obtain a remedy under it through court action

What do we mean when we say that the Statute of Frauds makes an oral contract unenforceable? The courts recognize that an **unenforceable contract** still exists even though one or both of the parties is unable to obtain a remedy under it through court action. Is this not the same as saying it is void? The answer is a definite "no," for although no action may be brought on the contract itself, it may still affect the legal relations between the parties in several ways.

Recovery of Money Paid Under a Contract

First, both parties to an unenforceable contract may, of course, choose to perform under it, but if they do not, recovery of any down payment made will depend upon which party repudiates the contract.

ILLUSTRATION 10.6

P orally agrees to buy Blackacre from *V* for $50 000 and gives a down payment of $5000, the balance to be paid in 30 days.

Suppose that *P* then sees a more suitable property and refuses to pay the balance. The Statute of Frauds applies and *V* cannot enforce the contract. On the other hand, *P* cannot by court action require *V* to return the payment. Although the contract is unenforceable, it is still valid and existing: *V* may retain the payment by claiming that it was properly owing and was paid under the contract.

---

14. Blackburn, *A Treatise on the Effect of the Contract of Sale*, p. 47. London: W. Benning & Co., 1845, as quoted in North Staffordshire Railway Co. v. Peek (1863), 120 E.R. 777, per Williams, J., at 782.

Suppose instead it is *V* who refuses either to complete the sale or to return the payment. *P* can sue successfully for the return of the payment. The court in these circumstances will not permit *V* to repudiate the contract and yet keep the payment received under its terms.

In the above illustrations we can see that the court will not permit the party who repudiates the contract to gain a further advantage, in Illustration 10.6 by allowing *P* to recover her payment after her own breach, and in Illustration 10.7 by permitting *V* to retain *P*'s payment after his breach. If the contract were found instead to be void, the problem of breach would not arise; there cannot be a "breach" of a void contract. Thus, if the contract had been void for, say, uncertainty (so that the requirement of offer and acceptance was not met), *P* could recover her payment whether it was she or *V* who refused to complete the transaction.

Recovery for Goods and Services

Second, a party who has accepted goods and services under a contract that is unenforceable because of the Statute is not permitted to retain the benefit received without paying for it.

In an oral agreement, *A* promised to do certain work for *B* over 18 months, and *B* promised to pay *A* $60 000 on completion. Since the contract would not be performed by either party within one year, it would be "caught" (affected) by the Statute. Before *A* began work, *B* could repudiate with impunity and *A* would have no right to sue *B*.

However, if after *A* had started working, *B* repudiated and refused to give *A* access to *B*'s premises where the work was being done, *A* could sue *B* *quantum meruit* for the value of the work done to that point. Although *B* could still repudiate the oral contract (and *A* would have no right to enforce the contract in court), *B* had nevertheless requested the work to be done and would be liable to pay a reasonable price for it, as was explained in Chapter 6.

Suppose that under the oral agreement in Illustration 10.8, *A* completed the work as agreed, with *B*'s acquiescence. The court would view *B*'s original promise to pay for the work as a continuing offer of a unilateral contract, which *A* accepted by completing performance. No contract was formed until *A* completed performance but at that moment the price became immediately payable.

In this view of the facts, the contract is clearly completed in less than a year after its formation—completion of the work—and it is not caught by the Statute. *A* could, therefore, sue *B* successfully for the agreed price of $60 000—another example of the lengths to which the courts will go in their reasoning to prevent the Statute from working an injustice. At the same time, we should note that the agreed price would bind *both* parties, as it would in any enforceable contract. *A* could not refuse *B*'s tender of $60 000 and sue *quantum meruit* simply because *A* believed the work to be worth more than the agreed price. The enforceable oral contract, now outside the Statute, governs the price *A* may recover.

Effect of a Subsequent Written Memorandum

Third, a written memorandum may come into existence *after* the contract has been formed and the memorandum will still satisfy the Statute. As long as the memorandum comes into existence before the action is brought on the contract, it provides the necessary evidence.

ILLUSTRATION 10.10

P agrees orally to buy Blackacre from *V*. *P* then refuses to complete the contract, and *V* sends her a letter outlining the contract and demanding that she carry out her obligations. *P* replies by letter saying that she has decided not to go through with the contract referred to in *V*'s letter and that she is not bound since the contract is not in writing. Even though the statements in *P*'s letter were intended as a denial of liability, the two letters taken together would amount to a sufficient memorandum to satisfy the Statute and make the contract enforceable.

Defendant Must Expressly Plead the Statute

Fourth, a defendant who is sued upon an oral contract must expressly plead the Statute as a defence to the action. If he fails to plead it, the court will decide the case without reference to the Statute. The plaintiff will then succeed if he establishes that the contract, though oral, was validly formed.

Effect on a Prior Written Contract

Fifth, an oral contract may effectively vary or dissolve a prior written contract even though the oral contract could not itself be enforced. An oral contract within the Statute is effective as long as a party does not have to bring an action to have it enforced.

ILLUSTRATION 10.11

P agrees to buy Roselawn from *V* under a written contract containing a promise by *V* to give vacant possession on a certain day. Subsequently, *V* has unexpected difficulty in removing his tenants; he informs *P* that he will not be able to give vacant possession. *P* then finds another property equally suitable to her and available with vacant possession. Rather than get into a dispute, the parties make a mutual oral agreement to call off the contract: *P* releases *V* from his promise to transfer Roselawn with vacant possession in return for a release by *V* of *P*'s promise to pay the purchase price. Afterwards *V* succeeds in removing his tenants and sues *P* to enforce the original written contract. *P* may successfully plead that the subsequent oral contract validly terminated the written contract.

Nonetheless, the oral contract cannot be sued upon directly. Suppose that in addition to terminating the prior contract *V* had orally agreed to give *P* an option on another property in settlement of *V*'s default in not giving vacant possession. Although the oral contract effectively dissolved the prior written contract, *P* could not sue upon the promise to give an option because otherwise the court would be enforcing an oral promise for an interest in land.[15]

Only the Party Who Has Signed Can Be Sued

Finally, as we have seen, a party to a contract who has signed a memorandum can be sued, but she cannot sue the other party who has not signed a memorandum; if the contract were void, neither party would have any rights under it.

THE DOCTRINE OF PART PERFORMANCE

We have seen how the courts have struggled to cut down the scope of the Statute of Frauds, severely limiting the circumstances in which it would apply. Nevertheless, in the common law courts even strict interpretation did not prevent the Statute from thwarting a large number of

---

15. See *Morris v. Baron*, [1918] A.C. 1 for a similar result.

contracts. The courts of equity were prepared to go further than the common law courts to enforce contracts concerning interests in land. Plaintiffs often sued in equity because of the courts' special power to grant the remedy of specific performance when they felt the circumstances warranted it.[16] Shortly after the Statute of Frauds was passed, the courts of equity developed and applied the doctrine of **part performance** to contracts concerning land: if the plaintiff could show that he had begun performance of the contract in reliance on it, the court would accept that performance as evidence of the contract in place of a written memorandum. Our modern courts still employ the doctrine in cases concerning an interest in land.

part performance
performance begun by a plaintiff in reliance on an oral contract relating to an interest in land, and accepted by the courts as evidence of the contract in place of a written memorandum

Not every act of performance under a contract qualifies as a substitute for a written memorandum. The following conditions must be satisfied before the court will enforce the contract:

(a) The contract must be one concerning land.

(b) The acts of performance must suggest quite clearly the existence of a contract respecting the land in question; they must not be ambiguous and just as readily explained as part of a quite different transaction. In Canada, a payment of a deposit on the price of land, by itself, while certainly an act of part performance, is not a sufficient substitute for writing: the payment could refer to almost any kind of contract between the parties—a contract for the sale of goods or for services to be rendered.[17] (Illustration 10.7 above shows that the purchaser may at least obtain the return of the deposit.) However, if a plaintiff has taken possession of the land with the acquiescence of the defendant and has begun to make improvements on it, the court considers this a sufficient act of part performance to satisfy the Statute. It would be extraordinary for an owner to allow a stranger to enter on his land and make improvements unless there was a contract in relation to the land to explain this behaviour.

(c) The plaintiff, not the defendant, must perform the acts, and must suffer a loss by the performance if the contract is not enforced. The plaintiff's performance in reliance on the oral contract and the defendant's refusal to carry out the contract combine to create a hardship that equity recognizes and seeks to remedy.[18]

Once an act of part performance is accepted by the court as sufficient evidence, the contract will be enforced. Even though the act of part performance does not disclose all the terms of the contract, the court will enforce the contract according to the terms orally agreed.

CASE 10.2

Ames entered into an oral contract for a 21-year lease of a flat and Rawlinson, the landlord, agreed to make certain alterations. During the course of the alterations (per-formed by Rawlinson), Ames inspected them and offered suggestions for further changes. Subsequently, she refused

continued

---

16. See Chapter 2 and Chapter 15.

17. See Ross v. Ross, Jr. et al. (1973), 33 D.L.R. (3d) 351. In England, however, shortly afterwards the House of Lords held that it is sufficient that the acts of part performance merely indicate the existence of a contract: Steadman v. Steadman, [1976] A.C. 536. In that case the court held that payment of arrears of maintenance by a husband to his wife was sufficient part performance of a contract to transfer land to him. The court admitted evidence of the full terms of the oral contract and ordered specific performance.

18. See Thompson v. Guaranty Trust Co. of Canada, [1974] S.C.R. 1023. The plaintiff had worked the farm of the deceased for over 40 years, receiving practically no remuneration during that time. On several occasions the deceased had stated to third persons that everything would go to the plaintiff if he remained with the deceased. The Supreme Court found that the years of work put in by the plaintiff were sufficient part performance to satisfy the Statute of Frauds.

to move into the flat, claiming that as the agreement was for an interest in land and required to be in writing and signed by her, it was unenforceable against her.

Rawlinson sued for specific performance of the lease and was able to offer evidence of his part performance in lieu of a written memorandum. He succeeded.[19]

CONTEMPORARY ISSUE

Should the Statute of Frauds Be Repealed?

The Statute of Frauds was passed in a particular historical situation, to deal with problems arising out of that situation. Over the three centuries since it was passed, the courts have seen injustices created by the application of a statute intended to prevent injustice. They have gone to considerable lengths to limit the Statute and soften its impact. Their efforts have created a confusing and seemingly contradictory set of exceptions and qualifications.

It has been argued that the historical reasons for creating the Statute of Frauds no longer exist. As you have seen, the Statute has been repealed or amended in some common law jurisdictions. Perhaps it is time to replace or amend it throughout Canada.

On the other hand, consider this recent statement from Mr. Justice Côté of the Alberta Court of Appeal:

> Over 20 years ago, it was fashionable to attack the Statute of Frauds, and indeed a number of jurisdictions have repealed large chunks of it. But Alberta has not touched s. 4. In my view, the trend of modern legislation is actually to call for more writing in contracts and commercial transactions. The idea that one can validly sell a valuable piece of land entirely by oral discussions runs contrary to the expectations of most lay people; one can almost say that absence of writing casts into doubt intention to create binding legal relations. So I feel no compulsion to undermine the Statute.

Sources: *Austie v. Aksnowicz*, [1999] 10 W.W.R. 713, 70 Alta. L.R. (3d) 154 (C.A.), at para. 55; Law Reform Commission of British Columbia, *Report on the Statute of Frauds* (1997); Manitoba Law Reform Commission, *Report on the Statute of Frauds* (1980); University of Alberta Institute of Law Research and Reform, *Background Paper No. 12: Statute of Frauds* (1979); *Report No. 44* (1985).

Questions to Consider

1. How are business relationships and commercial activity affected by complex legal rules about the enforceability of oral contracts?
2. Are there sound policy reasons for requiring some contracts to be in writing?
3. Do you think the distinction between a void contract and an unenforceable contract makes sense in a business context? Give your reasons.
4. Are amendments adequate to address the problems arising from the Statute of Frauds, or would it be better to repeal the Statute and replace it with legislation that meets contemporary needs?

---

19. Rawlinson v. Ames, [1925] 1 Ch. 96.

REQUIREMENTS OF THE SALE OF GOODS ACT

Until 1893, a provision of the English Statute of Frauds required as evidence of contracts for the sale of goods priced at £10 or more, either a written memorandum or one of three types of conduct. In that year, the provision was repealed and replaced by a similar one in the new Sale of Goods Act. When the Canadian provinces adopted the Sale of Goods Act, they followed the English example.

In 1954, when the English Parliament amended the Statute of Frauds, it also repealed the section in the Sale of Goods Act requiring special types of evidence to enforce contracts for the sale of goods, British Columbia followed suit in 1958, as did Ontario in 1994.[20] The requirements are still in effect for the other common law provinces in Canada.

What Constitutes a Sale of Goods Under the Act?

What is a sale of goods for the purposes of the Act? The question is not always easy. Is, for example, a contract to provide materials and erect a garage a contract for *the sale of goods* or one for *work and materials*? If it is one for work and materials, it is enforceable without satisfying the requirements of the Sale of Goods Act, but if it is one for the sale of goods, it must comply with those requirements. The problem of defining a sale of goods is also important for other provisions of the Act, and we shall consider it again in Chapter 16.

The various provinces have translated the £10 minimum into different amounts varying from $30 to $50.[21] Otherwise the wording is the same as the 1893 English wording.

CASE 10.3

In *Baldey v. Parker*,[22] Parker bargained for various articles in Baldey's linen shop. A separate price was agreed on for each, and no single item was sold for £10 or more, though the aggregate was much more than £10. Later a dispute arose about discounts, and when the goods were delivered, Parker refused them.

Baldey brought an action against him for breach of contract, claiming that: the price of the articles should be considered item by item; the amount of each sale was not large enough to come within the Act; consequently the contract, though oral, was enforceable. The court rejected the seller's argument and held that the total value governed the contract, making it unenforceable.

Accordingly, when a number of items are purchased at one time, the *aggregate* price of the order is the deciding amount for the purposes of the Act.

The Act states: "The price in a contract of sale may be fixed by the contract or may be left to be fixed in a manner thereby agreed, or may be determined by the course of dealing between the parties."[23] In other words, the Act permits consideration to be determined in other ways than by stating a fixed price.

---

20. Law Reform (Enforcement of Contracts) Act, 1954, 2 & 3 Eliz. 2, c. 34, s. 1 (U.K.); Statute Law Amendment Act, 1958, S.B.C. 1958, c. 52, s. 17; Statute Law Amendment (Government Management and Services) Act 1994, S.O. 1994, c. 27, s. 54.

21. The amount is $40 in Nova Scotia; $50 in Newfoundland, Saskatchewan, and Alberta; $30 in Prince Edward Island. These amounts are, of course, insignificant compared to their value over 100 years ago when the Sale of Goods Act was adopted.

22. (1823), 107 E.R. 297.

23. See, for example: Sale of Goods Act, R.S.B.C. 1996, c. 410, s. 12; R.S.O. 1990, c. S.1, s. 9; R.S.N.S. 1989, c. 408, s. 11.

Evidence That Satisfies the Act

Unlike the Statute of Frauds, the Sale of Goods Act states expressly that a party to a contract for the sale of goods who cannot produce the required memorandum may still enforce the contract if he can show one of the following kinds of conduct:[24]

   (a) "acceptance" and actual receipt of the goods by the buyer

   (b) part payment tendered by the buyer and accepted by the seller

   (c) something "by way of earnest" given by the buyer to the seller

"Acceptance"

"acceptance"

any conduct by the buyer in relation to the goods that amounts to recognition of an existing contract of sale

We have placed the word "**acceptance**" in quotation marks because the term has a special meaning in the Act. It means any conduct by the buyer in relation to the goods that amounts to recognition of an existing contract of sale. The buyer will have "accepted" the goods when he does anything tantamount to admitting that he has a contract with respect to them, and thus makes the contract enforceable. Although he may be neither satisfied nor willing to keep the goods, if he does anything that acknowledges them as the goods ordered, he will not be able to claim that the contract is unenforceable. For example, proof that the buyer has inspected the goods or sampled them to see if they are what he ordered establishes his "acceptance." Of course, he may still protest against the quality of the seller's performance; if the goods are not according to the terms of the contract, he may obtain remedies for breach of the contract. A buyer's remedies are examined later, in Chapter 16.

Part Payment

part payment

something tendered by the buyer and accepted by the seller *after* formation of the contract, to be deducted from the price

There may be doubt whether a buyer has made a **part payment**; the courts have to decide each case on its own merits. One point is clear: a part payment that has the effect of making the contract enforceable must be a separate act subsequent to the formation of the contract. Thus, if the buyer agrees to set off a present debt owed to her by the seller as the equivalent of a deposit on the goods, the court will not regard this arrangement as a part payment. In the words of Baron Alderson, "…[the buyer] must have done two things; first, made a contract, and next, he must have given something…in part payment or discharge of his liability. But where one of the terms of an oral bargain is for the seller to take something in part payment, that term alone cannot be equivalent to actual part payment."[25]

ILLUSTRATION 10.12

A orally offers to sell his old computer to *B* for $150. *B* accepts orally and then hands *A* a deposit of $10, which *A* accepts. The act of handing *A* the deposit immediately after the contract was formed is a sufficient act of part payment subsequent to the contract and satisfies the provisions of the Act.

Suppose, instead, *B* replies, "I'll buy your computer at that price if you will deduct the $10 you owe me from the price and consider it as a deposit." If *A* agreed to these terms, there would not be sufficient part payment.

We must contrast a sale of goods (moveable, tangible property) with a sale of an interest in land (including buildings). Part payment is acceptable evidence as a substitute for a written memorandum in contracts for the sale of goods, but may be insufficient in contracts for an interest in land.

---

24. R.S.N.S. 1989, c. 408, s. 7.

25. Walker v. Nussey (1847), 153 E.R. 1203 at 1205.

"Earnest"

"**Earnest**" differs from part payment in that it is not deducted from the price to be paid. Rather it is a token sum (or article) given to seal the bargain. Although the giving of something by way of earnest was common at one time, it is now rarely if ever done, and the reference to the practice remains as a relic in the Act.

When Both Acts Apply

Both the Sale of Goods Act and the Statute of Frauds may apply to the same contract. They both apply, for example, where there is an oral agreement to sell goods that are to be delivered and paid for by instalments over a period exceeding one year. The evidence may satisfy the requirements of the Sale of Goods Act if the buyer accepts some of the goods or makes part payment, but it does not comply with the Statute of Frauds because it is an oral contract that neither party can wholly perform within one year. Accordingly, it is unenforceable because of the Statute of Frauds, but not because of the Sale of Goods Act.

Criticism of the Sale of Goods Act

The requirement of a written memorandum in the Sale of Goods Act is open to the same criticism as the comparable provision in the Statute of Frauds. In 1937 the English Law Revision Committee complained:

> A man who by an oral contract buys or sells £10 worth of goods cannot...[subject to the special conduct accepted in lieu of a memorandum] enforce the bargain, yet a man who orally contracts to do work or to sell shares or to insure property...can enforce his bargain, and have it enforced against him *however great the amount involved*[26] (italics added).

Many other legal aspects of a contract for the sale of goods exist besides questions of evidence. We shall turn to these later, in Chapter 16.

CONSUMER PROTECTION LEGISLATION

For a number of years, growing concern for the protection of consumers in our increasingly complex market for goods and services resulted in much legislative activity: all the common law provinces have passed statutes varying both in name and application.[27] These statutes are concerned with the protection of only one party to a consumer contract, the buyer. An example is the Ontario Consumer Protection Act, which covers not only goods but also services. The significant sections of the Act with regard to the requirement of writing are found in section 1:

(d) "buyer" means a person who purchases goods for consumption or services under an executory contract and includes his or her agent, but does not include a person who buys in the course of carrying on business or an association of individuals, a partnership or corporation;

(i) "executory contract" means a contract between a buyer and seller for the purchase and sale of goods or services in respect of which delivery of the goods or performance of the services or payment in full of the consideration is not made at the time the contract is entered into;

---

26. The Law Revision Committee (U.K.), *Sixth Interim Report*, 1937 (Reprinted 1955), Cmd. 5449, p. 9.

27. See, for example: Consumer Protection Act, R.S.B.C. 1996, c. 69; R.S.O. 1990, c. C.31; R.S.N.S. 1989, c. 92; Direct Sales Cancellation Act, R.S.A. 1980, c. D-35.

and section 19, which states:

(1) Every executory contract...shall be in writing and shall contain...[detailed information about the subject-matter of the contract, details of credit arrangements and costs and any warranty or guarantee given].

(2) An executory contract is not binding on the buyer unless the contract is made in accordance with...[subsection (1) among other requirements] and is signed by the parties and a duplicate original copy thereof is in the possession of each of the parties thereto.

These sections are intended to give consumers wide protection in the form of complete disclosure by sellers.[28] Provinces have passed detailed regulations and set up agencies to hear consumer complaints as well as to investigate or even negotiate on the consumer's behalf. We will discuss consumer protection legislation in more detail in Chapter 32.

QUESTIONS FOR REVIEW

1. Distinguish among contracts that are unenforceable, voidable, and void.

2. Explain the criticism that "on the whole they [the provisions of the Statute of Frauds and Sale of Goods Act requiring written evidence] promote rather than restrain dishonesty." (The Law Revision Committee, (U.K.) *Sixth Interim Report*, 937.)

3. Explain the difference between a guarantee and an indemnity. Is there any policy basis for treating the two differently?

4. An accounting firm telephones *A* to offer her employment for the summer following the current academic year, and also for the following summer if she performs satisfactorily in the first summer. *A* accepts. Two weeks before the end of the academic year she receives a second call cancelling the job. Has she any legal remedy? What ironic aspect is there to this situation?

5. Give two examples of how it may be necessary to use more than one document to satisfy the requirements for a written memorandum.

6. What difference is there between part performance and part payment?

7. *X* writes a letter to *Y* stating, "The contract you included in your letter dated June 2, and that you claim binds us is unenforceable because I didn't sign it." Comment on *X*'s statement.

8. State which of the following contracts are affected by a statutory requirement that would permit the promisor to plead that the contract cannot be enforced against her because evidence of the terms is not available in the required form:

(a) *A* and *B*, having entered into a written agreement as purchaser and vendor respectively of a piece of land, later agree by telephone to call off the sale.

(b) *C* enters into an oral contract with *D*, a contractor, to build a house for *C*.

(c) *E* is the proprietor of a business that requires a bank loan. *E*'s father, *F*, tells the bank manager that if the bank will approve the loan and *E* does not repay it, he (*F*) will.

---

28. See, for example: Household Finance Corp. Ltd. v. McEllim *et ux.* (1970), 75 W.W.R. 187, where a husband and wife were joint signers of a promissory note. Only one copy of the detailed information on credit was given to the husband; the plaintiff (lender) thought this was sufficient. The action was dismissed against both parties because the wife had not received her own copy of the credit information.

(d) *G*, having just graduated from university, goes to work for a large Canadian manufacturing firm. In the exchange of letters between *G* and her employer, nothing is said about the duration of *G*'s employment.

(e) *H* agrees orally to buy six compact discs at $15 each from *J*.

9. Give an example of when a party to an unenforceable contract may nevertheless recover money he has paid to the other party.

10. Are there any circumstances in which an oral contract for the sale of goods may still be enforceable?

11. Regardless of the legal requirements, what are the practical advantages of a written memorandum?

12. Despite the criticisms of the writing requirements in the Sale of Goods Act, all common law provinces have passed statutes requiring detailed written consumer contracts. Why have they done so?

CASES AND PROBLEMS

1 On January 15, Tonino made a lease with Logan, signed by both parties, in which Logan agreed to rent her apartment to Tonino at $900 a month for three years, commencing February 1. In March of the same year Tonino and Logan agreed orally that Tonino would pay an additional $35 a month rent upon the completion of certain alterations and repairs to the premises within three months. Logan completed the alterations and repairs in April, but Tonino refused to pay anything but the $900 a month specified in the lease. In August, Logan sued Tonino for the additional rent.

What points must the court settle in reaching its decision, and what should the decision be?

2 Northern, a charter aircraft service, operated four aircraft including a Falcon 10 jet aircraft and a Metroliner 2, turbo-prop aircraft. The Falcon is a high-speed, fuel-efficient and highly sophisticated jet aircraft. In 1994–95 there were only two other Falcon aircraft operating in Canada. Pilots require specialized training to fly this aircraft, and to a lesser extent, also for the Metroliner. Gilbert had approximately seven years' experience as a commercial pilot on various other aircraft but had been laid off, along with many other pilots, when his airline merged with a larger carrier.

Northern offered Gilbert a job flying the Falcon and Metroliner. They discussed the terms of employment, and reached agreement orally. Northern agreed to pay moving and relocation expenses for Gilbert and his family from Edmonton to Yellowknife, and to arrange for all necessary professional training so that Gilbert could become qualified to fly the Falcon and Metroliner in Northern's charter operations; Northern would pay all the costs of his training, including payment of his salary while undergoing the training. Gilbert understood that the training was very expensive. To justify such an investment Northern insisted that Gilbert make a minimum commitment of two years' work for Northern. Gilbert agreed.

After less than 10 months, Gilbert gave two weeks' notice that he was leaving to take another position with a charter airline in Ontario. Northern sued him for breach of contract, and in particular to recover $53 000 in expenses, most of which was the cost of the training programs as well as the salary he received during the training periods. Gilbert defended by claiming that because his two-year contract was not in writing it was unenforceable.

Summarize the arguments for both sides and give your opinion of result.

3 M, N, O, and P each owned 25 percent of the shares in Resort Hotel Inc. As a result of a bad season, the hotel had a cash flow problem. M arranged to borrow $25 000 from a friend, Q, and to lend it to the hotel on condition that if the hotel did not repay the funds, his three co-owners, N, O, and P, would each pay $5000 to M. The three agreed to the arrangement. Subsequently, the hotel defaulted and M repaid the $25 000 to Q. He requested payment from N, O, and P but they refused to pay.

M sued the three for $5000 each; they defended claiming that their promises were "guarantees" and since they were not in writing they were unenforceable. M claimed that their obligations were part of a larger transaction to protect their shared interests in Resort Hotel and, therefore, were not mere guarantees. Whose argument should succeed? Give reasons.

4 The manager of Jiffy Discount Stores ordered a carload of refrigerators from Colonel Electric Company by telephone. When the refrigerators arrived at the warehouse, the transport employees and Jiffy's employees began unloading them. When about half of them were unloaded, the manager arrived and asked to examine one. An employee uncrated one refrigerator, and after looking it over, the manager stated it was not the right model and ordered the transport employees to take them back. The refrigerators were returned to Colonel Electric Company, and the company sued Jiffy Discount Stores for breach of contract. It was proved that the manager was mistaken, and the refrigerators did conform to the telephone order. What should the result be?

5 Carter left a position where he was earning $48 000 a year to accept a position as general manager of Buildwell Limited at the same annual salary. All negotiations leading up to his appointment were carried on orally between Carter and Webster, the president of Buildwell Limited. Both parties assured each other in various conversations that the employment would last "for life"; they agreed that each year Carter would receive a bonus, and that if he was not satisfied with it he could terminate his employment, but that the company could not terminate his employment unless he "did something wrong."

Over the succeeding few years Carter's salary was increased from $4000 to $5000 per month, and he received in addition annual bonuses of up to $4000. A letter to Carter announcing his last bonus was signed by both the president and vice-president of the company and included the words, "And we want you to know that with all the experiences we are going through in connection with the business, your efforts are appreciated."

Shortly afterwards Webster died, and immediately the company dismissed Carter without explanation, paying him one month's salary. Carter then attempted to go into business for himself but without success. He sued Buildwell Limited for wrongful dismissal, claiming breach of his employment contract. Can Buildwell Limited successfully plead the Statute of Frauds?

6 In February, Baldwin Co. Ltd., a woollen manufacturer, contracted to sell 500 pieces of blue serge to Martin Bros., tailors, at a price of $40 000, as stated in a written memorandum signed by both parties. After 220 pieces of the cloth had been delivered, a dispute arose between the parties: Martin Bros. complained of delay in delivery, and Baldwin Co. Ltd. complained of failure to pay for the goods delivered. Baldwin Co. Ltd. sued Martin Bros. for the price of the goods delivered, and Martin Bros. counterclaimed for damages for non-delivery.

In August, before the case came to trial, the parties orally agreed to a settlement and to substitute for the original contract a new one, in which Martin Bros. would have an additional three months to pay for the goods and have an option of buying the remaining 280 pieces at the prices in the earlier contract. The following November, Martin Bros. paid the amount due on the original 220 pieces of cloth and placed an order for the remaining 280 pieces under the option agreed to in the substituted contract. Baldwin Co. Ltd. refused to deliver these pieces, the agreed price being no longer profitable to them. Martin Bros. then brought an action against Baldwin Co. Ltd. for damages for breach of contract (failure to deliver). Should this action succeed?

7 John Brown, a retired widower, stated to Mrs. Adele Barber, that if he could find a suitable house and if she would move into it as a housekeeper, help operate it as a rooming house, and take care of him, he would give her the house on his death. Mrs. Barber agreed. Mr. Brown purchased a house that he operated as a rooming house until his death five years later. During this period Mrs. Barber served as housekeeper, making the necessary food and other household purchases and turning over to Mr. Brown the balance of the board money received from the tenants. She received no remuneration for her services other than her own board and an occasional allowance for clothing.

Mr. Brown made no provision in his will for Mrs. Barber, and following his death Mrs. Barber brought an action against the executors of his estate for specific performance of his promise. In evidence, Mrs. Barber offered the testimony of her two daughters, her son, and her son-in-law, who were present at the time of the original conversation between her and Mr. Brown. The executor contested the action.

(a) What legal considerations are relevant to a decision in this case? State whether Mrs. Barber's action would succeed.

(b) Suppose that instead of remaining in the house until Mr. Brown's death, Mrs. Barber and Mr. Brown had decided to part company after Mrs. Barber had served as his housekeeper for three years. At that time Mr. Brown wrote and signed a memorandum to Mrs. Barber that stated, "I hereby promise to pay you $5000 in consideration for the surrender by you of any rights to my house according to our earlier agreement." When Mr. Brown failed to pay the $5000 to Mrs. Barber, she sued him for this amount. What defence might Mr. Brown offer? Should Mrs. Barber succeed?

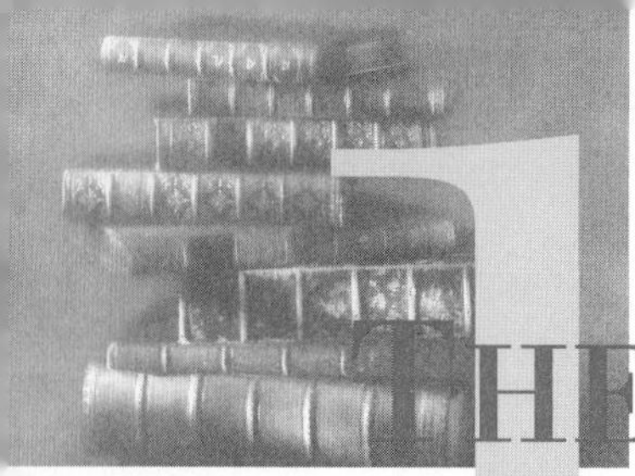

11 The Interpretation of Contracts

The Relationship Between Formation and Interpretation of Contracts

The Interpretation of Express Terms

The Parol Evidence Rule

Implied Terms as a Method of Interpretation

Once a contract has been formed, the parties may disagree about its meaning. We discuss here the nature of such disagreements and how they are resolved. In this chapter we examine such questions as:

- how do courts interpret express terms in a contract?
- what are the two main approaches to interpreting terms in a contract?
- how do courts choose between conflicting testimony of the parties?
- what is the parol evidence rule and how does it work?
- how do the courts avoid applying the rule?
- what are implied terms and how are they recognized?

The Relationship Between Formation and Interpretation of Contracts

In order to understand the nature of contracts we need to understand the elements required to form a valid contract. However, the large majority of disputes are not about the formation of contracts but about their meaning. Indeed, very often the reason a party disputes the formation of a contract is that he disagrees with its interpretation by the other party.

ILLUSTRATION 11.1

Smith offers to build a set of cabinets for Doe for $1000, and Doe accepts. The next day Smith appears and asks where the lumber is. Doe says, "You are supposed to supply it." Smith replies, "My price was for the work only, not for the materials."

At this point the dispute may take one of two different paths. In the first, one party may claim that the offer was too vague because it omitted an essential term indicating who should supply the lumber: such an ambiguous offer, is not capable of acceptance, and accordingly, no contract is formed. In the second approach, each side concedes that the agreement "to build a set of cabinets for $1000" is valid, but Smith claims the proper meaning to be that Doe should supply the lumber, and Doe will claim the contrary.

The problem of **construing** or *interpreting* the contract is the subject of this chapter. We are not dealing here with fraud or deceit, though each party firmly believes that his interpretation of the contract is the only sensible one and that the other party must be dishonest to suggest that there is any other. Often, a lawyer's most difficult task is to show the client that the view held by the other side has some merit. Only then may the lawyer broach the possibility of a compromise or, if the dispute goes to court, be in a position to counter the arguments of the other side.

construing
interpreting

A cynic may observe how strange it is that the interpretation by each party invariably favours itself. In response, we point out two characteristics of contracts. First, in the vast majority of cases, parties do not have conflicting interpretations because they have understood each other well enough to complete their bargain without dispute. Second, even when parties disagree, each party might well have rejected the terms at the outset had he realized they would be construed less favourably towards him. Words are at best inefficient vehicles for communicating thoughts: they can be ambiguous without the parties realizing it—and people tend to give themselves the benefit of the doubt even when they sense a possible ambiguity. Hence, disagreements about interpretation of contracts are not surprising but rather are a common risk in business arrangements.

When parties go to court to have a question of interpretation settled, the court seeks the most reasonable meaning that can be attributed to the words in the circumstances. This is no easy task. The difficulties courts experience with interpretation problems often lead to much criticism of the law. Learning that his "sensible and just" interpretation has been ignored, the losing party tends to blame the law, the judge, the dishonesty of his opponent, and his lawyer. The winning party regards the legal proceedings as superfluous and a waste of her time and money since they merely confirm the meaning of the contract that she accepted from the outset. To the outsider the dispute may appear as a mere quibbling over words. Yet the litigation arises because the parties could not agree on the meaning of the words they themselves used, leaving the dispute to be solved by the court. Difficulties may arise even in relatively simple contracts. In complicated and important contracts, prevention of ambiguity through the use of legal advice in drafting the terms is likely to be far cheaper than the cure.

To return to our example of the cabinets in Illustration 11.1 above, the misunderstanding might have been avoided had Doe asked Smith, "Does your offer include supplying the lumber?" She might also have asked, "When shall I pay you: in advance, in instalments, or after the work is completed?" It is understandable but unfortunate that people do not always think about all the important questions that may affect their contracts. The list of possible questions is a long one and while the parties can reduce the chances of a later dispute over interpretation by carefully discussing the implications of their contract before its formation, a risk of dispute remains.

THE INTERPRETATION OF EXPRESS TERMS

Two Approaches to Interpretation

What precisely did Smith promise when he agreed "to build a set of cabinets for $1000"? In attempting to answer such a question, it is sometimes argued that there are two approaches to the interpretation of words: the **strict** or **plain-meaning approach** and the **liberal approach**.

The plain-meaning approach restricts interpretation to the ordinary or dictionary meaning of a word. However, few words have a "plain" or "ordinary" meaning. Browsing through a dictionary will show that many words have two or more different definitions. In addition, the meanings of words change from time to time and place to place—or the context of the words in a contract may make it obvious that they have been used in a special sense.[1]

strict or plain-meaning approach
an approach that restricts interpretation to the ordinary or dictionary meaning of a word

liberal approach
an approach that looks to the intent of the parties and surrounding circumstances, and tends to minimize, but does not ignore, the importance of the words actually used

---

1. See Lewison, *The Interpretation of Contracts*. London: Sweet & Maxwell, 1989; Chafee, "The Disorderly Conduct of Words" (1942), 20 *Can. Bar Rev.*, p. 752. See also our discussion of the interpretation of statutes in Chapter 1 on the role of the courts as interpreters of legislation.

The liberal approach, by contrast, looks to the purposes of the parties in drafting their agreement: what did they intend? It stresses the circumstances surrounding the contract, the negotiations leading up to it, the knowledge of the parties, and any other relevant facts. It minimizes the importance of the words actually used. The liberal approach also has its limitations. In its extreme form, it too may lead to unsatisfactory results by inviting endless speculation about what the parties may have intended but never expressed. The particular words one chooses to use are a part of one's conduct in relation to the contract, and in law, conduct (including words) must continue to serve as the primary guide to one's intentions.

How the Courts Apply the Approaches

As a result there are not really two distinct approaches to interpretation, one of which is used to the exclusion of the other: rather than choosing between them, a court will emphasize one approach more than the other. In other words, the court must decide, in the circumstances of each case, how far it should look beyond the words used to explain their meanings.

In Illustration 11.1, about the cabinets, Smith promised "to build" them. Does "to build" include "to supply materials"? Literally, "to build" means only "to construct," but in many circumstances it may include "to supply materials." Thus, when a contractor undertakes to build a house, the price usually includes the price of materials. In the illustration, the words themselves are not conclusive either way. Since there is an ambiguity, the court will look outside the contract to the surrounding circumstances as a means of clearing up this ambiguity. For example, it will hear evidence of any past transactions between the parties to learn whether materials have been included in previous building contracts between them. It will hear evidence of the negotiations leading up to the contract: perhaps Smith had quoted different prices varying with the kind of wood to be used; perhaps Doe had made it clear earlier that she wanted an inclusive price. Any of these facts, if established in court, would support the claim that "to build" in this contract meant "to supply materials" as well as labour.

On the difficult problem of achieving a balance between the plain-meaning and liberal approaches to interpreting the words parties use in their contract, one of the great authorities on contract law commented:

> …[I]t can hardly be insisted on too often or too vigorously that language at its best is always a defective and uncertain instrument, that words do not define themselves, that terms and sentences in a contract, a deed, or a will do not apply themselves to external objects and performances, that the meaning of such terms and sentences consists of the ideas that they induce in the mind of some individual person who uses or hears or reads them, and that seldom in a litigated case do the words of a contract convey one identical meaning to the two contracting parties or to third persons.[2]

How the Courts Choose Between Conflicting Testimony

There is an inaccurate but widespread belief that when the two parties in a dispute give conflicting testimony in court and there are no other witnesses, the court will not accept either account but will apply the popular maxim, "One person's word is as good as another's." Normally reputable individuals have sometimes been tempted into making extravagant or distorted statements on the false assumption that a court has no choice but to accept their story on an equal footing with their opponents' testimony. True, a court is reluctant to accept direct testimony of one party rather than the other; it will seek corroboration of one of their versions if

---

2. Corbin, *Corbin on Contracts* (One Volume Edition), Pt. 3, Ch. 24, sec. 536, p. 499, St. Paul, MN: West Publishing Co., 1952.

possible from a third party or from the actions of the parties in relation to the contract. As a last resort, however, a court will choose between their versions, basing its decision on the credibility of the parties themselves, taking all the circumstances into account. In other words, it decides which story seems more reasonable. With their experience in this type of problem, judges, though certainly not infallible, develop an intuitive ability to assess the credibility of witnesses.

Special Usage of Words

To interpret the express terms of a contract, the court uses the dictionary definitions of the words used, their meaning in the context of the contract, the surrounding circumstances of the contract, and the judge's ability to weigh the evidence. Another important aid is evidence of special usage of words in particular trades and in particular areas of the country. In Illustration 11.1, Smith might produce expert witnesses who testify from their experience that in the carpentry trade standard usage of the word "build" means labour only. Or he might show that in that part of the country the word always has that meaning. In *Brown v. Byrne*, Mr. Justice Coleridge said:

> What words more plain than "a thousand," "a week," "a day"? Yet the cases are familiar in which "a thousand" has been held to mean twelve hundred, "a week" a week only during the theatrical season, "a day" a working day. In such cases the evidence neither adds to, nor qualifies, nor contradicts the written contract; it only ascertains it, by expounding the language.[3]

Evidence of special usage is not necessarily conclusive: a court may decide that the word was used in a general rather than a special way, perhaps because the user of the word was aware that the other party was not familiar with trade usage. In general, the courts construe words most strictly against the party who has suggested them, in order to prevent him from being able to select, among two or more possible meanings, the one that turns out to be to his advantage.[4]

Predicting the Likely Decision of a Court

There are no hard and fast rules of interpretation. At one time, the courts were quite mechanical in applying ancient rules of interpretation, but today they try to look for the most reasonable interpretation in the circumstances—an approach that requires flexibility and common sense. For a business person to be able to predict the decision a court is likely to reach if the meaning of a contract is challenged, she must know what a "reasonable interpretation" of it would be. Her personal interest deprives her of the ability to reach an objective conclusion about that meaning: she needs unbiased advice. A court, in searching for the objective meaning of words, seeks the advice of the mythical reasonable person—the informed, objective bystander. The business person's imperfect approximation of this legendary figure[5] must be her lawyer. If she finds her interpretation of a contract challenged, she should immediately obtain legal advice. By doing so she will have the benefit of an unbiased external opinion when it will be of most help to her. Her protection will be twofold: if her interpretation of the contract is correct, she will learn how best to enforce it; if it is incorrect, she may avoid a costly breach of contract.

The Goal of the Courts: To Give Validity to Contracts

Courts must render their decisions, difficult though they may be. Frequently, it may seem easier for them to declare an agreement unenforceable because of ambiguity in its wording; but if they

---

3. (1854), 118 E.R. 1304 at 1309.

4. See Manulife Bank of Canada v. Conlin, [1996] 3 S.C.R. 415.

5. For an amusing account of all the attributes of the "reasonable person" see Herbert, *Uncommon Law*, London: Methuen & Co., 1948, in the fictitious case of Fardell v. Potts.

took this attitude, the courts would not be performing their role of encouraging reliance on seriously made agreements. Consequently, they lean towards keeping an agreement alive rather than brushing it aside as being without force at law. If at all possible, courts assign to equivocal words a meaning that makes a contract enforceable. Lord Wright, one of the most respected of English judges in commercial law, gave a classic statement of the rule in a House of Lords decision:

> The object of the court is to do justice between the parties, and the court will do its best, if satisfied that there was an ascertainable and determinate intention to contract, to give effect to that intention, looking at substance and not mere form. It will not be deterred by mere difficulties of interpretation. Difficulty is not synonymous with ambiguity, so long as any definite meaning can be extracted.[6]

CONTEMPORARY ISSUE

Can Judges Really Assess Credibility?

When a dispute goes to court, each side presents the best evidence it has. In many cases, reliable documents or witnesses who are independent of either side are available to help determine the facts. However, sometimes the only evidence is the testimony of the disputing parties. The case then becomes a "credibility contest." The judge has to assess the credibility of the witnesses and decide whose version seems more reasonable. (Most trials are heard by a judge without a jury.) Credibility includes both truthfulness and reliability. One person may not have seen or heard clearly, may not remember well, or may have observed only part of an event. Even though a witness is honest, his testimony might not be reliable.

It is widely accepted in the legal system that the trial judge is in the best position to assess the witnesses' credibility. Appeal courts hesitate to question the trial judge's assessment because the judge had the opportunity to see and hear the witnesses and observe their demeanour. Both lawyers and judges seem to believe that years of experience on the bench equip judges to evaluate witnesses' credibility better than most people can.

Recent social science research does not support this belief. In particular, studies have shown that judges are no better than average at assessing the truthfulness of witnesses. Researchers have also pointed out cultural differences in people's behaviour that may affect perceptions of credibility. If the judge was raised in the belief that looking an authority straight in the eye is a sign of truth-telling, and the witness was raised in the belief that downcast eyes show respect—or vice versa—the judge may misinterpret the witness's demeanour and wrongly assess his credibility, without having any conscious bias against the witness.

Sources: Alvin Esau, "Credibility and Culture," Comments at Judicial Workshop, September 24, 1998, Webposted at <www.umanitoba.ca/faculties/law/Courses/esau/legal_system/LS-culture.html>; Gilles Renaud, Ontario Court of Justice (Provincial Division), "Evidence of Demeanour: Some Instruction Found in the Early Works of Georges Simenon," Webposted at <www.acjnet.org/capcj/renaudeng.html>.

Questions to Consider

1. If judges are not better than average at assessing the truthfulness of witnesses, what are the implications for the interpretation of contracts in which the parties' testimony conflicts and there is no independent evidence?

2. What steps might a business person take to reduce the likelihood of problems in interpreting contracts?

---

6. Scammel v. Ouston, [1941] 1 All E.R. 14 at 25.

THE PAROL EVIDENCE RULE

The Meaning of the Rule

Before a deal is made, the parties very often engage in a process of bargaining and negotiation, offer and counter-offer, with both sides making concessions until finally they reach a suitable compromise. The bargaining may be carried on orally or in writing. In important contracts, the parties usually put their final agreement into a more formal document signed by both sides. A party may later discover that the document does not contain one or more terms she believed were part of the agreement. The omission may have been due to a mistake in writing down the terms actually agreed upon—a typing error, for example. The equitable remedy of rectification, as explained in Chapter 8, may then be available.

When, however, there is no clear evidence that a term was omitted by error—as when the complaining party admits that she read the document over and approved it—she will be held to the contract as it is written. According to the **parol evidence rule**, a party cannot later add a term previously agreed upon between the parties but not included in the final form of the contract. In this context the word "parol" means *extrinsic to* or *outside of* the written agreement.[7] The rule applies both to an oral agreement that has been reduced to writing and to a written agreement that has been set out in a more formal document.

parol evidence rule
a rule preventing a party to a contract from later adding a term previously agreed upon but not included in the final written contract

The parol evidence rule operates to exclude *terms* that one party claims should be added to the contract. It does not exclude evidence about the formation of the contract such as its legality, the capacity of the parties, mistake, duress, undue influence, or fraud. In other words, it does not affect evidence of any of the circumstances surrounding the contract: it operates only to exclude the introduction of terms not found in the written document. As an example, we have seen that a court will admit oral evidence to prove that one of the parties made a material misrepresentation.

The Consequences of the Rule

Sometimes parties agree to omit a term from the final form of the contract, still intending it to be part of their whole agreement. They are most likely to do so when they are using a standard form contract, such as a conditional sale agreement, a short-term lease, a mortgage, or a grant of land. One party may persuade the other to leave a term out because it will be confusing or because his employer may object to it.

ILLUSTRATION 11.2

Sung offers to lease a computer system to Jeans, Inc., a small but prosperous manufacturer. An attractive part of the deal for Jeans is the promise by Sung that her firm will provide without charge a new software program for inventory and accounts receivable records. Sung explains that the contract contains no reference to this new software program because it is in its final stage of development and has yet to be publicly announced; her firm plans to introduce it with an advertising campaign.

Jeans' manager signs the contract without a term referring to the provision of the new software. The equipment is delivered several weeks later along with the promised program but the program does not function properly and proves to be a failure.

Jeans, Inc. would be unlikely to succeed in an action against Sung's firm for breach of her oral promise. It is doubtful that Jeans would be entitled to rescission for misrepresentation since Sung did not state as a fact that the program was fully developed and available at the time the contract was formed.

---

7. For a more extensive discussion of the meaning of the parol evidence rule, see Cross and Tapper, *Cross on Evidence* (7th ed.), pp. 695ff. London: Butterworth & Co., 1990.

The courts have been reluctant to relax the parol evidence rule even in circumstances where a party suffers hardship; they fear that to do so would tempt parties who are unhappy with their contracts to claim that favourable terms—discussed during negotiations but not agreed upon—are part of their contracts. The courts worry that they would create serious difficulties for the business community if they showed any tendency to upset written agreements deliberately made. For this reason, it is unwise to allow any term of importance to be omitted from the final written form of an agreement. If the term is important and the other side insists on excluding it from the final document, it is better to break off negotiations than to enter into the contract with that term excluded.

The Scope of the Rule

Does the Document Contain the Whole Contract?

We have seen that once the parties have reduced their agreement to a document in its final form, the parol evidence rule precludes either party from adding terms not in that final agreement. While at first sight the rule seems to apply, sometimes the court may conclude that the written document was not intended to embody the *whole* contract. In Chapter 10, we learned that the terms of a contract may be *partly* in writing and *partly* oral; if a party can show that the writing was *not* intended to contain the whole contract but was merely a part of it, then she may introduce evidence of those oral terms.[8]

ILLUSTRATION 11.3

A, the owner of a fleet of dump trucks, agrees orally with *B*, a paving contractor, to move 75 000 cubic feet of gravel within three months from Harrowsmith to Yarker for $15 000 and to provide any related documents that *B* may require for financing the project. To finance her paving operations *B* applies for a bank loan, and the bank requests evidence that the paving work can be started immediately. *B* therefore asks *A* to sign a statement to the effect that he will deliver 25 000 cubic feet of gravel from Harrowsmith to Yarker within the next month for $5000. Soon after *A* starts to make the deliveries, he discovers that he has quoted too low a price per cubic foot. He claims that his agreement with *B* has been reduced to writing and that he need move only the 25 000 cubic feet of gravel referred to in the writing.

The parol evidence rule does not apply. The written document for the bank was not intended to be a complete statement of the contract. Rather it was drawn up as part of *A*'s performance of his obligation under it. Accordingly, *B* may sue *A* for damages if *A* refuses to perform the balance of the contract, and for this purpose *B* may offer evidence of the terms of the original oral agreement.

Interpretation of the Contract

The parol evidence rule does not hinder the interpretation of express terms already in a contract. As noted in the preceding section, the court does accept evidence to explain the meanings of the words used in a written contract—to determine the meaning of the word "build" in the contract to build cabinets, for example. As one English judge has put it:

> There cannot be the slightest objection to the admission of evidence…which neither alters nor adds to the written contract, but merely enables us to ascertain what was the subject-matter referred to therein.[9]

---

8. DeLasalle v. Guilford, [1901] 2 K.B. 215, shows the lengths to which the courts will go in avoiding the parol evidence rule on these grounds. See also Gallen v. Allstate Grain Co. (1984), 9 D.L.R. (4th) 496, for a comprehensive review of the exceptions to the rule.

9. Macdonald v. Longbottom (1863), 120 E.R. 1177 at 1179.

Subsequent Oral Agreement

The parol evidence rule does not exclude evidence of an oral agreement that the parties may reach *after* they have entered into the written agreement. The subsequent oral agreement may change the terms of the written agreement[10] or, as we saw in the preceding chapter, may even rescind the prior contract altogether.[11] When such a claim is made, the court will hear evidence of a subsequent oral contract.

Collateral Agreement

An argument often used by a party is that there was a **collateral agreement** (sometimes called a collateral term or promise)—an entirely separate undertaking agreed on by the parties but not included in their written contract, probably because the written contract seemed an inappropriate place for it. The argument is that a collateral agreement may be enforced as a separate contract quite independent of the written document. If allowed much scope, this argument would easily circumvent the parol evidence rule. Our courts seem willing to accept such a claim only when a separate consideration can be found for the collateral promise.

collateral agreement
a separate agreement between the parties made at the same time as, but not included in, the written document

ILLUSTRATION 11.4

A offers to sell his residence, Rainbow End, to *B* for $90 000. *B* replies that she will buy Rainbow End for that price only if *A* will repair or replace a damaged, electronically operated garage door; *A* agrees. The parties draw up a written contract for the sale of Rainbow End but do not mention the garage door in it because they believe they should not do so in a formal contract. *A* fails to perform his promise regarding the garage door.

The consideration for the garage door repair or replacement is the payment of the $90 000 purchase price for Rainbow End, and thus the promise to include the item appears as an integral part of the contract:

unless the promise is mentioned in the written agreement, it is likely to be excluded by the parol evidence rule.

If, instead, *B* had agreed to pay *A* an extra $750 for the garage door, there would be a separate consideration for it. In effect there would be two separate contracts: a written contract for the sale of Rainbow End for $90 000 and a collateral oral contract for the repair of the garage door for $750. Because there would then be a separate consideration, the court would very likely consider the oral agreement outside the scope of the parol evidence rule and would enforce it.

Condition Precedent

A surprising historical exception to the parol evidence rule is the recognition given to a separate understanding about a condition precedent. A **condition precedent** is any set of circumstances or events that the parties stipulate must be satisfied or must happen before their contract takes effect. It may be an event beyond the control of either party, such as a requirement that a licensing board approve the transfer of a business. And it need not be in writing. If the party alleging that a condition precedent was agreed on and not met can produce evidence to support the claim, a court will recognize it despite the existence of a complete and unconditional written form of the contract, and will declare the contract void. The courts are prepared to recognize and enforce a condition precedent agreed to orally even when the subject-matter of the contract falls within the scope of the Statute of Frauds or the Sale of Goods Act.

condition precedent
any set of circumstances or events that the parties stipulate must be satisfied or must happen before their contract takes effect

10. See Johnson Investments v. Pagritide, [1923] 2 D.L.R. 985.
11. Morris v. Baron, [1918] A.C. 1.

ILLUSTRATION 11.5

B offers to sell a car to *A* for $14 000. *A* agrees orally to buy it provided he can persuade his bank to lend him $10 000. The parties agree orally that the contract will operate only if the bank makes the loan, and that otherwise the contract will be void. They then make a written contract in which *A* agrees to pay *B* $14 000 in 10 days and *B* agrees to deliver the car to *A* at that time. The writing does not mention that the contract is subject to *A* obtaining the bank loan. The bank refuses to lend the money to *A* who then informs *B* that the sale is off. *B* sues *A* for breach of contract and contends that their oral understanding about the bank loan is excluded by the parol evidence rule.

The parol evidence rule does not apply, and *B* will fail in his action. In his defence, *A* must show that there was an oral understanding suspending the contract of sale unless and until he could obtain the necessary bank loan.

The courts will admit evidence of an oral understanding about a condition precedent even when the written contract expressly states that the parties' rights and duties are governed exclusively by the written terms. Once a court accepts a contention that the parties did indeed intend to suspend the operation of their contract subject to a condition precedent, then the whole of the contract is suspended, including any term attempting to control the admission of such evidence. In support of this view, a court has said:

> This assertion as to the whole being in writing cannot be used as an instrument of fraud; the plaintiff cannot ignore the means by which he obtained the contract sued upon, falsify his own undertaking, and, by the help of the court, fasten an unqualified engagement on the defendant.[12]

Summary

It is not easy to convince a court that the parol evidence rule does not apply: usually, when one party has misunderstood the effect of an agreement and her later evidence about the alleged oral terms is in sharp conflict with the evidence of the other party, the court will limit the contract to the written terms. Although the rule has been relaxed recently in cases in which there is clear evidence that an orally agreed term is in conflict with the final written version,[13] it remains hazardous for a contracting party to count on the possibility of an exception to the rule. He will be taking a substantial risk either at the time a contract is being formed and put in writing or at a later time when he must decide whether to go to court over a difference of opinion about the terms of the contract.

IMPLIED TERMS AS A METHOD OF INTERPRETATION

Comparison with Interpretation of Express Terms

Courts are often confronted with disagreements that the parties did not foresee when they made their contract. As discussed earlier in this chapter, one approach the courts use in resolving such disagreements is to determine the most reasonable interpretation of express terms.

A second approach is to consider whether the intention of the parties can be achieved only by acknowledging the existence of an **implied term**, that is, a term not expressly included by the parties in their agreement but which, in the opinion of the court, they would *as reasonable people* have included had they thought of the possibility of the subsequent difficulty arising.

implied term
a term not expressly included by the parties in their agreement but which, as reasonable people, they would have included had they thought about it

---

12. Long v. Smith (1911), 23 O.L.R. 121, per Boyd, C., at 127.

13. Corey Developments Inc. v. Eastbridge Developments (Waterloo) Ltd. (1997), 34 O.R. (3d) 73.

Sometimes, the two approaches are simply different aspects of the same problem. In Illustration 11.1 about the contract to build cabinets, the court might choose to concentrate on the meaning of the express words "to build," or it might instead consider whether the contract taken as a whole implies a term that the carpenter is to supply the lumber necessary to build the cabinets. Here, the distinction between these two approaches is more apparent than real—the meaning of the word "build" is likely to be an important factor in deciding whether a term can reasonably be implied. In other instances, the *type* of contract will determine whether a term should be implied. Contracts for the sale of goods contain an implied term that the goods will be suitable for the purpose for which they have been purchased if that purpose has been made known to the seller and it is in the course of the seller's business to supply such goods;[14] but a contract for the sale of land carries with it no such implied term.

Terms Established by Custom

Implied terms usually result from long-established customs in a particular trade or type of transaction. They exist in almost every field of commerce and came to be recognized among business people because they made good sense or because they led to certainty in transactions without the necessity of spelling out every detail. In time, the courts fell into line with this business practice: when a party failed to perform in compliance with an implied term, the courts would recognize its existence and enforce the contract as though it had been an express term.

ILLUSTRATION 11.6

A asks B, a tire dealer, to supply truck tires for his five-tonne dump truck. B then shows A a set of tires and quotes a price. A purchases the tires. The sale slip merely sets out the name and the price of the tires. Later A discovers that these tires are not safe on trucks of more than three tonnes' capacity and claims that B is in breach of the contract.

On these facts, there was no express undertaking by B that the tires would be safe for a five-tonne truck or any other type of truck. Nevertheless, the court would hold that under the circumstances there was an implied term that the tires should be suitable for a five-tonne truck. It would say that in showing A the tires after he had made his intended use of them clear, B, as a regular seller of such tires, implied that they would be suitable for A's truck.

This approach applies to all kinds of contracts, but in some fields, especially the sale of goods, insurance, partnership, and landlord and tenant relations, a large and complex body of customary terms has grown up. In many jurisdictions, these customary terms have been codified in a statute that sets out in one place all the rules previously established by the courts for a particular field of law. Thus, court decisions in cases similar to Illustration 11.6 led to a specific provision in the Sale of Goods Act.

Reasonable Expectation of the Parties: The Moorcock Doctrine

Apart from those fields where customary terms are implied, the question remains: in what circumstances are the courts likely to find an implied term is appropriate to the interpretation of a contract? As a rule, the courts will imply terms reasonably necessary to give effect to a contract when otherwise the fair expectations of a party would be defeated. A case often cited on the subject of implied terms is *The Moorcock*.[15]

---

14. The various implied terms in a contract of sale are discussed Chapter 16.

15. (1889), 14 P.D. 64.

CASE 11.1

The defendants owned a wharf and jetty on the River Thames and contracted with the plaintiff, the owner of the steamship *The Moorcock*, that, for a fee, the ship would be loaded at the defendants' jetty. While the ship was docked there, the tide ebbed; the vessel came to rest on a hard ridge beneath the river mud and was damaged. The owner sued and recovered damages on the ground that the defendants must be taken to have implied that the facilities were reasonably safe for the ship at low tide, a necessary provision for carrying out the contract.

In giving his opinion Lord Justice Bowen said:

I believe if one were to take all the cases, and there are many, of implied warranties or covenants in law, it will be found that in all of them the law is raising an implication from the presumed intention of the parties, with the object of giving the transaction such efficacy as both parties must have intended that at all events it should have. In business transactions such as this, what the law desires to effect by the implication is to give such business efficacy to the transaction as must have been intended at all events by both parties who are business men.[16]

These famous words have been quoted and misquoted innumerable times by both judges and lawyers. The doctrine ensures that a court will not permit the legitimate and reasonable expectations of the parties to a contract to be defeated simply because the contract does not deal expressly with a serious contingency that affects the basis of the transaction.

The Limits of The Moorcock Doctrine

On the other hand, the court will not go further than is necessary and will not make a new contract for the parties. Nor will it imply a term that is contrary to the expressed intent of the agreement. Lawyers are sometimes inclined to resort to *The Moorcock* doctrine when all else has failed for their client. Consequently, the courts insist that the case for implying a term be made clearly. They tend to restrict the circumstances in which they rely on *The Moorcock* decision and find an implied term on grounds of business efficacy. Parties should therefore consider carefully what assumptions underlie the performance of a contract and bring as many of the important possibilities as they can think of into the open, so that they may reach an express understanding about the terms. In the words of Lord Justice Jenkins:

I do not think that the court will read a term into a contract unless, considering the matter from the point of view of business efficacy, it is clear beyond a peradventure that both parties intended a given term to operate, although they did not include it in so many words.[17]

CASE 11.2

M hires *D* Ltd. to drill a well on his property at $3 per foot plus the cost of pipe. *D* Ltd. drills to the depth of 385 feet, but stops when *M* refuses to pay for the work done and materials supplied because no water has been found. *D* Ltd. sues for the value of the work done and materials supplied, and *M* defends by claiming that the contract contains an implied term that he should have to pay only if clear water is obtained.

The court rejects this argument, holding that the contract contained no implied term to this effect either from trade custom or for reasons of business efficacy. Accordingly, *M* is liable for the work done and the materials supplied.[18]

---

16. *Ibid.*, at 68.
17. Sethia (1944) Ltd. v. Partabmull Rameshwar, [1950] 1 All E.R. 51 at 59.
18. Douglas Bros. and Jones Ltd. v. MacQueen (1959), 42 M.P.R. 256.

As a general rule, when parties deal explicitly with a matter in their contract, it precludes a court from finding an implied term that deals with the same matter in a different way. If the parties have been very diligent in canvassing the foreseeable possibilities for future dispute, a court may conclude that they intended to deal in a comprehensive way with all future eventualities, so that no further terms should be implied.[19]

QUESTIONS FOR REVIEW

1. Why does a dictionary definition of a word not always clarify its meaning in a contract? Give an example.

2. Explain and give an example of special usage of a word.

3. What are the primary goals of a court in interpreting a contract?

4. Describe some of the risks that may arise when parties have reached agreement orally about a contract and subsequently record it in writing. What role does the parol evidence rule play?

5. Name four ways in which a party may persuade a court that the parol evidence rule does not apply to the term or terms it asserts were part of the contract.

6. What is an implied term? Give an example.

7. Explain the purpose of *The Moorcock* Doctrine.

8. When a contract is subject to a condition precedent, does the contract, nevertheless, still exist? May either party simply withdraw from the contract before the condition precedent has been met?

9. *B* wishes to have a patio roof installed at the back of his house, facing west and overlooking a city park. In the Yellow Pages of his telephone directory, he finds an advertisement by Patio Specialists Inc. stating, "We have the expertise to design and build just what you need." *B* contacts the firm; they inspect his property and recommend a specific design. *B* signs a contract provided by the firm. On the reverse side of the document, in faint print, there is a clause stating, "Patio Specialists Inc. gives no warranties about the safety or otherwise of our product as installed." Three weeks after the patio roof is completed, a strong wind lifts a portion of the roof and the structure is substantially ruined. The strength of the wind was unusual but does occur once every two or three years. Does *B* have a claim against Patio Specialists Inc. that might succeed?

10. What did Lord Wright mean in his judgment in *Scammel v. Ouston* when he said, "Difficulty is not synonymous with ambiguity"?

11. "The normal contract is not an isolated act, but an incident in the conduct of business or in the framework of some more general relation." (Furmston, *Cheshire and Fifoot's Law of Contract* [8th ed.], p. 122.) Show how the idea expressed in this quotation is applied in the interpretation of contracts.

12. Clifton and Dealer sign a written contract in which Dealer is to deliver five fork-lift tractors to Clifton within two months, at the price stated in the contract. One month later,

---

19. See Cooke v. CKOY Ltd. (1963), 39 D.L.R. (2d) 209; Shaw Cablesystems (Manitoba) Ltd. v. Canadian Legion Memorial Housing Foundation (Manitoba) (1997), 143 D.L.R. (4th) 193.

Dealer telephones Clifton to say that because of a prolonged strike at the manufacturing plant in the United States, he will be able to deliver only three of the vehicles within the two months. He offers to deduct $4000 from the price if Clifton will accept three vehicles immediately with the other two to follow within the third month. Clifton agrees. The three vehicles are delivered at once, but one week after the two months have expired Clifton decides that he does not like the vehicles. He returns them to Dealer with a note stating that because of failure to deliver on time, Dealer is in serious breach of their written contract, which is the only arrangement binding them, and Clifton is justified in cancelling it and returning the vehicles. Do you agree?

CASES AND PROBLEMS

1 Chalmers had been employed full time as an auto mechanic by Pelham Motors for 16 years. He was 56 years of age and had been a certified mechanic for 20 years when Pelham's business suffered as a result of a downturn in the economy. He was laid off "temporarily," but his employer gave no specific duration for the layoff. Grudgingly Chalmers left work, but when he heard nothing for two weeks, he felt that the layoff amounted to wrongful dismissal and he sued Pelham Motors for severance pay.

In defence, Pelham Motors claimed that it was an implied term of Chalmer's contract of employment that he could be laid off periodically as a consequence of insufficient business. It claimed that such a term was normal in the auto mechanic trade. In reply, Chalmers asserted that: (a) there had never been any discussion of such a term of his employment with his employer, either when he was first hired or afterwards; (b) in 16 years he had never been laid off; (c) he was not aware of such a custom in the trade, even if it was the practice in some auto repair shops.

Should Chalmers succeed in his claim for severance pay? Explain.

2 Campbell offered to buy from Pym a three-eighths share in a machine invented by Pym, provided that two engineers, Ferguson and Abernethie, would recommend the invention. They arranged a meeting with the engineers to have them examine the machine and have Pym explain it to them. As a result of confusion about the time of the meeting, Abernethie did not attend; after waiting for some time they went ahead with the meeting without him. The other engineer, Ferguson, approved of the machine, and the three agreed that, since they might find it difficult to meet quickly with Abernethie, they would draft and sign an agreement that, if Abernethie later gave his approval, should be the final agreement. They drafted an agreement for the purchase of the three-eighths share and Campbell signed it: the agreement made no reference to the need for Abernethie's approval of Pym's invention.

Abernethie later refused to recommend the machine when he saw it and Campbell refused to proceed with the purchase. Pym sued Campbell to enforce the contract as written. Should he succeed?

3 To assist John Lees & Sons in buying cotton on credit from Haigh, Brooks gave the following guarantee to Haigh:

Messrs. Haigh:

In consideration of your being in advance to Messrs. John Lees & Sons in the sum of $10 000 for the purchase of cotton, I do hereby give you my guarantee for that amount on their behalf.

John Brooks

When the question of the validity of Brooks' guarantee arose at a later time, the court had to interpret the meaning of the words "in consideration of your being in advance." If the words "being in advance" meant "already being in advance" or "already having a sum owing to you from past credit purchases by John Lees & Sons," the guarantee would have been given for a past consideration (assuming, at any rate, that its purpose was not to obtain Haigh's forbearance from suing). If, on the other hand, the words "being in advance" meant "becoming further in advance," the debt to be guaranteed was a future debt, and there was consideration for the guarantee because Haigh, without the guarantee, might not have supplied goods to John Lees & Sons.

If no further evidence is offered to clarify the meaning of these words, what rule will the court follow in choosing between the two possible meanings?

4 Atkinson advertised her house for sale and Kirby made a written offer to purchase it for $124 000. The parties discussed the offer several days later, and Atkinson said that she would also like to sell her furniture. After discussion about the amount of furniture for sale and its price, Atkinson accepted, in writing, Kirby's offer to purchase the house. The offer had made no reference to the furniture and simply required Kirby's certified cheque for $8000 as an immediate payment towards the agreed price for the house. In fact, Kirby gave Atkinson a cheque for $24 950, the additional $16 950 being the price they had agreed upon orally for the furniture.

When Kirby took possession of the house, he found that Atkinson had taken the grand piano with her. He sued for breach of contract, alleging that their oral agreement about the furniture had specifically included the grand piano, and that he had even tried it out in her presence. In defence, Atkinson pleaded that she had never intended to sell the piano, and that, in any event, evidence of the oral agreement about the furniture would be inadmissible.

What issues must the court deal with before reaching a decision? Should Kirby's action succeed? Give reasons for your opinion.

5 In July, Saunders and Dimmock entered into a partnership for carrying on a grocery and butcher business on Dundee Street in Vancouver. They dissolved the partnership two years later: Dimmock sold his share to Saunders and agreed that Saunders would continue to operate the business by himself. Dimmock wrote out the agreement dissolving the partnership, and included his covenant as retiring partner that he would not "during a term of five years from the date hereof commence and carry on a butcher and grocery business, neither directly nor indirectly, nor…work as an employee in such business within a radius of one-half mile from said premises at 346 Dundee Street, in the City of Vancouver."

Shortly after, Dimmock opened a grocery and butcher business at 258 Dundee Street, less than a half-mile away, and operated it as sole proprietor. Saunders brought an action to restrain Dimmock from continuing to break the covenant. In defence, Dimmock admitted that the half-mile restriction on employment was a reasonable restraint. He also conceded that if the restriction on carrying on business (owning a business) were also limited to one half-mile, it would be a reasonable restraint, but he argued that the words "half-mile" applied only to *employment* and that there was no geographic limit to his covenant not to *carry on business*. Therefore, the first half of the covenant was void because it was an unreasonable restraint, and accordingly he was free to carry on business as owner. Did Dimmock break the contract?

6 Provinco Grain Inc. were in the business of selling seeds and buying and reselling the crops grown from the seeds they sold. Its sales manager approached Quinlan, a farmer in the Lower Fraser Valley in British Columbia, to grow an early crop of buckwheat for the Japanese market. Quinlan, who was an experienced farmer, was interested because it would be a valuable market. However, he had never grown the crop before and said he was worried about weeds; he understood they could be a serious problem. The sales manager replied that he need not worry—the buckwheat would smother any weeds. Quinlan bought seeds and signed a printed document stating that Provinco Grain Inc. gave no warranty as to "the productiveness or any other matter pertaining to the seed…and will not in any way be responsible for the crop."

Quinlan planted the seeds but weeds destroyed the crop and he suffered a substantial loss. He sued Provinco for damages on the basis that the sales manager's statement was a collateral warranty and a deliberate, material misrepresentation. With regard to the misrepresentation, the court found that the sales manager believed it to be true: he came from Saskatchewan where buckwheat did indeed suppress the weeds. Provinco further defended by claiming that the signed contract exempted it from all liability pertaining to the seeds and subsequent crop. Accordingly, any statement on this subject by the sales manager, would be excluded by the parol evidence rule.

In reply, Quinlan's lawyer claimed that the sales manager's warranty was about the risk of weeds and it did not contradict the terms of the signed contract pertaining to the seed itself. It was on the basis of that warranty that Quinlan signed the contract.

Give your view of each party's position and what the likely result would be.

7 Chénier sold the surface and minerals in her land in Alberta for $104 000 to Werner under an agreement for sale (an instalment sale that reserved the ownership in the property of Chénier until a specified amount of the price was paid). Werner defaulted payment, thus giving Chénier the right to recover possession by court action. Chénier started proceedings, but they were not yet complete when it became apparent that the land was very valuable. Werner entered into a petroleum and natural gas lease with Imperial Oil Ltd. and received a cash bonus of $110 000, which he intended to use to settle his debt to Chénier. About the same time Chénier, anticipating the recovery of her property by court order, entered into a similar lease of the same property with California Standard Oil Co. At the time Chénier gave her lease to California Standard Oil Co., she told the company's agent that her ability to lease the property depended upon a favourable outcome of her pending court action against Werner and that she could give the lease only if the company's agent would give her a signed statement acknowledging that she (Chénier) did not have any right to lease the mineral rights until the court action against Werner went through. The agent gave her a statement to that effect, and Chénier and California Standard Oil Co. entered into a lease of the mineral rights that made no reference to the proviso signed by the company's agent and, furthermore, contained a paragraph stating that the lease contained the whole of the agreement.

Werner tendered the balance of the purchase price to Chénier, but she refused it and proceeded with the court action. The court dismissed Chénier's petition for recovery of the property. She was, therefore, unable to lease the property to California Standard Oil Co. and that company sued her for breach of contract. Should the action succeed?

8 For several years, John Conrad Kent operated a very successful "pop" radio station, CROC, in Calgary. At the same time, a separately owned station in Edmonton, CRED, was languishing. Its policy of broadcasting classical music and book reviews to a small but higher-than-average-income audience was attracting very little advertising revenue. Finally, the desperate owner and principal shareholder of CRED Radio Limited approached John Conrad Kent to inquire whether he would act as a consultant in the operation of CRED. Soon afterwards the parties made a contract, in the form of the following letter:

CRED RADIO LIMITED

Edmonton, Alberta,
December 15, 1993

Mr. J.C. Kent,
400 Foothills Road,
Calgary, Alberta

Dear Mr. Kent:

This letter will confirm our recent discussions in which you expressed a willingness to act as a consultant to this Company on the terms set out below. If these terms continue to be acceptable to you, please acknowledge your agreement at the bottom of this letter and return one of the two enclosed copies to us.

1. You are to give us upon request such services and advice as we shall require and will consult with us in Edmonton at such times as may be reasonably required and are consistent with your duties elsewhere.

2. We are to pay you as remuneration for such services 40 percent of the operating profits of the Company. Operating profits shall mean the gross revenue from whatever sources before deducting your remuneration but after deducting all other operating and financial expenses, including depreciation expense and licence fees and taxes other than corporation income tax.

   Company's auditors shall prepare and deliver a statement of operating profits to you and to us as promptly as possible after December 31 each year, which statement shall be binding upon the Company and you. Payment of your remuneration shall be made by the Company within 30 days after the receipt of the auditor's statement.

3. Your employment shall be effective from January 1, 1994 and shall continue until terminated in the events and in the manner following:

   (i) Should the Company become bankrupt or go into voluntary liquidation, your employment shall forthwith be terminated without notice.

   (ii) In the event that the Company's broadcasting licence be cancelled for any cause whatever, your employment may be terminated forthwith by the Company by written notice to that effect.

   (iii) In the event that the annual net profits of the Company for the three business years preceding the year in which such notice is given have been on the average less than $20 000, your employment may be terminated by the Company at the end of the current business year by six months' written notice. "Net profits" shall mean the operating profits of the company as defined above after deducting your remuneration and corporation income tax.

Yours truly,

CRED RADIO LIMITED

Rosanna Smith

President

Approved and accepted:

John Conrad Kent

December 21, 1993

Kent had a free hand in the management of CRED, in making staff changes, in program planning, and in policy making. He introduced radical changes that resulted in a complete turnover in the station's audience. To banish its former image, the station's call letters were changed to CROL. At first, Kent went to Edmonton at least once a month and spent two or three days at the radio station; his visits were less frequent after the station was operating profitably, but he was always available and never refused his advice or presence when requested. Over the six-year period ending December 31, 1999, operating profits of CROL Radio Limited were $950 000.

At hearings of the Canadian Radio-Television and Telecommunications Commission (CRTC) in October 1999, criticisms were made about CROL's program format and its non-local "absentee" form of management. As a result, the CRTC approved a renewal of the station's licence for only one year instead of the usual three years.

In January 2000, Kent moved to St. John's, Newfoundland, to work with offshore oil-drilling interests there. CROL Radio Limited then decided to terminate its contract with him. It sent him a letter stating that his services would no longer be used after June 30, 2000.

Kent protested that he was still available to perform the contract; that when the contract was being negotiated he had resisted a suggestion that it contain a provision for termination on reasonable notice and would have refused to sign a contract containing such a term, and that none of the specific events had occurred for which the contract might, by its express terms, be terminated. He sued for breach of contract against CROL Radio Limited, claiming damages of $400 000, his estimate of the present value of his annual earnings from the contract for the balance of his expected active business career.

Develop a line of argument for the defendant company, CROL Radio Limited, and speculate on Kent's chances for success in his action.

PRIVITY OF CONTRACT AND THE ASSIGNMENT OF CONTRACTUAL RIGHTS

A contract creates rights and duties between the parties who enter into the agreement, and the rights may have an economic value that one party wishes to transfer to an outsider—a person who was not a party to the contract. Alternatively, a party may wish to arrange for her duties under the contract to be performed by another person. In this chapter we look at how the law of contracts accommodates these important needs, and we examine such questions as:

- novation—how may a new party be substituted for the original party to the contract?

- vicarious performance—how may an outsider perform a party's obligations under a contract?

- trusts—how may rights be created for the benefit of an outsider to a contract?

- what are the exceptions—the special types of contracts—that create rights for outsiders?

- how may rights be assigned and what are the consequences?

- what are negotiable instruments and why are they important in business?

PRIVITY OF CONTRACT

Limits on the Scope of Contractual Rights and Duties

When parties make a contract, they create a small body of law for themselves. It seems reasonable that the scope of a contract—its power to affect relations—should be confined to the parties who agreed to it; persons outside the contract, who had no say in the bargaining for its terms, should have neither rights nor duties under it.

In theory, this reasoning seems sound, and in fact it does represent the general attitude of the common law as well as of other legal systems. But in practice, many situations arise where the purposes of justice generally, and of business convenience in particular, require that a contract be allowed to affect persons outside it. In the law of contract, a person who is not a party to a contract is called a *third person* or **third party**, or sometimes a *stranger* to the contract. In this chapter, we explore the effect of contracts on third persons.

third party
a person who is not one of the parties to a contract but is affected by it

privity of contract
the relationship that exists between parties to a contract

The general rule is that a contract does not confer any benefits or impose any obligations on a stranger to the contract. To succeed in an action in contract, the plaintiff must therefore prove **privity of contract** with the defendant, that is, he must show that they are both parties to the same contract.

ILLUSTRATION 12.1

A, a carpenter, owes $4000 to *B*. *A* offers to renovate *C*'s kitchen if *C* will promise to pay off *A*'s debt to *B*. *C* accepts the offer, and *A* completes the renovation. As a third party to the contract for renovation *B* cannot enforce *C*'s promise; there is no privity of contract between them.[1] Consequently, if *C* fails to pay *B*, *B* cannot sue *C*, but may still sue *A* for the debt *A* owes her; *A* may then sue *C* for his failure to carry out his promise to pay *B*, and will recover damages of $4000 plus any costs he suffered as a result of *B* suing him.

FIGURE 12.1
Privity and Consideration

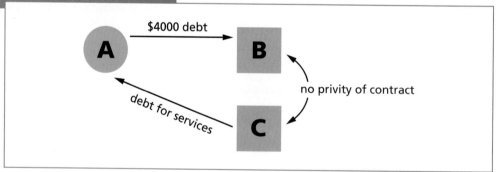

An additional argument against permitting a third person to sue on a contract is that he has not given consideration for the promise. Suppose in Illustration 12.1 that *B* also signed as a party to the contract between *A* and *C* to renovate the kitchen. There would now be privity of contract between *B* and *C* because *C* would have made his promise of payment to *B* as well as to *A*. However, *B* still could not sue *C* because he would not have given consideration for *C*'s promise. Not only must consideration for a promise be given by some party to the contract, it must be given by the party seeking to enforce the promise.

---

1. Price v. Easton (1883), 110 E.R. 518.

The privity of contract rule can have harsh consequences when it prevents a third person from enforcing a contract of which the whole object was to benefit him. Yet this was the decision in *Tweddle v. Atkinson.*[2]

CASE 12.1

The respective fathers of a young married couple made a contract: the father of the husband promised the father of the bride that he would pay £100 to the couple, and in return the father of the bride promised that he would pay them a further £200.

Before he had paid the £200, the father of the bride died and his executor, Atkinson, refused to pay it.

The husband, Tweddle, brought an action to enforce the promise. He failed because he was a stranger to the contract between the two fathers. The court rejected the argument that the plaintiff's kinship to one of the contracting parties made him something more than a "stranger" to the contract.

Comparison with Rights and Duties in Tort

Liability of Sellers of Goods

We have seen in the preceding chapter that a consumer who purchases goods from a merchant receives the benefit of an implied term that the goods are reasonably suited for the purpose for which they are sold. Thus, if a person buys a can of salmon that turns out to be poisonous and that seriously harms her, she may successfully sue the merchant for breach of the implied term that the fish was suitable to eat. But members of her family who were also harmed by eating the salmon cannot recover damages against the merchant because the contract of sale was with the buyer, and only she can sue successfully for breach of contract. Other members of the family have no privity of contract with the merchant and no rights under the contract.

Liability of Manufacturers

As we saw in Chapter 3, although members of the family have no rights against the merchant, the manufacturer may well be liable for negligence. After all, it is the manufacturer who has caused the product to be poisonous, and the merchant has no way of knowing that sealed goods are not up to standard. The buyer, too, may sue in tort since she has no contract with the manufacturer.[3] In perhaps the most famous case of the 20th century, *Donoghue v. Stevenson,*[4] the House of Lords decided that manufacturers are liable in tort for damages caused by their products when the products will likely be used without intermediate examination. In these circumstances, manufacturers are under a high duty of care to make their products safe. If they fail to meet the standards, they must pay damages for the loss suffered.

NOVATION

Novation occurs when the parties to a contract agree to terminate it and substitute a new contract. There are two types of novation:

novation
the parties to a contract agree to terminate it and substitute a new contract

---

2. (1861), 121 E.R. 762. The court based its decision on the rule that consideration must move from the promisee and that since the husband, Tweddle, could not show that he had given any consideration, his action must fail. But our definition of consideration also implies that the plaintiff to an action (in this case, Tweddle) must be a party to the contract; since he was not a party, he could not have given consideration in any event.

3. The idea of a "collateral warranty" that we shall shortly refer to in Shanklin Pier, Ltd. v. Detel Products, Ltd. is still regarded as a special concession in particular circumstances.

4. [1932] A.C. 562.

1. The parties may change the subject-matter of the contract. For instance, car dealer *B* may inform *A* that he cannot deliver the car *A* has ordered without a lengthy delay. They agree to cancel the contract and substitute a new one: for a favourable price offered by *B*, *A* buys a car that *B* has in stock.

2. One of the parties to the contract "leaves" and another replaces her. For example, *M* has a contract with *Q* to obtain advertising for her business. *M* arranges to sell her business to *N* who wishes to continue the advertising arrangement with *Q*. *M*, *N*, and *Q* meet and agree that *M* and *Q* will terminate their contract, each giving up all future rights under it, and that *N* and *Q* will sign a new contract under the same terms as the terminated contract between *M* and *Q*.

In 2 above, novation substitutes a stranger for an existing party to the contract. The new party may sue or be sued on the new contract, and the former party no longer has any rights or obligations; the result is consistent with the rule requiring privity of contract. This subject is discussed further in the next chapter.

VICARIOUS PERFORMANCE

How It Occurs

A promisor cannot escape his liability to the promisee by imposing a substitute for himself without the consent of the promisee. In other words, he cannot transfer or "assign" his liability by finding someone willing to assume the liability for him. If the promisee consents to a new contract with a change of parties, then the arrangement is no longer within the terms of the original contract—it is novation.

There are nevertheless many circumstances in which a party, without altering the terms of his contract, arranges for someone else to carry out his duties, though he remains accountable to the promisee for proper performance. Performance of this type is known as **vicarious performance**; typically, an employee of the promisor performs vicariously (that is, on behalf of the promisor). If the work is not done satisfactorily, the promisee may seek a remedy for breach of contract against the promisor, but not against his employee. In turn, the employee can look only to the employer (and not to the promisee) for payment for the work he has done under his employment contract with the employer. The results are consistent with the rule of privity of contract.

vicarious performance

a third party performs on behalf of the promisor who remains responsible for proper performance

When Is Vicarious Performance Allowed?

When may a promisor employ a third party to perform the work vicariously? He may do so if the work is of such a nature that personal performance by him was not the reason why the promisee entered into the contract.[5] The party entitled to performance generally cannot complain if someone other than the promisor turns up and does the work equally well. However, it would be unacceptable when personal performance is expected as, for example, when a pianist makes a contract to perform at a concert.

In many contracts, the understanding is that by their very nature they must be performed by a large number of persons who are not parties to the contract: contracts for the construction of buildings, the manufacture of goods, and the transport of people or goods. Moreover, when goods are shipped to a destination that requires the services of more than one carrier, both parties understand that not only employees of the first carrier but also of another carrier will perform: a shipment by rail from Toronto to New York City may be made by Canadian National

---

5. As we shall see in Chapter 27, corporations have no physical existence—personal performance is not possible, so all contracts with them must be carried out by their agents or employees.

Railways (CN) and the New York Central. The shipper contracts with CN, whose franchise area includes the point of shipment, and CN arranges for completion of the shipment with the connecting carrier operating beyond the CN area of franchise.

It may not always be clear, as in Illustration 12.2, whether a party is expected to perform personally or whether she may employ someone to perform vicariously.

ILLUSTRATION 12.2

A Co. Ltd. contracts with a public accountant, *B*, to have its accounts audited. *B* sends *C*, a senior accountant, to carry out the audit program. May *A* Co. Ltd. object? This is a type of work that can be carried out competently by a qualified accountant and ordinarily would not require *B*'s personal performance unless *A*

Co. Ltd. had expressly bargained for it. Consequently, the vicarious performance by *C* is permissible and *A* Co. Ltd. is not entitled to reject the tender of such performance. (We may, of course, assume that a final review of the audit would always be made by *B*.)

Sometimes a party arranges for its obligations to be performed vicariously when it should have performed personally, but the other party may have no opportunity to protest until the work is finished. In this situation, the promisor is guilty of a breach of a term in the contract (the implied or express promise to perform personally). The promisee may sue for damages to compensate for whatever loss he can show resulted from vicarious, rather than personal, performance.

Tort Liability

Suppose that in performing a contract vicariously an employee commits a tort: he negligently damages a valuable instrument belonging to the promisee. As we noted in Chapter 3 on torts, the promisee may sue both the employer for vicarious liability and the employee personally. Since the employer ordinarily has a "deeper pocket" than its employee, the promisee almost always sues the employer, but may sue the employee as well, in case the court should find that the employer is not liable because the damage did not occur *in the course of employment*.

ILLUSTRATION 12.3

Suppose that in Illustration 12.2 above, *C* does such an inadequate job that he fails to detect a material error in the accounts and as a result *A* Co. Ltd. suffers a loss. *A* Co. Ltd. must look to *B* for damages for breach of contract. In addition, if *C*'s poor work amounted to negligence, he would be personally liable to *A* Co. Ltd. in tort and *B* would also be vicariously liable in tort for *C*'s negligence.

If, while working in the offices of *A* Co. Ltd., *C* stole some valuable client records to sell to a competitor of *A* Co. Ltd., *C* would, of course, be guilty of a crime as well as of committing a tort. However, the theft would not be considered conduct in the course of employment and *B* would not be liable for *C*'s misconduct.

Exemption Clauses

Employers often protect themselves from tort liability. For example, carriers and storage companies usually insert exemption clauses in their standard form contracts to exclude or limit liability for negligence. By allocating the risk of loss to the promisee, a storage company lowers its costs and thus reduces its price to the promisee, which in turn obtains its own insurance against loss. While an exemption clause protects the storage company from liability for negligence,[6]

6. For a fuller discussion of the effect of exemption clauses, see Chapter 14.

until the 1990s its employees who were not parties to the contract were unable to claim its protection because of the traditional privity rule. In 1992, the Supreme Court of Canada reversed that position and granted protection to employees if they could show that the clause was intended to be for their benefit and the damage occurred in the course of their employment.[7]

Trusts

How a Trust Is Created

trust

property transferred to a person who administers it for the benefit of another person

trustee

a person or company who administers a trust

beneficiary

a person who is entitled to the benefits of a trust

beneficial owner

a person who, although not the legal owner, may compel the trustee to provide benefits to him

Suppose a mother wishes to provide for her son in the event that she should die while he is still an infant. In her will, she leaves a fund to be invested in securities, and directs that the income be used to care for her son. The fund will require someone to administer it, that is, to see that it is properly invested and that the income is paid out for the child's care. The fund is called a **trust**; the person—or perhaps a trust company—that looks after the fund is called a **trustee**. A trust has been defined as "any arrangement whereby property is transferred with the intention that it be administered by a trustee for another's benefit."[8] In this definition and in the above example, the trust is created by the transfer of some kind of *property* to the trustee.

Suppose that the mother dies and the fund is handed over to the trustee, but the trustee refuses to pay out the income for the benefit of the son. We know that the trust fund was set up by the mother for his benefit and not for that of the trustee. What rights has the child as **beneficiary** of the trust? Although under common law rules the trustee becomes the legal owner of the trust, the rules of equity recognize that the son has an interest: he is the fund's *true* owner—the **beneficial owner**—and equity has developed procedures by which a beneficiary may compel a trustee to carry out its duties diligently and faithfully.

The trust concept has important applications in business. When the creditors of a business convince the court that their debtor is no longer capable of paying its debts as they fall due, the court will order that the property of the bankrupt debtor be transferred to a trustee in bankruptcy for realization and distribution to the creditors. Another example occurs when a corporation transfers the title to its fixed assets to a trustee for the bondholders as security for the repayment of money borrowed by an issue of mortgage bonds; a corporation may pay annual instalments to a sinking fund trustee who will use the money to pay interest and to redeem and cancel a part of the bonds payable by the corporation.

The Relation of the Trust Concept to Third Parties: Constructive Trusts

constructive trust

the relationship that permits a third party to obtain performance of a promise included in a contract for his benefit

How is the concept of a trust related to contracts and the rights of third parties? The beneficiary of a trust is in a position analogous to that of a third party to a contract, being neither the person who created the trust nor the person who is appointed to administer it; yet, as we have seen, the beneficiary may enforce the trust in his favour. The rules of equity gradually developed an ingenious extension of the idea of the trust by recognizing that the legal right to demand performance of a promise in a contract is a thing of value—a type of property, in other words. The next step was to say that a promisee who has obtained a promise for the benefit of a third person can sometimes be regarded as a trustee for the third person of the benefit of that promise. The way was then open for permitting a third party to enforce the contract in his or her favour. A trust of this kind is called a **constructive trust**. When a court accepts this argument, the strictures of the privity of contract rule are avoided.

---

7. London Drugs v. Kuehne & Nagel International (1992), 97 D.L.R. (4th) 261. See also M.A.N.-B. & W. Diesel v. Kingsway Transports Ltd. (1997), 33 O.R. (3d) 355.
8. *Black's Law Dictionary* (6th ed.). St. Paul, MN: West Publishing Co., 1990.

CASE 12.2

A, B, and *C* entered into a partnership agreement, a term of which stated that if one of the partners should die, his widow would receive a share of the future profits of the firm. On the death of *A,* the surviving partners *B* and *C* refused to pay a share of the profits to *A*'s widow. Would she be successful in enforcing the term?

These facts are based on *Re Flavell,*[9] where the court held that while the widow was not a party to the partner-ship agreement, the agreement had created a trust in her favour. It decided that her husband as promisee of the term in the partnership agreement had become a trustee of her interest. On his death, his executor became the trustee in his place, and the executor was successful in obtaining the share for the widow.

Unfortunately, parties to a contract are not likely to be aware of the subtleties of a constructive trust, nor are they likely to create a trust expressly to ensure that a third party beneficiary will have rights enforceable in court. In an action by a third party to obtain a declaration that a trust was created, the court often must proceed only by inference from the contract: in many cases the party who intended to confer the benefit has died or is unavailable to give testimony of his intentions. As a result, the courts have had considerable difficulty in deciding when a constructive trust has been created; even when the facts have been ascertained, it is hazardous to predict the decision. Accordingly, it is wise to obtain legal advice to ensure that the wishes of the parties are made clear in the contract.

The Requirement That a Trust Cannot be Revoked

One of the main obstacles to finding a constructive trust is the rule that once created, a trust cannot be revoked by those who created it without the consent of the beneficiary. Before a court will find a constructive trust, it must be satisfied that the contracting parties intended that the benefit for the third party should be binding on them *without the possibility of later revision or revocation by them.* The courts have been reluctant to infer such an intention between contracting parties.[10] As a result, the constructive trust has not become a reliable means for avoiding the privity of contract rule.

EXCEPTIONS TO THE PRIVITY OF CONTRACT RULE

Insurance

Typically, in a contract (or policy) of life insurance, a person pays a premium in exchange for a promise from the insurance company to pay a sum of money on his or her death to a specified person, a spouse, say, who is not a party to the insurance contract. Each province has a statute that gives a beneficiary a right against the insurance company to enforce the insurance contract.[11] Similarly, in a contract of automobile insurance, the company may promise to indemnify not only the owner but also anyone driving with his consent. If a person driving with consent

---

9. (1883), 25 Ch. D. 89. For an interesting modern case, see Beswick v. Beswick, [1968] A.C. 58.

10. See Re Schebsman, [1944] Ch. 83.

11. See, for example: Insurance Act, R.S.O. 1990 c. I.8, s. 195; R.S.B.C. 1979, c. 200, s. 146; R.S.N.S. 1989, c. 231, s. 197.

injures a pedestrian and is required to pay damages, she may in turn sue the insurance company for indemnity against her loss, even though she was not a party to the insurance contract.[12]

The Undisclosed Principal

undisclosed principal
a contracting party who, unknown to the other party, is represented by an agent

A further modification of the rule requiring privity of contract occurs when one of the contracting parties, unknown to the other, proves to be an agent of someone else: the person for whom the agent was acting, known as an **undisclosed principal**, may sue or be sued on the contract. The subject is discussed more fully in Chapter 19.

Contracts Concerning Land

The idea of privity of contract does not apply generally in land law. If the owner of land leases it to a tenant who promises to pay rent and keep the property in good repair, and the owner subsequently sells it, the tenant must perform the promises for the new owner. The value of the land on the market would be substantially lowered if the tenant could ignore promises made to the former owner. Similarly, the new owner must respect the tenant's rights to remain on the property until the lease expires. Otherwise tenants would always be in jeopardy of being evicted when land is sold. Accordingly, persons who acquire interests in land often do so subject to earlier contracts that both create obligations and give benefits in relation to the property.

There has been some debate about whether liabilities arising out of the chartering of ships may affect subsequent purchasers of ships in a similar manner.[13]

Special Concessions to Commercial Practice

Collateral Contracts

Courts have sometimes been prepared to enlarge the sphere of a contract so that persons who are closely associated with a business transaction, though not strictly a party to it, may nevertheless find themselves subject to its terms.

CASE 12.3

Shanklin, the owner of a pier, consulted Detel Products, Ltd., paint manufacturers, about the best type of paint to use in repainting the pier. Detel recommended one of its own paints and promised that the paint would have a life of seven to ten years. Shanklin then made a contract with a contractor to do the work requiring it to use the paint recommended by Detel. The contractor purchased the paint from Detel. The paint proved unsatisfactory; it lasted only about three months. Shanklin sued Detel for breach of warranty regarding the quality of the paint.[14]

collateral contract
an implied contract that binds a party who made a representation or promise that induced a person to enter into a contract with another party

While there was an express contract between Shanklin and the contractor, and another between the contractor and Detel, there was no express contract between Shanklin and Detel. Nevertheless, the court found that there was an *implied* **collateral contract** between Shanklin and Detel on the following terms: Detel warranted that its paint was suitable for the pier in

---

12. See, for example: Insurance Act, R.S.O. 1990, c. I.8, s. 239; R.S.B.C. 1996, c. 226, s. 140.

13. See Lord Strathcona Steamship Co. v. Dominion Coal Co., [1926] A.C. 108, and Port Line Ltd. v. Ben Line Steamers Ltd., [1958] 2 Q.B. 146.

14. Shanklin Pier, Ltd. v. Detel Products, Ltd., [1951] 2 K.B. 854.

return for Shanklin requiring the contractor to purchase the paint from Detel. Shanklin recovered extensive damages.

In applying the principle of the *Shanklin Pier* decision, a Canadian court found that a manufacturer of farm machinery made a representation to farmers in the form of a "collateral warranty" when it published a promotional sales brochure used by dealers for the purpose of inducing farmers to buy its products.[15] Accordingly, a farmer recovered damages from the manufacturer for breach of warranty. Mr. Justice Reid of the Ontario High Court of Justice said:

> I can see no legal basis for differentiating between dealer and manufacturer in relation to collateral warranties. The manufacturer initiated the affirmations; it was the manufacturer who apparently prepared and certainly published the brochure. The dealer would perforce have to rely on the manufacturer.[16]

Exemption Clauses and the Allocation of Risk

We have seen that an exemption clause between the owner of goods and a storage or a transportation company may protect the employees who are not parties to a contract.[17] A related problem arises when an exemption clause is intended to allocate risk by protecting one or more other parties who may participate in the shipment of goods. For example, goods sent from Japan to Canada not only travel by ship but are moved on and off ship by stevedore firms in Japan and Canada, are perhaps stored for a short time in a warehouse, and then transported by rail or road carriers to their destination inland.

In these arrangements, the buyer usually obtains a single insurance policy to cover any loss that may occur after the goods leave the manufacturer until their arrival. The contract between the buyer and the principal carrier exempts the carrier—and all other carriers—from liability. In turn, the other carriers agree to perform their role and set their fees on the understanding that they are exempt from negligence. These arrangements are cost efficient and avoid the need for intermediate carriers to obtain insurance. But there is no contract between the intermediate carriers and the buyer. Can these carriers claim the benefit of the exemption clause if the buyer sues them?

The courts have struggled with this problem and the results are not entirely consistent. However, the prevailing opinion is that the intermediate carriers may successfully claim the protection of an exemption clause when the contract expressly states that they should be its "beneficiaries" and should be entitled to the protection of the clause, as set out in international rules (known as The Hague rules).[18] The cases illustrate the growing sensitivity of the courts to the substance of commercial transactions and an inclination to grant appropriate remedies.

ASSIGNMENT OF RIGHTS

The Nature of an Assignment

We have seen that, apart from land law, an assignment of liabilities to a third person is not possible. An assignment of contractual rights is, however, a common business transaction. Assignments are, in fact, the most important and long-established concession to commercial

---

15. Murray v. Sperry Rand Corp. et al. (1979), 23 O.R. (2d) 456, 96 D.L.R. (3d) 113. See also Cummings v. Ford Motor Co. of Canada, [1984] O.J. No. 431.

16. *Ibid.*, at 466. See also: Andrews v. Hopkinson, [1957] 1 Q.B. 229; Brown v. Sheen and Richmond Car Sales Ltd., [1950] 1 All E.R. 1102.

17. See *supra*, n. 8.

18. See New Zealand Shipping Co. Ltd. v. A.M. Satterthwaite & Co. Ltd., [1975] A.C. 154 (P.C.), followed by the Supreme Court of Canada in, ITO-International Terminal Operators Ltd. v. Miida Electronics Inc. and Mitsui O.S.K. Lines Ltd., [1986] 1 S.C.R. 752.

practice that our courts have recognized. Historically, such assignments became enforceable only as the courts became more willing to relax the privity of contract rule.

ILLUSTRATION 12.4

A Ltd., a building contractor, has erected a building for *B*. Under the terms of their contract, *B* still owes *A* Ltd. $10 000, to be paid one month after the completion of the building. *A* Ltd. has purchased $12 000 worth of materials from *X* Corp. In settlement of its debt to *X* Corp., *A* Ltd. pays $2000 in cash and assigns in writing its rights to the $10 000 still owing by *B*. *X* Corp. then notifies *B* that she should pay the money to it rather than to *A* Ltd. when the debt falls due.

assignor

a party that assigns its rights under a contract to a third party

assignee

a third party to whom rights under a contract have been assigned

assignment

a transfer by a party of its rights under a contract to a third party

choses in possession

rights to tangible property that may be possessed physically

choses in action

rights to intangible property such as patents, stocks, and contracts that may be enforced in the courts

In Illustration 12.4, the contractor *A* Ltd. is the **assignor** of its right to the payment of $10 000. It has assigned the right to *X* Corp., its **assignee**, for a valuable consideration. The consideration is *X* Corp.'s promise to accept the **assignment** in satisfaction of the balance of its claim against *A* Ltd. Given proper notice, the promisor *B* must perform for the assignee *X* Corp. instead of for the original promisee *A* Ltd.

As we noted in our discussion of constructive trusts, contractual rights are often valuable and may be considered a type of personal property along with the ownership of goods. The main difference is that tangible property, such as goods, may be possessed physically—it has a concrete existence; whereas a right to demand performance of a contract has no concrete existence—it is valuable only insofar as it is enforceable in the courts. The rights to tangible property that may be possessed physically are known as **choses in possession**; the rights to intangible property—to things that have value only because they may be enforced by action in the courts—are called **choses in action**. There are many types of choses in action, including such things as patents, copyrights, stocks, bonds, funds deposited in a bank account, rights to collect the proceeds of an insurance policy in the event the risk should occur, rights of action against persons who have caused injury, and rights under contracts generally.

The Importance of Assignments

A willingness to accept the ownership of choses in action as a form of personal wealth is an important mark of a modern industrial society. Choses in action give people the opportunity to retain valuable assets, say, their accumulated savings, and at the same time, through the ownership of shares and bonds, to put those assets to work as capital at the disposal of corporations; in other words, this device links personal saving to business investment. In some less developed countries, where citizens have little confidence in their legal system, it has been a major problem to persuade those who have assets to abandon their preference for investment in gold, jewels and real estate and to accept a portfolio of mortgages, shares and bonds as an alternative form of property. As a result, active capital markets in these countries have been slow to develop.

In this chapter, we are concerned with the assignment of rights arising under contracts generally; a discussion of the specific features of such choses in action as mortgages, shares, bonds and negotiable instruments is reserved for later chapters.

The Role of Equity

An assignment of rights (choses in action) and a sale of goods (choses in possession) are similar. In an assignment, the subject-matter is the transfer of contractual rights; in a sale the subject-matter is the transfer of ownership in goods. Unfortunately, the common law rules failed to give equal recognition to an assignment; unlike choses in possession, the common law viewed choses in action as personal rights that could not be transferred. But the need for recognition grew as commerce increased, and the courts of equity stepped in to recognize and enforce assignments of contractual rights.

Equity required only that a clear intention to assign a benefit be shown either orally or in writing by the assignor, and it would then permit the assignee to recover the benefit from the promisor. Because of the conflict between the rules of the common law courts and those of equity, the courts of equity required in every action by an assignee of contractual rights that the assignee make the assignor a party as well. The action then had three parties—the assignee, the assignor, and the promisor.

CheckList: Third Parties Who May Play a Role in a Contract

There are many ways in which a third party to the original contract may acquire rights under it and become subject to duties to perform:

- by novation, when a third party becomes a substitute for one of the original parties
- by vicarious performance, such as an employee carrying out the obligations of one of the parties to the contract
- by accepting responsibility as a trustee to confer benefits on a third party
- by an insurance contract under which the insurer promises to pay a third party in the event that a particular risk occurs, such as a motor vehicle accident
- by an agent making a contract on behalf of an undisclosed principal
- by a party acquiring an interest in land subject to rights and duties owed to a third person
- by a commercial contract containing an implied collateral contract binding a third party who made representations relied on by a party to the contract
- by an assignment of rights to a third party by a party to the contract

EQUITABLE ASSIGNMENTS

A basic principle of law is that a court will not decide a dispute unless all the persons directly affected by its decision have been made parties to the court proceedings and have had an opportunity to argue on their own behalf. Thus, if an assignor assigns *part* of her rights only, she remains vitally interested in the result of an action by the assignee against the promisor: if the court should decide that the promisor is not bound to perform any part of his obligations, its decision would adversely affect the assignor as well as the assignee.

ILLUSTRATION 12.5

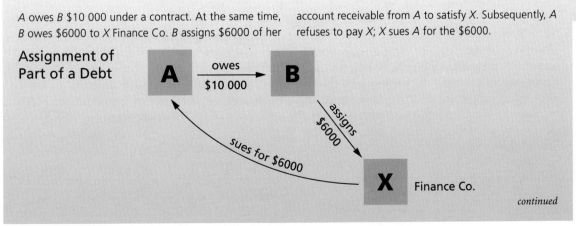

A owes B $10 000 under a contract. At the same time, B owes $6000 to X Finance Co. B assigns $6000 of her account receivable from A to satisfy X. Subsequently, A refuses to pay X; X sues A for the $6000.

Assignment of Part of a Debt

A — owes $10 000 → B

assigns $6000

X Finance Co.

sues for $6000

continued

If the court were to decide that *A* was not bound to pay anything on the debt because, say, the contract between *A* and *B* was within the Statute of Frauds and there was an insufficient memorandum of it, *B* would also be affected for she could not claim her remaining $4000 of the debt either.

The court requires that *B* be made a party to the action by *X* so that she may take part in it. In an assignment of part of a debt, both the assignee and the assignor are equally anxious that the court find the debtor (that is, the promisor) liable. Accordingly, the assignor *B* must have her own chance to argue and to adduce evidence. For example, it might well be that she would have in her possession a memorandum sufficient to comply with the Statute of Frauds, and her evidence might be decisive in holding the debtor liable.

Similarly, in an action brought by *B* against *A*, the court would require that *X* Finance Co. also be made a party.

For the purposes of Illustration 12.6 below, let us assume that the assignor assigns only part of its rights; the promisor is willing to perform his obligation, but he does not know what part he should perform for the benefit of the assignee and what part for the benefit of the assignor.

ILLUSTRATION 12.6

A owes $100 000 to *B* Inc., due in 12 months. *B* Inc. needs short-term financing and borrows $80 000 from *X* Bank, repayable in 12 months. Under their loan agreement, *B* Inc. gives *X* Bank a *conditional assignment* of its account receivable from *A* as security for repayment of the loan under the following terms:

> As long as *B* Inc. pays the interest on its loan every three months, the bank will not be entitled to notify *A* of the assignment; but if *B* Inc. fails to pay the interest or fails to pay the $80 000 on the due date, the bank may advise *A* to pay it that sum plus unpaid interest, in reduction of his debt to *B* Inc. In other words, the assignment is conditional upon the default of the borrower, *B* Inc.

If, at the end of the year, the bank notifies *A* that *B* Inc. has assigned his account and demands that *A* pay the bank, *A* cannot afford to do so until he has verified the default and the amount owing. He must check with *B* Inc. Suppose *B* Inc. claims that it has paid the bank $60 000 of the debt. *A* is in a quandary: he is aware of the competing claims and fears that if he pays one party and guesses wrong, the other may sue him successfully and collect the amount in dispute a second time. In such a case, *A* should hand the sum claimed by the bank over to the court as custodian and let *B* Inc. and the bank settle their dispute before a judge.

An equitable assignment also occurs when the subject of the assignment is an aggregate of book debts whose balances fluctuate over time.

ILLUSTRATION 12.7

Fribble Corp. owes $160 000 to Tower Bank under a demand loan. Fribble is required to make regular monthly payments on the loan and to provide the bank with semi-annual financial statements. Fribble reported substantial losses six months ago and was slow in making two subsequent interest payments. The bank threatened to call the loan unless it received additional security. Fribble then gave the bank a conditional assignment of its accounts receivable, including several large accounts, some of them running to tens of thousands of dollars.

Fribble receives frequent payments on these accounts from its customers, and also ships its products to them from time to time so that the account balances fluctuate substantially. Fribble promised to make its monthly interest payments without fail; otherwise the bank would call the loan and notify Fribble's customers of the assignment.

In these circumstances the assignment is conditional, not only because it depends on a future event (default by Fribble), but also because the value of the accounts receivable varies according to the state of accounts between Fribble and each of its customers at any given moment.

In Illustrations 12.5, 12.6, and 12.7, all the parties have a vital interest in the assignment, and it is necessary that all should be bound by the same court decision. Thus, the requirement of equity that the assignor and the debtor(s) should be made parties to the assignee's action is a just one in cases where the assignor retains an interest in the contract.

STATUTORY ASSIGNMENTS

The Need for Reform

In many business transactions, an assignor does not want to retain any rights under the contract; he assigns them entirely to the assignee. If later the assignee were to sue the promisor for failure to perform, the court-imposed requirement of making the assignor a party would be inconvenient and indeed might cause considerable hardship: the assignor might reside far away, or worse still, if he has died it would be necessary to make his personal representative a party. In any event, the requirement increases the expense of the action by bringing in a party who has no real interest.

The British Parliament remedied this defect in the 19th century when the Judicature Act amalgamated the courts of common law and equity. The Act permits an assignee to sue the promisor without joining the assignor to the suit provided: (a) the assignment was absolute (*unconditional* and *complete*), (b) it was in writing, and (c) the promisor received notice of it in writing. Most of the provinces in Canada have since passed similar statutes.[19] Assignments that comply with these requirements are known as **statutory assignments**. All other assignments are called **equitable assignments**. Note that the statute did not create a new type of assignment; it merely provided a streamlined procedure for hearing actions that meet the requirements laid down by statute.

statutory assignment
an assignment that complies with statutory provisions enabling the assignee to sue the other party without joining the assignor to the action

equitable assignment
an assignment other than a statutory assignment

Meeting the Requirements of the Statute

It is not always convenient in business to meet the requirements of the statute, and many assignments remain equitable rather than statutory. For instance, with regard to requirement (a), an assignment is not *complete* if a balance remains to be paid to the assignor after the assignee is paid—the assignor still has an interest in the contract. Nor is an assignment *unconditional* when the amount assigned varies according to the state of accounts between the assignor and his debtor; this situation exists when the balance of the account assigned fluctuates because the assignor continues to sell goods or services on credit to the debtor (the customer) or the debtor reduces the balance assigned by making payments on account to the assignor—the balance assigned is not fixed and may need to be verified from the assignor's records. In neither of these situations is the assignment "absolute."

The need for (b)–writing in support of the statutory assignment–is reasonable: if the assignment were oral, the assignee would have to call the assignor as a witness to prove that the assignment was actually made. As we noted in Chapter 2, evidence given by other persons of what the assignor said is *hearsay*, and for this reason the court will not allow such evidence when the assignor himself is able to testify. In most cases, a written assignment signed by the assignor is as good as his personal appearance in court. Only if there is a rare allegation of serious fraud, such as forgery, will further evidence be required to prove the assignment. Similarly, (c)–the requirement of notice of assignment in writing–simplifies proving that the promisor knew of the assignment. It is good business practice and common sense to send written notice by registered letter when important rights are in question in any transaction.

---

19. See, for example: Conveyancing and Law of Property Act, R.S.O. 1990, c. C.34, s. 53; Law and Equity Act, R.S.B.C. 1996, c. 253, s. 36; Judicature Act, R.S.A. 1980, c. J-1, s. 21; R.S.N.S. 1989, c. 240, s. 43(5). The statutory provisions are somewhat different in certain provinces. See, for example: Choses in Action Act, R.S.S. 1978, c. C-11, s. 2 and the Law of Property Act, R.S.M. 1987, c. L90, s. 31(1) and (5).

NOTICE TO THE PROMISOR

The Effect of Notice on the Promisor

To be effective, *all* assignments require that notice be given to the promisor. But that does not mean the promisor's consent is required. A promisor ignores a notice of an assignment at his peril. Confronted with a demand for payment from one who claims to be an assignee, the promisor should, of course, require proof of the assignment to protect himself against a possible fraud, but once he has had an opportunity to satisfy himself that there has been an assignment, he must make further payments to the assignee. If he persists in making payment to his original creditor, he can be sued by the assignee and required to pay the amount a second time.

CASE 12.4

Brian Wholesalers Ltd. buys a large quantity of goods on credit from Akron Manufacturing Inc. and defaults payment. Brian offers to pay Akron by assigning certain of its accounts receivable owed by retail merchants with excellent credit ratings. Akron agrees to this settlement and takes an absolute assignment of the debts, the largest of which is owed by Woolridge's Department Store. Akron sends to Woolridge's a notice, signed by an officer of Brian, stating that the account has been assigned to Akron, and encloses a request that Woolridge's pay Akron. Woolridge's inadvertently ignores the notice and request, and pays Brian, which shortly afterwards becomes bankrupt. Akron sues Woolridge's for payment of the debt again.

In these circumstances Akron would succeed in its action; Woolridge's paid Brian at its peril after receiving valid notice of the assignment.[20]

The Effect of Notice from Contending Assignees

The ability to assign contractual rights is an important modification of the doctrine of privity of contract: someone other than the original party to a contract is permitted to claim the benefit of rights under the contract. Indeed, more than one person may claim to be the assignee of the same right: an unscrupulous creditor might sell the right to collect the same debt to two different persons by assigning it to each of them. The debtor is then faced with two demands for payment. Which of the two innocent assignees is entitled to payment? And which is left only with an action for fraud against the assignor?

The law is clear: the assignee who first gave notice to the debtor is the one entitled to payment. This rule, like the rule that the debtor must at least receive some notice of assignment before it affects him, offers the only fair treatment to the debtor. Otherwise a debtor would be in a very insecure position, never being sure when he makes payment whether someone else to whom he should have paid the money may turn up later. An assignee who receives his assignment first may be slow in notifying the debtor, so that the second assignee notifies the debtor first.

The facts may be less clear: the second assignee is entitled to payment by the debtor, *unless* he knows of the prior assignment at the time of the assignment to him. If he knows of the prior assignment, he is a party to the fraud and cannot take payment ahead of the first assignee without becoming liable to him. In order to determine who is entitled to the debtor's performance, the court must ascertain the validity and extent of every right claimed by contending assignees.

Mercifully, the promisor need perform his obligation only once—provided he acts prudently when it is unclear whose claim should prevail. As is suggested in Illustration 12.6, it may be necessary to pay the money into court and leave it to ascertain the validity and extent of the claims by contending assignees.

---

20. See Brandt's Sons & Co. v. Dunlop Rubber Co. Ltd., [1905] A.C. 454.

THE ASSIGNEE'S TITLE

An Assignee "Takes Subject to the Equities"

A fundamental rule is that an assignee can never acquire a better right to sue the promisor than the assignor himself had. In legal terms, the assignee's claim is "subject to the equities": her claim is subject to any rights the promisor had against the assignor before the promisor received notice of the assignment; the assignee may be met by any defence that the promisor had against the assignor, with whom he originally contracted.

Thus, if a person takes an assignment of rights under a contract originally induced by the fraudulent misrepresentation of the assignor, the assignee will have no better chance to enforce her claim than if she had been the perpetrator of the fraud herself. In other words, if a debtor is the victim of fraudulent misrepresentation, the contract remains voidable at his option despite any assignment of the contractual rights. (The debtor cannot, however, sue the assignee for damages for the tort of deceit: he must sue the assignor, the person actually guilty of the fraud.) In addition to fraudulent misrepresentation, a promisor may use as a defence against an assignee: mistake, undue influence, duress, and the fact that he received no consideration for his promise.

The position of an assignee of a chose in action is in marked contrast to the position of a person who obtains title to goods under a similarly flawed contract. For instance, we have seen that, in spite of his fraud, a person may obtain title to goods so that, in turn, he may pass on valid title to a subsequent innocent purchaser, who may retain the goods against the claim of the person fraudulently persuaded to part with them.[21] But a person who obtains contractual rights by fraud does not, by assigning these rights, give an innocent assignee the right to enforce them against the defrauded promisor. An innocent assignee of a chose in action is in a much more vulnerable position than is an innocent purchaser of goods.

The Right to Set Off

An important defence of a promisor that requires further explanation is his right to **set off** a debt owed to him by the assignor at the time the assignment is made:

set off

the right of a promisor to deduct an existing debt owed to it by the promisee

ILLUSTRATION 12.8

A is employed by B at a salary of $550 per week, payable at noon Saturdays when the business closes. On Thursday, A borrows $200 from B. On Saturday, A fails to appear at work on time. When he telephones an hour late an argument ensues, and B informs A that he is fired and tells him not to bother coming back. On Monday, A sues B for $550 in the small claims court. B may set off both the $200 loan and the $50 A would have earned had he appeared at work on Saturday morning. A obtains a court judgment for $300.

Suppose, instead of suing B, A had assigned his claim for salary to his neighbour X for $500. X would take it subject to the equities between A and B, and even though X did not know of B's loan to A and of A's failure to work on Saturday, B would be able to set off these amounts in an action by X. Thus X would recover $300 from B, the same amount as A could recover.[22]

---

21. This result follows because fraud makes the contract voidable, not void. See Chapter 9 and King's Norton Metal Co. v. Edridge (1897), 14 T.L.R. 98; Lewis v. Averay, [1971] 3 All E.R. 907.

22. Provincial legislation may provide that an assignment of wages, or any portion, to secure payment of a debt is invalid. See, for example: Wages Act, R.S.O. 1990, c. W.1, s. 7(7); Assignment of Wages Act, R.S.S. 1978, c. A-30, s. 3; Labour Standards Code, 1972, R.S.N.S. 1989, c. 246, s. 89. In the authors' opinion, the reference is to amounts of wages coming due in future and not to wages already owing at the time of assignment. The policy underlying such a rule seems to be to prevent a creditor from depriving an employee of the means of livelihood, diminishing the employee's incentive to work and so undermining the employment relationship.

Until an assignee gives the promisor notice of the assignment, acts of either the assignor or the promisor or their agents may prejudice the assignee's rights. Thus, it is important for an assignee to give notice as soon as possible. If he delays, his rights may well deteriorate.

ILLUSTRATION 12.9

Williams owes Mehta $900. Mehta assigns the debt to Young on May 1. Young neglects to notify Williams, and on May 11 Williams, unaware of the assignment, pays Mehta $300 on account. Because of her failure to notify Williams, Young, the assignee, may now recover from Williams only $600 and must look to Mehta for the $300 already paid.

When a creditor, a building contractor, say, assigns rights to partial payment before it has completed performance, the assignee may be subject to an additional risk. Even when the assignee has given notice to the debtor (the party entitled to completion of the project), the debtor may be able to use defences based upon developments *after* the time of notice. The assignor's (builder's) subsequent failure to complete performance may cause the debtor damages which he can set off against the assignee's claim. In other words, an assignee's rights under a contract as yet incomplete are imperfect and subject to proper completion of the contract.[23]

A general assignment of book debts is an important business device for securing credit. The common law provinces each have statutes making such assignments void against the assignor's creditors unless the assignment is registered in a public office where its terms are available for inspection. The purpose of these statutes is to protect prospective creditors: they may inspect the registry to discover whether some assignee has a prior claim against the assets of a person who has applied to them for credit. We shall consider the reasons for providing public notice more fully in Chapters 23 and 30.

CONTEMPORARY ISSUE

Credit Cards

Credit cards are a very common way of paying for goods and services. There are several ways of setting up a credit card arrangement and organizing the legal relationships among the parties. Three-party credit card transactions (except when the card is issued by the merchant itself, such as a department store) are assignments of contractual rights: a business accepts a credit card and assigns its right to payment for goods or services purchased on credit to the credit card company. The credit card issuer pays the business for goods purchased with its card. The customer, by entering into a contract with the credit card company, consents to the assignment and agrees to pay the credit card issuer, rather than paying the business directly. The credit card industry is financed by charging businesses a small percentage of credit card sales, by charging cardholders an annual fee, and by collecting interest on unpaid balances.

The advantages of credit cards are shared by all three parties. Customers can make purchases on credit in places where they are not personally known. They can use their cards to take advantage of unanticipated bargains, to deal with emergencies, or simply to avoid carrying cash. Businesses shift the risk that some customers will fail to pay for goods or services purchased on credit to the credit card issuer. They are relieved of the trouble and expense of

continued

---

23. Young v. Kitchen (1878), 3 Ex. D. 127.

pursuing defaulting customers. They make sales they otherwise might lose. Credit card issuers earn revenue, employ people, and buy goods and services from other companies.

At the same time, credit cards tempt many consumers to take on unaffordable levels of debt. Consumer debt in North America is currently very high. The money used to pay interest on credit card debt is money that is not being saved, invested, or spent on other goods. Credit cards also offer opportunities to commit fraud.

Source: A.G. Guest and Eva Lomnicka, *An Introduction to the Law of Credit and Security*, Sweet and Maxwell, 1978, para. 366.

Questions to Consider

1. Cite two other everyday examples of assignment of contractual rights.
2. Are the benefits and costs of widespread credit card use properly balanced, in your view? What changes, if any, would you like to see made to the rules and practices concerning credit cards?

ASSIGNMENTS BY OPERATION OF LAW

Upon the Death of a Party

When a person dies, the law automatically assigns his or her rights and obligations under outstanding contracts to a personal representative. If the deceased person leaves a will naming a representative, the representative is called an **executor**. If he or she fails to name an executor in the will (or the executor refuses to assume the position) or else leaves no will (that is, dies **intestate**), the court will appoint a personal representative called an **administrator**. There is no obligation for a representative to perform a contract requiring personal services; the skill of the deceased cannot be demanded of the representative. We need only think of the executor of a deceased violinist to understand the reason for this rule.

The task of an executor or administrator is to pay all just claims against the deceased's estate, to complete performance of any outstanding contractual obligations of the deceased not requiring personal skill, to pursue all claims the deceased had against others, and then to distribute the assets according to the will—or in the case of an intestate person, to distribute them to the heirs according to statutory provisions.[24]

executor
the personal representative of a deceased person named in his or her will

intestate
a person dies without leaving a will

administrator
the personal representative of a person who dies intestate

Bankruptcy

A person carrying on business, who becomes insolvent, may realize that his position is hopeless, and may voluntarily apply for bankruptcy proceedings to avoid further loss to his creditors and injury to his name. Alternatively, creditors may commence bankruptcy proceedings against a reluctant debtor by petitioning the court for an order known as a **receiving order**. If the creditors satisfy the court that their debtor is insolvent, the court will declare him **bankrupt** and appoint a licensed trustee to take charge of his property. It is then the duty of a licensed trustee to liquidate the assets and to settle the creditors' claims.

We shall deal with bankruptcy again in Chapter 31. We raise the topic at this point simply to explain the relationship between a bankrupt person and the trustee in bankruptcy. In the

receiving order
a court order to commence bankruptcy proceedings

bankrupt
declared insolvent by the court

---

24. The way in which the estate of an intestate person will be distributed to the heirs is set down in provincial statutes. See, for example: Estates Administration Act, R.S.O. 1990, c. E.22; Intestate Succession Act, R.S.N.S. 1989, c. 236, s. 153; Estate Administration Act, R.S.B.C. 1996, c. 122, Part 7.

proceedings, the court assigns to the trustee the bankrupt person's assets, including his contractual rights and his liabilities.[25]

Assignments resulting from death and from bankruptcy proceedings started by creditors differ from other assignments in that they are involuntary; they take place "by operation of law." One's affairs are seldom completely in good order when either of these events occurs, and an assignment achieves an artificial extension of the assignor's legal existence until his affairs can be wound up.

NEGOTIABLE INSTRUMENTS

Their Nature and Uses

negotiable instrument
a written contract containing a promise, express or implied, to pay a specific sum of money to the order of a designated person or to "bearer"

A **negotiable instrument**—for example, a draft, promissory note, or cheque—is a written contract containing a promise, express or implied,[26] to pay a specific sum of money to the order of a designated person or to "bearer."

Generally speaking, a negotiable instrument arises from a contract that precedes it: a buyer delivers a negotiable instrument in payment for goods or services received. But delivery of the instrument does not complete the promisor's obligation. If he does not honour the instrument when it falls due and is presented to be paid, the promisee has the choice of suing under the original contract or for failure to honour the instrument. Often a promisee chooses to sue on the negotiable instrument, because the procedure is somewhat simpler.

The unique aspects of the law of negotiable instruments arise when a promisee assigns an instrument to a third party.

Negotiability Compared With Assignability

negotiation
the process of assigning a negotiable instrument

endorse
sign one's name on a negotiable instrument

holder
a party who acquires a negotiable instrument from the transferor

The process of assigning a negotiable instrument is known as **negotiation**. A promisee or payee of an instrument may negotiate it in one of two ways: if the instrument is payable to bearer, he need only deliver it to a third party; if the instrument is payable in his name, he must **endorse** his name upon it and then deliver it. Negotiation is really a special type of assignment in which the new **holder** of the instrument acquires from the transferor the rights that the instrument has to convey.

Chapter 21 of this book examines the law affecting negotiable instruments in more detail. Since, however, negotiation is a special application of assignments, we can better understand both concepts by reviewing their differences here. In a sense, negotiation is a privileged type of assignment that, for reasons of business convenience, is released from certain of the restrictions that apply to an ordinary assignment of contractual rights. It therefore differs from an assignment of rights generally in the following important respects.

Notice to the Promisor

We have seen that notice plays two important roles in assignment generally: first, written notice is necessary before an assignee may take advantage of a statutory assignment; second, notice protects an assignee against the consequences of the promisor being unaware of the assignment and paying the assignor or other assignees. However, notice is of no consequence in the transfer of a negotiable instrument—indeed, it is irrelevant—because the promisor is liable to pay only one person, the holder of the instrument for the time being. Thus, even if she receives notice of the assignment, neither she nor her bank will pay the assignee unless and until the

---

25. A licensed trustee may, however, with the permission of inspectors appointed by the creditors, disclaim any lease of property of the bankrupt debtor. Bankruptcy and Insolvency Act, R.S.C. 1985, c. B-3 (as amended), s. 30(1)(k).

26. According to the wording of a cheque, the drawer does not directly promise to pay its amount, but he does promise by implication that sufficient funds will be available in his account to pay it when it is presented.

assignee presents the instrument. The promisor pays her debt only once—to the holder of the instrument for the time being *and* in exchange for the instrument. In effect she pays for the return of her negotiable instrument. "The idea of 'embedding' legal rights in a document, such that the abstract rights move in unison with the physical certificate, has been very potent in commercial law, especially in regard to debt obligations."[27]

ILLUSTRATION 12.10

Steele receives his monthly paycheque of $3500 from Union Foundry Co. Ltd. He negotiates it to Comfy Furniture Mart for $2700 worth of furniture and $800 cash. Steele then tells his employer that he has inadvertently destroyed the cheque by throwing the envelope containing it into a fire, and he persuades Union to pay him a second time. When Comfy presents the original cheque for payment, Union must honour it even though Comfy gave no notice of the assignment.

If instead Steele had assigned to Comfy a claim against Union for arrears of wages (a contractual right not represented by any negotiable instrument) and if Comfy did not immediately notify Union of the assignment, Union could defeat the claim of Comfy, as assignee, by establishing that it had already paid Steele before receiving notice.

Defences of the Promisor

An assignee for value of a negotiable instrument may succeed in an action against the promisor where the assignor himself would not have succeeded. For example, even when a promisor is induced to sign a negotiable instrument because of fraud or undue influence, he may be sued successfully by a subsequent innocent holder who has given consideration for the instrument to the party guilty of the fraud; yet the rogue could not himself enforce the promise in the instrument.[28] A defrauder may transfer enforceable rights under a negotiable instrument in much the same way that he can pass valid title to goods to an innocent purchaser. Similarly, a person who has given a negotiable instrument in payment for an illegal consideration loses the defence of illegality against an innocent holder of the instrument for value. By contrast, in an ordinary assignment of rights, the assignee never acquires a better right than the assignor had; the debtor retains her defences against the assignee.

ILLUSTRATION 12.11

Bacchus contracted with Hermes for the illegal transportation of liquor into Saskatchewan and gave Hermes his cheque for $2000 for services rendered. The police discovered and confiscated the liquor, and Bacchus then asked his bank to stop payment on the cheque to Hermes.

In the meantime, Hermes had used the cheque to pay a debt to an innocent trade creditor, Argus, who knew nothing of the circumstances under which the cheque had been obtained. Argus learned that payment of the cheque had been stopped when he attempted to cash it at the bank. Argus sued Bacchus on the dishonoured instrument.

Bacchus might have used the defence of illegality in an action brought against him by the party with whom he contracted—Hermes. But he must pay the holder of the cheque, Argus, if (as appears probable) Argus can prove he took the instrument unaware of its illegal origin and gave value for it.

By contrast, if Hermes' claim for $2000 against Bacchus had remained simply in the form of an account receivable, no one to whom Hermes might have assigned the debt would have obtained a better right to collect it than Hermes himself had.

---

27. Baxter and Johnston, "New Mechanics for Securities Transactions" (1971), 21 *U.T.L.J.* 358.

28. But see The Bills of Exchange Act, R.S.C. 1985, c. B-4, restricting the rights of finance companies to assert the status of a holder in due course.

Form of Action

A holder of a negotiable instrument can sue in her own name; it is not necessary for her to join in the action any of the other parties who have signed the instrument.

Commercial Importance of Negotiability

For hundreds of years, merchants have found it to their advantage to recognize negotiable instruments as a special class of readily assignable promise, free from the formalities and many of the risks of an ordinary assignment of contractual rights. Business experience has shown that negotiability has a convenience far outweighing any cost of its abuse. We have noted that the law restricts the possibility of abuse in the face of such defences as fraud, undue influence, duress, and illegality by requiring a holder of a negotiable instrument to show that he was unaware of the origin of the tainted instrument, and that he or some previous holder of the instrument must have given value for it.[29]

Modern banking practice is based upon the relatively secure position of an innocent holder for value of a negotiable instrument. Banks are able to cash cheques or accept them for deposit without exhaustive inquiry into the background of the transactions out of which they arose since, as innocent holders for value, they are immune from the earlier flawed nature of the transaction. Without such a rule, banking facilities would be much less accessible to business and the public generally.

Currency

The familiar Bank of Canada note is a special type of instrument authorized by statute and designed to circulate with maximum ease of transferability. We shall refer to it again briefly in Chapter 21.

QUESTIONS FOR REVIEW

1. Define the following terms: third party, assignor, novation, constructive trust, beneficiary, chose in action.

2. Give an example of vicarious performance by a party other than an employee.

3. How has the privity of contract rule been modified with respect to insurance?

4. Describe the significance of exemption clauses in contracts for the storage and transportation of goods.

5. *P* contracted with *Q* to move equipment from one of *Q*'s buildings to another site. *R*, an employee of *P*, damaged some of the equipment. What facts must *Q* establish in order to hold *P* liable for *R*'s conduct?

6. Describe a collateral contract and the circumstances in which it may arise.

7. A debtor owed his creditor $2000. The creditor assigned her right to collect this debt to another person, *X*. The assignee, *X*, delayed in sending notice to the debtor that he was now the party entitled to payment. Before receiving any notice of assignment, the debtor paid his original creditor $750 on account. How have *X*'s rights been affected?

---

29. The requirements are somewhat more technical than we can conveniently describe here: the holder must be a *holder in due course*. See *infra*, Chapter 21.

8. Anderson, a skilled mechanic, agreed to do some car repair work for Bartlett. Anderson was busy when the car was delivered for repair and gave his friend Gauche the work to do, without consulting Bartlett. Gauche sent Bartlett a bill for the repair work. Bartlett refused to pay. Is he justified?

9. Give two examples of involuntary assignments.

10. What are the requirements for a statutory assignment? Describe the business advantages associated such assignments.

11. Explain the two types of assignment by operation of law.

12. Is notice required to assign a negotiable instrument? Explain.

CASES AND PROBLEMS

1 King, a building contractor, completed the construction of a house for Harris. At completion, Harris owed King a balance of $15 000. King then borrowed $10 000 from the Brandon Bank. In consideration for this loan, King assigned to the bank as much of his account receivable from Harris as should be necessary to repay the sum borrowed plus interest and any further sums for which he might become indebted to the bank. Is the bank, as assignee, entitled to sue Harris without the assistance of King's testimony?

Suppose instead that King had borrowed $20 000 from the Brandon Bank and in partial settlement assigned the whole of the $15 000 due to him from Harris. Are these changed facts in themselves sufficient to entitle the bank to sue Harris without joining King in the action?

2 The University of Ashcroft Business School offers one-week executive courses. For its October program on marketing strategies, Ashcroft's dean managed to make a deal with Professor Bertoff, a famous specialist in the field, to give the opening lecture and remain at the business school for two full days. Less than a week before the program was to begin, Bertoff sent an e-mail to the dean that his country's government had requested him to chair a crucial international meeting on trade policy; he would send his associate, Professor Colbert, a more junior but quite well-known person in the marketing field, to deliver the lecture prepared by Bertoff himself, and to remain on campus for the two days.

The dean is quite upset: he has no alternative but to allow Colbert to fill in. He wishes to know whether he has a good case against Bertoff. Give your opinion with reasons.

3 Garbutt was dismissed by her employer Carter Computers Inc. for allegedly dishonest conduct. She hired Harkin to be her lawyer and represent her in grievance arbitration for wrongful dismissal. Harkin was successful; the arbitrator found that Garbutt had been wrongfully dismissed and that she was entitled to be compensated for her losses.

During negotiations to settle the amount of compensation, Garbutt gave Harkin a signed direction to Carter Computers to pay 30 percent of the settlement proceeds to Harkin. He delivered a photocopy of the direction to Carter Computers' in-house lawyer, but she told him that Carter Computers would honour only an original signed copy.

The next day the parties reached a settlement of $20 000. Before the in-house lawyer received the original copy of the direction, she instructed the payroll department to issue a cheque to Garbutt for the full amount of the settlement proceeds. Harkin sued the defendant for failure to pay him the $6000.

Summarize the arguments of each side, and give your opinion of whether Harkin should succeed.

4 Keirson sold his taxi business to Martens, covenanting neither directly nor indirectly to carry on or be engaged in another taxi business within five miles of the place of business for five years from the date of sale. The agreement contained the usual clause extending the benefit of the contract to the "assigns" (assignees) of the parties. Two years later, Martens resold the taxi business to Nelman, and shortly afterwards Keirson entered into another taxi business within the five-mile area. Nelman brought an action against Keirson for an injunction to restrain him from operating a competing business within the five-mile area. Should Nelman succeed?

5 B. Flatt and F. Major made a $50 wager about the spelling of *Cavalleria Rusticana*. Flatt lost and he gave Major a cheque for $50. When Major attempted to deposit the cheque in her bank account, she learned that Flatt had instructed his bank to stop payment on it. What are Major's rights?

Would it make any difference if Major had cashed Flatt's cheque with her corner pharmacist and the pharmacist was then confronted with Flatt's stop-payment order?

6 Glashov purchased on credit from Brown a building for business purposes. In their agreement, Glashov covenanted that he would insure the property and assign the insurance to Brown, the vendor, as security for the amount that remained owing on the purchase price.

Glashov insured the property with the Standard Insurance Company but neglected to inform the company that the proceeds in the event of a claim should be paid to Brown. The building was later destroyed in a fire.

Immediately after the fire, three of Glashov's trade creditors sought payment of their claims and agreed to accept from him an assignment to them of the proceeds of the fire insurance. The trade creditors gave notice to Standard Insurance Company at once, before the amount of the loss had been established and before that company had admitted any liability under the policy. Brown, after learning what had happened, informed the insurance company that she wished to claim the insurance money due, and supported her claim by showing to the company the terms of the agreement for sale. The insurance company paid the money into court for settlement of the dispute.

What is the nature of the trade creditors' argument that they should have the insurance money instead of Brown? What possible defence or defences might Brown offer against this claim? To whom would a court order the payment of the insurance money?

7 York Bridge Co. Ltd. undertook construction work for the City of Vancouver. A month later, when the construction work was partly completed, York Bridge assigned to Southern B.C. Foundries & Steel Co. Ltd. the amount of $68 000 due to it for work completed by that time. When it took the assignment, the management of Southern B.C. Foundries was aware that the claim its company was acquiring arose from an uncompleted contract. Southern B.C. Foundries immediately notified the City of the assignment but delayed in pursuing its rights when the City was slow in paying.

York Bridge abandoned the contract in the following September, and its non-performance caused a loss to the City of $125 000. When Southern B.C. Foundries then attempted, as assignee, to collect $68 000 from the City, the City defended by claiming it no longer owed money for the construction work because the damages it had suffered from the breach of contract exceeded the sum owing for the part of the work that had already been done. Southern B.C. Foundries contended that the sum of $68 000 was due and payable at the time the City had been notified of the assignment.

Explain the issues raised by these facts and the applicable rules of law, and express an opinion whether Southern B.C. Foundries should be able to recover $68 000 from the City of

Vancouver. Explain also whether this would appear to be an equitable or a statutory assignment and indicate the significance that the type of assignment would have in this case.

 Norton responded to a campaign for funds by the National Association for the Preservation of Wildlife (NAPW) by signing the following statement, which she gave to a canvasser for NAPW:

$1250.00   Charlottetown, Nov. 2, 1998

To assist in the purchase of conservation area sites and in consideration of the subscriptions of others, I promise to pay to the Treasurer of the National Association for the Preservation of Wildlife the sum of twelve hundred and fifty dollars, payable $500 on February 1, 1999 and $750 on August 1, 1999.

Joan J. Norton

This and other similar agreements permitted the Association to acquire property for use as conservation areas.

In order to obtain cash immediately from some of the pledges made to it, including Norton's, NAPW sold (assigned) them to Simpson for an undisclosed cash sum. Simpson's secretary telephoned Norton to advise her of the assignment of her promise and Norton confirmed that she had made the pledge. Norton failed, however, to pay either of the instalments to Simpson. Simpson brought an action against Norton for payment of the $1250.

Express, with reasons, an opinion about the probable outcome of this action.

THE DISCHARGE OF CONTRACTS

The Ways in Which a Contract May Be Discharged

Discharge by Performance

Discharge by Agreement

Discharge by Frustration

Discharge by Operation of Law

When a contract comes to an end—is discharged—neither party has any obligations under it. Apart from breach, which is examined in the next chapter, we examine here the various ways in which a contract may be discharged. We discuss also the consequences of an event that makes performance impossible or pointless—a frustrating event—and its effects. In this chapter we examine such questions as:

- what is "tender of performance" and what are its requirements and consequences?

- what are the various ways in which a contract may be discharged by agreement?

- how may a contract provide for its own termination?

- what are the shortcomings of common law rules in their ability to deal with frustration?

- how have statutory reforms dealt with these problems?

- what special problems arise from frustration as it applies to the sale of goods?

- what is meant by "discharge by operation of law"?

THE WAYS IN WHICH A CONTRACT MAY BE DISCHARGED

discharge a contract
cancel the obligation of a contract; make an agreement or contract null and inoperative

To **discharge a contract** means "to cancel the obligation of a contract; to make an agreement or contract null and inoperative."[1] In this chapter, we shall consider four ways in which the discharge of a contract may occur: by performance, agreement, frustration, and operation of law. In addition, a contract is sometimes said to be "discharged" by its breach, but this topic is reserved for separate treatment in the following chapter.

---

1. *Black's Law Dictionary* (6th ed.), p. 463.

DISCHARGE BY PERFORMANCE

The Nature of Discharge by Performance

Parties who enter into a contract expect it to be discharged by performance. Their contract ends when they have performed their respective obligations satisfactorily. For a contract to be fully discharged, both parties—not merely one of them—must complete performance. A bilateral contract, formed by the offer of a promise for a promise, goes through three stages: first, when neither party has performed its promise; second, when one but not the other party has performed; and third, when both have performed. Only at the final stage is the contract discharged by performance. In a unilateral contract, formed by the offer of a promise for an act, the first stage is eliminated because the second takes place in the very formation of the contract through one party's performance; the last stage remains necessary for discharge by performance.

Performance may take several forms, depending on the contract. It may be services rendered, goods delivered, a cash payment made, or any combination of these.

Tender of Performance

One party may attempt to perform, but the other party refuses to accept the performance. An attempt to perform is called a **tender of performance**, whether accepted or rejected by the other party.

tender of performance
an attempt by one party to perform according to the terms of the contract

If a seller properly tenders delivery of the goods and the buyer refuses to accept them, the seller is under no obligation to attempt delivery again and may immediately sue for breach of contract.

A debtor who makes an unsuccessful but reasonable attempt to pay will be free from further liability for interest on the amount owing and generally will not have to pay court costs if he is later sued for the debt. To be sure of this result, he should offer the money in the form of **legal tender**. Legal tender consists of Bank of Canada notes (or "bills" as we call them) and silver coins to the limit of $10.[2] A creditor is legally within its rights to refuse to accept payment in silver of a debt of, say, $100; it may also refuse any negotiable instrument, including even a cheque certified by a bank. In practice, of course, payment is normally made in a form that is not legal tender; it may be made by cheque or other negotiable instrument, or increasingly often by electronic transfer of funds. Only when there is a risk of dispute does a legally correct tender of payment become important. The debtor will then make a formal legal tender of cash to the creditor to avoid any later claim that he was unwilling or unable to meet his obligations.

legal tender
Bank of Canada notes, and silver coins to the limit of $10

ILLUSTRATION 13.1

S agrees in writing to sell $10 000 worth of flour to B, cash on delivery. Before the date of delivery, the price of flour rises substantially. S becomes anxious to discover a means of avoiding the contract; hearing a rumour that B is in financial difficulties, he uses the argument that B may be unable to pay as a pretext for notifying B that he is terminating the contract. B, of course, wishes to proceed with the sale at the agreed price. She takes the contract to her bank and borrows sufficient cash (legal tender) to pay the purchase price. She then tenders the money to S in the presence of a witness. If S does not deliver the flour and B sues him for breach of contract, S cannot claim in defence that B was unable to pay.

If a creditor is foolish enough to refuse a legal tender of payment, any subsequent action to recover the money will be at the creditor's own expense. However, refusing a tender of payment does not discharge the debt itself. The debtor must still pay it, but no interest will accrue after

2. Currency Act, R.S.C. 1985, c. C-52, s. 8 as amended by R.S.C. 1985, c. 35 (3rd Supp.), s. 18.

the date of tender. If the debtor tenders payment in a reasonable fashion (though not strictly speaking in the form of legal tender), a court may, at its discretion, award the costs of any subsequent litigation against the creditor.

There is a legal maxim that the debtor must seek out her creditor. She is not excused from tendering payment because her creditor is slow or diffident about asking for it: the onus is on the debtor to find and pay her creditor.

DISCHARGE BY AGREEMENT

Waiver

The parties may agree between themselves not to perform their contract and thus discharge it. A **waiver** is an agreement not to proceed with the performance of a contract already in existence. If neither party has performed fully at the time both agree to call off the bargain, there is automatically consideration for the waiver of each party: each still has rights and obligations outstanding, and a promise by one party to waive its rights is sufficient consideration for it being released from obligations to the other.

On the other hand, if one party has already fully performed its part but the other has not, it receives no consideration for giving a waiver of the other party's duty to perform. To be enforceable, its promise to release the other party should be under seal.

ILLUSTRATION 13.2

Atwater agrees to install a sound system in the Kent Theatre for $5500. Kent's right, under the contract, is to receive the benefits of the work, and Kent's obligation is to pay for the work. Atwater's right is to receive the price, and his obligation is to do the work required. Consequently, if they should mutually agree to call off their contract before Atwater completes the work, there is consideration for the waiver. Atwater promises to abandon a claim for payment; Kent Theatre promises in return to abandon a claim for services. Each party's promise is a price paid for the promise of the other.

But suppose that Kent has paid Atwater the $5500 and that to date Atwater has only partly installed the system. At this stage, any undertaking by Kent that it will "require neither completion of the work nor a return of any money" is without consideration and, therefore, not binding unless under seal.[3]

Of course, neither party can impose a waiver on the other. A party who fails to perform without securing a waiver by the other commits a breach of the contract. As we shall see in the next chapter, the consequences of breach are quite different from discharge by agreement.

Substituted Agreement

Material Alteration of the Terms

If parties agree to a material alteration of the terms, one that goes to the root of the contract, they have in effect agreed to discharge their original contract and replace it with a new one. This amounts to novation, as discussed in the preceding chapter. Minor changes in the terms do not have this sweeping effect.

It is not always easy to decide whether an agreed alteration leaves the original contract intact or amounts to novation.

---

3. This statement remains subject to the discussion in Chapter 6, concerning the "Gratuitous Reduction of a Debt," and "Injurious Reliance."

CASE 13.1

P, a building contractor, agreed to pay a penalty if he did not have the construction work completed by a certain date. Before completion, *P* and the owner, *Q*, agreed that *P* should do some additional work on the same project. The changes made it impossible for *P* to complete the building by the original date. *Q* insisted that the penalty clause allowed him to deduct the penalty from the amount he still owed to *P*. The court held that the new agreement had discharged the old and that the penalty clause had disappeared with it.[4]

Accord and Satisfaction

Sometimes a party finds it cannot perform its obligation according to the terms of the contract or performance has become very difficult. It may offer the promisee a money payment or some other substitute if the promisee will discharge it from its original obligation. For example, a seller may find that it cannot obtain certain imported goods to fill an order and may offer other goods of equal quality, perhaps at a lower price, if the buyer will release it from its original promise. An aggrieved party may be preparing to sue the other before the settlement is agreed on. **Accord and satisfaction** often takes the form of a compromise out of court.

accord and satisfaction
a compromise between contracting parties to substitute a new contractual obligation and release a party from the existing one

The distinction between a material alteration of the terms and accord and satisfaction is in the purpose of the arrangement: in a material alteration, the parties are primarily concerned with a new arrangement—the discharge of the old contract is incidental; in accord and satisfaction the parties are seeking a way to discharge their existing contract—the new arrangement is for that very purpose.

A party may concede liability for damages although it and the other party still differ about the amount of the damages it should pay. Suppose the party admitting liability tenders payment of an amount in settlement but the other refuses it claiming that it is insufficient. The first party may then pay into court the amount offered. If the other party sues and the court awards it no more than the sum tendered in settlement, it will have to pay the court costs as a penalty for insisting upon litigation; in addition, the defendant will not be liable for interest on the sum due from the time it tendered the settlement. On the other hand, if the damages awarded are greater than the sum paid into court by the defendant, the judge may apportion the court costs between the parties, or if the sum tendered was unreasonably low, the judge may order the defendant to pay all the costs.

Novation

As noted in the preceding chapter, novation is another method of discharge: a replacement of one of the parties discharges the original contract and substitutes a new contract. A common example occurs when a party purchases a going business and assumes its outstanding liabilities as a part of the purchase price for the assets acquired. If the creditors accept the new owner as their debtor, either by an express agreement with it or by applying to the new owner for payment of claims against the former owner, the liability of the former owner is discharged and replaced by that of the purchaser. In the words of Mr. Justice Fisher:

> Where the business of a partnership is taken over by a new company [new owner] and the creditor of the partnership applies to the new company for payment, his claim is admitted and they promise to pay the debt, that is sufficient in my opinion to make the new company liable, as slight circumstances are sufficient to show an adoption by the creditors of the new company as their debtor.[5]

---

4. Thornhill v. Neats (1860), 141 E.R. 1392. See also Amirault v. M.N.R. (1990), 90 D.T.C. 1330.
5. Re Star Flooring Co. Ltd., [1924] 3 D.L.R. 269 at 272.

There must be, however, evidence of consent to the novation on the part of both the creditors and the new owner.[6] The evidence need not be in the form of an express agreement; it may be shown by examining the conduct of the parties. However, the burden is upon the party claiming that there was novation to show that the other party has assumed all liabilities under a pre-existing contract and has acted on that contract.[7]

In good business practice, neither the vendor nor the purchaser of a business relies on implied novation with creditors. The two parties to the sale agree on what debts the new owner should assume and then call in the creditors to obtain their express consent to the substitution of a new debtor. In addition, to protect itself, the purchaser of a business makes a careful examination of public records, requires the vendor to provide a declaration setting out the names of all its creditors and the amounts owing to them, and publicizes the sale. We shall examine the statutory reasons for these procedures more fully in Chapters 30 and 31, which discuss creditors' rights.

A Contract Provides for Its Own Dissolution

Before agreeing to a contract, one party may express concern about a possible event affecting its ability or willingness to perform. If the other party is agreeable, they may include an express term to allow for this eventuality. Sometimes, a similar term may be implied by trade usage or by the surrounding circumstances of the agreement. The term may be a condition precedent, a condition subsequent, or an option to terminate.

Condition Precedent

In Chapter 11, we noted that a condition precedent is a future or uncertain event that must have occurred before the promisor's liability is established. (The "occurrence" may be a "non-event," that is, a condition that the thing *not* happen before the time stipulated.) In that chapter, because we were concerned with the interpretation of contracts and the operation of the parol evidence rule, we referred to a condition precedent as the result of an oral understanding. It may, of course, be a term in a written contract.

ILLUSTRATION 13.3

A Co. Ltd., located in Moncton, writes to *B* in Winnipeg offering him a good employment position. *B* replies by letter that he will take the position if *A* Co. Ltd. will first find satisfactory living accommodation in Moncton for him and his family. *A* Co. Ltd. accepts *B*'s counter-offer by mail. The employer's act of finding the specified living accommodation is a condition precedent.

Alternatively, *B* might reply that he will take the position if his wife, who works for a different firm, is *not* offered a promotion for which she has already applied. The failure to receive the promotion is a condition precedent.

It has sometimes been argued that a contract does not even come into existence when there is a condition precedent, and that to be capable of discharge, a contract must first have existed. Yet there is a real sense in which a contract is formed from the time of the offer and the acceptance, even though a condition precedent is not resolved until later. A contract subject to a condition precedent *does* have a binding force from the outset, and the parties are not free to withdraw from their promises unless and until the condition precedent becomes impossible to fulfill. The arrangement is, therefore, much more than an outstanding offer that can be revoked

---

6. Toronto Star v. Aiken, [1955] O.W.N. 613.

7. See Pacific Wash-A-Matic Ltd. v. R.O. Booth Holdings Ltd. (1979), 105 D.L.R. (3d) 323.

prior to acceptance. Accordingly, in Illustration 13.3, if immediately after *B* received *A* Co. Ltd.'s acceptance he changed his mind and took a position with a different firm, he would be in breach of contract.

A contract may contain a series of conditions precedent:

ILLUSTRATION 13.4

Grey, the owner of a construction site, stipulates in her contract with the builder, Brown, that as work progresses on their construction project it must be approved at specified stages by a designated architect, Greene. If, after any stage of the work is completed, Greene states that he is not satisfied with the quality of performance, Grey's obligation to pay for that stage and for further work under the contract ceases: Greene's approval is a condition precedent to payment for the work completed and for continuing with the remaining stages.

A party that agrees to do work on these terms exposes itself to the judgment and reasonableness of a designated person who assesses the work. Unless it can show that there has been fraud or collusion between that person and the party for which it is to do the work, it is subject to the verdict reached; it cannot claim a breach of contract if the work is brought to an end prematurely when the designated person, acting in good faith, refuses to approve what has been done.

A promisor is in an even more difficult position if it gives the right to approve or disapprove of performance to the promisee itself rather than to a third party such as an engineer or architect. The promisee's opinion of what is satisfactory is far more likely to be prejudiced in its own favour. The courts have held that a promisee given such a power can withhold approval and avoid liability under the contract. It does not matter that the promisee's judgment is unreasonable, or that the judge or jury believe that in the circumstances they themselves would have approved of the performance: so long as they find that the promisee is honestly dissatisfied, the promisor has no rights against it.[8]

Condition Subsequent

A **condition subsequent** is an uncertain event that brings a promisor's liability to an *end* if it happens. Liability is established when the contract is formed but one of the parties has reserved for itself an "out" in certain circumstances. A buyer of a ticket for a baseball game has the benefit of a term in his contract that if the game is rained out before a stated inning he will be given a ticket for another game.

> **condition subsequent**
> an uncertain event that brings a promisor's liability to an end if it happens

ILLUSTRATION 13.5

Norton is the holder of a baseball season's ticket that, because of some of his habits known to the management, was sold to him on terms that he must watch his conduct at the games.

Norton attends a game and his conduct is an annoyance and nuisance not only to the operators of the ballpark but also to other fans and to those selling tickets. He has a loud, booming voice and insists on telling other fans things they do not want to know, and by moving about he obstructs the view of others. The management informs him that it is cancelling his season's ticket and tenders him a refund for the remaining games. Norton sues the management for breach of contract.

The contract contains a term relating to a condition subsequent—Norton's objectionable conduct. It is, therefore, discharged by agreement rather than by breach, and Norton's action will fail.[9]

---

8. Truman v. Ford Motor Co., [1926] 1 D.L.R. 960.
9. See North v. Victoria Baseball & Athletic Co., [1949] 1 W.W.R. 1033.

act of God
the raging of the natural elements

In contracts for the shipment of goods, an "**act of God**" (the raging of the natural elements) may be a condition subsequent if it results in the destruction of the shipment. When a railway, trucking line, airline, or marine shipping company accepts goods for shipment, it undertakes to be liable for any damage if the goods arrive at their destination in a poorer condition than they were received by the carrier; but there is also a term discharging the carrier from this liability if the goods are destroyed by an act of God. If the goods are only partly destroyed, the contract is not discharged completely; instead the carrier is absolved from liability to the extent that the damage was caused to the goods by an act of God and must deliver them as they are. Such a term is implied by trade custom, but most carriers take the added precaution of expressly stating the term in their bills of lading. Accordingly, it is wise when shipping goods at the owner's risk, to buy insurance against such loss.

Option to Terminate

A contract may include a term that gives one party, or perhaps both, the option of bringing the contract to an end before its performance has been completed, usually by giving notice. Exercising the option results in *discharge by agreement* because the means of discharge was agreed upon when drawing up the contract. For example, a contract of employment of indefinite duration usually contains an option clause, either express or implied, entitling the employer to dismiss an employee on giving the required notice, as explained in Chapter 20. Many mortgages have an option clause entitling the mortgagor to pay off the principal sum before maturity by tendering an additional payment of interest.

In a contract for the purchase of a business, a buyer may insist on a proviso allowing it to rescind the agreement if a current audit of the financial statements of the acquired business should result in the auditor being unable to give an unqualified opinion on their fairness. In these circumstances, an auditor's qualified opinion (or unwillingness to express any opinion) would give the purchaser an option to terminate the contract.

DISCHARGE BY FRUSTRATION

Effect of Absolute Promises

The common law originally held a party responsible without exception for a failure to perform her promise—even when the failure had not been her fault. Of course, a party could avoid such consequences, if she foresaw them, by insisting at the time of agreement on an express term absolving her from liability under stated circumstances. Indeed, the argument for holding a party responsible was that she could have provided for the event in the contract but did not do so. As a practical matter it is not possible to foresee all eventualities. In any event, the cost of administrative time and legal advice involved in adding extensive lists of exemptions that would excuse performance only in rare circumstances would normally exceed the benefits of such a procedure.

As the next section will explain, the courts now excuse persons for failure to perform their contracts in a wide variety of circumstances where they are not at fault. Nevertheless, courts remain reluctant to excuse performance in some types of contracts; historically, they have regarded these kinds of contracts as inviolable regardless of the reason for which they could not be performed.[10] Tenants' covenants in commercial leases to keep the property in repair and to pay rent are promises of this kind, with the result that tenants have found themselves liable for damages caused by fire, storms, and enemy action, and liable for rent for the duration of the

---

10. It is tempting to compare absolute liability for contractual promises with strict liability in tort law as discussed in Chapter 3. We should note, however, that their historical development and the policy underlying them vary greatly.

lease when the property was no longer of use to them.[11] However, in extreme cases where the whole point of the contract has disappeared, courts have become more willing to yield:

> I adopt the reasoning of Lord Simon in *Cricklewood v. Leighton's*[12]…and accept his conclusion that there is no binding authority in England precluding the application of the doctrine of frustration to contracts involving a lease of land. I believe the situation to be the same in Ontario.[13]

Even so, a party may choose to express his promise in such an absolute and unconditional way as to rule out any reservation for his benefit and thus forgo the defence of frustration.[14]

Several provinces have enacted legislation to overrule the common law and provide that the doctrine of frustration applies to tenancy agreements for residential premises.[15] The legislation does not, however, extend the doctrine to leases of commercial, as opposed to residential, premises.

Doctrine of Frustration

As we have seen, it is an essential principle that contracts in general should have binding force and effect: for the courts to condone a failure to perform on slight pretext would be to create uncertainty in business affairs. Since the doctrine of frustration qualifies this general proposition, judges have given much thought to the problem of defining the scope of the doctrine and the instances in which it can be applied. Sometimes the parties may have included in their contract a term to deal with the risk of a particular event occurring without providing adequate protection, in which case the courts will not accept the event as frustrating the parties' contract and will give only the limited protection provided in the contract.[16]

The courts have offered a variety of explanations for the **doctrine of frustration**. In *Davis Contractors Ltd. v. Fareham*, Lord Radcliffe said:

doctrine of frustration
the law excuses a party from performance when external causes have made performance radically different from that contemplated by the parties

> Frustration occurs whenever the law recognizes that without default of either party a contractual obligation has become incapable of being performed because the circumstances in which performance is called for would render it a radically different thing from that which was undertaken by contract…. It is not hardship or inconvenience or material loss itself which calls the principle of frustration into play. There must be as well such a change in the significance of the obligation that the thing undertaken would, if performed, be a different thing from that contracted for.[17]

In another case, Mr. Justice Goddard said:

> If the foundation of the contract goes, either by the destruction of the subject-matter or by reason of such long interruption or delay that the performance is really in effect that of a different contract, and the parties have not provided what in that event is to happen, the performance of the contract is to be regarded as frustrated.[18]

Lord Sumner put it this way:

> It is really a device by which the rules as to absolute contracts are reconciled with a special exception which justice demands.[19]

---

11. Paradine v. Jane (1647), 82 E.R. 897; Redmond v. Dainton, [1920] 2 K.B. 256; Foster v. Caldwell, [1948] 4 D.L.R. 70.
12. Cricklewood Property & Investment Trust, Ltd. v. Leighton's Investment Trust, Ltd., [1945] A.C. 221.
13. Capital Quality Homes Ltd. v. Colwyn Construction Ltd. (1975), 9 O.R. (2d) 617, per Evans, J.A., at 629. The application of the doctrine of frustration to these cases still remains limited: see Victoria Wood Development Corp. Inc. v. Ondrey (1977), 14 O.R. (2d) 723.
14. Budgett & Co. v. Binnington & Co., [1891] 1 Q.B. 35; Hills v. Sughrue (1846), 153 E.R. 844.
15. See, for example: Landlord and Tenant Act, S.M. 1981, c. L-70, s. 90; Tenant Protection Act, S.O. 1997, c. 24, ss. 11 and 12.
16. Teleflex Inc. v. I.M.P. Group Ltd. (1996), 149 N.S.R. (2d) 355.
17. [1956] A.C. 696 at 729.
18. Tatem Ltd. v. Gamboa, [1939] 1 K.B. 132 at 139.
19. Hirji Mulji v. Chong Yue Steamship Co., [1926] A.C. 497 at 510.

A decision that a contract has been discharged by frustration may be viewed, then, as a practical and reasonable solution imposed by a court under circumstances that were not anticipated by the parties.[20]

The simplest cases are those where performance becomes literally impossible, which explains why they were the ones first used by the courts to develop the doctrine of frustration.

CASE 13.2

The producer of a concert hired a music hall, but it was destroyed by fire before the scheduled date of the concert. No one was found to blame for the fire. The producer sued the owner of the hall for damages to compensate for losses sustained in having to cancel the concert. The court held that the contract had been discharged by frustration and refused to award damages. Had the court found instead that the owner of the music hall had broken the contract, it would have ordered him to pay damages.[21]

CASE 13.3

Robinson had engaged Davison, a pianist, to give a concert on an agreed date. Robinson incurred expenses in preparing for the concert: advertising, selling tickets, and hiring staff for the evening. About 9 a.m. on the morning of the concert date, he received word from Davison that a sudden illness would prevent her from performing. Robinson had further expenses in cancelling the concert. When he sued Davison for damages for his loss, the court held that the contract had been discharged by frustration, and the action failed.[22]

The doctrine was carefully adapted in later cases when actual performance remained physically possible but would have a very different meaning for the parties from that intended when they made their agreement.

CASE 13.4

In July 1914 in England, the contractors Dick, Kerr & Co. agreed to construct certain reservoirs for a local water board within six years at a specified price; they started work immediately. In February 1916, the Minister of Munitions, acting under wartime statutes, ordered the contractors to cease work. Most of their plant and materials were then sold under the Minister's directions.

After the war ended, the water board insisted that the contractors should resume their work under the original terms, but the contractors refused to comply. Prices and conditions of supply had changed drastically from what they had been in 1916. The court held that the contract had been discharged by frustration and the water board failed in its action.[23]

20. The theories underlying the doctrine of frustration are discussed in Furmston, *Cheshire, Fifoot and Furmston's Law of Contract* (13th ed.), Chapter 20; and in Guest, *Anson's Law of Contract* (27th ed.), Chapter 14.
21. Taylor v. Caldwell (1863), 122 E.R. 309. See also Laurwen Investments Inc. v. 814693 N.W.T. Ltd. (1990), 48 B.L.R. 100.
22. Robinson v. Davison (1871), L.R. 6 Ex. 269.
23. Metropolitan Water Board v. Dick, Kerr & Co., [1918] A.C. 119.

On the other hand, even a significant degree of hardship is not a sufficient excuse for failing to perform. The fact that contractual obligations prove to be more onerous than anticipated will not, by itself, discharge a contract by frustration. It follows that a business that finds itself, as a promisor, deprived of the most convenient or inexpensive method of performance is not excused if other means remain by which it may reasonably perform. To excuse a promisor in these circumstances would, in the words of Lord Wright, be

> to impair the authority of written contracts…by lax or too wide application of the doctrine of frustration. Modern English law has recognized how beneficial that doctrine is when the whole circumstances justify it, but to apply it calls for circumspection.[24]

Lastly, we note that for a contract to be discharged by frustration, its performance must become impossible or purposeless *after the agreement was made* for reasons beyond the control of the parties. We must distinguish this situation from one in which performance was impossible or purposeless at the very time the agreement was made. If the subject-matter has ceased to exist at the time of the agreement, the agreement is void for mistake, as Chapter 8 has shown; it is not discharged by frustration.

Self-induced Frustration

A party to a contract cannot willfully disable itself from performing and then claim successfully that the contract has been frustrated. Such **self-induced frustration** is a breach of the contract. In many circumstances, the distinction between true frustration and self-induced frustration is readily apparent.

self-induced frustration
a party willfully disables itself from performing a contract in order to claim that the contract has been frustrated

ILLUSTRATION 13.6

(a) *A* Inc. contracts to transport earth for *B*. On realizing that it has made a bad bargain, *A* Inc. sells its sole dump truck and claims that it cannot fulfill the contract because of frustration. We have no difficulty in deciding that *A* Inc. has broken the contract.

(b) *A* Inc. contracts to transport earth for *B* in an isolated northern community. Shortly after the contract is made, its truck (the only available one in

the area) is stolen and wrecked. The contract is discharged by frustration, and *A* Inc. is freed from its obligation to perform.

(c) *A* Inc. contracts to transport earth for *B*. Its dump truck breaks down because of an employee's negligence, and there will be a long delay in its repair as the parties are in a small northern community. Because the situation is attributable to *A* Inc.'s negligence, it will be liable for breach of contract.

Not every degree of fault or irresponsibility, however, will bar a party from claiming that the contract has been frustrated. As Lord Russell said in his judgment in a leading House of Lords case:

> The possible varieties are infinite, and can range from the criminality of the scuttler who opens the sea-cocks and sinks his ship, to the thoughtlessness of the prima donna who sits in a draught and loses her voice.[25]

---

24. Twentsche Overseas Trading Co. v. Uganda Sugar Factory Ltd. (1945), 114 L.J.P.C. 25 at 28. See also: Graham v. Wagman (1976), 14 O.R. (2d) 349: "I have never heard that impecuniosity is an excuse for non-performance of a promise." per Weatherston, J., at 352.

25. Joseph Constantine Steamship Line Ltd. v. Imperial Smelting Corp. Ltd., [1942] A.C. 154 at 179. See also Maritime National Fish Ltd. v. Ocean Trawlers Ltd., [1935] 3 D.L.R. 12; Kendall v. Ivanhoe Insurance Managers Ltd., [1985] O.J. No. 1725; Atcor Ltd. v. Continental Energy Marketing Ltd., [1996] 6 W.W.R. 274.

Perhaps the subtlest variation of the problem arises when the frustrating event is only partly in the hands of the promisor.

ILLUSTRATION 13.7

A Inc., a building contractor, makes a contract to erect a house for *B*. Before it begins actual construction, *A* Inc. follows the usual procedure of applying for a building permit from the municipality in which the house is to be built. *A* Inc. is informed that the town has just passed a by-law requiring any contractor intending to build within the town limits to deposit $40 000 in cash to ensure compliance with all local regulations. *A* Inc. refuses to make the deposit on the ground that it was not part of the contract and that the hardship involved would make it uneconomical for it to go through with the contract. Has the contract been frustrated? There appears to be no easy answer; the courts must decide each case on its own facts.

CONTEMPORARY ISSUE

Resolving Disputes Through the Court or Through Mediation?

Sometimes parties disagree about whether a contract has been discharged, or whether there has been complete performance, novation, or frustration. For example, a plumbing contractor may believe that it has fulfilled its promise under a contract to replace pipes in a building. The building owner may believe that the plumbing contractor has not fulfilled its obligations under the contract. The owner may believe that the contractor agreed to supply pipe of a different grade than what was used. To determine the issue, it may be necessary to take the matter to court. However, as we have seen, such a proposition may not always be financially feasible.

Many parties seek to resolve disputes and to avoid the courts through contractual resolution clauses. These clauses set out an alternative dispute resolution procedure for the parties in the event of a disagreement. One such method is arbitration, in which a neutral party or tribunal hears the dispute and renders a decision. Arbitration clauses frequently state that the arbitrator's decision cannot be appealed, so that the decision is quick and binding. Although arbitration clauses may be appropriate and useful in contracts between businesses, concern has been expressed that such clauses in consumer contracts could be seen as a way of taking advantage of consumers.

Some corporations are turning to the executive mini-trial for dispute resolution. In the mini-trial, senior executives and a neutral party listen to presentations of the issues by the lawyers, and reach an agreement by focusing solely on the business issues.

As we have noted in Chapter 2, mediation is another method of alternative dispute resolution. In recent years, it has become more popular in Canada than binding arbitration. In mediation, a neutral third party assists the parties in reaching their own dispute resolution. The parties can find a creative solution and are more likely to preserve their business or personal relationship. Mediation succeeds in 70 to 80 percent of cases, and the majority of mediations take less than a day. If the mediation is not successful, the parties can still go to arbitration or to court. A number of law firms offer mediation services; mediation firms, often staffed by retired judges, have also sprung up.

In Ontario, non-family civil cases subject to case management in Toronto and Ottawa-Carleton must go to mediation at an early stage. (Case management is a system of rigid

continued

scheduling that applies to all cases in Ottawa-Carleton and 25 percent of cases in Toronto.) The cost is shared between the parties. Mediation at reduced or no cost is available to disputants who meet financial criteria. Over time, the government intends to extend mandatory mediation throughout the province. In British Columbia, a pilot project at two courthouses sends all construction disputes for amounts under $10 000 to mediation.

Some critics have suggested that the Ontario rules require mediation at too early a stage in the process, before enough facts are known to decide whether settlement of the case is appropriate. Further, if the case is complex, the parties may be unwilling to speak frankly in mediation, for fear that if mediation fails and the case ends up in court, the other side will know the strengths and weaknesses of their opponent's case.

According to the federal Department of Justice, only about 2 percent of civil cases are actually tried before the courts; the rest are settled. Settlement can be reached at any time before the judge makes a decision. Some cases are settled "on the courthouse steps" or even after the trials have begun.

Sources: J. Melnitzer, "Contractual Resolution Clauses Must Be Cutting Edge," *Law Times*, February 24–March 2, 1997; Burstein, Greenglass and Brzezinski, "Avoiding Court: Alternative Dispute Resolution," Webposted at <webcom.net/~real/legal/bur.html>; J. Melnitzer, "Contracts Increasingly Stipulate Mandatory ADR," *Law Times*, August 24–30, 1998; J. Melnitzer, "Clients Prefer Mediation to Binding Arbitration," *Law Times*, August 24–30, 1998; P. Diane McDowell and Julie Dabrusin, "Preparing for Mediation Without Trepidation II," Webposted at <www.rogersmore.com>; Howard M. Wise, "Is Mandatory Mediation Required?" *Heavy Construction News*, June, 1997; Ontario Ministry of the Attorney General, Fact Sheet, "Ontario's Mandatory Mediation Program"; Department of Justice, *Canada's System of Justice*, "The Law in Action," Webposted at <canada.justice.gc.ca/Publications/Info_education/CSJ/CSJ_page19_en.html>.

Questions to Consider

1. What effect will the less adversarial atmosphere in mandatory mediation have on continuing commercial relationships?

2. Since most civil cases are settled anyway, what, if anything, is gained by requiring mediation?

3. How will the process of mandatory mediation be affected in situations where there is an imbalance of bargaining power between the parties?

The Effect of Frustration

Harshness of the Common Law

Until now, we have assumed that frustration discharges the contract and frees both parties from the duty of further performance. In the simple situation where neither party has performed at all, a complete discharge of both parties is a fair settlement. But often the circumstances are not so simple, and discharging both parties may lead to injustice. When, for example, performance is spread over a period and is to be paid for on completion, a frustration of the contract before its completion may cause serious hardship for the performer or his estate. The harsh results in the old case of *Cutter v. Powell*[26] serve as an illustration. A seaman was to be paid on completion of a voyage from Jamaica to Liverpool. He died en route when the voyage was nearly three-quarters complete. An action by his widow to recover a proportionate part of his wages failed on the grounds that he had not performed as promised.[27]

---

26. (1795), 101 E.R. 573.

27. The harshness of this rule has since been mitigated to some extent by the doctrine of substantial performance, discussed in the next chapter.

Early decisions concerning frustration were harsh in another respect: the frustrating event was considered to terminate the contract and future obligations under it from the time of the frustrating event, but any performance already due was still enforceable. A harsh decision was that in *Chandler v. Webster.*[28]

CASE 13.5

In London in 1902, the plaintiff rented a room to view the coronation procession of Edward VII. It was the first coronation in over 60 years (since that of Queen Victoria); the demand and price for locations with a view were very high—for this room £141 payable at once. The plaintiff was able to pay only £100 at the time and owed the remaining £41. The contract was frustrated when the king became ill and the procession was cancelled. The plaintiff not only failed to recover his £100, but the court held that since the remaining £41 was due and owing before the frustrating event occurred, he was still liable for that sum, too! The "solution" in this decision was to let the loss lie where it had fallen at the time of the frustrating event.

The Court's Attempt to Ameliorate the Harshness

The 1943 decision of the House of Lords in the *Fibrosa* case[29] altered the rule in *Chandler v. Webster*; it permitted a purchaser that had made an advance payment on equipment to recover its money since it had received no benefit from the other party before the frustrating event took place. This solution seems eminently reasonable from the purchaser's point of view—but is it always so from the point of view of the other party? While a seller may not have delivered any of the fruits of its labour, it may well have done considerable work towards the completion of the contract at its own expense; according to the *Fibrosa* decision, the buyer can still demand the return of its deposit in full. In fact, in the *Fibrosa* case, the defendant company had partially completed expensive, custom-built machinery, and not only was it unable to require the buyer to share in its loss, but it had to return the entire deposit it had received.

It follows from the *Fibrosa* decision that if a seller cannot succeed in retaining a deposit on the grounds that it has incurred expenses, it certainly cannot recover these expenses from a buyer that has made no deposit. On the other hand, the judgment stated that if the seller had conferred even the slightest benefit on the buyer (for example, if the seller had delivered a small advance shipment of spare parts), the seller could retain the whole deposit. The common law would do nothing to apportion the loss between the parties: it was a matter either of retaining the whole of the deposit or of returning it entirely.

Statutory Reform

At this point, it became apparent that only legislation could correct the law. In 1943, the English Parliament passed the Frustrated Contracts Act in an attempt to remedy the inequities. Subsequently, Prince Edward Island, New Brunswick, Ontario, Manitoba, Alberta, and Newfoundland passed similar acts with some improvement on the original English Act.[30] British Columbia passed its own act to the same effect but with major differences discussed below.[31]

---

28. [1904] 1 K.B. 493.

29. Fibrosa Spolka Akcyjna v. Fairbairn Lawson Combe Barbour, Ltd., [1943] A.C. 32.

30. Frustrated Contracts Act, R.S.P.E.I. 1988, c. F-16; R.S.N.B. 1973, c. F-24; R.S.O. 1990, c. F.34; R.S.M. 1987, c. F-190; R.S.A. 1980, c. F-20; R.S.N. 1990, c. F-26.

31. Frustrated Contract Act, R.S.B.C. 1996, c. 166.

On the occurrence of a frustrating event, the acts provide for the allocation of losses between parties where money was paid on account by one party to the other or was due but had not yet been paid.

> If, before the parties were discharged…[a party] incurred expenses in connection with the performance of the contract, the court, if it considers it just to do so having regard to all the circumstances, may allow the party to retain or to recover, as the case may be, the whole or any part of the sums paid or payable.[32]

In neither of these situations may the performing party retain or recover any money in excess of the payment made or already due, even when its loss has been greater. The other party may recover any amount by which its payment exceeds the performing party's allowed loss. In addition, the acts authorize a court to award the performer a just proportion of any valuable benefit *received* by the other party regardless of whether a deposit has been paid.

Unfortunately, when a party has expended time and money in performance of a contract, but the other party, which was eventually to have received the benefit of the work has (a) made no deposit, and (b) has not yet received any benefit—except in British Columbia—the first party is still without remedy and must bear the loss wholly itself.[33] The British Columbia Act states, "a 'benefit' means something done in the fulfilment of contractual obligations, whether or not the person for whose benefit it was done received the benefit."[34] Thus, expenditures made by the first party can be taken into account, and to the extent that the other party has received no benefit from them, the loss is divided equally.[35] This solution seems fair to both parties.

The Sale of Goods

Where the Sale of Goods Act Applies

In a contract for the sale of goods, where we might expect the doctrine of frustration to apply, we must first consult the Sale of Goods Act to see whether it deals directly with the particular situation. The Act states:

> Where there is an agreement to sell specific goods and subsequently the goods without any fault on the part of the seller or buyer perish before the risk has passed to the buyer, the agreement is thereby avoided.[36]

Three conditions must be present for this section to apply:

- First, the goods must be *specific*, that is "they must be identified and agreed upon at the time the sale is made."
- Second, the risk must still be with the seller, that is, the seller must still be responsible for the safety of the goods.
- Third, the cause of the frustration must be the perishing of the goods.

---

32. Frustrated Contracts Act, R.S.O. 1990, c. F.34, s. 3(2).

33. The point may be illustrated by the facts in Appleby v. Myers (1867), L.R. 2 C.P. 651, discussed in Chapter 15 under "*Quantum Meruit*." Even if the Frustrated Contracts Act had been passed at that time, it presumably would not have altered the decision.

34. Frustrated Contract Act, R.S.B.C. 1996, c. 166, s. 5(4).

35. *Ibid.*, s. 5(3).

36. R.S.B.C. 1996, c. 410, s. 11; R.S.O. 1990, c. S.1, s. 8; R.S.N.S. 1989, c. 408, s. 10.

ILLUSTRATION 13.8

A sends a fax to *B* offering to sell "the carload of number one flour sitting at our rail siding for $10 000, risk to pass to you on delivery of the shipping documents in seven days' time." *B* accepts by return fax. Three days later a shunting locomotive on adjacent tracks is derailed and knocks over the freight car containing the flour. The contents are spilled out and ruined by rain, frustrating the contract.

Both parties are immediately discharged from liability under the contract: *A* cannot sue for the price, nor can *B* sue for failure to deliver. *B* can recover any deposit it has made. *A*'s only remedy is against those responsible for the accident.

In Illustration 13.8, all three elements mentioned are present and the Sale of Goods Act applies; consequently the Frustrated Contracts Act does not.[37] But if any one of these elements is missing, the Sale of Goods Act does not apply.[38] The Frustrated Contracts Act applies in those provinces having the Act; in the remaining provinces the parties are left with the common law position up to and including the *Fibrosa* case. We may now discuss the position of the parties in each of these circumstances.

In Provinces Where the Frustrated Contracts Act Applies

The application of the Act is more easily understood if we begin with some examples.

ILLUSTRATION 13.9

(a) *A* sends a fax to *B* offering to sell "one thousand sacks of number one flour from our warehouse stock for $5000, risk to pass to you on delivery of the shipping documents in seven days' time." *B* accepts by return fax. Three days later, the warehouse and contents are destroyed by fire without any negligence on *A*'s part. The goods are not specific because they have not been segregated from the larger stock and earmarked for the buyer.

(b) *A* sends a fax to *B* offering to sell "the carload of number one flour sitting at our rail siding for $10 000, risk to pass to you on delivery of the shipping documents in seven days' time." *B* accepts by return fax. Three days later, the government requisitions all of *A*'s flour, including the carload sold to *B*, in order to help feed the victims of a flood disaster. Here the contract is frustrated by an event *other* than the perishing of the goods.

In neither of the above examples does the Sale of Goods Act apply. Under the Frustrated Contracts Act, if *B* had made a deposit and sued for its return, the court would consider whether *A* had incurred any expenses towards the completion of the contract and would take them into account in determining how much of the deposit *B* would recover. If *B* had made no deposit, *A* could only recover the value of any benefit already conferred upon *B*.[39] Thus, if *A* had delivered one sack of flour to *B* as a sample, it could recover the price of that sack, but no more.

The Frustrated Contracts Act also states that the courts shall give effect to any special provisions made by the parties in anticipation of a frustrating event.

---

37. Except in British Columbia, where s. 1(b) of the Frustrated Contract Act states expressly that the Act applies even in these circumstances.

38. See, for example: R.S.O. 1990, c. S.1, s. 2(2)(c).

39. Except, as already noted, in British Columbia, where the court could give recovery for part or all of the expenses incurred, whether or not a benefit was conferred.

ILLUSTRATION 13.10

A sends a fax to *B* offering to sell "the carload of number one flour sitting at our rail siding for $10 000, risk to pass to you upon acceptance of this offer. Delivery in seven days' time." *B* accepts by return fax. Three days later the flour is destroyed in a derailment accident. The risk has already passed to the buyer when the frustrating event takes place.

In the above example, the parties have agreed expressly that the risk should pass to the buyer, which seems to indicate that the buyer would be liable for any loss caused by a frustrating event after the risk has passed. The buyer must then pay the price to the seller. While both the Act and the express terms of the contract indicate this result, there are no reported cases directly on point. Ordinarily, buyers arrange to insure valuable goods not in their possession when the risk passes to them.

Where the Common Law Applies

Consider Illustrations 13.9 and 13.10 again as if they had occurred in a province without the Frustrated Contracts Act. In examples (a) and (b) of Illustration 13.9, the *Fibrosa* decision applies. If *B* had made a deposit, it could recover it in full regardless of whether *A* had incurred any expenses towards the completion of the contract. If, however, *B* had received the slightest benefit, such as one sack of flour as a sample, it could recover none of its deposit.

The *Fibrosa* case did not consider situations where the seller had conferred a benefit on the buyer (for instance, by an advance delivery of part of the goods) and where no deposit had been made. In these circumstances, the older cases would likely govern: both parties would be immediately discharged by the frustrating event, and the seller would have no right of recovery against the buyer for the goods already delivered when, by the contract, none are to be paid for until all are delivered. This result conforms to the law as stated in *Cutter v. Powell* and shows the value of the Frustrated Contracts Act in avoiding a harsh result.

The result in Illustration 13.10 is the same under the common law; the common law rule as well as the statute respects the intention of the parties as contained in their contract of sale.

When the Source of the Goods is Destroyed

Another way in which frustration may affect the sale of goods arises when the source of the goods, rather than the goods themselves, is destroyed. In a contract of sale containing no terms about how the goods shall be produced, the destruction of the *source* of the subject-matter will not frustrate the contract. If, for example, the parties do not specify where the goods will be made but the factory expected to be the source is destroyed by fire, the supplier will probably not be excused from liability for failing to deliver goods according to the contract.[40] The supplier must either purchase the goods elsewhere for delivery to the buyer or pay damages for non-delivery. On the other hand, if the parties specify a particular source and the source is destroyed, the contract will be frustrated, and the buyer cannot demand delivery. In *Howell v. Coupland*[41] the contract was for the sale of 200 tons of potatoes to be grown in a particular field. The crop failed. When the buyer sued for damages for non-delivery, the court held that the contract had been frustrated, and the action failed.

---

40. See Twentsche Overseas Trading Co., *supra,* n. 24. But see also Dow Votaw, *Legal Aspects of Business Administration* (3rd ed.), p. 165. Englewood Cliffs: Prentice-Hall, Inc., 1969. The authors note that in the United States, "there is an increasing trend in the courts towards implying an agreement that goods are to be manufactured in a particular factory which the parties reasonably understand is to be the source of the subject-matter of the contract."

41. (1876), 1 Q.B.D. 258.

The general rule is that a frustrating event must defeat the common intention of both parties. In *Blackburn Bobbin v. Allen*,[42] it was held that a contract of sale is not frustrated when the seller only (and not the buyer) has a particular source of supply in mind and that source fails.

CASE 13.6

Shortly before the outbreak of the First World War the buyer had ordered a quantity of Finnish birch timber to be delivered at Hull, England. He presumed, not unreasonably, that the seller would supply him from existing stocks in England; he was unaware that the seller had to obtain it directly from Finland and there was no discussion of the subject by the parties. The outbreak of war made it impossible for the seller to fill the order. In an action for damages for non-delivery, the English Court of Appeal held that there had not been frustration and that the action should succeed.

An interesting Canadian decision falls between the *Howell* and the *Blackburn Bobbin* cases.[43]

CASE 13.7

A trucker in Parkhill contracted with a Toronto corn merchant to deliver a quantity of corn to shipping points in the Parkhill area specified by the corn merchant. The parties appeared to have understood that the trucker was to purchase the corn from certain Parkhill farmers when the crop matured. Unfortunately, the trucker was unable to obtain the required quantity of corn because of a local drought. The corn merchant sued for damages for failure to deliver according to the contract. The Court of Appeal agreed with the defendant trucker that if the source of the goods formed a term of the contract, the failure of the crop would have amounted to a frustrating event, excusing the trucker from performance. The majority of the court found that the contract had not expressly stated that the corn should be from a particular source and it was unwilling to find an implied term to that effect. It held that the trucker should have obtained the corn from other suppliers and that it was accordingly in breach of contract.

In dissent, Mr. Justice Laskin (as he then was) took a more liberal view of the defendant's obligations. He said, in part:

> I cannot agree that these contracts should be viewed in the absolute terms in which the majority [of the court] has treated them. I think it is clear that the original attitude of the common law that a contract duty is absolute has been considerably modified over the past one hundred years as we have come to recognize that mutual assumptions by parties that underlie their commercial relations cannot be ignored, and that, in the enforcement of a contract, allowance must be made if a failure of those assumptions supervenes, without fault of the contracting parties, after the contract has been made....
>
> It is...material to the basis on which these contracts were concluded that the price to be paid by the defendant for the corn obtainable from the farmers was a price fixed by the plaintiff and the plaintiff also fixed the trucking charge that would be paid to the defendant for the transportation of the corn to the specified destinations set out in the written confirmations. It seems to me, therefore, that in the circumstances it would be changing the fundamental character of the contract to require the defendant...to obtain the grain from some other area and at the same time insist that it accept payment on the basis of a price and trucking arrangement

---

42. [1918] 2 K.B. 467.

43. Parrish & Heimbecker Ltd. v. Gooding Lumber Ltd., [1968] 1 O.R. 716.

which contemplated that the grain would come from the area about which the representatives of the parties had reached an understanding.[44]

DISCHARGE BY OPERATION OF LAW

The Bankruptcy and Insolvency Act operates to discharge a bankrupt debtor from contractual liabilities after the processes of bankruptcy have been completed. The debtor is discharged, however, only if he qualifies for a certificate stating that the bankruptcy was caused by misfortune and without any misconduct on his part.[45]

A debt or other contractual obligation that has been neglected by a creditor for a long time becomes **statute barred**, that is, the creditor loses the right to bring an action on it. Each province has a Limitations Act setting out the time at which a creditor loses its remedy.[46] The Limitations Act "bars" (rather than completely discharges) a right of action if the promisee fails to assert it within the time specified. In so doing, it gives effect to the legal principle that the public interest requires a definite end to the opportunity for litigation. The effect of the statute is really to banish the right of action from the courts rather than to pass a death sentence on it. The distinction is important because a claim may be rehabilitated and made enforceable by certain conduct of the promisor, as we shall see in Chapter 31.

statute barred
an action that may no longer be brought before a court because the party wishing to sue has delayed beyond the limitation period in the statute

QUESTIONS FOR REVIEW

1. What are the consequences for a creditor who refuses a tender of performance by the debtor?

2. Describe the nature of the consideration given by the parties to a waiver.

3. When a party admits liability for breach, what is his best course of action? Explain.

4. In what respect does the arrangement known as accord and satisfaction involve a discharge of a contract?

5. Describe the role of novation in the purchase of a going business.

6. Does a contract exist at all before a condition precedent has been satisfied? Explain.

7. Why may an "option to terminate" clause be described as a condition subsequent?

8. The principles of mistake and discharge by frustration may both relate to contracts in which the subject-matter is non-existent. How do these principles and their remedies differ?

9. What else, apart from physical destruction of the subject-matter of a contract, can result in frustration of the contract?

10. Is substantial hardship in performing sufficient to excuse a promisor from performing? Explain.

11. James had contracted to give a talk and demonstration on resolving human relations conflicts in small organizations for a management consulting firm. After dinner with his hosts the evening before his talk, he accepted a dare to slide down a lengthy banister on

---

44. *Ibid.* at 719–20.

45. R.S.C. 1985, c. B-3, s. 175.

46. See, for example: Limitation Act, R.S.B.C. 1996, c. 266, Limitations Act, R.S.O. 1990, c. L.15; Limitation of Actions Act, R.S.N.S. 1989, c. 258. For an explanation of the policy considerations underlying limitations, see "Adverse Possession" in Chapter 23 and "Limitations of Creditors' Rights" in Chapter 31.

the main staircase of the hotel. James fell off part way down and suffered a concussion and a badly sprained ankle. He was unable to give his talk and has been sued for breach of contract. Give a brief opinion of the likely result.

12. Give two examples of the shortcomings in the *Fibrosa* case.

13. In what important respect has the British Columbia Frustrated Contract Act provided a fairer solution when a contract is frustrated?

14. What three conditions are required for the Sale of Goods Act to apply to a frustrated contract? Does the Act apply to a case where the goods have been impounded by the government?

15. Suppose *P* contracts to buy 10 tonnes of corn grown in the county of Haldimand from *S*. Because of a local drought there is insufficient corn, but *S* can quite easily obtain corn of the same quality from the adjacent county of Frontenac. Has the contract been frustrated? Give reasons.

16. In what respect may bankruptcy bring about the discharge of contracts?

CASES AND PROBLEMS

1 Urban Construction Co. contracted with Mandel to build a small two-storey office building for $240 000. The contract contained a clause stating that the agreed price would be reduced by $500 for every business day the building was not completed after April 1. The price was to be paid on completion of the building.

During construction, Mandel asked Urban Construction Co. to alter certain specifications so that a complete air-conditioning system might be installed at a later time with a minimum of inconvenience and so that there would be an additional washroom on the second floor.

The building was completed April 17. Urban Construction Co. refused Mandel's tender of a cheque for $243 500 (comprising $240 000 less $6500 for 13 business days, plus $10 000, the agreed price for the extra work). Urban Construction Co. brought action for $250 000, the full price without deduction.

Examine the validity of the arguments Mandel might use in defending the action.

2 Twilight Properties agreed to purchase land on the Vancouver waterfront from the Harbour Commission, conditional upon no changes being made to the zoning by-law that permitted high-density development for building condominium units. Twilight then began negotiations with the city for a site plan for 650 units. Its chief executive officer, Moon, was very optimistic and immediately offered 500 units for sale. (He had a fallback plan to build only that number if the zoning and site plans were restricted by municipal authority.) Moon obtained agreements to purchase 110 units from individual purchasers, who paid deposits to Twilight of $20 000 per unit. Each contract contained a clause stating

if the development does not proceed in accordance with Twilight Properties' plans, Twilight retains the right to terminate the contract without liability on or before June 30, 1998.

This date corresponded with the closing date in the agreement with the Harbour Commission. Units were to be available and the deals closed one year later.

On June 30, 1998, Twilight completed the purchase of the lands but the date passed without any approval of the site plan by the city. At the end of July, the Planning and Development Department of the city approved the site plan and sent it on to the city council. However, in October the city council refused to approve the plan and stated that it intended reduce the number of units permitted on the property. The council instructed its secretary to write to

Twilight and ask it whether it would be willing to provide a guarantee to the original condominium purchasers that it would perform its commitments to sell the units if the development should be approved. Twilight replied that the city's request was inappropriate and an interference with its private contract rights. At its November meeting the city passed a more restrictive rezoning by-law that would permit only 400 units to be built.

Immediately afterwards Twilight returned the deposits of the purchasers and stated that their agreements were terminated; it was not possible to proceed with the project as planned. The unit purchasers sued for breach of contract. Twilight defended by claiming that their contracts were frustrated by the actions of the city. Summarize the arguments for each side and give your opinion about who should succeed.

3 In 1994, the Dryden Construction Co. contracted with the Ontario Hydro Electric Power Commission to build an access road seven miles long from its Manitou Falls generating station to provincial Highway No. 105. The contract contained the following clause:

> The contractor agrees that he is fully informed regarding all of the conditions affecting work to be done and labour and materials to be furnished for the completion of the contract and that his information was secured by personal investigation and research and not from the Commission or its estimates and that he will make no claim against the Commission.

In fact, the area over which the road was to be built was under heavy snow at the time and the temperature was very low. The description of the property proved to be inaccurate; there being much more muskeg than indicated. After these facts became known, the contractor claimed to be excused from the contract, alleging that it had been frustrated and that what was required amounted to an entirely different contract.

Is there a binding contract to build the road?

4 Howard rented a room to Kennedy along the route scheduled for the procession of the Royal Family for the day on which they would appear in Halifax. The agreement was in writing and the rent for the room was for a substantial sum, payable at the time of the procession. In the meantime, Howard redecorated the room for the occasion. Later it was announced that the route of the Royal Family through the city had changed and would not pass Howard's building. Kennedy then refused to pay the rent for the room, and Howard sued for the amount. Should Howard succeed? How would it affect the outcome if at the time Kennedy undertook to rent the room she had paid a $100 deposit?

Suppose that the place in which these events occurred had been Saint John, New Brunswick, instead of Halifax, Nova Scotia; would the result be different?

5 Gilman Steel Ltd. is a large fabricator of reinforcing steel. It makes its product from steel bars purchased from steel mills in accordance with engineers' specifications for particular projects. Universal Construction Corp. is an apartment construction company.

In September 1988, Gilman and Universal signed a contract for the supply of fabricated steel at a price of $253 per tonne for use in three apartment buildings to be built consecutively by Universal at different sites.

At the first building site, deliveries were made and paid for as agreed and construction of that building was completed. Then in July 1989, steel mill companies announced increases in the price of unfabricated steel, to take effect in two stages. The price to Gilman would increase on August 1, 1989, by $8.50 per tonne and a second increase of a then-unspecified amount would become effective as of March 1, 1990.

In the changed circumstances, Gilman suggested a new contract for the second and third apartment buildings. Universal agreed to reconsider because it found that it would not require as much fabricated steel for the remaining two buildings as it had initially contracted for. The parties signed a new contract for the supply of fabricated steel at a price of $257 per tonne, a price that only partially passed on the increase to Gilman. Universal had thus agreed to pay a higher unit price for a smaller quantity of steel. The parties did not include in the contract a clause providing for an escalation of price because Universal expected to complete the remaining buildings before the next round of price increases in March 1990.

Construction of the second apartment building began in August 1989 and Gilman made numerous deliveries of steel. Universal accepted all steel delivered and regularly paid the amount billed on each invoice at $257 per tonne. The second building was completed in January 1990 and construction of the third was started.

On March 1, while the third apartment building was still far from completion, the steel mills announced the anticipated second price increase. Officers of Gilman, hoping to agree on another new contract, met with a senior officer of Universal. They asked Universal to consider a new contract since construction had not progressed as expected. Universal agreed to accommodate Gilman on the understanding that Universal would be given favourable consideration in the supply of steel for the construction of additional apartment buildings.

Gilman then prepared an agreement dated March 1, 1990, and mailed it to Universal. It was a duplicate of the preceding contract in July except that the price of the steel was increased. Universal did not sign or return the document but it did accept deliveries of steel invoiced at the new rates without protest. Universal adopted a new method of payment, however, after March 1, 1990. It no longer paid by cheques based on the invoice amounts but in round figures that tended at first to overpayment; however, by the end of the construction this procedure led to a net balance of some $25 000 owing by Universal.

As construction of the third apartment building neared completion, the comptroller of Gilman asked for payment in full of the account. Universal informed him that it expected some new mortgage money to become available enabling it to pay the account in full soon. At about the same time officers of Universal met with Gilman's officers to discuss a contract for the supply of steel for a new apartment complex. Universal reminded Gilman that it had twice agreed to new contracts and asked whether Gilman could offer a good price. Gilman made an offer and Universal said it would consider it. The meeting was conducted and concluded in an atmosphere of goodwill without complaint about the March price increase. Shortly afterwards, Universal decided that the new offer was not attractive enough to accept and indicated for the first time that it would not pay the portion of the past due account that represented the increase in the March 1990 agreement.

Gilman Steel Ltd. sued Universal Construction Corp. for the balance owing according to its invoices.

(a) Outline the nature of the defence or defences available to Universal.

(b) Explain the nature of the argument or arguments that could be advanced for the plaintiff.

(c) Indicate with reasons what the court's decision would likely be. (If you perceive any difference between what the law is and what it ought to be in a case of this kind, set out your reasoning separately from your prediction of what the decision is likely to be.)

6 Parker's Automatic Laundry Services Inc. installed coin-operated washing machines and dryers in an apartment building owned by Mountbatten Estates Ltd. under a five-year contract dated June 1, 1985. The contract gave Parker's the exclusive right to install and maintain any laundry machines in the building. No one other than the employees of the laundry service company would be permitted to repair, remove, or replace any of the machines. A clause in the contract read:

> In the event the Proprietor [Mountbatten] sells or assigns its interest in the said premises, such Successor shall be fully bound by the terms of this agreement and before the Proprietor sells or assigns it shall obtain the consent in writing of the grantee or assignee to the terms of this agreement.

In return, Mountbatten was to receive 20 percent of the gross receipts collected from the use of the laundry equipment.

Six months later Mountbatten sold the apartment building to Baldoon Holdings Ltd. for $2 500 000. The lawyer acting for Baldoon drew up the agreement of sale, one clause of which read:

> The Vendor [Mountbatten] warrants to the Purchaser [Baldoon] that the 10 washing machines and 10 clothes dryers located in the apartment building have been placed there by Parker's Automatic Laundry Service Inc. pursuant to an agreement dated June 1, 1985, a copy of which is attached hereto.

Following its purchase of the apartment building, Baldoon continued for a time to operate the building much as before and retained the same manager. Parker's made the first quarterly payment to Baldoon three months after the purchase. At that time, Baldoon approached Parker's with a view to purchasing the 10 washing machines and 10 dryers and operating them itself, as owner of the building. Parker's refused and Baldoon then instructed Parker's to remove its machines within two weeks. When Parker's failed to do so, Baldoon moved the machines to a locked storage area in the basement of the apartment building and replaced them with new washing machines and clothes dryers of its own.

Parker's Automatic Laundry Services Inc. brought an action against Baldoon Holdings Ltd. for breach of contract. Indicate with reasons what the result of this action will likely be, leaving aside the question of what the amount of damages should be, if awarded.

7 Diehl owned some land on which she planned to have a house built that would be suitable for her retirement the following year. She made a contract with Summers, a building contractor, to build a house for $80 000, the price to be paid in full on completion. The contract contained an unqualified promise by the contractor to complete the house at that price. When the house was about three-quarters finished, Diehl stored some expensive furniture in a completed part and took out a $20 000 fire insurance policy on the furniture.

Two weeks later, before the house was completed, lightning caused a serious fire that did considerable damage to both the building and the furniture. Summers learned that Diehl would receive about $16 000 in insurance money. When Diehl asked him to go ahead and complete the house, Summers said, "I believe I'm no longer bound to go on and if you do not pay me the insurance money, I will ask a court to declare that the contract has been frustrated. I'm willing to compromise if you will pay me the insurance money." Diehl protested that she had lost considerably from the destruction of her furniture but finally said, "All right, go ahead and do the work."

When the house was completed Diehl paid Summers $80 000 but refused to pay anything more. Summers sued her for $16 000 on the ground that he had been led to believe he would receive this additional sum and would not otherwise have completed the contract.

At the trial, evidence was submitted that in contracts of this kind, builders frequently require an undertaking by the owner to insure the building during its construction against loss by fire and have the insurance company include a clause agreeing that, in the event of a claim, it would pay the insurance money first to the builder "insofar as his interest may appear." A copy of the written contract between Summers and Diehl was produced and showed that the contract did not include a term of this kind. The parties testified that neither of them had insured the building itself, as distinct from the contents. It was acknowledged that the contractor, Summers, would have had an insurable interest and could have insured the house himself to the value of the contract.

Develop the arguments for the plaintiff and the defendant, and offer an opinion about whether the action should succeed.

8

M Inc. chartered a vessel from *Q* Corp. under a five-year agreement that gave *M* an option to purchase the vessel at the end of the five-year term subject to "full performance of all its obligations under the agreement, including delivery of prompt payments in accordance with the schedule in the agreement." The agreement required seven monthly instalments each year on specified dates, "in cash, by way of Bank Transfer and/or certified cheques." The parties subsequently agreed informally that *M* would deliver seven post-dated, uncertified cheques to *Q* at the beginning of each operating season and they would be deposited on the specified dates.

There were no problems with the cheques for the first four years, but the cheque for the first payment in the fifth year was returned by reason of insufficient funds. The bank's refusal to honour *M*'s cheque was due to an error by a bank employee. *Q* immediately wrote to *M* stating that the option to purchase was void and of no further effect because of *M*'s failure to make the payment as required. *Q* also gave *M* instructions on how to remedy its late payment. *M* promptly made the payment with interest in accordance with *Q*'s instructions. All remaining payments were made on time.

As prescribed in the terms of their agreement, *M* gave notice to exercise the option to purchase the vessel. *Q* insisted that the failure to make the first payment in the fifth year on time was a precondition to exercising the option and that accordingly the option was void. *M* Inc. sued *Q* Corp. to enforce the option agreement. Give your opinion of which side should succeed.

THE EFFECT OF BREACH

N ot all breaches of contract occur in the same way nor have the same consequences. When one party commits a breach, the aggrieved party may have choices to make, and those choices depend on how the breach occurs and how serious it is. In this chapter we examine such questions as:

- what options are available to an aggrieved party when the other party
  expressly repudiates the contract?
  simply fails to perform at the agreed time?
  makes it impossible for itself to perform?

- how serious must the breach be to trigger various options?

- what role do exemption clauses play in affecting the aggrieved party's rights?

- what is the business significance of breach?

IMPLICATIONS OF BREACH

In our discussion of the ways in which a contract may be discharged, we noted that breach may sometimes become a method of discharge. We must qualify this statement in two ways:

First, not every breach may discharge a contract.

Second, breach does not discharge a contract automatically (as does frustration or completed performance, for example); even when a breach is sufficient to discharge the contract, only if the party that suffered the breach elects to treat it so will it be discharged.

An injured party cannot elect to treat every breach as discharging the contract and freeing it from its own obligation to perform. The breach must be of either the whole contract or an essential term of the contract so that the purpose of the agreement is defeated and performance by the aggrieved party becomes pointless. Breach of a minor term may entitle an aggrieved party to damages, but does not entitle it to abandon its obligations. It would do so at its peril, and the other party could in turn sue it successfully for failure to carry out its promises.

ILLUSTRATION 14.1

(a) *A* agrees to sell 10 000 bags of potatoes to *B* Wholesale Grocers and to deliver them in yellow paper bags with green labels. Through a mistake, the labels are printed in blue rather than green. The management of *B* may feel annoyed and believe that their merchandise display will not be as effective. *B* may sue *A* and collect damages for such loss as it can show the breach has caused but it cannot reject the potatoes without itself committing a breach that might make it liable for heavy damages.

(b) *A* agrees to sell 10 000 bags of potatoes to *B* Wholesale Grocers and to deliver them to *B*'s warehouse on Wednesday in time for *B* to distribute them to its supermarket chain for a weekend special. *A* makes no delivery until late Friday afternoon. By this delay *A* has committed a breach of an essential term of the contract—delivery on Wednesday. *B* may reject the potatoes and discharge the contract, freeing itself from any obligation to pay for them. In addition, it may sue *A* for damages caused by failure to deliver on time. In the alternative, *B* may accept the potatoes if *B* decides it still wants them. In this event, the contract is not discharged: *B* is liable to pay the price for the potatoes, subject to a deduction for damages caused by the failure to deliver them on time. If *B* should accept the potatoes and then refuse to pay for them, *A* could sue *B* for the price, and *B* could counterclaim for its damages.

Thus we see that breach itself does not discharge a contract: if the breach is of a minor term, the contract is still binding on both parties; if the breach is of a fundamental term, the party committing the breach is still bound, but the injured party may then elect to discharge the contract and free itself, or else to affirm the contract so that it continues to bind both parties.

We should note also that a major term may be broken in only a minor respect. Suppose in Illustration 14.1 that *A* delivers on time but is short by five bags. The *quantity* to be delivered is a major term, but delivering 9995 bags of 10 000 promised would be only a **minor breach** of that term and would not entitle *B* to reject the shipment. If however, *A* had delivered only 5000 bags there would be a **major breach** and *B* could elect to reject them.

It is not always easy to determine whether a term of a contract is essential to it or of lesser importance, or whether the breach of an essential term is a serious one. Nevertheless, in any dispute concerning a breach, the first task is to determine to which class the term in question belongs.

We must note an unfortunate development in terminology concerning essential and non-essential terms: for a variety of reasons stemming from 19th-century developments in contract law, essential terms became known as **conditions** and non-essential terms as **warranties**. These names are unfortunate because "condition" may easily become confused with "condition precedent" (where the word "condition" means a happening or event rather than a term of an agreement) and "warranty" may be confused with its special meaning in a sale of goods (where it means a guarantee of quality of the goods or of their ownership—usually an essential term). Despite the confusion, the use of "condition" and "warranty" to distinguish essential from non-essential terms has now become so common that we cannot ignore it. We must, therefore, take care to ascertain the meaning of these words each time we meet them.

minor breach
a breach of a non-essential term of a contract or of an essential term in a minor respect

major breach
a breach of the whole contract or of an essential term so that the purpose of the contract is defeated

condition
an essential term of a contract

warranty
a non-essential term of a contract

HOW BREACH MAY OCCUR

A party to a contract may break it

- by expressly repudiating its liabilities
- by acting in a way that makes its promise impossible to perform
- by either failing to perform at all or tendering an actual performance that is not equivalent to its promise

We shall discuss each of these ways in turn.

EXPRESS REPUDIATION

An **express repudiation** is a declaration by one of the contracting parties to the other that it does not intend to perform as it had promised. The promisee is entitled to treat the contract as being immediately at an end, to find another party to perform and to sue for whatever damages it sustains in delay and higher costs because the original contract will not be performed. Before substituting a new party to proceed with performance, it is prudent for the promisee to inform the repudiating party that it is treating the contract as terminated at once and is reserving its rights to sue for damages for breach.

express repudiation
a declaration by one of the contracting parties to the other that it does not intend to perform as promised

A promisee may, on the other hand, continue to insist on performance. If it chooses this option and does not receive performance by the latest time promised in the contract, it is still entitled to damages for breach of contract but it takes a chance that intervening events may provide the promisor with an excuse for not performing. *Avery v. Bowden*[1] shows what can happen when a promisee insists upon performance.

CASE 14.1

The defendant chartered a ship in England to pick up a cargo at Odessa. On arrival, the ship's master requested the cargo, but the charterer's agent refused to provide it. By custom a charterer was entitled to a period of grace to provide a cargo, but as soon as the charterer repudiated the contract, the ship's master could have treated himself as freed from further liability; he could have sailed immediately for England. Instead, he elected to wait out the usual grace period and continue to demand a cargo.

Before the period expired, war broke out between England and Russia, and it became impossible to complete the contract. The ship's owner was unsuccessful when he sued the charterer for damages caused by the futile trip: the contract had been discharged by frustration and *not* by breach. The court noted that the decision would have been different had the ship's master elected to treat the express repudiation as an immediate breach of contract.

Whenever breach occurs in advance of the time agreed for performance, it is known as **anticipatory breach**.

anticipatory breach
a breach that occurs in advance of the time agreed for performance of a contract

ILLUSTRATION 14.2

A Co. contracts with B Ltd. for the delivery to A Co. in six months of manufactured materials at an agreed price. A week later, B Ltd. discovers that it has agreed to a price that is much too low and informs A Co. that it will not deliver the materials as promised. B Ltd. has committed an anticipatory breach of its contract with A Co. and A Co. need not wait until the delivery date to sue B Ltd.

The courts have recognized that, as a promisee, *A* Co. is entitled not only to performance of the contract in six months' time but also to a *continuous expectation of performance* in the interim between formation of the contract and its performance. (In *Avery v. Bowden*, the charterer's repudiation was also an example of anticipatory breach.) The concept is a basic one; it asserts that a contract exists and has legal effect from the time of its formation, and not just from the time of its performance.

Major breach amounting to repudiation may also occur after performance has begun, and it will free the aggrieved party from further obligations.

1. (1855), 119 E.R. 647.

CASE 14.2

Atkinson's employment contract contained a clause that he would not work in competition with his employer, a billposting company, in the same town for two years after the termination of his employment. The employer dismissed him without cause in breach of the contract. Atkinson recovered damages for wrongful dismissal and then began to work within the district as a self-employed billposter. His former employer sought an injunction to restrain him from competition but failed. The court held that the company had by its dismissal repudiated the employment contract and entitled Atkinson to consider his own contractual obligations at an end.[2]

In these examples, repudiation takes the form of a declaration or of conduct affecting performance of the whole contract. In some business situations, however, one party repudiates only a minor term of the contract. As we have seen, such a breach does not entitle the other party to abandon the contract and declare it discharged. A wise manager will notify the other party that the firm is unable to perform exactly as promised as soon as she is aware of the situation so that the other party may take immediate steps to reduce any loss that the breach may cause.

ILLUSTRATION 14.3

X Inc., a wholesale distributor of electronic equipment, has agreed to supply B Ltd., a chain of retail stores selling home entertainment components, with a large quantity of new DVD players, along with sample demonstration discs of spectacular sound effects and advertising for the new product. Several days before delivery, the manager of X Inc. discovers that the DVD players are in stock but that the demonstration discs have not arrived and appear to have been lost during shipment. Knowing that B Ltd. plans to feature the new product, X Inc.'s manager would be wise to notify B Ltd. at once of the expected breach of this minor term. B Ltd. might then be able to arrange in advance for an alternative supply of good demonstration discs. If X Inc. were to deliver without prior indication of its inability to supply the discs, B Ltd. might suffer a greater loss for which X Inc. would be liable.

ONE PARTY RENDERS PERFORMANCE IMPOSSIBLE

Under this heading, only a willful or negligent act of the promisor constitutes a breach of contract—not an act that is an involuntary response to forces beyond its control. A deliberate or negligent act that makes performance impossible is tantamount to repudiation: the promisor may not have said so in words, but it is nonetheless implied. Such conduct is a form of the self-induced frustration considered in the preceding chapter. As with express repudiation, conduct that makes performance impossible may take place either before or during performance.

---

2. General Billposting Co. v. Atkinson, [1909] A.C. 118. This decision was followed in a preliminary hearing before trial in Gerrard v. Century 21 Armour Real Estate Inc. (1991), 4 O.R. (3d) 191, even where it was unclear whether there had been repudiation of the contract by the employer.

ILLUSTRATION 14.4

A agrees to sell her Ferrari sports car to B for $30 000, with car and registration to be delivered in three weeks. A few days later, X, unaware of the agreement between A and B, offers A $35 000 for the car. A accepts and delivers the car to X that day. A is in breach of the contract with B the moment she makes the sale to X, and B may sue her as soon as he learns of it. A is not permitted to argue that she can still deliver the car on time by buying it back from X; B is entitled to a continuous expectation of A's prospective performance until the day agreed for delivery arrives. The result would be the same if A's agent negligently sold the car to X.

FAILURE OF PERFORMANCE

Types of Failure

Unlike the other two types of breach, failure of performance usually becomes apparent only when the time for performance arrives or during the course of performance. A failure may be of various degrees: it may be a total failure to perform, it may be a grossly inadequate performance, or it may be a failure in a minor particular. It may also take the form of a satisfactory performance of all but one of the terms of the contract or of only part of a main term. The extent of a failure always has an important bearing on the nature of the remedies available to the injured party.

The problems created by failure of performance arise typically when the party guilty of the breach is required either by the terms of the contract or by usual trade practice to perform its part first. We have then to decide whether the injured party is excused from performance of its own part of the bargain. The question often arises in contracts calling for the delivery of goods by instalments when the quantity delivered fails to meet the amount called for in the contract. The issue is whether what is left undone amounts to a sufficient breach to free the injured party from its part of the bargain, or whether the breach is minor and entitles the injured party only to damages, while the agreement still continues to bind it. Partial delivery may be merely inconvenient, or it may be completely unsatisfactory.

ILLUSTRATION 14.5

(a) The seller contracts to deliver 6000 tonnes of coal in 12 monthly instalments of about 500 tonnes each. One of the terms is that the buyer will provide the trucks to take the coal away. In the first month, the buyer sends sufficient trucks to take away only 400 tonnes. The buyer's default would not likely be sufficient to discharge the seller from its obligation to stand ready to provide the remaining 5600 tonnes over the following 11 months.[3]

(b) The seller agrees to deliver 150 tonnes of iron per month but delivers only 21 in the first month. Its default is very likely sufficient to discharge the buyer, which may then turn to another source of supply and sue for damages resulting from the breach.[4]

Often, an innocent party is left in a quandary. If there is real concern about the seriousness of continuing defective performance, it is wise to seek legal advice before claiming to be discharged of one's own obligations; otherwise one risks being held liable for wrongful repudiation should a court find that the seller's default was only a minor breach.[5]

---

3. See Simpson v. Crippin (1872), L.R. 8 Q.B. 14, where, in a similar situation, the buyer took delivery of only 158 tonnes in the first month, and yet the seller was held to the contract.

4. Hoare v. Rennie (1859), 157 E.R. 1083.

5. For an example of the difficulties that a party claiming a major breach may encounter, see Agrifoods International Corp. v. Beatrice Foods Inc., [1997] B.C.J. No. 393.

In a contract where one party is to perform by instalments, the other may consider itself freed from liability only if it can offer convincing affirmative answers to both of these questions:

(a) Is there good reason to think that future performance will be equally defective?

(b) Is either the expected deficiency or the actual deficiency to date important relative to the whole performance promised?

The Doctrine of Substantial Performance

substantial performance

performance that does not comply in some minor way with the requirements of the contract

The courts have grown more willing than before to recognize substantial performance by the promisor, though defective or incomplete in some minor respects, as sufficient to bind the other party to its part of the bargain. The doctrine of **substantial performance** asserts that a promisor is entitled to enforce a contract when it has substantially performed, even though its performance does not comply in some minor way with the requirements of the contract. The promisor's claim is, however, subject to a reduction for damages caused by its defective performance. The effect of the doctrine is that a promisee cannot seize upon a trivial failure of performance to avoid its own obligations.[6] However, there can often be substantial disagreement about how serious or trivial a failure in performance turns out to be.[7]

When the Right to Treat the Contract as Discharged is Lost

Even when an aggrieved party would ordinarily have the right to treat its obligations as discharged by a serious breach, in two situations it will be entitled only to damages. The first occurs when the aggrieved party has elected to proceed with the contract and accept benefits under it despite the breach. In the second, the aggrieved party may have received the benefit of the contract and not learned of the breach until performance was complete.

CASE 14.3

A chartered a ship from *B* for £1550, for a voyage from Liverpool to Sydney. The contract specified that the ship should have a cargo capacity of at least 1000 tons. The vessel proved incapable of carrying that amount of cargo, but *A* allowed it to load what it could and made an advance payment on the freight. Subsequently, *A* refused to pay the balance, claiming the contract had been discharged for breach of a major term. In an action by *B* for the balance of the price, the court noted that while *A* could have treated the contract as discharged, refused to load the ship, and sued for its loss, *A*'s acceptance of performance by the smaller ship foreclosed the earlier option. Instead it had to pay the agreed price, less any counterclaim for damages it could establish.[8]

CASE 14.4

X Farms purchased seed from *Y* Nurseries, described by *Y* as "common English sainfoin." After it was sown, it proved to be "giant sainfoin," an inferior type. However, *X* could

continued

---

6. Dakin & Co. Ltd. v. Lee, [1916] 1 K.B. 566.

7. See Miller v. Advanced Farming Systems Ltd., [1969] S.C.R. 845.

8. Pust v. Dowie (1863), 122 E.R. 740 and 745.

not have learned of the breach until after the seed had been planted and came up, a time when it would be too late to reject the seed and treat the contract as discharged. *X*'s only remedy was to sue for damages for the breach.[9]

Cases 14.3 and 14.4 show that the right to consider a contract at an end may depend on an aggrieved party still being able to reject the substantial benefit of the contract. If it cannot, it will remain bound to perform its obligations, subject to a right to claim damages.

Exemption Clauses

Their Purpose

In business, a party that runs a significant risk of harm to the other party through some failure in the course of performing the contract must plan to cover its potential liability. There are several alternatives when striking a bargain:

(a) The party may obtain insurance against the risk and raise its price accordingly.

(b) It may be a "self-insurer," that is, charge a higher fee and build up a reserve fund to pay any claim that arises later from harm to a customer.

(c) It may insist on an **exemption clause** in the contract, in effect excluding itself from any liability for the risk and transferring the risk of harm to its customer.

exemption clause
a clause in a contract that exempts a party from liability for failing to perform some or all of its contractual obligations

As we noted in our discussion of the ticket cases in Chapter 5 on Offer and Acceptance, the last alternative is often the most attractive. We also discussed the use of exemption clauses in various business sectors under the heading "Vicarious Performance" in Chapter 12.

There are several advantages that make exemption clauses attractive—and widely used. First, they permit a supplier of goods and services to keep its prices low, since the supplier need not increase them to protect itself against the risk of liability to its customer. Second, if the supplier is sued for damages despite the exemption clause, it will completely disclaim liability and thus seek to avoid the difficult question of the extent of its liability for the harm done. Finally, if the supplier is in the position of using a standard form contract (especially if the contract is a detailed printed form with many other terms) it will in most circumstances have a distinct advantage over its customer; the customer may be quite knowledgeable about competitive pricing and drive a hard bargain, but may have little or no expertise in legal issues. A customer may gladly accept a lower price without fully realizing the implications of an exemption clause.

Exemption clauses usually make good sense and work reasonably well when the bargaining power and knowledge of the law is relatively equal between the parties. For example, one party may willingly assume a risk in return for a lower price; that party may already have adequate blanket insurance coverage. Or the activity may be extremely hazardous; a charter airline may be unwilling to fly a client into northern mountain regions in winter except at the client's own risk. Generally speaking, however, the party preparing the standard form contract drafts exemption clauses clearly to its own advantage, and the courts have developed techniques to cut this advantage down in egregious cases.

---

9. Wallis v. Pratt, [1911] A.C. 394. The buyer's remedy is confined to money damages "where a contract of sale is not severable and the buyer has accepted the goods or part thereof," by virtue of the Sale of Goods Act. R.S.O. 1990, c. S.1, s. 12(3); R.S.B.C. 1996, c. 410, s. 15(4); R.S.N.S. 1989, c. 408, s. 13(3).

Attitude of the Courts: Requirement of Adequate Notice

When an exemption clause appears in a document that a customer does not sign—such as a ticket or receipt or a sign displayed on a wall—the first defence against it is to deny adequate notice of the term. If this defence succeeds, then the term is not considered to be part of the bargain between the parties.

Even if a person signs a document, in the circumstances described in Chapter 8 on Mistake, he may plead *non est factum*; if successful, the entire document, including any exemption clause it may contain is void. As discussed in Chapter 9, a person may not be bound by a clause that is so unexpected and unfair that a reasonable signer would not think the contract contained such a term. This result is more likely if the contents of the document were misrepresented to the signer. A recent decision of the Ontario Court of Appeal has further enlarged the protection: for exemption clauses that absolve a defendant from liability for negligence, or limit its liability to a small portion of the harm suffered,

> ...*the defendant must establish* that it has specifically drawn the onerous limitation clause to the plaintiff's attention or has accurately stated its legal effect to the plaintiff *before* he signs the contract[10] [italics added].

This decision shifts the burden to the defendant to demonstrate that it adequately informed the plaintiff. However, where a person signs a contract that does not contain an unexpectedly onerous clause, he will be bound by all the terms it contains; this is true even with a document he is not expected to sign, if he actually knew or should reasonably have known its terms.

Strict Interpretations of Exemption Clauses

When adequate notice has been given, what effect does an exemption clause have if, apart from the clause, the party who has drafted it fails in some significant way to perform the contract as agreed? Exemption clauses are typically drawn in very wide terms. A supplier of machinery might exempt itself from all liability for defects in the product supplied, for any negligence of its employees, and for any guarantees implied by custom or trade usage—except for guarantees expressly set out in the contract, such as replacing any defective parts for three months. Courts have taken the view that exemption clauses should be very strictly construed against the party that draws them because they permit parties to evade legal responsibility ordinarily placed on suppliers of goods and services.

Even so, the courts respect the theory of freedom of contract, and in the absence of special rules (such as exist for common carriers) or special statutory protection (as in consumer protection legislation), they will not make a new contract for the parties to protect the one in a weaker position. If an exemption clause squarely excludes liability for the breach that has occurred, the injured party—subject to the discussion that follows—has no remedy. Thus, if one day after an express guarantee expires a piece of machinery breaks down for the first time, the supplier is not liable, even if at common law it would, in the absence of the clause, have been liable under an implied warranty of fitness.

Exemption clauses are strictly construed by the courts, in ways that are not at first apparent. Thus, a clause exempting a supplier from liability under the contract has been held not to exempt it from liability in tort.[11] Similarly, if a clause exempts a carrier from liability for negligence by its employees, the carrier will escape vicarious liability; however, the customer who has suffered injury or loss may still sue employees personally for their negligence unless, as decided in a recent Supreme Court of Canada case, the employees can show that the clause was clearly

---

10. Trigg v. MI Movers International Transport Services (1991), 84 D.L.R. (4th) 504, per Tarnopolsky, J.A., at 508.
11. White v. John Warrick & Co. Ltd., [1953] 2 All E.R. 1021.

intended to protect them as well.[12] Moreover, the courts will not enlarge the scope of the failure covered by an exemption clause.

CASE 14.5

Purolator undertook to deliver a tender document from Cathcart's office to the office of Ontario Hydro. The bill of lading contained a clause stating that Purolator would not be liable for "any special, consequential or other damages for any reason including delay in delivery." The tender document was never delivered to Ontario Hydro.

In an action by Cathcart to recover lost profits, Purolator admitted that had the bid been received, it would have been accepted and that the loss of profit by Cathcart was $37 000. However, Purolator claimed that the clause exempted it from any liability. Cathcart succeeded in its action. The court construed the clause strictly against the drafter of the term, Purolator, even though the parties were of equal bargaining power: the clause, on its "true construction," covered only damages rising from delay, not from a complete failure to deliver.[13]

Fundamental Breach

The most difficult cases for the courts arise when a breach has been so serious as to defeat the purpose of the contract; in the absence of the exemption clause, the aggrieved party could immediately have treated the contract as discharged and sued for damages. However, the clause is so broad that it appears to protect the wrongdoer from any liability. In a number of cases, courts have been reluctant to allow defendants to shelter behind such exemption clauses. In some instances, they have labelled the default a "fundamental breach" and have applied a hard rule using the following reasoning: if a breach is so serious that it amounts to a non-performance of the contract, it goes to the "core" of the bargain between the parties; to treat an exemption clause as excusing one party entirely from performance would be repugnant to the very idea of a binding contract; therefore, the clause must be struck down and the aggrieved party given a remedy in order to preserve the idea of a binding bargain. This rather doctrinaire line of reasoning means that once a court "identifies" a fundamental breach, it treats any exemption clause as ineffective to excuse that breach.

The above approach was seriously questioned by the English Court of Appeal:

> As to the question of "fundamental breach," I think there is a rule of construction [interpretation] that normally an exemption or exclusion clause or similar provision in a contract should be construed as not applying to a situation created by a fundamental breach of contract. This is not an independent rule of law imposed by the court on the parties willy-nilly in disregard of their contractual intention. On the contrary, it is a rule of construction based on the presumed intention of the contracting parties. It involves the implication of a term to give to the contract that business efficacy which the parties as reasonable men must have intended it to have. This rule of construction is not new in principle but it has become prominent in recent years in consequence of the tendency to have standard forms of contract containing exceptions clauses drawn in extravagantly wide terms, which would produce absurd results if applied literally.[14]

---

12. London Drugs v. Kuehne & Nagel International (1992), 97 D.L.R. (4th) 261, discussed in Chapter 12, Privity of Contract, under "Vicarious Performance." Traditionally, employees were third parties who were unable to claim the benefit of an exemption clause in the contract between carrier and customer, but under the London Drugs case, employees may be protected. London Drugs has been followed in a number of cases. See Madison Developments Ltd. v. Plan Electric Co. (1997), 36 O.R. (3d) 80.

13. Cathcart Inspection Services Ltd. v. Purolator Courier Ltd. (1982), 34 O.R. (2d) 187.

14. U.G.S. Finance Ltd. v. National Mortgage Bank of Greece, S.A., [1964] 1 Lloyd's Rep. 446, Pearson, L.J., at 453.

This statement was generally approved by the House of Lords in the *Suisse Atlantique* case.[15] As a result, an exemption clause may effectively protect a defendant from liability for fundamental breach if, in all the circumstances, it ought to be inferred that the parties so agreed. This opinion of the House of Lords was followed by the Supreme Court of Canada in a case where the defendant telegraph company failed to deliver a telegraphed tender, and the plaintiff contractor lost a construction contract it would otherwise have won.[16] The Court held that despite its failure to perform, the telegraph company was protected by the broad exemption clause printed on the telegram form. Subsequently, the House of Lords also allowed a very broad exemption clause to protect a defendant against liability for a deliberate act of destruction by one of its employees.[17]

The principle, stated as a rule of interpretation in the context of the whole agreement, is a sensible one, especially in transactions between businesses that agree to apportion the risks of a contract through the use of an exemption clause. For instance, a contractor for a large construction project may obtain insurance coverage at a better price than would be possible if each of its subcontractors had to take out separate policies. The subcontractors are thus able to make lower bids by exempting themselves from liability, with the agreement of the contractor. In these circumstances, if a court were to hold an exemption clause ineffective to protect a subcontractor, it would be defeating the bargain freely made by the parties.[18] We should note, however, that courts continue to examine these clauses very carefully, and to interpret them as not protecting the defendant when it would appear manifestly unfair to give protection.[19]

POSSIBLE CRIMINAL CONSEQUENCES OF BREACH

A breach of contract may be criminal when a party breaks the contract with the knowledge that the action will: endanger human life; cause bodily harm; expose valuable property to damage; deprive the inhabitants of a place of their supply of light, power, gas, or water; or delay or prevent the operation of a train by a common carrier.[20]

CONTEMPORARY ISSUE

Good Faith Required?

As we have seen in this chapter, breach of contract can occur by express repudiation, failure to perform, or inadequate performance. Some argue that an action for breach of contract should also lie when there has been bad faith or unfair dealing in carrying out obligations

continued

---

15. Suisse Atlantique Société D'Armement Maritime S.A. v. N.V. Rotterdamsche Kolen Centrale, [1967] 1 A.C. 361.

16. Linton v. C.N.R. (1974), 49 D.L.R. (3d) 548. Four of the justices dissented vigorously, protesting that the effect of the majority decision was to leave the telegraph company substantially without any obligation.

17. Photo Production Ltd. v. Securicor Transport Ltd., [1980] 2 W.L.R. 283.

18. For a full discussion of the problems raised with respect to the allocation of risk, see Waddams, *The Law of Contracts* (4th. ed.), pp. 338–51. In particular, at pp. 346–9, there is an interesting discussion of Harbutt's Plasticine case, in which the court disregarded an exemption clause protecting a defendant and as a result there was further litigation against an insurer that contested the unexpected liability of the defendant. See Harbutt's "Plasticine" Ltd. v. Wayne Tank & Pump Co. Ltd., [1970] 1 Q.B. 447, and Wayne Tank & Pump Co. Ltd. v. Employers Liability Assurance Corp. Ltd., [1974] Q.B. 57.

19. Monta Arbre Inc. v. Inter-Traffic (1983) Ltd. (1989), 71 O.R. (2d) 182.

20. Criminal Code, R.S.C. 1985, c. C-46, s. 422.

under a contract. Lawyer Stacey Reginald Ball argued in 1994 that an obligation of good faith and fair dealing should be a contractual term implied by law, particularly when discharging an employee, because it "would protect an employee's reasonable expectation of continued employment when job performance is satisfactory." Although some legal thinkers, like Ball, have argued for an implied duty of good faith, the Supreme Court of Canada disagreed in the case of *Wallace v. United Grain Growers Ltd.*, [1997] 3 S.C.R. 701. The Court stated:

> The law has long recognized the mutual right of both employers and employees to terminate an employment contract at any time provided there are no express provisions to the contrary....
>
> A requirement of "good faith" reasons for dismissal would, in effect, contravene these principles and deprive employers of the ability to determine the composition of their work force. In the context of the accepted theories on the employment relationship, such a law would, in my opinion, be overly intrusive and inconsistent with established principles of employment law, and more appropriately, should be left to legislative enactment rather than judicial pronouncement.

By contrast, the United States has legislated an obligation of good faith for all contracts. The *Uniform Commercial Code* section 1-203 provides that "every contract within this Act imposes an obligation of good faith in its performance or enforcement."

Sources: See S.R. Ball, "Bad Faith Discharge" (1994), 39 *McGill L.J.* 568; Kenneth Krupat, "Despite the Good Times, Jobless Worry Persists," *Toronto Star*, 18 December 1999, p. H6.

Questions to Consider

1. Do you agree or disagree with the Supreme Court of Canada that an implied obligation of good faith in employment contracts would be overly intrusive? Give your reasons.

2. If employment contracts were deemed to contain an implied obligation of good faith, would employees be bound by a duty of good faith when quitting their employment? What would such a duty mean in practical terms?

3. Should good faith be a statutory requirement for contracting parties as it is in the United States?

4. How would a statutory requirement of good faith and fair dealing affect the certainty and predictability of contracts? Are certainty and predictability so important that some degree of unfairness is a tolerable price for them?

THE BUSINESS SIGNIFICANCE OF BREACH

The vast majority of contracts are performed not because there are legal rules and courts to enforce them, but because the contracts make sense to the parties themselves. The parties must have seen a mutual economic advantage in forming their contract in the first place, or they would not have done so; the same advantage survives throughout the duration of most contracts to provide each side with an incentive to complete it. Few parties ever enter into a contract if they seriously suppose that they may later have to seek one of the remedies for breach through court action. Of course, the expected advantages from the bargain do not always materialize, and the benefits for one party may turn out to be losses; we cannot know how frequently that party may be persuaded, even if reluctantly, to perform because of a knowledge that the sanctions available to the other party would make breach at least as expensive as performing the unprofitable contract. The remedies for breach that we examine in the next chapter seem to play this type of supportive role, encouraging, in a small minority of cases, the performance of contracts and so assisting the other party to attain its expectations. To borrow from the words of Professor Macneil,

"…contracts are fundamentally mechanisms of cooperation and only mechanisms of conflict when things have gone wrong.…The law has thus to deal largely with pathological cases."[21]

QUESTIONS FOR REVIEW

1. Why does a major breach not automatically discharge a contract? Give an example.

2. Describe two ways in which anticipatory breach may occur.

3. In what types of contracts does it become particularly difficult to ascertain whether a breach is sufficient to allow the injured party to be freed from its part of the bargain? Explain.

4. Describe why the doctrine of substantial performance is of practical importance.

5. Even in the case of very serious breach, the aggrieved party may be unable to insist that he is discharged from his obligations. How does this occur?

6. What useful purpose is served by exemption clauses? Give an example.

7. Explain the attitude of the courts towards exemption clauses.

8. Give an example of strict interpretation of an exemption clause.

9. Explain the difficulties created by the doctrine of fundamental breach.

10. How have the courts modified its application?

11. What do you think Professor Macneil meant when he wrote, "The most important support for contractual relationships is not a sanction at all, but a continuation of the exchange motivations which led the parties to enter the relationship in the first place"? ("Whither Contracts" (1969), 21 *Journal of Legal Education* 403 at 410.)

CASES AND PROBLEMS

1 Stellar Construction Inc. agreed to build a new Olympic swimming pool for the Thomson Aquatic Centre for $450 000. The completion date was May 1. Thomson visited the pool on April 23, and was very disappointed with the quality of the tiles and caulking on the edges of the pool. She complained at once to Urqhart, Stellar's on-site manager.

Urqhart said that the tiles and caulking complied with the specifications, but if Thomson wanted them replaced there would be a delay of two weeks for completing the project. Thomson insisted that the quality was inadequate but that she needed to have the pool ready by May 3 when she had scheduled the grand opening celebration of the renovated Centre. Urqhart replied that she would have to choose between a delayed opening and accepting the tiles as is. Thomson then said, "Leave it. We'll settle it later."

Stellar continued its work and completed the project on May 2, in time for the grand opening. The final payment of $100 000 to Stellar was due May 15, but Thomson refused to pay it.

---

21. Macneil, "Whither Contracts" (1969), 21 *Journal of Legal Education* 403 at 408; reproduced in Swan and Reiter, *Contracts, Cases, Notes & Materials* (5th ed.), p. 995. Professor Macneil goes on to say, however, that "the rule of the pathological case governs the healthy case too."

She claimed that she had an independent appraisal of the tile work, that it would cost at least $50 000 to have the work done, and that the pool would have to be closed for two weeks, causing substantial losses in revenue to the Aquatic Centre.

Stellar sued Thomson for the $100 000, denying that Thomson's complaint was valid. It was established that the tiles failed to meet the specifications in the contract between the parties, that replacing them would indeed cost $50 000 plus the cost of business disruption. However, the diminished appearance of the pool caused by the tiles reduced the value of the pool by no more than $15 000.

Give your opinion whether it was Thomson's choice to replace or leave the tiles. In either case would Stellar's failure to perform amount to a minor or major breach?

2. O. Leander owns extensive greenhouses in which she grows flowers and plants for retail florists. On October 25, Jason, a retail florist, agrees to buy from Leander 1000 poinsettias for the Christmas trade, the plants to cost $1.00 each and to be available between December 10 and December 20. Jason requests delivery on December 11. At that time Leander advises him that she will not perform the contract, since she can obtain $1.25 each for the plants elsewhere. Jason refuses to pay more than $1.00 a plant and continues to insist upon delivery. On December 16, an extreme cold spell arrives, Leander's heating system breaks down and all the poinsettias she has on hand freeze. Jason then purchases the 1000 poinsettias from another wholesale florist but has to pay $1.30 a plant.

Has Jason any remedy? Discuss the arguments in his favour and the defences that Leander might offer. Would it make any difference if the contract had provided instead that the plants should be available between December 10 and December 15?

3. Fowler Engineering Co. agreed to supply Supreme Soap Co. with a specific machine for the manufacture of soap-chips from liquid soap. The essential terms of the contract were as follows:

Fowler agrees: To supply the machine and supervise its installation; to supervise the installation of all motors and pipes supplied by Supreme Soap; to test the machine and put it in good working order.

Supreme Soap agrees: To supply all necessary motors and pipes and labour; to pay $10 000 on delivery of the machine by Fowler; to pay the balance of $15 000 on completion of the installation.

When the machine was fully installed but had not yet been tested, Fowler demanded payment of the balance of $15 000. The manager of Supreme Soap Co. refused to pay until the machine had had a trial run and had proved satisfactory. Fowler said it did not want payment held up just because there might be some minor adjustments. Both parties were adamant. Supreme Soap Co. then employed another engineering firm to test the machine. The machine did not operate satisfactorily, although it was agreed that the defect could be remedied for about $250. The test also indicated that a different type of equipment would be better for the purposes of the soap company.

Supreme Soap Co. brought an action for return of the $10 000 deposit and for damages for breach of contract including the value of the floor space occupied by the machine, the value of the materials and labour it had supplied towards its completion, and the fees of the other engineering firm employed for the trial run. Fowler Engineering Co. counterclaimed for the balance owing on the price. What should the result be?

4. Three containers of equipment purchased by Bombardier Inc. in Japan arrived in Vancouver. Bombardier entered into a contract of carriage, using the standard bill of lading, with Canadian Pacific Ltd. (CP) to ship the containers by rail to Montreal. The contract contained a clause limiting CP's liability to $20 000 per container for any damage caused to the containers and their contents by CP's negligence while in transit.

The train carrying the containers derailed en route, but the accident was not caused by any negligence of CP. Two of the three containers were damaged by the derailment, but not seriously. (The third was unharmed.) However, during the salvage operation, CP's employees negligently set the two damaged containers on fire, causing much greater damage to their contents.

CP offered to pay $40 000 for the damage to the equipment in the two containers pursuant to the terms of the bill of lading. Bombardier rejected the payment and sued CP for $250 000, claiming that the damage done during the salvage operations was outside the contract of carriage; it argued that once the containers were thrown off the rails and were lying on the ground they were no longer "in transit." CP replied that salvage operations are an inherent part of a contract of carriage in case of accident, and that the clause limiting liability still applied.

Give your opinion of the arguments by each side and which would be likely to succeed.

REMEDIES FOR BREACH

Apart from treating a contract as discharged, an aggrieved party may need other remedies to compensate it for any harm caused by breach of contract. The usual remedy is an award of damages. However, when damages are not sufficient, other remedies may be available. In this chapter, we examine such questions as:

- what is the purpose of an award of damages?

- what are the limits placed on an award by the requirement that the aggrieved party minimize the harm it has suffered?

- what factors are taken into account in measuring the loss?

- what are the main problems involved in measuring non-economic losses?

- what approaches are used in measuring loss?

- what is the significance of, and the limits on, obtaining remedies of:
  - specific performance—ordering the wrongdoer to correct his wrong?
  - injunction—ordering the wrongdoer to cease his wrongful conduct?
  - rescission—returning the parties to a situation as if the contract had not existed?
  - *quantum meruit*—ordering payment for the value of goods or services received by the wrongdoer?

TYPES OF REMEDIES

In the last chapter, we discussed the remedy of termination, that is, the right to treat the contract as discharged as a result of breach. In addition, the injured party may have several other remedies available, depending on the type of breach and the subject-matter of the contract. They are as follows:

(a) damages

(b) equitable remedies—specific performance, injunction, and rescission

(c) *quantum meruit*

DAMAGES

The Purpose of an Award of Damages

damages

a money award to compensate an injured party for the loss caused by the other party's breach

An award of **damages** aims to place the injured party in the same position as if the contract had been completed. The award is intended only to compensate an injured party for the loss caused by failure to perform, not to punish the party liable for the breach. Of course, knowing that the injured party can force it to pay compensation usually deters a party from committing any breach it can avoid. In this respect, the purpose of an award of damages in contract is similar to that in the law of torts, that is, compensation and not punishment. The simple fact of liability acts as an economic deterrent.

The consequences of a solely economic approach may in some instances seem surprising. One can imagine circumstances in which a party to the contract could increase its total profits by deliberately breaking a contract.

ILLUSTRATION 15.1

X Inc. contracts to supply 100 000 widgets at $2.00 each to *Y* Corp. It expects to earn a profit of $20 000 on the contract. Shortly afterwards, *X* Inc. receives an offer to supply a different item to *Z* Ltd. at a profit of $60 000—but if it accepts the offer from *Z* Ltd., it will be unable to produce the 100 000 widgets for *Y* Corp.

X Inc. learns that a competing manufacturer can supply widgets of equal quality to *Y* Corp. at $2.25, that is, for $25 000 more than its own price. In these circumstances, *X* Inc. would gain financially if it were to forego its profit of $20 000 on the contract with *Y* Corp. and pay that company $25 000 in damages for breach while earning $60 000 on the new contract—a net gain of $15 000.

Such a strictly economic analysis of the purpose of damages leads to a controversial view of the nature of a contractual obligation. Some leading writers in the field have modified their views and no longer give unqualified support to this one-dimensional analysis. An American judge and leading writer in the field of economic analysis of law, states, with some reservations, that there is "a point" to

> Holmes's dictum, [as expressed in his "The Path of the Law"] *overbroad though it is...* that it is not the policy of the law to compel adherence to contracts but only to require each party to choose between performing in accordance with the contract and compensating the other party for any injury resulting from a failure to perform.[1]

This perception of contractual liability is morally neutral. It has been controversial precisely because it disregards any moral element in the legal obligation to perform one's promises.

We should note also that the arithmetic in Illustration 15.1 narrows and oversimplifies the nature of the decision that must be made. Additional intangible costs of a decision to break a contract are risk of harm to continuing good relations with the affected customer[2] as well as to one's general reputation for honouring commitments.

---

1. This analysis of Illustration 15.1 is based on Posner, *Economic Analysis of Law* (3rd ed.), p. 106. Boston: Little, Brown & Co. 1977, in which he refers to the classic article by Oliver Wendall Holmes, "The Path of the Law" (1897), 10 *Harv. L. Rev.* 462.

2. The existence of this intangible cost is recognized by Posner, *supra*, n. 1 at p. 81.

Mitigation of Damages

A party that has sustained a loss as a result of breach of contract is expected do what it can to mitigate the extent of the loss: the damages it can recover at law will not include what it might reasonably have avoided. In this respect, **mitigation** in contract law is analogous to the principle of contributory negligence in the law of torts. Thus, a business that has contracted to sell perishable goods and had them rejected upon tender of delivery will only prejudice itself by continuing to insist upon their acceptance. Instead, it is expected to dispose of them at the best obtainable price as quickly as it can if it wishes to recoup any resulting loss in an action for damages. Similarly, when a business has agreed to buy goods and the seller fails to deliver, the buyer should move to replace the goods from other suppliers as soon as possible. The same rule applies when a contract of employment is broken by the employer. An employee, in suing for damages for wrongful dismissal, should be able to show that he or she made every reasonable effort to find suitable alternative employment as a means of mitigating personal financial losses.

mitigation

action by an aggrieved party to reduce the extent of loss caused by the breach of the other party

In other words, an aggrieved party can recover only for such losses resulting from the breach *as it could not avoid by acting reasonably*. All the more then, a party that acts in a manner that aggravates and increases the resulting loss will be denied recovery for the alleged additional damages. A by-product of the mitigation rule is that it removes the incentive for conduct that is wasteful of economic resources.[3]

Prerequisites for an Award of Damages

To qualify for recovery, damage arising from breach of contract must "flow naturally from the breach." This principle has been interpreted to mean that a loss resulting from breach must be within the foreseeable boundaries of what the parties would have expected as a likely consequence of a failure to perform—had they thought about it when they drew up their contract. Damages are not generally awarded to compensate an injured party for some unusual or unexpected consequence of breach.

CASE 15.1

A carrier failed to deliver a vital piece of machinery promptly to the sawmill as instructed by an employee of the mill; as a result, the sawmill had to suspend operations until the part arrived. The sawmill company sued the carrier for the losses suffered by the shut down but the court refused to award damages because the employee had not told the carrier about the vital nature of the machinery when the carrier agreed to transport it, and the carrier had no reason to foresee the loss.

If the carrier had been told of the importance of the item it would likely have been liable for the loss—unless it exempted itself from liability and suggested that the sawmill insure the shipment against risk of delay or loss. Or it would have placed the item in a higher category of freight to ensure greater care in delivery, and charged a higher rate for its services.[4]

Sometimes a party does enter into a contract with knowledge of special liability if it fails to perform.

---

3. See Waddams, *The Law of Contracts* (4th ed.), pp. 553–63.

4. B.C. Saw Mill Co. v. Nettleship (1868), L.R. 3 C.P. 499. See also: Hadley v. Baxendale (1854), 156 E.R. 145; Koufos v. C. Czarnikow, The Heron II, [1969] 1 A.C. 350; Cornwall Gravel Co. Ltd. v. Purolator Courier Ltd. (1978), 18 O.R. (2d) 551.

CASE 15.2

An engineering company contracted to make a machine and deliver it by a given date. It then made a subcontract with the defendant firm to manufacture an essential part, clearly stating the date that the entire machine had to be completed for its customer. The defendant subcontractor did not manufacture the part on time and because of the delay, the buyer refused to accept the machine. The engineering company sued the subcontractor for damages, including the loss of profit on the main contract and the expenditure incurred uselessly in making the machine. It succeeded; the court agreed that the subcontractor should have foreseen the risk when the contract was made.[5]

In general, a seller or manufacturer of goods has a better idea of the consequences of late supply to the buyer than does a carrier of the goods. A supplier is more likely to know the needs of its customers in order to sell to them; a carrier usually knows only that the goods are to be picked up at one point and delivered to another according to the terms of the contract of carriage.[6]

A breach of contract may spark a chain of events that results in a significant "consequential" loss for the promisee. To an outsider, the logical relationship between the breach and the type of loss may be a tenuous one. The critical test, however, is to ask whether, from the past business dealings between the parties and the actual and supposed knowledge of the promisor *at the time of the contract*, not at the time the breach occurs, its managers should reasonably have expected such a loss to be a result of breach by the promisor. If so, damages may be awarded against it to compensate for the loss.

THE MEASUREMENT OF DAMAGES

Expectation Damages

Differences Between Tort and Contract

We have just noted that the relevant moment for determining whether damages were foreseeable is the time of making the contract and not when the breach occurs. Similarly, the relevant moment for determining the amount of damages that were foreseeable is also the time of making the contract. There is an important distinction between assessing damages for tort and assessing damages for breach of contract; in tort, the only conceivable time for measuring damages is the time of wrongdoing, that is, the moment the tort is committed. In breach of contract, the reason for referring to the earlier moment of formation is that from that moment, a promisor becomes liable to uphold the promise and the promisee becomes entitled to a continuous expectation of performance until the time for performance arrives; it is on the basis of this reasonably foreseeable liability that the promisor has bargained for the price.

Should a court include in its award of damages for breach an amount equal to the *expected profits* on the aborted transaction? The answer is yes, because that result is implicit in the objective of placing an aggrieved party in the position it would have enjoyed had the contract been performed. An award of **expectation damages** for breach of contract often contrasts sharply with the measurement normal in tort, where recovery is limited to harm suffered as a result of the tort.

expectation damages
an amount awarded for breach of contract based on expected profits

---

5. Hydraulic Engineering Co. v. McHaffie Goslett (1878), 4 Q.B.D. 670. See also Telecommander Corp. v. United Parcel Service Canada Ltd., [1996] O.J. No. 4664.
6. See Victoria Laundry (Windsor) Ltd. v. Newman Industries Ltd., [1949] 2 K.B. 528, per Asquith, J., at 537; United Oilseed Products Ltd. v. North American Car (Canada) Ltd., [1984] B.C.J. No. 409.

ILLUSTRATION 15.2

While examining a set of sketches in an art gallery, Jansen recognizes Took, a magazine art critic, and asks him what he thinks of the sketches. Took replies, "I like this one. I'm certain it is by Tom Thomson." As a result, Jansen immediately buys the sketch from the gallery at the asking price of $500. Took's assertion was a negligent misrepresentation and Jansen soon discovers the sketch is worth, at most, $100. Had it been a genuine Thomson, its value would have been at least $5000.

In a tort action against Took, the measure of damages would be Jansen's loss, the $400 extra she paid above the market value of the sketch. However, she could not recover the potential profit of $4500 that she could have earned on resale had Took's representation been true.

Suppose instead that Took was the gallery owner and sold the sketch to Jansen describing it on the bill of sale as a work by Tom Thomson. In these circumstances, Jansen could sue for the expectation loss of $4500.

Opportunity Cost

Why should there be this difference in the basis for recovery of damages? The main reason is the high value we place in our society on being able to rely on contracts from the moment we make them. If a contract breaker were liable to pay compensation only for losses actually suffered by the other party (such as out-of-pocket expenses), it could often ignore its obligations with relative impunity; the other party may not yet have made any actual expenditures, even though it may have forgone the opportunity to make a similar contract elsewhere. Indeed, the **opportunity cost**—the lost chance of making a similar contract with a different promisor—is an important reason for using expectation loss as a measure of damages. Many, if not most, business arrangements would otherwise lack an adequate sanction in law: a "deal" would not be a deal in any binding sense. In other words, the liability for expectation damages provides the essential background remedy for an effective system of contract law.[7]

opportunity cost
the lost chance of making a similar contract with a different promisor

Contracts of Sale

Contracts for the sale of goods provide a useful example of the approach taken by the courts in measuring expectation damages when one party is in breach. Suppose, first, that a buyer is in breach by refusing to accept delivery of the goods purchased. In an action for damages,[8] the first thing that we need to know is whether the seller's supply of goods exceeds the demand for them, that is, whether the seller can supply goods to all prospective customers. If so, the buyer's breach results in the seller's losing the profit on one sale, regardless of the resale of those same goods to a second buyer: the seller would still have made the second sale even if the first buyer had accepted the goods, and thus would have made two sales instead of one. Accordingly, the seller may recover damages from the first buyer amounting to the lost profits on their contract of sale.

However, when the seller's supply is limited and it could not have filled a second order if the first buyer had accepted the goods, the seller's damages will be measured by first, its additional expenses in taking reasonable steps to find a second buyer; and second, by any loss in revenue as a result of having to accept a lower sale price to dispose of the goods. The seller may sustain no damages at all if it resells for the full contract price (or more) without additional selling expenses.[9]

Suppose, instead, a seller breaks its contract by failing to deliver on time. If the buyer can obtain the goods elsewhere, the damages will be those reasonable expenses incurred in seeking an alternative supply and any additional price the buyer has had to pay above the original contract

---

7. See Waddams, *The Law of Contracts* (4th ed.), pp. 515–6. Also, West Coast Finance Ltd. and Booth v. Gunderson, Stokes, Walton & Co., [1974] 2 W.W.R. 428 at 434–5, and [1975] 4 W.W.R. 501.

8. As we shall see in Chapter 16, the Sale of Goods Act provides special rules that set out when title to goods passes to a buyer before delivery. (See section on "Title to Goods.") If title has passed, a seller may sue for the price instead of for damages.

9. In one sense, the first buyer's breach enabled the seller to make the second sale. See Apeco of Canada Ltd. v. Windmill Place (1978), 82 D.L.R. (3d) 1.

price. Of course, if the buyer obtains an alternate supply for the same or a lower price than that in the original contract, there will be no damages.

These principles for measuring damages are based on the premise that when buyer and seller agree on a price and time for delivery, each has taken into account, and therefore assumes, the risk of changes in the market price between the time of making the contract and the time of delivery. Whether the market price goes up or down in the interval, the seller must deliver and the buyer must accept delivery of the goods at the agreed time—or pay damages for failure to perform; they allocated the risk of change in price between them when they made the contract.

Consequential Damages

Consequential damages are in a sense secondary, one stage removed from the immediate effects of breach. Nevertheless, they may be both serious and reasonably foreseeable, so that a defendant will be liable to compensate for them. In our example of a seller that fails to deliver goods on time, suppose the buyer is unable to obtain suitable replacements from another source in time to use them for the intended purpose, for instance, to resell them or to utilize them as components in another product. The seller will be liable for those kinds of damages that it knew or ought to have known would flow "naturally" from the breach, that is, were reasonably foreseeable by the seller at the time the contract was formed. The measure is the lost profits on any resale transactions and may include damage claims against the buyer by its own customers as a result of its unavoidable default on contracts with them.

ILLUSTRATION 15.3

A Dairies Ltd. makes a written contract with B to supply B's restaurant with ice cream twice weekly, on Tuesdays and Fridays. A Dairies fails to deliver on a Friday at the beginning of a hot summer weekend. Other suppliers are busy servicing their own customers and refuse to supply ice cream to B. B runs out of ice cream Saturday morning and cannot obtain a fresh supply until Monday. B's loss is not the extra cost of obtaining ice cream elsewhere (which B was unable to obtain in any event); it is the loss of profits on ice cream sales over the weekend.

Instead of non-delivery, a seller's breach of contract may be in delivering defective goods. If so, other tests must be applied to assess the damages that would place the buyer in the same position as if the seller had performed the contract.

CASE 15.3

Lakelse Dairy Products purchased a new bulk-milk tank truck from General Dairy Machinery (GDM) to transport milk to its production facility. GDM was specialized in building such vehicles and warranted that it was fit for the purpose. However, the truck had serious flaws—there were cracks in the tank where milk remained in sufficient quantities that when it deteriorated and went bad, it infected new shipments of milk. Lakelse hired experts to find the source of the problem but it was confusing: was it the milk from the farms? was it the machinery in the production facility? was it the truck?

It took several months to uncover the source of the problem. Meanwhile, a substantial amount of milk had to be discarded and some had to be taken back from customers. When the source of the problem was discovered, Lakelse had to lease another tank truck. It sued GDM successfully, not only for the direct loss in value of the defective tank truck and the cost of leasing another truck but also for the lost profits that would have been made on the discarded milk if it had been sold by Lakelse at market value.[10]

---

10. Lakelse Dairy Products Ltd. v. General Dairy Machinery & Supply Ltd. (1970), 10 D.L.R. (3d) 277.

Consequential damages may arise from breach of a wide variety of contracts, not just the sale of goods. For instance, failure to repair the heating system of a concert hall as promised in time for a performance in midwinter could lead to the cancellation of the program, making the heating contractor liable for the losses due to cancellation, as well as for damage to the building by frozen pipes, since both are foreseeable harms.

General Damages

This term describes an estimated amount that a court may award over and above specific losses for harm that cannot be quantified in precise monetary terms, but that the court believes necessary to compensate the aggrieved party fairly. Thus, if a surgeon undertook to improve the appearance of a professional entertainer by performing plastic surgery on her nose, but the result was to disfigure the nose and give it a bulbous appearance, a court would have to decide what general damages, over and above specific out-of-pocket medical and hospital expenses, would compensate the plaintiff for the effects of this failure on her state of mind and professional morale. A U.S. court has, in fact, awarded general damages for breach of contract in such circumstances.[11]

Reliance Damages

Suppose that a management consultant contracts to spend three months advising a manufacturing firm on the reorganization of its operations. The contract term is to start two weeks later and in preparation for the project, the consultant spends the time assembling and preparing materials and reading the latest literature on the specialized business of the client firm. Just as she is about to start the consulting project on site, her client cancels the contract, saying it has decided to make no changes for the indefinite future. Fortunately, the consultant is able to take advantage of another consulting opportunity that can be easily substituted at the same fee. She could not, therefore, recover expectation damages for the fee she would have received if the manufacturing company had not cancelled the contract. However, she has still lost the time, effort, and expenditures involved in two weeks' preparation. Now it is merely wasted effort—not needed for the substituted job—effort she could have used more productively for other contracts. In these circumstances the consultant may recover as reliance damages the costs of all expenditures and wasted effort that were reasonably made in preparation for the first job.[12]

Liquidated Damages

Parties to a contract may agree in advance to terms stating an amount to be paid in damages if a breach should occur. The actual loss from breach may bear no relation to the agreed sum: it may turn out to be far greater or far less. Nevertheless, if the terms were a genuine attempt by the parties to estimate a loss, those terms will conclusively govern the amount of damages recoverable. Such provisions for **liquidated damages** can provide an economic incentive both to the promisor to perform (and so avoid incurring liability for the stated amount) and to the promisee to minimize its actual loss (since it will be entitled in any event to the stated amount and any savings will accrue directly to it).

liquidated damages
an amount agreed to be paid in damages by a party to a contract if it should commit a breach

---

11. Sullivan v. O'Connor, 296 N.E. 2d 183 (1973). Damages of $13 500 were awarded. For a later Canadian decision in which the plaintiff sued unsuccessfully in tort, see Lokay v. Kilgour (1984), 31 C.C.L.T. 177.

12. Anglia T.V. v. Reed, [1971] 3 All E.R. 690; Lloyd v. Stanbury, [1971] 2 All E.R. 267.

ILLUSTRATION 15.4

P Inc. agrees to construct an office building for *Q* Properties Inc., with a completion date of May 31. Both parties agree that any delay will cause a loss in revenue to *Q* from prospective tenants. A term of the contract states that for any delay in completion, *Q* may deduct $600 per day from its final payment of $100 000 to *P*, payable one month after *Q* obtains possession of the building. Such a term is binding upon both parties whether *Q* Properties Inc. should suffer a larger or smaller loss because of delay.

penalty clause
a term specifying an exorbitant amount for breach of contract, intended to frighten a party into performance

We must distinguish between a genuine attempt to anticipate or "liquidate" the consequences of a breach of contract and a **penalty clause**. If a term in the contract specifies an exorbitant amount, out of all relation to the probable consequences of breach, a court may find that it is intended merely to frighten a party into performance. Accordingly, the court will hold that it is a penalty clause and will disregard it in awarding damages based on an assessment of the actual loss suffered.

A sum paid as a deposit on the formation of a contract, to be forfeited on failure to perform, is a common type of liquidated damages provision, but it is treated somewhat differently. Partly because the money has already been paid as a guarantee of performance and partly because of a long history of deposits being forfeited, courts are reluctant to overturn such provisions even when they seem harsh: they are rarely recoverable. If, however, the sum is described as a part payment or a down payment, the courts are more willing to examine whether its forfeiture would be a penalty.

At the other extreme, a term limiting liquidated damages to a very small sum may be tantamount to an exemption clause. For instance, if a term states that $1 shall be payable as full compensation for breach, the issue for a court may be whether there has been a fundamental breach making the clause ineffective, as discussed in the preceding chapter; it is clearly not a penalty. We should note also that any clause that limits the maximum recovery but also allows a lesser recovery according to the damage suffered can never be a penalty clause, although it may amount to an exemption clause.

Nominal Damages

Occasionally, a court may award nominal damages to acknowledge a breach of contract where the loss sustained by the promisee is negligible. A court award of $1 will at least establish the validity of the plaintiff's claim where a question of principle is at stake. In general, when the amount in dispute is nominal, the likelihood that a "successful" plaintiff will still have to pay or share court costs discourages such litigation.

PROBLEMS IN MEASURING DAMAGES

Mental Anguish

The main basis for awarding damages is, of course, compensating for economic loss. There is, however, a range of contractual interests that are, at least in part, non-economic—illustrated in the preceding section by the case involving plastic surgery. As we noted in Chapter 3 on Tort Law, courts came gradually to recognize pain, suffering, nervous shock, and humiliation as harms for which they will grant limited recovery. The courts have now begun to follow the trend in contract in an increasing number of cases that recognize mental distress resulting from breach as a form of non-economic harm entitled to compensation.

Wrongful Dismissal

Mental anguish often may occur when an employee is wrongfully dismissed, especially after long years of service. Apart from direct financial loss, for which he or she is entitled to compensation, the dismissed employee may feel humiliated and suffer a serious loss of confidence. Until 1976, courts refused to allow any compensation for such upset, but in that year, an English court reversed this stand by awarding damages for mental anguish when an employer first urged the plaintiff employee not to accept an attractive position with another firm and a few months later wrongfully relegated him to an inferior position.[13] In the same year, a Canadian court awarded damages for loss of reputation in an action against a union by two of its members who had been wrongfully expelled.[14] Subsequently, Canadian courts have expanded the mental distress element of liability for wrongful dismissal.[15]

Lost Holidays

There are a large number of contracts, such as those for holiday travel and accommodation, that involve substantial sums of money but are not intended to confer an economic benefit on the vacationer. Unless courts take into account disappointment caused by the loss of an anticipated holiday, a vacationer would be without remedy apart from the return of any money paid. A return of that money would hardly be ample compensation to a vacationer who discovers at the airport that there is neither a flight nor any possibility of arranging an alternative holiday at the last minute. In 1973, an English court held, in the words of Lord Denning, "that damages for the loss of a holiday may include not only the difference in value between what was promised and what was obtained, but also damages for mental distress, inconvenience, upset, disappointment and frustration caused by the loss of the holiday."[16] This reasoning has been followed by Canadian courts.[17] A different example of recovery for mental distress arose in an action against an airline for breach of contract in transporting the plaintiffs' dogs.[18] The plaintiffs recovered damages for the mental suffering endured when they learned that their dogs suffocated while being carried in the baggage compartment of an airplane.

Attitude of the Courts

Apart from claims arising from wrongful dismissal, the relatively modest amounts that Canadian and English courts have awarded as damages for mental distress in actions for breach of contract[19] suggest that they are hesitant to give great monetary weight to highly subjective reactions that vary widely from person to person; they seem to have resolved their uncertainty by awarding damages, but only for limited amounts. In proposing a limit to the amount a plaintiff in a British Columbia case could recover for pain and suffering, the Supreme Court of Canada has indicated that the purpose of recognizing mental distress in an award of damages is "to substitute other amenities for those that have been lost, not to compensate for the loss of something with a money value…[and] to provide more general physical arrangements above and beyond those directly relating to the injuries, in order to make life more endurable."[20]

---

13. Cox v. Phillips Industries Ltd., [1976] 1 W.L.R. 638.

14. Tippett et al. v. International Typographical Union, Local 226 (1976), 71 D.L.R. (3d) 146.

15. In Pilato v. Hamilton Place Convention Centre (1984), 45 O.R. (2d) 652, the court awarded $25 000 in damages for mental distress for the severe and unfair manner in which the plaintiff was dismissed. In Ribeiro v. Canadian Imperial Bank of Commerce (1992), 13 O.R. (3d) 278, the court awarded $50 000 in punitive damages, and a further $20 000 for mental distress.

16. Jarvis v. Swan Tours Ltd., [1973] Q.B. 233. The quotation is Lord Denning's explanation of that decision in Jackson v. Horizon Holidays, [1975] 1 W.L.R. 1468 at 1472.

17. Elder v. Koppe (1974), 53 D.L.R. (3d) 705; Keks v. Esquire Pleasure Tours Ltd., [1974] 3 W.W.R. 406: Murray v. Triton Airlines Inc. (1994), 365 A.P.R. 131.

18. Newell v. C.P. Air (1976), 74 D.L.R. (3d) 574.

19. $500 for each of the two expelled union members; £125 for mental distress from loss of a holiday in the Jarvis case and £500 in the Jackson case; $500 for mental distress of the owners of the suffocated dogs.

20. Lindal v. Lindal (1981), 129 D.L.R. (3d) 263, per Dickson, J., at 272 and 273. See also Wilson v. Sooter Studios Ltd. (1988), 55 D.L.R. (4th) 361.

We have noted that a U.S. court awarded general damages for mental distress to a professional entertainer for the "wasted" pain and suffering she experienced when plastic surgery was unsuccessful.[21] Although the plaintiff also claimed compensation for disappointment in not obtaining the anticipated enhancement in her beauty, the court rejected such expectation damages as being too speculative. It relied on the opinion of noted authorities in contract law to the effect that, "the reasons for granting damages for broken promises to the extent of the expectancy are at their strongest when the promises are made in a business context, when they have to do with the production or distribution of goods or the allocation of functions in the market place."[22]

Cost of Performance Versus Economic Loss

The U.S. case *Peevyhouse v. Garland Coal & Mining Company*[23] provides a striking example of the difficulty of deciding on the appropriate criteria for measuring damages in circumstances that fall outside traditional categories of economic loss.

CASE 15.4

Owners of a farm containing coal deposits leased it to a mining company for five years. The operation was strip mining, in which coal is scooped from open pits on the surface, scarring the land. The owners insisted on including a term in the lease that the company would restore the surface at the expiration of the lease by moving earth in order to level the pits. At the end of the lease, the company vacated without restoring the land and the owners sued for damages.

Breach was admitted by the company. However, the court was faced with the following dilemma: the cost of restoring the land as promised would be $29 000, but the market value of the farm would increase by only $300 as a result of the restoration. The owners claimed damages of $29 000, measured by the "cost of performance," and the company countered that it was liable only for damages of $300, measured by the "diminution in economic [market] value" caused by the breach.

The majority of the court held that:

...under the "cost of performance" rule plaintiffs might recover an amount about nine times the total value of their farm. Such would be unconscionable and grossly oppressive damages, contrary to substantial justice...also, it can hardly be denied that if plaintiffs here are permitted to recover under the "cost of performance" rule they will receive a greater benefit from the breach than could be gained by full performance....[24]

Accordingly, the court found that an award of $29 000 to the plaintiffs would have given them a windfall of $28 700; it awarded damages of only $300.

The position taken by the majority of the court is supported by the following economic analysis: it encourages parties to decide whether to perform or break their contracts in strictly economic terms. Thus, it would discourage the coal company from committing $29 000 of labour, materials, and equipment to a project that would result only in an increase of $300 in value. If, instead, "cost of performance" was used to measure the damages, the company might have chosen to perform in order to avoid litigation.[25]

---

21. Sullivan v. O'Connor, *supra*, n. 11.

22. The reference is to Fuller and Perdue, "The Reliance Interest in Contract Damages: 1" (1936), 46 *Yale L.J.* 52, especially at 60–3. The authors offer as justifications for expectation damages "the loss of opportunity to enter other contracts" and "a policy in favor of promoting and facilitating reliance on business agreements."

23. 382 P.2d 109 (Okla. 1963). See also: James v. Hutton & J. Cool & Sons Ltd., [1950] 1 K.B. 9.

24. *Ibid.*, per Jackson, J., at 113.

25. See Posner, *Economic Analysis of Law* (3rd ed.), p. 109.

On the other hand, this strictly economic analysis ignores the owners' subjective interest in having the farm restored. For sentimental or esthetic reasons—suppose the farm had been in their family for generations and they occupied an adjacent farm—they may have bargained expressly for restoration. Was it legally impossible for them to bargain successfully for such a promise? Suppose that after losing their case, the owners nevertheless decided to proceed with restoration, and they paid a contracting firm $29 000 in advance to do the job. Could the contracting firm, having accepted the money, then refuse to perform, offering to pay damages of $300 as the measure of its breach? The *Peevyhouse* decision suggests that it could.

Even the economic argument can be stated differently: the approximate cost of restoration was known more or less accurately when the lease was entered into; this cost must have been taken into account in setting the price for access to the coal; the owners would probably have charged a higher price for the coal had they realized that the company could not be made to pay the cost of restoration; they could then have done the restoration using the extra revenue. In this sense, it is the company that has obtained a windfall of $28 700 in not having to pay the cost of what it had originally promised to do as part of the price of the lease.

It can be seen then that the *Peevyhouse* decision is debatable. The court was not unanimous in its opinion, and an opposite view was taken by another U.S. court.[26] While economic analysis is an important tool in both the understanding and the application of contract principles, it does not provide the exclusive basis for analysis. The legitimate expectations of parties may include non-economic interests, which are also entitled to the protection of the law.

EQUITABLE REMEDIES

Reasons for the Intervention of Equity

The old common law courts gave money damages as the sole remedy for breach of contract. But there are circumstances where money damages alone seem quite inadequate. For example, suppose a purchaser wishes to construct a large factory and for that purpose enters into contracts to buy adjoining lots from five different vendors. If one vendor, who owns a crucial middle lot, repudiates the agreement to sell, the purchaser will be left with four lots, now of no use, and will be unable to proceed with building. Damages suffered by the purchaser may be very large, perhaps many times the sale price of the lot the vendor refuses to transfer. The most sensible remedy would be to order the vendor to transfer the lot to the purchaser on payment of the purchase price. And that is exactly what the old courts of chancery (equity) did. They recognized the inadequacy of the common law remedy and intervened to grant one of their special remedies, that of *specific performance* (discussed below). Failure to comply with an equitable order places a defendant in "contempt of court" and can lead to a fine or imprisonment.

Reasons for Denying a Remedy

Equitable remedies are discretionary; that is, the court decides whether in view of all the circumstances there are good reasons to depart from the ordinary common law remedy of damages. However, the principles governing the exercise of this discretion have become well settled and a remedy is granted almost as a matter of course to a plaintiff that complies with the established principles of equity. The following are among the more important requirements:

(a) A plaintiff must come to court with "clean hands," that is, he must not himself be found to have acted unethically; if there is an element of sharp practice on his part, the court will leave him, at best, with his claim for money damages.

---

26. See Groves v. John Wunder Co., 286 N.W. 235, 123 A.L.R. 502 (1939). This decision is questioned by Posner, *supra*, n. 25, at pp. 108–9

(b) If, after learning of the defendant's breach, a plaintiff delays unreasonably in bringing an action, perhaps lulling the defendant into believing that no action will be brought, a court will deny an equitable remedy.

(c) As we noted in Chapter 8 on Mistake, a court will refuse to intervene on equitable principles when to do so would affect an innocent purchaser.

(d) A court will not grant a remedy in equity when the plaintiff has not paid a substantial consideration for the defendant's promise; if the promise is simply given under seal or in exchange for a nominal sum, money damages alone will be awarded.

(e) Finally, a plaintiff must ordinarily be a party against whom the remedy would be awarded were he the defendant instead; for example, because a court will not grant an equitable remedy *against* an infant defendant when a contract is voidable at his option, neither will it grant that remedy *in his favour* as a plaintiff. This insistence on symmetry is an ancient principle, hard to justify on grounds of fairness, and is no longer followed when an employee seeks reinstatement, as we shall see in Chapter 20.

Specific Performance

specific performance
an order requiring a defendant to do a specified act, usually to complete a transaction

A judgment for **specific performance** is an order requiring a defendant to do a specified act, most often to complete a transaction. When the subject-matter is land, the court orders the vendor to complete and deliver all documents necessary to the transfer of ownership, and to vacate the premises so that the purchaser may take possession on payment of the purchase price. In situations where the court might be obliged to supervise a defendant, specific performance will not be granted. As a result, performance that depends on the personal skill or judgment of a defendant does not lend itself to an order for specific performance. Thus, an artist who repudiates a contract to give a concert will not be ordered to perform; to do so would be to invite a disgruntled performance. The plaintiff will have to be content with an award of money damages.

The remedy of specific performance is most often applied to contracts for the sale of land. Courts granted specific performance originally on the argument that each piece of land is unique, and that consequently money damages are an inadequate remedy. The principle was firmly established that, when requested, specific performance would be granted almost as a matter of course in contracts for the sale of land. This appears no longer to be so: in *Semelhago v. Paramadevan* in 1996, Mr. Justice Sopinka of the Supreme Court of Canada stated that:

> While at one time the common law regarded every piece of real estate to be unique, with the progress of modern real estate development this is no longer the case. Both residential, business and industrial properties are mass produced much in the same way as other consumer products. If a deal falls through for one property, another is frequently, though not always, readily available….

> …It cannot be assumed that damages for breach of contract for the purchase and sale of real estate will be an inadequate remedy in all cases….

> …Specific performance should, therefore, not be granted as a matter of course absent evidence that the property is unique to the extent that its substitute would readily be available.[27]

The *Semelhago* decision has had a significant effect on legal claims for specific performance: in the short time since it was decided, several dozen decisions have referred to it—some courts relying on it to refuse specific performance and others finding that the land in question was suf-

---

27. [1996] 2 S.C.R. 415. For a critique of this case, see O.V. Da Silva, "The Supreme Court of Canada's Lost Opportunity: Semelhago v. Paramadevan" (1998), 23 *Queen's L.J.* 475.

ficiently unique to decree specific performance. There is now much greater uncertainty whether specific performance will be granted.

It may seem surprising that a vendor of land may also be entitled to specific performance. The reasons are, first, that the general principle giving parties mutual remedies wherever possible is followed; and second, that damages may be an inadequate remedy to a vendor. If damages were awarded, the vendor would still be left with the land; she would have to look after the land, pay taxes, maintain buildings, and would have to find another purchaser in order to rid herself of these burdens. Therefore, the court may order the purchaser to specifically perform the contract, that is, to pay the vendor the full sale price and accept the land.

Courts rarely grant specific performance of a contract for the sale of goods—damages are considered adequate compensation. Courts might grant specific performance of a contract for the sale of a chattel having a unique value. Antiques, heirlooms, rare coins, and works of art are possible examples. Shares in a corporation may also be considered property for which specific performance is an appropriate remedy, especially when a plaintiff's primary purpose is to obtain a controlling or substantial interest in the firm.

Injunction

An **injunction** is a court order restraining a party from acting in a particular manner; in relation to contract, it restrains a party from committing a breach. For the remedy to be available, the courts require the contract to contain a **negative covenant**, a promise not to do something. However, the covenant need not be stated expressly as a prohibition but may simply be a logical consequence of an express promise. Thus an *express promise* by a tenant to use leased premises for office space would likely be construed to contain an *implied promise* not to use them for a nightclub; the landlord could obtain an injunction prohibiting their use for a nightclub.

Sometimes a court may grant an injunction when it would not order specific performance, although the effect of the injunction may be almost the same as that of an order for specific performance. The court is willing to do so because it does not have the problem of continuing supervision when it grants an injunction; it simply orders the defendant to desist from committing further breaches. Thus, when a hotelkeeper promised to buy all the beer he required exclusively from one source of supply and then purchased some elsewhere, the court granted an injunction restraining him from making further purchases from other suppliers.[28] The court did not say, "You must buy all your supply from this source, and we will see that you do." Instead, it said in effect, "In future you must not buy from any other source, and if we hear of your doing so, you will be in serious trouble."

injunction
a court order restraining a party from acting in a particular manner, such as committing a breach of contract

negative covenant
a promise not to do something

Interlocutory Injunction

Contracts of the kind just described are common, and breach can lead to serious consequences for both supplier and buyer. In the typical case, the supplier is the one seeking an injunction. However, in *Sky Petroleum Ltd. v. VIP Petroleum Ltd.*,[29] the position was reversed.

CASE 15.5

The buyer, an owner of a chain of service stations, contracted for a long-term supply of petroleum products at fixed prices and promised to take all its requirements from the one supplier. The contract was entered into shortly before the 1973 energy crisis that created a shortage of

continued

28. Clegg v. Hands (1890), 44 Ch.D. 503.
29. [1974] 1 W.L.R. 576. See also Bentall Properties Ltd. v. Canada Safeway Ltd., [1988] B.C.J. No. 775.

fuel and a sharp rise in prices. During the crisis, the sup-plier claimed that the buyer was in default in payment and, by alleging breach, it tried to free itself from the obligation to continue delivering to the buyer's stations. Because of the severe shortage, the supplier's conduct would have left the buyer without any source of supply and forced it out of business before the courts could hear the dispute.

The buyer asked the court to take the exceptional step of granting a temporary injunction prohibiting the sup-plier from refusing to continue to deliver petroleum prod-ucts to it, in effect compelling specific performance by the suppliers in the interval before the full trial of the dispute. The court granted the injunction to prevent the bank-ruptcy of the buyer before it had a chance to present its case.

interlocutory injunction

a temporary restraining order

Thus, in some circumstances, a court will grant an **interlocutory injunction**—a temporary injunction—to restrain immediate harm from being done by a breach of contract, pending for-mal resolution of the dispute at trial. Courts are reluctant, however, to grant even a temporary injunction of this kind in personal service contracts.

Injunction Against an Employee

In contracts of employment, granting an injunction at the request of an employer against a for-mer employee may have unacceptable consequences. If an injunction prohibits an employee from working for any other employer, it may leave the person with the harsh alternatives of returning to work for the plaintiff in an atmosphere of hostility, or being without any means of earning a living. Accordingly, a court is reluctant to grant an injunction against an employee who has promised exclusive services to one employer but has broken the contract by working elsewhere.

Injunctions have been granted, however, when an employee in possession of trade secrets of great value left his employer in breach of his contract of employment and went to work for another in the same line of business,[30] and when a singer promised her exclusive services to an employer for a limited period and expressly undertook not to sing anywhere else.[31] The grant-ing of such injunctions is best regarded as an exception to the general rule that a court will not grant the remedy where the subject-matter of the contract is personal services and where the effect would be to leave the employee no alternative but to work for the original employer or remain unemployed.

Rescission

The Choice Between Damages and Rescission

Generally speaking, the primary purpose of remedies for breach is to place an aggrieved party as nearly as is practicable, in the position he would have been in *had the contract been completed*. But in some situations, another approach may be more advantageous to a plaintiff: she would prefer to return as nearly as she can to the position that would have existed *had the contract not been made at all*. In other words, she would prefer **rescission**—to have the contract *set aside* or *rescinded*.

rescission

setting aside or rescinding a contract to restore the parties to the positions they would have been in had the contract not been made at all

If a breach is serious enough to discharge the plaintiff from her own obligations, she may elect rescission, provided that it is feasible to return the parties substantially to their pre-contract positions. An aggrieved party must choose between an action for damages to obtain the benefit of the contract and one for rescission to return her to the position that she would have been in if a contract had never existed at all; she cannot have both remedies since they have contradic-tory purposes. Rescission is usually denied if the subject-matter of a contract cannot be returned

30. Robinson (William) & Co. Ltd. v. Heuer, [1898] 2 Ch. 451.

31. Lumley v. Wagner (1852), 42 E.R. 687; also Warner Bros. Pictures v. Nelson, [1937] 1 K.B. 209.

by the plaintiff to the defendant, as when it has been consumed or incorporated into other goods or sold to innocent third parties.

Perhaps the most common claim for rescission occurs when durable goods—equipment, machinery, or consumer products such as refrigerators or television sets—fail to perform as required in a contract of sale. A buyer who is unhappy with his acquisition rarely wants damages for the diminished value of the goods or even a replacement of the same brand; he would much prefer to return the goods and get his money back. If goods to be returned have been damaged or have deteriorated in value, a court may refuse to order rescission and instead leave a plaintiff with the remedy of damages. Since there may have been substantial use or deterioration of the goods while in the hands of the buyer, the remedy is often unavailable.

A less common but nonetheless important situation where rescission may be the preferred remedy arises in the sale of a valuable asset, such as land, when the purchaser defaults.

ILLUSTRATION 15.5

V agrees to sell Blackacre to P for $325 000, receiving a down payment of $25 000, the balance to be paid in quarterly instalments of $25 000. P is unable to make payment when the first instalment falls due and when he was also expected to take possession of the property. If V were to try to hold P to the contract, she would be entitled to some damages for the late payment, but she would have to give possession to P, and would remain uncertain about P's ability to meet future instalments. In these circumstances, V may well prefer to minimize her risks by obtaining rescission—returning P's down payment and retaining possession of Blackacre.

Opportunity Cost

When rescission is available, it may sometimes be more beneficial for a plaintiff than an action for damages.

ILLUSTRATION 15.6

Glenn Construction Inc. agrees to erect a warehouse for Hoyt Equipment Ltd. for a price of $1 000 000, payable in four equal instalments at specified stages of construction. When the work is half completed and the second instalment is due, Hoyt defaults payment because of financial difficulties and requests that Glenn cease work, effectively repudiating the contract. Since the making of the contract, construction costs have risen much faster than anticipated by the parties. In fact, it appears that had Hoyt not repudiated and Glenn had to complete the project, it would have cost Glenn $1 085 000 rather than an expected $900 000, causing a loss of $85 000 instead of a profit of $100 000. We shall assume that because of the increase in prices, the current value of the work completed by Glenn at the time of breach is $575 000.

In Illustration 15.6, if Glenn sued for breach of contract, it could collect damages of $250 000 for the missed instalment, but nothing for loss of profits because there would have been none. But if Glenn sues for rescission of the contract, that is, it elects to treat the contract as if it had never existed, then Glenn can make no claim *under the terms of the contract itself* and would even have to account for the $250 000 received as the first instalment. However, the work done by Glenn was at the request of Hoyt and created a substantial economic benefit. Consequently, Glenn could claim against Hoyt on a *quantum meruit* basis, as discussed earlier in Chapter 6, because valuable services were performed without a price having been settled by a binding agreement between the parties. Although there was an agreed price in the contract, it has no effect once the contract is rescinded—it ceases to exist along with the rest of the contract. Accordingly, the price will be set by the court at the fair market value of the work. As a result, Glenn may obtain judgment for $575 000 less the first instalment received of $250 000, leaving a balance of

$325 000. Thus, by seeking rescission and suing *quantum meruit* Glenn may obtain judgment $75 000 higher than the sum it would recover if it sued for damages under the contract.

The question arises, "Is Glenn merely being returned to the position that would have existed if the contract had never been made when it receives the market value of $575 000 for the work done, presumably including some element of profit?" In reply, it should be said that it is not possible to turn the clock back and place Glenn precisely in its pre-contract position, enabling it to seek an alternative contract and earn normal profits; the firm has lost that opportunity. Thus, payment of a normal profit margin on work done *quantum meruit*, by valuing the work at fair market value, can be viewed as reasonable compensation for the opportunity cost, as discussed earlier in this chapter.

Any advantage in suing *quantum meruit* on the facts of this case disappears if we change one important factor: suppose construction costs had not risen beyond those contemplated by the parties when they made the bargain. Glenn could then have expected a $100 000 profit on completion and, if it sued for expectation damages rather than rescission, it would be entitled to that sum in addition to the $250 000 missed payment.[32]

CONTEMPORARY ISSUE

When Are Legal Remedies Effective? What Alternatives Does an Aggrieved Party Have?

National Hockey League (NHL) players have sometimes refused to perform existing obligations under contracts with their teams unless those contracts are renegotiated to pay them more money. It doesn't seem to matter that the contracts were negotiated in good faith, and that the players, if they should perform poorly in one season, would still be paid an agreed increase in salary for the following year. As Jeffrey Simpson reported in *The Globe and Mail*, August 5, 1999, Pavel Bure refused to play and honour his contract with the Vancouver Canucks in 1998. Vancouver finally traded him to the Florida Panthers, where he received a higher pay: willful refusal to honour his contract paid off.

In 1999, it was Alexei Yashin of the Ottawa Senators who refused to play unless his salary in the fourth year of his four-year contract was renegotiated at twice the $3.6 million provided in the contract. As we go to press, this dispute has not been resolved. While his team could likely obtain an injunction to prohibit Yashin from playing for another team in the NHL, it might be very difficult to enforce such an injunction overseas—if sufficiently high salaries were paid there so as to lure Yashin.

Questions to Consider

1. What other remedies are available to the aggrieved party? Clearly, the team need not pay the player who refuses to carry out his contractual duties, but could it also have a valid claim for damages caused by loss of revenue, on the basis that fewer spectators will by tickets and some advertisers will likely lower their expenditures for televised games? If so, how could such a highly speculative loss be turned into a numerical calculation?

2. What dangers exist if this dispute cannot be resolved in the courts? What role is there in this dispute for the NHL Players Association and the NHL itself?

---

32. Indeed, if construction costs had risen by *less* than expected, the current market value of the work completed to the time of breach would probably also be lower, and a *quantum meruit* claim could provide a smaller sum than the amount of the missed instalment.

Quantum Meruit

We discussed in Chapter 6 how a *quantum meruit* claim arises for a valuable benefit conferred at the request of a promisee. We have also seen how *quantum meruit* may be utilized by a contractor who elects to rescind a contract when the other party repudiates before the contractor has completed performance. In either case, if the parties cannot agree on a price, the performing party may have the court assess the claim based on the fair market value of the benefit conferred.

A different question arises if the contractor decides to abandon the project before it is completed. Is it entitled to recover for the work done? In the absence of an express agreement to make progress payments, the normal presumption is that nothing is due until completion, and that a contractor that abandons after part performance, for whatever reason, cannot recover anything. There appears, however, to be one situation in which a worker who has abandoned a contract may still recover for the value of what has already been done. Blackburn, J. discussed the matter in *Appleby v. Myers* and stated as follows:

> Bricks built into a wall become part of the house; thread stitched into a coat which is under repair, or planks and nails and pitch worked into a ship under repair, become part of the coat or the ship; and therefore, generally and in the absence of something to show a contrary intention, the bricklayer, or tailor or shipwright is to be paid for the work and materials he has done and provided, although the whole work is not complete. It is not material whether in such a case the non-completion is because the shipwright did not choose to go on with the work.[33]

METHODS OF ENFORCING JUDGMENT

What happens when a party obtains a judgment for damages? How may he enforce his claim? When a plaintiff obtains judgment for a sum of money, he becomes a **judgment creditor**, and the defendant a **judgment debtor**. If the judgment debtor is financially sound, the force of the court judgment is usually sufficient: she will raise the money and pay it voluntarily. If, however, she is recalcitrant or in financial difficulty and unable to raise the money readily, the judgment creditor must then move to enforce payment. We must be clear that a judgment debtor is not considered a criminal. She cannot be imprisoned for debt as she once could, provided she does not attempt to commit a fraud, such as absconding and taking her assets with her. (Some jurisdictions provide for detaining a fleeing debtor temporarily to extract the assets she is escaping with.) There are legal procedures by which a judgment creditor may seize as much of the debtor's property as is necessary to satisfy the judgment. If the assets are insufficient, the creditor is without further remedy for the time being. He may wait in the hope that the debtor will obtain more assets in the future so that he may seize them as well. Generally, however, the creditor gets whatever he can soon after the judgment is obtained and writes off any expectation of further satisfaction at a future date.

The most usual procedure when the judgment debtor does not pay promptly is to register the judgment with the office of the sheriff of the county or district in which the debtor resides and to request the sheriff to **levy execution** against the assets of the debtor to satisfy the judgment. An **execution order** gives the sheriff authority to seize and sell various chattels and arrange for a sale of the debtor's lands after an appropriate grace period.[34] More complicated procedures are necessary to seize a bank account, the contents of a safety-deposit box, or an income from a trust fund. A creditor may also obtain a **garnishee order** against a debtor's wages. The order requires the employer to retain a portion of the debtor's wages each payday and surrender the sum to the creditor to be applied against the judgment.

judgment creditor
a party who has obtained a court judgment for a sum of money

judgment debtor
a party who has been ordered by the court to pay a sum of money

levy execution
seize and sell a debtor's chattels or arrange for a sale of his lands

execution order
an order that gives the sheriff authority to levy execution

garnishee order
an order requiring the employer to retain a portion of the debtor's wages each payday and surrender the sum to the creditor

---

33. (1867), L.R. 2 C.P. 651 at 660–1. Note that in this case the court did find an express agreement that no payment would be due until the whole work had been completed.

34. For a description of property exempt from seizure, see, for example: Execution Act, R.S.O. 1990, c. E.24, s. 2; Court Order Enforcement Act, R.S.B.C. 1996, c. 78, s. 71.

Besides money damages, a court may make two other types of money awards for breach of contract. As we shall see in Chapter 16, a seller may be awarded the price of goods sold instead of damages for non-acceptance. And a lender of money may be awarded the amount of the money lent plus accrued interest. Each of these awards is analogous to a decree of specific performance in which the performance is to take the form of a payment of money owed, except that the judgment debtor's failure to pay will not amount to contempt of court; a judgment creditor is left with the usual remedies described above.

QUESTIONS FOR REVIEW

1. Describe the controversy generated by a strictly economic view of the purpose of damages.

2. What is the reasoning behind the requirement that an aggrieved party mitigate its losses?

3. Explain why the consequence of a breach generally affects the liability of a carrier of goods differently from a manufacturer of the same goods.

4. Define expectation damages, opportunity cost, consequential damages, reliance damages, and specific performance.

5. When a buyer refuses to accept delivery of goods, explain the significance of supply and demand in determining the damages suffered by the seller.

6. Describe the nature of liquidated damages and how they are distinguishable from a penalty clause.

7. Jim goes to the airport at the peak of the holiday season to catch his flight for a one-week Caribbean holiday he has already paid for. His travel agent made an error in booking his flight: it left two days earlier and Jim is unable to obtain another flight. His agent offers to refund the cost of his holiday. Has Jim any additional claim? Explain.

8. Do you agree or disagree with the decision in *Peevyhouse*? Give reasons.

9. When will a court refuse to grant the remedy of specific performance to a purchaser of land?

10. In what circumstances might a court grant an interlocutory injunction?

11. When may it be to the advantage of a plaintiff to ask for rescission rather than damages?

12. When a judgment debtor refuses to pay his debt, what recourse does the judgment creditor have?

CASES AND PROBLEMS

1 The Complicated Machinery Co. Ltd. manufactures and assembles heavy equipment for industry. It accepted an order for a large machine from the Northern Paper Co. that would automate certain processes, one of the terms being that the machine was to be completed by October 31 of the same year. The contract further stated that if the machine was not completed by October 31, the Complicated Machinery Co. Ltd. would pay the Northern Paper Co. "liquidated damages" at the rate of $1000 a week for the duration of the delay. The manager of Northern Paper Co. had written in a letter accompanying the offer: "Until the machine is in full operation it is hard to say what our savings will be. A thousand dollars a week is a rough guess."

Complicated Machinery Co. Ltd. failed to deliver until December 26, eight weeks late. It billed the paper company for the full price less $8000 (eight weeks at $1000). The paper company discovered that the machine actually saved $2400 weekly in production costs. It therefore tendered as payment the full price less $19 200 (eight weeks at $2400). Which party is correct and why?

2 In December, Carvel Estates Ltd., a real estate developer, contracted to buy 24 large suburban lots from Dalquith Enterprises Inc., the transaction to close May 15. Carvel had hired an architect and intended to build expensive "up-market" homes. The plans for each house were at an advanced stage by late March, when without any prior notice, Dalquith sent Carvel a cheque refunding Carvel's down payment. Dalquith informed Carvel that it could not go through with the deal because Dalquith's parent corporation had applied for a zoning change and wished to construct luxury condominiums on the site. Dalquith also stated it had discussed the situation with the owner of land adjacent to the site Carvel had purchased, and the owner was willing to discuss selling an equivalent number of lots to Carvel.

Carvel's manager was very upset because the firm would have been ready to begin work immediately after the May 15 closing date. Dalquith refused to reconsider its repudiation when asked by Carvel. Carvel commenced an action, requesting specific performance and damages for any additional costs attributed to delay in the project. Explain whether it is likely that Carvel will succeed in its request for specific performance, and if not, what other remedies might be available to Carvel.

3 Malvern Enterprises Inc. invited tenders for a construction project. The invitation included an often-used "privilege" clause to the effect that "the lowest or any tender shall not necessarily be accepted." Granite Construction Ltd. submitted a tender that, as it turned out was the second lowest submitted. Another construction company made the lowest tender to which it added a condition that was not part of the invitation to tender. However, Malvern considered the condition to be a minor change and it accepted the tender.

When Granite learned of the change made in the tender by the added condition, it sued Malvern for breach of contract, for damages amounting to the profit Granite would have made had its tender been accepted. Granite claimed that upon submitting a tender, each of the tenderers entered into a customarily implied contract with Malvern that it would consider only tenders that conformed to the invitation. Malvern responded that the privilege clause protected it from having to accept any particular tender and, therefore, it was not in breach of any implied contract. It also claimed that in any event it was free to accept any other conforming tender—not just that submitted by Granite.

During the trial, evidence given supported the usual practice that if the lowest tender had been disqualified, the contract would probably have been awarded to the second lowest tenderer. The court found that there was an implied contract that only fully conforming tenders would be considered by Malvern, and also that the privilege clause did not excuse accepting a nonconforming tender. The problem remained whether Granite was in a stronger position than all the remaining tenderers and whether it was entitled in the circumstances to damages amounting to a lost profit or, indeed, to any other damages.

Give your opinion of the likely outcome with reasons.

4 In November, Tanton agreed orally with Marsh to cut and haul to Marsh's mill approximately 500 000 board feet of lumber at a price of $20 per thousand board feet delivered to the mill. The contract also stated that on completion of the contract,

Tanton should be reimbursed for the cost of the construction of camps and roads necessary for the lumbering operations.

In January next, after Tanton had delivered 200 000 board feet to the mill, he found himself in financial difficulties and unable to pay his employees. At the time Tanton had been paid for the logs delivered to date, but had not been paid for the camps and roads he had had to construct for the purpose. Tanton told Marsh that he was quitting and that he considered the contract as having been frustrated by his inability to pay his men. He then sued to recover the value of the work done in the construction of camps, roads, and bridges during the lumbering operations up to January.

Should Tanton succeed?

 Two students are trying after class to see what they can make of the legal significance of exemption clauses.

Harvey: *Exempting clauses are a cop-out. A promisor manages to put one in a contract and then is obligated to do nothing—only the other party is obligated.*

Lise: *But maybe the other party got a lower price because of the exemption clause.*

Harvey: *Often that's not so. Suppose the other party is a new Canadian and the exemption clause is in a standard form contract he's unfamiliar with?*

Lise: *But that must depend on whether the parties had equal bargaining power. Isn't that what the instructor said? One of the parties doesn't have to be exploited. Suppose the contract is between two established businesses?*

Harvey: *Then I still say there's no consideration on one side. What price does the business protected by an exempting clause pay for the other's promise?*

Lise: *The business may not be opting out of all its obligations. Then there's still consideration. Don't you remember, "It is not for the courts to concern themselves with the adequacy of consideration"?*

Harvey: *But suppose we're talking about a fundamental breach. Then what we have in effect is a total failure of consideration, even if technically we could find a little bit of consideration still there. Since you're quoting legal aphorisms, "The law does not concern itself with trivialities," either.*

Lise: *I think you have to assume business people know what they're doing and that such one-sided contracts are the exception. Maybe with a novice, yes, but with an established business, no.*

Harvey: *I'm beginning to get worried. Suppose a court decides an exemption clause shouldn't count because the breach is fundamental. If its reasoning is that there was a total failure of consideration, maybe there won't be any contract at all. Will that give the plaintiff what he wants? I thought he was suing for damages for breach.*

Lise: *Maybe we should go ask the instructor.*

Comment briefly on Harvey's last point. Would the remedies available to the plaintiff business be different if the court found that there was no consideration instead of there being a claim for damages for breach of contract?

On June 30, Sinkiewicz, a professional football player, signed a three-year contract with the Mariposa Football Club Ltd. The contract contained the following clause:

The Player promises and agrees that, during the term of this contract, he will not play football or engage in activities related to football for any other person, firm, corporation, or institution, except with the prior written consent of the Club, and that he will not, during the term of this contract, engage in any game or exhibition of basketball, baseball, wrestling, boxing, hockey, or any other sport that endangers his ability to perform his services hereunder without the prior written consent of the Club.

In July of the following year, Sinkiewicz accepted an offer from another professional football club, the Orillia Wildcats, and moved to Orillia intending to play with that club for the coming football season. He also arranged to play hockey in Orillia after the football season ended.

After learning about Sinkiewicz's breach, the officials of the Mariposa Football Club sued for damages and for an injunction restraining Sinkiewicz from continuing to break his contract. The Mariposa Club alleged that it had sustained irreparable injury in having to locate another player of Sinkiewicz's calibre, and that it had in the past spent considerable money in training Sinkiewicz as a professional football player. In defence, Sinkiewicz testified that he would be unable to earn his livelihood if prevented from playing football and hockey. Discuss the legal issues the court will consider in reaching its decision.

Brown, a painting contractor, made an oral contract with Hilton to paint the interior of Hilton's house for $1600, to be paid on completion of the work. Brown ran into difficulty when he painted the walls of the living room because the paint was pulled into the wall by the porous plaster. He had the same problem when he applied a second coat, then realized what was causing the trouble and applied what is known as a "sealer," so that the next coat might adhere properly. Leaving the living room until the sealer was dry, he began painting the dining room.

At that point, Hilton inspected the work and complained to Brown that the colour of the paint was not the colour she had selected. Brown became very annoyed and emphatically announced he would quit the job. Hilton urged him not to abandon the work without first seeing her husband, but in a huff he removed his materials and equipment. When he abandoned the work, Brown had still to finish painting the living room and had not begun to paint several other rooms in the house. It also appeared that the woodwork had been painted without having been sanded, and would have to be stripped and repainted. Brown brought an action against Hilton for $890, claiming $230 for materials and $660 for 33 hours work. Should he succeed?

On September 2, the Department of Government Services published an invitation to submit tenders for the supply of materials for construction of a large administrative building. Its advertisement specified that tenders were to be delivered on or before 3 p.m. on November 6 at the office of the Contracts Officer of the Department of Government Services in Ottawa.

Buttonville Brick, Inc. prepared an estimate of the cost of supplying brick for the project and then made out a tender for delivery to the Department of Government Services. The tender was for the supply of all the brick required at a price of $556 000—a price on which the company could expect to earn a profit of about $75 000.

On the morning of November 5, Buttonville's manager, Hodson, telephoned Bulldog Couriers Inc. to inquire whether it could deliver an important document in Ottawa by noon of the following day. He said, "A lot is at stake for us—maybe $100 000—and if you can't deliver our envelope by tomorrow noon, either I or one of the other people here is going to have to drive directly to Ottawa with it." Hodson was assured there would be no problem with delivery.

Bulldog sent a station wagon at once to pick up the envelope. Buttonville Brick completed a bill of lading on a form supplied by Bulldog. It read:

BULLDOG COURIERS INC.

BILL OF LADING

Date: November 5, 1999

Received at the point of origin on the date specified, from the shipper mentioned herein, the goods herein described, in apparent good order, except as noted (contents and conditions of contents of packages unknown) marked, consigned, and destined as indicated below, which the carrier agrees to carry and deliver to the consignee at the said destination. For other terms, see reverse side.

Point of origin
Buttonville Brick Ltd.,
100 Industrial Lane,
Buttonville, ON

Destination
Contracts Officer,
Department of Government Services,
100 Carling Drive,
Ottawa, ON

Contents	No. Pcs.	Weight	Charges

"Envelope—
  tender"
"Deliver before
  12 noon Nov. 6."
	"1"	"400 g"	"$15.00"

Declared value
(Maximum liability $3.00 per kg unless declared valuation states otherwise. If a value is declared see conditions on reverse hereof.)

(signed) "*Bernard Colley*
for Bulldog Couriers Inc."

(signed) "*S. Hodson*
for Buttonville Brick Ltd."

On the reverse side, the bill of lading stated:

VALUE

Unless otherwise specifically agreed to in writing, the carrier will not transport any goods declared to have a value in excess of $250. Enquiries for such service should be directed to the carrier's closest regional office.

APPLICABLE LAW

It is agreed that every service to be performed hereunder shall be subject to the laws relating to the terms and conditions to be contained in bills of lading applicable in Ontario under the Public Commercial Vehicles Act.

The van that took the envelope to Ottawa on its regular run was delayed because of a mechanical breakdown and the envelope was not delivered to its destination until 3:21 p.m. on November 6. As a result, it was rejected as an eligible tender. The contract was given to another bidder who, as it turned out, had submitted a bid of $590 000—$34 000 more than Buttonville's. Buttonville sued Bulldog Carriers, Inc. for consequential damages of $75 000.

At the trial the following excerpts from the Public Commercial Vehicles Act were cited:

12n (1) Except as provided in the regulations, every holder of an operating licence… shall issue a bill of lading to the person delivering or releasing goods to the licensee for transportation for compensation.

(2) A bill of lading shall contain such information as may be prescribed and shall include an acknowledgement of receipt by the carrier…therein described and an undertaking to carry such goods for delivery to the consignee or the person entitled to receive the goods and shall be signed by, or on behalf of, the issuing carrier…and by the consignor.

(3) The conditions set out in Schedule A shall be deemed to be a part of every contract for the transportation of goods for compensation.…

SCHEDULE A

1. The carrier of the goods herein described is liable for any loss thereof or damage or injury thereto, except as herein provided.

5. The carrier is not liable for loss, damage, or delay to any of the goods described in the bill of lading caused by an act of God, the Queen's or public enemies, riots, strikes, defect or inherent vice in the goods, the act or default of the shipper or owner.…

7. No carrier is bound to transport the goods by any particular public commercial vehicle or in time for any particular market or otherwise than with due despatch, unless by agreement specifically endorsed on the bill of lading and signed by the parties thereto.

9. Subject to paragraph 10, the amount of any loss, damage or injury for which the carrier is liable, whether or not the loss, damage or injury results from negligence, shall be computed on the basis of,

    (a) the value of the goods at the place and time of shipment including the freight and other charges if paid; or

    (b) where a value lower than that referred to in clause *a* has been represented in writing by the consignor or has been agreed upon, such lower value.

10. …the amount of any loss or damage computed under clause *a* or *b* of paragraph 9 shall not exceed $1.50 per pound [approximately $3.00 per kilogram] unless a higher value is declared on the face of the bill of lading by the consignor.

Develop arguments for the plaintiff and for the defendant in this action and express an opinion about the probable outcome.

PART

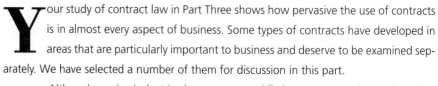

Special Types of Contract

Your study of contract law in Part Three shows how pervasive the use of contracts is in almost every aspect of business. Some types of contracts have developed in areas that are particularly important to business and deserve to be examined separately. We have selected a number of them for discussion in this part.

Although service industries have grown rapidly in recent years in number, size, and importance, the production and sale of goods remain central to the economy and to almost all retail business. In Chapter 16, we discuss the nature of sales contracts and their legal effects, particularly regarding ownership of goods and the risks assumed by the parties to a contract, the consequences of breach of contract, and the remedies available, for example, if a buyer fails to pay or if a seller delivers defective goods.

As Chapter 16 demonstrates, ownership of goods does not always coincide with possession. In Chapter 17, we examine two particular types of contract in which ownership and possession are necessarily separate—leasing and bailment. In recent years, leasing has become big business and the leasing of expensive equipment, as well as of items such as automobiles, has become an important alternative to sale. Bailment, of which leasing is but one special form, occurs in many business activities—for example, when articles are delivered to a person other than the owner for transportation, storage, or repair.

Chapter 18 discusses insurance law—an important aspect in the operation of every business. The general purpose of insurance is to protect a business from loss or damage to its property and from liability to others incurred in the operation of the business. The latter part of the chapter deals with the related topic of guarantees, that is, where a third person promises to perform a contract if the original promissor should default.

In Chapter 19 we examine two types of arrangement that are commonly used to expand a business—agency and franchising. Businesses, except the very smallest sole proprietorships, have always employed agents—to sell their goods, purchase supplies, and negotiate other types of contract. Franchising, by contrast, is a quite recent development but one that is of growing importance.

Most businesses (again, excepting the smallest sole proprietorships) also have employees. In Chapter 20 we concentrate on the employment relationship, the respective rights and duties of employers and employees, and the effects their conduct may have on third parties. We also examine the various laws that regulate employment relationships, such as workers' compensation, pay equity, and human rights.

Almost all business contracts, except contracts of barter or exchange, involve one party making payment to the other. To conclude this Part, Chapter 21 examines the use of negotiable instruments—cheques, promissory notes, and bills of exchange—and other methods of money transfer.

PART 4

Weblinks

The full texts of many of the statutes referred to in this Part can be accessed on the Internet, as follows:

gov.ab.ca/qp
Alberta

qp.gov.bc.ca/bcstats/
British Columbia

gov.mb.ca/che/statpub/free/index.html
Manitoba

gov.nb.ca/acts/
New Brunswick

www.gov.ns.ca/legi/legc/index.htm
Nova Scotia

www. attorneygeneral.jus.gov.on.ca/legis.htm
Ontario

Federal statutes may be accessed at <Canada.justice.gc.ca/STABLE/EN/Laws>.

In some cases the Act can be accessed directly; in others it must be accessed through an index of statutes.

Other Web sites of interest are:

www.ilrg.com/forms/busbillofsale.html
Contains a standard-form bill of sale

www.leasingcanada.com
The Canadian leasing resource page

www.cfla-acfl.ca
The Canadian Finance and Leasing Association

www.ibc.ca/English/legal/legal.htm
The legal division of the Insurance Bureau of Canada

www.cfa.ca
The Canadian Franchise Association

www.wwlia.org/ca-fran.htm
Franchise law in Canada

info.load-otea.hrdc-drhc.gc.ca/~weeweb/homeen.shtml
The Federal Government's Web site on workplace equity

www.droit.umontreal.ca/doc/biblio/en/bv/sources/travail.html
On employment law in Canada

www.acjnet.org/youthfaq/labour.html
Frequently asked questions on labour law

www.bank-banque-canada.ca
The Bank of Canada

16 SALE OF GOODS

The Sale of Goods Act

Terms in a Contract of Sale

Title to Goods

Remedies of the Seller

The Seller's Liability

Remedies of the Buyer

We begin our review of the more important types of commercial contracts with an examination of the contract of sale. Contracts for the sale of goods are the most common type of contract and the most readily understood. Nevertheless, perhaps because the contract of sale is so common, it generated a vast amount of case law, which was eventually codified into a statute—the Sale of Goods Act.

Unlike the preceding chapters in Part Three, which were primarily concerned with the *common law* of contracts, this chapter concentrates on the provisions of a *statute*. In it we examine such questions as:

- what is the scope of the Sale of Goods Act?
- what are the terms that it implies in a contract of sale?
- how is the ownership of goods transferred?
- to what extent is the seller liable for defective or unsatisfactory goods?
- what are the remedies available to buyers and sellers?

THE SALE OF GOODS ACT

History

When the term "contract" is used, the type of contract that probably springs to mind is the contract of sale. But in the long history of the common law, the law of sale of goods is a relatively recent development. The economic activity of medieval England was mainly agrarian, and much of the law was concerned with rules for holding land. Not until the late 18th century did the law governing the distribution and sale of goods become the subject of frequent decisions in the courts. In succeeding years, general principles began to emerge from the decisions of the courts, and by the latter part of the 19th century, these principles had become well established. By this time the body of case law was immense. In 1893, the British Parliament simplified the case law by codifying it into a comprehensive statute called the Sale of

Goods Act. All the common law provinces in Canada have since adopted this Act, almost word for word.[1]

The Sale of Goods Act, unlike most legislation, made no attempt to change the law; its purpose was to set out succinctly the law as it then existed, with clarification where necessary to resolve conflicts between competing principles. In particular, the cases decided before the Act was passed had recognized several important implied terms that formed a part of every contract for the sale of goods, unless those terms were inconsistent with the purposes of the contract or were expressly excluded by the parties. Such terms were *codified*: they are now implied under the Sale of Goods Act just as they were implied by case law before the Act was passed. We shall discuss these implied terms in the next section of this chapter.

Ownership and Possession

The words "ownership" and "possession" raise difficult analytical problems. We recognize the distinction in everyday activity, as when we lend possession of an object to a friend yet retain ownership of it. We correctly assume that if a friend refused to return our car, we would have a remedy in the courts against that person to protect our ownership or *title*. We have seen also in our discussion of mistake in Chapter 8 that, in English law, the distinction between possession and ownership of goods is carried to its logical conclusion, since the owner may recover stolen goods from a subsequent innocent purchaser.

The separation of ownership and possession occurs frequently in contracts for the sale of goods: when the contract is a sale that passes title to the buyer immediately, possession often remains with the seller or with a carrier for some time afterwards; as we shall see, under instalment sales contracts, a vendor often retains title to goods as security for payment of the price while possession passes to the buyer. Transactions other than sales, such as pledges, consignments, and rental arrangements, also separate ownership from possession. In this chapter, we shall often refer to the passing of title independently of possession and to a change in possession without a transfer of title.

Definition of Goods

For the Sale of Goods Act to apply, the subject-matter of the contract must be "**goods**," which the Act (section 1(1)) defines as meaning "all chattels personal, other than things in action and money...." As we shall see in Part Six, property is divided into two main classes: real property and personal property. Real property is confined to interests in land. All other property is called personal property, which in turn has two categories: choses ("things") in action, and goods or **chattels**. We have already discussed the nature of choses in action in Chapter 12 in relation to the assignment of contractual rights. In contrast to choses in action, which obtain their value because they represent binding obligations, goods derive their value intrinsically, that is, simply because people want the goods themselves, for the utility or satisfaction they provide.

goods
personal property, other than money and choses in action

chattels
tangible personal property

When discussing the requirement of writing in Chapter 10, we noted that a distinction is made between contracts for the sale of goods and other contracts, for instance those for work and materials. The distinction is not always an easy one to make. For example, in contracting to have a house constructed, a boat built, or a central heating system installed, the buyer agrees to pay for a finished product as well as for the labour that produced it. A court may have to decide whether it was the work or the materials that constituted the essence of the contract: if the final

---

1. Although the wording of the various provincial Sale of Goods Acts is virtually the same, the numbering of sections differs considerably. For simplicity of reference in the remainder of this chapter, we shall refer to the section numbers used in the Ontario act, R.S.O. 1990, c. S.1.

value is mainly the result of the skill and labour that have gone into its preparation, the contract will be one for work and materials and not for "goods" as defined by the Act.[2] In practice, the distinction is not always important, since many of the legal principles that apply to contracts for work and materials are much the same as provisions in the Sale of Goods Act. For example, a Canadian court has held that a contract for work and materials is also subject as a matter of common law to an implied condition of fitness, analogous to the condition of fitness implied in contracts for the sale of goods.[3] But that will not be so in every case.

CASE 16.1

The plaintiff was infected with HIV as a result of artificial insemination performed by her physician in 1985. The physician had screened the semen donors and taken the usual precautions according to the standard practice in Canada at that time (when no test was available to detect the virus in blood or semen). The trial jury found the physician negligent and awarded damages of $883 800, but the finding of negligence was overturned on appeal.

However, the plaintiff also based her claim on other grounds. The physician had supplied "goods," namely the semen; the semen was not fit for the purpose for which it was supplied. Thus, the plaintiff claimed, there was a breach of the "seller's" duty under the Sale of Goods Act.

The Supreme Court of Canada ruled

1. that the contract was one for the supply of services, not of goods.
2. that the courts should be wary of implying terms in contracts for the supply of services, especially when the contract involved the supply of products that carry inherent risks.

The physician had not been negligent and should not face a stricter liability for goods that are incidental to the service supplied than that imposed by the normal duty of care.[4]

Types of Contract of Sale

In the Sale of Goods Act, a contract of sale "is a contract whereby the seller transfers or agrees to transfer the property in the goods to the buyer for a money consideration, called the price." Money must form a part of the transaction; it follows that a straight barter of goods where no money changes hands does not come within the statute.

agreement to sell
a contract of sale in which the transfer of goods is deferred to some future time

The Act distinguishes between a sale and an **agreement to sell**. In a sale, the seller transfers ownership or title in goods to the buyer at the moment the contract is made. In an agreement to sell, the transfer is deferred until a future time; that time is either a specified date, or an indefinite date that depends on the fulfilment of a particular requirement. The Act applies to both sales and agreements to sell. An agreement to sell may be formed even when the goods are non-existent. A contract to sell goods to be manufactured in three months' time or to sell a crop at a stated price per bushel when it has grown in a certain field, are examples of agreements to sell. An agreement to sell is a binding contract just as are other contracts containing promises of future conduct.

---

2. The examples mentioned—a house, a boat, and a central heating system—have all been held to be contracts for "work and materials"; see Hodgkinson v. Hitch House Ltd. (1985), 60 O.R. (2d) 793. By contrast, a restaurant meal has been held to be "goods": Gee v. White Spot Ltd. (1986), 32 D.L.R. (4th) 238.

3. A.G. of Canada v. Laminated Structures & Holdings Ltd. (1961), 28 D.L.R. (2d) 92, per Macdonald, J., at 100–1.

4. ter Neuzen v. Korn (1995), 127 D.L.R.(4th) 577. See also Pitman Estate v. Bain (1994), 19 C.C.L.T. (2d) 1 (Ont. Gen. Div.), a case involving HIV-tainted blood.

We should also distinguish a contract of sale from a transaction known as a **consignment**. This is not always easy, since the word "consignment" is used in two different senses. In common usage, a consignment is simply a shipment of goods from one person or business to another in performance of a contract of sale; here, the consignor is a seller and the consignee a buyer. But in a more technical sense, a consignor may send goods to an agent (consignee) who will offer them for sale at their new location. In this instance, ownership in the goods does not pass between the consignor and consignee: if the consignee sells the goods, the title passes directly from the consignor to the purchaser. Expensive items displayed in the window of a jeweller's shop, for example, may not be part of the jeweller's own stock-in-trade but simply be held on consignment from a manufacturer or wholesaler. The distinction between sale and consignment may be important, since it may determine who bears the risk if the goods are damaged or destroyed.

consignment
the shipment of goods from one business to another for the purpose of sale

CASE 16.2

Win Sun Produce, a small family business engaged in importing fruit and vegetables, entered into an agreement with Pacific Produce, a large wholesale fruit and vegetable business, to supply Pacific with a container shipment of 950 boxes of pomelos imported from Thailand. The pomelos were delivered to Pacific, together with a "purchase order" invoicing the pomelos at $47 per box. A "load sheet," signed by the person at Pacific who took delivery, referred to the "consignment" as having been received.

Pacific had not previously stocked pomelos and found that they did not sell well. They asked Win Sun to take back 140 boxes, which they did, crediting Pacific with the

sum of $6580. Pacific was still unable to sell all the remaining pomelos and eventually many of them rotted. Win Sun claimed the balance of the price. Pacific contested this, claiming that the pomelos had been supplied on consignment and still belonged to Win Sun.

The trial judge held that the contract was one of consignment. On appeal, the British Columbia Court of Appeal ruled that the contract was one of sale. The word "consignment" in the load sheet had been used in the sense of "shipment." If the contract had been one of consignment, there would have been no need for Pacific to ask Win Sun to take some back or for Pacific to have been credited with part of the price.[5]

TERMS IN A CONTRACT OF SALE
The *Caveat Emptor* Principle

We encountered the Latin maxim *caveat emptor* briefly in Chapter 9 in our discussion of fraudulent misrepresentation. *Caveat emptor* means, literally, "let the buyer beware," that is, the risk is with the buyer. In other words, one must be reasonably cautious when buying goods in circumstances where a buyer can, and usually does, exercise personal judgment. *Caveat emptor* is, however, not a rigid rule but a flexible general principle, subject to the limits put on it by common sense and customary business practice.

The *caveat emptor* principle applies where the goods are in existence and are specific items that may be inspected by the buyer, and when the seller has made *no* misrepresentations about them. In these circumstances, *caveat emptor* is a sensible rule: the buyer has the opportunity to exercise her judgment by examining the goods; if she distrusts her own judgment or has doubts, she may choose to bargain for an express term stating that the goods have a particular quality she requires.

Caveat emptor encourages buyers to take care and to determine that the goods are what they want before they contract to buy them. However, there are circumstances in which the principle, if not qualified, would invite abuse by unscrupulous sellers. For example, a buyer must sometimes rely upon the knowledge or expert judgment of the seller, or by mutual consent, a buyer

---

5. Win Sun Produce Co. v. Albert Fisher Canada Ltd., [1998] B.C.J. No. 1091.

may sometimes place special confidence or trust in the seller. Accordingly, various implied terms to protect buyers were evolved in the decided cases and are now found in the Sale of Goods Act.

Statutory Protection for the Buyer: Implied Terms

Conditions and Warranties

In Chapter 14, we noted the unfortunate confusion caused by using the word "condition" in different senses. The Sale of Goods Act has used "condition" to mean a major or essential term of the contract, the breach of which relieves the injured party from further duty to perform the contract, if she so elects. The Act uses "warranty" to mean a minor or non-essential term, the breach of which does not relieve the injured party from the bargain—she must perform her side, but she may sue for damages. In this chapter, we use the two words with the meanings given them by the Act. Some terms implied by the Act are conditions and others are warranties; we must be careful to note which terms fall into each class.

In the remainder of this section, we discuss the more important terms of a contract of sale that are implied by the Act. It is important to remember, however, that these terms are only implied if there is no express provision to the contrary in the contract.

Seller's Title

Caveat emptor applies to the qualities of goods, not their ownership. Inspection by the buyer normally does nothing to indicate who owns the goods. In offering to sell goods, the seller impliedly represents that he has the right to do so. The Sale of Goods Act states (section 13):

13. In a contract of sale, unless the circumstances of the contract are such as to show a different intention, there is

    (a) An implied condition on the part of the seller that in the case of a sale the seller has a right to sell the goods, and that in the case of an agreement to sell the seller will have a right to sell the goods at the time when the property is to pass;

    (b) An implied warranty that the buyer will have and enjoy quiet possession of the goods; and

    (c) An implied warranty that the goods will be free from any charge or encumbrance in favour of any third party, not declared or known to the buyer before or at the time when the contract is made.

implied term as to title
it is implied that the seller has a right to sell the goods

An example of the **implied term as to title** is provided in Illustration 16.1.

ILLUSTRATION 16.1

Alberti purchases a second-hand refrigerator from Blake. It later turns out that Cowan, not Blake, was the owner of the refrigerator. Cowan retakes possession of the refrigerator from Alberti.

In the contract of sale between Alberti and Blake, there was an implied undertaking by Blake that he had a right to sell the refrigerator, that Alberti should have quiet possession of it (that is, not have physical possession of it interrupted), and that it would be free from any encumbrance in favour of a third person. None of these requirements was satisfied. Alberti is, therefore, entitled to recover money damages from Blake for breach of an *implied condition of title*.

Description

implied term as to description
it is implied that goods sold by description will conform to the description

The Act sets out the circumstances in which there is an **implied term as to description**, as follows (section 14):

14. Where there is a contract for the sale of goods by description, there is an implied condition that the goods will correspond with the description, and, if the sale is by

sample as well as by description, it is not sufficient that the bulk of the goods correspond with the sample if the goods do not also correspond with the description.

The word "description" applies to a generic characteristic of the goods (for example, that blouses offered for sale are cotton blouses instead of, say, nylon blouses) and not to words of praise about how good the blouses are (for example, that they will last a lifetime).

ILLUSTRATION 16.2

Bridges bought from ProMotors an electric motor for use in his workshop. The motor was described in ProMotors' catalogue as "heavy-duty, double bearing." In fact, the motor supplied had only a single bearing, although that was not apparent without taking the motor apart, and it burned out after only three months of use.

Bridges may sue ProMotors for damages based on the breach of an implied term to the effect that the goods will correspond with the description.

Suitability and Quality

The Sale of Goods Act makes two exceptions to the general rule that the buyer must exercise care as to the suitability and quality of the goods (section 15):

15. Subject to this Act and any statute in that behalf, there is no implied warranty or condition as to the quality or fitness for any particular purpose of goods supplied under a contract of sale, except as follows:

    1. Where the buyer, expressly or by implication, makes known to the seller the particular purpose for which the goods are required so as to show that the buyer relies on the seller's skill or judgment, and the goods are of a description that it is in the course of the seller's business to supply (whether he is the manufacturer or not), there is an implied condition that the goods will be reasonably fit for such purpose, but in the case of a contract for the sale of a specified article under its patent or other trade name, there is no implied condition as to its fitness for any particular purpose.

    2. Where the goods are bought by description from a seller who deals in goods of that description (whether he is the manufacturer or not), there is an implied condition that the goods shall be of merchantable quality, but if the buyer has examined the goods, there is no implied condition as regards defects that such examination ought to have revealed.

The **implied term of fitness** offers protection to a buyer who has a particular purpose in mind for the goods. To have the advantage of this provision, the buyer should declare this purpose specifically if it is not one of the general uses for such goods.

implied term of fitness
it is implied that the goods are of a type that is suitable for the purpose for which they are bought

ILLUSTRATION 16.3

Slack buys 30 m of clothesline wire from a hardware store and uses it as a cable for a homemade elevator in his barn. The wire breaks with him in the elevator, causing him injury. He sues the hardware dealer for damages.

Slack will not succeed because (1) he did not expressly state the particular purpose for which he intended to use the wire and so did not rely on the seller's skill and judgment, and (2) his damages were not of a kind that were a likely consequence of normal use of clothesline wire.

A purpose need not be stated in so many words if it is obvious; when buying buns in a bakeshop, one need not announce, "I propose to eat these." The essential requirement for Part 1 of section 15 noted above is that the buyer relied upon the seller's skill and judgment.[6]

CASE 16.3

Lavalin ordered 57 000 kilograms of welding electrodes from Carbonic for use in a project involving the fabrication of a cross-country buried gas transmission line. The electrodes turned out to be incapable of producing a satisfactory weld in the vertical down position. Lavalin had made known to Carbonic the fact that the electrodes were to be used in a gas transmission line, apparently assuming that Carbonic's engineers would know that the electrodes would have to be capable of functioning in a vertical position. In fact, Carbonic had no experience of pipeline work.

The court held that Carbonic had implied that it was familiar with pipeline work and that Lavalin had relied on Carbonic's skill and judgment. Lavalin was entitled to damages for the costs incurred with respect to the acquisition and handling of the useless electrodes.[7]

The Act provides that the implied condition of fitness does not apply when an article is sold under its trade name. In *Baldry v. Marshall*, the court had to consider the scope of this proviso. Lord Justice Bankes said:

> The mere fact that an article sold is described in the contract by its trade name does not necessarily make the sale a sale under a trade name. Whether it is so or not depends upon the circumstances....In my opinion the test of an article having been sold under its trade name within the meaning of the proviso is: did the buyer specify it under its trade name in such a way as to indicate that he is satisfied, rightly or wrongly, that it will answer his purpose, and that he is not relying on the skill or judgment of the seller, however great that skill or judgment may be?[8]

Part 2 of section 15 states when a seller is responsible for the *quality* of goods rather than for their suitability for any particular purpose. Under this part, to establish a breach of condition by the seller, the buyer need not show that she relied on the seller's skill and judgment.[9]

implied term of merchantable quality
it is implied that the goods are in reasonable condition and free from defects that would make them unsuitable for use

The **implied term of merchantable quality** needs explanation: to paraphrase an Australian decision, goods of merchantable quality should be in such a state that a buyer, fully acquainted with the facts and having found the goods in reasonably sound condition, would buy them without reduction below the current market price and without special guarantees.[10] The word "reasonably" needs to be emphasized; especially in the case of the sale of used goods, there is no warranty that the goods are entirely free from defect.

One problem is that the implied condition relates to the quality of the goods at the time of the contract, yet it may be some time later that the defect is discovered. Or it may be that the defect did not exist at the time of the sale but developed subsequently, perhaps due to misuse by the buyer or to some other reason. It is, consequently, a question of fact whether an article that

---

6. Chaproniere v. Mason (1905), 21 T.L.R. 633; McCready Products Ltd. v. Sherwin Williams Co. of Canada Ltd. (1985), 61 A.R. 234. The seller's failure to provide adequate instructions as to use of the product and to warn of possible dangers, may constitute a breach of the warranty: see Caners v. Eli Lilley Canada Inc. (1996), 134 D.L.R. (4th) 730.

7. SNC-Lavalin International Inc. v. Liquid Carbonic Inc. (1996), 28 B.L.R. (2d) 1.

8. [1925] 1 K.B. 260 at 266–7.

9. Wren v. Holt, [1903] 1 K.B. 610.

10. Australian Knitting Mills Ltd. v. Grant (1933), 50 C.L.R. 387, per Dixon, J., at 418; also Bristol Tramways v. Fiat Motors, [1910] 2 K.B. 831, per Farwell, L.J., at 841.

ceases to function properly was defective at the time of sale; a new car that develops transmission problems within a few months is likely to have been defective all along; one that runs well for several years before developing a fault may well have been in satisfactory condition at the time of sale.

CASE 16.4

McCann bought an electric blanket from Sears. More than 10 years later it caught fire, causing damage to McCann's bedroom. McCann brought action for breach of contract pursuant to the Sale of Goods Act on the ground that there was an implied condition that the electric blanket was reasonably free from defect. The court held that, in view of the time that had elapsed (during which the blanket had functioned without any problems), the buyer had failed to satisfy the burden of proving that the defect existed when the blanket was bought.[11]

In practice, which part of section 15 is the more relevant to a buyer's complaint is often uncertain as the two parts tend to overlap in their application. Professor Waddams has commented, "It is not inappropriate that a buyer who buys goods for their usual purpose and finds them unfit should be entitled to complain both of their general unmerchantability and also of their unfitness for the buyer's own purpose."[12]

CONTEMPORARY ISSUE

The Y2K Bug and the Sale of Goods Act

There has been much discussion of the "Y2K Bug," but relatively little has been written about the legal consequences of Y2K crashes. According to one legal commentator:

> The end of a century tends to be accompanied by a number of doomsday predictions, as various people predict the imminent demise of the world and any number of other unfortunate events. The end of a millennium increases the ranks of the prophets of doom, with large quantities of soothsayers predicting the end is near. The computer revolution has added another cause for end of century/end of millennium hysteria—namely the year 2000 date problem (referred to herein as "Y2K")....Estimates are circulating that the cost of dealing with Y2K worldwide is in the $600 billion range, with the cost in Canada alone totalling $7 billion....The Y2K problem raises a cluster of legal issues...a class action suit claiming $50 million in damages has been launched in California against a software firm that allegedly is unwilling to correct Y2K problems for free....Liability for a malfunctioning computer system as a result of Y2K could also arise under the various provincial *Sale of Goods Acts* across Canada....The user would have to prove, of course, that a non Y2K-compliant system was not of merchantable quality, which for some systems would arguably not be that hard to prove as it ground to an inglorious halt on 1-1-2000.

Source: George S. Takach, "Canada: Computer Law 1-1-2000—Legal Strategy and Tactics for the Millennium Date Problem," *Mondaq Business Briefing,* September 17, 1998.

continued

---

11. McCann v. Sears Canada Ltd. (1998), 43 B.L.R. (2d) 217.
12. Waddams, *Products Liability* (3rd ed.), p. 81. Toronto: Carswell Co. Ltd., 1993.

However, according to another legal expert:

> If it becomes a technical debate, then in my view the software vendor will win hands down because in most cases the court will accept that Y2K is not a hidden defect....I'm not sure how sympathetic a court will be to a sophisticated business....Defence lawyers will successfully argue that two-digit dated software was a "design limitation" that most programmers used until recently...and that it was foreseeable there would be a problem at or near the end of the century.

Source: Howard Solomon, "Courts Won't Buy Y2K as Defect," *Technology in Government*, Vol. 6, No. 1, p. 16 (January 1999).

Questions to Consider

1. Can a software or computer system that crashed on January 1, 2000, be said to be of "merchantable quality"?

2. Given that the Y2K problem has been well known for several years, should the onus be on the buyer or the seller to ensure that a computer system is suitable for the buyer's needs? Does it, perhaps, depend on when the system was purchased?

NOTE: For more information on the legal aspects of the Y2K problem, visit the web site of The Year 2000 Information Centre at **www.year2000.com**. The U.S. Federal Government also has a web site providing advice on Y2K issues at **www.ftc.gov/bcp/conline/edcams/y2k/index.html**.

Sale by Sample

implied term that goods correspond with sample
it is implied that, when a sample of the goods to be sold has been provided, the actual goods supplied will correspond to that sample in type and quality

The last of the implied terms recognized in the Act is the **implied term that goods correspond with sample.** The Act provides (section 16(2)):

16. (2) In the case of a contract for sale by sample, there is an implied condition

    (a) that the bulk will correspond with the sample in quality;

    (b) that the buyer will have a reasonable opportunity of comparing the bulk with the sample; and

    (c) that the goods will be free from any defect rendering them unmerchantable that would not be apparent on reasonable examination of the sample.

ILLUSTRATION 16.4

The plant supervisor at High Grade Printing Company examines a sample of choice quality paper supplied by Universal Paper Co. Ltd. and approves its purchase. When the paper is used in one of the books printed by High Grade, it turns yellow and the entire run must be done again. High Grade sues Universal Paper for damages for its loss. In defence, Universal Paper pleads that the paper supplied was exactly the same as the sample on which the purchase was based, and that a chemical test of the sample would have revealed the defect.

The printing company should succeed in its action if it can show that the defect would not have been apparent on an ordinary examination, and that an ordinary examination in this business would *not* include a chemical test.

Checklist: Implied Terms in a Contract for the Sale of Goods

Subject to certain exceptions and qualifications, the Sale of Goods Act implies the following contractual terms:

- an implied condition that the seller has (or will have) a right to sell the goods
- an implied warranty that the buyer will have and enjoy quiet possession of the goods
- an implied warranty that the goods will be free from any undisclosed charge or encumbrance
- an implied condition that the goods will correspond with the description under which they are sold
- an implied condition that the goods will be reasonably fit for the purpose for which they are required if that purpose was made known to the seller
- an implied condition that the goods will be of merchantable quality
- in the case of a sale by sample, an implied condition that the bulk will correspond with the sample

Exemption Clauses

The Sale of Goods Act contains the following provision (section 53):

> 53. Where any right, duty or liability would arise under a contract of sale by implication of law, it may be negatived or varied by express agreement or by the course of dealing between the parties, or by usage, if the usage is such as to bind both parties to the contract.

As a result, a seller may insist that a contract of sale contain an express term exonerating it from the liability normally imposed by implied terms. A prospective buyer may, of course, refuse to enter into a contract containing such an exemption clause; if she agrees to the clause, she loses the protection afforded a buyer by the Act.

In the belief that the terms implied by the Act are fair and equitable, the courts have restricted the circumstances in which a seller may absolve himself of liability under the Act. Clear and direct language must be used to contract out of statutory protections.

CASE 16.5

Syncrude orders 32 gearboxes from Hunter, a manufacturer, to drive its conveyor belts in the Alberta tar sands project. Syncrude provided specifications of what the gearboxes were required to do and Hunter designed them to meet those specifications.

The contract contained an express term guaranteeing the gearboxes for two years. When the period had expired, the gearboxes developed faults that were found to be due to faulty design. Syncrude could not succeed in an action on the express term, but the Supreme Court of Canada held that the implied term of fitness under section 15 of the Sale of Goods Act could still be relied on. The existence of an express warranty was not inconsistent with the statutory warranties.[13]

---

13. Hunter Engineering Co. v. Syncrude Canada Ltd. (1989), 57 D.L.R. (4th) 321. See also Fording Coal Ltd. v. Harnischfeger Corp. of Canada (1991), 6 B.L.R. (2d) 157.

If the words used in an exemption clause do not precisely describe the type of liability disclaimed, the courts will normally find that the implied liability is still part of the contract. Thus, if a seller includes an express term that "all warranties implied by statute are hereby excluded," the seller will avoid liability under all those implied terms that are *warranties* but not under those that are *conditions*.[14] Moreover, if the seller expressly promised that the goods would be of a certain quality or type, an exemption clause that refers only to *implied* terms will not free him from obligations under this *express* term.

CASE 16.6

Allan agrees to purchase a car from Lambeth Motors Ltd. In the contract the car is described as "a new, 190-horsepower, six-cylinder sedan." There is also a clause, inserted by the seller, that "all conditions, warranties, and liabilities implied by statute, common law, or otherwise are hereby excluded." After taking delivery, Allan discovers that the car is not new and has only four cylinders, and he sues for damages.

The exempting clause refers only to implied terms. The undertaking that the car is new and has six cylinders is an express term in the contract of sale. The seller has therefore failed to exempt itself from liability and must pay damages.[15]

The courts have declared, moreover, that a seller cannot so completely exempt himself from liability that he may default on his bargain with impunity. Consequently, the courts would not give effect to an exemption clause that gives a seller immunity from action if he delivers goods entirely different from those contracted for by the buyer or if he delivers goods to which he does not have good title.[16] In effect, the courts have held that a contract for the sale of goods would be deprived of all meaning if a seller's obligation were merely to deliver the goods, "if he felt like it." (We have already discussed the doctrine of fundamental breach in relation to exemption clauses in contracts generally in Chapter 14, and must keep in mind the policy of the courts in giving effect to an allocation of risk expressly agreed to between the parties.)

With respect to consumer sales, some provinces now prevent sellers from exempting themselves from liabilities under the implied conditions and warranties in the Sale of Goods Act. In these jurisdictions, the implied conditions and warranties continue to apply and provide a remedy for breach even when a customer has signed a contract expressly exempting the seller from liability. We shall discuss consumer protection legislation in Chapter 32.

Payment

Many contracts of sale set out the time of payment expressly; in others it may be implied from the terms of the contract and the particular circumstances. When the contract itself gives no guidance about when the buyer is to pay, the courts assume that delivery and payment are concurrent conditions; the transaction is presumed to be a cash sale. But this presumption may be rebutted by the circumstances in which the contract is made. For example, when payment from a customer is accepted by credit card, the buyer is normally entitled to delivery of the goods immediately, before payment by the credit card company.

The courts interpret the time set for payment as a warranty unless the parties have expressed themselves otherwise. Consequently, a seller is not entitled to rescind the contract of sale and have the goods back simply because payment is not made on time. He must be content

14. Gregorio v. Intrans-Corp. (1994), 115 D.L.R. (4th) 200 (Ont.C.A.).

15. Andrews Bros. Ltd. v. Singer & Co. Ltd., [1934] 1 K.B. 17.

16. Pinnock Brothers v. Lewis and Peat Ltd., [1923] 1 K.B. 690; Karsales (Harrow) Ltd. v. Wallis, [1956] 2 All E.R. 866; Canadian-Dominion Leasing Corp. Ltd. v. Suburban Superdrug Ltd. (1966), 56 D.L.R. (2d) 43.

with an action for the price of the goods. But the parties may agree on other terms. A seller may insist on a term entitling him to retake possession in the event of non-payment. This provision is characteristic of the instalment sale, to be considered separately in Chapter 30.

Delivery

The terms in a contract of sale relating to delivery are mainly of three kinds: terms relating to quantity to be delivered, the time of delivery, and the place of delivery. We shall deal with them in turn.

A term specifying the quantity of goods to be delivered is a condition. If the term is broken, that is, if the seller delivers a substantially different quantity, the buyer is free to reject the goods. Her right to do so exists whether a greater or lesser quantity than promised is delivered. The buyer may, of course, choose to treat the contract as not having been discharged by breach of condition and take all or part of what is delivered. If she does so, she must pay for what she takes at the contract rate.

The time specified for delivery is also usually a condition, so that if the goods are not delivered on time the buyer may rescind the contract. She is free to look elsewhere for the goods she needs as soon as she learns they will not be available. If the parties agree that the goods are to be delivered as soon as they are available without specifying a time, then delivery is to occur within a reasonable time, taking into account all the circumstances. What constitutes a reasonable time for delivery may vary according to the place of delivery: delivery may occur at the seller's place of business, the buyer's place of business, or some intermediate point.

Often, a commodity wholesaler or importer keeps its goods stored in the warehouse of a storage company, and a firm buying the goods may want to leave them there until it has arranged to store them itself or until it has resold them. In these circumstances, when the seller and buyer do not arrange a physical delivery of the goods, when does the delivery take place? The Sale of Goods Act states (section 28(3)):

> 28. (3) Where the goods at the time of sale are in the possession of a third person there is no delivery by the seller to the buyer unless and until such third person acknowledges to the buyer that the goods are being held on the buyer's behalf....

Thus, delivery takes place when the warehouse firm sends a notice to the buyer that it is holding the goods on the buyer's behalf.

The place of delivery is normally either the seller's place of business or wherever the goods happen to be located at the time of the contract. The parties may, however, express a different intention, or their intention may be implied from trade custom. Thus, when we order goods from a department store and give the clerk our address, the agreed place of delivery is our residence.

An offer for sale sometimes states, along with the asking price, the terms of delivery. It may, for example, quote wheat at so much per bushel *FOB Winnipeg*, or steel at so much for a shipment per tonne *CIF Hamilton*. There are other forms of quotations, but FOB and CIF are the most common. FOB means that the seller will place the goods at that location "free on board" the type of transportation specified; when a CIF (cost, insurance, freight) price is quoted, the seller undertakes to arrange insurance, ship the goods, and send an insurance policy, bill of lading, and invoice to the buyer. (These, and other, standard terms are widely used in international trade and are discussed further in Chapter 33.) Another common type of contract is the *COD* (cash on delivery) contract in which the seller's duty is to deliver the goods at the buyer's place of business or residence.

Risk of Loss

If buyer and seller do not expressly agree when the risk for loss caused by damage to or destruction of the goods will pass from the seller to the buyer, it becomes necessary to imply such a term from the contract as a whole. In FOB and CIF contracts, it is reasonably implied that the goods remain at the risk of the seller until they have been delivered to the carrier, and in COD contracts, until the seller or the carrier has delivered them to the buyer. Parties may not think to include an express term concerning the passing of risk, and it may often be impossible to discover an implied term on the subject from the terms of the contract. Such an omission, though unfortunate, is understandable, since the great majority of contracts of sale proceed without any loss occurring between the time of making the agreement and the receipt of the goods by the buyer.

When a loss does occur, however, it is possible that both parties may disclaim any interest in or responsibility for the goods. The reason for their disclaimers is that the risk of loss follows the title to the goods unless the parties have agreed otherwise: the party that has title ordinarily suffers the loss.[17] A first approach therefore is to consult the general rules used to determine who has title under the Sale of Goods Act.

TITLE TO GOODS

Specific Goods

specific goods
goods in existence and agreed on as the subject-matter of the sale

The first four rules set down in the Sale of Goods Act (section 19) for the passing of title relate to **specific goods**, that is, to goods in existence and identified and agreed on as the subject-matter of the sale at the time the contract is formed. These rules apply unless a contrary intention of the parties can be inferred from their conduct or from customary trade practice. Accordingly, we must always read the rule in the context of each transaction.

Rule 1

Where there is an unconditional contract for the sale of specific goods in a deliverable state, the property in the goods passes to the buyer *when the contract is made*, and it is immaterial whether the time of payment or the time of delivery or both is postponed.

ILLUSTRATION 16.5

Maple Leaf Appliances Ltd. is having its annual January sale. Late on a Saturday afternoon, Haag buys a new television set displayed on the floor and pays for it by a cheque post-dated five days later. The set is to be delivered on Monday. The parties never discuss which of them is to take the risk of loss before the set is delivered.

On the Sunday, burglars break into the seller's premises and steal the television set. Haag stops payment on the cheque. Maple Leaf Appliances sues Haag for the price of the set.

According to traditional analysis, title and risk are assumed to pass to the buyer at the same time and the action in Illustration 16.5 would succeed; title passed to Haag on Saturday and the loss would be hers. This traditional analysis is based on a typical transaction between two businesses; the purchaser would generally have insurance coverage for newly acquired goods. It bears little relation, however, to a modern consumer sales transaction. On the one hand, a consumer would think of the television set as being "hers" when she left the store and would object if the store were to resell it. On the other hand, she would assume that the retailer remained entirely responsible for the set until it was safely delivered. In other words, in the mind of a typical consumer, title and risk of loss or damage would be separate concepts. This separation is not unreasonable but the extent to which the courts will recognize it is uncertain.

If Maple Leaf Appliances had delayed delivery without Haag's request or consent and the theft had occurred instead on Monday night, so that the loss might have been avoided if the set had been delivered to Haag as agreed, Haag would not be liable to pay for the set.

---

17. For a recent example of this rule, see A.M.S. Equipment Inc. v. Case, [1999] B.C.J. No. 124.

Rule 2

Where there is a contract for the sale of specific goods and the seller is bound to do something to the goods for the purpose of putting them into a deliverable state, the property does not pass until such thing is done and the buyer has received notice.

ILLUSTRATION 16.6

During the same January sale described in Illustration 16.5, another customer, Oliveira, agrees to buy a second-hand television set that Maple Leaf is displaying, but a term of the agreement is that Maple Leaf will replace the picture tube. It had not done so when the set is stolen. The title has not passed to Oliveira, and she is not liable for the price.

Even if Maple Leaf Appliances had replaced the picture tube shortly after Oliveira left the store, she would not have the title unless she had also been *notified* that the replacement had been done before the set was stolen. Often, when a seller undertakes to deliver the goods, he will not communicate separately with the buyer to say that the goods are now in a deliverable state but will simply deliver them. In these circumstances, the required notice to the buyer is satisfied by delivery, and the title passes at the time of delivery.

Rule 3

Where there is a contract for the sale of specific goods in a deliverable state but the seller is bound to weigh, measure, test, or do some other act or thing with reference to the goods for the purpose of ascertaining their price, the property does not pass until such act or thing is done and the buyer has received notice.

ILLUSTRATION 16.7

McTavish, Frobisher & Co. agrees to buy a pile of beaver skins from Pond, a trapper, at an agreed price per skin. Before Pond counts the skins, most of them disappear mysteriously. Here, the title has not passed to the buyer, and in the absence of any special agreement between the parties, the loss is Pond's.

Rule 4

When goods are delivered to the buyer on approval or on "sale or return" or other similar terms, the property passes to the buyer

(a) when he signifies his approval or acceptance to the seller or does any other act adopting the transaction.

(b) if he does not signify his approval or acceptance to the seller but retains the goods without giving notice of rejection, then, if a time has been fixed for the return of the goods, on the expiration of such time, and if no time has been fixed, on the expiration of a reasonable time, and what is a reasonable time is a question of fact.

We can see from this rule that a buyer may accept goods and acquire ownership without having expressly communicated that intention to the seller. As our discussion of bailment in Chapter 17 will show, a prospective buyer who has custody of goods on approval owes a duty of care in looking after them; a possibility of liability therefore exists, but since there is as yet no agreed price under a contract of sale, the amount would be fixed by the court.

Unascertained Goods

unascertained goods
goods that have not been set aside and agreed upon as the subject of a sale

future goods
goods that have not yet been produced

The Sale of Goods Act sets out a separate rule for deciding when title passes in goods that are *unascertained* at the time of the contract. The extreme example of **unascertained goods** occurs when they have not yet been produced, that is, when they are **future goods**; but goods may also be unascertained even when they are in existence, provided they have not yet been selected and related categorically to a particular contract. Goods are ascertained once they have been set aside or earmarked and agreed on as the subject-matter of the sale. When unascertained goods are the subject of a contract, by definition the contract must be an agreement to sell, for title cannot pass to a buyer until the goods are ascertained. Nor can the parties effectively insert a term in their agreement purporting to pass the title before the goods are ascertained.

Rule 5

    (a) Where there is a contract for the sale of unascertained or future goods by description and goods of that description and in a deliverable state are unconditionally appropriated to the contract, either by the seller with the assent of the buyer, or by the buyer with the assent of the seller, the property in the goods passes to the buyer, and such assent may be expressed or implied and may be given either before or after the appropriation is made.

    (b) Where in pursuance of a contract the seller delivers the goods to the buyer or to a carrier or other bailee (whether named by the buyer or not) for the purpose of transmission to the buyer and does not reserve the right of disposal, he is deemed to have unconditionally appropriated the goods to the contract.

ILLUSTRATION 16.8

Prentice orders from Hall's automotive supply store four truck tires, size 750 × 20. Hall has a large number of such tires in his stockroom. Later in the day, a clerk removes four of them from the rack where Hall keeps his stock. He sets them aside in the stockroom, attaching a note, "For Prentice." The clerk's act of separating the tires from the larger bulk does not amount to an unconditional appropriation of the goods. If the contents of the stockroom were to be destroyed in a fire, the loss of the tires would still be the seller's because title has not yet passed to the buyer.

Unconditional appropriation of goods to a contract does not take place until a seller can no longer change his mind and substitute other goods for delivery to the buyer. In other words, some act must be done that conclusively determines what goods are appropriated to the contract. It seems that nothing less than delivery of the goods—or at least an act that virtually amounts to delivery—will constitute unconditional appropriation. If, in the above example, the tires had been installed on the truck, that would be tantamount to delivery and title—and risk would have passed to the buyer.

A buyer's assent to appropriation can be presumed from her prior order. Accordingly, title may pass to the buyer even before she receives notice of the unconditional appropriation, as would have been the case if the tires had been installed (in Illustration 16.8). In this respect, then, the rule for unascertained goods differs from some of the rules we discussed earlier for specific goods.

Rule 5 above refers to the possibility of a seller reserving "the right of disposal." We shall consider this right in the following section when we deal with bills of lading.

Checklist: The Passing of Title

Unless otherwise agreed, the Sale of Goods Act provides that title to goods passes from the seller to the buyer

- where there is an unconditional contract for the sale of specific goods in a deliverable state, when the contract is made.
- where there is a contract for the sale of specific goods and the seller is bound to do something to the goods to put them into a deliverable state, when the buyer has received notice that it has been done.
- where there is a contract for the sale of specific goods in a deliverable state but the seller is bound to do something to ascertain their price, when the buyer has received notice that it has been done.
- where goods are delivered to the buyer on approval or on "sale or return," when the buyer signifies his approval, or does some other act adopting the transaction, or when the buyer retains the goods beyond a reasonable time.
- where there is a contract for the sale of unascertained or future goods by description, when goods of that description and in a deliverable state are appropriated to the contract by one party with the assent of the other.

The Effect of Agency

When a business ships goods to its agent for the agent to sell, the effect of the consignment is to give the agent (the consignee) the appearance of ownership in the eyes of the public. Consistent with this appearance, statutes in the various provinces give the agent the same authority to deal with the goods as their owner has.[18] The agent may, therefore, validly pass title to anyone who purchases the goods in good faith, even though the sale may be on terms forbidden by the owner (the consignor). An agent, as a consignee of goods, may also pledge them as security for a loan, binding the owner to the transaction. We shall encounter the law on this point again in Chapter 19.

A similar though more complex problem arises when a seller gives a buyer possession but retains the title as security for payment, as it does in an instalment sale. We shall discuss the effect of an instalment sale in Chapter 30.

Bills of Lading

A **bill of lading** is an essential part of many commercial sales transactions and is important to the remedies of the seller, as we shall see in the next section. Recently, however, the written bill of lading has increasingly been replaced by computer transactions. A broadly similar result to that discussed below is now achieved through a process known as Electronic Data Interchange.[19]

We can best understand the nature of a bill of lading by considering its purposes:

bill of lading
a document signed by a carrier acknowledging that specified goods have been delivered to it for shipment

---

18. See, for example, Factors Act, R.S.O. 1990, c. F.1, s. 2; R.S.N.S. 1989, c. 157, s. 2; Sale of Goods Act, R.S.B.C. 1996, c. 410, ss. 58, 59; R.S.O. 1990, c. S.1, s. 25; R.S.N.S. 1989, c. 408, s. 28. See also Criminal Code, R.S.C. 1985, c. C-46, s. 325 for the circumstances under which a factor or agent does not commit theft by pledging or giving a lien on goods or documents of title to goods that are entrusted to him for the purpose of sale.

19. See Kindred, "Trading Internationally by Electronic Bills of Lading" (1992), 7 *Banking and Finance L. Rev.* 264. See further the discussion of Electronic Commerce in Chapter 34.

- It is a receipt issued and signed by the carrier, acknowledging that specified goods have been delivered to it for shipment.
- It provides evidence of the terms of the contract between the shipper and the carrier to transport the described goods to a stated destination.
- It may be evidence of title to the goods.

A bill of lading may be either a *straight* or an *order* bill of lading. By the terms of a straight bill of lading, the shipment is consigned directly to a designated party—usually the buyer, or sometimes the bank that is financing the buyer. By contrast, an order bill of lading is made out to the order of a specified party that has title to the goods in the course of transit and that may thus transfer title of the goods to someone else by endorsing it. The customary practice is for the seller to make out the bill of lading to his own order, thereby retaining the right of disposal during transit and enabling him to withhold title from the buyer until the buyer makes satisfactory arrangements for payment. When this is done, the seller endorses the bill over to the buyer. Alternatively, a bill may be *endorsed in blank*, that is, without specifying the party who is next to have title. An order bill of lading is, consequently, a useful device for transferring ownership of goods independently of their physical possession.

REMEDIES OF THE SELLER

Lien

lien

a right of a person in possession of property to retain that property against the claim of the owner

The primary objective of a business selling goods is to recover the contract price. One way of ensuring recovery is to withhold delivery until payment is made. While the goods remain in an unpaid seller's possession, the seller has a **lien** on the goods regardless of whether title has passed to the buyer; the seller has a claim or charge on them for their agreed price, and can refuse to part with them until the debt is satisfied. Once the seller delivers the goods to the buyer, however, he normally loses this special right to possession unless the buyer obtains them by theft or trickery. The right of lien is based upon possession and is extinguished when possession passes in good faith to the buyer.[20]

Not every contract of sale creates a right of lien for the seller. The remedy exists only in the following situations:

(a) where the contract does not state that the buyer is to have credit, so that payment may be required upon delivery

(b) where the goods have been sold on credit, the term of credit has expired without payment being made and the seller still has possession of the goods

(c) where the buyer becomes insolvent before delivery

In (c), a seller who refuses to deliver is excused only if the buyer is insolvent. A seller should be sure of the facts before exercising the right of lien; otherwise, he takes the risk that the buyer may subsequently sue for breach of the promise to deliver. It is not enough simply to hear that the buyer's financial position is questionable—it is necessary to be more specific and to show that the buyer is definitely unable to meet current debts as they come due. Otherwise, the seller must deliver as promised and will become an unsecured creditor of the buyer for the price of the goods.

A seller may waive his right of lien—and rely on the buyer's credit—in two ways. He may waive the right by implication, as in the usual credit sale, simply by agreeing to deliver before payment is due. Second, he may voluntarily deliver the goods before he needs to do so.

---

20. An exception to this rule applies when an unpaid seller repossesses goods under the provisions of the Bankruptcy and Insolvency Act; this exception is discussed below under the heading "Repossession."

Stoppage in Transit

If a buyer becomes insolvent after an unpaid seller has delivered goods to a carrier, the seller may still have time to order the carrier to withhold the goods from the buyer. If given notice in adequate time, the carrier is bound to obey these instructions. If the carrier delivers to the buyer in spite of notice, it is liable for damages for conversion.

The right of **stoppage in transit** (or *in transitu*—to use its Latin name) is an extraordinary one because it allows a seller who may have neither title nor possession to goods to exercise control over them. Like the right of lien, however, the remedy disappears once the goods are delivered.

A business may dispose of goods it has bought but not yet received if it holds an order bill of lading endorsed in its favour, or in blank, and it assigns the bill of lading to a customer or creditor. After the seller exercises a right of stoppage in transit, however, the buyer can no longer pass good title by means of a bill of lading to anyone who knows that stoppage in transit has occurred. On the other hand, a buyer can pass good title to an innocent assignee who is unaware that the right is likely to have been exercised and who has given value for the instrument.

stoppage in transit
the right of a seller to order a carrier not to deliver to the buyer

ILLUSTRATION 16.9

Lamb's Woollen Mills Ltd., Lancaster, England, ships a large order of women's sweaters to Byers Importers of Halifax, Nova Scotia. Since Byers is an old customer, Lamb's Woollen Mills forwards to it an order bill of lading for the goods, endorsed in blank. While the goods are still in transit, Lamb's Canadian agent learns that Byers is insolvent and notifies the carrier not to deliver the goods to Byers. In the meantime, Byers resells the goods to Premium Department Stores Ltd. by assigning the bill of lading. The officers of Premium Department Stores Ltd. are unaware of the exercise of the right of stoppage in transit or of Byers' impending bankruptcy.

In these circumstances, Premium Department Stores obtains the right to possession of the goods from the carrier. Lamb's ranks only as a general creditor of Byers, and in subsequent bankruptcy proceedings, would share in the available assets in common with the other general creditors. The available assets would include the money paid by Premium Department Stores for the sweaters.

A seller takes the same risk in exercising a right of stoppage in transit as he does in asserting a right of lien. If, as matters turn out, he has mistakenly assumed that the buyer is insolvent, the buyer may sue for damages for non-delivery.

Repossession

As stated above, once possession passes in good faith to a buyer, the seller loses the right to repossess the goods even if the buyer fails to pay for them. An important exception to the rule was introduced in 1992 by an amendment to the law of bankruptcy.[21] Where a seller has delivered goods to a buyer and the buyer, before having paid in full for the goods, becomes bankrupt or insolvent, the seller may make a written demand for the return of the goods. The demand must be presented, within 30 days after the goods were delivered, to the trustee in bankruptcy or receiver appointed to manage the debtor's affairs. The right to repossess applies only to goods that were delivered in relation to the buyer's business, not to consumer goods. The goods must still be in the possession of the buyer, must be identifiable, and be in the same condition as they were when sold. If the price has been partly paid, the seller has a choice between repossessing a portion of the goods in proportion to the amount still owing or of repossessing all of the goods and refunding the amount already paid. The right of repossession ranks above any other claim to the goods, except those of a subsequent purchaser who has bought the goods for value and in good faith, without notice of the unpaid seller's claim.

---

21. Bankruptcy and Insolvency Act, R.S.C. 1985, c. B-3, s. 81.1, as added by S.C. 1992, c. 27.

Resale

After exercising a right of lien or of stoppage in transit under the Sale of Goods Act, an unpaid seller may give notice to the buyer and resell the goods to a third party; the new purchaser obtains good title to them.[22] Although not expressly authorized under the Bankruptcy and Insolvency Act, it seems that an unpaid seller who repossesses goods under that Act also has the right to resell them. The right of resale is especially helpful when the goods are perishable, but is not confined to such emergencies.

The right of resale extends to other circumstances and is not limited to a lien or stoppage in transit. The right arises whenever a buyer commits a breach by refusing to accept goods. Resale is then the means by which a seller mitigates his loss. If the seller has made a diligent effort to obtain a good price on resale but obtains a lower price than that promised in the original contract, he may sue the original buyer for the deficiency.

Damages for Non-acceptance

We used the contract of sale to illustrate the measurement of expectation damages in Chapter 15. Our discussion assumed that the title to the goods had not passed to the buyer at the time of the buyer's breach. We saw that a critical factor in determining the appropriate amount of damages is whether the seller is in a position to supply more goods than prospective customers might order. If so, the seller's damages are measured by the profits lost due to the buyer's breach; if not, damages are generally measured by any deficiency in the resale price of the rejected goods compared with the original contract price.

ILLUSTRATION 16.10

Read examines a used accordion for sale in Crescendo Music Stores Ltd. She agrees in writing to buy it for $600 provided the bellows are repaired and gold monogram initials are affixed to it. Before the repairs are made, Read informs Crescendo that she has decided to take up the saxophone instead and refuses to accept the accordion. Crescendo sues Read.

The appropriate action is for damages for non-acceptance because the title has not passed to Read at the time of her repudiation. If the music store has more used accordions in stock than it has customers wanting to buy them, it has sustained damages equal to the profit it would have made had Read purchased the instrument as she promised.

If the store has no other used accordions and is able to resell the accordion, but for less than $600, it has sustained damages equal to the difference between the two prices. If the repairs and changes had been made but Read had not been notified before she repudiated the contract, title would still not have passed to her, and the seller might have a claim for additional damages equal to its expenses. That would depend on whether the required changes had enhanced the value of the instrument: Crescendo should be able to recover the cost of affixing the gold monogram, but not that of repairing the bellows.

Action for the Price

When title has passed to the buyer, a seller is entitled to its full price regardless of whether the buyer has taken delivery. If the buyer rejects goods after title has passed, she is rejecting what is her own.

---

22. See, for example: R.S.B.C. 1996, c. 410, ss. 44(1)(c) and 51(2); R.S.O. 1990, c. S.1, ss. 38 and 46(2); R.S.N.S. 1989, c. 408, ss. 41(1)(c) and 49(2) and (3).

ILLUSTRATION 16.11

Anderson buys a compact disc player on display at Burton's Appliance Store. The player is tagged "sold" with Anderson's name on it, and Anderson signs a form identifying the purchase and stating its price. On her way home, Anderson sees another model in the window of Modern Electronics Ltd., and decides that she would prefer it. She refuses the delivery of the player by Burton and Burton sues her for the full price of the machine.

The action will succeed. At the time Anderson attempted to repudiate the contract of sale, title had already passed to her. If Burton sues for the price, however, he must be willing and able to deliver the compact disc player.

The conclusion in Illustration 16.11 is based on the Sale of Goods Act. However, it has been criticized because a seller's right to sue for the full price may sometimes be hard to justify when the seller still has the goods; if the buyer is a consumer, the seller, as a dealer in the rejected goods, is normally in a better position to resell them. Accordingly, when a seller does not succeed in delivering the goods, it is arguable that its recourse should be limited to an action for damages even though title may have passed to the buyer. In jurisdictions in the United States that have adopted the Uniform Commercial Code, a seller may sue for the price only when the buyer has accepted the goods or when the seller is unable after a reasonable effort to resell the goods at a reasonable price; in virtually all other circumstances, a seller may sue only for damages for non-acceptance, regardless of whether title has passed.[23]

Many retail businesses make it a practice for reasons of goodwill to waive contracts of sale upon the customer's request and, even when the goods have already been delivered, to take them back. The waiver of the original contract revests title in the seller, who may then transfer the title to another buyer.

When a seller does sue, he usually sues for the price or, in the alternative, for damages for non-acceptance. This strategy is appropriate when the seller would prefer a simple action for the price (as it normally would), but when it is not clear whether title has passed to the buyer at the time of repudiation. If the court decides that title has passed, the seller will recover the price. If the court decides that title has not passed, the seller will still recover damages for non-acceptance.

Retention of Deposit

In a contract of sale, as in any contract, the parties may provide that, in the event of breach, the party in default shall pay the other a specified sum of money by way of liquidated damages. As we have seen in Chapter 15, the court will enforce such a term if the amount specified is a genuine estimate by the parties of the probable loss. Depending on the circumstances, an amount paid by a buyer as a deposit may be treated as liquidated damages in the event of her default. In many contracts of sale, the reason why the seller demands a deposit is to protect himself at least to that extent in the event of the buyer's non-acceptance; the intention is clear that the deposit will be forfeited upon breach by the buyer.[24]

deposit
a sum of money paid by the buyer to the seller, to be forfeited if the buyer does not perform its part of the contract

However, we must distinguish between a **deposit** intended primarily to provide a sanction to induce performance of the contract by the buyer, and a **down payment**, agreed upon primarily as a part payment of the purchase price and unrelated to the seller's probable loss in the event of breach by the buyer. If the title to the goods has already passed to the buyer at the time

down payment
a sum of money paid by the buyer as an initial part of the purchase price

---

23. For a discussion of the problems created by the rule that the seller is entitled to sue for the price when the buyer has rejected the goods, as long as title has passed, see Atiyah, *The Sale of Goods* (8th ed.), Chapter 24. London: Pitman Publishing, 1990. See also Uniform Commercial Code (U.S.), sec. 2-709.

24. See Stockloser v. Johnson, [1954] 1 Q.B. 476. If the contract provides for a non-refundable deposit but the deposit has not been paid, for example when the purchaser has stopped payment on the cheque, the vendor is entitled to recover the agreed sum: Vanvic Enterprises Ltd. v. Mark, [1985] 3 W.W.R. 644.

the buyer repudiates, the seller is entitled not only to retain the down payment, but also to sue for the balance of the price. If title has not yet passed, the seller is entitled to retain out of the down payment any damages for non-acceptance that he can prove and is accountable to the buyer for any remaining surplus.[25] If the seller can prove damages that exceed the down payment, he may retain that sum and sue for additional damage.

THE SELLER'S LIABILITY

Misrepresentation

We have considered the remedies for misrepresentation in Chapter 9; a review of that chapter is worthwhile at this point. We noted there that when a misrepresentation is innocent, the only remedy, rescission, is often impossible or at least impractical for the buyer; to have the more extensive remedies available for misrepresentation, the buyer must establish either fraud or negligence.

The type of statement that comes within the definition of misrepresentation has two important characteristics for our present purposes. First, the statement must be part of the preliminary bargaining and not be incorporated as a term in the contract of sale—if it were embodied in the contract, the buyer's recourse would be for breach of contract. Second, the statement made by the seller must be made as a statement of fact—the law provides no remedy for a buyer induced to enter into a contract by a mere expression of opinion or commendation of the goods.[26]

Advertising can be misleading but still not amount to misrepresentation as we have defined it. While the common law may seem inadequate in this respect, several factors help both to explain this state of affairs and to minimize potential abuse. First, most businesses act in a reasonably responsible way when dealing with the public, and any general rule sufficiently comprehensive to control and punish every type of deception would obstruct unduly the course of legitimate business. Second, no legal rule is an adequate substitute for a buyer's own care. A seller's superior position results largely from his knowledge about both his products and the limits of the law, and the only effective way for the buyer to minimize this advantage is to seek the knowledge for herself. Third, the common law can be, and has been, superseded by statute law in specific areas of abuse.

Apart from liability at common law, a variety of federal and provincial statutes regulate misrepresentations, especially in misleading advertisements, and impose penalties on those making them. This aspect of a seller's liability is dealt with, under the heading "Consumer Protection," in Chapter 32.

Breach of a Term

Generally, a breach of a condition entitles the injured party to discharge the contract as well as to sue for damages for any loss suffered. The Sale of Goods Act, however, sets down circumstances where a buyer will *not* be entitled to terminate the contract and return the goods even though the seller has been guilty of a breach of condition. The Act (section 12(3)) reads as follows:

> 12. (3) Where a contract of sale is not severable and the buyer has accepted the goods or part thereof, or where the contract is for specific goods the property in which has passed to the buyer, the breach of any condition to be fulfilled by the seller can only be treated as a breach of warranty and not as a ground for rejecting the goods and treating the contract as repudiated, unless there is a term of the contract, express or implied, to that effect.

This section means, first, that the buyer must keep the goods and be content with damages when the broken contract of sale does not contemplate delivery by instalments (is not severable)

---

25. Stevenson v. Colonial Homes Ltd. (1961), 27 D.L.R. (2d) 698.

26. In our discussion of negligent misrepresentation in Chapter 4, we noted that the expression of a professional opinion, as with expert opinion generally, may be regarded as a "fact" in the mind of the person influenced by it.

and the buyer has indicated an intention to keep the goods or treated them in a way inconsistent with the seller's ownership of them.

The section seems to contemplate a second situation where the right to repudiate would be lost when the contract is for specific goods, the property in which has passed to the buyer even though the goods are still in the seller's possession. However, when the seller has committed a breach of condition by allocating unsatisfactory goods to fill the contract, such a result would seem surprising; it is difficult to see how title would pass to the buyer in that situation, short of the buyer's acceptance of the goods. Courts avoid applying this part of the section and sometimes even seem to ignore it as inappropriate to modern selling practices.[27]

ILLUSTRATION 16.12

A sales agent for Agrarian Implements Ltd. shows to Macdonald, a farmer, a catalogue containing pictures of agricultural equipment that his firm has for sale. The agent tells Macdonald that they have just taken into stock "one brand new" combine of a type pictured in the catalogue. Macdonald agrees to buy it and signs the necessary papers.

When the combine is delivered, a neighbour of Macdonald recognizes it as the one which the same sales agent had earlier given him an extensive demonstration, and which the sales agent had referred to as "a demonstrator model that we could let you have at a bargain." Macdonald at once ships the combine back to Agrarian Implements and the firm then sues him for the price.

The combine was a specific article at the time Macdonald agreed to buy it. Nevertheless, he is entitled to treat the contract as discharged and refuse to accept the combine. Agrarian Implements has been guilty of breach of the condition as to description (that the combine was new), and the courts have reasoned that title did not pass to Macdonald.[28] If, however, Macdonald took delivery of the combine and used it for farm work, he could not subsequently, upon learning that it was not new when he bought it, insist he had a right to return it. He must be content with damages.

Even when the goods are specific and title has passed to the buyer at the time of sale, if the seller fails to deliver on time, the buyer may later refuse to take the goods and may terminate the contract. Section 12(3) concludes by stating that it does not apply where there is a term of the contract, express or implied, to the effect that the buyer can treat a breach of condition as grounds for rejecting the goods. When the parties specify a time for delivery, the courts may find that such an intention is implied.

In Case 16.7, we can see the consequences for the buyer when the seller is guilty of a breach of condition but the buyer has accepted the goods.

CASE 16.7

Leaf purchased a painting of Salisbury Cathedral that the seller, International Galleries, represented to him as the work of the famous artist Constable. When Leaf attempted to resell the picture five years later, it was discovered that it had not been painted by Constable but by a much less famous artist. Its value was consequently only a small fraction of what both the seller and buyer had thought.

Leaf tried to return the picture to International Galleries and recover the purchase price. The court held that the Sale of Goods Act applied, so that Leaf did not have the right to treat the contract as being at an end. Since he did not sue for damages, as he might have done, his action failed.[29]

---

27. See Waddams, *The Law of Contracts* (4th ed.), pp. 438–40.
28. See Varley v. Whipp, [1900] 1 Q.B. 513.
29. Leaf v. International Galleries, [1950] 2 K.B. 86.

It is interesting that the court regarded the representation as having been incorporated into the contract of sale as a term; its decision does not answer the question whether, had the case been treated as one of either innocent misrepresentation or mistake, the equitable remedy of rescission might still have been available at that late date.

Wrongful Withholding or Disposition by the Seller

wrongful detention

the refusal by the seller to deliver goods whose title has passed to the buyer

When the title to goods has already passed to the buyer, a seller who refuses to deliver them according to the terms of the contract is guilty of a tort: the buyer may sue the seller for damages for **wrongful detention**. Moreover, the buyer may occasionally obtain a court order for the delivery of the goods. If, in addition to a failure to deliver, the seller transfers the goods to a third party, he will have disposed of goods that do not belong to him; the buyer may sue for damages for the tort of *conversion*, that is, for converting the buyer's goods to his own use or purposes.

REMEDIES OF THE BUYER

A buyer has a range of possible remedies, in contract, in tort, and under consumer protection legislation. Remedies in tort, such as for conversion or for deceit, were discussed in Chapter 3. Consumer protection is dealt with in Chapter 32.

In contract, a buyer's usual remedy will be to claim damages. In Chapter 15 under the heading "Expectation Damages," we discussed the measure of damages available to a buyer when the seller fails to deliver. If delivery is merely delayed through the seller's fault and the buyer accepts the goods, the measure of damages is the value the goods would have had for the buyer if they had been delivered on time over their actual value when delivered.

A seller may be guilty of breach for reasons other than non-delivery: for example, failure to perform any of the implied terms as to title, description, suitability, and merchantability, or compliance with sample; or failure to perform an express term as to the quality or capability of the goods. Damages sustained by a buyer from the seller's breach of a term may sometimes, as we have seen, be greater than the price of the goods; to recover the loss, the buyer must take the initiative and claim it from the seller. When the damages amount to less than the contract price, the buyer may tender to the seller the price less the amount of the damages; if the seller refuses the tender and sues for the full price, the buyer may defend by claiming to set off her damages against the price. To reduce the risk of having to pay court costs, the buyer should promptly pay into court the amount tendered to the seller.

As an alternative to damages, a buyer may be able to claim the equitable remedy of specific performance or of rescission; both of these remedies were discussed in Chapter 15. The Sale of Goods Act gives the court discretion to order specific performance of a contract for the sale of goods, that is, to order the seller to deliver the goods to the buyer. Generally, the court does not grant this remedy when a seller refuses to deliver, because money damages are nearly always an adequate remedy. Where the goods have a unique value for the buyer, however, the court may exercise its discretion in her favour and order specific performance. As we have seen, in the preceding section under "Breach of a Term," the Sale of Goods Act restricts the right to rescind. Nevertheless, rescission remains a possible remedy for the buyer when the seller fails to deliver goods that have been prepaid in whole or in part.

QUESTIONS FOR REVIEW

1. What was the principal purpose of the original Sale of Goods Act?

2. Distinguish between ownership and possession.

3. How are "goods" defined in the Sale of Goods Act? What types of personal property are not within the definition?

4. Is a contract for the installation of a central heating system a contract for the sale of goods?

5. What is the distinction between a sale and an agreement to sell?

6. What is meant by a "consignment"?

7. When does the *caveat emptor* principle apply to the sale of goods?

8. What is meant by "quiet possession"?

9. Distinguish between the implied term as to fitness and the implied term of merchantable quality.

10. What is the significance of an article being sold under its trade name?

11. What terms are implied in the case of a sale by sample?

12. Why are exemption clauses in contracts of sale interpreted strictly?

13. What does it mean to say that the courts interpret the time set for payment as a warranty unless the parties have expressed otherwise?

14. If the seller delivers a greater quantity of goods than the buyer ordered, what choices does the buyer have?

15. What determines who bears the risk of loss when goods that are the subject-matter of a contract of sale are destroyed?

16. When does title pass in the case of specific goods that are in a deliverable state?

17. What is the distinction between unascertained goods and future goods?

18. What is a "bill of lading"?

19. When does an unpaid seller have a lien on the goods sold? When is there a right of repossession?

20. What is the appropriate measure of damages when the buyer refuses to accept the goods?

21. *A* offered to sell his goat to *B* for $10, and *B* accepted. *B* put a $10 note on the table and suggested they have a beer to celebrate the deal. While they were drinking the beer, the goat ate the $10 note. (News item, May 13, 1961.) Who owns the goat?

CASES AND PROBLEMS

1 Regal Motors Ltd. sold a car to Fox, whom they believed to be a prosperous and successful business person. They handed him the car, keys, and registration papers. In return, Fox gave Regal a personal uncertified cheque for the full price. The next day, Fox resold the car to Buck, for cash. One day later, Regal discovered that there were no funds to honour Fox's cheque.

The police traced the vehicle to Buck and seized it, but were unable to locate "Fox." Regal and Buck both claimed the vehicle.

Which of them should succeed?

2 Thrasher was an experienced farmer who, over more than 10 years, had successfully seeded and harvested several crops including wheat, canola, and barley. Three years ago he purchased a quantity of "QR5" granular herbicide from the manufacturer, Treflan Ltd. QR5 is a well-known product, widely used as an effective agent to control certain weed infestations, particularly those found in fields sowed to canola. The herbicide was labelled with the following warning (among others): "To cover the possibility of injury to rotational crops, seed the crops shallow into a warm moist seedbed."

In the fall of that year, Thrasher applied the QR5 by aerial spraying to 300 acres of his land, and sowed it to canola in the following spring. After the seed germinated, Thrasher noticed large areas of weed infestation choking out his crop. The canola crop produced at harvest only half as much as had been expected. Thrasher consulted Treflan, who advised him to sow the land the following year with wheat, as a rotational crop. He did so, but the crop was so poor that it had to be ploughed in.

Thrasher contended that the herbicide had been properly applied but failed to kill the weeds in the canola crop as it should have, and that it left a high residue that ruined the following year's wheat crop. Treflan's position was that Thrasher was at fault for the damage to the canola crop because he did not follow the application instructions properly, the herbicide was not applied uniformly, and the next year's wheat seed had been planted too deeply, contrary to the instructions and warnings that came with the herbicide.

Based on the evidence presented to it, the Court found that Thrasher had applied the herbicide correctly—it had failed to kill the weeds as it should have done and had contaminated the soil. However, Thrasher had ignored the manufacturer's warning and planted the wheat seed too deeply.

Should Treflan be held liable for the loss of (a) the canola crop, and (b) the wheat crop?

3 Horvat agreed to purchase a 1970 Cessna 180 aircraft from Balinder. Balinder explained that he no longer owned the Cessna, having just traded it in to Hidden Valley Aviation Ltd. in exchange for a newer model, but that he had agreed to find a buyer for the plane. In answer to questions from Horvat, Balinder assured her that the plane was a "little beauty" that had never given a minute of trouble, and that it had been regularly serviced. He invited Horvat to check the plane out thoroughly, but she replied that she was not a qualified mechanic and contented herself with a cursory inspection and a trial flight accompanied by Balinder.

A price was agreed on and Horvat handed over a certified cheque, made payable to Hidden Valley. The sales invoice showed Hidden Valley as the seller.

Horvat soon discovered that the Cessna's engine required major repairs to make it safe and airworthy. She brought an action against both Balinder and Hidden Valley, claiming damages for the cost of repairs.

Is Horvat entitled to recover?

4 Gabrieli bought a truck from a dealer, Transit Inc. Gabrieli signed a "purchase order" on May 12, at which time Transit ordered the truck from the manufacturer. It was agreed that the sale was subject to Gabrieli being able to arrange suitable financing.

Three weeks later, Gabrieli informed Transit that she had been able to obtain a loan from her bank and was in a position to let them have a bank draft for the full price. Transit confirmed that the arrangement was satisfactory. On August 2 the truck was delivered to Transit from the manufacturer. Transit called Gabrieli, telling her "your truck is here and ready for you to collect." Gabrieli went straight to the Transit premises, handed over the bank draft, and received the keys, papers, and the truck. At that time, Transit's sales manager also handed her a number of other documents, including one that the manager described as "your warranty," which he asked Gabrieli to sign. Gabrieli did so. The document gave a limited one-year warranty for defects but excluded implied warranties and excluded liability for consequential damages.

The truck proved to be defective and soon developed a number of faults. Gabrieli took the truck back to Transit on numerous occasions for various repairs, but these were mostly unsuccessful. Finally, after more than two years of unsatisfactory operation, Gabrieli returned the truck to Transit and demanded her money back.

Transit denied liability, pointing to the one-year warranty that excluded the statutory implied warranties.

Is Gabrieli entitled to any remedy?

5. Benner's Sawmill Inc. entered into a contract with Chen to purchase a quantity of timber growing on land leased by Chen. A price of $150 per cubic metre was agreed, and the quantity set at approximately 600 cubic metres. Chen was to cut and trim the timber ready for collection by Benner's, who paid an initial deposit of $15 000. Benner's asked its insurance company about insuring the timber and was told that the timber could not be insured until it had been felled, trimmed, and "timbermarked" (that is, marked with a provincially registered mark applied by swinging a timber hammer and striking the wood surface at both ends).

Some weeks later, Chen phoned Benner's and informed them that the timber had been cut, trimmed, and stacked. The total price was $94 000 (the quantity being a little more than 600 cubic metres). When asked if the timber had been timbermarked, Chen replied that it had not; he was going away on a short vacation but would see to it as soon as he returned. In accordance with the contract, Benner's sent Chen a cheque for the full price, less the deposit already paid.

Before Chen returned from vacation his sheds were destroyed by fire. When Benner's demanded the timber or their money back, Chen replied: "Sorry, but it was your timber that burnt."

Advise Benner's.

LEASING AND BAILMENT

In discussing contracts of sale in Chapter 16, we saw that ownership and possession of goods do not always go together. In this chapter, we examine two common types of contract in which ownership and possession are necessarily distinct: *leasing* and *bailment*. Leasing of personal property is a form of bailment, although from a commercial point of view, the two types of contract have very different functions. A lease of personal property—a *chattel lease*—is frequently regarded as an alternative to sale; a firm may choose to rent an expensive piece of equipment rather than buy it. By contrast, most types of bailment involve parting with possession of an item for a relatively short time—for storage, repair, or transportation. Legally, however, they share the same essential features.

In this chapter, we examine such questions as:

- what are the principal types of chattel lease?

- why are leasing contracts used, and why have they become so important?

- what are the terms that are commonly found in leasing contracts?

- what are the respective rights of the lessor and the lessee?

- what is the legal nature of bailment?

- what are the principal types of bailment contract?

- what are the rights and duties of a the parties to a contract of bailment?

LEASING

Leasing is a major growth industry and has become a multibillion dollar business in both Canada and the United States. At the consumer level, automobile leasing has become a common alternative to purchasing on credit; in business, more than 25 percent of capital equipment, such as heavy machinery and aircraft, is now leased.

The widespread use of leasing in business is a relatively recent development, although the concept of a **lease** is a very ancient one. Leases were known in Roman law and have been recognized since the earliest times in the common law. The essence of a lease is that the owner of an item of property, referred to as the **lessor**, leases the property to the **lessee**, that is, allows the lessee to have possession and use of the property for a stipulated period in return for the payment of *rent*. Leasing traditionally has been associated with real estate; leasing, or renting, a house or apartment, or leasing office space for a business, has always been an alternative to outright purchase. We shall consider leases of land in Chapter 24, under the heading "Landlord and Tenant."

Although the possibility of renting personal property, or chattels, has long existed and been recognized by the law, such contracts were comparatively rare until recently. A major reason, no doubt, was the risk that an owner ran when he parted with possession of personal property. A person who obtains a lease of land cannot remove it and, if she fails to pay the rent, the owner can repossess it. But chattels are transportable and there was, until modern systems of registration of property rights were developed, an obvious danger that a lessee might simply disappear with the leased property and stop paying rent for it.

The other factor that led to the great increase in the leasing of personal property was the realization that a lease could be used as a security device. This became understood in England about 100 years ago, in the leading House of Lords decision of *Helby v. Matthews*,[1] which recognized a hiring agreement with an option to purchase at the end of the hiring term as an effective method of selling goods on credit. It opened the way for the very popular type of transaction known in Britain as **hire-purchase**. In a typical hire-purchase agreement, the lessee/purchaser agrees to lease an item of property—for, say, a term of four years, paying a monthly rental—with an option to purchase it at the end of the term, provided the rent has been paid in full, for a purely nominal amount, such as $1.

This type of transaction is well known in Canada, principally as a means of marketing automobiles. In reality, it is a method of purchasing on credit, and as such is an alternative to the *conditional sale* and to the *chattel mortgage*.[2] But not all chattel leases are intended as security devices and in any event such leases have their own particular legal consequences.

Types of Chattel Lease

Two main types of chattel lease exist: *operating leases*, or "real" leases, where the intention is that possession will revert to the owner at the end of the term, and *purchase leases*, where it is anticipated that the lessee will eventually become the owner. Purchase leases can be further subdivided into *security leases*, where the credit is provided by the lessor/vendor, and *finance leases*, where a third party finances the transaction on credit.

Operating Leases

In an **operating lease**, since there is no intention to transfer ownership, the term tends to be relatively short—substantially less than the expected working life of the property leased. Examples include a car rental for a weekend or a month, the renting of specialized machinery for the duration of a construction contract, or of farm machinery for the harvest season.

lease
an arrangement where the owner of property allows another person to have possession and use of the property for a stipulated period in return for the payment of rent

lessor
the owner of the leased property

lessee
the person who takes possession of the leased property

hire-purchase
an agreement to lease an item of property with an option for the lessee to purchase it at the end of the stipulated term

operating lease
a lease under which there is no intention to transfer ownership

---

1. [1895] A.C. 471.
2. Those transactions are discussed in Chapter 30. For an interesting discussion see Kraus, "Leasing as an Alternative to Secured Financing" (1999), 62 *Sask. L. Rev.* 173.

Purchase Leases

In *Helby v. Matthews*,[3] the House of Lords distinguished between a "real" lease and a hire-purchase agreement according to whether the lessee/purchaser was obliged to pay the full price for the chattel and whether she became the owner on completing the payments. That test now appears to be too simplistic.[4] A more modern approach was adopted in Ontario by Henry, J., who considered that in order to determine the true nature of a lease, it is necessary to have regard to the position of the parties, their intention, and the true effect of the transaction.[5] In practice, however, this test has been difficult to apply and has led to contradictory results. The accounting profession has developed a more objective approach to determine whether to classify a lease as an operating lease or a **purchase lease**. A lease is treated as a purchase lease, or "capital lease,"[6] if one of three conditions exists:

> **purchase lease**
> a lease whereby ownership is intended to change hands at the end of the lease term

- Title passes automatically to the lessee at the end of the lease, *or* on the exercise of a "bargain purchase option."
- There is a non-cancellable term for at least 75 percent of the economic life of the asset.
- The present value of the minimum lease payments exceed 90 percent of the market value of the asset at the time the lease commences.[7]

The distinction between an operating lease and a purchase lease is important for a number of reasons. From an accounting perspective, if it is a purchase, or "capital," lease, the asset and the accompanying liability must be recorded in the balance sheet of the lessee/purchaser. From a taxation perspective, the distinction determines whether the lease payments are rental payments—and thus deductible by the lessee in determining the profits of the business—or are instalments of the purchase price and not deductible (apart from any interest element); it also determines which party is regarded as the true owner and thus entitled to claim capital cost allowances in respect of depreciation of the asset. From a legal perspective, the distinction may determine whether the lessor's interest must be registered under Personal Property Security legislation.[8]

Security and Finance Leases

In the typical purchase lease arrangement, it is the lessor who effectively provides the credit. The lessee pays what is, in reality, the purchase price by instalments—which are described as "rent." Until the price is paid in full, the lessor has a security interest by virtue of his continued ownership of the leased property—hence the expression **security lease**.

> **security lease**
> a purchase lease in which the lessor provides the credit

> **finance lease**
> an arrangement where a third person provides credit financing, becomes the owner of the property, and leases it to the lessee

An alternative that is becoming increasingly common is for a third person, such as a financial institution, to provide the credit financing. In this type of transaction, commonly known as a **finance lease**, the supplier of the goods sells them to the financer, who in turn leases them to the lessee. The financer is technically the owner of the goods, even though it probably has never had possession of them and will ultimately pass title to the lessee.

3. *Supra*, n. 1.

4. For a more sophisticated analysis see Ziegel (1990), 16 *C.B.L.J.* 369 at 379–86.

5. Re Speedrack Ltd. (1980), 1 P.P.S.A.C. 109. In Adelaide Capital Corp. v. Integrated Transportation Finance Inc. (1994), 111 D.L.R. (4th) 493 (Ont. Gen. Div.), the court attached particular importance to the fact that the lessor was in the business of providing credit financing.

6. That is, a lease that acquires a capital asset. Another term commonly used to describe the transaction is "lease-to-own."

7. *CICA Handbook,* section 3065. Somewhat different guidelines have been published by Revenue Canada in Interpretation Bulletin IT-233R.

8. Mitsui & Co (Canada) Ltd. v. Royal Bank of Canada (1995), 123 D.L.R. (4th) 449; Adelaide Capital Corp. v. Integrated Transportation Finance Inc., *supra*, n. 5. See the discussion of this issue in Chapter 30.

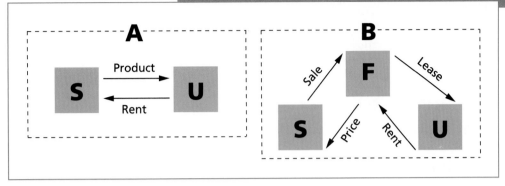

FIGURE 17.1
Comparing Purchase Lease and Finance Lease

In (A), a conventional purchase lease, the supplier, *S*, leases the property to the user, *U*, who pays rent in return. In (B), a finance lease, the supplier, *S*, sells the property to the financer, *F*, who in turn leases it to the user, *U*. *U* pays rent to *F*.

The major auto manufacturing companies commonly establish their own leasing companies to provide consumer financing in this manner.

Sale-and-Leaseback

A business with cash-flow problems may enter into a **sale-and-leaseback** transaction to raise working capital. The business sells assets for cash, and leases them back in return for future rental payments. The leaseback may take the form of an operating lease or of a purchase lease. In the latter case, the effect is similar to raising cash by mortgaging the asset.

sale-and-leaseback
a transaction in which the owner of property sells it and immediately leases it back from the new owner

REASONS FOR CHATTEL LEASING

The reasons for operating leases are obvious. A person is likely to be reluctant to go to the expense of purchasing an item that may be used only for a limited period, even though it may be possible to resell that item when it is no longer needed. Leasing will normally be a more convenient, and frequently less expensive, alternative to outright purchase.

The advantages of purchase leases and finance leases are less obvious. The lessor's perception may be that continued ownership of the asset, until payment has been made in full, provides more security in the case of default or insolvency of the lessee than would a conditional sale or chattel mortgage, though that view is questionable under modern Personal Property Security legislation.[9] The lessee may sometimes find it preferable to lease assets, as a form of *off-balance-sheet* financing; that is, since the asset is not owned by the business, it does not appear on the balance sheet, but neither does the future rental obligation appear as a liability. The net result is to record a lower debt-to-assets ratio than would be the case if the asset had been purchased with borrowed funds. Whether that is, in fact, the case depends upon the proper classification of the lease for accounting purposes.

Probably the main reason for preferring leasing lies in the way the transaction is treated for tax purposes. For the lessor, the principal tax advantage lies in the fact that, as owner of the asset, he is entitled to claim a deduction of capital cost allowance (i.e., depreciation) and may be eligible for an investment tax credit. Against that, he will be taxable on the rental payments. But

---

9. See Re Giffen, [1998] 1 S.C.R. 91. This issue is considered further in Chapter 30.

since the rental payments frequently remain constant over the term of the lease, whereas depreciation allowances are greatest in the early years of the life of the asset, there may be a substantial tax saving in those early years. That, in turn, makes it possible to charge a lower rental than might otherwise be the case. Some of these tax advantages have been countered by ever-stricter legislation, but it is nevertheless true that the rapid growth of leasing, and especially of international leasing, owes much to ingenious tax planning.

COMMON TERMS IN CHATTEL LEASES

What follows are the more important of the terms that are commonly found in chattel leases.

Duration

The lease normally sets out the duration for which it is intended to continue in force. In purchase lease arrangements, this is usually a fixed number of years. Operating leases may contain no fixed term, but rather provide for termination by one or other party on giving notice. If the term of the lease is shorter than the period for which the lessee is likely to want to use the asset, it is advisable to include an option for renewal.

Rent

Most leases provide for equal monthly or quarterly payments of rent, usually payable in advance. In a lease-to-own contract, the rent is calculated with reference to the normal selling price of the asset, with an additional "interest" element to take account of the period over which it is payable. Operating lease rentals take more account of the probable depreciation of the asset over the period of the lease and of the cost to the lessor of the asset, with an appropriate profit margin. Provision may be made for the payment of one or more month's additional rent in advance.

Insurance and Other Costs Payable by the Lessee

In short-term operating leases, the lessor normally insures the leased asset and bears the costs of maintenance and repairs. In longer leases, and especially in purchase leases, the lessee is usually required to covenant to keep the asset insured, to maintain it properly, and to pay the costs of maintenance and repairs. Sometimes the lessee is required to provide a "residual guarantee"; that is, a guarantee that the lessor will receive a minimum resale value at the end of the lease or if not, the lessee will be responsible for the difference.

Purchase Option

A purchase lease inevitably contains an option for the lessee to purchase the asset at the end of the term, usually for a relatively nominal amount. Operating leases sometimes also include a purchase option, at a price to be agreed, with the price reducing over the lease term to offset depreciation.

Early Termination—Minimum Payment

Where the leased asset is new, or relatively so, the decrease in its value due to depreciation will often be greater than the amount of rent payable, at least in the early part of the lease term. Consequently, it is usual for the lessor to insist on a minimum rental payment, to act as a deterrent against default or early termination. In England, hire-purchase agreements at one time contained harsh minimum payment clauses, requiring payment of two-thirds of the full price, or even the entire balance, if the lessee defaulted on even one monthly payment, with no reduction for the value of the asset that reverted to the lessor. Sometimes, such clauses were struck down as disguised penalties, but more effective protection to consumers was provided by statute.[10] In Canada, by contrast, very little statutory protection is provided. As one commentator observed, "large scale consumer leasing developed in Canada after consumer legislation ceased to be politically attractive."[11] In Ontario, the Consumer Protection Act[12] does not apply to consumer leases; in Alberta and Manitoba, there are disclosure requirements to ensure that lessees are made aware of the true costs of the transaction.[13]

Checklist: Terms in a Lease Contract

A lease contract will normally state

- the duration of the lease
- the rent payable
- the party responsible for maintenance and insurance
- whether there is an option to renew
- whether there is an option for purchase and, if so, the terms of the option
- what is to happen if the lease is terminated before the end of its prescribed term

Implied Terms

It is remarkable that there is very little "law" in Canada relating expressly to chattel leasing. Whereas England has its hire-purchase legislation going back to the 1930s and several U.S. states have legislation adopting article 2A of the Uniform Commercial Code, which applies to leases, there is no Canadian legislation specifically dealing with chattel leases. Nor, rather surprisingly, is there much case law. Perhaps this is because the lessors are mostly quite large concerns that use carefully drafted standard-form contracts. Since the contracts expressly cover most eventualities, there is little room for additional implied terms.

Nevertheless, it seems clear that the courts will, by analogy with the law on leases of real property, imply on the part of the lessor a warranty of **quiet possession**; that is, there will be no interference with the lessee's possession or use of the asset so long as the rent is paid and other terms are complied with. It is likely that, by analogy with sales, implied warranties, such as the warranty of fitness, should be equally applicable to purchase lease contracts.[14] It has been held that the lessor impliedly warrants that leased equipment is reasonably fit for the purpose for which it was hired.[15] Some doubt exists as to whether this warranty is limited to defects of which the lessor ought to have been aware; but if an analogy is drawn with the corresponding implied term in a contract of sale, a lessor, like a seller, should be liable even if the offending defect in the chattel is something it could not have detected.

quiet possession
a warranty that there will be no interference with the lessee's possession or use of the asset

The standard of care required of a lessee who hires equipment is to take such care as a prudent person would exercise in the use of her own property.

---

10. Initially in the Hire-Purchase Act, 1938, and subsequently in the Consumer Credit Act, 1974. In the United States, protection from unconscionable terms is provided by Article 2A of the Uniform Commercial Code (added in 1987) and under the consumer lease provisions of the Uniform Consumer Credit Code.

11. Cuming (1990), 16 *C.B.L.J.* 439.

12. R.S.O. 1990, c. C.31.

13. Consumer Credit Transaction Act, S.A. 1985, c. 22.5; Consumer Protection Act, R.S.M. 1987, c. 200. See further, Chapter 32.

14. This has been the case in England; see Astley Industrial Trust Ltd. v. Grimley, [1963] 1 W.L.R. 584.

15. Griffith S.S. Co. v. Western Plywood Co., [1953] 3 D.L.R. 29.

CASE 17.1

Roxburgh rented a portable steam engine from Reynolds to power a wood-cutting saw. The engine exploded immediately after it was put into use, killing one worker and injuring another. Reynolds sued Roxburgh for the value of the destroyed engine and boiler. He alleged that Roxburgh had not tested the steam gauge and safety valve before running the machine. The court applied the rule that "the hirer of a chattel is required to use…the degree of diligence which pru-

dent men use…in keeping their own goods of the same kind." The court held that this standard of care did not require the lessee to test the safety gauge and valve. Accordingly, the defendant was not in breach of his duty as a lessee and was not liable to pay for the destroyed steam engine.[16]

The question of who was liable for the injuries to the workers—the lessor or the lessee—was not raised in the case.

RIGHTS OF THE PARTIES

The Lessor

The rights of the parties under a lease contract are, of course, governed by the terms, express and implied, of the contract. The principal remedies available to the lessor are the right to sue for rent that is due and unpaid, and the right to retake possession of the leased property at the end of the lease or in the event of earlier default by the lessee. When a lessee contracts to hire a chattel for a given period, she remains liable for the whole rental even if she finds that she has overestimated the time needed to use the equipment. (In the same way, a tenant of a building is liable for rent for the full period of the lease whether she occupies or uses the premises or not.) A lessor may agree to take equipment back ahead of time and to reduce the rental charges; when he does so, he is consenting to a discharge of the original lease contract and to replacing it with a substituted agreement. But it seems that the lessor is entitled *both* to retake possession of the chattel *and* to sue for damages for loss of bargain in respect of the rent that would have been payable if there had been no default, or for any minimum rent stipulated in the contract.[17] Additionally, if the lessee is in breach of her duty to take proper care of the leased property, the lessor will have an action for damages for the loss.

The Lessee

As noted above, the lessor impliedly warrants that the lessee shall have quiet possession and, probably, that the goods are fit for the purpose for which they are hired. Consequently, the lessee is entitled to sue for damages if she is wrongfully dispossessed during the term of the lease, or if she suffers loss because of some defect in the goods.

The law is less clear in the case of finance leases where the supplier sells an article to the financer, who in turn leases it to the actual user, the lessee. The lessee's contract is thus with the financer, although most of her dealings will have been with the supplier, with whom she has no contract. Where the supplier has made express representations to the lessee to induce her to enter into the contract, a collateral contract may be implied between supplier and lessee; that is, in return for the supplier's warranty that the goods conform to a particular quality or have a particular characteristic, the lessee agrees to enter into the contract with the financer—a contract which is of benefit to the supplier.[18]

---

16. Reynolds v. Roxburgh (1886), 10 O.R. 649, per Armour, J., at 655.

17. Keneric Tractor Sales Ltd. v. Langille (1987), 43 D.L.R. (4th) 171 (S.C.C.).

18. See Hallmark Pool Corp. v. Storey (1983), 144 D.L.R. (3d) 56. This is consistent with the principle established in Shanklin Pier Ltd. v. Detel Products Ltd., discussed in Chapter 12, "Exceptions to the Privity of Contract Rule."

The lessee would have the usual contractual remedies against the financer, although in practice finance leases routinely exclude all implied warranties on the part of the lessor.

CONTEMPORARY ISSUE

Leasing or Fleecing?

There are many advantages to leasing as a means of acquiring capital assets of a business. However, as the following extract makes clear, leasing may also have its disadvantages.

> Leasing has been called fleecing because it's so profitable for dealers and can be so costly to consumers who don't know what they're getting into. Few lessees fully understand the real costs involved, focussing instead solely on the advertised low monthly payment.
>
> If lease payments look more attractive than loan payments, make sure you know why. The lower rates may be achieved by jiggling numbers—asking for more money up front, for example, or assigning the car a higher residual value (its preset buy-back worth as set out in the lease contract). As a result, lower rates don't necessarily represent real savings.
>
> In the past, leasing agreements have been confusing in the way they were laid out, and in the way they identified terms, costs and conditions. Since January [of 1997], the major manufacturers have worked to meet an industry commitment to simplify and clarify leasing contracts in all provinces. However, all the clarity in the world will not help if consumers don't pay attention to what they're signing.

Source: L.D. Cross, "The Economics of Auto Leases," *Financial Post*, October 1, 1997, p. 115.

Questions to Consider

1. Should there be legislation prescribing the information that must be provided and the manner in which it is presented in lease contracts?
2. Should such legislation apply only to consumer leases, or to all leases of personal property?

BAILMENT

Definition

A **bailment** is a transfer of possession of personal property without a transfer of ownership, usually on the understanding that the party receiving the property will return it at a later time or dispose of it as directed. The transferor of the property, usually its owner, is called the *bailor* and the party that receives the custody of it, the *bailee*. The concept embraces a wide variety of economic and social activities. Examples of bailment are: leaving an article with a railway for shipment; giving stocks and bonds to a bank as security for a loan; leaving a stereo with a repairer; storing furniture in a warehouse; and leasing a harvesting machine to a farmer.

bailment
a transfer of possession of personal property without a transfer of ownership

Non-Contractual Bailments

The above examples are all forms of *contractual* bailment, but a bailment can also occur without any contract between a bailor and bailee. The essential elements of bailment are delivery of possession without the intention to transfer title and with the intention that the property shall be returned to the bailor. All these elements may exist without a contract, as when the owner of a lawnmower lends it gratuitously to a neighbour. The intention that the object shall be returned need not be stated expressly between the parties but may be presumed from the circumstances. A bailment may also be *involuntary*; if a customer leaves a coat behind in a restaurant, the restaurateur becomes a bailee of the coat and cannot refuse to return it at the customer's request.

A person who finds a valuable object is not bound to take possession of it, but once she does so she becomes a bailee for the owner.

Bailment Compared With Sale

A bailment differs from a sale. A sale transfers ownership although, as Chapter 16 has shown, it need not involve a change in possession. By contrast, a bailment does not alter ownership but does require a change in possession. The subject-matter of a bailment need not be a chattel; it may be a document representing legal rights, such as a share or bond certificate, bill of lading, or title deed. And, as noted above, a bailment need not be contractual.

Bailment Compared With Trust

A transfer of property to a trustee for the benefit of one or more persons does not create a bailment. The creation of a trust gives legal ownership to the trustee and the beneficiary acquires an equitable interest in the subject of the trust. Thus, a receiving order transferring ownership of the assets of a bankrupt debtor to a trustee in bankruptcy for the benefit of creditors is not a bailment; nor does the transfer of property to an executor under a will constitute a bailment. The subject-matter of a trust may be real property as well as personal property, whereas bailment is confined to personal property.

Bailment Compared With Debt

A deposit of money in a bank or trust company creates a creditor–debtor rather than a bailor–bailee relationship.[19] By contrast, a deposit of specific items of personal property for safekeeping with a bank or trust company does create a bailment. The difference has important consequences if the recipient becomes bankrupt. A bailee has no title to articles entrusted to it: the articles do not form part of the assets available to creditors and must be returned to the bailor intact. Thus, a bailor is better off on the insolvency of the bailee than a creditor is on the insolvency of its debtor; the creditor must await its share in the available assets of the debtor, along with the other creditors.

Bailment Compared With Licence

The distinction between bailment and licence can be summarized as follows: bailments require a transfer of possession and a voluntary acceptance of the common law duty of safekeeping, while licences amount to no more than a grant of permission to the user of a chattel to leave it upon the licensor's land on the understanding that possession is not transferred and responsibility for guarding the chattel is not accepted.[20] For example, the owner of a parking lot normally does not accept responsibility for storage of the vehicle and grants only a licence to use the lot.[21]

The Benefit of Bailment

Bailments may be for the benefit of the bailor or the bailee, or for the benefit of both parties. By their nature, contractual bailments are intended to be of benefit to both parties: one party

---

19. For a case illustrating the importance of distinguishing between these relationships, see Royal Bank of Canada v. Reynolds (1976), 66 D.L.R. (3d) 88.

20. See Palmer, *Bailment* (2nd ed.), (1991), p. 382, quoted by Binder, J., in Dorico Investments Ltd. v. Weyerhaeuser Canada Ltd., [1999] A.J. No. 869. A licence has been described as the grant of authority to enter upon land for an agreed purpose where such entry would otherwise be a trespass: Heffron v. Imperial Parking Co. et al. (1974), 3 O.R. (2d) 722 at 727.

21. Bata v. City Parking Canada Ltd. (1973), 2 O.R. (2d) 446. The situation is probably different where the parking-lot operator parks the car and retains the keys: Heffron v. Imperial Parking Co. et al., *supra,* n. 20.

obtains the service desired and the other receives payment. Non-contractual, or *gratuitous* bailments, may be for the benefit of either party. Examples of those for the benefit of the bailor occur when a pet is left with a neighbour during vacation, or valuables are left in a relative's safe. Examples of bailments for the benefit of the bailee are the lending of a car for a trip, or a power tool to do a home repair. A **gratuitous bailment** may sometimes be for the benefit of both parties; for example, when a car is left with a friend for safekeeping but the friend has permission to use it from time to time, or when a loan of a camera is made in the hope that the borrower will buy it if satisfied with its performance.

gratuitous bailment
a bailment where one party provides no consideration, or where there is no intention to create a contractual relationship

RIGHTS AND DUTIES OF A BAILEE
Liability Under Contract and Tort

Sometimes bailed goods are lost, damaged, or destroyed while in the possession of a bailee. The question then arises whether the bailee is liable for the loss suffered. When the bailment is the result of a contract, its terms, either express or implied by trade custom, set out the duties and liabilities of the bailee for the goods in its possession. All bailees are, however, under a duty to take care of property bailed to them. The standard of care required by the law of torts applies in circumstances not covered expressly or impliedly by the bailment contract, and the standard applies also to gratuitous bailments involving no contract at all. The required standard of care does vary, as we shall see, according to the type of bailment.

Sometimes, a contract of bailment includes a term that the bailee shall not be liable for damage to the goods while in her custody, even when the damage is caused by negligence in the course of performing the contract. The courts construe this type of exemption clause very strictly against the bailee, just as we have seen them do against the seller in a contract of sale.[22] If the goods are damaged for any reason not related to the actual performance contemplated by the contract, the bailee is not protected by the exemption clause.

CASE 17.2

An army officer took his uniform to a firm of dry cleaners to be cleaned. The cleaners gave him a receipt in which they disclaimed all liability for damage arising in the course of "necessary handling." The uniform was never returned, and when the officer sued for its value, the cleaners pleaded the exemption clause. It was established that the loss arose when the cleaning firm had sent the uniform to someone else for cleaning; the court found that the wording of the contract required personal performance by the bailee. Thus, the damage had not taken place during "necessary handling" as contemplated in the exemption clause; the exemption clause did not apply and the cleaners were held liable for the loss.[23]

Although the law of bailment has elements of both tort and contract law, bailment is a distinct relationship governed by its own rules. For example, when goods are damaged or lost while in the possession of a bailee, it is often difficult for the bailor to ascertain exactly how the harm occurred. Since a bailee is better able to establish the facts, the law of bailment places on the bailee the burden of showing that she was not negligent; she must offer some reasonable alternative explanation for the loss. Consequently, it may be easier for a bailor to sue under the rules of bailment than under the ordinary rules of tort.

---

22. See *Baldry v. Marshall*, [1925] 1 K.B. 260, as discussed in Chapter 16, "Terms in a Contract of Sale."
23. *Davies v. Collins*, [1945] 1 All E.R. 247.

Sub-bailment

sub-bailee

a person who receives a bailment of property from a bailee

We have already noted that a relationship of bailment may exist without any contract between bailor and bailee. The relationship may also exist between a bailor and a **sub-bailee**, even when there has been no contract or communication between them.

CASE 17.3

Punch took her diamond ring, worth $11 000, to Savoy Jewellers in Sault St. Marie for repair. Savoy was unable to make the repair, so they sent it to Walker Jewellers in Toronto. Savoy sent the ring by registered mail and stated the value for insurance purposes as $100. Apparently, this was normal trade practice.

Since there was a postal strike when Walker had repaired the ring, it decided to return the ring to Savoy using a delivery service operated by Canadian National (CN). Again, the value was declared as $100. The contract between Walker and CN limited CN's liability for loss or damage to the declared value of $100. The ring was never delivered to Savoy. CN admitted a driver might have stolen the ring but it had not made a thorough investigation.

Punch sued Savoy, Walker, and CN. The court found that Savoy was a bailee, and both Walker and CN were sub-bailees. All three owed a duty of care to Punch, and the burden on each of them was to show it was not responsible for the loss, nor for inadequately insuring the ring.[24]

In *Punch v. Savoy Jewellers* (Case 17.3) the court held that the clause in the contract between CN and Walker, which limited CN's liability, could not be relied on by CN against either Savoy or Punch, since they were not parties to the contract. All three parties were found liable. The question of whether a sub-bailee may rely on a term of its contract with the (head) bailee against the original bailor, who was not a party to that contract, is not a straightforward one.[25] Suppose, for example, that Punch had agreed that Savoy's liability should be limited to $100 when it sent the ring by registered mail; why should CN and Walker not be entitled to rely on a similar limitation in their contracts? The Privy Council considered that question in *The Pioneer Container* (Case 17.4).

CASE 17.4

The plaintiffs contracted with a shipping firm, Hanjin Container Lines, to have goods shipped from the United States to Hong Kong. The contract with Hanjin contained a term that "the carrier shall be entitled to sub-contract *on any terms* the whole or any part of the handling of the goods"[italics added]. Hanjin contracted with the defendants, the owners of *The Pioneer Container*, to ship the goods on the last leg of their journey, from Taiwan to Hong Kong. The goods were lost in a collision off the coast of Taiwan. The bill of lading contract between Hanjin and the defendants contained a term that the contract should be governed by Chinese law and any dispute should be determined in Taiwan.

The plaintiffs sued the defendants in Hong Kong. The defendants objected that, under the terms of the bill of lading, they could be sued only in Taiwan. The court ruled that, although there was no contract between the plaintiffs and the defendants, the plaintiffs had authorized the sub-bailment and they had effectively consented to the terms of the sub-bailment.[26]

---

24. Punch v. Savoy Jewellers Ltd. (1986), 26 D.L.R. (4th) 546.

25. Contrast London Drugs Ltd. v. Kuehne and Nagel International Ltd. (1992), 97 D.L.R. (4th) 261, in which the Supreme Court of Canada held that employees of a warehouse firm, sued personally for negligently damaging goods stored in the warehouse, were entitled to the protection of a clause in the storage contract limiting liability to a stated amount. See the discussion in Chapter 12, "Vicarious Performance."

26. The Pioneer Container, [1994] 2 A.C. 324 (P.C.). For comment on the issue, see Bankes and Rafferty, "Privy of Bailment—Liability of Sub-bailee to Owner of Goods" (1997), 28 *C.B.L.J.* 245.

The Standard of Care

As noted above, the requisite standard of care varies according to the type of bailment. The standard is least exacting upon a bailee when the bailment is both gratuitous and for the benefit of the bailor, as when *A* permits *B* to store her car in *A*'s garage. In these circumstances, the bailee should not be under a particularly high duty towards the bailor for, after all, the bailee is doing the bailor a favour; but even a gratuitous bailee is liable for gross negligence.[27]

The standard of care is most exacting on a bailee when the bailment is gratuitous and for the benefit of the bailee, as when one borrows a friend's car for personal use. The bailor receives no valuable consideration, and so it is fair that, in such circumstances, the bailee should compensate the bailor when damage to the goods results from even slight carelessness on the bailee's part. A gratuitous bailment for the benefit of both parties is, at least in part, for the bailee's benefit and it would appear that the higher standard of care applies here as well.

In bailments for value, the standard of care falls between that of gratuitous bailments for the benefit of the bailee and of those for the benefit of the bailor. (Thus, a bailee who allows a friend to leave her car in the bailee's garage is not under as high a duty of care as would a warehousing firm being paid to store the car.) Generally, a bailee for value is expected to take the same care of goods as a prudent and diligent person should take of goods belonging to those with whom she transacts business—a standard of care that is at least as high and probably higher than she might choose to apply to her own goods.

The standard also varies according to the type of goods bailed and the extent of the promise to look after the goods. In interpreting both express and implied promises of the bailee, the courts consider all the circumstances. Thus, if the property is very valuable and easily damaged, lost, or stolen, the standard of care required will be higher: one must take greater care with expensive jewellery than with a bicycle stored in one's shed. In the words of one judge, "The substantial question must always be, whether that care has been exhibited which the special circumstances reasonably demand."[28]

Two special classes of bailee are subject to very high standards of care because they deal with the public generally. These are common carriers and hoteliers or innkeepers, whom we shall discuss later in this chapter.

Remedies of a Bailee for the Value of Services Rendered

Damages and *Quantum Meruit*

In a contractual bailment, the bailee, as a party to a contract, has the usual contractual remedies for breach by the bailor. Because of the character of bailment, rescission of the contract is rarely practical or even possible: it is too late to rescind a contract for storage or safekeeping or for the shipment of goods once the bailee has performed her duties; in most cases repairs already made to goods cannot be undone. Consequently, the main concern of a bailee is to receive compensation for services rendered.

When a bailee has completely performed her part of a contract, as when a warehouse returns goods that have been stored with it, the usual remedy is an action for the contract price. Occasionally a bailee may not be able to complete performance, as when a carrier has contracted to transport goods in several instalments but the bailor (shipper) delivers only part of the goods for shipment. The carrier may then sue *quantum meruit* for the value of the services it has performed and for damages compensating it for its loss of profits because the bailor failed to deliver all the goods for shipment. We have discussed these remedies for breach of contract in Chapter 15.

---

27. See Munroe v. Belinsky, [1995] M.J. No. 168.

28. Fitzgerald v. Grand Trunk Railway (1880), 4 O.A.R. 601, per Moss, C.J.A., at 624.

Lien

An important additional remedy available to a bailee for non-payment by a bailor is a *lien* on the bailed goods in its possession. This gives the bailee a right to retain possession of the goods until the bailor pays what is due for the services; the bailor cannot repossess the goods until he has paid the sum due. Generally, a right of lien arises only when the services have been performed and payment is already due. If payment is not due when the goods are to be repossessed, no lien exists, and the bailee is under a duty to return the goods.

ILLUSTRATION 17.1

Pliable Plastics Ltd. has very little storage space for its manufactured products. It enters into an arrangement with Stately Storage Limited whereby Pliable Plastics delivers its products for storage on a daily charge basis, and when they are sold, picks them up again for delivery to the buyer. Storage charges are billed and become payable every three months.

Stately Storage has no lien upon the goods stored with it until the end of the three-month period and until it has billed Pliable Plastics. If, after two and one-half months have passed, Pliable Plastics sells a portion of the stored goods, Stately Storage must surrender the goods on demand to Pliable Plastics or to a buyer who presents proper documents. When three months have expired and Stately Storage bills Pliable Plastics, Stately Storage has a lien for all the accrued storage charges upon the goods remaining in the warehouse at that time.

In our discussion of the rights of an unpaid seller in Chapter 16, we saw that a lien is a possessory remedy: an unpaid bailee loses her lien on the bailed goods as soon as the bailor obtains possession of them without deceit or fraud.

A right of lien under common law rules is available to bailees who perform services in the nature of repairs or improvements to goods bailed with them, to innkeepers, to common carriers, who are under a duty to accept goods from anyone so long as they have space for them, and also to professional people like lawyers and bankers, who have a common law right of lien over documents in their possession when they have performed services related to the documents. However, the common law did not give a right of lien to a bailee for simply storing goods. Various statutes have created liens in other types of bailment and, even though they may have a common law or statutory right of lien, many businesses acting as bailees for value expressly provide for the right as a term in their contracts with customers. We shall discuss these rights of lien as they arise in the remaining sections of this chapter.

The Right of Sale

The right of lien is valuable to a bailee because the bailor usually needs to recover his goods and to do so he must first pay off overdue charges. If, however, the bailor is unable to pay off the charges, as when he becomes insolvent, the bailee is left with goods she cannot use because she has no title to them, and yet she has the burden of storing them. Various statutes give bailees with a lien upon goods stored with them an additional right to sell the goods. Bailees that do not have the statutory right to sell bailed goods may acquire that right as a term of the bailment contract just as they may acquire the right of lien.

The provisions of the statutes vary in detail, but generally they require first, that a certain time elapse after payment falls due; second, that advance notice be given to the bailor of the bailee's intention to sell; third, that the sale be advertised; and fourth, that it be held by public auction. Until the time of sale, the owner of the goods (or other person entitled to possession) is usually entitled to recover them on payment in full of the bailee's charges.[29] The proceeds of

---

29. For example, Warehouse Lien Act, R.S.B.C. 1996, c. 480, s. 7; Repair and Storage Liens Act, R.S.O. 1990, c. R.25, s. 22.

the sale are used, first, to reimburse the bailee for her costs of holding the sale, and, second, to pay the overdue charges for her services; any surplus belongs to the bailor.

Special Types of Bailment

Storage and Safekeeping

A warehousing firm that accepts goods for storage, or a bank that rents a safety-deposit box, are bailees for storage or safekeeping and are under a duty to take care of the goods stored with them. The express or implied authority that a bailment contract gives the bailee for dealing with the bailed goods may affect her liability for them. Thus, a warehousing company may or may not have implied authority to subcontract for the storage of the goods with another warehouse; this may depend upon the nature of the goods stored.[30] The terms of a contract may reduce liability; for example, if the bailor overrides a warehouse keeper's usual discretion in handling the goods by directing where the goods are to be placed, the liability of the warehouse keeper will be restricted to complying with those instructions.

A warehouse firm is not customarily obliged to insure goods stored with it against loss by fire;[31] but when it has expressly contracted to do so and fails, it is liable to the bailor for the insured value of the goods if they are destroyed. Ordinarily, a bailee must return to the bailor the exact goods stored. When, however, the goods stored are **fungible** (that is, replaceable with identical goods also in storage), the bailee's liability is discharged when she returns to the bailor goods of the exact description in the warehouse receipt. For example, when a quantity of grain of a specific grade is stored in a grain elevator in bins containing other grain of the same grade, the elevator company is bound to deliver not the exact grain that was bailed with it, but an equivalent quantity of the same grade.

> **fungible goods**
> goods that may be replaced with different but identical goods

At common law, a warehousing firm did not obtain a right of lien on goods stored with it unless it had specifically bargained for the lien. In Canada, however, we have legislation passed by all the common law provinces giving a warehouse a right of lien on goods stored with it for the amount of its charges. The statutes state that "every warehouseman has a lien on goods deposited with him for storage whether deposited by the owner of the goods or by his authority or by any person entrusted with the possession of the goods by the owner or by his authority."[32] The statutes further provide that "a warehouseman may sell by public auction in the manner provided in this section any goods on which he has a lien for charges that have become due."[33] The warehouse must give notice to the owner, the debtor (if different), and to any other persons known by the warehouse managers to have a claim on or an interest in the goods, stating that unless the charges are paid within the allotted time, the goods will be advertised for sale and sold by public auction at a time and place specified in the notice. The statutes set out the details of the type of advertisement and the way in which the sale is to be held. The aim is to give adequate protection to the bailor or owner while giving the bailee a reasonably prompt method of obtaining payment.

---

30. An English court has held that in a contract for the storage of furniture, it is implied that the bailee shall perform the contract itself and that sub-bailment amounts to a breach of contract: Edwards v. Newland, [1950] 1 All E.R. 1072.

31. See Neff v. St. Catharines Marina Ltd. (1998), 155 D.L.R. (4th) 647. But the warehouse firm's failure to install alarm and sprinkler systems may amount to failure to exercise due care of the goods: Hogarth v. Archibald Moving & Storage Ltd. (1991), 57 B.C.L.R. (2d) 319.

32. See, for example: Warehouse Lien Act, R.S.B.C. 1996, c. 480, s. 2; Warehousemen's Lien Act, R.S.N.S. 1989, c. 499, s. 3. In Ontario, the former Warehousemen's Lien Act has been repealed and replaced by the Repair and Storage Liens Act, R.S.O. 1990, c. R.25. Section 4(1) gives a similar lien to a "storer" of goods.

33. R.S.B.C. 1996, c. 480, s. 4; R.S.N.S. 1989, c. 499, s. 5. In Ontario, a storer has a similar right: Repair and Storage Liens Act, R.S.O. 1990, c. R.25, s. 4(7).

Repairs and Work on a Chattel

Bailment is often a normal consequence of contracts made for the maintenance of various kinds of business equipment, as when a truck is delivered to a garage for repair, when an electronics firm receives business machines for servicing, or when a laundry picks up factory uniforms for cleaning. A repairer who works on these articles on its own premises is a bailee for value. In accepting the work, the repairer undertakes to do it in a competent manner employing the skill it professes to have and to have it done by the time it promises. Failure to do these things is a breach of contract on its part;[34] depending on the circumstances, a breach may entitle the bailor to not pay for work already done or to sue for damages. The bailor is also entitled to the return of the chattel. The standard of care required of a worker towards chattels bailed with him is similar to that required of a warehousing company.

CASE 17.5

Duckworth owned a classic sports car that was damaged in an accident. He took the car to Superior Autobody to have repairs done, and left a deposit of $500. The shop did not have an alarm system and did not have padlocks on the latches of the overhead doors. The shop's practice was also to leave the keys in cars to allow easy removal. Thieves broke in and stole the car, which was never recovered. The court held that the repairers were bailees for reward and were liable for the loss since they had failed to take the appropriate care of the car while it was in their charge.[35]

Ordinarily, by leaving an article for repair, a bailor gives the repairer implied authority to order the parts necessary to carry out the repairs and include the cost of parts in the charges. A bailor who wishes to limit expenses may make it a term of the contract that the repairer shall not make repairs beyond a stated sum, or may prohibit the repairer from proceeding with the repairs at all if parts and labour exceed a specified amount.

As noted earlier, the common law gives a repairer a lien for the value of the work done upon goods left with him. The common law right does not extend to the right to sell the goods, but some of the provinces give an additional statutory right to the repairer to sell the goods when the repair charges are three months overdue.[36]

Transportation

Types of Carriers

The law distinguishes three types of carriers. A *gratuitous* carrier is anyone who agrees to move goods from one place to another without reward. A *private* carrier is a business that undertakes on occasion to carry goods for reward, but reserves the right to select its customers and restrict the type of goods it is willing to carry. A **common carrier** is a business that holds itself out to the public as a carrier of goods for reward. The essence of its status is that it does not discriminate among those who request its services, nor does it reserve the right to refuse an offer of goods for shipment when it has the means of shipping them. However, it may be a common carrier on the terms that its services are restricted to a certain area and to those kinds of goods that are suitable for carriage by its equipment. Most railway and steamship companies are common carri-

common carrier
a business that holds itself out to the public as a carrier of goods for reward

---

34. Alternatively, the bailor may sue in tort. In practice, there would seem to be little or no difference in the standard of care required: Morrison v. McCoy Bros. Group, [1987] A.J. No. 134.

35. Duckworth v. Armstrong (1996), 29 C.C.L.T.(2d) 239.

36. See, for example: Repairers' Lien Act, R.S.B.C. 1996, c. 404, s. 2; Repair and Storage Liens Act, R.S.O. 1990, c. R-25, s. 3(3).

ers, as are some trucking companies and even gas and oil pipeline companies. Airlines may repudiate the status of a common carrier by reserving the right to refuse goods.

A carrier's liability for damage to goods in the course of transit depends upon the type of carrier it is. A carrier is a bailee and always has *some* responsibility for the goods under its control. Even a gratuitous bailee must exercise at least the diligence and care to be expected of a reasonable person in handling his or her own property. The duty of care required of a private carrier is greater. It owes a degree of care commensurate with the skill reasonably expected of a competent firm in its line of business. The liability of a common carrier is still greater, although it may take advantage of certain recognized defences that we shall examine.

Liability of a Common Carrier

A common carrier undertakes to indemnify the shipper (the bailor) against loss whether the loss occurs through the carrier's fault or not. The carrier is, therefore, an insurer as well as a bailee. The historical reason for this special liability was to prevent the practice, once frequent in England, of collusion between carriers and highwaymen: the highwayman would "rob" the carrier of the shipper's goods and the carrier would plead that it was not its fault that the goods were taken. Although these reasons seem amusing when applied to the modern railroad, steamship, and trucking companies, there is good sense in the rule itself: its practical effect is to relieve the shipper of any burden of producing evidence that it was the common carrier's lack of reasonable care that caused the damage to the shipper's goods en route. In most circumstances, it would be impossible for the carrier to gather this evidence. The shipper need only prove (1) that the carrier received the goods in good condition, and (2) that the carrier delivered them in bad condition or failed to deliver them at all. The burden is then on the carrier, if it is to avoid liability, to establish that the cause of the loss was within one of the recognized defences available to common carriers.

It is not enough for a common carrier to show that it was not negligent. Its only defences are an act of God,[37] an **inherent vice** in the goods, or default by the shipper. Fire is not an act of God unless caused by lightning, and a common carrier, unlike other bailees for value, is liable for damage to goods caused by fire, although there is no negligence provable against it. Even when the cause of the loss is a natural catastrophe, the carrier may still be liable if it has negligently contributed to the loss, for example by putting to sea during a severe storm.[38] A common carrier may also avoid liability if it can show that the goods had an inherent vice at the time of shipment; for example, the goods may have been in a combustible condition or may have had latent defects that made them more susceptible to breakage than is typical of goods of their category. This defence by the carrier also includes inadequate packing of the goods by the shipper, regardless of whether the carrier was aware of the inadequate packing.[39]

A common carrier can offer a third defence: that the shipper has been guilty of a breach of duty. A contract for the transportation of goods includes an implied promise on the part of the shipper that the goods are safe to carry; the term exists regardless of whether the shipper is aware of the danger.[40] It is possible therefore for the shipper itself to be in breach of contract and so to release the common carrier from its part of the bargain. Indeed, if the goods cause damage to the carrier's equipment, for instance by exploding, the carrier may successfully sue for damages.

Unless otherwise agreed, a common carrier is liable for the full value of goods lost or destroyed. However, the carrier may, and frequently does, limit the amount of its liability when the shipper does not declare the value of the goods. Thus, a bill of lading commonly states, "Liability limited to $50.00 unless higher value is declared by the shipper and inserted herein."

inherent vice
a latent defect or dangerous condition of goods

---

37. That is, a natural catastrophe: see the discussion in Chapter 13, under "Condition Subsequent."

38. Nugent v. Smith (1875), 1 C.P.D. 423.

39. Gould v. South Eastern & Chatham Railway, [1920] 2 K.B. 186.

40. Burley Ltd. v. Stepney Corp., [1947] 1 All E.R. 507 at 510.

This term requires the shipper to declare a higher value when necessary and to pay a correspondingly higher rate for the greater liability undertaken by the common carrier. Where the shipper declares less than the full value of the goods to the carrier, in order to pay a lower freight charge than it would have paid had it declared their true value, the carrier is not released from its duty, but its liability is limited to the declared value.

Contractual terms limiting the liability of carriers who operate interprovincial or international routes are enforceable only if approved by the Canadian Transport Commissioners; thus there is some public control over the extent to which common carriers may contract themselves out of their special liability. Terms limiting liability, when subject to public control, often make good sense between the parties: the common carrier bases its freight charges on all the terms of the contract and the other contracting party (the shipper) knows the extent to which it should contract separately for insurance. While these terms are a type of exemption clause, they seek to limit rather than eliminate the carrier's liability. As with other types of contract, the courts have been unwilling to construe an exemption clause as freeing a party to a contract from liability for default when the default amounts to a total failure to carry out the contract.[41]

Remedies

All carriers, whether common carriers or not, have the usual remedies for breach of contract when a shipper is in default. There is, however, a distinction between common carriers and other carriers regarding the right of lien. A common carrier is bound to accept goods for shipment if it has space available; in return, the common law gives it a lien on goods shipped for the amount of unpaid freight. Although some doubt exists, the general opinion is that the common law does not give a private carrier a similar lien, though it may acquire a right of lien as a term of the contract. Neither the common law nor any statutes of general application give either common carriers or private carriers the right to sell goods retained under a lien. Both types of carriers, however, usually stipulate for an express right to sell the goods in case of default.

Hotelkeepers and Innkeepers

Definition of an Innkeeper

A distinction similar to that between private carriers and common carriers exists between innkeepers (or hotelkeepers) and others who also offer various forms of accommodation to the public. The traditional word "**innkeeper**," like the more modern term "hotelkeeper," or simply "hotel," refers to a person or firm that maintains an establishment offering lodging to any member of the public as a transient guest. For this purpose, a hotel differs from a boarding-house keeper, who may pick and choose whom he or she is willing to accommodate, and also from a restaurant owner, who does not offer lodging to guests. The proprietor of a tourist home or a motel that does not offer restaurant facilities is apparently not an innkeeper.

innkeeper
a person who maintains an establishment offering lodging to any member of the public

Liability

Businesses other than hotels or inns offering accommodation to the public are under a duty to take reasonable care of the belongings of their guests and patrons. Like warehousing firms, they are liable for damage or loss caused by their negligence or the negligence of their employees. Under the common law, however, innkeepers are under a much higher liability. They are liable as insurers for the *loss or theft* of their guests' goods. The historical reason is similar to that for the liability of a common carrier—to prevent collusion between the innkeeper and thieves. There is, however, an important difference between goods bailed to a common carrier and goods left in the room of a hotel guest: the bailor of goods to a common carrier gives them over com-

---

41. Firchuk v. Waterfront Investments & Cartage Ltd., [1970] 1 O.R. 327. See the discussion in Chapter 14, "Failure of Performance."

pletely to the care of the carrier, whereas the hotel guest shares the responsibility with the hotel, since he or she has control over the goods when occupying the room. Accordingly, a hotel may avoid liability if it can show that the disappearance was due to the carelessness of the guest. It may be difficult to decide the cause of the loss in any given case. Leaving a door unlocked in a small country hotel may not amount to negligence, and the hotel might be liable if the guest's goods were stolen. The same act in a large city hotel might well amount to carelessness that absolves the hotel.

For a similar reason, the considerations that make a common carrier an insurer of *physical damage* to goods bailed with it do not necessarily apply to a hotel: the guest may be in a position to ascertain whether there was negligence on the part of the hotel. Accordingly, a hotel is liable for damage to the goods of its guests—as distinct from its liability for their disappearance through loss or theft—only if the damage was caused by the negligence of the hotel's employees.

The Innkeepers (or Hotelkeepers) Act

A hotel may limit its liability as an insurer for the loss or theft of the goods of guests by complying with the provisions of the Innkeepers Act or Hotelkeepers Act in its province. Depending on the province, the legislation either reduces a hotel's liability to a maximum amount varying from $40 to $150 or eliminates its liability as an insurer entirely.[42] A hotel does not have the benefit of this protection "where the goods have been stolen, lost or injured through the wilful act, default or neglect of the innkeeper or a servant in his employ," or "where the goods have been deposited expressly for safe custody with the innkeeper." If a hotel refuses to accept the goods of a guest for safe custody, it loses the benefit of the reduced liability under the statute and is subject to the full common law liability of innkeepers.

The various statutes require hotels to display conspicuously a copy of the section of the Act that limits liability to take advantage of the section. If a hotel fails to comply with this requirement, it loses that protection.

Remedies

A hotel, like a common carrier, owes a duty to the public generally. As we have seen, it is restricted in its right to refuse guests. Accordingly, the common law gave it a lien over the goods of guests for the value of its services.[43] The right was only a lien, however, and did not include the right to sell the goods. However, the Innkeepers Act of the various provinces usually give the right to sell the goods of guests by public auction if their bills remain unpaid for a specified period.

Pledge or Pawn

While these two terms have the same legal significance, a pawn has a colloquial usage that restricts it to transactions with a pawnbroker. A **pledge** or **pawn** is a bailment of personal property as security for repayment of a loan. The borrower is the *pledgor* and the creditor the *pledgee*. The subject-matter of a pledge may be goods left with a **pawnbroker**, for example, or share certificates left with a bank. As with other forms of bailment, the basis of the transaction is that the title to the thing bailed remains with the borrower (bailor), although the possession passes to the lender (bailee).

A pledgee is a bailee for value and must exercise such care as is reasonable in the ordinary and proper course of its business. A bank is expected to store negotiable bonds in its vault and

pledge or pawn
a bailment of personal property as security for repayment of a loan where possession passes to the bailee

pawnbroker
a business that loans money on the security of pawned goods

---

42. See, for example: Hotelkeepers Act, R.S.B.C. 1996, c. 206, s. 3; Innkeepers Act, R.S.O. 1990, c. I.7, s. 4(1); Tourist Accommodation Act, S.N.S. 1994-95, c. 9, s. 11.

43. Boarding-house keepers and proprietors of restaurants had no such right to a lien, but provincial statutes usually give such a right: R.S.B.C. 1996, c. 206, s. 2; R.S.O. 1990, c. I.7, s. 2; S.N.S. 1994–95, c. 9, s. 10.

is liable for their loss if they are left out of the vault and stolen. A pledgee obtains a lien on the personal property pledged with it, and the pledgor cannot recover possession of the goods until it repays the debt for which they are security. In addition, by pledging the goods, the pledgor gives authority to the pledgee to sell the pledged goods upon default. The lender (pledgee) may reimburse itself out of the proceeds of the sale for any costs incurred as a result of the default and for the amount of the unpaid loan. The surplus, if any, belongs to the borrower. If the property does not bring enough in the sale to liquidate the debt, the borrower remains liable as an ordinary debtor for the deficiency.

The rule is different for pawnbrokers, where the legal effect is governed by provincial statute. A pawnbroker may obtain absolute ownership of the pledged goods after retaining them for a specified period, sending notice of a last opportunity to redeem to the pawner, and publishing a final notice in a newspaper.[44]

QUESTIONS FOR REVIEW

1. What is the principal difference between an operating lease and a purchase lease?

2. Distinguish between a security lease and a finance lease.

3. What warranties will normally be implied in a chattel lease?

4. What are the main perceived advantages of leasing capital assets as opposed to borrowing in order to purchase them?

5. Why would a business enter into a sale-and-leaseback transaction?

6. If a lessee defaults in paying the rent, is the lessor entitled to retake possession of the leased property as well as to sue for the rent owing?

7. Give an example of (a) a non-contractual bailment, (b) an involuntary bailment.

8. Distinguish between a bailment and a licence. In what circumstances is the distinction especially important?

9. What factors determine the standard of care to be expected of a bailee?

10. What is a "sub-bailment"?

11. In what circumstances may a bailee claim a lien on bailed goods?

12. What does it mean that goods are "fungible"? How does that affect a bailee's liability?

13. Who normally bears the loss if goods left in a warehouse are stolen or destroyed?

14. Distinguish between a common carrier and a private carrier.

15. What does it mean to say that a common carrier "is an insurer as well as a bailee"?

16. What are the principal defences available to a common carrier when goods in its possession are damaged or lost?

17. Is a hotelkeeper liable if a guest has property stolen from his or her room?

18. What is meant by a "pledge"?

---

44. See, for example: Pawnbrokers Act, R.S.O. 1990, c. P.6, ss. 20–2.

CASES AND PROBLEMS

1 Cabinco entered into an agreement with Steamboat, whereby Cabinco would construct a prefabricated log cabin and deliver it to a site in a river valley close to Edmonton. Because of the size of the cabin, it was not possible to deliver it directly to the proposed site and arrangements were made to store it temporarily on a 20-acre secured site owned by Waldhauser used for the storage and distribution of forest products. Initially, no charge for storage was contemplated; Waldhauser was simply doing Cabinco a favour, since the owners of the two corporations had a long-standing business relationship.

A dispute arose between Cabinco and Steamboat when it became apparent that Steamboat was unable to pay the price for the cabin. The dispute dragged on, and Cabinco agreed to pay Waldhauser $2000 in return for continuing to store the cabin. Waldhauser was aware of the dispute with Steamboat.

About two years later, Waldhauser received a phone call from a man called "Collins," who said he was ready to come and remove the cabin. Waldhauser informed him that he was welcome to do so, provided he brought a certified cheque for $2000. A few days later, Collins appeared with the cheque and disappeared with the cabin. Collins had no authority from Cabinco and was not known to them.

Cabinco brought an action against Waldhauser for breach of its duty as bailee. Should the action succeed?

2 Intrepid Exploration Inc. is a comparatively small corporation engaged in exploring and drilling for oil in shallow coastal waters, usually as a subcontractor for major companies. Intrepid's owners recently entered into a contract with Globres Inc., one of the majors, to provide specialized drilling services in a project off the New Brunswick coast. They anticipated making a substantial profit on the contract.

Intrepid found that, to perform the contract, it would need a high-pressure drilling unit of a particular type that it did not own. Normally such units are custom made, cost about $500 000, and take about six months to construct. Fortunately, Intrepid was able to locate such a unit, which was owned by Banditoil, a rather larger corporation in the same line of business as Intrepid. The unit was not in use at the time and was unlikely to be needed by Banditoil for at least 18 months.

Intrepid negotiated a contract with Banditoil, under which it would lease the drilling unit for 12 months, with an option to extend the lease for a further 6 months, at a monthly rental of $15 000. Shortly thereafter, and before Intrepid took delivery of the drilling unit, Globres informed Intrepid that it was unwilling to have Intrepid do the work contracted for, and was awarding the contract to another corporation, Cutprice Inc. Globres claimed to be entitled to do so under a clause in the contract; a claim that Intrepid contested. Intrepid immediately informed Banditoil that it no longer needed the drilling unit. Banditoil acknowledged receiving the information and replied that it was considering what action, if any, to take.

Intrepid has now received a demand from Banditoil for payment in full of the sum of $180 000 under the lease contract. Intrepid has also learned that Cutprice has agreed to rent the same drilling unit.

What is the extent of Intrepid's liability towards Banditoil?

3 Thames Pharmacies Ltd. (Thames) entered into a contract with Koenig & Nebel Inc. (K&N) to have a large three-tonne transformer stored in the K&N warehouse for a few weeks, until the transformer could be installed in Thames's own new premises, which were still under construction. A written contract was drawn up, which contained the following provision:

> The warehouse's liability on any one package is limited to $40 unless the holder has declared in writing a valuation in excess of $40 and paid the additional charge specified to cover warehouse liability.

Thames chose not to declare a higher value and pay the extra charge, relying instead on its own insurance.

When the time came to deliver the transformer to Thames' new premises, two employees of K&N, Kupfer and Vanwijk, were instructed to load the transformer on to a truck. They attempted to do so using two forklift trucks, when safe practice would have required the transformer to be lifted in chains from above and lowered on to the truck. The transformer toppled over, causing extensive damage.

Thames then discovered that its own insurance did not cover the damage and brought an action against K&N, and against Kupfer and Vanwijk personally, alleging breach of their duty of care and claiming damages of $34 000.

Is Thames entitled to succeed?

4 Mortensen has been an owner and driver of trucks for about 20 years. Last year he purchased a new truck of a type that he had not operated before, which allowed him to attach a dump trailer. Some weeks later, he was able to buy a used dump trailer for $3000 at an auction. The trailer had obviously seen heavy use—a new trailer of that type would have cost $22 000.

Mortensen took the trailer to McKays Trucks Ltd., where he had always had his vehicles serviced in the past. He asked them to check the trailer thoroughly and to carry out whatever repairs seemed necessary to "make sure the trailer is ready to go to work." McKays carried out some repairs and replaced some worn parts. McKays' foreman told Mortensen that the trailer was now in fairly good working order; in particular, he mentioned that the hinge pins looked "OK," and "probably had another year's wear in them."

Three weeks later, when Mortensen was using the trailer to haul asphalt, the trailer collapsed while tipping its load, causing the truck to overturn into a ditch. The evidence was that the cause of the accident was the failure of the hinge pins, which were loose and badly worn.

Mortensen brought an action for damages against McKays, claiming that they had been negligent in carrying out the repairs and that, in particular, he had relied on their representation that the trailer was in working order and that the hinge pins were okay. Should he succeed?

5 Nerdley is a skilled interior designer, who decided to go freelance after years of being employed by a large construction company. Although accustomed to using a computer in her work, she understands very little about their characteristics and specifications, having always relied in the past on other specialist employees of the company for advice and assistance.

Nerdley realized that she would need to acquire her own computer equipment. She was told by a friend that Millennium Electronics had "the best prices in town," and a competent sales staff. She visited their local store, briefly explained what she perceived to be her needs to Boffin, a salesperson, and eventually decided to acquire two computers, a printer, and various other items of equipment. Boffin assured her that they were "state of the art," and should be able to do everything she needed them to do.

The total price came to around $11 000. Nerdley then asked about credit and was told that Millennium recommended a leasing agreement with a finance company that it normally used in such cases. Under the agreement, Millennium sold the equipment to the finance company for $10 500, and Nerdley entered into a lease agreement with the finance company under which she agreed to make 36 monthly payments of $400, with an option at the end of the 3-year period to buy the equipment for a further $400. The lease was on a standard printed form, and included the following clause:

The lessee acknowledges that the equipment hereby leased was personally selected by the lessee for business purposes and purchased by the lessor at the lessee's request from a supplier designated by the lessee. The lessee takes full responsibility for such selection and waives all defences predicated on the failure of the said equipment to perform the function for which it was designed or selected and further acknowledges that such failure shall not be deemed to be in breach of this lease.

Nerdley very soon discovered that the computer did not have sufficient memory to operate some of the sophisticated design programs that she used, and that the printer did not have sufficiently high definition to reproduce her designs adequately.

When she attempted to take the equipment back to Millennium she was told that it was nothing to do with them and she should take it up with the finance company. Advise her.

6. Moriera's car had broken down with transmission failure. She wanted it towed 40 km to the dealership in Winnipeg where she had bought it the previous year but was surprised to discover how much the tow would cost. Her nephew suggested she could save the expense by having it towed by his friend, Brodsky. Brodsky agreed to deliver the car to the dealership "as a favour," and instructed one of his drivers, Petrides, to pick up the car where it had broken down and tow it to the dealership.

When Petrides reached Winnipeg, he realized that he did not know which dealership to take the car to. He phoned Brodsky, who admitted that he also did not know. As it was getting late, Brodsky told Petrides to leave the car at the premises of a scrap merchant with whom they did business from time to time.

The next day, Moriera phoned Brodsky to ask if her car had been delivered safely. Brodsky told her where it had been left. When she went to the scrap yard, the car was nowhere to be found and the scrap merchant said he knew nothing about it.

Advise Moriera.

18

INSURANCE AND GUARANTEE

This chapter deals with two types of contract that have in common the fact that their aim is to distribute *risk*. A contract of insurance enables a business to shift the risk of loss—from damage to its property or from being held liable for damage to someone else's person or property—to an insurance company. In return the business pays for that protection. A contract of guarantee allows a lender or creditor to reduce the risk of non-payment by obtaining a promise from a third person to pay the debt if the debtor defaults.

In this chapter we examine such questions as:

■ what is the nature of the contract of insurance?

■ how is insurance law regulated?

■ what types of insurance are available to protect against loss or damage to business premises and assets?

■ what types of insurance protect against liability or loss in the operation of a business?

■ what is the legal nature of a guarantee?

■ how may a guarantee be discharged?

■ what are the rights and liabilities of a guarantor?

THE NATURE OF INSURANCE

A contract of insurance is a method of purchasing protection against a possible loss. Not only does insurance *shift* the risk of loss from the person purchasing the protection, it also *spreads* the risk among several parties who have agreed to take a share in the risk.

ILLUSTRATION 18.1

Fifty farmers agree at a meeting to form a contract of mutual fire insurance with one another: each promises to pay 1/50th of any loss suffered by fire by any other of the 50 in return for the promises of the others to pay collectively the whole of any loss suffered by him through fire (less his own 1/50th). Thus, when farmer *A* sustains a loss of $100 000, each of the other 49 will pay him $2000 for a total of $98 000.

Such an agreement contains all the usual elements of an insurance contract, but it would have two great disadvantages: (1) it would require the farmer who suffered the loss to collect 1/50th from each farmer, an impractical task; and (2) the potential loss each farmer could suffer would vary greatly according to the value of his property, and the relative safety of the property because of its construction, use, or proximity to fire-fighting equipment. A farmer whose property consisted of $400 000 worth of fire-resistant buildings would not be happy to exchange his promise with a neighbour who had $1 000 000 worth of hazardous buildings; he would be taking a much greater chance of having to pay his neighbour $20 000 in a total loss than of receiving from him only $8000 in a less likely total loss of his own buildings.

The two disadvantages in the above illustration may be overcome in the following ways: (1) the money can be collected in advance to form a fund available to pay claims for losses suffered, and used for investment until it is required to pay claims; and (2) the amount of money collected from each insured can be calculated so that it bears a direct relationship to the risk being assumed, that is, the total possible amount of loss and the probability of that loss occurring. Insurance business proceeds on just these principles. The only remaining difference of importance is that instead of a group of risk-bearers getting together and agreeing on a cooperative basis to insure one another, an insurance company operates independently as a central agency for insuring risks and administering the funds collected. The insurance company calculates the payment required to insure a particular risk based on experience with the type of risk in question, as summarized in actuarial tables. The amount it charges is also calculated to produce a surplus: it aims for an excess of money received for insuring risks over amounts paid out in claims and amounts set aside as reserves to meet unexpectedly large claims. The surplus may be paid out in dividends to shareholders or, in the case of a mutual insurance company, returned to policy holders.

We see, then, that insurance achieves a pooling of risks so that a large number of lucky participants subsidize the losses of a relatively few unlucky ones, and that typically an insurance company acts as intermediary in this process. Indeed, the need to spread the risk operates even among insurance companies themselves. When an insurance company contracts to provide insurance protection for a particularly large single risk, the insurance company may *re-insure* a part of this risk with one or more other insurance companies. In the event of a claim, the loss is then spread among a number of insurance companies. Some international financial institutions have specialized in providing re-insurance of this kind for smaller insurance companies.

INSURANCE TERMINOLOGY

An **insurance policy** is written evidence of the terms of an insurance contract. The insurance company providing the protection is called the *insurer*; the party contracting for the insurance protection is the *insured*.[1] The **premium** is the price paid by the insured for the insurance coverage specified in the policy. The premium may be paid in a single sum, but more usually it is paid yearly or at some other shorter interval throughout the term of the insurance.

insurance policy
the written evidence of the terms of a contract of insurance

premium
the price paid by the insured to purchase insurance coverage

---

1. In life insurance we must distinguish between the *insured* and the *life insured* when the subject of the insurance is the life of someone other than the party contracting for insurance.

The four basic aspects of an insurance contract are:

- the nature of the risk covered
- the amount for which it is insured
- the duration of the protection
- the amount of the premium

The terms of a policy may require the insurer to pay the insurance money, in the event of a claim, either to the insured, to the insured's estate, or to some other person designated as **beneficiary**. When an insured requires supplementary coverage, that is, wider protection than is available under the insurer's standard form policy, additional clauses are incorporated in the contract by attaching them to the policy in a separate insertion called a **rider**. When the parties agree to a change in the terms of an existing insurance contract, they may do so without rewriting the entire policy by attaching a separate paper or **endorsement** to the face of the policy.

An **insurance agent** is an employee or agent of the insurance company whose function is to arrange contracts with persons seeking insurance protection for themselves. By contrast, an **insurance broker** conducts an independent business and generally acts for the insured rather than for the insurer.[2] As we shall see, a business is exposed to many types of risk and often finds it worthwhile to consult a specialist in insurance problems—a broker—who will advise on the coverage required and arrange insurance with the companies best suited to provide it at a minimum cost to the insured. However, the distinction between an agent and a broker is not always a clear one. In practice an insurance agent often renders a service to the insured by offering advice about the appropriate coverage, and it is possible in some cases for an agent/broker to be considered to be acting as agent for both the insurer and the insured.[3]

beneficiary
the person entitled to receive insurance monies

rider
additional provisions attached to a standard policy of insurance

endorsement
written evidence of a change in the terms of a policy

insurance agent
an agent or employee of the insurance company

insurance broker
an independent business that arranges insurance coverage for its clients

CASE 18.1

Miller was injured in a motor vehicle accident caused by the negligence of a person who was underinsured. Miller had purchased an insurance policy from an agent of the Guardian company. He had requested full coverage, but the agent did not suggest that the policy should contain an "underinsured motorist endorsement," which was available at a modest premium. As a result, Miller was not fully covered for the accident that occurred.

The court held that the agent had a duty to advise the insured on suitable coverage, and since the agent was acting as the agent of the insurance company, the company was also liable.[4]

insurance adjuster
a person who appraises property losses

personal insurance
insurance against death, injury, or ill health of an individual

property insurance
insurance against damage to property

term insurance
personal insurance that provides coverage for a limited period only

An **insurance adjuster** is an expert in the appraisal of property losses and offers these services to insurance companies for a fee. When a claim has been made, the adjuster gives an opinion to the insurer about whether the loss is covered by the insurance contract and, if so, what the amount of the loss is.

Insurance falls into two main classes: **personal insurance** and **property insurance**. Personal insurance includes life insurance, medical insurance, accident and sickness disability insurance, and workers' compensation. All other types of insurance are property insurance. Life insurance is unique in that the risk insured against is certain to materialize eventually, though in the case of **term insurance**, it may not occur during the period covered by the policy.

2. See Adams-Eden Furniture Ltd. v. Kansa General Insurance Co. (1996), 141 D.L.R. (4th) 288.
3. For a fuller discussion see Tuytel (1991–92), 3 *Can. Insurance L. Rev.* 115.
4. Miller v. Guardian Insurance Co. of Canada (1997), 149 D.L.R. (4th) 375.

REGULATION OF INSURANCE BUSINESS

Each province has one or more statutes regulating the practice of insurance business within its borders. The main purposes of these statutes are to protect the public by requiring responsible operation on the part of insurance companies and others in the business. Among other matters, the statutes authorize the appointment of a superintendent of insurance to oversee the operations and financial responsibility of licensed insurers within the province, describe the terms that must be included in insurance policies, and define the extent to which an insurer may limit its liability. In addition to these provincial statutes, the federal Insurance Companies Act[5] provides for compulsory registration of federal and foreign insurance companies wishing to carry on insurance business in Canada and for voluntary registration of provincial insurance companies. Its aim is to ensure financial stability in the insurance industry by providing a system of inspection and by requiring statements and returns from these companies.

In the next two parts of this chapter, we shall describe briefly those types of insurance that are most commonly used in business.

INSURANCE OF BUSINESS PREMISES AND OTHER ASSETS

Fire, Accident, and Theft Insurance

While fire insurance affords protection against loss by fire damage to buildings and contents (inventory, fixtures, and equipment), it is important to understand that the liability of the insurer sometimes does not extend to a variety of losses incidental to the fire, nor to fires attributable to certain specified causes. Thus, a fire insurance policy may not cover some of the following types of risk:

- losses of books of account, business papers, money, and similar items
- theft of money or merchandise during the fire
- loss of property belonging to others, kept on the premises
- medical expenses of persons injured by the fire
- loss of profits caused by suspended business operations while the property is being restored
- increased hazard from a subsequent vacancy of the premises
- fire loss resulting from explosives kept on the property
- damage caused by riots or invasion of which the fire may be a part
- damage intentionally caused by the insured[6]

An insured should check precisely which risks are covered in the insurer's standard policy and obtain protection against additional risks by having special terms to that effect inserted in the policy and paying a higher premium.

In addition to fire insurance, it is usually advisable to arrange supplementary coverage against loss by water (rain, snow, or flood), storm, and (in some parts of the world) earthquake. Farmers commonly buy insurance against damage to their crops by wind, storm, and hail and also participate in government-supported schemes to insure against crop failure caused by

---

5. S.C. 1991, c. 47.

6. This exclusion may prevent recovery for damage intentionally caused by any other person whose property is also insured under the policy; see Scott v. Wawanesa Mutual Insurance Co. (1989), 59 D.L.R. (4th) 660, where the fire resulted from arson committed by the son of the named insured.

drought or blight. Businesses often make extensive use of plate-glass, which is costly to replace. Fire insurance covers the cost of replacement of plate-glass if the breakage is caused by a fire, but not otherwise, and many businesses take out separate plate-glass insurance.

Theft insurance provides protection against the unlawful taking of property of the insured. The policy may limit the liability of the insurer to a relatively small amount—well below the total amount of the policy—for losses of items that are easily stolen, such as cash, negotiable securities, and jewellery, to encourage their proper safekeeping.

Rather than issue a variety of policies, each providing protection against specific risks, the modern tendency has increasingly been to issue *comprehensive* general accident insurance. Such insurance frequently also covers liability incurred by a business towards others—a topic discussed in the next part of this chapter. Because of its broader scope such insurance tends to be expensive, though it may well turn out to be cheaper than purchasing a series of separate policies insuring against specific risks. The great advantage to the insured lies in the comprehensiveness of the coverage; unexpected risks are insured against rather than falling between the cracks of two or more separate policies.

CASE 18.2

Goderich had insured grain stored in their elevator under an "all risks" insurance policy, which covered "all risk of direct physical loss or damage...except as excluded." The policy excluded "loss or damage caused directly or indirectly by...dryness of atmosphere, changes of temperature, heating, shrinkage, evaporation...." Some grain was found to contain an excessive quantity of damaged grain, known as "heated grain," which was of less value. The cause of the heated grain could not be established, but there was no evidence of external causes. It might have been due to spontaneous internal causes such as slightly excessive moisture content of the grain.

Goderich's claim under the insurance policy was contested by the insurance company. The court held that the loss was covered by an "all risk" policy, and the insurance company had not shown that the cause was specifically within the exclusion.[7]

In most instances, an insurer is liable either for the cost of repairing damaged property or for the value of the destroyed property. Value takes into account the condition of the property immediately before destruction. One may purchase insurance for full replacement value, but this higher protection is more expensive. In any event it is sensible to review the replacement value from time to time in order to make sure that protection is adequate; inflation or changes in building by-law requirements may make existing insurance inadequate.

mortgage clause
a clause in a policy of property insurance requiring that the proceeds be used first to pay off the mortgage

When a debtor mortgages insured property to a lender as security for a loan, the lender (mortgagee) should see that the policy contains a **mortgage clause**. This clause requires that in the event of a claim the proceeds shall be paid first to the mortgagee "as his interest may appear," with the balance payable to the insured, and that insofar as the mortgagee has an interest, the insurance shall not be invalidated by any act or neglect of the insured.

Vehicle Insurance

A business normally insures separately against loss of, or damage to, its vehicles; it also insures against injury to third persons and their property caused by the operation of those vehicles.

---

7. Goderich Elevators Ltd. v. Royal Insurance Co. (1999), 169 D.L.R. (4th) 763. The court applied one of the "general principles of interpretation of insurance policies" set out by McLachlin, J. in Reid Crowther & Partners Ltd. v. Simcoe & Erie General Insurance Co. (1993), 99 D.L.R. (4th) 741 (S.C.C.), namely that "coverage provisions should be construed broadly and exclusion provisions narrowly."

Such insurance against third-party liability is now compulsory and most provinces have introduced compulsory systems of "no fault" automobile insurance. This type of system provides for automatic compensation of automobile accident victims, regardless of who is to blame for the accident.

A vehicle insurance contract typically contains a **deductible clause** stating that the insured shall pay the first $500 (or some higher amount) in respect of each claim. A deductible feature gives the insured a greater incentive to take care of the insured property and, by eliminating a large number of small claims, makes the insurance much cheaper.

deductible clause
a clause requiring the insured to bear the loss up to a stated amount

Marine Insurance

This type of insurance protects against loss of a ship, its cargo, or equipment caused by perils at sea, including sinking, stranding, burning, collision, contact with sea water, and even piracy and mutiny. Marine insurance may be written for a specific voyage or a fixed period, depending on the nature of the risk. Although marine insurance is primarily intended to cover loss or damage at sea, it may also cover transportation by inland waterway or even by rail and road, for example, when part of a journey is by sea and part by land. Marine insurance is one of the oldest forms of insurance and has developed somewhat independently from other forms; certain rules or principles apply that are not found in other branches of insurance.

INSURANCE ON THE OPERATION OF A BUSINESS

Business Interruption Insurance

As we have seen, insurance payable for damage caused to business property does not necessarily include compensation for the loss of profits that ensues when a firm is unable to operate for a time following the fire or for the costs of moving to temporary quarters. Business interruption insurance protects an insured business against these risks by paying compensation for loss of profit, expenses that necessarily continue even when the business is not operating, and money expended to reduce business losses (for example, the cost of moving to temporary accommodation). The insured may also choose to insure the payment of all employees' wages and salaries for the same period as the business interruption or for some shorter maximum period.

Credit Insurance

A business may obtain protection against bad debt losses by insuring the collection of its accounts receivable with a commercial credit insurance company. The insurer's assessment of the creditworthiness of the customer-debtors whose accounts it insures determines the cost of the insurance. A form of credit insurance may also be obtained by selling accounts receivable to a **factor**. A factoring business sometimes discounts book debts **without recourse**—that is, if the accounts it buys prove uncollectable, it has no recourse against the business from which it bought them.

factor
a business that provides a form of credit insurance by buying accounts receivable

without recourse
a provision that, where accounts that have been sold prove to be uncollectable, the buyer shall have no claim against the seller of the accounts

Fidelity Insurance

Fidelity insurance protects against losses caused by the fraud or theft of employees of the insured. The policy is called a **fidelity bond**, and the insurer is usually called a *bonding company*.

fidelity bond
insurance against loss caused by fraud or theft committed by employees of the insured

Key-Person Insurance

A business may have a considerable investment in the training and development of its management and, in the event of the premature death of one of its officers, must often incur further expense in training and developing a replacement. For this reason the business has an insurable interest in its executives and may insure their lives. The insurance premiums are a business expense, and the proceeds of the insurance paid on death belong to the business.

In a partnership, each partner's interest in the firm is a part of the partner's personal estate and becomes payable to the deceased partner's estate after his or her death. To assist in settling with the estate of any one of them who dies, partners frequently carry life insurance on each other's lives. This form of insurance provides a fund enabling the surviving partners to pay to the estate the value of the deceased partner's share in the firm. A partnership may thus avoid the risk of having to liquidate valuable assets to raise the money needed for settlement. Similar arrangements are also common in small corporations, where principal shareholders insure each other's lives for the same purpose.

Insurance for Employees

Frequently, a business will arrange medical and dental insurance for its employees. The premiums for this type of insurance are sometimes a joint responsibility of employer and employee, with the employee contributing through regular payroll deductions. Although the employer may contribute towards the premiums, claims are payable by the insurer to the employee. Plans of this kind usually cover members of the employee's family, and may include group life insurance coverage.

As we shall see in Chapter 20, an employer's liability to employees for injuries sustained in the course of employment has now been resolved over a wide area by statutes providing for compulsory workers' compensation insurance. The provincial government is in effect the insurer, though it delegates the administration of the insurance to a workers' compensation board. Employers to whom the legislation applies must make payments—in effect, premiums—to the board on behalf of their employees, who are beneficiaries of any claims made.

Public Liability Insurance

Businesses continuously face possible liability for injury to members of the public or their property. The harm may result from defective equipment or from the negligent acts of the proprietors or employees in the ordinary course of business. The liability of an employer for employees' torts is discussed in Chapters 3 and 20.

product insurance
insurance to protect against liability for damage caused by defective products

Various forms of insurance are available to indemnify a business for the liability it may incur in many situations. As we saw in the preceding section, automobile and marine insurance normally protect against liability to third parties. Manufacturing and distributing companies may also obtain **product insurance** to protect against liability to members of the public who sustain injury in their use of the product sold. Storekeepers, too, may be liable for injuries sustained by customers visiting their premises. And, as we saw in the preceding chapter, a bailee, such as a carrier, repairer, or warehousing firm, may be liable for loss or damage to property in its care, and consequently may seek insurance protection. A bailee may decide to insure only its own liability, or may insure for the full value of the goods so that in the event of a total loss the customer will be fully compensated. The cost of additional insurance is ordinarily passed on to the customer. As in the case of general accident insurance, the modern tendency in all of these cases is to effect comprehensive general liability insurance rather than to insure separately against liability resulting from different causes. Frequently, the same policy covers both accident and liability insurance.

professional liability insurance
insurance for professionals against liability for loss resulting from negligence or other breach of duty

Practising members of a profession may, and in some professions are required to, obtain **professional liability insurance** to indemnify themselves for losses payable to clients or patients as damages awarded against them for negligence. Similarly, the directors of companies may obtain liability insurance as protection against the possibility of actions brought against them by shareholders or creditors for breach of their duty of care, diligence, and skill.

CONTEMPORARY ISSUE

Inadequate Coverage?

According to high-tech insurance expert, Thomas R. Cornwell:

> Too many electronics companies, especially software developers, are leaving themselves open to liability risks few of them are prepared to deal with. If high-tech vendors do not understand their insurance options and to what extent their product is covered should it malfunction, they will pay for it in court.... Too often companies assume they are fully covered without first looking at all the facts. Traditional product liability insurance protects companies in the event a product causes property damage or injury. What many vendors do not realize, however, is that it does not provide coverage for "intangible" damages, such as data loss or loss of production time. The consequences of such loss can be as serious as a fire....Also not covered are damages incurred when a company sells software based on false or mistaken claims.

Cornwell told of a client who had led a customer to believe his software package could perform certain functions when, in fact, it could not. The plaintiff sued, and the loss to the business was roughly US$1 million. Cornwell advises software companies to purchase errors and omissions insurance tailor-made for the high-tech industry, designed to cover failure to perform, damage to intangible property, and the potential of computer viruses. Larger software companies are usually aware of errors and omissions insurance, but smaller vendors often are not. And in an industry where small businesses play such a crucial function, Cornwell said it is important to spread the message.

Source: Michael MacMillan, "Protect yourselves well, software vendors warned," *Computer World Canada*, December 19, 1997, p. 1.

Questions to Consider

1. Whose duty should it be to ensure that small businesses are advised as to the appropriate insurance coverage for their particular activities?
2. Should "comprehensive" insurance be required to cover all foreseeable risks?

SPECIAL ASPECTS OF THE CONTRACT OF INSURANCE

Legality of Object—Wrongful Act of the Insured

It is a general principle of insurance law that the courts will not enforce a contract of insurance when the claim arises out of a criminal or *deliberate* tortious act of the insured.[8] Two reasons are commonly given for this rule: it would be contrary to public policy to allow the insured to profit from his own crime and it would be contrary to the purpose of insurance to allow the insured to recover compensation for a loss that he had deliberately caused himself. Thus, a beneficiary under a life insurance policy who murders the person whose life is insured is not entitled to

---

8. Beresford v. Royal Insurance Co., [1938] A.C. 586; Acklands Ltd. v. Canadian Indemnity Co. (1985), 8 C.C.L.I. 163.

claim,[9] and an arsonist is not entitled to recover under a policy of fire insurance.[10] However, the courts have been careful to restrict the scope of the public policy exception.

CASE 18.3

Maria Oldfield owned a policy that insured the life of her husband, Paul, and named her as the beneficiary. Paul also owned two policies, each of which insured his life, and named Maria the beneficiary. The Oldfields subsequently separated.

About a year after the separation Paul died while on a trip to Bolivia. An autopsy revealed a number of condoms filled with cocaine in his digestive tract. One of the bags had burst, causing his death. The circumstances indicated the death was accidental. It was agreed that the husband's ingestion of the cocaine amounted to possession of a narcotic and was a crime under the laws of Bolivia and of Canada.

Mrs. Oldfield claimed the benefits of the policies. The insurers refused to pay on the ground that the claims resulted from a criminal act of the life insured. The court allowed the claim, holding that the public policy rule against persons benefitting from their crimes does not apply where the owner of the policy insures his life and designates another person as the beneficiary before the crime; the death was accidental and the beneficiary had no involvement in the crime.[11]

Insurable Interest

In Chapter 7 we distinguished an insurance contract from a wager by the fact that the insured has an *insurable interest*, so that the contract shifts a genuine risk of loss from the insured to the insurer. An insurable interest is the measure of loss that may be suffered by the insured from damage to or destruction of the thing insured. This is not always easy to determine. In a leading English case, the House of Lords held that a shareholder who owned most of the shares in a company had no insurable interest in its principal asset, a quantity of timber destroyed in a fire; the loss was solely that of the company itself.[12] However, the Supreme Court of Canada has since held that a sufficient insurable interest exists where an insured can demonstrate a relation to or concern in the insured property so that damage to it will cause a loss to the insured. Thus, a person who owned all the shares in a corporation was held to have an insurable interest in the property of the corporation, because damage to that property would necessarily reduce the value of his shares.[13] Similarly, a tenant may have an insurable interest in leased premises that he uses for his business, since he may suffer financial and other loss if the premises are destroyed or damaged.[14]

When must the insurable interest exist? The answer depends upon whether the insurance is on property or on a life. When a contract is for property insurance, the insured must have an insurable interest at the time the contract was formed; otherwise the contract is void. Since the purpose of insurance is to indemnify for loss suffered, the insured must still have an interest at the time the claim arises; otherwise there will be no loss to be recovered by the insured.[15]

9. Demeter v. Dominion Life Assurance Co. (1982), 132 D.L.R. (3d) 248, where the husband who was convicted of the murder of his wife was the owner and beneficiary under personal policies issued on the life of his wife. See also Brisette Estate v. Westbury Life Insurance Co., [1992] 3 S.C.R. 87; Lachman Estate v. Norwich Union Life Insurance Co. (1998), 40 O.R. (3d) 393.

10. See Scott v. Wawanesa Mutual Insurance Co., *supra*, n. 6.

11. Oldfield v. Transamerica Life Insurance Co. of Canada (1998), 43 O.R. (3d) 114.

12. Macaura v. Northern Assurance Co., [1925] A.C. 619.

13. Kosmopoulos v. Constitution Insurance Co. (1987), 34 D.L.R. (4th) 208. The Court's reasoning suggests that any person holding a substantial proportion of a corporation's shares would have an insurable interest in its property; it is unclear whether a holder of only a small proportion would be found to have an interest.

14. Evergreen Manufacturing Corp. v. Dominion of Canada General Insurance Co. (1999), 170 D.L.R. (4th) 240.

15. Howard v. Lancashire Insurance Co. (1885), 11 S.C.R. 92.

When the contract is for life insurance, the person buying the insurance must either (a) obtain the written consent of the person whose life is to be insured, or (b) have an insurable interest at the time the contract is formed, though not necessarily at the time of death of the person whose life is insured.[16] Thus, if a creditor has insured the life of its debtor for the amount of the debt and that sum proves to be more than the balance owing at the time of the debtor's death, the policy is valid and the creditor remains entitled to the full value of the policy.[17] This arrangement, however, is not as common as one where a creditor requires its debtor to obtain life insurance, pay the premiums, and make the creditor a beneficiary for the amount of the debt. If at the death of the debtor the amount owing is then less than the value of the policy, the balance is paid to the debtor's estate.

Formation of the Contract

A *proposal* drafted by an insurance agent is usually a mere invitation to treat, not an offer; the offer to purchase insurance coverage is made by the party seeking the insurance protection—the prospective insured—by signing an application form. What constitutes acceptance by the insurer? We need to know so that we can tell when the insurance is in force.

Life Insurance

With life insurance, the applicant's offer is not accepted until the insurance company delivers the policy; moreover, it is a condition precedent to delivery of the policy that the first premium shall be paid by the insured.[18] But it may take some time for the head office of an insurance company to prepare the policy for delivery; is the insured protected in any way in the interval between signing the application form and taking delivery of the policy? The answer depends upon the wording of the application form and related form for acknowledging receipt of the premium. Many life insurance companies include an *interim insurance* provision as a term in the receipt form given for the payment of the first premium. This provision gives the insured protection from the time of signing the application, provided that medical information or the results of any medical examination would be acceptable to the company on the terms proposed in the application. Such interim insurance expires once the insurer delivers the policy to the insured.

Property Insurance

Making contracts for property insurance is typically less formal than for life insurance. An agent dealing in property insurance may have an agency contract with each of several insurers. Each such contract gives the agent authority to sign and deliver policies and renewal certificates and generally to bind the insurer concerned; a business seeking property insurance can obtain the desired protection immediately, before paying the premium or receiving a policy. The agent need only prepare a memorandum or *binder* for the agency's records as evidence of the time and nature of the request for insurance. When immediate protection is required, an insured should be satisfied that the agent has an agency contract with the proposed insurer.

Renewal

Property insurance is written for a limited period (usually for one year). Frequently, the intention is that the insurance should be renewed at the end of the period, and it is not uncommon for the insured to fail to renew it in time. What is the situation in the meantime? A common

---

16. See, for example: Insurance Act, R.S.B.C. 1996, c. 36(2)(b); R.S.O. 1990, c. I.8, s. 178(2)(b); R.S.N.S. 1989, c. 231, s. 180(2)(b). In subsequent footnotes in this chapter, references to B.C., Ont., and N.S. will be to these statutes.

17. Dalby v. India & London Life Assurance Co. (1854), 139 E.R. 465.

18. See, for example: B.C., s. 38; Ont., s. 180; N.S., s. 182.

practice is for an insurance company, or its agent, to prepare a renewal policy or memorandum and send it to the insured shortly before the current policy expires; this acts as a reminder that the insurance protection is about to cease if not renewed. But unless there is evidence of an agreement between the company and the insured that they intend the mere delivery of a renewal policy or memorandum to create a new contract of insurance, or such an agreement can be inferred from their past dealings with one another, the act of delivering the renewal policy amounts to no more than making an offer to the insured. No contract is formed until the insured communicates acceptance, and because the offer is open at most for a reasonable time, the insured cannot wait indefinitely to express assent.

CASE 18.4

The insured's auto insurance policy expired on February 5, 1989. About a month before, the insurance company sent him an offer to renew if the premium was paid before February 5, and a "pink slip" certifying that the insurance was in effect until August 5, 1989. The insured did not pay the renewal premium and was injured in an accident on February 20.

The Supreme Court of Canada held that the pink slip did not amount to a renewal of the contract. It was sent to the insured for convenience only and did not bind the company.[19]

CASE 18.5

Under a life insurance policy, a premium payment became due on July 26, 1984. The grace period expired and the company sent a "late payment offer," offering to receive late payment under certain conditions. Four months later, the company sent a letter to the insured, saying that the policy was "technically out of force," and that immediate payment of the premium was required. In February 1985 the company sent a further letter, stating that the insurance had lapsed. The letters did not come to the insured's attention until April 1985, and in July, he sent a cheque. By then, his life had become uninsurable and he died a month later.

The Supreme Court of Canada held that the July payment was too late. The company had offered to renew the policy, but that offer was open only for a reasonable time.[20]

Terms of the Contract

Chapter 5 referred to an insurance policy as an example of a standard form contract since it is prepared unilaterally in advance by one of the contracting parties (the insurer). To offset this advantage for insurers, the courts subject such contracts to a strict interpretation of the words they contain: they construe words most strongly against the party using them, as we noted in Chapter 11. They take the attitude, for example, that clauses exempting an insurer from liability in specific circumstances must be stated in clear and unambiguous terms to be binding.[21]

Disclosure

In our discussion of misrepresentation in Chapter 9, we noted that an insurer may avoid liability if it can show that the insured did not exercise the *utmost good faith* in the application for

19. Patterson v. Gallant (1994), 120 D.L.R. (4th) 1.

20. Saskatchewan River Bungalows Ltd. v. Maritime Life Assurance Co. (1994), 115 D.L.R. (4th) 478.

21. See, for example: British Columbia Ferry Corp. v. Commonwealth Insurance Co. (1985), 40 D.L.R. (4th) 766.

insurance. The requirement of utmost good faith on the part of the insured has traditionally been particularly strict: early cases held that an insured may be unable to collect for a claim even when it arose from causes unrelated to facts that the insured should have disclosed, but had not disclosed.[22] However, some recent Canadian decisions have mitigated that rule. For example, a statement by the insured that a night watchman would be present on the premises every night was held not to be material when the loss occurred in the afternoon,[23] and the insured need not disclose information of a general nature that should be well known to the insurer: an asbestos manufacturer was not required to inform its insurer that there were health risks related to working with asbestos, so long as the likelihood of exposure to asbestos was disclosed.[24]

In *Coronation Insurance Company v. Taku Air Transport Ltd.*,[25] the Supreme Court of Canada took a significant further step, holding that the utmost good faith principle should not apply at all in the highly regulated field of aviation insurance. The requirement that air carriers should have insurance for their passengers was primarily intended for the benefit of the public, whose protection should not be depend entirely on the good faith of the carrier. Consequently, the failure of a carrier to fully disclose its past safety record did not invalidate the policy. The insurance company had a duty at least to check its own files and the public records.[26]

An insurer may insert terms in an insurance contract to extend the obligation of the insured even beyond that imposed by the requirement of utmost good faith. The application form signed by the party seeking insurance may contain a provision that the applicant warrants the *accuracy*—not merely the *truthfulness*—of any declarations made. If in these circumstances an applicant for life insurance replies in the negative to the question, "Have you any disease?" and proves later to have had a disease of which he or she was unaware, the insurer may avoid its liability. The courts, however, regard this type of provision with disfavour and insist on strict proof by the insurer that the question was answered inaccurately.

Insurance contracts other than for life insurance contain a statutory term that the insured shall notify the insurer promptly of any change that is material to the risk and within the control or knowledge of the insured. Such a term then gives the insurer the option of either cancelling the insurance and returning the unexpired portion of the premium, or of informing the insured that the insurance will continue only on payment of an increased premium. Prompt notice by the insured in these circumstances is a condition precedent, so that the insurer is absolved from liability under the policy if it does not receive such notice. Such insurance contracts normally also contain a term requiring the insured to notify the insurer promptly of any loss that occurs. Failure to give notice promptly may free the insurer from liability to pay the claim.

Assignment

A life insurance policy of the type that accumulates a cash surrender value is an item of property—a chose in action—which the insured may assign for value, for example, by giving a conditional assignment of the policy to a bank as security for a loan. If the insured defaults on the loan, the bank is entitled to the cash surrender value up to the amount due on the loan. The insurer's consent to an assignment of life insurance is not necessary, although the insurer is entitled to notice. The risk of the insurer is not affected by an assignment of the benefits of a life insurance contract.

---

22. See Lachman Estate v. Norwich Union Life Insurance Co. (1998), 40 O.R. (3d) 393.

23. Case Existological Laboratories Ltd. v. Century Insurance Co. (1982), 133 D.L.R. (3d) 727.

24. Canadian Indemnity Co. v. Canadian Johns-Mansville Co., [1990] 2 S.C.R. 549.

25. [1991] 3 S.C.R. 622.

26. Unfortunately, the crash victims still did not recover compensation. The aircraft was carrying more passengers than provided for in the policy, and the policy was consequently void.

In contrast, property insurance is not assignable without the consent of the insurer; in fact, novation is necessary. The reason for this rule is that an assignment substitutes a new person as the insured, and the personal qualities of the insured may be relevant to the risk assumed by the insurer. When a person sells a house or an automobile, there is usually unexpired insurance on the property; the purchaser must therefore renegotiate the insurance with the insurer, possibly at different premium rates. On the other hand, *after* a risk materializes and an insurance claim is established, an insured may assign the claim (say, to creditors) without the consent of the insurer.

Subrogation

If a storeowner has obtained fire insurance for her premises and suffers a loss because of a fire negligently caused by her neighbour, she can recover from her own insurance company without having to sue the neighbour. On the other hand, she cannot recover twice over: if she were subsequently to sue the neighbour and recover damages that, when added to her insurance compensation, would give her a sum in excess of her loss. She would hold that excess in trust for her insurer. As a result, as long as she is fully insured, she will have no incentive to sue her neighbour. If that ended the matter, many torfeasors would escape liability for their careless acts. However, under general principles of insurance law, when an insurer has paid a claim it is entitled to "step into the shoes of the insured," and sue the person liable for the loss. But the right of subrogation cannot place the insurer in a better position than the insured.

CASE 18.6

A fire broke out in leased premises, apparently due to the negligence of the tenant. The landlord was fully indemnified by its insurer who brought an action for damages against the tenant by way of subrogation. In the lease, the landlord had covenanted to insure against damage by fire, and the tenant had agreed to pay a proportionate share of the landlord's cost of insuring. The tenant covenanted to repair the premises, except for insured fire damage.

The court held that the terms of the lease indicated that the tenant had bargained for the right to be free of liability for fire arising from its negligence. Regardless of the terms of the policy between the insurer and the landlord, the insurer could have no better claim against the tenant than the lease gave to the landlord.[27]

subrogation

the right of an insurer who has paid a claim to "step into the shoes" of the insured and sue the person responsible for the loss

The right of **subrogation** does not apply to all cases but, unless it is expressly excluded, it will generally be presumed to apply.[28]

Co-Insurance

Fires and accidents rarely result in a total loss. Consequently, a person or business might think of saving premium costs by insuring the property for only a part of its total value. Insurance companies often insert a clause in the contract stating that an insured that does not purchase coverage of at least a stated percentage of the value of the property (usually 80 percent) will become a co-insurer proportional to the lower coverage, along with the insurance company, for any loss that results. The insured would not then recover the total loss, even though the loss itself was less than the face value of fire insurance policy.

27. Amexon Realty Inc. v. Comcheq Services Ltd. (1998), 155 D.L.R. (4th) 661.

28. See M.G. Baer, "Rethinking Basic Concepts of Insurance Law," in *Insurance Law*, p. 210. Special Lectures of the Law Society of Upper Canada. Toronto: Richard de Boo, 1987.

ILLUSTRATION 18.2

A building owned by *X* Company Ltd. is insured for $80 000, but the insurance contract contains an 80 per-cent co-insurance clause. The building is damaged by fire to the amount of $30 000. The depreciated replacement value of the insured property at the date of the fire is $150 000. The insurance company will then pay

($80 000 ÷ 80% of $150 000) × $30 000 = $20 000

and *X* Company Ltd., as insured, must absorb $10 000

in a total loss of $30 000

GUARANTEE

The Nature of a Guarantee

A **guarantee** usually arises in one of three common business situations. First, a prospective creditor may refuse to advance money, goods, or services solely on the prospective debtor's promise to pay for them. Second, a creditor may state that it intends to start an action against its debtor for an overdue debt unless the debtor can offer additional security to support a further delay in repayment. Third, a prospective assignee of rights under a contract may be unwilling to buy these benefits if it has nothing more to rely on than the undertaking of the promisor in the original contract.

guarantee
a promise to perform the obligation of another person if that person defaults

In each of these circumstances, further assurance sufficient to satisfy the creditor or assignee, is often supplied by a third party who promises to perform the obligation of the debtor if the debtor should default in performance. The debtor is then called the *principal debtor*, and his obligation is known as the *principal* or *primary debt*. The person who promises to answer for the default of the principal debtor is called the *guarantor* or *surety*, and her promise is a *guarantee* or *contract of suretyship*.

ILLUSTRATION 18.3

(a) Crown Autos Ltd. agrees to sell a sports car to Tomins provided that her uncle, Gilmour, will guarantee payment of the instalments. Gilmour agrees to assist his niece, and both join in signing an instalment-purchase agreement whereby Tomins promises as principal debtor to make all payments promptly, and Gilmour promises as guarantor to pay off the debt if Tomins defaults payment.

(b) Arthurs purchases a delivery truck from Bigtown Trucks Ltd. under an instalment agreement. After Arthurs has made more than half his payments, he defaults because of business difficulties. Bigtown Trucks Ltd. threatens to retake possession of the truck. Arthurs states that if Bigtown Trucks Ltd. takes the truck, his business will lose all chance of recovery. He asks the company to give him an extra six months to pay if he can obtain a satisfactory guarantor. The company agrees, and Arthur's friend Campbell signs a contract of guarantee, promising to pay the balance in six months if Arthurs fails to do so.

(c) Perez buys a commercial freezer from Quincy and gives a promissory note payable in 60 days for the full purchase price. Quincy is in need of cash and takes the note to her banker who agrees to give her cash for it less a 5 percent charge. Quincy endorses the note in favour of the bank, that is, she places her signature on it when assigning it to the bank, and thereby guarantees payment if Perez should default.

We may note three important characteristics of a guarantee. First, a guarantor makes a promise to the *creditor*, not to the principal debtor. A promise made to a debtor to assist in the event of default is not a guarantee, and since the promise is not made to the creditor, the creditor cannot recover on it. Second, a guarantee is a secondary obligation arising only on default of the primary debt. For this reason it is a *contingent* liability in contrast to the absolute liability of the principal debtor. A creditor has no rights against the guarantor until default by the principal debtor.[29] Third, a guarantor's duty to pay arises immediately on default by the principal debtor. The creditor need not first sue the debtor. Strictly speaking, the creditor need not even notify the guarantor of the default before starting an action to enforce the guarantee. As a practical matter, however, the creditor always does make a demand on the guarantor before suing. Of course, when giving a guarantee, a guarantor may stipulate as a condition precedent to liability that the creditor must first have sued the debtor and have failed to recover, but it is unusual for a guarantor to do so.

FIGURE 18.1
Liability on a Guarantee

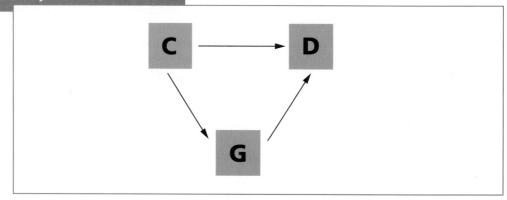

The creditor, *C*, may sue either the principal debtor, *D*, or the guarantor, *G*, once *D* has defaulted. Normally, *G* will be entitled to sue *D* to recover what she has paid on *D*'s account.

ILLUSTRATION 18.4

Jenny Williams tries to rent a launch from Boat Rentals Ltd. but is refused because of her youth. Williams' father, a reputable businessman, informs the manager of Boat Rentals Ltd. that if the company will rent the launch to his daughter, he will be responsible for any damage caused by her negligent acts if his daughter does not reimburse the company for any such damage. Boat Rentals Ltd. accepts his offer.

In Illustration 18.4, the guarantee is rather like a contract of insurance in which the father is the counterpart of an insurer and the boat-rental firm of the insured. If Williams' father had undertaken absolutely (without reference to a failure by his daughter to make good the loss herself) to assume any costs of his daughter's possible negligence, his promise would have been an indemnity and even more like a contract of insurance.

We have seen (in Chapter 10) that the distinction between guarantee and indemnity is important with respect to the requirement of writing in the Statute of Frauds. The distinction is also important in that the liability of a guarantor depends on the continuing existence of the liability of the principal debtor, whereas the liability under a promise of indemnity stands alone. Thus, if a person guaranteed the debt of a consumer debtor and the obligation was not binding under consumer legislation (for example, for failure to deliver a written statement of the terms of credit) the guarantor would not be bound to pay either. On the other hand, a promise of indemnity is independent of any obligation of the person who benefits from that promise. Thus,

---

29. See Chapter 11 for the distinction between a guarantee and an indemnity; an indemnifier promises absolutely to pay the debt of another person.

if *A* said to a seller, "If you will supply *B* with a 20-inch portable colour television set, I promise to pay the price," *A*'s liability would not depend on whether *B* has contracted a binding debt; so long as the seller carried out *A*'s wishes, *A* would be bound to indemnify it.

Continuing Guarantee

A continuing guarantee covers a series of transactions between a creditor and its principal debtor. A guarantor may, for example, agree to guarantee *X* Co.'s account with supplier *Y* up to an amount of $5000. In a series of purchases by *X* Co. and payments by it, *X* Co.'s indebtedness to *Y* will fluctuate considerably; at any given date during the currency of the guarantee, the guarantor is contingently liable for the debt, to a maximum of $5000. A continuing guarantee is often given for a specific length of time and debts contracted afterwards are not the liability of the guarantor. In any event, the death of a guarantor ends liability with respect to further transactions, although the guarantor's estate remains contingently liable for the debt existing at death.

A guarantor may limit liability under a continuing guarantee until a specified date: if the principal debtor has not defaulted by that date, or has defaulted but the creditor has not yet started an action to enforce the guarantee, then the guarantor's liability terminates. The variety of terms of a guarantee is virtually limitless, and they depend only on the ability of the parties to reach agreement.

Consideration

We have said that a guarantee is a promise, and we know that a promise is not enforceable unless it is given either under seal or for a consideration. Occasionally a guarantor does make the promise under seal but generally does not. What then constitutes the consideration for a guarantee?

The consideration is clearest when the guarantor receives an economic benefit—when she obtains a higher price as an assignor of an account receivable because she is willing to guarantee payment by the debtor. More frequently the guarantor does not receive any economic benefit for her promise; but as we have already noted (Chapter 6), consideration need confer no economic benefit on a promisor. The essential element of consideration is simply that the promisee pays a price for the promise of the other party. The creditor gives sufficient consideration for the promise of the guarantor by performing some act or forbearing to do some act at the request of the guarantor. The guarantor's request need not even be express; it may be implied from the circumstances.

ILLUSTRATION 18.5

Creely threatens to sue Dobbs for his past-due debt. Dobbs asks for 60 days more to raise the money, but Creely refuses to give the extra time unless Dobbs obtains a guarantee from his cousin Guara. Dobbs takes a form of guarantee to his cousin, explains the situation, and requests her signature. Guara signs the guarantee and mails it to Creely. Creely forbears to sue Dobbs for 60 days. When Dobbs defaults payment again, Creely sues Guara. She defends on the ground that she has received no consideration for her guarantee.

Guara's defence will fail. The court will accept the argument that she impliedly requested Creely to forbear to sue Dobbs for 60 days and that Creely gave consideration by complying with this request. Accordingly, Creely's action will succeed.

Similarly, when a person guarantees a contract by which the debtor obtains goods or services on credit, it is usually quite easy to imply a request by the guarantor to the creditor that the creditor enter into a contract it would otherwise have refused.

Discharge of Guarantee

The liability of a guarantor may be discharged by subsequent acts of the creditor. In a recent decision of the Supreme Court of Canada, Iacobucci, J., reviewed the numerous authorities and stated the following propositions:[30]

1. The guarantor will be discharged if the creditor breaches the contract of guarantee. For example, where the creditor bank commences proceedings against the principal debtor without giving notice to the guarantor and making it a party to the proceedings, as required by the contract of guarantee, the guarantor was discharged.[31]

2. The guarantor will be discharged if the principal contract between the creditor and the debtor is varied without the guarantor's consent and in a manner that is not obviously to the benefit of the guarantor. For example, in *Holland-Canada Mortgage Co. v. Hutchings*[32] a group of individuals jointly guaranteed a loan to a charity. Subsequently the loan was renewed, at a higher rate of interest. Some of the guarantors learned of the change and refused to agree to it, and so were released. The other guarantors were not told of these developments, but when the charity defaulted on the loan they were sued on their original guarantee. They were held not liable; the terms of the original contract had been changed materially and their risk had been increased by the withdrawal of some of their co-guarantors.

CASE 18.7

Conlin guaranteed a mortgage to a bank for a three-year term. Prior to the end of the term, the mortgagor and the bank renewed the mortgage for a further three-year term at a higher interest rate and without notice to respondent. Conlin did not sign as guarantor on the renewal form. The mortgagor subsequently defaulted and the bank obtained a summary judgment against the mortgagor and the respondent. On appeal, the court set aside the judgment and dismissed the action against Conlin. The contract had been materially altered without notice to him and he was relieved from liability.[33]

The rationale for this rule is that the guarantor has undertaken to underwrite a particular risk and is entitled not to have that risk materially altered to his detriment. Thus, if the creditor gives the principal debtor an extension of time in which to repay the debt without expressly reserving the rights of the guarantor (thus enabling the guarantor to sue as soon as the debt falls due if he chooses to do so), the guarantor is discharged from his obligation. However, mere delay in commencing proceedings against the debtor does not discharge the guarantor.

3. If the creditor acts in breach of its contract with the principal debtor, and that breach materially affects the risk assumed by the guarantor, the guarantor will be discharged. Thus, where a bank, having agreed to give a family company more time to pay off its debt, in return for a personal guarantee from its principal shareholders, made a demand for immediate payment and put the company into receivership, the guaran-

---

30. Pax Management Ltd. v. Canadian Imperial Bank of Commerce, [1992] 2 S.C.R. 998. For an extensive review, see Perell (1994), 73 *Can. Bar Rev.* 121.

31. Bank of British Columbia v. Turbo Resources Ltd. (1983), 23 B.L.R. 152 (Alta C.A.).

32. [1936] 2 D.L.R. 481.

33. Manulife Bank of Canada v. Conlin (1996), 139 D.L.R. (4th) 426 (S.C.C.). See also Royal Bank of Canada v. Bruce Industrial Sales Ltd. (1998), 40 O.R. (3d) 307.

tors were held to be discharged.[34] But in another case, where a bank appointed a receiver without first demanding repayment from the debtor, the guarantor was held not to be discharged since, on the evidence, there was nothing the debtor could have done even if it had been given proper notice. There was consequently no prejudice to the guarantor.[35]

4. Finally, when the creditor does something that impairs the value of any security given by the principal debtor, but without materially affecting the guarantor's risk under the original contract of guarantee, the guarantor is entitled to be partially discharged from her obligation, but only to the extent that the value of the security is reduced.[36]

Rights of the Guarantor on Default

Defences

A guarantor may generally defend an action by the creditor on any grounds that would be open to the principal debtor. Thus, if a debtor has a good defence because of the misrepresentation of the creditor in selling the goods, the guarantor may take advantage of this defence. A guarantor may also set off against the creditor, in reduction of the debt, any claim the debtor has against the creditor, as when the debtor has performed services for the creditor for which he has not yet been paid.

If the principal contract is void, as for example in the case of a prohibited loan to a company, then any purported guarantee will also be a nullity.[37] It is uncertain whether a guarantor can plead the principal debtor's infancy as a defence on the grounds that if, as guarantor, she were to pay the debt to the creditor, she could not herself succeed in an action to recover it from the principal debtor.[38] However, as we saw in Chapter 7, the general rule is that a contract made with an infant is not void but merely unenforceable against the infant and might not necessarily prevent the enforcement of a guarantee.

Subrogation

We noted earlier in this chapter that an insurer, upon paying a claim made by an insured, becomes subrogated to the rights of the insured and may pursue any remedies that the insured would have against the party responsible for the loss. Similarly, a guarantor who pays off the creditor becomes subrogated to the rights of the creditor against the debtor and the debtor's assets. She may sue the debtor for the amount she has paid the creditor and for any expenses she has incurred because of the debtor's default; if the creditor holds shares or bonds or other property pledged as security for the debt, the guarantor is entitled to have these assets transferred to her in mitigation of her loss.[39]

A guarantor may choose to pay off the creditor and become subrogated to its rights as soon as the debt falls due: she need not wait for the creditor to make a demand or to sue. The guarantor may wish to act even when the creditor is content to wait because it believes the guarantor

---

34. Bank of Montreal v. Wilder (1986), 32 D.L.R. (4th) 9 (S.C.C.).

35. Royal Bank of Canada v. Nobes (1982), 49 N.S.R. (2d) 634.

36. Rose v. Aftenberger (1969), 9 D.L.R. (3d) 42.

37. Communities Economic Development Fund v. Maxwell, [1992] 1 W.W.R.193. In William E. Thompson Associates Inc. v. Carpenter (1989), 61 D.L.R. (4th) 1, the principal debtor's obligation was held to be unenforceable because the interest rate exceeded the maximum permitted under the Criminal Code. Nevertheless, the guarantee of repayment of the principal sum only was held to be severable and enforceable.

38. The argument in favour of enforcing such guarantees is that it would be unconscionable for the guarantor to have persuaded the creditor to lend to the minor and then to plead the debtor's infancy when the minor defaulted.

39. See Royal Bank of Canada v. Dickson (1973), 33 D.L.R. (3d) 332 at 343–4.

is financially sound and able to make payment. The guarantor may have ascertained that the debtor is failing and may wish to take action before the debtor becomes insolvent—if she waits until the creditor demands payment, it may no longer be worthwhile suing the debtor.

Requirement of Writing

Chapter 10 has shown that a contract of guarantee must be in writing and signed by the guarantor to be enforceable against him; we noted that this requirement has been retained even in those jurisdictions where the Statute of Frauds has been largely repealed.[40] Most guarantees, such as those given to a bank, are in writing, regardless of whether writing is required by law. It is generally considered that if oral guarantees were binding, there would be a real danger of inexperienced people being induced to undertake obligations that they did not really understand.

QUESTIONS FOR REVIEW

1. How does insurance both shift and spread the risk of loss?

2. What is "re-insurance"?

3. Distinguish between an insurance agent and an insurance broker.

4. What are the advantages and disadvantages of "comprehensive" insurance?

5. What is a "mortgage clause"?

6. What is meant by an "insurable interest"?

7. Does a shareholder have an insurable interest in the property of his or her corporation?

8. What is the legal position where an insured fails to renew an insurance policy by the due date?

9. Is it necessary for an insured to notify the insurer of changes of circumstance that occur after the policy enters into force?

10. Can an insurance policy be assigned to a third person?

11. What is "subrogation"?

12. In what business circumstances are guarantees commonly required and given?

13. To whom does a guarantor give his or her promise?

14. What normally constitutes the consideration for a guarantee?

15. How may a guarantee be discharged?

16. Is a guarantee of a minor's debt valid?

17. Does a contract of guarantee have to be in writing?

---

40. Only Manitoba does not require a guarantee to be in writing: Act to repeal the Statute of Frauds, R.S.M. 1987, c. F-158. In Alberta, the requirement is more stringent; a guarantee by an individual must also be acknowledged before a notary public: Guarantees Acknowledgement Act, R.S.A. 1980, c. G-12.

CASES AND PROBLEMS

1 Whitehorse Furniture Ltd. took out a fire insurance policy on their premises with Kansafe Insurance Co., the coverage being arranged through an insurance broker, J&H Ltd. Whitehorse did not inform J&H that they had made a previous substantial claim against another insurance company (for a fire in which arson was suspected) and that there had also been two previous fires at their premises that had caused little or no damage. Consequently, Kansafe were also unaware of those facts.

A further fire occurred at the Whitehorse premises. Kansafe initially denied liability because of the non-disclosure. Whitehorse claimed that they had not thought the earlier fires were relevant. Since J&H had not asked any questions about previous fires or claims, Whitehorse had not mentioned them. Kansafe eventually agreed to settle the Whitehorse claim and made a payment of $550 000, without admitting liability.

Subsequently, Kansafe brought an action against J&H, alleging that they had been negligent in not making proper inquiries of Whitehorse and failing to disclose important information when they applied for the insurance coverage on behalf of Whitehorse.

Should Kansafe succeed against J&H?

2 Perennial Manufacturing Inc. carried on a foundry business in premises leased from Sharbo Investments Ltd. Perennial arranged a contract of fire insurance with the Commonwealth Insurance Co.; the insurance covered equipment, business interruption, and the value of the building. At the time when the insurance was arranged, a Mr. Vandervelde was the controlling shareholder of both Perennial and Sharbo; he subsequently sold his shares in Perennial and no longer had an interest in that corporation.

The building burned down. Perennial claimed on the insurance policy and Commonwealth paid out $700 000 for the loss of stock and equipment, business interruption, and extra expenses. It refused to make any payments for the loss of the building on the ground that the building was not owned by Perennial. (It was not insured by Sharbo.)

Is that a valid defence to the claim?

3 Two years before her death, Desai took out a term life insurance policy for $400 000 on her own life. Her friend, Trumble, was named as beneficiary.

In her application for the insurance, Desai described her occupation as "business administrator," Trumble was described as her "business associate," and she stated that her net financial worth was $100 000. None of those statements was entirely accurate. Although she had studied business administration, she was then working as an office cleaner. She did not have a business relationship with Trumble, and her net worth was considerably less than $100 000.

Desai was subsequently murdered by Trumble. Desai's sister claimed on the policy as executrix. The insurance company refused to pay.

What defences are available to the insurance company?

4 Blackgold Investments Limited required additional financing if it was to exploit some apparently attractive opportunities. Its directors decided to assist the company by raising the sum of $500 000 on their own credit. The corporation then applied for a loan with Merchants' Bank, on the terms that a guarantee would be signed jointly by all the directors. The guarantee was on a standard form provided by the bank and included the clause:

> This guarantee shall be binding upon every person signing the same, notwithstanding the non-execution thereof by any other proposed guarantor.

Four directors signed the guarantee in the office of the bank manager in Calgary. Then it was sent to Edmonton, where four other directors signed it together. They noted the absence at the time of the signature of Fowler, the corporation's president (also a director), and agreed among themselves that they were signing only on the condition that the guarantee would not be delivered to the bank until Fowler had signed as well.

When the guarantee was returned to one of the directors in Calgary, she gave it to the bank manager with instructions that it was not to be treated as having been delivered to the bank as an operative instrument until Fowler had signed. In the end, Fowler refused to do so because he did not want to diminish his own line of credit at the bank. Nevertheless, the bank manager advanced the corporation $500 000 and the corporation gave the bank its promissory note for that amount.

Blackgold subsequently defaulted on the note and the bank claimed the sum owing from those directors who had signed the guarantee. They refused to pay on the grounds that the guarantee would not operate unless and until all directors had signed. The bank sued them to enforce the guarantee.

Explain whether this action should succeed.

5. Bellini and Franck were employees and shareholders of Arachne Enterprises Inc. In 1989, to assist their corporation in raising additional funding, they signed limited guarantees for the principal sum of $128 000, with interest at bank prime plus 1.5 percent in favour of the Monarch Bank.

The guarantees were to secure a line of credit for Arachne and were provided for (1) a $100 000 term loan with interest at bank prime plus 2.25 percent and (2) a revolving demand loan for general operating purposes. The revolving loan was not to exceed the principal sum of $125 000 and the lending was subject to an accounts receivable margin requirement. Interest under the revolving loan was at prime plus 1.5 percent. The revolving loan contained a provision under which the bank agreed to apply specified credit balances to repay the loan.

In 1991, Bellini and Franck had their employment terminated, at which time they notified the bank in writing that they were determining their liability in accordance with the guarantee. (Their understanding was that this fixed their maximum liability at the amount then outstanding under the loan.) At the time of the notice, their liability under the revolving loan was $95 000.

After receiving the notice, the bank converted the revolving loan into a fixed loan without the knowledge or consent of Bellini and Franck. In 1992, Arachne renegotiated its loan arrangements to comprise (1) a $100 000 term loan with interest at prime plus 2.5 percent and (2) a fixed operating loan with interest at prime plus 2 percent and with more flexible margin requirements. On March 28, 1993, the bank demanded payment. Arachne proved to be insolvent, and the bank sued Bellini and Franck to enforce the guarantees.

Bellini and Franck consider that they are no longer liable on the original guarantee. Are they correct?

AGENCY AND FRANCHISING

Two types of contract that allow a business to expand its operations are *agency* and *franchising*. The contract of agency has ancient origins and was well known in Roman law. Franchising, by contrast, is a relatively recent phenomenon.

In this chapter we examine such questions as:

- ■ what is the nature of agency?

- ■ how is an agency relationship created?

- ■ what are the duties of the agent and the principal?

- ■ what is the extent of the liability of the principal and of the agent to third parties?

- ■ how is an agency relationship terminated?

- ■ what is the legal nature of franchising?

- ■ what are the usual contents of a franchising agreement?

- ■ what are the rights and duties of the parties to a franchising agreement?

THE NATURE OF AGENCY

Agency is a relationship in which one person, known as an **agent**, is authorized to bring another party for whom she acts, known as a **principal**, into contractual relations with third parties. The relationship between agent and principal is usually a contractual one, with the agent being remunerated for her actions on behalf of the principal, but a person may also volunteer gratuitously to act as an agent. A promise to do so is not binding, but once a person begins to act as an agent in a particular transaction, that person is bound by all the duties of an agent under contract.

agent
a person acting for another person in contractual relations with third parties

principal
the person on whose behalf the agent acts

dependent agent

an agent who acts exclusively, or mostly, for a single principal

independent agent

an agent who carries on an independent business and acts for a number of principals

A distinction is sometimes made between **dependent agents** and **independent agents**. A dependent agent is one who acts exclusively, or mostly, for a single principal. Most insurance agents—though by no means all—are dependent agents. Agency may be created by the terms of an employment contract in which an employer (as principal) delegates to an employee (as agent) the task of negotiating and making some or all of its contracts. However, the functions of agency and employment may be entirely separate: an agent need not be an employee, just as not all employees are agents. Sometimes it is difficult to determine whether an agent is an employee; usually, a self-employed agent is remunerated solely by commissions and does not receive any salary, but that is not always conclusive. The distinction is important in employment law and is discussed further in Chapter 20; it is also very important for income tax purposes.

An independent agent is not an employee and acts on behalf of several principals or clients. Lawyers frequently act as agents for their clients in the purchase or sale of land and buildings. Stockbrokers are agents for clients who place orders with them to buy or sell shares. Auctioneers and commission merchants in possession of goods have authority to sell them for their principals. Insurance brokers act as agents for the clients on whose behalf they arrange insurance. A person may be a **commission agent**, that is, one who sells on behalf of a principal to third parties and receives remuneration through commissions for whatever contracts she does make on behalf of her principal.

commission agent

one who sells on behalf of a principal to third parties and receives remuneration through commissions

Sometimes the term "agency" is used in a broader sense and is not restricted to entering into contracts on behalf of the principal. The so-called real estate "agent" does not have authority, as such, to sell the property of a client—her role is to introduce prospective purchasers, and the client contracts directly with the purchaser. In this chapter, most of our references will be to instances in which an agent's role is to enter into contracts for her principal.

The agency relationship is widely used in business affairs. A corporation, as an entirely artificial "person," can enter into contractual relations only when its officers and employees act as agents on its behalf. In partnerships, too, agency plays an important role. Each partner is presumed by law to be an agent of the other partners, with very wide authority to act on behalf of the firm.

CREATION OF AN AGENCY RELATIONSHIP

The Parties to the Relationship

In discussing the law of principal and agent, we must keep in mind two levels of relationship: first, the relation between principal and agent, usually expressed in the form of an **agency agreement**; and second, the relation between the principal and third parties with whom the agent makes contracts on the principal's behalf.

agency agreement

the agreement between principal and agent, whereby the agent undertakes to act on behalf of the principal

Any person who has the capacity to contract may engage an agent to contract on his behalf. An agent's power to contract on behalf of her principal is limited to the capacity that the principal possesses. Accordingly, if a minor engages an agent, the contracts made for him by the agent are as voidable at his option as if he had made them personally. However, a minor may act as an agent and bind her principal in contracts with third parties, even where she would not bind herself.

Express Agreement

An agency agreement may be oral, written, or in writing under seal. If an agency agreement is to extend beyond one year, it must be in writing to be enforceable in those provinces where the relevant section of the Statute of Frauds continues to apply. In any event, each party should have a copy of the agency agreement in writing and signed by both of them in order to minimize future misunderstandings about the scope of the agent's authority and other terms of the arrangement.

The contract setting out the relationship between a principal and its agent should clearly define the limits of the agent's authority: how far she can go in making a contract with a third party without obtaining further instructions from the principal. An agency agreement may confer on an agent a very wide and general authority to make contracts, an authority narrowly restricted to making a specific contract, or any degree of authority between these extremes.

An agent should always have authorization in writing if she wishes to issue promissory notes, accept drafts, and draw cheques in the name of her principal, and she should sign them in a way that makes it clear that she is acting in a representative capacity; otherwise she may be personally liable on the instrument.[1]

A **power of attorney** is a special type of express agency agreement. Normally, a power of attorney is issued under the seal of the principal, since an agent who does not receive authority under seal cannot be authorized to sign documents under seal on behalf of the principal. A power of attorney, for example, must be given under seal to an agent who is expected to carry through a real estate transaction.

power of attorney

a type of agency agreement authorizing the agent to sign documents on behalf of the principal

A contract of agency, like any other contract, frequently contains implied terms; these terms may supplement the express authority in the contract. Thus, when a principal expressly authorizes an agent to make a purchase, say, of Irish linen in Belfast, the agent would also have implied authority to make a contract for shipment of the goods to Canada.

Ratification

Sometimes a person purports to act as an agent knowing she has no authority but hoping that the proposed principal will later adopt the contract. Subsequent adoption by the principal is called **ratification**. The need for ratification may arise for either of two reasons: first, because the person purporting to act as agent is not an agent at all for the principal on whose behalf she purports to act; or second, because she has only a limited authority and has exceeded it. If a principal does not ratify, questions of reliance by third parties and estoppel may arise. These issues will be discussed in the next section of this chapter.

ratification

subsequent adoption by the proposed principal of a contract made by an agent acting without authority

When a principal does ratify, the effect is to establish the contract with the third party retroactively, as if the agent had possessed the needed authority at the time she made the contract. The principal, agent, and third party are then in the same position regarding the contract as if the agency agreement had existed from the beginning.

A named principal need not state his ratification expressly. It may be implied from the fact of his assuming the benefits of the contract. Ratification cannot be partial: a principal cannot accept the benefits without also reimbursing the agent for her costs, nor can he ratify only those aspects of the transaction that prove to be to his advantage but refuse to ratify the balance of the contract. A principal must also ratify within a reasonable time to be able to claim the benefit of a contract.[2]

Not all contracts made by an agent without authority may be ratified by the principal; a principal may not be able to ratify a contract made for him if, at the time the contract was made he would have been unable to enter into the contract himself.[3] Nor may the principal ratify a contract if, at the time he purports to ratify it, he could not have made that contract himself.

ILLUSTRATION 19.1

A arranges on behalf of *P*, but without *P*'s authority, to insure *P*'s buildings against fire loss, with the entire insurance payable to *P*. The buildings burn down, and *P* then purports to ratify the contract of insurance. The ratification will not be effective because at the time *P* attempts to ratify, the buildings are already destroyed, and it would be too late for *P* to insure them.[4]

---

1. See Bills of Exchange Act, R.S.C. 1985, c. B-4, s. 51(1).
2. Metropolitan Asylums Board Managers v. Kingham & Sons (1890), 6 T.L.R. 217.
3. At common law, a corporation could not ratify a contract made in its name before it was incorporated. This rule has been changed by legislation in nearly all of the provinces; see Chapter 29. As was seen in Chapter 7, contracts made by a minor may sometimes be ratified after he reaches the age of majority.
4. See Portavon Cinema Co. Ltd. v. Price and Century Insurance Co. Ltd., [1939] 4 All E.R. 601 at 607.

Again, a principal cannot ratify when the rights of an outsider are affected.

ILLUSTRATION 19.2

A, without authority from *P*, purports to accept *T*'s offer to sell a large quantity of canned goods to *P*. Subsequently, before the delivery date, *T* learns that *A* had no authority. Because the market is uncertain, *T* is afraid to wait for *P*'s ratification and makes a contract to sell the same goods to *X*. Ratification by *P* will now be ineffective because an outsider, *X*, has acquired rights to the goods.

Illustration 19.2 raises a further problem. Suppose the market value of the goods is rising rapidly at the time *T* learns that *A* had no authority to buy them. Can *T* revoke its offer to sell and retain the goods for later sale to another party at a higher price? The answer turns on the legal significance of *A*'s acceptance. If *A*'s acceptance is ineffective until ratification by *P*, then *T* can revoke its offer before that time. If *A*'s acceptance creates a binding contract, we are confronted with the paradox that *T* is bound while *P*, not yet having ratified, has a choice to bind himself or not. This situation arose in *Bolton Partners v. Lambert*[5] where *T*'s offer was accepted by *A* on behalf of *P* but without authority, and *T* then attempted to withdraw the offer before *P*'s ratification. The court held that the revocation was ineffective and *T* was bound by *P*'s subsequent ratification.

The decision has been followed in a few English cases although it has been criticized.[6] In *Fleming v. Bank of New Zealand*,[7] Lord Lindley noted that the decision in the *Bolton* case "presents difficulties," and suggested that the court might reconsider the authority of the case in the future. These misgivings are reflected in the position taken by courts in the United States, where revocation is held to be effective if it precedes ratification. The point has not often come before the Canadian courts, but in one case the court referred to Lord Lindley's statement and impliedly disapproved of the decision in the *Bolton* case.[8] As a result it is questionable whether the *Bolton* decision applies in Canada. Even if it does apply, it is subject to the important qualifications that ratification must not prejudice the rights of an outsider and that the principal must ratify within a reasonable time.

Finally, a principal cannot ratify if, at the time the agent made the contract, she failed to name her intended principal or at least mention the existence of a principal whose identity can then be ascertained. This rule prevents a person from entering into a contract simply in the hope that she may subsequently find a principal to ratify and so relieve her of her rights and duties. An *undisclosed principal* cannot afterwards ratify a contract made without his authority. On the other hand, as we shall see, when a contract is made *with* the authority of an undisclosed principal, the principal may intervene and enforce the contract, or may be held liable on the contract once the third party learns of his existence and identity.

When an agent purports to accept an offer "subject to the ratification of my principal," the later ratification will not be retroactive. This apparent exception is simply an application of the rules of offer and acceptance: a conditional acceptance by an agent is not acceptance at all. The offeror may revoke the offer at any time before acceptance. In these circumstances the eventual "ratification" of the principal is really only an acceptance of the original offer.

---

5. (1889), 41 Ch. D. 295.

6. See Fridman, *The Law of Agency* (7th ed.), p. 100. Toronto: Butterworths, 1996.

7. [1900] A.C. 577.

8. Goodison Thresher Co. v. Doyle (1925), 57 O.L.R. 300.

Estoppel

When one party allows another to believe that a certain state of affairs exists and the other person relies upon that belief, the first party will be prevented from afterwards stating that the true state of affairs was different.[9] This rule of law is called *estoppel*: a party is *estopped* from stating the actual facts when it has induced another to rely on an entirely different version. The rule has relevance to the law of agency in two types of case.

Apparent Authority

Agency by estoppel arises when the agent's authority is merely apparent, not real. An agent may acquire **apparent authority** from a past manner of transacting business by the principal or from trade custom. The circumstances may make it appear to third parties that an agent has authority to make the bargain when, in fact, she does not have any real authority for the purpose; there exists no understanding between her and her principal, express or implied, granting this authority.

apparent authority
authority that is not real but is acquired from a past manner of transacting business or from trade custom

An agent may exceed her real authority by venturing into sideline activities, or she may act within the limits usually ascribed to agents of her type but in violation of a special restriction placed on her activities by the principal. In either of these situations the principal may not want to perform the contract. When may the principal legally refuse to perform and when will he be bound by the contract?

The test is whether the third party should have been aware of the agent's lack of authority— or at least have had reason to be suspicious—or whether it could reasonably assume from the kind of business in which the agent is engaged that the agent had authority for the contract in question. A third party is expected to act with a reasonable measure of business acumen and common sense. If the proposed contract is not within an area ordinarily entrusted to such agents, or if its consequences are of relatively great importance for the principal and the third party, a third party should first check with the named principal about the agent's authority. For example, an agent does not usually have authority to borrow money in the principal's name or to commit the principal to new lines of activity. An agent who is authorized to sell goods is not necessarily authorized to accept the purchase money, particularly where payment to the agent is not customary trade practice or where the principal has sent an invoice to the third party requesting payment. If the third party pays the money to the agent and the agent absconds, the third party may have to pay the money again to the principal.[10]

On the other hand, it would be impractical in day-to-day business for third parties to have to check an agent's authority in every instance. A presumption of authority is established by trade usage for various types of agency. A principal that seeks to restrict abnormally his agent's authority takes the risk that the agent will have, in the eyes of third parties, an apparent authority exceeding her real authority and may make contracts in excess of that authority. The principal will be estopped from denying liability on contracts made for him within the range of that apparent authority. It is sometimes said that a principal "clothes" his agent with apparent authority; third parties are entitled to judge by appearances.

CASE 19.1

Garrod and Parkin entered into a partnership to run a car repair and maintenance business. Parkin was to be the active partner; Garrod provided most of the financing.

When the partnership agreement was drawn up, Garrod insisted that an express provision be included that the

continued

---

9. See the discussion in Chapter 6 under "Injurious Reliance (Equitable Estoppel)."
10. Butwick v. Grant, [1924] 2 K.B. 483.

business of the firm should not include the buying or selling of cars. Parkin later sold a car belonging to a customer who had left it with the firm for repairs, without the knowledge of the owner, and disappeared with the proceeds. The car was later recovered by the owner, and the purchaser, who had innocently bought the car from Parkin, brought an action against Garrod (for breach of the implied condition in the contract of sale that the seller has title). The court ruled that, in selling the car, Parkin was acting as agent for Garrod since, in partnership law, each partner is an agent for the other partners. Parkin had no actual authority to sell the car, because of the express provision in the partnership agreement, but he did have apparent authority. Selling used cars is a common part of car repair businesses.[11]

A firm that especially restricts its agent's authority should consequently ensure that the third parties with whom the agent is likely to deal receive actual notice of the restriction.

Holding Out

A principal may also be estopped from denying liability on contracts with third parties because of conduct known as **holding out**: when a business represents someone to be its agent, either by words suggestive of that relationship or by acquiescing in similar contracts made for it by that person in the past, it will not be permitted to deny the existence of an agency. For example, if a corporation describes someone as a "director," it will not be permitted to claim that that person had never been properly appointed and was consequently not an agent.

CASE 19.2

Pickering authorized a broker, Swallow, to buy hemp for him. After the purchase, Pickering left the hemp on deposit at a wharf in Swallow's name. Swallow, without any authority, sold the hemp and delivered it to the buyer. The buyer became bankrupt, and the trustee, Busk, acting for the bankrupt buyer obtained title to the hemp.

Pickering claimed that he was not bound by the contract of sale made by Swallow and should be able to recover the hemp from Busk. The court held that Pickering's conduct in leaving the hemp in the broker's name had given the broker apparent authority to sell as well as to buy. Accordingly, Pickering failed to recover the hemp from Busk and could only claim as a creditor of the bankrupt.

As we shall see, Pickering might also have had a claim against Swallow for breach of their contract of agency.[12]

The question of holding out may also arise when an agency agreement ends. If an agent continues to enter into contracts for the principal after the agency has ended, and third parties have had no notice of the termination, the principal is bound by the contracts. This is of practical importance, as we shall see, when a partner retires from a partnership firm, since partners customarily act as agents for the partnership in contracts with outside parties such as suppliers.

The transaction known as a *consignment* may for some purposes create an agency by estoppel. As we noted in Chapter 16, the effect of a consignment is to transfer physical possession of goods from their owner, the consignor, to a consignee. While the consignor continues to own the goods, the possession of them gives the consignee the appearance of ownership and implied authority to sell them as agent for the consignor. The Factors Act states that a mercantile agent

---

11. Mercantile Credit Co. Ltd. v. Garrod, [1962] 3 All E.R. 1103.

12. Pickering v. Busk (1812), 104 E.R. 758.

(for example, a retail shopkeeper or commission merchant) who holds articles for sale on consignment may effectively sell the goods or use them as security for a loan even when she exceeds her authority.[13] The third party (the buyer or lender) thus obtains valid title to the goods against the consignor, provided the third party accepted the goods innocently and in good faith, that is, without knowledge that the owner had forbidden their sale or pledge.

Agency by Necessity

As a rule, English law does not recognize agency by necessity. There may be circumstances where one person enters into a contract on behalf of another without authority and where the party receiving the benefit of the contract has a moral duty to ratify, but as a general rule our law does not force a liability on a person against his will. There are a few exceptions to this principle; for example, the owner of a ship salvaged at sea is bound to compensate the rescuer.[14] The situation may be different where an agency relationship already exists. An agency of necessity arises when an agent with restricted express authority has to take prompt action in excess of her instructions; for example, a carrier of perishable goods usually has authority as an agent by necessity to dispose of them at a reasonable price if it is unable to communicate with their owner for instructions.[15]

THE DUTIES OF AN AGENT TO THE PRINCIPAL

Duty to Comply With the Contract

The duties of an agent are determined by the terms—express and implied—of the contract. Custom and trade usage have introduced a number of rights and duties for both agent and principal as implied terms of the agency agreement. Any of these implied terms may, of course, be incorporated expressly in the agency agreement or may be excluded by an express term or even by the special circumstances surrounding the particular agency agreement. The breach of any term, whether express or implied, gives the aggrieved party the usual remedies against the other for breach of contract. For example, an agent may have private instructions restricting her authority, and if she exceeds that authority but acts within her apparent authority, her principal will be bound by the resulting contract. Nevertheless, the principal will be able to recover from the agent any loss that results from her breach of duty.

The courts generally regard notice to an agent as being the equivalent of notice to her principal: what an agent knows the principal is deemed to know. An agent therefore has a duty to be diligent in keeping her principal informed about all important developments affecting their relationship.

Duty of Care

An agent owes a duty of care to the principal. The degree of skill that the principal can expect depends on the nature of the agent's task and her known competence for the purpose. An agent ought not to agree to represent a principal in complicated and technical transactions for which she is not qualified, but she has a better chance of avoiding liability for the consequences if she can show that the principal was fully aware of her lack of qualifications.

---

13. See, for example: Sale of Goods Act, R.S.B.C. 1996, c. 410, s. 59; Factors Act, R.S.O. 1990, c. F.1, s. 2; R.S.N.S. 1989, c. 157, s. 3. Note that the Factors Act retains a now obsolete definition of *factoring*. When the act was passed, a *factor* was one who sold merchandise shipped to him on consignment by the owner and, generally, received a commission based on the amount received from sales. In recent years, factors have abandoned their selling and merchandising function and have concentrated on credit and collection activities.

14. The Five Steel Barges (1890), 15 P.D. 142 at 146. See also Canada Shipping Act, S.C. 1993, c. 36 Sched. V.

15. Couturier v. Hastie (1856), 10 E.R. 1065.

An agent may promise to act for her principal without receiving payment for her services. Before performing such a gratuitous promise, she may withdraw. Nevertheless, if she does proceed to act on behalf of the principal, she is bound to use reasonable care, diligence, and skill.

Personal Performance

Because of the high degree of confidence and trust implicit in an agency relationship, the general rule is that an agent cannot delegate her duties. An agent's usual terms of reference include the personal exercise of her judgment, skill, and discretion on the principal's behalf. For this reason, there are relatively few situations in which an agency agreement can properly be performed vicariously by a sub-agent. An agent who wrongfully delegates her responsibilities is guilty of a breach of duty to her principal.

There are some circumstances where the nature of the agency relationship or trade usage will give the agent an implied authority to delegate all or part of her duties. Thus, when a stockbroker agrees to buy or sell shares, the broker will have implied authority to make the actual purchase or sale through a sub-agent on the floor of the stock exchange. Again, when a bank acts as agent for its customers, it may sometimes require the services of other banks to represent it in countries where it has no branches itself. Indeed, whenever a corporation is appointed as an agent, it must perform through sub-agents, namely its directors or employees. Finally, a principal may give express consent to performance by a sub-agent, or may subsequently ratify that type of performance.

When an agent has implied authority to perform through a sub-agent, there is generally privity of contract only (1) between the principal and the agent, and (2) between the agent and the sub-agent; in other words, no privity of contract exists between the principal and the sub-agent. Accordingly, the principal may recover from the agent for the consequences of an improper performance by the sub-agent, but the principal has no claim in contract against the sub-agent. The agent may in turn recover from the sub-agent. A third party may enforce the contract against the principal if the sub-agent has express authority to act for it, makes contracts that the principal subsequently ratifies, or acts in circumstances where the principal is estopped from denying its authority.

Good Faith

Fiduciary Relationship

The duty of good faith arises from the fact that parties are in a special relationship of trust, a *fiduciary* relationship, of which principal and agent is only one example. The law also imposes a duty of the same high degree of good faith and loyalty on members of a partnership and participants in joint business ventures,[16] as well as on members of professions in their relations with clients and patients; fiduciary duties of this nature were considered in Chapter 4.

Money that comes into an agent's possession in respect of contracts made for the principal belongs to the principal, although the agent may be entitled to withhold amounts due to her as commission. She should keep separate records so that she can account to the principal for money received. Thus, an agent who fails to keep proper accounts may be liable to her principal for any unexplained shortfalls.[17] The money should be put in a separate bank account, so that property in an agent's possession that belongs to the principal is not confused with the agent's own assets.

The duty of good faith requires that an agent inform the principal of any information coming to her attention that might influence the principal's decisions. If she has been authorized to

---

16. See Lac Minerals Ltd. v. International Corona Resources Ltd. (1989), 61 D.L.R. (4th) 14.

17. See Killoran v. RMO Site Management Inc. (1997), 33 B.L.R. (2d) 240.

buy property at a certain price and learns that it can be obtained for a lesser sum, she is bound to inform the principal. If she buys at the lower price, she must pass on the savings to the principal, rather than make a secret profit for herself.[18]

Acting for Two Principals

An agent can act for both parties in a transaction if they are aware of the arrangement and have agreed to it. However, ordinary business prudence suggests the each party should normally hire his own agent. In most circumstances, an agent will not be acting in good faith when she serves two principals in the same transaction without their knowledge and consent. The two principals will normally have conflicting interests, as each will want to get the best possible bargain. The most common breach of faith by an agent consists of accepting a commission from a third party as well as from the principal. Such conduct is tantamount to taking a bribe to secure something less than the best possible bargain for the principal.

In *Andrews v. Ramsay*,[19] a real estate agent had agreed to assist in selling property on a commission basis. Subsequently, the agent accepted a commission from the purchaser. The court held that he was liable to his principal not only for the return of his regular selling commission but also for the commission he had received from the third party. Probably, had he chosen, the principal might also have avoided the contract of sale with the third party on grounds of fraud: a third party that offers a payment in these circumstances is as guilty as the agent and is a party to the fraud.

In *Salomons v. Pender*,[20] a real estate agent arranged a sale of land for the owner to a corporation of which the agent was a director and shareholder. The court held that he was not entitled to a commission because he had also an interest in the business of the other contracting party.

Contracts Between Agent and Principal

An agent's loyalty to her principal is also compromised when she makes herself the other party to the contract without prior notice to, and approval of, the principal—by buying property from or selling it to the principal. In such a case, an agent places her own interest in conflict with that of her principal. She will be concerned to get the best of the bargain for herself and not for her principal.

CASE 19.3

A client gave a broker an order to buy tallow. The broker already held some tallow on his own account, and simply sent this tallow to the client. The court held that the client did not have to accept or pay for it. There was no evidence that the broker had obtained either the best tallow or the best price for the principal. Indeed, there is a presumption in these circumstances that the broker would obtain as much personal profit as possible.[21]

CASE 19.4

A solicitor agreed to sell property for a client and then decided that he would like to own it himself. He bought it ostensibly in the name of someone else. The court held that he could not enforce the purchase.[22]

18. McCullough v. Teniglia (1999), 40 B.L.R. (2d) 222.

19. [1903] 2 K.B. 635.

20. (1865), 195 E.R. 682.

21. Robinson v. Mollett (1874), L.R. 7 H.L. 802.

22. McPherson v. Watt (1877), 3 App. Cas. 254. See also Aaron Acceptance Corp. v. Adam (1987), 37 D.L.R. (4th) 133.

It should be noted that the Criminal Code provides that an agent commits a criminal offence when she corruptly demands or accepts any remuneration from a third party in the conduct of her principal's business affairs.[23] The third party that offers such a bribe or kickback is equally culpable.

THE DUTIES OF THE PRINCIPAL TO THE AGENT

Remuneration

Usually an agency agreement sets out how an agent's fee or commission is to be determined. In the absence of an express term, an agent is entitled to a reasonable fee to be determined by reference to the fees of other agents who perform comparable services. A request by a principal for services of a kind for which an agent would normally expect to be paid implies a promise to pay a reasonable fee—another example of *quantum meruit*.

The terms on which a principal retains a real estate agent raise special problems about the principal's liability to pay a commission. Placing property for sale with a real estate agent is essentially an offer to pay a fee to the agent in return for a strictly defined service. The prospective seller's offer to pay a commission will take effect only when the agent does what she has been engaged to do. Many agreements between prospective sellers and real estate agents state that the agent is entitled to commission when she introduces a prospective purchaser who is "ready, willing, and able to purchase"—the fact that the sale is not completed by reason of the seller's refusal to perform will not deprive the agent of this right.[24] The seller may, however, withdraw his offer at any time before a satisfactory purchaser is introduced, and will not be liable to pay commission. He might even sell the property on his own, and he will not be liable to pay the real estate agent a commission unless the real estate agent was instrumental in introducing the purchaser to him. Real estate agents do, however, often urge a client to sign an **exclusive listing agreement** to operate for a stated period: the client undertakes to pay a commission on any sale of his property during the period whether it is sold by the client himself, the agent, or any other real estate agent. A client is not, of course, obliged to enter into such a contract, but if he does, he will be bound by its terms.

In other cases, a prospective seller insists that the listing agreement contain a term that the agent is not entitled to commission unless and until a sale is completed. Such a term governs the rights of the agent; she is not entitled to her commission even when she introduces a suitable purchaser whose offer the seller refuses.

A number of provinces have statutes rendering a contract to pay commission to a real estate agent unenforceable unless it is in writing and signed by the prospective seller of the property. In these provinces, when an agreement for an agent's services is entirely oral, the agent does not acquire an enforceable right even though she may have introduced a willing and able purchaser to the client.[25]

Expenses

Even if an agency agreement does not say so directly, there is an implied term that the principal will reimburse the agent for all reasonable expenses incurred within the scope of her real authority. An agent should consequently keep proper accounts and records to substantiate her claim. The principal is under no obligation to reimburse an agent for unauthorized acts unless he ratifies them.

exclusive listing agreement
an agreement by the client of a real estate agent to pay commission on any sale of a property whether it is sold by the client, the agent, or some other agent

---

23. R.S.C. 1985, c. C-46, s. 426.

24. Columbia Caterers & Sherlock Co. v. Famous Restaurants Ltd. (1956), 4 D.L.R. (2d) 601.

25. See, for example, Real Estate and Business Brokers Act, R.S.O. 1990, c. R.4, s. 23; Real Estate Act, S.A. 1995, c. R-4.5, s. 22; Real Estate Trading Act, S.N.S. 1996, c. 28, s. 26.

LIABILITY OF PRINCIPAL AND AGENT

When an agent makes a contract on behalf of her principal with a third party, the question arises as to who is liable on the contract—the agent or the principal? The answer depends upon a number of factors; was the agent acting within the scope of her authority in making the contract? Was the identity or existence of the principal disclosed to the other party? There are three possible solutions:

- the principal alone is liable on the contract
- the agent alone is liable
- either the principal or the agent may be held liable

The Principal Alone Is Liable on the Contract

An agent incurs no liability on contracts made for her principal when the agency relationship is functioning as intended. Having brought the contract into being, the agent steps out of the picture: her principal is liable for performance and is the one able to enforce it against the third party. Further, an agent has no liability to the third party even when she acts outside her real authority so long as she acts within her apparent authority and thus binds her principal; but she may, as we have seen, be liable to the principal for breach of the agency agreement.

To ensure that she has no liability in contracts made for her principal, an agent should indicate that she acts as agent and should identify the principal.[26] The following are examples of signatures that accomplish this purpose:

"The Smith Corporation Limited, per W.A. Jones"

or

"W.A. Jones, for The Smith Corporation Limited."

By identifying her principal, an agent makes it clear to the third party that she is acting only as agent. If an agent does not name her principal, it may be more difficult for her to prove that the third party regarded her as merely an agent; she adds to the risk that the third party may be entitled to look to her for the actual performance of the contract.

Sometimes, an agent may persuade a third party to enter into a contract with an unidentified principal. She may describe herself as agent for a party that does not want for the time being to disclose his name. For example, an agent may negotiate in this way in order to obtain options for the purchase of individual pieces of land intended for assembly into a large block. The reasoning is that if the prospective purchaser is a large developer, the disclosure of his identity and purpose might induce some owners to hold out for much higher prices. In this situation, although the principal was not named in the contract, it was nevertheless made on his behalf and with his authority, and he alone is liable on, and entitled to enforce, the contract. The third party has no rights against the agent.[27]

Where the principal is liable under a contract made on his behalf, he does not discharge his liability by handing over the contract price, or goods, to his agent for transmission to the third party; if the agent absconds with the money or the goods, the principal remains liable.[28]

The Agent Alone Is Liable on the Contract

When an agent describes herself as a principal, though she is in reality acting or intending to act for an undisclosed principal, the agent alone has rights and liabilities relative to the third party. The

---

26. See Hills v. Swift Canadian Co., [1923] 3 D.L.R. 997.

27. See QNS Paper Co. v. Chartwell Shipping Ltd. (1989), 62 D.L.R. (4th) 36.

28. Irvine & Co. v. Watson & Sons (1880), 5 Q.B.D. 414.

principal can neither sue nor be sued on the contract.[29] If the agent describes herself (incorrectly) as the "owner" of a building or a ship, the third party is entitled to regard the contract as confined to itself and the agent.[30] The agent must, however, do something more than merely fail to disclose the existence of a principal; she must also contract on terms that she herself is the real principal.

Either the Principal or the Agent May Be Held Liable on the Contract

Sometimes a person who is an agent makes no mention of her status, and deals with a third party without it being apparent that she is acting as an agent. The third party is entitled to sue the agent on the contract. This is fair, since it may have been influenced by the personal credit and character of the agent. However, alternative liability of agent and principal does *not* apply when the third party knows that the contract is being made on behalf of the principal.[31]

What are the third party's rights when it discovers the existence and identity of the principal? If the contract was one that the agent had authority to make, the third party has the option of holding *either* principal *or* agent liable for performance of the contract, but not both. If the third party sues and obtains judgment against the agent before it learns of the real principal, it has no rights against the principal.[32] If, however, the fact of agency emerges during litigation, the action may be discontinued and fresh proceedings taken against the principal. In that case, the principal may treat the contract as being made with him and has all of the defences, as well as the liabilities, of a contracting party.

The Undisclosed Principal

In the preceding section, we saw that a party who contracts with an agent for an undisclosed principal may enforce the contract against the principal when his existence is discovered. Can an undisclosed principal enforce a contract made on his behalf and with his authority? Generally, the answer is "yes"; he may normally intervene and enforce the contract against the other party. To that rule, there is one major exception. An undisclosed principal is not permitted to enforce a contract that is essentially personal in nature; for example, a contract to purchase shares in a family corporation.[33]

To succeed, however, an undisclosed principal must show that the contract was made with his authority. If the agent had no real authority, the undisclosed principal cannot ratify the contract and enforce it. If he were allowed to do so, he would be in a position to choose whether to be bound by the contract. But can the third party hold the principal liable?

CASE 19.5

A was employed as manager of an alehouse by *P* Co., a firm of brewers. *P* Co. had expressly forbidden *A* to purchase certain articles for the business, even though the normal practice of the trade was to give managers such authority. *A* contracted to buy such articles from *T*, without disclosing that he was *P* Co.'s manager. On the licence above the door of the alehouse, only *A*'s name appeared, suggesting that he was the owner rather than just a manager. When *T* discovered the agency relationship, he sued *P* Co. for the price of the goods.

29. Note, however, that the principal may still acquire rights under the contract as an assignee from the agent.

30. Humble v. Hunter (1848), 116 E.R. 885. Contrast the decision in Watteau v. Fenwick, *infra*, n. 34.

31. Lang Transport Ltd. v. Plus Factor International Trucking Ltd. (1997), 143 D.L.R. (4th) 672.

32. Kendall v. Hamilton (1879), 4 App.Cas. 504.

33. See Collins v. Associated Greyhound Racecourses, [1930] 1 Ch. 1.

In Case 19.5, the English Court of Queen's Bench held the brewery firm liable[34] on the basis that the contract was one that a manager would normally have power to make and was thus within his apparent authority. The fallacy of this reasoning, however, has been pointed out by several commentators:[35] if the principal was not disclosed, how could the agent have *apparent* authority to contract on his behalf? In a later Canadian case, the court declined to follow the English precedent.

CASE 19.6

A Co. was a management company controlled by the owner of a shopping mall. It had entered into a contract to rent an electronic sign from T for use in the shopping mall. In 1983, P Co. acquired the ownership of the mall; A Co. continued to manage the mall as its agent. T was unaware of the change of ownership. In 1985, T entered into a new contract with A Co. to renew the rental of the sign. At the time, no mention was made of P Co.'s ownership. The contract was one that A Co. had no authority to make. P Co. refused to honour the contract and was sued by T.

The British Columbia Court of Appeal held that P Co., the undisclosed principal, was not liable on the contract. The agent had no authority, and the plaintiff had no knowledge of the principal's existence. The plaintiff's right of recovery was limited to A Co.[36]

FIGURE 19.1
Liability on Agency Contract

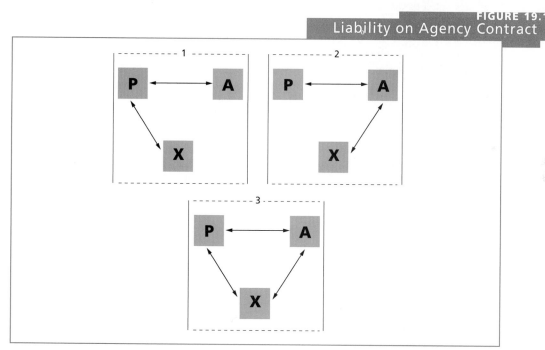

In the most common type of case (1), an agency contract exists between the principal (P) and the agent (A). A, acting within her authority, actual or apparent, negotiates a contract with a third person (X). But that contract is one between P and X. In case (2), A describes herself as principal and does not disclose the existence of P. The result is that the contract is between A and X. In case (3), A says nothing about her status as agent. X is entitled to assume that A was acting on her own account and can sue A. But if A was in fact acting on behalf of P, X can choose to sue P instead.

---

34. Watteau v. Fenwick, [1895] 1 Q.B. 346.

35. See the comments of Fridman (1991), 70 *Can. Bar Rev.* 329.

36. Sign-O-Lite Plastics Ltd. v. Metropolitan Life Insurance Co. (1990), 49 B.C.L.R. (2d) 183.

Liability for Misrepresentation

When an agent is guilty of fraudulent misrepresentation in making a contract, even though the principal did not authorize the misrepresentation or had forbidden it, the third party may rescind the contract. Furthermore, if the agent was acting within her apparent authority, the third party may successfully sue the principal as well as the agent for the tort of deceit.[37] If the principal was innocent of the fraud, he may in turn successfully sue his agent for damages to compensate for the loss, but if he participated in the misrepresentation, he is a co-conspirator and has no rights against the agent.

More generally, a principal is jointly and severably liable with his agent for torts committed by the agent while acting within the scope of her actual or apparent authority.[38] As we have seen in Chapter 3, the actual tortfeasor (in this case the agent) remains liable for her torts, even though the principal is liable as well. An agent may also be liable to a third party for negligent misrepresentation. For example, Canadian courts have held that a real estate agent, though engaged and paid by the vendor, also owes a duty of care in the statements she makes to the purchaser.[39]

Breach of Warranty of Authority

There is no contract when a person holds herself out to be an agent but has no authority, actual or apparent, and the named principal does not ratify. The situation may arise because the alleged agent has acted fraudulently; for example, a rogue may give the name of a reputable party as principal to obtain goods on credit. The seller will have an action in tort for deceit against the fraudulent agent, but that will only be worth pursuing if the rogue has assets of her own. An action in tort will also lie where an agent makes a *negligent* misrepresentation that she has an authority that she does not possess.[40]

An agent may innocently act without authority when, unknown to her, her principal has become bankrupt or insane or has died. No contract between a third party and the principal can be formed after the principal has lost contractual capacity or has ceased to exist. And no contract is formed between the agent and the third party either, because the agent has acted *as agent*. The

warranty of authority
a person who purports to act as agent represents that she has authority to contract on behalf of the principal

remedy of the third party lies not in the ineffectual contract but in an action against the agent for *breach of **warranty of authority***. It does not matter that when the agent acted for the principal, she was unaware of the principal's misfortune. It is therefore advisable for an agent to communicate frequently with her principal.

We have seen that an agent may be liable if she acts in anticipation of a ratification that she never receives or if she contracts on behalf of a non-existent principal. These are two further instances of breach of warranty of authority.

It is not entirely clear whether breach of warranty of authority is a tort or a wrong to be redressed within the law of contract. If the remedy is contractual, it is not related to the abortive contract between the third party and the principal; rather, it is regarded as a breach of a separate *implied* contract between the agent and the third party in which, in return for the third party agreeing to contract with the principal, the agent impliedly promises that she has authority to act. Alternatively, if it is a tort, it seems to be a type of negligent misrepresentation. In either case, it seems that the measure of damages will be that which is necessary to put the other party in the position in which he would have been had the representation been true.[41]

---

37. Lloyd v. Grace, Smith & Co. Ltd., [1912] A.C. 716.
38. Fridman, *The Law of Agency* (7th ed.), p. 315. If the agent is an employee, the principal may also be vicariously liable.
39. See Avery v. Salie (1972), 25 D.L.R. (3d) 495.
40. Alvin's Auto Service Ltd. v. Clew Holdings Ltd., [1997] S.J. No. 387.
41. Delta Construction Co. Ltd. v. Lidstone (1979), 96 D.L.R. (3d) 457.

CASE 19.7

The plaintiff owned a block of shares in a corporation of which he was the treasurer. He was dismissed from that position and, in the course of negotiations, the defendant, a solicitor, purportedly acting on behalf of the majority shareholders, made an offer to buy out the plaintiff's shares. The solicitor did not have authority to make the offer and the majority shareholders refused to go through with the purchase. In the meantime, the shares were delisted and became worthless.

The solicitor was held to be in breach of his warranty of authority and the plaintiff was entitled to damages representing his loss of bargain—namely the difference between the price offered and their new value, which was zero.[42]

TERMINATING AN AGENCY RELATIONSHIP

An agent's authority may be terminated on any of the following occasions:

- at the end of a time specified in the agency agreement
- at the completion of the particular project for which the agency was formed
- upon notice by either the principal or the agent that he or she wishes to end the agency
- upon the death or insanity of either the principal or the agent
- upon the bankruptcy of the principal
- upon an event that makes performance of the agency agreement impossible

Where no specific time is fixed for an agency relationship, it is implied that either party may end the relationship by notice to the other. In other words, an option clause is implied that may be used to discharge the contract by agreement and without breach. If, however, the agreement is for a specified time, premature withdrawal by either principal or agent without the consent of the other constitutes a breach of contract.

Occasionally, an agency agreement may be discharged by frustration. An example of an agency that becomes impossible to perform occurs when an owner of goods has engaged an auctioneer to sell them and the goods are destroyed by fire before their sale.

When an agency arrangement ends for any reason other than the bankruptcy, death, or insanity of the principal, the principal may be bound by the former agent continuing to act within her apparent authority. In his own interest, a principal ought to bring the termination to the attention of all third parties likely to be affected. This precaution is especially important when a partnership is dissolved and will be discussed in Chapter 26.

As noted at the beginning of this chapter, it is sometimes difficult to determine whether an agent is also an employee of the principal. Courts are increasingly willing to infer that a principal–agent relationship contains elements of an employer–employee relationship, and when such an inference is drawn, each party is entitled to reasonable notice before termination becomes effective,[43] as will be discussed in the next chapter.

FRANCHISING

Superficially, agency and franchising appear to have much in common. Both are methods that permit a business to expand rapidly. In both, the proprietor of the original business—the

---

42. Salter v. Cormie (1993), 108 D.L.R. (4th) 372 (Alta. C.A.).
43. See Martin-Baker Aircraft Co. v. Canadian Flight Equipment, [1955] 2 Q.B. 556.

principal or the franchisor—employs the assistance of other persons or business entities in order to reach out to a wider public. Independent agents are engaged to market the principal's products, just as franchisees are used to market the franchisor's products. In law, however, there are significant differences between the two relationships.

The Growth of Franchising

Franchising has become a major business form in Canada with about 1400 franchise systems, 76 000 franchise operators, and $100 billion in sales. Franchises now account for more than 40 percent of all retail sales and business services provided in North America, and international franchising is growing rapidly. When people are asked about franchising, most think of fast food, especially a particular brand of hamburger, yet franchising has become common in many sectors—from hotels and restaurants to office supplies, real estate agencies, and video stores.

Nature of Franchising

Despite its economic importance, there is remarkably little "law" on the subject in Canada. In most provinces, the law applicable to franchising must be found in the general principles of contract and tort law and more specific areas of law, such as consumer protection and intellectual property law.

The essential characteristic of the franchising relationship is that one party, the *franchisor*, grants a *licence* to the other party, the *franchisee*, to market its product and use its name and trademark in return for payment of a *franchise fee*. However, a franchise normally amounts to considerably more than the mere granting of a licence: it involves a substantial degree of control by the franchisor over the franchisee's business. The franchisee nevertheless operates as an independent business and is not simply an employee or agent of the franchisor. As described by one judge:

> …franchising promises to provide the independent merchant with the means to become an efficient and effective competitor of large integrated firms. Through various forms of franchising, the manufacturer is assured qualified and effective outlets for his products, and the franchisee enjoys backing in the form of know-how and financial assistance.[44]

Typical Contents of a Franchising Agreement

A franchise is created when the franchisor and franchisee enter into a contract, referred to as the **franchise agreement**. Since the franchisor normally makes a substantial number of such agreements—McDonald's has more than 3000 franchises in North America alone—whereas the franchisee normally enters into only one such agreement, the agreement is usually the franchisor's standard-form contract, often accompanied by an operating manual for the franchisee. Typically, the agreement will deal with the following subjects.

Consideration Provided by the Franchisor

The essential feature of the agreement is the grant to the franchisee of a right, or licence, to market goods supplied by, or made to specifications provided by, the franchisor. The agreement further allows the franchisee to use trademarks, trade names, logos, secret processes, and so on that belong to the franchisor.

While the above features are also found in simple licensing agreements, a franchise agreement goes further: it normally provides for training the franchisee in the operation of the busi-

franchise agreement
an agreement under which a franchisor grants to the franchisee a right to market the franchisor's products

---

44. Stewart, J. of the U.S. Supreme Court, in United States v. Arnold, Schwinn & Co., 388 U.S.365, at 386 (1967), quoted by Stark, J. in Jirna Ltd. v. Mister Donut of Canada Ltd. (1970), 13 D.L.R. (3d) 645, at 646 (Ont. H.C.).

ness, and for ongoing supervision, assistance, and management services. The franchisor frequently assists in the design of the business premises—usually to a standard design—and in establishing accounting, inventory control, and purchasing systems. It is also common for the franchisor to provide financial assistance to the franchisor, through loans or guarantees.

One of the main purposes of franchising is to enable a comparatively large number of small, independent entrepreneurs to take advantage of well-known and widely recognized trade names and reputations. Thus the franchisor invariably undertakes to provide advertising and promotion on a national or regional scale.

Consideration Provided by the Franchisee

For its part, the franchisee is required to provide an initial contribution of capital to what is, after all, the franchisee's own business. The size of the contribution varies widely, according to whether premises and equipment are purchased (and perhaps custom built), or leased from the franchisor or from some other person. Additionally, the franchisee agrees to pay for the services and assistance provided by the franchisor. Normally, there is a basic franchise fee and ongoing payments, which may take the form of a percentage of the revenues of the franchise, rentals for premises or equipment, payments for management services, or contributions to the cost of advertising campaigns.

A further source of profit to the franchisor is often derived from exclusive supply arrangements. In some types of franchise, the franchisee essentially acts as a retailer for products manufactured or supplied by the franchisor; the franchisee normally undertakes to sell only the franchisor's products. In other types of franchise, the franchisor is primarily selling an idea or a process; the actual goods sold to the public may be manufactured locally according to a set formula, and usually the franchisee may purchase the components only from suppliers approved by the franchisor.

Conduct of the Business

As noted above, a franchise agreement commonly provides for a substantial degree of supervision by the franchisor. The franchisee must consequently agree to give the franchisor right of access to carry out inspections and to provide proper accounts and regular information. Usually, the franchisee is required to covenant that the business will be carried on only in accordance with the franchisor's regular operating instructions and that no other competing business will be carried on by the franchisee. Since it is the franchisor's reputation that is the basis of the entire arrangement, the franchisee further covenants to protect the goodwill, trademarks, and trade secrets of the franchisor.

CASE 19.8

Robin's Foods was a franchisor of donut stores. One of its franchises was held by a numbered Ontario corporation. The numbered corporation, in addition to operating the franchise, supplied wholesale donuts to other shops for resale. The packaging did not identify the donuts as Robin's donuts, and the donut mix used was not the same mix required by Robin's. The sale of the wholesale donuts was done secretly on a cash basis and not recorded in the accounts provided to Robin's.

The court ruled that the secret activity constituted a breach of the franchising agreement, entitling Robin's to treat the agreement as terminated.[45]

---

45. 1017933 Ontario Ltd. v. Robin's Foods Inc., [1998] O.J. No. 1110.

Termination of the Franchise

As Case 19.8 illustrates, it is common to provide that serious breaches of the franchising agreement constitute a repudiation of the agreement, allowing the other party to treat it as terminated. Additionally, the agreement normally contains detailed provisions regarding the duration and termination of the relationship. Franchising usually involves a substantial investment by both parties and an expectation that the relationship will continue for a number of years. Consequently, one would expect the agreement to provide for a substantial fixed duration, normally with an option to renew, and to require a substantial period of notice to terminate, with penalties for premature termination.

However, it is an unfortunate fact that not all franchises are successful and that not all franchisees are capable of running successfully what should be a viable business. As a result, some franchises change hands quite regularly. To protect the franchisor against assignment of the franchise to an unsuitable operator, it is normal for the franchise agreement to stipulate that any assignment of the franchisee's interest may only be made with the consent of the franchisor.[46]

Restrictive Covenants

Franchises are usually territorial in nature: a franchisee is assigned a particular area—a county, city, or part of a city—in which to operate and the franchisor undertakes not to grant any other franchise within the same territory. In return, the franchisee agrees not to carry on business outside that territory.

An obvious risk taken by franchisors is that their franchisees, having operated a franchise successfully, will have acquired valuable experience and information, and have established relationships with customers and suppliers that they could put to their own use in an independent business. To guard against this danger, the franchisee is normally required to covenant that it will not, for a given number of years after termination of the agreement, carry on a similar or competing business within a stipulated radius from the franchise location. As we have noted in Chapter 7, such covenants may be unenforceable if they constitute an unreasonable restraint on trade.

CASE 19.9

Hohnjec had been the holder of a franchise granted by Yesac Foods to operate a restaurant in Barrie, Ontario. Subsequently, after termination of the franchise, Hohnjec opened a restaurant in Toronto. The new restaurant was not similar in concept to the Yesac franchise.

Yesac sought to enforce a provision in the franchise agreement, which purported to prevent the franchisee from engaging "in any other business...related to the food, beverage or restaurant business." The court held that the clause, which had no time or geographical limitations, was invalid and unenforceable.[47]

Dispute Resolution

Franchising agreements are intended to run for a number of years and contain a substantial number of provisions, each of which could become the subject of dispute. To avoid the expense and the possible ill will involved in litigation, it is not uncommon for franchise agreements to contain a provision establishing a procedure for resolving disputes that may arise during the

46. For an interesting example, see Kentucky Fried Chicken Canada v. Scott's Food Services Inc. (1998), 41 B.L.R. (2d) 42.

47. Yesac Creative Foods Inc. v. Hohnjec (1985), 6 C.P.R. (3d) 398. See also Kardish Food Franchising Corp. v. 874073 Ontario Inc., [1995] O.J. No. 2849; Cash Converters Pty. Ltd. v. Armstrong, [1997] O.J. No. 2659; Nutrilawn International Inc. v. Stewart, [1999] O.J. No. 643.

operation of the franchise. Such a provision may, for example, oblige the parties to submit to mediation before the contract may be terminated for alleged breach by one of the parties.[48]

Checklist: Contents of a Typical Franchise Agreement

Franchise agreements usually cover the following:

- nature and location of franchise
- services to be provided by franchisor (training, management services, advertising, etc.)
- licensing of trademarks, know-how, etc.
- provision of financial assistance
- capital to be provided by franchisee
- franchise fee
- ongoing payments by franchisee (percentage of receipts, payments for services, etc.)
- arrangements for supply of materials and inventory
- provisions governing conduct of business (supervision, accounting, etc.)
- duration of relationship
- termination of relationship (notice, restrictions on assignment, penalties, etc.)
- restrictive covenants
- procedures for resolving disputes

Legal Relationships Created by Franchising

The relationship between franchisor and franchisee is a contractual one between independent entrepreneurs. It would seem that no fiduciary obligations exist between them as a result of the franchise itself,[49] though such a relationship could arise in particular cases, especially where the franchisor exercises a substantial degree of control over the operation of the business. It seems that, apart from the legislation to be discussed in the final part of this chapter, there is no duty on the franchisor to disclose material information about the franchise, such as past profitability, or about other comparable franchises. However, as we saw in Chapter 9, non-disclosure—or partial disclosure—may constitute misrepresentation and give a right to rescission or compensation.

CASE 19.10

Neish entered into a franchise agreement with Melenchuk. He was provided with financial statements that purported to be historical records for the franchise. In fact, the records did not relate to the particular outlet but rather consisted of reconstructed records of other outlets. The records significantly misrepresented the profit and loss sit- uation of the outlet. Neish's bank provided financing based upon the financial records provided.

Subsequently, Neish found that he had to borrow more money to keep the business alive. When he could not

continued

---

48. See, for example, Toronto Truck Centre Ltd. v. Volvo Trucks Canada Inc. (1998), 163 D.L.R. (4th) 740.

49. Jirna Ltd. v. Mister Donut of Canada Ltd. (1973), 40 D.L.R. (3d) 303 (S.C.C.). The Alberta Franchises Act (s. 7) requires the parties to a franchise agreement to deal fairly with each other; see "Fair Dealing" in the next section.

borrow any further he simply walked away from the business. He brought an action seeking compensation for his losses.

The court found that there was no evidence that Melenchuk knew that the records put together were actually misleading so as to constitute fraud. However, he had been negligent in putting the records together and was liable for negligent misrepresentation and breach of contract. Neish was entitled to damages for his lost investment.[50]

With respect to customers, it is important to remember that franchising is entirely different from agency. The franchisee contracts with members of the public on its own behalf, not as agent for the franchisor. There is thus no contract between the customer and the franchisor, though the franchisor might be considered, in some cases, as having held the franchisee out as having authority to act on its behalf and consequently be estopped from denying an agency relationship. When defective goods have been manufactured or supplied by the franchisor it may, of course, be liable in tort.

CONTEMPORARY ISSUE

Reducing the Risks of Franchising

Franchises offer the investor an opportunity to reduce the risk of business failure by providing a proven business concept. Franchises tend to fail less frequently than independent businesses that are started from scratch. But franchising is not a guarantee of success. Potential investors need to do their homework carefully and, as one recent report put it, there are "some predators who specialize in selling dreams and churning franchises, separating one would-be entrepreneur after another from their life savings." The report instances a demonstration of ex-franchisees at a pizza parlour near Maple Leaf Gardens that changed hands 5 times in 18 months.

According to another report:

Fereshteh Vahdati and her husband spent more than $100 000 to buy a Toronto pizza franchise, invested thousands more on various fees—and worked 17 hours a day. Their payoff? "We didn't make any money," a despondent Vahdati said yesterday. "Everything goes to [the chain]....These people cheat us and we've lost everything."...Vahdati said she and her husband spent $100 000 on legal costs in a fruitless court fight against the pizza-chain owner....The owner...asked them to pay a 10 per cent royalty and 4 per cent of sales for advertising, Vahdati said. But after they bought the stores, they were told they also had to spend $65 000 a year to buy flyers from the owner. They eventually ran out of money and the company seized the stores from them, Vahdati said.

Sources: "Ontario introduces bill to protect franchisees: Law to require full disclosure of all fees, costs," *Toronto Star,* December 4, 1998, p. C5; John Deverell, "New franchising law called sales job," *Toronto Star,* December 5, 1998.

So far in Canada, only Alberta and Ontario have introduced legislation specifically to protect franchisees.

continued

---

50. Neish v. Melenchuk (1993), 120 N.S.R. (2d) 239. See also Nutrilawn International Inc. v. Stewart, *supra*, n. 47.

Questions to Consider

1. How far should the law go to protect franchisees against bad bargains?
2. Given that most franchisors are large corporations with "deep pockets," while franchisees are mostly small businesses, is there a need for some special procedure to resolve disputes that arise in franchise situations?

FRANCHISE LEGISLATION

To date, only Alberta has enacted legislation expressly regulating franchising,[51] though it seems likely that similar legislation will take effect in Ontario during 2000. The most important features of the Alberta law are as follows:

Disclosure

The Franchises Act (section 4) requires franchisors to give every prospective franchisee a copy of the franchisor's *disclosure document* at least 14 days before the signing of any agreement or the payment of any consideration. The disclosure document must comply with the requirements of regulations and contain detailed information about the business and the franchise system, including financial statements and reports. The proposed Ontario law is essentially similar. Failure to provide a disclosure document as required gives the franchisee the right to rescind the agreement within two years (section 13), and misrepresentation in the document entitles the franchisee to compensation (section 9). The disclosure requirements generally do not apply in the case of a sale of a franchise by a franchisee (section 5), and the Act makes provision for the adoption of regulations granting further exemptions (section 6). It has been suggested, for example, that certain sectors—such as hotels and airlines—might be exempted, since franchisees in these sectors are normally large concerns that ought to be able to look after their own interests without statutory protection.

Fair Dealing

The Alberta Act (section 7) provides:

> Every franchise agreement imposes on each party a duty of fair dealing in its performance and enforcement.

This appears to establish a fiduciary relationship between franchisor and franchisee. A similar provision has been proposed in Ontario.

Right to Associate

In the past, some franchisors have tried by various means to prevent their franchisees getting together to "compare notes" and, perhaps, to take concerted action against what are perceived to be unfair practices. The Franchises Act (section 8) expressly recognizes a "right of association" among franchisees; a franchisor may not prohibit or restrict its franchisees from forming an organization and may not penalize them in any way for doing so.

---

51. Franchises Act, S.A. 1995, c. F-17.1. New Brunswick has legislation relating to motor vehicle franchising; Motor Vehicle Franchise Act, S.N.B. 1987, c. 70. In Ontario the Franchise Disclosure Act was introduced in 1999 and is expected to become law in 2000.

Industry Self-management

The Act (section 21) allows for the passing of regulations establishing a governing body for the franchising industry in Alberta, but it seems that no such move has been made yet.

Enforcement and Dispute Resolution

Although the various associations of franchisees generally have welcomed the Alberta law and the proposed Ontario legislation, one criticism is that franchisees must still resort to the courts in order to enforce their rights. Here, they face the problem that franchisors are often large, multinational corporations while franchisees are usually quite small businesses that are unable to afford protracted litigation. Consequently, there have been some demands for compulsory arbitration or mediation to be made part of the legislative framework.

QUESTIONS FOR REVIEW

1. Distinguish between dependent agents and independent agents.

2. Is a "real estate agent" a true agent?

3. What is a power of attorney?

4. What is the effect when a principal ratifies a contract made on its behalf by an agent who lacked the authority to enter into the contract?

5. Are there contracts that cannot be ratified?

6. What was decided in the English case of *Bolton Partners v. Lambert*? Would Canadian courts reach the same decision?

7. How does an agent acquire "apparent authority"?

8. What is meant by "holding out"?

9. Does the law recognize an "agency by necessity"?

10. Is an agent entitled to delegate his or her duties to some other person?

11. Why should an agent not act for both parties to a transaction? What are the probable legal consequences of doing so?

12. In what circumstances may an agent be held liable on a contract that he or she has negotiated?

13. Can an undisclosed principal enforce a contract made on his or her behalf?

14. What is meant by "breach of warranty of authority"?

15. Distinguish between a franchise and a licence.

16. What restrictions are usually placed on a franchisee carrying on other business activities?

17. What is the relationship between a franchisor and the eventual customer of the franchisee?

18. Is the relationship between franchisor and franchisee a fiduciary relationship?

CASES AND PROBLEMS

1 Halloran entered into a contract with Scallop Petroleum Ltd. to manage one of Scallop's gas stations. The contract set out detailed arrangements for the operation of the station. It provided that all inventory should be the property of Scallop until sold, and that all proceeds of sale belonged to Scallop, out of which Halloran was to receive a fixed percentage as commission. Halloran was required to maintain two bank accounts, to pay all sales receipts into one of those accounts, and to provide Scallop with regular records of all transactions.

At first, the relationship seemed to be working well. Then Halloran became less diligent in furnishing accounts, and Scallop began to notice various other irregularities. Halloran's records were inadequate, and an investigation revealed a shortfall in the sales account of about $80 000, which appeared to have accrued over more than a year. Scallop suspected Halloran of theft and the police were called in. Their investigation was inconclusive; it seemed probable that the money had been stolen by a former employee of Halloran, who could not be traced.

Halloran was cleared of all involvement in the theft. However, it became clear that he had not been operating the station in accordance with the instructions set out in the contract. For example, he had been keeping cash and credit card receipts in a freezer and in a locked tin box, instead of paying them into the bank as required.

Scallop gave Halloran notice that it was terminating their relationship; it refused to pay Halloran commission on the previous month's sales, and brought an action against him for the balance of the $80 000.

Is Scallop entitled to succeed?

2 Da Silva entered into a franchising agreement with Snacks Unlimited, Ltd. to operate a fast-food outlet in Regina. Under the contract, the store was to make and sell hot dogs and hamburgers, the ingredients to be of a specified quality and the products made to uniform standards. The premises were to be equipped and maintained according to a prescribed format and would have the decor and distinctive sign of "Snacks." Large sales were anticipated since Snacks was already a well-known operation and carried on extensive advertising.

The franchising agreement signed by Da Silva required him to do five things:

- pay a franchise fee of $40 000
- pay a royalty of 2 percent on gross sales
- pay an annual fee of $10 000 for advertising services provided by Snacks
- buy his store equipment from Snacks
- buy his ingredients from sources indicated by Snacks

The agreement set out detailed provisions as to how the business was to be conducted and concluded with the words, "The relationship between the parties is only that of independent contractors. No partnership, joint venture, or relationship of principal and agent is intended."

Da Silva operated the business successfully for two years and showed a reasonable profit. Last year, he discovered that the firms from whom he was required to purchase his supplies were paying substantial rebates to Snacks. On the question of whether he had paid prices higher than the prevailing market prices for comparable supplies, it was difficult to generalize. For some materials, this was true; for others he paid much the same price and in some instances even a somewhat lower price. In any event, Snacks had instructed all the suppliers to have no dealings or negotiations with its franchisees that might indicate the true nature of the arrangements made with them for rebates.

Da Silva sued Snacks for an accounting of these undisclosed profits and rebates and an order requiring them to be paid over to him. Discuss the merits of his case and indicate with reasons whether his action should succeed.

3 Keycorp was an insolvent corporation that had defaulted in payment of its mortgage to its banker, the Lusitania Bank. Keycorp instructed the bank to try to find a buyer for its commercial premises. A real estate agent engaged by the bank approached Carl's Cars Ltd. as a potential purchaser of the building. Carl's Cars submitted an offer to purchase, and a counter-offer was returned to them; in each case Lusitania Bank was described as the vendor (although the property still belonged to Keycorp). Over the next two weeks, there were further negotiations, and a price was finally agreed.

The bank was about to approach the chief executive officer of Keycorp to obtain her approval of the deal when it received a substantially higher offer from another corporation, Lockley Ltd. The bank put both offers to Keycorp, which accepted the Lockley offer and sold the property to it.

Carl's Cars eventually found another building, but its planned business relocation was delayed for several months, resulting in lost profits.

Does Carl's Cars have any cause of action against (a) Keycorp or (b) Lusitania Bank?

4 On a number of occasions over the past two years, Longhaul Transport Ltd. had carried goods belonging to Factorplus Products Inc. The shipments were arranged by a broker, Transshipments Inc. Longhaul invoiced Transshipments, which in turn invoiced Factorplus. The normal procedure was for Transshipments to pay Longhaul out of funds received by it from Factorplus. Longhaul was aware that the goods belonged to Factorplus and was under the mistaken impression that Transshipments was simply a division or subsidiary of Factorplus, rather than an independent broker.

Following one major shipment, Longhaul invoiced Transshipments but was not paid; Transshipments had received no payment from Factorplus in respect of the shipment and refused to pay the shipping charges.

Advise Longhaul whether it should sue (a) Transshipments, (b) Factorplus, or (c) both.

5 Strauss, an experienced business administrator, became unemployed six years ago when his firm "downsized." He was unable to find suitable similar employment and decided to set up his own business. He was especially attracted to the lawncare business, which he considered to have excellent growth potential. He also thought that a franchised operation provided the best chance of establishing a successful business quickly.

After examining a number of lawncare franchises, Strauss concluded that a firm called Sodmaster Inc. was the franchisor best suited to his requirements. Strauss contacted Sodmaster and had several discussions with their area manager for Eastern Ontario. Strauss was provided with a vast amount of information about Sodmaster's operations, including various projections of costs and profits based on the operation of other Sodmaster franchises. Strauss also visited other franchisees and talked with them about their experiences.

According to the financial projections in the booklet given to him by Sodmaster, a franchise with a gross annual revenue of $200 000 would normally make a small loss (after allowing for a modest management fee); one with revenue of $400 000 would show a reasonable profit, and one with revenue of $800 000 or more would show an excellent profit. Potential franchisees were warned that it was unusual to break even in the first year of operation. The projections were essentially accurate, based on the actual experience of Sodmaster franchises, though the booklet omitted to point out that only one of the franchises actually grossed more than $800 000 per year.

Strauss also made his own projections of his probable revenues and decided to go ahead and purchase a franchise for Frontenac County, Ontario. He agreed to pay a franchise fee of $40 000

($25 000 payable immediately and the balance after two years) and to pay royalties of 6 percent on gross revenues. He also entered into the usual restrictive covenants not to carry on a competing business within 30 km of the franchise area for a period of five years after termination of the franchise. In order to get started, Strauss borrowed money on the security of his home and, in all, invested about $100 000 of his own money.

The business did not work out nearly as well as Strauss had expected. In his first year he had sales of only $60 000 (when he had anticipated twice that figure) and he made a loss of $75 000. The second year's sales reached $100 000 (with a loss of $12 000); by the third year, sales had risen to $180 000, still with a small loss; in the fourth and fifth years, Strauss' sales levelled out at a little more than $200 000, and he was still making a loss.

Because of his financial problems, Strauss never paid the remaining $15 000 owing on the franchise fee, and he also fell behind early on in the payment of the royalties. Relations between Strauss and Sodmaster became strained and eventually Sodmaster informed Strauss that they would not be prepared to renew the franchise at the end of its five-year term. Strauss then abandoned the franchise and set up his own lawncare business in the same area.

Sodmaster brought an action against Strauss, claiming payment of the balance of the franchise fee, the unpaid royalties, and an injunction to restrain the breach of the restrictive covenant. Strauss counterclaimed for damages, alleging that he had been misled into entering into the franchise agreement in the first place.

Who should succeed?

20 THE CONTRACT OF EMPLOYMENT

We review the extensive area of employment law both for individual employees and for those who are members of trade unions that bargain terms of employment on their behalf. We begin by distinguishing employment from other arrangements, such as agency, and describing the nature of the employment relationship at common law. We next examine legislation that protects workers. Finally, we discuss trade unions, the collective bargaining process, and the system of regulation in place to facilitate resolving disputes. In this chapter we examine such questions as:

- what is the difference between an employer's liability in contract and in tort?

- what are the grounds for dismissal "with cause"?

- what is "wrongful dismissal" and what are its consequences?

- what are the effects of human rights requirements, and pay and employment equity statutes?

- what are the consequences of regulation on general working conditions?

- how is mandatory retirement affected by the Canadian Charter of Rights and Freedoms?

- how are employment conditions affected by workers' compensation and occupational health regulation?

- what are the implications of a collective agreement for the individual employee?

- what is the legal status of trade unions?

DEVELOPMENT OF THE LAW GOVERNING EMPLOYMENT

Before the middle of the 19th-century, the law relating to employment was almost entirely composed of common law rules defining the **relationship of master and servant**. This law developed in an early business environment where the employer (master) had a separate contract with each employee (servant); welfare legislation and trade unions were unknown. Today, the individual contract of employment remains the most common employment relationship, and the law of master and servant continues to be important. Nevertheless, the economic and social changes of the past century and a half have greatly affected the common law in two respects:

- *First*, statutes have been passed to establish minimum standards of working conditions; we shall refer to this branch of the law as employee welfare legislation.

- *Second*, the emergence of trade unions has led to the evolution of the collective agreement—a whole separate body of law known as the law of collective bargaining—to govern the relationship between employers, trade unions, and their members.

In this chapter we shall discuss the relationship at common law of master and servant (in current language that of employer and employee), employee welfare legislation, and collective bargaining.

We begin with a note of caution. In our treatment of welfare legislation and collective bargaining, we cannot cite all the relevant statutes in the space available, and in any event it might be dangerous to do so: this part of the law frequently changes and statutes may soon become obsolete. The purpose of the chapter is simply to acquaint the reader with the general approach of the law in another main area of business administration. For further discussion of specific labour problems, the reader should consult the works that have been specially prepared in this field, cited from time to time in footnotes.[1]

relationship of master and servant
the contractual relationship between an employer and an employee

RELATIONSHIP OF EMPLOYER AND EMPLOYEE

Compared With Agency

The relationship of employer and employee is established by a contract that gives one party, the employer, authority to direct and control the work of the other party, the employee. The services that are contracted for may or may not include making contracts with third parties as agent for the employer.

The distinction between agent and employee, then, is one of function. The same person is often both an employee and an agent. Indeed an employee's chief duty may be to make contracts with third parties on behalf of the employer: for example, a purchasing agent for a company has a duty to order goods on the company's credit and has authority to do so within the limits of her agency. She is nonetheless also a company employee and subject to the direction of its senior officers. Other employees may have very limited duties as agents of their employer: the driver of a delivery truck is an employee who may act as an agent when taking the truck into a garage for servicing, thereby binding the employer to pay the charges. In many types of employment, an employee has no occasion to enter into contracts on behalf of the employer and no authority, express or implied, to do so—a stenographer or lathe operator, for instance. Indeed, as we noted at the beginning of the preceding chapter, the functions may be completely separate, as when a business engages an agent who is not an employee at all.

---

1. See, especially, Adams, *Canadian Labour Law* (2nd ed.). Toronto: Canada Law Book, 1993.

In Chapter 19 we learned that when an agency agreement is of indefinite duration, an agent may have no recourse against a principal that terminates the agreement without notice. An employee, as we shall see, often has a right of action for damages for wrongful dismissal in comparable circumstances.

Both principals and employers may be liable in tort for the acts of their agents and employees respectively. However, for various reasons, some historical and some related to the different functions of agents and employees, the scope of liability of an employer may be wider than the corresponding liability of a principal; in any event the basis for vicarious liability is not the same for principals and employers. Accordingly, when a third party is injured, it may be important to establish whether the wrongdoer was acting as an employee or as an agent of a firm.

Compared with an Independent Contractor

An independent contractor undertakes to do a specified task such as building a house. The contract between the parties does not create an employer–employee relationship because the contractor is not subject to the supervision of the person engaging him. His job is to produce a specified result, and the means he employs are his own affair.

It is not always easy to distinguish between an independent contractor and an employee. Occasionally the two functions are combined in a single person: the owner of a building may hire a building contractor to do certain repairs for a fixed price, but the agreement may also require the repairs to be made under the supervision of the owner. It may be difficult to decide whether the person doing the work is primarily an independent contractor or an employee.

When a firm undertakes work as an independent contractor, liabilities incurred by it in the course of accomplishing its task are almost entirely its own.

ILLUSTRATION 20.1

Imperial Contractors contracted with Parkinson Corp. to erect an administration building. During the construction work, Miss Chance, a passerby on the sidewalk far below, is injured by a falling brick. The accident is attributable to the inadequate protection for pedestrians provided by Imperial Contractors. Imperial Contractors and not Parkinson Corp. would generally be liable for the injury so caused.

On the other hand, Parkinson does have a duty to take reasonable care to hire a competent contractor. Also, if by the nature of the work undertaken, the possibility of damage to adjoining property is apparent—for example, through blasting with dynamite[2]—or if the work is inherently dangerous to third parties, Parkinson has an obligation to see to it that the contractor takes reasonable precautions to avoid such damage.

As we shall see in Chapter 31, a business engaging a building contractor may have to follow certain procedures in paying the contractor in order to avoid having its land and buildings subject to liens filed by employees of the contractor or by subcontractors such as suppliers of materials. Apart from this complication, a person engaging an independent contractor is not generally responsible for the contractor's obligations.[3]

The Relationship at Common Law

In defining the relationship of employer and employee, the courts have developed rules about

- employer's liability to third persons
- the notice required to terminate the relationship

---

2. Savage v. Wilby, [1954] S.C.R. 376; Sin v. Macioli (1999), 43 O.R. (3d) 1.
3. See Vic Priestly Landscaping Contracting Ltd. v. Elder (1978), 19 O.R. (2d) 591 at 601–5.

- grounds for dismissal
- assessment of damages for wrongful dismissal

These rules are part of the common law as it continues to apply to individual employment contracts, and we shall deal with them in turn.

THE EMPLOYER'S LIABILITY

Liability in Contract

As we noted in Chapter 12 under the heading "Vicarious Performance," parties to a contract often understand that they will not perform personally—corporations cannot do so—and that either employees or an independent contractor will perform. The promisor remains liable for satisfactory performance when a construction firm undertakes to erect a building according to specifications, although it hires a subcontractor to put up the structural steel and the subcontractor does defective work. So, too, will it be liable for breach of contract should its own employees do improper work.

Liability in Tort

In our discussion of vicarious liability in Chapter 3, we noted that a business is liable for damages to a third party for the consequences of any tort an employee may commit in the course of employment. The employer need not have authorized the wrongful act: it is liable even though it has forbidden such conduct. All the injured party need establish is that the employee caused the damage while engaged at work. If, however, the harm results while the employee is not engaged in the employer's work, as when he takes time off from his duties to attend to some personal matter, the employer is not liable: the employee alone is liable. Nor is the employer liable if the employee delegates the work to someone else without the employer's consent.

ILLUSTRATION 20.2

Adair is employed by Magnum Computers as a sales agent. While driving a company van on his rounds, he negligently collides with another vehicle. He has committed a tort in the course of his employment; the owner of the damaged car may sue both Magnum Computers and Adair.

CASE 20.1

Adair injures a pedestrian as a result of negligent driving while using the company van to take his family to the theatre after hours, without permission or knowledge of his employer. In the words of a Nova Scotia judgment in a similar case, Adair has "departed from the course of his employment and...embarked upon an independent enterprise—'a frolic of his own'—for purposes wholly unconnected with his master's business."[4] He alone is liable; Magnum Computers is not.

---

4. Hall v. Halifax Transfer Co. Ltd. (1959), 18 D.L.R. (2d) 115, per MacDonald, J., at 120. See also Longo v. Gordie's Auto Sales Ltd. (1979), 28 N.B.R. (2d) 56.

CASE 20.2

While delivering a computer, Adair becomes embroiled in an argument with a customer about the quality of the product. He pushes the customer who falls and injures himself. Is Magnum Computers vicariously liable to the customer for the assault?

Of the three examples in Illustration 20.2, Case 20.1, and Case 20.2, the last is the most difficult to resolve. As one judge put it, "Before the employer can be held liable the blow complained of must be closely connected with a duty being carried out in the authorized course of employment and not delivered at a time when the servant has divested himself of his character as a servant."[5] We must ask whether the unauthorized and wrongful act of the employee is "so connected with the authorized act as to be a mode of doing it" or whether it is "an independent act."[6]

If having conversations about his employer's product at the time of delivery is an authorized incident of Adair's employment so as to be a way of carrying out his duties, his employer is also liable for the assault; but if his conversation is an independent act, Adair alone is liable. The court will hear evidence of trade practice in this matter before reaching its decision.

When an employer has been held liable for the negligence of an employee, it has a right to be indemnified by the employee;[7] it may, if it deems it worthwhile, sue the employee.

NOTICE OF TERMINATION OF INDIVIDUAL EMPLOYMENT CONTRACTS

When an employer has hired an employee for a stated period and that time has elapsed, no notice of termination is necessary on the part of either party. Neither one has a right to expect anything more from the other at the end of the specified time: each has been on notice from the beginning, as for example, where a student accepts summer employment to terminate on the Friday before Labour Day.[8]

Often employers and employees do not discuss when the employment relationship is to end, nor do they expressly agree on the length of notice required to terminate employment. They may intend the hiring to be by the week, the month, or some other length of time, renewable for successive periods and possibly lasting for many years; or as more often happens, they may simply regard the employment as a general or indefinite hiring.

In the absence of an express term about notice in a contract of employment, the common law rule is that reasonable notice shall be given. Sometimes a court can determine the length of reasonable notice from evidence of an established customary practice followed by the particular employer for the type of employee in question. In other circumstances, the court will ask what type of hiring the parties intended when they made the employment contract. The usual minimum reasonable notice for a weekly hiring is one clear work week, and for a monthly hiring, one clear work month.[9] If the hiring is general or indefinite—and is not related to the time when the employee receives pay—reasonable notice depends on all the circumstances of the

---

5. Wenz v. Royal Trust Co., [1953] O.W.N. 798, per Aylen, J., at 800.

6. Salmond, *The Law of Torts* (20th ed.), p. 457, Heuston and Buckley, eds. London: Sweet & Maxwell Limited, 1992.

7. Finnegan v. Riley, [1939] 4 D.L.R. 434.

8. See, for example: Employment Standards Act, R.S.O. 1990, c. E.14, s. 57(10)(a).

9. The notice required to terminate a weekly or monthly hiring is similar to the notice required to terminate a weekly or monthly tenancy. For a fuller explanation, see Chapter 24 under "Termination and Renewal of a Tenancy."

employment; it has usually varied between three and six months and occasionally as long as one year or more.[10] Executive compensation settlements have more recently been for as much as several years' salary.[11] In most provinces and at the federal level as well, the minimum length of required notice is specifically set down by statute, and any attempt by an employer to impose a term shorter than the minimum is void.[12] Since the provisions are minimum requirements only, customary notice periods in a particular trade or in express contractual terms may be substantially longer.

When no other evidence about the intention of the parties is given to the court, it may infer a weekly or a monthly hiring from the mere fact that the employee receives pay by the week or the month. A court is, however, perfectly free to find other considerations that outweigh any inferences one might draw from the length of the pay period. The court may rule, for example, that a hiring is indefinite even though the employee is paid by the week. As stated in *Lazarowicz v. Orenda Engines Ltd.*:

> Upon all the circumstances of this case I have come to the conclusion that the plaintiff, despite the fact that his wages were stated to be a weekly sum only, was employed upon a general or indefinite hiring only, and for these reasons: Firstly, the plaintiff was a graduate engineer....At the time he was employed by the defendant corporation [he] had been employed...at a monthly salary of $450. He was secure in that position and there seems little reason to conclude that he would have left that position to accept one with the defendant company if he were to be merely a weekly servant. A more important circumstance is the actual work performed by the plaintiff....The evidence...shows that he was in a position of some considerable importance, requiring a great deal of mechanical and technical experience.[13]

An employer is not in breach of the employment contract if in dismissing the employee without notice, it tenders an additional amount of pay for a period equal to the time required for reasonable notice. In the *Lazarowicz* case, the court held that reasonable notice in the circumstances was three months; since the employee had been given only one week's salary in lieu of notice, it held that the employee was entitled to the balance of three months' salary.

An employee who decides to leave voluntarily has a contractual obligation to give the employer the same amount of notice as he himself would be entitled to receive for dismissal. If he does not do so, the employer may, if it considers it worthwhile, sue the employee for damages equal to the loss caused by this breach of contract.

An employee is justified in leaving without giving the usual notice if he can show that he was obliged to work under dangerous conditions that the employer refused to correct. Here the employer has broken the contract, freeing the employee from his obligations, for it is an implied term in the contract that the employer will maintain a safe place to work. An employee also has grounds for leaving immediately if he is ordered to do an illegal act.

GROUNDS FOR DISMISSAL WITHOUT NOTICE

The Contractual Basis

An employer need not give notice when it can show that the employee was dismissed for cause. **Dismissal for cause** is an example of the general law of contract: when an employee's conduct

dismissal for cause
dismissal without notice or further obligation by the employer when the employee's conduct amounts to breach of contract

---

10. See Bardal v. The Globe and Mail Ltd. (1960), 24 D.L.R. (2d) 140; Stevens v. Globe and Mail et al. (1992), 86 D.L.R. (4th) 204; Minott v. O'Shanter Development Company Ltd. (1999), 42 O.R. (3d) 321.

11. See Kilpatrick v. Peterborough Civic Hospital (1998), 38 O.R. (3d) 298.

12. See, for example: Labour Standards Act, R.S.S. 1978, c. L-1, ss. 43–44; Labour Standards Code, R.S.N.S. 1989, c. 246, s. 72; Employment Standards Act, R.S.O. 1990, c. E.14, s. 57, as applied in Machtinger v. HOJ Industries Ltd. (1992), 91 D.L.R. (4th) 491 (S.C.C.) and Rizzo & Rizzo Shoes Ltd. (Re), [1998] 1. S.C.R. 26.

13. (1960), 22 D.L.R. (2d) 568, per Robertson, C.J.O., at 573; Affirmed on appeal (1962), 26 D.L.R. (2d) 433.

amounts to a breach of the contract of employment, the employer may be entitled to consider itself discharged from any further obligations and to terminate the contract at once. As we know, in contract law, generally not every petty breach would have this result.[14] However, the frequently unequal bargaining power between an employer and an individual employee may encourage an employer to impose its idea of what an important breach is. To counterbalance this inequality, the common law has tended to classify the kinds of breach that are sufficient grounds for dismissal without notice, and the collective bargaining process has developed the idea further. In some jurisdictions, employees have gained additional protection by statute.[15]

Misconduct

In the times of Henry VIII and Elizabeth I the law treated any violence by a servant against her master as a minor form of treason and subjected the employee to the grisly methods of execution reserved for that most heinous of offences.[16] Even wishful thinking by an employee was hazardous while witchcraft remained an offence. This attitude of the law, demanding of employees the utmost in subjection and loyalty, lingered on; until as late as the end of the 19th century a strike was regarded as a form of conspiracy.

Today, misconduct against an employer, while it may be grounds for a dismissal, is not a crime in itself. An employee guilty of such grossly immoral conduct as might bring the employer's business into public disrepute, disturb the morale of other employees, or cause the employer direct financial loss may be summarily dismissed. Conviction for a crime, especially when it involves moral turpitude such as stealing or embezzlement, may also be grounds for summary dismissal.

A firm is entitled to place confidence in its employees, and, depending on the nature of the employment, evidence of a lack of integrity is often grounds for instant dismissal. An employee's deception need cause no financial loss to his employer: it is enough that the employer can no longer trust him.[17]

Disobedience

Willful disobedience of a reasonable and lawful order from an employer is grounds for immediate dismissal without notice. The definition is broad enough to include situations where the employee does not directly disobey but acts in a manner inconsistent with the usual devotion to duty expected of employees of that kind. In the old case of *Ridgway v. Hungerford Market Co.*[18] a clerk entered in a company minute book a protest, in his own handwriting, against a resolution of the directors calling a meeting to appoint his successor. He was dismissed at once and forfeited the right to any reasonable notice that would normally have been implied in the directors' resolution.

Incompetence

The degree of skill an employer may demand depends partly on the representations of the employee when seeking the position and partly on the degree of skill ordinarily to be expected of an employee of that category and rate of pay. If an employee accepts a position on the understanding that he is capable of doing a particular kind of work and it becomes apparent that he

14. See Chapter 14, "The Effect of Breach."

15. See, for example, Employment Standards Act, R.S.O. 1990, c. E.14, s. 57(10)(c).

16. See Smith, *A Treatise on the Law of Master and Servant* (6th ed.), p. 390, E.M. Smith, ed. London: Sweet & Maxwell Limited, 1906. We have followed the classification of grounds for dismissal outlined by Smith at pp. 102–15.

17. Werle v. Saskenergy Inc. (1992), 103 Sask. R. 241.

18. (1835), 111 E.R. 378. See also Hodgkin v. Aylmer (Town) (1996), 23 C.C.E.L. (2d) 297.

cannot, in fact, do this work satisfactorily, the employer may then dismiss him without notice. On the other hand, incompetence as a cause for dismissal becomes more difficult to justify the longer an employee has been retained.[19]

Illness

Permanent disability or constantly recurring illness entitles an employer to consider the contract at an end, independently of any terms in the contract requiring notice. An employer cannot, however, recover damages from an employee for breach of contract in these circumstances: the contract is discharged by frustration and not by breach.

Effect of Dismissal

Any of the four grounds for dismissal set out above permits an employer to treat the contract of employment as discharged. Misconduct, disobedience, or incompetence amount to discharge by the employee's breach, whereas illness discharges the contract by frustration. Discharge for any one of these personal failures of performance by an employee relieves the employer of the duty to give notice but it must nevertheless pay the dismissed employee any wages earned until the time of dismissal.

Adverse Economic Conditions

Adverse economic conditions do not excuse an employer from its implied obligation to give employees reasonable notice of termination. An employer might overcome this implied obligation by getting his employee to agree expressly that in adverse economic conditions he may be dismissed without notice. However, when a right to notice is required by statute, even an express agreement to give it up is ineffective; the statute prevails, and the employer must still give notice or wages in lieu of notice.

Neither does an employer have the right to temporarily lay off employees for economic reasons without notice. Yet some statutes now permit an employer to do so for periods as long as three months, under conditions prescribed by regulation.[20]

WRONGFUL DISMISSAL

Damages

For an employee to succeed in an action against her employer for damages for wrongful dismissal, she must show that the employer has broken the contract, as when it fails to give the employee the notice to which she was entitled. An employer often defends its actions either by claiming that the employee was dismissed for cause, or that adequate notice was given. If the employer's defence fails, the court is left with the task of assessing damages.

The measure of damages for wrongful dismissal is a particular application of the rules for assessing damages in contracts generally. In Chapter 15, we saw that the purpose of an award of damages is to place an injured party in the position it would have been in if the contract had been completed. In an employment contract, we must ask what amount of damages will compensate the employee for failure to receive the required notice of termination.

---

19. See Duncan v. Cockshutt Farm Equipment Ltd. (1956), 19 W.W.R. 554; Bardal v. The Globe and Mail Ltd., *supra*, n. 10.
20. Canada Labour Code, R.S.C. 1985, c. L-2 and Canada Labour Standards Regulation, C.R.C. 1978, c. 986, s. 30; Employment Standards Act, R.S.O. 1990, c. E.14, ss. 57–58 and R.R.O. 1990, Reg. 327.

The first task for the court is to determine what length of time would have been reasonable notice in the circumstances. We have noted that the court has considerable discretion when the contract is for a general or indefinite hiring:

> There can be no catalogue laid down as to what is reasonable notice in particular classes of cases. The reasonableness of the notice must be decided with reference to each particular case, having regard to the character of the employment, the length of service of the servant, the age of the servant and the availability of similar employment, having regard to the experience, training and qualifications of the servant.[21]

In the past two decades, a large number of wrongful dismissal cases have discussed this classic quotation from the *Bardal* case with approval and have expanded its scope, especially in circumstances where the employer had been found to have acted in bad faith. When bad faith has added to the harm caused—as where the employer has made it appear that the employee was dismissed for serious misconduct—additional damages may be assessed against the employer.[22]

To assess the loss in remuneration, the court then multiplies the employee's rate of pay and the value of fringe benefits by the length of reasonable notice.

We must remember that a party injured by breach of contract is expected to act reasonably in order to mitigate her loss. Accordingly, the court asks whether the employee has made a serious attempt following her dismissal to obtain reasonably comparable work elsewhere. If the employer shows that the employee had such an opportunity to work elsewhere but declined it, the court will reduce the award of damages by the amount the employee might have earned during the required term of notice. However, a dismissed employee is not required to take any work simply to mitigate her loss; if the only work available is substantially below what she might reasonably expect based on her qualifications and experience, she may refuse it without fear that the court will reduce an award of damages. If she does accept a lower-paid job, she will be entitled to the lost difference in remuneration during the term of notice.

Finally, the court will consider other damage that flows naturally from the employer's breach. The employee may have incurred travelling expenses in seeking other employment, or even become physically ill. As we noted in Chapter 15, courts in recent decisions have been willing to give damages for pain and suffering caused by wrongful dismissal.

Sometimes an employer has such a general dissatisfaction with or mistrust of an employee that it dismisses him apparently without cause. If the employer should later discover that there were in fact specific grounds for dismissing the employee without notice, it could use these grounds to defeat an action by the employee for wrongful dismissal.[23]

There is an increasing tendency to view an employee's interest in a job as being something more than merely contractual; in particular, the growing remedy of reinstatement, discussed in the next section, suggests that the interest is almost a proprietary one. This view has been put forward to claim that before an employee can be dismissed—and thus deprived of an "interest" in his job—he is entitled to a fair hearing. Accordingly, it has been argued that before dismissing an employee, the employer should be required to confront him with a charge of misconduct and give the employee an opportunity to clear himself or at least to explain his acts and minimize their significance.[24]

---

21. Bardal v. The Globe and Mail Ltd., per McRuer, C.J.H.C., *supra*, n. 10, at 145.

22. For a detailed discussion by the Supreme Court of Canada of additional factors affecting damage awards for wrongful dismissal, see Wallace v. United Grain Growers Ltd., [1997] 3 S.C.R. 313.

23. The courts admit such evidence even if it becomes known after the action has been started. See, for example: Lake Ontario Portland Cement v. Groner (1961), 28 D.L.R. (2d) 589; Bannister v. General Motors of Canada Limited (1998), 40 O.R. (3d) 577.

24. See: Reilly v. Steelcase Canada Ltd. (1979), 26 O.R. (2d) 725; Pulsifer v. GTE Sylvania Canada Ltd. (1983), 56 N.S.R. (2d) 424; Pilato v. Hamilton Place Convention Centre (1984), 45 O.R. (2d) 652.

Reinstatement

The emphasis on damages for wrongful dismissal as the sole remedy of employees implicitly denies the availability of other remedies such as *reinstatement*—a form of specific performance by which the court orders the employer to continue to employ the aggrieved employee. We noted in Chapter 15 the great reluctance of courts to order specific performance of contracts of service against an employee. Based on common law principles alone,[25] they are as unlikely to award reinstatement. However, the impersonal nature of most employment in large business enterprises has diminished the strength of argument against reinstatement based on the personal nature of services. Unions have long bargained for arbitration procedures in cases of dismissal and for reinstatement in appropriate cases. Indeed, reinstatement has become the norm as the remedy for wrongful dismissal under collective agreements. Another example of the use of reinstatement occurs at universities; professors who have been wrongfully dismissed are ordinarily entitled to reinstatement.

Similar protection has become available to non-union employees in industries within the legislative jurisdiction of the federal Parliament. The Canada Labour Code provides that

245 ...any [dismissed] person

  (a) who has completed twelve consecutive months of continuous employment by an employer, and

  (b) who is not a member of a group of employees subject to a collective agreement may make a complaint....["26]

If an adjudicator decides that the person has been "unjustly dismissed," she may order the employer to reinstate the employee. This provision, first introduced in 1978, has been used with increasing frequency as available alternative jobs for dismissed employees have declined. The Québec Labour Standards Act and the Nova Scotia Act create a similar right in for employees, but in Québec, only after four years of uninterrupted service with one employer, and in Nova Scotia, only after 10 years.[27] Specialists in the field expect to see this type of legislation in other provinces in the near future.

CONTEMPORARY ISSUE

The Growth in Self-Employment

Self-employment has grown significantly in Canada in recent decades. According to Statistics Canada, the number of self-employed Canadians more than doubled between 1976 and 1998, from 1.2 million to 2.5 million. Self-employed persons made up 18 percent of the work force in 1998. Although many people assume that the rise in self-employment is a response to poor economic times and high unemployment, recent Statistics Canada studies suggest that this assumption is false. Since 1976, the rate of self-employment has risen, regardless of whether the economy was in recession or expansion.

Self-employment involves a wide range of occupations: professionals such as lawyers, accountants, and physicians; freelancers such as musicians, editors, and writers; small-business

continued

---

25. For an exception arising out of unusual circumstances, see Hill v. Parsons, [1971] 3 All E.R. 1345.

26. R.S.C. 1985, c. L-2, s. 245.

27. Labour Standards Act, R.S.Q. 1991, c. N-1.1, ss. 124–28; Labour Standards Code, R.S.N.S. 1989, c. 246, ss. 71(1) and 26(2)(a).

owners; contract workers in business and industry, from clerical staff to truck drivers; and many others. Some self-employed people enjoy interesting work and make good incomes; others earn considerably less than paid employees with full-time, regular jobs. The reasons given for choosing self-employment include freedom, flexibility, control over one's work, and the pursuit of a dream. The disadvantages include long hours, unpredictable income, lack of the legal protections such as statutory notice periods enjoyed by full-time employees, and lack of non-wage benefits such as employment insurance and pension plans.

From an employer's point of view, one advantage of replacing some regular, full-time employees with freelancers and contract workers ("independent contractors") is the ability to expand or reduce the work force quickly as staffing needs change. Another advantage is reduced costs for non-wage benefits and other expenses connected with full-time employees. However, the advantages of a stable work force with a collective fund of experience and knowledge can be lost.

Some employers might be tempted to get around their legal duties by treating workers who are actually full-time employees as if they were independent contractors. However, the courts have established legal tests to determine who is an employee and who is an independent contractor. The factors they consider include the degree of control an employer has over how the work is performed, whether the worker is subject to the employer company policies, and whether the worker is economically dependent on one company. If control and other factors indicate an employer–employee relationship, that status will not be affected even when the worker is paid through a personal corporation. An employer wishing to hire a worker as an independent contractor should eliminate any ambiguity in the worker's status with a well-crafted contract.

Sources: See "The Dynamics of Self-Employment," Statistics Canada, *The Daily*, June 8, 1999; "Working Together: Self-Employed Couples," Statistics Canada, *The Daily*, December 1, 1999; Tom Arnold, "Self-Employed Numbers Twice as High as in 1976," *National Post*, 2 December 1999; Steven Theobald, "Jobless Rate Dips to 6.9%," *Toronto Star*, December 4, 1999; Ron Walton, "Legally Speaking: When is an Independent Contractor an Employee?" Webposted at <www.canadaone.com/magazine/law021698.html>.

Questions to Consider:

1. What do you think the long-term implications of this trend towards more self-employment are for business? Consider both positive and negative implications.

2. According to Statistics Canada, in the 1980s, nearly two-thirds of the newly self-employed hired others to work for them. In the 1990s, nine-tenths of the newly self-employed worked on their own without hiring any help. What factors do you think might account for the difference?

3. If the trend towards more self-employment does not result from a poor economy, what do you think does account for it?

EMPLOYEE WELFARE LEGISLATION

History

In the social upheaval that came with the industrial revolution and before the emergence of trade unions, employers held nearly all the advantages in bargaining: often, workers had to either accept the proposed terms of employment or see their families starve. The movement for reform in working conditions stressed the economic inequality between employer and employee. Reformers urged that society had a duty to protect the weaker contracting party.

The arguments of the reformers, however, went directly against 19th-century ideas of freedom of contract as a pillar of a larger political philosophy of *laissez faire*. This philosophy asserted that society functions most efficiently when contracting parties are left free to obtain whatever advantage their bargaining power will command, and that a society will come closest to realizing its economic potential when individuals are left to their own resources in resolving their conflicts of interest without the intervention of any outside arbiter.

The reform movement therefore had to proceed against formidable opposition by the proponents of freedom of contract. Nevertheless, the pressures of a changing society were irresistible: they resulted in a series of acts of Parliament commencing just before the mid-19th century. These statutes marked a new role for the state—active intervention on the side of the employees.

Initially, reform statutes specified the minimum age of workers, maximum hours of work, the presence of safety devices for machinery, the maintenance of safe premises in which to work, and the definition of the liability of employers when an employee was injured in the course of employment. These statutes were only a beginning. A review of the statute law we shall consider briefly in this section illustrates the degree to which our legislatures have qualified the freedom of contract between individual employers and employees.

A number of statutes also provided special rules affecting women in respect to both working hours and working conditions; some have been repealed in the name of equality between the sexes, and it is yet to be seen how the remainder will be judged in relation to the guarantees of equality in section 15 of the Canadian Charter of Rights and Freedoms.

To the extent that employees are now represented by trade unions, the disparity in bargaining power between employer and employees has been largely redressed. There remain, however, important categories of work in which employees typically are not unionized. In these types of work, employees still negotiate contracts of employment on an individual basis with their employers. Accordingly, legislation enacted for the welfare and protection of employees continues to provide a minimum standard of working conditions for many people.

Legislative Jurisdiction

In Canada, the activities of a comparatively small but very important group of businesses bring them under federal jurisdiction, and for them the rights and duties of employers and employees are governed by federal labour legislation. These industries include shipping, air transport, inter-provincial transportation and telephone systems, radio, banking, and the operations of federal Crown corporations.[28] The remainder of our economic activity, comprising the bulk of what we think of as industrial and commercial enterprise, is subject to provincial rather than federal legislation.

Employee Rights

Human Rights

Enhancing the rights of employees through human rights legislation began in the 1970s, and preceded the Canadian Charter of Rights and Freedoms. However, the process was accelerated by the words in section 15 of the Charter:

> Every individual…has the right to the equal protection and equal benefit of the law without discrimination and, in particular without discrimination based on race, national or ethnic origin, colour, religion, sex, age or mental or physical disability.

Section 28 emphasized that Charter rights "are guaranteed equally to male and female persons."

As we noted in Chapter 1, the Charter has not been applied to the private sector but human rights legislation passed by every province and the federal Parliament does apply to the private

---

28. Constitution Act, 1867, s. 91.

sector. Most complaints under the legislation relate to employment. The wording varies considerably but, generally speaking, the acts make it an offence to engage in

> a discriminatory practice…to refuse to employ or continue to employ an individual, or…to differentiate adversely…on a prohibited ground,[29]

that is, on the basis of

> race, national or ethnic origin, colour, religion, age, sex, sexual orientation, marital status, family status, disability and conviction for which a pardon has been granted.[30]

Human rights legislation has had a considerable educational effect on both public and private sector employers. To employers who are sensitive to the issues of non-discrimination, there is little or no additional cost of doing business. Indeed, it has been argued that employers who seek the most competent people and comply with the legislation by ignoring the personal listed characteristics of prospective employees benefit in terms of increased efficiency.

Pay Equity

Pay equity legislation is directed towards redressing gender discrimination in remuneration. There are two ways of assessing the wage gap between men and women. The more traditional is through the principle of "equal pay for equal work." The law prohibits differential pay for substantially the same kind of work performed in the same establishment, the performance of which requires substantially the same skill, effort, and responsibility, and performed under similar working conditions.[31]

comparative value
"equal pay for work of equal value"

The second approach requires a focus not on the similarity of the jobs done by women and men, but on their **comparative value** to the employer—the concept of "equal pay for work of equal value" or "comparable worth."[32] The legislation requires employers to pay employees performing jobs traditionally done by women the same as those performing jobs done by men if the jobs are of equal or comparable value. The main task is to attribute a meaning to the word "value." It must mean something more than current market value of work, for if women are being hired at a traditionally lower wage than men receive, then an employer can argue that the market shows it can hire women at that lower wage: according to this argument, they are already being paid what they are "worth." Instead, the effort and training of the worker must be taken into account. Thus, while a secretary's job may require less physical effort and she may have better working conditions than a groundskeeper, her job may require taking more responsibility, applying more mental effort, and having greater skills training. Assessing the relative value of different kinds of work can be the subject of much debate.

Once a job evaluation results in a finding that one group of employees is paid too little in comparison with another, almost invariably it is unacceptable to reduce the wages of the more highly paid group. The pressure to increase the wages of the lower paid group may substantially raise the labour costs of an employer; thus the employer is likely to contest the finding because of perceived increases in costs.

Under traditional legislative reform, someone must file a complaint in order to trigger enforcement of the legislation's general prohibitions. An important difficulty with implementing pay equity results from reliance on a complaints system because such a system assumes that

---

29. Canadian Human Rights Act, R.S.C. 1985, c. H-6, s. 7 (a) and (b).

30. *Ibid.*, s. 3 (1), amended to include "sexual orientation," by S.C. 1996, c. 14.

31. In most jurisdictions, pay equity legislation distinguishes between the public and private sectors. At present, the standard of "equal pay for equal work" applies in Alberta, British Columbia, and Ontario in both sectors, and to private sector employers in Manitoba, New Brunswick, Newfoundland, Nova Scotia, Prince Edward Island, and Saskatchewan.

32. This standard applies to both sectors in areas of federal jurisdiction and in Québec. See *Canadian Pay Equity Compliance Guide* (North York: CCH Canadian Ltd., 1990).

violations are the exception, not the rule; it is effective only if breaches of the legislation are infrequent. However, if wage discrimination is *systemic* and pervasive throughout the economy, then a complaints system of enforcement may easily be overwhelmed. To overcome this problem, the most recent pay equity legislation is based on **systemic discrimination**. It abandons the complaint system of enforcement in favour of a regulatory model that not only prohibits wage discrimination but also places positive obligations on employers to scrutinize their pay practices and ensure that these practices comply with the legislation.

systemic discrimination discrimination that is pervasive throughout an employer's work force

At present, the latest regulatory model applies to the public sectors in Manitoba, New Brunswick, Newfoundland, Nova Scotia, and Prince Edward Island, and in Ontario to the public sector and to private sector employers who employ 10 or more persons. Throughout the rest of Canada, the complaints system alone remains in force.

Employment Equity

The newest development in employment rights goes beyond requiring employers to treat equally individual applicants for jobs, regardless of personal characteristics. Employers may be required to strive towards making their work force reflect the various underrepresented classes of disadvantaged persons in the general population.

In 1986, the federal Parliament passed the Employment Equity Act,[33] which applies to all employers with 100 or more employees, "in connection with federal work, undertaking or business as defined in section 2 of the *Canada Labour Code....*" Employers are required to conduct a "workforce analysis," that is, to obtain relevant information about the personal characteristics of their current employees, in order to determine underrepresentation of designated groups—women, visible minorities, aboriginals, and persons with disabilities—in the work force generally. In addition to information from their current employees, employers must seek the same information from job applicants before determining whether certain applicants should be given preference. Employers are required to review their formal and informal hiring policies in order to remove all systemic discrimination against the designated groups, and to set goals and timetables for achieving representation based on the working-age population within each employer's community. Finally, they must prepare a plan to implement their goals, including monitoring systems to assess their progress.

There was debate about intrusiveness in obtaining information about the personal characteristics of both employees and job applicants, and also about the weight employers will be required to give to the designated characteristics in making hiring decision, but the federal legislation has remained in force. In December 1993, the Ontario legislature passed a bill similar to the federal Act,[34] which applied to all public sector employment and to private sector employers with more than 50 employees. It became a major issue in the 1995 provincial election; the Progressive Conservative Party vowed to repeal the legislation, and did so after it was elected to power.[35] At the time of writing, no other provinces have passed similar legislation.

Regulation of Working Conditions

General Working Conditions

Each province has enacted a variety of statutes prohibiting child labour, regulating the hours of work of young persons, and providing for the health and safety of employees while at work. Provinces may appoint inspectors to see that these requirements are complied with. Other statutes specify a minimum age at which children may leave school and accept full-time employment.

---

33. S.C. 1986, c. 31.

34. Employment Equity Act, S.O. 1993, c. 35.

35. Job Quotas Repeal Act, S.O. 1995, c. 4.

All provinces and the federal government provide by statute for minimum-wage rates, and grant discretionary power to designated government agencies to fix a minimum wage that varies with the industry. The legislation provides for limited working hours, with some exceptions, of eight hours a day and a maximum of 44 or 48 hours a week. These statutes also require overtime rates if the number of hours worked exceeds the specified maximum.

All but two provinces have given formal statutory approval to agreements among employers and employees in a particular trade or industry within a specified geographic zone, when all agree to minimum rates of wages and maximum hours of work and days of labour.[36] This approval is subject to the provisions of other statutes dealing with hours of work, minimum wages, and working conditions. The agreements must be reached at a properly convened conference of the employers and employees affected. Recognition of agreements of this kind is an important qualification of the negative attitude of the law towards restraint of trade.

All provinces now provide for annual vacations with pay. The most frequent requirement is for employers to grant their employees one week's paid vacation after one year of work. Some provinces also provide for public holidays with pay.

Mandatory Retirement and the Charter of Rights and Freedoms

For many years, Canadians have accepted mandatory retirement schemes as desirable and humane social institutions: workers were expected to leave their jobs, usually at age 65, and enjoy retirement on an adequate pension. However, increasing good health and life expectancy have meant that many people approaching their 65th year, who feel vigorous and enjoy their work, wish to continue working. Moreover, rapid inflation over a 30-year period until the 1990s has led to an unexpected diminution of pensions available to many people reaching retirement age who feel they must continue to work to maintain a reasonable standard of living. On the other hand, employers and others—especially young people seeking work—want employees to retire at the established compulsory retirement age. Some employers have insisted that they do so.

Since section 15 of the Charter of Rights and Freedoms guarantees "equal protection and benefit of the law without discrimination…based on…age," many employees wishing to remain in their jobs have challenged mandatory retirement provisions. They claim that basing mandatory retirement solely upon a particular age, without regard to the health or competence of an employee, is arbitrary and discriminatory and therefore offends the Charter. A similar argument was made successfully under the Manitoba Human Rights Code in 1981, before the Charter was made part of the Constitution; the court held that a mandatory retirement provision at the University of Manitoba offended the provincial Code and was void.[37] The province of Québec abolished compulsory retirement by statute in 1982.[38] The federal government in the autumn of 1985 abolished mandatory retirement in its civil service.

Defenders of mandatory retirement schemes claim that, because the schemes are socially desirable, under section 1 of the Charter they are valid because they are a "reasonable limit prescribed by law" and "can be demonstrably justified in a free and democratic society." Human rights statutes, such as those of British Columbia and Ontario, prohibit discrimination based on age but only between the ages of 18 and 65 years, thus allowing mandatory retirement at 65. The Supreme Court of Canada allowed such schemes in a group of four decisions dealing with com-

---

36. See, for example: Municipal Act, R.S.B.C. 1996, c. 323, ss. 682–691; Industrial Standards Act, R.S.O. 1990, c. 216; Labour Standards Code, R.S.N.S. 1989, c. 246, ss. 44–47.

37. McIntyre v. University of Manitoba (1981), 119 D.L.R. (3d) 352, followed by Newport v. Government of Manitoba (1982), 131 D.L.R. (3d) 564. Both cases held that s. 6(1) of the Human Rights Code, S.M. 1974, c. 65, made mandatory retirement provisions void.

38. Abolition of Compulsory Retirement Act, S.Q. 1982, c. 12.

plaints made by employees of hospitals, community colleges, and universities.[39] The issue is a good example of the important effects that the Charter can have not only on individuals but also on the workplace and society generally.

Employment Insurance

The Employment Insurance Act[40] manages an employment insurance fund to which employers and employees must contribute according to a published schedule of rates. Coverage is very wide, with only such limited exceptions as persons receiving retirement pensions, self-employed by a spouse, and employed by provincial governments, foreign governments, and international organizations.[41] Both employers and employees, through payroll deductions, contribute to the fund. The employer must account for all employee contributions and, along with its own contributions, regularly remit them to the government. Employment insurance benefits are payable out of the fund to workers who have contributed in the past and are currently unemployed. These benefits are not available in several circumstances, one of which is loss of work caused by a labour dispute in which the employee is on strike. Other employees, not on strike but "locked out" because a plant or business is shut down by a strike, remain eligible for benefits.

Workers' Compensation

Harshness of the Common Law

While the common law recognized that an employer could be liable to an employee for injury sustained in the course of employment, it was notoriously difficult for the employee to recover damages. The employer might defend the action successfully if it could show that the injury resulted from the contributory negligence of the employee, the negligence of a fellow employee, or the fact that the employee had assumed a risk of injury as a customary incident of the type of work he had contracted to do.

The doctrine of contributory negligence as discussed in Chapter 3, prevented an employee from recovering damages if the evidence showed that he was partly responsible for the accident, even in a small degree. Nor was an employer liable for injury to an employee caused by the negligence of a fellow employee (or **fellow servant**), provided the employer took reasonable care to hire competent workers: the usual result was that the employer escaped liability for the negligence of one employee that caused injury to another. Finally, the defence of **assumed risk**, broadly interpreted, might itself defeat almost any action by an employee, for it could be argued that every risk is a risk an employee assumes in accepting a particular employment.

An action at common law also suffered from the fact that the burden lay with the employee to prove negligence on the part of the employer; he might find it exceedingly difficult to do so, especially if he suffered shock from his injury that limited his ability to recall what happened. In addition, the dependants of an employee who had been killed rather than injured in the course of employment had no cause of action—the right to sue for personal injury caused by a tort died with the injured person at common law.

fellow servant
fellow employee

assumed risk
risk assumed by an employee in accepting a particular employment

---

39. McKinney v. University of Guelph, [1990] 3 S.C.R. 229; Harrison v. University of British Columbia, [1990] 3 S.C.R. 451; Stoffman v. Vancouver General Hospital, 3 S.C.R. 483; Douglas/Kwantlen Faculty Association v. Douglas College, 3 S.C.R. 570. Provincial human rights codes, and the federal Human Rights Act, apply to *all* employment contracts within their jurisdiction, both in the public and in private sectors. In contrast, s. 15 of the Charter applies to all employment contracts made in the *public sector*—contracts made by governments at all levels, by Crown corporations, school boards, community colleges, etc.; it does not bind the *private sector*, including universities (see the McKinney case), even though they may receive a high proportion of their funding from governments.

40. Employment Insurance Act, S.C. 1996, c. 23 E-5.6.

41. *Ibid.*, s. 3(2).

Statutory Reform

It was not until the latter part of the 19th century that legislation was enacted in England to permit action against an employer by the relatives of an employee killed while on the job. The legislation also clarified and extended the liability of employers; but the burden of proof remained with an employee or the dependants to prove negligence on the part of the employer. Similar statutes were passed in the Canadian provinces. The final step was the enactment of the Workmen's Compensation Act. This statute made substantial improvement in the rights of injured employees, or of their immediate dependants in the event of death caused by accident while at work. The Act was passed in England in 1906 and later enacted in each of the provinces of Canada with various modifications.[42]

Each of these Acts creates a Workers' Compensation Board to hear employees' claims. Each Act also establishes a fund to which employers subject to the Act must contribute regularly and out of which claims are paid. Payment out of the fund replaces any personal action against an employer. To succeed, an employee need only show that the injury was caused by an accident in the course of employment. The defences of contributory negligence, negligence of a fellow servant, and assumed risk no longer apply. An employee's claim will fail only if it is shown that the accident was caused substantially by his willful misconduct. Even then, the employee or the dependants will recover if the accident has caused death or serious disablement. The requirement of proving negligence on the part of the employer, so long a barrier to compensation for injury, no longer exists. There is a major advantage because the costs and hazards of litigation are avoided. Also, since an employee claims recovery from a compensation board and not from his employer, he need not fear prejudicing his future with the employer by making the claim.

Variations in Provincial Reforms

Coverage varies somewhat among the provinces. Generally included are workers in the following industries: construction, mining, manufacturing, lumbering, fishing, transportation, communications, and public utilities. Industries are classified according to the degree of hazard. Exemptions may include casual employees and employees of small businesses employing fewer than a stated number of workers. For employees excluded from the usual workers' compensation benefits, several provinces have added a second part to their legislation defining the employer's liability for injuries caused by defective plant or equipment, or by the negligence of other employees, and granting employees a right to damages in spite of contributory negligence on their part. In other jurisdictions, the common law rules still apply to casual employees and to those in small businesses.

Occupational Health

An area of growing concern and controversy closely related to occupational safety is occupational health. There are several reasons for the increasing prominence of health standards in the work place. First, the general concern over environmental hazards to health has made the public much more sensitive to the special problems of the work environment: if a chemical dispersed in the atmosphere can harm people at a great distance, how much more dangerous is it for the workers who handle it and are directly exposed? Second, improvement in the general level of public health has drawn attention to the fact that persons in particular occupations suffer from certain illnesses to a greater degree than does the general public. Third, improvement in the quality of medical records and the sophistication of medical diagnosis has made it easier to connect certain diseases with some occupations. This last aspect has received great prominence in reference to industries where large numbers of workers can be seen to have very high incidences of specific ailments 20 or 30 years after starting work.

---

42. See, for example: Workers' Compensation Act, R.S.B.C. 1996, c. 492; R.S.N.S. 1989, c. 508; Workplace Safety and Insurance Act, S.O. 1996, c. 16.

Many questions concerning occupational health in the work place remain unanswered. Should the general system of workers' compensation be responsible for research into potential health hazards, for policing work conditions in plants, and for financial aid to affected workers? Should special legislation be enacted to make industries legally responsible for specific illnesses (keeping in mind that it may be very difficult to prove in a court that the work place actually caused a particular illness)? Should certain industrial activities such as the processing of asbestos be banned completely (as has been done in some European countries)? Will other economic activities wither away because of the costs of imposing liability for their consequences? Could the country lose its comparative advantage in international trade by imposing such high standards of health on certain industries that they cannot compete with those in countries requiring lower standards? How economically important would the lost jobs be? It is likely that these and other questions relating to occupational health will continue to be debated extensively and that there will be no easy answers to them socially, economically or legally.

COLLECTIVE BARGAINING

The Process

The process of establishing conditions of employment through negotiations between a business and the bargaining agent for its employees is known as **collective bargaining**. For those industries within federal jurisdiction, a federal statute regulates collective bargaining.[43] Statutes passed by each of the provinces regulate all other industries.[44] These acts state that all employees are free to belong to trade unions and that membership in a trade union does not provide the employer with grounds for dismissing an employee. The acts also require employers to recognize the representative union as the bargaining agent for employees for determining the general terms of their employment.

If an employer is unwilling to recognize a trade union voluntarily, as often happens, the union may have to apply to be certified before it can proceed to bargain for the employees. **Certification** is an acknowledgment by an administrative tribunal (called in some provinces a **labour relations board**) that a particular union commands sufficient membership to justify its role as exclusive bargaining agent for the employees. The arrangement has the practical advantages of confining the negotiations to a single representative of the employees and avoiding the confusion of rival unions claiming the right to act as bargaining agents for a group of employees. We must distinguish between a bargaining agent and a bargaining unit: a **bargaining agent** is a union that has the exclusive right to bargain with the employer on behalf of the bargaining unit: the **bargaining unit** includes a specified group of employees eligible to join the union, whether they join or not.

Content of a Collective Agreement

When an employer and union conclude their bargaining, they place the terms agreed on in a contract called a *collective agreement*. The terms usually include a definition of the employees covered, an acknowledgment by the employer that the contracting union is their recognized bargaining agent, an outline of the steps that both parties must take in settling grievances, seniority provisions in the promotion and laying off of employees, wage rates, hours, vacation periods and other fringe benefits, the duration of the collective agreement, and the means by which it may be amended or renewed. Often there is a clause acknowledging that the maintenance of

collective bargaining
establishing conditions of employment by negotiation between an employer and the bargaining agent for its employees

certification
an acknowledgment by an administrative tribunal that a particular union commands sufficient membership to justify its role as exclusive bargaining agent for the employees

labour relations board
an administrative tribunal regulating labour relations

bargaining agent
a union that has the exclusive right to bargain with the employer on behalf of the bargaining unit

bargaining unit
a specified group of employees eligible to join the union

---

43. Canada Labour Code, R.S.C. 1985, c. L-2.

44. See, for example: Labour Relations Code, R.S.B.C. 1996, c. 244; Labour Relations Act, S.O. 1992, c. 21; Trade Union Act, R.S.N.S. 1989, c. 475.

discipline and efficiency of employees is the sole function of the management of the company, subject to the right of an employee to lodge a grievance. The agreement almost invariably forbids strikes or lockouts as long as the agreement continues to operate; indeed, most provinces require that such a term be included. The employees covered do not generally include those employed in a confidential capacity, those who have managerial responsibilities such as the authority to hire or discharge others, or those employed as guards or security police in the protection of business property. Some provinces have also excluded certain professional groups such as engineers, although the recent tendency has been to include more of the professions.

The terms of a collective agreement generally prescribe in detail the procedure for dismissing employees, displacing the common law rules for notice of dismissal and grounds for dismissal. To the extent that the collective agreement prescribes working conditions above the level required by existing legislation, it replaces employee welfare legislation as a protection for the interests of workers.

First Collective Agreement

Experience has shown that frequently the most difficult collective agreement to reach is the first one after certification: the union is new and its local members are inexperienced (even if they have advice from other union officials); management is unaccustomed to working with a union; often there has been some hostility and bitterness between employer and employees during the certification campaign. In response to the problem, first British Columbia in 1973, followed by the federal government, Québec, Manitoba, and Ontario, passed legislation providing for "first contract arbitration."[45] If the parties cannot reach agreement on a contract within the time specified in the Act, then the provincial or federal labour board concerned may, after hearing the parties in an arbitration, impose a first contract on them.

LABOUR DISPUTES

Types of Disputes

We may identify four major types of disputes affecting trade unions: jurisdictional disputes, recognition disputes, interest disputes, and rights disputes.

jurisdictional dispute
two or more unions compete for the right to represent a particular group of employees

recognition dispute
an employer refuses to recognize the union as the employees' bargaining agent

interest dispute
an employer and the union disagree about the particular terms to be included in the collective agreement

rights dispute
an employer and the union differ in their interpretation of terms in an existing collective agreement

1. A **jurisdictional dispute** is a disagreement between competing unions for the right to represent a particular group of employees; the type of work they do may have two aspects, each of which seems to bring it within the terms of reference of a different trade union. Such a simple operation as drilling a hole through both metal and wood might raise a question of whether the worker should belong to the metalworkers' or the woodworkers' union.

2. A **recognition dispute** arises between an employer and a union when the employer insists on negotiating employment contracts directly with its employees and resists a union demand that it be recognized as the employees' bargaining agent.

3. An **interest dispute** arises when an employer and a union cannot reach agreement about the particular terms to be included in a collective agreement.

4. A **rights dispute** is a difference of opinion between employer and union on the interpretation of terms in a collective agreement already in existence.

45. R.S.B.C. 1996, c. 244, s. 55; R.S.Q. 1991, c. C-27, s. 93.1; R.S.M. 1987, c. L-10, s. 75; S.O. 1992, c. 21, s. 41.

Legislative Regulation

As we noted at the outset, the regulation of labour disputes is a field of study in its own right, and we cannot do more than indicate a few of the basic methods used. For an adequate treatment of the law, one must consult recognized works in the field; a few are listed in the bibliography at the end of this book.

Statutes now provide machinery that either eliminates or minimizes the need to resort to strike action in each of the four main types of dispute mentioned above. Certification procedure, briefly considered in the preceding section, has done much to resolve jurisdictional disputes and is the only legal means of settling recognition disputes.

Provincial statutes require both employer and employees to follow a series of procedures designed to aid in the settlement of interest disputes:

- First, they require a genuine attempt over a specified period to bargain to reach agreement.[46]

- Second, if the parties fail to agree, they must submit to **conciliation procedure**, that is, bargain further with the help of a conciliation officer or board.

- Third, if the parties still fail to agree, the employer cannot declare a lockout or the union begin strike action until a further specified **cooling-off period** has elapsed.

For the fourth type, a rights dispute, the law imposes **arbitration procedure**: the parties are bound to accept the interpretation placed on the collective agreement by an arbitrator. In conciliation procedure, the parties are not bound to accept the solution proposed by the conciliation officer, but in arbitration procedure, the decision of the arbitrator is binding.

In summary, we can see that *only* in interest disputes does the possibility of lawful strike action exist, and then only after the prescribed conciliation procedure and cooling-off period. A strike is "illegal" if the preliminary grievance procedures set down by statute have not been followed or, even when they have been followed, if the strike is not conducted according to carefully defined rules. The conduct of a strike by the union must be free of compulsion, intimidation, or threat. Furthermore, a strike may become unlawful if it is undertaken with an intent to injure another party and not with the intent of furthering the trade interest of the strikers.

Although strikers are entitled to picket at or near the place of the employer's business, they must do so peaceably and only for the purpose of obtaining or communicating information. Statements made on placards or in literature distributed at the scene of the picketing must be correct and factual. Mr. Chief Justice McRuer of the Ontario Supreme Court outlined the scope of these rights as follows:

> It is one thing to exercise all the lawful rights to strike and the lawful rights to picket; that is a freedom that should be preserved and its preservation has advanced the interests of the labouring man and the community as a whole to an untold degree over the last half-century. But it is another thing to recognize a conspiracy to injure so that benefits to any particular person or class may be realized. Further, if what any person or group of persons does amounts to a common law nuisance to another what is being done may be restrained by injunction.[47]

conciliation procedure
bargaining with the help of a conciliation officer or board

cooling-off period
a time during which the employer cannot lock out nor the union begin a strike

arbitration procedure
the procedure in a rights dispute that binds the parties to accept the interpretation of the collective agreement by an arbitrator

---

46. In Canada, an employer need not bargain with a union that has not been certified and with which it has not previously made a collective agreement. In the United States, an employer must bargain with a union representing the majority of its employees, whether it is certified or not.

47. General Dry Batteries of Canada Ltd. v. Brigenshaw, [1951] O.R. 522, per McRuer, C.J.H.C., at 528. See also O.K. Economy Stores v. R.W.D.S.U., Local 454 (1994), 118 D.L.R. (4th) 345.

IMPLICATIONS OF THE COLLECTIVE AGREEMENT FOR THE INDIVIDUAL EMPLOYEE

The parties to a collective agreement are the employer and the representative union; generally, each party is a large organization or institution and the individual employee does not actively participate in negotiating the terms of employment. Since nearly all the bargaining is done by the union, comparatively little ground is left for an employee to negotiate with the employer at the time of making his or her individual contract of employment.

Labour unions have, of course, been a means by which workers collectively have achieved a bargaining power that they cannot have individually, and unions have secured many improvements in conditions of work. On the other hand, the process is one that necessarily subordinates individual employee preferences to the collective goals of an organization. An individual's terms of employment are determined by virtue of his status as a member of the bargaining unit, rather than by virtue of any personal bargaining efforts:

> …contract becomes largely the technique of group manipulation and use. Professional managements speak for the large corporation, and professional labor leaders speak for workers; the contract thus arrived at becomes a contribution to a code of administrative behavior by which the individual's personal right to contract is considerably diminished. As a working proposition, then, we are prepared to assert that contract is meaningful today more in terms of its use by organizations and less in terms of its use by individuals.[48]

The Province of Québec has a unique piece of legislation that takes this process a stage further: the terms of a collective agreement may apply even to workers who are not members of the bargaining unit for which the union was entitled to negotiate.[49] Under the legislation, when a union has bargained for a certain rate of pay with one or more large employers within the industry, the parties may apply to the Minister of Labour for a decree extending the provisions of the collective agreement to all other employers and employees within the industry or trade in the province or within a region of the province. To succeed, the application must establish that the collective agreements already written have acquired a dominant significance and importance for establishing conditions of labour within the industry or region. The effect is to establish a minimum wage law within the area covered by the decree, and to extend the terms of the collective agreement to workers not represented in the formation of the contract.

Not only do unions have the dominant role in bargaining on behalf of individual workers; often workers do not have the freedom to choose whether to belong to the union. In *Bonsor v. Musicians' Union*[50] the plaintiff, who had been wrongfully expelled from the union and found it impossible to earn a livelihood as a musician without being a member, testified as follows:

> I would like to tell his lordship that if I could earn my living forthwith without being a member of this so-called Musicians' Union I would not want to join it, but I have got to join it in order to work because it is a closed shop. I will always pay my subscriptions, but I will not take any active part in union matters. I will be a member by force because I am forced to be a member.[51]

After quoting the above statement of the plaintiff, Lord Denning commented:

---

48. Eells and Walton, *Conceptual Foundations of Business* (2nd ed.), pp. 260–1. Homewood, IL: Richard D. Irwin Inc., 1969.

49. Collective Agreement Decrees Act, R.S.Q. 1991, c. D-2.

50. [1954] Ch. 479. (The dissenting judgment of Denning, L.J., was approved on appeal to the House of Lords: [1956] A.C. 105.)

51. *Ibid.*, at 485.

When one remembers that the rules are applied to a man in that state of mind, it will be appreciated that they are not so much a contract as we used to understand a contract, but they are much more a legislative code laid down by some members of the union to be imposed on all members of the union. They are more like by-laws than a contract.[52]

Trade unions are, of course, only one of the modern institutions that have this effect on contract. Contracts between existing businesses that restrict competition by fixing prices or output effectively diminish the freedom of contract of the consuming public; we shall consider the law dealing with this problem in Chapter 32. In addition, as we have seen, many financial institutions (insurance companies and finance companies, for example) present those to whom they sell their services with a standard form contract. It contains the terms of the agreement set down in advance on a take-it-or-leave-it basis, thereby diminishing or even eliminating the opportunity for the other contracting party to bargain for terms it would prefer.

THE LEGAL STATUS OF TRADE UNIONS

We touched briefly on the legal status of trade unions when discussing capacity to contract in Chapter 7. We noted that trade unions are recognized as legal entities before labour relations boards in order to bind them to the board's rulings; but this recognition is for a limited purpose, and we must not infer from the fact that unions have a separate existence before an administrative tribunal that they necessarily have comparable standing before the courts. We noted also that the technique of representative action provides a possible means by which unions may sue or be sued in the courts.

For various reasons, our legislatures have avoided the otherwise obvious path of requiring trade unions to come within existing legislation for corporations, and so conferring on them a corporate existence comparable with that of other business organizations. Nevertheless, the legislatures seem to be moving in that direction and when there is no decisive statutory authority, the courts are able to cite the reasoning in the famous *Taff Vale* case, a decision handed down by the House of Lords in 1901.[53]

CASE 20.3

During a strike, two agents of a union "put themselves in charge…and…illegally watched and beset men to prevent them from working for the company, and illegally ordered men to break their contracts." The court interpreted the strike as a conspiracy in restraint of trade under the then existing law of England. As a result, the company suffered business losses and sued the union. But even though there was an admitted wrong, could the union as such be sued for damages? The House of Lords found the trade union to be a "quasi-corporate" body that could be sued. It held the union liable in damages for the company's losses.

Although the result of the *Taff Vale* case was nullified shortly afterwards by an act of Parliament,[54] and although this act was adopted by provinces in Canada, the *judicial reasoning* concerning the legal personality of trade unions survived and persisted.

---

52. *Ibid.*

53. Taff Vale Railway Co. v. Amalgamated Society of Railway Servants, [1901] A.C. 426.

54. See Trade Disputes Act, 1906, 6 Ed. VII, c. 47, s. 1, declaring that actions of a trade union in furtherance of its interests would not thenceforth be interpreted as a restraint of trade.

The Supreme Court of Canada in 1960 made extensive use of the *Taff Vale* decision in the case of *International Brotherhood of Teamsters v. Thérien.*[55]

CASE 20.4

Thérien was the owner of a Vancouver trucking business and had been doing business with City Construction Company for some years when the company entered into a collective agreement with the Teamsters' Union requiring, as one of its terms, that all employees should be union members (a **closed-shop agreement**). Thérien agreed then to hire only union members for the operation of his trucks. However, he declined to join the union personally because he wished to maintain his relationship as an independent contractor in dealings with City Construction. He further claimed that in the capacity of an employer in his own right he was forbidden by the Labour Relations Act of British Columbia from participating in union activities.

The union opposed that view and because of its threats to picket City Construction, the general manager of the company informed Thérien that the company must dispense with his services. Thérien suffered a significant loss of business and he sued the union, claiming damages for its wrongful conduct. The union defended on the grounds that it was not a legal entity and so could not be sued and, second, that in any case it had not been guilty of conduct that might constitute a tort.

closed-shop agreement

a collective agreement requiring all employees to be union members

On the first argument of the union, the court noted that the union had been certified as a bargaining agent under the terms of the Labour Relations Act, and stated:

> It is necessary for the exercise of the [statutory] powers given that such unions should have officers or other agents to act in their names and on their behalf. The Legislature, by giving the right to act as agent for others and to contract on their behalf, has given them two of the essential qualities of a corporation in respect of liability for tort since a corporation can only act by its agents.[56]

The court quoted with approval the remarks of Lord Halsbury in the *Taff Vale* case:

> If the Legislature has created a thing which can own property, which can employ servants, and which can inflict injury, it must be taken, I think, to have impliedly given the power to make it suable in a Court of Law for injuries purposely done by its authority and procurement.[57]

Having identified the union as a suable legal entity, the court then found, first, that the union had threatened to resort to picketing instead of following the grievance procedure set out in the collective agreement, and second, that the consequence of its conduct was the injurious termination of Thérien's arrangement with City Construction Company. The court awarded damages to Thérien and ordered an injunction restraining the union from interfering with him in the operation of his business.

The *Thérien* decision is one of a succession of Canadian cases developing the common law on the subject of the legal status of trade unions.[58] It does not apply, of course, in provinces whose statutes specifically define the circumstances in which trade unions may be sued. In par-

---

55. (1960), 22 D.L.R. (2d) 1. This decision has been followed in a Manitoba case: Dusessoy's Supermarket St. James Ltd. v. Retail Clerks Union Local No. 832 (1961), 34 W.W.R. 577.

56. International Brotherhood of Teamsters v. Thérien, *ibid.*, per Locke, J., at 11.

57. Taff Vale Railway Co. v. Amalgamated Society of Railway Servants, *supra*, n. 53, per Halsbury, L.C., at 436.

58. See for example, U.N.A. v. Alberta (Attorney-General) (1990), 89 D.L.R. (4th) 609.

ticular, Ontario has a statutory provision that restricts the possibility of an action against a trade union for torts.[59]

QUESTIONS FOR REVIEW

1. Briefly describe two employees each of whom has varying degrees of responsibility as agent.

2. How does an independent contractor differ from an employee?

3. Give an example of circumstances where an employee commits a tort but his employer is not liable. What element is necessary to make the employer liable?

4. After earning his B.Comm. degree, Bruce was hired as a junior accountant by Cargo Wholesale Inc. He received favourable assessment letters and salary increases after year one and year two. At the end of his third year, he received his final pay cheque with a letter stating that he was dismissed for incompetence. What points might Bruce argue to show that he was wrongfully dismissed?

5. Norman is hired as a waiter in a restaurant at a summer resort without any discussion about the length of his employment contract. He receives a weekly pay cheque. He is let go without notice at the end of the summer. Explain whether he has been wrongfully dismissed.

6. On what grounds is a business justified in dismissing its employees without notice?

7. What are the main factors to be taken into account when assessing damages for wrongful dismissal?

8. When is reinstatement an unlikely remedy for wrongful dismissal?

9. Why is it not effective to define pay equity solely in terms of the market value of comparable jobs?

10. Describe briefly the benefits of and problems with compulsory retirement.

11. Why was it difficult before the passing of the Workers' Compensation Act for an employee injured at work to obtain a remedy against her employer?

12. Under workers' compensation legislation, who pays compensation to an injured employee? How are the funds raised?

13. Describe some of the main elements in a collective agreement.

14. In certain provinces and in federal jurisdiction, what happens when the parties do not succeed in making a deal for their first collective agreement?

15. What is the difference between a jurisdictional dispute and an interest dispute?

---

59. Rights of Labour Act, R.S.O. 1990, c. R.33, s. 3. For legislation expressly making unions suable entities, see Labour Relations Code, R.S.B.C. 1996, c. 144, s. 154; Labour Relations Act, R.S.M. 1987, c. L-10, s. 127; Industrial Relations Act, R.S.N.B. 1973, c. I-4, s. 114(2); Trade Union Act, R.S.S. 1978, c. T-17, s. 29, as amended by S.S. 1983, c. 81, s. 9.

16. Collective agreements have been described by some commentators as being more like legislation for individual workers. Explain.

17. Quality Meat Packers Ltd. has major factories and warehouses from coast to coast. How does this fact complicate the company's collective bargaining with its employees?

CASES AND PROBLEMS

1 Savard was a helicopter pilot working for the provincial government fire-fighting brigade. After a long summer day inspecting small fires that had broken out in the region, Savard returned to the government base with his supervisor, Torman. They agreed that after Savard took a short break to get something to eat, he would fly to his home in a small village 25 kilometres away. He could spend the night with his family and be closer to the next site inspection the following morning.

As Torman was leaving the base, he was approached by three tourists who asked if they could arrange a flight aboard the helicopter. Torman replied, "That's a government helicopter, and besides, it would be too expensive for you." The tourists thanked him and continued walking around the base. As he was unlocking his car, Torman saw the tourists approach Savard. The tourists and Savard then began walking towards the helicopter. Torman assumed that Savard was merely showing it to them. He got into his car and left. A few minutes later, he saw the helicopter in the air. As it turned out Savard had agreed to take the tourists along. Tragically, the helicopter crashed a few minutes later and all four were killed.

The families of the tourists sued both Savard's estate and the provincial government for damages claiming both were responsible for the accident. Evidence established that Savard had indeed operated the helicopter negligently, perhaps because he was tired. Savard's estate was not large enough to meet the claims. Should the families' claims succeed against the provincial government?

2 Benson had been manager of the Kilnnok Pub for 10 years. The owner, James, learned that Benson had behaved inappropriately at work, insulting several customers after he had had too much to drink. James made it clear to Benson that if he drank alcohol again during work, it would be grounds for dismissal. Two years later, there was another incident at work when Benson was rude to customers. James had had enough: he dismissed Benson and gave him three weeks' severance pay.

Benson sued James for damages for wrongful dismissal, claiming 12 months' salary.

James did not defend by pleading that he dismissed Benson for drinking while on duty; in fact, James was not aware of such conduct. However, at the trial, evidence of other employees and patrons of the pub established that Benson had been drinking on duty on many occasions. Should Benson's action succeed?

3 C.W. Jonas was a conductor employed by the East-West Railway Company. While the passenger train on which he was working was standing in a railway station, it was struck by another train. Because of the negligent operation of the train, Jonas was severely injured. He sued the East-West Railway Company for damages for negligence.

In defence, the railway company produced its copy of an employment contract signed by Jonas. The contract included the following clause:

The employee, C.W. Jonas, agrees that in consideration of employment and wages by the Great East-West Railway Company, he will assume all risks of accident or casualty incident to such employment and service whether caused by the negligence of the Company or of its employees or otherwise, and will forever release, acquit, and discharge the said Company from all liability. The employee waives all rights to worker's compensation that might otherwise arise under this contract.

Without rendering a decision, discuss the public policy considerations inherent in a dispute of this kind.

4 Devellano operated a retail food supermarket that bought 60 percent of its merchandise from Prairie Wholesale Grocers Limited. Because of a wage dispute the employees of Prairie Wholesale Grocers who were members of the Office & Shop Clerks Union, went on strike. An official of that union then telephoned Devellano to enlist her support and apply economic pressure on Prairie Wholesale Grocers by reducing purchases from it. When Devellano refused, members of the union picketed her supermarket. They stopped cars on their way into the parking lot of the supermarket and distributed leaflets, intimating, inaccurately, that Devellano's store was controlled by Prairie Wholesale Grocers. The placards used while picketing contained the words "Devellano's Supermarket" and "Strike" in large letters, although none of Devellano's own employees were on strike. As a result, Devellano lost customers and sued the union for damages and an injunction to restrain the picketing of her premises. Discuss the defences available to the union and state whether they would succeed.

5 Lucy Anang was hired as a chemist by the Plastic Toy Co. Her employment contract stated that, following termination of her employment with the company, she would not work for any competitor in the province for five years nor at any time in the future disclose to anyone any information about secret processes used by Plastic Toy Co. Anang had worked in the laboratory of the company for a period of about three years when she was given two months' notice of dismissal.

After her dismissal, Anang tried to earn a living as a consulting chemist. The plant supervisor at Plastic Toy then learned that she was disclosing certain information about manufacturing processes to one of the company's chief competitors. Specifically, it appeared that she had disclosed secret processes related to the production of equipment used in the colouring of toys, processes of value to the company.

Plastic Toy Co. sued Anang for damages and for an injunction restraining her from disclosing further information. One of Anang's defences was that no injunction could be granted to deprive her of the right to practise her profession as a chemist. What is the likelihood that the action will succeed?

Suppose instead that Anang had left Plastic Toy Co. because she had received an offer of a higher salary from a competitor of Plastic Toy. The management of Plastic Toy had no evidence that she disclosed any of its secret processes to her new employer, but was concerned that she might do so. Is it likely that Plastic Toy could obtain an injunction restraining Anang from working for its competitor. What conflicting policy issues must the court resolve?

6 In May 1983, the directors of Universal Printing Co., publishers of an evening newspaper with a large circulation, approached Bell to persuade him to become their assistant advertising manager. They suggested that if he accepted, he would probably succeed the present advertising manager upon his retirement. At the time, Bell held a responsible position with an advertising agency and was 42. During the discussions Bell emphasized that his present position was a very satisfactory one, that it was important at his age that his employment should be permanent, and that he would not consider a change that did not offer the prospect of a position lasting for the balance of his working life.

After careful consideration Bell accepted the position offered at a salary of $65 000 a year. He was promoted to advertising manager in 1991, and in the period from May 1983 to July 1999, his salary was increased regularly until it reached an annual sum of $160 000. In addition, every year he received a discretionary Christmas bonus approved by the directors and a special distribution pursuant to a profit-sharing plan confined to selected employees and made under the sole direction of the principal shareholder of Universal Printing Co. Ltd. Bell's receipts under the profit-sharing plan were $23 600 in 1996, $20 400 in 1997, and $17 000 in 1998.

In August 1999, the President of the Universal Printing Co. Ltd., T. G. Dodds, called Bell into his office and after some opening pleasantries about Bell's prowess in golf, told Bell that he thought another advertising manager he had in mind could produce better results for the company. Dodds told Bell that if he could see his way clear to resigning forthwith, he might have three months' salary in lieu of notice. Bell replied that he could not afford at this stage in his career to admit to the incompetence implied in a resignation and refused. Later in the afternoon, his secretary brought him the following letter:

August 8, 1999

Dear Mr. Bell:

This is to confirm the notice given to you today of the termination of your employment with Universal Printing Co. Ltd. as of this date. Enclosed is a cheque for your salary to date. Your pension plan has been commuted to a paid-up basis that will pay you $3500 a month commencing at age 65.

T. G. Dodds.

Bell at once made efforts to secure other employment, and by December 8, 1999, found a position with an advertising agency at a salary of $42 000 a year. If he had remained a further year with Universal Printing Co. Ltd., the paid-up value of his pension would have increased to $6500 per month.

Bell brought an action against Universal Printing Co. Ltd. for damages for wrongful dismissal. What amount of damages, if any, should he recover? Are there any additional facts you would like to know?

7 In September, Knowles, the owner of a professional hockey club, began negotiations with Meyer, a professional hockey player, for Meyer's services for the following two years. The two agreed orally to a salary of $3000 a week for Meyer during the training and playing seasons. At the time, Meyer asked whether players would be covered by workers' compensation insurance if injured. Knowles replied that the club's lawyer had advised that players were not covered, but that in any event he was having written contracts drawn up by the lawyer in which a clause would provide that every player would be insured against injury and that if a player were disabled he would be looked after.

Written contracts were subsequently prepared and presented to all the players (including Meyer) for signing. The contracts in their written form specified the agreed salary for each individual player, and outlined the usual conditions regarding the player's obligations to the club, but there was no reference to insurance protection against injury or to the employer's obligation in the event of a player being disabled.

Meyer played for the team for six weeks and then received a serious injury to his eye during a hockey game. He was immediately taken to the hospital. At the end of the game, Knowles announced to Meyer's teammates in the dressing room that he would pay Meyer's salary to the end of the season.

Knowles paid Meyer's salary to the date of his injury and refused to pay any additional sum. Meyer brought an action for damages claiming $45 000 representing his salary for the remaining 15 weeks of the playing season; $500 for the cost of an artificial eye; and $100 000 general damages as compensation for the loss of his eye.

Discuss the issues raised by these facts and explain whether Meyer's action is likely to succeed.

21 NEGOTIABLE INSTRUMENTS

For centuries negotiable instruments have been the main method of paying debts and financing transactions in both domestic and international business. We shall discuss the nature and uses of these devices under the Bills of Exchange Act. In this chapter we examine such questions as:

- what types of negotiable instrument are governed by the Act and how are they utilized?

- what is meant by negotiability?

- what are the methods, purposes, and consequences of endorsement?

- what is the liability of various parties to a negotiable instrument?

- what is a "holder in due course"?

- what are the three defences available to the parties?

- how do these defences differ?

- how are consumer bills and notes treated differently?

HISTORY

In the last section of Chapter 12, we outlined the special nature of negotiable instruments; that section should be reread before proceeding with the present chapter.

Negotiable instruments began as a form of **bill of exchange**, a document made by a merchant or "banker" in one city instructing a colleague elsewhere to make a payment to a certain person or to the bearer of the document. They were probably used by the merchants of ancient Greece and Rome, and the practice was passed on to the medieval Islamic world. Later they came into wide use to meet the needs of merchants in the great age of discovery and trade.

bill of exchange
a written order by one party to another party to pay a specified sum of money to a named party or to the bearer of the document

By means of a bill of exchange a merchant in London, for instance, who had bought goods from a merchant coming from Hamburg, could arrange for the goods to be paid for by a banker in Hamburg, making it unnecessary for the Hamburg merchant to risk carrying coins or bullion back with him. The London merchant would pay a sum to a London firm dealing in bills of exchange, and the firm would draw a bill on its agent in Hamburg instructing him to pay the Hamburg merchant in local currency on a certain date. The Hamburg merchant would accept the bill in exchange for his goods.

With trade taking place in both directions, the credits collecting in Hamburg would be set off by similar credits in London through goods sold by English merchants to others in Hamburg. In place of purely bilateral settlements, money-changing firms and merchants later learned to set off credits on a multilateral basis among several of the great trading cities. At regular intervals, usually at annual fairs held in the trading cities, they would get together and tally the paper they had honoured and pay each other any difference owing. The money-changers were able to charge fees because of the savings to merchants who would not have to transport gold back and forth. Today, this form of setting off credits still exists in a much more sophisticated form through "clearing house" arrangements.

The rules governing negotiable instruments developed as part of the Law Merchant,[1] and as economic activity increased, the ordinary courts also adopted the rules. Eventually, a very large and complex body of case law developed around the subject. The British Parliament codified the rules in the Bills of Exchange Act (1882). In Canada, the subject of negotiable instruments is within federal jurisdiction. Our Bills of Exchange Act[2] follows the English act closely.

FUTURE DEVELOPMENTS

The recent burgeoning use of electronic transfer of funds is discussed in Chapter 34 on electronic commerce. The question naturally arises, "Will electronic banking displace negotiable instruments?" The answer to this question is complex: for certain purposes electronic transactions will certainly do so, particularly for the instantaneous transfer of funds among businesses. We should recall, however, that the encroachment of one method of transfer upon another has been an ongoing process over the centuries: first, negotiable instruments became an important substitute for transporting coins and other valuables; then, transmitting funds by telegraph, cable, and later by telex grew to take over a significant portion of transfers in business-to-business transactions.

Beginning in the 1950s and 1960s, largely in consumer transactions, credit cards began to replace both cash and cheques—particularly for paying bills while travelling; as online systems developed, merchants preferred credit cards because they could be more easily assured that funds were available than if they accepted payment by cheque. In the past decade, direct debit cards have displaced credit cards in an increasing proportion of transactions; more and more consumers prefer to use these cards rather than to carry cash with them.

As more people gain Internet access, we can expect that an increasing proportion of financial transactions will occur on the Internet. However, as we shall see in Chapter 34, many difficult problems have been recognized with electronic transactions. In particular, both domestic and international systems of regulation have barely been developed and there is broad opportunity for unfair practices, especially in consumer transactions. The greater certainty in using negotiable instruments will continue to make them attractive in many transactions. In addition, as we shall see in this chapter, negotiable instruments play an important role in many credit

---

1. *Supra*, Chapter 2, "The Sources of Law."
2. The Bills of Exchange Act, R.S.C. 1985, c. B-4. When a footnote mentions a section only, the reference will be to this Act.

arrangements though the use of drafts, promissory notes, and post-dated cheques. At present there is no equivalent system for use on the Internet.

While the law governing negotiable instrument is rather technical, it functions efficiently and causes few problems. We shall limit our discussion to a broad outline of what the law aims to do and how it accomplishes its purpose.

NATURE AND USES OF NEGOTIABLE INSTRUMENTS

As Personal Property

In Chapter 12 we discussed the rights to intangible property—*choses in action*—and noted that negotiable instruments are a special kind of chose in action. In this chapter we shall consider the distinctive characteristics of negotiable instruments that have made them a significant and useful business tool.

Every negotiable instrument contains an express or implied promise made by one or more parties to pay the amount stated in the instrument. In the absence of evidence to the contrary, the promisee is presumed to have given good consideration for it. Thus, a negotiable instrument is normally a self-contained contract with all the necessary written evidence of its terms stated on its face. As a practical matter, a negotiable instrument is usually a part of a contract in which one side satisfies its promise to pay for goods or services by giving the other side an instrument. Delivery of the instrument is only a **conditional discharge** because if the debtor dishonours it, the promisee's rights remain under the original contract. Promisees generally choose to sue on the negotiable instrument rather than on the original contract because it is simpler to do so.

conditional discharge
the debtor is discharged under the original contract only if the negotiable instrument given in payment is honoured

Types of Instruments

The Bills of Exchange Act governs three common types of negotiable instrument: bills of exchange (or drafts), promissory notes, and cheques. There are other kinds of instruments with the special quality of negotiability, but disputes concerning them are resolved by common law and not by the Bills of Exchange Act. For instance, bearer bonds have been held also to be negotiable instruments.

Following U.S. practice, there is a growing tendency to treat share certificates as negotiable instruments. Jurisdictions using the certificate of incorporation system, explained in Chapter 27, state expressly that a share certificate whose transfer is not restricted by words printed on its face is a negotiable instrument.[3]

We shall confine our discussion to the three common forms of negotiable instruments governed by the Bills of Exchange Act.

Bill of Exchange (Drafts)

A *bill of exchange* (see Figure 21.1) is a written order by one party, the **drawer**, addressed to another party, the **drawee**, to pay a specified sum of money to a named party, the **payee**, or to the bearer, at a fixed or determinable future time or on demand. A bill of exchange originates with a creditor (drawer) that requests its debtor to acknowledge indebtedness and to agree to pay according to the terms stated in the instrument. A drawer sometimes designates itself as a payee; at other times it may direct that some other person or business to whom it owes money shall be the payee instead. The drawer expects the debtor (drawee) to consent by signing the instrument together with the word "accepted" and the date; the drawee then becomes an **acceptor**. A bill of

drawer
the party who draws up the bill of exchange

drawee
the party who is required to make payment on the bill of exchange

payee
the party named to receive payment on the bill of exchange

acceptor
the drawee who consents to the bill of exchange by signing it together with the word "accepted" and the date

---

3. Canada Business Corporations Act, R.S.C. 1985, c. C-44, s. 48(3).

exchange may circulate among a number of holders as an item of valuable personal property even *before* it has been accepted. It has value for a holder because the drawer, by drawing and delivering it, has made an implied promise guaranteeing its payment.[4] Its subsequent acceptance adds the express promise of the acceptor.

An acceptor may indicate that the bill be paid out of its bank account. The drawer (or a subsequent holder) may then leave the instrument with its own bank for collection and have it deposited in its account; that bank will present the bill to the acceptor's bank for payment out of the acceptor's account. After the amount is deducted from the acceptor's account, the cancelled bill of exchange is returned to the acceptor as evidence of payment just as cancelled cheques are returned.

FIGURE 21.1
A Bill of Exchange (Accepted Time Draft)

```
ACCEPTED                        DUE    Nov. 5. 2001              NO. 531
OCT. 4, 2001
  Payable at                    The Sterling Bank
  The Regal Bank                Norwich Branch
  Tower Branch,
  London                        Norwich, Ontario              Oct. 3, 2001
  G. Fawkes                     Thirty days after date _____ pay to the order of
  for G. Fawkes & Co.           the undersigned drawer           $150.00
                                                                          XX
                                One hundred and fifty .................  ---
                                                                         100

                                value received and charged to the account of

                                TO  G. Fawkes & Co.           THE CROWN CO. LTD.

                                    Parliament Street         Per
                                                               Edward Cole
```

There are three types of bill of exchange, depending upon the time at which they are to be paid:

(a) **Demand drafts,** payable immediately upon presentation without the addition of any days of grace. The cheque is the leading example of a demand draft, and we treat it separately below.

(b) **Sight drafts,** which the drawee is ordered to pay "at sight." In Canada, three days of grace for making payment are allowed after presentment for acceptance.

(c) **Time drafts,** payable a stipulated number of days, months, or other period "after date" (after the date stated on the instrument) or "after sight" (after presentment for acceptance). Three days of grace should be added in fixing the maturity of a time draft. A bill payable at a given time after sight is a time draft, not a sight draft.

Presentment for acceptance is necessary whenever a bill is payable at sight or after sight, so that the time at which payment is due may be determined.[5]

Sight drafts can be used as a collection device. Instead of employing a collection agency to recover its slow accounts, a business may draw sight drafts on recalcitrant customers and have

demand draft
a bill of exchange payable immediately upon presentation without any days of grace

sight draft
a bill of exchange payable "at sight"—three days of grace are allowed after presentation

time draft
a bill of exchange payable within a stipulated period after the date stated on the instrument or after presentation

---

4. S. 129.

5. S. 74.

the drafts presented for acceptance and payment through the bank. The drawees will have a new incentive to accept and pay, not wanting to become known to the bank as poor credit risks.

Time drafts can be used as a means of finance for the business drawing them. By discounting them at a bank or by pledging them as security for a bank loan, the drawer can obtain cash in advance of the time when payment is due from the customer. Instead of waiting to be paid until the credit term granted to a customer expires, a business may draw a time draft on the customer immediately following the sale and discount or pledge the draft. As we see in Chapter 30 however, there are other means of achieving this result. For example, a business may borrow from a bank by conditionally assigning its accounts receivable, it may sell its accounts to a factor, or it may assign them to a finance company.

Drafts and bills of lading often complement one another when goods sold on credit are shipped to the buyer by common carrier. Their joint use permits the seller to withhold possession of the goods from the purchaser when they reach their destination until the purchaser accepts a draft drawn on it for the price. The purchaser may examine the goods but cannot obtain possession from the carrier until the seller or its agent transfers the bill of lading to the purchaser.

Promissory Note

promissory note

a written promise to pay a specified sum of money to another party at a fixed or determinable future time or on demand

maker

the party who signs and delivers a promissory note

A **promissory note** (see Figure 21.2) is a written promise by one party, the **maker**, to pay a specified sum of money to another party, the payee, at a fixed or determinable future time or on demand. The maker is usually a debtor of the payee, and takes the initiative in preparing the instrument, though it may do so at the urging of the payee.

Unlike a bill of exchange, a promissory note is not presented for acceptance. From the outset, it contains an express promise to pay. To a subsequent holder, a promissory note that has been endorsed by the payee has the same effect as an accepted bill of exchange. The Bills of Exchange Act applies both to accepted bills and to notes, but the provisions relating to the acceptance of bills of exchange do not apply to promissory notes.

A maker of a note may word it so that it will be payable out of the maker's bank account at maturity; it is then paid through its bank and returned cancelled to the maker.

FIGURE 21.2
A Promissory Note

$250   Fredericton, N.B., April 26, 2001   **after date I promise to pay**

to the order of Wholesale Grocers Limited

the sum of Two hundred and fifty $\frac{xx}{100}$ **DOLLARS**

payable at The Maritime Bank, Fredericton, N.B.

The Corner Group
Per

DUE July 29, 2001   *John Henry*

Cheque

A **cheque** (see Figure 21.3) is a bill of exchange drawn against a bank and payable on demand. From the point of view of the holder, a cheque contains the implied promise of its drawer that the drawer has funds on deposit at the bank sufficient to meet its amount, or that the amount is within the terms of a line of credit granted by the bank. For this reason it is sometimes convenient to think of the drawer of a cheque as a "promisor." The bank on which the cheque is drawn is called the *drawee bank*.

cheque
a bill of exchange drawn against a bank and payable on demand

FIGURE 21.3
A Cheque

SUPERIOR PRODUCTS LIMITED		**No. 80013**
Calgary, Alberta		April 26, 2001

To
THE STERLING BANK
  Lethbridge, Alberta

Pay to the order of   C.B. BOWEN & CO. LTD.   **$** 400.00

FOUR HUNDRED   **DOLLARS**

. . . . .XX/100

SUPERIOR PRODUCTS LIMITED
J. B. Riches
J.B. Walker

Certification

Since a cheque is payable on demand, the payee does not ordinarily present it to a bank for acceptance, but cashes it or deposits it to the credit of its own account. The Bills of Exchange Act does not expressly authorize the acceptance of cheques, nor does it refer specifically to the current banking practice of "certifying" cheques.[6] **Certification** amounts to an undertaking by the bank to pay the amount of the cheque to its holder when later presented for payment and, to ensure this result, the bank forthwith deducts the amount of the cheque from the drawer's account. Certification takes the form of the bank's stamped acknowledgment, with date, on the face of the cheque.

certification
an undertaking by the bank to pay the amount of the cheque to its holder when later presented for payment

Occasionally a supplier will refuse to release goods until paid by certified cheque. The buyer prepares a cheque payable to the supplier, has the drawee bank certify it, and then delivers it to the supplier. Alternatively, a payee may receive the cheque uncertified and before releasing the goods will have the bank certify it; if the payee is returning to another city, such a cheque is safer to hold than cash—a thief would have to forge an endorsement before being able to cash it. In addition, certification *at the request of the holder* also forestalls any attempt by the drawer to stop

---

6. See Falconbridge, *The Law of Negotiable Instruments in Canada*, p. 43. Toronto: The Ryerson Press, 1955.

payment on the cheque: since the payee could have cashed it instead of having it certified, the act of certifying makes the drawee bank liable directly to the payee.[7]

For most practical purposes, certification of a cheque is comparable to the acceptance of other types of bills of exchange.[8] The bank concerned is the drawee to whom the instrument is addressed; once having undertaken certification, it assumes a liability to the holder for the amount of the cheque.

Postdated Cheques

postdate

give a cheque a date later than the time when it is delivered to the payee

The drawer may "**postdate**" a cheque by giving it a date later than the time when it is delivered to the payee. A cheque is an order addressed to a bank, and the bank must follow the instructions given to it on the face of the cheque: the bank is therefore not entitled to pay the instrument before its date. While a cheque is by definition payable "on demand," a holder's right to demand payment is not effective until the date arrives; in the meantime the instrument operates like a time draft, though without the benefit for the drawer of three days of grace. Postdating is a convenience for a drawer who expects to be unavailable at the time a debt is due and who does not wish to pay in advance. It is common for a drawer to give a series of postdated cheques to meet instalment payments.

"Stop Payment"

stop payment

an instruction from the drawer of a cheque to the bank not to pay the cheque

After delivering a cheque, the drawer may learn that the payee is in serious breach of the contract between them. Before the cheque has been charged against its account, the drawer may countermand or "**stop payment**" by instructing its bank not to pay the cheque. The bank may require the drawer to agree that it will not be held responsible if, through its inadvertence, the cheque is paid out of the drawer's account in spite of the countermand.

Even a cheque certified at the request of its drawer and not yet delivered to the payee may be countermanded and the amount returned to the drawer's account at the bank. Since the bank has a liability on the certified cheque, it will reject the countermand unless the cheque is surrendered by the drawer for cancellation or the drawer agrees to indemnify the bank should the bank be sued for refusing to honour the cheque.

The Predominant Use of Cheques

Although payments can be made from current bank accounts by means of sight drafts, time drafts, and promissory notes, cheques have largely superseded them. This development is due to the practice of paying accounts once each month. Suppliers that once relied heavily upon the acceptance of drafts as immediate acknowledgments of indebtedness now depend upon the creditworthiness of their buyers. In any event, they can easily monitor the reliability of their buyers on a monthly basis. A good credit reputation is a prized business resource, and its reputation is quickly lost when a business issues cheques that prove to be "n.s.f." (not sufficient funds). The comparative simplicity of payment by cheque has proved to be justified in all but a few instances. There are still a few trades in which the routine use of sight and time drafts persists by tradition, and in the field of international trade, where the parties are often unknown to one another and have to deal at great distance, drafts retain some advantage. The promissory note, particularly the demand note, survives as the common method by which a borrower provides evidence of its indebtedness for a bank loan.

---

7. When a cheque is certified at the request of the holder, the drawer is entirely discharged by its implied promise that the bank will honour the cheque. See Crawford and Falconbridge, *Banking and Bills of Exchange* (8th ed.), B. Crawford, ed., p. 1791. Toronto: Canada Law Book Inc., 1986.

8. The difference between certification and acceptance is confined to the circumstance where the drawee bank fails, and even then relates only to certification at the request of the holder (rather than of the drawer).

Most people have become accustomed to expect payment, including their wages, by cheque. The old pay envelopes have almost entirely disappeared, and employers now issue paycheques, often deposited directly in employees' personal bank accounts. The risks inherent in handling large amounts of cash on payday are eliminated. Cheques also afford an easy and relatively safe method of making payments by mail.

A cheque, even one certified by a bank, is not legal tender. Strictly speaking, a creditor is entitled to payment in Bank of Canada notes and in coins up to the designated amounts for each denomination. However, to insist upon payment in cash would be inconvenient to both parties, and if a creditor refused a reasonable tender of payment by cheque and sued for payment in cash, court costs would likely be awarded against it.

Checklist: Classes of Negotiable Instruments

There are two classes of negotiable instruments:

1. Those governed by the federal Bills of Exchange Act
   - bills of exchange (or drafts)
   - promissory notes
   - cheques

2. Those governed by other statutes and common law rules in some jurisdictions
   - bearer bonds
   - share certificates

PREREQUISITES FOR LIABILITY

Until an instrument is delivered, the drawer, acceptor, or maker, as the case may be, has no liability, and even after signing it may reconsider and tear it up before delivering it. A drawee has no liability in respect of a bill of exchange before accepting and delivering it.

Delivery may be "actual"—the instrument being issued directly by the promisor to the payee; or it may be "constructive"—simply by notice to the payee that the instrument is complete and ready for delivery.[9] Once an instrument has been delivered, the term "negotiation" describes any subsequent transfer of it by the payee to a new holder as well as any later transfers to other holders.

NEGOTIABILITY

Meaning of Negotiability

Negotiability is the special quality possessed by negotiable instruments as a distinct class of assignable contract. As noted in Chapter 12, their transfer is distinguished from ordinary assignments of contracts by three features:

negotiability
the special quality possessed by negotiable instruments as a distinct class of assignable contract

(a) A negotiable instrument may be transferred (or assigned) from one holder to another without the promisor being advised about each new holder; the promisor becomes liable to each successive holder in turn.

---

9. S. 38.

   (b) An assignee may sometimes acquire a better right to sue on the instrument than its predecessor (assignor) had.

   (c) A holder may sue in its own name any other party liable on the instrument without joining any of the remaining parties.

The above legal qualities give a high degree of transferability to negotiable instruments. As a practical matter, lease of transfer enables negotiable instruments to meet business needs, because on their face they are sufficiently reliable for transferees to accept them without hesitation.

For negotiable instruments to acquire these desirable qualities they must meet the following criteria:

   (a) The promise or order must be set out in writing—otherwise the transferee would hold no evidence of the promise.

   (b) The obligation must be for a money payment only, requiring no further inquiry into its value. Other types of obligation—to render services or transfer ownership of a chattel—would require a prospective assignee to investigate the value of what is being promised.

   (c) The money promised must be a "sum certain." It may be repayable in instalments or with interest and still be a "sum certain."[10] But a promise to pay "the balance owing to you for services rendered" is insufficient because it is not possible from the face of the instrument to quantify the value of the promise.

   (d) The promise or order must be unconditional so that the holder need not look outside the instrument to learn the implications of some qualifying phrase such as, "if the goods are delivered in good condition" or "subject to an allowance for poor material." A contract subject to a condition, though it may be valid between the immediate parties, lacks the certainty needed for a negotiable instrument: any attempt to transfer rights under it would be a mere assignment.

   (e) The negotiable instrument must be payable at a fixed or determinable future time or on demand.[11] The value of a contractual right can be appraised only when it indicates the time at which it is to be performed.

   (f) Negotiation must be of the whole instrument, not for part of the amount.

   (g) The negotiable instrument must be signed by the drawer (or authorized signing officers of a drawer business)[12] if it is a draft or cheque, or by the maker if a promissory note.

Consequences When a Document Is Not Negotiable

Suppose *A* Co. draws a bill on *B* Ltd. payable to *C* Inc. and *B* Ltd. refuses to accept. Does drawing the bill nevertheless serve as notice to *B* Ltd. that it must now pay *C* Inc. instead of *A* Co.?

---

10. Ss. 27 and 186. Problems arise where the instrument provides for payment of a fixed sum plus a variable or "floating" rate of interest, for example, "prime rate plus 2 percent." The Supreme Court of Canada has held that the sum must be capable of being ascertained by numerical calculation from the information contained in the instrument itself: MacLeod Savings & Credit Union Ltd. v. Perrett, [1981] 1 S.C.R. 78. The courts have had difficulty in applying this test with consistency. See also Canadian Imperial Bank of Commerce (CIBC) v. Morgan (1993), A.R. 36.

11. It is hard to justify the uncertainty introduced by the definition of "determinable future time" in s. 23(b), *viz.*, "on or at a fixed period after the occurrence of a specified event which is certain to happen *though the time of happening is uncertain*" (italics added). It seems that a promissory note payable "at my death" would be a valid negotiable instrument. The provision is of little practical importance in business.

12. The signer is personally liable unless he states that he signs in a representative capacity: s. 51. The usual practice for a corporation is for its name to be printed on the instrument and for the officer to sign "per *X*" or "*X*, director." For an interesting case, see Allprint Co. Ltd. v. Erwin (1982), 136 D.L.R. (3d) 587.

The Bills of Exchange Act states that the act of presenting an instrument for acceptance does not of itself amount to notice of an assignment of the stated sum.[13] Accordingly, if *B* Ltd. refuses to accept, it owes nothing to *C* Inc.

Although a document may not amount to a negotiable instrument (where, for example, the order or promise is conditional), it may still be enforceable between the original parties and be capable of assignment as an ordinary contractual right. In these circumstances, the Bills of Exchange Act does not apply and the parties' rights are subject to the general rules governing contractual assignments. Accordingly, a holder of the instrument cannot enforce the promise until the condition is met.

METHODS OF NEGOTIATION

By Endorsement and Delivery

An order instrument is one expressed to be payable "to *A*," "to *A* or order," or "to the order of *A*." To negotiate it, *A* must endorse as well as deliver it to a new holder. Endorsement may take a number of forms, which we shall examine below, but essentially it is the signature (traditionally on the reverse side of the instrument) of the payee.

A party that purchases an order instrument without the proper endorsement on it acquires a very limited legal right, probably confined to recourse against the transferor, and has no rights against any prior parties.[14] In any event, a new holder cannot acquire a better legal right than the transferor had until it has obtained the transferor's endorsement on the instrument. A new holder has a right to require the transferor to make the needed endorsement.[15]

By Delivery Only

Endorsement is not necessary for an instrument in "bearer" form. It is in bearer form when initially it is made payable "to bearer," or "to *A* Co. or bearer," or when no payee has been named and a space is left blank for the insertion of a name. It is also in bearer form when it is payable to an abstraction (for example, "Pay to Petty Cash"). Moreover, an order instrument becomes a bearer instrument when the specified payee endorses it without any qualifying words. Unless and until a subsequent payee endorses it payable to order, it may be negotiated by delivery alone.

An order instrument is safer because any attempt to negotiate it dishonestly amounts to the criminal offence of forgery.[16] The Bills of Exchange Act makes forgery one of the exceptions to the rule that a holder may acquire a better right than the transferor had. Forgery is a defence to the parties liable on an order instrument. By contrast, because a bearer instrument may be negotiated by delivery only, a thief may successfully negotiate it without resorting to forgery. Thus, even if a bearer instrument was lost or stolen at some previous time, its holder can require the party liable to pay, provided he can show that he acquired the instrument without knowledge of the loss or theft.[17]

Businesses rarely prepare negotiable instruments in bearer form although, as we have noted, order instruments may be converted into bearer form by their holders. An employee, for example, may endorse her paycheque before taking it to the bank. If her endorsement is simply her signature, she has converted the cheque into a bearer instrument and it becomes subject to the risks discussed above.

---

13. S. 126.

14. See Crawford and Falconbridge, *supra*, n. 7, p. 1503.

15. S. 60.

16. The Criminal Code, R.S.C. 1985, c. C-46, s. 374.

17. Megrah and Ryder (eds.), *Byles on Bills of Exchange* (26th ed.), pp. 228 and 431. London: Sweet & Maxwell, 1988.

Bank notes were formerly promissory notes in bearer form, but now they simply state that they are legal tender and are freely negotiable by virtue of the Bank of Canada Act.[18]

ENDORSEMENT

Types of Endorsement

Endorsement in Blank

The payee on an order instrument signs his name—and nothing else—by way of endorsement, thus making it payable to bearer.

Special Endorsement

The payee specifies the next person to whom payment is to be made. For example:

Pay to Prometheus

(*signed*) *M. Zeus*

Restrictive Endorsement

By endorsing an instrument "for deposit only", the payee makes it non-negotiable. There is a risk that, if an instrument is stolen from a payee, the thief may forge the payee's endorsement and sell the instrument to a new holder, for example, by cashing it at a bank. When endorsed "for deposit only", an instrument can then only be deposited to the credit of the payee's account at the bank; it is no longer possible for a thief to cash the stolen instrument.

Conditional Endorsement

The payee specifies a party to whom payment is next to be made, provided he has lived up to the terms of a contract between them as, for example, "pay to the order of Bacchus if sober". Such a condition differs from a condition written into the instrument by a drawer, acceptor, or maker because it does not make the original promise in the instrument conditional. The party primarily liable may disregard a conditional endorsement in making payment, but the endorser may recover from the endorsee (Bacchus) if the condition was not satisfied.

Qualified Endorsement

The payee transfers rights in a way that denies liability as an endorser, for example, "Jane Bond, without recourse". Anyone giving value for the instrument is on notice that no remedy is available against Ms. Bond should the party primarily liable default; as we shall see, in the absence of a qualified endorsement, an endorser normally is liable to subsequent endorsees. Manufacturers or wholesalers that "factor" their accounts receivable sometimes use a qualified endorsement. A **factor** may be willing to purchase drafts drawn on customers and endorsed over to it "without recourse"; the factor bears the risk of collection, without recourse to its client (the manufacturer or wholesaler).

factor
a party who purchases drafts drawn on customers at a discount and then collects directly from the customer

Anomalous Endorsement

Suppose a party to a negotiable instrument is not sufficiently creditworthy to persuade a prospective holder to buy it. For instance, a purchaser starting up a new business wishes to pay for goods by draft but the seller is unwilling to accept the purchaser's signature alone. The purchaser then obtains the signature of his sister; as a person with a recognized credit standing she signs the instrument solely to add her liability, as endorser (guarantor), to that of her brother

---

18. Bank of Canada Act, R.S.C. 1985, c. B-2, s. 25.

who is primarily liable. The endorsement is "**anomalous**" or exceptional because it is not added for the purpose of negotiating the instrument; the endorser was not a holder in her own right.

Bills, frequently endorsed in this manner, are called "**accommodation bills.**" The acceptor or endorser usually signs to accommodate the drawer, that is, to make it easier for the drawer to obtain credit on the bill. An anomalous endorser contributes to negotiability because of her good credit standing.

Purposes of Endorsement

An endorsement may be the means of

    (a) transferring title to an instrument payable to order

    (b) giving increased security to the payee (or subsequent holder)

    (c) identifying the party entitled to payment

    (d) acknowledging a partial payment

We examined the first of these purposes above when we looked at the methods of negotiation and the types of endorsement. Most endorsements serve simply as the method of transferring ownership in the instrument.

We have also seen that an anomalous endorsement can make a negotiable instrument more marketable because the endorsement makes the endorser liable if the party with primary liability defaults. This is so though the endorser has never owned the instrument and has not negotiated it to someone else.[19] An anomalous endorsement is a means of guaranteeing a debt, with the endorser in the role of guarantor.[20]

A holder of a negotiable instrument has no claim against the drawer if an intermediate holder has forged a signature. When a bank has cashed a cheque containing an endorsement forged by the person cashing it, the bank becomes a holder with no right to claim the amount from the drawee customer's account. To protect itself, a bank may occasionally require an endorsement from someone known to it for the purpose of identifying the person seeking to cash a cheque. For instance, it may require an endorsement in the following form:

T. Smith is hereby identified

(signed) *R. Jones*

As endorser, Jones is not liable for payment as are other endorsers should the party primarily liable default. Her liability is limited to the loss that would follow from having identified someone as T. Smith who later proved not to be that person.

If the maker of a note is to pay her debt by instalments, it is up to her to see that every time she makes a partial payment she obtains an endorsement on the instrument by its holder for the amount paid. Otherwise she remains liable for the full face amount of the instrument if it is subsequently negotiated to a holder who is unaware of the partial payments. An example of this type of endorsement is

May 12, 2000

Received in part payment, $175.00

(signed) *B. Brown*

---

19. S. 130. The endorser is liable to the payee even though the payee has not himself endorsed. *Robinson v. Mann* (1901), 31 S.C.R. 484. Also, *Byles on Bills of Exchange, supra,* n. 17, p. 204.

20. The same effect may be had without endorsement if both the guarantor and debtor sign in the first instance as joint makers of a promissory note.

As an alternative arrangement, the debtor may make a series of separate notes bearing the dates of the various instalments and require the surrender of the related note each time she pays an instalment.

LIABILITY OF PARTIES

An Endorser

dishonour

the failure by the party primarily liable to pay the instrument according to its terms

"**Dishonour**" is the failure by the party primarily liable to pay the instrument according to its terms. If the instrument is a draft, dishonour may take the form of either the drawee's refusal to accept or, if he accepts, of his later refusal to pay.[21] We have noted that an endorser is liable to any holder for the amount of the instrument should the party primarily liable dishonour it, but this statement needs to be qualified. If an endorser does not receive prompt notice of the dishonour from the holder, the endorser will be freed from liability.

In the rare event that an order instrument is negotiated several times, a particular endorser's liability extends to any *subsequent* endorser as well as the current holder; he has no liability to *prior* endorsers—indeed, they are liable to him. The holder has a choice of endorsers to require payment from when the instrument is dishonoured, provided each of them has received the necessary notice of dishonour.[22] In turn, an endorser who is held liable has recourse against any prior endorser but not against any subsequent one.[23] Assuming he cannot recover from the party primarily liable, the ultimate loser will be the first endorser (or the drawer if the instrument is a draft).

When an instrument contains a forged endorsement, the drawer and any endorser prior to the forgery are freed of liability. The only holder who can recover from an endorser in these circumstances is one who has satisfied the conditions for qualifying as a "holder in due course," as explained later. When such a holder suffers a loss arising from a forged endorsement or the forged signature of the drawer, unless the forger can be caught and made to pay, the loss will ultimately be borne by the person who acquires the instrument immediately following the forgery.[24]

ILLUSTRATION 21.1

A knew that *C* maintained an account at the *B* Bank. *A* drew a cheque on the *B* Bank payable to herself, forging *C*'s signature as drawer. *A* then endorsed the cheque with her own signature and cashed it at a hotel operated by *D*. *D* endorsed the cheque and deposited it in the hotel account at the *X* Bank. The *X* Bank presented the cheque for payment to the *B* Bank through the bank clearing system. The *B* Bank recognized the forgery and refused to pay the cheque out of *C*'s account. The cheque was then returned to the *X* Bank.

The *X* Bank is entitled to recover the amount that it had previously credited to *D*'s account in respect of the cheque. The *X* bank is the holder (in fact, a holder in due course) and *D*, as the endorser immediately after the forgery, is liable.[25] In this illustration there is no other endorser between *D* and *A*, the perpetrator of the fraud. The loss must fall upon *D* unless *A* can be apprehended and the funds recovered from her.

---

21. S. 132(a).

22. Alternatively, the holder may sue all the endorsers as co-defendants in a single action and leave them to work out their individual liability among themselves.

23. S. 100. Each endorser has, after receiving notice of dishonour, the same period for giving notice to earlier endorsers that the holder had after dishonour.

24. S. 132(b).

25. S. 49(1) and (2).

An endorser also warrants to any later party that he had a good title to the instrument.[26]

Finally, unless a holder "duly presents" the instrument for payment endorsers will not have any liability to him. Accordingly, an instrument payable on demand must be presented for payment within a reasonable time after its endorsement, and an instrument that is not payable on demand must be presented on the day it falls due.[27]

A Drawer

The drawer of a draft undertakes that on due presentment the draft will be accepted and paid according to its terms, and that if it is dishonoured the drawer will compensate the holder or any endorser who is compelled to pay it.[28] The drawer of a cheque undertakes that the cheque will be paid from his account on demand: if there are insufficient funds in his account, he is liable to the holder or to any endorser from whom the holder may recover. Because the parties to a cheque do not ordinarily contemplate a formal acceptance of it by the drawee bank, the drawer of the cheque becomes for practical purposes "the party primarily liable" comparable to the acceptor of a draft or the maker of a note.

A bank follows instructions from its customer in disposing of the funds on deposit with it. Its authority to pay a cheque ends when its customer stops payment or when it receives notice of the customer's death.[29] While a holder cannot then hold the bank liable, his rights against the drawer remain unaffected by the countermand. By stopping payment a drawer dishonours the instrument and may be sued by the holder. The death of the drawer makes the amount of the cheque a charge against the drawer's estate, and it becomes one of the debts the personal representative (executor or administrator) must settle.

Notice of Dishonour

We have noted that neither an endorser nor a drawer will be liable in the absence of prompt, express notice of dishonour from the holder[30]—it is not enough for the holder to show that the endorser or drawer heard about the dishonour from some other source.[31] Notice must be given not later than the business day next following the dishonour.[32] If notice is mailed, the time limit applies to the time of depositing it in the post office and not to the time it is received.[33]

No special form of notice is required as long as it conveys the essential message. In two instances, however, a special form of notice of dishonour known as *protest* is prescribed. Protest is required if the instrument is drawn or payable or accepted in Québec[34] or outside Canada.[35] The services of a notary public, or justice of the peace where no notary public is available, are required to confirm the dishonour, prepare a notice of the protest in prescribed form[36] and deliver it to the endorsers and drawer within the same time as for a notice of dishonour generally.[37] The holder is responsible for contacting a notary public and is entitled to be reimbursed

---

26. S. 132(c).

27. S. 85.

28. S. 129.

29. S. 167.

30. S. 105(1)(b).

31. S. 98. See also Crawford and Falconbridge, *supra*, n. 7, p. 1576.

32. S. 96. Under some circumstances, a delay in giving notice may be excused (s. 104).

33. S. 102(2).

34. S. 113.

35. S. 111.

36. The prescribed forms are set out at the end of the Act.

37. S. 125.

the notary's fee by the endorser or drawer to whom the notice of protest is delivered.[38] An endorser may waive the right to any notice of dishonour, and avoid the expense of the fee, by including the words, "No Protest," in his endorsement.[39]

A Transferor by Delivery

The term "transferor by delivery" describes anyone who negotiates an instrument in bearer form. Since no endorsement is required, a transferor by delivery is not liable on the instrument *as an endorser* if the party primarily liable simply proves financially incapable of paying it.[40] However, he may be liable to the one person to whom he has negotiated the instrument, his *immediate transferee*, but only for such loss as that transferee would sustain if the instrument were not genuine, that is, if the instrument is not what the transferor purported it to be or he was aware that it was valueless or if he had no right to transfer it.[41]

An Acceptor or Maker

By accepting a bill, a drawee undertakes to pay it according to the terms of his acceptance.[42] Similarly, the maker of a promissory note undertakes to pay it according to its terms.[43] On the death of either the maker or acceptor, his liability passes to his personal representative.

Statute of Limitations

We have seen that the holder of a negotiable instrument must duly present the instrument for payment and, when necessary, give the required notice of dishonour in order to establish his legal rights against all prior parties to the instrument. He must then also prosecute his legal rights, by court action if necessary, within six years (five in Québec) because thereafter an action on a negotiable instrument is barred by the Statute of Limitations.[44] The period of six or five years dates from the maturity of the instrument, the time of the most recent payment made in respect of it, or the date of any written acknowledgment from which a promise to pay may be implied, whichever date is the latest. The lapse of this period of time does not, however, extinguish the liability of the parties completely. Chapter 30 contains a discussion of how such a liability may be revived.

HOLDER IN DUE COURSE

Negotiation Compared with Assignment of a Chose in Action

In Chapter 8 we learned that an innocent purchaser of goods can often retain them even when the transferor, who had obtained them fraudulently, would have had to surrender them to the original vendor. We have also noted that an innocent transferee of a negotiable instrument may

---

38. S. 123.

39. S. 105(1)(b).

40. S. 136(2).

41. S. 137.

42. S. 127.

43. S. 185. If the party seeking payment is a "holder in due course" as defined below, the maker of a note cannot refuse to pay on the grounds that the payee whom he has named in his note either does not exist or lacks capacity to endorse.

44. See, for example: Limitation Act, R.S.B.C. 1996, c. 266, ss. 3 and 4; Limitations Act, R.S.O. 1990, c. L.15, s. 45(1)(g); Limitation of Actions Act, R.S.N.S. 1989, c. 258, s. 2(1)(e).

be able to enforce payment when the transferor himself could not do so. Thus a transfer of a negotiable instrument more closely resembles a transfer of title to goods than an assignment of a chose in action—negotiation is an exception to the general principle governing assignment of choses in action that an assignee takes no greater rights than the assignor had. Accordingly, a negotiable instrument may become *more* valuable when it is transferred. The greater rights available to innocent third-party holders of negotiable instruments encourage reliance on these instruments and make them useful tools of commerce.

Requirements to Become a Holder in Due Course

For the holder of a negotiable instrument to acquire something more than the transferor himself had, the holder must satisfy four conditions.[45]

(a) The holder must have taken the instrument complete and regular on its face.

(b) She must have acquired it before it was overdue and without notice of any prior dishonour.

(c) She, or someone through whom she claims, must have given consideration ("value") for the instrument.[46]

(d) She must have taken the instrument in good faith and without notice of any defect in the title of the person who negotiated it.

A holder who satisfies these conditions becomes a *holder in due course*.[47] Business experience has shown that the concept of negotiability has a convenience far outweighing the cost of its occasional abuse. In any event, the possibility of abuse is greatly reduced by confining the legal advantage to a holder in due course.

Purpose of the Requirements

Notice

The rule that a person cannot be a holder in due course if she has taken the instrument with knowledge of its previous dishonour, or in bad faith, or with notice of a defect of title in the transferor, has one purpose: to deprive a holder of any advantage in conspiring with a transferee to take the instrument from him with a view to outflanking the defences of the party liable. Such a transferee does not qualify as a holder in due course and can be defeated by any of the defences that the party liable might have used against the transferor: the transferee can gain nothing by the maneuver.

When the instrument is a time draft or note, a prospective holder of it can tell at a glance whether it is overdue or not. If it is already due, an obvious question to ask is why the present holder is trying to negotiate it instead of presenting it for payment. A prospective holder will have more difficulty deciding whether a demand draft is overdue. If it has been outstanding for an "unreasonable" length of time (which varies with the circumstances), it is deemed to be overdue,[48] and a new holder does not then become a holder in due course.

An outstanding demand note may have a different significance from a demand draft. A demand note is sometimes given as evidence of long-term indebtedness and may remain outstanding a long time without necessarily raising doubts about its collectability. Consequently,

---

45. S. 55.

46. S. 56 requires that she shall have taken the instrument "for value" but s. 53 states that where value has been given at any time for a bill, the holder is deemed to be a holder for value.

47. A subsequent holder will succeed to the rights of a holder in due course whether or not he himself satisfies all the essential conditions, unless he was a party to fraud or illegality affecting the instrument: s. 56.

48. S. 69(2).

the criterion of an unreasonable length of time used in other areas of the law may be unsuitable in determining whether a demand note is overdue.[49]

Advantages

An important benefit of the concept of a holder in due course is that banks are willing to discount drafts and cash cheques drawn on other banks with relatively little delay and at much reduced risk to themselves, since they acquire the instruments in the capacity of a holder in due course. If the law did not recognize the concept, banks would be reluctant to purchase negotiable instruments and hold them as assets; they would first have to make exhaustive inquiries to be sure that valuable consideration was given for an instrument and that it was free of fraud, illegality, duress, or undue influence. Banks would not risk acquiring instruments that might be subject to such defences when the time came to collect from the party primarily liable.[50]

DEFENCES

Meaning of Defence

The term "defences" is a legal description for the various arguments that a party liable on an instrument may put up against a holder who demands payment. In determining whether a defence will succeed, there are two aspects to consider: (a) the status of the holder relative to the party liable; and (b) the type of defence of the party liable. We shall examine these aspects in the context of a legal action in which the plaintiff is the holder of the instrument and the defendant an acceptor, maker, drawer, or endorser.

immediate parties
the holder of an instrument and the party alleged to be liable on it who have had direct dealings with each other

remote parties
parties to an instrument who have not had direct dealings with one another

Types of Holders

We must first examine the relationship between the holder and the party alleged to be liable on the instrument. When a holder has had direct dealings with that party, the two of them are **immediate parties**. If they have not had direct dealings with one another and yet are parties to the same instrument, they are **remote parties**. Since a holder in due course must acquire the instrument by negotiation from the payee or from a subsequent endorser, he is *always* a party remote from the acceptor of a draft, maker of a note, or drawer of a cheque.

ILLUSTRATION 21.2

A draws a cheque in favour of *B*. *B* endorses it to the order of *C*. *C* endorses it to the order of *D*. *D* is the present holder of the cheque.

A and B, B and C, and C and D are immediate parties. The remote parties are *A* and *C*, *A* and *D*, and *B* and *D*. Whether the present holder, *D*, is a holder in due course will depend upon whether he satisfies the four essential conditions.

---

49. S. 182. See also Crawford and Falconbridge, *supra*, n. 7, pp. 1510–1.

50. As an additional protection, a bank will require the endorsement of the person from whom it acquires the instrument; but recourse against endorsers is at best a second resort, which banks naturally wish to avoid.

Types of Defences

A holder's chance of success in collecting from an immediate party is no better than his contractual rights under the agreement between them. The negotiable instrument does not increase the holder's rights. Against an immediate party, the party liable can use a line of *mere personal defences*, usually not available against remote parties.

By contrast, a remote party who is a holder in due course has the best chance of success in collecting payment. The party liable has a greatly reduced list of possible defences, termed *real defences*, with which to resist the demands of a holder in due course.

If a remote party fails to meet the standards of a holder in due course, his position lies *between* an immediate party and a holder in due course: he is subject not only to real defences but also to *defect of title* defences. He is not, however, subject to mere personal defences. We shall discuss all three of these classes of defences.

Mere Personal Defences

All the defences—real, defect of title, and mere personal—are available to the defendant when the contestants are immediate parties, but the mere personal defences, apart from the exception noted in the next paragraph, are available *only* when they are immediate parties. Defences good only against an immediate party are (a) lack of consideration and (b) the right of set-off.

Lack of Consideration

When a promisor makes a gift of a negotiable instrument it is, of course, a gratuitous promise not yet performed. As with such promises generally, the promisor may plead lack of consideration and refuse to perform.[51] She may use the defence of lack of consideration where she gave the instrument to pay the price stated in the contract, and the underlying contract proves void or voidable for reasons of mistake, provisions in a statute or public policy.[52] The Bills of Exchange Act makes it clear that a prior debt or liability constitutes valuable consideration for the instrument.[53]

Right of Set-off

Suppose a buyer of goods pays for them with a negotiable instrument. If the goods are deficient in quality or quantity, the defences available to her against enforcement of the instrument will depend on whether the supplier has transferred the negotiable instrument.

ILLUSTRATION 21.3

May Dental Supplies Ltd. sells $500 worth of supplies to Dr. Nichols and receives a cheque in payment. Shortly afterwards, Dr. Nichols discovers that the shipment is short of several items, worth in total $225, so that the dental supply company is in default.

Dr. Nichols then tells the supplier that she has stopped payment of the cheque at her bank. The supplier sues her on the instrument. Dr. Nichols can use the defence of set-off and the supplier can recover only

continued

---

51. While it is unlikely that a negotiable instrument would change hands more than once without consideration being given at some stage, if no party has given "value" for it, the party liable can continue to plead a lack of consideration, even when the plaintiff is a remote party. To enforce payment against the maker of a gratuitous instrument, the holder *or someone through whom he claims* (that is, a prior party) must have given value for the instrument.

52. Lack of consideration is a reason for refusing to honour a negotiable instrument. It is a different matter if the promisor has already honoured the instrument and then seeks to recover its amount in a separate action. Thus, if a person makes a gift of money by cheque, he cannot recover the amount by court action unless he can offer additional reasons such as duress or undue influence.

53. S. 53. See also English Law Revision Committee, *Sixth Annual Report*, pp. 17–8.

$275 by court action. Here the parties are immediate parties.

Suppose instead that the supplier has already deposited Dr. Nichols' cheque and it has been charged against Dr. Nichols' account at her bank. The defence of set-off is lost to Dr. Nichols. The bank where Dr. Nichols keeps her account, having paid the supplier's bank, is entitled to keep the full $500 it has taken from her account. The dentist and her own bank are remote parties in respect of the transaction. By her act of drawing and delivering her cheque, the dentist has "cast her instrument upon the world" and has become accountable to any subsequent holder for its full amount if the payee has succeeded in negotiating it for value to a third party.[54] Dr. Nichols' only recourse is to claim a refund from the supplier.

The defence of set-off illustrates the difference between the effect of an ordinary assignment of a debt and the negotiation of a negotiable instrument. In the law of negotiable instruments, the defence is good between immediate parties but is lost when the party seeking to enforce the instrument is a remote party to the defendant. In an ordinary assignment, the defence of set-off remains available against an assignee.

Defect of Title Defences

We have seen that a holder in due course must have taken the instrument without knowledge of any defect in title and, when he has done so, defences based on such defects will fail. Generally speaking, when an instrument is regular on its face, there is no defence against a holder in due course.[55] But if a holder takes the instrument *with* knowledge of one or more defects, or when there is an irregularity on the face of the instrument, he is *not* a holder in due course and a defence based on a defect will be successful.[56] Such defects are:

(a) incapacity to contract as a result of drunkenness or insanity[57]

(b) discharge of the instrument by payment, or renunciation of a holder's rights in it

(c) absence of delivery when the instrument was complete at the time

(d) fraud, duress, undue influence, illegality

(e) want of authority in an agent to complete the instrument on behalf of the party primarily liable

Incapacity as a Result of Drunkenness or Insanity

We are already familiar with this type of defence as it applies to contracts generally, as discussed in Chapter 7. The defence is confined to drunkenness and insanity. Only if the subsequent holder was aware of the incapacity at the time the instrument was negotiated to him will the defence be effective. This type of incapacity must be distinguished from the incapacity of a minor as discussed (on page 458) under "Real Defences."

---

54. In practice, the bank where May Dental Supplies Ltd. deposited the cheque would not sue Dr. Nichols if it found she had countermanded the cheque at her own bank. It is much easier for this bank to charge the amount back to May Dental Supplies Ltd., as it is entitled to do on the strength of the dental supply company's endorsement at the time of deposit.

55. These observations restate conditions (b) and (d), under the heading "Requirements to Become a Holder in Due Course," *supra*.

56. Ss. 55 and 57(2).

57. Depending upon the circumstances, insanity might instead be interpreted as a real defence. See Falconbridge and Crawford, *supra*, n. 7, pp. 1348–51.

Discharge or Renunciation

Suppose a party pays the amount due on an instrument on or after its maturity but does not require it to be returned to her. Although it is fully discharged,[58] if the payee transfers it to an innocent holder—and it remains regular on its face and does not appear to be overdue (as with a draft or time note) or to have been outstanding for an unreasonable length of time (as with a cheque)—the holder in due course can still enforce the instrument. However, if the holder takes the instrument with the knowledge that it has already been paid, he is *not* a holder in due course and cannot enforce it.

We can see that if a party paying an instrument fails to cancel it, she takes the risk that it will find its way into the hands of a holder in due course and she will be liable to pay it again. The usual way to cancel an instrument is by writing or stamping the word "paid" (with the date) across its face.

A holder, by renouncing his right to payment, discharges the instrument.[59] For instance, suppose *A* says to *B*, "I shouldn't have charged you so much for that job. I am cancelling the balance of your debt and you don't have to honour the last cheque you gave me." As with a discharged instrument, any remote party who takes the instrument with notice of the renunciation cannot enforce it, but an innocent holder can.

Absence of Delivery

We have noted that delivery is a necessary step in establishing the liability of the party primarily liable. Suppose the treasurer of a business expects to be on a business trip when goods are to be delivered and paid for. She signs a completed negotiable instrument before leaving and delivers it to the supplier subject to the condition that it must not be used in any way until the supplier delivers the goods. The defence of "absence of delivery" includes such circumstances where there is physical delivery to a payee, but subject to a condition that must be satisfied.[60] If the condition is not satisfied, neither the payee nor any subsequent holder who acquires the instrument with knowledge of the defect can enforce payment. However, one who acquires it without notice of the defect may be able to enforce payment.

Fraud, Duress, Undue Influence, Illegality

These defences were discussed in detail as they relate to the law of contracts in Chapters 7 to 9. When a party has signed a negotiable instrument, for example, after being defrauded he will have a good defence against a holder who takes the instrument with knowledge of the circumstances.

ILLUSTRATION 21.4

Conn offered to sell Mark a shipment of pure silk men's ties for $2000. After examining several samples Mark agreed and drew a cheque in favour of Conn for $2000 in full payment. In fact, virtually all the ties were made of polyester and were worth only a fraction of the price. Conn had deliberately defrauded Mark. Brad, a friend of Conn, was present during the sale and was aware of Conn's deceitfulness. He paid Conn $1500 in cash in return for the endorsed cheque. However, before Brad was able to take it to the bank, Mark, on advice from the police, directed his bank to refuse payment.

Although Brad is a remote party he is not a holder in due course because he took the instrument with notice of the defect (Conn's fraud). Mark, therefore, has a good defence against the holder, Brad.

---

58. S. 138.

59. Ss. 141(2) and (3); 142(2) and 145(1).

60. S. 39(1)(b).

Want of Authority to Complete a Signed Instrument

Want of authority may arise when a party has signed an instrument but has left some of the details blank, and then delivers it with instructions for completing it. No problem arises if the person in possession completes it in strict compliance with instructions; the instrument then has the same effect as though the party liable had completed it. As in agency law, the defence of want of authority will fail with respect to both an immediate transferee and any subsequent holder if the agent had apparent authority to sign on behalf of the principal.[61]

Any abuse of authority, however, creates a defect of title, and the party liable may refuse payment to the party guilty of the abuse and to any holder who takes the instrument with notice of the defect. Since, however, a holder in due course can enforce the instrument in the form in which it was completed,[62] it is risky to leave it to someone else to fill in the details.

Real Defences

Categories

The following defences are good against any holder, even a holder in due course:

    (a) incapacity to contract because of infancy

    (b) cancellation of the instrument

    (c) absence of delivery where the instrument is incomplete when taken

    (d) fraud as to the nature of the instrument when the promisor is blind or illiterate

    (e) a forged signature on the instrument

    (f) want of authority, in someone who has represented himself as an agent, to sign on behalf of the party liable

    (g) alteration of the instrument

Incapacity Because of Infancy

The incapacity to contract of a person under age is a real defence even when the instrument is given in payment for necessaries. A minor cannot be sued successfully on his negotiable instrument. A supplier may sue the minor for a reasonable price of necessary goods, but this remedy has to be distinguished from an action on the instrument itself. While no holder will have any recourse against a minor who is a prior party on the instrument, the holder's recourse against other parties is not affected.[63]

Cancellation

When cancellation is apparent on the instrument itself, the party liable has a good defence against everyone.[64] If a cancellation made before maturity is not apparent, an artful and dishonest holder may negotiate the instrument for value. The party liable may then find that he must honour his instrument a second time—in favour of a holder in due course.

Absence of Delivery of an Incomplete Instrument

We have noted that absence of delivery when an instrument is complete at the time is a mere defect of title defence and of no avail against a holder in due course. So too is a mere abuse of authority by an agent of the signer when the instrument has been delivered to him only for the

---

61. See explanation of the creation of an agency by estoppel in Chapter 19.

62. S. 31.

63. See Crawford and Falconbridge, *supra*, n. 7, pp. 1344–5. But see Soon v. Watson (1962), 33 D.L.R. (2d) 429, where an infant was held liable on a note. No authority is cited in the judgment and the law remains uncertain.

64. S. 142.

purpose of completing it and transferring the property in it to someone else.[65] However, if an instrument is *both incomplete and undelivered* when it is intercepted by the wrongdoer, the signer will have a real defence, good against all holders. "Absence of delivery" requires *both* (a) prior abuse of signing authority or abuse of an incomplete document supplied by the signer for a special purpose only *and* (b) failure to satisfy a condition to which the delivery of the instrument was subject—for example, a failure to supply specified goods.

ILLUSTRATION 21.5

X told Y, his employer, that the bank had asked him to procure a new specimen of his employer's signature for its files. X persuaded Y to give him Y's signature on a blank piece of paper. X then completed the paper in the form of a demand note payable to the order of himself with Y's signature in the space for the maker of the note. X told an acquaintance, Z, that Y was away on a trip and that he needed money at once for a family emergency. Z discounted the note for X and shortly afterwards presented it for payment to Y, who refused to pay it.

First, Y gave no authority to X to convert the paper into a complete negotiable instrument; the "instrument" was incomplete at the time, consisting of nothing but a signature on a piece of paper. Second, there was an absence of delivery; the "note" was not delivered to Z by X as an authorized agent of Y. Y had given the specimen signature to X for the special purpose of supplying it to the bank. As a result, and despite his carelessness, Y has a real defence, good against any holder, even a holder in due course such as Z. Z's only recourse is to sue X (if he can be apprehended and has sufficient assets to satisfy a court judgment). In addition to his fraud, X would be liable to Z on the strength of his endorsement.

CONTEMPORARY ISSUE

Debit Card Fraud

In December 1999, Canadians were shocked to learn that according to an RCMP technological expert, the entire debit-card system had been compromised by new methods of electronically stealing the encrypted data in the cards, loading them onto phony cards, and emptying unsuspecting cardholders' bank accounts. Within a day of the initial reports, the RCMP and the banking industry were hastening to reassure consumers that electronic banking was still safe—but not everybody was convinced.

Canadians are the world's heaviest users of ABM (automated bank machine) transactions, averaging 52.7 transactions per resident in 1997. Canada has the largest number of debit-card terminals per capita and is second in the number of annual transactions. There are about 34 million debit cards in circulation for an adult population of 22 million. In 1998, Canadians used debit cards 1.3 billion times; 320 000 merchants offered the Interac direct payment system. According to Interac, 57 percent of cardholders use debit or credit cards as their preferred method of payment, contrasted with 39 percent preferring cash and 3 percent preferring cheques. This preference for electronic banking and payment methods gives security of card transactions great importance while arguably reducing the significance of cheque forging.

Debit (and credit) card data can be stolen in a number of ways. Credit card numbers can be copied from a transaction slip or from the card itself. Card numbers can also be acquired

continued

65. S. 39(1)(b).

over the telephone and the Internet. Debit and credit cards can be double-swiped by a dishonest sales clerk: once in the legitimate machine and once in a second machine that reads the information in the magnetic strip and stores it in a computer. The data can then be uploaded onto any card with a magnetic strip. PIN numbers can be recorded by a hidden camera or by someone watching over the customer's shoulder.

The dire warnings in December 1999 resulted from a raid in which the police seized two examples of a new type of device: a debit-card machine with an extra set of wires leading to a computer chip concealed in a power bar. This gadget is capable of recording the PIN number as the customer punches it in. Initial reports stated that only one swipe of the card was needed and that the card never had to leave the customer's hand; later, police said that the card had to be clandestinely swiped a second time. With the PIN number and a fake card bearing the magnetic data, the thieves could raid the customer's bank account—then load new data onto the card and raid another account. While bank customers are protected against losses resulting from fraud, getting reimbursement can involve a great deal of time and trouble.

It is not clear whether these machines were actually used; they were found in a home, not in a business. However, the episode focused new attention on the security of electronic transactions.

Sources: See Interac, "1999 Annual Tracking—Consumer Research," Webposted at <www.interac.org> Robert Cribb, "We're a Nation of Button Pushers," *Toronto Star*, September 3, 1999; Timothy Appleby, "Chilling Debit-Card Scam Uncovered," *Globe and Mail*, December 10, 1999; Robert Carrick, "Police, Bankers Rush to Reassure Card Holders," *Globe and Mail*, December 11, 1999; Stewart Bell, "Despite PIN Scam, Debit Card System Safe, Police Say," *National Post*, December 11, 1999; Rob Carrick, "More Straight Talk Needed From Banks," *Globe and Mail*, December 14, 1999.

Questions to Consider

1. How risky do you think debit cards really are for customers and for merchants compared with the risks associated with cash, cheques, and credit cards?

2. What precautions can or should merchants take to prevent their employees from participating in debit-card scams?

3. Who should bear the losses of debit card fraud? How easy or difficult should it be for bank customers who have lost money to fraud to get reimbursement?

Fraud

As noted in the preceding section, fraud is usually a defect of title defence, giving the victim no protection against a holder in due course. Even when the instrument itself was misrepresented to him and he was not found to be negligent, the promisor is very likely to be held liable *except* in one instance: if he is a blind or illiterate person[66] he may successfully plead the real defence of *non est factum*, as discussed in Chapter 8.

Forged Signature

Liability for a Forged Signature

A forged signature may be that of either the party primarily liable or of an endorser. Either type of forgery is a real defence for persons who have assumed liability on the instrument *prior* to the forgery. Apart from situations of estoppel, as discussed below, the real defence of forgery pro-

---

66. And perhaps persons unable to read the majority language (English or French) in their region of Canada.

vides the alleged drawer of a cheque with grounds for refusing to honour the instrument attributed to him. Since the funds out of which his cheque is to be paid are on deposit at the bank named as drawee on the cheque, the bank is necessarily involved as a result of the forgery.

Insofar as the *drawer's* signature is concerned, a bank is supposed to know the signatures of all its customers[67] and for this purpose keeps their specimen signatures on file. It has an obligation to detect a forgery of the drawer's signature and to restore any amount it mistakenly pays out of the drawer's account.

In Canada, a bank's liability extends also to the payment of instruments bearing forged *endorsements*.[68] To understand a bank's liability in this respect we must distinguish between a presenting bank and a drawee bank. A **presenting bank** is any bank where a payee or a subsequent endorsee presents a cheque to receive payment; a **drawee bank** is the bank where the drawer keeps his account. With a forged endorsement, the presenting bank and not the drawee bank has the primary obligation to detect the forgery. For this reason a presenting bank takes special precautions when asked to cash a cheque for a person who has no account there or who is not otherwise known to it.

presenting bank
a bank where a payee or a subsequent endorsee presents a cheque to receive payment

drawee bank
a bank where the drawer keeps his account

ILLUSTRATION 21.6

(a) A drew a cheque on the Merchants Bank payable to the order of B and delivered the cheque to B. X stole the cheque from B, presented it for payment at a branch of the Crown Bank and forged B's signature.

The Crown Bank would refuse to cash the instrument for X unless X could produce identification papers purporting to show that he is the payee, B. If the Crown Bank were persuaded to cash the cheque for X, the loss would fall upon it and would probably come to light along the following lines: the Crown Bank would stamp its name and the date on the cheque and clear it to the Merchants Bank branch against which it is drawn; the Merchants Bank would charge the amount against A's account there; B, discovering the loss of the cheque, would ask A for a duplicate; A would then ascertain that the cheque charged against his account bore the forged

endorsement of B; A (because of his real defence) would require the Merchants Bank to restore the amount to his account; the Merchants Bank would recover the amount from the Crown Bank because the Crown Bank's stamp on the cheque acts as its implied guarantee of the authenticity of prior endorsements, such as X's forgery of B's signature.

(b) The circumstances are the same as in (a) except that, instead of taking the cheque to the Crown Bank, X persuaded a pharmacist, C, to cash it for him. C then deposited the cheque in his account at the Crown Bank after endorsing it as required by the bank.

The Crown Bank, when all the facts are ascertained, may recover the amount from C on the strength of his liability as endorser.[69] It would normally recover the amount by charging it against C's account.

Limits to the Defence of Forgery

A bank's liability for cheques bearing a forged endorsement does not extend to cheques where the payee is "fictitious or non-existing." As noted previously under "Methods of Negotiation," such a cheque is treated as being payable to bearer[70] and the bank as bearer would become entitled to enforce it against the drawer.

---

67. Bank of Montreal v. The King (1908), 38 S.C.R. 258; Canadian Imperial Bank of Commerce v. Bank of Credit & Commerce Canada, [1989] 4 W.W.R. 366.

68. S. 48(1) and (3).

69. Banks normally require their customers to endorse the cheques they present for cash or deposit, even if the cheques are in bearer form. However, even if C had not endorsed, he would, as a transferor by delivery, have warranted to the Crown Bank (his immediate transferee) that he had a right to transfer the cheque; he would not have this authority because of X's forgery.

70. S. 20(5).

CASE 21.1

In *Royal Bank v. Concrete Column Clamps,*[71] a dishonest payroll clerk of the drawer company fraudulently secured the signature of a company officer on a number of pay-cheques, some payable to former employees and some to fictitious persons. He subsequently forged endorsements and cashed all the cheques. The Supreme Court of Canada held that the bank could be held liable only for those fraudulent cheques made payable to former employees (existing persons) and that the drawer company would have to bear the loss for the remaining cheques made payable to fictitious persons.[72]

Where the drawer of a cheque has a right to recover funds deducted from her account because the endorsement was forged, she must advise the bank of the forgery, within a reasonable time, not to exceed one year from the time she learns of it.[73] The Act does not specify a similar time limit for notice when the signature of the drawer herself has been forged, but she has a duty to inform any holder or prospective holder of the facts as soon as she learns of them. If she does not do so, she may be estopped from using the real defence of forgery.[74] Although not a party to the instrument, she must take reasonable steps to avoid a loss for those who would be deceived by the forgery of her signature.

Want of Authority to Sign an Instrument

When someone purporting to be an agent signs a negotiable instrument without any real or apparent authority, the party described as principal can deny liability on the grounds that the instrument is not his; it is a form of forgery.[75]

We must distinguish want of authority *to sign* from want of authority *to complete an already signed instrument* (for example, to fill in the amount on behalf of the party liable). As we have seen, an instrument completed in an unauthorized manner may be negotiated to a holder in due course who may then require the party liable to pay.

Alteration

To provide a real defence, an alteration of a negotiable instrument must be apparent to the naked eye. No holder who takes an instrument bearing an apparent alteration can expect to recover from any party *prior* to the alteration, but he may recover from a party who *subsequently* endorsed the instrument for the altered amount. If, however, the alteration is not apparent, the instrument may be negotiated to a holder in due course who can sue parties prior *according to the original terms* of the instrument, as well as parties subsequent to the alteration for the *altered sum.*[76]

---

71. (1976), 74 D.L.R. (3d) 26. See also Canadian Imperial Bank of Commerce v. Bank of Credit & Commerce Canada, *supra,* n. 67.

72. For a criticism of this decision, see B. Geva, "The Fictitious Payee and Payroll Padding" (1978), 2 *C.B.L.J.* 418. See also, Fok Cheong Shing Investments Ltd. v. Bank of Nova Scotia, [1982] 2 S.C.R. 488; Boma Manufacturing Ltd. v. Canadian Imperial Bank of Commerce (1996), 140 D.L.R. (4th) 463.

73. S. 48.

74. *Ibid.*, which establishes forgery as a real defence and recognizes that a party liable may be estopped from using that defence. A party is estopped only if it has actual notice and fails to act: Canadian Pacific Hotels Ltd. v. Bank of Montreal, [1987] 1 S.C.R. 711. A good example of a case where a party acted promptly: Armstrong Baum Plumbing & Heating v. Toronto-Dominion Bank (1994), 15 B.L.R. (2d) 84.

75. In Don Bodkin Leasing Ltd. v. Toronto-Dominion Bank (1998), 40 O.R. (3d) 262, a bank that had paid almost $1 million on forged cheques was held not liable to its customer. Although the cheques had been forged by the customer's accountant who had no actual authority, he did have apparent authority.

76. S. 144.

The drawer of a cheque owes a duty to his bank to prepare it in such a way as to make its alteration difficult; if he leaves spaces blank or otherwise invites alteration, he, not the bank, must absorb any loss resulting from alteration.[77]

CONSUMER BILLS AND NOTES

The modern concept of negotiability is a highly refined one, developed over the centuries and adapted to the convenience of business. Its advantages have had to be restricted, however, because of certain abuses. A select committee of the Ontario Legislature described a common abuse as follows:

> Cases were brought to the Committee's attention where the seller in an instalment sales transaction misrepresented to the purchaser, in some cases dishonestly and fraudulently, the terms of the contract. Yet the purchaser was compelled to pay the whole debt because the discounter of the promissory note (the finance company) which formed part of the contract was a holder in due course with no knowledge, or provable knowledge, of the representations made.
>
> The promissory note is a statement of obligation by which the signer promises to pay the holder an amount of money, but there is nothing in the note to the effect that there is any contractual obligation which must be fulfilled by the vendor of the goods or services before the money is payable....
>
> If the paper was negotiated and had been bought by a finance company, a dissatisfied customer's refusal to pay because of the dealer's failure to fulfil his promise was no defence in an action on the note. Even if the dissatisfied customer went to court, the court, if it held that the finance company was a holder in due course, had to find in favour of the finance company and the disillusioned customer had to pay not only the purchase price but court and legal costs. The customer had a right of action against the dealer for non-performance, but this remedy was valueless with "fly-by-night" dealers.[78]

In some circumstances, the courts had held that a finance company and dealer were so closely related as to preclude the finance company from claiming to be a holder in due course.[79] In most cases, however, where no special relationship existed between conditional seller and finance company, the courts felt unable to restrict the rights ordinarily afforded to a holder in due course. As a result, Parliament amended the Bills of Exchange Act to remove the protection otherwise accorded to a holder in due course in consumer credit arrangements where a finance company acts in concert with a seller of goods on the instalment plan. After defining a consumer transaction, the statute states:

> 190 (1) Every consumer bill or consumer note shall be prominently and legibly marked on its face with the words "consumer purchase" before or at the time the instrument is signed by the purchaser or by anyone signing to accommodate the purchaser [that is, a guarantor].[80]

The penalties for failure to comply with this section are severe: the instrument is void in the hands of either the seller or the finance company[81] (although they might negotiate it to an innocent holder in due course). In addition, everyone who normally participates in obtaining such

77. Crawford and Falconbridge, n. 7, p. 989.

78. Ontario, *Final Report of the Select Committee of the Ontario Legislature on Consumer Credit*, Sessional Paper No. 85, pp. 19–21.

79. See Federal Discount Corp. Ltd. v. St. Pierre (1962), 32 D.L.R. (2d) 86, and Range v. Corporation de Finance Belvédère (1969), 5 D.L.R. (3d) 257.

80. S. 190(1).

81. *Ibid.*, s. 190(2).

an instrument without the appropriate marking is guilty of an offence and subject to a fine.[82] Most important, even when the instrument is properly marked on its face,

> 191 the right of the holder of a consumer bill or consumer note...to have the whole or any part thereof paid by the purchaser or...[a guarantor] is subject to any defence or right of set-off, other than counterclaim, that the purchaser would have had in an action by the seller on the consumer bill or consumer note.[83]

Thus, a buyer on consumer credit can now raise against a finance company that sues him as holder of his promissory note all the personal defences formerly available only against the seller.

QUESTIONS FOR REVIEW

1. Describe the nature of "clearing house" arrangements.

2. In addition to bills of exchange, promissory notes, and cheques, describe two other types of negotiable instruments.

3. Describe briefly the respective uses of demand drafts, sight drafts, and time drafts in commercial practice.

4. What is the difference in legal effect between a drawer having her cheque certified and a payee later having the cheque certified?

5. Describe the three qualities of negotiable instruments that distinguish them from ordinary assignments and how these qualities make them commercially useful.

6. Donna draws a cheque payable to Edgar for "a maximum of $1000 for carpentry work." Edgar completes the work while Donna is out of town, and takes the cheque to his bank to cash it. The bank refuses. Is the bank correct? Explain.

7. Describe the difference between a "bearer" instrument and an "order" instrument.

8. Explain the significance of a party transferring a negotiable instrument endorsed "without recourse." When is this type of endorsement used?

9. J delivers a cheque for $500 in payment for a second-hand computer purchased from K. K inadvertently leaves the cheque on a restaurant table. Q picks it up from the table, forges K's name and cashes the cheque at the L Bank. K reports the loss of the cheque to J who immediately informs her bank to stop payment. What rights does the L Bank have?

10. W delivers a cheque for $1000 in payment of a debt owed to X. X endorses the cheque to Y Second Hand Shop to purchase a "surround-sound" television set. Y endorses the cheque to her landlord Z, in part payment of her monthly rent. When Z takes the cheque to his bank, the teller recognizes W's signature and has heard that he is in financial difficulty; she contacts W's bank and learns that there are not sufficient funds in W's account. What should Z do to protect his claim?

11. Describe the requirements to be considered a holder in due course.

12. What are the three types of defences that a party liable on an instrument may raise, depending on the relationship between that party and the holder.

---

82. *Ibid.*, s. 192.
83. *Ibid.*, s. 191.

13. You are the maker of a note in which you undertake to pay $500 to a moneylender on demand. Subsequently you pay an instalment of $200 to the moneylender on this liability. What steps should you take to ensure that you will not have to pay a further $500 at some later time?

14. Gower has drawn a time draft on Cohen payable three months after sight to Jenkins. The draft is complete and regular with the possible exception of a clause that Cohen, the drawee, is "to pay the amount of this draft out of money due me on December 31 for professional services rendered." If Cohen refuses to accept the draft, does he owe its amount in future to Gower or to Jenkins?

15. The endorsements appearing on the back of each of three negotiable instruments are reproduced below. An asterisk following a name indicates an actual signature. Identify each of the endorsements by type and explain its effect for the parties concerned:

    (a) Pay to John Factor, Without Recourse
        The Synthetic Textile Co. Ltd.
        per Terry Lean,*/Manager.
        John Factor*

    (b) Pay to James Hawkins,
        S. Trelawney*
        For deposit only,
        James Hawkins*

    (c) Pay to Archibald Grosvenor only
        No Protest
        Reginald Bunthorne*
        Archibald Grosvenor*
        Archibald Grosvenor is hereby identified,
        Ralph Rackstraw*

16. *P* drew a cheque for $100 in favour of *Q*. *P* has his account at the *R* Bank. In drawing this cheque, *P* left a blank space before the words "one hundred" and *Q* added the words "two thousand and." The *R* Bank paid *Q* $2100 and the latter left the country with the proceeds. Can *P* insist that the *R* Bank make good his loss of $2000? Why or why not?

17. Wilma purchased a used mini-van, including a three-month warranty on parts and labour, from Xenon Used Cars Inc. for $10 000. She paid $1500 down and signed a promissory note for $8500, payable in monthly instalments of $285 for three years. If any payment is missed by Wilma, the entire sum will fall due at once because of her default. Xenon immediately transferred the note to Yarrow Finance Corp. and received payment of $7750. Wilma received notice of the transfer with a request to make her monthly payments direct to Yarrow Finance. The van broke down repeatedly within the first month and Wilma was unable to obtain proper repairs from Xenon. She refused to make the payments to Yarrow Finance and it sued her for the full sum due. Describe the nature of Wilma's defence against Yarrow Finance and whether she will succeed.

CASES AND PROBLEMS

On April 28, the University of Penticton made a note payable to the Baroque Construction Co. Ltd., three months after date. The amount of the note was expressed simply as "the balance due to you for construction of our Arts Building."

On May 2 following, the Baroque Construction Co. Ltd. sold the note to a private financier, R. Jay, for $47 500, having shown him accounts and vouchers indicating a balance of $50 000 due from the university. On July 31, R. Jay presented the note to the treasurer of the university for payment and was advised by him that the construction contract with the Baroque Construction Co. Ltd. contained a guarantee clause and that serious defects had developed in the foundation of the Arts Building. The treasurer stated that the university was not prepared to pay the note for this reason. R. Jay countered with the argument that the defective work was not the slightest concern of his, and that the proper officer of the university had signed the note. He then sued the University of Penticton on its note. Should he succeed? Give reasons.

2 On the afternoon of October 27, Connor supplied office furniture valued at $48 000 to Osmond. When the furniture was delivered, Connor received a certified cheque for $48 000 from Osmond. The cheque, drawn on Osmond's account at the Kelsey Bank, had been certified earlier that afternoon by the bank at Osmond's request. That morning Osmond had deposited a cheque from a customer for $76 000; the cheque had not yet been cleared, but the bank took the risk that it would be honoured by the Portage Bank, where Osmond's customer had his account.

On October 28, after having been informed by Portage that it would not honour the $76 000 cheque, the Kelsey Bank called Connor to say that certification had been revoked and that she should not attempt to negotiate the cheque. The next day, Connor presented the certified cheque for payment. The Kelsey Bank refused payment, and Connor sued the bank.

Is the Kelsey Bank legally bound to honour the cheque? Explain.

3 Elston owned all the issued common shares of Ham Ltd. He lent Ham Ltd. $160 000 of his personal funds and obtained in return a promissory note from the company payable to his order.

For personal reasons Elston subsequently had to borrow money on his own account from the Atlas Bank. To secure this loan he delivered the Ham Ltd. promissory note to the bank, but without endorsing it. The bank gave no notice to Ham Ltd. that it was the transferee.

Two months later, Elston sold his shares in Ham Ltd. to new owners who had no knowledge of the existence of the note. At the same time Elston gave Ham Ltd. a general release of all claims he had against it in terms wide enough to include the company's obligation to him on the $160 000 note.

Elston defaulted on his personal loan from the Atlas Bank and it then demanded payment of the note from Ham Ltd. Ham Ltd. refused to pay, and the bank brought an action against it for $160 000.

Give reasons whether or not this action should succeed.

4 Allison opened a chequing account with the Picton Bank and signed an "Operation of Account" agreement; she agreed to notify the bank of any discrepancies and errors in her bank balance within 30 days of receiving her monthly statement and to notify the bank of any forgeries or frauds within her organization as soon as she became aware of them. Soon after, she hired Ralph, a new bookkeeper. Just two weeks later Ralph forged four cheques, worth $24 000, on Allison's chequing account. Ralph was very shrewd; he had done this while Allison's general manager, who was in charge of dealings with the bank, was on vacation. Each of the four cheques was made out to a fictitious payee named Quigley and each was marked "for deposit only." Ralph had set up an account for Quigley in another bank, deposited the cheques, and within a few days withdrew all the money.

The general manager discovered Ralph's fraud on the day he returned; he immediately told Allison about it and she phoned the bank at once—but it was too late. Ralph had absconded. The Picton Bank refused to return the funds to Allison's account, claiming that she had been negligent. In reply, Allison claimed she had complied with the Operation of Account agreement.

Outline the legal argument that Allison would use, and the defence of the Picton Bank. Give your opinion on whether she should succeed.

5 As accountant at a branch of the Crown Bank, Cole misappropriated rent of $3000 due to the bank. When the bank inspector discovered these facts, the bank notified the Flin Flon Fidelity & Guarantee Co., which had previously bonded Cole for the bank, and claimed the $3000. The bonding company told Cole that it preferred not to prosecute if it could avoid it, and a possible way out would be for Cole to get his friends to come to his assistance. Cole then prevailed on his friend Smith to sign a promissory note payable 12 months after date in favour of the bonding company. When Smith dishonoured his note at maturity, the bonding company sued him. Should it succeed? Would the result be different if the bonding company had discounted Smith's note at its bank and Smith had refused to pay the bank at the note's maturity?

6 VanWyck drew a cheque payable to Lockhart but decided not to send it until he had examined the goods purchased from Lockhart to see whether they were satisfactory. VanWyck's clerk, Anderson, inadvertently gave the cheque to Lockhart without first getting permission from VanWyck. (Anderson normally had nothing to do with the preparation or delivery of VanWyck's negotiable instruments.) Lockhart endorsed the cheque for value to Snider, who took it without notice of the circumstances. When Snider attempted to cash the cheque, she discovered that VanWyck had requested his bank to stop payment on it. Snider sued both VanWyck and Lockhart for the amount. State with reasons the rights of the respective parties and the probable result of the action.

7 Andrews, a clerk, placed on the desk of his employer, Barton, a number of mimeographed circular letters that required the employer's signature at the foot. Andrews arranged the letters so that, except for the first copy, no more was visible than the blank space for the signature at the bottom. One sheet in the pile was not a copy of the letter but a completed form of promissory note for $1000 payable to the order of Andrews. Having by this ruse obtained Barton's signature as maker of the note, Andrews negotiated it to Cartier. Cartier, not knowing about Andrew's fraud, paid $990 for it since 30 days remained until its maturity date. When Cartier later presented the note for payment, Barton refused to pay it. Cartier then sued Barton on the note. Who should succeed? Give reasons for your decision, citing any relevant cases.

8 Originals Inc. held an auction of antique furniture and received a winning bid of $18 000 from Parker. Parker gave his cheque drawn on the Regal Bank to Originals Inc. and asked that the furniture be delivered to his warehouse the next day. Originals' clerk deposited the cheque at its bank the afternoon of the auction.

When the furniture arrived the following morning, Parker examined the items on the delivery truck and realized that most of them did not meet the description provided by the auctioneer. He rejected them and the deliverer returned them to Originals Inc. Parker immediately telephoned his bank to stop payment on the cheque and then telephoned Originals to inform them of what he had done. Originals protested but accepted the furniture and said it would sue Parker.

Regal Bank's employee erroneously overlooked Parker's stop payment order and paid the cheque to Originals. When the error came to light the Regal Bank credited the amount of the cheque to Parker and brought an action against Originals Inc. to recover the amount of the payment. Originals claimed it was entitled to hold onto the funds because of breach of contract.

Summarize the arguments of both sides. Who should succeed?

PART

5

Property

The third and fourth parts—Chapters 5 to 21, comprising almost half of this book—have been devoted to the law of contracts generally and to special types of contracts that are especially important to businesses. The emphasis on contracts should not be surprising since the making of contracts for the buying and selling of goods and services is fundamental to the conduct of business.

As we have seen, a party to a contract acquires the right to have the promises the contract contains performed or to be compensated for non-performance. We have noted in Chapter 12 that certain contractual rights may be regarded as a form of property called a chose in action, which may be transferred to a third person. Two examples of property created by a contract are insurance policies and negotiable instruments, discussed in Chapters 18 and 21.

Of course, not all types of property originate in a contract. One may acquire an interest in land, or real estate as it is frequently called, by gift or inheritance. A person may also acquire property by a creative act: for example, copyright is a form of property that results from the act of creating a work of art or literature—or a computer program. As we shall see, any of these property interests may subsequently be transferred to other persons.

Traditionally, in the common law system, property is divided into real property and personal property; civil law systems recognize a corresponding though not identical distinction between "immoveables" and "moveables." Real property consists of interests in land; all other forms of property are personal property. Personal property in turn is subdivided into two classes: choses in possession—such essentially tangible things as automobiles, furniture, machinery, and jewellery; and choses in action—intangible or incorporeal "things," their essence being an enforceable legal right against another person.

We shall discuss several of these forms of property in the next four chapters. Chapter 22 deals with intellectual property—a subject of increasing concern to modern business—and in particular, with trademarks, copyright, patents, and industrial designs. Chapter 23 to 25 are concerned with various interests in real property, including mortgages, leases, condominiums, and real estate transactions.

Most forms of intellectual property are regulated by federal statutes. The full text of those statutes may be accessed at

canada.justice.gc.ca or at
cbsc.org/ontario/buslinks/pubip.htm
This is the Ontario Business site, with links to the following statutes: Copyright Act, Patent Act, Integrated Circuit Topography Act, Industrial Design Act, and Trade-marks Act.

Among the many other interesting and useful sites, the following can be especially recommended:

www.wipo.org
The World Intellectual Property Organization

cipo.gc.ca
The Canadian Intellectual Property Office

dsp-psd.pwgsc.gc.ca/dsp-psd/Reference/f-IP-e.html
A Canadian Government site on intellectual property, with links to federal information on intellectual property law

www.ipww.com
Intellectual Property Worldwide: a site on intellectual property law in the United States and the rest of the world

www.efc.ca
Electronic Frontier Canada: has links to recent news articles relating to intellectual property issues

www.strategis.ic.gc.ca/sc_mrksv/cipo/learn/sn/sn_hp_e.html
Strategis site with questions and answers about intellectual property

www.wwlia.org/ca-re1.htm
Canadian Real Estate Law Centre

www.lsuc.on.ca/public/public_law_realestate_en.shtml
Law Society of Upper Canada: has links to real estate law including landlord and tenant responsibilities and information on purchasing a house or a condominium

catalaw.com/topics/LandlordTenant.shtml
Links to Landlord and Tenant Acts

www.unbc.ca/housing/renting/tenant.htm
University of British Columbia: includes lists of tenant responsibilities and landlord responsibilities under Residential Tenancy Act and questions to ask prior to renting

www.firstottawa.on.ca/firstottawa/Terms.htm
Realty Organization: explains contract terms relating to real estate contracts

www.canmortgage.com
Canada Mortgage information web site with mortgage calculator

mortgagecentre.com
Links to Canada's leading lenders, and a glossary, mortgage news, and mortgage calculator

www.quicken.ca/eng/calculators/index.html
Quicken calculators for mortgage, car deductions, retirement, exchange rates

www.cba.ca/eng/statistics/fastfacts/mortgages_then_and_now.htm
Canadian Banker's Association: compares mortgages and options in the 1970s and 1990s

www.orea.com/about.htm
Ontario Real Estate Association

www.bcrea.bc.ca
B.C. Real Estate Association

realtors.mls.ca/crea
Canadian Real Estate Association

www.chip.ca
Canadian Home Insurance Plan: information on reverse mortgages

INTELLECTUAL PROPERTY

I n this chapter we review the various forms of intellectual property—trademarks, copyright, patents, and industrial designs. We examine the following questions:

- what is "intellectual property"?

- how is intellectual property acquired?

- what types of intellectual property are protected by law?

- what constitutes an infringement of intellectual property?

- what are the remedies for infringement?

- how does intellectual property law adapt to new technologies?

- how should the rights of inventors and innovators be balanced against the general public interest?

THE NATURE OF INTELLECTUAL PROPERTY

Industrial Property and Intellectual Property

The terms *industrial property* and *intellectual property* have been used more or less interchangeably to describe the same legal concept. Until recently "industrial property" tended to be used in reference to trademarks, patents, and industrial designs, and "intellectual property" described copyright—the work of authors and artists. Neither term is entirely satisfactory. Industrial property conjures up images of tangible assets, such as machines and smokestacks, rather than the intangible rights to which it is intended to refer, while trademarks and trade names are not always noted for their high intellectual content. Nevertheless, the word "intellectual" does better convey the notion that the various types of property included in the description are essentially the product of mental activity. Today the single term "intellectual property" normally encompasses all of these forms of property.

The feature common to trademarks, copyright, patents, and industrial designs—apart from the fact that they are all forms of intangible property—is that they are all concerned with ideas or inventions of which individuality or originality is an essential feature. But not all ideas, information, or knowledge qualify as "property": confidential information, trade secrets, and what is commonly referred to as "know-how," though in some ways protected by law, are not regarded as forms of property.

Should Intellectual Property Be Protected?

The proposition that ideas should receive legal protection as a form of property has not always been universally accepted. In particular, most socialist countries and many developing countries initially strongly opposed such protection, though in recent years they have generally been obliged to concede it in order to attract foreign investment, especially in the more technologically advanced sectors. Nevertheless, while many countries have signed international agreements to harmonize intellectual property laws, the scope and extent of protection still varies considerably from one country to another.

Advocates of greater protection claim that creators, such as writers, inventors, and designers, have a moral right to the rewards arising from their efforts, and furthermore, that without protection, creativity is discouraged. Thus, it has been said:

> In most countries it is generally accepted that creators are entitled to a degree of protection for their works, on the grounds that a creator should benefit from the fruits of his labour. If creators are guaranteed a minimum of protection, they will be encouraged to create new works, thereby enriching the cultural life and fabric of the country and adding to the store of information.[1]

By contrast, opponents of protection claim that ideas and inventions, or at least some ideas and inventions—especially those concerning matters such as health, medicine, food production, and education—properly belong to the whole world. They point to the heavy social costs of protection: not only higher prices and payment of royalties and licence fees, but also inefficient use of resources resulting from restrictions on the use of new techniques and from the exercise of monopoly power. Excessive protection, as much as lack of protection, may hinder economic and social progress. The problem, especially for a country such as Canada, which is both an exporter and importer of cultural and technological innovation, is to find the right balance.

FORMS OF INTELLECTUAL PROPERTY

There are four distinct types of intellectual property recognized in Canada: trademarks, copyright, patents, and industrial designs. Each category comprises a particular type of property, protected according to its own rules. In addition, as we shall see in the final part of this chapter, there are some recently introduced statutory rights that do not fit easily into any of these categories.

As a result, we are presented with a very complicated subject: some property rights are protected solely by statute, whereas others are also protected by common law rules; for some interests, registration is essential, while for others rights exist independently of registration; some types of intellectual property may fall within two different categories; others may fall into gaps between the categories so that no protection is provided at all. In addition, since intellectual property is essentially concerned with knowledge, information, and above all, innovation, it is inextricably linked to technological progress. In the fields of information and communication technology, progress has been especially fast. New methods of storing, presenting, and

---

1. *Copyright in Canada: Proposals for a Revision of the Law*, p. 2. Ottawa: Consumer and Corporate Affairs Canada, 1977.

transmitting information and ideas are constantly being devised, and some of these techniques do not fit neatly into the traditional categories of intellectual property that were established 100 or more years ago. In Chapter 34 we consider some of the ways in which intellectual property law is affected by the Internet and by the growth of electronic commerce.

Before examining the categories of intellectual property in greater detail, a word of warning is necessary: of all the different areas of law, intellectual property law is one of the most complex and technical, and perhaps the most specialized. The registration of trademarks and patents, for example, is normally dealt with by a small and select body of experts. For this reason, this chapter does not provide a detailed account of the law. Nonetheless, the subject is one of such increasing importance in business that we need to have a general understanding of which intellectual property rights may be protected, and how of to protect those rights, and avoid infringing the rights of others.

Checklist: Forms of Intellectual Property

The following forms of intellectual property are recognized in Canadian law:

- trademarks
- copyright
- patents
- industrial designs
- plant breeders' rights
- integrated circuit topography rights

TRADEMARKS

Passing-off

passing-off
misrepresenting goods, services, or a business in such a way as to deceive the public into believing that they are the goods, services, or business of some other person

goodwill
the benefit and advantage of the good name, reputation, and connection of a business

At common law a person commits the tort of **passing-off** by misrepresenting goods, services, or a business in such a way as to deceive the public into believing that they are the goods, services, or business of some other person, and thus cause damage to that person. The main purpose of a passing-off action is to protect the other trader from what is, in effect, a misappropriation of goodwill.

Goodwill is not an easy concept to describe. It refers to an important asset of a successful business. A widely accepted legal definition is that given by Lord Nacnaughten of the House of Lords, in *Inland Revenue Commissioners v. Muller*:[2] "[Goodwill is] the benefit and advantage of the good name, reputation and connection of a business. It is the attractive force which brings in custom." A useful approach is to consider goodwill as the difference between the market value of a business as a going concern and its break-up value, that is to say, the sum that could be obtained by selling off all of its fixed assets and inventory. The difference in the two sums can be attributed to the income of the business based on its reputation and established relationships with customers and clients. The name of the business, any mark clearly associated with it, or some "get-up" such as a particular method of packaging or presenting its goods, all form part of that reputation and thus part of the goodwill.

---

2. [1901] A.C. 217 at 223.

CASE 22.1

Ray Plastics Ltd. manufactured a successful tool—a combined snow brush, ice scraper, and squeegee—called "Snow Trooper." It supplied the tool to a number of large retailers, including Canadian Tire. Canadian Tire suggested to another of its suppliers, Dustbane Products Ltd., that Dustbane might consider producing a similar type of tool. Dustbane did so, producing a tool that was virtually identical, at a lower price, and thereby obtained all of Canadian Tire's snow-brush business.

The court found that the design of the "Snow Trooper" was very distinctive, that it had been intentionally copied, and that this constituted the tort of "passing-off." It awarded an injunction and damages to Ray Plastics.[3]

A number of distinct elements generally comprise the tort of passing-off:

- The plaintiff's goods, services, or business must enjoy a reputation that is of some value worth protecting.
- The defendant must have misrepresented its goods, service, or business as those of the plaintiff.
- There must either be actual confusion or a likelihood of confusion in the public's mind between the goods, services, or business of the plaintiff and those of the defendant.
- The plaintiff must have suffered damage in consequence of the passing-off.[4]

In a number of recent cases, attempts have been made to propose a "modern view" of passing-off: this view argues that passing-off occurs when one person makes use of a well-known trade name or mark in order to obtain a benefit, even though no damage can be shown to have resulted to the owner of the name or mark and there is no likelihood of confusion in the minds of the public. To date, this view has not found much favour with the courts.

CASE 22.2

The defendants named their new hotel in Edmonton the "Fantasyland Hotel." An injunction was sought by Walt Disney Productions, which had for some years used the name "Fantasyland" in connection with its amusement parks. The Alberta Court of Appeal confirmed the trial judgment, dismissing the action. According to the court:

> Passing-off cases fall into two broad categories. In the first are those where competitors are engaged in a common field of activity and the plaintiff has alleged that the defendant has named, packaged or described its product or business in a manner likely to lead the public to believe the defendant's product or business is that of the plaintiff. The second, and nowadays perhaps more common type of passing-off, is where it is alleged that a defendant has promoted his product or business in such a way as to create the false impression that his product or business is in some way approved, authorized or endorsed by the plaintiff or that there is some business connection between the defendant and the plaintiff. By these means a defendant may hope to cash in on the goodwill of the plaintiff. The appellant says this case is of the second type because the respondent in using the name "Fantasyland" for its

continued

---

3. Ray Plastics Ltd. v. Dustbane Products Ltd. (1994), 57 C.P.R. (3d) 474.

4. See Ciba-Geigy Canada Ltd. v. Apotex Inc. (1992), 44 C.P.R. (3d) 289 (S.C.C.), per Gonthier, J. However, where the passing-off deliberately suggests an association with another's product it may not be necessary to show damage. For example, an advertising campaign that incorrectly associates a product with another's product may actually benefit that other product: see National Hockey League v. Pepsi-Cola Canada Ltd. (1995), 122 D.L.R. (4th) 412.

hotel, is creating the false impression that it is authorized or connected with the appellant, in other words, the respondent is "cashing in" on the appellant's goodwill. The appellant's theory of the law of passing-off contains a fatal weakness. Even the "more common type of passing-off" referred to requires proof of the essentials of goodwill: misrepresentation or confusion, which the trial judge found, as a fact, did not exist in this case. In other words, the allegation or even the belief that the respondent is benefitting from the use of the name "Fantasyland" is not enough to found the tort of passing-off.[5]

Section 7 of the Trade-marks Act

In addition to the common law, section 7 of the Trade-marks Act[6] provides statutory causes of action that are closely related to, though not identical to, the action of passing-off. Section 7 prohibits

- making a false or misleading statement tending to discredit the business, wares, or services of a competitor
- directing public attention to one's wares, services, or business in such a way as to cause or be likely to cause confusion in Canada between those wares, services, or business and the wares, services or business of another
- passing-off other wares or services as and for those ordered or requested
- making, in association with wares or services, any description that is false in a material respect and likely to mislead the public as to their character, quality, origin, or mode of production
- doing any other act or adopting any other business practice contrary to honest industrial or commercial usage in Canada

Section 7 appears to give wider protection in some respects than does the common law. For some years there were doubts about the validity of section 7 and, although the constitutionality of the provision has now been established,[7] it is still sometimes unclear whether the rights of a trademark holder are best protected under the statute or the common law.

Business Names

The name of an established business is normally an important asset and part of the goodwill of the business. The choice of a business name is important, not only in order to provide the right sort of image for a business but also to avoid inadvertently becoming involved in potentially expensive proceedings for passing-off or for infringing another person's trademark.

Two types of business names can be distinguished: those of unincorporated businesses and those of corporations. In the case of unincorporated businesses, there is no general rule requiring the registration of business names. Most provinces have legislation that requires at least some unincorporated businesses to register; in Ontario, an individual who carries on business under a name *other* than his or her own name is required to register, as must a partnership

---

5. Walt Disney Productions v. Fantasyland Hotel Inc. (1998), 85 C.P.R. (3d) 36. Similarly, the use of a trademark "Playboy," in connection with magazine and hotels, was held not to be confusing with the same name for hair stylists: Playboy Enterprises Inc. v. Germain (1978), 39 C.P.R. (2d) 32.

6. Trade-marks Act, R.S.C. 1985, c. T-13. (Unless otherwise stated, statutory references in this part of the chapter are to that Act.)

7. The doubts arose from the decision of the Supreme Court of Canada in MacDonald v. Vapor Canada Ltd., [1977] 2 S.C.R. 134. The constitutional validity of s. 7 was affirmed in Asbjorn Horgard A/S v. Gibbs/Nortac Industries Ltd., [1987] F.C. 544.

unless the firm name consists solely of the names of the individual partners.[8] The legislation is far from comprehensive and tends not to be strictly enforced; thus when we have selected a name, we cannot be sure, simply by making a search of the relevant provincial register, that no other business with the same, or a confusingly similar, name does not already exist.

The registration of corporate names is much more strictly regulated. Before a corporation can be incorporated certain information must be provided, including the name of the proposed corporation.[9] The appropriate government office must first approve the name and will refuse to register the corporation if it falls within certain prohibited categories (in particular, those that falsely suggest an association with the government or with certain professional bodies, or that are scandalous or obscene); if it is not sufficiently distinctive; or if it is likely to be confused with the name of some other corporation or other business entity. In order to avoid the inconvenience and delay caused by the rejection of a chosen name, intending incorporators normally first make a "name search" to check that no existing corporation is registered with a similar name; of course, the government office responsible for registration also makes its own check. Records of corporations are now computerized, which greatly facilitates such checks, and if the name is not important to the incorporators, the problem can be avoided by using a "number name."

The fact that a corporation has been incorporated under a particular name does not, however, give it the right to carry on business under that name if to do so would infringe upon the registered trademark of some other business entity or would amount to the tort of passing-off. Thus, approval of the application to register does not of itself afford protection to a corporation. The approval may be challenged by some other corporation and the new corporation may be ordered to change its name.[10] Confusion may also exist with the name of an existing *unincorporated* business, which may not be registered at all. In addition, there may be confusion with the registered trademark of another business where the trademark is not the same as the name of its owner. It may therefore be advisable when incorporating to make a search of the Trade Marks Register as well as the register of corporate names. It may also happen that two companies, one incorporated provincially and the other federally, operate in the same province using confusingly similar names; for this reason, both provincial and federal registers should be searched. Similar problems arise in connection with the use of "domain names" on the Internet; these problems are discussed in Chapter 34.

Registered Trademarks

As we have seen, business names and trademarks are protected at common law through the passing-off action, without the need for any registration. Nevertheless, registration of trademarks does secure certain advantages over and above those that exist under the common law.

When a registered mark is used there is no need to indicate that it is registered, but it has become common practice, on labels and in advertisements, to so indicate by use of the symbol ® or ™, frequently accompanied by words such as "…is the registered trademark of XYZ Inc."

Rights Obtained by Registration

The Trade-marks Act (section 19) gives the owner of a valid registered trademark the exclusive right to its use throughout Canada in respect of the wares and services for which it was registered. No unauthorized person may then sell, distribute, or advertise any wares or services in association with a confusing trademark or trade name (section 20), or otherwise use the mark

8. Business Names Act, R.S.O. 1990, c. B.17, s. 2. The requirements for partnership registration are considered further in Chapter 26.

9. See, for example, Canada Business Corporations Act, R.S.C. 1985, c. C-44, s. 6.

10. See Canadian Motorways Ltd. v. Laidlaw Motorways Ltd., [1974] S.C.R. 675. At the time of the 1988 Winter Olympic Games in Calgary, a number of companies were required to remove the word "Olympic" from their names to avoid infringement of the trademark of the International Olympic Committee.

in a manner that is likely to have the effect of depreciating the value of the goodwill attached to it (section 22). An exception to this exclusive right arises when, after a trademark has been registered, it is discovered that some other person had been using a confusingly similar trademark before the registered owner.

When the mark has been registered for less than five years, the prior user may bring proceedings to have the registration expunged, on proof that the prior use has not been abandoned (section 17(1)). However, when the registration occurred more than five years before the proceedings commenced, it will not be expunged unless the prior user shows that the registered owner had actual knowledge of the prior use when adopting the mark (section 17(2)). If the registered owner had no such knowledge the court may make an appropriate order to allow the prior user to continue to use the mark, perhaps restricted to a given geographic area or in a modified form (section 21).

Registration confers other advantages on the owner; normally it applies to the whole of Canada so that the right of exclusive use is not restricted to the area in which its owner actually does business and has established a reputation. A trademark that has been registered in Canada may also be registered in other countries that adhere to the International Convention for the Protection of Industrial Property. Procedurally, the registering of a trademark creates a presumption that it is valid and distinctive and is indeed owned by the registered owner.

Duration

A trademark registration is valid for a period of 15 years, and may be renewed. Thus unlike copyright, patents, and industrial designs, a trademark can be preserved indefinitely. The Registrar may from time to time request evidence that the trademark is still being used, and if it has been abandoned or is not renewed at the end of the 15-year period, it may be expunged from the register (sections 44, 45).

Registration

The Mark

Section 2 of the Trade-marks Act defines a trademark as

    (a) a mark that is used by a person for the purpose of distinguishing or so as to distinguish wares or services manufactured, sold, leased, hired, or performed by him from those manufactured, sold, leased, hired, or performed by others

    (b) a certification mark

    (c) a distinguishing guise

    (d) a proposed trademark

mark or trademark
any visual characteristic of products or their presentation distinguishing them from products that do not have the same trade connection

Although the Act does not define the word **mark**, it is generally accepted that virtually any visual characteristics of goods or their presentation that serve to distinguish them from goods that do not have the same trade connection can fairly be described as a "mark." A **trademark** may be and frequently is part of a business name, but that name is not itself a trademark. For example, the word "Ford" is a trademark of the Ford Motor Company, but the full name is not.

certification mark
a special type of trademark used to identify goods or services that conform to a particular standard

A **certification mark** is a special type of trademark used to identify goods or services that conform to a particular standard, a typical example being the "Good Housekeeping Seal of Approval" mark. The owner of the certification mark may register it and license its use to other persons whose goods or services meet the defined standards.

distinguishing guise
the shaping of goods or their containers, or a distinctive mode of wrapping or packaging

A **distinguishing guise** usually refers to the shaping of goods or their containers, or to a mode of wrapping or packaging that is distinctive—a Coca-Cola bottle, for example.

proposed trademark
a mark that the owner proposes to use

A **proposed trademark**, as the name implies, is a mark that the owner proposes to use; the advantage of applying to register such a mark is that it can be protected without its actual use having been first established. Although the United States also permits registration of a proposed trademark, most countries require actual use before any rights may be acquired.

Requirements for Registration

In order for a trademark to be registered it must satisfy a number of additional conditions (section 12). In particular, the mark must *not* be

(a) a word that is primarily merely the name or surname of an individual who is living or died within the preceding 30 years

(b) clearly descriptive or deceptively misdescriptive of the character or quality of the wares or services, or of their place of origin

(c) the name of any of the wares or services in connection with which it is used

(d) likely to be confused with a registered trademark

(e) a mark that is prohibited by section 9 or section 10 of the Trade-marks Act

These prohibitions serve a number of purposes. Given the exclusive nature of trademark rights, prohibitions (a), (b), and (c) seem primarily designed to ensure that the names of people and places, and descriptive words that are in common usage, are not in effect taken out of circulation through registration by giving a monopoly of use to the registered owner. The intention of prohibition (d) is to carry out the main purpose of the Act: trademarks are designed to be distinctive, and such distinctiveness would be lost if two or more persons were allowed to register confusingly similar marks. Finally, sections 9 and 10 prohibit registration of marks that suggest an association with royalty, the government, certain international organizations or professional groups, or that are scandalous or obscene.

Selecting and designing a suitable trademark is a difficult operation. Ideally, the mark will be distinctive and eye-catching and will quickly become associated in the public mind with the goods or services of its owner. It must be original so that it does not offend against condition (d) by being confusingly similar to some other registered mark, but should not be one that is likely to be rejected under one of conditions (a), (b), or (e). The normal practice is to make a search of the records of the Canadian TradeMarks Office for other marks that are visually or phonetically similar to the mark being proposed for registration; in some cases it may also be advisable to make searches in the United States. In practice, the application to register is normally prepared and filed by a specialist trademark agent, who will give advice on the likelihood of an application being accepted; such advice is important, since the case law on this subject is extremely complicated.

ILLUSTRATION 22.1

(a) A mark consisting of the name of a historical figure, such as "William Shakespeare" or "John A. MacDonald" would probably be acceptable, even though it is very likely that there are living persons with those names. Similarly, fictitious names, such as "Captain Kirk" or "Darth Vadar," are registrable because the public would not identify the names with living individuals. In one instance, a coined name, "Marco Pecci," was held to be registrable in the absence of evidence that such an individual actually existed, despite the possibility that there might somewhere be a person of that name.[11]

(b) Words, especially adjectives, that are merely descriptive (or misdescriptive) of the quality of the goods are not acceptable. "Instant" or "Super" would be rejected though "Kold One" has been accepted when applied to beer[12] and the word "Golden" was held not to be descriptive of a beer and therefore acceptable.[13]

continued

11. Gerhard Horn Investments Ltd. v. Registrar of Trade Marks, [1983] 2 F.C. 878.

12. Registrar of Trade Marks v. Provenzano (1978), 40 C.P.R. (2d) 288.

13. Molson Cos. v. John Labbatt Ltd. (1984), 1 C.P.R. (3d) 494.

(c) The use of a place name as descriptive of the quality or origin of goods is normally not permitted. The mark "Toscano," applied to wine, was disallowed since that is the Italian name for wine from a famous region.[14] In another case, however, a producer was permitted to register the mark "Oberhaus" in relation to wine, despite the fact that there is in Germany a small village called Oberhausen where wine is produced. It was considered unlikely that the Canadian wine-buying public would know of the place.[15]

The Owner

Registration alone does not make a person the owner of a trademark; that person must already be the owner at the time of registration. This is so, even in the case of applications based upon proposed use, for the mark will be registered only after the applicant has filed a declaration that it has commenced to use the mark in Canada.

The application to register may be based upon any one of the following grounds (section 16):

- the mark has been previously used or made known in Canada
- the mark has been registered and used abroad, in a country that is a party to the convention
- it is proposed to use the mark in Canada

Generally, the mere advertising of a trademark is not sufficient to constitute "use"; the goods or services to which the mark relates must have been sold or performed. However, advertising alone may be sufficient to amount to "making known" the mark in Canada.

Opposition Proceedings

The initial obstacle in registering a trademark is to satisfy the Registrar that the chosen mark is eligible for registration. If the Registrar refuses registration, the owner may appeal that decision to the courts. If there is no objection by the Registrar, or an objection has been overcome, the Trade Marks Office issues a notice that the application has been approved for advertisement in the Trade Marks Journal and, subsequently, the application must be advertised. Once the trademark has been advertised, any person may, within two months, file a notice of opposition. Registration may be opposed on any of the following grounds:

- the application did not comply with the various formal requirements for filing
- the mark is not registrable
- the applicant is not the person entitled to registration
- the mark is not "distinctive" (sections 37, 38)

The opponent must specify the ground or grounds upon which the opposition is based in sufficient detail to enable the applicant to reply to the objection. However, the onus of satisfying the Registrar that the trademark should be registered still rests on the applicant. This is so, even though the Registrar has in effect already reached a preliminary decision in favour of the application by permitting it to be advertised. Opposition proceedings are determined in the first place by Hearing Officers, with appeal to the Trial Division of the Federal Court.

---

14. Jordan & Ste Michelle Cellars Ltd. v. Gillespies & Co. (1985), 6 C.P.R. (3d) 377. In that case the words were also deceptively misdescriptive, since the wine was Canadian.

15. Stabilisierungsfonds fur Wein v. T.G. Bright & Co. Ltd. (1985), 4 C.P.R. (3d) 526.

An objection that the mark is not registrable includes all the elements set out in section 12 of the Act—that the mark is primarily merely a name of an individual or that it is descriptive of the character or quality of the goods or their place of origin, or that it comes within the categories of prohibited use. The motivation behind a challenge is usually to prevent a business competitor from gaining an advantage by being granted the exclusive right to use the mark. The other common reason is that the objector claims already to have rights, whether registered or not, to the use of a mark that is identical or confusingly similar. Determining what is, or is not, "confusing" depends very much upon the nature of the business concerned and of the goods or services supplied.[16]

Remedies for Infringement

Unauthorized Use

As we have seen, a trademark may be infringed at common law by passing-off, and a registered trademark may in addition be infringed by any unauthorized use of that mark, or a confusingly similar mark, by some other person.

What constitutes "use" is sometimes difficult to determine. Sections 2 and 4 of the Act indicate that a trademark is "used" when it distinguishes someone's wares or services from those originating from someone else. To appropriate another's name or mark, even without any intent to deceive, is to "use" another's mark.[17] It is not necessary for the defendant to have attempted to pass off its products as those of the owner of the mark. Thus, comparative advertising, where one firm attempts to demonstrate that its product is superior to a rival's, may constitute a "use" of the rival's mark if the advertisement refers to the name or mark of the rival product.[18] An infringement may be accidental or deliberate; it is not necessary to show an intention to damage the goodwill of the owner of the mark,[19] though such an intention may persuade a court to award punitive damages.

An important recent decision was that in *Coca-Cola Ltd. v. Pardhan*.[20] The well-known soft-drink company brought an action alleging infringement of its trademark on the ground that the defendant had bought quantities of the beverage in Canada and then exported it for resale without the consent of the manufacturer. The intention of the manufacturer was to use its ownership of the trademark to control the marketing of its product and to prevent "parallel exports." Coca-Cola argued that the defendant "used" the trademark, because section 4(3) of the Act deems any export of goods bearing a trademark to be "use" of that trademark. The Federal Court of Appeal rejected that argument, holding that the purpose of section 4(3) is not to equate exporting with "use," but rather to enable Canadian producers who do not make local sales but simply ship their goods abroad, to establish "use" in Canada for the purposes of obtaining Canadian trademark registration.[21] Strayer, J. cited the Federal Court of Appeal in *Smith & Nephew Inc. v. Glen Oak Inc. et al.*,[22] where it was held that "goods which originate in the stream of commerce with the owner of a trademark are not counterfeit or infringing goods simply because they may have arrived in a particular geographical market where the trademark owner does not wish them to be distributed."

---

16. Pink Panther Beauty Corp. v. United Artists Corp. (1998), 80 C.P.R. (3d) 247. See also n. 5, *supra*.

17. Walt Disney Productions v. Triple Five Corp. (1993), 113 D.L.R. (4th) 229.

18. Eye Masters Ltd. v. Ross King Holdings Ltd. (1992), 44 C.P.R. (3d) 459. Contrast, Future Shop Ltd. v. A & B Sound Ltd. (1994), 55 C.P.R. (3d) 182.

19. Even a "spoof" upon a trademark may be actionable: see Source Perrier S.A. v. Fira-Less Marketing Co. Ltd. (1983), 70 C.P.R. (2d) 61.

20. (1999), 85 C.P.R. (3d) 489.

21. See also Molson Cos. v. Moosehead Breweries Ltd. et al. (1990), 32 C.P.R. (3d) 363.

22. (1996), 68 C.P.R. (3d) 153.

Action for Infringement

The trademark owner may bring an action for infringement in the appropriate provincial court, in which case common law as well as statutory remedies are available, but a successful judgment can be enforced only within that province. On the other hand, if an action is brought in the Federal Court, the judgment is enforceable anywhere in Canada. However, the Federal Court has jurisdiction only to hear actions brought under the Trade-marks Act. Normally, that should not cause any difficulty since, as we have seen, section 7 of the Act generally provides even greater protection to trademark owners, whether registered or not, than does the common law.

Whether the action is one at common law, for passing-off, or is a statutory action, the remedies that the court may order are essentially the same. If there is injury to the goodwill of the owner, then damages may be awarded; if the defendant has profited from the infringement, an account of profits may be ordered. In any event, the defendant may be restrained from further infringement by an injunction and may be required to deliver up or dispose of infringing materials. The court may also order the defendant to allow the plaintiff to search for and seize offending wares and relevant books and records,[23] and in a statutory action, may impose a ban upon further imports of offending products.[24]

Assignment, Licensing, and Franchising

At common law, a trademark was considered to be a part of the goodwill of a business and therefore inseparable from the business itself. Consequently, the owner could not assign a trademark except where the transferee also took over the business. Nor was it possible to retain the use of a trademark while granting a licence to another person to use it as well; the essence of a trademark is its distinctiveness, a quality that is lost once it is used by two or more different persons. Section 48 of the Trade-marks Act substantially modifies these rules so that the owner may now transfer a trademark (a) whether or not it is registered, (b) either as part of or separately from the goodwill of the business, and (c) in respect of either all or some of the goods and services in association with which it has been used. An owner may also license the use of a registered trademark, the licensee being permitted to use the mark under conditions prescribed by the licence (section 50).

Special care must be taken when assigning or licensing a trademark to ensure that the rights of either or both parties are not lost. Generally, when a business is sold, the rights in a trademark with which it is associated pass to the purchaser; thus, a transfer of the business operates to assign the trademark. If the mark is registered, the fact of the assignment may be entered on the register, but an assignment may be valid even if unregistered. If a mark is unregistered the new owner may seek to register it after having commenced to use it. A more difficult situation occurs when an owner keeps the business but assigns the trademark, perhaps because the business is to discontinue production of the particular line of goods with which the mark is associated. An example occurs when a foreign company that has previously marketed its goods in Canada and has established rights to a trademark here, forms a subsidiary company in Canada to take over the manufacture or distribution of its goods. The difficulty arises because, in the eyes of the public, the trademark may remain distinctive of the goods of the previous owner rather than those of the new owner, who consequently will not immediately have an established right to it.[25]

When licensing a trademark, the owner often desires to continue to use the mark and also to permit concurrent use by one or more other businesses, usually in return for payment of a fee or royalty. The former system, whereby licensed users could be registered, has been abandoned

---

23. This is the so-called "Anton Piller" relief: see Anton Piller KG. v. Manufacturing Processing Ltd., [1976] Ch. 55.

24. The power to ban imports has been restricted by the North American Free Trade Agreement Implementation Act, S.C. 1993, c. 44, s. 234.

25. See Wilkinson Sword (Canada) Ltd. v. Juda, [1968] 2 Ex. C.R. 137.

and it is now sufficient to give notice to the public that use is under licence; in that case use by the licensee is then deemed to be that of the registered owner itself so as to preserve the distinctiveness of the mark.[26] A registered user cannot transfer the right to use a mark, and a breach of any of the terms of the licence will normally constitute an infringement of the trademark.

Although a *franchise agreement*, as we saw in Chapter 19, usually involves much more than the licensing of a trademark, the franchiser will in most cases require that the franchisee market goods or services under the franchiser's trademark. Franchisers normally insist on strict conditions in the franchise agreement, relating to such matters as quality control, purchasing of supplies and equipment, advertising, and the use of trademarks, trade names, designs, and the like. Breach of the agreement by a franchisee normally terminates its right to use the trademark, so that continued use would amount to infringement.

COPYRIGHT

Statutory Origin

Unlike the law of trademarks, copyright is entirely the creation of statute; there is no common law action for infringement of copyright. Copyright is a comparatively modern concept. It was unknown in the ancient world and began to be considered only after the invention of the printing press in the 15th century. Even then, it took a couple of centuries to evolve; the first known copyright law was the Statute of Queen Anne, adopted in England in 1709. For many years copyright was associated almost exclusively with the written word, though its scope was later extended to cover drawings, paintings, and musical scores. In recent years, with the advent of motion pictures, sound recording, radio and television broadcasting, and computer software, it has become a central feature of several major industries.

In Canada, the law of copyright is governed by the Copyright Act,[27] originally adopted in 1924 and substantially amended in 1988, 1993, and most recently in 1997.

International Treaties

Canada is a signatory to the Berne Convention, an agreement to which more than 60 countries adhere. An author who is a citizen of a Convention country has copyright protection in Canada, and Canadian authors enjoy protection in other Convention countries. Canada also adheres to the Universal Copyright Convention. The Universal Copyright Convention enables a citizen of a contracting state to enjoy the same copyright protection in another contracting state as does a national of that state. Thus, a Canadian national can obtain protection in the United States simply by following the American practice of marking the work with the symbol ©, or the word "copyright," followed by the name of the copyright owner and the year of first publication. Similar benefits are also provided by a number of reciprocal agreements that Canada has entered into with other countries, and the Copyright Act itself extends far beyond the boundaries of Canada, since it applies to the original works of all British subjects or residents within Her Majesty's Realms and Territories, and thus gives protection in Canada to citizens of the United Kingdom and the Commonwealth countries. In 1997, Canada also became a signatory of two treaties developed by the World Intellectual Property Organization; further legislation is being prepared to implement those treaties, which are especially concerned with the impact of new technologies and the use of the Internet.[28]

---

26. Trade-marks Act, s. 50, as amended by the Intellectual Property Law Improvement Act, S.C. 1993, c. 15, s. 69. See Linehan (1993), 10 Canadian Intellectual Property Rev. 537.

27. R.S.C. 1985, c. C-42. Unless otherwise stated, references in this part of the chapter are to that Act, as amended.

28. Copyright issues arising from the Internet are considered further in Chapter 34.

Nature of Copyright

What is commonly referred to as "copyright" is really a collection of distinct rights conferred by statute. The basic rights of the owner of copyright are:

- the right to produce or reproduce the work in question, or any substantial part of it, in any material form
- the right to perform or deliver the work in public
- the right to publish an unpublished work

There are also a number of more specific rights:

- the right to translate the work
- the right to convert the work from one form into another (e.g., to convert a novel into a play, or vice-versa)
- the right to make a recording or film of the work
- the right to communicate the work by radio communication (including television)
- the right to exhibit the work in public
- the right to authorize any of the above (section 3)

The essence of copyright is perhaps better understood, however, when expressed in terms of limits; its importance lies in the power of the author or owner of the copyright to restrain others from doing any of those things that only the author or owner has the right to do. In all works in which it exists, copyright arises automatically and without any registration simply by the act of creation, whether the work is published or not. The author or creator of the work is the original owner and may assign the copyright. Thus, copyright may be owned by the author of a book or by the firm that publishes it, by the composer of a piece of music or by the recording company, or it may be owned by some person not connected in any way with the creation or production process, such as an heir or creditor of the author. However, there are other rights, generally referred to as **moral rights**, that are personal to the author or creator and that cannot be assigned. These include

moral rights
the rights of an author or creator to prevent a work from being distorted or misused

- the right to integrity of the work
- the right to prevent its being distorted or mutilated
- the right to prevent it from being used in association with some product, service, cause, or institution
- where the work is copied, published or performed, the right to be associated with the work as author by name or pseudonym, or to remain anonymous

Thus, the author of a play is entitled to have the authorship properly attributed to her when it is performed or, if she wishes to remain anonymous or use an alias, the right not to have her true identity revealed. An artist who paints a picture is entitled not to have it defaced.

CASE 22.3

A sculptor who created a flock of flying geese, to be displayed in a shopping centre, is entitled not to have them decorated with red ribbons at Christmas time.[29] This is the case whether or not he still owns the copyright.

---

29. Snow v. Eaton Centre Ltd. (1982), 70 C.P.R. (2d) 105.

Limits to Copyright

We have noted that copyright exists in unpublished as well as published works. However, there can be no copyright in any work unless and until it has been created. Thus, there is no copyright in a mere idea, but only in the expression of an idea in a material form. As was stated in one leading case:

> It is...an elementary principle of copyright law that an author has no copyright in ideas but only in his expression of them. The law of copyright does not give him any monopoly in the use of the ideas with which he deals or any property in them, even if they are original. His copyright is confined to the literary work in which he has expressed them.[30]

Thus, a playwright could "borrow" the plot from another person's novel, provided the play was expressed entirely in his own words. Such conduct might be considered to be unprofessional, and to amount to *plagiarism*, but it would not by itself constitute an infringement of copyright.

Works in Which Copyright Exists

Copyright exists in every original literary, dramatic, musical, and artistic work (section 5). It must be emphasized that the requirement of *originality* applies to each of these four categories. "Originality" is used here in the sense that the work must have originated from the author; there is no requirement that it must be particularly imaginative, novel, or skillful. Nevertheless, for a work to be "original," it must be work independently created by its author, and must display at least a minimal degree of skill and judgment; the fact that it may have involved substantial effort is not by itself determinative of originality.

CASE 22.4

Tele-Direct Publications Inc., an affiliate of Bell Canada, brought an action against American Business Information Inc., claiming copyright on its "Yellow Pages" directories because of the extra work it did to arrange phone number information from Bell Canada and add other data, such as fax numbers. The Federal Court of Appeal ruled that compilations of this nature, which simply rearrange existing data do not make it subject to copyright.

According to the court, the Yellow Pages, taken as a whole and given the visual aspects of the pages and manner of their arrangement, are protected by copyright. The information that they contain is not. The court concluded that Tele-Direct had exercised only a minimal degree of skill, judgment, or labour in its overall arrangement, which was insufficient to support a claim of originality in the compilation so as to warrant copyright protection.[31]

Literary Works

The Copyright Act gives a very broad meaning to "literary work." The expression includes any work that is reduced to writing or printing, and includes maps, charts, plans, tables, and compilations. There must, however, be some reduction into a tangible form, such as writing, film, or sound recording; there is no copyright in mere spoken words.

---

30. Moreau v. St. Vincent, [1950] Ex. C.R. 198, per Thorson, P., at 202.
31. Tele-Direct (Publications) Inc. v. American Business Information, Inc., [1998] 2 F.C. 22. Prior to the 1993 amendments to the Copyright Act (introduced to implement NAFTA, Art. 1705), compilations were protected only in so far as they could be characterized as literary works. Compilations may now also be related to artistic, dramatic, and musical works. In the Tele-Direct case, the court warned that earlier cases regarding compilations should be applied with caution.

CASE 22.5

A book was published about the late classical pianist, Glenn Gould. The book was largely based on private interviews between Gould and the author, Jock Carroll. Gould's estate sued claiming, among other things, that copyright in the interviews belonged to Gould. The court held that Carroll was the sole author and owner of the copyright in the notes and recordings of his interviews of Gould, and that Gould (and his estate) had no copyright in the spoken words.[32]

As well as the obvious items such as books, and magazine and newspaper articles, the term literary works has been held to include income tax tables, street directories, examination papers, insurance forms, parts catalogues, and the like. From this list it is apparent that, for the purposes of the Act, literary merit is not an essential element of a "literary work." Machine drawings and sketches have sometimes been treated as literary works, though it is more common for them to be classified as artistic works; the actual classification is usually unimportant.

Computer Software

Amendments to the Act made in 1988 added computer programs to the list of protected literary works. Prior to that year, the situation in Canada regarding computer programs had been somewhat uncertain. A program is usually first written in a computer "language," such as "Java" or "C++." This "source code" is humanly readable. It is then translated into an "object code," consisting of a series of "0s" and "1s," readable by the computer. The object code may in turn be embodied in a "chip." It is reasonably clear that the humanly readable source code qualifies as a literary work. However, in *Apple Computer Inc. v. Mackintosh Computers Ltd.*[33] the defendants were accused of copying the plaintiff's chips and, in doing so, substantially reproducing the programs embodied in the chips. The defendants argued that the program is merely a "specification" and that by copying the chip the defendants were simply carrying out the specification, just as is done when one makes a pie from a recipe. The plaintiffs responded that the defendants' conduct should more properly be compared to copying the recipe itself. The Supreme Court of Canada agreed and held that copyright subsists in computer programs embodied in a chip, or in other machine-readable form, and that the copying of a chip constitutes an infringement of the copyright in the program itself. The 1988 amendment reinforces this position, defining "computer program" to mean instruction or statements expressed, fixed, embodied, or stored in any manner, for use directly or indirectly in a computer in order to bring about a specific result. The new provisions contain certain exemptions, permitting the making of single copies for a specific purpose, such as making a back-up copy or reproducing the program in another form in order to render it compatible with a particular computer.

Dramatic Works

A "dramatic work" is defined to include any piece for recitation, choreographic work, or entertainment in "dumb show," the scenic arrangement or acting form of which is fixed in writing or otherwise, and any cinematographic production where the arrangement or acting form, or the combination of incidents represented give the work an original character (section 2). The category is sufficiently wide to include not only the older forms of drama, such as plays, operas, and

32. Gould Estate v. Stoddard Publishing (1998), 161 D.L.R. (4th) 321. Contrast, Hager v. ECW Press Ltd., [1999] 2 F.C. 287.

33. (1990), 71 D.L.R. (4th) 95. See the detailed review of the issues raised in this case by Hayhurst (1987), 19 *Ottawa L. Rev.* 137; Morgan (1994), 26 *Ottawa L. Rev.* 425. The litigation in the U.S. between these two corporations reputedly cost $30 million in legal expenses!

ballets, but also most new forms of entertainment. The key words in the definition are "fixed in writing or otherwise." The text of a play, or the libretto and score of a musical comedy, are protected since they are fixed in written form. But so also are films, video recordings of dramatic works, or a sound recording of an interview or of a poetry reading.

Although an event such as a street riot or a plane crash, or perhaps even a football game, occurs independently of a person making a record of it, and is not itself a "dramatic work," recording such an event, for example on film, can constitute the dramatic work of the photographers and film editors; copyright can subsist in such a film, and to copy the film would constitute an infringement of copyright. Before 1988, a "live" broadcast of such an event was considered not to be protected by copyright, because it was not "fixed."[34] This rule has been amended, in part to comply with Canada's obligations under the Canada–U.S. Free Trade Agreement, and in large measure to deal with a number of problems relating to cable retransmissions of television signals. The amendment states that it shall be an infringement of copyright to communicate a work to the public by any form of telecommunication unless the retransmission complies with the Broadcasting Act.[35] The new rule deals with the problem of "live" broadcasts by providing that a work is considered to be "fixed" even if it becomes fixed simultaneously with its transmission.

Musical Works

A "musical work" is defined as any combination of melody and harmony, or either of them alone, that is printed, reduced to writing, or otherwise graphically produced or reproduced. The important word here is "graphically," for copyright extends only to the music in written or notational form; a performance of a musical work is not within the definition. However, separate protection is given to records or other "contrivances" that mechanically reproduce sound (section 5(3)). The contrivance or recording is itself regarded as a work in which copyright subsists, whether or not the work being performed also has its own copyright. Thus, a recording of a live performance by a jazz pianist or trumpeter, in which a new work is improvised, is protected by copyright even though the music itself was never reduced to written or graphic form. A recording of a symphony by Beethoven is similarly protected, even though any copyright in the symphony itself would long ago have expired.

Artistic Works

An "artistic work" is defined by section 2 of the Copyright Act to include paintings, drawings, maps, charts, plans, photographs, engravings, sculptures and artistic craftsmanship, and architectural works of art, which in turn are defined as any building or structure, or model of such building or structure. For architectural works, copyright is restricted to the artistic character and design and does not extend to the processes or methods of construction. Some overlap exists between "artistic" works and "literary" works, since the definition of the latter also includes maps, charts, and plans.

We should note that a trademark of distinctive design may also qualify as an artistic work and be protected by copyright. In addition, plans and drawings of machinery or other devices may be protected by copyright as artistic works, and at the same time may depict or describe an invention protected by *patent*. It is also frequently difficult to determine whether a particular piece of work is an artistic work, protected by copyright, or an *industrial design*, which may receive a different form of protection.

---

34. Canadian Admiral Corp. v. Rediffusion Inc., [1954] Ex. C.R. 382. In the leading Australian case of Victoria Park Racing and Recreation Grounds Co. Ltd. v. Taylor (1937), 58 C.L.R. 479, it was held that no copyright was infringed when the defendants broadcast a radio commentary on horseraces organized by the plaintiffs from a platform erected on land adjoining the racetrack.

35. Canada–United States Free Trade Agreement Implementation Act, S.C. 1988, c. 65, s. 63.

Excluded Works

Copyright was never intended to protect mass-produced items, and until 1988 the Copyright Act expressly excluded designs capable of being registered under the Industrial Design Act, where those designs were intended to be used as models or patterns to be reproduced by some industrial process. The Act now provides that there is no copyright in three-dimensional articles that are functional, or in drawings or plans for such articles. However, as noted earlier, an artistic work may take a three-dimensional form, such as a sculpture or an architect's model, and have the benefit of copyright.

Public policy in Canada does not appear to prohibit copyright in works that are obscene, immoral, or otherwise offensive, but as a matter of public policy the courts would likely refuse to grant damages to an author of such a work whose copyright was infringed.

The Protection of Copyright

Duration of Copyright

Generally, a work is protected by copyright during the life of its author and for a further period of 50 years after the author's death (section 6). The deceased author's estate or an assignee of the copyright, for example a publisher, may use the protection. The Act prescribes different terms for the following:

- photographs and phonograph records are protected for 50 years from the making of the original negative, plate, or master tape
- posthumous works—works not published before the death of the author—are protected for 50 years from the date of first publication
- jointly authored works are protected for 50 years after the death of the last surviving author
- Crown copyright persists for 50 years from the date of first publication

Ownership of Copyright

Normally, copyright belongs initially to the author or creator of a work. Copyright in a work may be jointly owned by two or more authors, such as the joint authors of a book. However, it is also possible for separate copyrights to exist in different parts of the same complete work; for example, the writer of the lyrics of a song may hold copyright in the words (as a literary work) and the composer may hold copyright in the music.

There are a number of exceptions to the general rule. When photographs have been commissioned, copyright belongs to the person who ordered the photograph to be taken rather than to the photographer, unless otherwise agreed. Works that have been prepared or published by or under the direction of the government belong to the Crown, subject to contrary agreement. Most important is the rule that where the author of a work was employed by some other person and the work was made *in the course of employment*, copyright belongs to the *employer*—again, unless otherwise agreed. Thus, copyright in an examination paper or a set of lecture notes would belong to the university or college, rather than to the teacher who authored them.[36]

As mentioned earlier, and as discussed in the next section, copyright may be assigned by the original owner to some other person. The Act provides that, when an author has assigned a work, copyright in it reverts automatically to the author's estate 25 years after the death of the author. This rule cannot be varied by agreement. However, the rule applies only in cases of sole authorship where the original copyright belonged to the author.

---

36. In Hanis v. Teevan (1998), 162 D.L.R. (4th) 414, copyright in computer software developed by an employee was held to belong to the employer university.

Assignment and Licensing

An owner of copyright may assign it, for value or by way of gift, or it may pass under the will or intestacy of the owner. The so-called "moral rights" of an author, as already noted, are not capable of being assigned. An owner may also assign only part of a copyright in a work, or may divide it territorially. For example, one person might own the copyright of a book in Canada and another in the United States; copyright could even be divided between Western and Eastern Canada. Authors often assign the copyright in a book to their publishing company in return for the payment of a royalty—for example, 10 percent of total sales revenue. The parties may attach a variety of conditions to an assignment, dealing with such matters as publication in other countries, translations, and reproduction in other forms.

Alternatively, an author may retain the copyright in a work but give the publisher a licence to print or reproduce and sell it, again normally in return for a royalty. Licences may also be much more restricted: an author may grant a licence for the single performance of a play or musical work, on a specified date at a particular theatre, or for the reproduction of an extract from a work in some other work, for example, in an anthology of poetry, a collection of essays, or a set of teaching materials.

In some circumstances, a person wishing to perform or reproduce a copyrighted work may do so without obtaining the consent of the owner by paying a prescribed royalty. This may be done, for example, when the author has been dead for 25 years and copyright has reverted to the author's estate, or when the author cannot be traced.

A special arrangement is available for musical and musical-dramatic works. An author may assign the performing rights of the work to a **performing rights society**; there are three such societies in Canada at present. In turn, the society grants licences for performance for a fee, pays part of the fee to the author and retains the remainder to cover the society's costs. A Copyright Board has authority to regulate the rates set by their collectives.

performing rights society
a society to which authors of musical and dramatic works assign performing rights, and which grants licences for performances

Registration

Copyright comes into existence automatically on the creation of a work. Registration of copyright is not necessary, but the Act provides for registration (section 54) and it does confer certain advantages on the registered owner. In particular, the certificate of registration creates a presumption that copyright subsists in the work and that the person registered is the owner of the copyright. Still, the advantages to be gained from registration are relatively small and the practice is not widely used except by performing rights societies.

Infringement of Copyright

What Constitutes Infringement?

Copyright consists of a number of exclusive rights vested in the owner. An infringement occurs when another person, without the consent of the owner, does an act that only the owner has the right to do. Thus, the unauthorized public performance, publication, or reproduction of a copyrighted work constitutes an infringement, as does the translation of a work or its conversion into some other form, or recording, broadcasting, or exhibiting it in public. A person who purports to authorize some other person to do any of those acts, without the owner's consent, is also guilty of infringing copyright.

It is not necessary for the entire work to be copied to constitute an infringement of copyright; the unauthorized copying of a substantial part is sufficient. What amounts to a "substantial" part is a question of fact and of degree. A quotation of a few lines from a written work, especially if attributed to its author, does not constitute an infringement, but the quotation of several pages might. The offending copy need not be identical to the original work, and one cannot avoid liability simply by arranging the copied work in a different format or by making minor changes.

CASE 22.6

Hager was the author of a book about famous Canadians of aboriginal heritage, which included a nine-page chapter about country music star Shania Twain. The chapter was based on Hager's interviews of Twain, and included many quotations from those interviews. Subsequently, Holmes was commissioned by ECW Press to write a book about Twain. The ECW book was found to contain substantial portions of Hager's work, including most of the direct quotations from the interviews with Twain. Hager sued ECW for breach of copyright.

ECW argued that the quoted words of Twain were not protected by copyright, because they were not the original work of Hager. They also claimed that the copying was not substantial (it amounted to about one-third of the Hager chapter) and that it constituted fair dealing for research purposes.

These defences were rejected and Hager was awarded damages, plus an accounting equal to 10 percent of ECW's profits from the sale of their book. The court held that Hager's work was protected by copyright because it was a product of her skill, judgment, and labour. Twain's quoted words were in response to Hager's questions, and had been selected by Hager for inclusion in her book. The copying was substantial and could not be said to have been done for research purposes.[37]

A person may also infringe copyright by reproducing a work in an altogether different form. For example, making a three-dimensional object from a designer's drawings may infringe the copyright in those drawings.[38]

The person who actually makes the copy is not the only one who may be liable for infringement of copyright. A theatre owner who permits her theatre to be used by a group of actors or musicians for a performance that infringes the author's copyright is as guilty of infringement as are the performers. Also, a bookseller who imports and sells a "pirated" edition of a copyrighted book is as guilty as the illegal publisher. It is an infringement of copyright to authorize a person to do something that the owner of the copyright has the sole right to do. Thus a person who buys a book and lends it to a friend for the purpose of photocopying it infringes the copyright in the book as much as does the friend. However, to manufacture and sell tape recorders that have a facility for "dubbing" pre-recorded tapes onto blank tapes has been held not to constitute authorizing an infringement.[39]

"Fair Dealing" and Other Permitted Uses

Certain acts that would otherwise amount to infringements of copyright are expressly permitted by the Copyright Act, and the exemptions have been expanded by the 1997 amendments to the Act. The most important exemption allows the fair use of copyright works for the purpose of research or private study (section 29), for criticism and review (section 29.1), or for news reporting (section 29.2). Subject to a number of conditions, educational institutions are permitted to copy and reproduce works for purposes of instruction (section 29.4).[40]

Remedies for Infringement

The usual civil remedies are available in cases of infringement of copyright:

---

37. Hager v. ECW Press Ltd., *supra*, n. 32.

38. Hanfstaengl v. H.R. Baines & Co., [1895] A.C. 20; Bayliner Marine Corp. v. Doral Boats Ltd. (1985), 5 C.P.R. (3d) 289.

39. CBS Songs Ltd. v. Amstrad Consumer Electronics, [1988] 2 All E.R. 484. The 1997 amendments to the Copyright Act now impose a levy on the sale of blank cassette tapes and compact disks.

40. It does not permit the reproduction of an entire work, or a substantial portion thereof: see Boudreau v. Lin (1997), 150 D.L.R. (4th) 324.

- *damages* for profit or income lost by the owner, or for conversion of the owner's property[41]
- *account* for profits made by the defendant as a result of the infringement (normally an alternative to damages)
- *injunction*, to restrain the defendant from further infringement and to require the delivering-up of any offending copy

The new rules, adopted in 1999 pursuant to the 1997 amendments to the Act, also provide for fines up to $20 000 to deter bootlegging and pirating of copyrighted materials.

Of course, many infringements of copyright go unpunished. While it may be a breach of copyright to photocopy a book or article other than for purposes of study or research, or to videotape a television broadcast of a copyrighted work for later viewing,[42] it is most unlikely that the offences will be discovered or, if they are, that it will be worthwhile for the owner to sue the offender.

PATENTS

At common law, an inventor had no inherent right to the fruits of his or her creation and no law was broken by merely making use of another's invention. Thus, like copyright but unlike trademarks, the law of patents is entirely based upon statute. However, a patent differs fundamentally from copyright: while copyright comes into existence *automatically* as a result of the act of creation, a patent exists only by virtue of being granted by the appropriate government body.

In England, the law of patents is usually traced back to the Statute of Monopolies of 1623; it gave the sovereign the sole right to issue *letters patent* for the exclusive "working or making of any manner of new manufacture." The law of patents evolved slowly in Britain, the first general statute being adopted only in 1852; by that time a substantial body of patent law had already evolved in the United States, following the adoption of a federal patent law in 1790.

Patent legislation was introduced as early as 1824 and 1826, in Lower and Upper Canada respectively. The first federal Patent Act was adopted in 1869, based largely upon the existing American legislation. This American influence prevailed until just a few years ago. The current Patent Act,[43] originally enacted in 1935, was substantially amended in 1987,[44] in part to bring Canada's law into conformity with international practice under the Patent Cooperation Treaty. The 1987 amendments changed a number of the specifically American features of our law. These amendments came into effect on October 1, 1989; patents granted or applied for prior to that date remain subject to the earlier law. Further substantial amendments, notably in respect of pharmaceutical products, were introduced in 1992 and 1993.[45]

The concept of a patent is now almost universally recognized. Well over 100 countries belong to the Paris Union and adhere to the International Convention for the Protection of Industrial Property, which dates back to 1883, and close to 100 countries now adhere to the Patent Cooperation Treaty adopted by the World Intellectual Property Organization. Canada belongs to both.

---

41. Improper copies are deemed to be the property of the copyright owner. However, they are essentially worthless, so that where an offending publisher destroyed improper copies it was not liable for additional damages in conversion: Editions JCL Inc. v. 91439 Canada Ltee (1994), 120 D.L.R. (4th) 225.

42. Tom Hopkins Int'l. Inc. v. Wall & Redekop Realty Ltd. (1984), 1 C.P.R. (3d) 348.

43. R.S.C. 1985, c. P-4. (Unless otherwise stated, references in this part are to that Act, as amended.)

44. R.S.C. 1985, c. 33 (3rd Supp.).

45. S.C. 1993, c. 2; S.C. 1993, c. 15.

The Nature of Patents

An inventor, or the legal representative of an inventor, may obtain a patent that gives the applicant exclusive property in the invention for a period of 20 years (section 44).[46] This property comprises the "exclusive right, privilege and liberty of making, constructing and using the invention and selling it to others to be used" (section 42).

In return for this right, the inventor must make the invention public, by filing an adequate description of the invention, so that others will be able to duplicate the invention freely when the statutory period of monopoly has expired. Thus, an inventor has a choice: he or she can keep the invention entirely secret and continue to exploit it indefinitely but run the risk that some other person will sooner or later stumble upon the same invention or will unravel the secret; or the inventor can reveal it and enjoy exclusive rights for a limited period only. Given the speed at which technological advances are now being made, and the perhaps over-generous period of protection, applying for a patent would seem advisable for inventions that are likely to prove lucrative. However, obtaining a patent is a complex and fairly expensive business and if an invention is likely to have only a short productive life, secrecy may be the better option. The alternatives of registering the invention as an industrial design or relying upon copyright protection of the plans or specifications should also be considered. But it must be remembered that while copyright provides protection for a much longer period, the protection is more limited, since it extends only to the method of expression and not to the idea itself.

Patentable Inventions

Only "inventions" qualify for patent protection. What qualities must they have? The Act defines an invention as "any new and useful art, process, machine, manufacture or composition of matter, or any new and useful improvement in any art, process, machine, manufacture or composition of matter" (section 2). Thus, three elements in the definition must be present for an invention to be patentable. It must be:

- an art, process, machine, manufacture, or composition of matter or an improvement to such
- new
- useful

As well, inherent in the notion of an invention is the requirement that it is something that possesses the quality of ingenuity and is not simply an obvious step any person with ordinary skill in the field may have taken.

Art, Process, Machine, Manufacture, or Composition of Matter

For an invention to be patentable, it must fall within one of these categories. The word "art" refers to the manual or productive arts, as distinct from the fine arts. A "process" means a method of manufacture or operation designed to produce a particular result, for example, a new process for the chemical cleaning of fabrics. "Machine" and "manufacture" are given their usual meanings, and a "composition of matter" refers to such things as chemical formulae that produce new compounds and substances.

A patent will not be issued solely for a scientific principle or abstract theorem, such as a mathematical formula (section 27(8)). For these purposes, a computer program is equated to an abstract theorem and is *not* by itself patentable,[47] though a patent may be granted for an invention that involves the use of a computer program as an essential part to achieve a particular result.

---

46. For patents issuing from applications filed before October 1989 the period is 17 years.
47. Schlumberger Canada Ltd. v. Commissioner of Patents, [1982] 1 F.C. 845.

CASE 22.7

A researcher at Harvard College developed a method of genetically altering mice to make them more susceptible to cancer formation following exposure to chemicals. This made the mice valuable for experimentation purposes. The invention was registered as a patent in the United States (and in a number of European countries) by the college. The college subsequently attempted to register a patent for the "Harvard mouse" in Canada.

Registration was refused by the Patent Appeal Board and the refusal was upheld by the Federal Court. The court considered that the insertion of the foreign gene into the genetic fabric of the mouse was largely uncontrollable and unpredictable. The process lacked the element of reproducibility required of a patent.[48]

The "Harvard mouse" decision does not necessarily mean that genetically modified life forms can never be patented in Canada,[49] but there does seem to have been a reluctance to date on the part of the authorities and the courts to accept that such processes constitute a patentable "invention."[50]

"Substances"

Until the 1987 reforms, no patent might be issued for any "substance" intended for food or medicine, but the process for producing it could be patented. A patent may now be issued in respect of substances themselves, prepared or produced by microbiological processes and intended for food or medicine, as well as for the particular method by which the substance is prepared or produced.[51]

For pharmaceutical products protected by patent in other countries, a system of **compulsory licensing** existed that allowed Canadian firms to manufacture or import drugs upon payment of a low royalty to the patentee. This system led to the development of a thriving generic drug industry in Canada, to the economic benefit of the Canadian consumer but to the detriment of foreign pharmaceutical companies. It also arguably acted as a deterrent to research and development of pharmaceutical products within Canada. It became a controversial issue that featured prominently in the debates on the Free Trade Agreement between Canada and the United States and in the subsequent NAFTA negotiations; American pressure has in part been responsible for the changes that have been made in the law.

The 1987 and 1993 amendments to the Act replaced the compulsory licensing scheme for patented medicines with special regulations that established a framework for allowing generic drug companies to obtain the right to produce patented drugs on payment of a royalty to the patent owner. The regulations are extremely complex and have produced one of the most hotly contested areas of litigation.[52] In part due to the problems highlighted by this litigation, the regulations were amended in 1999, but further amendments may become necessary since the present Canadian scheme has been challenged by a number of countries as being contrary to the rules of the World Trade Organization.

compulsory licensing
granting a licence to a person to work a patent without the consent of the owner of the patent

---

48. Harvard College v. Canada (Commissioner of Patents) (1998), 79 C.P.R. (3d) 98.

49. Genetically modified yeast has been patented; see Re Application of Abitibi Co. (1982), 62 C.P.R. (2d) 81.

50. See Pioneer Hi-Bred Ltd. v. Canada (Commissioner of Patents) (1987), 14 C.P.R. (3d) 491 (F.C.A.); affd (1989), 25 C.P.R. (3d) 257 (S.C.C.) in which it was held that a soybean variety developed by traditional plant cross-breeding was not patentable subject matter. The rights of plant breeders may be protected under the Plant Breeders' Rights Act; see below, under the heading "Technological Change and Intellectual Property Law."

51. Patent Act Amendment Act, S.C. 1993, c. 2.

52. See the decisions of the Supreme Court of Canada in Eli Lilly and Co. v. Novopharm Ltd. (1998), 161 D.L.R. (4th) 1; Merck Frosst Canada Inc. v. Canada (1998), 161 D.L.R. (4th) 47.

Novelty

An essential element of an invention is that it be "new." A patent will not be granted for a machine or process that is already known or in use, even if it has not been patented by some other person.

Until 1989, Canada was one of the few countries—along with the United States—to apply a "first-to-invent" system; that is to say, if two or more persons applied for a patent for the same invention, only the first inventor was considered the true inventor and entitled to the patent. The new law adopts the more common "first-to-file" system; in cases of conflicting applications, the application with the earlier filing date prevails.

An invention for which a patent is claimed must be one that has not been disclosed to the public anywhere in the world before the filing date. There is an exception to this rule when the inventor himself makes the disclosure, but even then he must file the application within one year of making the disclosure.

Utility

For an invention to qualify as "useful" it must possess industrial value, for example, by making a process easier, cheaper, or faster. Also implied is that it be usable; that is to say, it should be reproducible and operable, so that a skilled worker, by following the specifications published in the patent, should be able to reproduce the invention and obtain the desired result.[53]

Ingenuity

An invention requires an element of ingenuity; as we have noted, it must be more than an obvious step. As has been said:

> The question to be answered is whether at the date of invention...an unimaginative skilled technician, in light of his general knowledge and the literature and information on the subject available to him on that date, would have been led directly and without difficulty to [the] invention.[54]

In reaching such a conclusion, the patent office or court must be careful not to be influenced by hindsight: great inventions often seem deceptively simple and obvious in retrospect.

Obtaining a Patent

Only the inventor, or the legal representatives of the inventor, may apply for the grant of a patent. "Legal representatives" include not only heirs and executors, but also persons claiming through the inventor. If an inventor has assigned the rights to an invention to another person or to a corporation, the assignee may apply. An employer usually owns inventions made by its employees, and thus is entitled to apply for a patent.

Applications for patents are made to the Commissioner of Patents and are processed by the Patent Office, located in Hull, Québec. Individual inventors may pursue their own applications, but any other applicants must use the services of a registered **patent agent**. In practice, making an application is a highly complex and specialized matter and is almost invariably handled by a patent agent.

The agent first makes a search of the register of patents, and frequently also a search at the U.S. Patent Office, to ensure that no patent has already been granted in respect of the invention. The next major task is to draft the application, in a form prescribed by the Patent Rules. The most important part of the application has two elements: (a) the **specification**, providing a full description of the invention, its use, operation, or manufacture; and (b) the **claim**, setting out

patent agent
a registered agent who pursues applications for patents on behalf of individual inventors

specification
the description of the invention, its use, operation, or manufacture

claim
a statement of the features claimed to be new and in respect of which the applicant claims an exclusive right

---

53. This was the principal reason for refusing the application in the "Harvard mouse" case, *supra*, n. 48.

54. Beecham Canada Ltd. v. Proctor & Gamble Co. (1982), 61 C.P.R. (2d) 1 at 27, per Urie, J.A.

the features claimed to be new and in respect of which the applicant claims an exclusive right. Particular care must be taken to ensure that the claim is sufficiently broad to obtain the maximum benefit from the invention. At the same time it must not be excessively wide so as to include matters that are obvious or already known, and thus render the claim invalid.

When an application has been filed, a further application must be made for the claim to be examined. The Patent Office then appoints an Examiner to consider the application. The Examiner makes searches of patents, and frequently of technical publications, to ensure that the claimed invention is indeed novel and otherwise complies with the requirements of the Patent Act. The Examiner scrutinizes the specification and claim to ensure that complete disclosure has been made and that the invention is described in a way that would enable other persons to utilize it once the period of protection has elapsed. During this stage the applicant may make amendments to the application in order to satisfy objections raised by the Examiner. When the process is complete, the Examiner determines whether or not a patent shall be granted. An appeal from a rejection of the application may be made to the Patent Appeal Board and then to the courts.

When the application is successful, the Patent Office issues a "Notice of Allowance," and on payment of a fee (which is additional to the application fee) it issues the patent. Since 1989, the Act requires that a further yearly fee be paid in order to maintain the patent. The fees, however, are relatively modest: for an applicant that qualifies as a "small entity"[55] the total fees to obtain a patent and to maintain it for the full 20-year period could be less than $2500. The cost of protection for a five-year period could be as little as $500. However, the services of a skilled patent agent will cost considerably more than the fees paid to the Patent Office.

Protection of Patent Rights

As we have seen, patent rights may now be preserved for a period of 20 years, so long as the yearly maintenance fee is paid. A patent confers on its owner the exclusive right of constructing and using the invention and selling it to others to be used. An owner may assign patent rights to others, or grant a licence for their limited or exclusive use. An assignment must be in writing and registered with the Patent Office, as must a grant of an exclusive licence.

Any unauthorized act that interferes with the full enjoyment of the exclusive rights conferred by the patent is an infringement. The usual remedies of damages, injunction, and accounting for profit are available to the patentee and to anyone (for example, an assignee or licensee) claiming under him. An action to protect or enforce a patent right may be brought in the Federal Court or in the appropriate provincial court.

Patents and the Public Interest

The granting of a patent is a serious matter, since giving an exclusive right to use and exploit an invention, for a period of up to 20 years, in effect creates a *monopoly*. The result is to confer a considerable advantage over business competitors and sometimes, if the patentee chooses not to exploit the invention, to deprive the public of the use of the invention. There are many stories—most of them probably fabrications—of large corporations buying up inventions (such as everlasting light bulbs) that threaten their business in order to suppress the invention.

Patent legislation attempts to protect the public in a number of ways, which are discussed below.

Scope of the Claim

The law seeks to ensure that only genuine inventions qualify for the grant of a patent, and disallows claims that are too broad in scope. One of the most important functions of the patent

---

55. A "small entity" means an individual inventor or a business concern that employs 50 or fewer persons, or is a university, and that meets a number of other conditions. The fees payable by other applicants are twice as high.

action for impeachment
an action challenging the
validity of a patent

examiner is to enforce these policies. In addition, third parties, such as business competitors or rival researchers, may challenge the validity of a patent by bringing an **action for impeachment** in the Federal Court. The Attorney General of Canada may also bring such an action.

For patent applications filed after October 1, 1989, an alternative form of challenge is available: any person may apply to the Commissioner of Patents for re-examination of any claim of a patent. Upon receiving such a request, the Commissioner establishes a Re-examination Board to examine the request.

Abuse of Patent Rights

Another form of protection allows the Attorney General, or any interested person, to apply to the Commissioner of Patents when it is alleged that patent rights are being abused. An abuse occurs, for example,

- if demand for the patented article in Canada is not being met to a reasonable extent and on reasonable terms
- if the patentee is hindering the creation of new industries or damaging the public interest by refusing to grant licences
- if any trade, industry or person engaged therein is unfairly prejudiced by the conditions attached to a patent
- if the existence of a patent has been used so as to unfairly prejudice in Canada the manufacture, use or sale of any materials

Compulsory Licensing

The aim of patent law is not only to encourage new inventions by protecting them, but also to encourage the working of those inventions in Canada without undue delay. Thus, a patentee cannot simply hold a patent for the purpose of blocking trade; if it does not exploit the invention itself in a reasonable manner, it must sell it or grant a licence on reasonable terms. Where there is abuse, some other person who wishes to make use of the invention may apply for the grant of a compulsory licence, which may be ordered on terms that allow the applicant to work the patent while giving the patentee a fair return. Normally this arrangement involves the payment of a stipulated rate of royalty on products manufactured under the licence.

Competition Law

The Competition Act[56] provides a further form of protection of the public interest. It prohibits the exploitation of a patent in such a way as to unduly restrain trade or prevent or lessen competition, and authorizes the Federal Court to grant appropriate relief.

CONTEMPORARY ISSUE

The Generic Drugs Dilemma

Manufacturers of generic drugs say a bid to extend federal patent protection beyond 20 years...could "devastate" the industry and cost the health system billions of dollars. The European Union will go before the World Trade Organization...in an attempt to throw out provisions of Canada's drug patent law that allow generic manufacturers to hit store shelves with new products the day a patent expires....A study done for the CDMA [Canadian Drug

continued

56. R.S.C. 1985, c. C-34. See further Chapter 32.

Manufacturers Association] last year suggested a five-year increase in patent protection to 25 years would cost the health-care system $6 billion. Generic manufacturers have total revenue approaching $1 billion and employ 5000. Many of those jobs could disappear if the EU is successful....

This is just the latest battle over drug patent protection in Canada, which reached a recent peak just last year when the government reviewed the legislation. The generic manufacturers worked hard to get the patent period reduced but were unsuccessful when Ottawa decided to make no major changes. Canada is home to a handful of generic-drug makers and more than 60 publicly traded biotech companies. But it is still a branch-plant location for brand-name pharmaceutical companies.

Source: Ian Jack, "EU pushes Canada to toughen drug patents," *National Post*, November 13, 1998, p. C1.

The dilemma is that, if patent protection is increased, Canada may well lose its highly competitive generic drug industry. If protection is not increased, Canada will be a less attractive location for the major multinational pharmaceutical companies and for their research activities. A further factor is that

Jobs for science graduates are welcome. But they need to be balanced against the cost Canadians pay in higher drug prices. They are the fastest-rising component of the nation's medical bill. They hit low-income working people (who make up most of the 3.6 million Canadians without drug insurance) especially hard.

Source: Editorial, "Consumers lose in drug price battle," *Toronto Star*, January 23, 1998, p. A20.

Questions to Consider

1. How should the various interests of the multinationals, the "generics," and the public be balanced?

2. Is extended patent protection really necessary to promote research on drugs? Will international competition not have that effect?

INDUSTRIAL DESIGNS

Industrial designs comprise a fourth type of intellectual property, registrable under the Industrial Design Act.[57] Originally enacted in 1868, the Act has been amended on a number of occasions. Despite the amendments, the Act remains a somewhat archaic and rather unsatisfactory piece of legislation.

Meaning of "Industrial Design"

Until the Act was amended in 1988, it contained no definition of an industrial design. The Act (section 2) now states that "industrial design" means:

features of shape, configuration, pattern or ornament and any combination of those features that, in a finished article, appeal to and are judged solely by the eye.

Features that are solely utilitarian or functional are not protected, nor is any method or principle of manufacture or construction. For many years it was thought that the Act referred only to designs placed on an article, such as a decorative design on a dinner service, a crest or emblem on a sports shirt, or a design on a roll of wallpaper. More recently, however, it has been held to apply also to the design of the shape of the article *itself*, insofar as the design is ornamental and not

---

57. R.S.C. 1985, c. I-9. (Unless otherwise stated, references in the part are to that Act, as amended.)

dictated by the function of the article. Thus, the shape of a stacking chair, or of a knife handle, may be registered, but in order to secure registration some degree of originality is also required.

Protection by Registration

The Industrial Design Act permits the proprietor of an industrial design to register it and obtain exclusive rights to its use in Canada for a term of five years, with the possibility of renewing the registration for one further term of five years. At common law there is no property in an industrial design, except insofar as it may qualify for protection as a trademark. Protection is consequently dependent upon registration. A proprietor may apply to register a design with the Commissioner of Patents, in Hull. Application must be made within one year of the first publication of the design.[58] "Publication" in this sense means making the design available to the public, for example, by selling an article to which the design has been applied.

The only person entitled to apply for registration is the "proprietor," who is usually the designer, but if a client or customer commissioned and paid for the design, that person is considered to be the proprietor. If the design was produced by the employee in the normal course of employment, the employer will normally be the proprietor.

Registration gives the proprietor the exclusive right to apply the design to any article for the purpose of sale. However, in order to protect the design each article to which the design is applied must be marked with the name of the proprietor, the word "Registered" or its abbreviation, "Rd," and the year of registration. A proprietor may assign or grant a licence for the use of a registered design, but the assignment or licence must be recorded on the register in order to preserve the exclusive right.

During the existence of the exclusive right, no other person may apply the design, or any imitation of it, to any article for the purpose of sale without the written consent of the proprietor. The usual remedies of damages, injunction, and account for profits are available to the proprietor and, in addition, the Act prescribes a number of summary offences, punishable by fine, for infringement of industrial design rights.

As we have seen, both industrial designs and patents may be protected only by prompt registration. Normally, it will not be difficult to decide whether a design qualifies for patent protection or should be registered as an industrial design. Industrial designs are essentially ornamental, whereas a patentable invention must be useful. In cases of doubt, the advice of a qualified patent agent should be sought.

Industrial Designs, Trademarks, and Copyright

The same design or logo that may be applied to an article as an industrial design may also be considered a trademark. Similarly, the ornamental shape of a container or wrapper may be registered as an industrial design as well as be protected under trademark law as a "distinguishing guise." Protection as a trademark is clearly superior, since property rights in a trademark are not dependent upon registration and are not limited to a maximum period of 10 years. However, the two forms of protection do not conflict: a proprietor may register an industrial design and still claim protection for the design as a trademark.

The situation with respect to copyright is more complex. The Copyright Act originally refused copyright protection for designs capable of being registered under the Industrial Design Act. An exception was made for designs that were not used or intended to be used as models or patterns to be multiplied by any industrial process. This provision was revised in 1988,[59] though the intention of the new provision remains essentially similar. Now, if the design is applied to a useful article and the article is reproduced in a quantity of more than 50, some other person

---

58. S.C. 1992, c. 1, ss. 47–52. Previously actual registration had to occur within one year of first publication in Canada.

59. Copyright Act, R.S.C. 1985, c. C-42, ss. 64 and 64.1, as amended by S.C. 1988, c. 15, s. 11.

does not infringe copyright in the design simply by reproducing the article. Thus, protection for the design can only be secured by registering it under the Industrial Design Act.[60]

CONFIDENTIAL INFORMATION, TRADE SECRETS, AND KNOW-HOW

The description "intellectual property" should properly be restricted to the four forms—trademarks, copyright, patents, and industrial designs—that we have discussed in this chapter. Mere ideas or knowledge, however valuable, are not regarded as "property" in the strict sense of the word. Thus, the Supreme Court of Canada has ruled that confidential information is not property that can be the subject of theft under the Criminal Code.[61]

Such information may nevertheless have commercial value: a secret manufacturing process—if it *can* be kept secret—may be more valuable not patented than patented; and a uniquely efficient way of operating a business, though not capable of being patented at all, may be worth millions in extra profits to its owner. Similarly, a list of customers or clients may constitute an important part of the goodwill of a business. Information can be valuable to people other than its owner; although not property in the strict sense, information can still be sold to others as, for example, where data is made available to subscribers to a computerized data-retrieval service.

The possessor of confidential information, trade secrets, or know-how is not entirely without legal protection, though such protection normally arises out of a contractual or fiduciary relationship rather than from any proprietary interest. Thus, a seller may supply machinery or equipment to a buyer and at the same time license the buyer to use the seller's know-how or some secret process; it is usual to stipulate in the contract that the buyer will not divulge the secret to anyone else.[62] Similarly, some contracts of employment include a restrictive covenant restraining the employee, if she leaves the employment, from making use of the employer's confidential information or divulging it to someone else. In addition, employees, company directors, partners, and parties to a joint venture stand in a *fiduciary relationship* to their employers, corporations, or co-partners. To misuse or divulge confidential information acquired in the course of such a relationship may constitute a breach of trust, which can be restrained by injunction or punished by an award of damages or an accounting for profits made as a result of the breach.[63]

CASE 22.8

A former employee of Apotex took up a new position with a competing firm, Novopharm. He brought with him confidential information about a process for making the drug, Lovastatin. Apotex brought an action for an injunction restraining Novopharm from carrying out further research on the drug, and for damages against the employee and against Novopharm.

The court held both the employee and the new employer liable. Novopharm knew, or ought to have known, that the information was confidential and had been obtained from Apotex. They were consequently liable for the breach of trust of their new employee.[64]

---

60. See Bayliner Marine Corp. v. Doral Boats Ltd. (1986), 10 C.P.R. (3d) 289.

61. R. v. Stewart, [1988] 1 S.C.R. 963.

62. In Cadbury Schweppes Inc. v. FBI Foods Ltd. (1999),167 D.L.R. (4th) 577, the Supreme Court of Canada held that a manufacturer under licence who produced a competing product after the termination of the licence, using confidential information, was liable in damages for the loss suffered by the licensor.

63. See Lac Minerals Ltd. v. International Corona Resources Ltd. (1989), 61 D.L.R. (4th) 14. Misuse of confidential information by corporate directors or officers is discussed further in Chapter 28.

64. Apotex Fermentation Inc. v. Novopharm Ltd. (1998), 162 D.L.R. (4th) 111.

TECHNOLOGICAL CHANGE AND INTELLECTUAL PROPERTY LAW

Although a number of important statutory changes have been made recently, the basic principles of the statutes governing Canadian intellectual property law are generally well over a century old. Yet few aspects of society have changed so much as those that are affected by intellectual property law. Firms and nations now spend vast amounts on research and development, aware that inventiveness is the key to competitiveness in the international economy. Entertainment, of which copyright is the raw material, is a multibillion-dollar industry. In corporate mergers and takeovers, trademarks and brand names are frequently valued in millions. Information, it seems, knows no frontiers: of the total number of patents now registered each year in the United States, approximately one half are registered by foreign inventors. Intellectual property has become internationalized.

New technologies have created new problems, not all of which are easily solved by analogy to old situations. That this is so is illustrated by two relatively recent statutes, enacted to protect the rights of plant breeders and the designers of integrated circuits, respectively. The Plant Breeders' Rights Act[65] provides exclusive rights, similar to patent rights in respect of new varieties of plants, including genetically modified plants. To qualify, a plant variety must be clearly distinguishable from all other commonly known varieties of the species, be both stable and homogeneous, and be of a variety not yet sold in Canada. Application is made to a Commissioner of Plant Breeders' Rights, who may require or conduct such tests as are necessary to establish the novelty of the variety. A grant is for a term of 18 years, subject to payment of an annual fee, and confers the exclusive right to sell, produce, and use the variety.

The Integrated Circuit Topography Act[66] also provides exclusive rights similar to patent rights in the "topography" or design of integrated circuits (semiconductor chips) and in the circuits that incorporate such designs themselves. Registration is required, and protection is for a period of 10 years.

New technologies have not only given rise to the creation of new types of intellectual property and new rights, the ways in which existing rights may be exercised and infringed is also changing. The advent of sound recording and television, not to mention direct broadcasting by satellite, cable transmission, and computer databanks, have greatly widened the concept of "publication." At the same time, tape and video recorders and photocopiers have made it very easy to infringe intellectual property rights. New questions are constantly being raised, to which simple answers cannot be given; for example, to what extent does trademark and copyright law apply to material accessible through e-mail or the Internet? (This issue is discussed further in Chapter 34.) As we observed at the beginning of this chapter, intellectual property law raises important issues of public policy. We conclude by quoting the Economic Council of Canada:

> ...new technology and the movement towards an increasingly knowledge-based economy and society are throwing up issues of such scale and significance that no part of the existing policy structure can remain unaffected.[67]

QUESTIONS FOR REVIEW

1. What types of intellectual property are protected by law?

---

65. S.C. 1990, c. 20.

66. S.C. 1990, c. 37.

67. *Report on Intellectual and Industrial Property.* Ottawa: Economic Council of Canada, 1971, pp. 5–6.

2. What are the principal costs and benefits of protecting intellectual property?

3. What are the essential elements of the tort of passing-off?

4. Are there any advantages to be gained in registering a trademark?

5. What precautions should be taken in selecting the name of a new corporation?

6. What is a "certification mark"?

7. On what grounds may the registration of a trademark be opposed?

8. What are the principal rights possessed by an owner of copyright?

9. In relation to copyright, what are "moral rights"?

10. Does copyright exist in computer software?

11. For how long does copyright usually last?

12. In what ways may a person become an owner of copyright?

13. What constitutes "fair dealing"?

14. What qualities must an invention have in order to be patented?

15. Why might an inventor choose not to register a patent?

16. What is meant by an "industrial design"?

17. How may "know-how" be protected?

CASES AND PROBLEMS

1 In 1955, a highly successful novel entitled *Lolita*, authored by Vladimir Nabokov, was published. The novel recounts the story of how a middle-aged man, Humbert Humbert, becomes infatuated with his 12-year-old stepdaughter, Lolita, eventually descending to rape, murder, and madness. The story is narrated by Humbert himself.

In 1995, the Italian author Pia Pera wrote a book entitled *Lo's Diary*, which was subsequently translated into English. The book purports to tell the story of the affair as experienced by Lolita herself. The principal events of the earlier parts of the story are the same as described in the Nabokov book, though described from the very different perspective of the young girl. (Ms. Pera's book goes on to describe events that occurred after the parting of the two protagonists.)

The late Mr. Nabokov's son and executor threatened action for infringement of copyright. Should the action succeed?

2 A small Ontario corporation, Pink Panther Beauty Corp., applied to register the name "Pink Panther" as a trademark for hair-care and beauty supplies that it proposed to market.

The application was opposed by United Artists, the well-known movie studio that owns the Pink Panther movies, the Pink Panther cartoon character, and the accompanying music. United Artists has its own "Pink Panther" registrations for movie-related services. It argued that the application by the Ontario corporation should not be granted because of the risk of confusion with its existing marks. Further, it claimed that the applicants were simply trying to cash-in on their famous name.

Is the objection a valid one?

3 Shamrock Homes Inc. is a major construction company that specializes in the construction of large residential developments. Brendan, their chief engineer, has worked out an entirely new method of planning a development, requiring the construction of a factory in which prefabricated components for houses are manufactured and assembled to speed up the construction of houses. The factory is specially designed to be converted into a shopping mall when all the houses are completed. Shamrock estimates that the new method reduces construction costs by as much as 15 percent.

Shamrock wishes to patent this new method, fearing that competitors will easily be able to copy it otherwise. Give your opinion as to whether the method is patentable.

4 Bouchard was a part-time university student in an MBA program. As part of his work for one course, he wrote a term paper based on his experience of a particular problem he had dealt with in his full-time employment, using data that he had collected there. His employer consented to his use of that material.

Without Bouchard's knowledge, Lam, the professor who had supervised the paper, had it published (with some revisions) in a casebook sold by the university to MBA students. In the casebook, Lam was named as the author and no mention was made of Bouchard.

When Bouchard saw his paper in the casebook, he brought an action for infringement of copyright. Should his action succeed? What defences might be raised by Lam?

5 McCoy's Restaurants Ltd. is a large firm incorporated under the Canada Business Corporations Act. It operates a chain of some 60 restaurants across Canada under the name of "McCoy's," and is very well-known nationally due to its extensive advertising campaigns.

Angus McCoy recently bought a restaurant, previously known as "Sam's Diner," situated at a busy truck stop near Brandon, Manitoba. He formed a company under the name of Angus McCoy (Brandon) Ltd., incorporated under the Manitoba Business Corporations Act, and renamed the restaurant "The Real McCOY's." The decor and furnishings of Angus's restaurant are not at all like those of the McCoy chain, but the external appearance bears some similarity.

The president of McCoy's Restaurants Ltd. is angry because she has been planning to open a branch in that particular location. She alleges that Angus is attempting to deceive the public, is trading on her company's reputation, and is benefitting from its advertising. She has written to Angus, insisting that he change the name of his company and of his restaurant, otherwise McCoy's Restaurants will commence legal proceedings.

Angus maintains that no one is confused, that he chose the name "The Real McCOY's" deliberately to distinguish his restaurant from those of the chain, and that, since the principal owners of McCoy's Restaurants Ltd. are called Angelotti and Zbigniewsky, they are the ones who are trading under false colours.

Advise Angus what legal actions might be taken against him and whether or not they might succeed.

6 Dolphin Marine Ltd. is a well-established firm with an excellent reputation for building racing boats. It has recently produced a new 12-metre model, the DM35X, with a fibreglass hull of novel design, which has been highly successful in a number of important races.

Kopikat Inc. is a small firm that has been building catamarans for a number of years with little success, either sporting or financial. Kenny, the controlling shareholder and president of Kopikat, buys one of the new Dolphin models, constructs a mould of the hull, and commences to produce a racer with a hull identical to the DM35X and with other features that are very similar. Kopikat is planning to market it at a price $8000 lower than the DM35X.

Has Kopikat infringed any right of Dolphin?

Interests in Land and Their Transfer

Since land remains the "ultimate platform of human activity," the ownership of interests in land is a primary concern both in private life and in carrying on business. It is, therefore, important to understand the background to ownership. In this chapter we examine such questions as:

- what are the various "estates" in land?

- what are their legal characteristics and consequences?

- what are "interests less than estates"?

- what is "adverse possession"?

- how are interests in land transferred and protected?

The Nature of Interests in Land

Real Property

The Meaning of "Property"

We usually refer to land as *real property*, an important term that needs some explanation. The word **property** itself has two closely related meanings. The more common one defines property as "everything which is the subject of ownership…everything that has exchangeable value or which goes to make up wealth…."[1] By this definition, property means *the thing itself*, whether it be a piece of land, a piece of cheese, or a bill of lading, a share certificate, or the tangible things these documents represent. The lesser-known meaning of property is not the thing itself but *the legal interest* in the thing—the right or rights that the law will recognize and protect. Property in this sense has been called "ownership, the unrestricted and exclusive right to a thing; the right to dispose of a thing in every legal way, to possess it, to use it, and to exclude everyone else from interfering with it."[2] A common synonym for the term "property" in the sense of ownership is the word **title**: the expressions "ownership *of* a thing," "title *to* a

property
everything that is the subject of ownership, that has exchangeable value or that goes to make up wealth, *or* the legal interest in the thing

title
ownership of, or property in, a thing

---

1. *Black's Law Dictionary* (6th ed.), p. 1216. St. Paul: West Publishing Co., 1990.
2. *Ibid.*

thing," and "property *in* a thing" are used interchangeably. Although the first meaning of property—the thing itself—is of general importance in law, it is in the second sense that we use the word in the present chapter.

The Meaning of "Real"

real
historically, the legal remedy a party could get when rights to land had been interfered with

real action
an action to repossess an interest in land that had been interfered with

personal action
an action for money damages

Historically, the word "**real**" referred to the kind of remedy a party could get in court when property rights had been interfered with. Certain types of interests in land gave the owner a remedy by way of **real action**—an action to repossess the interest interfered with—rather than a remedy by way of **personal action**, an action for money damages without a right to have the interest back again. Real actions were available only when one of a carefully defined class of interests was interfered with; but in time the term "real property" came to refer to interests in land generally, whether or not a real action would lie for the recovery of the interest, and we shall so use the term.

The Meaning of "Real Property"

The law of real property has special concepts and terms of its own, and we must take great care to use the terms accurately. The reasons for this special terminology are partly historical and partly attributable to the peculiar qualities of land. Land is permanent, except on the rare occasions when a piece of it slides into the sea and is lost, or is permanently flooded by a large hydro development, as occurred along the St. Lawrence Seaway. Otherwise a given piece of land exists perpetually: it remains long after its temporary owners are gone, and it has a fixed location. An interest in land recognized by law may affect that land and the people concerned with it long after the temporary owner who created the interest has died. Thus, if the owner of land grants to a city the right to lay watermains across the land and maintain and repair them, the right could affect a subsequent owner who would like to tear up the pipes and erect a building. If over many years successive owners of the land were to grant away more of their rights, eventually there would be a complex bundle of rights held by various persons. Each subsequent owner would own the land minus the rights granted away. In this manner, land may easily be the subject of many complicated interests.

The Definition of Land

land
comprises the surface, all that is under the surface, including the minerals and oil, and everything above the surface, including buildings

The word *land* has a special meaning in the law of real property. Ordinarily, when we think of land, we think of the surface and its contours. For everyday usage this concept is sufficient, but a purchaser who buys land must know more accurately what the term includes. In law, **land** includes not only the surface but all that is under the surface, including the minerals, oil, or whatever else is present within the boundaries of the lot, and everything above the surface, including the buildings on the land and the column of air as well. It used to be said that land included all the earth to the centre of the globe and all the air up to the heavens. For all practical purposes, the owner of land today does have ownership extending below the surface as far as people can penetrate with mine shafts and oil wells. But it is a different matter with the column of air above the land: various statutes, international treaties concerning air travel, and municipal by-laws limiting the use of land have cut down ownership of the column of air considerably. Aircraft may pass freely over the land at a safe height, and the owner is often restricted in the height of buildings that may be erected.

Perhaps most important to remember is that land includes all things permanently affixed to it—trees, buildings, fences. Thus, when *A* transfers her house and lot to *B*, the document describes the land only, according to its location and dimensions, but it is nevertheless presumed that everything affixed to the land goes with it. Lawyers do not draw a distinction between land and buildings as do businesses and accounts. Although for business purposes we report the depreciation of buildings but not of land, the two are lumped together in law when ascertaining ownership or transferring the title to land.

Restrictions on the Use of Land

Historical Restrictions

The owner of a chattel may do as she pleases with it—she may even destroy it, and no one has the legal right to interfere. Land is not regarded in this way, especially when it is situated in a community where people live quite close to one another. From very early times, communal governments have assumed the power to regulate and prohibit dangerous activities in populous areas. If a landowner sets off explosives or lights fires that spread sparks on to a neighbour's lands, the danger is obvious. Accordingly, community regulations limit a landowner's right to use his land for dangerous activities.

Nuisance

The courts have long recognized further restrictions on the use of land that seriously affect an owner's freedom of activity: a user of land may be restrained from committing the tort of **nuisance**. A nuisance is an activity that interferes with the ordinary comfort and enjoyment of land of others in the vicinity. The interference may take the form of smoke, noxious vapours, noise, polluted water, or other harmful liquids flowing in streams or percolating through the earth—things that escape from the land of the user and affect other lands. A person who has sustained injury from a nuisance may obtain money damages for the loss and also an injunction from the court restraining the offender from continuing the conduct responsible for the nuisance.

nuisance
an activity that interferes with the ordinary comfort and enjoyment of land of others in the vicinity

Public Regulation of Land Use

Community regulation has grown rapidly in the last half century and is likely to continue growing. Early regulations covered only such nuisances as fire and health hazards, but the increased density and size of urban centres and the growing complexities of city life have forced municipal governments into large-scale regulation of land use. Zoning by-laws prescribe the use and type of buildings that may be erected in various districts of a municipality; building regulations prescribe minimum standards of quality for materials and the size of all parts of structures erected within an area; planning by-laws set out requirements for roadways and for water and sewage services, and often prescribe the amounts of land a land developer must give to the municipality for use as school and park areas.

Growing public awareness and concern about long-term environmental hazards, such as those created by chemicals formerly considered safe, have led to the passage in all jurisdictions of environmental assessment and protection legislation. Another area of concern has been the protection of historical, architectural, and archeological buildings and sites, a concern reflected in "heritage" statutes. Consequently, we are witnessing the growth of a large body of public law, imposing various limits on the use owners may make of their land. These restrictions are important for industrial enterprises and redevelopment projects in urban centres and increasingly in rural and forested regions.

The Development of Strict Rules in Land Law

In feudal times land was the most valuable asset because it contained the principal sources of wealth—crops, animals, timber, and serfs. Before industry or merchant trade grew, land represented the wealth of the country. In England, the king learned early to utilize a system of land-holding to consolidate his strength. In feudal England no one *owned* land except the Crown. A lord **held** land from the Crown, subject to certain rights and duties. So long as the lord performed his duties, he and his heirs continued to hold the land. In turn, each lord granted portions of his estate to vassals, who held the land from the lord subject to various rights and duties. The vassals often granted their land to sub-vassals, subject to further rights and duties.

held
possessed land from the Crown, subject to certain rights and duties

In later feudal times these relationships became extremely intricate and technical. The king objected to the complexities because they made it difficult for him to enforce his own feudal rights and collect taxes. Parliament passed statutes and the courts handed down decisions to cut down the number of interests in land. Gradually, a strict set of legal rules grew up for recognizing a limited number of interests in land. If a holder of land tried to create a type of interest not already recognized by the courts, the interest would be void. In contrast with the law of contract where rules generally grew to meet business convenience and fairness, rules for the recognition of classes of interests in land often had no relation to convenience or fairness; rather they were rules, arbitrarily made, for the purpose of limiting the number of interests in land and keeping them within manageable proportions. Even so, the variety of interests that can arise in relation to just one piece of land is great. Many if not most of the old rules have been repealed or modernized by various statutes, but comparatively speaking, the old concepts have been very slow to die in this field of the law.

The strictness of the courts is understandable when we consider how imaginative and resourceful were the medieval landowners and their lawyers in developing concepts of land ownership. The courts carved up ownership in two main ways:

(a) according to the *time* during which the holder of the interest would have the right to exclusive possession of the land—interests called *estates in time*

(b) according to the *kind of use* permitted or restricted upon the land—called *interests less than estates*

We shall discuss these interests in the following two sections.

ESTATES IN TIME

Freehold Estates

freehold estate

an interest in land that is indeterminate in time

A **freehold estate** is indeterminate in time; it cannot be predicted how long the interest of the owner will last.

Fee Simple Estate

fee simple

an interest in land closest to complete ownership, held for all time, subject only to the owner dying without having transferred it by a will and without having relatives to inherit it

This estate, usually referred to as the **fee simple**, is the greatest interest a person can own in land and is as close to the idea of complete ownership as English law comes. Thus, when we speak of a person owning land, we mean that he holds the fee simple in it. The holder of the fee simple holds it for all time present and future, subject only to its return to the government in the event of his dying without having relatives to inherit it and without having made a will giving it to some person. He may grant the whole of the fee simple away; he may grant away a lesser interest keeping the rest for himself; or he may grant the whole of it in various portions to different persons.

ILLUSTRATION 23.1

(a) *A*, the holder of the fee simple in Blackacre, may grant it to an older brother *B* for the rest of *B*'s life. At *B*'s death it returns to *A*, or to *A*'s heirs if *A* dies before *B*.

(b) *A* may grant Blackacre to a brother for life with the rest of the fee simple going to a niece *C* at the brother's death.

The holder of a fee simple may carve up the estate in other ways and grant them to other persons; the above situations in Illustration 23.1 serve merely as examples.

Life Estate

life estate

an estate in land held for the life of one person

A **life estate** is an estate in land for the life of one person—usually for the life of the person who holds the estate, but not necessarily: a person may hold an estate, measured by the life of *another* person. Thus *A* may grant Blackacre to *B* for the rest of *A*'s own life—if *A* dies within a few months, the life estate ends; *B* retains no interest in Blackacre. This type of life estate, however, is quite rare. The more usual life estate, for the life of the person to whom the interest is given, often arises under the terms of a will. Thus, for example, the owner of a fee simple may by the terms of her will give a life estate in the family home to her brother, who becomes the **life tenant**; or a widow may give a life estate to her eldest child. In either of these situations she may also direct that the rest of the fee simple pass, let us say, to the grandchildren.

life tenant
a holder of a life estate

The balance of the fee simple, after a life estate has been carved out, is called either a *reversion* or a *remainder*. It is called a **reversion** when the grantor of the life estate reserves the balance of the fee simple for herself and her heirs (that is, it *reverts* to the grantor or her heirs after the life estate ends). It is called a **remainder** when it goes to some third person. The balance of the estate in example (a) in Illustration 23.1 above is a reversion and in example (b) a remainder.

Unfortunately, life estates create many problems.

reversion
the balance of a fee simple reserved to the grantor and her heirs at the end of a life estate

remainder
the balance of a fee simple that goes to a third person at the end of a life estate

- *First*, it is very difficult to sell land subject to a life estate: very few people will buy only the remaining years of a life tenant's interest, an uncertain period of time; similarly, they will rarely buy a reversion or remainder, because it is impossible to tell how long the life tenant will live, thus delaying a purchaser's right to make use of the land. Only if both the *life tenant* and the **remainderman** join in the sale and together grant the whole of the fee simple will it be relatively easy to sell the land.

remainderman
a person who holds the reversion or remainder in a fee simple

- *Second*, a life tenant is limited in the changes she can make on the land without the consent of the remainderman: she cannot tear down buildings or cut down trees without the permission of the remainderman even if she wishes to replace them with something more valuable; she must leave the land to the remainderman substantially as she received it. On the other hand, she is under no duty to make repairs, and may let buildings decay.

- *Third*, she cannot compel the remainderman to contribute anything to the cost of substantial repairs and maintenance needed on the land though they will ultimately be of great benefit to the remainderman in preserving its value.

Life estates were much more common until the end of the 19th century when land was still perhaps the most important measure of wealth of individuals. In our society today, land is no longer so major a portion of a person's wealth. Assets in the form of shares and bonds, bank accounts, life insurance, jewellery, and automobiles may add up to a larger portion. This change in the form of wealth has led to a different method of providing a life income for a surviving dependant.

Instead of creating a *life estate in land* a person may give a *life interest* in a sum of money. She directs in her will that a portion of her assets be liquidated into a fund of money and invested, the income to be paid to the dependant for life. On the dependant's death, the principal sum is paid to those who would formerly have been remaindermen of real property.

Rights in the Matrimonial Home

For many centuries a widow's principal security on the death of her husband was a right to **dower**, that is, a right to a life interest in one-third of the real property held by her husband in fee simple during their married life. As we have just noted, that form of financial security no longer makes practical sense. Legislation has reformed and expanded property rights of spouses to include assets nominally held in the name of the other spouse, both during their joint lives and after death of one of them.

dower
a widow's right to a life interest in one-third of the real property held by her husband in fee simple before his death

Dower has now been abolished in all provinces, but the new legislation still recognizes the special interest that a spouse has in the family home. Statutory rights go much farther than the ancient right to dower, and include the right to refuse consent to any change in the family home or to its sale (a sale without consent is void), as well as a life estate in the *whole* of the family home to the surviving spouse.

The legislation varies greatly from province to province and has been changing so frequently in recent years that it would not be useful to attempt a summary. However, some of the main features are as follows: in some provinces, the claim to a matrimonial home must be registered in the land registry office; in others it arises as soon as husband and wife establish a home within the meaning of the statute; in some provinces with older legislation, the right accrues only to the wife and not to either spouse; some legislation protects only one matrimonial home while others make it a question of fact whether a couple also has a second family home such as a cottage.

Claims to the matrimonial home are so important that no transaction involving residential property should be entered into without taking into account the relevant matrimonial property legislation.

Leasehold Estates

leasehold

an interest in land for a definite period of time

A **leasehold** estate is an interest in land for a definite period of time—a week, a month, a year, a hundred years, or any other specific period. Here we find the great distinction between a freehold and a leasehold estate: a freehold estate is either for an *infinite* time (the fee simple) or an *indefinite* time (the life estate), whereas the leasehold is for a definite time. In a leasehold estate, the person to whom the interest is granted is called the **lessee** or **tenant** and the grantor of the interest is called the **lessor** or **landlord**.

lessee or **tenant**

a person to whom an interest in a leasehold estate is granted

lessor or **landlord**

a grantor of an interest in a leasehold estate

Historically, leaseholds have always been considered lesser estates than freeholds. This was so even though it was obvious that leases for 100 years would almost invariably last longer than a life tenancy, a freehold estate. However, a leasehold interest must be derived from a freehold interest and cannot last longer than the freehold from which it is derived.

ILLUSTRATION 23.2

By will *T* gives *A* a life estate in Blackacre with the remainder after *A*'s death to *X* in fee simple. *A* leases Blackacre to *B* Inc. for 100 years. Several months later *A* dies. *X*, the remainderman, can take possession of Blackacre and put *B* Inc. out. *X* is not bound by the lease because *A* could not create a leasehold interest in Blackacre to last longer than *A*'s own life estate.

The above result is an application of the rule that a person cannot grant to another a greater interest than he himself holds.[3]

Leasehold interests share an important characteristic with freehold interests: a lease gives a lessee the right to exclusive possession of the land described in the lease. Thus a lessee has the right to keep all persons off the leased land *including* the lessor himself, unless the lessor has reserved the right to enter the property for inspection and repairs. The law concerning leasehold interests is the meeting-place of the strict concepts of real property and the flexible concepts of contract. Leases play an important role in commerce and industry, and in finance as an alternative to the traditional method of borrowing money on the security of mortgages. Leaseholds are discussed more fully in Chapter 24 "Landlord and Tenant" and Chapter 30 "Secured Transactions".

Concurrent Interests in Estates

Tenancy in Common

Two or more persons may become owners of the same estate in land at the same time. They are concurrent holders of the estate whether it be a fee simple, a life estate, or a leasehold estate. In

---

3. In 1877 England passed the Settled Estates Act creating an important exception to the rule. The statute was later enacted only in British Columbia and Ontario. Under the statute a life tenant may lease his estate for a term not exceeding 21 years, and the lease will be valid against the remainderman. If the life tenant dies, the lessee pays the rent to the remainderman for the balance of the lease, and may stay in possession. The statute also provides that the rent bargained for by the life tenant must be the best reasonably obtainable.

the absence of any special agreement between them or of special terms set out in the grant by which they acquired the interests, concurrent holders are deemed to be tenants in common. **Tenants in common** hold equal shares in the estate; that is, each is entitled to the same rights over the property and an equal share of the income. Each interest is an *undivided* interest: one tenant cannot fence off a portion of the property for her exclusive use—each is entitled to the use of the whole property. However, tenants in common may agree expressly to hold unequal shares, transfer the share of one to another, or divide and fence the property into exclusive lots. In addition, a tenant in common may transfer her interest to any third party without the consent of the others: the transferee becomes a tenant in common with them. When a tenant in common dies, her interest goes to her heirs, who continue to hold the interest with the other tenants in common.

tenants in common
concurrent holders of equal shares in an estate

Joint Tenancy

Another form of concurrent interest is the joint tenancy. Two or more persons become **joint tenants** only when expressly created at the time the estate is granted to them or afterwards by an express agreement among them. The feature that distinguishes a joint tenancy from a tenancy in common is the **right of survivorship**. Under the right of survivorship the interest of a deceased joint tenant passes on his death to the surviving tenant or tenants instead of to the heirs of the deceased tenant. Thus, if *A*, *B*, and *C* own Blackacre in joint tenancy, upon *C*'s death his interest will pass to *A* and *B*, who will continue to own Blackacre in joint tenancy between them; *C*'s interest does not go to his heirs.

joint tenants
concurrent holders each of whom has a right of survivorship

right of survivorship
the right of a surviving tenant to the interest of a deceased joint tenant

Husband and wife often take title to their family home in joint tenancy. On the death of either spouse the survivor automatically receives full title to the property. Joint tenancy is an advantage to the survivor because the house does not form part of the deceased partner's estate, thus becoming entangled in problems of **probate** (administration and settling of deceased person's estate). Legal fees and probate costs are significantly reduced. Formerly, a capital gains tax advantage was available for not having family real property owned in joint tenancy where the family owned two properties (for example a city residence and a country residence or cottage) and each spouse could separately own one of the properties. Since now only one principal residence is allowed per couple as a capital gains tax exemption, joint ownership of a family home by husband and wife has become an attractive and popular arrangement.

probate
the process of administering and settling the estate of a deceased person

Severance

A joint tenant may destroy the right of survivorship at any time before his death without the consent of the other joint tenants. By a procedure called **severance**, he may turn his joint tenancy into a tenancy in common with the other tenant or tenants. If there are two or more other tenants remaining, they continue as joint tenants with each other but are tenants in common with the one who has severed his joint tenancy. The most common method of severance is by a joint tenant granting his interest to a third party; the grant automatically turns the interest transferred into a tenancy in common with the remaining interests. A joint tenancy is also severed by giving a mortgage on one's share. However, a joint tenant cannot sever his share by disposing of it in his will: the courts have held that a will speaks only at the moment a testator has died, and at that moment his share has already passed to the surviving joint tenant or tenants.

severance
a procedure that turns a joint tenancy into a tenancy in common

Condominiums

Condominiums are a modern response to a shortage of housing and recreational areas in large urban centres; it is claimed that they provide the occupiers with the satisfaction of home ownership and communal access to recreational areas that they could not hope to purchase for their own exclusive use. Nearly all the common law provinces have enacted legislation permitting the granting of an estate in fee simple in individual **units** of multiple-unit developments, such as high-rise apartments, row housing, or groups of single-family semi-detached, or duplexes, or

condominium unit
a unit in a multiple-unit development, such as a high-rise building or row housing, that may be owned in fee simple

similar residences.[4] The legislation is not restricted to residential housing and applies equally to the development of commercial and industrial buildings.

The Nature of Ownership in a Condominium

common elements

structures and areas external to a condominium unit, including communal facilities

An owner of a unit is entitled to exclusive possession of that unit and also obtains an undivided part ownership, in common with other unit owners, of **common elements** including structures and areas external to the unit such as entrances, stairs and elevators, and communal facilities such as laundries, recreation rooms, garages, swimming pools, tennis courts, playgrounds, and so forth. Each unit can be bought and sold, mortgaged, and passed to successors on death. It is separately assessed and taxed and may be sold for unpaid taxes. Such transfers do not affect the ownership of other units. A purchaser acquires a unit subject to several important conditions: in a multiple-unit building he must, like a tenant, allow entry to make necessary repairs to services; contribute to the operation, upkeep, and in some degree to the restoration of the common property; and insure his own unit. In addition, he becomes a member of the **condominium corporation** charged with responsibility for management of the property as a whole and given statutory powers for that purpose, and he is subject to the rules and regulations governing the development. Although the corporation is not the owner of the common elements, it may own one or more units and thus share in that ownership. For example, it may own units rented for janitorial and supervisory staff as well as for its own offices.

condominium corporation

a corporation—whose members are the condominium owners—that is responsible for managing the property as a whole

Responsibility for Maintaining Units

The legislation has done away with the technical difficulties that the common law found in granting ownership of a freehold entirely separated from the ground by other units of freehold below. However, condominium law does leave a number of practical problems that necessarily arise in complex high-rise buildings. For example, the definition of a unit is a matter of critical importance: does a unit-owner's property extend beyond the surface of the walls of the rooms? If a piece of plaster two centimetres thick is knocked out of the wall, is the damage to the property of the unit-owner or to the common elements, and thus the corporation's responsibility to repair? If the description of a unit included ownership of, let us say, the space eight centimetres beyond the surface of the wall, and plumbing in that space immediately behind the plaster failed, would the unit-owner be responsible for repairs even if the plumbing served an adjoining unit and not his own? We can see that it may be a serious disadvantage to own much of the area beyond the surface of the inner walls. Responsibility for repairs and maintenance is generally in the hands of the corporation, but where services are within the unit, it is important to set out clearly where responsibility lies.

Investment Risks

The equivalent of condominium ownership has long existed in many parts of the world, especially where buildings are expected to have a very long life, often calculated in hundreds of years. A modern apartment building of low quality, constructed for rental accommodation, may have an expected life of only 40 to 50 years. Its conversion to a condominium may have pitfalls for an unwary buyer who purchases a rapidly deteriorating asset. For example, if such an apartment building, already 15 years old, were converted to a condominium and a purchaser bought a unit with an instalment mortgage over a 25-year period, the building might well be in a state of great disrepair by the time the buyer had paid the mortgage off. Instead of acquiring an appreciating asset, as is usually the case with the purchase of a residential home, the condominium unit-owner might find that the unit had lost a substantial part of its value. Accordingly, it is important for a prospective purchaser of a unit to take great care in assessing the quality of construction in a condominium building and its life expectancy.

---

4. See, for example: Condominium Act, R.S.B.C. 1996, c. 64; R.S.O. 1980, c. 84; R.S.N.S. 1989, c. 85.

Maintenance and Management of a Condominium

In a good-quality rental apartment building, a competent landlord is interested in maintaining this asset in good condition and will have the necessary management and technical expertise to do so. In a condominium, when the last unit has been sold the purchasers of condominium units become the owners of the complex. If the entrepreneur who built the condominium retains no further interest, the tasks of maintaining the condominium in a good state of repair, paying its bills, and having generally efficient management become the collective responsibility of unit-owners through the condominium corporation. Ordinarily, it would not be possible for individual owners to run a large development, and they would authorize the corporation to hire an expert to oversee the operation. Frequently the entrepreneur, while still controlling the condominium corporation as the owner of the unsold units, will arrange a management contract for, let us say, five years. Thus, even after selling off the last unit, the entrepreneur may stay on as manager at a substantial fee. Accordingly, it is important for a prospective buyer of a unit to assess the reputation of the entrepreneur and the quality of management it is likely to provide for the condominium development. Even when management is in competent hands, a unit-owner cannot sit back as a house-owner ordinarily can and attend to her own property. She must remain concerned about the sound management of the condominium corporation on a continuing long-term basis.

Financing and Insurance

The financing and sale of condominium units are more complicated than those of privately owned residences because of the continuing obligation of a unit-owner to pay charges levied by the condominium corporation and because of the relationship between a master mortgage of all the common elements, including the ground on which the condominium development is located, and the mortgages of the individual units. So too the nature and amount of insurance required for a condominium presents special problems. If a high-rise apartment building is destroyed by fire, the apportionment of loss between each unit and common elements and the responsibility for subsequent reconstruction present considerable difficulty. The most common method of dealing with the problem is through an "insurance trust." A trustee insures the entire building for the benefit of both the condominium corporation and every individual unit-owner; each pays part of the premium proportionate to its interest.

We can see then, that while there are many attractive features in the development of condominiums, there are also new problems confronting prospective purchasers that must be weighed against the advantages.

CONTEMPORARY ISSUE

Fair Sharing of Expenses in a Condominium

While the word "condominium" probably means "residence" to most people, industrial and commercial properties can be set up as condominiums. Mixed-use residential and commercial condominiums also exist.

One of the issues that arises in a condominium is how the utilities—water, gas, electricity—should be paid for. In high-rise residential condominiums, the cost of utilities consumed by the common elements and all the units is apportioned among the units, generally in proportion to their floor space. It would be unduly costly and complicated to meter each unit and to levy one charge for the unit's own consumption and another for its share of the common consumption. As a result, some units may pay for more water, heat, or power than they

continued

actually use, and some for less. The possibility of being slightly overcharged is one of the trade-offs for the benefits of this type of ownership. In low-rise condominiums such as townhouse developments, the common elements consist largely of grounds and building exteriors. Where there are no elevators, lobby, or shared hallways, it is more feasible and more obviously fair to meter each unit separately for the utilities it actually consumes. Separate metering is often more feasible in commercial and industrial condominiums as well.

Sometimes, conflict can arise over payment for utilities. In a case decided in the Ontario courts, the owner of a commercial unit in a mixed commercial and residential condominium operated a successful restaurant. The restaurant used special methods of food preparation, involving lengthy washing and soaking of dried ingredients in running water. Because of these food preparation methods, along with the usual uses of water in a restaurant, that one unit consumed three times as much water as all rest of the complex. Its budgeted share of the common expense for water was only 6.0501 percent. Although the restaurant and a few of the other retail units were separately metered, the rest of the units were not metered and there was a master meter for the whole development.

The condominium corporation's expense for water vastly exceeded the budgeted amount. It sought to have the restaurant pay for its water consumption in excess of normal cooking and household requirements. The restaurant owner resisted on the basis that the condominium declaration required individual owners to pay for their water consumption only if "each unit" was separately metered. The court found, looking at all the documents, that the condominium corporation intended in its declaration that retail units would pay for any excessive use of water. It interpreted the disputed clause of the declaration to mean "any unit" rather than "each and every unit." The court found it would not be just to allow the restaurant to keep a benefit for which it had not paid, and ordered that it pay for its excess water use.

Source: See York Region Condominium Corp. No. 771 v. Year Full Investment (Canada) Inc. (1993), 12 O.R. (3d) 641 (C.A.).

Questions to Consider

1. Do you think the court's interpretation of the phrase "each unit" in the declaration was reasonable? Do you think the result was fair?
2. Could this situation have been prevented from arising? How?
3. In general, what do you think are the advantages for a business of locating in a mixed-use condominium? The disadvantages? How much does it depend on the type of business?

Cooperative Housing

An alternative to condominiums is cooperative housing. In a cooperative housing development a member merely buys a share in the cooperative organization and, by virtue of his equity in it, becomes entitled to occupy one of the units in the development. A risk of this type of home ownership, however, is that the whole cooperative venture may flounder because of bad management and insolvency: all members are affected equally by the failure, and may lose their equity investment even though they may personally have been honouring their obligations and paying the required contributions for taxes and upkeep. Financing a share in cooperative housing presents difficulties of its own. A member buys an equity share and has rights, similar to a leasehold interest, to occupy a unit. The method of borrowing money on the value of a share in a cooperative, combined with the right to occupy a unit, is more complicated than a straight loan by way of mortgage on a private residence, but on the other hand, a share is often available to prospective tenants who have less capital than is usually required to buy a condominium unit.

A cooperative venture usually requires a high degree of commitment to a community project and more direct involvement in management than is typical of condominium ownership. A high level of involvement in the management of the cooperative is probably the best assurance of sound management and survival.

INTERESTS LESS THAN ESTATES

Easements

At Common Law

In addition to estates in land divided according to time, there are other interests distinguished by the use or benefit they confer upon the holder. None of these interests gives the right of exclusive possession as do freehold and leasehold estates.

At the beginning of this chapter we referred to an example of a landowner granting a right to a city to lay watermains over her land and to maintain and repair them. This right belongs to the class of interests called easements. An **easement** is a right enjoyed by one landowner over the land of another, for a special purpose rather than for the general use and occupation of land. The most common type of easement is a **right-of-way**: the holder of a right-of-way may pass back and forth over the land of another in order to get to and from her own land. She does not have the right to remain on the other's land or bring things on the land and leave them there or to obstruct others from using the land, but she can maintain an action against anyone who interferes with her right to pass. Other examples of easements are the right to string wires and cables across land, to hang eaves of a building over another's land, to drain water or waste materials from one piece of land over a watercourse on another's land. Once granted, an easement attaches to the land and binds subsequent owners—they cannot interfere with the exercise of the easement. Similarly, purchasers of the land benefiting from the easement acquire the former owner's easement rights.

An essential requirement of an easement is that there must be a **dominant tenement** (a piece of land that is to benefit from the easement) and a **servient tenement** (the land subject to the easement). The location of the dominant tenement has presented difficulties. It has long been decided that the dominant tenement need not directly adjoin the servient tenement, but it must be reasonably close to it. This qualification is vague, but the law has not been able to devise a more exact definition. It is highly unlikely that if Blackacre is 30 km from Whiteacre, the owner of Blackacre can acquire a right-of-way over Whiteacre; but it is not clear what the answer would be if a kilometre separated the lands and if it were shown that the proposed easement would be of great benefit to the use and enjoyment of Blackacre.

"Statutory Easements"

The term "easement" is sometimes used to describe certain statutory rights such as the right granted a telephone company to run wires and cables either underground or overhead on poles. The telephone company has the right to leave wires where they have been installed and to inspect and repair them when necessary—rights very similar to easements. But often the telephone company owns no land in the area. The nearest land that could be considered a dominant tenement may be many kilometres away. Strictly speaking, the right is not an easement: it owes its existence to a statute. If a telephone company were to attempt to buy an easement to lay cables over long distances without the authority of a statute, no easement would come into existence because there would be no dominant tenement reasonably close by. Although it might have contractual rights against the person who sold the right, the company would have no real property interest in the cables. A subsequent purchaser of the lands would not be bound to let the company use the land or even to let it take the cables away.

easement
a right enjoyed by one landowner over the land of another for a special purpose but not for occupation of the land

right-of-way
an easement that gives the holder a right to pass back and forth over the land of another in order to get to and from her own land

dominant tenement
the piece of land that benefits from an easement

servient tenement
the land subject to the easement

Easements by Prescription

A landowner may acquire an easement over adjoining land without a written grant from the owner of the servient tenement. The method by which the adjoining owner may do so is called **prescription**. In medieval England, a custom grew that if an individual habitually exercised a right over the land of another for a very long time and if that right *could* have been granted to him as an easement, it was presumed that he had received a grant of easement at one time but had subsequently lost the grant. This fiction was merely a convenient way of permitting a person to rely on a right he had exercised for a very long time. From this fiction developed a rule that if a person continuously exercised a right, openly, notoriously, without fraud or deceit, without using force or threats against the owner of the land, and at no time acknowledged the right of the owner in writing or paid for the use of the land, he would acquire an easement by prescription after 20 years. The right had to be exercised continuously, that is without interruption by the owner's exerting of his rights of ownership through exacting a fee or keeping the prospective easement holder off the land.

An easement by prescription is as valid as an easement by grant and is fully recognized in the four Atlantic provinces and in parts of Manitoba and Ontario. Easements by prescription are not recognized in the three westernmost provinces or in those parts of Manitoba and Ontario covered by *land titles* registration, a system of recording interests in land that will be discussed in the last section of this chapter. In areas where easements by prescription may arise, a landowner must guard against them. One great danger is that a former owner of the land may have permitted the exercise of a right for many years. The prescription period continues to run from the moment that the right was exercised regardless of a transfer of ownership of the land. Thus, there may be only a small part of the 20 years to go when the current owner obtains title. While a prospective easement may seem inoffensive to the current owner, there is a risk that the easement may later reduce the market value of the land.

ILLUSTRATION 23.3

X obtains an easement by prescription over a three-metre strip of Servacre by using it as a right-of-way to his garage on Domacre for over 20 years. During this period Servacre contains only a single family dwelling. Later it becomes suitable for erecting a large apartment building, but municipal building regulations for the construction of apartments require that the three-metre strip be used for a parking area. Without the three-metre strip there would be insufficient parking area to comply with the regulations. The owner of Servacre will be unable to develop the property or sell it to another party interested in developing it unless and until he can buy a release of the easement from the owner of Domacre.

Covenants

The Consequences of a Covenant

An owner of land may wish to sell part of it yet control or restrict the use of the part she proposes to sell. We can understand her motives: she may wish to see the property kept in good repair so that the area does not deteriorate; she may wish to prevent the carrying on of a noisy business that would interfere with her privacy; she may wish the purchaser to improve the land by planting trees and shrubs, to enhance the beauty of the area. She may, of course, require the purchaser to do any or all of these things as part of the consideration for the sale of the land. If the purchaser does not abide by his promise, the vendor has her normal contractual remedies for breach. But if the purchaser resells the land to a third party, there is no privity of contract between the vendor and the third party, and the third party need not fear a contractual action by the vendor if he chooses to ignore his predecessor's promise. The vendor has a remedy only if the purchaser's promise has created *an interest in land* that the law recognizes as binding upon all subsequent holders. Recognition of such interests would create further complexities.

ILLUSTRATION 23.4

V, owner of Blackacre and Whiteacre, sells Whiteacre to *P*. As part of the consideration he obtains a promise that *P* and all subsequent owners of Whiteacre will keep in repair all buildings on both Whiteacre and Blackacre. So long as *P* owns Whiteacre, he is bound by his promise. Subsequently *P* sells Whiteacre to *A*, who is aware of that promise. *A* refuses to carry it out, and *V* sues *A* for breach. The court would have no difficulty dismissing the promise to repair buildings on Blackacre as not binding *A*: *A* has no connection with *P*'s promise insofar as it affects Blackacre—he has no interest in that land nor was he a party to the contract between *V* and *P*. Thus, *A* is not bound to repair the buildings on Blackacre.

The promise concerning Whiteacre is more troublesome. It may seem reasonable for *V*, who still owns adjoining lands, to require Whiteacre to be kept in good repair so that the area will remain at high market value. The courts have held, however, that it is too onerous to subject subsequent owners to such positive duties, and that as a matter of public policy it would be dangerous to permit the creation of interests in land requiring a subsequent owner to personally perform promises in perpetuity. Lands might eventually be tied up by an interminable series of such promises or covenants for the benefit of surrounding lands.

Restrictive Covenants

In spite of constant discouragement from the courts over the centuries, vendors continued to extract promises from purchasers, some highly desirable and some injurious and spiteful. In the middle of the 19th century one of these covenants was questioned in the English Court of Chancery in the famous case of *Tulk v. Moxhay*.[5] The court decided that it was too onerous to require a subsequent holder to act positively in order to carry out covenants (as in Illustration 23.4), but if the covenant were purely *negative*, that is, if the holder were required to refrain from certain conduct or certain use of the land, then the court would hold the covenant valid and enforceable. These negative covenants became known as **covenants running with the land**, or **restrictive covenants**. Restrictive covenants are subject to a rule similar to that concerning easements—there must be a piece of land subject to the covenant and another piece that receives the benefit of the covenant. A covenant recognized by the courts as running with the land is enforceable *by* any subsequent holder of the land benefiting from it *against* any subsequent holder of the land subject to it.

There are a number of rules governing the types of conduct that may be regulated by restrictive covenants, how the benefits of the covenants may be transferred, and how they may be enforced.[6] Covenants found to be highly unreasonable or against public policy will not be enforced by the courts against subsequent holders.

covenant running with the land or restrictive covenant
a covenant requiring the holder of the land to refrain from certain conduct or certain use of the land

Remedies for Breach of a Covenant

Suppose an owner of land subject to a restrictive covenant acts quickly in defiance of it, for example, by erecting a high wall or cutting a doorway through an existing wall, before an aggrieved adjacent owner manages to obtain an injunction. Is the adjacent owner without remedy? The court may exercise its discretion, especially when a deliberately provocative breach of covenant has occurred, to grant a *mandatory injunction* requiring the wrongdoer to tear down the prohibited wall, or block the doorway and restore the wall. If it is too late to restore the

---

5. (1848), 41 E.R. 1143.

6. See Preston and Newsome, *Restrictive Covenants Affecting Freehold Land* (7th ed.). London: Sweet & Maxwell Limited, 1982. An Ontario court has held that for a restrictive covenant to be enforceable, not only must the party seeking to enforce it (the covenantee) own land to be benefited by the covenant but the land must also be identified in the instrument creating the covenant. Re Sekretov and City of Toronto (1973), 33 D.L.R. (3d) 257; Canada Safeway v. Thompson (City), [1997] 7 W.W.R. 565. For statutory authority to modify or discharge a restrictive covenant see, for example: Conveyancing and Law of Property Act, R.S.O. 1990, c. C.34, s. 61(1).

damage, as when the wrongdoer has cut down a row of 100-year-old oak trees, the court may award damages in lieu of an injunction.

Building-scheme Covenants

Restrictive covenants are widely used in residential areas to regulate the uses to which land may be put. Typical restrictive covenants prohibit the use of land for other than residential purposes, limit building on the land to one-family dwellings, require minimum frontage per house, and specify minimum distances at which buildings may be erected from the sidelines of lots or from street lines.

If over the years the character of an area has changed and a once reasonable covenant has become unduly restrictive, an affected landowner may apply to the court to have the covenant terminated. The court will require that the owner of the land for whose benefit the covenant was made be served with notice and given an opportunity to defend the covenant.

building-scheme covenant
a restrictive covenant that regulates land use over an entire neighbourhood or a shopping centre

Restrictive covenants that regulate land use over an entire neighbourhood or a shopping centre are referred to as **building-scheme covenants**. In a building scheme each owner mutually agrees with all other owners to be bound by the covenant in return for the promise of all neighbouring owners to be similarly bound. In order to have the court remove the covenant for the benefit of one owner, all adjoining owners must be served with notice and given a chance to state their opinions. As a result, it may be very difficult to have a restrictive covenant under a building scheme terminated.

Covenants are gradually being replaced by municipal regulations in the form of zoning and building by-laws, especially in newly developed areas. Nevertheless, covenants still play an important role in older settled parts of our cities and towns; sometimes they unduly restrict the development of an area.

Other Interests

Oil, Gas, and Mineral Leases

There are several other interests in land that are less than estates, but we leave most of them to be described in treatises on real property. One interest deserves special mention—the right to take minerals, oil, and gas from under the surface of land occupied by others. The right to remove materials is usually found in an agreement commonly called a *lease*. An oil, gas, or mineral lease bears little similarity to a true leasehold interest. Rather, it combines several interests in land in one agreement.

- *First,* to the extent that the agreement permits the lessee to occupy a portion of the surface area of the land (often only a very small proportion of the area from which the oil, gas, or mineral is taken) it has elements of a true lease.

- *Second,* to the extent that it grants the lessee the right to travel back and forth over the owner's land, lay pipes and move equipment, it is similar to an easement.

- *Third,* to the extent that it permits the lessee to remove materials extracted from the ground (previously the real property of the owner and now the personal property of the lessee), it is similar to an ancient interest in land known as a ***profit à prendre***.

profit à prendre
an interest in land permitting the lessee to remove material extracted from the ground

The law concerning mineral, oil, and gas leases has become highly specialized in recent years. It will suffice to know that such agreements are more than mere leases and that they form a highly developed field of study of their own.

Licences

A "licence" given to another person by an owner to use his land is not, strictly speaking, an interest in land at all. Thus, if *B* gives his friend, *A*, permission to hold a garage sale on his front lawn, *A* becomes a "licensee" on *B*'s land during the garage sale; she is not a trespasser. However, she has no "right" to remain on *B*'s land and if he should revoke permission, something he may do at any time, *A* would have only a reasonable minimum time to remove her goods and herself from *B*'s lawn. Suppose, however, that parties enter into a contractual licence.

ILLUSTRATION 23.5

The city of Brockville charges the Jazz Theatre Company a fee to use its municipal auditorium—a licence to perform a play for one week; the city also provides box-office facilities and janitorial services. Revocation of permission to use the auditorium for that week would be a breach of contract: if the breach were sufficiently serious Jazz Theatre might well obtain an injunction preventing the city from removing its stage settings and players until the end of the week. An injunction—or any other remedy—would be a contractual right enforceable only against the city. If the city sold the auditorium before the week scheduled for the performances, Jazz Theatre would have no rights against the purchaser; its only remedy would be for damages against the city.

However, such breaches are rare. Contractual licences between enterprises that have entered into long-term and stable relations can have substantial business value, and they do create rights binding between the original parties. Their relative simplicity when contrasted with the formalities of creating an interest in land has made licences a useful business tool.

ADVERSE POSSESSION

The Reasons for Limitation Periods

Suppose that 20 years ago *A* stole ten dollars from a corner store. Had he been caught at the time, he might well have been charged with theft. But if 20 years later this fact is discovered and throughout that time *A* has been a law-abiding person, almost everyone will feel that it would be morally, if not legally, wrong to pursue the matter. Similarly, if someone had left several pieces of furniture with a friend while she travelled around the world, the friend would probably return them without question a few months later. But if the owner did not ask for their return until a dozen years later, her friend would probably have come to think of the pieces of furniture as his own and resent having to part with them. This desire to leave things undisturbed, as they have been for a very long time, finds its expression in the **law of limitations**. The policy of the law is that a person who has a right of action against another must pursue it within a definite period of time or lose the right: he must not keep the other party in indefinite jeopardy of being sued.[7] In Chapter 30 we shall discuss when a creditor who does not sue to collect a debt within the time permitted will lose that right to sue. Limitation statutes are not concerned with the merits of the plaintiff's claim: they require only that he pursue his claim within a definite time or abandon it.

law of limitations
a person who has a right of action against another must pursue it within a definite period of time or lose the right

Application of Limitation Periods to Land

Limitation rules apply to interests in land. They might arise as an issue, for example, in the following circumstances:

(a) *A* occupies land owned by *B*. He treats it as his own and improves it. His family continues to occupy the land for many years after his death. After several generations, the heirs of *B* try to dispossess the heirs of *A*.

---

7. In Chapter 13, we discussed limitation periods in relation to pursuing remedies for breach of contract. In matters of criminal law, however—in theory at least—a person should be prosecuted and punished regardless of the time that has elapsed since he committed an offence. The state is the prosecutor, and limitation statutes generally do not apply to it.

(b) *A* mistakenly puts up a fence that encloses not only his own land but part of *B*'s land. He erects a costly building covering a portion of *B*'s land that he had enclosed. Years later the mistake comes to light, and *B* insists on the destruction of the building so that he may get his land back.

These circumstances present difficult problems for the court. In each case *B* owned the land; but to dispossess *A* or his successors would work hardship and injustice. In medieval times, when there were many large estates and absentee landowners, squatters who entered and stayed on their lands for long periods were very common. In recent times, with speedy means of transport and communication and with accurate surveys available, the number of squatters has become smaller. Even so, disputes frequently occur; modern statutes in England, in the Atlantic provinces, and in parts of Ontario and Manitoba set out limitation periods beyond which an owner loses the right to regain possession of his land.[8] By adverse possession an occupier of land can **extinguish the title** of the owner; the possessor becomes in effect the owner of the land.

The three westernmost provinces and parts of Manitoba and Ontario have a modern land titles system governing the recording of interests in land. In the belief that this advanced system of registration, combined with modern methods of surveying, can eliminate almost all errors, and with a policy of having all interests in land recorded exclusively in the official registry, all these jurisdictions have provided by statute that the title of the registered owner cannot be extinguished by adverse possession.[9] But the attitude of people towards reviving long-dormant claims, as we have discussed above, has caused resistance to the new rules. There have been cases where the courts of some of these jurisdictions were unwilling to accept the full implications of the statutory provisions. In some cases they have avoided the provisions, and in effect recognized possessory interests.[10]

Elements of Adverse Possession

Most instances of possession of the land of another are not adverse possession but rather are the result of an arrangement between owner and occupier. The most common example is that of a tenant in possession under a lease. The terms of the lease govern the relations between landlord and tenant: though the lease may run many years longer than the time needed for adverse possession to destroy an owner's title to land, the lease continues to govern their relations, not the statutory rules on limitation periods.[11] But if the tenant were to stop paying rent due under the lease and ignore his other obligations, treating the land as if it were his own, he would then be in adverse possession, and the limitation period would begin to run from the time of his breach. The landlord could, of course, sue the tenant for breach of the lease and have him evicted; but if she failed to pursue her remedies within the time set out in the statute, she would lose all her rights. Here then, we see the elements needed for **adverse possession**: the possessor stays in exclusive possession using the land like an owner and ignoring the claims of other persons including the owner.

A further element of adverse possession is that it must be *open and notorious*—a person who furtively creeps into a deserted house each night and sleeps there for a period equal to the limitation period would not extinguish the title of the owner. A court takes various facts into account in deciding whether a person has established possession that is exclusive, and open and notorious.[12] By showing that he has paid the municipal taxes, made improvements to the prop-

---

extinguish the title

bring to end the title of the owner and the owner's right to regain possession

adverse possession

the exclusive possession of land by someone who openly uses it like an owner and ignores the claims of other persons including the owner

---

8. See, for example: Limitations Act, R.S.O. 1990, c. L.15, s. 4 (10 years); Limitations of Actions Act, R.S.N.S. 1989, c. 258, s. 10 (20 years).

9. See, for example: Land Titles Act, R.S.A. 1980, c. L-5, s. 64(1); Real Property Act, R.S.M. 1987, c. R-30, s. 61(2).

10. See Boyczuk v. Perry, [1948] 1 W.W.R. 495; Tooke v. Eastern Irrigation District, [1993] 3 W.W.R. 329.

11. The Supreme Court of Canada has recently confirmed this rule: Bovey v. Ganonoque (Town), [1992] 2 S.C.R. 5.

12. See, for example: Wallis's Ltd. v. Shell-Mex and BP, [1974] 3 All E.R. 575; Teis v. Ancaster (Town) (1997), 35 O.R. (3d) 216; Leichner v. Canada Attorney General (1996), 31 O.R. (3d) 700.

erty, fenced the property, or performed other acts normally done by an owner, a possessor may strengthen his claim of adverse possession.

Adverse possession ceases to be effective if it is interrupted by the owner before the limitation period has elapsed. Thus, if the owner demands and receives rent from the possessor in acknowledgment of the owner's superior rights to the land, the adverse possession is terminated. However, if the possessor remains in possession after the rent period expires, a new limitation period will begin; but it must run the full duration to extinguish the owner's title—it is not added to the previous period. When the owner has not interrupted possession, the adverse possessor may pass possession directly to another person, and the limitation period continues to run against the owner from the time of the entry into adverse possession by the first possessor.

When the Owner Is Presumed to Be in Possession

Unless another person establishes adverse possession, the law *presumes* the owner of land to be in possession of it. This rule has two consequences: first, an owner's title is not prejudiced merely by the fact that he has not occupied the land or leased it to a tenant—land abandoned for an indefinite period remains the property of the owner; second, when an adverse possessor abandons land before the limitation period has expired, the law regards possession as returned to the owner—the limitation period must start afresh if the possessor returns, or if someone else goes into adverse possession.

THE TRANSFER OF INTERESTS IN LAND

On Death of the Owner

An interest in land may be transferred in any one of several ways. If the holder of an interest dies *intestate* (without leaving a will), the interest passes according to statutory rules of inheritance to the holder's heir or heirs; that is, the interest passes automatically to the closest relatives. If, for example, a widow holds a fee simple in Blackacre and at her death she is survived by two daughters, they will become the owners of the fee simple.

A person need not allow her wealth to go automatically according to the rules of intestate succession. She may dispose of her property by *will* according to her wishes and the claims she feels she should satisfy. Thus, a second way that land may be transferred is by will.

By Compulsory Sale

The holder of an interest in land may be compelled to transfer it against her will. A creditor may obtain judgment against her in court and eventually have the land sold in order to satisfy the debt. A common type of compulsory transfer of land is **expropriation**. When a public body such as the federal government or a local school board requires land for its activities, it may proceed under statute to force the transfer of land to itself. It must, of course, pay compensation for taking the land, and if the parties cannot agree upon a price, the statute provides for arbitration or judicial proceedings to determine the price to be paid.

expropriation
a compulsory sale and transfer of land to a public body under statute

By a Voluntary Grant

The most common way of disposing of an interest in land is by a voluntary transfer between living persons in performance of a contract for the sale of land. The methods used to transfer land have developed over hundreds of years; by the middle of the 19th century, a comparatively uniform method had evolved in the use of a *grant*. It contains a description of the grantor, the grantee, and the interest being transferred, and is signed and sealed by the grantor before a witness. Since the document is under seal, it is often called a **deed of conveyance**—frequently shortened to **deed**. We should recall, however, that every document under seal is a deed, and

deed of conveyance
or **deed**
a grant, a document under seal that transfers an interest in land from the owner to another party

transfer
under the land titles system the equivalent of a grant; not required to be made under seal

many deeds are not concerned with transfers of land at all. The equivalent of a grant under the land titles system, used in some areas as described in the next section, is called a **transfer** and is effective without being made under seal.

A holder of an interest may grant the whole of it or only part, reserving the rest of it to himself. When he grants only part of it, the balance remains his. For example, when a landlord grants a lease for five years he retains the *reversion*; possession returns to him at the end of the lease—just as we have already seen, when the holder of a fee simple grants a life estate, the reversion stays with him and his heirs. When a person grants an easement over his land, he retains the remaining interest in the land (the servient tenement).

The transferor of an interest may wish to transfer almost all his interest, retaining only a small part for himself. In these circumstances, the *form* of the grant changes: he conveys away his whole interest except that he expressly reserves the part he wishes to keep. Thus, if *A* owns both Blackacre and Whiteacre and wishes to sell Whiteacre to *B* but retain an easement over it in order to get to and from Blackacre, *A* will grant Whiteacre to *B*, at the same time *reserving* a right-of-way over it. Such **reservations** are quite common in grants of land.

reservation
that part of an interest in land expressly retained by the transferor

In summary, a transfer of an interest in land can have two results: first, if it is a transfer of the *whole interest*, then the interest remains unaltered but is in the hands of another person; second, if it is a transfer of only *part of an interest*, the interest is divided into two parts and there are two holders—the grantee with the interest he has obtained under the grant, and the grantor with the interest he has retained because he did not transfer it by the grant.

THE RECORDING OF INTERESTS IN LAND

The English System

We have seen that interests in land are varied and complex and also that they may be transferred in a variety of ways. How is a prospective purchaser to discover what interest a vendor really holds in the land he offers to sell and what claims others might have? Ordinarily, under the terms of a contract to sell land, the vendor sets out the interest he is selling and gives the purchaser the right to examine all the title documents in order to see whether the vendor really has the interest claimed. In England, until recent times, owners kept all the title documents to their land going back many years, often centuries. The system worked quite well, but it placed a very high value on these title documents as evidence of an owner's interest. Thus, an accidental loss or destruction of the documents could create serious problems in proving ownership. And, of course, such documents deteriorated over the years.

Systems in Canada and the United States

In Canada and the United States a more reliable method of ascertaining title was developed. Each transfer of an interest in land is recorded in a public registry office. The usual practice is for the grantor to deliver to the grantee the original document and a duplicate copy. The grantee files both of them with the registrar. The original is then recorded (formerly by hand or typewriter, but now on microfilm or computer storage systems), assigned a number, and filed away. The duplicate is stamped and certified by the registrar with the number of the original recorded on it and is returned to the grantee. Registry office records are stored in a fireproof structure—both the original document and the microfilm of it—and in addition the purchaser keeps the duplicate copy of the original. Thus the danger of loss or destruction of a record of transfer is virtually eliminated. This method has now come into use in many parts of England also.

Registry Systems

Generally, there is a registry office for each regional political division within a province or state. For example, each county or district within a province usually has a land registry office located in the county or district town, the seat of regional government. A purchaser **searches** (examines) the title to the particular piece of land she is buying only in the local registry office. Any person with an interest in the land is protected by provincial statute only if that interest is registered. If the interest is not registered he takes the risk that a **bona fide purchaser**, that is, a purchaser who buys the land without knowledge of an unregistered claim, will buy free of that claim. In turn, the purchaser, the new owner, must register her interest in order to protect it.

Before the introduction of the registry system, if *V* granted a fee simple in Blackacre to *X* and subsequently *V* made a second grant of the same interest to *P* who did not know of the first grant, *X* would have title to Blackacre and *P* would have nothing. For when *V* granted Blackacre to *X*, he sold all that he had—he had nothing more to give to *P*. Accordingly, the grant to *P* was a nullity. But under the registry system, if *P* registers her deed before *X* registers his, *P* will effectively cut out *X* and obtain title to Blackacre. The result of this rule is of course that a purchaser will register her grant immediately on receiving it. Prospective purchasers rely on records in the registry office: they buy interests according to these records and need not worry about other interests that may have been granted but not recorded.

Reflecting the rules of the statutes of limitations, some registry systems limit to 40 years the period in the records that a purchaser must search for evidence of good title.[13]

ILLUSTRATION 23.6

X is considering the purchase of Red Oaks from *Y*. The records in the registry office show that *A* sold Red Oaks to *B* in 1930, but *B*'s name does not appear again. The next entry on the record is a grant in 1953 by *M* to *N*, and from then on there is a continuous chain of title to the present holder, *Y*.

X need not worry about the transfer from *A* to *B*, nor any subsequent transfer by *B*. In all probability *B* transferred title to *M*, and *M* neglected to register the grant, but it is not necessary to establish this link. The fact that *M* conveyed the land to *N* more than 40 years ago and that there is no subsequent difficulty with the title establishes a title upon which *X*, as an intending purchaser, can rely.

Searching the title to a piece of land under the registry system can be a labourious and sometimes a hazardous task. An error in one of the documents that has gone undetected may later be discovered and disclose an outstanding interest, creating serious consequences for the current owner. If harm results through the negligence of a lawyer, he or she must compensate the client. Lawyers take out liability insurance to compensate clients in case such an error occurs.

Land Titles Systems

The risks inherent in the registry system we have just described encouraged the adoption of a newer system in the mid-19th century. The new system is called the **land titles** or the **Torrens** system, named after an officer in the Australian marine shipping-registry department. He adopted the system of ship registration directly for land registration. The distinctive feature of the system is that as each new transaction concerning a piece of land is submitted for registration, the land titles office carefully examines and approves the document before recording it. At the time of recording, the office brings all outstanding interests in the land up to date and certifies them as being correct. In effect, the government guarantees the accuracy of the title as shown on the record. There are variations from jurisdiction to jurisdiction in the methods of recording and in the type of guarantee given by the government. The great advantage of the system is that a purchaser need not search through 40 or more years of records to discover the state

---

13. Registry Act, R.S.O. 1990, c. R.20, s. 112(1); Limitations of Actions Act, R.S.N.S. 1989, c. 258, s. 20.

of the title. The land titles office will give her a complete statement, valid to the moment the statement is issued.

The Two Systems Compared

As we have seen, the land titles system attempts to do away with the risks of adverse possession and to give absolute and concise information on the state of the title. The older registry system makes no attempt to do this: its purpose is simply to give a complete record of all title documents and let the searcher judge their validity. The registry system exists in the older settled parts of Canada—the four Atlantic provinces and throughout most of southern Ontario and parts of Manitoba. The land titles system is used in the three westernmost provinces, most of Manitoba, throughout most of northern Ontario, and in a number of southern Ontario districts.

Claims That Are Not Registered on Title

Adverse Possession

We must not assume that a careful search of the recorded documents will assure a purchaser that the land is free from all other claims. We have already noted that in the provinces using the registry system, a purchaser cannot rely solely on the records because the vendor's title may have been extinguished by adverse possession. The purchaser should personally inspect the property to see if there is evidence of a third party that appears to be asserting a right of exclusive possession over the whole or any part of the lands. Otherwise the interest purchased, or a part of it, may already have been extinguished.

Arrears of Taxes

Two other claims against lands not ordinarily recorded under either the registry or the land titles system are arrears of municipal tax on the land and, in some provinces, arrears of tax against corporations accruing while they hold the land. If any of these claims comes to light after a purchaser has paid the vendor, the purchaser must satisfy them in order to protect her interest in the land. Thus, a prospective purchaser should obtain evidence from the municipality of any taxes outstanding and evidence from the provincial government of any arrears of corporation taxes. This information cannot be obtained from the registry or land titles office but only from the government concerned.

Creditor's Claims

A claim against land may arise when the vendor is a judgment debtor at the time of the sale, that is, he has been sued successfully by a creditor who has registered its judgment with the sheriff for the county or district. If a claim of this kind is outstanding (unpaid) at the time the land is sold, the judgment creditor may still require the sheriff to **levy execution** against the land, that is, seize and hold a sale of the land in order to realize the amount due under the judgment. The purchaser will then have to pay the debt to save the land. Accordingly, a purchaser should also make a search for executions in the sheriff's office to ensure that there are none before completing the sale. Various other claims against a vendor, such as debts owed to public bodies for fines or taxes may be registered in the sheriff's office, according to each province's own rules. In order to facilitate a search for these claims the sheriff's office and the land registry office are often in the same building, or special facilities are provided in the registry office to search the execution records.

levy execution
to seize and hold a sale of land in order to realize the amount due under a judgment registered against the owner

Tenant in Possession

Another hazard to a purchaser may be created by a tenant in possession of the land. In most jurisdictions, short-term leases—usually for three years or less—need not be registered or even be in writing and are valid against purchasers that buy the interest of the landlord. Thus, a purchaser must inspect the property to see whether there are any tenants, and if there are, she should obtain an acknowledgment from them of the type of tenancy they claim to hold.

ILLUSTRATION 23.7

Victor agrees to sell Paula a retail store that is currently occupied by a tenant, Todd. Victor assures Paula that Todd is only a monthly tenant who can be given one month's notice to vacate. After the sale is completed, Paula serves Todd with a month's notice to vacate, but Todd shows Paula a two-year lease from Victor, signed seven months earlier, and he refuses to vacate for a further 17 months. Paula is unable to put the tenant out even though she has bought the premises for the purpose of obtaining possession for herself and carrying on business there.

However, if Paula had approached Todd before completing the sale and had obtained a signed acknowledgment from him that he is a monthly tenant only, the court would not permit him to claim later that he held a two-year lease. A purchaser may thus rely upon a signed statement of the tenant.

Summary

We can see that the sale of an interest in land is a complex transaction requiring careful examination of the records at the local registry or land titles office, the offices of municipal and provincial governments, the local sheriff's office, and an inspection of the land itself. We should remember that a sale of land is completed and title passed to a purchaser when she obtains delivery of the deed or transfer. The purchaser becomes full owner of her newly acquired property at that moment in time. Prompt registration or recording of a transfer of land gives protection against subsequent fraudulent acts by an unscrupulous vendor.

QUESTIONS FOR REVIEW

1. Define the terms title, real action, land, and nuisance.

2. What factors have encouraged the growth of public regulation of land use?

3. Describe the two main classifications of interests in land. Distinguish between freehold and leasehold estates.

4. How does the existence of a life estate hamper the sale of land?

5. Describe the nature of the interest that a spouse has in the family home. How did this interest evolve?

6. In what ways may title to land be acquired?

7. In what situation are there advantages in holding land in joint tenancy rather than tenancy in common?

8. Describe the two elements of ownership in a condominium and how they affect responsibility for maintenance.

9. What is the special nature of insurance for a high-rise condominium building?

10. In cooperative housing, who owns the property?

11. What are the reasons for limitation periods generally? How do they apply to land?

12. Distinguish the circumstances under which an easement may be obtained by prescription and a title may be extinguished by adverse possession. Need the required periods of time be the same?

13. Describe the three typical characteristics of oil, gas, and mineral leases.

14. Distinguish a restrictive covenant in a grant, a building-scheme covenant, and a zoning by-law.

15. For decades, each winter Timson has openly entered the fields of an uninhabited farm adjoining his home, and cross-country skied several times a week. He knows the Abel family that used to farm there, but they have moved to a town 25 kilometres away. The Abels have just sold the farm to Belsen and he has erected a sign at the gate, "No Trespassing." Does Timson have a right to continue his cross-country skiing?

16. What is expropriation and how does it take place?

17. Describe the old English system of recording interests in land. What were the risks?

18. What is the main difference between registry and land titles systems?

19. What must a prospective purchaser of land do to ensure that the vendor has the right to transfer the property clear of any claims? Describe the types of claims that might arise.

CASES AND PROBLEMS

1 Rumford College was established in the centre of the city in the late 19th century when the city was still small. It was granted 20 acres at the time—about nine hectares—and occupied two hectares with its buildings and lawns, expanding to about four hectares over the years. By the 1960s, as the city grew, the remaining five hectares became extremely valuable, and Rumford ultimately agreed to sell certain portions for commercial development. It sold one hectare to each of three developers, including a restrictive covenant with each grant limiting the height of any buildings to 20 metres so as to protect the view of Rumford's college towers. Two of the three developers erected buildings complying with the restriction. The third, Townhouse Inc., kept the land vacant.

Savvy Developers Inc. wished to erect a 25-storey luxury apartment building in the area to a height about five times more than the 20-metre limit. In addition to paying market value to Rumford for one-half hectare of land, it offered to donate $500 000 to the college's endowment fund if it would forego the restrictive covenant to allow the construction of the apartment building. Rumford agreed and sold the land. When Townhouse learned about the deal with Savvy, it resold its hectare to Upper Developments Ltd., deliberately omitting the restrictive covenant from the grant.

Upper Developments then sought a declaration from the court that the restrictive covenant no longer applied because of the concession made to Savvy. How do you think this dispute should be resolved by the court?

2 Peter Green owned and operated Green's General Hardware as well as the lands and buildings where he carried on business. His younger brother John worked for him as manager, as did his daughter, Susan. Peter died leaving a will in which he gave the business and real property to John for life, with the remainder to Susan at John's death. John and Susan could not agree on how to run the business: John wanted to push sales and expansion as quickly as possible; Susan feared that such action would make the business unstable—she preferred to build more slowly, consolidating the gains of the business. The dispute became heated, and John fired Susan. Within a few years the business was in serious financial difficulty; John had allowed several buildings, including a warehouse, to fall into disrepair. Susan sought by court action to force John to keep the buildings in good repair. Should she succeed? Why?

John died and left a will giving his whole estate including the business and buildings to his wife. Who is entitled to the business and why?

3 Ferrand owned a summer cottage near Fredericton, New Brunswick. He sold it and delivered a grant to Simpson in exchange for $35 000 cash on June 10. On June 11, Simpson received a telephone call to return home to Newfoundland where her mother was seriously ill; she left without registering her grant to the cottage. When Ferrand learned that Simpson had left the area he called an acquaintance, Entwistle, and asked him whether he was interested in buying the cottage at a bargain price of $26 000. Entwistle had offered Ferrand that amount several months before and Ferrand had refused. Entwistle eagerly accepted the offer on June 20 and paid Ferrand. On the same day, Entwistle received a grant to the cottage and registered it without knowledge of its prior sale to Simpson. Ferrand then absconded with the money from both sales.

Several weeks later, Simpson returned to find Entwistle occupying the cottage. When Entwistle refused to move, Simpson brought an action to have Entwistle put out and herself declared the owner.

The Registry Act, R.S.N.B. 1973, c. R-6, contains the following provision:

19. All instruments may be registered in the registry office in the county where the lands lie, and if not so registered, shall…be deemed fraudulent and void against subsequent purchasers for valuable consideration whose conveyances are previously registered.

Will Simpson succeed in her action? Would the result be different if Entwistle had heard that Simpson had purchased the cottage before he paid Ferrand the $26 000? Give reasons.

4 Don Wellman owned his own home, subject to a mortgage, when he married Victoria Selva. The two lived in the house for 20 years. Since Victoria earned a higher salary than Don she made most of the payments on the house mortgage and also financed various improvements as well as an addition to the house. They had two children. Don suffered from severe depression and as he aged he became violent during arguments with Victoria. One day, during a fit of rage, he killed her and was convicted of manslaughter and sentenced to prison.

Her estate sued Don, claiming a transfer of one-half the value of the house for the benefit of her heirs, including the two children. Give your opinion of the arguments that might be made for both sides and whether the action would succeed.

5 For over 30 years Montgomery owned two farms: Green Gables, on which he lived, and Wildwood. The two were separated by a farm owned by Cavendish. Montgomery continually used a road across the Cavendish farm to go to and from Green Gables and Wildwood. The access to the road was through a gate on the boundary of the Cavendish property. During most of these years Montgomery gave Cavendish a large turkey for New Year's, presumably as a gesture of good will and appreciation for the use of the road.

Three years ago Montgomery sold Wildwood to Radoja. Radoja made relatively little use of the road over the Cavendish property (going across twice yearly to visit Montgomery with mortgage payments) until last year, when she also bought Green Gables. The old road then became valuable to Radoja as the most convenient access between her two properties. In the meantime, however, the Cavendish family had extended their lawn across the roadway and Radoja's suddenly increased use of the road led to a dispute about her rights.

Cavendish sought a court injunction to restrain Radoja's use of the alleged right-of-way. Indicate, with reasons, whether the court will grant the injunction.

6 Running southerly from Halifax along the Atlantic is a provincial highway approximately 300 metres from the shoreline, where Essex Oil Ltd. has owned a service station on the east side of the road since 1953. The Essex Oil property extends about 300 metres along the east side of the highway and 100 metres east to a right-of-way owned by the province for a proposed scenic highway that would run closer to the seacoast parallel to the existing highway. The oil company's land was unfenced except along the existing highway, beside the station. On the other side of the provincial right-of-way and running down to the Atlantic shore is the Webster Trailer Court and Campsite, a business that was operating there for some years before Essex Oil opened its station.

The province continually deferred construction of the new road, and the right-of-way, a strip about 50 metres wide, lay vacant. The trailer court obtained a licence from the province to use the right-of-way but made no request of Essex Oil Ltd. to use that portion of its land not occupied for the business of the service station. Beginning in 1954, without any communication with Essex Oil, Webster's employees cut the grass on both the provincial right-of-way and the oil company's land, cleared litter, planted flowers, and painted the fence on the far side of the oil company's land, adjacent to the existing road. The employees converted the whole of this land into a playground for guests, putting up tennis courts and a baseball diamond, and during the winter flooding part of the land for a skating rink.

Finally, in 1973, some 19 years after the trailer court had begun to make use of this land, the province announced that it had abandoned all plans to build a road on the proposed site. Essex Oil Ltd. then decided to dispose of its unused land and wrote to Webster Trailer Court and Campsite, offering to sell the land for $25 000.

Mr. Webster, owner of the trailer court, consulted his solicitor, who checked the title deed and confirmed that the disputed land belonged to Essex Oil Ltd. The solicitor also advised him, however, that if the trailer court were to remain in possession for another two months it would have been using the land for 20 years and would then, under Nova Scotia law, have obtained title by adverse possession and without any payment to Essex Oil Ltd.

The Webster Trailer Court and Campsite did not reply to Essex Oil's offer and continued to make use of the land for the enjoyment of its guests. Essex Oil Ltd. wrote again in three weeks and received no reply. A week later, the local manager of Essex Oil Ltd. attempted to reach Mr. Webster by telephone. His secretary said he was out of town for another four weeks, but had left word that on his return he would be glad to discuss the offer in the oil company's first letter.

The full 20-year period had elapsed by only two or three days when the management of Essex Oil Ltd. became suspicious of what was going on and immediately had a fence constructed around the unfenced sides of its strip of land, right across a number of tennis courts and through the baseball diamond. It had no sooner done so than it received a letter from the Webster Trailer Court and Campsite solicitor stating that his client had a "possessory title" to the disputed land. Webster Trailer Court and Campsite then brought an action against Essex Oil Ltd. for a court order to the effect that it had acquired title to the land.

Discuss the validity of the plaintiff's case and the nature of the argument, if any, that might be offered by the defendant.

LANDLORD AND TENANT

There are many reasons why someone leases real property—vacant land, entire buildings and surrounding land, or just space within a building. The premises may be used for residential, recreational and social, or business purposes. In this chapter we examine such questions as:

- what is the nature of the landlord-and-tenant relationship?

- what classes of tenancies may be created?

- what are the typical covenants put into leases and what is their effect?

- how are tenancies terminated and renewed?

- what are "fixtures" and why are they important?

- what are the consequences of a landlord transferring his or her interest?

- what are "leasebacks" and how are they used?

- why are residential tenancies treated in a special way?

THE NATURE OF THE RELATIONSHIP

Definition of a Tenancy

A leasehold interest is created when a landlord (lessor) grants, and a tenant (lessee) accepts, a term. A **term** is an interest in land for a definite period. The landlord thus divides the interest in the land between himself and the tenant by giving a term to the tenant and retaining the reversion. At the end of the term, the tenant must give up the land: the right to possession reverts to the landlord. The word **lease** is used both as a short form for leasehold interest and to refer to the agreement between landlord and tenant creating the leasehold.

term
an interest in land for a definite period of time

lease
the short form for leasehold interest, and also the agreement between landlord and tenant creating the leasehold

As we have seen in the preceding chapter, a leasehold interest is an estate in land. When parties create a leasehold, certain rights and duties automatically accrue to both the landlord and the tenant. But the requirements of land law for creating an estate are strict and do not take into account the intentions of the parties; although the parties clearly intend to create a leasehold interest, if they fail to fulfill these requirements no estate in the land comes into existence, and the usual rights and duties between landlord and tenant do not arise. The consequences may be serious for either party but especially for a would-be tenant: she may be evicted by the owner at once; she has no right herself to evict strangers; she cannot acquire further interests in land such as easements, which may be annexed only to a freehold or a leasehold estate. For these reasons the essentials for the creation of a leasehold interest deserve emphasis. They are, first, that the tenant must obtain the right to exclusive possession, and second, that the tenancy must be for a definite or ascertainable period of time.

In this chapter it is important to bear in mind that most provinces now distinguish *residential tenancies* as a special class of tenancy in their landlord and tenant legislation. They do so in order to recognize the special importance of basic shelter for individuals who lease apartments and houses as their residence. We shall deal separately with these special aspects in the concluding section of this chapter under the heading "Residential Tenancies." The discussion through the major part of the chapter applies to *commercial tenancies*; its relevance for residential tenancies must be qualified by reference to the specific statutory provisions that we discuss in the final section.

Exclusive Possession

Exclusive possession defines the historic distinction between estates in land and lesser interests in land. It distinguishes control over the land from a mere right to use the land in common with others. A person who has a right to use land in common with others may have an easement, as we have discussed in the preceding chapter, or may be merely a *licensee*. A licensee enters upon land with the consent of the owner, as for example when he goes fishing in a farmer's stream; he is on the land lawfully, not as a trespasser, but he has no interest in the land. He does not have the right to put others off the land or to object if the activity of others interferes with his use and enjoyment of it. Moreover, in some circumstances the owner may put him off the land even when the owner has given him a contractual right to be there. The rights of a contractual licensee can be quite complicated and are better left for a treatise on land law.[1]

A tenant's right to exclusive possession gives her far greater power than she would have as a contractual licensee. She may keep anyone off the land, and her landlord has no right to put her off the land until the term ends. A tenant may keep even the landlord from entering the land unless she has agreed to the landlord's right to enter for a specific purpose, such as to view the state of repair of the property and to make repairs. The right to exclusive possession of land gives a tenant the ability to acquire other lesser rights—a tenant may acquire an easement over adjoining land for the duration of her tenancy in the same manner as may the holder of a fee simple.

There have been numerous cases about what constitutes exclusive possession. The main problem is whether a person is considered to have exclusive possession if under the terms of the lease others are given limited rights to use or access over the land. Thus, if a business contemplates obtaining a lease that reserves to the landlord or other persons the right to make special use of the premises at the same time, it exposes itself to serious risk. It should obtain legal advice about the matter. Generally, it is not wise under the terms of a lease to grant a right for the use of the premises to a third person or the landlord, except that the landlord may be given the right to enter for the limited purpose of inspecting the premises and making repairs.

---

1. For example, Burn (ed.) *Cheshire and Burn's Modern Law of Real Property* (14th ed.), pp. 555–75. London: Butterworths, 1988.

Definite or Ascertainable Period

A lease must begin on a fixed date, and it must end on a fixed or ascertainable date; the final date need not be stated if the period itself is definite. Thus, a lease that begins on March 1 of a certain year to run for a week, a month, a year, five years, or 500 years is a valid leasehold interest because the date of expiry can always be worked out accurately. If the parties attempt to create a term for an uncertain period, the term is void and no leasehold interest comes into existence. It has been held that a lease "for the duration of the war" or "until the tenant becomes insolvent" is void. However, parties who wish to have a lease of such a nature can accomplish their purpose by a comparatively simple change in the wording. The requirement of certainty is satisfied if a lease must end *at the latest* upon a certain date, but may be brought to an end *at an earlier date* upon the happening of a particular event. Thus a lease of Blackacre from *A* to *B* for 100 years that is to be terminated earlier if and when "hostilities between country *X* and country *Y* should formally come to an end," or "should *B* become insolvent" is a valid lease. This requirement illustrates the strict formalism that remains part of land law.

CLASSES OF TENANCIES

Term Certain

A **term certain** is a tenancy that expires on a specific day, the term ending without any further act by either the landlord or the tenant. A lease of a restaurant at a summer resort "from May 24 to September 15" of a particular year or a long-term lease of a cold-storage plant "from March 1, 1980, to February 28, 2000" are examples of typical commercial leases for a term certain. The tenant is expected to vacate before the end of the last day of the tenancy unless it has made new arrangements with the landlord. If it stays on without making any arrangements, it becomes an **overholding tenant** and may be put out by the landlord. If, however, the landlord accepts further rent without protesting, a new tenancy may be created, as explained below.

term certain
a tenancy that expires on a specific day

overholding tenant
a tenant who remains on the premises without a new agreement with the landlord after the term of the lease expires

Periodic Tenancy

A **periodic tenancy** is a leasehold interest that renews itself automatically on the last day of the term for a further term of the same duration, unless either the landlord or the tenant serves notice—as discussed later in this chapter—to bring the tenancy to an end. A periodic tenancy may be created by a formal agreement, but in Canada it arises more often in an informal way when a tenant moves into possession and pays an agreed rent to the landlord at regular intervals as agreed between them, either in writing or orally. If, for example, a business pays rent on the first day of each month, the tenancy renews itself for another month without further agreement between the parties. A periodic tenancy also comes into existence when a tenant remains in possession after its tenancy for a term certain has expired, and pays further rent to the landlord. The most common type of periodic tenancies are weekly, monthly, and yearly. The yearly tenancy is often called a **tenancy from year to year**.

periodic tenancy
a leasehold interest that renews itself automatically on the last day of the term for a further term of the same duration

We may note here the contrast between a term certain and a periodic tenancy: a term certain ends automatically unless the parties make an arrangement to continue it; a periodic tenancy renews automatically unless either of the parties serves notice to end it. We shall discuss the requirements of notice below, under "Termination and Renewal of a Tenancy."

tenancy from year to year
a periodic tenancy that renews itself yearly

Tenancy at Will

A tenancy at will is not a true leasehold interest because it does not last for a definite period, nor does the tenant have any right to exclude the landlord and remain on the premises. The tenant is there merely at the landlord's will, and the landlord may demand possession at any time without notice. The tenant does, however, have a reasonable time to gather up possessions and leave.

On the other hand, a tenant at will is under no obligation to remain in possession and pay rent; it may vacate possession at any time without notice. Such a tenancy may exist when the owner of real property allows a prospective purchaser to occupy the premises pending the conveyance of the title to it, or when a landlord permits a tenant to remain on a day-to-day basis pending the wrecking of the building to make way for new construction. A tenancy at will may be gratuitous, or the landlord may exact a payment without turning the arrangement into a leasehold.

Tenancy at Sufferance

A tenancy at sufferance is not a tenancy at all. The typical example is that of an overholding tenant that entered into possession rightfully under its lease but now stays in possession wrongfully after the term has expired. Since it came into possession lawfully, it is not treated as a *trespasser* unless the landlord orders it to leave and it refuses. (Ordinarily, a **trespasser** is one who enters without consent or lawful right on the lands of another or who, having entered lawfully, refuses to leave when ordered to do so by the owner.) We should contrast the position of a tenant at sufferance with that of a tenant at will. Although a tenant at will has no estate in the land and can be put out by the landlord, it is nonetheless there lawfully, by agreement. A tenant at sufferance has no agreement with the landlord: its occupation of the land is merely suffered by the landlord until the landlord acts to put the occupier out.

trespasser
one who enters without consent or lawful right on the lands of another or who, having entered lawfully, refuses to leave when ordered to do so by the owner

COVENANTS
To Pay Rent
The Price Paid for a Definite Term

The covenant to pay rent is easily understood when we recall the nature of a leasehold interest. A leasehold is a specific period "carved out" of the fee simple and sold for a fixed sum. Very often leases recognize this fact by stating the total rent to be paid during the whole of the lease, and then describing how this sum is to be paid. The transaction is similar to an instalment purchase of a chattel. For example, the tenant may promise to pay the sum of $120 000 to lease a suite of offices for five years in 60 monthly instalments of $2000 per month. Thus, when the leasehold is transferred to the tenant, it becomes the holder or owner of that period of five years somewhat like the purchaser of a car on instalments becomes the owner of an interest in the car; each is to pay for the purchase over the succeeding few years.[2]

The Unqualified Nature of the Promise

We may carry the analogy further: if the car is destroyed, the buyer must still pay for it. Similarly, if leased premises are destroyed—in the absence of a specific term in the lease dealing with the problem—the tenant is still liable for the rent; it has purchased a leasehold interest consisting of a certain geographically defined area, and must pay for it whether or not the building and amenities continue to exist for the full term. It would seem, then, that the doctrine of frustration has no application to commercial leaseholds, with perhaps the exception of leasehold interests above the ground floor in a multi-storey building. If, for example, a 10-storey building burns down, can the landlord insist that a firm on the ninth floor continue to be liable for rent because it could employ a surveyor to show it exactly where its office suite used to be, and so it may still use the space if it wishes? To the present time, there are no decisions on this problem, but probably the tenant would be released from its obligation to pay rent. A leading treatise states:

2. We shall discuss the nature of a purchaser's interest in an instalment plan purchase in detail in Chapter 30.

If the subject-matter [of a lease] is destroyed entirely, it is submitted that the lease comes automatically to an end....There being no such thing in law as a [lease]...of a volume of space above the surface of the earth...it is submitted that no [lease]...of part of a building without any of the soil upon which the building stands, can survive such a destruction of the building as leaves no physically defined subject-matter....[3]

The Limited Range of Relief from Payment

In addition, it is generally the duty of the landlord to provide access to leased premises on upper floors by means of staircases or elevators, and failure to do so might in itself relieve the tenant from liability to pay rent.

When a tenant leases only a portion of the landlord's building, the landlord usually retains control over heating, repairs, and maintenance. In these circumstances it is common to state in the lease that liability to pay rent shall be suspended if the leased premises are substantially destroyed by fire or other cause, and not by the tenant's own negligence. Such a provision is not automatically implied, however, and unless it is expressly stated in the lease, the tenant remains liable for the rent—subject to our discussion above concerning leases of premises above the ground floor.

A tenant's covenant to pay rent is independent of any express promise by the landlord to make repairs to the property, and the tenant is not excused from paying rent on the grounds that the landlord has not performed her part of the bargain. A tenant is not, however, liable for further rent when the acts of the landlord amount to an eviction, as we shall see when we consider the covenants of "repairs" and "quiet enjoyment" below.

The Landlord Is Also Bound by the Covenant

The terms of the covenant to pay rent are binding on both parties. During the term, the landlord cannot increase the rent unless express provision has been made, as in the case where the parties agree that the landlord may increase the rent by an amount equal to any increase in property taxes. If the landlord wishes to increase the rent, she cannot do so until the term expires: she may, of course, bargain for an increase in any subsequent lease.

Assignment and Subletting

Freedom to Assign

A tenant may wish to assign the balance of the term of a tenancy before it expires. For example, a firm's business may have become so successful that it requires larger premises, or it may be offered a large sum for goodwill to sell the business as a going concern provided, of course, that it assigns the balance of the lease to the purchaser so that the business may continue at the same location. A tenant, as owner of a leasehold interest, has (subject to the terms of the lease) the right to assign it, just as the owner of a fee simple or a chattel has the right to sell or transfer those forms of property. A tenant does not, however, terminate its contractual obligations to the landlord by assigning: the landlord may still hold it accountable for performance of those obligations if, after the assignment, the assignee does not perform them. For this reason a tenant always makes it a term of the assignment of its tenancy that the assignee shall carry out all of the tenant's covenants in the lease and indemnify it against any loss caused by default in that respect.

A Term Requiring the Landlord's Consent

When leasing premises a landlord is often concerned with the reputation of the tenant as well as with its ability to pay the rent: it may be a matter of prestige, for instance, to have the head

3. Blundell and Wellings, *Woodfall's Law of Landlord and Tenant* (27th ed.), pp. 966–7. London: Sweet & Maxwell Limited, 1968.

office of a large corporation as a tenant in a new building in order to encourage other prospective tenants of good quality. A landlord may also be concerned about the type of business to be carried on for one or more of several reasons: the prestige or reputation of the building; unprofitable competition with the business of other tenants or with that of the landlord herself—a problem often arising in large business blocks and shopping centres; noise, fumes, or traffic interfering with other tenants; or the wear and tear certain businesses may inflict upon the premises. Various combinations of these reasons may determine whether or not a landlord will accept a particular tenant. Yet if a tenant were free subsequently to assign to whomever it pleased it might, by assigning, defeat the landlord's objectives. For this reason, a landlord almost invariably requires a tenant to covenant that it will not assign the lease without leave (permission) from the landlord.

Withholding Consent

If a landlord were free to grant leave or withhold it as she chose, the tenant might be placed in a difficult position. A landlord could arbitrarily refuse to give consent to an assignment that is in no way harmful to her. Accordingly, tenants often stipulate that the words "but such consent shall not be unreasonably withheld" be added to the covenant. In the provinces of Manitoba, New Brunswick, Prince Edward Island, and Saskatchewan, these words are implied by statute as part of the covenant unless they are expressly excluded.[4] It is both harsh and unusual for them to be expressly excluded; a tenant should be cautious about entering into a lease in the provinces mentioned above when the landlord excludes the implied words—or in the other provinces when the landlord refuses to permit the addition of these words to the covenant requiring her consent to an assignment.

Subletting

A sublease differs from an assignment as follows: an assignment is a transfer of the *whole* of the remainder of the tenant's term to the assignee; so long as the assignee performs all its covenants, the tenant has no further right or interest in the lease. A sublease is a transfer of *part only* of the tenant's term to the subtenant. If the term given the subtenant expires just one day before the expiration of the main lease (leaving the tenant with a reversion of one day), the tenancy of the subtenant is created *not* by an assignment but by a sublease, and the tenant becomes the landlord of its subtenant. The sublease may differ materially from the main lease in the rent payable, in any of the covenants given by either party, and in the extent of the premises sublet (the subtenant may hold only a portion of the premises leased to the tenant). In a sublease, just as in an assignment, the tenant remains liable to the landlord to perform all the covenants under the main lease. The discussion concerning the requirement of consent of the landlord for assignment applies equally to subleases—the covenant usually refers to subletting as well as to assignment.

Restriction on Use of Premises

We have noted that a landlord is usually concerned with both the reputation of a tenant and the use to which the premises are to be put. Once a landlord has accepted a tenant, she can do nothing about the tenant's manner of conducting its affairs. However, by requiring a covenant in the

---

4. The right to assign a leasehold interest, when it is subject to consent that may not be unreasonably withheld, is now considered to be a major term of the lease. If a landlord unreasonably withholds consent, his doing so will be a major breach; the tenant may end the relationship by cancelling the lease without further liability: Lehndorff Canadian Pension Properties Ltd. v. Davis Management Ltd. (1989), 59 D.L.R. (4th) 1 (B.C.C.A.). However, justifiable reasons for withholding consent may include economic ones, such as a prospective assignee (or a subtenant) competing with the landlord's interests. See Windsor Apothecary Ltd. v. Wolfe Group Holdings Ltd. (1996), 148 Sask. R. 234.

lease that restricts the use of the premises to particular trades, the landlord acquires important control. Such covenants are also enforceable against the tenant's assignees and subtenants.

A tenant may, in turn, insist that the landlord not rent adjoining premises to a competing business, and may obtain a covenant to that effect. If, however, the landlord should commit a breach by renting adjoining premises to an innocent third party unaware of the covenant, the tenant would have no rights against the third party. Its remedy would be limited to an action for damages against the landlord.

Even in the absence of an express covenant, there is an implied covenant by the tenant to treat the premises in a tenant-like manner, that is, use them only for those purposes for which they are reasonably intended. Thus, a tenant could not turn a cold-storage plant into a glue factory, or a restaurant into a hotel. In other words, a tenant may be prevented from carrying on activities for which the premises were not intended and that would cause excessive wear and tear.

Fitness for Occupancy

At common law, there is generally no covenant of fitness implied by a lessor in granting a lease. "The lessee takes the…premises as he finds them and at his own risk."[5] Until recent years, unless a tenant obtained an express covenant in the lease concerning the fitness of the premises for its particular use, or unless the landlord made a misrepresentation— thus giving the tenant the usual remedies in contract and tort for misrepresentation—the tenant was responsible for its own investigation of the premises and had to take them as it found them.[6] However, courts have suggested that the course of dealing between the parties may create an implied covenant that the premises will be fit for the lessee's purposes as disclosed to the lessor, much as the implied condition of fitness arises in a sale of goods.[7]

As we noted in Chapter 12, a landlord is not liable to a tenant or the tenant's customers, family, or guests for injuries caused by the unsafe condition of the premises, unless the landlord was, or ought to have been, aware of the dangerous condition when the lease was entered into and failed to warn the tenant who was unaware of the danger until a mishap occurred. Suppose, however, the landlord covenants to make repairs; if after receiving notice of a danger, she fails to make the repairs and the tenant sustains a loss, the landlord will be liable. In all other circumstances the tenant, as the party in exclusive possession of the property, bears any responsibility that arises from injuries caused to persons on the property.

Repairs

The General Rule

As a general rule, a landlord is not liable to make repairs to the property unless she expressly covenants to do so. Quite apart from law, of course, a landlord has an economic incentive to maintain her property in rentable condition.

The Landlord's Duties in Particular Circumstances

In some circumstances, she may be liable to repair structural defects that develop, particularly if failure to repair would amount to an indirect eviction of the tenant and consequently a breach of the covenant for quiet enjoyment, as we shall see in the next subsection. For example, if the failure of a landlord to repair a leak in the roof of an office building results in the soaking and

---

5. Foa, *Outline of the Law of Landlord and Tenant* (4th ed.), p. 71. London: The "Law Times" Office, 1928.

6. Long before the recent legislation affecting residential tenancies, the courts had made an exception to this common law rule: they held that when a landlord rents premises as a furnished house or furnished apartment, he gives an implied warranty that they will be in a habitable state at the beginning of the lease.

7. Telex (A/Asia) Proprietary Ltd. v. Thomas Cook & Sons (A/Asia) Proprietary Ltd., [1970] 2 N.S.W.R. 257 (C.A.).

eventual crumbling of the ceiling and walls in an office suite, the tenant has an action against the landlord even where no covenant to repair has been given. In addition, when rented premises are in a large building, the landlord is responsible to the tenants for the maintenance of corridors, stairways, and elevators.

The Tenant's Duties in Particular Circumstances

The general rule is that a tenant also is not liable to make repairs to the premises unless he has expressly covenanted to do so. The rule is subject to two exceptions. First, as we have already noted, the tenant must not make such use of the premises as will cause excessive wear. Second, he is liable for committing **waste**. Waste may be either *voluntary*—as when a tenant pulls down part of a building or otherwise damages it, or makes alterations that reduce its value—or *permissive*, that is negligent, as when a tenant is aware of some small damage such as a leak in the roof and realizes that more serious harm will result if he does not correct the problem, and yet neglects to do so. The law concerning permissive waste is complex and rather uncertain, but fortunately of little consequence today, since parties to a lease generally make an express agreement about which of them shall keep the leased premises in good repair.

waste

damage to the premises that reduces its value, caused by a tenant's voluntary destructive acts, by alterations or by negligence

The Usual Covenants in the Lease of an Entire Building

When a tenant leases an entire building or property, the landlord frequently obtains a covenant from it to keep the property in good repair, reasonable wear and tear excepted. As tenant, it thus agrees to make such repairs as are necessary to keep the property in the same condition as when the lease began, except for normal depreciation. The tenant is not liable for rot caused by faulty construction or for deterioration in the property due to a normal and progressive action of the forces of nature. Unless the lease exempts the tenant, however, the tenant's covenant to repair includes liability to make good any loss by fire or storm. Often a tenant exempts itself from liability in this respect by qualifying the covenant to repair with the words "loss by fire, lightning, and tempest excepted."

The Usual Covenants in the Lease of Part of a Building

When a tenant leases only part of a building, the landlord usually undertakes to provide various services such as heat, water, and elevator service, and also to keep the premises in good repair.

We should note that there is an important difference between a covenant to repair given by the tenant and one given by the landlord: a tenant is in possession of his premises and should be aware of their falling into disrepair—he is in breach of the covenant the moment he permits the premises to fall into disrepair, and it is not up to the landlord to remind her tenant.

In contrast, the landlord, not being in possession of the tenant's premises, is not presumed to be aware of any state of disrepair in them and her duty to repair does not arise until the tenant gives her notice. A landlord who undertakes to repair the premises often reserves the right to go on the premises at reasonable hours and inspect and view the state of repair. Reserving this right, however, does not place any duty upon her to make inspections or to repair until she has received notice from the tenant.

Quiet Enjoyment

The whole purpose of a tenant in acquiring a lease is to obtain possession and to "enjoy" the premises during the term of the lease. Accordingly, the landlord covenants to give **quiet enjoyment** either impliedly, simply by granting the lease, or expressly, in a specific covenant for that purpose. The covenant has two aspects: first, it is an assurance against the consequences of the landlord's having a defective title at the time she gives the lease; and second, it is a covenant that the landlord will not subsequent to the making of the lease herself interfere, or permit anyone obtaining an interest in land from her to interfere with the tenant's enjoyment of the premises.

covenant of quiet enjoyment

a landlord's promise that she has done and will do nothing to interfere with the tenant's possession and use of the premises

ILLUSTRATION 24.1

(a) Greer owns a large tract of land including certain warehouses. A mining company survey shows valuable ore deposits; she grants the company a long-term mining lease, and the company undertakes extensive mining excavations. Subsequently, she leases the warehouses to Atkins Inc., which wishes to use them to store heavy machinery. Atkins discovers that the mining operations have undermined the foundations of the warehouses, making them unsafe for use. Since the mining company is conducting its activities properly, and Greer cannot prevent its operations because she had validly granted it a mining lease before granting Atkins Inc. its lease, Greer's title was defective; therefore, she committed a breach of her covenant to Atkins Inc. for quiet enjoyment.

(b) Mendoza leases a suite of offices to McAdam and McCollum, a firm of practising accountants. Subsequently, he leases the area on the floor directly above to a machine shop. The machine-shop operations create noise and heavy vibrations, making it impossible for the accountants to carry on any aspect of their practice with adequate care. Mendoza is in breach of his covenant.

The courts have moved from their former position that breach of the covenant of quiet enjoyment requires physical interference with the enjoyment of the premises. Although there are some conflicting judgments, it appears that now substantial noise or vibration that interferes with the comfort or convenience of a lessee will be recognized as a breach of the covenant of quiet enjoyment. Accordingly, a court may reduce the rent of the tenant during the period of interference.[8]

Insurance

Who Takes Responsibility for Obtaining Insurance?

In the absence of an express provision, neither landlord nor tenant is under a duty to insure the premises for the benefit of the other. In most cases, of course, the landlord insures the premises to protect her own investment. If the leased property consists of an entire building or group of buildings under the complete control of one tenant, especially if the lease is for a very long term, the rent may be set on the basis that full responsibility for the premises including obtaining insurance passes to the tenant.

The complexity of liability and insurance problems increases when there is a large number of business tenants, each with its own employees, as in a large office building or a shopping mall. Who is liable for the loss if an employee should negligently cause a fire that substantially destroys a mall? Providing insurance protection and allocating risk through the use of exemption clauses requires great expertise.[9]

The Consequences of Severe Damage to Leased Premises

The question of insurance is closely tied to the problem of what should happen to the tenancy in case of severe damage to the premises by fire, flood, or storm. Unfortunately, parties often fail to consider these possibilities carefully. Failure to make proper provision can lead to great hardship, particularly for the tenant. A lease stating that if the premises are substantially destroyed,

---

8. For a full review of the law in this area, see Caldwell v. Valiant Property Management (1997), 145 D.L.R. (4th) 559. A tenant's right to quiet enjoyment extends to non-interference with the guests whom she might invite to visit her: Cunningham v. Whitby Christian Non-Profit Housing Corp. (1997), 33 O.R. (3d) 171.

9. See Greenwood Shopping Plaza Ltd. v. Beattie, [1980] 2 S.C.R. 228, where employees were held personally liable and could not take advantage of an exemption clause as third parties. The subsequent Supreme Court decision in London Drugs v. Kuehne & Nagel International Ltd. (1992), 97 D.L.R. (4th) 261, appears to overturn, or at least limit, the restrictive view taken in the Greenwood case. See also Laing Property Corp. v. All Seasons Dispal Inc. (1998), 53 B.C.L.R. (3d) 142.

the liability to pay rent is suspended until the building is repaired, may not be a benefit to the tenant; indeed, such a clause may place a tenant at the mercy of a capricious or simply undecided landlord. While the landlord decides what to do, the tenant, although not paying rent, is temporarily out of business. If it leases premises elsewhere, it may find when the building is repaired that it is liable to pay rent for both locations. A fair term of a lease should state that the repairs must be made within a certain time and that if they are not made within that time, the tenant then has the option of terminating the lease rather than waiting until the premises are restored. A further variation gives the tenant the right to make the repairs itself and deduct the costs from future rent.

Provision of Services and Payment of Taxes

Once more, a distinction must be made between tenancies for a whole building and those for a suite or a portion of a building. When a tenancy is for a portion of a building only and the landlord retains control over the building as a whole, it is usual for her to covenant to provide a reasonable amount of heat during the colder months of the year, water, sometimes electric power, and occasionally even telephone service. When the tenancy is for the whole of the building, it is usual for the tenant to provide all these things itself.

Generally, property taxes are paid by the landlord when the tenant leases only a portion of the building. If it leases the whole of the building, the taxes may be paid by either party. As long as the agreement is clear, it is not important who pays: if it is the landlord, the rent is that much higher; if the tenant, then it is that much lower. In the absence of an agreement on the matter it is the landlord's duty to pay the taxes.

Checklist: Covenants in a Lease

This is *not* a complete list of covenants; there may be other important ones depending on the circumstances of the lease. In every lease, however, covenants that should be checked carefully by both parties are those concerning

- payment of rent
- restrictions on assigning or subletting the premises
- restrictions on the use of the premises
- fitness for occupancy
- responsibility for repairs
- quite enjoyment of the premises
- responsibility for insurance
- responsibility for provision of services such as access (e.g., elevators), heating, electricity, etc.
- responsibility for payment of property taxes

REMEDIES OF THE LANDLORD FOR BREACH OF COVENANT

Damages and Rent at Common Law

A landlord may sue for damages caused by a tenant's breach of any covenant other than the covenant to pay rent. The right to recover rent requires further discussion. Suppose without excuse a tenant abandons the premises and pays no further rent. According to long established rules concerning interests in land, the landlord is then in a predicament. On the one hand, by leaving the premises vacant and insisting on her rights under the lease, she can claim the entire rent due under it. But the tenant may be impecunious at the time and unable to pay the full amount due. (In land law, apart from any statutory provisions to the contrary, there is no duty to mitigate damages as there is in contract law.) On the other hand, the landlord may occupy the premises or lease them to another tenant at a lower rent in order to reduce her loss, but she will then be presumed to have accepted the **surrender** by the tenant, freeing it from further obligations to pay rent.

surrender
abandonment of the premises by the tenant during the term of the lease

Relevance of the Contract Duty to Mitigate

While a lease creates an interest in land, it is also a contract between the parties. The courts could look to the principles of contract law for a solution, but it was not until recently that they conceded this possibility. They now give the landlord a way out: if she wishes both to resume possession and to continue to hold the tenant liable for rent, she must inform the tenant that she regards it to be in breach and that she will hold the tenant responsible for any loss during the remainder of the tenancy even if she relets the premises to a new tenant at a lower rent. Thus a landlord may now mitigate her losses without losing her rights against the defaulting tenant. But if the landlord chooses not to mitigate, it has become unclear whether the tenant still remains liable for the full rent.

To clarify the law with respect *only* to residential tenancies, Ontario and several other provinces amended their landlord and tenant laws, as follows:

> Where a tenant abandons the premises in breach of the tenancy agreement, the landlord's right to damages is subject to the same obligation to mitigate his damages as applies generally under the rule of law relating to breaches of contract.[10]

Does this amendment lead to the implication that no similar rule exists for commercial tenancies? In 1971, the Supreme Court of Canada affirmed the rule that a landlord has no duty to mitigate if she chooses not to do so.[11] However, a number of recent cases have left the law in the area confused, some holding that a landlord is always expected to mitigate losses,[12] and others holding that a landlord need only mitigate if she chooses to sue for damages rather than for unpaid rent with the premises left empty.[13]

Effect of the Bankruptcy and Insolvency Act

Under the Bankruptcy and Insolvency Act, a landlord has priority over other creditors in the event of the tenant's bankruptcy to the amount of three months' rent in arrears.[14] For rents due in excess of this sum, she ranks only as a general creditor. The purpose of the three months' preference is to encourage landlords to be a little more patient with a defaulting commercial tenant. Inability to pay rent may be only temporary, but eviction will close the business down, probably causing greater hardship to both the tenant and other creditors of the tenant. Provincial landlord and tenant acts recognize the right of a trustee in bankruptcy to repudiate an outstanding lease

---

10. Residential Tenancy Act, Landlord and Tenant Act, R.S.M. 1987, c. L-70, s. 94. The wording of the latest version of the Ontario and B.C. acts are different but with the same legal effect; Tenant Protection Act, S.O. 1997, c. 24, s. 13; R.S.B.C. 1996, c. 408, s. 80(5) and (6).

11. Highway Properties Ltd. v. Kelly, Douglas & Co. Ltd. (1971), 17 D.L.R. (3d) 710.

12. See for example, Smith v. Busler, [1988] B.C.J. No. 2793 (S.C.); Globe Convestra Ltd. v. Vucetic (1990), 15 R.P.R. (2d) 220 (Ont. Gen. Div.).

13. See, for example, Transco Mills Ltd. v. Percan Enterprises Ltd. (1993), B.C.L.R. (2d) 254 (C.A.); Jade Agencies Ltd. v. Meadow's Management Ltd., [1999] B.C.J. No. 214.

14. R.S.C. 1985, c. B-3, s. 136(1)(f), as amended by S.C. 1992, c. 27. In the absence of bankruptcy proceedings, a landlord's priority under provincial legislation is usually greater than three months.

without further liability or, with proper notice, to continue to use the premises for so long as may serve the purpose of liquidation and pay rent at the rate specified in the lease.[15]

Eviction

right of re-entry

a landlord's remedy of evicting the tenant for failure to pay rent or breach of another major covenant

This remedy is sometimes called the landlord's **right of re-entry**. The right of re-entry for failure to pay rent is a term implied by statute if not expressly included in the lease. The period for which rent must be in arrears before a landlord is entitled to re-enter and evict the tenant varies considerably from province to province and is longer in the case of residential tenancies. Before evicting a tenant in default, the landlord must follow the procedure laid down in the legislation of the province.

Leases often provide that the landlord may re-enter and evict the tenant for breach of any of the other covenants in the lease. Since eviction amounts to a *forfeiture*, that is, to the penalty of forfeiting the remainder of term to the landlord, the court is very reluctant to permit eviction for breach of any covenant other than one relating to payment of rent, use of the property, or assignment of the lease. The court grants a tenant relief against forfeitures either under the general principles of equity or under various statutory reliefs found in provincial legislation.[16] Generally speaking, so long as the tenant subsequently makes good its breach, the court will restrain the landlord from evicting it and will declare the lease to be valid under its original terms.

Distress

distress

the right of the landlord to *distrain*, that is, to seize assets of the tenant found on the premises and sell them to realize arrears of rent

The landlord has a power of **distress** or the right to *distrain* for rent; that is, she may seize assets of the tenant found on the premises and sell them to realize arrears of rent. Usually, the landlord authorizes a bailiff to distrain on the property of the tenant. The right to distrain does not arise until the day *after* the rent is due and a demand for payment has been made. A landlord cannot prevent the tenant from removing goods from the premises even as late as the day the rent is due; she may, however, object if the tenant is clearly removing the goods in order to avoid the landlord's power of distress. If the tenant removes the goods in spite of the landlord's objection or later removes them fraudulently to prevent the landlord from asserting her rights, after the right has arisen, the landlord may follow the goods and have them seized in another location, provided that they have not been sold in the meantime to an innocent purchaser. The time limit within which a landlord may seize goods in this fashion varies from province to province.

It should be noted that a landlord cannot exercise the right of eviction and simultaneously or subsequently exercise a right of distress. The right to distrain is limited to situations where the relationship of landlord and tenant still exists.[17]

Certain personal property is exempt from seizure: necessary household furniture, a limited supply of food and fuel, and mechanic's tools. If the landlord by mistake seizes the goods of third parties such as customers or consignors, they must be released on proof of ownership. The landlord may also seize equipment or appliances purchased on the instalment plan and not fully paid for, but before selling them he must first pay the balance owing to the seller.[18] A commercial lease may contain a term by which the tenant "contracts out" of its right to exemptions should the landlord distrain for rent; the result, in the words of the Ontario Law Reform

---

15. See, for example: Commercial Tenancy Act, R.S.B.C. 1996, c. 57, s. 29; Commercial Tenancies Act, R.S.O. 1990, c. L.7, ss. 38(2) and 39(1); Landlord and Tenant Act, R.S.M. 1987, c. L-70, ss. 46(2) and 47(1).

16. Courts of Justice Act, R.S.O. 1990, c. C.43, s. 98; Law and Equity Act, R.S.B.C. 1996, c. 224, s. 24.

17. Mundell v. 796586 Ontario Ltd. (1996), 3 R.P.R. (3d) 277.

18. The priority of a landlord may be superior to that of a chattel mortgagee, that is, of a different type of secured creditor. Chattel mortgages are discussed in Chapter 30, "Methods of Securing Credit."

Commission, is that "a successful seizure can leave the tenant with nothing but the clothes on his back."[19]

Injunction

If a tenant proposes or has begun to use the premises in a manner that would be in breach of a covenant restricting use, the landlord may obtain an injunction ordering the tenant to cease the prohibited use. An injunction may be obtained against certain types of use even when they are not expressly prohibited under the terms of the lease, if they are inconsistent with the general design and ordinary use to which the property would be put. For example, a landlord could obtain an injunction to prevent a house ordinarily used as residential property from being turned into a medical clinic.[20]

Generally speaking, wherever a landlord may obtain an injunction, she also has the right to re-enter the property and evict the tenant. Which of these remedies she chooses depends largely on the circumstances, and in particular, on whether the lease is an otherwise desirable one from the point of view of the landlord.

REMEDIES OF THE TENANT FOR BREACH OF COVENANT

Damages

A tenant may recover from the landlord for damages arising from breach by the landlord of any of her covenants. A landlord, believing the tenant has committed a breach, may wrongfully infringe the tenant's rights. For instance, she may evict the tenant mistakenly believing that the tenant was in arrears of rent and had been served with notice. The wrongful eviction by the landlord is a breach of the covenant for quiet enjoyment. Similarly, if a landlord distrains upon more goods than were reasonably necessary to satisfy a claim for arrears of rent, the tenant may recover damages. If the landlord or her bailiff, in attempting to distrain upon the goods of the tenant, enters the premises illegally, that is by use of force, she will be liable for damages for trespass. A tenant is entitled to prevent an exercise of the power of distress by keeping the premises continually locked; but in these circumstances the threat of distress can be a continuing harassment to the tenant.

If a landlord has expressly covenanted to keep the premises in good repair or rebuild if they are destroyed, her failure to do so will be a breach not only of the covenant to repair but also of the covenant for quiet enjoyment.

Injunction

A tenant may also obtain an injunction to restrain a landlord from a continuing breach of the covenant of quiet enjoyment: a court will grant an injunction against a landlord for interfering with quiet enjoyment caused by a continuing nuisance, such as vibrations, noise, or fumes escaping from the landlord's premises. The court will not grant an injunction, however, where it would be futile to do so, for example, where vibration caused by the landlord has so damaged the structure that it has been condemned as unsafe for occupation, thus destroying its usefulness to the tenant; the tenant's remedy is in vacating the premises and seeking damages.

---

19. *Interim Report on Landlord and Tenant Law Applicable to Residential Tenancies*, p. 14. Toronto: Ontario Law Reform Commission, 1968. We shall see in our discussion below that many of the provinces have now abolished the remedy of distress for residential (though not for commercial) tenancies.

20. McCuaig v. Lalonde (1911), 23 O.L.R. 312.

We have already noted that an important covenant often given by a landlord to a retail tenant is a promise not to lease premises in the same building or shopping centre to a competing business. When a breach occurs, an injunction restraining the second tenant from carrying on the competing business will be granted only if the second tenant was aware of the covenant.

Termination of the Lease

When a landlord's breach of the covenant of quiet enjoyment has made the premises unfit for the tenant's normal use and occupation, the tenant, in addition to any other remedy, may terminate the lease and vacate the premises. Upon so doing, it ceases to have any further liability to the landlord. The landlord's breach must render the entire premises unfit for the tenant's use—amounting to a total eviction—before the tenant will have this option.

If the landlord's interference is only with part of the premises or only a nuisance or inconvenience rather than amounting to a total eviction, the tenant remains bound to pay the rent and cannot terminate the lease. Its remedies are then an action for damages for the injury suffered and an injunction to restrain further breach. Even in residential tenancies where tenants have been given greater rights than in commercial tenancies, the courts have not supported a group of tenants who collaborated to withhold rent in the face of the landlord's neglect to complete promised amenities in a new apartment building (such as elevators, garage, parking lots, pool, sauna, laundry room, and landscaping).[21]

TERMINATION AND RENEWAL OF A TENANCY

Surrender

As we noted under "Classes of Tenancies" earlier, a commercial tenancy for a term certain expires automatically without notice. Although not required by law, a landlord often serves a reminder on the tenant that the lease is about to expire and that it must vacate on the date of expiry. Upon vacating the premises, the tenant surrenders them to the landlord.

A surrender may also take place during the term of a tenancy by express agreement between landlord and tenant, as when a tenant no longer desires to keep the premises and pays the landlord a sum of money to release it from obligations for the balance of the term. A landlord may also bargain for the tenant's surrender of the remainder of its term when she needs vacant possession in order to sell the property or wishes to make substantial alterations or demolish the building.

Suppose a tenant abandons the premises without making an agreement to surrender to the landlord. As we have seen, a landlord may be presumed to have treated an abandonment as a surrender of the premises when she re-rents to another tenant or takes possession of the premises herself to make use of them for her own purposes. Often it may be difficult to decide from the circumstances whether the landlord has accepted an abandonment and thus released the tenant from further obligation to pay rent. Since abandonment is usually committed by an impecunious tenant, the landlord's rights against the tenant may have little practical value.

Forfeiture

In our discussion of a landlord's remedies, we noted that breach of certain covenants by a tenant (such as failure to pay rent) entitles the landlord to evict the tenant and thus impose a forfeiture of the lease. Once such a forfeiture takes place, the relationship of landlord and tenant is

---

21. C. Jowell, "Comments—Landlord and tenant relations—rent-withholding in Ontario" (1970), 48 *Can. Bar Rev.* 323 at 328, and reference to In the Matter of Vivene Developments Ltd. v. Jack K. Tsuji, an unreported case, transcript, County Court Reporters, Toronto, March, 1969, cited by Jowell.

terminated: the tenant has no further obligations under the lease, although it may be liable because of its breach before forfeiture for damages suffered by the landlord. Similarly, if a landlord has attempted to impose forfeiture by improperly evicting her tenant—entitling the tenant to consider its obligations under the lease at an end—the relationship of landlord and tenant is terminated, but the tenant may still recover damages for the landlord's breach of covenants.

Termination by Notice to Quit

Periodic Tenancies

A periodic tenancy renews itself automatically unless either the landlord or the tenant serves **notice to quit** on the other party, that is, serves notice of an intention to bring the tenancy to an end. Notice to quit served by a tenant is sometimes called notice of intention to vacate. In weekly, monthly, or quarter-yearly tenancies, the length of notice required to bring the tenancy to an end is *one clear period of tenancy*. In other words, one party must give the other notice *on or before the last day of one tenancy period* for the tenancy to come to an end *on the last day of the next period*.

notice to quit
notice of an intention to bring the tenancy to an end, served by either the landlord or the tenant on the other party

ILLUSTRATION 24.2

West Side Corp. rents a small warehouse from Bernstein on a monthly basis, commencing March 1, at a rent of $1250 per month. The following September, West Side buys a warehouse building with possession available on November 1. West Side must serve Bernstein with notice to quit on or before September 30 if it wishes to terminate the tenancy on October 31. October is then a clear month. If, however, it does not serve notice until after September 30—say, on October 3—October is no longer a clear month, and West Side Corp. is not able to terminate the tenancy until November 30. In these circumstances, November will be the clear month.

The English rule that six clear months' notice is necessary to terminate a *yearly tenancy* at the end of the first year or any succeeding year of the tenancy applies to commercial leases in all provinces except New Brunswick, Nova Scotia, and Prince Edward Island. In these provinces only three clear months' notice is required.

ILLUSTRATION 24.3

Bok leases the Greenbrier summer hotel in Alberta from O'Brien at a yearly rental of $30 000, commencing April 1, 1992. The yearly tenancy will renew itself automatically each April 1 unless either party gives six clear months' notice before April 1, that is, on or before September 30 of the preceding year. If Bok wishes to vacate the property by March 31, 2001, he must serve notice on or before September 30, 2000. If he serves notice on October 1, 2000, it is too late; the tenancy will automatically renew itself on April 1, 2001, and continue to March 31, 2002. Thus, the maximum time that may elapse between giving notice and terminating the tenancy may be 18 months less a day, that is from October 1, 2000, to March 31, 2002.

Tenant That Remains in Possession After the Expiration of a Term Certain

We have already noted that if a tenant remains in possession after the expiration of a term certain, it becomes a tenant at sufferance and may be evicted by the landlord at any time on demand. If, however, the landlord accepts further rent from the tenant, a periodic tenancy then arises on all the terms of the original lease except those repugnant to a periodic tenancy. An example of a repugnant term would be a covenant by the landlord to redecorate the premises every three years during a term certain of 12 years. This covenant would not become part of a subsequent periodic tenancy.

Generally speaking, if a periodic tenancy arises after the expiry of a *term certain expressed in years* (for example, a lease for five years at an annual rental of $8400 payable in instalments of $700 per month), then the periodic tenancy created will be a *yearly tenancy*. If instead the term certain is stated as a *term of months* (say, a lease for eight months at a monthly rent of $700), then the periodic tenancy created will be a *monthly* one; similarly, if the term certain is expressed in terms of weeks or quarter-years, a succeeding periodic tenancy will be weekly or quarter-yearly respectively.

The wording used to describe the term in the original lease may be ambiguous and can result in a difficult question of interpretation about what type of succeeding periodic tenancy is created when the landlord accepts further payment of rent. Suppose, for example, in the original lease a *term certain is granted for one and a half years at a monthly rent* of $700, and the tenant remains in possession and continues to pay rent after the expiry of the original term. Is the term thus created one expressed in years or months? There has been conflict in the Canadian cases.[22] If such a problem should arise, it is best to seek legal advice at once: if the periodic tenancy following the original lease is held to be a yearly one, it may be impossible for either party unilaterally to bring the tenancy to an end for a period of almost 18 months; whereas if the periodic tenancy is a monthly one, the maximum period of notice would be just under two months.

Parties May Set Their Own Terms for Notice

The requirements for a valid notice to quit discussed above are those that apply in the absence of express agreement; the parties to a lease may agree to vary them to suit their own needs. Thus, landlord and tenant may agree that some period less than six months, say two months, is sufficient notice for either party to terminate a yearly tenancy. Similar variations may be agreed upon for any length of tenancy.

Renewal

A lease for a term certain, particularly a lease of premises for a retail store, often provides for a renewal at the option of the tenant. Asking for such an option makes good business sense: in taking the risk of operating a retail outlet in a particular area, the tenant may not want the added burden of a long-term lease for fear that the venture may prove unprofitable. On the other hand, if it takes only a short-term lease and the venture proves to be a success, it cannot count on successfully negotiating for a new lease at the expiry of the original lease. An option permits it to terminate the tenancy at the end of the original lease if it does not wish to continue, yet it has the security of exercising the option if business proves successful. A typical option arrangement would be an initial lease for three or perhaps five years, with an option for a further five or 10 years. Landlords are usually quite willing to grant options provided they receive some protection against inflation and sufficient notice to obtain a new tenant if the option is not exercised.

The various forms of protection a landlord may seek are numerous. In general, a landlord will require that the rent in any renewal be increased by the amount of any increase in taxes that occurs during the original lease, and sometimes will also require either a fixed increase in rent or a series of percentage increases at various intervals during the term of the renewal, commonly tied to the consumer price index or some other measure of the rate of inflation. A landlord will usually require notice of at least three months from the tenant that it intends to exercise the option, and probably six months if the renewal is for a long period, such as 10 years.

---

22. See Williams and Rhodes, *The Canadian Law of Landlord and Tenant* (6th ed.), pp. 4:11–3. Toronto: The Carswell Co. Ltd., 1988.

FIXTURES

As we noted in Chapter 23 in our introduction to real property, land includes everything fixed to it. Trees, fences, and buildings form part of the land, but they are distinguished from the land itself in that they are called **fixtures**. Technically, then, an oil derrick, a grain elevator, a stand of timber, and a large office building are all fixtures, although in the everyday language of business they are not commonly called fixtures. An object that is affixed to a fixture (such as a furnace installed in a building) is itself a fixture. It is in this more restricted sense that the word is commonly used, and may become the source of disagreement.

General Rules for Ownership of Fixtures

Whether an object is held to be a fixture may determine who is its owner. Generally, an object permanently affixed to a building becomes a part of the building and of the real property itself. In a sale of land the vendor cannot remove fixtures that were attached at the time of the contract of sale; they belong to the purchaser. Similarly, since fixtures belong to the landlord a tenant cannot remove them.

The question of what is or is not a fixture does not often arise in a sale of land because the purchaser and vendor usually agree between them what fixtures remain with the land. If the vendor wishes to take certain fixtures away, he expressly reserves that right in the agreement of sale and the sale price may be adjusted accordingly. In tenancy, however, a problem may arise *after* the lease begins: the tenant may attach objects to the premises for its own benefit without any agreement with the landlord. The question then arises whether it may take them away when it vacates the premises.

The result would be very harsh if a tenant temporarily attached very valuable objects to the building, unaware of the consequences of so doing, and later discovered it could not remove them under any circumstances; and the landlord might well reap an unjust benefit. Understandably, the law has developed more flexible rules in these circumstances than in a sale of land. To apply the rules we must decide, first, whether the object has become a fixture and, second, if it has, whether it belongs to those classes of fixtures that may be removed by a tenant.

Determining Whether an Object Is a Fixture

To determine whether an object has become a fixture, we may ask a number of questions.

- Has the object been fastened to the building with the intention that it become a fixture?
- What use is to be made of it?
- How securely and permanently is it attached?
- How much damage, if any, will be caused to the building by its removal?

A picture hanging on a hook in the wall is quite obviously not attached. A partition nailed and bolted to the walls of the building is quite clearly a fixture. But what would we conclude about the following: a table that has been bolted to the floor to prevent delicate machinery on it from being jarred; machinery bolted to the floor to prevent vibration; a display stand tacked to a wall so that it will not topple over; a neon sign held in place by guy wires bolted to the roof of the building?

Ordinarily, objects not bolted or anchored in any way but merely resting on their own weight are presumed not to be fixtures. Objects affixed even comparatively flimsily create a presumption that they are fixtures, although this presumption may be rebutted by asking what a reasonable person would intend when attaching the object, for instance the display stand mentioned above. When objects are held not to be fixtures they may be removed by the tenant at any time. If the tenant should inadvertently forget to remove them from the premises when the lease expires, they still remain the property of the tenant and may be claimed afterwards.

Tenant's Fixtures

Even when it is decided that an object was affixed in such a manner that it has become a fixture, the tenant may still have the right to remove it if it can show either (a) that it was attached for the convenience of the tenant or for the better enjoyment of the object, as when it is purely ornamental, or (b) that it was a **trade fixture**, that is, an article brought onto the premises for the purpose of carrying on some trade or business, including manufacturing. Both these classes of fixtures are commonly called **tenant's fixtures**. A tenant may remove them before the end of its tenancy, provided that in doing so it does not cause permanent damage to the structure of the building and it repairs what damage is done. If, however, a tenant leaves without removing its fixtures and the term expires, they are presumed to become part of the premises and the property of the landlord. We might add that tenant's fixtures include *only* those fixtures brought onto the premises by the tenant itself. Fixtures installed by the landlord or left by preceding tenants are the landlord's property from the time of installation or from the beginning of the tenancy and may not be removed.

trade fixture
an object attached to the premises for the purpose of carrying on a trade or business

tenant's fixture
a trade fixture or any other fixture attached for the convenience of the tenant or for the better enjoyment of the object

Advantages of an Express Agreement About Fixtures

From the above discussion, we can see that it is difficult to state precise and predictable tests to determine whether objects attached to the premises by a tenant remain its property or become a part of the building. The problem can often be avoided in advance by making an agreement concerning specific fixtures. If the parties expressly agree that a particular object—one that would otherwise undoubtedly be a fixture—is to remain the property of the tenant, the agreement is conclusive: a difficult decision arising from the facts will never have to be made. It is, of course, wise to make such an agreement in writing.

ORAL LEASES

In most jurisdictions, when a tenant is in possession under a short-term lease of three years or less, the lease need not be in writing in order to satisfy the Statute of Frauds, although, of course, a written lease is wise in any event.[23] Leases of longer than three years are usually unenforceable if they are not in writing. If, for example, a tenant enters into an oral lease for five years and the landlord later changes his mind and refuses to let the tenant into possession, the tenant is without remedy. If, however, the tenant is already in possession and has paid rent, the doctrine of part performance as discussed in Chapter 10 under the Statute of Frauds will apply; under the rules of equity the court will order the landlord to give the tenant its lease in the terms originally agreed between them. A landlord too may obtain specific performance and hold the tenant bound to a long-term lease if, after taking possession, the tenant should wish to avoid the lease and vacate the premises.

TRANSFER OF THE LANDLORD'S INTEREST

Relationship Between a Tenant and a Purchaser of the Landlord's Interest

As we noted at the beginning of this chapter, a landlord grants away a present right to possession of her land for a term and reserves to herself the right to possession at the end of the term,

---

23. The enforceability of oral short-term leases may depend upon the amount of rent to be paid. See, for example: Statute of Frauds, R.S.O. 1990, c. S.19, s. 3, and R.S.N.S. 1989, c. 442, s. 3; Carter v. Irving Oil Co., [1952] 4 D.L.R. 128, per MacDonald, J., at 131; Williams and Rhodes, *The Canadian Law of Landlord and Tenant, supra,* n. 22, pp. 2:1–2.

that is, the reversion. She also receives the benefit of the tenant's covenants. When a landlord sells land subject to a lease, she parts with both the reversion and the benefits of the covenants given by the tenant. Accordingly, a purchaser acquires the whole interest in the land subject to the outstanding lease, and succeeds to both the rights and duties of the former landlord. We may well ask, "How can a purchaser receive both the rights and duties of the landlord when the tenant was not a party to the sale and there is no privity of contract between purchaser and tenant?" The answer is that between the tenant and the new landlord who has purchased the reversion there is **privity of estate**. The doctrine of privity of estate is much older than the doctrine of privity of contract. It dates from feudal times, from the relationship between lord and vassal. Although the archaic aspects of this doctrine have been abolished, privity of estate between a new landlord and the tenant has been retained and is eminently sensible: neither landlord nor tenant can destroy the stability of the relationship by claiming that the original contract of lease does not bind them. Their respective interests in the land create the relationship between them.

privity of estate
the relationship between tenant and landlord created by their respective interests in the land and that passes to a transferee of the interest

Privity of Contract With the Former Landlord

The creation of *privity of estate* with a new landlord does not bring to an end *privity of contract* with the former landlord. Although a landlord may sell his reversion, he still remains personally liable on his covenants to his tenant, in particular the covenant for quiet enjoyment. Thus, if the new landlord should interfere with the covenant for quiet enjoyment in an irreparable manner, the tenant, if it chose, could sue the original landlord in contract. It might well have to do so if the new landlord had subsequently become insolvent or had little in the way of assets. The doctrine of privity of estate is a concept of real property and does not apply to personal property, with the possible exception of ships.[24]

Relationship Between a Tenant and the Landlord's Mortgagee

The leasehold estate acquired by a tenant, like other interests in real property, is valid against parties that subsequently acquire an interest in the land. Thus, if *after* leasing his land the landlord borrows against it under a mortgage, the mortgagee's (that is, the creditor's) title will be subject to the rights of the tenant. If the mortgagor (the landlord-borrower) defaults, the mortgagee may claim the reversion, but is not entitled to evict the tenant. So long as the tenant observes the terms of the lease, the mortgagee is bound by it and cannot obtain possession except as provided under the lease.

On the other hand, when the landlord mortgages his land *before* leasing it—unless the mortgagee concurred in the lease at the time it was given—the tenant is, in theory at least, at the mercy of the mortgagee if the landlord defaults. However, it is almost always in the best interest of the mortgagee to collect the rent rather than put the tenant out and try to obtain a new tenant. The risk to a tenant is greater if the lease is a long-term one, and at the time of default the value of the premises for leasing purposes has increased substantially beyond the current rent. For this reason, it is wise for a tenant to obtain the concurrence of the mortgagee before entering into a long-term lease.

The Need to Register a Long-term Lease

To protect its interest, a tenant should register a long-term lease in the land registry office. Otherwise the interest may be destroyed if the landlord fraudulently sells to a bona fide purchaser

---

24. See Lord Strathcona Steamship Co. v. Dominion Coal Co., [1926] A.C. 108; Port Line Ltd. v. Ben Line Steamers Ltd., [1958] 2 Q.B. 146. See also "Contracts Concerning Land" in Chapter 12 under "Exceptions to the Privity of Contract Rule."

who has no notice of the tenancy. The need for registration varies from province to province. In some provinces, leases as short as three years must be registered, while in others, only leases over seven years need be. Leases under three years need not be registered in any province.

CONTEMPORARY ISSUE

Commercial Condominium Ownership: An Alternative to Leasing?

Leasing premises is not the only option when a business does not wish to purchase or construct a building. Non-residential condominiums are increasingly being used for professional, office, retail, commercial, and even industrial purposes. Mixed-use condominiums might have retail stores and services at ground level, perhaps offices above them, and residential units on the higher levels.

There are several advantages to buying a commercial condominium unit rather than leasing. Among them are stability and security of tenure (no need to worry about large increases in rent or being refused renewal when the lease expires), the opportunity to own a specific location, the benefits of a sound capital investment, tax advantages of ownership, the opportunity to have a say in the operation of the building without being solely responsible for its management, and ownership of improvements. In a mixed-use condominium, the residents on the upper floors are a potential "captive audience" for the businesses below.

Nevertheless, the disadvantages of owning a non-residential condominium should also be considered. The initial capital investment and the carrying costs may be unaffordable. If the business grows and requires more space, adjacent units may not be available. Resale potential may not be good. A wise choice of location is very important; selling in a poor real estate market could be disastrous. In a mixed-use development, the developer may not have structured voting rights and cost allocations equitably. Conflict and bad feeling between residential and non-residential owners and poor management of the development might result.

Source: See Margaret Fairweather and Lynn Ramsay, Q.C., *Condominium Law & Practice in British Columbia* (looseleaf), Continuing Legal Education Society of British Columbia, paragraphs 1.8–1.9.

Questions to Consider

1. What kinds of business would benefit most from locating in a commercial condominium? What kinds would be better off leasing space? Give your reasons.

2. What sorts of business might be best suited to a mixed-use condominium development?

3. From an urban planning point of view, what are the benefits of mixed-use developments? The drawbacks?

LEASEBACKS

Long-term Leases in the United Kingdom

In the United Kingdom, it has long been common practice for the owner of a fee simple to grant a long-term lease and retain the reversion, whereas in similar circumstances in North America he would sell the fee simple outright. Several factors have contributed to this difference, but perhaps the main one is the strictly limited amount of land available in the United Kingdom and accordingly the significance attached to retaining the ultimate reversion. In North America, where until recently land has been relatively cheap and almost unlimited, it has not been valued so highly. In England, leases for 21 years, 49 years, or 99 years are very common, and sometimes leases for as long as 999 years are granted. For practical purposes, the longer the term of the lease, the more the position of the tenant approximates that of an owner in fee simple: only the remote reversionary interest of the landlord's heirs and the regular payment of rent serve to remind the tenant of its status.

The Growth of Long-term Leases in North America

In North America, the supply of land no longer appears limitless; particularly is this so in and around large cities. A lease is a flexible and adaptable tool of finance, especially to the investor desiring a secure, long-term income. Consequently, the use of relatively long-term leases of commercial properties has grown rapidly throughout North America. An established company with a good record of earnings is often able to arrange with a financial institution, usually an insurance company, to finance its acquisition of a new building by a long-term leasing device known as a **leaseback**, which forms part of a larger transaction. The business and the insurance company arrange the entire transaction in advance. First, the business obtains a short-term loan, usually from a bank, to finance construction of the building. As soon as the building is completed, the business sells it to the insurance company and pays off its bank loan. The insurance company then leases the building back to the business. The lease is usually for a period of 20 or 25 years, with the lessee business receiving an option to renew for two or three additional five-year periods. The lessee business acts very much as the owner of the property rather than as a tenant, paying for all repairs, maintenance, insurance, and property taxes during the currency of the lease.

leaseback
a financial arrangement enabling a business to buy a building and sell it to a financial institution that in turn gives a long-term lease of the property back to the business

Business Incentives for the Use of Leasebacks

The leaseback device has several advantages for the lessee business. First, the business need not go through the relatively more expensive and elaborate procedure of issuing securities in the capital market as a means of financing its expansion. The arrangements for a leaseback are relatively simple, once a willing financial institution is found to undertake the project. Second, in terms of financing a leaseback may be more advantageous than buying the property and mortgaging it, because a mortgagee will not generally provide the full value of the project, leaving the company to raise the balance, whereas under a leaseback a financial institution provides the whole amount required. Third, the lessee business may be able to claim a larger deduction for expenses in computing its taxable income than it could claim as capital cost allowance and interest on borrowed funds, had it purchased the building instead and financed it by a bond issue or a mortgage.

From the point of view of a lessor financial institution, rented property represents an investment of funds that not only provides regular rental revenue that includes the amortization of the cost of the property, but also gives the lessor the reversionary interest and possession of the entire property at the expiration of the lease. Thus any improvements in the building added by the tenant and any inflation in land values accrue to the benefit of the landlord. In addition, if the lessee business gets into financial difficulty, the legal formalities in evicting it are simpler and quicker than those required for a mortgagee to foreclose on a mortgage. This advantage is seldom a major concern, however, since the leasebacks are confined in practice to large businesses with good earning records.

The leaseback, as compared with other leases, is a relatively long, detailed, and complex document, often carefully setting out the rights a tenant has in making alterations and adding fixtures to the building, as well as in the types of trade it may carry on. Sometimes the lessor may impose restrictions on the future borrowing of the lessee business, as a means of insuring that it will not enter into obligations so great as to impair its ability to pay the rent.

Options to Purchase in Leasebacks

Sometimes a leaseback includes an option for the lessee business to purchase the premises at the end of the term or the last renewal of the term. The price at which the option may be exercised by the lessee may be determined in a variety of ways; it may be simply a specified sum of money, or it may be calculated by a formula taking into account, for example, whether the option is exercised at the end of the original term or the end of a renewal.

RESIDENTIAL TENANCIES

The Changing Needs of Residential Tenants

Rapid urbanization after the Second World War caused Canadian cities to grow very quickly and raised dramatically the cost of buying housing. Cities also attracted the vast majority of immigrants as well as Canadians from declining rural areas. Much of this influx was met by rental accommodation, especially in high-rise apartment buildings, as the newcomers to the cities did not have adequate capital to invest in the purchase of private homes. The typical city tenant now lives in a large apartment complex, knows few of his neighbours, and is remote from his corporate landlord. He has come to regard himself as a consumer of housing and to think of his relation with his landlord as based on a contract for services rather than an acquisition of an estate in land. Beginning in 1969, most provinces enacted legislation that reflected this changed attitude towards housing. The legislation repealed a number of the rules of landlord and tenant law that differ from the rules of contract law—but it did so only for residential tenancies; it does not affect the leasing of premises for business purposes. We shall briefly review major changes in residential tenancy law.

Legislated Protection for Tenants

Restrictions on Security Deposits

The landlord in a residential tenancy is prohibited from requiring any security deposit in excess of one month's rent, and even that sum may only be applied to the payment of rent for the last rent period under the tenancy agreement; the landlord must also pay interest on the amount of the deposit at a specified rate.[25] Formerly, landlords used security deposits to reimburse themselves for damage to the premises during a tenancy agreement; and if a landlord refused to return any or all of the deposit the burden lay with the tenant to sue for it. While the abolition of security deposits removes the landlord's advantage, the benefit may be illusory in a time of chronic housing shortages. Landlords may simply raise their rent by an amount adequate to cover the risks that used to be met by security deposits.

Landlord's Obligation to Maintain Premises

Under common law, a residential tenant was deemed to have accepted the property in its state at the time of entering into the lease: the landlord had no liability for repairs or injury caused even by hidden dangers about which the tenant could not reasonably have known. (A landlord was liable for repairs only when renting furnished premises.) The legislation makes the landlord liable for maintaining residential premises in a good state of repair fit for habitation and further states that the tenant's knowledge of the lack of repair before the lease is irrelevant.[26]

---

25. Tenant Protection Act, S.O. 1997, c. 24, ss. 117 and 118. The protection afforded tenants with respect to security deposits varies considerably from province to province. See, for example: Residential Tenancy Act, R.S.B.C. 1996, c. 406, ss. 2 to 23; R.S.N.S. 1989, c. 31, s. 12 (1) to (4) as amended, S.N.S. 1992, c. 27.

26. Residential Tenancy Act, R.S.B.C. 1996, c. 406, s. 10(1) and (2); Landlord and Tenant Act, R.S.M. 1987, c. L-70, s. 95 (1).

Freeing a Tenant From Further Performance After a Landlord's Breach

There are several other important statutory reforms. Formerly, the failure of a landlord to perform its own covenants, even if they were major terms, did not release the tenant from the obligation to pay rent unless the landlord's breach amounted to an eviction of the tenant. The new legislation makes a number of promises or covenants in a residential lease interdependent, so that breach by one party of a condition entitles the other to regard himself as freed from his own obligations.[27]

Freeing a Tenant From Further Performance by Applying the Doctrine of Frustration

The doctrine of frustration is now declared to apply to residential tenancies.[28] It replaces the common law rule that a contract for a leasehold estate in land contained an absolute promise by the tenant to pay rent and keep the property in repair. As we noted in Chapter 13, a tenant was liable to pay rent for the balance of the term even when the premises became uninhabitable through no fault of his own, and also to restore the property if it was destroyed for any reason during the tenancy. It should be noted that this requirement for restoration of the property was customarily expressly excluded in leases in multi-storey buildings.

Abolition of the Remedy of Distress

The amending legislation has abolished the landlord's remedy of distress.[29] This change was made in response to criticism by the Ontario Law Reform Commission, which described distress as "an extra-judicial remedy for the recovery of rent," and complained that in many leases a tenant was required to waive his usual rights to retain necessary goods against an exercise of this remedy.[30]

Landlord's Duty to Mitigate

We have already noted under "Remedies of the Landlord for Breach of Covenant" that when a tenant wrongfully breaks his lease by quitting the premises and failing to pay the rent, the landlord's right to damages is subject to an obligation to mitigate damages by re-renting the property as quickly as he reasonably can.

Assignment, Subletting, and Termination by Notice to Quit

The legislation eases the requirements when a tenant wishes to move from the premises: a landlord may not arbitrarily or unreasonably withhold consent to an assignment or subletting.[31]

Nor can a tenant be evicted as easily: termination by notice to quit has been changed to require notice even for a term certain tenancy that would otherwise end without any act by either landlord or tenant;[32] in the absence of notice to quit, a tenancy is deemed to continue as a periodic tenancy. In addition, the notice has been lengthened in some provinces. In Ontario, probably because the shortage of rental accommodation in large cities is so widespread, legislative protection of tenants is highest. All tenancies other than weekly tenancies require at least 60

27. R.S.B.C. 1996, c. 406, s. 83(1) and (3); S.O. 1997, c. 24, ss. 11 and 24; S.M. 1987, c. L-70, ss. 91 and 98.

28. R.S.B.C. 1996, c. 406, s. 78(2); R.S.M. 1987, c. L-70, s. 87; S.O. 1997, c. 24, s. 10.

29. R.S.B.C. 1996, c. 406, s. 80(1); R.S.M. 1987, c. L-70, s. 88; S.O. 1997, c. 24, s. 31.

30. See *Interim Report on Landlord and Tenant Law Applicable to Residential Tenancies*, Chapter 2, Ontario Law Reform Commission, 1968, and preceding discussion in this chapter under "Remedies of the Landlord for Breach of Covenant."

31. R.S.B.C. 1996, c. 406, s. 17(2) and (3); R.S.M. 1987, c. L-70, s. 90(1) and (3); S.O. 1997, c. 24, s. 17(5) .

32. For example: S.O. 1997, c. 24, s. 47(2), (3), and (4); R.S.B.C. 1996, c. 406, s. 32(1)(a).

clear days' notice prior to the termination date[33] and weekly tenancies require 28 days, on the part of both landlord and tenant.[34] Landlords are precluded from terminating tenancies and evicting tenants except for a serious breach of the lease by a tenant;[35] or because at the end of the current lease the landlord wishes to repossess the premises for occupation by himself or his immediate family; or because the premises are going to be torn down or substantially altered in order to be used for different purposes such as conversion to commercial premises.[36]

Municipalities May Establish Mediation and Arbitration

The legislation also makes provision for a local municipality to establish a residential landlord and tenant advisory bureau to receive complaints and mediate or arbitrate disputes between the parties.[37]

QUESTIONS FOR REVIEW

1. Define tenancy at will; term certain; overholding tenant; subletting; eviction; forfeiture; surrender; quiet enjoyment.

2. To what extent is it common for a tenant to limit her right to exclusive possession of the premises? Explain.

3. Should a leasehold interest be shown as an asset (with an equal and offsetting liability) on the balance sheet of a business? If so, at what amount?

4. Describe the difficulty caused by the strict covenant to pay rent as it relates to frustration in contract law.

5. What are the concerns of a landlord with respect to a tenant's right to assign the remainder of a leasehold interest?

6. Lewis owns a five-bedroom house next to his own home in Niagara-on-the-Lake, a major tourism centre, and rents it to Tessa for three years. Tessa then applies for a licence to operate a bed and breakfast on the premises. Lewis objects to such use of the house. Would he have any legal recourse against Tessa?

7. Describe the usual responsibilities of a landlord for repairs when a tenant leases only part of a building. How does this situation differ from a lease of an entire building?

8. Turner rented a store from Lauren on the ground floor of a multi-storey building as an art gallery to sell paintings and small statues. Turner's hours of business were normal retail business hours. A few months later, Lauren leased the adjoining store to Rockbar Inc. It played very loud music from noon until Turner's closing time. The music, especially the

---

33. S.O. 1997, c. 24, s. 47(2), (3), and (4).

34. *Ibid.*, s. 47(1). British Columbia requires notice of "at least one month" for all tenancy agreements that are not for a term certain: R.S.B.C. 1996, c. 406, ss. 33 and 34 (2) and (3). See also R.S.N.S. 1989, c. 401, s. 10(1)(c)(i) and (ii) as amended, S.N.S. 1992, c. 31. Nova Scotia requires the landlord to give four weeks' notice but the tenant need give only one week's notice.

35. R.S.B.C. 1996, c. 406, ss. 35, 36 and 38; S.O. 1997, c. 24, ss. 62 to 67 inclusive.

36. R.S.B.C. 1996, c. 406, s. 38(4) and S.O. 1997, c. 24, s. 53(1)(a) to (c). Both require 120 days' notice in case of demolition but in any event not before expiration of the current lease. In Ontario, notice of forfeiture is required under s. 106 even for non-payment of rent.

37. R.S.B.C. 1996, c. 406, s. 18 and Part 4; R.S.M. 1987, c. L-70, ss. 95(6) and 99(16); S.O. 1997, c. 24, s. 181.

thumping sounds, could be heard clearly in Turner's store and interfered with normal conversation. Does Turner have any remedies?

9. How would you suggest that responsibility for insuring the premises be allocated in a large shopping mall? Describe the most difficult aspects of the problem.

10. What is the historical position of the landlord when a tenant abandons the premises during the term of the lease?

11. Describe the three different positions that courts have taken with respect to landlord's duty to mitigate after a tenant abandons the premises.

12. In what way may a tenant be in a difficult position when the premises burn down, even if the lease states that the rent is suspended until the premises are rebuilt?

13. What property is exempt from a landlord's right to distrain?

14. Under the traditional English rule, how long a period of notice must be given to terminate a yearly tenancy? Give an example.

15. Oscar leased Blackacre from Brenda for five years at a monthly rent of $1200. Neither of them seemed to notice when the lease had expired: for several months, Oscar continued to pay his rent on the first day of each month. Brenda now needs to take possession of Blackacre for a large construction project. How much notice must she give to Oscar?

16. Explain the importance of renewal clauses in business leases.

17. Thomson has rented a restaurant. He bolts a large shelf to the wall and places a television screen on the shelf. In the kitchen he bolts a small partition to the floor to separate his stoves from the refrigerator and freezer area. Define which of these objects are fixtures and if so, the types of fixture they may be.

18. How is the relationship of a tenant affected by her landlord's sale of his interest to a purchaser? What is the nature of the new relationship?

19. Stroll leases a warehouse for a term certain of five years. During the second year of the lease the landlord, Vernon, mortgages the land. At the end of the fifth year of the lease Stroll and Vernon enter into another lease for a further five years. Explain the difference, if any, in Stroll's position the first term and in the second term insofar as the mortgage is concerned?

20. What are three reasons that make leaseback arrangements attractive to lessee businesses?

21. What are the reasons that make them attractive to lessor financial institutions?

22. Describe briefly the reasons for treating residential tenancies differently from commercial tenancies.

CASES AND PROBLEMS

1 Ms. Bone, the owner of a downtown block of stores, rented one of them to Mr. Bull, who opened a retail china shop on the premises. Bull's tenancy was from year to year. He had a number of display cases built with glass doors to keep their fragile contents out of the reach of curious customers. The cases were secured to the wall by one-inch nails. Bull also purchased and installed heavy-duty air-conditioning equipment, which was connected to the water supply and anchored to the floor.

Several years later, Bull was adjudged bankrupt on a petition of his creditors. At the time he owed Bone $3600 for three months' rent. The trustee in bankruptcy remained in possession of the store pending liquidation of the business assets. The trustee claimed the display cases and air-conditioner for the benefit of Bull's general creditors, but Bone claimed them as lessor of the store.

Discuss the respective rights of Bone and of the trustee in bankruptcy.

2 Kruger leased a warehouse to Pool Corp. for a term certain of eight months at a rent of $3000 per month, commencing January 1 and expiring August 31. Pool did not move out on August 31 and tendered its cheque for $3000 to pay the rent for September. It was accepted by Kruger. On October 1, Pool's manager appeared at Kruger's office with another cheque for $3000. Kruger said he had inspected the warehouse and was disappointed by the rough treatment the building was receiving from Pool's employees. When the manager replied that he could hardly expect otherwise in a busy operation, Kruger stated it was not worth his while to rent it under those conditions unless he received at least $4000 per month. The manager refused to pay that much and tendered the company's cheque for $3000. Kruger refused the cheque and ordered Pool to "clear out of the warehouse at once." The manager left and mailed the cheque to Kruger, who simply held it and did not cash it.

On November 1, Kruger called Pool by telephone and asked if the company would pay $4000. The manager replied, "No." Kruger said that he was at the end of his patience and had given Pool a full month to change its mind. He sent a bailiff to evict Pool that very day, cashed its cheque for the previous month, and sent it a demand for "the $1000 still owing."

Pool was forced to move its stock to a more expensive warehouse at once and suffered some damage to its goods when they were moved into the street by the bailiff. It sued Kruger for losses of $8000 caused by the eviction. Should it succeed? Give reasons for your opinion.

3 Rogers, a dance teacher, was looking for space to operate a dance studio. She visited premises on the second floor of Hart's building four times with other people who concluded that the premises were suitable for the purposes intended. Rogers signed a lease and, with Hart's approval, she had installed a special dance floor, cabinets, dance bars and mirrors, did painting and electrical work, including installation of light fixtures. She then began her classes.

Hart immediately noticed that the building began to vibrate. Within 24 hours, he had a special beam installed but the vibrating continued. Hart hired a structural engineer at once to examine the building. The engineer concluded that the vibration was caused by harmonic pressure created by the coordinated movement of the dancers. He stated that the vibration could not be avoided by structural changes and it could ultimately cause the building or parts of it to collapse. Hart worried about the safety of the patrons of the restaurant situated under the dance studio, as well as of Rogers herself and her students. Three days after classes had begun, he told Rogers that the classes had to stop.

Rogers immediately began to look for new premises and took the position that by preventing her from continuing dance classes, Hart terminated the lease without notice. She sued Hart for damages for the cost of all the improvements she had made, the cost of moving and general damages for loss of business. She argued that because the defect in the premises was latent and did not become apparent until after she had begun the dance lessons, it was unreasonable to ask her to ensure the soundness and safety of the premises. It was Hart's problem as landlord to deal with.

Give your opinion of Rogers claims and whether they should succeed.

4 Allgate Realties Ltd. constructed a new building suitable for a restaurant in a suburb of Calgary. Streeter, the manager, invited Kratinsky to examine it. Kratinsky already owned and operated a restaurant in the city and was hesitant. Streeter assured him that the suburb was growing rapidly with new businesses about to open, as well as new housing developments. He offered Kratinsky a five-year lease including a sale to him of the building at the end of the lease. Kratinsky finally accepted; he opened the restaurant three months later.

Almost no new construction took place in the area; the restaurant was isolated and business was very poor. Within six months Kratinsky closed the restaurant and refuse to pay further rent, claiming that Allgate had made serious misrepresentations and was in breach of the contract. Allgate responded that there were no covenants in the lease referring to future development in the area and that Kratinsky remained bound by the lease and sale of the property.

Whose argument do you think will prevail?

5. Ivan Drugs Inc., a drugstore chain, leased premises from Hay Investments Ltd. in its shopping mall. The lease was for 10 years, at a "base" rent of $46 200 per year in monthly instalments of $3850, plus Ivan's share of the taxes, insurance, and common expenses of the mall. Ivan also agreed to pay an additional 6 percent of gross annual sales as rent, to the extent that its gross sales exceeded $770 000 for the year ($46 200 represents 6 percent of $770 000). The lease also contained a usual covenant allowing Ivan to assign the lease with consent of Hay.

In the first three years, Ivan's sales exceeded $1 500 000, and it duly paid the additional sums to Hay. However, during the third year a much larger shopping mall was opened across the street from Hay's mall. Ivan, fearing its sales at the current location would suffer, leased larger premises at the new mall and moved from its old premises, leaving them vacant. Ivan continued to pay the "base" rent and its share of the taxes, insurance, and common expenses, but paid no additional rent based on its sales in the new mall.

Partly as a result of receiving diminished rent, Hay was unable to obtain extensions of its mortgages or new financing for the mall and was in financial difficulty. Hay served notice on Ivan to enforce the original agreement according to its terms and to pay rent based on sales that could be attributed to Ivan's business if it had remained in Hay's mall. Hay Investments Ltd. asserted that Ivan Drugs Inc. had impliedly promised to carry on business for the full term of the lease.

Give your opinion of the validity of Hay's claim and what you think the result should be.

6. John Perini purchased a house and then called on his widowed daughter-in-law, whom he admired, and said, "Mary, I want you to look at the house I have bought for you. You won't have to worry about rent any more." Mary was very pleased, and moved into the house with her children within a few days. During the first three years after he purchased the house, Perini frequently visited his daughter-in-law and grandchildren in the house but then moved into a senior citizens' home where, except for a few special family occasions at the house, they came to visit him.

Perini died 14 years after he had purchased the house. Mary had always paid the municipal taxes and looked after the house but paid no rent to her father-in-law. Perini regularly paid the fire insurance premiums himself under a policy that specified that any claims would be paid to him as the insured. He never conveyed the title to Mary, apparently because he had once bought a house for another member of his family who had soon after sold it, wasted the proceeds, and returned to him destitute, asking for money.

An officer of the trust company that was executor for Perini's estate found the duplicate copy of the deed in Perini's name, among his papers. The executor then claimed the house from Mary as part of the Perini estate to be given to other beneficiaries under the will. Mary did not understand the legal arrangements; she could only state that she believed the house had been bought in her name and that she had lived in it continuously from the time of its purchase. She needed the house for her family and resisted the executor's demand. The trust company, as executor for the estate, sued her for possession of the property.

During the trial the court was referred to the Limitations Act of the province. The sections referred to read in part as follows:

4. No person shall make entry…or bring an action to recover any land or rent, but within ten years next after the time at which the right to make such entry…or to bring such action…first accrued to the person making or bringing it.

5. Where a person is in possession…as tenant at will, the right of the person entitled subject thereto…to make an entry…or to bring an action to recover the land or rent shall be deemed to have first accrued either at the determination of the tenancy, or at the expiration of one year after the commencement of the tenancy, at which time the tenancy shall be deemed to have determined.

8. No person shall be deemed to have been in possession of any land within the meaning of this Act merely by reason of having made an entry thereon.

Express an opinion, with reasons, about the probable outcome of this action.

Frost Investments Limited owned three adjoining buildings downtown that it rented to various tenants as office space. All three buildings were heated centrally from a single heating plant in Building No. 1. The Generous Loan Company occupied offices in Building No. 3 under a lease in which the lessor, Frost, covenanted to maintain the heat continuously above 60 degrees from October 1 to May 24, except for weekends. In January a serious fire occurred in Building No. 2 breaking the heating connections between Buildings No. 1 and No. 3. The damage was so serious that Frost decided to demolish Building No. 2 and rebuild.

In the meantime, Generous Loan Company suffered a significant drop in business because of very low temperatures in its offices. It eventually vacated the premises and leased other quarters at a higher rent. It then sued Frost claiming damages of $1750 for the additional amount of rent it had to pay the new landlord for what otherwise would have been the balance of the term of its lease with Frost, and $6000 for its estimated loss of profits. Frost counterclaimed for rent for the balance of the term of the lease, seven months at $2150 per month. What do you think the decision should be?

Tagom rented a service station from Oil Can Limited for a term of 12 months commencing July 1, at a rent of $975 per month payable on the first day of each month. The lease contained the following clause:

If the lessee shall hold over after the term…the resulting tenancy shall be a tenancy from month to month and not a tenancy from year to year, subject to all the terms, conditions and agreements herein contained insofar as same may be applicable to a tenancy from month to month.

On May 28 of the following year, Oil Can sent Tagom a notice stating that he must give vacant possession on the expiry of the lease. On June 30, Oil Can representatives visited Tagom and asked him what he intended to do. He replied that he would not leave the premises "peacefully." Tagom remained in possession on July 1, and sent a cheque by registered mail to Oil Can as rent for that month. Although the area superintendent had given instructions to the accounting department not to accept any rent from Tagom, a junior clerk deposited it in the company bank account. Soon afterwards, a senior officer discovered the error, informed Tagom that the act of the clerk in accepting the cheque had been inadvertent and against instructions, and delivered a refund cheque from the company to Tagom for $975. Tagom returned the cheque.

Was a new tenancy created or could Oil Can obtain a court order for immediate possession?

MORTGAGES OF LAND AND REAL ESTATE TRANSACTIONS

A purchaser of land rarely has the resources to pay the full price at the time of completing the purchase; a mortgage plays a central role in financing the transaction. We discuss the development of mortgage law and the various stages of a typical real estate transaction. In this chapter we examine such questions as:

- what is the concept of a mortgage and how has it evolved?

- what are the rights of the mortgagor and mortgagee?

- what remedies are available to the mortgagee?

- what is a "second mortgage" and how is it used?

- in what ways are a mortgagee's rights different from those of other creditors?

- what is an "offer to purchase"?

- what are the necessary steps in proceeding with a real estate transaction?

- what is the process of "closing" the transaction?

THE CONCEPT OF THE MORTGAGE

The history of the word "mortgage" helps us to understand its meaning. Mortgage is derived from the Norman French words **mort**, meaning dead or passive, and **gage**, meaning pledge. In the Middle Ages the Church condemned the lending of money for interest as the sin of

mort
dead or passive

gage
pledge

usury. Nevertheless, even in a simple economy some form of credit was often needed, and people simply would not lend money and assume the risk that it might not be repaid unless they received some benefit for taking the risk. To evade the usury laws an individual would lend money on the condition that the borrower would pledge his land as security. The lender would actually take possession of the borrower's land (a "*live*" gage rather than a mortgage) and retain it until the loan was repaid. Meanwhile he would be entitled to keep any of the crops or rents earned from the land. These benefits derived from the land would be the equivalent of interest, but since the lender was in possession he was considered to be entitled to the benefits: the courts did not consider the transaction usurious. If the borrower did not repay the debt on the appointed day, he lost all right to claim his land—it became the land of the lender absolutely.

This ancient form of live gage was very cumbersome, first because it meant that the borrower had to give up possession of his land (the best means he might have of earning the money for repayment), and second because the lender had to take possession in order to obtain the benefits (an arrangement that might be inconvenient or impossible for him). As England grew commercially, so did the need for more sophisticated means of obtaining credit; the law changed to meet these needs. Eventually, the lender was permitted to exact interest on the loan without going into possession, that is, to take his security as a *mort* gage.[1] He had a right to the interest as well as to the principal sum as a debt owed by the borrower. The lender retained the right to go into possession and take the land absolutely upon default by the borrower. This latter right, the right to take the land absolutely, was the cause of the main development in the law of mortgages.

THE DEVELOPMENT OF MORTGAGE LAW

Harshness of the Common Law

mortgage

a conveyance of an interest in land as security for a debt, with a condition that if the debt is repaid by an appointed day the conveyance becomes void and the interest reverts to the mortgagor

mortgagor

a borrower who conveys the interest in land as security for a debt

mortgagee

a lender who accepts the interest in land as security for the loan

Under the common law, a **mortgage** is a conveyance of an interest in land (usually the fee simple) by the **mortgagor** (the borrower) to the **mortgagee** (the lender) as security for a debt, with a condition that if the debt is repaid by an appointed day the conveyance becomes void and the interest in the land reverts to the mortgagor. If the appointed day passes without the debt being repaid, the condition then expires, and the mortgagee owns the interest absolutely. The common law courts construed the condition strictly: if a mortgagor was delayed by a storm or by illness and arrived with the money the day after the final day for payment, it was too late—the mortgagee could take possession of the land and keep it. Moreover, the mortgagee was still entitled to repayment of the debt: he could sue the unfortunate mortgagor and collect the debt even while retaining the land. The gross unfairness of this position was soon remedied by the court of equity: if the mortgagor appealed to that court, it would restrain the mortgagee from suing for the debt unless he agreed to reconvey the land to the mortgagor on payment of the full sum owing. At this point in the development of the law a defaulting mortgagor did not, at least, lose his money as well as his land. He could keep one or the other, depending on whether the mortgagee chose to keep the land and not sue for the debt, or to sue for the debt on condition that he would reconvey the land.

The Mortgagor's Right to Redeem

A mortgagor was still in an unfair position, because the choice lay with the mortgagee. If the mortgagor had borrowed only a small sum of money on the security of land worth many times as much, it would be small comfort to know that he would not be sued but that the mortgagee would keep his land instead. Thus if a mortgagor, delayed by a severe storm, arrived the morn-

---

1. For a more detailed history of mortgages, see Rayner and McLaren, *Falconbridge on Mortgages* (4th ed.), pp. 3–7. Toronto: Canada Law Book Co. Ltd., 1977.

ing after the last day to pay off his mortgage, he could not demand the return of an estate worth many thousands of pounds even though he had borrowed only a few hundred pounds and now tendered payment. The court of equity eventually granted a remedy in these cases of hardship as well. If the mortgagor petitioned the court and pleaded hardship and also tendered payment of the debt in full, the court would acknowledge his interest in the land and permit him to **redeem** it; it would order the mortgagee to reconvey the land to him. This right of redemption obtained by the mortgagor from a court of equity has become known as the **equity of redemption**; it is often called simply the **equity**. We see here the derivation of the modern business term "equity" meaning the interest of the proprietors of a business in its total assets after allowing for creditors' claims.

redeem
have the land reconveyed to the mortgagor

equity of redemption or equity
the right of the mortgagor to redeem mortgaged land on payment of the debt in full

The Mortgagee's Right to Foreclose
Need for the Foreclosure Remedy
Gradually, over a long period, the chancery courts entertained petitions of hardship based on weaker and weaker excuses, longer and longer after the day for payment had passed, until finally they accepted almost any excuse provided full payment was tendered. The scales were then tipped in favour of the mortgagor. A mortgagee who was quite willing to accept payment for a long time after the due date might finally despair of ever obtaining payment and begin to improve the land, treating it as his own. Years later, the mortgagor could appear and force him to reconvey upon tendering the full amount of the debt. In a turnabout, mortgagees now began to appeal to the chancery courts for a declaration that the mortgagor had had every reasonable opportunity to redeem and that if he did not do so within a fixed time set by the court his right to redeem would be forever foreclosed. The mortgagee could then safely treat the land as his own. By the 19th century, the **foreclosure** period became generally accepted as six months from the date of the hearing in the case.

foreclosure
an order by a court ending the mortgagor's right to redeem within a fixed time

Why Mortgagees Rarely Take Possession
In practice, a mortgagee rarely takes possession until after it has obtained foreclosure, unless it believes that the mortgagor has no intention of trying to redeem and will allow the premises to become dilapidated. There are three main reasons for not going into possession:

- *First*, a mortgagee generally wants its money rather than the mortgagor's property, and it would prefer to encourage the mortgagor to pay off the debt.
- *Second*, its possession would be uncertain, since the mortgagor might at any moment tender payment and demand possession.
- *Third*, it must account for any benefits it receives from occupation of the land and deduct it from the amount owing if the mortgagor tenders payment, thus losing any material advantage gained from taking possession.

The Consequences of These Developments
In summary then, under rules developed by the courts and apart from statutory reforms, a mortgage is a conveyance of an interest in land as security for a debt. If the debt is repaid as promised, the mortgage is discharged and the mortgagor has the title to the land returned to him. If he defaults, the land becomes the property of the mortgagee subject to the right of the mortgagor to redeem. Most mortgages today call for repayment, not in a lump sum on the last day, but in a series of instalment payments of principal and accrued interest. Mortgages almost always contain an **acceleration clause**, which states that upon default of any instalment, the whole of the principal sum of the mortgage and accrued interest immediately falls due; default accelerates the maturity date, and the mortgagee may pursue all its remedies.

acceleration clause
a clause stating that upon default of any instalment, the whole of the principal sum of the mortgage and accrued interest immediately falls due

Upon default the mortgagee may put the mortgagor out and take possession itself. It may also ask the court for an order of foreclosure. The mortgagor may repay the loan at any time before the deadline specified in the court order and obtain the return of his land, but if he does not do so, the land becomes the mortgagee's absolutely.

Even after the final day for redemption the mortgagee may successfully sue the mortgagor for the debt until the period prescribed by the Statute of Limitations runs out,[2] provided of course it can still reconvey the land to the mortgagor.[3] Following foreclosure, once the mortgagee sells the land to a third party it loses the right to sue for any deficiency, even though the mortgagor may subsequently become very wealthy. The courts presume that by selling the land the mortgagee has elected to accept the receipts of the sale in full satisfaction of the debt. On this basis it may also retain any profit made on the sale.

Under the land titles system (covering the areas discussed in Chapter 23) mortgages are called *charges*.[4] Charges are not, strictly speaking, conveyances of the legal title. Rather, they are liens upon the land, for which the ordinary remedy is to force a sale of the land and then apply the proceeds towards repayment of the debt. We discuss the mortgagee's remedy of sale more fully below.

As in earlier times, real estate mortgages still frequently arise out of a private transaction between two individuals. However, a very large proportion of mortgage lending to individual borrowers is now done by financial institutions—insurance companies, trust companies, and banks, for example—that have assumed the role of corporate mortgagees.[5]

RIGHTS OF THE MORTGAGEE AND MORTGAGOR UNDER COMMON LAW AND EQUITY

The Mortgagee

legal title
an interest in land recognized by the common law

equitable title
an interest in land recognized by equity

Although the courts of common law and equity are merged, the interests of the mortgagee and mortgagor are still interpreted according to the remedies available before the merger. In the absence of statutory reform,[6] a mortgagee is considered to be the holder of the **legal title**, and the mortgagor to have the **equitable title**; that is, his interest is recognized by equity and will be enforced against the mortgagee under the circumstances we have already described. The remedies of a mortgagee upon default by the mortgagor are as follows:

(a) It may sue the mortgagor on his personal covenant to repay, just as a creditor may sue any debtor who is in default.

(b) It may dispossess the mortgagor and occupy the land itself (or put in a tenant).

(c) It may sell the land, as explained below.

(d) It may proceed with an action for foreclosure and eventually destroy the mortgagor's right to redeem.

---

2. The limitations periods vary from six to thirty years among the provinces. The matter is complicated by the number of parties that may be involved in a mortgage transaction and the variety of problems that may arise.

3. Except in Manitoba and Saskatchewan, where a final order of foreclosure extinguishes the right to sue on the personal covenant of the mortgagor: Mortgage Act, R.S.M. 1987, c. M200, s. 16; Limitation of Civil Rights Act, R.S.S. 1978, c. L-16, s. 6.

4. Since 1984, mortgages throughout Ontario, including those regions under the registry system, have been converted to charges: Land Registration Reform Act, R.S.O. 1990, c. L.4, s. 1.

5. The reverse situation, where the mortgage borrower is a corporation and the lenders individuals (bondholders), is also common, as we shall see in our discussion of the nature of corporate securities in Chapter 27 and of floating charges as security devices in Chapter 29.

6. Despite these reforms and the fact that the mortgagor who gives a charge on his land retains legal title, the old terminology concerning legal and equitable title remains in common use.

(e) Subsequent to foreclosure it may again sue on the covenant to pay the debt, always provided it is willing and able to reconvey the land.

A mortgagee frequently chooses a combination of these remedies.

The Mortgagor

The remedies of a mortgagor after default are as follows:

(a) He may repay the mortgage loan together with interest and all expenses incurred by the mortgagee up to and including the date of the order of foreclosure and obtain a reconveyance of his land.

(b) He may obtain an accounting for any benefits obtained from the land by the mortgagee and deduct them from the amount owing on redemption.

(c) If sued on his covenant to repay after foreclosure, he may require the mortgagee to prove that it is ready and able to reconvey the land upon repayment.

(d) He may also obtain relief against the consequences of an acceleration clause: if he pays all prior accrued payments, performs all other terms of which he may have been in default and pays all costs incurred by the mortgagee, a court will permit him to continue to make regular payments under the original terms of the mortgage.[7]

THE MORTGAGEE'S REMEDY OF SALE UPON DEFAULT

As we have seen, once a mortgagee forecloses and disposes of the land, it no longer has any right to demand payment. Two alternative remedies have developed whereby the land may be sold and the mortgagee still maintain an action to recover the balance of the debt if the sale has not produced a sufficient price to repay the debt completely. These two remedies are described below.

Sale by the Court

A mortgagee may request to have the land sold under the supervision of the court (or in some of the western provinces, under the supervision of the registrar of titles), the sale to be either by tender or by auction. Some jurisdictions permit the mortgagee or its agent to bid; others prohibit such bidding. The sale must be advertised for a specified period and carried out according to provincial statutes and regulations. In some jurisdictions the court or registrar sets a reserve price below which no tenders will be accepted. The reserve price is not disclosed: when the tenders are opened, the highest one is accepted if it is over the reserve price. If no bid is above the reserve price, then the land remains unsold and the mortgagee may resort to its other remedies.

When a sale produces a successful bid, the mortgagee is entitled to recover the principal sum owing, accrued interest, and expenses of the court action and the sale. If the sale produces a smaller sum, the mortgagee may obtain judgment against the mortgagor for the deficiency. If the sale is for a larger sum, the surplus is returned to the mortgagor or his other secured creditors of the land.

In some jurisdictions, when a mortgagee starts a foreclosure action and the mortgagor believes that the land is worth more than his mortgage debt, the mortgagor or a subsequent secured creditor may request the court to hold a sale. We shall return to this topic when we discuss provincial variations later in this chapter.

---

7. Mortgages Act, R.S.O. 1990, c. M.40, ss. 22(1) and 23(1).

Sale by the Mortgagee

power of sale
a right upon default to sell mortgaged land, given to the mortgagee by the terms of the mortgage or by statute

Many mortgages, and in some jurisdictions the statutes governing mortgages, give the mortgagee a contractual **power of sale** that may be exercised privately without court action or supervision, although advance notice to the mortgagor is generally required. A mortgagee may exercise its power of sale at any time after default, subject to any statutory period of grace. By executing a proper grant and declaring that the grant is made in pursuance of a power of sale, it may validly transfer the title to the land to any third party. The sale must, however, be a genuine sale and not amount to a fraud upon the mortgagor. A mortgagee may not sell to itself either directly or through an agent. If the mortgagee is a private lender, she may sell the land to a company of which she is a shareholder or officer, but such sales will be zealously scrutinized by the court and may be easily upset if there is any evidence of taking unfair advantage by selling at an unreasonably low price. Whenever a mortgagee exercises a power of sale, it is under a duty to take reasonable steps to obtain a fair price for the land. If the mortgagor can show that the mortgagee sold for an unreasonably low price, the court will reduce the deficiency accordingly or give the mortgagor judgment for any surplus he should have received.

The same rules concerning the proceeds of a sale apply here as in a sale by the court: if there is a deficiency, the mortgagee may still sue the mortgagor for the sum; if there is a surplus, it must be returned to the mortgagor or to the remaining secured creditors.

SALE BY A MORTGAGOR OF HIS INTEREST

Financial Arrangements

A mortgage transaction is, as we can see, a sophisticated credit arrangement. When it concerns but two parties, it is reasonably straightforward. The transaction becomes more complex, however, with the addition of a third party to the relationship.

ILLUSTRATION 25.1

A, the owner of Blackacre, mortgages it to *B* Trust Co. for $100 000. Subsequently she sells Blackacre to *X* for $160 000. How is the price to be paid by *X*? There are three possibilities. First, *X* may pay *A* the full $160 000 and obtain an undertaking from *A* that she will pay off the mortgage to *B* Trust Co. Second, *X* may pay $60 000 to *A* for *A*'s equity of redemption and a further $100 000 to *B* in full payment of the mortgage. Third, *X* may pay *A* $60 000, as above, and accept Blackacre *subject to the mortgage*; that is, *X* will himself assume responsibility for paying off the mortgage. We can see that the third possibility is really a variation of the second: instead of paying the mortgage off at once, *X* simply pays it off as it falls due.

In circumstances like those in Illustration 25.1, the first possibility rarely occurs, because *X* takes the risk that *A*'s other creditors might obtain the purchase money through court action or *A* might abscond so that the funds never reach *B* Trust Co., leaving *X* to pay *B* in order to redeem the mortgage. He might end up paying $260 000 for Blackacre instead of $160 000. The second possibility does not occur very frequently either, for two reasons: first, by the terms of the mortgage the mortgagor may not have the right to pay off the mortgage before the due date; second, purchasers rarely pay the full purchase price up front for land. Land transactions are almost invariably financed by a credit arrangement, usually in the form of a mortgage. Therefore, it is often most convenient for *X* simply to pay $60 000 to obtain Blackacre and to *assume* the mortgage liability for making payments.

Sometimes, especially where the mortgagor (vendor) has significantly reduced the first mortgage by instalment payments, the purchaser may not have the resources to pay fully for the vendor's equity. Accordingly he will arrange through a financial institution for a new mortgage for a larger sum of money. He will then use the proceeds of the new mortgage to pay off the existing mortgage, with the balance going towards the cash portion of the purchase price.

Effect of Default by the Purchaser

What would happen if the purchaser, X, should default on payment of the original mortgage? The fact that A has sold her equity of redemption to X does not affect B's rights as mortgagee holding the legal title to Blackacre; B retains all its rights against the land. It may also recover from A, the mortgagor, on her covenant—her contractual obligation—to repay the debt. If B sues A, what rights does A have upon paying off the mortgage? A may successfully sue X for the full sum of money she was required to pay to B. One reason for this result is that as part of his purchase price for Blackacre, X assumed the mortgage and agreed to pay it off. The law implies that the promise to pay off the mortgage includes a promise to indemnify A, that is, save A from any liability under it. A second reason is that by paying off the mortgage A has in effect purchased the mortgagee's rights. She becomes *subrogated* to the mortgagee's rights and is in effect the mortgagee to whom X is now a mortgagor. At this point A may invoke all the remedies against X that B Trust Co. might itself have utilized against the land and the mortgagor.

Instead of suing A, may the mortgagee B sue the purchaser X directly? There is no contract between B and X giving B this right. Nor do the courts recognize any privity of estate between a mortgagee and the purchaser of the equity as they do in landlord and tenant. Under common law rules, B may successfully sue X only if it can obtain an assignment of A's right to indemnity discussed in the preceding paragraph. As a practical matter A will often agree to assign her right in order to avoid having the mortgagee sue her on her covenant in the mortgage. In Ontario, the Mortgages Act gives the mortgagee a statutory right to sue the purchaser X directly, without obtaining an assignment from A, the mortgagor, but only while X holds the equity.[8] If he sells it to yet another purchaser Y, then Y becomes liable to pay the mortgage, and X is released from his statutory obligation to the mortgagee.

SECOND MORTGAGES

Uses of a Second Mortgage

A prospective purchaser often finds he does not have sufficient money to buy the equity in land already subject to a mortgage, or sometimes the owner of land already subject to a mortgage may wish to raise an additional sum by using his equity as security. Although there is only one legal title to the land and it is already held by the mortgagee, the mortgagor or his successor may nevertheless mortgage the equity and still retain an equity of redemption; equitable title may be divided up as many times as the holder of the equity wishes to do so and can find creditors willing to take an interest in the remaining equity as security for the debts owed to them. Second mortgages (that is, mortgages of the equity of redemption) are quite common. Less common are third and fourth mortgages (further mortgages of the equity of redemption).

closing date
the date for completing a sale of property

ILLUSTRATION 25.2

V offers Hillcroft for sale for $230 000 subject to a mortgage for $150 000 to M Co. Ltd. P would like to buy Hillcroft, but she has only $55 000 in cash, and she needs $80 000. She arranges to borrow $25 000 from her business associate M2 and to give M2 a second mortgage on Hillcroft. Having made these arrangements P accepts V's offer to sell, and they arrange a **closing date** (a date for completing the transaction).

continued

---

8. Mortgages Act, *ibid.*, s. 20(2), (3).

On the closing day the following transactions take place: (a) *V* delivers a transfer of Hillcroft to *P*; (b) *P* delivers a mortgage of Hillcroft to *M2*; (c) *M2* gives *P* $25 000; (d) *P* gives *V* the total sum of $80 000 and also assumes the exiting first mortgage given by *V* to *M* Co. Ltd. These transactions usually take place simultaneously in the office of one lawyer or in the registry office; the parties trade the necessary documents and sums of money and *P* and *M2* immediately register the transfer and mortgage. The net result of the transaction is as follows: *P* holds the equity in Hillcroft subject to the first mortgage to *M* Co. Ltd. for $150 000 and the second mortgage to *M2* for $25 000. She is indebted in the sum of $175 000.

Rights of a Second Mortgagee

A second mortgagee has rights similar to those of a first mortgagee except that

(a) his interest is in the equity of redemption, not the legal title, and,

(b) he ranks behind the first mortgagee in priority of payment.

Thus, in Illustration 25.2, if *P* defaults payment on both mortgages, the first mortgagee may start an action for foreclosure. The second mortgagee may decide to stand by and do nothing. If the first mortgagee completes the foreclosure against the equity in Hillcroft, the interest of both *P* and the second mortgagee is destroyed. The second mortgagee loses his security in Hillcroft and is left with only a right of action for debt against *P*, who may be insolvent. If the first mortgagee proceeds with a sale under power of sale or sale by the court, the proceeds will be paid *first*, to satisfy the first mortgage debt and expenses of the sale, and *second*, to satisfy the second mortgage debt. The second mortgagee will be paid only to the extent that there is any surplus after paying off the first mortgagee. Of course, the sale may bring in more money than the total amount owed on both mortgages, and the excess will go to *P*.

When the first mortgagee begins a foreclosure action, the second mortgagee may choose to redeem, that is, to pay off the first mortgage himself and receive an assignment of it. But then he will have invested an additional sum in the land: in Illustration 25.2 above, *M2* would have to pay about $150 000. With *P* insolvent, *M2* would have little hope of collecting by suing for the debt. He may in turn commence a foreclosure action, and in effect buy Hillcroft for about $175 000 (which may or may not be a good buy depending on the current real estate market); or he may proceed with either of the two remedies of sale, taking the risk that a sale may not bring in enough to pay off the sums he has invested.

Risks for a Second Mortgagee When the Mortgagor Defaults

A second mortgage invariably provides that default on the first mortgage is also immediate default on the second mortgage, that is, a breach of the mortgagor's obligation to protect the second mortgagee's interest in the land, and he may immediately act upon the usual remedies. In the absence of such protection a second mortgagee might find himself in the following position:

(a) Payment of the second mortgage is not yet due and thus there is no default on it.

(b) The first mortgage, having an earlier due date, is in default and the first mortgagee promptly pursues one of its remedies against the land—foreclosure, sale by court, or exercise of the power of sale.

(c) The result of either of these remedies would be to destroy the second mortgagee's interest in the land.

In a sale either by the court or by the first mortgagee, to the extent that the sale brought in more than the debt due on the first mortgage, the second mortgagee would receive compensation, but he might well recover only a part of the debt. To avoid these risks a second mortgagee may himself act promptly to pursue his remedies.

Sometimes a mortgagor defaults on only the second mortgage, or if he has defaulted on the first as well, the first mortgagee may be quite satisfied with the adequacy of its security and is willing to "sit tight" and see what the subsequent mortgagees and creditors intend to do. The first mortgagee need not worry since it has the prime interest in the land and no one can affect its position. In this situation, the second mortgagee may proceed with foreclosure or a sale, and thus destroy the interest of the mortgagor in the equity of redemption without affecting the first mortgagee. If the second mortgagee forecloses, he becomes the sole holder of the equity of redemption, subject to the prior interest of the first mortgagee. Similarly, when the second mortgagee proceeds by sale, the purchaser obtains the whole of the equity of redemption clear of the mortgagor's interest, though of course still subject to the first mortgage. In either case the new holder of the equity of redemption must make satisfactory arrangements with the first mortgagee; he may redeem the first mortgage or else assume the obligations under it by agreement with the first mortgagee.

Subsequent Mortgages After a Second Mortgage

When a mortgagor places successive mortgages upon her equity, each ranks in priority according to its creation in time. Each subsequent mortgage gives all the usual remedies to the mortgagee, subject to the prior rights of any earlier mortgagee. Each subsequent mortgagee takes a greater risk as creditor for several reasons:

- *First*, the land is subject to a greater financial debt and any drop in price will injure the security of the latest mortgagee first.
- *Second*, a succession of mortgages on one piece of land usually indicates financial instability and poor management on the part of the borrower.
- *Third*, failure by a subsequent mortgagee to act reasonably promptly in case of default may result in the destruction of its secured interest in the land, if a prior mortgagee exercises its power of sale.
- *Fourth*, the cost of redeeming prior mortgages may be too high—in order to prevent foreclosure of its interest a subsequent mortgagee may have to lay out more money than it can afford.[9]

MORTGAGEE'S RIGHTS COMPARED WITH RIGHTS OF OTHER CREDITORS

A creditor that has no security other than its debtor's promise is a **general creditor**, and its claim ranks as a general claim. A creditor that has collateral security, that is, a prior claim against one or more specified assets of the debtor, is a **secured creditor**. If the debtor becomes insolvent, the general creditors must wait until the claims of the secured creditors have been satisfied out of the assets against which they have their claims. When the sale of an asset brings in more than the amount owing the secured creditor, the excess becomes available for the settlement of general claims. Here we may see the relation of the mortgagee's remedy of sale to other creditors' claims: as we noted earlier in this chapter, after a sale of the mortgaged land by the mortgagee any surplus is returned to the mortgagor; if the mortgagor is insolvent, the surplus goes to his creditors. However, if there is a deficiency, that is, the particular security realizes *less* than the amount of the secured creditor's claim, to the extent of that deficiency the secured creditor then ranks as a general creditor along with all the general creditors.

general creditor
a creditor that has no security other than the debtor's promise to pay

secured creditor
a creditor that has collateral security in the form of a prior claim against specified assets of the debtor

---

9. Subsequent mortgagees frequently demand additional security, such as mortgages on other lands or personal property, before advancing a mortgage loan.

ILLUSTRATION 25.3

(a) Harper is the proprietor of a successful small retail business with a building worth about $320 000. He has mortgaged the building for $250 000 to Commerce Trust Co. Unfortunately his area suffers a serious recession when a large local industry closes; he has meagre working capital and cannot weather the indefinite loss in sales. He becomes insolvent and is declared bankrupt. A trustee is appointed, and in due course the building is sold; the remainder of Harper's assets are also sold. The following is a statement of Harper's financial position after all the assets are liquidated:

Assets		Liabilities	
Bank balance from:		Commerce	$247 000
sale of building	$270 000	Trust Co.	
sale of other		General	85 000
assets	38 000	Creditors	
TOTAL	$308 000	TOTAL	$332 000

The assets would distributed as follows:

Commerce Trust Co.	$247 000
General Creditors	61 000
	$308 000

We see that the mortgagee receives 100 cents on the dollar of debt owed to it from the sale of the building. In addition the sale produces a surplus of $23 000. This sum is added to the $38 000 realized from all other assets, and is paid out rateably to the general creditors. Here they receive $\frac{61\,000}{85\,000}$ of each dollar of indebtedness—about 72 cents on each dollar.

(b) Suppose, however, that the sale of the building brings a much smaller sum because of the depressed market—say, $200 000. The assets and liabilities are now as follows:

Assets		Liabilities	
Bank balance from:		Commerce	$247 000
sale of building	$200 000	Trust Co.	
sale of other		General	85 000
assets	38 000	Creditors	
TOTAL	$238 000	TOTAL	$332 000

The assets would now be distributed as follows:

Creditors

	Secured	General	Total
Commerce Trust Co. $200 000			
plus $\frac{47\,000}{132\,000} \times 38\,000$		$13 530	$213 530
General Creditors			
$\frac{85\,000}{132\,000} \times 38\,000$		24 470	24 470
	$200 000	$38 000	$238 000

Note: We obtain the figure of $132 000 by adding the deficiency of $47 000 on the mortgage debt to the total unsecured debt of $85 000. In these circumstances the mortgagee receives a total of over $213 000 from a debt of $247 000—about 86 cents on each dollar of debt. On the other hand the general creditors suffer much more severely: they receive about $\frac{24\,500}{85\,000}$ of each dollar of indebtedness—about 29 cents on each dollar. We may note that their position is worsened by the fact that the mortgagee joined them to rank as a general creditor for that portion of the debt unsatisfied by the sale of the building, thus dividing the assets among a larger group of claims.

THE MORTGAGE AS A CONTRACT AND AS A TRANSFER OF AN INTEREST IN LAND

The Mortgage as a Contract

A mortgage document—as well as transferring an interest in land to the mortgagee—is a contract containing a number of important terms, the most important being the personal covenants of the mortgagor to pay off the debt and of the mortgagee to discharge its interest in the land upon repayment. It is useful to set out the more important covenants of each party. The mortgagor covenants

(a) to pay the debt and accrued interest, either at maturity date or in instalments as agreed by the parties[10]

(b) to keep the property adequately insured in the name of the mortgagee

---

10. Except in Alberta and Saskatchewan, where a mortgagor cannot be sued personally for the mortgage debt. See the section dealing with provincial variations, below.

(c) to pay taxes on the land and buildings

(d) to keep the premises in a reasonable state of repair

The mortgagee covenants

(a) to execute the necessary discharge of the mortgage upon repayment in full

(b) to leave the mortgagor in possession and not interfere with his use and enjoyment of the mortgaged premises so long as the mortgagor observes all his covenants

The mortgagor signs the mortgage, and the mortgagee merely accepts the document without signing it. Since the mortgagee's promises are set out as provisos—some are simply implied by the principles of mortgage law—its acceptance of the document binds it to the terms. We can see that contractual obligations form a large part of a mortgage transaction.

The Mortgage as a Transfer of an Interest in Land

A mortgage is both a transfer of an interest in land in the same way as a grant is and also a contract containing terms that govern the transfer. As a transfer, it must comply with the usual requirements by adequately describing the parties and the land being transferred and must be in the proper form required for registration in the registry office of the jurisdiction. Our discussion in Chapter 23 concerning the recording of interests in land applies equally to interests created by mortgage. Thus, if a mortgagee fails to register its mortgage, a subsequent purchaser from the mortgagor, unaware of the mortgage, will acquire title free from it upon registering his own grant. Similarly a subsequent mortgagee, unaware of the first mortgage, will establish priority over the first mortgage if it registers first. We can see, then, that failure to register may result in the complete loss of the land as security where there is a transfer to an innocent purchaser, or to loss of priority against another secured creditor of the mortgagor that registers its claim first. Our concern here is only with establishing the mortgagee's interest in the land: failure to register does not wipe out its other rights as a creditor against the mortgagor.

Assignment

When a mortgagee is a private lender, he may wish to obtain cash by selling the mortgage rather than by waiting for the mortgage debt to fall due in order to collect. The mortgage may be a sound investment, having good security and a reliable debtor, or it may be a risky investment. In either case, the mortgagee may sell his mortgage at the best price he can get for it. The sale of a mortgage is a transaction involving both its contractual and real property aspects. The mortgagee *assigns* his rights to the covenants made by the mortgagor, and *grants* or transfers his interest in the land to the purchaser (assignee) of the mortgage. Sometimes, in order to obtain a higher price an assignor-mortgagee guarantees payment—that is, if the mortgagor defaults in payment the assignor, on the assignee's demand, will pay off the mortgage and take back an assignment of it. In most sales, however, a mortgagee sells the mortgage outright, and the purchaser takes the risk of default together with all the usual remedies of a mortgagee.

A purchaser of a mortgage, as an assignee of contractual rights, is bound by the usual rules of assignment in contract. As we have seen in Chapter 12, the debtor, in this case the mortgagor, is not bound by the assignment until receiving notice of it, and the assignee takes the mortgage subject to the equities and the state of the mortgage account between mortgagor and mortgagee.

Discharge of Mortgages

Effects of a Discharge

When a mortgagor, or a subsequent purchaser of her equity, pays off the whole of the mortgage debt at maturity of the loan, she is entitled to a discharge from the mortgagee. A discharge operates both as an acknowledgment that the debt has been paid in full and as a reconveyance of the legal title from the mortgagee to the holder of the equity. To protect herself, the holder of the equity of redemption promptly registers the discharge in the land registry office; by registering she conclusively becomes the holder of the legal title. A fraudulent mortgagee cannot then successfully exercise a power of sale and grant the legal title to an innocent purchaser on the pretence that the mortgage is unpaid and in arrears. A fraudulent mortgagee has been known to do just that and to deprive a mortgagor of the land when the mortgagor has neglected to obtain a discharge and register it.[11] In areas under the land titles system, a discharge from the mortgagee operates to dissolve the charge upon the mortgagor's land.

Arrangements for Prepayment of Mortgage Debt

A mortgage usually contains a contractual term permitting the mortgagor to repay the mortgage and to obtain a discharge even before the debt matures. The term permitting such repayment may have various conditions attached to it. Often a mortgagee requires a period of notice, usually three months, before it need accept the money; such a requirement gives it time to find a new borrower so that the money received does not lie idle until it finds a new investment. A mortgagee usually requires payment of a bonus, for example three months' interest in lieu of notice, or it may require both notice and a bonus. Flexible mortgage-prepayment clauses often contain various other prepayment possibilities. A mortgagor may be permitted to prepay part of the debt rather than all of it, simply to make good use of extra earnings and to reduce the interest payable on the mortgage loan. Certain types of mortgages, particularly second mortgages and short-term mortgages, permit repayment "at any time without notice or bonus." Mortgages containing such a term are usually called **open mortgages**.

Partial Discharges

A mortgage may also permit the mortgagor to prepay a specified portion of the mortgage debt and to obtain a **partial discharge**, that is, a discharge of a definite portion of the mortgaged lands. Partial discharges are common when the mortgagor is a land developer: the developer may own a large piece of undeveloped land and wish to sell off a part free from any encumbrance; or it may wish to erect a large building on a particular part of the land and require financing in the form of a large new mortgage—which it cannot obtain except as a first mortgage. These various methods of prepaying part or all of a mortgage debt play an important role in the credit financing of land development.

PROVINCIAL VARIATIONS

The remedies available to mortgagees and mortgagors developed, as we have seen, over a long period. The various provinces of Canada adopted existing English law at the date each province obtained its first legislative body; the dates range from 1758 in Nova Scotia to 1870 in Alberta, Manitoba, and Saskatchewan. Accordingly, the variations in the mortgage law received by each province may be considerable. Subsequent to its adoption of the English law, each province developed its own procedures and made statutory amendments to meet its own needs. The needs differed widely according to the economy of the province and the character of business within it. The result is a rather confused and sometimes inconsistent pattern of remedies for both mortgagee and mortgagor. We present here a brief summary of the main variations among these remedies.

---

open mortgage
a mortgage permitting repayment of the debt at any time without notice or bonus

partial discharge
a discharge of a definite portion of the mortgaged lands

---

11. Dicker v. Angerstein (1876), 3 Ch. D. 395.

The Mortgagee's Rights

In Alberta, British Columbia, and Saskatchewan, a mortgagee's right to sue on the covenant to repay has been restricted by statute. A mortgagee may sue only mortgagor's that are corporations and have waived the statutory protection[12]

In British Columbia, in that portion of Manitoba under the registry system, and in Ontario, New Brunswick, Prince Edward Island, and Newfoundland, a mortgagee may foreclose the equity of redemption in the manner we have already discussed. In Alberta, Saskatchewan, and that portion of Manitoba under the land titles system, the usual remedy is sale by the court: if the sale does not produce any satisfactory bids then the mortgagee may proceed to foreclose, but foreclosure appears to be a rare remedy in practice. In all provinces, a mortgagee may request the court or registrar to hold a sale of mortgaged land, and except in Nova Scotia, may sell under a power of sale if it is provided for either by statute or under the terms of the mortgage. In Nova Scotia, although the court issues an order of "foreclosure and sale," foreclosure is not really permitted: the court must hold a sale.

The Mortgagor's Rights

With the exception of New Brunswick, those provinces permitting a mortgagee to start an action for foreclosure also allow the mortgagor to request the court to hold a sale, provided he deposits a sum of money (usually under $100) as security for the costs of the sale in the event of its producing no acceptable bids. A mortgagor may thus prevent the mortgagee from acquiring the mortgagor's interest in the land; this right of the mortgagor can be an important protection when the land is worth substantially more than the mortgage debt. We should remember, however, that if the market value of the land does exceed the mortgage debt by a significant amount, the mortgagor, unless he is considered a bad personal credit risk, should be able to refinance the land by obtaining an extension of his mortgage or arranging for a new mortgage and paying off his old mortgagee to whom he has defaulted. In any event, he should be able to sell the equity of redemption at its market value. In all jurisdictions a mortgagor has the right to redeem the land by paying off the entire debt before foreclosure or sale.

REVERSE MORTGAGES

A recent development in Canadian law has been the adoption from Europe of the concept of the **reverse mortgage**. It can be a benefit, mainly to senior citizens who are retired and have been described as "house rich and cash poor."[13] Typically, a homeowner purchased a house many years earlier and during her career paid off the mortgage debt on the property; she owns it without debt. However, her employment did not make provision for a generous retirement pension and she now has a meagre income. Meanwhile her house has increased substantially in market value.

reverse mortgage
a form of mortgage given in return for a monthly payment; no repayment is due until the mortgagor sells or dies

Using the reverse mortgage concept, she may give a mortgage on her house, and receive a monthly payment based on the market value of the property, prevailing interest rates, and actuarial calculations of her life expectancy. She remains in possession of the house while the principal and interest on the reverse mortgage accrue; no repayment is due until she sells the house or dies. When one of these two events occur, and if the market value of the house is greater than the accrued debt, the lender pays the excess to the owner or her estate. If the value of the house is less than the accrued debt then the lender absorbs the deficiency.

12. Law of Property Act, R.S.A. 1980, c. L-8, s. 41, amended by S.A 1982, c. 24, s. 3 and s. 43, amended by S.A. 1983, c. 97, s. 2, S.A. 1984, c. 24, s. 3 and S.A. 1994, c. 23, s. 27; Property Law Act, R.S.B.C. 1996, c. 377, s. 32; Limitation of Certain Civil Rights Act, R.S.S. 1978, c. L-16, s. 2(1) and (2). See National Trust Co. v. Mead, [1990] 2 S.C.R. 410.

13. For a useful discussion of the reverse mortgage, see Mary Beggan, "Reverse Mortgages: Ahead of Our Time," 99:5 *Canadian Banker* 45.

As our population ages and the number of persons who may find themselves in the financial position we have just described increases, the reverse mortgage seems likely to become more common. Financial institutions may well begin to promote this new area. There are wide variations in the design of reverse mortgages and at present no systems of regulation.

Concern has been expressed that seniors should seek advice before undertaking a reverse mortgage and consider alternatives such as selling the house and buying or renting smaller accommodation.

CONTEMPORARY ISSUE

A Two-lawyer Rule for Private Mortgages?

In 1999, as part of a process of revising the Rules of Professional Conduct, the Benchers of the Law Society of Upper Canada (the governing body for lawyers in the province of Ontario) considered recommendations for a "two-lawyer" rule in certain mortgage transactions. The rule would prohibit a lawyer, or two lawyers practising as partners or associates, from representing both borrower and lender. The rule would apply to private mortgage transactions, but would not apply where the lender is an institution that lends money in the ordinary course of its business (such as a bank, insurance company, trust company, credit union, or pension fund). Exceptions would also be made for lawyers practising in remote locations where another lawyer is not available, vendor take-back mortgages, mortgages for small amounts ($15 000 is the proposed ceiling), and situations where the lender and borrower are not "at arm's length" as defined in the *Income Tax Act* (for example, a loan from a parent to a child).

The stated purposes of the rule are to protect mortgagee/investor clients from conflict of interest and fraud and to reduce claims on the Lawyers' Fund for Client Compensation, which helps people who have lost money because of a lawyer's negligence or misconduct. Staff at the Fund estimated in 1997 that if a two-lawyer rule had been in place during the previous nine years, the Fund would have saved $7.1 million in grants paid.

The Law Society of British Columbia has had a two-lawyer rule for over 10 years, and has had only two incidents of mortgage fraud in that time. A similar rule exists in England and Wales.

Critics of the proposed rule suggest that it might be seen as a cash grab by lawyers, and that some borrowers will have no legal representation at all because they will not be able to afford a separate lawyer.

Sources: See The Lawyers Fund for Client Compensation Committee, Report #2 to Convocation, March 26, 1999, Webposted at <www.lsuc.on.ca/conv.mar1999/lawyers0.pdf>; Elizabeth Raymer, "Real Estate Lawyers Term Rule Changes 'Drastic'," *Lawyers Weekly*, October 15, 1999, p. 15.

Questions to Consider

1. How much impact do you think a two-lawyer rule for private mortgages would have on the ability of business people to raise financing? Would the impact be positive or negative?

2. If the rule is a good idea, should it be extended to institutional lending situations? (This is being considered in England and Wales.) Give your reasons.

3. Might the exception to the two-lawyer rule for transactions that are not at arm's length leave open the possibility of undue influence? See *MacKay v. Bank of Nova Scotia* (1994), 20 O.R. (3d) 698 (Gen. Div.). Note that the lender in this case was a bank.

A Typical Real Estate Transaction

The Circumstances

A real estate transaction can best be understood by following a typical sale in some detail from start to finish. We shall use for an example a fictional piece of land in Oshawa, Ontario. John Vincent owns the land and building on Main Street described in his grant as Lot 27, Plan 7654 in the City of Oshawa. The building fronting on Main Street consists of a large store at ground level and three suites of offices on the second floor. Vincent occupies the store himself and runs a men's wear shop. The offices are rented to three tenants, one to Dr. A. McAvity, dentist, the second to Happy Auto Insurance Company, and the third to C. McCollum, chartered accountant. Business has been poor; Vincent is 70 years old and wishes to retire. He has advertised without success to find a buyer of his business. He has received many inquiries about purchasing the building, a prime location, but no one is interested in buying his rather old-fashioned stock and fixtures. He has finally decided to run a selling-out sale and then sell the building.

The Offer to Purchase

Hi-Style Centres Ltd., a firm selling women's wear, operates a chain of stores and is anxious to have an outlet in Oshawa. It approaches Vincent with the proposal that he rent the store to them. Vincent has decided to leave Oshawa and retire to Victoria, B.C.; he wishes to break all business connections in the East. He says he would consider an offer to purchase but not to rent. Hi-Style makes two offers to purchase, both rejected by Vincent as too low. It now makes a third offer that Vincent is considering seriously. The essential terms are:[14]

(a) Hi-Style offers to buy the premises for $645 000, payable as follows: tender $25 000 as a deposit by certified cheque attached to the offer; assume the first mortgage of about $375 000 held by the Grimm Mortgage Company; give back to Vincent a second mortgage of $125 000 (interest and other terms set out in detail); pay the balance on *closing date* (completion date).

(b) The sale is to be closed 60 days after the date of the offer.

(c) Hi-Style may search the title and submit **requisitions** (questions concerning claims against Vincent's title) within 20 days of acceptance of the offer. Vincent promises to deliver a copy of the survey of the lot, which he has in his possession, for examination by Hi-Style. If serious claims against Vincent's title are raised and Vincent cannot answer them satisfactorily, the contract will be terminated and the deposit returned to Hi-Style. If requisitions are answered satisfactorily or no requisitions are submitted within 20 days, it is presumed that Hi-Style accepts Vincent's title as satisfactory.

requisitions
questions concerning claims against a seller's title to property

(d) Vincent is to remain in possession and the building is to remain at his risk until closing. He promises to keep the building insured to its full insurable value. He also undertakes to give possession of the building in substantially the same condition as it was at the time of making the contract. If the building is destroyed or seriously damaged, Hi-Style may elect to take over the premises and to receive the proceeds of all insurance, or it may elect to terminate the contract, with Vincent to suffer the loss, if any.

---

14. An offer to purchase may also include other terms, the importance of which varies according to the circumstances, in particular the nature of the property. For example, the vendor might be required to give a warranty that the heating plant conforms to regulations; to produce a certificate of inspection of boiler or gas installations; to warrant that the premises do not violate existing zoning by-laws; to identify all encroachments or easements in respect of which the property is either a servient or a dominant tenement; and to allow the prospective purchaser access to the premises for the purpose of checking the land survey.

(e) Vincent is to pay all taxes and insurance until closing and deduct from the amount due at closing all outstanding current expenses, such as accrued water and electric bills, unpaid taxes, and insurance. He will transfer all insurance policies to Hi-Style, provided the insurance companies are willing to accept Hi-Style as a satisfactory risk, and Hi-Style will pay for the prepaid unexpired portion of such policies. Alternatively, Hi-Style may arrange its own insurance to commence on the day of closing.

(f) Vincent warrants that his three suites of offices are leased to tenants as stated at rents of $1250 monthly per suite under leases expiring two years after date of closing for Suite No. 1, two years four months after closing for Suite No. 2, and Suite 3 as a monthly tenancy only. He will deliver the original of the two leases and assignments of the leases on closing, an acknowledgment from the third tenant that she is only a monthly tenant, and signed notices to the tenants that Hi-Style is the new landlord to whom they are to pay their rent.

(g) The offer is open for two days and acceptance must be communicated to the office of the lawyer for Hi-Style in Oshawa before 5 p.m. on the second day.

Preparations for Completing the Transaction

Accepting the Offer

Vincent has two copies of the offer. He decides to accept it and sends one signed copy to Hi-Style's lawyer, Harmon, retaining the other copy for his own lawyer, Vale. He also sends a copy of the survey of his lot to Harmon. The manager of Hi-Style has taken the careful step of having Harmon draw up the offer in the first place. Thus Harmon is familiar with its terms; in particular, she has made a special note in her file of the last day to submit requisitions concerning title to the land, as well as the date of closing the transaction.

Verifying Title and Possession

Harmon now takes the following steps:

1. She sends a junior member of her law firm to the registry office to search the title to the lot and also to compare the survey received from Vincent with the plan of the whole area as filed in the registry office, to make sure there are no discrepancies in the boundaries of the lot and to learn whether there are any outstanding claims registered for unpaid corporation taxes.

2. She writes to the city tax department asking for a certificate showing the state of real property taxes, both arrears and current, and encloses the small fee usually required for the certificate.

3. She writes to the Grimm Mortgage Company and asks them to prepare and forward a mortgage statement showing what the exact amount outstanding on the mortgage, including accrued interest, will be on the date of closing.

4. She examines the zoning by-law and checks with the office of the building inspector for any outstanding work orders and deficiency notices under municipal by-laws.

5. She asks her client to examine the premises carefully to confirm that the building is occupied by the tenants and by Vincent as stated in the contract and that there are no other persons who appear to be exercising an adverse claim over any part of the premises. In the case of valuable commercial property on main streets, the boundaries are very important, especially if demolition and reconstruction are even remotely contemplated. Harmon advises Hi-Style to hire a surveyor to make a new survey and compare it with the old, thus checking whether adjacent owners are in possession of any part of the lot and have perhaps extinguished Vincent's title to portions they have occupied.

6. She checks with the sheriff's office for any claims that may be filed there against the vendor.

Preparing the Documents for Closing

Within a few days Vincent's lawyer, Vale, prepares a **draft deed**, that is, a copy of the grant that Vincent will later sign for delivery on closing. He sends a copy to Harmon, who examines it and approves of its content. Harmon prepares a draft copy of the second mortgage to be given by Hi-Style to Vincent on closing and sends it to Vale. To avoid any confusion about names or initials and the description of the land to be conveyed, both lawyers check very closely to see that all details are described in identical terms in the following documents: the grant received by Vincent when he originally bought the land; the first mortgage by Vincent to Grimm Mortgage Company; the draft deed by Vincent to Hi-Style; and the draft second mortgage from Hi-Style to Vincent.

draft deed
a copy of the grant that the seller will later sign for delivery on closing

Preparing the Accounts for Closing

Harmon finds that Vincent's title to the land is in good order and that there are no outstanding corporation taxes or municipal taxes except for the current year. She receives a mortgage statement from Grimm Mortgage Company, and it agrees with the statement made by Vincent concerning the amount outstanding. A few weeks before the date of closing, Vale prepares a document called a **statement of adjustments** (see below) setting out all the items, both credits and debits, that must be adjusted between the parties to arrive at the correct amount to be paid by Hi-Style to Vincent on the date of closing. The closing date is to be April 15.

statement of adjustments
a document setting out all the items—both credits and debits—that must be adjusted between the parties to arrive at the correct amount to be paid on closing

---

Re: Lot 27, Plan 7654, in the City of Oshawa
Hi-Style Centres Ltd. purchase from Vincent

STATEMENT OF ADJUSTMENTS

1. SALE PRICE		$645 000.00
2. Deposit paid by purchaser		$ 25 000.00
3. First mortgage to Grimm Mortgage Company to be assumed by purchaser	$373 580.60	
Plus interest, April 1 to 15 at 10.5%	$ 1 612.03	
		$375 192.63
4. Second mortgage back to vendor		$125 000.00
5. Unpaid taxes for current year, $5695.00, charged to vendor to April 15— 3½ months		$ 1 661.04
6. Rent received in advance:		
Suite #1: 1½ months	$ 1 875.00	
Suite #2: 1½ months	$ 1 875.00	
Suite #3: ½ month	$ 450.00	
		$ 4 200.00

continued

7. Union Hartford Fire Insurance
   Policy no. 8953744, three years,
   expires Nov. 1, current year.
   Amount: $450 000
   Premium: $1 870.
   Unexpired portion: $ 1 012.92

8. Full tank of furnace oil –
   2000 litres @ 43.4¢ $ 868.00

9. BALANCE DUE ON CLOSING $115 827.25

                                       $646 880.92 $646 880.92

The Closing

Trading Documents

On the morning of April 15, Vale and Harmon meet at the registry office. Harmon checks again with the sheriff's office to search for executions and finds none. She also brings her search of the title up to date to make sure no new documents have been registered against it. She gives Vale the properly executed mortgage for $125 000 made out in duplicate, and a certified cheque for $115 827.25. On behalf of the vendor, Vale delivers the following documents to Harmon:

(a) properly executed grant in duplicate

(b) original copy of leases to Suites No. 1 and No. 2

(c) properly executed assignments of each lease

(d) acknowledgment of tenant in Suite No. 3 that she is a monthly tenant at a rent of $900 payable in advance

(e) notice signed by Vincent to each tenant of Suites No. 1, No. 2, and No. 3 informing them of the change of ownership and requesting them to pay all future rent to Hi-Style

(f) current tax bill

He also hands to Harmon, for the purpose of inspection, a certified copy of the insurance policy on the building and a transfer noting both the interest of Hi-Style as purchaser and Vincent as second mortgagee. Vale will subsequently send these to the insurance company himself. After trading documents, Harmon registers the grant from Vincent to Hi-Style, and Vale registers the second mortgage from Hi-Style to Vincent.

Delivering Possession

Vale agrees not to release the funds he has received until Vincent delivers possession to Hi-Style. The mechanics of delivering possession to a purchaser sometimes cause great friction and even court action. To avoid such friction the vendor should arrange to be completely out of the premises by the time the deal is closed and deliver the keys to the purchaser. If this is not done, the purchaser may understandably be very upset and demand that the money not be released. Once anger replaces common sense both vendor and purchaser may become obstinate, and the vendor's lawyer holding the cheque is caught between them. In the present case, however, all goes smoothly: Vincent has vacated the premises the day before and delivers the keys to Vale who now hands them over to Harmon. On returning to her office, Harmon calls the manager of Hi-Style to tell her that the keys are available. The manager picks up the keys, goes to the building, and finds the store vacant. She calls Harmon and informs her that Hi-Style is now in possession. Harmon calls Vale and tells him that he may release the cheque to Vincent. The sale has now been effected.

After the Closing

Each lawyer still has several things to do besides submitting a bill. Vale will write to Grimm Mortgage Company to inform it of the sale and name the purchaser. He will also write to the city tax office to inform them of the change of ownership. He will write to the insurance company enclosing the copy of the policy and the transfer, and request the return of the policy with an endorsement noting the change of ownership and the interest of the second mortgagee in the property. He will also request that a copy of the policy be sent to the purchaser.

Harmon will communicate with Vale to see that all these things have been completed. She will also write to Grimm Mortgage Company and to the city tax office asking each of them to send all further notices to the head office of Hi-Style. She will write to each of the tenants to inform them of the change of ownership, enclosing Vincent's notice and giving them the address at which Hi-Style would like the rent to be paid.

Only after all these things have been done, when the lawyers are able to return all the documents to their respective clients and to make a full written report of all details, will the transaction be complete.

The Distinctiveness of Each Transaction

It is important to stress that each sale of land is a separate and distinctive transaction: the terms should be tailored to meet the specific requirements of the parties in the circumstances. Perhaps we see the greatest degree of standardization in contracts for the sale of similar houses in a subdivision. Even there, however, significant variations in such standard contracts occur because of special credit arrangements, extra features installed by the builder, or arrangements for completion of the house after possession. In the sale of commercial property, the variations are far greater: often, possession does not pass to the purchaser on closing, as where the whole premises are already rented to tenants and are purchased for their investment value, or where the vendor stays on as a tenant. Sometimes when the sale of a business is involved, the purchaser covenants to buy goods from the vendor, or the vendor covenants to refrain from opening a competing business in the same neighbourhood. Our fictional illustration set out above is not a model for other transactions, nor does it deal with every detail that might arise in the circumstances. Rather it is intended to give a picture and an understanding of a typical real estate transaction.

QUESTIONS FOR REVIEW

1. What were the two main disadvantages of a "live" gage? What major change in the law permitted the growth of the mortgage in place of the "live" gage?

2. Describe the two harshest of the common law rules for mortgagors. How did equity remedy this?

3. Why does a mortgagee rarely take possession immediately on default by the mortgagor?

4. Define foreclosure; acceleration clause; legal title; charge; power of sale.

5. In a sale of mortgaged land by the court, what are the consequences for the mortgagor if there is a deficiency? If there is a surplus?

6. When a purchaser acquires land from the mortgagor and defaults, whom may the mortgagee sue? Why? Are there any exceptions to this rule?

7. What are the main options open to a second mortgagee when the mortgagor defaults?

8. In addition to timely repayment of the loan, what other duties does a mortgagor assume?

9. *M*, a mortgagee, wishes to sell you a $20 000 mortgage on Blackacre. *M* states that *Q*, the mortgagor, is in already default, but *M* needs money quickly to proceed with another transaction. *M* offers to assign the mortgage to you for $16 000. Before accepting the offer, name the two most important things you would need to verify.

10. Distinguish between a general creditor and a secured creditor.

11. Greenacre, a five-hectare field in a new subdivision, is available for sale. You would like to divide it into 20 lots, develop eight of them yourself and eventually sell off the remaining 12 lots. Describe an important term you would want in the mortgage you need to finance the purchase.

12. Why would a mortgagor who has defaulted request the court to hold a sale of his property rather than allow the mortgagee to foreclose?

13. What is the appeal of a reverse mortgage on their home to a retired elderly couple?

14. In our "Typical Real Estate Transaction," explain why Vincent would agree to take back a second mortgage.

15. Before closing the real estate transaction, there are a number of tasks that the purchaser's lawyer must complete, checking with various public and private offices. What reasons are there for visiting the premises themselves?

CASES AND PROBLEMS

1   Four years ago Azoic Wholesalers Ltd. purchased a warehouse building for $550 000. To finance the purchase the company paid $75 000 in cash, gave a 7.5 percent first mortgage to the Reliable Insurance Company for $315 000, and an 11 percent second mortgage of $160 000 to the vendor. The vendor subsequently sold the second mortgage to Sharpe Realties Ltd. for $145 000. All documents were duly registered. For the next few years Azoic Wholesalers Ltd. managed to pay interest on both mortgages and somewhat reduce the principal.

Azoic Wholesalers Ltd. subsequently became insolvent and was declared bankrupt. A trustee in bankruptcy was appointed, and all the assets of the company sold. The following statement shows its financial condition after all assets were liquidated:

Azoic Wholesalers Ltd.			
STATEMENT OF CONDITION AT DATE OF DISTRIBUTION			
Assets		**Liabilities**	
Bank balance from:		Reliable Insurance Co.	
sale of building	$425 000	(first mortgage)	$296 000
sale of all other assets	78 000	Sharpe Realties Ltd.	
		(second mortgage)	151 000
Total available cash	503 000		
Deficiency of assets	83 000	General creditors	139 000
	$586 000		$586 000

Calculate how the available cash will be distributed to the various creditors.

2. Fedorkow purchased a 100-hectare farm on the St. John River in New Brunswick for $90 000. He paid $12 000 cash and gave back a mortgage of $78 000 to the vendor, Bowes. The mortgage was payable over a 15-year period with interest at 8.5 percent in instalments of about $630 per month. Within a year, Bowes fell ill and decided to retire to a warm climate. She sold the mortgage to Manor Mortgage Co. with only a slight discount on the amount then outstanding because she personally guaranteed payment by Fedorkow.

A year later Fedorkow received an offer to purchase his frontage on the St. John River, an area of about 5 hectares, for $32 000. He visited the offices of Manor Mortgage Co. and asked if they would be interested in giving a discharge of the mortgage over the 5 hectares. Manor Mortgage Co. agreed to do so provided Fedorkow would give a $1000 bonus and a further $12 000 in reduction of the mortgage debt. The parties carried out the arrangement, and the 5 hectares were discharged from the mortgage, leaving the mortgage on the remainder of the farm. Subsequently, Fedorkow defaulted on the mortgage, having also let the farm fall into disrepair. Manor Mortgage Co. sued Bowes as guarantor of the mortgage debt for the balance of $31 560 then outstanding.

Should Manor Mortgage Co. succeed? Explain.

3. Expecting to make a quick profit, Pender purchased two hectares of land in a suburban community outside Fredericton for $85 000. He paid $15 000 in cash and obtained a loan for $65 000 by mortgaging the property to Quincy for two years with interest at 11 percent. Under the terms of the mortgage Pender was to make quarterly payments of $5000 plus interest, with balance of the principal sum and interest due at the end of two years. Pender's attempts to sell the land failed because the suburb did not develop as he had hoped. He paid the first quarterly instalment but missed the second.

Quincy took possession shortly after the default in payment and applied for foreclosure. The market for land in the area continued to weaken and shortly after he obtained a final order of foreclosure, Quincy advertised the property for sale "under the mortgagee's power of sale." He accepted the highest offer of $50 000 and sued Pender for the deficiency of $10 000 plus accrued interest and the costs of obtaining foreclosure and conducting the sale, for a total of $15 600.

Pender defended by claiming that Quincy had given up all rights against him when he foreclosed Pender's equity of redemption, unless he could return the land. Quincy argued that he retained the choice to exercise his power of sale with a claim for any deficiency.

Which argument do you believe is sounder? Explain.

4. Keller owned and operated the Serene Bed & Breakfast near Sarnia for many years. It was a small business and her health was not good; she decided to sell but found the market very limited. Jepson agreed to purchase Serene Bed & Breakfast from her for $195 000 if she agreed to take back a second mortgage. On March 31, Jepson paid Keller $30 000 on closing, assumed the first mortgage of $150 000 held by Huron Co-op Inc., and gave Keller a second mortgage for the balance of $10 000.

The spring and summer tourist seasons were very poor and Jepson lost money during the first six months. He defaulted on payments to both mortgagees and informed them that he could not carry on. Huron replied that it intended to commence foreclosure proceedings immediately. Both Jepson and Keller then met several times with the manager of Huron at his office, to try to work out the most convenient arrangement and keep expenses to a minimum, avoiding court costs. They agreed to avoid court proceedings by Jepson conveying the property to Huron—and Keller would also transfer her interest as second mortgagee to Huron in return for the nominal sum of $100.

Several months later Keller learned that Jepson owned a substantial interest in a large retail hardware store; he earned a good salary there as manager. She requested that he pay the unpaid debt on the second mortgage, but he refused on the basis that Keller could no longer reconvey the interest she held, having already transferred it to Huron. Keller believed that she was entitled to repayment and sued Jepson.

Give your opinion of the defence raised by Jepson and whether Keller should succeed.

5. Lawlor purchased a small house from Cloutier at a price of $80 000. She paid $15 000 in cash and gave Cloutier a first mortgage for the balance. A year later, when Lawlor had reduced the principal amount of the mortgage to $52 000, she suffered financial reverses that made it impossible for her to continue to repay mortgage principal as required. Cloutier brought an action against Lawlor and on May 15 obtained an order for foreclosure with the deadline for payment by Lawlor specified as November 15.

On July 10, the insurance of $50 000 on the house expired and Lawlor renewed it while she was seeking to refinance with a new mortgagee. A few weeks later the house was seriously damaged by fire; the insurance adjuster appraised the loss at $35 000.

Both Cloutier and Lawlor immediately claimed the insurance money. The insurance company refused to pay Cloutier on the grounds that the insurance policy contained no mortgage clause that would have assigned to him rights in any claim "in so far as his interest may appear." The insurance company also refused to pay any part of the loss to Lawlor on the grounds that she had no insurable interest in the property.

Discuss the validity of the claims of Cloutier and Lawlor. Assume that there is no evidence to show that the fire was other than accidental in its origin.

6. Three years ago, the Lister Co. Ltd. borrowed $200 000 from the Hi-Rise Bank. The Lister Co. was in the textile business and gave a real estate mortgage on one of its buildings as collateral security for the bank loan: the mortgage provided security in the land, building, and fixtures in the building.

The company was later adjudged bankrupt on a petition of its creditors. A question arose about whether certain expensive machinery in the mortgaged building was in fact a fixture against which the bank would retain priority in liquidation. The trustee in bankruptcy, representing the general creditors, claimed it was not a fixture, so that the proceeds from its sale would be applied to all creditors' claims and not solely to that of the bank as mortgagee.

An officer of the bank and the trustee in bankruptcy went personally to inspect the machine, but were unable to agree whether it could be described as being "permanently" affixed. The bank then started legal action to have its claim as mortgagee of the machine confirmed. At this point, the trustee offered as a compromise to recognize the bank's priority to the extent of $20 000, a sum much less than the probable resale value of the machine; the bank accepted the offer and withdrew its action.

A few days later the bank learned that at the time it took the mortgage on the building the machine in question had been affixed to a cement floor in the plant in a permanent way, but that the building had since been renovated and the machine was reattached much less securely to the new floor. Neither the bank nor the trustee had this information when they contracted to substitute $20 000 in cash for the mortgage claim. The trustee refused to waive the agreement, however, and the Hi-Rise Bank brought an action asking the court for rescission of that contract and an order acknowledging its claim as a secured creditor with respect to the machine.

Discuss the nature of the argument on which the bank would base its claim and indicate whether its action should succeed.

7. Joseph Bator and Cecilia Potter met in 1986 and went out together for the next seven years. From time to time they discussed marrying but always delayed. In 1990 Joseph bought a large old residence that he converted into a rooming house.

While on a trip in the summer of 1993 Joseph met another woman and they made plans to marry. When Joseph broke this news to Cecilia, it proved to be a traumatic occasion for both of them. To soothe his conscience, Joseph promised Cecilia he would give her the rooming house. He consulted his lawyer, who reminded him that capital gains tax would become payable because of the proposed gift but that his tax liability might possibly be deferred if Joseph were to convey the house to Cecilia and take a mortgage back for its total value of $100 000. His lawyer drafted a mortgage for $100 000 stating that the principal sum of $100 000 would be repayable without interest in instalments of $4000 per annum. Both Joseph and Cecilia understood that, as mortgagee, Joseph would not enforce payment of the annual $4000 instalments due under the mortgage; they were to be his gift to Cecilia. Cecilia gave up her apartment and moved into the rooming house and proceeded to manage it.

Joseph was married in late 1993 and a year later Cecilia also married someone else. In the late 1990s, Joseph's fortunes declined significantly; Cecilia and her husband prospered. By November 1999, Joseph was pleading with Cecilia that she begin paying him the annual instalments on the mortgage. Cecilia was sympathetic but her husband insisted that she not do so. Joseph then sued Cecilia for the full unpaid principal sum of $100 000, which, by a standard acceleration clause in the mortgage, became due upon default.

Give an opinion on the probable outcome of this litigation with reasons.

8. Victor Contractors Ltd. financed the construction of a high-rise apartment tower in Hamilton by receiving "draws" on first mortgage financing as work progressed. Rail Canada Pension Fund held the first mortgage for $10 700 000. The mortgage contained the following clause:

> The Mortgagor [Victor Contractors Ltd.] covenants and agrees with the Mortgagee [Rail Canada Pension Fund] that, except with the prior consent of the Mortgagee (which consent shall not be unreasonably withheld), it will not enter into any agreement for the sale, transfer or other disposition of the mortgaged premises.

On May 31, Victor Contractors agreed to sell the apartment building to Steel City Developers Corp. for $16 000 000. Steel City Developers paid a deposit of $75 000 and agreed to assume the existing first mortgage. The closing date was December 1, with the balance due on closing. The contract included the following clause:

> This Agreement is conditional upon the Vendor [Victor Contractors Ltd.] being able to obtain within thirty days following this date the consent of the first mortgagee [Rail Canada Pension Fund] to this sale and to the assumption of the first mortgage obligations by the Purchaser [Steel City Developers Corp.].

When Victor Contractors requested consent from Rail Canada Pension Fund, its manager stated that he would have to be satisfied with the financial capability of Steel City Developers and wished to see its audited financial statements. The secretary-treasurer of Steel City Developers refused to produce the statements on the grounds that her company had a firm policy of never disclosing its financial affairs to anyone except its bank because this policy gave it an advantage over its competitors.

With matters at an impasse, the solicitors for Steel City Developers finally wrote on June 28, informing Victor Contractors that since, as vendor, it had been unable to obtain the consent of the first mortgagee as required, "This Agreement is now null and void." In reply, Victor Contractors wrote, "It is clear that your letter of June 28 written on behalf of your client constituted a wrongful renunciation of the contract of sale and purchase."

Victor Contractors then sued Steel City Developers for specific performance or, alternatively, for damages for breach of contract. Steel City Developers counterclaimed for the return of the deposit of $75 000.

Outline what you consider to be the main issue that the court will have to resolve in this case and offer with reasons an opinion about the probable outcome. Why would Rail Canada Pension Fund have insisted upon a right to satisfy itself of the financial capability of any purchaser of the apartment building?

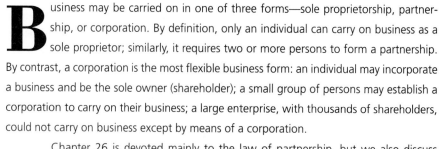

PART

6

usiness may be carried on in one of three forms—sole proprietorship, partnership, or corporation. By definition, only an individual can carry on business as a sole proprietor; similarly, it requires two or more persons to form a partnership. By contrast, a corporation is the most flexible business form: an individual may incorporate a business and be the sole owner (shareholder); a small group of persons may establish a corporation to carry on their business; a large enterprise, with thousands of shareholders, could not carry on business except by means of a corporation.

Chapter 26 is devoted mainly to the law of partnership, but we also discuss briefly the place of sole proprietorships. While there is no separate body of law regulating sole proprietorships and no special formalities are required to begin operations, they remain subject to many regulations of general application to business. For example, the owner may be required to obtain a licence in order to carry on a particular type of business. In most provinces, if business is carried on under any name other than the actual name of the proprietor, that name must be registered. By contrast, each province regulates partnerships under its Partnership Act. These acts govern not only the relationship among partners but also their relations with the rest of the community.

The much more complex law of corporations is the subject of Chapters 27, 28, and 29. In Chapter 27, we examine the nature and significance of corporations and their formation and composition. In Chapter 28, we concern ourselves with the relations between directors and shareholders, and the management of a corporation's internal affairs. Chapter 29 deals with the external business relations of a corporation—with its customers, its creditors, its potential investors, and with the general public.

Business Organizations

Their Forms, Operation, and Management

PART 6

Weblinks

Chapter 26 is primarily concerned with the application of the various provincial Partnership Acts. The full texts of some of those statutes can be accessed on the Internet, as follows:

gov.ab.ca/qp
Alberta

qp.gov.bc.ca/bcstats/96348 01.htm
British Columbia

gov.nb.ca/acts/acts/p-04.htm
New Brunswick

www.gov.ns.ca/legi/legc/index.htm
Nova Scotia

www.attorneygeneral.jus.gov.on.ca/legis.htm
Ontario

In some cases the Act can be accessed directly, in others it must be accessed through an index of statutes.

Chapters 27, 28, and 29 examine in depth the Canada Business Corporation Act, which can be accessed at

canada.justice.gc.ca/FTP/En/Regs/Chap/C/C-44/index.html

Provincial corporate statutes are available at

www.qp.gov.bc.ca/bcstats/96062_00.htm
British Columbia

www.gov.ns.ca/legi/legc
Nova Scotia

209.195.107.57/en/index.html
Ontario, which also gives access to the Ontario Securities Act

Other useful Web sites are:

canada.gc.ca/programs/pgrind_e.html#business
Links to most federal government business sites

ic.gc.ca
Industry Canada, with many useful links

www.strategis.ic.gc.ca/SSG/c100150e.html
The Industry Canada corporate law policy information page

www.cbsc.org/main.html
The Canadian Business Service Centre

www.cdn-news.com
Canadian Corporate News homepage

www.electriclawyer.com/lawinfo/businesslaw.html
Electric Lawyer: information on business law

British Columbia, Nova Scotia, and Ontario have particularly good sites on setting up a business, at

www.osbr.sb.gov.bc/ca

www.gov.ns.ca/ecor/infocent/startbus.htm

www.gov.on.ca/MBS/english/business/index.html

26 SOLE PROPRIETORSHIPS AND PARTNERSHIPS

This chapter examines *unincorporated* business entities—sole proprietorships and partnerships. A sole proprietorship cannot really be described as an "organization," since it involves only one person. Consequently, the main emphasis of the chapter is on partnerships. In the chapter we examine such questions as:

■ why are partnerships formed?

■ what is the legal nature of a partnership?

■ why is it important to establish whether a partnership exists between persons carrying on a business?

■ how are partnerships created?

■ what are the usual contents of a partnership agreement?

■ to what extent are partners liable for the acts of their co-partners and for the debts of the firm?

■ what are the duties owed by partners to one another?

■ how are partnerships terminated, and what happens when they are?

■ what are "joint ventures"?

■ what are limited partnerships?

Choosing the Appropriate Form of Business Organization

Almost all businesses in Canada are carried on in one of the following forms:[1]

- sole proprietorship
- partnership
- corporation

A sole proprietorship or a partnership may come into existence without formality, that is, simply by the actions of the individual or group setting up a business. However, a corporation may only be formed under a statute in a prescribed manner and registered with the designated government department. Although for many years the procedure for incorporation was relatively expensive and cumbersome, a corporation can now be formed quickly and for a few hundred dollars. In addition, almost all provinces currently permit a corporation to be created with a single shareholder, so that corporations are a viable alternative not only to partnerships but also to sole proprietorships. Accordingly, when an individual or a group of persons contemplate establishing a business, an initial decision must be made whether or not to incorporate. At this point professional legal, accounting and management advice should be sought. Many small businesses decide to incorporate at the outset while others make the decision to do so later, or they remain unincorporated. There are now more than one million corporations registered in Canada, representing close to one-third of all businesses, most of them small and medium-sized enterprises.

In the next chapter we shall consider the reasons why a person, or group of persons, might decide to incorporate their business. The subject of this chapter is those businesses that operate without incorporating.

Sole Proprietorships

An individual who sets up a business has, simply by doing so, created a **sole proprietorship**; no formalities are necessary. While there is no distinct body of law regulating sole proprietorships, they are subject to many regulations that apply to all forms of business. Laws regarding public health, zoning, and, of course, taxation, apply to all businesses, whether sole proprietorships, partnerships or corporations. A sole proprietor may have to obtain a licence to carry on a particular type of business. For example, a municipal licence is normally required before one may start business as an electrician, plumber, restaurateur, or taxi-driver. Provincial licensing and registration may be required for a car dealer, insurance broker, or employment agency. The proprietor must keep proper accounts for income tax purposes; she must make payroll deductions for employee income tax, employment insurance and Canada Pension Plan; in hiring staff, she must observe human rights legislation and must comply with health and safety regulations.

In most provinces, statutes require that if business is carried on under a name other than the actual name of the owner, whether the owner is a sole proprietor, a partnership or a corporation, the name must be registered.[2]

sole proprietorship
an unincorporated business owned by a single individual

---

1. A few businesses are carried on by cooperatives, trusts, and other types of unincorporated association but because of their limited importance we shall not consider them.
2. See, for example, Business Names Act, R.S.O. 1990, c. B.17, s. 2(2), and the discussion in Chapter 22.

PARTNERSHIPS

Advantages and Disadvantages

partnership
the relationship between two or more persons carrying on a business with a view to profit

A **partnership** may be formed by two or more persons, who may be natural persons (individuals) or legal persons (corporations). There are obvious advantages in carrying on a business venture as a joint undertaking. Working together, members of a group can pool their knowledge and skills, and their physical and financial resources. There are also obvious disadvantages: disagreements may lead to stalemate; dishonesty or incompetence of one member may lead to losses suffered by other members; when a group wishes to make important decisions, it may lose valuable time in arranging a meeting. None of these problems exists when a person acts solely on his or her own behalf.

The Partnership Act

Although partnerships may be established without formality, their affairs are governed by a well-developed body of laws. This is because, until the 20th century, partnership was the accepted way for two or more persons to carry on an enterprise; problems concerning almost every aspect of partnership arose and became the subject of legal decisions, starting about the middle of the 18th century. By the 1880s, there was a virtually complete body of rules that were well settled, but the mass of decisions on detailed points made it difficult to discover the broader principles. To remedy this situation, the British Parliament in 1890 passed the Partnership Act,[3] which brought together the numerous cases under more general principles and codified the law as the experts in the field then believed it to be. The English Act has been adopted in substantially the same form by all the common law provinces.[4] With one important exception,[5] the Act has remained virtually unchanged from its original form and there have been comparatively few cases on its interpretation, so that it can be taken as an accurate representation of the state of partnership law today.

THE NATURE OF PARTNERSHIP

The Definition of Partnership

"Partnership is the relation which subsists between persons carrying on a business in common with a view of profit."[6]

Checklist: Elements of a Partnership

There are four basic elements in the definition of "partnership": a partnership is

- a relationship,
- between persons,
- carrying on business in common,
- with a view to profit.

---

3. 1890, 53 & 54 Vict., c. 39 (U.K.).

4. In Ontario it is referred to as the "Partnerships Act" (in the plural): R.S.O. 1990, c. P.5.

5. The creation in Ontario of limited liability partnerships, considered later in this chapter.

6. Partnership Act, 1890, s. 1(1). The same wording is used in Canadian versions of the statute. See, for example: Partnership Act, R.S.B.C. 1996, c. 348, s. 2; R.S.N.S. 1989, c. 334, s. 4: Partnerships Act, R.S.O. 1990, c. P.5, s. 2. Subsequent references in this chapter to B.C., Ontario and N.S. are to these statutes.

This definition of partnership is extremely important because of the consequences that may follow from a finding that a person is a partner. Whether two or more persons are partners depends upon all the circumstances of a case.

The Partnership Relationship

Partnership is a consensual, and contractual, *relationship*. Normally a formal written partnership agreement is drawn up and is signed by all the partners. However, persons may be found to be partners although no written or even oral agreement exists. In the absence of an express agreement they may still be held to be partners if they have acted as such. The courts look at the substance of the relationship, and are not necessarily guided by what the parties may themselves choose to call it.[7]

The Business Nature of Partnership

The Partnership Act defines partnership as a relation between persons carrying on a *business*. Under our system of law, the word "partnership" refers exclusively to joint business enterprises carried on for profit. It does not refer to other associations, such as charitable enterprises, joint trustees of an estate, or public boards.

The term "business" is an imprecise one. It includes "every trade, occupation, or profession," but it does not include every activity carried on for a profit. For instance, owning property and collecting rent from tenants does not necessarily amount to carrying on a business. The joint ownership of property does not of itself make the owners partners. Similarly, if a group of investors forms a syndicate to hold a portfolio of securities, that arrangement does not amount to carrying on a business unless the investors engage in the trade of dealing in shares, rather than merely retaining them for investment income.

CASE 26.1

A group of persons, including a corporation (Kamex), joined together to purchase a piece of development property with a view to reselling it at a profit. One of the co-owners, March, entered into an exclusive listing agreement with a real estate agent (Le Page); in doing so, he was acting without the agreement of his co-owners.

The group sold the property, and Le Page sued the members of the group for its commission. It claimed that they had formed a partnership and that they were consequently jointly liable on the contract made by March.

The court held that there was no partnership. The members of the group were not carrying on a business, but were merely co-owners of the property. Consequently, March alone was liable for the commission.[8]

Although a partnership must be a business relationship, not every business relationship makes the parties to the relationship partners with each other. The Act speaks of "carrying on" a business. Isolated transactions engaged in jointly do not by themselves establish the parties as partners. For example, if two merchants in the Atlantic provinces pool an order of goods purchased in Montréal so that they can fill one freight car and obtain a lower freight rate, that arrangement does not by itself make them partners. However, a partnership may exist for even a single venture, depending on the circumstances.

---

7. In Lansing Building Supply (Ontario) Ltd. v. Lerullo (1990), 71 O.R. (2d) 173, co-developers of land entered into a "joint venture" agreement that specifically provided that they were not to be considered partners. Nevertheless, the court held that the true nature of their relationship was one of partnership.

8. A.E. Le Page Ltd. v. Kamex Developments Ltd. (1977), 78 D.L.R. (3d) 223.

The Profit Motive

The definition requires that the business be carried on with a view to *profit*. Those words might seem redundant, since profit—or the hope of it—is what business is all about. But the words have generally been taken to mean that a *sharing* of profits is an essential element of partnership.

Generally, the sharing of *gross receipts* does not create a partnership: if an owner of a theatre were to rent it to a drama group and one of the terms of the contract was that she would receive 10 percent of the gross receipts, such an arrangement would not make the owner a partner in the venture of producing a play. Similarly, in our example of the two merchants pooling an order to reduce shipping charges there is a sharing of costs, but not of profits.

The receipt of a share of the profits of the business is strong evidence tending to establish a partnership, though it is not by itself conclusive. In particular it does not by itself amount to a partnership if the sharing of profits is part of an arrangement to

- repay a debt owed
- pay an employee or agent of the business as part of his remuneration
- pay an annuity to a widow, widower, or child of a deceased partner
- repay a loan under which the lender is to receive a rate of interest varying with the profits
- pay the seller of a business an amount for goodwill that varies according to the profits[9]

Apart from the above situations, it is difficult to imagine circumstances in which the only evidence of a partnership would be the fact that a person is sharing in the profits of a business. A person receiving a share of profits has usually contributed property or money to the business. Even though partners sometimes share profits according to a ratio that is not based on capital contribution, the courts consider profit sharing that coincides with the ratio of capital contribution strong evidence of partnership.

Another important factor is whether the person receiving the profits has taken part in the management of the business. Evidence showing that she has taken some active role in the business, particularly in making decisions on important matters, when added to the fact that she has shared in the profits, will usually suffice to establish her as a partner.

The Legal Nature of Partnership

Legal Personality

In the next chapter, on corporation law, we shall discuss in considerably more detail the significance of legal personality. As a matter of law a corporation does have a separate personality of its own. In the law of partnership the position is less clear. The Act defines a partnership as a "relation" between persons; strictly, a partnership has no independent existence and merely represents the collective rights and duties of all the partners. Logically, this means that whenever a partner dies or retires, or a new partner is admitted, the partnership comes to an end and is replaced by a new relationship. In actual practice, however, and in some of its legal implications, a partnership does have a semi-separate existence of its own. Certainly, as an accounting matter, a partnership is treated as a separate entity with its own assets, liabilities, and financial statements.

The Continuing Relationship Between Partners

The Partnership Act itself recognizes, in a number of places, the concept of a "firm,"[10] which members join or leave. It speaks of a person being admitted as a partner into an existing firm,

---

9. B.C., s. 3; Ont. s. 3.; N.S., s. 5.

10. B.C. s. 5; Ont., s. 5; N.S., s. 7.

or retiring from a firm, or being expelled from a firm, and of the composition of a firm being changed. And while it provides that the death (or insolvency) of a partner dissolves the partnership, the Act accepts that the partners may agree that the partnership should continue between the survivors.[11] It is consequently possible, and normally advisable, for partners to agree expressly that, on the death, bankruptcy or retirement of one of them the partnership relation among the others will continue.

Partnership Property

Again, it is clear from the Act that a partnership may have property that is distinct from the property of the individual partners. In particular, real property held by a partnership is treated according to the usual rules governing real property as far as the partnership is concerned, but insofar as the individual partners are concerned their interest in the real property is considered personal property.

Creditors of the Firm

Partnership creditors have first call against partnership assets before the personal creditors of an individual partner. This is so because until the creditors of the partnership have been paid, it is impossible to identify and distribute the share of an individual partner. If, after these creditors are paid, no assets remain, then the partner has no share for personal creditors to seize.

Another instance of the separate existence of the firm occurs in the rule that a deceased partner's personal creditors have first call against the personal assets of her estate.[12] Thus, if the partnership assets are insufficient to pay off the partnership creditors, they must wait for the personal creditors to be paid out of the personal estate of the deceased partner before they can take what is left in order to satisfy their debt. Under the Bankruptcy and Insolvency Act, this rule applies also to the estate of a living partner who becomes bankrupt.[13]

Legal Proceedings

For the purposes of court action, a partnership may be treated as if it were a separate entity. The partnership may bring an action in the name of the firm without naming all the partners as plaintiffs, and an outside party may sue a partnership in its firm name without naming all the partners as defendants. It is, in fact, wise to sue a partnership in the firm name rather than in the names of the individual partners, as we shall see when we consider the question of the liability of partners.

THE CREATION OF A PARTNERSHIP

The Partnership Agreement

A partnership comes into existence by the agreement, express or implied, of the partners. A **partnership agreement** may be wholly oral and yet be valid and enforceable provided it does not come within one of the sections of the Statute of Frauds. The Statute of Frauds affects a contract of partnership only if by its terms it extends beyond one year and performance has not begun. Once a partnership begins to operate, the statute has no effect.[14] As we know, of course, an oral agreement is subject to the lapses of memory of the parties to the agreement, and if only for certainty it is important to have a written record of it.

partnership agreement
an agreement between persons to create a partnership and (usually) setting out the terms of the relationship

---

11. B.C., s. 36(1); Ont., s. 33(1); N.S., s. 36(1).

12. B.C., s. 10; Ont., s. 10; N.S., s. 11.

13. R.S.C. 1985, c. B-3, s. 142.

14. Burdon v. Barkus (1862), 45 E.R. 1098. As noted in Chapter 10, the Statute of Frauds has been abolished in some provinces.

Generally speaking, partners may agree to whatever terms they wish, provided the terms are not illegal and do not offend public policy. Business partnerships, like marriages, can be perilous ventures, and probably because dissolution of a partnership is somewhat easier, a higher proportion of them break up after a very short time. The reasons for dissolution are extremely varied. Many are dissolved because the business venture has proved unprofitable, others because the venture has proved very profitable and the partners have gone on to form a corporation. Still others dissolve because of a conflict of personalities that the parties cannot resolve. A substantial number of profitable partnerships are destroyed by misunderstanding or mistrust. The failure to decide important issues in advance often leads to the kind of misunderstanding and mistrust that in turn creates an eventually irreparable breach between the parties.

Drafting an Effective Agreement

The main purpose of a partnership agreement is to set out, as carefully and as clearly as possible, the entire terms of the relationship.

Checklist: Contents of a Partnership Agreement

Normally, a partnership agreement will deal with the following matters. Depending upon the individual circumstances, there are likely to be other matters that should be covered as well.

- identity of the partners
- name of the firm
- nature of the business to be carried on
- duration of the relationship
- method of terminating the partnership
- rules for introducing new partners
- what is to happen on the retirement or death of an existing partner
- participation in management and in making major decisions
- contribution of each partner in terms of work and responsibilities
- capital contribution of each partner
- ownership of property used in the business
- sharing of profits and losses
- procedure for resolving disputes

As we shall see in a later part of this chapter, the Partnership Act sets out a number of implied terms in the absence of any provision in the agreement to the contrary. It is normally advisable, however, for the parties to make express provision in respect of the matters covered by the Act.

In order to draft an effective partnership agreement, the parties must consider the most likely events that might lead to disagreement and upset the partnership or change its course of action. A well-drafted, carefully thought-out partnership agreement is of itself no guarantee of a successful partnership. The other elements—a sound business idea, reasonably good luck, mutual trust and good faith, and diligent application—must be present for a partnership to succeed: but a well-drawn agreement minimizes one major hazard.

If only because of subjective bias, it is virtually impossible for partners to draft their own agreement. The usual problems of ambiguous words and unconscious interpretations favourable to oneself can create the same misunderstandings that arise in the law of contracts. In addition, individual partners may be unaware of many of the pitfalls that accumulated experience in business and learning in partnership law may avoid. For these reasons a partnership agreement is, perhaps more than any other type of agreement, one that should be drafted with expert advice and assistance. If the parties to the agreement are investing large sums in the venture, then each should have his or her own legal counsel to help protect that investment.

Registration

No particular formalities are required in order to form a partnership; by contrast, as we shall see in the last part of this chapter, a *limited partnership* is formed by registration. However, almost all provinces do require the filing, in a local registry office, of a declaration giving such essential information as the names and addresses of each partner and the name under which they intend to carry on business. Declarations must also be filed when there is any change in membership or when a firm is dissolved. The registration requirements do not necessarily apply to all partnerships. For example, in British Columbia only partnerships engaged in trading, manufacturing or mining are required to register, and in Ontario a partnership is not required to register if it carries on business under a name that is composed solely of the names of the partners.[15]

There are penalties for failure to carry out the requirements of the statute, which vary from province to province, but non-registration in no way affects the existence of the partnership as such. The purposes of this registration system are quite clear. The register is open to the public and provides the minimum of essential information about a partnership and particularly about the partners in the firm, thus enabling a plaintiff to serve each partner with notice of an action if she wishes to do so. It is also helpful to prospective creditors or other suppliers in checking the accuracy of information given by a member of the partnership concerning the membership of the firm.

THE LIABILITY OF A PARTNER

What is the significance of deciding that a particular venture is a partnership and identifying a person as a partner in the venture? The significance lies primarily in the partner's personal liability to outsiders who have dealt with the partnership. Generally speaking, a person who is held to be a partner becomes personally responsible for the debts and liabilities of the partnership.

Contractual Liability

Agency Principles

Probably the greatest risk of liability to which a partner subjects himself results from the contractual obligations of the partnership. "Every partner is an agent of the firm and his other partners for the purpose of the business of the partnership, and the acts of every partner who does any act for carrying on in the usual way business of the kind carried on by the firm of which he is a member, bind the firm and its partners,"[16] unless the authority of the partner has been restricted by an agreement with the other partners and the third party knows of this restriction. Any acts done by a partner within the scope of his *apparent authority* and relied upon by an outsider bind the firm and all the partners. Thus, a restriction placed upon the authority of a

---

15. Partnerships Act, R.S.B.C., 1996, c. 312, s. 81; Business Names Act, R.S.O. 1990, c. B.17, s. 2(4). An Ontario limited liability partnership must register under the Business Names Act: see Partnerships Act, R.S.O. 1990, c. P.5, s. 44.3 (added by Partnerships Statute Law Amendment Act, S.O. 1998, c. 2).

16. B.C., s. 7; Ont., s. 6; N.S., s. 8.

partner has the same effect as a restriction placed upon the authority of an agent by his principal: it affects only those outsiders who have knowledge of the restriction.[17]

The notion of apparent authority was discussed in Chapter 19, in the context of the law of agency, and need not be repeated here.[18]

Joint Liability

joint liability

the situation where each of a number of persons is personally liable for the full amount of a debt

"Every partner in a firm is liable jointly with the other partners for all debts and obligations of the firm incurred while he is a partner...."[19] The chief effect of this rule of **joint liability** is that each partner is personally liable for the full amount of the firm's debts. When the liabilities of a partnership exceed its assets, a creditor or injured party, having obtained judgment against the partnership and exhausted its assets in trying to satisfy judgment, may look to the personal assets of any partner or partners until the judgment has been satisfied. Accordingly, it is important for a person advancing credit to a firm to determine whether it is a partnership and, if so, who are the partners.

Another consequence of this rule is that only one cause of action arises from the obligation. If by carelessness or ignorance of the facts a plaintiff brings action against some of the partners and obtains judgment against them, her rights will be exhausted: if their assets are insufficient to satisfy the judgment and she later discovers that there are other partners, she will not be able to sue those others for the deficiency. This risk is eliminated if she sues the defendants in the firm name, as was suggested above, since that has the effect of suing all the persons who were partners at the relevant time.

If a partner pays the firm's debts in full, he is entitled to be reimbursed by his co-partners for their shares of the debt.[20] But if they are insolvent, one partner may be left with payment of the full debt; it is consequently crucial to choose one's partners carefully.

FIGURE 26.1
Joint Liability

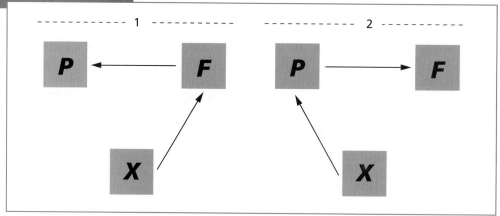

(1) If the outsider (*X*) sues the firm (*F*), then any partner (*P*) is liable to contribute his share to the firm, and may be sued by the firm for that share.

(2) If *X* instead sues *P*, *P* is fully liable but is entitled to be indemnified by the firm; that is, *P* can sue *F*, or his co-partners personally.

17. B.C., s. 10; Ont., s. 9; N.S., s. 11.

18. See, in particular, the case of Mercantile Credit Co. Ltd. v. Garrod, [1962] 3 All E.R. 1103, discussed in Chapter 19.

19. B.C., s. 11; Ont., s. 10; N.S., s. 12.

20. B.C., s. 27(a), (b); Ont., s. 24.1, 24.2; N.S., s. 27(a), (b).

Apparent Partners

In principle, a person is liable only for the obligations of a partnership incurred while he is a member of the firm. Hence, "a person who is admitted as a partner into an existing firm does not thereby become liable to the creditors of the firm for anything done before he became a partner," and "a partner who retires from a firm does not thereby cease to be liable for partnership debts or obligations incurred before his retirement."[21] The only way he may free himself from his obligations is by novation between the partners remaining in the firm, its creditors, and himself.[22]

A person who, not being a partner, represents himself to be, or allows himself to be represented as, a partner in a firm, is liable to any person who has given credit to the firm on the faith of that representation.[23]

CASE 26.2

A was a salaried lawyer, employed by another lawyer, S. A was not in partnership with S, and did not share in the profits of the practice. However, A's name was on the "firm's" letterhead and there was a bank account in the firm's name.

The plaintiff engaged S to lend some of its funds in a mortgage transaction. S did not register the mortgage and misappropriated the money. He was subsequently disbarred and sent to prison.

A did not perform any work for the plaintiff, but had been introduced to its senior officers, apparently as a partner of S.

The court held that A had allowed himself to be represented as a partner, and consequently could have been liable. However, the plaintiff had enjoyed a long personal relationship with S, and had not been induced to deal with the "firm" by A's holding out. A was therefore not liable.[24]

Although a partner who retires is generally not liable for debts of the firm contracted after he ceased to be a partner, he may be liable by estoppel to third parties who reasonably believe he is still a member of the firm and advance credit to the firm in reliance on his membership. A retiring partner may free himself from this liability by carrying out the requirements of the Partnership Act.[25] An advertisement in the Official Gazette of the province is adequate notice to persons generally who had not dealt with the firm before the retiring partner left the firm, but all persons who have dealt with the firm before the partner's retirement should receive actual notice of the retirement if the retiring partner is to be fully protected. It is customary, therefore, to send notices to all those persons who have dealt with the firm more or less recently, depending on the nature of the business. A further important precaution is to ensure that, where particulars of the partnership have been registered, the retiring partner's name is removed from the list of partners.[26]

Estoppel does not apply when a partner dies. His estate is not liable for credit extended to the firm after his death, even though the creditors do not know he has died.

---

21. B.C., s. 19; Ont., s. 18; N.S., s. 20.

22. See Chapter 13 under "Discharge by Agreement" (Substituted Agreement).

23. B.C., s. 16; Ont., s. 15; N.S., s. 17.

24. Bet-Mur Investments Ltd. v. Spring (1994), 17 B.L.R. (2d) 55.

25. B.C., s. 39; Ont., s. 36; N.S., s. 39.

26. The precise legal effects of registration are somewhat uncertain. The Nova Scotia statute provides that a statement in the register that a person is a partner is "incontrovertible"; Partnerships and Business Names Registration Act, R.S.N.S. 1989, c. 335, s. 11. The Ontario statute formerly contained the same rule, but no such provision appears in the current statute.

Checklist: Steps to Be Taken on Retirement From a Partnership

To protect himself against possible liability for future acts of his partners, a retiring partner should

- ensure that all existing clients of the firm are notified
- place a notice in the Official Gazette of the province (and perhaps also in the local newspaper)
- ensure that his name is removed from the register
- ensure to the best of his ability that any letterheads are destroyed or altered to remove his name

Tort and Breach of Trust

The liability of a firm, and of its partners, is not restricted to contracts. The Act makes the firm liable for "any wrongful act or omission of any partner acting in the ordinary course of the business of the firm." (B.C., s. 12; Ont., s. 11; N.S., s. 13) Thus the firm, and the other partners, would be liable for injuries or damage caused by a partner when driving on the firm's business, for a defamatory statement made by him in business correspondence, or for negligence in dealing with a client's affairs.[27] The principle is similar to that of vicarious liability, discussed in Chapter 3. The firm is also liable for breaches of trust committed by a partner, in particular for any misapplication by a partner of funds that have been placed in the care of the partner while acting within the scope of his apparent authority, or that have been entrusted to the firm.[28] The Act (B.C., s. 13; Ont., s. 12; N.S., s. 14) envisages two situations: see Figure 26.2.

FIGURE 26.2
Misapplication of Funds

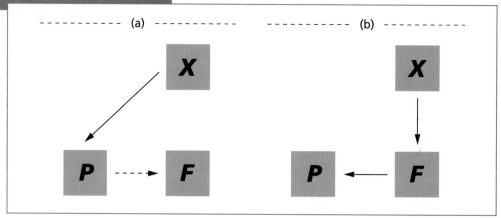

In situation (a), *X* entrusts *P* with money or property to be handed over to the firm (*F*); instead, *P* keeps the money or property for himself. In the second situation, (b), *X* entrusts money or property to the firm, and it is subsequently misappropriated by *P*.

---

27. McDonic v. Hetherington (1997), 142 D.L.R. (4th) 648.
28. See Ernst & Young v. Falconi (1994), 17 O.R. (3d) 512.

CASE 26.3

A partner in a law firm undertook (privately) the administration of his aunt's estate. The firm's letterhead was used, and funds belonging to the estate passed through the firm's bank accounts.

The partner defrauded the estate and transferred funds to his own account.

In an action against the firm, it was held that firm was liable, even though the other partners were not aware of the activities in relation to the estate. The partner had been acting within the scope of his apparent authority, since the administration of estates is a matter normally undertaken by lawyers.[29]

Limited Liability Partnerships

After remaining virtually unchanged for more than 100 years, Ontario's partnership law saw a radical change in 1998 with the introduction of the **limited liability partnership** (LLP). Although the LLP has only a very limited application for the present, the implications of the change are substantial.

As we have noted above, the Ontario statute, like those of the other common law provinces, makes a partnership liable for torts committed by a partner in the ordinary course of the business (section 11), and makes each partner jointly liable for the debts and obligations of the firm (section 10). The new Ontario legislation[30] qualifies section 10, providing:

> …a partner in a limited liability partnership is not liable…for debts, obligations and liabilities of the partnership or any partner arising from the negligent acts or omissions that another partner or an employee, agent or representative of the partnership commits in the course of the partnership business while the partnership is a limited liability partnership.[31]

A partner remains liable for his own negligent acts or omissions, and for those of a person who is under the partner's direct supervision or control.[32] It also appears that the firm itself remains liable, but an injured party may not look beyond the assets of the firm to the assets of the individual non-negligent partners.[33] The protection of non-negligent partners extends only to the *negligent* acts or omissions of a partner—it does not apply to other torts or to breaches of trust, nor does it affect the contractual liability of partners.

The provision applies only to LLPs (which are not to be confused with *limited partnerships*, discussed in the last part of this chapter). An LLP is formed when two or more persons enter into a *written* agreement that designates the partnership as a LLP and states that the agreement is governed by the (Ontario) act.[34] An LLP must register its firm name under the Business Names Act, and the name must contain the words "limited liability partnership" or the abbreviations LLP or L.L.P. (or the French language equivalents).

The most important restriction is that an LLP may carry on business in Ontario only for the purpose of practising a *profession* governed by statute. In addition, that statute must expressly permit an LLP to practise the profession, and the governing body of the profession must require the partnership to maintain a minimum amount of liability insurance.

limited liability partnership
a partnership in which non-negligent partners are not personally liable for losses caused by the negligence of a partner

---

29. Public Trustee v. Mortimer (1985), 16 D.L.R. (4th) 404; see also Korz v. St. Pierre (1988), 43 D.L.R. (4th) 528.

30. Partnerships Statute Law Amendment Act, 1998, S.O. 1998, c. 2.

31. *Ibid.*, s. 10(2).

32. *Ibid.*, s. 10(3).

33. *Ibid.*, s. 10(4).

34. *Ibid.*, s. 44.1. An existing partnership may be converted into a LLP if all the partners agree in writing.

To date, the only professions to which the new provisions apply are those of chartered accountant,[35] and lawyer.[36] Ontario is the only province to have introduced the LLP concept. Consequently, partners in an Ontario LLP do not enjoy any exemption outside the province. However, the new legislation does recognize the likelihood that other jurisdictions will follow Ontario's lead, and if so Ontario would apply the law of the other jurisdiction, regarding liability, to extra-provincial LLPs.[37]

CONTEMPORARY ISSUE

Limited Liability for Professionals

Ever since the *Hedley Byrne* decision (see Chapter 4), professionals—and especially accountants—have been concerned about the size of damages awards in negligence actions and the fact that the negligence of one partner makes all partners potentially liable. In Ontario they now have a chance to limit their liability. According to a recent report:

> Chartered accountants in Ontario are about to get relief from one of the nightmares that haunt their business. On July 1, the provincial government is expected to proclaim a bill allowing CAs to form limited liability partnerships. Under the law today, all the partners in a firm are liable for the firm's debts. That liability extends to their personal assets—their stake in the partnership, their houses, their RRSPs. With the big lawsuits that have been filed against accounting firms in major corporate disasters, partners who had nothing to do with the failed company could lose everything if the firm lost the case. But Ontario's bill, the first of its kind in Canada, will protect personal assets of accountants from successful legal action taken against their partners....The Canadian Institute of Chartered Accountants expects other provinces—perhaps Nova Scotia, Alberta or British Columbia—will follow Ontario's example within a year....

Source: "Ontario accountants get break on liability," *Financial Post*, June 19, 1998, p. 9.

Questions to Consider

1. Should limited liability apply only to accountants and lawyers?
2. Should professional firms be allowed to incorporate, with full limited liability?

THE RELATION OF PARTNERS TO ONE ANOTHER

Partnership is a contractual relationship, and the relations of partners to one another is essentially governed by the terms of their contract. These terms may be found in the partnership agreement, they may be inferred from the conduct of the parties or, as we are about to discuss, they may be implied from the Partnership Act. A partner who acts in a manner that is contrary to the partnership agreement commits a breach of contract and may be liable to compensate the other partners for any damage resulting from the breach.[38]

---

35. The 1998 Act amends the Chartered Accountants Act, 1956 to expressly allow for the creation of LLPs.

36. By-Law 26 of the Law Society of Upper Canada.

37. S. 44.4(4).

38. See, for example, Ernst & Young v. Stuart (1997), 144 D.L.R. (4th) 328 (partner leaving firm without giving proper notice and joining competitor).

Implied Terms

The Act sets out a number of terms that will be implied if those matters are not expressly covered in a partnership agreement. The main terms that are implied are summarized below, with explanatory comment where necessary.[39] It is important to remember that the parties to a partnership agreement may, and frequently do, vary these terms either at the time of the original agreement or later by unanimous consent.[40]

Partnership Property

"All property and rights and interests in property originally brought into the partnership stock or acquired, whether by purchase or otherwise, on account of the firm or for the purposes and in the course of the partnership's business are called ... 'partnership property' and must be held and applied by the partners exclusively for the purposes of the partnership and in accordance with the partnership agreement." (B.C., s. 23(1); Ont., s. 21(1); N.S., s. 23(1).) Additionally, the Act provides that, unless the contrary intention appears, all property bought with money belonging to the firm is deemed to have been bought on account of the firm and is available only for the use of the firm (B.C., s. 24; Ont., s. 22; N.S., s. 24).

It is not always clear whether a particular item of property is "brought into the partnership stock"; property that is used in the business is not necessarily partnership property, but may remain the property of the individual partners. Consequently, the partnership agreement should make clear precisely what property is to be considered to have been contributed as "capital."

ILLUSTRATION 26.1

A and *B* decide to go into partnership in a local delivery business. *A* owns a warehouse, valued at $50 000; *B* owns two vans, also valued at $50 000. Two years later the partnership is dissolved. The warehouse is now worth $70 000 and the vans are worth $20 000. How much is each entitled to?

(a) If the warehouse and vans were brought in as partnership property, then the total value of the assets—$90 000—would be divided equally between them and each would receive $45 000;

(b) If the assets brought into the business remained the individual property of *A* and *B*, then *A* would recover the warehouse ($70 000) and *B* only the depreciated vans ($20 000).

Either result might be fair, depending on the original intentions of the parties, but in the absence of a clear agreement, one party might receive a windfall of $25 000 at the expense of the other.

Financial Arrangements

The Act sets out a number of basic presumptions with respect to capital and profits, which apply "subject to any agreement express or implied between the partners." It should be emphasized that these rules are more often than not varied by agreement.

(1) "All the partners are entitled to share equally in the capital and profits of the business and must contribute equally towards the losses, whether of capital or otherwise, sustained by the firm." (B.C., s. 27(a); Ont., s. 24.1; N.S., s. 27(a)).[41] Partners commonly vary this term: they contribute different proportions of capital and share profits based on other criteria such as time spent on partnership business.

(2) If a partner incurs expenses or personal liabilities "in the ordinary and proper conduct of the business of the firm," or in doing anything to preserve the business or

---

39. The passages quoted are from the Ontario statute; the British Columbia and Nova Scotia versions differ very slightly in a few cases.

40. See B.C., s. 21; Ont., s. 20; N.S., s. 22.

41. In Ontario, an exception is made in the case of losses of an LLP.

property of the firm, the firm must indemnify him for these expenses or liabilities (B.C., s. 27(b); Ont., s. 24.2; N.S., s. 27(b)). Thus, as we have seen, if one partner is sued for the firm's debts, he is entitled to a contribution from his fellow partners.[42]

(3) A partner is not entitled, before the ascertainment of profits, to interest on the capital subscribed by him (B.C., s. 27(d); Ont., s. 24.4; N.S., s. 27(d)). In other words, if the agreement provides for the payment of "interest" on a partner's capital, the payment is not regarded as an expense of the firm, but rather as an appropriation of profits. But if a partner contributes to the firm a sum of money or other valuable consideration in excess of what he has agreed to subscribe under the partnership agreement, he is entitled to interest at the rate of 5 percent on the value of the excess contribution while it remains with the firm. Excess contributions are usually called "advances"; where there is an express agreement that a partner will make an advance, a different rate of interest may be fixed.

(4) "No partner is entitled to remuneration for acting in the partnership business" (B.C., s. 27(f); Ont., s. 24.6; N.S., s. 27(f)). Partnership agreements frequently do provide for the payment of a "salary" to one or more partners. Sometimes, one partner is the managing partner who hopes to derive his livelihood from the partnership business, whereas the other partner or partners are merely investing partners. Their partnership agreement will likely state that the managing partner is to be paid a salary. Entitlement to this "salary" is normally considered as a first call on the partnership profits. The agreement may state that the sum shall be deducted from his share of the profits, or more usually that it be his prior share before any further division of profits among all the partners. A partner, however, is not an employee, and his salary is not an expense of the firm. Like interest on capital, it is considered to be a distribution of profits.

CASE 26.4

M was described as a "salaried partner" in a law firm. He was to be paid a fixed salary of £1200 per year out of profits, plus one-third of the profits of the branch office that he ran.

The firm suffered a substantial loss, due to defalcations by the senior partner. M claimed he was still entitled to his salary of £1200, which should be paid by the other partners.

It was held that M was entitled to nothing. He was a partner, not an employee. His "salary" was a first charge on the profits of the firm. Since there were no profits, his share was nothing.[43]

Normally, partners are not willing and able to wait until some time after the end of the firm's accounting year, when the year's profits have been ascertained, before enjoying any of the fruits of their labour. It is common, therefore, to provide that a partner may "draw" up to a specified amount each month out of his prospective share of profits. Such an amount will be considered merely an advance on his share of the projected profits, repayable to the firm to the extent that it exceeds his share of the actual profits.

Conduct of the Business
The Act provides that, unless there is agreement to the contrary:

(1) "Every partner may take part in the management of the partnership business" (B.C., s. 27(e); Ont., s. 24.5; N.S., s. 27(e)). In small partnerships, this implied term is occa-

---

42. Again, there is an exception in the case of an Ontario LLP.
43. Marsh v. Stacey (1963), 103 Sol. J. 512 (U.K.).

sionally varied. For example, a parent who takes a child into partnership may wish to reserve the management of the firm to himself. Very large partnerships, such as large law firms, often have two or three classes of partners, and it may be that only the senior partners take part in the management of the firm.

(2) "Any difference arising as to ordinary matters connected with the partnership business may be decided by a majority of the partners, but no change may be made in the nature of the partnership business without the consent of all existing partners" (B.C., s. 27(h); Ont., s. 24.8; N.S., s. 27(h)). In cases of a serious disagreement this provision can be troublesome. The minority may insist that the particular decision did not concern an ordinary matter but affected the nature of the partnership business. It may be advisable, therefore, to spell out clearly which matters may only be decided unanimously.

(3) "The partnership books are to be kept at the place of business of the partnership or the principal place if there is more than one and every partner may, when he thinks fit, have access to and inspect and copy any of them" (B.C., s. 27(i); Ont., s. 24.9; N.S., s. 27(i)).

Membership

Partnership is a personal relationship, a fact that is underlined by two further provisions of the Act:

(1) "No person may be introduced as a partner without the consent of all existing partners" (B.C., s. 27(g); Ont., s. 24.7; N.S., s. 27(g)). Two common variations occur: where there are senior and junior partners, and the consent of only the senior partners is required; where a partner has reserved the right to have a son or daughter join the firm at a later date.

(2) No partner may assign his share in the partnership, either absolutely or by way of mortgage, so as to permit the assignees to take over his duties or "to interfere in the management or administration of the partnership business or affairs, or to require any accounts of the partnership transactions, or to inspect the partnership books." An assignee may, however, "receive the share of profits to which the assigning partner would otherwise be entitled and the assignee must accept the account of profits agreed to by the partners" (B.C., s. 34; Ont., s. 31; N.S., s. 34).

Fiduciary Duties

The Act contains three provisions that, together, set out the fiduciary duties of partners to one another.[44] It is probably erroneous to describe these as "implied terms," since the rules are not stated to be subject to contrary agreement and, indeed, it is doubtful to what extent partners may contract out of these duties.

Information

"Partners are bound to render true accounts and full information of all things affecting the partnership to any partner or his legal representatives" (B.C., s. 31; Ont., s. 28; N.S., s. 31).

Thus, information regarding the firm's business that is provided to any of the partners must be made available to all of them.[45] The only circumstances under which this term might be varied would be in a partnership having several classes of partners. It is possible that by

---

44. The B.C. Act (s. 22(1)) also contains a general rule that "a partner shall act with the utmost fairness and good faith towards the other members of the firm in the business of the firm."

45. See Dockrill v. Coopers & Lybrand (1994), 111 D.L.R. (4th) 62. Legal advice on how to "downsize" the firm must be made available to the partner being "downsized."

express agreement the most junior group of partners might not have access to all the books and records of the partnership. Even such a reservation, however, would be restricted to a narrow class of information.

Secret Benefits

"Every partner must account to the firm for any benefit derived by him without the consent of the other partners from any transaction concerning the partnership or from any use by him of the partnership property, name or business connection" (B.C., s. 32; Ont., s. 29; N.S., s. 32). A partner may be given permission by his co-partners to use partnership property for his own purposes, or to take advantage of an opportunity offered to the firm. But without full disclosure and authorization, any benefit belongs to the firm.

Duty Not to Compete

"Where a partner without the consent of the other partners carries on any business of the same nature as and competing with that of the firm, he must account for and pay over to the firm all profits made by him in that business" (B.C., s. 33; Ont., s. 30; N.S., s. 33). These terms are varied occasionally according to the circumstances of the partnership. For example, an entrepreneur might be carrying on a retail business in the downtown area and subsequently enter into a partnership to carry on a similar business in a suburban shopping centre. Since the two businesses might well be considered "of the same nature and competing with" each other, the partner owning the downtown business would require, as a term of the partnership agreement, that the partners in the suburban business consent to his continuing the downtown business.

The duty to account for secret profits and the duty not to compete sometimes overlap.

CASE 26.5

Davis and Ouellette formed a partnership to secure certain mining claims. The scheme fell through, but the partnership was never formally dissolved. Ouellette subsequently acquired the opportunity to buy the shares of a corporation that owned some of the claims. He notified Davis that he was terminating the partnership and then purchased the shares on his own behalf.

It was held that when Ouellette acquired the opportunity to buy the shares he was still a partner. The opportunity belonged to the firm and he had derived a benefit without the consent of his partner. He was liable to account for the profit that he made.[46]

CASE 26.6

Olson and Gullo were partners involved in property development and speculation. Gullo acted fraudulently: he bought a piece of land and resold it at a profit of $2.5 million. (Apparently, he also attempted to have Olson killed—which was presumably a breach of his fiduciary duty!) The trial judge awarded the whole profit to Olson. On appeal

by Gullo's estate it was held that he was accountable for only half of the profit. It was incorrect to say that this allowed him to profit from his own wrong. As a partner, half of the profit should have belonged to him anyway. It was the other half that should go to the plaintiff.[47]

---

46. Davis v. Ouellette (1981), 27 B.L.R. 162.
47. Olson v. Gullo (1994), 113 D.L.R. (4th) 42.

TERMINATION OF PARTNERSHIP

Express Provision

It is advisable for the partnership agreement to make express provision for what is to happen on termination—in particular on the retirement or death of a partner. What events justify termination? How much notice must a partner give to terminate the arrangement? Will the partnership among the remaining members continue? How is the retiring partner's share to be valued? What are the arrangements for the continuing partners to buy out the share of a deceased or retired partner? These are among the most important matters that should be settled in advance.

Implied Statutory Rules

In the absence of express agreement, the Partnership Act sets out a number of rules to govern termination.

Termination by Notice or Expiry

"Where no fixed term is agreed upon for the duration of the partnership, any partner may determine the partnership at any time on giving notice of his intention so to do to all other partners" (B.C., s. 29; Ont., s. 26; N.S., s. 29). The notice so given may be oral or in writing, unless the partnership was originally formed by deed, in which case notice in writing is necessary.

A partnership may be entered into for a fixed term, or may simply be a partnership at will, that is, so long as the partners wish to continue. Where a partnership was entered into for a fixed term, but is continued after the term has expired and without any express new agreement, the rights and duties of the partners remain the same as they were at the expiration of the term (B.C., s. 30; Ont., s. 27; N.S., s. 30). Without such continuing conduct, however, the partnership is dissolved by the expiration of a fixed term. Similarly, if it was entered into for a single venture or undertaking, it expires by the termination of that venture or undertaking.

Termination on Death or Insolvency

Since partnership is a personal relationship, it automatically terminates on the death of a partner, at least so far as the relationship between the deceased and the other partners is concerned. The Act, however, goes further and provides that, subject to any contrary agreement, "every partnership is dissolved *as regards all the partners* by the death or bankruptcy or insolvency of any partner" (B.C., s. 36(1); Ont., s. 33(1); N.S., s. 36(1)).

This term, perhaps more than any other, is varied by the partnership agreement. In a partnership having substantial assets and many members, the operation of this implied term dissolving the partnership could be disastrous. Accordingly, the partnership agreement usually provides that the partnership will continue in existence upon the death or insolvency of any partner. The partnership agreement usually provides that the surviving partners will buy out the share of a deceased partner, often using life insurance purchased on the life of each partner.

Even in a simple partnership between two persons their agreement should provide for some means of ascertaining the value of the partnership on the death of either of them; although the partnership will be terminated, the survivor may wish to continue the business as a sole proprietor—or find a new partner—and to buy out the share of the deceased partner.

The problem is primarily financial rather than legal. The arrangements must take into account the ability of the remaining partners to pay for the share of the deceased or insolvent partner, methods for ascertaining the value of that share, and the tax consequences of a particular method.

The Act further provides that, if a partner causes his share of the partnership property to be charged as security for his personal debts, the other partners are entitled to terminate the relationship (B.C., s. 36(2); Ont., s. 33(2); N.S., s. 36(2)).[48]

Dissolution by Law

A partnership is dissolved by any event that makes it unlawful for the business of the firm to be carried on or for members of the firm to carry it on in partnership (B.C., s. 37; Ont., s. 34; N.S., s. 37). The results here are in keeping with the general law of contract concerning illegality.

Even when there is disagreement amongst the partners concerning dissolution, or where dissolution at a specific time would be contrary to the terms of the partnership agreement, the court may on an application by one or more partners order the partnership dissolved under the following circumstances:

- where a partner is found to be mentally incompetent
- where a partner becomes permanently incapable of performing his part of the agreement
- where a partner has been guilty of conduct likely to prejudicially affect the business
- where a partner commits a breach of the agreement or otherwise conducts himself in such a manner that it is not reasonably practicable for the other partners to carry on the business in partnership with him
- where it is just and equitable that the partnership be dissolved (B.C., s. 38; Ont., s. 35; N.S., s. 38)

Effects of Dissolution

On the dissolution of a partnership, the property of the partnership is applied in payment of the debts and liabilities of the firm and the surplus assets are applied in payment of what is due to the partners respectively (B.C., s. 42; Ont., s. 39; N.S., s. 42). The Act further provides that, subject to any contrary agreement, in settling accounts between the partners after a dissolution of the partnership, losses (including losses and deficiencies of capital) are to be paid first out of profits, next out of capital, and lastly, if necessary, by the partners individually in the proportion in which they were entitled to share in the profits. The Act (B.C., s. 47; Ont., s. 44; N.S., s. 47.) also prescribes the sequence in which the liabilities of the firm must be met.

Checklist: Sequence of Payments on Dissolution

The assets of the firm must be applied in the following sequence:

(1) payment of the debts of the firm owed to non-partners
(2) repayment of loans made to the firm by partners
(3) repayment of the capital contributed by partners
(4) sharing any surplus among the partners according to their entitlement to share in profits

---

48. Under the B.C. Act, where there are three or more partners this terminates the relationship only as between the partner whose share is charged and the other partners. The relationship between the other partners remains intact (s. 36(2)).

The above provisions may be varied, though not so as to affect the rights of non-partners. It could, for example, be agreed that any loss be borne by the wealthier partner, even though he was not entitled to all of the profits. What is important to note is that deficiencies of capital are treated as a loss of the firm; this is in contrast to the situation of shareholders in a corporation, as we shall see in the next chapter.[49]

JOINT VENTURES

A **joint venture** is an agreement that two or more parties (often corporations) make to contribute a part of their respective resources (particular assets and expertise) to a specific project. Sometimes a project requires a greater capital outlay than any one corporation may be prepared to put at risk. A joint venture spreads the risk among the participants. In the oil and gas industry, large corporations have found it practical to undertake exploration expenditures jointly to discover and develop oil and gas reserves, as in the Arctic and Atlantic continental shelf explorations.

joint venture
a business venture undertaken jointly by two or more parties

Legally, a joint venture may take a variety of forms. Its simplest form is just a contractual relationship among the participants for a specific undertaking, and is sometimes referred to as a **contractual joint venture**. An alternative method is for the parties to incorporate a separate corporation (a joint subsidiary) for the venture with each participant holding shares in it. This type of arrangement is known as an **equity joint venture**, and is subject to the general rules of corporation law.

contractual joint venture
a joint venture effected by agreement without the creation of any separate legal entity

equity joint venture
a corporation formed by, and jointly owned by, the parties to a joint venture for the purpose of carrying on the venture

Participants typically regard a contractual joint venture as an extension of their own operations and a collaboration with other parties, rather than as a separate business. The venture is for a specific project or series of explorations, and of limited duration. Normally, profits are not retained jointly for investment in other projects, but are distributed to each of the participants in proportions set down in the joint-venture agreement. The parties may also try to limit their liability by providing that their only contribution will be those things specifically set out in the agreement, that the agreement shall not be construed as a partnership, and that their liability will not be joint and several. They may also try to limit the authority of members to act as agents for one another in the operation of a joint venture and may identify one of themselves (or an independent party) as the "operator" of the joint venture. Whether such an arrangement will be effective to limit the agency of each participating member remains a question of fact to be determined by the court if a dispute arises with an outside third party. Such restrictions may not be effective if it is determined that the venture was as a matter of fact a partnership.[50]

Co-venturers in a joint venture are in a fiduciary relationship with each other with respect to the purposes of the undertaking. They are much like partners with a continuing duty of utmost good faith in the conduct of the affairs of their joint enterprise.

LIMITED PARTNERSHIPS

All provinces have either a Limited Partnership Act or a set of provisions in their Partnership Act permitting the carrying on of business under certain very restricted conditions, with limited liability. These Acts came into force at about the same time that the private limited company (discussed in the next chapter) also became available for general use. Since for most business ventures, incorporating a company is a more effective way to obtain limited liability, very little use has been made of limited partnerships.

---

49. See Garner v. Murray, [1904] 1 Ch. 57, for an interpretation of this section when partners make unequal capital contributions or share losses unequally. In Ontario, s. 44 is modified in the case of an LLP.

50. Central Mortgage and Housing Corp. v. Graham (1973), 43 D.L.R. (3d) 686; Lansing Building Supply (Ontario) Ltd. v. Ierullo, *supra*, n. 7.

limited partnership
a partnership in which some of the partners limit their liability to the amount of their capital contributions

general partner
a partner in a limited partnership whose liability is not limited

limited partner
a partner in a limited partnership whose liability is limited to the amount of his or her capital contribution

The major requirement for the formation of a **limited partnership** is that there must be one or more general partners. A **general partner** has unlimited liability, while a **limited partner** has a liability limited to the amount paid by her to the limited partnership as capital. That is, she stands to lose what she has invested in the business but is not liable to contribute further.

All the Acts prohibit a limited partner from taking an active part in the management of the partnership. If she does so, she becomes liable as a general partner. The words of prohibition vary considerably in each of the statutes.[51] A limited partner would be "taking an active part" if she were personally to transact any business for the firm or be employed for that purpose as an agent or as a lawyer; but she can examine the records of the firm, inquire into its progress and advise on its management without incurring the liability of a general partner. The result is that a limited partner who attempts to take part in the management of the firm does so at a considerable personal risk. She may find herself in the dilemma that if she does not interfere, the business may fail completely; yet if she chooses to exercise some control in order to save the business, she will incur unlimited liability. For this reason more than any other, limited partnerships have been rarely used, except for tax planning purposes.

The limited partnership provisions set out more stringent regulations for registration than are demanded of ordinary partnerships. Failure to comply with requirements of detailed essential information also results in the loss of limited liability.

A limited partnership is not to be confused with an Ontario *limited liability partnership* (LLP), discussed in an earlier part of this chapter. A LLP makes no distinction between general and limited partners, and does not restrict contractual liability.

QUESTIONS FOR REVIEW

1. What laws are sole proprietorships subject to?

2. Is it necessary to have a written agreement in order to create a partnership?

3. What are the advantages and disadvantages of partnerships as opposed to sole proprietorships?

4. What are the basic elements of the partnership relationship?

5. What is the difference between sharing profits and sharing gross receipts?

6. In what circumstances may a person receive a share of the profits of a partnership business without herself being a partner?

7. Why is it important to distinguish between partnership property and the personal property of the individual partners?

8. When is it necessary for a partnership to be registered?

9. What does it mean to say "every partner is an agent of the firm"?

10. What is meant by "apparent authority"?

11. What is "joint liability"?

12. What steps should a partner take to protect herself against ongoing liability when she retires?

---

51. See, for example: Partnership Act, R.S.B.C. 1996, c. 348, s. 64; Limited Partnerships Act, R.S.O. 1990, c. L.16, s. 12; R.S.N.S. 1989, c. 259, s. 17.

13. What is a "limited liability partnership"? How does it differ from a "limited partnership"?

14. Can a partner receive a "salary" from the firm? What is the real nature of a partner's salary?

15. What are the three principal fiduciary duties imposed on partners?

16. How is partnership property distributed on the dissolution of a partnership?

17. Is there any difference between a partnership and a "joint venture"?

18. What are the principal forms that a joint venture may take?

19. What are the principal advantages and disadvantages of being a limited partner?

CASES AND PROBLEMS

1 Angus had been a partner for some years in the accounting firm of Harty & Old, and was the head of their Vancouver insolvency department. According to the terms of the partnership agreement, each partner was required to give 12 months' notice in writing to terminate the relationship. The partnership agreement also contained a provision whereby each partner undertook not to enter into any business that was in direct competition with Harty & Old for a period of five years after leaving the firm.

Unknown to his fellow partners at Harty & Old, Angus entered into negotiations with Sandersons, a rival accounting firm. He negotiated an agreement with them to join their insolvency department, and then informed Harty & Old that he was leaving them immediately.

Harty & Old commenced an action against Angus for breach of the partnership agreement, and also sued Sandersons for inducing the breach.

Ought they to succeed (a) against Angus; and (b) against Sandersons? What would be the most appropriate remedy?

2 Giovanni and Leporello were in partnership together under the registered name "Adventures Unlimited." The partnership was formed for the purpose of providing guided adventure vacations for rich clients. Under a clause in the partnership agreement it was provided that neither partner might incur expenditures on behalf of the firm in excess of $500 without the approval of the other partner.

Giovanni purported to enter into a contract—in the name of "Adventures Unlimited"—with Elvira Sails Ltd. (a corporation engaged in selling and leasing boats), to rent a large cabin cruiser for a period of three months, at a rent of $10 000 per month. He signed the rental agreement in his own name, paid a deposit for $1000 by a cheque drawn on the partnership's bank account, took delivery of the cruiser, and has not been seen since. The cruiser was reportedly last seen in the Virgin Islands.

What rights (if any) do Elvira Sails have against Leporello?

3 Crawford and McDougall were sisters of relatively advanced years. For some years they had entrusted their financial affairs to Watson, a lawyer, who was a partner in the firm of Heather & Co. Due to some disastrous investments that they made, on Watson's advice, they lost almost $250 000.

The loss was discovered when they learned that Watson had been disbarred for misconduct. It was evident that their loss had been caused either by fraud or by negligence on the part of Watson, though it was less clear which.

The sisters brought an action against Heather & Co, claiming damages for their loss.

Should they succeed? What particular circumstances might be relevant?

Albinoni, Bonporti, and Corelli were partners.

According to the partnership agreement, the following provisions applied:

a) Capital

Albinoni and Bonporti each contributed $20 000; Corelli contributed no capital.

b) Advances

Albinoni advanced $10 000 to the firm by way of loan, repayable on six months' notice or on dissolution.

c) Profits

Profits were to be shared in the following proportions:

Albinoni,	40 percent
Bonporti,	40 percent
Corelli,	20 percent

They were to contribute in the same proportions (40/40/20) to make up any loss or deficiency.

d) Drawings

The partners were entitled to draw, by way of an advance on their prospective shares of profits, up to $60 000 in any year.

Since the end of the last accounting period, the following drawings were made:

Albinoni,	$ 8000
Bonporti,	$ 7000
Corelli,	$15 000

The partnership has now been dissolved. At the time of dissolution, the total value of the firm's assets, including undrawn profits, was $100 000. (This does not include the $30 000 already drawn by the partners.)

Calculate how the surplus, or deficiency, should be shared, if the total liabilities to the firm's *external* creditors (i.e., not including debts owed to partners) is

1. $10 000

2. $90 000

3. $150 000

The Nature of a Corporation and Its Formation

This is the first of three chapters concerned with corporations. In it we discuss some of the most fundamental issues concerning the nature of the corporation and examine such questions as:

- what is a corporation?
- what are the consequences that flow from incorporation?
- what is meant by "limited liability"?
- how is a corporation formed?
- what are the usual provisions of the "corporate charter"?
- what is corporate "capital"?
- what are "shares"?
- what are the main distinctions between shares and bonds?

THE NATURE OF A CORPORATION

The corporation, or limited company, has become the dominant feature of the modern business world. Not only is it the main instrument of big business, it also rivals sole proprietorship and partnership as a means of carrying on smaller enterprises.

legal person
an entity recognized at law as having its own legal personality

A corporation is a person in the eyes of the law; that is, it is a **legal person**. A legal person is an entity[1] recognized by law as having rights and duties of its own. A distinction is commonly drawn between legal persons and natural persons. Natural persons, that is, human beings, automatically have rights and obligations; their rights and obligations may vary, according to age, mental capacity, and other factors,[2] but they are all "persons." By contrast, a legal person is entirely a "creature" of the state. A legal person has rights and duties under the law, but it cannot insist on those rights or carry out its duties except through human agents.

corporation
a legal person formed by incorporation according to a prescribed legal procedure

Although legal systems create other legal entities, for our purposes the most important one is the **corporation**. The corporation evolved from the need to look after the common interests of a group of natural persons. Whether a group can have a "personality" distinct from each of its individual members is still a matter of philosophical debate, but the legal principle is firmly established, in both common law and civil law countries, that a corporation may be created as a separate and distinct legal person apart from its members.[3]

There are numerous types of corporations: publicly owned corporations created by governments to carry on special activities (for example, the Bank of Canada, the Canadian Broadcasting Corporation, Central Mortgage and Housing Corporation, Canadian National Railway); municipal corporations to run local government; charitable corporations—the Red Cross, the Heart and Stroke Foundation, the Ford Foundation; educational institutions; and business corporations—the most numerous type of all. For the purposes of this book, we are concerned only with business corporations.

CHARACTERISTICS OF CORPORATIONS AND PARTNERSHIPS

The significance of the legal personality of a business corporation can best be understood when compared with partnership, under the subheadings below.

Liability

As we saw in Chapter 26, in a partnership each partner is normally liable for the debts of the firm to the limit of his or her personal assets. A corporation is liable for its own debts. If, as is usually the case, a shareholder has paid the full price for his shares, he can lose no more in the event that creditors seize the corporation's assets. It is for this reason—the limited liability of their *shareholders*—that business corporations are referred to as limited companies, although this is really something of a misnomer since the corporation itself is liable to the full extent of its assets.

limited liability
the liability of shareholders is limited to the amount of their capital contributions

Limited liability is widely regarded as one of the main advantages of incorporation. However, the benefits of limited liability are sometimes over-estimated since, for a small corporation to obtain credit, its directors or shareholders are often required to give personal guarantees or to pledge their own property as collateral security. In addition, as we shall see in the next two chapters, when shareholders become directors—as they often do in smaller enterprises—they are subject to a wide and increasing range of liability to other shareholders, to those doing business with the corporation, and to society as a whole.

---

1. The expression "legal entity" is also commonly used in the same sense.
2. The contractual capacity of minors and persons of unsound mind was considered in Chapter 7.
3. See Bonham and Soberman, "The Nature of Corporate Personality," in *Studies in Canadian Company Law*, Ziegel, ed. Vol. 1, Ch. 1. Toronto; Butterworth & Co., 1967.

Transfer of Ownership

A partner cannot release herself unilaterally from her liabilities—to her partners, to the firm, and to its clients—simply by retiring. She must bargain for her release with both her partners and her creditors; she may even be liable for debts contracted after her retirement, unless she has given notice to persons who habitually deal with the firm and has fulfilled the other requirements of the Partnership Act. Since a shareholder has no liability for corporate debts even while he retains his shares, creditors of the corporation have no interest and no say in what he does with his shares. The shareholder may sever all connections with the corporation simply by transferring his shares to another person. Anyone may buy the shares and is entitled to all the rights of a shareholder upon registration of the transfer at the corporation's office. However, as we shall see later in this chapter, it is usual in closely held corporations to impose special restrictions on the transfer of shares.

Management

A partnership is unsuitable for a venture involving a large number of investors. Each partner, as an agent of the firm, may enter into contracts on behalf of the firm, and as the number of partners increases, the risk of unwise contracts is correspondingly greater. By contrast, shareholders have no authority to bind their corporation to contractual obligations—only officers of the corporation may do so.

A partnership usually requires unanimity on major business decisions, a requirement that could stalemate a firm with a large number of partners. In a corporation, management is delegated to an elected board of directors that normally reaches decisions by simple majority votes. Major decisions that are referred back to the shareholders do not require unanimity, but at most a two-thirds or three-quarters majority, depending on the issue and on the requirements of the corporation law statutes in the jurisdiction.

This separation of ownership and management ranks with limited liability as a primary feature of the business corporation. These two features permit the raising of large amounts of capital: they enable an investor to invest a specific sum of money and receive a return on it, without either taking any additional risk beyond the sum invested or having to take an active part in management of business affairs. Of course, the investor may choose to take an active role in the corporation by becoming a director, or he may sell his interest if he becomes dissatisfied with the operation of the corporation; but it is primarily the possibility that he may limit his risk and is not required to take an active part in management that has made corporate investment so attractive to investors.

Although at one time the leading shareholders in a corporation were usually its managers as well, there has been an increasing separation between those who invest and those who manage.[4] The separation is, however, less pronounced in Canada than in the United States because many large Canadian corporations are still controlled by a single individual or by members of a family, or are wholly owned subsidiaries of foreign parent corporations.

Duty of Good Faith

As we saw in Chapter 26, partners owe each other a duty of good faith. Thus it would normally be a breach of duty for a partner to carry on another business independently without the consent of her other partners (especially if it were a competing business), or to enter into contracts with the firm on her own behalf. A shareholder owes no such duty to the corporation: he may

---

4. The classic study of this subject is that by Berle and Means, *The Modern Corporation and Private Property.* New York: Macmillan, 1932.

carry on any independent business himself and may trade freely with the corporation as if he were a stranger.[5]

Continuity

We have seen that in the absence of special provisions in the partnership agreement, the death or bankruptcy of a partner dissolves a partnership. Even when provisions are made in advance to continue the partnership and to buy out the share of the deceased or bankrupt partner, the procedure is often cumbersome and expensive. A corporation, by contrast, exists independently of any of its shareholders.[6] A person's shares may be transferred by gift or by sale, by creditors seizing them, by will or by statute transmitting them to the personal representative on death, yet none of these events affects the existence of the corporation. A corporation continues in existence perpetually unless it is dissolved by order of a court or by a voluntary resolution of its shareholders, or it is struck off the register for failure to comply with statutory regulations.

Checklist: Partnerships and Corporations Contrasted

	PARTNERSHIP	CORPORATION
legal personality	no	yes
personal liability of participants	yes*	no
transferability of ownership	no	yes
participation of owners in management	yes	no
continuity	no	yes
taxable entity	no	yes

*There are exceptions; see Chapter 26.

CONSEQUENCES OF SEPARATE CORPORATE PERSONALITY

Capacity

A corporation is created by the legal system and has the characteristics that the legislators give it. At one time, the legal capacity of corporations was relatively limited; they were formed for specific purposes and could act only for those purposes. Even when incorporation became more widely available, their constitutions were required to state the objects for which they were created; any act outside the scope of those objects was ***ultra vires***—beyond the powers—of the corporation. Contracts made for an unauthorized purpose were invalid, resulting in inconvenience and hardship, especially for outsiders dealing with corporations.

ultra vires
beyond the powers

The *ultra vires* doctrine, as it applied to corporations, has now been abolished throughout Canada. Under the federal Canada Business Corporations Act,[7] and most of the provincial statutes under which business corporations are formed, a corporation has the capacity and all the rights, powers, and privileges of a natural person (section 15).

---

5. As we shall see in Chapter 28, *directors* owe a duty of good faith to their corporation.

6. It survives even the death of all its shareholders: Re Noel Tedman Holdings Pty. Ltd., [1967] Qd. R. 561 (Queensland S. C.).

7. R.S.C. 1985, c. C-44, referred to hereafter as the CBCA.

As an artificial person, a corporation can, of course, act only through its human agents—its directors and officers. Thus, when a corporation purports to make a contract it is always necessary to determine whether its agent had authority; the law of agency has been considered in Chapter 19, and we shall return to it in Chapter 29, when we examine the question of the liability of corporations.

Separate Existence

Salomon's Case

As we noted in the previous section, a corporation is a legal entity distinct from its shareholders. The classic case on the existence of the corporation as a separate entity came before the House of Lords in 1897 in *Salomon v. Salomon & Co. Ltd.*[8] It is probably the most widely quoted decision in the whole of corporate law.

CASE 27.1

Salomon had carried on a successful business as a shoe manufacturer for many years. In 1892 he formed a corporation in which he held almost all the shares (20 001 out of 20 007—the remaining six shares being held by members of his family, in order to meet what was then the statutory requirement of seven shareholders) and sold his business to the corporation. Soon afterwards a downturn in the shoe industry, caused by loss of government contracts and a series of strikes, drove the corporation into insolvency and a trustee was appointed to wind it up. The trustee claimed that the corporation was merely a sham, that Salomon was the true owner of the business and the true debtor—and as such he should pay off all debts owed by the corporation. The lower courts supported the trustee's position, but the House of Lords decided in favour of Salomon. The Lords said that either the corporation was a true legal entity or it was not. Since there was no fraud nor any intention to deceive, all transactions having been fully disclosed to the parties and the statutory regulations complied with, the corporation was duly created and was solely responsible for its own debts.

The decision in the *Salomon* case was important because it recognized the separate legal personality of the so-called "one-man company" at the time when it was becoming a common form of doing business.[9] Some writers believed that the court had gone too far in giving independent existence to the corporation. Nevertheless, as a leading writer on the subject has said, "Since the *Salomon* case, the complete separation of the company and its members has never been doubted."[10]

Implications of Salomon's Case

For the most part, the principle of separate legal personality has worked well in the commercial world, but some later cases have carried the logic of Salomon's case to extreme lengths, producing what appear to be unfair results. For example, it has been held that the owner of a business who transferred all its assets to a corporation of which he was the sole owner, but who neglected to transfer the benefit of the fire insurance policy on the assets as well, could recover nothing when those assets were destroyed by fire.[11] The assets were owned by the corporation, and a shareholder has no direct ownership in these assets but only in the corporation itself, and

---

8. [1897] A.C. 22.

9. The CBCA, s. 5, now allows a corporation to be formed with only one shareholder, as do the laws of almost all provinces.

10. Davies, *Gower's Principles of Modern Company Law* (6th ed.), pp. 79–80. London: Sweet & Maxwell Ltd., 1997.

11. Macaura v. Northern Assurance Co., [1925] A.C. 619.

therefore (it was reasoned) has no insurable interest in the assets. This decision was followed for a number of years by Canadian courts, but in 1987 was rejected by the Supreme Court of Canada in the *Kosmopoulos* case. The court accepted that a shareholder, even one who owns all the shares of a corporation, does not own its assets, but rejected the contention that he has no insurable interest in those assets. If they are destroyed, his shares will diminish in value; consequently, he should be entitled to insure against their destruction.[12]

It remains unclear how far the principle in the *Kosmopoulos* case can be taken and whether it is restricted to insurance claims. Certainly, it does not seem to follow that, where an injury is done to a corporation, a shareholder will always have a claim for the consequent reduction in the value of his or her shares. As the Ontario Court of Appeal ruled in a recent case, the fact that the plaintiff was the principal shareholder and directing mind of corporations that were defrauded did not entitle him to personal compensation for the losses suffered by the corporations. To hold otherwise would enable him to jump in front of the queue to the prejudice of other corporate creditors. Where a wrong is done to a corporation, a shareholder has no claim for damages in respect of that wrong.[13]

CASE 27.2

An oil exploration company had formed two subsidiaries, apparently to take advantage of government financing. One subsidiary owned a drilling rig, the other contracted to provide drilling services. The rig was damaged due to the alleged negligence of the defendant. The defendant was *prima facie* liable to the corporation that owned the rig, but not for the economic loss sustained by the service corporation; the two corporations were separate entities and the loss to the service corporation was too remote.[14]

In other cases, the hardship is suffered not by the owners of the corporation but by the persons who deal with it.

CASE 27.3

K, a Toronto lawyer, had incorporated a real estate company, Rockwell, of which he effectively owned almost all the shares. Rockwell became involved in a contractual dispute with another corporation, Newtonbrook, and eventually brought an action against Newtonbrook for specific performance of the contract. Rockwell lost the action and Newtonbrook was awarded costs of $4800. When Newtonbrook sought to recover the costs, it found that Rockwell's entire assets consisted of $31.85 in its bank account.

Newtonbrook's attempt to recover from *K* personally failed.[15]

12. Kosmopoulos v. Constitution Insurance Co. of Canada (1987), 34 D.L.R. (4th) 208. The concept of insurable interest is discussed in Chapter 18.

13. Martin v. Goldfarb (1998), 163 D.L.R. (4th) 639.

14. Bow Valley Husky (Bermuda) Ltd. v. Saint John Shipbuilding Ltd. (1997), 153 D.L.R. (4th) 1. The question of recovery for economic loss was considered in Chapter 3.

15. Rockwell Developments Ltd. v. Newtonbrook Plaza Ltd. (1972), 27 D.L.R. (3d) 651.

Limitations on the Principle of Separate Corporate Existence

When application of the *Salomon* decision leads to unfair results, should the courts refuse to follow it? Should legislation disregard the principle of separate legal identity?

Exceptions to Limited Liability

The limited liability of shareholders is not absolute. We have already noted that, in practice, shareholders of small private companies are often required to provide security or personal guarantees for loans made to their corporations. The Canada Business Corporations Act (CBCA) provides a further exception to the principle: where shareholders have received an improper distribution of corporate assets, for example, where a dividend has been paid although the corporation had made no profits, they are liable for the corporation's debts to that extent (section 45).[16] Other statutes, such as the federal Bankruptcy and Insolvency Act,[17] require shareholders who have received property from a corporation before it became insolvent to repay the amounts received in certain circumstances.

It is also important to note that the principle of limited liability does not protect the owners of corporations from *personal* liability. For example, a director who drives dangerously and causes an accident while on company business is not absolved from liability in tort, even though the corporation may also be vicariously liable.[18] And directors who make negligent misrepresentations regarding the affairs of their corporation may be personally liable for any resulting loss.[19]

Other Statutory Provisions

There are numerous examples, especially in taxation and labour law, where statutes require the separate personality of corporations to be disregarded. For example, Canadian-controlled private corporations are taxed at a lower rate on the first $200 000 of their annual income; but it is not possible to multiply this concession by forming several distinct corporations, because **associated corporations** are only entitled to a single concession between them.[20] Again, employers are not allowed to avoid statutory employment standards by transferring their assets to an associated corporation, thereby leaving the employer unable to meet employee claims for unpaid wages, vacation pay and other benefits.[21]

associated corporations
corporations that are related either (a) vertically, as where one corporation controls the other, or (b) horizontally, as where both corporations are controlled by the same person

Lifting the Corporate Veil

There have also been cases—although in Canada they have been very rare—where the courts have been prepared to disregard the separate existence of corporations and "lift the veil" of

---

16. There are also several provisions that make *directors* liable for the debts of their corporation; these are considered in Chapter 29.

17. R.S.C. 1985, c. B-3. See Chapter 31.

18. See Berger v. Willowdale (1983), 41 O.R. (2d) 90. The situation is not entirely clear. It seems that where directors commit a tort or offence in the course of performing their duties, without being *personally* at fault, they are not liable; see Montreal Trust Co. v. Scotia McLeod (1994), 15 B.L.R. (2d) 160. But the fact that they are acting in the corporation's interest does not by itself protect them from personal liability; see ADGA Systems International Ltd. v. Valcom Ltd. (1999), 43 O.R. (3d) 101.

19. NBD Bank of Canada v. Dofasco Inc. (1997), 34 B.L.R.(2d) 209; contrast Scotia McLeod Inc. v. People's Jewellers Ltd. (1995), 26 O.R. (3d) 481.

20. Income Tax Act, R.S.C. 1985, c. 1 (5th Supp.), s. 125. Corporations are associated where one corporation controls the other (parent–subsidiary relationship), or where both corporations are controlled by the same person or group of persons (affiliates).

21. See, for example, Employment Standards Act, R.S.O. 1990, c. E.14, which defines "employer" to include any associated corporation.

incorporation to see what lies beyond it. It seems that, in order to identify an individual with a corporation, three conditions must be met:

- The individual must control the corporation.
- That control must have been exercised to commit a fraud, a wrong, or a breach of duty.
- The misconduct must be the cause of the plaintiff's injury.[22]

Rather than equate a controlling shareholder with the corporation that he controls, Canadian courts have generally preferred to seek other routes to secure a just result. Thus, as we saw in the *Kosmopoulos* case,[23] the Supreme Court of Canada refused to lift the veil and to hold that the corporation and the individual who owned all of its shares were one and the same person, but reached the same result by finding that he had an insurable interest in the corporation's property.

CONTEMPORARY ISSUE

Lifting the Corporate Veil

As details emerged following the historic filing for bankruptcy protection by the T. Eaton Company, news stories examined various aspects of Eaton's financial situation. This is the headline from one such story:

Credit card operation no sinkhole for Eaton's:
Unit saw a $55-million profit, but is out of creditor's grasp

The report goes on to point out that, while the main Eaton's company apparently owes more than $300 million to suppliers and lenders, the profits of its credit card division is not, in law, available to meet those claims. The credit card division is operated by a separate corporation.

Source: *The Globe and Mail*, March 9, 1997, p. B1.

Questions to Consider

1. Should the "corporate veil" be lifted in such circumstances?
2. Should parent companies be liable for the debts of their subsidiaries and vice-versa?

METHODS OF INCORPORATION

Early Methods of Incorporation

royal charter

a special licence given by the Crown to form a corporation for the purpose of carrying on a particular activity

The oldest method of incorporation in the common law system—dating back to the 16th century—is by **royal charter** granted by the sovereign. Until the 19th century, all corporations were created by charter, some of which are still in existence—the best known to Canadians being the Hudson's Bay Company founded in 1670. A few royal charters are still issued today to universities, learned societies, and charitable institutions, but none to business corporations.

---

22. W.D. Latimer Co. Ltd. v. Dijon Investments Ltd. (1992), 12 O.R. (3d) 415.

23. *Supra*, n. 12.

From the end of the 18th century, corporations began to be created by **special Acts of Parliament**, especially for large projects of public interest—railroads, canals, waterworks, and other public utilities. Today, special acts are still used to create such corporations as Bell Canada and Canadian Pacific, and also to create special government corporations like Central Mortgage and Housing Corporation, the Canadian Broadcasting Corporation, and Air Canada. Parliament and the provincial legislatures have also passed statutes setting out procedures for the incorporation of particular types of businesses, such as banks and trust and loan companies. Such businesses may be incorporated only under these acts.

special Act of Parliament
a legislative act creating a particular corporation

Incorporation Statutes

Today, however, almost all business corporations are incorporated under the provisions of a statute of general application. Under a statute of this type any group of persons who comply with its requirements may form a corporation. In Canada we have had a unique development in that different types of general acts have evolved and the system varies from one province to another.

The Memorandum and Letters Patent Systems

In 1862, a new system was introduced in England that depended on Parliament rather than on the royal prerogative, and this system was adopted by five provinces; it now remains in force in only two—British Columbia and Nova Scotia. The system requires applicants to register a document that sets out the fundamental terms of their agreement, called a **memorandum of association**. If the memorandum and certain other prescribed documents comply with the statute and the registration fee is paid, the authorized government office issues a **certificate of incorporation** and the corporation comes into existence. We shall call corporations incorporated in this manner "memorandum corporations."

memorandum of association
a document setting out the essential terms of an agreement to form a corporation

certificate of incorporation
a certificate that a corporation has come into existence

Originally the other five provinces and the federal government employed a different system under their general acts, but the system remains in force only in Quebec and Prince Edward Island. There the incorporating document is called the **letters patent**, an offspring of the royal charter, but issued under the authority of the Crown's representative in each jurisdiction. Under the letters patent system, a general statute regulates the conditions under which the letters patent may be issued. Although in theory the granting of letters patent is discretionary, in practice, the steps taken by applicants do not differ greatly from those for registering a memorandum under the English system. Since the great majority of corporations operating in Canada were at one time incorporated by letters patent under either federal, Ontario, or Quebec acts, and since their business operations and the sale of their securities extend throughout the country, one still encounters these corporations frequently in all parts of Canada.

letters patent
a document incorporating a corporation, issued by the appropriate authority, and constituting the "charter" of the corporation

The Articles of Incorporation System

In 1970, Ontario passed a substantially different Business Corporations Act, creating a new method of incorporation adapted from a system in use in the United States. In 1975, the federal Parliament adopted the same system in its new statute, although many of the provisions of the federal act were quite different from those of the Ontario version. The CBCA has become the model for the new system: Manitoba, Saskatchewan, New Brunswick, Alberta, Ontario, and Newfoundland have followed with acts based on the federal scheme, although with local variations. Under the articles of incorporation system, persons who wish to form a corporation sign and deliver **articles of incorporation** to a government office and in turn are issued with a certificate of incorporation.

articles of incorporation
the basic constitutional document of corporations incorporated in most Canadian jurisdictions

The system combines features of both the memorandum and letters patent systems. Unfortunately, the terminology chosen is unnecessarily confusing in the Canadian business and legal context; the new statutes have adopted terms used in various parts of the United States, in particular the word "articles," which has a different meaning in those Canadian provinces still using the memorandum system, as well as in Britain and most Commonwealth countries.

As the articles of incorporation system is now the widely used one in Canada, our discussion will focus on it. However, we must keep in mind the three different methods of incorporation; wherever the differences have important consequences we shall point them out.

Checklist: Methods of Incorporation

MEMORANDUM	LETTERS PATENT	ARTICLES OF INCORPORATION
British Columbia	Prince Edward Island	Canada
Nova Scotia	Quebec	Alberta
		Manitoba
		New Brunswick
		Newfoundland
		Ontario
		Saskatchewan

The Choice of Jurisdiction

The first decision to be made in forming a corporation is whether to incorporate federally or provincially. The CBCA is especially suitable for large businesses that carry on their activities nationwide; but even a small, local, one-person business may incorporate under it.[24]

The activities of a business incorporated under provincial jurisdiction are not restricted to that province; it may carry on business anywhere inside or outside Canada. However, corporations *not* incorporated within a province—and this includes federally incorporated corporations as well as those incorporated in other provinces—must comply with certain registration requirements in order to carry on business there.[25] A corporation is, of course, subject to the general laws of any province in which it carries on business, as well as federal regulations, as discussed in Chapter 29. Nevertheless, the act under which it was incorporated governs its *internal* operating rules for holding shareholder meetings, electing directors, declaring dividends, and other matters to be examined in Chapter 28.

THE CONSTITUTION OF A CORPORATION

Articles of Incorporation

Almost all commercial corporations are incorporated under a general act and, as we have seen, most are now incorporated under the articles of incorporation system. The articles of incorporation are often referred to as the "charter" of the corporation; they set out essential information about the corporation. The precise requirements for such essentials vary from one province to another. In those provinces that have not adopted the articles of incorporation system, the corresponding "charter" document is the letters patent or the memorandum of association.

---

24. The incorporation fee under the CBCA ($500) is a little higher than that under most provincial statutes; the corresponding Ontario fee is $315.

25. See, for example, the Ontario Extra-Provincial Corporations Act, R.S.O. 1990, c. E.27. The formalities that must be complied with vary to some extent according to whether the corporation is incorporated federally, elsewhere in Canada, or abroad; for example, only non-Canadian corporations require a licence to do business in Ontario. The Corporations Information Act, R.S.O. 1990, c. C.39, requires registration of certain information, for example, place of registered office, names of directors, place within the province where notice may be served.

Checklist: Contents of the Articles of Incorporation

- name of the corporation
- place where the registered office is situated
- classes and any maximum number of shares that the corporation is authorized to issue
- if there are two or more classes of shares, the rights and restrictions attached to each class
- any restriction on the transfer of shares
- number of directors
- any restrictions on the business that may be carried on
- other provisions that the incorporators choose to include

Occasionally, to suit the special requirements of a closely held corporation, matters not usually found in a charter will be placed there; this may be done in order to give certain "entrenched" rights to minority shareholders. Normally, the charter can only be altered by a special resolution, requiring the approval of a two-thirds majority of the shareholders,[26] and the filing of the amended charter. In most circumstances, however, the charter is an unsuitable instrument for reflecting special arrangements among the shareholders. Instead, shareholders enter into a separate shareholders' agreement outside the corporate constitution, setting out how they will exercise their powers. This topic will be discussed further in the following chapter.

By-laws

Nature of By-laws

Incorporators generally keep the incorporating documents as short as possible to gain flexibility in the operation of the corporation. The corporation still needs detailed operating rules for its day-to-day affairs; under both the articles of incorporation and letters patent systems these operating rules are called *by-laws*, but for a memorandum corporation they are called *articles of association*. We shall refer to them as **by-laws**, since what we say about by-laws generally applies to the articles of association, but with this important exception: all articles of association are specially entrenched and cannot be amended except by a special resolution.[27] By-laws are more flexible, requiring confirmation by only a simple majority of shareholders, although corporations acts do specify some matters that must be dealt with by special resolution requiring an increased majority.

by-laws
the internal working rules of a corporation

Another difference is that, under the memorandum system, both the memorandum and articles of association must be registered and they form part of the corporate constitution; under the other two systems it is not strictly necessary to have by-laws at all. Of course, it is normal and convenient to have them and they may be amended, or new by-laws may be adopted, as and when required, with a minimum of formality. Usually, the directors amend by-laws or adopt new ones, but the new or amended by-laws need confirmation at the next general meeting of shareholders to remain valid. Under the articles of incorporation system, shareholders themselves have the power to propose and adopt by-laws.

---

26. The procedures for altering letters patent or a memorandum tend to be more cumbersome than those under the newer articles of incorporation system.

27. In the memorandum system, a special resolution requires a three-quarters majority.

Content

By-laws fall into two main categories. The first category provides general operating rules for the business of a corporation that are usually passed at the first meeting of the shareholders. The first by-laws are often quite long and elaborate, dealing with such matters as the election of directors; their term of office; the place and required notice for meetings of directors; the quorum necessary (that is, the minimum number who must be present) before a meeting of directors can act on behalf of the corporation; the categories of executive officers; provisions for the allotment of shares and for the declaration of dividends; and procedures for holding the annual general meeting and other meetings of shareholders.

Checklist: Provisions Included in Typical By-laws

- The qualification of a director shall be the holding of at least one share in the capital stock of the corporation.
- A director shall hold office until the third annual general meeting following his appointment.
- Notice of a meeting of directors shall be given in writing to each director not less than seven days before the meeting.
- Three directors shall constitute a quorum for the transaction of any business, except as otherwise provided in these by-laws.
- Questions arising at any meeting of directors shall, except as herein provided, be decided by a majority of votes: in the event of an equality of votes, the Chair of the meeting shall have a second or casting vote.
- Any contract entered into by the corporation that involves the expenditure, or the incurring of a liability, in excess of $10 000 must be approved by a majority of all the directors.
- Written notice of not less than 28 days, in the case of an annual general meeting, and 21 days, in the case of other shareholder meetings, shall be given to all shareholders entitled to vote at the meeting.
- A quorum is present at a general meeting of shareholders if not less than 10 shareholders, together holding a majority of the shares entitled to vote at the meeting, are present in person or by proxy.
- Shares in the corporation shall be allotted by resolution of the board of directors, approved by not less than two-thirds of all directors, on such terms, for such consideration, and to such persons as the directors determine.
- The directors may at any time by resolution, approved by not less than two-thirds of all directors, declare a dividend, or an interim dividend, and pay the same out of the funds of the corporation available for that purpose.

Authorization to Directors

Before the introduction of the articles of incorporation system, by-laws were used to give the directors express authority from the shareholders to carry out transactions that require shareholder approval, according to statute or the corporation's own constitution. The particular matters requiring this type of approval vary from province to province, but most statutes now do not make it necessary (unless the corporation's own constitution so requires) for a by-law to be passed in order to confer any particular power on the directors.[28] Certain matters, such as the sale of substantially all of a corporation's property or the amalgamation with another corporation are required to be approved by special resolution of the shareholders, and although directors now normally have the power to borrow money on the security of the corporation's assets without special authorization, it is common for them to ask the shareholders to confirm a major loan transaction, because creditors may insist upon such confirmation. Shareholder resolutions of this type are still sometimes referred to as "by-laws."

WIDELY HELD AND CLOSELY HELD CORPORATIONS

Public and Private Corporations

When the first general statutes permitting incorporation of business enterprises were passed in England and Canada in the mid-19th century, the legislators believed limited companies would be used primarily for large undertakings having many shareholders. These acts required at least seven incorporators who signed the original application to establish the corporation. Following a number of fraudulent schemes, it became evident that investors in publicly held corporations needed to be protected, and various statutory requirements were enacted to ensure the disclosure and publication of a corporation's financial position, both in soliciting prospective investors and in reporting to shareholders.

By the end of the 19th century it had become evident that incorporation was also a useful and fully effective tool for family businesses. Since these small corporations did not seek investment from the general public, the disclosure and publication requirements were unnecessary, as also was the requirement to have at least seven shareholders; the latter was merely a technical requirement that could be satisfied by giving one share each to six employees or relatives while the true controlling shareholder held all the remaining shares—as in *Salomon's Case*.

These facts were recognized in 1908 when the British Parliament enacted provisions to permit the formation of **private companies**, which were not permitted to offer shares to the public and in which the right to transfer shares had to be restricted in some manner. Those provisions found their way into Canadian incorporation statutes, but now exist only in Prince Edward Island and Nova Scotia. The CBCA and other provincial statutes now permit even a single shareholder to form a corporation, and do not maintain a formal distinction between public and private corporations. Instead, a more realistic distinction is made between those corporations that issue their shares to the general public and those that do not; the two types of corporation are commonly referred to, respectively, as "widely held" and "closely held."

private company
a corporation with a restricted number of shareholders prohibited from issuing its shares to the general public

Widely Held Corporations

Incorporation statutes, such as the CBCA, apply to both widely and closely held corporations but draw a number of distinctions between them with respect to such matters as proxy solicitation, the number of directors, and the need for an audit committee. These requirements are considered further in Chapter 28. But the most important difference is that widely held corporations are subject also to regulation under the relevant securities acts in those provinces in which their securities are issued or traded: this topic is considered in Chapter 29.

---

28. See CBCA, s. 16(1).

Closely Held Corporations

As suggested, the main use of the closely held corporation is to incorporate small- and medium-sized business enterprises where the number of participants is small. Closely held corporations have often been described as "incorporated partnerships." Although the description is sometimes apt, we must not be misled by it: a closely held corporation is a true limited company with the same legal significance and corporate independence as the widely held corporation. In fact, when a large corporation creates a subsidiary, it usually does so by incorporating a closely held corporation. Many large U.S. and other foreign corporations operate wholly owned subsidiaries in Canada that are closely held: all the shares are held by the parent corporation, except for a few that may be held here by corporate officers. A number of these subsidiaries rival our own large public corporations in size.

The vast majority of corporations are closely held—over 90 percent in Canada. It may therefore seem surprising that they are largely neglected as a subject of study in business administration. The literature of economics, finance, accounting, and management directs its attention to widely held corporations in the securities market and the related need for financial disclosure. Until recently, at least, closely held corporations have been permitted the luxury of operating in an atmosphere of relative privacy. In a closely held corporation, the owners are usually the managers as well, thus focusing questions of management and ultimate decision making within a small group. We shall examine the legal implications of this characteristic of closely held corporations in the next chapter.

CORPORATE CAPITAL

Equity and Debt

There are two principal ways in which a corporation can raise funds: by issuing shares (equity), or by borrowing (debt). A third method—financing the corporation's activities out of retained profits—is really akin to the first, since the shareholders are effectively reinvesting part of their profit. Although borrowing increases the funds that are at the disposal of the corporation's management, it is really erroneous to speak of "debt capital," since borrowing increases both assets and liabilities. Thus, a corporation's true capital is its "equity capital" or "share capital."

Share Capital

authorized capital
the maximum number (or value) of shares that a corporation is permitted by its charter to issue

issued capital
the shares that have been issued by a corporation

paid-up capital
the shares that have been issued and fully paid for

stated capital account
the amount received by a corporation for the issue of its shares

share
a member's proportionate interest in the capital of a corporation

Every business corporation must have a share capital.[29] The word "capital" has different meanings in different contexts. In letters patent and memorandum jurisdictions, when a corporation is incorporated, its charter places an upper limit on the number or money value of shares it may issue. This limit is called the **authorized capital**. A corporation need not issue all its authorized share capital. The **issued capital** and **paid-up capital** of a corporation are, as their names indicate, the parts of the authorized capital that have been issued and that have been paid for.

In articles of incorporation jurisdictions, by contrast, a corporation may state the maximum number of shares that can be issued if it so wishes, or it can simply leave matters open-ended. A corporation must, however, still keep a **stated capital account** disclosing the consideration received for each **share** issued. Shares must be fully paid for at the time of issue;[30] consequently there is no difference between issued capital and paid-up capital.

The issued capital of a corporation is the result of a series of contracts—contracts of subscription—between the corporation and its shareholders. We should bear in mind that there are several ways of becoming a shareholder: by being one of the original applicants for incorpora-

---

29. Charitable and non-profit corporations need not have a share capital.

30. CBCA, s. 25(3). Previously, shares could be issued "partly paid," with the corporation being able to make a subsequent "call" for the remainder of the price. In British Columbia this is still possible with certain types of shares.

tion; by buying additional shares issued by a corporation subsequent to its incorporation; or by acquiring (by purchase or gift) shares that have already been issued to another shareholder. The first two ways result from contracts between the shareholder and the corporation; the transactions increase the issued capital as shown in the accounts of the corporation. The third way is the result of a transfer to which the corporation is not a party at all; such a transfer does not affect its accounts.

Par Value

Until the early part of the 20th century, all shares had a nominal or **par value**, that is, a fixed value placed upon them like a bank note or a bond. Usually, these shares were in large denominations such as $100, $500, or $1000 and were issued by the corporation at their par value. Within a short time after issue, however, a share rarely had a market price identical with its par value. If the corporation was successful its shares would increase in value and command a "premium" price on the market; if it had suffered losses or was a poor earner, its shares might fall below their par value. Thus par value provided little or no indication of the real value of shares.

par value
a nominal value attached to a share at the time of issue

    Par value also created a hardship. A corporation was prohibited from issuing its shares for less than their par value (i.e., at a "discount"). If a corporation's shares were selling on the market at below their par value and the corporation required additional capital, investors would not purchase a new issue at par. In order to make an issue, the corporation would be compelled to reduce the par value of the shares to a more realistic figure and to reduce its capital accordingly by obtaining an amendment to its charter, causing delay and expense.

    In the United States, the idea evolved of issuing **no par value shares**, that is, shares that represent a specific proportion of the issued capital of the corporation, rather than a fixed sum of money. The advantages of no par value shares, in particular the fact that they may be issued from time to time at prices that correspond to their current market value, resulted in their adoption by all the jurisdictions in the United States and soon afterwards they were permitted in Canada. The articles of incorporation system has now abolished par value shares entirely.

no par value share
a share that has no nominal value attached to it

ILLUSTRATION 27.1

Pliable Plastics Inc. is incorporated under the articles of incorporation system. Its articles contain no restriction on the total number of shares that may be issued and its shares have no par value. Initially, it issued 50 000 shares at $100 each, giving it a stated capital of $5 000 000. The directors wish to raise a further $3 000 000.

If the current market price of the shares has fallen to $60, they can raise $3 000 000 by issuing 50 000 new shares at that price. On the other hand if the market price has risen to $120, they will need to issue only 25 000.

Until the introduction of the articles of incorporation system, **preferred shares** were almost always issued with a par value. They paid a preferred dividend expressed as a percentage of the par value and the corporation could redeem them at par value: for example, a share had a par value of $100 (and was redeemable at that price) and paid a dividend of 8 percent (i.e., $8 per share). With the abolition of par values, preferred shares are now stated to have a redemption price ($100), with a preferred dividend expressed simply as a sum of money ($8).

preferred share
a share carrying preferential rights to receive a dividend and/or to be redeemed on the dissolution of the corporation

CORPORATE SECURITIES

The Distinction Between Shares and Bonds

A corporation may borrow money in a number of ways, but when it borrows substantial sums on a long-term basis it normally does so by issuing **bonds**. The classic distinction between

bond
a document evidencing a debt owed by a corporation

shares and bonds (or "debentures," as they are sometimes called) is that the holder of a share is a member of, and owner of an interest in, the corporation; a holder of a bond is a creditor. In the business world, there is no such clear-cut distinction. In the language of modern business the true *equity* owner of a corporation, and the person who takes the greatest risk, is the holder of **common shares.** From this end of the scale, we proceed by degrees to the person who is a mortgagee or bondholder, where the holder takes the least risk. In between we may have the holders of preferred shares. Today, most larger corporations have, in addition to an issue of common shares, one or more classes of bonds or debentures and probably also a class of preferred shares.

common share
a share carrying no preferential right

When deciding whether to invest in the shares or the bonds of a corporation, an individual usually does not make a conscious choice between becoming a member (i.e., an equity owner) and becoming a creditor. She regards herself in both instances as an investor. Her investment decisions are determined primarily by economic considerations. Bonds provide a fixed and guaranteed return (provided the corporation remains solvent), in the form of regular interest payments, and the right to be redeemed in full at their maturity date. Common shares carry no guarantee that their holders will receive anything, either in the form of dividends or on dissolution; but their holders participate in any "growth" of the corporation. Preferred shareholders come somewhere in between; they are entitled to receive dividends and to have their shares be redeemed on the dissolution of the corporation, before payments are made to the holders of the common shares, but those rights are often restricted to a fixed dividend and a fixed amount payable on redemption.

The line between shareholder and bondholder is nonetheless a distinct and important one in its legal consequences for a corporation. First of all, since bondholders are creditors, interest paid to them is a debt of the corporation. It must be paid whether the corporation has earned profits for the year or not. Shareholders are not creditors and receive dividends only when the directors declare them. One consequence, especially important for taxation, is that interest payments are normally an expense of doing business and are deducted before taxable income is calculated; dividends, on the other hand, are payable out of after-tax profits. Second, bonds are usually secured by a mortgage or charge on the property of the corporation (see the discussion in Chapter 30 under "Floating Charges"). If a corporation becomes insolvent, its bondholders are entitled to be repaid not only before the shareholders but also before the general creditors: they are secured creditors, and the trustee acting for them can sell the corporation's assets to satisfy the debt owed to them.

Rights and Privileges of Security Holders

Bondholders

Bondholders do not normally have a direct voice in the management of the corporation unless it is in breach of the terms of the trust deed or indenture under which the securities were created. Only when a corporation gets into financial difficulty or is in breach of the trust deed may the trustee, acting on behalf of the bondholders, step in and take part in management. It is true, however, that bondholders do exert an indirect form of control over management in the restrictive clauses commonly written into bond indentures, which may place a ceiling on the further long-term borrowing of the corporation, on the amount of dividends it may pay, and even, in smaller corporations, on the salaries it pays to its officers.

Common Shareholders

By contrast, common shareholders have, in theory at least, a strong voice in the management of the corporation. As we shall see in the next chapter, it is they who elect the board of directors, and who must approve major changes in the corporation's activities. Otherwise, however, their rights are limited: they have no entitlement to a dividend and can receive one only after bondholders and preferred shareholders have been paid; and, on the liquidation of the corporation, their entitlement is to share what is left after the claims of creditors and preferred shareholders have been satisfied.

Preferred Shareholders

Preferred shareholders are in an intermediate category. Usually, they are entitled to be paid a fixed dividend before any dividend is paid to the common shareholders, and they are entitled to be paid the fixed redemption price of their shares on liquidation of the corporation before any surplus is distributed to the common shareholders. Frequently, they have no right to vote unless the payment of dividends to them is in arrears. In this respect they are more like creditors than investors. However, payment of preferred dividends is not a contractual commitment of a corporation as is bond interest; a preferred shareholder must enforce her rights as an individual and is not dependent upon a trustee taking action, as a bondholder normally is.

Class Rights

Where a corporation issues more than one class of shares—for example, common shares and preferred shares—the precise rights of each class must be set out in its constitution.[31] The various combinations of rights and privileges that may attach to a class of shares are extensive and may relate not only to dividend rights and rights of redemption, but also to voting rights, rights to appoint directors, and sometimes to the right to convert a security of one class into a security of another class.

Problems of interpretation arise in the drafting of rights for various classes of shareholders just as they do in the drafting of statutes, contracts, and wills. Two questions with respect to preferred shareholders' rights to dividends are particularly important. The first is whether the rights are **cumulative**: if the full preferred dividend is not paid in one year, do the arrears accumulate so that they must be paid in a subsequent year or on winding up the corporation, before the common shareholders are entitled to anything? The second is whether on winding up, their rights are **participating**: if after the preferred shareholders have been fully paid, do they still participate in any remaining surplus along with the common shareholders? This uncertainty makes it all the more important to draft class rights with the greatest care.

cumulative right
the right of the holder of a preferred share to be paid arrears from previous years before any dividend is paid on the common shares

participating right
the right of a holder of a preferred share to participate in surplus profits or assets of the corporation in addition to the amount of the preferred dividend or redemption price

Checklist: Priority of Payment on Liquidation of a Corporation

On liquidation of a corporation its assets must be distributed in the following sequence. (Note that bondholders are creditors—and usually they are secured creditors.)

1. secured creditors
2. unsecured creditors
3. preferred shareholders
4. common shareholders

THE TRANSFER OF CORPORATE SECURITIES

Negotiability

We have seen in Chapter 12 that share and bond certificates are a type of personal property subject to different rules of transfer and ownership from those that apply to sales of goods. We noted further in Chapter 21 that these choses in action may in some circumstances be treated as negotiable instruments. Thus, bond certificates in bearer form may be considered as a type of

---

31. See CBCA, s. 6(1)(c).

negotiable instrument at common law. Articles of incorporation statutes expressly treat share certificates in bearer form as a type of negotiable instrument.

In theory, if bonds and shares are to serve the purposes of a capital market they should be readily transferable (that is, "liquid") and this purpose is promoted when the risks of owning them are minimal. When bonds and shares are treated as negotiable instruments, an innocent holder for value may often acquire a better title than his predecessor had, as, for example, when he purchases bonds or share certificates that have been stolen. However, two unfortunate results have also flowed from this development: first, there has been an increased temptation to indulge in theft as it is easy to sell stolen certificates; second, it has become easier to pass off forged (and therefore worthless) certificates on purchasers. The innocent holder of a forged negotiable instrument, as we have seen, obtains no title.

Restrictions on Share Transfer

In a widely held corporation, shares are almost always freely transferable; if they are not, the shares will not be accepted for listing on a stock exchange. In contrast, closely held corporations almost invariably restrict the transfer of shares, for otherwise it would be difficult for them to remain closely held.

Restrictions on share transfer are required to be set out in the corporation's constitution,[32] and can take almost any form. In practice, the most common restriction is to require the consent of the board of directors to any transfer, but there are other varieties, such as giving the right of first refusal to existing shareholders or directors before a shareholder can sell to an outsider, or giving a major shareholder the right of veto. Requiring the consent of directors gives them the discretion to approve or reject a proposed member of the corporation, much as partners determine whether they will admit a new partner.

QUESTIONS FOR REVIEW

1. What is meant by a "legal person"?

2. What is meant by "limited liability"? Whose liability is limited?

3. What are the principal differences between partnerships and corporations?

4. What were the principal arguments made by the creditors in *Salomon's Case* in attempting to make Salomon personally liable?

5. In what ways may two or more corporations be said to be "associated"?

6. What is meant by "lifting the corporate veil"?

7. How does the articles of incorporation system of forming a corporation differ from (a) the letters patent system and (b) the memorandum and articles system?

8. What information *must* be set out in articles of incorporation?

9. What is the main function of a corporation's by-laws?

10. What are the principal characteristics of closely held corporations?

---

32. See, for example, CBCA, s. 6(1)(d).

11. What is the function of a corporation's stated capital account?

12. In what way are par values for shares likely to be misleading?

13. What special rights are normally carried by preferred shares?

14. What are the usual rights of bondholders?

15. What factors influence an investor's choice between shares and bonds?

16. In what sequence should a corporation's assets be distributed on liquidation of the corporation?

CASES AND PROBLEMS

1 Oakdale Motors Inc. is a corporation, incorporated under the Canada Business Corporations Act, engaged in the selling, repairing, and servicing of automobiles. All of its shares are owned by Faulkner, who is also the sole director. Faulkner acts as the general manager of the corporation and supervises its day-to-day operations.

One day last winter, Hill visited the premises of Oakdale Motors to look at a used car that she had seen advertised and that she was interested in purchasing. The area outside the sales office was extremely slippery, being covered by ice that was, in turn, covered by a thin layer of snow that had fallen overnight. Faulkner was working at the Oakdale premises that day and knew of the dangerous state of the premises, but had made no effort to have the danger removed.

Hill slipped on the ice, fell, and broke her leg. The injury was a serious one and has left her with a permanent disability.

She has learned that Oakdale Motors Inc. is in severe financial difficulties and is likely to be made bankrupt. However, Faulkner appears to be quite wealthy. *See 607.*

Would Hill have any claim against Faulkner?

2 Macbeth, the owner of 20 hectares located on the outskirts of Niagara Falls, decided to sell, and on January 2 signed an exclusive listing agreement with Ross, a real estate broker. Macbeth agreed to pay Ross a commission of 5 percent on the sale of the property, which he listed at $350 000.

On January 19, Ross filed articles of incorporation for a new corporation, Burnam Woods Properties Ltd., of which he was the sole shareholder. He appointed his friend Lennox as general manager.

Several weeks later, Ross introduced Macbeth to Lennox as general manager of Burnam Woods but said nothing to suggest that he, Ross, had any interest in the corporation. Within a few days Lennox submitted an offer on behalf of the corporation to purchase Macbeth's property for $240 000. Macbeth rejected the offer but made a counter-offer to sell at $290 000. Burnam Woods accepted the counter-offer, and the deal was closed on March 15, when Macbeth paid Ross his commission of $14 500.

Shortly afterwards, Burnam Woods entered into negotiations with another corporation, Castle Hall Developments Ltd., and sold the 20 hectares to it for $450 000, realizing a quick profit of $160 000.

On April 24 following, Macbeth learned of the resale by Burnam Woods and also learned about Ross's share ownership in the Burnam Woods company. Macbeth immediately sued Ross and Burnam Woods jointly for recovery of the real estate commission of $14 500 and for the $160 000 profit realized on the second sale by Burnam Woods Properties Ltd. to Castle Hall Developments Ltd. *See 608 Corporate Veil.*

Examine the validity of Macbeth's claim and offer an opinion about its chances for success.

3 Rosina has recently developed a highly original computer program that, she claims, will revolutionize the practice of landscape architecture. She has been advised by a consultant that marketing the software is likely to be a highly profitable venture. However, to develop and market the project will require working capital, which Rosina does not have. Fortunately her uncle, Bartolo, has agreed to put $100 000 of his savings into the project.

With the help of a lawyer friend (who has advised them that they should each obtain independent legal advice) they have worked out a rough structure for their project, as follows:

(a) They will form a corporation, of which they will be the sole shareholders.

(b) Rosina will assign her copyright in the program to the corporation and will work full-time in developing and marketing it.

(c) Bartolo will contribute $100 000 in cash as working capital and will participate in major management decisions but will not be responsible for the day-to-day running of the business.

Since Rosina will be giving up a fairly well-paying job in order to develop the new business, she is concerned that she should not be left entirely without income during the initial period (when there would be no sales revenue). In turn, Bartolo would like there to be some sort of guarantee of a reasonable return of income on his investment.

What form of capital structure for the corporation, and what other possible arrangements, would you consider to be appropriate?

THE INTERNAL AFFAIRS OF CORPORATIONS

28

This chapter and the next discuss, respectively, the internal and external affairs and the business of a corporation. In this chapter we examine such questions as:

- how is a corporation managed?
- what is the function of the board of directors?
- how are they appointed and removed?
- what are the duties of directors?
- what are the rights and duties of shareholders?
- how are the rights of minority shareholders protected?

BUSINESS AND AFFAIRS OF A CORPORATION

The Canada Business Corporations Act (CBCA),[1] and the corresponding provincial statutes, draw a broad distinction between two aspects of a corporation's activities. Section 102 states that "the directors shall manage the *business* and *affairs* of a corporation"[italics added]. The difference between these two terms is explained in section 2 (1), where "affairs" are defined as "the relationships among a corporation…and the shareholders, directors and officers…but *does not include the business carried on* [by the corporation]…" [italics added]. The distinction, which is helpful in understanding the complex activities of corporations, is between

    (a) the *affairs*: the internal arrangements among those responsible for running a corporation and its main beneficiaries—the shareholders—which we discuss in this chapter, and

---

1. R.S.C. 1985, c. C-44. Unless otherwise stated, statutory references in this chapter are to that Act.

(b) the *business*: the external relations between a corporation and those who deal with it as a business enterprise—its customers, suppliers, and employees—as well as relations with government regulators and society as a whole; discussed in Chapter 29.

There is at least one major area, the sale of securities, where the distinction becomes blurred: an invitation to the public to invest in a corporation is directed towards those who are not yet part of its internal relations, but if they accept an offer to buy shares they will subsequently become involved in its "affairs." Because of the strong public interest in regulating the sale of securities, we shall discuss distribution of securities as a subject in Chapter 29.

THE STRUCTURE OF THE MODERN BUSINESS CORPORATION

Business corporations differ greatly from one another in their size and composition. Modern legislation tries to take these differences into account and permits widely differing corporate structures although, as we shall see, there are certain elements that are essential to all corporations.

The two basic organs common to all corporations are the general body of shareholders and the **board of directors**. In closely held corporations, such as family companies or "incorporated partnerships," it often happens that most, or even all, of the shareholders are also directors. But although in practice the distinction between shareholders and directors may sometimes become blurred—for example, when they get together to discuss business does the group constitute a directors' meeting or a shareholders' meeting?—it remains important legally.

In a large corporation, by contrast, the board of directors may have as many as 15 or 20 members. Generally, in such cases the board will appoint a *chief executive officer* (or "CEO"—also often called the "president" or "managing director") or a smaller committee of directors (the *management committee* or *executive committee*) to direct the affairs and business of the corporation and to supervise its full-time officers and employees; the CEO or committee refers only the more important policy matters to the less frequent meetings of the full board. In turn, the board of directors usually calls no more than the required annual meeting of shareholders, at which it reports to them on the state of the corporation's affairs and holds elections for the coming year. Thus we see that the directors function, at the business level, in somewhat the same manner as a cabinet of government functions at the political level.

board of directors
the governing body of a corporation, responsible for the management of its business and affairs

FIGURE 28.1
Corporate Structure

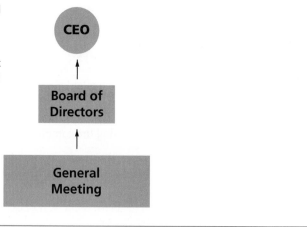

Power originates with the general meeting of shareholders. The shareholders appoint a board of directors to manage the corporation. The directors in turn appoint a chief executive officer, who is in charge of day-to-day running of the corporation.

CEO

Board of Directors

General Meeting

DIRECTORS

The Role of the Directors

Section 102 of the CBCA provides that the directors shall manage the business and affairs of the corporation. In addition to the general power of management, the Act confers a number of specific powers on the directors. The most important of these are:

- to issue shares—subject to the corporation's constitution, the directors may issue shares at such times, to such persons, and for such consideration as they may determine (section 25)
- to declare dividends—the directors determine whether, or to what extent, profits should be distributed to the shareholders or retained in the corporation
- to adopt by-laws governing the day-to-day affairs of the corporation—the directors may adopt new by-laws or amend existing ones; although they must submit them for approval at the next meeting of shareholders, the by-laws remain effective until then (section 103)
- to call meetings of shareholders (section 133); the directors must call an annual general meeting each year, but may call additional meetings whenever they wish

Checklist: Powers of Directors

In relation to the *internal* affairs of the corporation, the most important powers given to the directors are:

- to issue shares
- to declare dividends
- to adopt by-laws
- to call meetings of shareholders

A corporation is required to have one or more directors.[2] A corporation whose shares are issued to the public must have not fewer than three directors, at least two of whom must be "outsiders"; that is, they must not be officers or employees of the corporation.

Where a corporation has more than one director, decisions of the board of directors are normally taken by majority vote, unless the corporate constitution requires a higher special majority or unanimity. Usually, the by-laws make provision for the holding of meetings of the board, the election of a chairperson, rules on voting, quorums, and like matters.

Shareholders, as such, play little or no part in management. They have certain rights, the most important being to vote at meetings, but generally, once the shareholders have elected a board of directors they have no further power to participate in management. If they do not like the way the directors are running the corporation's business and affairs, they cannot interfere; legally their only course is to dismiss them and elect new directors in their place.[3] It is

---

2. Even a corporation with only a single shareholder must have one or more directors, though there is no reason why the shareholder should not also be the sole director. The articles of incorporation are required to state the number of directors that the corporation is to have; s. 6(1)(e).

3. If dissatisfied shareholders hold a sufficient proportion of the shares, they need not wait until the next meeting called by the directors; they may requisition a meeting (s. 143) to elect a new board.

consequently of vital importance that the shareholders should select competent and trustworthy individuals as their directors.

CASE 28.1

The majority shareholder of a corporation wanted the corporation to sell its main asset. At his request the directors called a general meeting of shareholders, which passed a resolution (over the opposition of some of the minority shareholders) instructing the board of directors to go ahead with the sale.

The board refused to do so, believing that the sale was not in the best interests of the corporation. The majority share-holder sought a declaration that the board was bound to carry out the instructions of the general meeting of shareholders.

The court refused to grant the declaration, ruling that it is the directors who manage the business of a corporation and, until such time as they are replaced, they must act as they think best for the corporation and are not bound to follow instructions from the shareholders.[4]

One very important effect of this rule is that the shareholders cannot compel the directors to declare a dividend, unless there is an express requirement in the corporation's constitution that a dividend be paid in particular circumstances.

Appointment and Removal of Directors

Any individual may be appointed director of a corporation, unless he or she is under the age of 18, has been found to be of unsound mind, or has the status of bankrupt (section 105). However, a majority of the directors of a corporation must be resident Canadians.[5] Unless required by the articles of incorporation, a director need not hold shares in the corporation.

A corporation's first directors are appointed at the time of incorporation and hold office until the first meeting of shareholders, which must be held not less than 18 months after the corporation comes into existence (section 133). Subsequently, directors are elected, re-elected, or replaced on a regular basis; normally this occurs at the annual general meeting of the corporation, but elections may be held at any time at a special meeting called for that purpose. Casual vacancies on the board—for example where a director dies or becomes seriously ill—may normally be filled by the remaining directors.

Directors are elected by ordinary resolution of the shareholders (section 106(3)); that is, a simple majority vote is sufficient. The effect of this rule is that a single shareholder, or a group of shareholders, holding anything more than 50 percent of the total votes, is able to elect the entire board of directors. (Conversely, complete equality between two competing groups can lead to deadlock—as sometimes happens when two equal partners incorporate their business.) An exception to the general rule may be made by providing, in the articles of incorporation, that directors be elected by a system of **cumulative voting**—a form of proportional representation designed to ensure that any substantial minority of shareholders will be represented on the board. Such systems, however, are quite rare in Canadian corporations.

cumulative voting
a method of electing directors by a form of proportional representation

As we have already mentioned, once they have elected the board of directors the shareholders have virtually no say in the management of the corporation's business and affairs. At one time, the position of the directors could be even more strongly entrenched—for example by providing in the corporate constitution that they should hold office for life, or that an incumbent director might be replaced only by a special majority or unanimous vote of the shareholders. This type of provision is no longer permitted. A director's term of office may now not

---

4. Automatic Self-Cleansing Filter Syndicate Co. Ltd. v. Cuninghame, [1906] 2 Ch. 34 (U.K.C.A.).

5. S. 105(3). A landed immigrant counts as "Canadian," but only until one year after she becomes eligible to apply for citizenship: see the definition of "resident Canadian" in s. 2(1).

exceed three years, and even during that term a special meeting may be called to vote on the removal of a director (section 109). Except where cumulative voting is provided for, an ordinary resolution (simple majority) is sufficient for the removal of any director, and the articles may not prescribe a greater majority (section 6(4)).

DUTIES OF DIRECTORS

To Whom are Directors' Duties Owed?

According to section 122 of the CBCA

(1) Every director and officer of a corporation in exercising his powers and discharging his duties shall

    (a) act honestly and in good faith with a view to the best interests of the corporation; and

    (b) exercise the care, diligence and skill that a reasonably prudent person would exercise in comparable circumstances.

(2) Every director and officer of a corporation shall comply with this Act, the regulations, articles, by-laws and any unanimous shareholder agreement.

To the Corporation

Although the Act does not expressly say so, it is implicit, especially in the words "with a view to the best interests of the corporation," that the duties of directors are owed, at least primarily, to the corporation. But do directors owe duties to anyone other than the corporation?

To the Shareholders

Although directors are elected and can be removed by a majority of the shareholders, it would be wrong to conclude that their first duty is to those shareholders who have elected them—as was demonstrated in Case 28.1, above. Just as the first duty of an elected member of Parliament is to the country as a whole rather than to his or her constituency, so too, the courts have stated, is the duty of a director owed to the corporation as a whole. The interests of "the corporation" are normally taken to mean the interests of the general body of shareholders, *present and future.* Thus, directors may—and should—consider the long-term interests of the corporation and not merely the present interests or wishes of the shareholders. But this does not answer the question whether, in addition to the duties owed to the corporation as a whole, any duty is owed to *individual* shareholders. The traditional English and Canadian answer is "no."

CASE 28.2

P wished to sell his shares in a private corporation. He wrote to the directors asking them if they knew of anyone who might be willing to buy them, quoting a price based on an independent valuation that he had recently obtained. *W*, the chair of the board of directors, replied that he was prepared to buy the shares at that price. After further negotiation, *P* sold his shares, at a slightly higher price, to *W* and two other directors.

The directors did not disclose during the negotiations that they had been having talks with another person, who was interested in acquiring control of the corporation. (In the event, those discussions came to nothing.)

When *P* learned of the discussions he brought an action to have the sale of his shares set aside. It was held that the directors owed no duty to the shareholder to reveal the fact of the discussions, and the sale was valid.[6]

---

6. Percival v. Wright, [1902] 2 Ch. 421. As noted below, such conduct might now be forbidden by statute.

The above case is usually taken as authority for the proposition that directors generally owe no duty to individual shareholders under corporate law. Only if the directors offer to act on behalf of other shareholders, thereby creating an agency relationship, or if they stand in some other fiduciary relationship, will they be under a duty to them.[7]

To the Public

Recent literature on corporate governance often refers to the "stakeholder" concept of the corporation; that view holds that the conduct of a corporation's business affects not only shareholders but many other sectors of the public. If a large corporation is badly managed, the well-being of many people and even the national interest may be seriously affected: creditors of a bankrupt corporation go unpaid; employees may lose their jobs, as may other members of the community where the corporation carries on business; a corporation that produces defective products may injure consumers; and one that does not take effective measures to prevent pollution may cause severe damage to the environment. Consequently, the public in general has a "stake" in good corporate management.

This public interest is reflected in the enormous body of legislation to which modern corporations are subject. Some of that legislation will be discussed in Chapter 32, and in Chapter 29 we examine other aspects of the external relations of corporations. As we shall see, corporate directors must manage their corporations in conformity with the law, and may incur personal liability if they fail to do so. But, apart from statutory obligations, the courts have generally resisted the notion that directors owe a *duty* to the public or to any sector thereof. Their duties are owed solely to the corporation.[8]

That does not mean that directors should never consider other interests. A corporation that promotes good labour relations by considering the welfare of its employees, that enjoys good customer and community relations, and that is perceived as socially responsible and responsive to environmental concerns is likely to prosper better in the longer term than one that does not. A corporation's management rightly devotes considerable attention to its public image and relations; it may even be argued that directors owe a duty to the corporation to do so, but that duty is owed to the corporation and not to the public.

Duties of Care and Skill

Negligence

As already noted, section 122 of the CBCA requires directors to exercise the care, diligence, and skill that a reasonably prudent *person* would exercise in comparable circumstances. A director owes a duty to the corporation not to be negligent in carrying out her duties. In this respect no greater diligence is required of a director than is required of the average person; she is placed under no higher standard. We have not as yet developed standards for a professional class of directors. By contrast, a director who is also *employed* by a corporation, for example as its chief executive officer, its treasurer, or its chief engineer, will normally owe a professional duty of care, but that duty is owed in respect of the employment, not as a director.

A director is not expected to give continuous attention to the affairs of the corporation and, unless there are suspicious circumstances, she is entitled to rely on information received from the officers of the corporation, such as its president, company secretary, or treasurer.[9] However, she may not willfully close her eyes to mistakes and misconduct. If she acquiesces in such matters, she may be liable in damages to the corporation for any losses that result.

---

7. Allen v. Hyatt (1914), 17 D.L.R. 7. Under securities legislation directors are required to disclose to the shareholders information relating to takeover offers; see the discussion in Chapter 29.

8. There may be special circumstances in which directors owe a fiduciary duty to others—for example, to clients of the firm; see Air Canada v. M & L Travel Ltd. (1993), 108 D.L.R. (4th) 592.

9. Dovey v. Corey, [1901] A.C. 477.

Strict Liability

Directors are more likely to be held liable for their acts than for their omissions. The CBCA and corresponding provincial statutes make directors liable to their corporation when they vote at meetings of the board on specified matters that cause financial losses to the corporation, such as the improper redemption of shares or the payment of a dividend in circumstances that leave the corporation unable to meet its liabilities (section 118(2)). In addition, if the corporation becomes insolvent the directors are personally liable to all employees of the corporation for up to six months' unpaid wages for services performed while they were directors.[10] Directors may also become liable for failure to comply with other statutes; for example, if the corporation is insolvent, the federal government may collect from the directors income tax that the corporation was required to withhold from the wages and salaries of employees.[11] Even the volunteer directors of a non-profit corporation have been held liable under this provision.[12]

Fiduciary Duties

In contrast to the standards of care and skill, the duty of good faith towards the corporation imposes a high standard of conduct on a director. The CBCA requires that directors and officers shall "act honestly and in good faith with a view to the best interests of the corporation" (section 122(1)). This duty takes a number of forms. All of them involve, in one way or another, a director putting herself in a position where there is a conflict, at least potentially, between the director's personal interest and that of the corporation. Indeed, one can probably assert that there is a general duty on directors to avoid any *conflict of interest* with their corporation. This duty finds a parallel in the duty of good faith that partners owe to each other, discussed in Chapter 26. We should note that this duty is imposed not only on directors of a corporation but also on its other officers and senior employees who owe it a fiduciary duty.[13]

Contracts With the Corporation

Perhaps the most important fiduciary obligation is the duty to disclose any interest that the director may have in contracts made with the corporation. This duty arises where a director negotiates the sale of her own property to the corporation, or the purchase of property from the corporation. It often arises in more indirect ways: a director may be a shareholder in another corporation that is selling to or buying from her corporation, or the person making a contract with her corporation may be acting as agent or trustee for her or for a member of her family. The problem occurs frequently among related corporations, as where a director of one corporation is a shareholder and perhaps a director of a second corporation.

ILLUSTRATION 28.1

Brown holds a large number of shares in each of World Electric and Universal Shipbuilding, and is a director of each of these corporations. Universal Shipbuilding requires expensive turbo-generator sets for two large ships under construction. World Electric is one of several manufacturers of turbo-generators. Brown is faced with an obvious conflict of interest: can she encourage or even support a contract between the two corporations? On one side, it is in Brown's interest to see Universal Shipbuilding obtain the equipment at the lowest possible price. On the other side, it is in her interest to see World Electric get the contract and obtain the highest possible price.

---

10. S. 119. This section is unique, in that liability for unpaid wages is unqualified; it is no excuse that a director acted with proper care and skill in carrying out her duties.

11. Income Tax Act, R.S.C. 1985, c. 1 (5th Supp.), s. 227.1. A director may raise the defence of due diligence, showing that she had used reasonable care in the circumstances.

12. R. v. Corsano (1999), 172 D.L.R. (4th) 708.

13. See MacMillan-Bloedel Ltd. v. Binstead (1983), 22 B.L.R. 255.

To look after the type of situation described in Illustration 28.1, the courts evolved a set of rules that have been codified and form a part of corporation legislation. Thus, under section 120 of the CBCA, a director who has an interest in a contract must disclose this fact at a meeting of the board of directors that considers the contract, and must not vote on the matter. If, after learning of the interest, the remaining independent members of the board still wish to go through with the contract, then a subsequent vote of them alone will create a binding contract. Failure by a director to disclose her interest gives the director's corporation the right to rescind the contract upon learning of her interest in it. Alternatively, it may affirm the contract on the terms on which it was made. Sometimes almost all the directors of a corporation are interested in a contract, and the remaining independent directors are not enough to form a quorum. In those circumstances, the contract should be presented to a general meeting of the shareholders for their ratification after full disclosure has been made to them.

Interception of Corporate Opportunity

In the preceding paragraphs we discussed the duty that arises when a director has an interest in a contract proposed to be made with the corporation. In this section we shall discuss a director's duty to the corporation in a transaction she makes with a third person.

If it appears in the particular circumstances that it is a director's duty to acquire a particular item of property for the corporation, or to give the corporation the chance of first refusal, and if instead she acquires the property for herself, then she has *intercepted* an opportunity belonging to the corporation and has committed a breach of duty.

The Director's Mandate

The duty of a director to acquire property on behalf of a corporation arises chiefly in two situations. The first situation occurs when she has received a mandate to act as agent either in the purchase of a specific piece of property or in the purchase of a class of property generally. In these circumstances she is under a duty ordinarily placed upon any agent to acquire property for her principal. If a director buys property for herself after she has received an express mandate to acquire such property for the corporation, she is clearly guilty of a breach of duty.

CASE 28.3

R was a director of a large corporation that was in the process of expanding its chain of retail grocery stores. A major part of his duties was to travel around the country looking for suitable independent stores for the corporation to purchase. *R* entered into an arrangement with a friend to buy those stores that seemed especially good bargains and to resell them to the corporation, concealing the fact of his ownership. When this was later discovered, the corporation brought proceedings against him.

The court held that *R* was under a duty to acquire the stores for the corporation, and did so as its agent.[14]

Corporate Information

A second situation with respect to a director's duty to acquire property on behalf of a corporation occurs when a director receives information about a profitable venture or an opportunity to buy property at an advantageous price. If this opportunity has arisen because of her corporate office, that is, if she has received the information as a director of the corporation, then it is

---

14. Canada Safeway Ltd. v. Thompson, [1951] 3 D.L.R. 295. Note that in reselling the stores to the corporation, the director was also in breach of his duty to disclose his interest. The corporation could have chosen instead to rescind the contracts. See also Slate Ventures Inc. v. Hurley (1998), 37 B.L.R. (2d) 138.

her duty to give the corporation first chance at acquiring an interest in the venture or property. If the corporation decides not to acquire the property, the director is probably free to do so. But she makes a dangerous decision if she assumes that the corporation would not want the property anyway, and then acquires it in her own name without consulting the corporation. In practice, it may be difficult for a court to decide whether in the circumstances the information came to the director personally or in her role as a director of the corporation. Nevertheless, once the court decides that the opportunity belonged to the corporation, the result is quite clear: purchasing on her own behalf is a breach of duty.

CASE 28.4

C was a director of a corporation involved in exploration and natural resource development. C was approached by a prospector, who asked if the corporation would be interested in acquiring certain claims. He reported this at a meeting of the board of directors. A majority of the board considered that the corporation was already over-committed financially and decided against taking up the offer.

When the prospector approached C again, C decided to take up the claims for himself. He later left the corporation, after a disagreement. The corporation learned of his acquisition of the claims and brought proceedings against him.

The court held that, once the corporation had rejected the opportunity, it no longer belonged to the corporation and C was free to take advantage of it.[15]

In contrast to the situation in Case 28.4, in a case where a majority of the directors (and shareholders) of a corporation purported to pass a resolution rejecting a contractual opportunity offered to the corporation and then took it for themselves, that was held to be a breach of their duties.[16]

Competing With the Corporation

Another aspect of the conflict of interest principle is the rule that a director may not carry on a business competing with that of her corporation, except with the permission of the corporation.

CASE 28.5

O'Malley was a director of Canaero, a corporation specializing in aerial surveying. He had been engaged on a project for the corporation in Guyana, during which he learned a lot about the terrain and made some useful contacts. He subsequently resigned from Canaero, formed his

own corporation, and successfully tendered for a surveying contract with the government of Guyana.

O'Malley was held to be in breach of his duty to Canaero and accountable to them for his profit on the contract.[17]

Case 28.5 can be regarded as an illustration of the rule that a director may not compete with her own corporation—and it also demonstrates that the rule cannot be circumvented simply by resigning. Alternatively, it serves as another example of the principle that a director will not be permitted to make personal use of information obtained in the capacity of director.

15. Peso Silver Mines Ltd. v. Cropper (1966), 56 D.L.R. (2d) 117 (S.C.C.).

16. Cook v. Deeks, [1916] A.C. 554.

17. Canadian Aero Service Ltd. v. O'Malley (1973), 40 D.L.R. (3d) 371 (S.C.C.).

Consequences of a Breach of Fiduciary Duty

A director who has breached her fiduciary duty to the corporation may be liable in damages for any loss sustained by the corporation as a result of that breach. In addition, as we have seen, a corporation is entitled to rescind a contract in which a director has a material interest that she did not disclose.[18] The position of a director who acquires an interest in property or a venture while under a duty to act for the corporation is the same as that of any agent who acquires an interest on behalf of her principal: although she may have formal or legal ownership of the property, she holds it for the benefit of the principal, the beneficial or equitable owner. On discovery of the transaction the corporation may force the director to transfer the interest to it while reimbursing her for her cost of acquiring the interest; she is not entitled to any profit. If, when the corporation discovers the transaction, the director has already sold the property to a bona fide purchaser, then she must account to the corporation for any profits that she made as a result of the transactions. A director will also be liable to account for any profits derived from improperly competing with her corporation, and an injunction may be obtained to restrain her from continuing to do so.

Insider Trading

In addition to the categories of directors' duties considered above, there is a further type of conduct for which English and Canadian courts were reluctant to impose liability, but where the legislatures have intervened to create a duty—that of **insider trading**.

insider trading
the use of confidential information relating to a corporation in dealing in its securities

Insider trading occurs when a director or officer of a corporation, or some other person (for example, a major shareholder of the corporation), buys or sells the corporation's shares or other securities, making use of confidential inside information in order to make a profit or avoid a loss.

ILLUSTRATION 28.2

(a) The directors of a small family company are approached by a large public corporation that offers to buy all the shares of the family company at a price considerably above that at which the shares had previously been valued. The next day, one of the directors is approached by her uncle, who is a shareholder, and who offers to sell some of his shares to her. Without disclosing the proposed takeover, she buys the shares at a price well below that of the offer.

(b) The directors of a mining corporation receive a confidential report from their surveyor that very valuable mineral deposits have just been discovered. One of the directors immediately instructs her broker to buy as many of the corporation's shares as possible on the stock exchange, before the good news is released and forces up the price.

(c) The directors of a corporation learn that their major customer has just declared bankruptcy, owing the corporation a large sum of money. Default on the account by their customer is likely to result in the corporation showing a substantial loss in the forthcoming half-yearly accounts. One of the directors promptly sells her shares just before the news becomes public and the shares drop in value.

In each of the hypothetical cases in Illustration 28.2, a director has made use, for her own benefit, of information that came to her in her capacity as a director.

At common law, there were two problems in holding the director liable. First, as we have seen, the courts have consistently held that a director's duty is owed to the corporation and not to individual shareholders. Absent fraud or other special circumstances—such as where directors could be regarded as acting as agents or trustees for the shareholders in negotiating a takeover—a director owed no duty to disclose confidential information to a shareholder.

---

18. So long as rescission is still possible: see the discussion in Chapter 15.

Second, no harm appears to have been done to the corporation; in the illustrations above, the confidential information affected the value of the corporation's shares, but in no sense could it have been used for the corporation's benefit. Thus, although the cases might be regarded as further examples of a director misusing confidential information belonging to the corporation, there is no appropriation of corporate opportunity.

In the absence of common law remedies the legislatures stepped in to fill the void. As we shall see later in this chapter and in Chapter 29, securities legislation has made insider trading a criminal offence, punishable by fines or imprisonment or both, and imposes strict disclosure requirements whenever a director, or other insider, trades in the securities of her own corporation. These provisions apply principally to corporations whose securities are publicly traded. However, section 131(4) of the CBCA provides that, even in the case of a private corporation, an insider who, for her own benefit or advantage, makes use of specific, confidential, price-sensitive information in connection with a transaction in securities of her own corporation, or any of its affiliates, is liable

(a) to compensate any person for any direct loss suffered as a result of the transaction

(b) to account to the corporation for any benefit or advantage obtained.

For the purposes of the legislation, "insider" includes a director or officer, an employee, any shareholder who holds more than 10 percent of the corporation's securities, and a "tippee"—that is, a person who knowingly receives confidential information from an insider.

Checklist: Directors' Liability

A director faces the following types of liability for breach of her duties:

1. To the corporation
   - damages for loss suffered by the corporation as a result of the breach
   - accounting for amounts paid on the improper redemption of shares or payment of a dividend
   - rescission of a contract in which a director has an undisclosed interest
   - constructive trust of property acquired under the director's mandate
   - accounting for profit improperly obtained by a director
   - injunction to restrain breach of duty

2. To others
   - liability to employees for unpaid wages
   - liability for unpaid taxes
   - compensation to persons suffering direct loss as a result of insider trading

3. Criminal liability
   - for insider trading
   - for other statutory offences (see Chapter 29)

RIGHTS OF SHAREHOLDERS

The Role of Shareholders

In Widely Held Corporations

In most large, publicly traded corporations, shareholdings are widely distributed, frequently with no single shareholder or group holding more than 5 percent of the voting stock. No

632 **Part Six** Business Organizations: Their Forms, Operation, and Management

majority or controlling group of shareholders can be discerned; only in exceptional circumstances can a group be mobilized to try to overturn the rule of the existing managers. In such corporations management is largely self-perpetuating, even when it is inefficient, and management—the senior executive officers—operates almost entirely independently of the board of directors. Those decisions that are referred to the board are usually rubber stamped when the CEO speaks in their favour.

Paradoxically, poor managers are supported in their position by a sensible piece of practical advice to investors: "If you don't like the management, sell!" In other words, "Do not get into costly corporate struggles; cut your losses by getting out and re-investing in a corporation more to your liking." In such circumstances, the takeover bid may turn out to be the shareholders' best protection. Poorly managed corporations—especially those in which the rate of return to investors is low in relation to the value of the business or assets—become obvious targets for takeovers. It is this threat rather than any fear of a successful shareholders' revolt that tends to keep corporate managers on their toes.

In Closely Held Corporations

In closely held corporations, the problem is radically different. The usual problem is a serious disagreement among the principal shareholders, who are frequently also directors and senior employees of the corporation. In the absence of careful contractual arrangements providing safeguards, a minority shareholder in a closely held corporation may find himself "locked in" and "frozen out" at the same time.

The minority shareholder is "locked in" in the sense that he probably cannot sell his shares except at a small fraction of what he believes they should be worth. There are two reasons for this state of affairs: first, in most closely held corporations the transfer of shares is restricted, usually requiring the consent of the board of directors. It is the controlling majority on the board who have made the minority shareholder's life miserable, and they may be unwilling to agree to the transfer of his shares except to someone of their own choosing. Second, even if the minority shareholder is free to sell the shares, he will have great difficulty in finding a buyer who would consider acquiring a minority position in a private corporation.

The minority shareholder may be "frozen out" in the following manner: first, the majority directors may fire him from his job with the corporation, or at the very least refuse to renew his employment contract when it expires; second, they may remove him from the board of directors, or elect someone else in his place at the next election; and third, they may increase salaries to themselves, so that the corporation itself earns no apparent profit. Even if a profit is shown, it may be retained by the corporation, since dividends are payable only at the discretion of the board of directors. Thus, it can happen that a minority shareholder with his life savings invested in a corporation may find himself deprived of his salary-earning position, his directorship, and his prospect of any dividends on his investment. Worse, as we noted above, he is often left without a marketable security.

In these circumstances the majority shareholders may not have broken any law, and no remedy existed at common law. However, a number of statutory provisions empower the courts to give relief to minority shareholders. We shall discuss these, as well as ways of avoiding the problem, under "Rescuing the 'Locked-in' Shareholder," below.

Rights Attached to Shares

Shareholder rights derive from two principal sources: the rights attached to their shares by the articles of the corporation and any additional rights conferred on them by the relevant corporate legislation.

As we saw in Chapter 27, the corporate constitution sets out the rights attached to each class of shares. For example, the CBCA requires that the articles state the classes of shares that may be issued and, if there are to be two or more classes of shares, the rights, privileges, restrictions, and conditions attaching to each class (section 6(1)(c) and section 24(4)). If there is only one class of shares, the rights of the shareholders include the rights

- to vote at any meeting of shareholders
- to receive any dividend declared
- to receive the remaining property of the corporation (after payment of its debts) on dissolution (section 24(3))

Additional rights may be attached to shares, and if there are different classes of shares, rights may be granted to some shares and not others; but the three basic rights must exist and be exercisable by one or other class of shares.

Voting: A Voice in the Affairs of the Corporation

Notice and Attendance at Meetings

If shareholders wish to voice their objections about the management, they need a forum to do so. The forum provided under all statutes is the **general meeting of shareholders**. The corporation may hold other meetings of shareholders in the course of the year, but it is required by statute to hold at least one **annual general meeting**.[19] Shareholders are entitled to advance notice of all general meetings and are entitled to receive copies of the financial statements before the annual general meeting. They may attend the meetings, question the directors, and make criticisms of the management of the corporation.

general meeting of shareholders
a formal meeting of shareholders at which they are able to vote on matters concerning the corporation

annual general meeting
the general meeting of shareholders that is required by law to be held each year to transact certain specified business

The Right to Requisition Meetings

Occasions may arise where the shareholders wish to call a meeting and the board of directors refuses to do so. All the provinces provide in their statutes that the shareholders themselves may call the meeting. However, these provisions require a comparatively large proportion of the shareholders to petition in order to compel the calling of the meeting, a requirement virtually impossible to meet in large corporations where even a relatively large group of shareholders may hold a very small percentage of the total shares.[20] The right to requisition a **special meeting** is therefore of limited use in large corporations, but is still especially valuable in the smaller closely held companies.

special meeting
any general meeting of shareholders other than the annual general meeting

The Right to Vote

The right to attend meetings and to criticize must ultimately be backed by some form of sanction in the hands of the shareholders. This sanction is found in the right to vote. The collective power of the shareholders is exercised through the passing—or defeating—of resolutions; an **ordinary resolution**, which is adopted by a simple majority of votes cast, and a **special resolution**, which requires a two-thirds majority.[21] The CBCA sets out a number of matters that must be approved by either an ordinary or a special resolution, the most important being

(a) the approval of alterations to the articles of incorporation (section 173)

(b) the approval of certain other fundamental changes, such as amalgamation with another corporation (section 183) or the sale of all, or substantially all, of the corporation's property (section 189)

ordinary resolution
a resolution adopted by the general meeting and passed by a simple majority

special resolution
a resolution of the general meeting required to be passed by a special (usually two-thirds) majority

---

19. CBCA, s. 133. The Act requires that an annual meeting be held not more than 15 months after the previous annual meeting; thus it is possible for a calendar year to pass without a meeting.

20. CBCA, s. 143, requires a requisition to be made by 5 percent of shareholders, and this is the requirement in most provinces. Prince Edward Island specifies the impossibly high figure of 25 percent.

21. S. 2. In memorandum companies a special resolution requires a three-quarters majority.

(c) the approval of any amendments made by the directors to the by-laws (section 103)

(d) the election of the auditor (section 162)

(e) the election, or removal, of directors (sections 106, 109)

Items (a) and (b) require a special resolution; the other items, and any other matters that might be put on the agenda, may be effected by ordinary resolution. Except in the relatively rare case where a fundamental change is proposed in the corporate constitution, or in the nature of its business, the most important matter voted upon by the shareholders is the election of directors since, as we have seen, it is the directors who control the management of the corporation's affairs.

Class Voting Rights

Not all shareholders necessarily have the right to vote. A corporation's shares may be divided into different classes, with different voting rights. Common shares almost invariably carry the right to vote; preferred shares often carry a right to vote only in specified circumstances, such as when preferred dividends are in arrears. The founders of a corporation may create several classes of shares and weight the voting heavily in favour of a small group of shares held by themselves. For example, they could give class A shares 100 votes per share and class B, issued to a broader group of shareholders, only one vote per share. It would be virtually impossible for a publicly listed corporation to have such a share structure today: securities commissions, stock exchanges, and underwriters would probably refuse such an issue, and without their concurrence a public offering is impossible. Virtually all common stock offered on the market today carries one vote per share. By contrast, in closely held corporations there is no restriction upon the different rights that may be attached to various classes of shares, provided at least one class has voting rights; within a particular class, however, all shares must enjoy the same rights (section 24).

class rights
special rights attaching to a particular class of shares

Class rights, which may relate not only to voting but also to other matters such as rights to priority in payment of dividends or to receive the surplus on liquidation of the corporation, must be set out in the articles of incorporation. Consequently, they may only be varied by special resolution of the shareholders. In addition, to alter the rights of a particular class requires approval by the votes of two-thirds of that class and of any other class that may be adversely affected (section 176).

Proxies

In most widely held corporations, only a small proportion of shareholders actually attend general meetings. All corporations statutes permit a shareholder to nominate a **proxy** to attend a general meeting and to cast that shareholder's votes at the meeting as instructed. This is done by signing a form, naming the proxy, and sending it to the corporation before the meeting. Most jurisdictions now go further and require all corporations, except the smallest closely held ones, to send a **proxy form**, the contents of which are prescribed in detail, to all shareholders at the same time as notice of a meeting is given.

proxy
a person appointed to attend a general meeting of shareholders and to cast the votes of the shareholder appointing him or her

proxy form
a form required to be circulated to shareholders before a general meeting, inviting them to appoint a proxy if they so wish

In the event of a proxy fight between two groups of shareholders—usually the board of directors and a dissenting group—each group solicits all the shareholders by mail in order to persuade them to give their proxy forms to the group making the solicitation. The dissentient group may go to the corporation's head office to obtain lists of all the shareholders from the share register in order to make their solicitations. Here the board of directors has a great advantage: as a matter of practice, they include proxy forms, offering one of themselves as the proposed proxy, with the mailed notice of the annual general meeting.[22] In this manner, the costs

---

22. This advantage is only partly offset by disclosure requirements and by compelling management to provide shareholders with a means to nominate a different proxy.

of compiling the list and addressing and mailing the notices are borne by the corporation, whereas a group of dissentient shareholders, in order to solicit proxy forms, must bear all these costs themselves. In very large corporations, the costs may be prohibitive. The larger the corporation, the more difficult it is to dislodge an incumbent board of directors, but there have been a few instances of dissatisfied shareholders voting out the entire board of directors and in turn, removing the senior management of large corporations.

CONTEMPORARY ISSUE

Shareholder Democracy

"The speeches are tiresome, the videos are silly, the eyes are glazed. And the questions? Pretty dumb....Welcome to the corporate annual meeting, Canadian style....Could we stop meeting like this?" These were the observations made in one newspaper article.

The article continues: "...almost nothing said or done at an annual meeting changes the course of corporate history."

Source: *The Globe and Mail*, March 15, 1997, p. B-1.

Another recent article looks at the annual reports of corporations:

> Nortel Networks seems to have turned back time with this year's annual report. No glossy, 56-colour, monument to corporate public relations for 1998. Nortel is mailing out to shareholders just the bare bones required by law: an unembellished, black-and-white package containing financial statements, auditor's report, management discussion and analysis, and proxy circular. But, there on the front page, in type that can't be missed, is Nortel's Internet address. Go there and you'll find all the glitz and glamour usually associated with the company's annual report.
>
> Nortel, this year, has chosen to dramatically reduce the costs of producing its annual report by letting print handle the statutory basics and its Web site the corporate PR. Nortel, designers, consultants and printers say, probably reflects the future of the annual report....

This seems to part of a trend. The article goes on:

> "It's a question of why kill all those trees to mail people information they don't want," says Ron Blunn of Blunn & Co. Inc. in Toronto. His small—four people—company has acted as annual report consultant to about half the Toronto Stock Exchange's top 60 firms during the past five years, by his own reckoning.

Source: *National Post*, May 15, 1999, p. E1.

Questions to Consider

1. How can "shareholder democracy" be promoted?
2. How long will it be before "electronic" shareholder meetings become the fashion?
3. Does shareholder democracy really matter if shareholders can simply "vote with their feet"?

Financial Rights

Shareholders expect to receive a return on their investment in one or both of two forms: earnings distributed regularly in the form of dividends and growth that can be realized by selling the shares or on dissolution of the corporation. Holders of common shares may be satisfied with smaller dividends if there is capital appreciation in the corporation's assets or if a significant part of the profits is retained within the business and has the effect of increasing the value of the shares. Preferred shares, as we saw in Chapter 27, often do not participate in growth and their holders are primarily concerned with receiving dividends.

Dividends

dividend
a distribution to shareholders of a share of the profits of the corporation

A fundamental right attached to shares is the right to receive any **dividend** that is declared by the corporation. Whether dividends are declared is a matter entirely within the discretion of the board of directors; shareholders normally have no right to be paid a dividend even when the corporation makes large profits.

There can be no discrimination, however, in the payment of dividends among shareholders of the same class; each is entitled to such dividends as are declared in proportion to the number of shares of that class held. In addition, directors are bound to pay dividends in the order of preference assigned to the classes of shareholders. Thus, they may not pay the common shareholders a dividend without first paying the whole of any preferred dividends owing to preference shareholders.

Distribution of Surplus

On the dissolution of a corporation, provided it has assets remaining after paying off all its creditors, shareholders are entitled to a proportionate share of the remaining net assets. The distribution of these net assets among the various classes of shareholders must also be made in accordance with the respective priorities of each class; this has also been discussed in Chapter 27.

Pre-emptive Rights

One of the more important powers given to the board of directors is the power to issue shares. The issue of new shares involves two possible risks for existing shareholders. First, the issue of shares to some other person will necessarily reduce the proportion of the total number of shares that a shareholder holds in the corporation. Thus a shareholder who holds 51 percent (or 34 percent) of all the corporation's shares would find that he could no longer secure the adoption of an ordinary resolution (or prevent the passing of a special resolution) if sufficient new shares were issued to someone else. Second, there is the risk of "stock watering"; if new shares are issued for a price that is less than the value of the existing shares, the value of those shares will be diluted.

ILLUSTRATION 28.3

A owns 34 out of the total of 100 shares issued by *XYZ* Inc. The assets of *XYZ* Inc. are worth approximately $1 million. The directors wish to raise additional capital and resolve to issue 20 new shares to *T*, at a price of $5000 per share. As a result, *A* will now own only 28.3 percent of the total shares and can no longer block the adoption of a special resolution. *A*'s shares, previously worth $10 000 each, will be worth only $9167.

pre-emptive right
a right to have the first opportunity to purchase a proportionate part of any new shares to be issued

United States courts have held that at common law a shareholder has a **pre-emptive right** to retain his proportionate holdings in a corporation, but this right is subject to various qualifications. When a corporation proposes to issue more shares it must normally offer each shareholder a proportion of the new issue equal to the proportion he holds of the existing shares. A shareholder who has 3 percent of the issued shares of a corporation is entitled to purchase 3 percent of any further issue. A right of pre-emption preserves the balance of power in the corporation. It also ensures that, if the new shares are issued at a price that is less than the value of the existing shares, the existing shareholders are not prejudiced, at any rate if they exercise their right of pre-emption. Any reduction in the value of their existing shares will be exactly balanced by the gain they receive in buying the new shares at an undervalue.

Canadian courts have never recognized a general principle of pre-emption. In limited circumstances, however, they have recognized rights somewhat similar to pre-emptive rights. Thus, although the directors have the right to issue authorized share capital of the corporation at their discretion, they must issue shares only for the purpose of raising capital or for purposes that are in the best interest of the corporation. If they have a bona fide intention to raise capital, they may distribute the shares to whomever they wish upon payment of a fair price. But if directors issue shares not for the benefit of the corporation but to affect voting control, the issue may be declared void. For example, if directors were to issue shares to themselves for the purpose of out-voting shareholders who, up to that point, had a majority of the issued shares, the extra share issue could be set aside by the court.

CASE 28.6

Bonisteel was a director of Collis Leather Co., and the owner of 458 out of a total of 1208 issued shares. He entered into an agreement with another shareholder to buy that shareholder's 150 shares. The purchase would have given him control of the corporation. Collis, the general manager and the person most responsible for the corporation's success, threatened to leave if Bonisteel took control. In order to forestall Bonisteel, the directors resolved to issue 292 new shares, and each director was asked how many shares he wished to subscribe for. Most of the new shares were taken up by directors other than Bonisteel, with the result that he would be left with less than 50 percent of the total shares. Bonisteel brought an action to restrain the directors from making the allotment.

The court held that such an allotment would be invalid. The corporation was not in need of additional funds, and it was improper to issue new shares for the purpose of altering the balance of control.[23]

CASE 28.7

Afton was a "junior" mining company, incorporated in British Columbia. As was common in the industry, it was looking for a "major" company to help finance a large drilling program. Teck, a large resource corporation, became interested in Afton and made an offer to buy a controlling block of its shares. The directors of Afton, led by its chief engineer, Millar, rejected the offer and preferred to enter into an arrangement with Canex, the subsidiary of another Canadian corporation, even though Canex was not prepared to match the Teck offer.

Following the rejection, Teck started buying Afton shares on the stock exchange, and soon announced that it had acquired more than 50 percent of the issued shares. The Afton directors then entered into a long-term contract with Canex, which involved issuing a large block of new shares to Canex. This arrangement diluted the Teck holding to less than 50 percent.

The share issue was challenged by Teck, but upheld by the court. The Afton directors had entered into the arrangement with Canex, and had issued the new shares, because they genuinely believed that the interests of Afton would be better served as a "partner" of Canex than as a subsidiary of Teck.[24]

While not required to do so, a corporation often does give its shareholders a pre-emptive right. When it proposes to issue further shares it may first issue subscription rights or share rights to all existing shareholders, giving each shareholder one right for each share held. The shareholder then has an option to purchase a new share at a specified price for a specified number of subscription rights. For example, a shareholder owning 50 shares may receive 50 rights entitling him to buy 10 shares (one share for every five rights) at a specified price per share. Subscription

---

23. Bonisteel v. Collis Leather Co. Ltd. (1919), 45 O.R. 195.
24. Teck Corp. v. Millar (1973), 33 D.L.R. (3d) 288.

rights are normally made transferable, and if the market value of the existing shares significantly exceeds the specified price for the new shares, the rights themselves will have a market value; they may be sold to anyone who wishes to purchase them and exercise the option.

The Right to Information

An underlying principle of modern corporate legislation is that shareholders—and potential investors—should be given sufficient information to enable them to decide whether to buy or sell shares, and how to vote at shareholder meetings. Disclosure of relevant information enables investors to evaluate the effectiveness of management and publicity may be an effective deterrent to high-handed behaviour or misconduct in management.

The Financial Statement

financial statement
annual accounts that are required to be presented to the shareholders at the annual general meeting

Of the information that must be disclosed, probably the most important is the annual **financial statement**, which must be presented to the shareholders at the annual general meeting. All corporation acts require that a certain minimum of information be part of the financial statement, though the detailed requirements vary. Generally, the basic items required are the income statement, showing the results of operations for the financial year; the balance sheet, showing the corporation's assets as of the financial year-end (including details of changes in share capital during the year); a statement of changes in financial position, analyzing changes in working capital; a statement of retained earnings showing changes during the year, including the declaration of dividends; and a statement of contributed surplus. The annual financial statement should be in comparative form, showing corresponding data for the preceding financial year. In addition, some statutes require that shareholders be sent a comparative interim quarterly financial statement.

The Auditor

To assist in the analysis and evaluation of the financial statement, and to ensure their accuracy so far as is possible, the acts provide for the appointment of an independent auditor by the shareholders: smaller closely held companies may dispense with this requirement, but only if the shareholders unanimously agree to do so. The auditor represents the shareholders' interests and must be an independent person who is not employed by the corporation.[25] She has the duty to investigate all the records and accounts of the corporation so that she may check on the fairness of the financial statement in advance of the annual general meeting of shareholders. Her task is to present to the shareholders her opinion of the financial statement issued by the directors. She must state whether in her opinion the statement fairly presents the financial position of the corporation in accordance with generally accepted accounting principles.[26] Both the auditor's report and the financial statement must be sent to all shareholders before the corporation's annual general meeting; the period usually specified is at least 21 days before the meeting. These items are included in the corporation's **annual report** to shareholders.

annual report
the report on the business and affairs of the corporation, which the directors are required to present at the annual general meeting

The financial statement is prepared from the books of account. Only the auditor, as representative of the shareholders, and the directors have the right to examine these books; shareholders as such do not have access to them. If a shareholder suspects that something is wrong, he may communicate his information to the auditor, but the auditor has no duty to undertake a special examination at the request of a shareholder. Or again, a shareholder may communicate with a director who would be sympathetic to his point of view and who may be willing to check the information against the books of account. As a last resort, a shareholder may apply to a court for the appointment of an inspector.

---

25. However, the auditor's duty is owed to the corporation, not to the shareholders who appointed her: see Hercules Managements Ltd. v. Ernst & Young (1997), 146 D.L.R. (4th) 577 (S.C.C.).

26. See section 5400, *CICA Handbook* (Canadian Institute of Chartered Accountants) for a complete statement of the form and content of the auditor's report.

Appointment of Inspector

All the jurisdictions, with the exception of Prince Edward Island, have statutory provisions enabling shareholders to apply to the courts to appoint an **inspector** to investigate the affairs of the corporation and to audit its books. The statutes give inspectors sweeping powers of inquiry, and the remedy can be a very effective one. In some jurisdictions there are a number of obstacles that undermine this effectiveness; in particular, a substantial proportion of shareholders may be required to join in the application, and the applicant may be required to give security to cover the costs of an investigation, which may be very high. However, the CBCA, and most of the provincial acts based on it, now permit a single shareholder to apply and they expressly state that the applicant is not required to give security for costs (section 229). A concerned shareholder may choose either of two options: he may request the Director—a government official appointed to supervise the affairs of corporations—to apply to the court to order an investigation, or he may apply directly to the court himself. In either event, it is necessary to make out a *prima facie* case, that is, produce sufficient evidence of the probability of serious mismanagement to warrant further investigation.

inspector
a person appointed by the court to investigate the affairs of a corporation

Documents of Record

In addition to the annual report, a corporation must maintain certain documents of record at its head office, which may be inspected by any shareholder during usual business hours. These **documents of record** include minute books of the proceedings at meetings of the shareholders; a register of all transfers of shares, including the date and other particulars of each transfer; a copy of the corporation's charter; a copy of all by-laws (or articles) and special resolutions; a register of shareholders; and a register of the directors. These documents may often be useful to a minority group of shareholders attempting to collect evidence to support a claim of misconduct or ineffectiveness on the part of the directors. Access to the share register permits a dissentient group to obtain the names and addresses of all other shareholders so that they may communicate with them, explain their complaints and attempt to enlist their support.

documents of record
documents that a corporation is required to keep and make available to shareholders

Another document of record is the minute book of the proceedings at meetings of the board of directors. Unlike the other documents of record, however, directors alone, not the shareholders, have a right of access to it.

Record of Insider Trading

In 1966, Ontario substantially amended the disclosure requirements of the Corporations Act and passed a new Securities Act, requiring detailed information of dealings in a corporation's securities by directors and other insiders to be filed with the provincial Securities Commission. The Act was further revised in 1978 and again in 1987, giving greater administrative supervision to the Commission. Most of the other provinces have enacted securities acts similar to the Ontario provisions; we shall return to the subject of securities regulation in the next chapter.

DUTIES OF SHAREHOLDERS

We have seen that directors of corporations are under strict duties of good faith. At least in theory, they must also use their own best judgment as to what is in the best interests of the corporation and are not bound to follow the instructions of the shareholders. However, when there is a controlling shareholder (or group of shareholders)—with the power to call a general meeting, dismiss directors, and appoint new ones in their place—it is usually the controlling shareholder who determines corporate policy and the directors merely act as a "rubber stamp." That being the case, one must ask whether shareholders—and especially controlling shareholders—owe any duty to their corporation.

Unlike some U.S. courts, Canadian courts have consistently held that a majority shareholder owes no positive duty to act for either the welfare of the corporation itself or the welfare of his fellow shareholders.[27] His obligation ends when he has paid the full purchase price for his shares. He has no obligation to attend meetings or to return proxy forms, and he is free to exercise his vote in whatever way he pleases and for whatever purposes he desires. His share is an item of property that he is free to use as he pleases, even if that is against the interests of the corporation or of his fellow shareholders. This seems to be so even where the shareholder is himself a director of the corporation. Although a director owes a duty to act honestly and in good faith with a view to the best interests of the corporation (section 122), when he votes as a shareholder he is entitled to consider his own personal interests.[28]

THE PROTECTION OF MINORITY SHAREHOLDERS
Oppression of Minority Rights

At the very least, a shareholder's freedom to use his vote as he chooses means that the courts will not substitute their judgment for his when his actions are based upon business considerations. As a consequence, a controlling group of shareholders, through its ability to determine the composition of the board of directors, to approve their actions or decline to do anything about their misdeeds, and even (if they have a two-thirds majority) to amend the corporation's constitution, could ensure that the affairs of the corporation were managed entirely for their own benefit and to the detriment of the minority. As we saw when we considered the dilemma of the "frozen-out" shareholder, these things can happen without any law being broken.

ILLUSTRATION 28.4

A, *B*, *C*, and *D* are the equal shareholders and directors of a corporation, Traviata Trattoria Ltd. The articles of incorporation restrict the business of the corporation to the operation of one or more restaurants. Contrary to *D*'s wishes, *A*, *B*, and *C* decide to sell the restaurant to a property developer and to invest the proceeds in a casino business. They use their votes to pass two special resolutions: (1) approving the sale of the restaurant (substantially the only asset of the corporation) and (2) amending the articles to remove the restriction on the business that may be carried on by the corporation.

In this example, no wrong has been done to the corporation and the majority has acted within its rights. Nevertheless, *D* may justifiably feel aggrieved since the whole basis upon which he became a shareholder in the corporation has been changed.

ILLUSTRATION 28.5

Sixty percent of the shares of Figaro Ltd. are held by Almaviva Inc., a large public corporation, and 40 percent by its original founder, Susanna. Following a disagreement over company policy with Susanna, Almaviva used its majority voting power to appoint three of its own directors to be directors of Figaro. The new directors subsequently sell an important piece of Figaro's property to Bartolo Ltd, a corporation wholly owned by Almaviva. The sale is at a gross undervalue.

Here, the directors of Figaro have probably been in breach either of their duty of care and skill or their duty to act in good faith and in the interests of their corporation. The corporation, Figaro, has been injured, since the value of its assets has been reduced, but the loss falls entirely on its minority shareholder, Susanna, since the majority shareholder, Almaviva gains more as shareholder of the purchaser, Bartolo (100 percent of the undervalue), than it loses as shareholder of the vendor, Figaro (60 percent of the undervalue). Consequently, Almaviva, as controlling shareholder of Figaro, will not complain about any breach of duty by its directors.

---

27. See *Brant Investments Ltd. v. Keeprite Inc.* (1991), 3 O.R. (3d) 289.
28. *North-West Transportation v. Beatty* (1887), 12 App. Cas. 589.

ILLUSTRATION 28.6

The shares in Jenufa Ltd. are held in equal proportions by *A*, her husband *B*, and his two sons by a previous marriage, *C* and *D*, all of whom had until recently been directors. After an acrimonious divorce, *B*, *C*, and *D* use their majority voting power to remove *A* from the board. Subsequently, they greatly increase their own salaries as full-time officers of the corporation, which consequently reduces the corporation's profits. Instead of distributing the remaining profits as dividends, they decide to reinvest them in a fund to provide for the long-term capital needs of the corporation. They also refuse to consent to *A* transferring her shares to any third party.

In this example, *A* is locked-in and frozen-out, as we have described earlier in this chapter. But the corporation has not been injured and, unless it can be shown that *B*, *C*, and *D* acted in bad faith, there may have been nothing improper in their actions.

Under traditional principles of corporation law, the aggrieved minority shareholders, in the above illustrations, received little or no help from the courts. However, special statutory remedies, introduced during the past 20 or 30 years, have greatly improved the situation of the minority. In examining the more important of these, we shall concentrate upon the remedies provided in the CBCA; almost all of the provinces have adopted essentially similar rules.

The Appraisal Remedy

In some situations, where the majority shareholders make fundamental changes to the corporation, section 190 offers a procedure whereby a dissenting shareholder need not go along with the change; he may elect instead to have his shares bought out by the corporation. If a price cannot be agreed, the court will fix a fair price. However, this **appraisal remedy** is limited to specific actions by the majority, the most important of which are:

- changing any restriction on the issue, transfer, or ownership of shares
- changing any restriction on the business that the corporation may carry on
- amalgamating or merging with another corporation
- selling, leasing, or exchanging substantially all of the assets of the corporation

While the remedy can be important in closely held corporations, where no ready market exists for minority shareholdings, the procedure is a complicated one, and the dissenter must comply with every step prescribed by the Act in order to take advantage of it. If instead, the shareholder can show that his interests have been "unfairly disregarded" he is more likely to resort to the "oppression remedy" discussed below. A dissenter in a widely held corporation would normally just sell his shares on the market.

appraisal remedy
the right to have one's shares bought by the corporation at a fair price

The Derivative Action

When a corporation has suffered an injury, as in Illustration 28.5 or, for example, where directors have made a secret profit for themselves by exploiting a "corporate opportunity," the corporation may sue the wrongdoer in the same manner as may a natural person.

Ordinarily, an action on behalf of the corporation must be started by its directors—it is part of the management function. However, if the directors are the wrongdoers they are hardly likely to commence an action against themselves. At common law a minority shareholder was permitted to start an action on behalf of the corporation in the name of himself and all other aggrieved shareholders—a representative or class action derived from the injury to the corporation, and frequently called a **derivative action**—but the courts surrounded this right with so many procedural requirements that the right was of little value.

The modern statutory derivative action (section 239) overcomes most of those procedural barriers. It permits a shareholder to obtain leave from the court to bring an action in the name

derivative action
proceedings brought by one or more shareholders in the name of the corporation in respect of a wrong done to the corporation

and on behalf of the corporation: to do so he need only establish that the directors refuse to bring the action themselves, that he is acting in good faith, and that it appears to be in the interests of the corporation or its shareholders that the action be commenced. If he establishes these things, then the court may make an order to commence the action. The acts prohibit the court from requiring the shareholder to give security for costs. Indeed, "the court may at any time order the corporation…to pay to the complainant interim costs, including legal fees and disbursements…" (section 242(4)), and may make "an order requiring the corporation…to pay reasonable legal fees incurred by the complainant in connection with the action" (section 240(d)). The court may also direct "that any amount adjudged payable by a defendant in the action shall be paid, in whole or in part, directly to former and present shareholders of the corporation…instead of to the corporation…" (section 240(c)). Thus in our Illustration 28.5, above, Susanna could receive direct compensation for her loss, rather than being compensated only indirectly through an increase in the assets of the corporation.

Although the statutory derivative action has substantially improved the position of minority shareholders, the remedy has been somewhat overshadowed by the oppression remedy, discussed below.

Rescuing the "Locked-in" Shareholder

We briefly described the plight of the locked-in minority shareholder under common law rules: his former business associates have frozen him out of the corporation but have been scrupulously careful not to break any rules or to be guilty of harming the corporation itself.

Winding Up

In a partnership, the rules of equity give considerable protection to a minority member; she is entitled to an accounting of profits and to receive her share of them regularly; if the impasse is total between the partners she can insist on a dissolution and sale of the assets and receipt of her proportionate part of the proceeds. Since the other partners cannot continue to use the partnership assets for their sole benefit, they must either face dissolution and sale or else come to a reasonable settlement. Not so in a closely held corporation: in the absence of a separate agreement among the shareholders, a minority shareholder has none of the rights of a partner.

Corporation statutes have, however, followed partnership law in one important respect: they give the courts discretion to make an order **winding up** a corporation where it is "just and equitable" to do so.[29] But because of the drastic nature of the remedy the courts have been reluctant to use it if the corporation is flourishing or is fairly large. Typically, the remedy is available where the corporation is a small family business or an "incorporated partnership," where there is deadlock, where relations between the participants have broken down, or where a "partner" has been frozen out. In these cases, the remedy has proven quite effective, since the mere threat of its use has often been sufficient to persuade the majority to reach a compromise.

winding up
the dissolution (or liquidation) of a corporation

The Oppression Remedy

More recently however, an alternative remedy—usually called the **oppression remedy**—has been introduced and widely adopted in Canada. It provides far greater flexibility since it allows a court, where the complainant has been treated unfairly or oppressively, to make any order it considers just and appropriate to remedy the situation. Typically, it is the remedy sought where a minority shareholder is "frozen-out," as in our Illustration 28.6,[30] but it has also been applied in cases of deadlock or breakdown in the relations between shareholders or directors, which for-

oppression remedy
a statutory procedure allowing individual shareholders to seek a personal remedy if they have been unfairly treated

---

29. CBCA, s. 214(1)(b)(ii). The "just and equitable winding up" rule has been a feature of English and Canadian company law statutes since around the end of the 19th century.

30. Re Ferguson and Imax Systems Corp. (1983), 150 D.L.R. (3d) 718; Daniels v. Fielder (1989), 52 D.L.R. (4th) 424.

merly might have led to a just and equitable winding up;[31] in a few cases, the oppression remedy has been used where a wrong has been done to the corporation, and a minority shareholder has suffered in consequence, even though a derivative action would seem to be more appropriate in such circumstances. Thus it is possible that Susanna, in Illustration 28.5, might seek an oppression remedy rather than bring a derivative action.[32]

To justify the making of an order under section 241, a complainant must show that the action complained of has been "oppressive or unfairly prejudicial or…unfairly disregards the interests" of the complainant. However, the courts have emphasized that the conduct need not be wrongful or in bad faith, though this will be a factor to take into account.[33]

Section 241(3) allows the court to make any order it thinks fit. By far the most common remedy granted has been to require the majority to buy out the minority interest at a fair price, but a wide range of other orders may be made. Because of its great flexibility, and the absence of technical obstacles, the oppression remedy is quickly becoming the most widely used shareholder remedy in Canada; it has largely replaced both the derivative action and "just and equitable" winding up.

SHAREHOLDER AGREEMENTS

Advantages

Although the oppression remedy has greatly increased the protection given to the minority shareholder, he still must depend on the court exercising its discretion in his favour—and it may decline to do so if the majority have complied with the corporation's charter and are not in breach of their duties to the corporation. Thus, a shareholder is still in a less secure position than is a partner.

This uncertainty is a factor to be considered if a small group of equal partners propose to transform their business into a corporation. It may make good business sense to incorporate because of the nature of the business, its growth, and its tax position. Yet each of the partners, if aware of the dangers of being a minority shareholder at odds with the others, might well hesitate to give up the protection of partnership law.

Fortunately it is possible to devise an agreement among the shareholders themselves—outside the constitution of the corporation—as well as an employment contract with the corporation that together approximate the protection available to partners. The process is not simple because, as we have seen, directors owe their primary duty to the corporation: they must not fetter their duty to exercise their discretion bona fide in the best interests of the corporation. Thus, subject to an important exception to be discussed below, any agreement among shareholders must be restricted to their role as shareholders and must not impinge on their role as directors.[34] This danger can be avoided in a well-drafted **shareholder agreement**. Each agreement must be custom-tailored to the needs of the individual business, just as in partnership, but it may be useful to examine briefly the chief elements normally used to protect minority shareholders.

shareholder agreement
an agreement between two or more shareholders that is distinct from the corporation's charter and by-laws

Right to Employment

Each shareholder may enter into a long-term employment contract with the corporation at a stipulated salary. There may be a provision that, in addition to the salary, he will receive an employee's bonus equal to a specified proportion of the corporation's profits each year.

---

31. Eiserman v. Ara Farms (1989), 52 D.L.R. (4th) 498; Tilley v. Hailes (1992), 7 O.R. (3d) 257.

32. See, for example, Journet v. Superchef Food Industries Ltd. (1984), 29 B.L.R. 206. For discussion of this issue, see MacIntosh, "The Oppression Remedy: Personal or Derivative?" (1991), 70 *Can. Bar Rev.* 29.

33. Brant Investments Ltd. v. Keeprite Inc., *supra*, n. 27; Westfair Food Ltd. v. Watt (1991), 79 D.L.R. (4th) 48.

34. Motherwell v. Schoof, [1949] 4 D.L.R. 812.

Right to Participate in Management

The shareholders promise to elect each other to the board of directors at each annual meeting and not to nominate or vote for any other person. They may agree not to sell their shares to an outsider without giving the right of first refusal proportionately to the remaining shareholders. They may also promise not to vote for any major change in the corporation's capital structure or in the nature of its business except by unanimous agreement.

The Right to a Fair Price for a Share Interest

The shareholders may agree to a regular method of valuation of their shares. If one of them commits a major breach of the shareholder agreement and remains unwilling to remedy it, on notice he can be required to sell his interest to the others at the appraised value. In addition, if any shareholder is wrongfully expelled or dismissed by the others, he may require them to buy out his interest at the appraised value. This provision may also state that in the event of a dispute about appraisal a named person, usually the auditor, will arbitrate and assess the value of the interest.

Unanimous Shareholder Agreements

unanimous shareholder agreement

a shareholder agreement to which all shareholders are parties

Articles of incorporation statutes formally recognize **unanimous shareholder agreements** and expressly permit them to govern relationships among shareholders in a closely held corporation in much the same manner as in a partnership. The CBCA states that "an agreement among all the shareholders...that restricts in whole or in part the powers of the directors to manage the business and affairs of the corporation is valid" (section 146(2)), and that a shareholder who is party to such an agreement "has all the rights, powers and duties of a director...to the extent that the agreement restricts the discretion or powers of the directors,...and the directors are thereby relieved of their duties and liabilities to the same extent"(section 146(5)).

The Act also states that "a transferee of shares subject to an unanimous shareholder agreement is deemed to be a party to the agreement" (section 146(4)). Thus, on the sale of a share interest in a closely held corporation that is subject to such an agreement, the transferee not only receives an assignment of rights as a shareholder but is also bound to carry out the duties of the transferor. A unanimous shareholder agreement must be "noted conspicuously" on the face of a share certificate in order to bind subsequent transferees (section 49(8)).

These provisions modify the common law rule that no agreement may fetter the discretion of directors. However, only *unanimous* agreements have special status under the acts. Accordingly, these agreements cannot be utilized in corporations using employee profit-sharing schemes where employees receive a share interest, unless the employees also are made parties to the agreement.

The CBCA makes frequent reference to unanimous shareholder agreements and treats them almost as if they were part of the corporate constitution, rather like by-laws. In doing so, it has provided the opportunity to develop a new, flexible device for business planning in closely held corporations.

QUESTIONS FOR REVIEW

1. What is the distinction between the "business" and the "affairs" of a corporation?

2. What are the principal powers given to the board of directors of a corporation incorporated under the CBCA?

3. How are directors appointed? How may they be removed?

4. To whom are directors' duties owed?

5. When a director enters into a contract with his or her own corporation, what precautions should be taken to ensure the validity of the contract?

6. What is meant by "intercepting a corporate opportunity"?

7. What is "insider trading"?

8. Who is an "insider"?

9. What is meant when one says that a minority shareholder is (a) "locked-in" and (b) "frozen-out"?

10. What are the principal rights attached to shares in a corporation?

11. What is the difference between an ordinary resolution and a special resolution?

12. What are "class rights"?

13. What is a "proxy"? How are proxies appointed?

14. Do shareholders have any right to receive a dividend if the corporation is profitable?

15. What are "pre-emptive rights" in relation to a corporation's shares?

16. Are there any restrictions on the directors' powers to issue new shares?

17. What information must be provided in a corporation's annual financial statement?

18. What is the role of a corporation's auditor? To whom is the auditor's duty owed?

19. What are a corporation's "documents of record"?

20. Do shareholders owe any duty to their corporation?

21. What is the "appraisal remedy"?

22. What is meant by a "derivative action"?

23. What matters are commonly dealt with in shareholder agreements?

CASES AND PROBLEMS

1 Ten years ago, Davidson and Farmer formed a corporation to develop a fishing lodge that they had bought (in the name of the corporation). They each owned 50 shares in the corporation: there were no other shareholders and Davidson and Farmer were the only directors.

They worked hard to develop the business, which became quite successful. No dividends were ever paid by the corporation but Davidson and Farmer had paid themselves generous salaries for their work as directors.

Last year, Davidson died. In his will he left his entire estate to his sister, Eriksen. Before her marriage she had occasionally worked at the lodge (for a salary), but recently had not been involved in the business.

Shortly after Davidson's death, Farmer (as the sole surviving director) purported to appoint his niece, Greenberg, as a director to fill the vacancy on the board. Next, Farmer and Greenberg passed a resolution issuing one share in the corporation to Greenberg for a consideration of $10 000 (which was estimated to be approximately 1 percent of the value of the business).

In response to requests from Eriksen, Farmer has agreed to register the transfer of Davidson's shares to her, but has made it clear that he will not agree to her becoming a director and that he intends to continue running the business together with Greenberg.

Does Eriksen have any remedy?

2 Petrescu is a director of Dracula Fashions Ltd., a small but successful corporation operating a boutique in Calgary. She also owns 25 percent of the corporation's shares.

Petrescu recently inherited some property from her aunt, including a bookstore in downtown Calgary. The bookstore was not very successful, but Petrescu realized that the store premises would be ideal for Dracula, which was seeking to expand.

At the next board meeting she informed her fellow Dracula directors that she had heard of a suitable property that had just come on the market. The chief executive officer, Vlad, agreed to inspect the property and, when he reported back that the property seemed very suitable and was reasonably priced, the board unanimously approved the purchase of the property from the estate of Petrescu's aunt.

Petrescu at no time disclosed the fact that the estate was that of her aunt or that she was the main beneficiary under the aunt's will. However, Vlad has since discovered that fact.

Was Petrescu in breach of her duty to the corporation? Does the corporation have any remedy?

3 Until three years ago, Slater was the sole shareholder and director of Lockley Quarries Ltd., a small corporation that owned a quarry and produced trimmed limestone blocks. Then an opportunity arose to purchase a second quarry at a very good price. Slater did not have sufficient funds and persuaded Mason to come into business with him and to help finance the purchase of the new quarry. As a result, Mason became a 40 percent shareholder and a director of Lockley Quarries. Slater and Mason got on well together and the business prospered.

A few months ago, Slater was approached by an old friend, Chalker, who proposed that they—Chalker and Slater—should purchase and operate a gravel pit that had come on the market. Slater agreed and a new corporation was formed to acquire the gravel pit, with Chalker and Slater as equal shareholders and directors.

Mason has learned of the dealings between Slater and Chalker. He considers that he should have been given the opportunity to participate in the new gravel pit venture. Do you agree? Does Mason have any remedy against Slater?

4 Normin Inc. is a large mining corporation, incorporated under the CBCA, the shares of which are publicly traded and are listed on the Toronto Stock Exchange. It has recently been conducting extensive exploration on land acquired in the Canadian Arctic.

Late in the afternoon of March 31, Normin's chief executive officer, Baffin, received a fax from the mineralogist in charge of the explorations. The fax, headed "Highly Confidential," informed Baffin that a giant deposit of tin had been discovered. It appeared that it would be fairly easy to extract and would be extremely profitable.

Baffin at once informed as many of the directors and senior officers as he could contact. After some discussion they agreed to prepare a press release the next morning. However, on the evening of March 31:

(a) One of the directors, Banks, telephoned his broker, Charles, and without giving any reason instructed Charles to buy as many Normin shares on his account as he could, provided the price did not exceed $30 per share. The following morning, Normin shares opened on the exchange at $28.75. Charles bought 10 000 shares for Banks, at prices between $28.75 and $29.50.

(b) Another director, Melville, contacted her brother, Parry, and offered to buy his shares in Normin. Parry had acquired the shares some years before, but had since lost interest in the investment and had several times asked Melville if she would like to buy them. Melville offered to pay $29 per share, and Parry accepted and transferred his 15 000 shares to his sister.

(c) Hudson, a senior executive of Normin, told his bridge partner, Frobisher, that she should tell no one, but should buy Normin shares as soon as possible. Frobisher bought 2000 shares on the exchange the following morning, at $29.25 per share.

At midday on April 1, the press release was published, giving details of the find. Trading on the exchange became brisk, and by the end of the day the price of Normin shares had reached $47.50.

Discuss the possible liability of any of the individuals mentioned, and the remedies, if any, which Parry and other shareholders who sold their shares before midday on April 1 might have.

5 For many years Sergei (a widower) owned and ran a large farm, initially by himself and later with the help of his four children. Eight years ago, on the advice of his accountant and his lawyer, he decided to transfer the farm to a corporation and, with a view to keeping the farm in the family (and to saving taxes), to make his children shareholders in the corporation.

A corporation, Eisenstein Farms Inc., was formed with two classes of shares. As consideration for the transfer of the farm to the corporation, Sergei received 1000 Class 'A' preferred shares, each share carrying one vote. The four children, Galina, Ivan, Oleg, and Tanya, each received 100 Class 'B' common shares, also carrying one vote per share, for which they paid $10 per share. Two of the children—Galina and Ivan—had left home and no longer took an active part in running the farm. The other two—Oleg and Tanya—continued to live with their father and work on the farm, and were made directors and employees of the corporation along with Sergei. No dividends were paid by the corporation in respect of the common shares (Sergei received dividends on his preferred shares), but Sergei, Oleg, and Tanya all received salaries.

A year ago things started to turn sour. Oleg got married, and neither Sergei nor Tanya got on with his wife. They complained that he was neglecting the farm and spending most of his time helping his wife with her business. (Oleg denied this.) After a series of heated arguments Oleg threatened to resign from the board of directors and to quit his employment with the corporation. Sergei and Tanya immediately accepted his "resignation." Since then, relations between them have deteriorated further. Oleg is no longer receiving any remuneration from the corporation, either as a director or employee, has been excluded from directors' meetings and has been given no information about the corporation's business or affairs.

Oleg considers that he has been treated unfairly. Does he have any remedy?

6 Aldeburgh Inc. is a corporation incorporated under the CBCA. It has never issued shares to the public. It owns a large piece of land, and a number of vacation cottages, fronting on a lake some distance north of Queensville, Ontario. The property has produced relatively little income in the past.

Until recently, Aldeburgh had four shareholders—Balstrode, Crabbe, Orford, and Swallow—who each owned 25 percent of the issued shares. Balstrode, Crabbe, and Orford are the directors of the corporation. Swallow is retired and has taken little interest in the business.

A few months ago, the three directors received a tip from Grimes (a friend of theirs and a prominent local politician) that a large corporation, Maltings Developments Inc., was proposing to establish a major recreational complex along the lake and was almost certain to get permission for the development. When the news became public, he suggested, the price of land in the area would soar.

Balstrode, Crabbe, and Orford held a directors' meeting and resolved that Aldeburgh should try to buy up as much property in the area as possible. They did not tell Swallow the good news. Aldeburgh borrowed as much money as it was able to and bought a number of lots.

During the same period, the following events occurred:

(a) Balstrode approached Swallow and persuaded Swallow to sell her his shares. She said nothing about the proposed development.

(b) Crabbe personally bought one lot for herself (without disclosing the fact to anyone), which she was later able to resell to Maltings at a large profit.

(c) Orford bought one lot (in the name of a numbered company) that she resold to Aldeburgh at a quick profit, without disclosing that she was the beneficial owner.

(d) Grimes bought several lots himself, which he later sold to Maltings at a large profit.

Soon afterwards, Maltings offered to buy all of the land owned by Aldeburgh or, alternatively, to buy all of its shares. An agreement was reached to sell the shares, with the result that all of the Aldeburgh shares are now owned by Maltings, and the shareholders of Aldeburgh all made large profits on the sale of their shares.

Maltings has now discovered the secret activities of Balstrode, Crabbe, Orford, and Grimes. Swallow has learned about the profit that Balstrode made on the resale of his shares.

Who is liable for what? to whom? on what grounds? How can liability be enforced?

THE EXTERNAL RESPONSIBILITIES OF A CORPORATION

This chapter examines the relationship between the corporation and the outside world—its customers, creditors, potential investors and the general public. We must remember that a corporation is an *artificial person*; it can act only through its directors, officers, and agents. In this chapter we examine such questions as:

- to what extent is a corporation liable for the acts of its directors, officers, and agents?

- how do corporations enter into contracts?

- can a corporation be negligent?

- can it commit a crime?

- to what extent may directors, officers, or agents be held personally liable for acts done, or not done, in the name of the corporation?

- what liability is imposed on corporate officers under environmental legislation in particular?

THE CHANGING NATURE OF BUSINESS RESPONSIBILITIES

In the classic 19th-century view, the duty of directors was to protect the corporation's capital and to produce profits for the shareholders. There were very few restrictions on the activities of business enterprises and liabilities arose mainly through contract and tort. In the 20th century, duties owed by enterprises—and by their directors and officers—began to expand to employees, in terms of legislation concerning health and safety and general working conditions; to consumers, in terms of product liability and safety standards; and to the general public, most notably in terms of environmental legislation.

Today, even to operate a small corner store the proprietor will find that she must comply with a large number of regulations. At the level of the small business, both government regulation and general tort liability tend to resolve themselves into issues of higher overhead costs—whether in the form of insurance premiums or the time taken to do the required paperwork. However, it is manufacturing, natural resource, and transportation enterprises that now feel the major effects of the vast increase in regulation.

In this chapter we shall discuss the liability of corporations at common law and under various regulatory schemes—liability both for enterprises themselves and for their directors and senior officers.

LIABILITY OF A CORPORATION FOR ACTS OF ITS AGENTS

Generally speaking, a corporation is liable for the acts of its agents under the ordinary rules of agency. A director or an officer of a corporation acting within her actual authority binds the corporation to contracts made with third parties. A corporation may ratify acts made by unauthorized agents on its behalf. Further, where a director or officer acts within the scope of her usual, or apparent, authority, even though she has no actual authority to do so, the corporation will be bound unless the third party knew (or ought to have known) of the lack of authority.

indoor management rule
the principle that a person dealing with a corporation is entitled to assume that its internal procedural rules have been complied with unless it is apparent that such is not the case

What is the effect upon an innocent third party if a contract has been made in an irregular manner? The courts have held that in the absence of notice of the irregularity or of suspicious circumstances, everything that appears regular on its face may be relied upon by an outsider and will bind the corporation.[1] That principle is often referred to as the **indoor management rule**,[2] and is really just an application of the apparent authority principle in agency law: an innocent third party may rely on the regularity of a corporate act, just as he may rely on the apparent authority of an agent, if it is reasonable for him to do so in the circumstances.

ILLUSTRATION 29.1

W, the chief executive officer of *A* Ltd, negotiates a contract to buy equipment from *B* Inc. for $1 million. The by-laws of *A* Ltd provide that any contract involving expenditure of more than $50 000 must be approved by the board of its Japanese parent company. That approval had not been obtained. Consequently, *W* was acting outside the scope of her actual authority. Can *B* Inc. enforce the contract?

The answer is "yes" unless *B* Inc. knew of the restriction in the by-laws and that the approval of the parent board had not been obtained.

As we saw in the preceding chapter, certain corporate documents must be filed in a government office and are available to the public for examination, in a manner similar to the registration of title documents concerning land. At one time, the public was deemed to have notice

---

1. Royal British Bank v. Turquand (1856), 119 E.R. 886.

2. This rule receives statutory recognition in articles of incorporation jurisdictions: see, Canada Business Corporations Act, R.S.C. 1985, c. C-44, s. 18 (hereafter CBCA). Subsequent references in this chapter are to the CBCA unless otherwise stated.

of the contents of those documents whether they had read them or not. Hence, if the documents prohibited either the corporation or one of its officers from carrying out certain acts, a third party could not rely upon what otherwise might be the officer's apparent authority to perform those acts. That rule could lead to substantial injustice and has now been abolished by statute. For example, section 17 of the Canada Business Corporations Act (CBCA) provides:

> No person is affected by or is deemed to have notice or knowledge of the content of a document concerning a corporation by reason only that the document has been filed by the Director or is available for inspection at an office of the corporation.

Of course, a contracting third party who actually has read or knows the contents of a restriction will be bound by it, but in saying this we are merely restating the common law rule of agency: a third party who knows of an express restriction between the principal and agent cannot claim to rely on an apparent authority that ignores the restriction.

PRE-INCORPORATION CONTRACTS

We noted in Chapter 19 that, at common law, a corporation could not ratify a **pre-incorporation contract**—that is, a contract made on its behalf before it came into existence. If a "contract" was made in the name of a corporation even one day before it came into existence the purported contract was of no effect and a new contract would have to be negotiated once the corporation was formed. Further, the individual who purported to contract on behalf of the corporation could not be held to the contract either, since the intention was to contract with the corporation.[3]

The CBCA, and the provincial statutes based on it, largely remedied the deficiencies of the common law. The CBCA provides that:

pre-incorporation contract
a purported contract made in the name of a corporation before it comes into existence

> A corporation may, within a reasonable time after it comes into existence, by any action or conduct signifying its intention to be bound thereby, adopt a written contract made before it came into existence in its name or on its behalf, and upon such adoption
>
> (a) the corporation is bound by the contract and is entitled to the benefits thereof as if the corporation had been in existence at the date of the contract and had been a party thereto; and
>
> (b) a person who purported to act in the name of or on behalf of the corporation ceases…to be bound by or entitled to the benefits of the contract.[4]

If the corporation does not adopt the pre-incorporation contract, the CBCA expressly makes the person who signed the contract bound by it and entitled to any benefits under it. The clear intention is that, whether the contract is adopted or not, it will be enforceable by the other party.[5] The Act also seeks to prevent unfair manipulation by a corporation and a contractor. For example, a contractor may make a contract on behalf of a corporation that he himself will subsequently incorporate and control and to which he plans to give virtually no assets. If, after incorporation, he decides that the contract is a bad bargain, he might cause the corporation to adopt the contract and thereby seemingly escape any personal liability as its agent-contractor. To prevent this abuse, the Act goes on to state:

> …whether or not a written contract made before the coming into existence of a corporation is adopted by the corporation, a party to the contract may apply to a court for an

---

3. See Delta Construction Co. Ltd. v. Lidstone et al. (1979), 96 D.L.R. (3d) 457. The individual may be liable for breach of warranty of authority: this is discussed in Chapter 19.

4. S. 14(2). There are some variations from province to province. For example, Ontario does not restrict the rule to written contracts.

5. S. 14(1). See, however, Westcom Radio Group Ltd. v. MacIsaac (1989), 70 O.R. (2d) 591, which casts some doubt on the effectiveness of this provision. Contrast Sherwood Design Services Inc. v. 872935 Ontario Ltd. (1998), 158 D.L.R. (4th) 440.

order fixing obligations under the contract as joint or joint and several or apportioning liability between or among the corporation and a person who purported to act in the name of or on behalf of the corporation and upon such application the court may make any order it thinks fit.[6]

The CBCA also states that a promoter acting on behalf of a corporation before it comes into existence may avoid personal liability and waive any benefits under the contract when the contract includes an express term that the promoter will not be bound by the agreement.[7]

FIGURE 29.1
Pre-incorporation Contracts

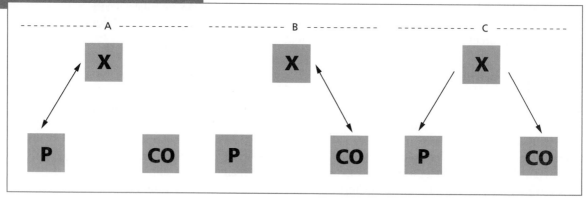

In situation A, the promoter, *P*, has entered into a contract with a third party, *X*, in the name of corporation *CO*, before it has come into existence. The effect is to create a contract between *P* and *X*. In situation B, the corporation has since been formed and has adopted the contract. There is now a contract between *CO* and *X*, and *P* is no longer a party to it. In situation C, the court has, on an application by *X*, apportioned liability and both *P* and *CO* are liable.

PROTECTION OF CREDITORS

Implications of Limited Liability

We have seen that when a sole trader or partnership becomes insolvent, the creditors are entitled to whatever assets are available and that if a deficiency remains they may look to the personal assets of the trader or partners. In these forms of business organization, a debtor's liability is not limited to her business assets: her personal assets may be seized as well. In a corporation, however, a creditor's rights are limited to the assets held by the corporation. If those assets are inadequate, it normally has no further remedy against the shareholders.[8] Accordingly, a creditor's only protection is the fund of assets owned by the corporation itself. For this reason, legislatures and courts have tried to evolve rules to assure creditors that those assets will not be wasted.

Minimum Capital Requirement

Except for such financial institutions as banks, insurance companies, and trust and loan companies, the law requires no minimum issued capital for corporations.[9] Legally, a corporation may carry on business with a share capital of $1. Of course, a corporation would find it difficult

---

6. S. 14(3).

7. S. 14(4). To be effective, there must be an express exclusion of liability: see Szecket v. Huang (1999), 168 D.L.R. (4th) 402.

8. There are a few limited exceptions to this principle: see the discussion under "Exceptions to Limited Liability," in Chapter 27.

9. In most countries outside North America corporations must have a minimum capital prescribed by law.

to obtain credit with only a nominal equity investment, but even so, such a corporation might become liable to pay a large sum of money as a result, say, of the negligent conduct of one of its officers or employees.

Preservation of Capital

It is not possible to devise legal rules that will protect creditors from the risk of extending credit to a corporation whose management runs it badly and impairs its capital through business losses. The primary concern of the law has been to ensure that a corporation's stated capital is not improperly reduced by preferring the rights of shareholders over those of creditors.

As we have seen, a consequence of the principle of limited liability is that the creditors of a corporation may look only to the assets of the corporation for payment of what is owed to them. On the winding up of a corporation its creditors are entitled to have the assets applied in satisfaction of their claims before any surplus is returned to the shareholders. From this rule evolved the principle that a corporation's capital could not be returned to its shareholders except on a winding up, after all creditors had been paid in full. That principle resulted in the following rules:

- Dividends could be paid only out of profits.
- A corporation was not allowed to buy back its own shares.
- A corporation was not allowed to lend money to assist a purchaser to acquire its shares.
- A corporation could not normally lend money to its shareholders.

Over time these rules gave rise to much confusing, and sometimes conflicting, case law. For example, if a corporation incurred losses for several years and then made a profit in one year, could it pay a dividend in that year or was it required to first make good the losses incurred in earlier years? Could a corporation create a "profit" simply by reassessing—and increasing the book value—of its assets? Some of the exceptions to the rules also created problems: a corporation could make loans to its employees (even if they were also shareholders) to enable them to purchase housing; and in some cases the courts could approve a **reduction of capital**.

The rules also proved inflexible and made legitimate restructuring of a corporation's capital difficult and expensive—or even impossible—to achieve.

reduction of capital
writing down the stated amount of a corporation's capital

Protection of Capital Under the CBCA

Happily, the difficulties have been largely eliminated in most of Canada; the CBCA (and those provincial statutes modelled on it) now set out rules that are relatively simple to understand and to apply. The CBCA rules are essentially of two kinds: rules that prohibit any payment by the corporation to its shareholders that renders the corporation's liquid assets insufficient to pay the then outstanding claims of creditors, or any such payment when the corporation is already insolvent; and rules that prohibit or restrict the "return of capital" to shareholders even when the corporation might still be left with sufficient liquid assets to pay its creditors.

The Solvency Test

After a corporation has received assets from shareholders by an issue of share capital, subsequent transactions with those shareholders will be confined largely to payments of dividends, and in certain circumstances to the redemption or repurchase by the corporation of its own shares. If payments by the corporation in either of these instances is made when the corporation is insolvent or would have the effect of making the corporation insolvent, the directors may become personally liable to the corporation for the deficiency.[10]

---

10. See, for example: CBCA, ss. 42 and 118(2)(c).

insolvency

having liabilities in excess of the realizable value of one's assets or being unable to pay one's debts as they fall due

The effectiveness of this test depends upon the definition of **insolvency** that is used. For the purposes of the corporations acts, two factors must be considered: a corporation is deemed insolvent if the realizable value of its assets has become less than its total liabilities, or if it is unable to pay its debts as they become due.[11]

The Maintenance of Capital Test

The theory underlying provisions for the maintenance of capital requires more than a solvency test; it requires that assets paid into the corporation by shareholders be preserved as far as possible within the corporation as a "capital fund," available for absorbing business losses so that creditors (and in some cases, preferred shareholders) may still be paid in full. The maintenance of capital test therefore goes beyond the solvency test. It applies in the following cases.

Dividends

The CBCA, section 42 provides that a corporation may not pay a dividend if there are reasonable grounds for believing that (a) the corporation is, or would after the payment be, unable to pay its liabilities as they become due, and (b) if the realizable value of the corporation's assets would thereby be less than the aggregate of its liabilities *and* its stated capital of all classes. In other words, after the dividend has been paid the corporation's net assets must not be less than the amount of its stated capital. This rule effectively restates (in a less ambiguous manner) the old rule that dividends may only be paid out of profits. A corporation's net assets will only exceed its stated capital if either it has undistributed profits or its assets have increased in value.

ILLUSTRATION 29.2

A corporation originally issued shares for a total of $5 million. For several years it has traded at a profit, in the sense that its revenues exceeded its expenditures. However, its capital assets have depreciated in value. It now has net assets of exactly $5 million. Despite having a trading profit, it cannot pay a dividend.

Return of Capital

A corporation may return a part of its capital to its shareholders either by making a *pro rata* payment to each shareholder—in which case the effect is essentially the same as the payment of a dividend—or by buying back the shares of some of its shareholders. A return of capital, like the payment of a dividend when there are no profits or capital gain out of which to pay it, reduces the funds available to meet the claims of creditors and, if the corporation should subsequently become insolvent, would give a preferred repayment to shareholders before the creditors' claims are met.

As described above, the statutes in both letters patent and memorandum jurisdictions had very strict rules about maintenance of capital; a corporation could not return any part of its capital to its shareholders except with the consent of its creditors or by leave of the court, nor could it purchase its own shares (apart from redeeming preferred shares as provided in the corporation's charter), or enable a subsidiary to hold shares in its parent. The rules were vigorously applied by the courts and could sometimes cause unreasonable hardship.

Although some or all of the rules remain in force in a few jurisdictions, they have mostly been repealed or replaced with more practical rules better suited to business needs. Under the CBCA, for example, a corporation may repay capital to its shareholders provided that it will still

---

11. The federal Bankruptcy and Insolvency Act provides, additionally, an "after the fact" test that permits a trustee in bankruptcy to apply for a court inquiry in respect of dividends paid within 12 months preceding bankruptcy to determine whether the dividend rendered the corporation insolvent, and that authorizes the court to give judgment to the trustee against the directors, jointly and severally, in the amount of such dividend: R.S.C. 1985, c. B-3, s. 101.

be able to satisfy both parts of the solvency test.[12] This rule is reasonable, since shareholders may have contributed substantially more capital than, as it turns out, the corporation really needs; so long as creditors are amply protected there is no reason to insist that excess—and unutilized—capital remain in the corporation.

Corporations may also redeem or purchase their own shares for a number of specified reasons, subject to solvency requirements to protect creditors.[13] Since the prohibition against a corporation holding its own previously issued shares has been relaxed, the rule against giving financial help to any person to buy shares has also become unnecessary.[14]

An actual return of capital to its shareholders must be distinguished from a reduction in the amount of a corporation's stated capital. A reduction generally does no more than recognize a state of affairs that has occurred: the corporation's net assets have decreased in value. As such it is not objectionable.[15]

Loans to Shareholders, Directors, and Employees

The old rules against return of capital were reinforced by a prohibition against a corporation making loans of any kind to its shareholders, directors, or employees. The idea behind the prohibition was that such loans might amount to an indirect return of capital and might deprive the corporation of liquidity. A common exception was to permit loans to employees to help them buy housing or to buy shares under a share purchase plan. The CBCA has relaxed the rules considerably: loans to shareholders, directors, and employees are prohibited only if they would endanger a corporation's solvency, or reduce the value of its assets—not counting such loans as an asset—to less than the amount of its stated capital.[16]

PROTECTION OF INVESTORS

Securities Legislation

In Canada, securities legislation is substantially within provincial jurisdiction,[17] in contrast with the United States where the related controls are divided between federal and state jurisdictions. Each Canadian province has a Securities Act or Securities Fraud Prevention Act, under which a government board is created, known in most of the provinces as a **securities commission**. The securities commission operates as the enforcing agency charged with ensuring that the requirements of the Act are complied with.

securities commission
the statutory authority appointed to supervise the issue of securities to the general public and the operation of the securities industry

Objectives of Securities Legislation

Two main objectives of securities legislation are common to all provinces: (1) to prevent and punish fraudulent practices in the securities industry, and (2) to require full disclosure of financial information to prospective buyers of shares and bonds offered for the first time to the

---

12. CBCA, s. 38. To do so requires a special resolution.

13. Ss. 30–37.

14. It remains illegal, of course, to lend money for this purpose if to do so would make the corporation insolvent: s. 44(1).

15. S.38(1)(c), and (3).

16. S. 44. The section seems to produce the strange result that a loan may be made to an employee for a house or share purchase, or to a parent or subsidiary corporation, even if the loan would put the corporation in a position where it was unable to pay its debts as they fell due.

17. Federally incorporated companies, in addition to being subject to provincial securities acts, must file any prospectus with the federal government; *ibid.*, s. 193. In 1971, the securities regulatory authorities in the provinces of Alberta, British Columbia, Manitoba, New Brunswick, Ontario, Prince Edward Island, Quebec, and Saskatchewan agreed to a number of "National Policies" that include, for example, an agreed procedure by which an underwriter may clear a prospectus in more than one province. In additional, the five westernmost provinces (British Columbia to Ontario) agreed upon a further number of "Uniform Act Policies."

public. These objectives are related to the policy of increasing the efficiency of the capital market, first by maintaining the confidence of investors, and second by providing information for rational investment decisions. A basic purpose of securities legislation is to make the capital market an efficient medium for allocating available funds among competing investment opportunities; according to this theory, improving investors' ability to make intelligent choices gives the most deserving projects a priority. However, the efficacy of many aspects of securities regulation has been seriously questioned by some economists and finance theorists.[18]

Traditionally, Canadian securities legislation has used two devices for achieving the objectives described above: (1) registering or licensing those engaged in various aspects of the securities business, and (2) requiring the issuer of securities to the public to file a prospectus with the securities commission.

Licensing

The registering of persons engaged in the securities industry is an important device for ensuring a reasonable measure of ethical conduct. Licensing is on an annual basis, and each securities commission has authority under its provincial statute to revoke, suspend, or refuse to renew the licence of anyone when in its opinion such action is in the public interest. Operating without a licence is a criminal offence. Depending upon the jurisdiction, a licence may be required of persons engaged in a wide variety of activities. Those affected include brokers (who buy and sell securities as agents), investment dealers (who buy and sell securities as principals), broker-dealers (who may act as either principal or agent in the promotion of companies), securities issuers (companies issuing their securities directly to the public without the intermediate services of investment dealers), salespeople employed by any of these businesses, and investment counsel and securities advisers.

Prospectuses

prospectus

the document that a corporation is required to publish when inviting the public to subscribe for its securities

The filing of a **prospectus** with a securities commission is not merely a formality. The commission will refuse to approve a prospectus if, after a thorough review of the contents, its staff concludes that the prospectus is misleading or omits required data, and no one may issue securities to the public unless and until the prospectus has been approved. Prospectus requirements are an attempt to ensure that prospective investors have access to the pertinent facts about a corporation before deciding whether or not to invest in it. In many instances, an investor is entitled to a copy of the prospectus before buying securities and may rescind the contract of subscription if he or she does not receive the prospectus and acts to repudiate the contract within a specified period. The minimum detail required in the prospectus is prescribed by statute, or in regulations appended to the act, and is too comprehensive to set out here in full. It is sufficient to note that the prospectus must, among other things, include

- a full description of the securities to be offered (either shares or bonds) with a statement of their voting rights, preference, conversion privileges, and rights on liquidation, if any
- the nature of the business carried on
- the names, addresses, and occupations of the directors
- the proposed use of the proceeds from the issue of securities
- details of any share options to be given by the corporation[19]

---

18. See, for example, articles in Manne (ed.), *Economic Policy and the Regulation of Corporate Securities*; Posner, *Economic Analysis of Law* (3rd. ed.), pp. 571–7. Boston: Little Brown and Company, 1986.

19. A share option is a right to subscribe for shares in the corporation at a fixed price within a specified time, given by a corporation as consideration for the payment of money, the rendering of services (often the services of directors), or any other valuable consideration. The option becomes valuable at any time before expiry that the market price exceeds the option price.

- the remuneration of the underwriter
- the dividend record of the corporation
- the particulars of property and services to be paid for out of the proceeds of the issue
- recent audited financial statements

Continuing Disclosure

The enactment of revised securities acts in the various provinces, commencing in 1966, has ushered in a new era of public control over the securities industry in Canada. In addition to licensing and prospectus provisions, the legislation has introduced important forms of control, largely inspired by experience in the United States since the establishment of the Securities and Exchange Commission in 1934.[20] One of the most important innovations gives the securities commission control over the stock exchanges within the province (in Ontario, for example, over the Toronto Stock Exchange).[21] The significance of the provision is that control by the regulatory body extends not only to issues of new securities but also to trading in already outstanding securities: the act specifies the minimum of financial information that must be disclosed, on a regular basis, to shareholders of all companies whose shares are traded on the stock exchange.[22] In addition, the legislation contains provisions designed to make the proxy a more effective means of registering shareholders' opinions.[23] As we noted Chapter 28, the legislation also requires publication of insiders' transactions in their corporation's shares,[24] authorizes actions against insiders, and makes insider trading a statutory offence.[25]

Takeovers and Reorganizations

Another important objective of securities legislation is to give shareholders who have received a **takeover bid** for their shares sufficient information and time to assess the merits of the bid.[26] Takeover provisions include a requirement for disclosure of the number of shares in the offeree corporation held by the offeror corporation and its officers, and details of recent trading in those shares. In addition, the directors of an offeree corporation are required to issue a **directors' circular** to the shareholders setting out, among other things, their own intentions with respect to the takeover offer, and details of any arrangements made with the offeror corporation concerning their continuance in office or compensation for loss of office. However, this legislation does not apply to all corporations; in particular, takeovers of small private corporations are not regulated.

takeover bid
an offer by one corporation to acquire all or a substantial part of the shares of another corporation

directors' circular
a document required to be issued to the shareholders by the board of directors when a takeover of a widely held corporation is proposed

Both corporate and securities legislation contain detailed and complex rules dealing with mergers, with various types of corporate reorganization, and with winding up. These are fields requiring the talents of experts, both financial and legal. Needless to say, no one faced with the problem of making a decision in one of the above areas should undertake a course of action without expert assistance from beginning to end of the project. The problems involved usually concern creditors' rights, the effects of taxation, the relevance of competition legislation, and the rights of various classes of shareholders, in addition to the general economic consequences for the corporations involved.

---

20. It is not possible to do justice to this important area in the present chapter. For a complete discussion see Alboini, *Securities Law and Practice* (2nd ed.). Toronto: Carswell, 1984.

21. Securities Act, R.S.O. 1990, c. S-5, s. 23.

22. *Ibid.*, ss. 75 to 83.

23. *Ibid.*, ss. 84 to 88.

24. *Ibid.*, ss. 106 to 109.

25. *Ibid.*, ss. 76, 122(1)(c), and 134.

26. *Ibid.*, ss. 89 to 105.

PROTECTION OF THE PUBLIC INTEREST

We have already noted how a number of areas of regulation to which businesses are subject have expanded in recent years. Apart from the benefits that may be secured to organized employees through collective agreements under a carefully regulated system of labour relations, individual employees are protected by workers' compensation legislation, employment standards acts and, most recently, by human rights codes and pay equity legislation, as noted in Chapter 20. The increasing complexity of consumer products and the inability of distributors and retailers to assure the quality and safety of products has, of necessity, led to increased liability for producers through safety, health and labelling standards, and consumer protection legislation. There are other important areas of regulation, notably the Competition Act, to prohibit collusive business arrangements contrary to the public interest and legislation for the protection of the environment. These are discussed in Chapter 32.

Environmental regulation, in particular, has evolved rapidly in recent years and provides a helpful example of the growing responsibilities of business and the consequences of failure to comply with regulatory requirements. Questions of corporate liability arise in breaches of many types of statutory regulations, but for the remainder of this chapter we shall focus mainly on environmental regulations.

THE NATURE OF CORPORATE LIABILITY

To help us in discussing regulatory schemes generally, we should first note an important distinction between

- *civil liability*—liability towards a plaintiff, typically to pay damages for harms done through committing a tort or breaking a contract; and
- *criminal liability*—conviction for an offence, typically punished by imprisonment or payment of a fine or both.

Regulatory Offences

Schemes of government regulation resemble traditional criminal law because, in order to protect the public interest, they almost invariably prohibit certain kinds of conduct and punish those who ignore the prohibitions. While most types of government regulations are not primarily concerned with punishing wrongdoers they nevertheless derive their standards from criminal law.[27] Accordingly, we shall begin by describing the elements that traditionally the prosecution must prove in order to obtain a conviction.

The Requirement of Fault

In general, the prosecution must prove beyond a reasonable doubt not only that an accused actually committed the offence with which he is charged, but also that he was "at fault": it must establish that the accused had *mens rea* (a guilty mind), that is, a guilty intention or guilty knowledge. The offence of "possession of stolen goods" provides a useful example: a person who is found to be in possession of stolen goods has not committed an offence if he did not know that they were stolen, even if he were naive about their source. Only when a court is persuaded that the accused knew the goods were stolen will he be found guilty.

---

27. Some statutory regulations also create civil liability, so that a wrongdoer may have to compensate a party harmed by its breach. See, for example, liability for insider trading, discussed in Chapter 28. Section 131 of the CBCA makes "insiders" (usually directors or employees of a corporation) who use confidential information to profit from a transaction in the corporation's securities liable to compensate any person who suffered loss and accountable to the corporation for the profits. In addition, such regulations almost invariably authorize the appropriate government agency to prosecute and to exact punishment. Section 251 of the CBCA makes a person who contravenes s. 131 "guilty of an offence punishable on summary conviction."

The Presumption of Fault

As we move away from the traditional criminal offences towards what are sometimes called regulatory offences such as careless driving, we find that the courts—and, as we shall see, more and more often the statutes that create new offences—broaden the definition of *mens rea*; it may be enough to show that if any ordinary person would or *should* have realized that his conduct was an offence, the wrongdoer will be convicted. For instance, if a person drove his car at 100 km/h through a crowded shopping area in a city, he would very likely be convicted of a provincial offence of "careless driving" or even the more serious Criminal Code offence of "dangerous driving," despite his own belief that he was not endangering anyone.

The broader definition of the guilty mind principle as applied in the careless driving case results from public policy concerns—the need for deterrence; for reasons of road safety we do not want people who drive dangerously to avoid conviction easily. Consequently, for a number of offences, the courts now hold there is a *presumption* that the accused, in committing the wrongful act, had the requisite guilty mind in a broad sense—that he was careless and did not make a diligent effort to avoid the breach. However, the accused can overcome the presumption by persuading the court that he acted with reasonable care in the circumstances.

Absolute Liability

As early as the middle of the 19th century, the courts went even further. They held that for certain regulatory schemes where public health and safety were paramount, no *mens rea* at all was required for a conviction; it was enough for the prosecution simply to prove that the accused had committed the wrongful act. As a result, under some statutes, but not many, accused persons may be convicted without any proof of *mens rea*, for example, a driver in a new vehicle with a faulty speedometer who is unaware that he is exceeding the speed limit.[28]

Checklist: Classification of Offences

The issue of whether the prosecution must establish that the accused had a guilty mind within the narrower traditional definition of intention or actual knowledge, or within a broader definition, or indeed, whether there is need to establish a guilty mind at all, remains a controversial problem in criminal law. In a 1978 case in which a municipal government was charged with breach of an environmental regulation, the Supreme Court of Canada divided criminal offences into three classes, which may be summarized as follows:[29]

- *Mens rea offences*, where the prosecution must demonstrate the existence of a "guilty mind," consisting of some positive state of mind such as intent, knowledge, or recklessness.
- *Offences of strict liability*, where there is no necessity for the prosecution to prove the existence of *mens rea*; the doing of the prohibited act raises a presumption that an offence has been committed, leaving it open to the accused to avoid liability by proving that he took all reasonable care.
- *Offences of absolute liability*, where it is not open to the accused to excuse himself by showing that he was free of fault. Simply doing the act makes one guilty of the offence.

continued

mens rea offence
an offence where the prosecution must establish a "guilty mind" on the part of the defendant

strict liability offence
an offence where there is a presumption of guilt unless the defendant can show that he or she took reasonable care

absolute liability offence
an offence where the absence of fault is no defence

---

28. See R. v. Hickey (1976), 70 D.L.R. (3d) 689. At least in some provinces, exceeding the speed limit is still considered such an offence: Motor Vehicle Act, R.S.B.C. 1996, c. 318, s. 146; Highway Traffic Act, R.S.O. 1990, c. H.8, s. 128 (14).

29. See R. v. City of Sault Ste Marie (1978), 85 D.L.R. (3d) 161 (S.C.C.).

It is generally agreed that the third class remains a very limited one; our courts are reluctant to punish an accused where no evidence of carelessness has been presented. Indeed, the Supreme Court of Canada has decided that an absolute liability offence is unconstitutional when conviction may lead to an accused being imprisoned.[30]

Liability of Corporations

Can Corporations Commit Crimes?

We have seen earlier in this chapter that corporations may incur *civil* liability as principals for the acts or omissions of their agents and employees. Corporations are also liable to be punished under *criminal law*, subject to the principles we have just discussed. However, the characteristics of corporations present special problems:

(a) As we have seen, most offences require the prosecution to prove both that the accused actually committed the offence and also that at the very least he has been negligent—but a corporation has neither a physical body with which to carry out the offence, nor a "mind" of its own that could be considered guilty or negligent.

(b) If convicted, a guilty person's punishment is often imprisonment—but a corporation cannot be imprisoned.

The consequences of (b) merely limit sanctions against a corporation to fining it, or to ordering it to refrain from certain conduct, or in some cases to dissolving the corporation, a relatively painless form of capital punishment. The prosecution may also lay charges personally against directors and senior officers of a corporation, a topic to which we shall soon return.

With regard to (a), the courts did not find it easy to apply the principles of criminal law to corporations. First, there was the question of whether a corporation could "commit" an offence, that is, whether it could actually carry out an act, since it has no physical presence—no finger to "pull the trigger." Nevertheless, for the very limited number of absolute liability offences, the courts seemed to ignore this issue and simply convicted a corporation when an agent or employee committed the offence in the course of her employment. However, for crimes that required a guilty mind, until early in the 20th century the courts generally held that a corporation could not itself be guilty even when it was clear that the individuals involved were acting for the corporation. The individuals who committed offences might be convicted, but not the corporation.

The "Directing Mind" Principle

A leading case in 1915 altered this principle and allowed courts to come to the conclusion that a corporation could commit an act requiring a guilty mind, at least in some circumstances. In *Lennard's Carrying Company*,[31] a ship owner was sued for damages under a statute that stated an owner would not be liable for harm caused by his vessel "without his actual fault." Speaking for the House of Lords, Viscount Haldane found that a Mr. Lennard was "the active director" of the corporation, and that it was "impossible...to contend...that he did not know or can excuse himself for not having known" that the ship was unseaworthy. He went on to call the director "the active spirit," the "directing mind and will," and "*the very ego and centre of the personality* of the corporation" (italics added). Viscount Haldane then made an important statement of policy:

> [Mr. Lennard's] action must, *unless a corporation is not to be liable at all*, have been an action which was the action of the company itself.... [italics added]

---

30. Reference re s. 94(2) of the B.C. Motor Vehicle Act, [1985] 2 S.C.R. 486, per Lamer, J., at 514.

31. Lennard's Carrying Co. Ltd. v. Asiatic Petroleum Co. Ltd., [1915] A.C. 705.

Accordingly, although the owner was a corporation, the House of Lords found that it was "actually" at fault and therefore liable. While this was a civil case and not a criminal prosecution, it was seen as opening the door for courts to find the actions of senior officers and directors of corporations to be those of the corporation itself both with regard to the actual committing of the acts and the required guilty or negligent mind.

A further problem arises when the wrongful act is committed not by a senior officer or director, but by a person lower down in the hierarchy. Canadian courts have generally tended to find an act committed by an employee who has significant responsibilities, such as being the head of an important department or a branch, to be an act of the corporation itself.[32] But the courts would not hold the act of a low-level employee, for example, of a clerk who cheated a customer—in the absence of evidence that a senior employee was aware of and permitted the conduct—to be the act of the corporation itself. However, drawing the line between those employees and officers whose acts will be identified as acts of the corporate employer and those whose acts will not be so identified is not an easy task; in one recent case it was held that a truck driver employee of a waste disposal corporation was not a "directing mind" of the corporation, and his conduct did not make the corporation liable for an offence that required *mens rea*.[33]

Personal Liability of Directors and Senior Officers

As we noted in Chapter 27, the principle of limited liability does not protect directors from liability for torts or breaches of fiduciary duty that they personally commit. The question we address here is whether directors (and officers) should be held criminally liable for offences committed by their corporation under their supervision.

One view is that simply holding corporations liable is not in itself a strong enough deterrent to assure effective enforcement of regulatory schemes. A large corporation with sufficient assets might consider the penalty merely a "licence"; it pays the fine and carries on with its activities; the corporation's manager thus often passes the costs on to the ultimate consumer through higher prices, or to the corporation's innocent shareholders through lower dividends; at the other extreme, a corporation may be merely a "shell" with virtually no assets to pay its fine; those who control the enterprise walk away from it and start up a similar activity using a new corporation.

Accordingly, a strong argument has been made that effective deterrence requires that, as well as the corporation, the individuals responsible for the offence be punished directly. Hence, directors and senior officers have more and more been held personally liable for offences found to have been committed by their corporation. In addition, particularly in the United States, the generally accepted view is that criminal sanctions are necessary as a deterrent. As has been said, "…the threat of jail sends a clear message to corporate executives that they are not immune to criminal sanctions.…Incarceration is one cost of business that you can't pass to the consumer."[34]

Even when it is agreed that, in addition to the corporation, its human actors ought to be held liable for breaches, problems remain in attempting to prosecute individuals. In complex organizations, where responsibility is diffused among a number of persons, each in charge of a narrow, perhaps ill-defined task, it is often difficult to identify with any certainty who is "responsible," that is, who can—and should—be convicted of committing an offence. The task is particularly difficult when, in order to obtain a conviction, the prosecution must prove beyond a reasonable doubt that the accused was the person who committed the offending act. (Of course, whenever a director or officer of a corporation has been found personally to have committed an offence, the courts do not hesitate to find the wrongdoer guilty and to punish accordingly.)

---

32. See R. v. Waterloo Mercury Sales Ltd. (1974), 18 C.C.C. (2d) 248, where a used-car sales manager, who was neither a director nor a signing officer of the corporation, illegally turned back the odometers on used cars. His corporation was found guilty.
33. R. v. Safety-Kleen Canada Inc. (1997), 145 D.L.R. (4th) 276. The corporation was found guilty of another, strict liability, offence.
34. See Nelson Smith, "No Longer Just a Cost of Doing Business…" (1992), 53 *La. L. Rev.* 119 at 126.

These two factors, a belief that human agents and not just corporations should be made liable, and that it is often difficult to obtain convictions, have led legislatures

- to enact express provisions making senior officers and directors liable
- to make the grounds for individual liability much broader

As a recent Canadian book on the subject states, "An impressive number of statutes expressly impose personal liability upon officers and directors for offences by the corporation."[35]

CONTEMPORARY ISSUE

Directors Still on the Hot Seat

Directors increasingly are placed in a dilemma when their corporations get into financial difficulty. Should they quit when the going gets rough, or try to pull things round and risk incurring increased personal liability? The following extract highlights the problem:

> One of the thorny problems impeding the restructuring of insolvent companies is the vulnerable position of their directors. The proliferation of provincial and federal legislation that imposes personal liability on directors for the failure of the company to remit taxes or pay wages puts directors in a position of personal jeopardy, which impairs their ability to lead insolvent companies through a restructuring. While a business is healthy, its directors feel secure. As long as the company is able to pay wages, tax remittances and other accruing liabilities from cash flow, the directors feel that they are not at any personal risk. This feeling of security quickly fades when the company begins to encounter financial difficulties. If the company becomes insolvent and is no longer able to meet its obligations as they come due, tax remittances and accruing employee obligations, for which the directors may be personally liable, may remain unpaid.
>
> Directors seeking to avoid personal liability for these accruing obligations are left with few choices. They can resign, hoping to limit their personal exposure to the director liabilities that accrued up to the date of their resignation, or they can continue as directors and take the risk that the company can resolve its financial difficulties and restore its ability to meet its obligations in the ordinary course.
>
> Many directors of insolvent companies decide to resign, believing that resignation is the only way they can control their own fate. While the directors of the insolvent company are central figures in any restructuring process, they do not control the outcome, and many directors resign rather than increase their personal risk of liability trying to save an insolvent company. Mass resignation, however, dooms a company to failure and liquidation, unless the directors can be replaced by competent new directors....
>
> The various federal and provincial statutes that imperil directors of insolvent companies put directors' personal interest in avoiding liability at odds with their general duty to act in the best interests of the company. Instead of pursuing the interests of the company with objectivity, directors either resign at the first sign of trouble or, instead of resigning, participate in the restructuring process as parties with a personal stake in the outcome of the restructuring process.

Source: K. McElcheran, "Directors still on hot seat following BIA Amendments," *The Lawyer's Weekly*, Vol. 17, No. 48, May 1, 1998.

Questions to Consider

1. Is the possibility of personal liability likely to make directors act more responsibly and thus improve the quality of management?

2. Or will the prospect of personal liability be more likely to deter qualified persons from taking on directorships?

---

35. Thompson, McConnell and Huestis, *Environmental Law and Business in Canada*. Aurora: Canada Law Book, 1993, p. 299. In an accompanying footnote, the authors point out that there are at least 80 federal statutes of this type, 62 in British Columbia, 98 in Alberta, 45 in Manitoba, 126 in Ontario, and 19 in New Brunswick.

THE BASIS FOR LIABILITY IMPOSED ON ENTERPRISES AND THEIR HUMAN AGENTS: ENVIRONMENTAL LEGISLATION

In the following section we concentrate on liability for environmental offences; this topic provides a good illustration of the wider general issue of corporate liability, as well as being a question of major practical concern to corporations and their officers.

What Standard of Skill and Care Must Be Met?

When an offence such as improper disposal of hazardous wastes occurs, a presumption arises that the activity was carried on negligently. An enterprise as well as any of its directors and officers charged with an offence can overcome the presumption by showing that they used "due diligence" in carrying out their duties. The challenge for the accused is to meet what is generally acknowledged to be a steadily rising standard of care. The enterprise must demonstrate that it has an effective system to prevent offences, must monitor the results of the system and must improve the system if problems occur. Thus a corporation cannot escape liability simply by delegating responsibility to an employee. If the employee is sufficiently senior to be a "directing mind" of the corporation, his actions will be treated as those of the corporation itself; if not, the corporation will have failed to put in place an effective system of control.[36]

Since science and technology are advancing steadily, it is difficult to rely on yesterday's standards. Each enterprise whose activities may pose a risk must show that it reviews its current monitoring system frequently and makes reasonable efforts to keep up to date on technological change in the field.

The Expertise Required of Directors and Senior Officers

Another aspect of the problem relates to the expertise of directors and senior officers. Are they held to higher standards of care and skill if they have expertise in the area where a hazardous activity is carried on? Suppose a senior officer is an engineer with long experience in the field. Would she be expected to take precautions against a risk that an accountant would unlikely be aware of? A common-sense view would say yes, and there is some support for it in a 1983 case, *R. v. Placer Developments Ltd.*,[37] where the accused corporation allowed diesel fuel to escape into fishing waters. The court seemed to expect greater diligence from the corporation's experienced senior officers:

> The accused was required to possess, and did possess sufficient expertise to be aware of the potential risk to the environment posed by a fuel system in northern mining camps....[T]he accused had the opportunity and knowledge in the field, through their employees Mr. Morganti with thirty-two months' field experience and Mr. Goddard with twenty-five years' experience, to influence the offending conduct on the site.[38]

On the other hand, the court suggested that even if the accused firm did *not* possess that expertise it would still be liable for the offence:

> The greater the likelihood of harm, the higher the duty of care....Anyone choosing to become involved in activities posing danger to the public or to the environment assumes an obligation to take whatever measures may be necessary to prevent harm....Unless equipped with appropriate professional skills, no one ought to undertake any activity involving a danger to the public....Mining in the north requires not only an expert knowledge of mining, but equally

---

36. *Supra*, n. 33.

37. (1983), 13 C.E.L.R. 42 (Y.T. Terr. Ct.).

38. *Ibid.*, at 49.

important, an expert appreciation of the special problems caused by remote operations in northern environments.[39]

These observations appear to suggest that the accused corporation was caught in one of two ways: either it failed to employ the expertise it ought to have known that it needed in order to manage the hazardous activity, or if it did employ the necessary expertise, then the person having that expertise failed to use the professional care and skill attributed to him. Perhaps an unskilled employee who had been sent to the site would not be found personally liable because he could not have been expected to anticipate the risk, but the employer enterprise would be caught by its failure to send an employee with the necessary skills to carry out the task.

A Uniform Standard?

A recent decision of the Supreme Court of Canada suggests that, at least in the absence of explicit regulatory standards for specific categories of persons, a standard must not vary according to the special knowledge and training of an individual. In *R. v. Creighton*,[40] Madam Justice McLachlin, for the majority of the Court, stated:

> The first concept is the notion that the criminal law may properly hold people engaged in risky activities to a minimum standard of care, judged by what a reasonable person in all the circumstances would have done. This notion posits a uniform standard for all persons engaging in the activity, regardless of their background, education or psychological disposition.

She then stated:

> The second concept is the principle that the morally innocent not be punished....

These two statements may be in conflict. On the one hand, there appears to be a uniform standard, but on the other, we ought not to punish the innocent, presumably even if they do not meet the standard.[41] McLachlin, J. explained the apparent conflict as follows:

> A person may fail to meet an elevated *de facto* standard of care in either of two ways. First, the person may undertake an activity requiring special care when he or she is not qualified to give that care. Absent special excuses like necessity, this may constitute culpable negligence. An untrained person undertaking brain surgery might violate the standard this way. Second, a person who is qualified may negligently fail to exercise the special care required by the activity. A brain surgeon performing surgery in a grossly negligent way might violate the standard in this second way. *The standard is the same, although the means by which it is breached may differ.* [italics added]

This analysis may still present difficulties for courts to determine liability in situations where a person without special training could not reasonably be expected to foresee a risk, while another person with expertise in the field would be expected to foresee that same risk. The law in this area is changing quickly, making it all the more important for enterprises whose activities involve any significant environmental risks to make diligent efforts to comply with standards or care as described below.

Who Should Be Found Liable?

Those in Charge of an Activity?

We have already noted that, apart from the liability of an enterprise itself, any person who actually commits an offence is personally liable, even when he was acting within the scope of his

---

39. *Ibid.*, at 52.
40. (1993), 105 D.L.R. (4th) 632.
41. *Ibid.*, at 678 and 679.

authorized activities and a senior officer acquiesced or ordered him to perform the act. The issues become more difficult when legislatures enact regulations to make senior officers and directors liable because they are considered to be in charge of an activity, even though they have not participated directly in the offence. The task is to find appropriate language, sufficient to capture those who should bear the blame and yet absolve those who were innocent. With this purpose in mind, our legislatures have tended to use two phrases: the first makes liable those who "cause or permit" a hazardous substance to be discharged;[42] the second makes liable, "any officer, director or agent…who directed, authorized, assented to, acquiesced in or participated in the commission of an offence."[43]

So, who are these persons? In order to "permit" or "acquiesce in" an activity such as disposing of hazardous materials, one must have a significant role in controlling those who actually carry it out. Permitting or acquiescing has no meaning if the person charged is merely one who learned about the activity but could do nothing to affect it. Accordingly, the prosecution must first persuade a court that a person charged had effective powers and responsibility. A senior officer and director who is personally in charge of a hazardous procedure (that is, she is the person to whom those performing the activity report on a regular basis), presents a clear case of effective control and responsibility for the activity.

Outside Directors?

But what of an "outside" director—a person who was elected to the board because of his experience in financial services and who faithfully attends board meetings twice a year? He reads all the material sent to him and asks probing and useful questions at meetings. However, when it comes to environmental concerns he relies on the reports and assurances given by the senior officer, the "inside" director, who is in charge. Should the outside director also be considered to share in control? Did he "permit" or "acquiesce in" an offence that occurred under the supervision of the inside director?

The Difficulty of Determining Responsibility

Since the law is not intended to punish innocent and reasonably diligent people, it would seem that ordinarily an outside director in those circumstances ought not to be held personally liable for the offence. This view seems to be confirmed by the current case law: virtually all of the charges brought under Canadian legislation have been against inside directors. However, in many situations there is not a clear-cut division between insider and outsider: for instance, did the outsider receive any reports that disclosed questionable practices to a reasonable person in his position? Were answers to his questions evasive? What should an outsider do when he feels uneasy with the information provided?

We should also note that not all insiders are in control of an operation, or directly involved in it, simply because they are directors and senior officers within the enterprise. Should an inside director who learns secondhand about a potential problem in another branch of the enterprise be expected to undertake a personal investigation, outside her normal responsibilities? These questions remain very difficult and depend on the particular facts. As a result it may be a number of years before the courts provide clear guidance as to what they find to be sufficient control for a person to be convicted of an offence.

---

42. See, for example: Fisheries Act, R.S.C. 1985, c. F-14, s. 36(3); Health Act, R.S.B.C. 1996, c. 179, s. 15.

43. Canadian Environmental Protection Act, R.S.C. 1985, c. 16 (4th Supp.), s. 122.

CASE 29.1

A corporation's premises contained a large, toxic, chemical waste storage site with many decaying, rusting, and uncovered containers; soil samples revealed concentrations of various dangerous chemicals. The prosecution charged the corporation with permitting the discharge of liquid industrial waste that could impair the quality of the groundwater and contaminate the environment. Charges were also laid against three directors.

All the defendants argued that they had shown due diligence in carrying out their duties. Ormston, J., found that the corporation—Bata Industries—did not establish a proper system to prevent to prevent the escape of toxic substances and did not take reasonable steps to ensure the effective operation of even their faulty system. The corporation was found guilty.[44]

With respect to the directors, the court provided a useful summary of the questions that should be asked in assessing a director's defence of having shown "due diligence" in his particular circumstances:

(a) Did the board of directors establish a pollution prevention "system," that is, was there supervision or inspection?

(b) Did each director ensure that the corporate officers have been instructed to set up a system sufficient within the terms and practices of the industry of ensuring compliance with environmental laws, to ensure that the officers report back periodically to the board?

(c) The directors are responsible for reviewing the environmental compliance reports provided by the officers, but are justified in placing reasonable reliance on reports.

(d) The directors should substantiate that the officers are promptly addressing environmental concerns brought to their attention by government agencies or other concerned parties including shareholders.

(e) The directors should be aware of the standards of their industry and other industries which deal with similar environmental pollutants or risks.

(f) The directors should immediately and personally react when they have notice the system has failed.

Of the directors, Mr. Thomas Bata was found to be "the director with the least personal contact with the plant" where the offence occurred. His responsibilities were at other plants and "he attended on site...once or twice a year to review the operation and performance goals...." Although Mr. Bata did not personally review the operation when he was on site:

> He responded to the matters brought to his attention promptly and appropriately. He had placed an experienced director on site and was entitled in the circumstances to assume that...[the on-site director] was addressing the environmental concerns....He was entitled to rely upon his system...unless he became aware the system was defective.[45]

Accordingly, Mr. Bata was acquitted.

In contrast, another director, Mr. Douglas Marchant, was found to have more responsibility than Mr. Bata but less than a third director who was held to be "on-site." Mr. Marchant came to the facility once a month and toured the plant. The court found that the problem was brought to his "personal attention" and that:

> ...he had personal knowledge. There is no evidence that he took any steps after having knowledge to view the site and assess the problem....[D]ue diligence requires him to exercise a degree of supervision and control that demonstrate that he was exhorting those whom he may be normally expected to influence or control to an excepted standard of behaviour.

Mr. Marchant was found guilty.

From this example, we can see that a finding of guilt will depend on the degree of involvement of a director in the particular circumstances of each case.

---

44. R. v. Bata Industries Ltd. (1992), 9 O.R. (3d) 329 at 362.
45. *Ibid.*, at 364.

What Should Be the Punishment?

A further question is: what punishment should a court impose? Generally, corporations are fined according to the seriousness of the breach and the harm caused. Directors and officers receive somewhat smaller fines, but in extreme cases, they may be sentenced to prison terms.[46]

CASE 29.2

A corporation, Varnicolor Chemical Ltd., reprocessed and disposed of industrial wastes. Waste materials escaped from its toxic disposal site into the groundwater, and moved towards a river that was used as a source of drinking water for downriver communities. The corporation took no action to clean up the spill; rather it was the Ministry of the Environment that did so at an estimated cost of $2.5 million. Both the corporation, Varnicolor, and one of its directors, Severin Argenton, were charged with offences.[47]

Since Mr. Argenton was "the only officer and director to take an active part in the operations and actual management of...[Varnicolor]. He was clearly, at all relevant times, the sole directing mind of the company...." Accordingly, his actions were the actions of the corporation. Mr. Argenton pleaded guilty. Charges against the corporation were stayed. The court discussed in detail the criteria for sentencing Mr. Argenton.

It stated that the purposes in sentencing are:

- to protect the public
- to deter and rehabilitate offenders
- to promote compliance with the law
- to express public disapproval of the act

It summarized the factors that should affect the severity of a sentence as follows:

- *The nature of the environment affected*: The concern is both with the sensitivity of the environment affected and the gravity of the risk. In this case, the drinking water of residents in the area would be contaminated.
- *The extent of the damage actually inflicted*: Here, there was a high cost of cleanup.
- *The deliberateness of the offence*: In considering this factor, the court stated:

Not only was Mr. Argenton involved on site in the operations of the company, but he was as well involved in the negotiations which preceded the issuance of the certificate of approval by the Ministry...for the Varnicolor site....Therefore, as a result of this active involvement and in-depth knowledge of the business operations, it is clear that Mr. Argenton was uniquely in a position to be aware...of...the requirements of the Ministry. Mr. Argenton has indicated that he found these requirements to be unclear and ambiguous; however, it was at all time open to... [him] to seek clarification....There is no indication...that he made any attempts to do so. In a number of respects, Mr. Argenton acted in defiance of the requirements....Such violations are in effect a breach of trust on the part of the person to whom such a certificate has been granted and, as such, jail terms are an appropriate penalty to ensure compliance with the law by both the person being sentenced and society in general.[48]

- *The attitude of the defendant*: In this case, Mr. Argenton did not voluntarily report the escape of toxic waste, nor did he show a co-operative attitude.
- *Attempts to comply with the regulations*: There was no evidence of a cleanup at the site by Varnicolor or by Mr. Argenton, and indeed, the corporation had become inactive.

The maximum sentence under the Environmental Protection Act was 12 months. The court found that the conduct of the defendant amounted to a serious breach of the Act, and sentenced him to eight months in jail. We can see then, that the courts are prepared in egregious cases to imprison those who ignore environmental regulations.

---

46. For a case in which both a fine ($76 000) and a jail sentence (30 days) were imposed, see R. v. Romaniuk (1993), Sask. R. 129 (Q.B.).

47. R. v. Varnicolor Chemical Ltd. (1992), 9 C.E.L.R. (N.S.) 176.

48. *Ibid.*, at 180–1.

The Business Consequences

What conclusions can we draw from these developments and how will they affect the conduct of business? Clearly, there is a public consensus that protecting the environment is a high priority; in response to public concern legislatures have created extensive regulatory schemes. Meeting the standards under these schemes imposes substantial costs on many businesses, especially on resource industries and manufacturing and transportation enterprises. The most important challenge is to meet the requirements effectively and efficiently.

How may this be done? First, businesses need to review their practices to learn whether any of their activities, especially disposing of waste materials, create a concern about health or safety or the breach of regulations. They must seek the best advice available and keep up to date with current technology; they are expected to take every reasonable precaution to meet the latest standards.

Second, once they are well informed about the risks, they should review their insurance coverage with a view to obtaining the maximum risk protection that is available *and* affordable. The cost of insurance coverage leads to the third stage: if after obtaining the best advice for implementing safety systems and obtaining insurance a particular business activity ceases to be competitive, then it becomes necessary to decide whether to continue that branch of operations.

QUESTIONS FOR REVIEW

1. What is meant by the "indoor management rule"?

2. Is a person dealing with a corporation expected to know the contents of the corporation's articles of incorporation? Or its by-laws?

3. Can a corporation adopt a pre-incorporation contract? What is the effect of its purporting to do so?

4. Is a corporation required to have any minimum amount of capital?

5. Are there any restrictions on a corporation paying dividends to its shareholders?

6. Why are there restrictions against a corporation returning capital to its shareholders?

7. What are the principal objectives of securities legislation?

8. What is a prospectus?

9. What is the difference between strict liability and absolute liability?

10. Can a corporation be convicted of a criminal offence? How?

11. Should directors be held personally liable for environmental offences committed by their corporation?

12. What standard of care and skill is expected of corporate directors in relation to environmental offences?

13. Is any distinction made (in relation to environmental offences) between "inside" and "outside" directors? Should there be any difference in their treatment?

CASES AND PROBLEMS

About a year ago, MacIntosh, a qualified accountant with substantial business experience, met Kellerman, the owner of a nightclub and a number of other business ventures. Kellerman persuaded MacIntosh that her experience would be very valuable to him in his own business activities, which he was seeking to expand. He persuaded MacIntosh to invest a substantial proportion of her savings in his ventures, in return for which it was agreed that she would become a shareholder and director of Kellerman's corporation, "AJP Enterprises Inc." In the course of their discussions, MacIntosh was shown books of account and other records that purported to relate to AJP Enterprises.

MacIntosh transferred $50 000 into a bank account in the name of AJP Enterprises Inc. In return, Kellerman gave her what appeared to be a document assigning to her one-half of his shares in that corporation.

Soon afterwards, MacIntosh negotiated an arrangement with an advertising agency, Occidental Broadcasts Ltd., to provide radio and television advertising for the AJP nightclub in return for monthly payments of $2000. Occidental were paid (out of the AJP Enterprises bank account) for the first three months, but have not been paid since then although they continued to provide advertising services for a further five months.

When Occidental eventually demanded payment of a further $10 000, MacIntosh discovered that

(a) the AJP Enterprises bank account contained only $1.73.

(b) Kellerman had disappeared.

(c) there was no record of any corporation by the name of "AJP Enterprises Inc.," or any similar name, having been incorporated in any jurisdiction in Canada.

Can MacIntosh be held personally liable for the $10 000 claimed by Occidental?

2 Rainbow Sails Ltd. is a corporation incorporated under the CBCA. It has three shareholders, Brown, Green, and White, who are also the directors of the corporation. White acts as chief executive officer, though he has never been formally appointed to that position. The articles of the corporation contain (*inter alia*) the following provisions:

- The business of the corporation is restricted to the manufacture, buying, and selling of sailboats, and under no circumstances is the corporation to engage in the manufacture, buying, or selling of mechanically powered boats or other craft.

- Any contract or proposed contact involving an expenditure in excess of $5000 must be approved unanimously by the Board of Directors.

Some months ago, White sold on behalf of Rainbow a new sailboat that they had manufactured to a customer, Mermaid Marinas Inc. White agreed to accept from Mermaid a small motor boat in part exchange. Although White had no difficulty reselling the motor boat, Brown and Green were angry when they learned of the transaction since they both had an aversion to powered boats. They warned White not to enter into any other similar transactions, otherwise they would deprive him of his powers as chief executive officer.

Some weeks later, Mermaid's sales manager asked White if Rainbow would be interested in buying a floatplane that Mermaid no longer had much use for. White thought the plane was an excellent bargain and agreed to pay $15 000 for it. White took delivery of the plane, and the next day crashed it.

Brown and Green are again very angry. They both refuse to countersign any cheque to Mermaid, and Mermaid are now threatening to sue for the price of the plane.

Is Rainbow liable to pay for the plane? If so, does Rainbow have any right of action against White personally?

3 Queensville Quality Cars Ltd. is a large automobile dealership specializing in the sale of both new and used cars and light trucks. Until recently its used car division was managed by Murphy, who was in charge of a dozen salespersons and mechanics. Murphy was not a director of the corporation.

Following several complaints from customers, alleging among other things that the odometers on used cars appeared to have been altered, the managing director of the corporation, Patel, sent written instructions to all division heads (including Murphy) warning them that tampering with odometers is a serious offence and that any officer or employee of the corporation found doing so would face instant dismissal.

Notwithstanding the warning, Murphy instructed one of his mechanics, Ferreira, to change the odometer on a car that the corporation had recently obtained as a trade-in. Ferreira did so, the car was resold, and the purchaser subsequently complained about the condition of the car.

When questioned, Ferreira admitted having changed the odometer and was dismissed. At about the same time, Murphy disappeared, taking with him a substantial amount of cash belonging to the corporation. Patel reported both the theft and the tampering with odometers to the police.

Queensville Quality Cars Ltd. have now been charged with an offence under the Criminal Code in respect of altering an odometer. Should they be convicted?

4. Gigantic Forestry Inc., one of Canada's largest pulp and paper enterprises with 12 mills in various locations across the country, operates a pulp mill on the Grizzly River in British Columbia. It has a government permit to discharge up to 18 200 kg of suspended solids per day into the river. The main suspended solids consist of a lime mud, ash, wood bark, clay, sand, and pulp fibre. Gigantic was charged with exceeding the permitted levels of discharge and pleaded guilty. There had been a previous conviction 18 months earlier, with a fine of $50 000 against the corporation. Two directors, described below, were also charged.

On February 27, Gigantic discharged suspended solids at a level significantly in excess of its permit. The spill resulted from a mechanical failure causing an overflow of lime mud from the storage tank into an emergency spill pond. The pond being near to capacity when the emergency occurred overflowed to the river. The suspended solid emission was 35 483 kg per day, more than double the permitted level.

Aggravating factors are: (1) Prior to the spill, Gigantic had prepared a "response manual" to deal with spills but no specific guidelines in place to deal with this type of event. Since then guidelines have been created including reduction of production in relevant areas and, if machinery cannot be repaired, shutting down production completely. (2) The emergency spill pond had not been cleaned for five or six days. (3) The high level alarm in the storage tank was not working that evening.

On the day of the spill, during the day shift, it was noted that the mud filter drive tripped out three times. The night shift supervisor checked the filter at approximately 19:45 hours that day, just after the start of his shift. The filter drive was not working. Millwrights were called and they set to work to repair the mud filter drive at 20:30 hours, and by 04:25 hours the next day, February 28, mud was again being pumped from the storage tank to the mud filter.

Initially during the shutdown of the mud system, mud continued to flow from the mud washer to the storage tank. The shift supervisor instituted procedures to minimize the flow of mud from the mud washer to the storage tank. He had noted a large amount of clear liquid in the pond when he came on shift. The shift supervisor then made certain that everything was done to minimize the overflow of the storage tank to the pond. The shift supervisor's judgment that mud was not escaping from the pond to the sewer was unfortunately incorrect. To the recollection of the plant people interviewed following this incident, this was the first time the pond had overflowed to the sewer.

Blinkov is a director and president of Gigantic. He resides in Vancouver where the corporation has its head office and visits the Grizzly River site several times a year, but spends most of his workdays in Vancouver or visiting the other 11 mills. His assistant, Crowe, is in charge of environment control systems at all 12 mills and regularly prepares detailed reports on each plant for Blinkov to review. Charbonneau is a director and manager of the Grizzly River mill.

She lives in a nearby town and spends most of each day at the mill. The supervisors report to her at least once each month and are instructed to report any problems immediately. She had not personally examined the storage tank or emergency spill pond for several months before the spill. At 22:00 hours the day of the spill, the night shift supervisor telephoned Charbonneau and told her of the problem. She said she would examine the situation the following morning.

The court fined Gigantic $200 000. Should either or both directors, Blinkov and Charbonneau be found guilty? If so, suggest what the penalty might be.

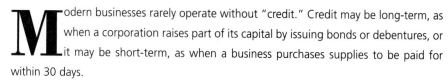

PART

7

odern businesses rarely operate without "credit." Credit may be long-term, as when a corporation raises part of its capital by issuing bonds or debentures, or it may be short-term, as when a business purchases supplies to be paid for within 30 days.

A reputable business generally has little difficulty obtaining credit to purchase its normal day-to-day needs. For purchases of more substantial items the firm granting credit may require "security" beyond the buyer's contractual promise to pay. The creditor may require collateral security in the form of a mortgage of the buyer's land, as discussed in Chapter 25. More often, a buyer will give collateral in the form of a security interest in other types of property—the items purchased from the creditor, other chattels, or stocks and bonds.

In Chapter 30 we discuss the different methods of securing credit. Most provinces have now adopted comprehensive legislation called Personal Property Security Acts, regulating various kinds of credit arrangements. In addition, special rules apply to certain types of bank loans under the federal Bank Act. The relationships and conflicts that may arise among these different forms of security is one of the issues we consider in this chapter.

Some businesses inevitably fail. They may become insolvent and be unable to meet the claims of all their creditors. In Chapter 31 we consider the rights of creditors when a business becomes bankrupt—an area under federal legislation—and we also examine the protection given to creditors by provincial legislation, in particular by statutes dealing with mechanics' liens.

Creditors and Debtors

PART 7

Weblinks

The full texts of many of the statutes referred to in this Part can be accessed on the Internet, as follows:

gov.ab.ca/qp
Alberta

qp.gov.bc.ca/bcstats/
British Columbia

gov.mb.ca/che/statpub/free/index.html
Manitoba

gov.nb.ca/acts/
New Brunswick

www.gov.ns.ca/legi/legc/index.htm
Nova Scotia

www.attorneygeneral.jus.gov.on.ca/legis.htm
Ontario

Federal statutes may be accessed at

canada.justice.gc.ca/STABLE/EN/Laws

The following statutes are especially relevant:

canada.justice.gc.ca/STABLE/EN/Laws/Chap/B/B-3.html
The Bankruptcy and Insolvency Act

canada.justice.gc.ca/STABLE/EN/Laws/Chap/B/B-1.01.html
The Bank Act

canada.justice.gc.ca/STABLE/EN/Laws/Chap/C/C-36.html
The Companies' Creditors Arrangement Act

Other useful Web sites are:

www.natlaw.com/pubs/overview.htm and
www.wwlia.org/ca-ppsa.htm
Overviews of Canadian Personal Property Security law

strategis.ic.gc.ca/sc_mrksv/bankrupt/engdoc/superint.html
The Office of the Superintendent of Bankruptcy

www.wwlia.org:80/ca-bankr.htm
The WWLIA Bankruptcy page

30 SECURED TRANSACTIONS

The Meaning of "Security"

Methods of Securing Credit

Personal Property Security Legislation

Effect of Security Interests on Purchasers

Effect of Security Interests on Other Creditors

Security for Bank Loans

Almost all business operates on credit to some extent. Most businesses have debts, and most have accounts receivable. As we shall see in this chapter, an important distinction is drawn—in law and in business practice—between *secured* and *unsecured* credit. In this chapter we describe the various legal devices for securing credit and examine such questions as:

■ what is meant by "security"?

■ what is the nature of a conditional sale?

■ what is a chattel mortgage and how does it differ from a conditional sale?

■ how are consignments and leases used as security devices?

■ what is a floating charge?

■ how do the Personal Property Security Acts operate to protect secured creditors?

■ how are secured creditors' rights enforced?

■ how do secured interests affect the rights of innocent third parties?

■ what additional protection is given to banks as secured creditors?

THE MEANING OF "SECURITY"

Types of Security Interest

collateral security

an interest in property of a debtor to which a creditor may look in the event of non-payment of the debt

The best security for a debt is the good reputation and the earning power of the debtor. But over and above a debtor's willingness and ability to pay back the debt, various legal devices give a creditor "backup" or additional assurance that debts owing will be repaid. Most of these devices are agreed to in advance as terms in the contract by which they are created; they are often called *consensual security interests* and typically give a creditor **collateral security**, that is, a right to take possession of and to sell specified assets of the debtor in satisfaction of the debt. Security agreements can be very widely drawn, and modern legislation makes it theoretically possible to cover virtually all existing and future property owned by a debtor.

There are also security interests that arise as a normal consequence of a transaction, not because the parties to a credit transaction have bargained for them, but because of rules of the common law or express statutory provisions. They may be described as *non-consensual security interests*. We have examined examples of such interests as rights of lien and resale available to unpaid sellers of goods and repair services in earlier chapters[1] and will examine others in the next chapter. In this chapter our main concern is with consensual security interests.

Security Practices

Suppliers generally do not require collateral security when extending credit to trade customers: unsecured transactions are simpler and cheaper to record; their risk is relatively small because trade credit is usually short-term and competition may make it unwise for a supplier to offend customers by demanding security. If a supplier loses only a small proportion of its sales revenue by defaults in payment, it may well be better off accepting the loss than incurring added administrative costs and perhaps losing sales by requiring security for each sale and then having to take possession of and sell the secured assets if default occurs.

In any event, collateral security is not a good substitute for a sound debtor; suppliers or lenders would be unlikely to extend credit at all if they thought it probable that they would have to use their remedies to recover the secured assets. Security is nonetheless a risk-reducing device and is widely resorted to in large transactions and in consumer sales; in particular, it establishes a creditor's *priority* relative to other creditors in the event of a debtor's insolvency.

In consumer transactions, security devices are used primarily as a form of incentive to pay the money owing and to thus avoid repossession of the article sold. When a right of repossession is actually exercised, it is most likely to be used against expensive durable goods; even then, the realizable value for the secured creditor will probably be disappointing. It is common for goods in the hands of a defaulting debtor to have deteriorated considerably before repossession.

Rights of a Secured Creditor

An **unsecured creditor**, that is, a general creditor with no security interest in any of the debtor's assets, may ultimately acquire an interest rather like a security interest through a court action to collect an overdue debt. When a creditor obtains judgment for the amount of the debt and the debtor fails to pay, the creditor can then obtain an execution order authorizing the seizure and sale of certain of the debtor's assets.[2] By contrast, a **secured creditor** need not invoke the rather lengthy judicial machinery required to obtain an execution order, but can proceed on its own to enforce its rights over the security. In this sense, a security interest provides a creditor with a self-help remedy. More important, as we shall see, an unsecured judgment creditor generally has no right to seize any assets already subject to a security interest of another creditor; the secured creditor has **priority**.

However, even when a debt is stated to be payable "on demand," the debtor must normally be given time to raise the funds to repay the debt; if the creditor seizes property without giving reasonable notice it may be liable in damages.[3]

unsecured creditor
a creditor who has no security interest in any of the debtor's property

secured creditor
a creditor who has a security interest in the property of the debtor

priority
a first, or prior, right to be repaid out of the debtor's property

---

1. See Chapter 16 for an explanation of an unpaid seller's rights of lien and resale and Chapter 17 for similar rights available to warehousing and repair service businesses and common carriers.
2. See the discussion of "Methods of Enforcing Judgment" in Chapter 15, *supra*.
3. Ronald Elwyn Lister Ltd. v. Dunlop Canada Ltd. (1982), 135 D.L.R.(3d) 1. At least 10 days' notice must be given before enforcing security in the property of an insolvent debtor; see Chapter 31, below.

CASE 30.1

Murano operated a video store, the business being financed in part by a loan from the Bank of Montreal. The bank became concerned about the financial affairs of the store and wrote to Murano, indicating their intention to liquidate if adequate arrangements were not made within the next six weeks. In fact, the bank took no further steps for three months, when the parties met to discuss a request by Murano for a new financing arrangement. The bank agreed to consider the request but one week later,

without giving notice, it appointed a receiver and took possession of the store. It also informed other creditors of Murano of its actions.

Murano lost his entire business, including another store that was not included in the bank's financing arrangement. The court held that the bank had failed to give reasonable notice, that it was in breach of duty to its client in disclosing information to other creditors, and that it was liable in damages to Murano.[4]

Unfortunately for the creditor, when a debtor's financial position has deteriorated to the point that the creditor decides it must act, the secured assets in the possession of the debtor may already be in a rapidly deteriorating condition or even in the process of mysteriously disappearing, and other creditors may also have designs on them. Accordingly, security agreements frequently require a debtor to waive any right to notice of the creditor's intention to exercise security rights. After a creditor takes possession, however, statutes generally require the creditor to give notice to the debtor of the time and place at which the goods are to be sold in order to satisfy the debt.[5]

METHODS OF SECURING CREDIT

Credit Devices Previously Considered

Mortgages

This chapter is concerned with collateral security in the form of *personal* property rather than real property. Nonetheless, the concept of priority in relation to land mortgages and to other creditors' claims explained in Chapter 25 remains relevant, and readers may find it helpful to review the section entitled "Mortgagee's Rights Compared with Rights of Other Creditors" in that chapter. Historically, the law affecting credit devices has been drawn from a combination of real estate mortgage law and the law of the sale of goods.

Leases

We have examined leases of equipment as an instance of bailment in Chapter 17, and leases of land as an interest or estate in real property in Chapter 24. As we saw in Chapter 17, leases may also serve as a type of security device, where expensive items of personal property, such as aircraft, automobiles, and photocopiers, are acquired on credit. A close parallel exists between a lease and an instalment purchase (conditional sale) contract: the hirer (lessee) undertakes to pay rent for a specified period and at the end of that period can elect to buy the item, applying rent already paid towards the purchase price.

---

4. Murano v. Bank of Montreal (1998), 163 D.L.R. (4th) 21.
5. See, for example: Personal Property Security Act [hereafter PPSA], R.S.O. 1990, c. P.10, s. 63(4); S.M. 1993, c. 14, s. 59(6); S.S. 1993, c. P-6.2, s. 59(6).

Consignments

We distinguished briefly between a consignment of goods and a sale of goods in the opening section of Chapter 16. A consignment may also amount to an indirect type of secured credit. As we have seen, retailers of expensive items such as jewellery may not have sufficient capital to carry inventory for display and sale to customers. They may instead bring in a stock of goods shipped on consignment by a manufacturer or wholesale distributor. The arrangement is based on a consignment contract in which a retail business (consignee) acknowledges that the merchandise remains the property of the manufacturer or wholesale distributor (consignor).

The retailer, as agent of the consignor for the purpose of selling the goods, is accountable for all money received on the sale of the merchandise up to its wholesale price. Goods held on consignment are not part of the retailer's inventory and are not, therefore, generally available for the payment of other creditors' claims. The consignor effectively provides financing in the form of goods rather than money, and the consignee "owes" the consigned merchandise (to the value of its wholesale price) to the consignor.

Other Credit Devices

Earlier chapters have also dealt with assignments of book debts and with pledges—both of which can be considered to be methods of securing credit. A third-party guarantee (considered in Chapter 18) is rather different in that the "security" consists of a promise by a person, rather than a legal interest in an item of property. Credit cards perform a rather similar function. Customers use the cards to make purchases from retailers who have agreed in advance with the bank to accept cards as a means of payment. While no security is required by banks from cardholders, the arrangement does provide a form of security for the retailer. Banks in effect guarantee the credit of cardholders to retailers, and pay retailers the price of goods and services sold to cardholders, less a percentage commission. Sellers are thus relieved of concern about collecting customers' accounts.

Among the more important forms of security we have yet to consider are those created by conditional sale contracts, chattel mortgages, and floating charges, and by section 427 of the federal Bank Act; these are dealt with in the following sections.

Conditional Sales

Nature of the Security

Contracts for the sale of goods frequently take place on credit with provision for the seller to retain an interest in the goods until the price is paid. A familiar form of transaction provides that the transfer of title to the buyer is conditional upon the buyer's completion of a series of scheduled instalment payments. In the meantime, the buyer has possession of the goods and the seller retains the title to them as security for the full payment of the purchase price. In our discussion we refer to the parties as the *conditional seller* and the *conditional buyer*.

In the business world, a conditional sale contract serves two main functions as a security device: first, it gives the secured party a right to look to the goods in satisfaction of the debtor's obligation; and second, it gives the secured party priority in the goods over the interests of third parties, especially other creditors.

Obligations of a Conditional Buyer

The essential feature of a conditional sale agreement is the creation of a debt: the conditional buyer promises to pay a sum of money, usually in instalments. During the term of the conditional sale contract, the conditional buyer has possession of the goods; she is thus a *bailee* for value and has those obligations discussed in Chapter 17. A conditional sale contract, however, often places the conditional buyer under a higher duty by making her responsible for damage to the article whether caused by her or not; that is, the contract places the conditional buyer under strict liability. Frequently, too, the contract requires her to insure the article.

Remedies of a Conditional Seller

What are a conditional seller's remedies on default? First, as a creditor, the conditional seller has the ordinary contractual remedy of suing the debtor for the unpaid balance of the debt. Second, a conditional seller invariably makes it a term of the agreement that he may retake possession of the goods on default by the buyer. **Repossession** does not affect the ownership of the goods since the seller has retained title from the outset.

repossession
the act of taking back possession of property that has been in the possession of another

A conditional seller is not entitled to use force in recovering the goods. If a conditional seller encounters resistance in retaking possession, therefore, he should not persist. The proper course of action is to obtain a court order authorizing the necessary steps to regain possession. In some provinces a seller is not entitled to repossess goods except by court process. A conditional buyer who resists in the face of the court order is then guilty of contempt of court.

A majority of the provinces permit a conditional seller not only to repossess the goods upon a conditional buyer's default but also to sue the buyer for any deficiency arising because the amount still owed by the buyer exceeds the amount realized on resale of the goods.[6] In other provinces a conditional seller has to make a choice—either to sue the conditional buyer for the amount owing or to repossess the goods but not both.[7] Moreover, consumer protection legislation in some provinces provides that a term in the conditional sale contract allowing the conditional seller to repossess and resell the goods on default is unenforceable after the conditional buyer has paid a certain proportion (for example, two-thirds) of the purchase price.[8]

Rights of the Conditional Buyer

Does a conditional buyer acquire an accumulating "equity," entitled to protection, as she pays progressively more instalments towards total payment of the price agreed upon? Does she have any rights once she has defaulted and the conditional seller has repossessed the goods? Does the conditional buyer have a right to redeem (recover) the goods by paying the debt within a given period following default? Does she have a right to an accounting for any surplus if the conditional seller realizes more from the resale of the goods than she still owes? Would she remain liable for any deficiency after resale of the goods?

acceleration clause
a provision whereby the full outstanding amount of a debt becomes immediately payable if the debtor defaults in making any instalment payment

Unfortunately, the various provincial legislatures provide different answers to these questions. Some provinces permit a conditional buyer to redeem within specified periods upon payment of the instalments in arrears plus interest and costs incurred by the seller in repossessing.[9] Other provinces require a conditional buyer who has defaulted to pay the whole unpaid balance of the price—not merely the amounts in arrears—when an **acceleration clause** is included in the conditional sale contract.[10] In most jurisdictions a conditional buyer has a statutory right to receive any surplus realized by a conditional seller that repossesses and resells the goods for more than the amount owed by the buyer plus costs of reselling.[11] This right hardly balances the conditional buyer's corresponding liability for a deficiency should the proceeds of resale be inadequate, since the resale of used goods seldom brings in more than the amount owing on them. Possession and resale of chattels is notoriously "value destructive."

Assignment of the Conditional Seller's Interest

Many merchants who sell goods on the instalment plan do not finance the credit transactions themselves. Instead, they sell or assign their conditional sale agreements to finance companies

---

6. For example: PPSA, S.N.S. 1995–96, c. 13, s. 61(6); s. 63(5)(f) (Ont.).

7. For example: PPSA, R.S.B.C. 1996, c. 359, s. 58.

8. For example: Consumer Protection Act, R.S.O. 1990, c. C.31, s. 23; PPSA, s. 58(3) (B.C.). However, a court may still grant the right to repossess and resell on special application by the conditional seller.

9. For example: PPSA, s. 62(1) (Man. and Sask.).

10. For example: PPSA, s. 66(2)(a) (Ont.).

11. For example: PPSA, s. 64 (Ont.).

that collect the instalments and administer the contracts. A finance company acquires, as assignee, an asset in the form of a *retail instalment account receivable*; in return, the merchant, as assignor, gains revenue in the form of cash (less a discount) very quickly after he makes a credit sale. Under the terms of most conditional sale assignments to finance companies, however, conditional sellers remain liable for payment if their conditional buyers should default. When an assignee has recourse to the assignor for payment if an assigned account proves uncollectable, the arrangement is known as **recourse financing**.

Conditional sale contracts also play an important role in financing wholesale purchasers: a retailer or dealer may finance its purchases of stock-in-trade from a manufacturer by buying them from the manufacturer under a conditional sale contract. This practice is common in the automobile business. As a conditional seller, the manufacturer acquires an asset in the form of a *wholesale instalment account receivable*, which it almost invariably assigns to a finance company. As an assignee, the finance company stands in the position of the manufacturing company, with title in the goods withheld from the dealer or merchant (the conditional buyer) until the account is paid in full.

Recall from Chapter 12 that an assignee of a conditional seller takes "subject to the equities," that is, subject to personal defences that the buyer has against the conditional seller. For example, a buyer might protest that the goods were defective, or that the seller was not honouring his warranty or had been guilty of a misrepresentation. The buyer might then successfully resist action by an assignee finance company to recover the balance owing.

To avoid this result, finance companies often required conditional sellers to obtain promissory notes from their conditional buyers for the total amount due under the contract. The conditional seller would then endorse these notes in favour of the finance company and send them to the company along with a copy of the assigned conditional sale contract. Until the courts and legislatures intervened, this practice put consumers at a disadvantage: a finance company had the rights of a holder in due course (see Chapter 21) and did not need to worry about the personal defences of a conditional buyer. The use of promissory notes to make finance companies holders in due course was widely criticized, principally because the practice placed consumers at the tactical disadvantage of having to seek redress in the courts against the conditional seller, rather than being able simply to withhold payment. Growing concern for consumer protection led to a 1970 amendment to the Bills of Exchange Act expressly removing the protection of a holder in due course in consumer sales.[12] As a result, the use of promissory notes has become less common, since they no longer improve the position of assignee finance companies.

A conditional seller usually assigns all his conditional sale contracts to the same finance company. It would be tempting for the finance company to collaborate with the conditional seller in designing a standard form conditional sale contract with terms to meet their common interests at the expense of consumers. The contract might well include a type of exempting clause by which conditional buyers agreed that an assignee acquired rights against the buyers free from any of the buyers' personal defences against sellers—a result similar to that which a promissory note formerly produced. Such a term is sometimes called a **cut-out clause**. Consumer protection acts seek to make such clauses ineffective.[13]

recourse financing
where the assignee of a debt is entitled to look to the assignor (the original creditor) for payment if the debtor defaults in making payment

cut-out clause
a provision whereby an assignee of a contractual debt takes free of any defences that the original debtor may have against the original creditor

Chattel Mortgages

Nature of a Chattel Mortgage

As we saw in Chapter 25, in discussing mortgages of land, a mortgage is a transfer of an interest in property by the mortgagor (borrower) to the mortgagee (lender) as security for a debt, with

---

12. See now, R.S.C. 1985, c. B-4.

13. For example: Consumer Protection Act, R.S.O. 1990, c. C.31, s. 31; R.S.B.C. 1996, c. 69, s. 3(1); R.S.N.S. 1989, c. 92, ss. 21, 25, 28.

a condition that if the debt is repaid by a specified date the interest in the property reverts to the mortgagor. However, it is not only interests in land that may be the subject of a mortgage; an interest in personal property may be similarly charged, by what is commonly referred to as a **chattel mortgage**.

chattel mortgage
a mortgage of personal property

As with mortgages of land, there are two basic uses of chattel mortgages. In the first type of case, the vendor of an article of property "takes back" a mortgage on the property sold; the effect is essentially similar to a conditional sale, except that in a conditional sale the article remains the property of the vendor until the debt is paid, whereas in a chattel mortgage it is transferred to the buyer and immediately re-transferred to the vendor. In the second type of case, the owner of the article mortgages it to the lender—usually a bank or financial institution—as security for a loan; that loan may be used either to pay for the article that is being mortgaged, or to purchase some entirely different article.

A chattel mortgage may be contrasted with a pledge. In a chattel mortgage, the borrower retains possession of the property and the lender's security interest is in the title to specific goods or in after-acquired property. By contrast, a pledge is a form of bailment: the lender takes possession of the assets or of documents evidencing the borrower's ownership, while the title remains with the borrower.

Business Uses of a Chattel Mortgage

We have seen that in a purchase of real property, the vendor frequently takes back a mortgage as part of the consideration offered by the purchaser. In contrast, commercial sellers of goods and equipment seldom take back chattel mortgages; they usually prefer to sell on short-term credit, leaving it to buyers to borrow longer-term capital from financial institutions. When commercial sellers do find it necessary to offer longer-term financing to buyers, they prefer using conditional sale contracts or leasing the assets. However, in two types of transaction it is quite common for a vendor to take back a chattel mortgage.

A chattel mortgage is often used in the sale of a business as a going concern where office equipment, machinery, or vehicles are included in the sale transaction. If the purchaser does not have all the cash required, the vendor may agree to take a chattel mortgage on specific equipment or machinery or on the stock-in-trade as security for the unpaid balance. In other words, the vendor receives his price partly in cash and partly in a promise to pay secured by a chattel mortgage.

Another common use of the chattel mortgage occurs in the sale of a building with equipment, such as a furnished office building or apartment building. Frequently the price includes both real property and equipment in the building. Not only may the vendor take back a real estate mortgage for the unpaid balance of the purchase price, but he may also take back a concurrent chattel mortgage on all moveable equipment. By so doing, the vendor obtains better security for the debt should it become necessary to foreclose or sell. In addition to prohibiting the mortgagor from disposing of any of the equipment, the chattel mortgage (so long as it is duly registered) avoids any question about whether certain equipment is a fixture; a real estate mortgage would cover only fixtures, but with a concurrent chattel mortgage covering furniture and equipment the question becomes irrelevant.[14]

More commonly, chattel mortgages are used as security for loans made by financial institutions. In particular, banks use chattel mortgages as a device for securing credit in the field of consumer financing. However, they are not restricted to chattel mortgages in the kinds of collateral they may require in granting personal or consumer loans; when lending money for the purchase of a new car a bank may, for example, obtain a guarantee of a third party, a pledge of shares or bonds, or a conditional assignment of the cash surrender value of a life insurance policy.

---

14. For full discussion of this issue see MacDougall (1993), 72 *Can. Bar Rev.* 496.

The Security

When a person borrows to finance a purchase of goods and gives a chattel mortgage, the effect may not seem much different from buying the goods under a conditional sale contract. The borrower will make regular payments to the lender in either situation, and under either device the creditor may repossess the goods if the borrower defaults. However, as noted above, a chattel mortgagee and a seller of goods are ordinarily entirely separate parties; the borrower consequently has no legal excuse to refuse to pay instalments to the mortgagee because of a seller's breach of the contract of sale.

As we have also noted, in a conditional sale, it is the actual goods purchased that comprise the collateral; in a chattel mortgage, the debtor (chattel mortgagor) may give security in a variety of other personal property and even in property acquired after the chattel mortgage has been executed.

A chattel mortgage that includes **after-acquired property** is a very flexible device. It may cover inventories that fluctuate during its term, as some goods are bought and added to inventory while others are sold and subtracted from inventory. The mortgage does not transfer title to specific goods to the creditor, and buyers acquire good title to goods sold by the debtor in the ordinary course of business. The creditor's security interest remains as a suspended priority against general creditors; if the debtor defaults the secured creditor may then seize whatever property is covered by the chattel mortgage and sell it to satisfy the debt. A chattel mortgage may also cover goods not yet in a deliverable state, such as goods in production and growing crops.

The terms of chattel mortgages vary with the type of goods used as security. When a mortgage is on particular assets, the mortgagor usually covenants not to sell or dispose of the goods without the prior consent of the mortgagee and not to permit them to be seized to satisfy the claims of other creditors. Any default in these covenants gives the mortgagee the power to seize the assets. A chattel mortgage usually differs from a real estate mortgage since a chattel mortgagee ordinarily prohibits the sale of the mortgaged property without consent, but a land mortgagee usually does not. A chattel mortgagor usually covenants to keep the mortgaged goods insured against loss by theft and damage by fire, to pay the insurance premiums, and to make the insurance payable to the mortgagee "in so far as his interest may appear."

after-acquired property
property acquired by the debtor after the debt has been incurred

Remedies of a Chattel Mortgagee

A chattel mortgagee has remedies similar to those of a conditional seller. First, as a creditor he may sue on the mortgagor's covenant to pay the debt. Second, he may take possession of the mortgaged goods upon default by the mortgagor. If the mortgagor refuses to give up possession voluntarily, the mortgagee may follow the same procedure as a conditional seller in repossessing goods. So long as the goods remain in the possession of the mortgagee, the mortgagor may redeem them by paying the balance of the debt with interest and costs.

A chattel mortgagee invariably reserves the right upon default to resell the goods to a third party. In exercising this right of sale, he must act reasonably and fairly to obtain a good price for them. If he fails to do so, he may be accountable to the mortgagor for the difference between the price obtained and what would have been a fair price for the goods. If on selling at a fair price, the mortgagee obtains less than the debt outstanding, he may obtain judgment against the mortgagor for the deficiency, but if there is any surplus he must return that surplus to the mortgagor.

A chattel mortgagee, like a mortgagee of real property, may foreclose the interest of the mortgagor by court proceedings and have the chattel declared to be his property absolutely. In contrast with a real estate mortgagee, however, a chattel mortgagee seldom resorts to this measure.

Bills of Sale

A bill of sale is a written contract of sale in which a seller acknowledges the transfer of ownership of specified goods to a buyer for a stated price. It provides evidence of ownership for a buyer who does not acquire immediate possession and leaves the goods for the time being with the seller. Used in this way, a bill of sale is a document evidencing title rather than a credit device. The buyer may resell the goods simply by written assignment of the bill of sale.

A bill of sale may also be used as an instrument of credit much like a chattel mortgage. A person wishing to borrow money may be able to "sell" the title to goods for cash, while still retaining possession and use of them; the "buyer" is in fact a lender who obtains title to goods as security for repayment of the sum lent (the price of the goods). The true intention of the bill of sale can readily be inferred from a term providing for a transfer of the title back to the original owner upon repayment in full of the price. The courts regard such a bill of sale as a chattel mortgage for the purposes of personal property security legislation.

Floating Charges

As we saw in Chapter 27, it is common for a corporation to borrow money for a long term by issuing bonds to the public, using its land and buildings as security. Each certificate issued to a bondholder is evidence of an interest in a **trust deed**—an elaborate form of mortgage on the lands and buildings of the company. The parties to a trust deed are the borrowing corporation (as mortgagor) and a trustee for the bondholders (as mortgagee); the bondholders themselves are beneficiaries of the mortgagee's rights, and the trustee administers these rights for their benefit. Generally, a trust company acts as trustee for the bondholders.

Bonds issued by Canadian corporations frequently provide additional security over and above the mortgage of real property through the creation of a **floating charge**. A floating charge adds those remaining corporate assets not already mortgaged or pledged to the security. When a trust deed includes a provision for a floating charge, the trustee for the mortgage bondholders also has access to business assets, including chattels and choses in action, ahead of the unsecured creditors of the corporation.

A floating charge nicely complements a mortgage of real property because it provides security over the whole of the assets as a working unit. If the corporation defaults in the payment of its bond obligations, the trustee may then more easily place the corporation in the hands of a receiver and manager who can operate it in the interest of the bondholders. A sale of the mortgaged lands and buildings alone may be an ineffective remedy for the bondholders; if the buildings and fixtures are of a highly specialized nature, they will have relatively small realizable value on a forced sale. Such value as they possess is best realized through continued operation of the corporation.

Canadian corporations sometimes issue bonds secured by a floating charge alone and without a mortgage of specific assets. Such bonds are referred to technically as *floating charge debentures* or *contingent debentures*, although they are commonly called simply "debentures." Strictly speaking the term "**debenture**" alone describes corporate bonds that are just a promise to repay the stipulated sum, and are not secured either by a mortgage or a floating charge; however, in common usage, it refers to all types of corporate bonds.

All provinces require mortgages and floating charges contained in trust deeds to be registered. As with conditional sales and chattel mortgages, failure to register makes the trust deed void against creditors and subsequent purchasers or mortgagees. The statutory registration requirements vary from province to province. Some are found in corporations acts, while others are in separate acts. In addition, the interests that are secured by floating charges fall within the general scope of personal property security legislation and are protected by registration in the normal way (see below).[15]

trust deed

a document evidencing a mortgage on the property of a corporation

floating charge

a form of mortgage on all of the assets of a corporation other than those already specifically charged

debenture

an alternative term to describe a corporate "bond"

---

15. In Ontario it was for some time unclear whether a floating charge on a corporation's assets needed to be registered under the Corporate Securities Registration Act (CSRA), the PPSA, or both. Since 1989, registration under the PPSA alone is required and the CSRA was repealed. However, charges registered under the CSRA prior to October 10, 1989, remain protected: S.O. 1989, c. 16, s. 84; PPSA, s. 78.

Checklist: Types of Personal Property Security Interests

Personal property security interests may take any of the following forms:

- conditional sales
- chattel mortgages
- floating charges
- chattel leases
- consignments
- pledges
- assignments of accounts receivable

PERSONAL PROPERTY SECURITY LEGISLATION

Jurisdiction and Application

Section 92 of the Constitution Act, 1867 assigns "Property and Civil Rights in the Province" to provincial jurisdiction. Until relatively recently, the legislatures of the various provinces dealt with legal arrangements for securing credit in quite different ways. Since Canadian businesses often seek a national market for their goods and services, the effect of having to comply with widely varying provincial laws added substantially to the cost of doing business. However, in 1976, Ontario introduced a Personal Property Security Act (PPSA), modelled rather loosely on the provisions of the U.S. Uniform Commercial Code, and since then all of the common-law jurisdictions have followed suit.[16] Each of the provinces and territories has repealed its statutes dealing separately with corporate securities registration, conditional sale contracts, chattel mortgages, and assignments of book debts. Instead, a single act now applies "to every transaction…that in substance creates a security interest";[17] it governs not only conditional sale contracts, chattel mortgages, and assignments of book debts but also floating charges, pledges, leases and consignments intended as security, and other less common forms. The act does not apply, however, to non-consensual security interests; nor does it apply to interests in real property. Unfortunately, although all the laws adopt essentially the same approach, they differ in detail. Additionally, as we shall see, conflicts may arise between the relevant provincial legislation and federal laws, such as the Bank Act.

Purpose of PPSA Legislation

When parties create a security interest, they create a relationship that may often prejudice the interest of others. The degree to which legislatures and courts should support security interests at the expense of innocent third parties is an important policy question.[18] We see here two conflicting goals: that of encouraging lenders to advance credit by lessening their risks through security devices; and that of encouraging others to engage in trade by enabling them to rely on the certainty of title in transactions.

---

16. At the time of writing, the Newfoundland and North West Territories legislation had not entered into force. The revised Quebec Civil Code, which came into effect in 1994, contains broadly similar provisions to the PPSAs.

17. PPSA, s. 2 (Ont.).

18. For a review of this question, see Goode, "Is the Law too Favourable to Secured Creditors?" (1983-4), 8 *C.B.L.J.* 53.

PPSA legislation attempts to achieve those goals by adopting two fundamental principles:

1. All forms of security interests in personal property should be treated in the same manner.

2. All should be subject to a comprehensive system of registration.

The acts themselves are complex, technical, and present a number of problems of interpretation.[19]

A serious problem is caused by the diversity of legal rules that still persists across Canada and by the possibility of conflicts arising between two or more applicable laws. Although PPSA legislation now applies throughout almost the entire country, differences persist between the various provincial laws. Even if there were no differences, there still may be problems determining which provincial law applies to a particular transaction.

CASE 30.2

Gimli Autos, a corporation with its head office in Alberta, leased three trucks from a Manitoba dealer and a car in British Columbia for use by a member of its staff in that province. At that time, Manitoba law did not require registration of pure leases and the truck leases were not registered there; the lease of the car was registered in British Columbia. None of the leases was registered in Alberta.

Gimli became bankrupt. Because of the failure to register in Alberta, the leases were not effective against the trustee in bankruptcy.[20]

Uniform Treatment of Security Interests

Two principal benefits may be gained from rules that are consistent from one type of security device to another. First, the rights and remedies of both debtor and creditor in the event of default should be uniform, and in particular, legislation should recognize and protect a buyer's remaining equity in the security in the same way regardless of the security device used. Second, third parties should have a single form of warning of the existence of a security interest for all types of security.

The acts recognize that all security devices have the same purpose—to secure repayment by the debtor. They set out to establish a single unified system with common rules for the following purposes:

- to define a secured party's remedies against the debtor
- to create one system of registration for all secured interests
- to define priorities between a secured party on the one hand, and third party purchasers, subsequent secured parties, and general creditors on the other

Financing Statement

financing statement
the document setting out details of a security interest that must be filed in order to protect that interest

The diversity of existing security interests makes it impossible to set out a simple system of priorities, but the legislation does attempt to develop a consistent set of principles for ascertaining priorities. The system does not distinguish the particular form of security interest registered; all are reduced to a common form of **financing statement**. The legislation does not, however, prohibit businesses from using their old contract forms to create security interests or from continuing to refer to them by such traditional labels as "conditional sale contracts" or "chattel mortgages."

---

19. For a discussion of the problems and proposals for reform see Ziegel and Cuming (1981), 31 *U.T.L.J.* 249; Ziegel (1991), 70 *Can. Bar Rev.* 681.

20. Gimli Auto Ltd. v. BDO Dunwoody Ltd. (1998), 160 D.L.R. (4th) 373.

Leases and Consignments as Security Interests

The acts recognize that both leases and consignments of goods can be used as forms of security. However, as we saw in Chapters 16 and 17, these arrangements are frequently used quite apart from any intention to create a security interest. In recognition of this, the registration provisions in Ontario apply only to leases and consignments intended as security.[21] The application of registration requirements to a particular transaction will thus turn on whether the parties truly intended to create a security interest. Cases 30.3 and 30.4 illustrate the inquiry needed to ascertain the intention of the parties.

CASE 30.3

Anglo-Oriental Rugs Ltd. was a wholesale distributor delivering expensive carpets to retailers under consignment contracts giving the retailer (consignee) an unrestricted right to return consigned carpets at any time prior to their sale, and requiring the retailer to account to Anglo-Oriental for the proceeds of each rug sold up to its wholesale cost. The arrangement was described as "usual and customary in…the sale of oriental rugs throughout the world." For a number of years Anglo-Oriental and Stephanian's did business on this basis. Anglo-Oriental did not register consignment contracts as security interests under the Personal Property Security Act.

When Stephanian's became bankrupt, the trustee in bankruptcy claimed 14 carpets on consignment from Anglo-Oriental for the benefit of general creditors. The trustee argued that the consignment contract had been intended to create a security interest, not perfected by registration, and was therefore subordinate to the interest of the trustee. The court held on the fact that the consignment of rugs had not been intended as security; the fact that unsold rugs remained in the inventory of Stephanian's did not provide any "security" to Anglo-Oriental, since the rugs belonged to them in any event. As a result, registration was not required to protect their ownership and the court ordered the trustee to return the rugs to Anglo-Oriental.[22]

CASE 30.4

A lease of a photocopier, with an option for the lessee to purchase the machine for 10 percent of its original price at the end of the term of the lease, was held to have been intended as a security agreement rather than as a true lease. The lessor had no real interest in retaining title to the copier at the end of the term, since it would already have received the full price in rent and would not be able to re-lease the used machine. Since the agreement had not been registered the lessor's interest was subordinate to that of the trustee in bankruptcy when the lessee became insolvent.[23]

As these cases illustrate, it is not always easy to determine whether a lease or consignment is intended as security. The courts will have regard to various factors—in particular, whether the agreement contains an option to purchase, and if so on what terms, and whether the lessor is in the business of providing credit.[24]

All of the other provinces have adopted an approach that effectively avoids this difficulty. As in Ontario, a consignment or a lease that secures payment or performance of an obligation

---

21. R.S.O. 1990, c. P.10, s. 2(a)(ii). Manitoba had adopted a similar approach, but this was changed in 1993.

22. Re Stephanian's Persian Carpets Ltd. (1980), 1 P.P.S.A.C. 119.

23. Standard Finance Corp. v. Coopers & Lybrand Ltd., [1984] 4 W.W.R. 543.

24. See Adelaide Capital Corp. v. Integrated Transportation Finance Inc. (1994), 111 D.L.R. (4th) 493. For a discussion of the issue see Ziegel, "Characterization of Equipment Leases and other PPSA Problems" (1994–5), 24 *C.B.L.J.* 141.

is within the scope of the act;[25] additionally, the act applies to "commercial" consignments and to leases for a term in excess of one year, whether or not they are intended to create a security interest.[26]

CASE 30.5

Telecom Leasing leased a car to the B.C. Telephone Company, which in turn leased the car to one of its employees, Giffen, who subsequently became bankrupt. The lease was for a term of more than one year and gave the lessee the option of purchasing the vehicle. Telecom failed to register a financing statement under the (B.C.) PPSA.

It was accepted that the lease was a genuine lease, rather than a security arrangement. Nevertheless, the lessor's interest was required to be perfected under the PPSA, and since it had not been, Telecom had no right to retake possession of the vehicle.[27]

After-acquired Property

PPSA legislation recognizes that assets subsequently acquired by a debtor can be added to a security interest already created and permits the use of chattel mortgages to cover after-acquired goods such as inventories.[28] However, in consumer transactions the security interest of sellers or creditors is confined to the goods financed and does not extend to any other assets of the consumer.

The acts recognize not only inventories as an acceptable form of security interest but also permit proceeds from the sale of inventory in the course of business—*cash or accounts receivable*—to join the security interest.[29] In doing so, the acts acknowledge a long-standing security practice in the financing of inventories.

Registration

If security interests are to be protected by the law, then an effective early warning system alerting third parties to those interests, whatever their form, should be an important corollary. The acts establish a centralized registration system within each province for recording security interests. By using computer facilities to record and revise security information and by enlarging the geographic area over which a search can be made, a very large data base is established and maintained; however, there seems to be little prospect at present of a comprehensive nation-wide system of registration being developed.

Beyond mere creation of a security interest by the agreement of creditor and debtor alone, the legislation requires two further events:

1. the security interest must attach to the asset

2. it must be perfected

attachment
the moment in time when a debtor's property becomes subject to a security interest

Attachment occurs only upon performance of the security agreement by both debtor and creditor. A security interest cannot attach to an asset until the debtor has acquired an ownership interest in it. Nor does a security interest attach until the creditor has performed his part of the bargain by giving the value promised to the debtor.

---

25. For example, s. 1(1) (B.C.); s. 4(1)(b) (N.S.); S.N.B. 1993, c. P-7.1, s. 3(1)(b).

26. *Ibid.*, s. 3(b),(c) (B.C.); s. 3(2) (N.B.); s. 4(2) (N.S.).

27. Re Giffen, [1998] 1 S.C.R. 91.

28. *Ibid.*, s. 12.

29. Consequently, a secured creditor will be able to trace the proceeds into the debtor's bank account: Massey-Ferguson Industries Ltd. v. Bank of Montreal (1983), 4 D.L.R. (4th) 96.

Perfection of a security interest may occur when the secured party takes possession of the assets—as in a pledge—thus ending any false impression of ownership given by the debtor's possession. Perfection occurs most often, however, when a secured party files a financing statement within the registration system. The financing statement gives details of the security interest and provides public notice of the creditor's interest.[30]

perfection
the moment in time when a creditor's security interest becomes protected

The system adopts an insurance method from the land titles system of recording interests in land; the provincial government maintains a fund to reimburse losses caused by incorrectly processed information. The central registry office provides a guaranteed certificate of search. A search under this system is made against the name of a particular debtor whereas under the land titles system it is made against a described parcel of land.[31]

Competing Interests

The three stages of creation, attachment, and perfection are necessary to protect the security against competing interests of others.

ILLUSTRATION 30.1

X Co. borrows money from *Y* Bank in order to buy a truck, gives *Y* Bank a chattel mortgage on the truck, and takes delivery of it. The security interest is created by the loan contract and chattel mortgage; the interest attaches when *Y* Bank hands over the money to *X* Co. and *X* Co. uses it to obtain delivery of the truck from the dealer. The interest is perfected when *Y* Bank registers a financing statement.

Suppose that one secured party finds himself competing for priority with another claiming security in the same asset. The legislation assigns priority to the creditor that first perfects his interest; in practice this generally means that priority goes to the first to register. Thus a creditor that first creates and attaches his interest may nevertheless lose his priority if he delays perfecting that interest and a subsequent creditor perfects first. The subsequent creditor might be aware of the unperfected security interest of the first creditor; even so, by registering first, that interest is perfected and obtains priority.

CASE 30.6

BMP Corp. sold the assets of its donut business to a numbered corporation and took back a chattel mortgage. The mortgage was guaranteed by a Mr. Trafford, whose wife was the sole shareholder of the numbered corporation. Due to an oversight, the financing statement was not registered. Subsequently, Mrs. Trafford registered a financing statement regarding shareholder advances, to protect herself against any unsecured creditors of the purchaser. She had actual notice of the guarantee given by her husband and of BMP's security interest. When BMP discovered the oversight, it registered its financing statement and brought an application for an order setting aside Mrs. Trafford's financing statement, or postponing her interest.

The court held that, notwithstanding her knowledge of the chattel mortgage, Mrs. Trafford's interest had priority.[32]

---

30. The two alternatives are not available for every form of security interest. A security interest in negotiable instruments is perfected only by possession (holding) of the instrument and a security interest in book debts is perfected only by registration.

31. A search may also be made against the property charged. In particular it is advisable to search against the V.I.N. of any vehicle that may be subject to a security interest; see Re Lambert (1994), 119 D.L.R. (4th) 93. This provides additional protection in cases where the debtor's name is incorrectly spelt.

32. BMP & Daughters Investment Corp. v. 941242 Ontario Ltd. (1993), 7 B.L.R. (2d) 270.

The legislation attempts to clarify the priorities among secured creditors who claim competing interests in the same assets. Suppose one creditor takes security in after-acquired property and a subsequent creditor supplies new assets to the same debtor, taking back a security interest in them. Although the new assets become after-acquired property of the debtor, a good case can be made for giving the one who supplies later credit a priority over existing creditors; otherwise a business in financial straits will find it difficult to obtain additional credit needed to rehabilitate itself and survive. In any event, the debtor's assets have been increased by the value of the assets financed by credit, so that the first creditor has not had his security diminished.

purchase-money security interest

the interest that arises when goods purchased by a debtor are charged as security for a loan made to enable those same goods to be acquired

In recognition of this problem, the acts give special priority to a **purchase-money security interest**. This interest arises when a seller (for example, a conditional seller) *reserves* a security interest in the very goods sold to the debtor and when a lender (for example, a chattel mortgagee) finances a debtor's acquisition of the very assets used as collateral. The rule is a necessary qualification to a system that makes it easy to include after-acquired assets and their proceeds in a security interest.

Relations among competing priorities are potentially very complex, especially for the financing of business inventories. Fortunately, in practice a business often has only a single source of financing for its inventories, in which case the need to establish priorities does not arise. In financing other business assets, however, competition is more likely between one secured creditor claiming a charge on after-acquired assets and another claiming a purchase-money security interest, as when a company gives a floating charge over all its assets and then acquires new equipment under a conditional sale contract. In these circumstances, the legislation gives priority to the interest of the conditional seller.[33]

EFFECT OF SECURITY INTERESTS ON PURCHASERS

Separation of Possession and Ownership

The existence of security arrangements typically separates possession of property from formal legal ownership of it. For example, a consignor ships goods to a consignee while retaining title under a consignment contract; a conditional seller gives possession of goods to a conditional buyer while retaining title under a conditional sale contract; a mortgagee acquires title but leaves possession of the goods with a mortgagor under a chattel mortgage. Since possession of goods usually creates an appearance of ownership to a third party, the effect of a credit device may be to mislead an innocent third person; a debtor left in possession of goods may appear to own assets that she in fact does not own.

Under the common law, a seller cannot transfer title to goods that she does not own; a creditor whose existence is not known to the buyer may have legal title to the goods and subsequently assert his right to repossess them from the buyer. The buyer is thus unaware of the risk of not acquiring title and of losing the goods.

Legislatures have generally been more sympathetic to the interests of innocent purchasers than have the courts of common law. A measure of protection is provided under the Factors Act and the Sale of Goods Act,[34] but the principal safeguard for purchasers now lies in the PPSA, in requiring that a security interest be "perfected" by registration.

---

33. Provided, of course, that that interest has been perfected; see Canadian Imperial Bank of Commerce v. Otto Timm Enterprises Ltd. (1995), 130 D.L.R. (4th) 91.

34. See Chapter 16, under the heading "Title to Goods."

Effect of Registration

A properly registered security interest is generally effective against third parties, except for specified classes of bona fide transferees.[35]

ILLUSTRATION 30.2

Peng purchases a video cassette recorder (VCR) from Federchuk's Stereo Stores Ltd. under a conditional sale agreement. He makes a down payment and agrees to pay the balance plus finance charges in 18 equal monthly instalments. Two months later Peng sells the recorder to Tse without disclosing the existence of the conditional sale contract. Can Federchuk's gain possession of the VCR from Tse despite the fact that she is an innocent purchaser?

According to the Personal Property Security Acts, in Illustration 30.2 Federchuk's would be able to recover the VCR from Tse if it had properly registered its security interest before Peng resold the machine to Tse, since she would have had the opportunity to find out about the security interest before making the purchase by making the appropriate search. She is not in a stronger position because of her ignorance. Federchuk's claim takes priority because it was perfected before the purported sale to Tse. The same effect would be achieved if, instead of buying on credit by means of a conditional sale, Peng had borrowed the money from a bank, given a chattel mortgage as security, and used the proceeds of the loan to buy the VCR. The bank would then have been in a position analogous to Federchuk's for the purposes of registration and of maintaining its rights of repossession against third parties.

The Mercantile Agency Rule

There is one common type of business transaction in particular in which a conditional seller clothes a conditional buyer with an appearance of ownership: as we noted in our discussion of trade practices, manufacturers of certain goods often sell them to dealers or merchants under wholesale conditional sale contracts. Suppose that a retail business finances its inventories under a wholesale conditional sale contract registered by the manufacturer. Is the retailer able to give a good title to its customers when it does not itself have title? A negative answer would fly in the face of consumer expectations. This type of financing arrangement invites consumers to rely on a merchant's apparent ownership of its inventories. Hence the PPSA provides that when a conditional seller delivers goods to a conditional buyer who resells them *in the ordinary course of business*, a retail buyer acquires a good title to the goods.[36] Should the dealer fail to meet its obligations, the manufacturer or a finance company holding a registered wholesale instalment account receivable cannot seize the goods from the retail buyer.

The above rule does *not* protect buyers of goods from someone who is not a regular seller of those goods. An unfortunate buyer may find that the conditional seller or his assignee can lawfully seize the goods purchased. The buyer's only remedy is to sue the seller for breach of an implied promise to convey good title. Unfortunately, a seller's warranty in a private sale is likely to be of little value—probably of less value than would be the warranty of an established business selling goods as a mercantile agent. It can be argued that an innocent purchaser in a private sale needs more protection than she would have in a sale by a regular dealer. Yet she has less protection; in this respect it seems that the law is unsatisfactory.

Registration Practice

PPSA legislation does not *require* registration in the sense that failure to register is an offence; nor does it invalidate the creditor's interest. If a secured creditor (or his assignee) chooses not to

---

35. See, for example, ss. 9(1), 25 and 28 (Ont.).

36. For example, s. 28(1) (Ont.).

register, he simply takes a risk that third parties may acquire interests that prevail over his own. Why might a creditor choose not to register? The answer turns on the nature of the creditor's business. Suppose that a creditor's business is primarily one of selling relatively low-value goods to many different customers. He may not find it worthwhile to trace goods wrongfully disposed of by a debtor and then to sue in order to recover them from an innocent purchaser. Instead, he may decide to save the trouble and expense of registering the security interest in the first place. In practice, disputes do not often arise between a secured creditor and a subsequent transferee of goods. Accordingly, except for more expensive consumer durable goods, retail conditional sellers (or finance companies as their assignees) may decide not to register conditional sale contracts.

On the other hand, sales by a manufacturer or wholesaler often involve taking a security interest in assets of a debtor business that has other creditors as well. For instance, a truck manufacturer may sell an expensive fleet of vehicles under a conditional sale agreement to a large retail business. The retail business purchases stock-in-trade from suppliers who also provide credit. If the business should become insolvent, a dispute may arise over the truck manufacturer's claim to repossess the vehicles and thus to deprive the other creditors of an important asset from which to realize their own claims. Risk of this kind of dispute provides the main incentive for registration; registration of a security interest is essential for a creditor to maintain priority against other creditors.[37]

EFFECT OF SECURITY INTERESTS ON OTHER CREDITORS

Assignment of Book Debts

In this chapter we have thus far examined two of the principal ways in which a security interest may arise: as a result of a sale of goods on credit, and as a result of a loan to purchase goods. In these circumstances a debtor's increased liabilities are offset by the newly acquired assets. A third use of security devices arises when an existing creditor requires additional collateral as a condition for leaving a loan outstanding. For this purpose, businesses often provide a conditional assignment of book debts to a bank or other creditor. As we saw in Chapter 12, an assignment of this kind is conditional in two respects: first, the amount of the accounts receivable used as security fluctuates with the state of accounts between the borrowing business (assignor) and its customers; second, the assignment is only a potential one as long as the borrowing business keeps its loan in good standing: the security arrangement does not materialize in an actual assignment, with notice to the borrowing business' customers, unless the borrowing business defaults on its loan.

Should default occur, however, the lender, as assignee, may realize directly on the book debts owed to the assignor in priority to the assignor's general creditors. Thus, an assignment of book debts may seriously prejudice the position of those general creditors, and prospective general creditors need a means of ascertaining whether an assignment has been made. Again, registration of a creditor's security interest provides the necessary information.

Under the PPSA, an assignment is ineffective against creditors of an assignor and against subsequent assignees of the book debts unless it is properly registered.[38] The object is to assure prospective creditors of a business that, unless there is registered public notice to the contrary, the assets of the business in the form of accounts receivable will be available to meet their claims. Registration provides public notice that those accounts are not available.

---

37. For example, s. 20 (Alta., B.C. and Ont.); s. 21 (Sask.).

38. An assignment of book debts is also void as against a trustee in bankruptcy unless it has been properly registered: Bankruptcy and Insolvency Act, R.S.C. 1985, c. B-3, s. 54.

While registration of an assignment may provide information to assist the decisions of a prospective creditor, it does nothing for existing *unsecured* creditors whose decisions to give the debtor credit have already been made. The effect of an assignment is to deprive them of a part of the assets to which they might otherwise have been able to look for payment of their claims; knowledge of the assignment does not help them. Thus, when a major creditor such as a bank insists on obtaining and registering an assignment of book debts, unless the assignment provides a significant benefit to the debtor in exchange, the assignee obtains its new priority at the expense of the general creditors, for whom no relief is available.

Priorities

We have seen that other creditors of a debtor may be affected by a security interest claimed by a particular creditor. Priorities among creditors become of crucial importance when the proceeds from a liquidation of all the assets of a debtor are insufficient to pay in full the claims of all creditors, as we have seen in our discussion of land mortgages. Information about the existence of security interests is therefore essential in making decisions about granting credit: a prospective creditor needs to know the extent to which an applicant has already given collateral security to other creditors before deciding whether to grant further credit of his own.

The Personal Property Security Acts (PPSAs), by extending to a wide variety of methods of securing credit and by adopting a simple "first to register" system, have done much to make the necessary information available though, as we have seen, there may still be problems in interprovincial situations. Unfortunately, the acts do not cover the entire field of personal property security, and conflicting claims between different types of creditors remain all too common and are often difficult to resolve.[39] Conflicts may arise, for example, where a landlord of premises distrains for arrears of rent and claims fixtures that are subject to a security interest that has been registered under the PPSA.[40] Or the conditional seller of a vehicle may have an interest, protected by the PPSA, that conflicts with the lien of a repairer.[41] As we shall see in the next chapter, conflicting claims to priority frequently arise in bankruptcy proceedings,[42] and, as we shall see in the final part of this chapter, conflicts exist between provincial PPSA laws and the federal Bank Act.

SECURITY FOR BANK LOANS

Loans Under the Bank Act

The right to lend to primary producers against the security of their natural products has long been a distinctive feature of Canadian banking practice and, in fact, antedates Confederation. The production of raw materials dominated the early Canadian economy. Typically the producers—usually small-scale farmers—have always required short-term financial assistance to help defray costs through the growing season; farmers must wait several months to recoup costs through sales of their produce, and generally they lack sufficient capital to finance themselves in the meantime. Appropriate financing is a short-term *self-liquidating loan*, that is, a loan that must be repaid from the proceeds from sale of the goods whose production the loan is financing. Over the years, successive revisions of the Bank Act have expanded the types of assets that

---

39. See, for example, Rich-Wood Kitchens Ltd. v. National Trust Co. (1995), 121 D.L.R. (4th) 278, in which a conflict existed between the (Ontario) Mortgages Act, the Registry Act, and the Personal Property Security Act (PPSA).

40. 859587 Ontario Ltd. v. Starmark Property Management Ltd. (1999), 42 B.L.R. (2d) 16.

41. See Canadian Imperial Bank of Commerce v. Kawartha Feed Mills Inc. (1998), 41 O.R. (3d) 124; General Electric Capital Canada Inc. v. Interlink Freight Systems Inc. (1998), 42 O.R. (3d) 348; VFC Inc. v. Tomax Corp., [1998] O.J. No. 5100.

42. See, for example, Royal Bank of Canada v. Sparrow Electric Corp. (1997), 143 D.L.R. (4th) 385, in which the trustee in bankruptcy was faced with claims under the Alberta PPSA, the federal Bank Act, and the Income Tax Act.

may serve as security and the types of borrowers who may qualify for this type of bank loan, but their underlying self-liquidating character has remained substantially the same.

Section 427 of the current federal Bank Act,[43] which came into effect in 1992, is the successor to section 178 of the previous Bank Act, that in turn replaced section 88 of an earlier act in 1980. It is common to encounter, in the literature on this subject, the expression "section 178 loan," or even "section 88 loan." Section 427 empowers Canadian chartered banks to lend to the following types of borrower:

- wholesale or retail purchasers or shippers of, or dealers in (i) products of agriculture, the forest, the quarry and mine, the sea, lakes, and rivers; and (ii) wares and merchandise whether manufactured or not
- manufacturers
- aquaculturalists
- farmers
- fishermen

The types of security that banks are authorized to take vary with the type of borrower and have become quite diverse. At the retail and wholesale level, a bank may take primary produce or manufactured items of inventory held in stock pending resale. Thus, a grain-elevator company may borrow under section 427 to permit it to pay farmers on receipt of their grain for storage. Manufacturers may borrow under the section on the security of inventories of raw materials, work-in-process, and finished goods; a significant proportion of loans is to manufacturing companies. When lending to farmers, a bank may accept as security crops growing or produced on the farm, livestock, or agricultural equipment. The section permits advances to a farmer for the purchase of seed, fertilizer, or pesticides with future crops serving as security for the loan; the purchase of feed with the livestock as security; the purchase of agricultural equipment with the equipment itself as security; and repairs, improvements, and additions to farm buildings on the security of agricultural equipment. Fishermen may obtain loans on the security of fishing vessels, equipment, supplies, or products of the sea. Similarly, forestry producers can borrow on the security of fertilizer, pesticide, forestry equipment, or forest products.

Rights of a Lending Bank

The security taken by a bank is neither a pledge nor a chattel mortgage. It is not a pledge because the borrower does not physically transfer the assets to the bank as security; indeed, the security may not even be in existence when the loan is made—it may be a crop yet to be grown. Nor does the security amount to a transfer of ownership, because the bank does not acquire title to the property as security: to realize the security the bank must have a power of attorney from the borrower.

A borrower under section 427 signs an agreement containing the following promises:

- to keep the property insured and free from claims
- to account to the bank for the proceeds of sales
- to give the bank a right to take possession in the event of default or neglect
- to grant a power of attorney to the bank
- to consent to the sale of the security without notice or advertisement if the borrower defaults

While the loan is in good standing the borrower must apply the money realized from the sale of the goods towards a reduction of the loan. As a further assurance that the proceeds from

---

43. Bank Act, S.C. 1991, c. 46.

sales are applied against the loan, a bank frequently takes a conditional assignment of the borrower's accounts receivable. If the borrower defaults and the bank takes possession of the goods in the borrower's hands and sells them, the bank is entitled to retain out of the proceeds whatever amount will repay the balance owing on the loan plus costs;[44] any surplus belongs to the borrower, and any deficiency represents a debt still due.

To protect its security against a borrower's unsecured creditors and subsequent purchasers or mortgagees in good faith, a bank must insist that the borrower file a standard form of notice expressing an intention to give this type of security. Filing of a notice of intention constitutes constructive notice of the bank's interest to other persons dealing with the borrower and preserves the bank's authority.[45] The place for filing is the local or nearest office of the Bank of Canada.[46] In order to protect the value of the security itself, a bank may also require borrowers other than farmers or fishermen to submit at frequent intervals a statement showing the current value and location of the goods comprising the security.

Other Forms of Collateral Security for Bank Loans

The Bank Act also authorizes chartered banks to employ many of the devices for securing credit that we have considered earlier in this chapter. In addition to, or instead of, security under section 427 a bank may require any of the following types of security as a condition for granting credit:

- an assignment of a warehouse receipt, representing title to goods while held in storage, or of an order bill of lading representing title to goods while in the course of transit
- a pledge of shares or bonds, accompanied by a power of attorney signed by the borrower authorizing the bank to sell them as the borrower's agent if need be
- a pledge of drafts drawn by the borrower against his customers
- an assignment of book debts
- an assignment of the cash surrender value of a life insurance policy
- a chattel mortgage
- a real estate mortgage[47]
- a guarantee by a third party

While the right is not expressly granted by the Bank Act, Canadian judicial decisions permit a bank, in addition to holding collateral security provided by the borrower, to exercise a right of lien on other personal property belonging to the borrower in the bank's possession.[48] A bank may apply against a loan any draft that the borrowing business has left with it for collection.[49] It may apply in settlement of the loan any deposit balances kept with it by the borrowing business if it has not previously earmarked these balances for some particular purpose.[50] A bank lien does not extend to property left with the bank for safekeeping.[51]

---

44. Employees of the borrower take priority over the bank to the extent of three months' arrears of wages. Bank Act, S.C. 1991, c. 46, s. 427(7).

45. See Royal Bank of Canada v. Lions Gate Fisheries Ltd. (1991), 76 D.L.R. (4th) 289.

46. Bank Act, s. 427(4), (5).

47. Normally a mortgage loan is limited to 75 percent of the value of the property; further restrictions apply to loans made on the security of residential (as opposed to commercial) property: Bank Act, s. 418(1).

48. Re Williams (1903), 7 O.L.R. 156.

49. Merchants Bank v. Thompson (1912), 26 O.L.R. 183.

50. Riddell v. Bank of Upper Canada (1859), 18 U.C.Q.B. 139.

51. Leese v. Martin (1873), L.R. 17 Eq. 224.

Conflicts Between the Bank Act and Personal Property Security Acts

As the preceding sections have shown, banks may utilize a wide range of security devices: they can take advantage of the provisions of section 427 of the Bank Act, or can use the more common forms of security such as chattel mortgages and floating charges. The range of options available, however, can pose a dilemma for banks and can lead to conflicting claims between them and other creditors.

One problem is that a degree of overlap exists between section 427 of the Bank Act and the credit devices more generally available. For example, while section 427 does not extend to all forms of property that can be the subject of a security interest under personal property security acts, it is unclear to what extent security interests under section 427 fall within the scope of the provincial acts and are protected by registering under those acts.[52]

Second, the Bank Act and the provincial acts each have their own system of registration, which can result in conflict between creditors, each claiming priority under a different scheme.[53]

Third, since the Bank Act is federal legislation but other personal property security legislation is within provincial jurisdiction, neither level of government can resolve the problems alone. Although the operation of section 427 cannot be made subject to provincial legislation,[54] the respective spheres of operation of the different laws remains unclear.

CONTEMPORARY ISSUE

Too Much Security

It is interesting to speculate what would happen to the business community if all forms of security...were abolished overnight. Would this herald the end of capitalism as we know it? Would the financial markets collapse? Or...would life go on very much as before?

These question are posed by Professor R.M. Goode, in an article entitled "Is the Law too Favourable to Secured Creditors?" Professor Goode goes on to state that "the question now being asked in many common law jurisdictions is whether the law has not swung too far in favour of the secured creditor...."

His concerns are echoed by Professor R.C.C. Cuming, who states that "nowhere in the world is there a system for the regulation of secured financing that is more accommodating to secured creditors than the Canadian PPSAs."

Source: R.M. Goode, "Is the Law too Favourable to Secured Creditors?" (1983–4), 8 *C.B.L.J.* 53; and R.C.C. Cuming, "Canadian Bankruptcy Law: a Secured Creditor's Heaven" (1994–5), 24 *C.B.L.J.* 17 at 21.

Questions to Consider

1. Is this degree of protection—for secured creditors—justified?
2. Does it make credit easier to obtain and thus promote economic growth?
3. Whose interests suffer as a consequence of protecting secured creditors?

---

52. See Rogerson Lumber Co. Ltd. v. Four Seasons Chalet Ltd. and Bank of Montreal (1980), 113 D.L.R. (3d) 671; Re Bank of Nova Scotia and International Harvester Credit Corp. of Canada Ltd. (1990), 73 D.L.R. (4th) 385. For full discussion of this issue see Cuming (1992), 20 *C.B.L.J.* 336.

53. For example, Bank of Montreal v. Pulsar Ventures Inc. and City of Moose Jaw, [1988] 1 W.W.R. 250; Royal Bank of Canada v. Sparrow Electric Corp. (1997), 143 D.L.R. (4th) 385.

54. Bank of Montreal v. Hall, [1990] 1 S.C.R. 121.

QUESTIONS FOR REVIEW

1. What is meant by "collateral security"?

2. Why might a creditor choose *not* to take security for a debt?

3. In what way do security devices act as an incentive to repay one's debts?

4. What are the principal types of security interest?

5. Why is a lease of personal property commonly treated as a security interest?

6. What is an "acceleration clause"?

7. What is meant by "recourse financing"?

8. What does it mean when a person is said to "take subject to the equities"?

9. Why are "cut-out clauses" considered to be unfair?

10. Distinguish between a chattel mortgage and a pledge.

11. What is the principal difference, in practice, between a conditional sale agreement and a chattel mortgage?

12. How can a creditor obtain a security interest in property that the debtor does not yet possess?

13. What is a "floating charge"?

14. What are the fundamental principles upon which the Personal Property Security Acts are based?

15. What is the function of a "financing statement"?

16. What does it mean that a security interest must be "perfected"?

17. What is a "purchase-money security interest," and why is it given special priority?

18. What is a "self-liquidating loan"?

19. What types of loan receive special protection under the Bank Act?

20. How is a security interest protected under the Bank Act?

CASES AND PROBLEMS

1 In May 1994, SIS Ltd. leased two large, portable, tent-like structures to Cansaw Services Inc. for a term of 24 months, at a monthly rental of $11 000. In December of the same year, Cansaw negotiated a loan from the Regal Bank and executed a general security agreement, which gave the Bank a security interest in:

> ...the undertaking of Cansaw and all of Cansaw's present and after-acquired personal property including, without limitation, in all goods, intangibles, money, and securities now owned or hereafter owned or acquired by or on behalf of Cansaw...and in all proceeds and renewals thereof, accretions thereto and substitutions therefore..., and including, without limitation, all of the following now owned or hereafter owned or acquired by or on behalf of Cansaw: all equipment (other than inventory) of whatever kind and wherever situate, including, without limitation, all machinery, tools, apparatus, plant, furniture, fixtures, and vehicles of whatsoever nature or kind....

The Bank registered its security interest under the (Alberta) Personal Property Security Act on the same day.

By May 1996, Cansaw's business was in severe financial difficulties. It had not paid rent to SIS for almost six months and owed them $65 000 in arrears. Its debts to the Bank now totalled almost $1 million.

On May 3, 1996, the Bank delivered a written notice to Cansaw that it was in breach of the financing agreement and gave it one week to remedy its breach. On May 16, 1996, the Bank demanded payment of the outstanding debt and delivered a notice of intention to enforce its security (under section 244 of the Bankruptcy and Insolvency Act). A few days later, the directors of SIS learned of Cansaw's problems with the Bank and gave instructions to a civil enforcement company to enter Cansaw's premises and to dismantle and repossess the structures. At the same time, acting on the advice of their lawyer, SIS registered a security interest in the structures.

The Bank demanded that SIS return the structures, claiming that their general security agreement covered the structures and had priority over the claim of SIS. SIS replied that they were the owners of the structures and were entitled to repossess them since Cansaw had defaulted on payment of the rent. Who has the better claim?

2 Clarkson purchased an automobile from Easyprice Autos for $17 000, under a conditional sale agreement. Easyprice assigned the conditional sale contract to CVF Inc., which advanced Clarkson the bulk of the purchase price. CVF immediately registered its security interest under the (Ontario) Personal Property Security Act.

Six months later, Clarkson entered into a second conditional sales contract with Sonmax Corp. for the purchase and installation of stereo equipment in the vehicle at a cost of $3500, including financing charges. CVF were not informed of this second contract. Sonmax promptly registered a lien against the vehicle under the Repairs and Storage Liens Act.

A few months later, when Clarkson fell into arrears with his repayments, Sonmax repossessed the vehicle, and gave Clarkson notice of its intention to sell the vehicle to secure repayment of what was owed them. At that point, CVF learned of the action by Sonmax and also claimed the vehicle.

Which firm has the prior claim?

3 Silver was the proprietor of the "Sick Parrot," an exotic but eventually unsuccessful restaurant. The premises were originally leased from Desai, who sold the property to Ramesh in 1996.

In order to finance the purchase of new furniture and fittings, Silver had borrowed $20 000 from McTavish in 1995; in doing so he had entered into a general security agreement, giving McTavish a security interest in "…all inventory, furnishings, and fitments…" of the business. McTavish did not register her interest at the time, and Ramesh was unaware of the interest when he purchased the property.

Around the end of 1997, it became clear to Silver that the restaurant business had failed. He was six months in arrears with his rent and still owed McTavish $15 000. He decided simply to abandon the business and has disappeared. When Ramesh learned that the restaurant had gone out of business, he re-entered the premises and took possession of all the inventory, furniture, and so forth. A few days later, McTavish also learned of Silver's departure. She immediately registered her security interest and demanded that Ramesh return all the items he had seized.

Ramesh agreed to return the inventory and furniture, which were worth very little, but claimed that, as the landlord, he was entitled to keep the bar, shelving, refrigerators, light fitments, and other "fixtures." Is Ramesh correct?

4 Avila purchased a second-hand Cadillac from Better Buy Motors Ltd. under a conditional sale agreement. She used the car for several months in her work as a sales representative and paid her instalments regularly. When she had only two instalments left to pay, the car was towed out of her driveway and delivered to Fancy Finance Corp., on instructions of that company. Avila had never heard of Fancy Finance before. It informed her that it had "repossessed" the car under a prior, properly registered chattel mortgage that it held, and that the chattel mortgagor had fraudulently sold the car to Better Buy Motors.

Examine the nature of Avila's rights and indicate against whom they are available. What factors should be taken into account in assessing her loss?

31 CREDITORS' RIGHTS

In this chapter we examine the various ways in which the rights of creditors are protected and enforced. The main focus is on the Bankruptcy and Insolvency Act, but consideration is also given to other statutes, in particular the various provincial laws regarding mechanics' liens—known also as builders' liens or construction liens in some provinces. We consider such questions as:

- what are the principal objectives of bankruptcy law?

- how does bankruptcy law distinguish between different types of debtors—and why?

- what constitutes an "act of bankruptcy"?

- what principles govern the administration of a bankrupt's assets?

- what is a mechanics' (or builder's or construction) lien?

- how are the interests of contractors and subcontractors protected?

- what is the effect of limitation periods on creditors' rights?

STATUTORY ARRANGEMENTS FOR THE PROTECTION OF CREDITORS

In Chapter 15 we examined two of the most important methods by which a creditor's rights may be enforced—levying execution against the goods of the debtor and garnishing his wages. These methods work more or less satisfactorily where the debtor has sufficient assets or income to satisfy the debt and where there is only one creditor. We also considered, in Chapter 30, the rights of a secured creditor to recover what is owing by taking possession of the debtor's property that constitutes the security for the debt and selling it. We noted that where there are a number of creditors, with conflicting claims, problems of priorities arise.

The great majority of business persons are honest and pay their debts reasonably promptly if they are able to do so—resorting to legal procedures to collect money owed by solvent debtors is comparatively unusual. But in some cases a debtor's financial position may become so hopeless that it is unwise or impossible for him to continue to carry on business, as when he becomes insolvent. A person becomes insolvent when he is unable to pay his debts as they fall due or when his liabilities exceed his realizable assets. When a debtor finds himself in that condition, at least some of his creditors will share the loss with him.

A number of statutes have as their main purpose the protection of creditors' claims. These acts set out the rights of creditors both against their debtor and against each other. In this chapter, our main concern will be with the ways in which the Bankruptcy and Insolvency Act and the Mechanics' Lien Acts assist in this purpose.

THE BANKRUPTCY AND INSOLVENCY ACT

Background

Jurisdiction over bankruptcy is assigned to the federal Parliament under the Constitution Act, 1867. The first federal Bankruptcy Act was adopted in 1919 and remained in force until replaced by the Bankruptcy Act of 1949. That Act remains the basis of our current bankruptcy law, though it has been substantially amended on a number of occasions, most notably in 1992, when it was renamed the Bankruptcy and Insolvency Act.[1] Further substantial amendments to the Act were made in 1997.[2]

In the period prior to 1919 some provinces passed legislation governing procedures for "assignments" and prohibiting certain types of fraudulent conduct by debtors,[3] but no legal machinery existed for the compulsory division of an insolvent debtor's property among his creditors, nor were there any means for giving an honest debtor a formal discharge from his obligations once all his assets had been distributed to his creditors; they could continue to pursue him for payment, subject only to limitations statutes.

The Bankruptcy and Insolvency Act performs a number of functions:[4]

- It establishes a uniform practice in bankruptcy proceedings throughout the country and attempts to do so as inexpensively as possible.
- It attempts to provide for an equitable distribution of the debtor's assets among his various creditors.
- It provides a framework for preserving and reorganizing the debtor's business or affairs by working out an arrangement with the agreement of his creditors, thus avoiding a total liquidation of a debtor's estate, if possible.
- It provides for the release of an honest but unfortunate debtor from his obligations and so permits him to make a fresh start free of debts.

1. Bankruptcy and Insolvency Act, R.S.C. 1985, c. B-3, as amended by S.C. 1992, c. 27. Unless otherwise stated, statutory references in this part of the chapter are to that Act.
2. S.C. 1997, c. 12.
3. Some provincial legislation remains in effect; see for example the Assignments and Preferences Act, R.S.O. 1990, c. A.33. In case of a conflict between provincial and federal legislation dealing with insolvency, the latter prevails: British Columbia v. Henfrey Samson Belair Ltd. (1989), 59 D.L.R. (4th) 726.
4. For a detailed account of bankruptcy law, see Houlden and Morawetz, *1997 Bankruptcy and Insolvency Act*. Toronto: Carswell, 1996.

Policy Issues

It is helpful in bankruptcy law to distinguish the public interest from that of the parties to a bankruptcy proceeding, even though their interests often coincide. Business confidence and respect for the law are reinforced if creditors are able to recover what is lawfully owing to them. But their interests may diverge from that of society generally in a number of ways. The chief concern of most creditors is to recover promptly as much as possible of what is owed to them. They will normally have little interest in whether a debtor's business can be saved and turned around. Bankruptcy law, however, contains provisions whereby creditors may be encouraged, and sometimes compelled, to accept an arrangement designed to save a business. Similarly, a creditor normally wishes to preserve the possibility of recovering in full what is owed, even if this is not possible in the debtor's present financial circumstances. However, it is in the public interest to allow an honest but unfortunate debtor to be discharged from his debts once he has paid as much as is possible and to give him a fresh start. It is important to keep economic initiative alive, rather than to stifle it on account of a past misfortune.

In other circumstances, where a debtor has virtually no assets available to meet his debts, the natural instinct of his creditors may be simply to cut their losses and not waste time and money in a fruitless attempt to recover something. One of the aims of bankruptcy legislation, however, is to promote an atmosphere of confidence in business relations, and confidence would be undermined were bankruptcy frauds to go unpunished. The Act consequently contains provisions to punish dishonest debtors and to prevent them from re-engaging in business activities.

There are, of course, limits to what even well-drafted legislation can achieve. In many situations, the damage done to creditors' claims by the time bankruptcy occurs is largely irreparable. The best protection for creditors is their own astuteness in granting credit. Careful creditors check the credit rating of prospective borrowers and, where appropriate, require collateral security. To assist prospective creditors by making more information available to them, the Act requires certain information to be filed concerning bankrupt debtors and the directors and officers of bankrupt corporations.

Government Supervision

The Act (section 5) creates the position of Superintendent of Bankruptcy, who keeps a record of all bankruptcy proceedings in Canada and has a general supervisory function over all bankrupt estates. The Superintendent is responsible for investigating the character and qualifications of persons applying for licences to act as trustees and has the power to suspend or cancel a trustee's licence. He or she may issue directives to trustees or receivers regarding the administration of a bankrupt estate, may intervene in any court proceeding, and may investigate situations where a bankruptcy offence may have been committed (section 10(1)).

official receiver
a public official responsible for the supervision of bankruptcy proceedings

For the purposes of administration, the Act makes each province and territory a bankruptcy district; each district may be divided into two or more divisions, according to the size of the province. For each division, one or more **official receivers** is appointed. Official receivers are officers of the court and are required to report to the Superintendent all bankruptcies originating in their divisions (section 12).

The Act designates the highest trial court in each province or territory as the court for hearing bankruptcy proceedings (section 183). Usually a particular judge or judges of the provincial court are designated to deal with bankruptcy matters, and their courts are commonly referred to as the Bankruptcy Court, though strictly speaking no separate bankruptcy tribunal exists. The courts hear creditors' petitions for the bankruptcy of their debtors and determine whether a debtor should be discharged after his affairs have been wound up.

trustee in bankruptcy
the person appointed to administer the property of a bankrupt

The actual administration of a debtor's estate is placed in the hands of a licensed **trustee in bankruptcy**, who is normally an accountant and is appointed by the court or, in the case of a voluntary assignment in bankruptcy, by the official receiver. In either case, in appointing the trustee regard must be paid to the wishes of the creditors, who retain the power to appoint a substitute trustee (section 14). The creditors also appoint one or more (but not exceeding five) inspectors to instruct and supervise the trustee (section 116).

Persons to Whom the Act Applies

Bankrupts and Insolvent Persons

The Act applies, in general, to debtors who are individuals, partnerships, and corporations—apart from banks, insurance companies, and trust, loan, or railway companies (section 2). A "**bankrupt**" is defined as a person who has made an assignment or against whom a receiving order has been made; that is, a formal legal step must be taken in order to declare a person bankrupt. A distinction is made between debtors who voluntarily declare bankruptcy and those who are forced into bankruptcy by their creditors.

> **bankrupt**
> a person who has made a voluntary assignment in bankruptcy or against whom a receiving order has been made

The Act, as its new title indicates, applies to insolvent persons as well as to bankrupts. An **insolvent person** is defined, for the purposes of the Act, as a person who is not bankrupt, whose liabilities to creditors amount to at least $1000, and who either

> **insolvent person**
> a person who is unable to meet (or has ceased to pay) his or her debts as they become due, or whose debts exceed the value of his or her realizable assets

- is unable to meet his obligations as they generally become due
- has ceased paying his current obligations in the ordinary course of business as they generally become due
- has debts due and accruing due, the aggregate of which exceed the realizable value of his assets (section 2)

The Act thus distinguishes between two basic types of person—those (insolvents) who are potential candidates for bankruptcy and those (bankrupts) who have been declared bankrupt. A person may be insolvent without having been declared bankrupt, and a bankrupt may turn out not to be insolvent.

Consumer Debtors

An important distinction is drawn in the Act between "consumer debtors" and other debtors. It defines a **consumer debtor** as an insolvent natural person (i.e., an individual) whose aggregate debts, excluding any debt secured by the person's principal residence, do not exceed $75 000 (section 66.11). Thus, despite the name, the true distinction is not that between non-business and business debtors but rather between small, individual, debtors and others.

> **consumer debtor**
> an individual who is insolvent, but whose aggregate debts do not exceed $75 000

The relevance of the distinctions—between insolvent persons and bankrupts, and between commercial and consumer debtors—will be considered when we discuss the various procedures provided for under the Act.

Corporations

The application of bankruptcy law to corporations is somewhat problematic since, as we saw in Chapter 27, the principle of limited liability means that the shareholders of a corporation are not liable for its debts. The corporation is liable for its own debts to the full extent of its assets, but these may be very few. Notions of punishment and rehabilitation have little meaning for a bankrupt corporation. A group of individuals may form a corporation with a very small capital sum and, if the corporation becomes bankrupt, they lose very little (unless they have personally guaranteed its debts). To make a fresh start in business they may simply form a new corporation. However, the worst abuses—for example, where the assets of a corporation are "creamed off" by the payment of excessive dividends or by redeeming shares—are governed by provisions that allow such transactions to be reviewed and set aside. Further, where a corporation commits a bankruptcy offence, any director or officer who authorized, participated in, or acquiesced in the offence is liable to punishment for the offence (section 204).[5]

PROCEDURES UNDER THE ACT

The Act makes provision for three distinct types of procedure, applicable in different circumstances and each with its own special consequences:

proposal
a procedure whereby a debtor, by agreement with the creditors, reorganizes his or her affairs without being made bankrupt

assignment
a voluntary declaration of bankruptcy

receiving order
a court order made in proceedings instituted by creditors, whereby a debtor is declared bankrupt

1. a **proposal**—a procedure to avoid formal liquidation of the debtor's estate, at least temporarily, by allowing the debtor time to attempt to reorganize and save a viable business or, in the case of a consumer debtor, to reorganize his affairs

2. an **assignment**—a voluntary application by a debtor to institute bankruptcy proceedings

3. a **receiving order**—initiated by creditors to have their debtor declared bankrupt by the court

We shall examine each of these procedures in turn.

Proposals

The Act makes provision for two types of proposal—commonly referred to as *commercial proposals* (Division I) and *consumer proposals* (Division II)—the latter being a simplified procedure available to individual consumer debtors. For corporations, an alternative method of avoiding liquidation is provided under the Companies' Creditors Arrangement Act; that Act is considered later in this chapter, under the heading "Other Methods of Liquidation and Reorganization."

Commercial Proposals

A Division I proposal may be made by an insolvent person, a liquidator of an insolvent person's property, or by a receiver in relation to an insolvent person; a proposal may also be made by a bankrupt, or by the trustee of a bankrupt's estate, provided the estate has not yet been wound up (section 50(1)).

A proposal constitutes an offer made by the debtor to his creditors, providing for the orderly repayment of his debts, or of some part of his debts,[6] over a period of time. If the proposal is accepted by a sufficient proportion of the creditors, application may be made to the court to have it declared binding upon all the creditors.

Where a proposal is made before bankruptcy, the debtor files a copy of the proposal with the official receiver in the debtor's district. The proposal must be accompanied by a statement showing the debtor's financial position, verified by affidavit of a licensed trustee. An insolvent person can gain additional time by filing a notice of intention with the official receiver, stating his intention to make a proposal (section 50.4). If the debtor has already been made bankrupt, the proposal and statement of financial position are delivered to the existing trustee. Such a proposal must be approved by the inspectors (appointed by the creditors to supervise the trustee), before any further action is taken.

The next stage is to obtain approval for the proposal at a meeting of the creditors. One of the most important changes introduced in the 1992 amendments was to bring secured creditors within the scope of the Act. Now, a proposal may be made to secured creditors, or to one or more classes of secured creditors, as well as to unsecured creditors. Acceptance of a proposal

---

5. An individual who is a bankrupt is not permitted to be a director of a corporation; see, for example, Canada Business Corporations Act, R.S.C. 1985, c. C-44, s. 105(1).

6. Certain debts, notably those to the Crown and to employees, must be paid in full; s. 60(1.1), (1.3).

requires the approval of a majority in number, and two-thirds in value, of the unsecured creditors, and a similar proportion of each class of secured creditors. Secured creditors not included in the proposal, or whose class has rejected the proposal, continue to enjoy the protection provided by their security.

If the proposal is accepted by a sufficient proportion of creditors, the next step is for the trustee to apply to the court for approval. Although the court will be reluctant to refuse approval to a proposal that is acceptable to the majority of creditors, it must be satisfied that the terms of the proposal are reasonable and for the benefit of the general body of creditors (section 59(2)). In particular, it may withhold approval if the proposal fails to provide reasonable security for repayment of at least 50 cents on the dollar to unsecured creditors, or if the debtor has been guilty of a bankruptcy offence.

Once approved by the court, the proposal is binding on all unsecured creditors and on all secured creditors of a class that has given its approval. Unless the proposal provides to the contrary, the debtor retains control of his property. However, monies payable under the proposal must be paid to the trustee for distribution to the creditors. Where the debtor defaults in the performance of any provision of the proposal the trustee is required to notify all creditors and the official receiver. Application may then be made, by any creditor or by the trustee, to have the proposal annulled (section 63). The effect of annulment is that the debtor is deemed to have made an assignment (see below).

Consumer Proposals

An insolvent individual who owes no more than $75 000, not counting any debt secured by mortgage on a principal residence, may make a proposal to his creditors for the reduction or extension of time for the payment of his debts (section 66.12). It should be noted that the provisions do not apply to individuals who have already been declared bankrupt; bankrupt consumers are subject to the general provisions of the Act, though they presumably may make a proposal under Division I.

A Division II proposal must be prepared with the assistance of an "administrator"—a licensed trustee or other person appointed by the Superintendent to administer consumer proposals. The administrator is responsible for investigating the debtor's financial affairs and for providing counselling. Procedures are simplified, and a formal meeting of creditors is not required unless requested by creditors representing 25 percent in value of the proven debts. Where no meeting is requested, the proposal is deemed to be accepted by the creditors. A proposal that has been accepted, or deemed to be accepted, does not require approval of the court.

An important consequence of filing a consumer proposal is that the debtor also obtains protection against lease terminations, acceleration of instalment payments, or having utilities shut off (section 66.34).

Assignments

By making an assignment an insolvent person may voluntarily declare himself bankrupt. A debtor who is no longer able to meet his debts as they fall due may prefer to initiate bankruptcy proceedings himself, rather than wait for his creditors to do so. By making an assignment he puts an end to an unsatisfactory situation and makes an earlier rehabilitation possible. Also, to continue to carry on a business once he knows he is insolvent might well involve him in the commission of a bankruptcy offence, and thus prejudice his eventual discharge (section 173(1)(e)).

A debtor makes an assignment by filing a petition with the official receiver, accompanied by a sworn statement of his property and of his debts and creditors (section 49). (As we saw above, a person who defaults on a proposal may also be deemed to have made an assignment.) When the official receiver files the petition, she appoints a trustee, who becomes responsible for the administration of the debtor's estate and to whom the debtor's property is assigned. From that point on, the debtor ceases to have any right to dispose of or deal with his property.

The estate of a bankrupt who has made an assignment is administered in the same manner as one administered under a receiving order; the procedure will be dealt with in the next section of this chapter. However, a special simplified form of summary administration is provided in the case of an individual bankrupt who has made an assignment and whose realizable assets, after deducting the claims of secured creditors, do not exceed $5000 in value (section 49(6)).

Receiving Orders

A creditor, or group of creditors, may file a petition with the court in the judicial district where the debtor is located in order to have the debtor declared bankrupt, provided the creditor (or group) is owed not less than $1000, and the debtor has committed an **act of bankruptcy** within the previous six months (section 43). A secured creditor may initiate a petition, but to the extent that she makes a claim in bankruptcy she is considered to have abandoned her security.

act of bankruptcy
a prescribed act of a debtor that must be proved before the debtor may be declared bankrupt

It should be noted that, unlike the rules for making proposals and assignments, there is no requirement that the debtor be insolvent; it is sufficient that he has committed an act of bankruptcy. An act of bankruptcy, as we shall see in the next section of this chapter, may be committed by a person who is not insolvent. However, in the great majority of cases where a receiving order is made, the debtor is likely to be insolvent.

Subject to a few exceptions, a petition may be filed in respect of any debtor, whether an individual, partnership, or corporation. No petition may be made against an *individual* who is engaged solely in fishing, farming, or the tillage of the soil, or against a wage earner who does not earn more than $2500 a year and does not carry on any business on his own account (section 48).[7]

Bankruptcy proceedings are considered penal in nature, and the burden of proving the facts alleged is on the petitioning creditors, who must comply with all the formalities required by the Act. The petition may be opposed by the debtor, who may dispute the existence of the debt or of an alleged act of bankruptcy. Even where the petitioning creditors succeed in establishing facts that would justify the making of a receiving order, the court has a general discretion to refuse to make the order or to grant a stay of proceedings. For example, it may decline to make an order if it considers that, given a fair chance, the debtor will be able to meet his obligations within a reasonable period. It may also decline to make an order where the debtor has no assets to divide among the creditors and there is no likelihood that he will have assets in the future.

Where a receiving order is made, its effect is to vest the bankrupt's property in the trustee appointed by the court to administer the estate.

Acts of Bankruptcy

We have noted that before creditors can succeed in having their debtor adjudged bankrupt and a receiving order issued, they must prove that he has committed an act of bankruptcy. The Bankruptcy and Insolvency Act sets out in detail the various types of conduct that constitute an act of bankruptcy by a debtor (section 42). In summary they are as follows:

- An assignment of assets to a trustee—If a debtor makes an assignment of his property to a trustee for the benefit of his creditors, whether it is an authorized assignment or not, and the arrangement is not satisfactory to the creditors, they may cite the assignment as an act of bankruptcy and petition to have a receiving order issued. They might choose to do so, for example, when the debtor has transferred his assets to a trustee who is not acceptable to them.

- A fraudulent transfer of assets to a third party other than a trustee—A transfer of property by a debtor in anticipation of bankruptcy in order to withhold assets

---

7. Such an individual may, however, make a voluntary assignment. A corporation engaged in farming or fishing may be petitioned.

from distribution to creditors is a fraudulent transfer. As we shall see when discussing "Powers and Duties of the Trustee" below, any attempt to deprive creditors of access to assets by transferring them to a third person (including the debtor's spouse or child) is void if the transfer takes place within a specified period prior to bankruptcy.

- A fraudulent preference—Any payment by a debtor that has the effect of settling the claim of one creditor in preference to the outstanding claims of other creditors is a fraudulent preference.
- An attempt by the debtor to abscond, with intent to defraud creditors.
- A failure to redeem goods seized under an execution issued against the debtor[8]— as we have seen in Chapter 15, a creditor may sue a debtor, obtain judgment, and seek to satisfy the judgment by having the debtor's assets seized. When a debtor's assets are few, a seizure may well benefit the judgment creditor to the disadvantage of other creditors; accordingly, if a debtor fails to take steps to prevent the sale of his property under an execution order, he commits an act that entitles his creditors to apply to the court for his bankruptcy. If they do so, all the debtor's property, including the property subject to the execution order, is put in the hands of a licensed trustee for distribution to all the creditors.[9]
- The presentation at a meeting of creditors of (a) a statement of assets and liabilities disclosing the debtor's insolvency, or (b) a written admission by the debtor that he is unable to pay his debts.
- An attempt to remove or hide any of his property, with intent to defraud creditors.
- Notice to any of the creditors that the debtor is suspending payment of his debts.
- A default in any proposal that the debtor has previously persuaded the creditors to accept as a means of forestalling bankruptcy proceedings.
- A failure to meet liabilities generally as they become due.

The most common of these acts of bankruptcy are failing to pay debts as they become due, and failing to redeem goods seized under an execution.

ADMINISTRATION OF A BANKRUPT'S AFFAIRS

Powers and Duties of the Trustee

The appointment of a trustee is the first step in establishing creditor control. The trustee takes possession of the assets of the bankrupt debtor and of all books and documents relating to his affairs. She becomes in effect a temporary manager of the business, subject to the supervision of inspectors appointed by the creditors. She may carry on the business, or alternatively, sell the assets. She can do such things as employ a lawyer, borrow further money for the business by pledging or mortgaging its remaining free (unsecured) assets, and negotiate with creditors for the acceptance by them of specific assets in lieu of money settlement of their claims. She may even engage the bankrupt debtor himself to assist in the administration of the bankrupt estate. To do these things she must have specific authority from the inspectors (section 30). The

---

8. More specifically, a debtor commits an act of bankruptcy if he permits an execution to remain unsatisfied for fourteen days after seizure by the sheriff, or until within four days of the time fixed for sale by the sheriff, or in a variety of other circumstances set out in section 42(1)(e).

9. It is possible that, instead of petitioning for a receiving order, all the debtor's major creditors might choose to obtain individual judgments and execution orders. In Ontario, the Creditors Relief Act, R.S.O. 1990, c. C.45, provides for a scheme of rateable distribution of the proceeds of sale among execution creditors.

principal duties of a trustee, however, are to recover all property that under bankruptcy law should form part of the debtor's estate, and to apply that property in satisfaction of the claims of creditors (sections 16(3), 25).

Recovery of Property

The trustee takes possession of those assets of the debtor that are in the debtor's possession, and also seeks to recover any other assets, for example by collecting debts owed to the debtor. As a general rule, the trustee cannot obtain a better title to property than the debtor himself possessed in that property. Consequently, the trustee's interest is subject to the claims of persons who own property that is in the possession of the debtor, or of secured creditors who have interests in that property. However, the Personal Property Security Acts (PPSAs) have introduced an exception to the general principle. Thus, for example, if someone has leased personal property to the debtor and has failed to register that interest, the security interest is ineffective and is subordinate to the claim of the trustee.[10]

In addition, there may be property that the debtor has disposed of and that by law should form part of his bankrupt estate to be available to satisfy the claims of creditors. Thirteen sections of the Act under the heading "Settlements and Preferences" are needed to set out the complex rules for the recovery of property (sections 91–101.2).

Settlements

settlement
a gift of property made by a debtor before becoming bankrupt

The term "**settlement**" refers to gifts of property made by the debtor before becoming bankrupt. The intention of the rules is to prevent a person who is insolvent, or on the verge of insolvency, from prejudicing the claims of his creditors by giving his property away—usually to members of his family or to friends.

In general, any gratuitous transfer of property[11] by a debtor that occurred within a year before his bankruptcy becomes void and recoverable by the trustee. In addition, the trustee may impeach a transfer of property made as long as five years before the bankruptcy, but the burden is then on the trustee to show that at the date of the transfer the debtor was unable to pay his debts in full without the aid of such property (section 91).[12]

fraudulent transfer
a transfer of property by a debtor (usually to a related person) with the intention of putting that property out of the reach of creditors

In realizing the assets of the debtor, the trustee in bankruptcy may demand the property, or its value, from the party who received it. The trustee may also recover payments of money by the debtor to or for the benefit of a spouse or child and transfers of property under a marriage contract, if made within six months preceding bankruptcy or at any time when the debtor was unable to pay his debts without the aid of that money or property (sections 92, 93).[13]

A settlement may be attacked not only under the provisions of the Bankruptcy and Insolvency Act but also under provincial laws dealing with **fraudulent transfers;**[14] it is not unusual for a trustee in bankruptcy to pursue both kinds of remedies.

---

10. Re Giffen, [1998] 1 S.C.R. 91.

11. The rule does not apply to transfers of property that would otherwise be exempt from execution, such as a RRIF; see, for example, Royal Bank of Canada v. North American Life Assurance Co. (1996), 132 D.L.R. (4th) 193 (S.C.C.).

12. In practice it is almost impossible for a trustee to establish the exact financial status of a bankrupt debtor at a time as long as a year or more before the bankruptcy.

13. The onus is upon the recipient to show that the transferor was solvent at the time.

14. See, for example, Fraudulent Conveyances Act, R.S.O. 1990, c. F.29.

CASE 31.1

A husband and wife had jointly owned their matrimonial home since 1974. In 1978, the husband gave a personal guarantee to a bank in respect of a debt owed by the corporation of which he and his wife were the sole shareholders. In 1990, the husband transferred his half-interest in the home to his wife for $1. Shortly thereafter the bank demanded repayment of the debt and, when the husband was unable to meet the guarantee it appointed a receiver. The husband died insolvent in 1991.

The bank successfully claimed that the transfer of the interest in the home was a fraudulent conveyance and was consequently void under the (Ontario) Fraudulent Conveyances Act. The bank was entitled to a 50 percent interest in the property.[15]

Preferences

A solvent debtor is entitled to pay his creditors in any order he pleases; he may choose to pay one creditor before he pays another, that is, to give *preference* to the claim of the first creditor over the second—perhaps because he depends on the prompt services or delivery of goods from the first creditor. (Another reason, if the debtor is a corporation, is that the directors may have given personal guarantees of one or more of the debts.) By contrast, in bankruptcy the guiding principle is that creditors of the same class should be treated equally.

A debtor facing imminent bankruptcy should consequently not be permitted to unfairly favour certain creditors over others. The Act deals with this situation by providing that (a) a payment of money or a transfer of property to a creditor, (b) by an insolvent debtor within three months preceding bankruptcy, (c) with a view to giving that creditor preference over other creditors, amounts to a **fraudulent preference** and is recoverable (section 95). The time limit extends to 12 months where the creditor who received the preference is a related person (section 96). The provisions are intended to nullify transactions that would otherwise defeat the legitimate claims of creditors; they do not invalidate payments made in good faith to creditors who were unaware of the impending bankruptcy, nor other transfers of property such as the sale of inventory or other business assets in the normal course of business (section 97).

fraudulent preference
the payment of money or transfer of property to a creditor with a view to giving that creditor preference over other creditors

CASE 31.2

Green Gables Manor Inc., a corporation operating a nursing home, made payments of $13 000 to each of its two controlling shareholders and directors. The payments were stated to be in respect of management fees owed to them. It also executed a general security agreement in their favour in respect of outstanding claims. The following day, a receiving order was granted and Green Gables was declared bankrupt.

The trustee claimed repayment of the sums and a declaration that the security agreement was void. The court found that the two directors were "related" to the corporation for the purposes of the Bankruptcy and Insolvency Act, that the transactions represented a "preference," and that they should accordingly be set aside.[16]

15. Bank of Montreal v. Bray (1997), 36 O.R. (3d) 99. See also Mutual Trust Co. v. Stornelli (1999), 170 D.L.R. (4th) 381.

16. Re Green Gables Manor Inc. (1998), 41 B.L.R. (2d) 299. Contrast Sheraton Desert Inn Corp. v. Yeung (1998), 168 D.L.R. (4th) 126.

Reviewable Transactions

A third source of potential abuse is that category of transactions where a debtor has entered into a contract with a relative or a corporation in which he has a major interest. Since he was not dealing at **arm's length** with that other party, there is a risk that the interests of his creditors may have been harmed. The debtor may have sold property at an undervalue, or bought at an excessive price; the effect is as if he had made a gift of the difference between the sum actually received or paid and the fair market value of the property. Persons related to each other are deemed not to deal at arm's length. The Act defines "related" broadly, so that it includes not only personal relationships through blood, marriage, or adoption, but also the relationship between a corporation and its controlling shareholders or between two or more corporations with a common controlling person or group (section 4.)

Under the Act, transactions that were not at arm's length are reviewable; if entered into by the debtor within 12 months preceding bankruptcy, the trustee may apply to the court for an inquiry into whether or not the debtor gave or received, as the case may be, fair market value for the property or services that were the subject of the transaction (sections 3, 100).[17] If the price paid in the transaction was conspicuously greater or less than fair market value, the court may award the difference gained by the other party to the trustee in bankruptcy.

Payment of Claims

Having taken possession of a bankrupt's property, the trustee's duty is to apply the property in payment of the lawful claims against the bankrupt estate. However, not all of the bankrupt's property is subject to seizure. Section 67 provides that "the property of a bankrupt divisible among his creditors shall not comprise…any property that…is exempt from execution or seizure under the laws of the province within which the property is situated and within which the bankrupt resides." Provincial laws provide exemption from seizure for such items as household furnishings and appliances, and for insurance policies and RRSPs, though these exemptions vary considerably from one province to another.

Having taken possession of the bankrupt's property, the trustee's duty is to apply that property in satisfaction of the claims of creditors. That normally involves selling the property and distributing the cash proceeds among the creditors. In appropriate cases the trustee may distribute **liquidating dividends** (payments on account) to the creditors from time to time as required by the inspectors and as realization of the debtor's assets permits. In doing so she must, of course, be careful to take account of the claims of the secured and preferred creditors.

Because the assets are almost certainly insufficient to satisfy all the claims in full, the priority of claims is important. A trustee must act with great care in the administration and liquidation of the debtor's affairs; she may be personally liable to creditors for losses caused them by her failure to pay the claims in the proper order of priority. As we saw in Chapter 30, the determination of priorities can be an extremely difficult matter, especially where the claims of secured creditors are involved. The trustee must determine whether a claim to a secured interest is effectively protected (for example, by registration under the PPSA);[18] where there are two or more such claims, the trustee must determine their respective priority. That may prove especially difficult where the claims are made under different statutes, such as a provincial PPSA and the federal Bank Act.[19]

In such cases, it is normally advisable for the trustee to seek a ruling from the court.

---

17. A similar inquiry may be made where a bankrupt corporation has paid dividends to its shareholders or has redeemed shares; s. 101.

18. See Re Giffen, *supra*, n. 10.

19. See, for example, Royal Bank of Canada v. Sparrow Electric Corp., [1997] 1 S.C.R. 411; Abraham v. Canadian Admiral Corp. (1998), 39 O.R. (3d) 176.

Two of the more important changes introduced by the reforms of 1992 concern the rights of *unpaid sellers* and of *secured creditors*; these have been mentioned already, in Chapters 16 and 30 respectively.

Unpaid Sellers

An unpaid seller now has a right to repossess goods sold and delivered to a bankrupt in relation to his business (section 81.1). The supplier must make a demand within 30 days of the delivery of the goods, and the goods must still be in the possession of the purchaser, be identifiable, and be in the same condition as when sold. The claim ranks above any other claim to the goods, except that of a bona fide purchaser of the goods for value without notice of the supplier's right. A supplier who repossesses goods cannot subsequently claim against the bankrupt for any deficiency in respect of those goods.

CASE 31.3

Thomson Electronics had supplied a substantial quantity of goods to Consumers Distributing, for which it had not been paid. Consumers Distributing was declared bankrupt and Thomson claimed recovery of the goods that it had supplied in the preceding month. The goods were not in the possession of Consumers Distributing but were being stored in a warehouse belonging to Tibbett and Britten Inc., which was also a creditor of Consumers Distributing.

The court held that for section 81.1 to apply, the goods had to be in the actual physical possession of the bankrupt. Thomson's claim to recover the goods accordingly failed.[20]

An additional priority is created for farmers, fishermen, and aquaculturalists who have supplied their products to a bankrupt and have not been paid. The claims of such suppliers extends not only to the goods supplied but also are secured by a charge on the entire inventory of the purchaser; this charge ranks above any other claim against that inventory, except that of an unpaid seller of specific goods (section 81.2).

Secured Creditors

The 1992 amendments also bring secured creditors within the scope of the Act. Secured creditors, as we have seen, may be included in a proposal made by an insolvent person and may also be affected by the rights of unpaid sellers and of agricultural suppliers. The Act now requires a secured creditor to give at least 10 days' notice to an insolvent person before enforcing her security, (section 244) and contains provisions governing the conduct of a receiver, appointed by a secured creditor, in so far as that conduct relates to the administration of a bankrupt estate (sections 245–7).

Subject to these provisions, however, a secured creditor is entitled to enforce her security to obtain payment of what is owing. A secured creditor must pay to the trustee any surplus if the security she holds is worth more than the debt owing to her. When the trustee and secured creditor cannot agree on the value of the security, it may be necessary to sell it and pay the secured claim out of the proceeds (sections 127–34). The bankrupt estate is entitled to any surplus for the benefit of other creditors. When the value of the security is less than the secured debt, the creditor receives the full value of the security and in addition ranks as a general claim along with other unsecured creditors for the deficiency. When the trustee and secured creditor agree on the value of the secured assets without having to sell them, the creditor may accept the security in

20. Thomson Consumer Electronics Canada, Inc. v. Consumers Distributing Inc. (1999), 170 D.L.R. (4th) 115.

settlement of her account, either by paying any excess value to the trustee or by making a claim against the trustee as a general creditor for the deficiency.

Preferred Creditors

preferred creditors
unsecured creditors whose claims are given preference over those of other unsecured creditors

Out of the free assets remaining after payment or settlement of secured claims, the trustee must next pay the **preferred creditors**. Preferred creditors are listed in section 136 of the Act. The following is a summary of preferred claims, in the order of their priority:[21]

(1) When the bankrupt debtor is deceased, his reasonable funeral expenses and legal expenses related to his death.

(2) Expenses and fees of the licensed trustee in bankruptcy and her legal costs.

(3) A levy for the purpose of defraying the expense of the supervision of the Superintendent in Bankruptcy.

(4) Up to six months' arrears of wages of employees of the bankrupt debtor to the extent of $2000 for each employee. (The Act postpones all claims for wages by spouses, former spouses, parents, children, brothers, sisters, uncles, and aunts of the debtor until all other claims have been satisfied.)

(5) Municipal taxes levied within the two years preceding bankruptcy.

(6) Arrears of rent due to the landlord for a period of three months preceding bankruptcy.

(7) The costs of the first execution or attachment creditor. (A creditor obtains an execution order against tangibles, such as land or goods, and an attachment against choses in action, such as accounts receivable or bank deposits.)

(8) Indebtedness of the bankrupt under the Canada Pension Plan, the Employment Insurance Act, and the Income Tax Act for amounts required to be deducted from employees' salaries.

(9) Claims for certain injuries sustained by employees.

General Creditors

general creditors
creditors whose claims are not secured or preferred

After settling the secured and preferred claims, the trustee pays the **general creditors** rateably to the extent of the funds remaining.

Checklist: Priority of Payment of Claims

Claims against the property of a bankrupt debtor are paid in the following sequence:

1. secured creditors
2. preferred creditors
3. general creditors

Proving Debts

To rank as a claim against the bankrupt estate, all creditors must "prove" their debts. They do so by submitting declarations to the trustee outlining the details of their accounts and specifying

---

21. The 1997 amendments introduced a new category of preferred claims, claims for spousal or child support, ranking between (4) and (5); s. 136 (d.1).

the vouchers or other evidence by which they can substantiate these claims. The declaration states whether or not the claim is a secured or preferred claim.

Duties of the Bankrupt Debtor

Following a receiving order or authorized assignment, the debtor must submit himself for examination by the official receiver to explain his conduct, the causes of his bankruptcy, and the disposition of his property. He must submit a sworn statement of his affairs to the trustee, together with a list of the names and addresses of his creditors and the security held by them, attend the first meeting of creditors, and give the information they require. He must also deliver up possession of his property to the trustee, cooperate with the trustee, and "aid to the utmost of his power in the realization of his property and the distribution of the proceeds among his creditors" (section 158(k)).

Bankruptcy Offences

A bankrupt debtor and any other person who commits an offence listed in the Act, is liable to imprisonment or to a substantial fine. These offences include failing to perform any of the duties we have considered above, making a fraudulent disposition of his property before or after bankruptcy, giving untruthful answers to questions put to him at an examination, concealing, destroying, or falsifying books or documents, and obtaining any credit or property by false representations before or after bankruptcy (section 198).

Discharge of the Bankrupt Debtor

As we have noted, an important object of our bankruptcy legislation is to clear an honest but unfortunate debtor of outstanding debts and to leave him free to resume business life. The **discharge** of a bankrupt debtor usually cancels the unpaid portion of his debts remaining after they have been reduced by payment of liquidating dividends, and gives the debtor a clean slate with which to start business again.[22]

discharge
a court order whereby a person who has been declared bankrupt ceases to have the status of a bankrupt person

The discharge of a debtor is an official act of the court. In deciding whether to grant or refuse a debtor's application for discharge, the court consults the report of the trustee (sections 170–2). One of the more important reasons why a court may refuse or suspend the debtor's discharge is that his assets have proved to be insufficient to pay the unsecured creditors at least 50 cents on the dollar; he may still obtain a discharge, however, if he can show that he cannot justly be held responsible for this circumstance. Other reasons for refusing to give a discharge are that the bankrupt debtor neglected to keep proper books; that he continued to trade after he knew he was insolvent; that he failed to account satisfactorily for any loss or deficiency of assets; that he caused the bankruptcy by rash speculation or extravagant living; that within three months preceding bankruptcy he gave an undue preference to a creditor; that he was bankrupt or made a proposal to his creditors on a previous occasion; that he is guilty of any bankruptcy offence or has failed to perform his duties, as explained above. Other related reasons are set out in the Act (section 173).

Until obtaining his discharge, a bankrupt debtor is liable to fine or imprisonment if without disclosing his status he obtains credit of $500 or more for a purpose other than the supply of necessaries for himself and his family, or if he recommences business and fails to disclose to those with whom he deals that he is an undischarged bankrupt (section 199).

---

22. The Act specifies, in s. 178, those types of debt that are not released by an order of discharge—for example, fines and alimony. Certain student loans were added to this category by the 1997 amendments.

OTHER METHODS OF LIQUIDATION AND REORGANIZATION

Corporate Winding Up

We have seen that the Bankruptcy and Insolvency Act provides a means for liquidating insolvent corporations, partnerships, and sole proprietorships. There are, in addition, a variety of ways in which the affairs of a solvent corporation may be wound up, but it is shareholders rather than the corporation or creditors who initiate proceedings.

Each of the provinces has a separate statute or a part in its corporations act to provide a means of winding up solvent corporations with provincial charters.[23] The legislation may authorize the shareholders to appoint a liquidator, who may be a director, officer, or employee of the corporation, to wind up the affairs of the corporation without recourse to the court, or alternatively it may authorize them to apply to the court for a winding-up order and the appointment of a liquidator.

In addition, the federal Winding-Up Act[24] outlines a procedure by which the shareholders of a solvent, federally incorporated corporation may petition the court to issue a winding-up order. The court may issue a winding-up order if the capital of the corporation has been impaired to the extent of 25 percent, or if a substantial proportion of the shareholders petition for winding up because of a lack of integrity or responsibility on the part of the corporation's management.

A corporation may also surrender its charter, apart from proceedings under either the Bankruptcy Act or a Winding-Up Act. For example, the Canada Business Corporations Act permits dissolution, if a corporation has no property and no liabilities, by special resolution of the shareholders. "Articles of dissolution" are then sent to the director of the federal government office that regulates federally incorporated corporations and she issues a certificate of dissolution.[25] A corporation may wish to dissolve in this way when it has sold all its assets to another corporation and distributed the proceeds to its shareholders, and when the purchasing corporation has with the consent of creditors assumed all its liabilities.

The Companies' Creditors Arrangement Act

compromise and arrangement

an agreement made by a debtor corporation with its creditors whereby arrangements are made for repayment of debts without liquidating the corporation

As we have already noted, the Bankruptcy and Insolvency Act provides an alternative to the formal liquidation of a debtor's estate by means of a "proposal." For corporations, an alternative method of avoiding liquidation is by means of a **compromise and arrangement** with the creditors, approved by the court, under the Companies' Creditors Arrangement Act (CCAA).[26] That Act and the Bankruptcy and Insolvency Act are distinct statutes and provide alternative procedures, though many of their provisions are broadly similar.[27]

The CCAA allows a corporation in financial distress to seek court protection in order to reorganize its affairs and to avoid what might be an unnecessary and undesirable bankruptcy. If the going concern value of a corporation exceeds its break-up value, a reorganization of its debts is economically preferable to the corporation itself, its creditors, its employees, and soci-

---

23. See, for example: Company Act, R.S.B.C. 1996, c. 62, ss. 267–96; Corporations Act, R.S.M. 1987, c. C225, Part XVII; Business Corporations Act, R.S.O. 1990, c. B.16, Part XVI; Companies Winding-Up Act, R.S.N.S. 1989, c. 82.

24. R.S.C. 1985, c. W-10.

25. R.S.C. 1985, c. C-44, s. 210. Some provincial statutes also provide for dissolution of companies formed under their acts. See, for example: Corporations Act, R.S.M. 1987, c. C225, Part XVII; Business Corporations Act, R.S.O. 1990, c. B.16, s. 239.

26. R.S.C. 1985, c. C-36. Although a federal statute, this act applies to both federally and provincially incorporated corporations.

27. The 1997 Act (S.C. 1997, c. 12) made amendments to both the Bankruptcy and Insolvency Act and to the Companies' Creditors Arrangement Act, bringing the provisions of the two acts much closer to each other.

ety at large. The Act was used infrequently until the mid-1980s, when the benefits of reorganizations and workouts become more widely appreciated. The mechanism is somewhat similar to that found in Chapter 11 of the U.S. Bankruptcy Code.

The purpose of the CCAA is to permit a corporation to restructure its affairs so that it can eliminate some of its debt and resume business in a leaner, more efficient form that will have a greater chance of returning to profitability. During the reorganization, the corporation's creditors are restrained from taking action except through the reorganization process.

A relatively recent development has been the emergence of "**vulture funds**"—large investors that are prepared to purchase substantial portions of the debtor corporation's debts, or of its shares, at a heavily discounted price, hoping that the reorganization will be successful. This development seems in some ways to be contrary to the true intention of the Act, since these investors are clearly far more concerned with realizing a quick profit on their investment than in securing the rehabilitation of the debtor. However, one advantage is that the process provides a market in which smaller creditors may sell their claims without having to wait for the reorganization to be completed.

vulture funds
large investors that purchase the debt or shares of a corporation in the course of its reorganization

Since the 1997 amendments, the differences between the CCAA and the proposal procedures under the Bankruptcy and Insolvency Act have been substantially lessened, though some significant differences remain. In particular, the CCAA applies only if the total of creditor claims exceeds $5 million. When a court grants a stay of proceedings under the CCAA, it appoints a **monitor** to supervise the business and financial affairs of the debtor corporation. The position of the monitor is essentially similar to that of a trustee in bankruptcy. The final arrangement must be approved by the creditors; the majority required for approval was decreased from three-fourths (in value) of the creditors to two-thirds by the 1997 amendments to the Act.[28]

monitor
a person appointed to supervise the reorganization of a debtor corporation under the Companies' Creditors Arrangement Act

CONTEMPORARY ISSUE

Bankruptcy: Death or Life Support?

The following extracts from press reports of the Eaton's bankruptcy highlight the differences between the various procedures that exist for dealing with the affairs of insolvent corporations.

> Insolvent T. Eaton Co. is now operating under the protection of the Companies' Creditors Arrangement Act. An Ontario court approved the retailer's request yesterday to switch from the Bankruptcy and Insolvency Act. The move was a condition of Sears Canada Inc.'s offer to buy Eaton's shares and up to 13 of its stores. The CCAA protection also gives Eaton's more flexibility in arranging its affairs and putting together a plan to pay back creditors at least some of $330 million owed. In granting the transfer, the court also agreed to concessions to landlords as some were concerned they would have fared better under provisions of the bankruptcy act.

Source: "Court lets Eaton's switch," *Calgary Sun*, September 30, 1999, p. 64

> As bargain hunters descended on Eaton's for yet another day, angry creditors were in court to try to put an end to the fun. Mall owners want the sales moved out of the chain's stores and the landlords and rival retailers asked a packed Ontario Superior Court yesterday to prevent Eaton's from bringing in any new merchandise. As well, some suppliers are asking to get back recently shipped merchandise....Another key issue debated yesterday is the fate of the goods that suppliers had shipped 30 days before Eaton's sought court protection from creditors, on Aug 23.
>
> If Eaton's had declared bankruptcy instead of issuing a proposal under the bankruptcy act the suppliers would have the right to get that merchandise back. If they can't get the goods

continued

---

28. CCAA, s. 6, as amended by S.C. 1997, c. 12.

back, the suppliers told the court they want to get paid for them. Court documents show that Eaton's received $19 million worth of 30-day goods.

Source: Steven Theobald, "Landlords fight Eaton's sales," *Toronto Star*, August 28, 1999.

T. Eaton Co. has filed for protection from its creditors before—but not like this. When the 130-year-old retailer opted to file under the Bankruptcy and Insolvency Act (BIA) Friday, it was a sign the end is near, experts say. It was different two years ago, when Eaton's sought protection under the Companies' Creditors Arrangement Act, known as CCAA, which offers floundering firms a kind of stay of execution, says Laurence Booth, a finance professor at the University of Toronto. In that instance, the parties involved agreed that the company as a whole is worth more than just breaking it up and selling the parts. But by filing under the BIA, it's like 'they're admitting that there's no value to the Eaton's brand name, there's no point keeping these stores going,' Booth says.

....It's important to remember that technically, Eaton's is not bankrupt, it's in liquidation. There's a legal difference, explains labour lawyer Susan Rowland. "Bankruptcy means that legally the old company dies and the trustee in bankruptcy now owns everything that Eaton's did. If you're in a proposal, the company is still alive. It's sort of like it's on life support," Rowland says.

Source: Madhavi Acharya, "Grand Old Firm on Life Support," *Toronto Star*, August 22, 1999.

Questions to Consider

1. Whose interests are affected when a large corporation becomes insolvent?

2. When those interests come into conflict, what should be the primary objective of the law?

3. Should the law provide a variety of procedures, each of which produces a different result? Who is most likely to benefit from this?

MECHANICS' LIENS

Nature of Mechanics' Lien

We noted in Chapter 17 that a bailee who makes repairs or improvements on goods bailed with her obtains a possessory lien on the goods for the value of her services. She may keep them in her possession until the bailor or the owner pays the amount due her. In addition, in some provinces a bailee may sell the goods to satisfy her claim. By contrast, when a person extends credit by performing work or supplying materials in the construction of a building or other structure affixed to land, it is physically impossible for him to exercise a possessory lien. In any event, under the law of real property, when goods are affixed permanently to land they become fixtures: the supplier of the goods is not permitted to sever them from the property. In these circumstances, a creditor had no recourse at common law except to sue for the debt owing and obtain judgment and an order for execution against the land. However, a substantial degree of protection is provided by statute.

mechanics' lien

an interest that builders and others involved in construction work may have in a building as security for money owed to them for work done (also known as a **builders' lien** or **construction lien**)

Contractors and Subcontractors

In all provinces of Canada, persons who have extended credit in the form of goods and services to improve land now have a statutory remedy under **mechanics' lien** legislation. Although the title and wording of the acts vary from province to province,[29] each act provides substantially the same protection for creditors. Its basic purposes are to give creditors who have provided work and material for the improvement of land an interest in the land as security for payment and "to

---

29. In Alberta and British Columbia the statute is called the *Builders' Lien Act*, and in Ontario, since 1983, the *Construction Lien Act*.

prevent multiplicity of actions for small claims, in which the cost would be enormously out of proportion to and in excess of the sums claimed...."[30]

The provisions of mechanics' lien acts operate in two somewhat different ways which can best be understood by an example.

ILLUSTRATION 31.1

O Co owns a piece of land on which it plans to have an apartment building constructed. O Co hires C Co to erect the building for an agreed price. C Co in turn subcontracts to various firms the specialized tasks of sup-

plying and erecting the structural steel, installing the plumbing and heating systems and electrical wiring, and supplying and installing elevators, to various firms specializing in these trades.

In Illustration 31.1 we have two types of contracts, a master contract between O Co, the owner of the property, and the main contractor, C Co, and a series of subcontracts between the main contractor, C Co, and the various specialized firms. In respect to the master contract, O Co is liable for the whole amount of the contract price as a contractual debt; C Co has a mechanics' lien, that is, an interest in O Co's land and building as it is erected, for the total value of work and materials (to the maximum of the contract price) provided by C Co and its subcontractors. In turn, the subcontractors and suppliers have a right of action against C Co for the value of the work and materials supplied for the project under the terms of the subcontracts. There is, however, no privity of contract between the subcontractors and suppliers and O Co. Nevertheless, the Mechanics' Lien Act also gives liens against the land to the subcontractors and suppliers.

"Holdback"

The value of these liens is limited by the Act to a specified proportion of the price due from the owner, O Co, to the main contractor, C Co, under the master contract. This proportion, called a **holdback**, varies somewhat from province to province but is generally from 10 to 20 percent.[31] Where the value of the work and materials exceeds the holdback, the subcontractors and suppliers have no security in the land for the excess sum.

O Co fully protects itself against liens of the subcontractors and suppliers by retaining the holdback during construction and for a specified period afterwards. If C Co should become insolvent during this period, O Co would pay the holdback into court for the benefit of the lienholders. The court would then supervise the payment of this money among the lienholders, and neither O Co nor its land would be subject to their claims.

holdback
an amount that the owner who contracts for construction work may withhold from payments made to the principal contractor to protect against claims from subcontractors and suppliers

Who Is Protected?

A mechanics' lien is available only to creditors who participate directly as workers or supply material for use directly in the construction work. In *Brooks-Sanford Co. v. Theodore Tieler Construction Co.*, the court said:

> While the objects and policy [of the Mechanics' Lien Act]...is to prevent an owner from obtaining the benefits of the labour and capital of others without compensation, it is not the intention to compel him to pay his contractor's indebtedness for that which does not go into or benefit his property.[32]

---

30. McPherson v. Gedge (1883–4), 4 O.R. 246, per Wilson, C.J., at 257.
31. See, for example: Builders' Lien Act, S.B.C. 1997, c. 45, s. 4(1); Construction Lien Act, R.S.O. 1990, c. C.30, s. 1(1); Mechanics' Lien Act, R.S.N.S. 1989, c. 277, s. 13(2). (Subsequent references to these particular acts in footnotes will be simply to B.C., Ont., and N.S. followed by section number.)
32. (1910), 22 O.R. 176, per Moss, C.J.O., at 180.

The courts have held that an architect who prepares the plans for a building comes within this definition and is entitled to a lien. Some provincial statutes give a lien to a lessor who rents equipment for use on the contract site for the price of the rental of the equipment.[33] On the other hand, a party that sells tools or machinery to a contractor is not entitled to a lien against a building constructed with the use of the tools or machinery it has supplied; the tools and machinery remain the property of the contractor and can be used in other projects as well.[34] Nor can suppliers obtain a lien against property where the contractor has ordered materials for the building and has had them delivered to its own premises, unless the supplier can prove that the supplies were later used in the construction of the building. Where, however, a supplier delivers the goods directly to the building site, it obtains a lien immediately, whether the materials are eventually used in the structure or not.[35] The reason for this provision is that a supplier that delivers materials to the building site reasonably assumes that they will be used there and relies upon the property as security for its claim.

Suppliers of materials may, if they choose, waive their right of lien by contract. They may find an advantage in doing so when the effect is to persuade a mortgagee to lend additional funds for the completion of a project: the suppliers may then realize their claims out of the proceeds of a sale of the completed building.

Employees' Rights

Provincial legislatures have acknowledged that the bargaining power of wage earners (or at least of those who receive low rates of pay) may be unequal to that of builders and contractors who employ them, and that these wage earners may not fully understand the nature of their rights. As a result, the various provincial acts contain a provision that a term in a contract of employment waiving the employee's right of lien is void. However, in some provinces this provision does not apply to employees whose wages exceed a specified amount per day.

Provincial acts give wage earners a priority for approximately one month's arrears of wages over all other liens derived through the same contractor or subcontractor.[36] This priority recognizes the fact that wages often provide the sole means of subsistence of wage earners, while suppliers of materials and lessors of equipment probably carry on business with several construction projects at once, and usually have larger capital funds to depend on if a single contractor or owner defaults in payment.

Procedures Under a Mechanics' Lien Act

Registration

A mechanics' lien arises immediately upon work being done or materials being used in the improvement of property or (in some provinces) upon the supply of rented equipment for use on a contract site. To make a lien legally actionable, the lienholder must register it. It may be registered during the performance of the work or services or supply of material or within a specified period (usually 45 days) of time after completion or abandonment of performance. If a lien is not registered within the time specified it ceases to exist. Registration gives a lienholder a period within which it must commence a legal action—usually 90 days after the work has been completed or the materials have been placed or furnished, or after the expiry of the period of

---

33. This type of lien is available in Ontario, Alberta, Newfoundland, and Saskatchewan: see, for example, Ont., ss.1(1) and 14(1).

34. Crowell Bros. v. Maritime Minerals Ltd., [1940] 2 D.L.R. 472.

35. Ont., s. 15; N.S., s. 6(1).

36. B.C., s. 37; Ont., s. 81; N.S., s. 16.

credit.[37] For this purpose provinces have interpreted "completion of the contract" to mean "substantial performance of the contract."[38] Registration also gives a contractor or subcontractor a lien against the property itself.

In most of the provinces, an action brought by one lien claimant is deemed to be brought on behalf of all other lien claimants, and it is unnecessary even to name other lien claimants as participants since they must be served with notice of the trial.[39]

A lien may be registered against land in the same way and same place as are other interests in land. Registration provides public notice of a lienholder's claim and establishes the lienholder's priority over unsecured creditors of the owner of the property and over subsequent mortgagees and purchasers of an interest in the property. After registration, a lien expires unless the lienholder brings an action to enforce the claim within the prescribed time and registers a certificate stating that the action has been started, or unless another lienholder starts an action within this period.

Lienholders' Rights

A mechanics' lien does not give a lienholder the right personally to take possession of or to sell land and buildings to realize a claim. In fact, if the lienholder is a subcontractor and if the owner pays the statutory holdback into court, the lienholder's rights are limited to its share in this fund: it has no rights against the land and buildings of the owner. Even if an owner fails to pay the statutory holdback into court, the lienholder's claim against the land is limited to the amount the owner should have paid into court. To realize its claim against the land, a lienholder, whether a main contractor or a subcontractor, must first bring an action and obtain a court order appointing a trustee. The trustee then has the power to manage the property and to sell it for the benefit of the lienholder and other creditors.

If eventually the trustee does sell the property, she must pay the proceeds to satisfy first, the claims for municipal taxes; second, those of mortgagees who have prior registered mortgages; third, lienholders' claims for wages regardless of the order in which they filed their liens; fourth, all other lienholders' claims regardless of the order in which they filed their liens; fifth, subsequent mortgagees or other persons who have a secured interest in the land; and, finally, if there are any proceeds left, claims of the general creditors of the owner.[40] After all creditors are paid, any balance remaining belongs to the owner.

Progress Payments

During the construction of a building and for the specified statutory period afterwards, the owner may safely make progress payments to the contractor for all amounts except the statutory holdback.[41] However, if the owner receives notice from subcontractors or suppliers that liens are outstanding and unlikely to be paid by the contractor, she should cease payments to the contractor at once and ascertain the extent of the liens. If there is some doubt whether the holdback is sufficient to satisfy the claims for liens, she should seek legal advice immediately; as soon as she has knowledge of these claims, she loses the protection of the Mechanics' Lien Act to the extent that she continues to make payments to the contractor. On the other hand, she must not

---

37. B.C., s. 14 (one year); Ont., s. 36; N.S., s. 26(1).

38. B.C., s. 1; Ont., s. 2.

39. Ont., ss. 50(3) and 59; N.S., s. 34(4) and (5).

40. The problem of priorities, particularly those respecting lienholders as opposed to prior and subsequent mortgagees, is complex and technical. See Macklem and Bristow, *Construction and Mechanics' Liens in Canada* (6th ed.), Chapter 8. Toronto: Carswell, 1990.

41. B.C., s. 6(3); Ont., s. 22(1); N.S., s. 13(5).

make the error of wrongfully withholding payment due to a solvent contractor because of an unfounded claim for a lien.

In some jurisdictions, all money received by contractors and subcontractors on account of the contract price are deemed to be trust funds held for the benefit of those who have performed work or services or furnished materials. The contractor or subcontractor, accordingly, cannot divert those funds to its own use until all of the claims against it are satisfied.[42]

Once the statutory period has elapsed and no claims have been registered, the owner may pay the amount withheld to the contractor and so complete her obligations under the contract.

Practical Application of Mechanics' Liens

Mortgage Lenders

An owner of land usually finances a construction project by mortgaging the land to a mortgagee who advances the mortgage money as work progresses on the building. Some mechanics' lien laws require a mortgagee to withhold from the mortgage advances an amount equal to the sum that the owner should withhold from the contractor. Even if the Act does not have such requirements, it is sensible for a mortgagee to do so to protect the mortgagor (owner), who is liable to subcontractors and suppliers for the amount of the holdback if the contracting firm does not pay its accounts.

Tenants

When a tenant contracts to have a building erected on his landlord's property or, perhaps more commonly, to have improvements made to existing buildings, a mechanics' lien is not enforceable against the landlord's interest in the property unless the lienholder can establish that the work was undertaken either expressly or impliedly at the request of the landlord.

General Contractors

The party that takes the greatest risk in the construction industry is normally the general contractor. Most large contracts are awarded by tender to the lowest bidder with a sound reputation. In this highly competitive business, contractors often cut their margin both for errors and profit to a very small sum in order to win a contract. Bad luck in the form of unexpectedly difficult foundation work, bad weather delaying the project, a breakdown of essential equipment, an accident seriously injuring key personnel, or a labour dispute may leave a contractor in a deficit position. Mismanagement or inadvertence, such as making a mistake in calculating an important cost figure in the contract or underestimating the cost of subcontracts, may also bring failure to a contractor.

Subcontractors

Even when her contractor is in financial difficulty, an owner incurs no liability herself if she follows the procedures of the Mechanics' Lien Act. The subcontractors, on the other hand, take the risk that the holdback will not be sufficient to pay their claims. Where the subcontract is for a large sum of money, they generally protect themselves by receiving progress payments from the contractor: they do not let themselves get too far ahead in the work without being paid a proportion of the price.

---

42. Ont., s. 8(1). See Rudco Insulation Ltd. v. Toronto Sanitary Inc. (1998), 42 O.R. (3d) 292.

Contractors Who Own the Land

Contractors often undertake to construct buildings on land owned by themselves, especially residential buildings. Usually a builder erects such a building with a view to selling it soon after its completion. If bad luck or mismanagement should cause his insolvency, his "subcontracts" with specialized trades are really main contracts with himself as owner. Accordingly, the land is subject to liability for the total value of the liens, and the holdback provisions do not apply. Often a builder will have obtained mortgage money on the land; the mortgagee will have priority over the lienholders for the money already advanced to the builder before the liens arise. When a mortgagor becomes insolvent, his mortgagee usually stops making progress payments immediately. If the lienholders and mortgagee can come to an agreement, the mortgagee may advance the rest of the money to permit the completion of the building, thus making it easier to sell and realize sufficient funds to pay off the lienholders, and perhaps to obtain a sound buyer who will manage the property successfully and honour the mortgage commitments.

OTHER STATUTORY PROTECTION OF CREDITORS

Provisions protecting the rights of creditors, or of particular types of creditors, are found in many statutes, in most of which creditor protection is merely incidental to the main aim of the statute. In addition to the measures discussed above, two other statutes merit a brief mention.

Bulk Sales Acts

Until relatively recently, all of the common law provinces had a statute called the Bulk Sales Act, modelled on legislation commonly adopted in the United States. The purpose of the statute is, or was, to protect the creditors of a person making a "**bulk sale**"—that is, a sale of all, or substantially all, of the inventory of a business or of the fixtures and goods with which the business was carried on. In 1985, British Columbia abolished its Bulk Sales Act, and subsequently most of the other provinces have followed that lead, apparently taking the view that with the adoption of comprehensive Personal Property Security Acts, the Bulk Sales Act no longer served any useful purpose. In addition, the relation between the provincial Bulk Sales Act and the federal Bankruptcy and Insolvency Act was complicated and technical and resulted in uncertainty.

bulk sale
a sale of all or substantially all of the assets of a business

The main exception to this trend has been Ontario, which still retains its Bulk Sales Act,[43] though even there the Act is rarely used. Consequently, it will be described very briefly.

The underlying philosophy of the Act is that the sale of all, or a large portion, of the assets of a firm usually denotes the cessation of active business and may seriously impair the interests of the existing creditors of the firm. If a bulk sale merely caused a change in the composition of the business assets—inventory or equipment exchanged for cash—the creditors would have no cause for concern, since the business would be at least as capable of paying its debts as formerly. The danger for creditors is, however, that the proceeds of the sale may not be retained within the business. The solution provided by the Act is to place the onus on the buyer in a bulk sale to take certain steps to inform the seller's creditors of the proposed sale, to obtain their consent to the transaction without having their accounts paid, or, if they demand the payment of their accounts, to make sure to pay the necessary portion of the purchase money to the creditors before paying the balance to the seller. If the buyer does not meet the statutory requirements, the

---

43. R.S.O. 1990, c. B.14.

sale is voidable (within a specified period after the sale) and the buyer becomes liable to the seller's creditors for the value of the goods.

Business Corporations Acts

A comparative recent development has been the use by a corporation's creditors of the "oppression remedy," provided in the Canada Business Corporations Act (CBCA) and the various provincial Business Corporations Acts. The oppression remedy was discussed in Chapter 28, under the heading "The Protection of Minority Shareholders," and it is clear that the primary intention behind the remedy was to protect shareholder rights. However, the CBCA[44] includes, in the definition of a "complainant" who may seek a remedy for oppression, the holder of a "security" of the corporation (which includes a debt obligation) and "any other person who, in the discretion of the court, is a proper person to make an application" under that Part of the Act.

The remedy may be granted where the court is satisfied that the actions of a corporation have been oppressive or unfairly prejudicial to the interests of "any security holder, creditor, director or officer" of the corporation. The various provincial statutes contain essentially similar provisions.

In a number of cases, most notably in the Ontario courts, it has been held that creditors, both secured and unsecured, have standing to complain of oppression by the managers of their debtor corporation, and are entitled to seek any of the wide range of remedies that the court has discretion to order.[45]

CASE 31.4

SCI Systems had advanced money to GTL Co in return for a promissory note in the amount of $800 000. GTL defaulted when the note fell due and SCI obtained a default judgment against GTL. GTL still failed to pay, claiming that it was unable to do so. SCI discovered that, shortly before the note became due, GTL had paid dividends amounting to $850 000 to its three directors, who were also its sole shareholders, and had also transferred to them further assets worth $250 000.

In an action under section 248 of the (Ontario) Business Corporations Act, the court held that the conduct of the directors had resulted in protecting the company from its payment obligation to SCI Systems. The acts of GTL Co's directors were oppressive to SCI, and the directors were personally liable for the full amount of the judgment.[46]

Although the courts have occasionally warned that debt actions should not be routinely turned into oppression actions,[47] the practice of using the oppression remedy as a means of enforcing creditors' rights is growing rapidly. This trend is perhaps unfortunate, since it seems that the oppression remedy can be used to allow one creditor to gain an advantage over other creditors with competing claims, who are not parties to the action and whose interests are not

44. R.S.C. 1985, c. C-44, ss. 238 and 241.

45. See, for example, Sidaplex-Plastic Suppliers Inc. v. Elta Group Inc. (1995), 131 D.L.R. (4th) 399; Levy-Russell Ltd. v. Shieldings Inc., [1998] O.J. No. 3932. See also the learned judgment of Macdonald, J. in First Edmonton Place Ltd. v. 315888 Alberta Ltd., [1988] A.J. No. 511 (Alta. Q.B.).

46. SCI Systems, Inc. v. Gornitzki Thompson & Little Co. (1997), 147 D.L.R. (4th) 300. The applicant also relied on the provisions of the Fraudulent Conveyances Act, R.S.O. 1990, c. F.29, and the Assignments and Preferences Act, R.S.O. 1990, c. A.33, but having found oppression the court considered it unnecessary to deal with that issue.

47. See Royal Trust Corp. of Canada v. Hordo (1993), 10 B.L.R. (2d) 86.

required to be considered by the court. It also adds yet another form of action to the already bewildering confusion of potentially conflicting creditors' remedies.

LIMITATIONS ON CREDITORS' RIGHTS
The Effect of Limitations Statutes

We noted in Chapter 13 that when a promisee has a right of action against a promisor who defaults payment on a debt or who is in breach of contract, the promisee must begin an action within a prescribed period or lose the right to sue. In the common law provinces the remedy for breach of ordinary contracts is barred when six years have elapsed from the time the right of action arose.[48] A plaintiff must start court proceedings within the six-year period or lose the right to resort to the courts. Such limitations on actions are justified as being in the public interest: the opportunity for litigation should end after a certain defined period because first, a person who neglects to pursue a claim leaves the other party in a state of uncertainty that ought not to continue perpetually; and second, as the years pass it becomes more difficult to adduce the evidence concerning the facts of the case—memories may fade and witnesses die and important records may be lost.

It is important to ascertain when a right of action "arises" in order to calculate the limitation period. A right of action does not arise until there has been a breach or default. Thus, in a contract for the sale of goods on credit, the seller's right of action does not arise at the time of the making of the contract nor even at the time of the delivery of the goods, but only when the price falls due and the buyer fails to pay. A trade account receivable often comprises a number of charges for goods or services invoiced at different times in the past and since paid in part. A customer (debtor) is entitled to specify the particular purchases against which a payment on account is to be applied, but in the absence of such instructions the supplier (creditor) is entitled to treat each payment as discharging the oldest outstanding purchases and so to keep the debt current.

Ways in Which the Limitation Period is Extended

We noted in Chapter 23 in our discussion of adverse possession that if at any time after the statutory limitation period begins, a person in adverse possession acknowledges the owner's right by paying rent, he ceases to be an adverse possessor. The limitation period stops running; an entirely new limitation period begins to run if the tenant remains in possession after the period for which he has paid rent expires. In a similar manner, the limitation period for an action for breach of contract starts over again if the debtor makes a part payment or delivers a written promise to pay; the creditor has six years to bring its action from the time of the making of the part payment or delivery of the written promise.

An important difference exists, however, between limitation periods regarding possession of land and limitations of actions in contract. When a limitation period runs out against the owner of land, her title is extinguished—it is completely gone. When a limitation period against a contractual right of action expires, the debt is not extinguished—only the legal remedy is barred. The statute has provided the debtor with a shield, but he may, if he chooses, throw it aside. If the debtor makes a new promise to pay the debt, he is bound by his promise and may be sued upon it. In these circumstances the creditor sues not on the original claim but on the new promise to

---

48. See, for example: Limitation Act, R.S.B.C. 1996, c. 236, s. 3; Limitations Act, R.S.O. 1990, c. L.15, s. 45(1)(g); Limitation of Actions Act, R.S.N.S. 1989, c. 258, s. 2(1)(e).

pay. We see here a modification of the doctrine of consideration: the still-existing but statute-barred debt provides good consideration for the subsequent promise of the debtor. Since the creditor's right of action is derived from the new promise, the creditor has no greater rights than the new promise bestows. Thus, if the debtor promises to pay the debt out of the proceeds of a particular transaction if it should produce a profit, or if he promises to pay only half the sum in satisfaction of the whole debt, the creditor's rights are limited to suing on these terms.[49]

To be enforceable by a creditor, limitations statutes required a promise to pay a statute-barred debt to be in writing; the creditor could not sue on an oral promise alone. Although this requirement appeared in early limitation acts in England, courts of equity ignored it when the oral promise was accompanied by a part payment of the debt; they permitted the creditor to sue on the oral promise. This exception to the requirement of writing is now formally recognized in most of the limitations statutes.[50]

A debtor need not make an express promise to pay; his promise to pay may be implied from the circumstances of the part payment. Generally speaking, a presumption of a new promise to pay arises from the mere fact of making a part payment without other evidence to contradict the presumption. But if a debtor should say, "Take this—it is all you are going to get," then, of course, no such presumption arises, and the creditor has no right of action for the balance. The reasoning applies as well to a written acknowledgment of a debt. A written acknowledgment is not an express promise to pay, but usually such a promise is implied in the debtor's acknowledgment. The terms of the acknowledgment itself or the surrounding circumstances may, however, contradict such an implication—as when a debtor writes to a creditor, stating: "I know I owe you $1000, but the debt is barred by the Limitations Act. Since I believe you overcharged on the contract price anyway, I have no intention of paying this balance." Quite clearly, no implied promise to pay arises from such a statement.

Limitations in Other Types of Actions

The limitation period for actions on negotiable instruments is the same as for ordinary contracts, six years. When a cause of action arises from breach of a promise under seal, the limitation period is considerably longer, usually 20 years, but it may vary according to the subject-matter of the promise. For example, the personal covenant of a mortgagor in a mortgage of land is discharged after 10 years in some provinces.

Each province has a general limitations statute governing limitation periods for a number of different classes of actions. In addition, numerous other statutes, both federal and provincial, prescribe limitation periods for various rights of action under them. Some of these statutes extinguish the cause of action; others only bar recourse to the courts. The limitation periods vary from a few days to many years, according to the purposes that the statute serves. For this reason, when considering starting an action or defending one under the provisions of a statute, a lawyer first checks to see if a limitation period may affect the rights of the parties.

QUESTIONS FOR REVIEW

1. What objectives does the Bankruptcy and Insolvency Act seek to achieve?

2. What are the functions, respectively, of the Superintendent of Bankruptcy, the Official Receiver, and the Trustee in Bankruptcy?

---

49. See Phillips v. Phillips (1844), 67 E.R. 388, per Sir James Wigram, V.C., at 396.
50. See, for example: Limitation Act, R.S.B.C. 1996, c. 266, s. 5(2)(a)(ii); Limitations Act, R.S.O. 1990, c. L.15, s. 50.

3. Distinguish between a bankrupt and an insolvent person.

4. How is a "consumer debtor" defined?

5. What is the difference between an assignment and a receiving order?

6. What is the effect, in bankruptcy law, of a proposal?

7. Distinguish between an act of bankruptcy and a bankruptcy offence.

8. Distinguish between a fraudulent transfer and a fraudulent preference.

9. What is a "reviewable transaction"?

10. What special right does an unpaid seller of goods have when the buyer is bankrupt?

11. What is a "preferred creditor"? What are the principal categories of preferred claims?

12. How does a bankrupt become "discharged"?

13. What is the aim of the Companies' Creditors Arrangement Act?

14. What is the purpose of a "holdback" under mechanics' lien legislation?

15. Whose interests are protected by a mechanics' lien?

16. What is a "bulk sale"?

17. How do the Business Corporations Acts protect creditors of corporations?

18. In what ways may limitation periods be extended?

CASES AND PROBLEMS

1 Griffiths entered into a contract with Vic's Karsales Ltd. under which it was agreed that she would lease a new Moskvitch saloon car for a period of three years, at a monthly rent of $350. The contract contained an option for Griffiths to extend the term of the lease or to purchase the car at the end of the term for $5000. Both parties were under the impression that Griffiths intended to keep the car for no more than three years and to lease another new car at the end of the lease period.

One year later, Griffiths became bankrupt. By that time, she had missed three monthly payments on the lease. Vic's Karsales demanded the return of their car. The trustee in bankruptcy refused, on the ground that Vic's had not registered a security interest.

Who is entitled to the car?

2 Leung was in serious financial difficulties. She owed $150 000 to Desert Rose Inc., in respect of a business venture. She also owed $100 000 to Kwan. She entered into an agreement with Kwan whereby she sold her house to Kwan for $500 000, which was approximately its fair market value. The debt of $100 000 was set off against the purchase price, and it was further agreed that Kwan would lease the house back to Leung for a period of two years at a rent of $30 000 a year. That sum of $60 000, was also set against the purchase price. The balance of $340 000 was paid on completion of the transfer and was mostly used by Leung to pay off debts to her other creditors.

When Desert Rose sought to collect the debt owed to it, Leung was unable to pay. Does Desert Rose have grounds for impugning the transaction between Leung and Kwan?

3 On April 1, Greenfingers Garden Centre Ltd. was declared bankrupt as a result of a petition entered by the Agricultural Bank Ltd. The Bank was owed $250 000 by Greenfingers and had registered a security interest pursuant to a general security agreement that covered all of Greenfingers inventory and other business assets.

On the preceding March 1, Snow White Ornaments Inc. had supplied Greenfingers with 120 garden gnomes, to the value of $2500. On March 12, Bauer, a farmer, supplied a number of fruit trees to Greenfingers for $1000. And on March 15, Spreaders Inc. supplied Greenfingers with a quantity of bags of fertilizer for $800. None of them has been paid. Some of the trees and fertilizer, and almost all of the gnomes, remain unsold.

What claims do the respective creditors have?

4 Buckhouse Inc. is the owner of a large office building in the downtown area of a major Canadian city. It entered into a 10-year lease, at a monthly rental of $8000, with Justitia Ltd. As an inducement to enter into the lease, Buckhouse granted Justitia an 18-months rent-free period, a leasehold improvement allowance of $100 000, and a cash payment of $150 000.

Justitia Ltd. is a corporation formed by two lawyers, Straight and Narrow, as a management company for their law practice. Straight and Narrow are the sole shareholders and directors of Justitia.

The law practice occupied the premises for a period of 21 months, though Straight and Narrow never entered into a written lease with Justitia Ltd. At the end of that period, rent having been paid for only three months, they moved out of the building and found other premises.

Justitia has ceased to pay rent to Buckhouse and, apart from the lease, has no assets. The inducement payment of $150 000 was paid out as a dividend to Straight and Narrow.

Does Buckhouse have any claim against Straight and Narrow?

5 The N.S.F. Manufacturing Co. Ltd. was adjudged bankrupt on a petition of its creditors, and the trustee in bankruptcy realized the following amounts from the sale of its business assets:

Cash in bank	$ 1 000
Accounts receivable	12 000
Inventories	25 000
Land and buildings	74 000
	$112 000

The liabilities of the business were as follows at the time of the receiving order:

Bank loan secured under section 427 of the Bank Act	$ 40 000
Trade accounts payable	65 000
Municipal taxes payable	5 000
Wages payable (five months at $3 000 per month for one employee)	15 000
First mortgage on land and buildings	50 000
Second mortgage on land and buildings	25 000
	$200 000

The expenses of liquidation were $5000. The trustee's fee was $3000.

How many cents on the dollar should the general creditors receive? Show the order in which the trustee in bankruptcy made payments to the various types of creditors. Assume that all secured creditors had taken the necessary steps to protect their security.

6. Yorkville Construction Inc. was the main contractor on a large construction project on land owned by Mayfair Properties Ltd. Yorkville engaged Rodwell Ltd. to provide piping insulation services for the project. Yorkville received a series of payments from Mayfair under the contract, and used all of the monies to pay its general overhead expenses, including advertising and promotion expenses, bank charges, insurance, lease payments on its vehicles, office rent, and utilities. It did not pay Rodwell for its work.

Yorkville became insolvent.

Does Rodwell have any claim against (a) Mayfair, or (b) the directors of Yorkville?

PART

The preceding parts of this book have been concerned primarily with *private law*—in particular with the law of torts, of contracts, and of property, and with the forms of business organization. But business is increasingly becoming a matter of *public law* and of *international law*. In the following chapters we look at two of the most important influences on modern business activity: the ever-increasing scope of government regulation and the impact of globalization. We conclude our study with an examination of some legal aspects of electronic commerce.

One of the most onerous tasks for modern business managers is to keep up with the never-ending flow of new government regulations, and to ensure that the firm complies with those regulations. Despite the adoption, in the 1980s, of policies of "deregulation" in many countries, there was little if any reduction in the production of new legislation regulating business. Government may, to some extent, have removed itself from actually running business, but it certainly did not refrain from telling business what it might and might not do. Chapter 32 examines the process of regulation, and looks at some of the more important specific aspects of regulation—consumer protection, competition, and environmental law.

Chapter 33 is concerned with international business transactions. Such transactions are primarily contractual in nature, and we might have included them in Part Four, under the title "Special Types of Contract." However, as we shall see, when a business operates internationally it must be concerned with far more than just its contractual relationships with its customers and suppliers. International business is extensively regulated by governments, so that the legal relationship between an importer or exporter and the governments of the countries concerned in the transaction is often at least as important as is that between the private parties involved. International business consequently has both a private law and a public law dimension. But there is also a third dimension to consider—international law: the treaties and agreements made between governments are also an important factor in international business, as are the rules of such bodies as the World Trade Organization (WTO) and the North American Free Trade Association (NAFTA).

In Chapter 33 we deal both with foreign trade and with foreign investment, examining the private relationships between parties to contracts, the public relationships between those parties and the governments concerned, and the international relationships among governments. The final section is devoted to a topic of increasing concern to business everywhere—the resolution of international business disputes.

In our final chapter we take a look at the rapidly growing use of electronic commerce (e-commerce) and examine some of the legal implications of the Internet and of doing business in cyberspace. Electronic commerce is a very new development, and there is as yet very little clear indication as to how legal systems will adapt to the challenges that it poses. What is clear is that the business community, and the legal community, are only just beginning to appreciate the complexity of the subject.

The Modern Legal Environment for Business

PART 8

Weblinks

The full texts of many of the statutes referred to in this Part can be accessed on the Internet, as follows:

gov.ab.ca/qp
Alberta

qp.gov.bc.ca/bcstats/
British Columbia

gov.mb.ca/che/statpub/free/index.html
Manitoba

gov.nb.ca/acts/
New Brunswick

www.gov.ns.ca/legi/legc/index.htm
Nova Scotia

www. attorneygeneral.jus.gov.on.ca/legis.htm
Ontario

Federal statutes may be accessed at
canada.justice.gc.ca/STABLE/EN/Laws

For Chapter 32, the following statutes are especially important:
canada.justice.gc.ca/STABLE/EN/Laws/Chap/C/C-34.html
The Competition Act
canada.justice.gc.ca/STABLE/EN/Laws/Chap/C/C-15.3.html
The Canadian Environmental Protection Act

Other useful sites relating to government regulation of business are:
strategis.ic.gc.ca/engdoc/main.html
Industry Canada's main site
strategis.ic.gc.ca/sc_consu/engdoc/homepage.html
Industry Canada's consumer information
www.ccr.gov.on.ca
The Ontario Ministry of Consumer and Commercial Affairs
strategis.ic.gc.ca/SSG/ct01250e.html
The Competition Bureau
www.ec.gc.ca
Environment Canada

There are very many Web sites dealing with international business—the subject of Chapter 33:
investcan.gc.ca/index.htm

The main site of Investment Canada, which provides information about the Investment Canada Act at
investcan.gc.ca/en_doc_a.htm

The text of the Investment Canada Act can be found at
canada.justice.gc.ca/STABLE/EN/Laws/Chap/I/I-21.8.html

Other important sites are:
www.dfaif-maeci.gc.ca
The Department of Foreign Affairs and International Trade
www.ccib.org
The Canadian Chamber of Commerce

citt.gc.ca
The Canadian International Trade Tribunal

Important international organizations may be found at
www.wto.org
The World Trade Organization
www.nafta.net
NAFTA
www.dfaif-maeci.gc.ca/nafta_alena
The Canadian government's NAFTA online site
infoexport.gc/ca/ftaa/menu_e.asp
The Free Trade Area of the Americas
www.oecd.org
The Organisation for Economic Cooperation and Development (OECD)
www.iccwbo.org
The International Chamber of Commerce
www.doc.gov
The U.S. Department of Commerce

An excellent source of general international business links is the Michigan State University's International Business Resources on the World Wide Web at
ciber.bus.msu.edu/busres/inttrade.htm

Not surprisingly, there are very many Web sites relating to e-commerce, several of which are concerned with legal issues. Readers may find the following sites especially useful:
e-com.ic.gc.ca
This is a special section of the Industry Canada Web site, devoted to the activities of the Task Force on Electronic Commerce. It contains up-to-date information on e-commerce developments in Canada, and useful links to other Web sites in Canada and abroad.
www.law.ualberta.ca/alri/ulc/current/eee98il.htm
Provides access to the Uniform Law Conference of Canada's electronic commerce site
www.oecd.org/subject/e_commerce
A special section of the OECD Web site giving access to news on international developments and to articles on e-commerce. In September 1998 the OECD held a major conference on e-commerce in Ottawa: information about that conference and subsequent developments is available from a separate Web site, published at
www.ottawaoecdconference.org
by the Canadian government
www.doc.gov/ecommerce/governme.htm and
www.doc.gov/ecommerce/internat.htm
Published by the United States government and provides information about, respectively, U.S. and international developments in e-commerce
gse.ucla.edu/iclp/hp.html
The Web site of the Institute for Cyberspace Law and Policy, at the University of California, Los Angeles, provides a wealth of U.S. and international material on legal issues relating to e-commerce

32 GOVERNMENT REGULATION OF BUSINESS

The Legal Framework for Doing Business in Canada

The Power to Regulate Business

Regulation of Various Business Sectors

Judicial Review of Government Regulation

Consumer Protection

Competition

Environmental Protection

G overnment regulation affects many aspects of business activity. In this chapter we examine the regulatory framework within which Canadian business must operate, concentrating on three of the most important areas of regulation from the point of view of business. We examine such questions as:

- who has the power to regulate?

- how are specific business sectors regulated?

- what control do the courts exercise over the regulators?

- what are the consequences of consumer protection law for the consumer and for business?

- how does competition law affect business arrangements?

- what are the main consequences of environmental protection law?

THE LEGAL FRAMEWORK FOR DOING BUSINESS IN CANADA

As we noted in Chapter 1, for business to operate effectively it is necessary to have an adequate legal and regulatory framework in place. Clearly then, all regulation is not bad; but excessive regulation can impose heavy and unnecessary costs and inhibit business activity. The need, as always, is to strike an appropriate balance.

During the 1980s and early 1990s, "deregulation" was a popular notion; business should be freed from excessive government control. The movement towards privatization of industry and commerce and the disengagement of government from the actual running of business were primary examples. But in many instances direct government interference was replaced by a different sort of regulation: while governments stopped controlling businesses themselves, increasingly they prescribed what businesses are permitted, or not permitted, to do.

A distinction is sometimes made between *direct* regulation and *social* regulation. Direct regulation occurs when the government controls such matters as prices, rates of return, and production levels. Social regulation, on the other hand, lays down standards that business must observe, in such areas as health, safety, and the environment. In this chapter we examine some of the more important aspects of both types of regulation.

THE POWER TO REGULATE BUSINESS
Division of Powers Under the Constitution

In Canada—as in other federations such as the United States and Australia—all three levels of government—federal, provincial, and municipal—regulate business activities according to the powers allocated to them by the Constitution. Most of these powers are allocated by sections 91 and 92 of the Constitution Act, 1867, although some are found in other sections.[1] Section 91 sets out the areas assigned to the federal Parliament, and section 92 assigns jurisdiction to the provinces. Since municipalities are created by the provinces, they may receive only such powers as the provinces themselves have been granted. Inevitably there is overlap and sometimes even conflicting rules, making it difficult for businesses and their lawyers to determine which regulations apply in a particular situation, especially when business is carried on in more than one province.

When a party wishes to challenge the validity of a particular law, it begins by asking whether the legislature that passed the law had jurisdiction. It is not always an easy question to answer, since some of the powers in section 91 overlap those listed in section 92. For example, Parliament has jurisdiction over "the regulation of trade and commerce," and provinces have jurisdiction over "property and civil rights in the Province." The courts have interpreted the latter phrase to mean virtually the whole body of private law, including contracts and most business transactions—matters that we might well think are included in federal jurisdiction over "trade and commerce." Accordingly, a law may fall within both a federal and a provincial area of jurisdiction.

As we saw in Chapter 1, the courts are the arbiters of the Constitution. They have adopted a two-stage approach to this question. First, they identify the true subject-matter—the "pith and substance"—of the law in question, and second, they assign it to the appropriate area or "head" of legislative power. If a court decides that the subject-matter of a provincial law more properly belongs under a federal head of jurisdiction, then it will declare the law invalid. The converse may happen to a law passed by the federal Parliament.

The question is not always easily resolved: over a century ago, the Judicial Committee of the Privy Council restricted the meaning of "trade and commerce" to matters of international and interprovincial trade, even though the Constitution does not so limit the phrase.[2] As a result, the Privy Council ruled that a provincial statute regulating fire insurance was within the provincial power; it did not affect the federal trade and commerce power because the federal power did not extend to matters wholly within the boundaries of a single province.[3] It is interesting to note that

---

1. For example, s. 95 provides that both the federal and provincial governments have concurrent jurisdiction over agriculture and immigration, and s. 92A (added in 1982) gives the provinces concurrent powers to make laws regulating the export of natural resources.

2. Citizen's Insurance Co. v. Parsons (1881), 7 App. Cas. 96.

3. The Supreme Court of Canada has continued to question the federal power to legislate in general commercial matters where the application of a law falls within the boundaries of a province. See, for example, MacDonald v. Vapour Canada, [1977] 2 S.C.R. 134, and Labatt Breweries v. Attorney-General of Canada, [1980] 1 S.C.R. 914.

in the U.S. Constitution, its equivalent to our trade and commerce provision is "commerce among the several states"; the U.S. Supreme Court has given these words a much wider interpretation and has expanded the powers of Congress, despite the interstate requirement of the words themselves.

concurrent powers

matters in which both the federal and provincial governments have power to legislate

In some instances, the Constitution expressly confers **concurrent powers** on both levels of government, as in section 95, which grants shared jurisdiction over agriculture and immigration. More often, both levels of government will have passed laws in the same area, relying on their respective powers in section 91 and section 92. The court may find that the subject-matter has a "double aspect," that is, it clearly falls within both a federal and a provincial head of power. If there is no conflict between the federal and provincial laws, then both are valid.[4]

federal paramountcy

a federal law prevails over a conflicting provincial law

But what if there is a conflict? In that event, the principle of **federal paramountcy** applies: in order to preserve the same law across the country in an area of federal jurisdiction, the federal law prevails over a contrary provincial law.[5]

Restrictions on Government Powers: The Charter

As we noted in Chapter 1, the rights entrenched in the Canadian Charter of Rights and Freedoms cannot be infringed by legislation, federal or provincial; to the extent a law offends a right in the Charter, it will be declared invalid.

CASE 32.1

A firm was prosecuted for opening its store on a Sunday, contrary to the federal Lord's Day Act. In its defence it claimed that the law was unconstitutional. The Supreme Court of Canada first considered whether the law should be characterized as criminal law (and therefore within federal powers), enacted for a religious purpose (preserving "the sanctity of the Christian Sabbath"), or as a law regulating business (and accordingly within provincial powers

over property and civil rights in the province) to ensure that workers enjoyed "a uniform day of rest."

The Court concluded that the purpose was religious, and the law was properly within federal power to enact criminal law. However, it struck the law down as being contrary to the Charter, which prohibits discrimination on the basis of religion.[6]

As a general rule, the Charter is intended to protect the rights and freedoms of individuals. However, as Case 32.1 illustrates, there are occasions when corporations may invoke its protection. In particular, a corporation should be allowed to rely on the Charter where it is charged with an offence, or is the defendant in civil proceedings instigated by the state or a state organ, under legislation that it alleges to be unconstitutional. Just as no one should be convicted of an offence under an unconstitutional law, no one should be subject to any proceedings or sanction authorized by an unconstitutional law.[7]

---

4. See, for example, Multiple Access v. McCutcheon, [1982] 2 S.C.R. 161. The court found no conflict between federal and provincial laws dealing with insider dealing in corporate securities.

5. See, for example Bank of Montreal v. Hall, [1990] 1 S.C.R. 121, which was considered in Chapter 30.

6. R. v. Big M Drug Mart, [1985] 1 S.C.R. 295. Subsequently, in R. v. Edwards Books and Art, [1986] 2 S.C.R. 713, the court held that an Ontario law prohibiting stores from opening on Sundays was a valid exercise of the province's power over property and civil rights, since the purpose of the law was to ensure that workers had a uniform day off each week. Sunday opening has since been legalized in Ontario.

7. Canadian Egg Marketing Agency v. Richardson, [1998] 3 S.C.R. 157. In that case, a national egg marketing scheme was held (by the Supreme Court of Canada) not to be contrary to the Charter.

Although Charter rights are essentially personal in nature, they nevertheless do have an important application to some business situations. In particular, the fundamental freedoms of expression and of association may be invoked to protect business activities.[8] Thus the Supreme Court of Canada has ruled, on a number of occasions, that "commercial speech" is protected under section 2(b).[9]

Restrictions on advertising, of products or of professional services, are *prima facie* contrary to the Charter, though such restrictions may be justified under section 1 provided they are reasonable and do not go beyond what is necessary to promote a legitimate objective.[10]

CASE 32.2

In 1988, the federal government introduced legislation prohibiting all advertising and promotion of tobacco products. The prohibition was challenged by one of the leading cigarette manufacturers.

The Supreme Court of Canada held that the legislation violated section 2(b) of the Charter and was not justifiable under section 1. The objective of the legislation—to discourage the use of tobacco—was legitimate, but there was no direct scientific evidence showing a causal link between advertising bans and decreased tobacco consumption. The government had failed to show that a partial advertising ban would be less effective than a total ban. The impairment of the complainant's rights was more than minimal and the offending provisions of the legislation were declared to be of no force and effect.[11]

The freedom of association, protected by section 2(d) of the Charter, may also have some applications to business situations.

CASE 32.3

Pursuant to the Optometrists Act, R.S.B.C. 1996, c. 342, the Board of Examiners in Optometry promulgated rules prohibiting business associations between optometrists and non-optometrists. Two optometrists, who had been cited by the board for violating the prohibition, petitioned for judicial review of the validity of the board's rules. They argued that the rules violated their freedom of association guaranteed by section 2(d) of the Charter.

The court held that the rules were of a public nature. Section 2(d) applies to a wide range of associations, including those of an economic nature, and a business relationship is an association protected under the section. The prohibition could not be justified under section 1 of the Charter. The board had failed to establish that the rules were proportional to the objective of maintaining high standards of professional conduct and independence free of any real or apparent conflicts of interest that would undermine the public's confidence in the profession. The absolute prohibition against any business relationship between optometrists and non-optometrists was overly broad.[12]

---

8. Charter of Rights and Freedoms, s. 2(b) and (d). By contrast, in Canadian Egg Marketing Agency v. Richardson, *supra*, n. 7, the mobility rights (under s. 6) were held to be essentially private in nature; they do not extend to the right to conduct one's business anywhere in Canada without restriction.

9. Irwin Toy Ltd. v. Quebec (1989), 58 D.L.R. (4th) 577; Rocket v. Royal College of Dental Surgeons of Ontario (1990), 71 D.L.R. (4th) 68.

10. See Griffin v. College of Dental Surgeons of British Columbia (1989), 64 D.L.R. (4th) 652; contrast Carmichael v. Provincial Dental Board of Nova Scotia (1998), 169 N.S.R. (2d) 294.

11. RJR-MacDonald Inc. v. Canada, [1995] 4 F.C. 3.

12. Costco Wholesale Canada Ltd. v. British Columbia (1998), 157 D.L.R. (4th) 725.

REGULATION OF VARIOUS BUSINESS SECTORS

The allocation of powers in the Constitution was decided in the 1860s, when Canada was mainly an agrarian society. Their subsequent interpretation by the courts has often left both levels of government dissatisfied. However, agreeing on constitutional changes satisfactory to both sides has proven elusive and perhaps impossible. In any event, the complexity and rapid change in the business environment make it unrealistic to expect that a magic formula to allocate powers between the two levels can be found.

Both the federal and provincial legislatures have created regulatory schemes in many areas. Provinces normally have the power to regulate those business activities that take place within their own boundaries, while federal jurisdiction applies to the same types of activities when they regularly cross provincial boundaries. In other words, provinces regulate *intra*provincial business and the federal government regulates *inter*provincial and international trade. Despite this conceptual divide, business activities in many sectors fall within both federal and provincial jurisdiction. There are some important exceptions: section 91 has been interpreted to give the federal government exclusive jurisdiction over banks and banking, deep sea, coastal, and Great Lakes shipping and navigation, air transportation, radio and television broadcasting, and atomic energy. The production, storage, sale, and delivery of oats, barley, and wheat is in federal hands through the monopoly given to the Canadian Wheat Board by Parliament on the basis that its major activity is international. Energy resources generally, because so large a proportion of the product is exported from the extracting province, are under the supervision of the federal National Energy Board.

We can see that the type of business activity usually determines which level of government dominates; those that by their very nature regularly cross provincial boundaries fall primarily under federal jurisdiction. Examples are: virtually all telephone systems, since even small telephone companies interconnect with larger interprovincial systems; and railway lines. On the other hand, two sectors with a large interprovincial element remain almost exclusively within regulatory schemes of the provinces: road transportation including trucking, and stock exchanges and securities transactions in general. The federal government has stayed out of these areas and left them to the provinces.

JUDICIAL REVIEW OF GOVERNMENT REGULATION

Legislation that confers regulatory powers on government ministers or agencies frequently also expressly provides for review of, and appeals against, executive decisions and actions; in many cases, the legislation establishes special boards or tribunals for that purpose, and may also make provision for appeals to the courts from decisions of the board or tribunal. As well, federal and provincial legislation commonly give the courts a power of review. Thus the Federal Court has a general jurisdiction to review the exercise of powers by federal boards and commissions,[13] and several of the provinces have enacted similar provisions with respect to provincial boards.[14] Even without such legislation, the courts have traditionally asserted a general right to review the legality of administrative acts and decisions.

An administrative act or decision may be challenged on a number of grounds:

- *Constitutionality*—As noted above, the legislation on which the act or decision is based may lie outside the jurisdiction of the federal or provincial legislature that enacted it or may be contrary to the Charter.

---

13. Federal Court Act, R.S.C. 1985, c. F-7, s. 18.

14. For example, Judicial Review Procedure Act, R.S.B.C. 1996, c. 241; R.S.O. 1990, c. J.1.

- *Lack of authority*—Although the relevant legislation itself is valid, the official or agency acted outside the scope of the authority conferred by the statute.
- *Procedural irregularity*—The official or agency proceeded in a manner inconsistent with the requirements of the statute; for example, public meetings required by the legislation were not held, or the prescribed notice was not given.
- *Procedural unfairness*—Even when the legislation does not prescribe appropriate procedures an official or agency is not entitled to act in a purely arbitrary manner. As Professor Mullan states:

> In general, whenever a person's 'rights, privileges or interests' are at stake, there is a duty to act in a procedurally fair manner.[15]

This means that persons likely to be affected have a right to be heard and to have access to relevant documents, that adequate notice must be given of any public hearings, and that the decision-maker must act impartially and not have a personal interest in the subject-matter.

CONSUMER PROTECTION

Background

The concept of consumers as a class of people to be protected by the courts and legislatures is a relatively recent one. Specific laws to remedy abuses by merchants and moneylenders may be found in ancient codes, and from time to time since the Middle Ages governments have acted to give relief from harsh treatment by creditors. Until the late 19th century, specific measures probably sufficed. Retail trade was carried on by relatively small local merchants who dealt directly with customers in an ongoing relationship: if sellers did not treat their customers fairly, customers would go elsewhere. Goods were simpler and most buyers could check the quality of what they bought. Even in this simpler trading environment, there was opportunity for misleading conduct and sharp practice, but the available remedies were more or less adequate: actions for the tort of deceit in cases of fraud, and remedies for failure to supply goods of merchantable quality and reasonably fit for the purpose for which they were bought. We have considered these remedies in Chapters 3 and 16.

Modern Developments

Several modern developments made these simpler remedies inadequate. First, the concentration of manufacturing and distribution in the hands of large enterprises has virtually ended any equality of bargaining power between individual buyers and sellers. In the words of Lord Denning:

> …the freedom was all on the side of the big concern.…The big concern said 'Take it or leave it.' The little man had no option but to take it.[16]

Second, many manufactured goods have become so complex that even a competent retailer cannot detect defects or, if they are discovered, remedy them—the goods can only be returned to the manufacturer when a customer complains.

Third, economies of distribution dictate that many goods formerly shipped in bulk and divided by quantity at the retail level are now shipped in sealed packages that cannot be examined either by the retailer or the shopper until taken home and opened for use. This marketing system applies to everything from a package of wood screws to many items of fresh and frozen food. The

---

15. D.J. Mullan, *Administrative Law* (3rd ed.), p. 200. (Toronto: Carswell, 1996).
16. George Mitchell (Chesterhall) Ltd. v. Finney Lock Seeds Ltd., [1983] 1 All E.R. 108 at 113.

result may be that the goods (sometimes) reach the consumer at lower prices, but there is no opportunity for assessing the quality of a product or its suitability for the consumer's intended use.

Fourth, a highly developed system of advertising through the mass media creates expectations of product performance that play an important part in inducing consumer purchases and is often more influential than the retailer with whom the consumer deals.

Fifth, in the purchase of expensive goods such as cars, large appliances, and furniture, the use of credit has become the norm. Sophisticated and complex schemes for determining the cost of borrowing make it difficult for the ordinary buyer to understand the effective rate of interest being charged.

Our legislatures have not developed a systematic theory or policy about consumer protection and legislation has grown in response to specific, perceived problems, generally without much thought to the broader consequences of regulation. The current movement towards consumer protection really began in the 1960s.[17] Since then each Canadian province, as well as the federal government, has pursued legislative reform with little if any consultation, although with some copying of the legislative efforts of the pioneers in each field.

During the 1980s and the first half of the 1990s, it seemed that governments were taking a relatively passive attitude to consumer protection, causing one leading commentator to observe that there had been a dramatic reversal in the influence of the consumer voice in the councils of government.[18] More recently, however, the federal government has introduced strict new legislation, especially with respect to "telemarketing" (discussed later in this part), and has begun to enforce existing laws more aggressively. In May 1999, a Quebec court imposed a record $1 million fine against a telemarketer convicted of misleading advertising offences, fined the firm's president $100 000, and sentenced him and several of the firm's sales agents to prison terms of up to six months.

The wisdom of legislative attempts to protect consumers against exploitative contractual arrangements has proved to be a controversial topic. Legislative intervention on the side of consumers may be justified by demands for a more equitable economic system: consumers are perceived as typically having less bargaining power than businesses with which they deal. But consumer protection regulation is criticized as ineffective—consumers are rarely aware of their rights, and government agencies make little effort to enforce the law. Moreover, consumer protection is seen by some as paternalistic—overruling consumer preferences, substituting the government's view of what is in the consumer's best interest, and adding to the cost of doing business. This cost may be absorbed by sellers and creditors, in reduced profits, or is more likely passed on to consumers in the form of higher prices.

Principal Types of Consumer Legislation

Some of the provisions of consumer protection legislation can best be understood in the context of discussions of other topics. Thus we have dealt in Chapter 9 with the prohibition on charging excessive rates of interest; with the requirement of written evidence of the terms of consumer sales contracts in Chapter 10; and with the prohibition of exempting clauses in consumer sales contracts in Chapter 15. We have dealt with changes in the law affecting residential tenancies in Chapter 24 and with restrictions on the repossession of goods purchased under instalment contracts in Chapter 30. The purpose of the present section is to provide an overview of the main categories of consumer protection. We have identified the following five classes of consumer protection legislation, and we shall examine them in turn:

---

17. There are isolated earlier examples of consumer protection legislation; for example, provisions against false and misleading advertising were introduced in the Criminal Code as early as 1914.

18. See Ziegel, "Is Canadian Consumer Law Dead?" (1994–5), 24 *C.B.L.J.* 417.

- regulation of misleading advertising
- regulation of quality standards affecting labelling, safety, performance, and availability of servicing and repairs
- regulation of business conduct towards consumers
- disclosure of the effective cost of credit
- supervision of businesses that deal with the public through licensing, bonding, and inspection

We should note that virtually all consumer protection statutes apply both to the sale of goods to consumers and to the sale of services such as home repairs, carpet cleaning, and the preparation of income tax returns.

Misleading Advertising and Other Representations of Sellers

The law affecting misleading representations by sellers of goods and services is steadily becoming more codified—a trend that probably reflects reservations about the ability of the courts to adapt and apply the common law to new and ingenious selling practices. Statutes not only govern the representations that can be made about particular products, but also provide for inspection of the industry and regulation of the quality of goods sold. The best known of these statutes is the Food and Drugs Act, which prescribes penalties for the sale of any article of food or any drug that is adulterated or that is manufactured, packaged, or stored under unsanitary conditions. The Act also provides in part:

> No person shall label, package, treat, process, sell or advertise any food in a manner that is false, misleading or deceptive or is likely to create an erroneous impression regarding its character, value, quantity, composition, merit or safety.[19]

Sellers must also take into account the growing body of legislation regulating advertising. The federal Competition Act contains a section[20] that begins with a general prohibition of misleading representations made for the purpose of promoting the supply or use of a product or of any business interest. More specifically, the section makes it an offence to make false or misleading representations about the qualities of a product, or the "regular" price at which it is sold. When reading the section we should also bear in mind that the Act defines the word "product" as referring equally to goods and services. The section, as amended in 1999, reads as follows:

52. (1) No person shall, for the purpose of promoting, directly or indirectly, the supply or use of a product or for the purpose of promoting, directly or indirectly, any business interest, by any means whatever, knowingly or recklessly make a representation to the public that is false or misleading in a material respect....

    (2) For the purposes of this section, a representation that is

        (a) expressed on an article offered or displayed for sale or its wrapper or container,

        (b) expressed on anything attached to, inserted in or accompanying an article offered or displayed for sale, its wrapper or container, or anything on which the article is mounted for display or sale,

        (c) expressed on an in-store or other point-of-purchase display,

---

19. R.S.C. 1985, c. F-27, s. 5(1). Other provisions regulating labels and advertising are found in the Weights and Measures Act, R.S.C. 1985, c. W-6. An identical provision applies to deception in the sale of drugs. There are separate federal statutes regulating the sale of meat, livestock, fruit, vegetables, and honey.

20. Competition Act, R.S.C. 1985, c. C-34, s. 52, as amended by S.C. 1999, c. 2.

(d) made in the course of in-store, door-to-door or telephone selling to a person as ultimate user, or

(e) contained in or on anything that is sold, sent, delivered, transmitted or made available in any other manner to a member of the public,

is deemed to be made to the public by and only by the person who causes the representation to be so expressed, made or contained....

A new subsection (2.1) extends the prohibition to persons outside Canada who market their products in Canada and is clearly aimed at American telemarketers who target Canadian consumers.

An offence against this section carries a possible maximum penalty of five years imprisonment or a very substantial fine or both. However, criminal prosecution is likely to be reserved for egregious misconduct or for repeat offenders. By contrast, several of the advertising-related offences under the Act have been decriminalized by the 1999 amendments and have been included in a category of reviewable "deceptive market practices."[21] These include misleading advertising, **bait and switch advertising**, making performance claims that lack proper substantiation, and making misleading savings claims. Such practices are subject to review by the Competition Tribunal, which may order the offender to refrain from such conduct for up to 10 years and may impose fines of up to $100 000.

The provinces have also passed various forms of protection legislation dealing with misleading advertising. The earliest versions gave government agencies the power to prohibit such advertising and imposed fines against sellers who continued to mislead. Later, new remedies were given directly to consumers who were affected by the misleading statements. For instance, Ontario's Business Practices Act declares it to be an "unfair practice" to make "a false, misleading or deceptive consumer representation" which may include a wide variety of representations about the "sponsorship, approval, performance characteristics, accessories, uses, ingredients, benefits or quantities" that the goods or services do not have.[22] There follows a long list of examples of deceptive representations. The Act also creates "an unconscionable consumer representation" as a type of unfair practice that includes such conduct as simply asking a price that "grossly exceeds the price at which similar goods or services are readily available to like consumers."[23] A consumer subjected to an unfair practice may terminate the contract and "where rescission is not possible…the consumer is entitled to recover the amount by which the amount paid under the agreement exceeds the fair value of the goods or services received under the agreement or damages, or both" (section 4(1)(b)). In addition, the court is expressly authorized to award exemplary or punitive damages against the wrongdoer. Similar statutes have been passed in other provinces.[24]

The above provisions illustrate the overlap of federal and provincial jurisdictions in the Constitution; both levels of government seem to have concurrent powers to regulate these types of selling practices, and this has resulted in a considerable degree of constitutional uncertainty.[25]

bait and switch advertising

advertising a product at a bargain price but not supplying it in reasonable quantities

Regulation of Labelling, Product Safety, and Performance Standards

The federal Parliament has legislated extensively in prescribing public health and safety standards that the sellers of consumer products must meet. We shall review briefly the requirements of the most important of these statutes.

---

21. S. 74 of the Act, as amended.

22. Business Practices Act, R.S.O. 1990, c. B.18, s. 2(1)(i).

23. *Ibid.*, s. 2(1)(ii).

24. For example: Trade Practice Act, R.S.B.C. 1996, c. 457; Unfair Trade Practices Act, R.S.A. 1980, c. U-3.

25. For further consideration of the overlap between federal and provincial consumer legislation see Nielson, (1992) 21 *C.B.L.J.* 70.

The Consumer Packaging and Labelling Act[26] sets out comprehensive rules for packaging and labelling consumer products, including requirements for identifying products by their generic names and stating the quantity of the contents. The Act also provides for standardized package sizes to avoid confusion. The list of products sold in standardized packages is added to from time to time by federal regulation after consultation with affected industries.

The Textile Labelling Act[27] requires labels bearing the generic name of the fabric to be attached to all items of clothing. The federal care-labelling program encourages manufacturers to include recommended procedures for cleaning and preserving the fabric. In view of the pervasive use of synthetic fibres, these labels give us important information.

The Hazardous Products Act[28] divides products into two classes. Part I lists products considered so dangerous that their manufacture is prohibited in Canada. The list includes such items as children's articles painted with liquid containing lead. Part II lists products that must be manufactured and handled in conformity with regulations under the Act and includes such items as bleaches, hydrochloric acid, and various glues containing potent solvents. The Minister of Industry[29] has broad discretion in banning products deemed to be a threat to public health or safety.

The Food and Drugs Act[30] is a compendious statute regulating many aspects of foods and medical and cosmetic products, since virtually all of them, if improperly processed, manufactured, stored, or labelled, may adversely affect consumers' health or safety. Provisions deal with such matters as conditions of sanitation in production, measures to prevent adulteration of food and medicines, the listing of ingredients contained in products, and the dating of products having a shelf life of less than 90 days.

The Motor Vehicle Safety Act[31] provides for the adoption of regulations setting national safety standards for motor vehicles whether manufactured in Canada or imported. It also requires manufacturers to give notice of defects in vehicles to the Department of Transport and to all purchasers of the defective vehicles.

Provincial statutes provide further protection for consumers. As we have noted in Chapter 16, implied terms under the Sale of Goods Act with respect to merchantability and fitness are made binding on sellers in contracts with consumers; sellers cannot escape liability by requiring buyers to sign exemption clauses.[32]

This approach, of imposing liability on sellers by inserting compulsory terms in consumer contracts, has been taken further in the Saskatchewan and New Brunswick statutes, which imply additional warranties and extend protection to third persons who were not parties to the contract, such as members of the buyer's family.[33]

Regulation of Business Conduct Towards Consumers

Pressure Selling

As a response to the excesses of high-pressure door-to-door selling methods, most provinces have enacted legislation giving a buyer the right to rescind certain types of contract of sale.[34]

---

26. R.S.C. 1985, c. C-38.

27. R.S.C. 1985, c. T-10.

28. R.S.C. 1985, c. H-3.

29. The former Department of Consumer and Corporate Affairs was merged with the Department of Trade, Industry and Technology in 1993.

30. R.S.C. 1985, c. F-27.

31. S.C. 1993, c. 16.

32. For example: Consumer Protection Act, R.S.N.S. 1989, c. 92, s. 26(3); R.S.O. 1990, c. C.31, s. 34(2).

33. Consumer Protection Act, S.S. 1996, c. C-30.1; Consumer Product Warranty and Liability Act, S.N.B. 1978, c. C-18.1.

34. For example: Consumer Protection Act, R.S.B.C. 1996, c. 69, s. 11; R.S.O. 1990, c. 87, Direct Sales Cancellation Act, R.S.A. 1980, c. D-35, s. 6, as amended by S.A. 1981, c. 44, s. 2.

cooling-off period

a specified period following a contract of sale during which a buyer may terminate the contract by giving written notice to the seller

Unfortunately, there has been virtually no cooperation among the various governments and the resulting provisions vary in the extent and nature of the remedies they provide for the buyer. The legislation was inspired by an act in the United Kingdom giving consumers a **cooling-off period** after door-to-door sales. A buyer may terminate the contract during this period by giving written notice to the seller. Upon doing so, he or she has no further obligation under the contract and may recover any money already paid. This marks an important departure from the common law rule that the rights and liabilities of the parties are established at the time the contract is formed.

In these statutes the cooling-off period varies from two to ten days. In some provinces it is based on the time when the contract is entered into; in others, from the date on which a written memorandum of the contract is received by the buyer. The legislation applies to both goods and services but in some provinces it does not apply to sales under $50.

Unsolicited Goods

Pressure selling can take the form of sending goods not ordered by the consumer, hoping to induce the recipient to pay for them. Consumer protection statutes expressly state that use of the goods by the recipient does not amount to an acceptance of the seller's offer. Accordingly, a recipient of unsolicited goods may use them without becoming liable for their price. The purpose of the provision is to discourage sellers from sending unsolicited goods to consumers, and it seems to have been quite effective. Some provinces have taken a similar approach to unsolicited credit cards.[35]

Telemarketing

telemarketing

the use of telephone communications for promoting the supply of a product or for promoting a business interest

Recent concerns about fraudulent **telemarketing** led to major amendments in the Competition Act, which took effect in March 1999.[36] "Telemarketing" is defined as "the practice of using interactive telephone communications for the purpose of promoting, directly or indirectly, the supply or use of a product or for the purpose of promoting, directly or indirectly, any business interest."[37] Deceptive telemarketing is made a criminal offence, punishable by a maximum of five years in prison and a fine within the discretion of the court; a fine of up to $200 000 may be imposed on summary conviction. The new provisions also extend criminal responsibility to directors and officers of a corporation when its employees are found guilty of deceptive telemarketing.

The new rules require agents to disclose the name of the company they represent, the purpose of the call, the kind and value of the product or service being promoted, the terms or restrictions relating to delivery of the product to customers, and other specified information. Additionally, the provisions prohibit telemarketers from conducting contests where the participant can receive prizes only after they make some kind of prior payment, or from offering gifts or prizes for buying a product unless the value of the gift is disclosed. It is also illegal for telemarketers to offer a product for sale at a price grossly in excess of its fair market value, where delivery of the product is conditioned on prior payment by the customer.

Repossession

A standard form consumer contract may contain a term asserting that the lender or seller has some form of self-help remedy should the consumer default. For example, the contract may authorize the seller to repossess the goods from the consumer if instalment payments are not kept up, or to sue for the entire balance due under the contract if the consumer defaults in one

---

35. See Consumer Protection Act, R.S.B.C. 1996, c. 69, s. 47; R.S.N.S. 1989, c. 92, s. 23; R.S.O. 1990, c. C-31, s. 36.

36. S.C. 1999, c. 2, which introduces a new s. 52.1.

37. Internet communications, automated pre-recorded messages, and consumer-instigated calls to a customer relations line are not covered.

instalment payment. Consumer protection statutes in some provinces state that the seller's remedy of repossession is lost once the buyer has paid a specified proportion (for example, two-thirds) of the purchase price, and other statutes limit the circumstances in which a seller or creditor can enforce an **acceleration clause**. A further example occurs in the law of landlord and tenant, where some provinces have abolished a landlord's self-help remedy of seizing a residential tenant's goods for arrears of rent.[38]

acceleration clause
a contractual provision whereby the unpaid balance of the price becomes payable immediately in the event of default by the buyer

Financing Arrangements

Many merchants who sell durable goods to consumers on the instalment plan, "discount" their consumer credit contracts to finance companies. Typically, a merchant assigns the contract to a finance company and receives immediate payment of a sum that is less than the full amount to be paid by the buyer. The buyer then receives notice of assignment and makes the instalment payments to the finance company. The general rule about assignment of contractual rights, as we have seen in Chapter 12, is that an assignee "takes subject to the equities" and acquires no more enforceable claim than the assignor had. There is little doubt that a merchant can more readily (and probably more cheaply) find an assignee to buy its instalment receivables if the assignee acquires rights against the buyer that are *not* subject to any complaints the buyer (consumer) may have about the goods.

Merchants and finance companies found a way around the general rule about assignments by using a negotiable instrument: a buyer was required to sign a promissory note for the balance of the purchase price plus finance charges, and this note, along with the conditional sale contract, was endorsed by the merchant to the finance company. The finance company thus became a *holder in due course* of the note, immune to any "personal defences" the buyer might have against the merchant. Until the matter was corrected by legislation in the late 1960s, a consumer might be liable to a finance company with no opportunity to refuse to pay for the goods if they proved defective or if the dealer refused to perform its warranties. An amendment to the Bills of Exchange Act made finance companies subject to consumers' defences against sellers.[39]

Another way around the rule was to use the contract of sale itself to waive the consumer's rights by a rather special kind of exempting clause: the consumer was asked to sign a standard form contract of sale containing a clause (sometimes referred to as a "cut-out clause") agreeing that any assignee of the contract (for example, a finance company), when seeking to enforce the debt, would not be subject to the defences that the debtor (consumer) might have against the assignor (dealer). As noted in Chapter 30, most consumer protection acts now state that an assignee of a consumer credit contract shall have no greater rights than the assignor and is subject to the same obligations.[40]

Disclosure of the True Cost of Credit

Consumer protection statutes of the 1960s, which dealt with door-to-door sales, also contained disclosure requirements for all contracts where a buyer of goods or services or a borrower of money repays the debt by instalments. They require sellers and lenders to give their customers a detailed statement of the terms of credit in dollars and cents and in percentage terms as an effective annual rate of interest, as well as any charges for insurance and registration fees. A customer is not bound by the contract if the seller fails to comply with the requirements.[41]

---

38. See, for example, Residential Tenancy Act, R.S.B.C. 1996, c. 406, s. 80.

39. R.S.C.1985, c. B-4, s. 191.

40. For example: Consumer Protection Act, R.S.B.C. 1996, c. 69, s. 3(1); R.S.N.S. 1989, c. 92, s. 25; R.S.O. 1990, c. C.31, s. 31.

41. For example: Consumer Protection Act, R.S.B.C. 1996, c. 69, s. 41; R.S.O. 1990, c. C.31, s. 19.

The purpose of this legislation was to make the costs of obtaining credit clearer to the prospective debtor, who would then find it easier to compare offers of credit and to shop prudently for the lowest effective rate of interest. However, it is doubtful if it has proved very effective.

Regulation of Businesses by Licensing, Bonding, and Inspection

Consumer protection through licensing of businesses has been a method long in use. We have discussed the licensing of many professions in Chapter 4. Licensing is also used to regulate the providers of a variety of goods and services. A familiar example is the inspection and licensing of restaurants by municipal authorities to ensure sanitary conditions in the preparation of food.

Consumer legislation affecting door-to-door sales, to which we have already referred, led not only to cooling-off periods but also to the registration of door-to-door sellers. In addition, consumer protection acts may enable regulatory boards to suspend or revoke registration and to hear complaints. All provinces prohibit door-to-door traders from continuing to sell unless they are registered so that the sanctions, if actively pursued, can be very effective. Collection agencies—accused from time to time of using high pressure tactics and harassment to collect outstanding debts—are also subject to similar registration requirements.

After some highly publicized failures of travel agencies in the 1970s in which consumers who had paid for holiday packages lost their money, some provinces passed legislation to license travel firms in much the same way as door-to-door sellers and collection agencies. In addition, they required travel agents to be bonded in order to guarantee consumers against loss of prepaid travel and accommodation, or established Travel Assurance Funds to accomplish the same purpose.

COMPETITION

Background

The underlying belief of what may be termed the "deregulation movement" is that the market allocates resources more efficiently than do governments. Thus governments should interfere as little as possible with the conduct of business. The essential characteristic of an efficient market economy is competition. If consumers and customers have a choice between the goods or services of competing firms, prices will be lower or quality better or both. But an entirely unregulated market has within it the seeds of its own destruction. The most efficient firms will ultimately drive the less efficient out of business—at least in certain sectors of the market. They will then enjoy a *monopoly*, there will be no competition, and the benefits of a free market will be lost. The same may occur where two or more firms, ostensibly in competition with each other, coordinate their actions and strategies in such a way as to divide up the market. Where such market imperfections exist, or are likely to occur, governments must intervene in order to preserve competition.

The Common Law

As we saw in Chapter 8, the common law has long recognized the desirability of promoting free and fair competition, in particular by refusing to enforce contracts that are unreasonably in restraint of trade. Typically, the courts have struck down provisions in contracts whereby one party agrees not to compete with the other and where the scope of that restriction is unreasonably wide. Provisions of that nature restrict a former employee from establishing his own business or working for a competitor firm during a certain period after termination of the employment; similarly, restrictions placed on franchisees, partners, shareholders in small corporations, or vendors of businesses to prevent them from competing with their former associates or with the new owners of their businesses. Such provisions are not necessarily invalid, but the courts will strike them down if they unreasonably restrict competition and are contrary to the public interest. However, the common law principle operates only to prevent a party from enforcing a contract that is in restraint of trade; it has no application to situations where the parties voluntarily enter into and abide by contracts that operate against the public interest.

The torts of conspiracy and of unlawful interference with trade may also provide a remedy for a business injured by unfair competition, as noted in Chapter 3. The actions are very limited in scope, applying only where two or more parties deliberately conspire to cause injury to another's business, or where one person uses unlawful means to induce another to breach a contract with a third person; such actions are very rare in Canada.[42]

The Competition Act

The perceived inadequacy of the common law to protect the public interest against anti-competitive behaviour led to the enactment of the Combines Investigation Act—which also proved relatively ineffective—and its successor, the Competition Act.[43] The Competition Act, as we saw in the preceding part of this chapter, also contains various provisions relating to matters such as misleading advertising and abusive marketing practices, and to consumer protection generally. As for anti-competitive practices, the provisions of the act can be grouped under three main headings, dealing respectively with

- conspiracies
- monopolizing
- mergers

Before examining these provisions, two other aspects of the Act should be considered briefly.

Exemptions

The Act does not apply to certain classes of persons, nor to certain types of restrictive practice. In particular, the basic prohibition against conspiracies generally does not apply to the professions; thus, governing bodies of professions such as law, medicine, and public accountancy may establish agreements among their members with respect to such matters as qualifications, so long as these are reasonably necessary for the protection of the public. Also exempt are agreements or arrangements among underwriters and others involved in the distribution of securities, and among members of a shipping conference.

Enforcement

The administration of the Act is in the hands of the Director of Investigation and Research, assisted by the Bureau of Competition Policy, a division of the Department of Industry. Matters may be referred by the Director to the Competition Tribunal, a specialized tribunal with power to order a variety of civil remedies, or in serious cases involving criminal offences may be referred to the Attorney-General of Canada for prosecution. The Act sets out a number of criminal offences, punishable by heavy fines and by imprisonment of up to five years. During 1999, for example, fines totalling almost $90 million were imposed on a number of producers of vitamins participating in a international price-fixing cartel; a Swiss business man was personally fined $250 000 and, in another case, a Canadian business man was jailed for nine months.

Normally, a person who is adversely affected by conduct that is prohibited by the Act lodges a complaint with the Director, leaving it with the Director to investigate and take the appropriate procedure. However, section 36 also provides that an individual may bring an action for

---

42. For an interesting (unsuccessful) action see Ed Miller Sales & Rentals Ltd. v. Caterpillar Tractor Co. (1996), 30 C.C.L.T. (2d) 1 (Alta. C.A.).

43. R.S.C. 1985, c. C-34. References to section numbers in this part of the chapter are to this Act, as amended.

damages resulting from prohibited conduct or from contravention of an order of the Tribunal.[44] In view of the difficulties of proving that an offence has been committed and of proving damage—and the very expensive nature of such actions—they are only rarely entertained.

Conspiracies

Section 45 of the Competition Act

cartel

an agreement or arrangement between enterprises to lessen competition

Section 45 of the Act sets out the basic prohibition against **cartels,** or "trusts" as they are known in the United States—hence the expression *anti-trust* law. (The expression "trust," when used in this sense, is not to be confused with the equitable concept of the trust, described in Chapter 12.)

Section 45 provides:

(1) Every one who conspires, combines, agrees or arranges with another person

    (a) to limit unduly the facilities for transporting, producing, manufacturing, supplying, storing or dealing in any product,

    (b) to prevent, limit or lessen, unduly, the manufacture or production of a product, or to enhance unreasonably the price thereof,

    (c) to prevent or lessen, unduly, competition in the production, manufacture, purchase, barter, sale, storage, rental, transportation or supply of a product, or in the price of insurance upon persons or property, or

    (d) to otherwise restrain or injure competition unduly, is guilty of an indictable offence and is liable to imprisonment for a term not exceeding five years or to a fine not exceeding ten million dollars or to both.

The section creates a criminal offence and, consequently, in order to secure a conviction it is necessary for the prosecution to prove that the conduct of the accused was intentional; that is, that there was *mens rea*.[45] It was initially uncertain whether a dual intent had to be proved—to conspire or enter into an agreement with another person *and* to unduly lessen competition. An amendment, in the form of a new subsection (section 45(2.2)), was introduced in 1985, ostensibly to the effect that a single intention, to conspire or agree, was all that is required. That requirement was subsequently clarified when the Supreme Court of Canada established that, for an offence to have been committed, (i) the accused must have intended to conspire or agree, and (ii) it must have been objectively apparent to the accused that the likely effect would be to lessen competition.[46]

"Conspires, Combines, Agrees or Arranges..."

The essential requirement of section 45 is that two or more persons conspire together; that is, that they enter into some sort of agreement. The great difficulty lies in proving it. Restrictive agreements are rarely in writing. There would be little point in drawing up a formal written agreement since it would not be enforceable and would constitute damning evidence of a criminal conspiracy. In investigating suspected offences under the Competition Act, the Director has wide powers to search premises and computer records, and to seize documents (sections 15 and 16). Consequently, the existence of an agreement must usually be inferred from the actual behaviour of the parties and surrounding circumstances, unless one of the conspirators can be induced to testify. Section 45(2.1), added in 1986, allows the court to infer the existence of an agreement from circumstantial evidence, with or without direct evidence of meetings between the alleged parties, but adds that the existence of the agreement must still be proved beyond rea-

---

44. The constitutionality of this provision was upheld by the Supreme Court of Canada in City National Leasing Ltd. v. General Motors of Canada, [1989] 1 S.C.R. 641.

45. For a fuller discussion of *mens rea*, see Chapter 29.

46. R. v. Nova Scotia Pharmaceutical Society, [1992] 2 S.C.R. 606.

sonable doubt. Circumstantial evidence of an agreement might take the form of sudden, identical, changes in prices by apparent competitors, or unexplained secret meetings.

CASE 32.4

Members of the Canadian Steel Pipe Institute were concerned about the lack of price stability in their market, following a period during which there had been wide fluctuations and various attempts by some firms to undercut their competitors and fellow members. Public meetings were held and industry reports circulated, urging members to adopt an open pricing policy. The policy involved publication of price lists and notification of price changes.

The Institute emphasized that the policy was a voluntary one, and each member was free to adopt its own pricing policy. Nevertheless, the evidence was that after the open price policy was instituted, bids submitted by members of the institute were frequently identical.

The only evidence to support the existence of an actual agreement was

(1) the various public statements that had been made

(2) the publication of price lists

(3) the fact of identical pricing

(4) a communication from one firm to another to the effect that a third firm, which had been awarded a contract at a substantially lower price, was "not playing ball"

On that evidence the court inferred that a tacit agreement had in fact existed among the members of the Institute.[47]

A distinction must be drawn between a tacit agreement and conduct that is sometimes described as "conscious parallelism." The fact that prices among competitors in a particular industry tend to go up or down at the same time, and by approximately the same amount, does not necessarily mean that there is a conspiracy or agreement. Within the industry, prices of competitors will tend to be similar for similar products, otherwise those with higher prices would lose sales; one firm may tend to be the "price leader," so that if it raised or reduced its prices, the others would quickly follow suit even though they had made no commitment to do so. Thus **parallel pricing** by itself is not evidence of conspiracy.

parallel pricing
the practice, among competing firms, of adopting similar pricing strategies

Undue Lessening of Competition

One method of reducing or eliminating competition, as Case 32.4 demonstrates, is parallel pricing. Other common examples of anti-competitive practices are:

- imposing limits on production (i.e., setting quotas)
- market-sharing, where firms agree to divide up the market on a territorial basis
- product specialization, where firms agree that each will manufacture, or sell, a different type of product

The Competition Act requires not only that there should be a lessening of competition, but that it be lessened "unduly." This rather vague provision suggests that *some* lessening of competition is acceptable. But how much? The courts have interpreted it to mean that there must be a serious or significant reduction in competition.[48] In order to determine the seriousness of the effect, the relevant market must first be defined, with regard both to the product and to its geographical scope; then, the court must determine whether the accused parties possessed a sufficiently large share of that market ("market power") to injure competition. For example, a

47. R. v. Armco Canada Ltd. (1976), 70 D.L.R. (3d) 287.

48. R. v. Nova Scotia Pharmaceutical Society, *supra*, n. 46.

number of small firms could legitimately combine together to protect their share of the market from one or more larger competitors without unduly limiting competition.

CASE 32.5

A number of pool car operators entered into an agreement whereby each agreed not to undercut prices charged by other members of the cartel to existing customers on shipments from Toronto to the West. The question was whether their agreement was likely to reduce competition unduly.

The court accepted that there was a significant reduction of competition among pool car operators. However, that was only one method of shipping goods. There were substitute methods, such as trucking and intermodal freight forwarding, to which potential customers could easily switch. Consequently, competition was not significantly affected.[49]

Other Specific Offences

Apart from the general conspiracy offence, under section 45, the Act expressly specifies a number of types of anti-competitive behaviour that constitute separate offences. In particular, it is an offence

bid-rigging
agreeing not to submit a bid or agreeing in advance what bids will be submitted in response to a call for bids or tenders

- to agree not to submit a bid, or to agree in advance what bids will be submitted in response to a call for bids or tenders (**bid-rigging**) (section 47)
- to limit unreasonably the opportunities for any person to participate in professional sport or to play for the team of her or his choice in a professional league (section 48)
- to implement in Canada a directive or instruction from a person outside Canada, giving effect to a conspiracy that, if it had been entered into in Canada, would constitute an offence under the Act (section 46)

This last provision is aimed at multinational corporations carrying on business in Canada, where the Canadian subsidiary carries out improper instructions from a foreign parent.

Monopolizing

The offence of conspiracy requires that two or more persons agree to restrict competition. However, a single person or firm that enjoys a monopoly, or even a very powerful position, in a particular sector of the market may also abuse its power in a manner that is contrary to the public interest. The Act deals with such conduct in a variety of ways. Certain types of conduct, especially in relation to pricing and distribution, are made illegal; more generally, the Act identifies some anti-competitive behaviour as an **abuse of dominant position,** which, though not a criminal offence, may be prohibited by order of the Tribunal.

abuse of dominant position
taking an unfair advantage of possessing a monopoly or dominant position in the marketplace

Pricing Practices

Section 50 prohibits three types of pricing practices: discriminatory pricing, regional price discrimination, and predatory pricing. **Discriminatory pricing** occurs where a seller knowingly makes a practice of discriminating between purchasers who are in competition with each other, with respect to the price charged for goods of like quality and quantity, and at the same time. To constitute an offence, there must be a systematic pattern of behaviour. Practices such as granting volume discounts and loyalty bonuses or rebates are allowed, so long as they are made avail-

discriminatory pricing
where a seller makes a practice of discriminating between purchasers with respect to the price charged for goods or services

---

49. R. v. Clarke Transport Canada Inc. (1995), 130 D.L.R. (4th) 500.

able to all competing customers on the same terms; vendors are, of course, permitted to change their prices from time to time.

Regional price discrimination occurs where a vendor of products charges lower prices in one part of Canada than elsewhere in the country, with the effect or tendency of significantly lessening competition or eliminating a competitor. **Predatory pricing** involves selling products at unreasonably low prices, again with the effect or tendency of significantly lessening competition or eliminating a competitor. Although the statute does not expressly say so, an essential element of both offences is that the vendor must possess substantial market power; in order to be able to reduce competition, or to drive out a competitor, by artificially lowering the price of one's product, a firm needs to have both a large share of the market and deep pockets. This was certainly so in the *Hoffmann-LaRoche* case,[50] in which the manufacturer of "Valium" distributed the drug to Canadian hospitals free of charge for a period of a year. The court held that this constituted an attempt to prevent other manufacturers of tranquillizers from entering the market.

> **regional price discrimination**
> where a seller charges lower prices in one region than it charges elsewhere, with the aim of eliminating competition

> **predatory pricing**
> where a seller temporarily reduces prices to an unreasonably low level with the aim of driving competitors out of business

Section 61 applies to the practice of **resale price maintenance**. It is an offence for the supplier of a product, "by agreement, threat, promise or any like means," to attempt to influence upwards, or to discourage the reduction of, the resale price of the product. Usually the offence takes the form of a refusal to supply, or some other form of sanction against, cut-price and "discount" retailers. Manufacturers or wholesalers are entitled to suggest or recommend to their customers a particular resale price, but if they do so they should make it clear that the customer is under no obligation to follow that suggestion and will not be prejudiced by a failure to do so. A supplier may raise a number of defences specifically recognized by section 61; in particular, that the customer has used the products as "loss leaders," has engaged in "bait-and-switch selling," has been guilty of misleading advertising, or has provided poor service to its own customers.

> **resale price maintenance**
> where a supplier of goods attempts to control their resale price

Distribution Practices

In addition to the pricing practices outlined above that constitute offences, the Act deals less strictly with other types of distribution practices. Generally, a supplier is entitled to choose its customers and is free to decide whether to supply a particular person or not, except where that refusal is part of a conspiracy or is related to a pricing offence. However, in circumstances where a product is not in short supply, and a potential customer is willing to meet the usual trade terms and cannot otherwise obtain adequate supplies of the product because of a lack of competition among suppliers, the Tribunal may order a supplier to supply that customer (section 75).

Other distribution practices, such as **exclusive dealing**, **tied selling**, and **market restriction**, are also reviewable. A supplier may make it a condition that the buyer deals only or primarily in the supplier's products; it may be a condition for the supply of one type of product that the buyer also deals in other products of the supplier; or it may be a condition of supplying a customer that the customer markets the product only within a prescribed area. Such practices are not forbidden, but section 77 provides that the Tribunal may, on application by the Director, make an order prohibiting the practice or requiring it to be modified.

> **exclusive dealing**
> where a supplier of goods makes it a condition that the buyer should deal only or primarily in the supplier's products

> **tied selling**
> where a supplier makes it a condition that, to obtain one type of product, the buyer must also deal in other products of the supplier

> **market restriction**
> where a supplier makes it a condition that the buyer markets the product only within a prescribed area

Abuse of Dominant Position

Although, under the former Combines Investigation Act, monopolizing was a criminal offence, the statute was worded, and interpreted, in such a way that it was all but impossible to secure a conviction. The Competition Act decriminalized monopolizing (apart from certain specific offences considered above), and introduced the concept of reviewable conduct amounting to an abuse of a dominant position.

To obtain an order remedying an abuse of dominant position, the Director must show that the firm against which the order is sought is in substantial control of a particular business sector and has engaged in an anti-competitive practice that has prevented, or is likely to prevent or

---

50. R. v. Hoffmann-LaRoche Ltd. (1980), 28 O.R. (2d) 164.

substantially lessen competition (section 79). Section 78 sets out a non-exhaustive list of practices that are regarded as anti-competitive, such as the buying up of products to prevent the erosion of existing price levels, the pre-emption of scarce facilities or resources, and the requirement that a supplier refrain from selling to a competitor or sell only to certain customers.

The applicability of section 79 depends largely upon the identification of the relevant product and market; the firm usually argues for a broad definition, while the Director proposes a narrower definition so that fewer products or a smaller geographic area will be taken into account.[51]

CASE 32.6

Nutrasweet accounted for more than 95 percent of all sales in Canada of the sweetener aspartame—a product used mainly in the soft drinks industry. One other firm, Tosoh, accounted for the rest of the market.

Tosoh complained to the Director that Nutrasweet had entered into exclusive purchasing contracts with its customers: if they wished to buy aspartame from Nutrasweet they had to agree to buy only from Nutrasweet.

This raised the question of defining the relevant market; was it the market for aspartame, or for sweeteners generally, and was the market Canada, or the world?

The Tribunal considered the evidence of cross-elasticity of demand between the various types of sweeteners and concluded that there was at most only weak evidence of

competition between aspartame and other sweeteners. Customers were unlikely to switch to other sweeteners on account of the conditions imposed by Nutrasweet. Similarly, although aspartame was available in other countries, transportation costs were low, and there were no tariff barriers, the Tribunal concluded that the relevant market was Canada; prices in Canada differed significantly from prices in other countries, suggesting that Canada was a distinct geographic market and that customers were unlikely to switch to imported aspartame.

Having thus defined the market, the Tribunal found that Nutrasweet had used its market power to keep other suppliers out of Canada, with the effect of lessening competition significantly.[52]

Checklist: **Restricting Competition**

Competition may be restricted by *conspiracies* between a number of producers, or by *monopolizing* on the part of a single producer (abuse of dominant position).

Common examples of conspiracies are

- price fixing
- parallel pricing
- bid-rigging

Common examples of monopolizing are

- discriminatory pricing
- predatory pricing
- regional price discrimination
- resale price maintenance
- exclusive dealerships
- "tied selling" arrangements
- marketing restrictions

51. See Canada (Director of Investigation and Research, Competition Act) v. Southam Inc., [1997] 1 S.C.R. 748.

52. Director of Investigation and Research v. NutraSweet Co. (1990), 32 C.P.R. (3d) 1.

Mergers

One way to combat monopolizing is to try to prevent monopolies coming into existence in the first place. To this end, section 92 of the Competition Act gives the Tribunal power to prevent a merger from proceeding, in whole or in part, and to make various other orders, where it concludes that the merger is likely to prevent or significantly lessen competition in Canada. The Tribunal may act only on a reference from the Director, after the Director has carried out a full investigation of a proposed merger or of one that has taken place.

"**Merger**" is broadly defined (by section 91) to include the acquisition, by the purchase of shares or assets, or by amalgamation, combination, or other means, of control over, or of a significant interest in, the business of a competitor *(horizontal merger)*, supplier or customer *(vertical merger)*, or other person *(conglomerate or diversification merger)*. "Control" apparently means legal control, that is, ownership of more than 50 percent of the shares or voting rights of another corporation, but a "significant interest" may be something less than legal control.[53] Most likely to lessen competition are horizontal mergers between competing firms, since the number of competitors is effectively reduced when one such firm obtains control over another. But vertical mergers, where a firm takes control of its suppliers or of its distributors, may also reduce competition by increasing the market control of large firms. Diversification will only rarely have an anti-competitive effect.

merger
the amalgamation of two or more businesses into a single business entity

In determining whether a merger is likely to have a significant effect on competition, the Tribunal is required (by section 93) to have regard to a variety of factors: in particular, it should consider whether

- the existence of foreign competition is likely to ensure that a reduction of competition within Canada will not have adverse consequences
- the "target" firm is in poor economic health and would likely not have continued in business
- acceptable substitutes exist for the products affected
- there are barriers that might prevent new competitors entering the market
- effective competition will still exist after the merger
- the merger will eliminate a vigorous, effective, and innovative competitor

Even where it is determined that a proposed merger will substantially and detrimentally lessen competition, it may still be justified on grounds of economic efficiency (section 96). The creation of a larger firm, pooling the assets and skills of the parties, may produce gains—such as improved products, increased exports, or reduced reliance on imports—that offset any detrimental effects resulting from a reduction in competition.

Although the Tribunal has the power to "unscramble" a completed merger, such an event is unlikely for two reasons. First, there are pre-notification requirements for large mergers, involving firms whose combined revenues exceed $400 million per year, or whose assets exceed $35 million. A party proposing a large acquisition must inform the Bureau before proceeding with the transaction.[54] Consequently, the mergers most likely to affect competition are reviewed before they take place. Secondly, where it is reasonably clear that a merger will not have anti-competitive consequences, the review process can be avoided by obtaining an advance ruling from the Director.

---

53. From the Merger Enforcement Guidelines, published by the Director in 1991, it appears that an interest of 10 percent or less will not be considered significant.

54. As noted in the next chapter, additional requirements, under the Investment Canada Act, apply in the case of acquisition of a Canadian firm by a foreign firm.

CONTEMPORARY ISSUE

Airline Mergers

Onex Corp. says it will not resurrect its bid to gain control of Canada's airlines, saying it is simply facing too many hurdles to conclude a deal in a timely fashion. Onex terminated its $2.2 billion offer [on November 5, 1999] after a Quebec Superior Court judge rules its bid for 31 percent of Air Canada shares was illegal.

Source: "Onex says it won't resurrect airline deal," *The Globe and Mail*, November 8, 1999, p. B1.

The proposed takeover of Canadian Airlines and its merger with Air Canada sparked a major national and international controversy. At issue was whether the Canadian government would, or should, remove a restriction that prohibited any person owning more than 10 percent of Air Canada shares, whether it was appropriate to suspend the operation of the Competition Act, and whether Canada really needs a "national" air carrier. Also interested in the issue were the United States and the European Union, whose own competition policies were involved.

Question to Consider

1. Who should determine such issues—the Courts, Parliament, or the shareholders of the corporations involved?

ENVIRONMENTAL PROTECTION

If, as was suggested earlier in this chapter, the influence of the consumer lobby has declined in recent years, that of the environmental lobby has increased dramatically. Environmental law is probably the fastest growing area of law and regulation in Canada. The total volume of regulations is immense: one law publisher has produced a complete set of Canadian regulations together with a digest of recent cases; the materials fill six, thick, loose-leaf volumes![55] Municipalities also pass by-laws to provide local environmental protection and to restrict activities deemed to be harmful. As a result, a large proportion of enterprises must now seek professional advice about which regulatory schemes may apply to their industry.

Growing Concern for the Environment

The common law, in particular the tort of nuisance, has a very limited application to pollution problems, as we saw in Chapter 3: generally, an owner was entitled to do as he chose on his land, subject only to being liable to compensate persons who could prove that they had been injured as a result of the escape of some harmful substance stored on the land. Except in the most direct of injuries, the burden of proof was insuperable.

A few regulatory schemes were introduced many years ago in order to prevent the most obviously harmful disregard of the environment; in the 19th century there were laws prohibiting the dumping of dangerous substances into our rivers, lakes, and harbours. However, at that time, and indeed until quite recently, there was limited appreciation of the cumulative effects of pollution; governments made very little effort to enforce the early schemes and offending industries often ignored them entirely.

---

55. Cook and Lucas, *Canadian Environmental Law*, (2nd ed.). Toronto: Butterworths, 1991.

Increased awareness made enforcement a major public issue, and the need for legislation and regulation to remedy the deficiencies of the existing statutory and common law became very apparent. Major environmental disasters, such as the running aground of the *Exxon Valdez* off the coast of Alaska, the Bhopal chemical spill in India, and the worldwide concern about the "greenhouse effect" and depletion of the earth's ozone layer, made the public much more aware of the dangers associated with many activities in industry, in transportation, and in the field of natural resources such as logging.

The Modern Legislative Framework

Environmental law is another of the areas in which the federal Parliament and provincial legislatures have concurrent jurisdiction. The protection of the environment is clearly within the competence of the provinces, but matters such as air and water pollution are national problems and require national solutions.

CASE 32.7

The Manitoba government established a scheme to compensate fishermen for loss suffered as a result of mercury contamination. In addition to Manitoba firms, corporations operating in Ontario and in Saskatchewan were found to have discharged mercury into rivers that drained into Manitoba. The Supreme Court of Canada held that Manitoba did not have power to impose liability in respect of acts done outside the province.[56]

Federal Legislation

The most important federal legislation is contained in the Canadian Environmental Protection Act (CEPA);[57] it is augmented by a number of separate statutes relating to particular types of pollution or dangers to the environment.[58]

The CEPA applies to all elements of the environment—air, land, and water, all layers of the atmosphere, all organic and inorganic matter and living organisms, and any interacting natural systems that include components of the foregoing. The Act requires the Minister of the Environment to formulate environmental quality objectives, guidelines, and codes of practice relating to the environment in general and to such specific matters as recycling, storing and disposing of substances, and activities for the conservation of natural resources and promotion of sustainable development (section 8). Separate parts of the CEPA deal with subjects such as toxic substances, hazardous wastes, nutrients, international air pollution, and ocean dumping. The amendments proposed in Bill C-32 aim to introduce stricter controls over the use of toxic substances and to give significant new powers to enforcement officers to deal with polluters. The Bill has nevertheless been widely criticized as being too weak to deal with many serious pollution problems.

---

56. Interprovincial Corp. Ltd. v. R., [1976] S.C.R. 477.

57. R.S.C. 1985, c. C-16 (as amended). The act consolidated and repealed a number of earlier statutes, among them the Clean Air Act, the Environmental Contaminants Act, the Ocean Dumping Control Act, and parts of the Canada Water Act. Substantial amendments to the Act have been proposed by Bill C-32, but as at December 1999 the Bill had not yet passed.

58. Most notably in the Atomic Energy Control Act, R.S.C. 1985, c. A-16; the Fisheries Act, R.S.C. 1985, c. F-14; the Pest Control Products Act, R.S.C. 1985, c. P-9; and the Transportation of Dangerous Goods Act, R.S.C. 1985, c. T-19.

Provincial Legislation

All of the provinces have a "general" environment protection law,[59] supplemented by various statutes referring to specific types of environmental protection; examples are statutes relating to air pollution,[60] water conservation and pollution,[61] transportation of dangerous goods,[62] and waste management.[63]

Environmental Impact Assessment Review

An important recent development has been the introduction of review processes to examine proposed major projects that are likely to have an impact on the environment; it is much better to prevent injury to the environment than to try to remedy it after it has occurred. Environmental impact assessment review processes have been introduced, in one form or another, at the federal level and in all provinces. Usually, the initiator of a development project is required to undertake an environmental assessment of the project, and submit it to the appropriate government agency. Major projects are subject to public review, by an independent review board, and public hearings are held in the communities likely to be affected. The review board submits its findings to the minister responsible, or to the whole Cabinet, which makes the final decision.

The scope and the procedures of the review process vary from one jurisdiction to another. In some, the process applies to both the private and the public sector; in others, only public authorities are required to comply with the process. However, that is not as important an omission as it might seem, since few if any major private development projects can occur without the involvement of one or more government agencies. For example, the federal Environment Assessment and Review Process applies only to "federal projects," but federal projects include not only those initiated by federal departments and agencies, but also those for which federal funds are solicited and those involving federal property.

Enforcement and Liability

Although private enforcement of the duties imposed by environment protection statutes is possible through the common law tort of nuisance, and although failure to comply with the standards required by statute may constitute evidence of negligence, the enforcement of environmental laws is primarily a public matter. Legislation usually provides public authorities with a wide variety of enforcement mechanisms. Polluters may be ordered to refrain from harmful activities, to remedy existing situations, and to pay for the costs of cleanup. Owners of contaminated property may be forbidden from dealing with that property, even where they were not responsible for causing the contamination. Most important, environmental legislation normally creates a number of offences, punishable by fines and, in serious cases, by imprisonment. And, as we saw in Chapter 29, since most major polluters are corporations, which cannot be sent to prison, the statutes frequently provide for the punishment of corporate directors and officers who are personally responsible for pollution offences.

---

59. For example, Environment Management Act, R.S.B.C. 1996, c. 118; Environment Protection Act, R.S.N.S. 1989, c. 150; Environment Protection Act, R.S.O. 1990, c. E.19.

60. For example, Clean Air Act, S.S. 1986–87–88, c. 12.1; Environmental Protection and Enhancement Act, S.A. 1993, c. E-13.3.

61. For example, Environmental Protection and Enhancement Act, S.A. 1993, c. E-13.3; Environment Act, S.N.S. 1994–5, c. 1.

62. For example, Dangerous Goods Handling and Transportation Act, R.S.M. 1987, c. D-12; Dangerous Goods Transportation Act, R.S.O. 1990, c. D.1.

63. For example, Waste Management Act, R.S.B.C. 1996, c. 482; Dangerous Goods and Hazardous Waste Management Act, R.S.N.S. 1989, c. 118.

QUESTIONS FOR REVIEW

1. Distinguish between "direct regulation" and "social regulation."

2. How does the Constitution divide the power to regulate business among the various levels of government in Canada?

3. What is meant by "concurrency" and by "paramountcy"?

4. Which provisions of the Charter have particular application to business activity?

5. What are the principal grounds on which the courts may review the legality of decisions and actions of government departments and agencies?

6. Who bears the costs of consumer protection measures?

7. What are the principal forms of misleading advertising that are prohibited by the Competition Act?

8. What is the purpose of a "cooling-off period"?

9. How do the new (1999) rules seek to prevent fraudulent telemarketing?

10. What is a "cartel"? How do cartels operate against the public interest?

11. What is "conscious parallelism"?

12. Give examples of the principal types of abuse of dominant position.

13. Why is it thought necessary for governments to control mergers?

14. Why are "horizontal" mergers more likely to affect competition than other types of merger?

15. Why is the determination of the relevant "market" essential to the application of competition law?

16. What is the purpose of environmental impact assessment review?

CASES AND PROBLEMS

1 Dr. Carpenter relocated her dental practice to premises in a new shopping mall and placed an advertisement to that effect in the local newspapers. The notice conformed with the advertising standards of the dental profession in the province, but one of the newspapers decided to print a "human interest" story and did an interview with Dr. Carpenter. The story was printed without first having been shown to Dr. Carpenter, and a number of advertisements for dental supplies appeared on the same page. At the same time, Dr. Carpenter ordered a sign announcing the change of premises, which she intended to be displayed in the window of her old premises. Instead, by mistake, the sign was displayed in a public area of the shopping mall.

The professional association considered that the sign, and the advertisements that accompanied the newspaper article, constituted breaches of the professional advertising code, and gave notice to Dr. Carpenter of a disciplinary hearing, which could result in the cancellation or suspension of her licence to practice.

On what grounds, if any, can the validity of the disciplinary hearing and the professional regulations be challenged?

2. Ebrahim bought a used car from Cival Autos Inc., for $8000. The car was described by Cival as "one careful owner only, low mileage, excellent condition." In fact, Cival's manager was aware that the car had had three previous owners, the most recent of whom had been convicted of dangerous driving following a collision in which the car had sustained serious damage. He also knew that the odometer had been altered and that the car was generally in very poor condition.

Very soon after Ebrahim took delivery, the car started to develop problems. At first he took the car back to Cival, where he was told that the problems were minor and that they had "fixed" them. After three such visits to Cival, Ebrahim took the car to an independent garage, and the true facts about the car became known.

Apart from the normal remedies in contract and tort, is there any other legal action that Ebrahim can take against Cival?

3. Red Square Records Inc. is a Canadian corporation holding the sole rights to import and distribute in Canada discs and tapes produced by a Russian company, Krasnayadisk. For some years Red Square has been importing two labels that have proved very popular, partly because of their low price. It has been selling the discs to dealers at $4.99 each and they are retailed at prices ranging from $6.99 to $8.99.

Recently, Krasnayadisk introduced a new label, on which it is releasing previously unavailable archive recordings that are of great interest to collectors. Red Square has started to import the discs and makes them available to retailers at $18.99 each.

Steve's Records Inc., a Canadian firm that owns a large chain of record stores across Ontario, had been selling large quantities of the cheaper Krasnayadisk recordings, and its customers had shown a lot of interest in the new label. However, many were deterred by the high price. Steve's found another source for the new label—a dealer in the U.S., who was prepared to supply Steve's at a price of $11.99 per disc. This enabled Steve's to sell the new label at a much lower price than any of its competitors.

Some months ago, Steve's received a letter from Red Square informing it that, if Steve's did not stop purchasing the new label from the U.S., Red Square would no longer be willing to supply it with the two cheaper labels. Steve's ignored the warning and continued to import the new label.

A few weeks ago, Steve's ordered some discs from Red Square and was informed that Red Square would no longer supply Steve's. The cheaper labels are also available in the U.S., but at the same price of $4.99, and with higher shipping costs.

Is there any action that Steve's can take against Red Square's refusal to supply it?

4. Truenorth Press Inc. owned both of the daily newspapers in Bayville. The papers were relatively unsuccessful compared to Truenorth's other dailies throughout Canada and faced stiff competition for advertising revenue from a large number of small community newspapers that circulated in the same distribution area. Those community newspapers contained local news stories, as well as advertisements from mainly local firms, appeared once or twice a week, and were distributed free of charge.

Truenorth embarked on a campaign to acquire the community papers and, within one year, obtained control of 20 publications, including the two papers with the largest circulation.

A group of citizens—readers, who feared that there would be fewer "local" stories, and small firms, who feared that their advertising rates would be increased once Truenorth gained control of the remaining papers—held a number of public meetings to express their concern.

Is there any legal action that they could take?

INTERNATIONAL BUSINESS TRANSACTIONS

Canadian Business in a Global Economy

Law and International Business

Foreign Trade

Foreign Investment

The Resolution of International Business Disputes

Thus far our book has been concerned with law and business administration in Canada. But neither law nor business is restricted to a purely national dimension. Increasingly, the world is becoming a single giant marketplace in which firms from different countries compete against and sometimes cooperate with each other. This chapter provides an overview of the legal framework within which international business is conducted, discussing various aspects of foreign trade, foreign investment, and the resolution of international business disputes. We examine such questions as:

- what are the common features of export contracts?

- how are such contracts interpreted and enforced?

- how do governments regulate international trade?

- how is international trade affected, and promoted, by international bodies such as the World Trade Organization (WTO) and the North American Free Trade Association (NAFTA)?

- what are the legal forms available to foreign investors?

- how do governments regulate foreign investment?

- in what ways does international law apply to investment?

- how are international business obligations enforced by the courts?

- what is the role of international commercial arbitration?

- how are trade disputes resolved within NAFTA and the WTO?

CANADIAN BUSINESS IN A GLOBAL ECONOMY

For Canada, more than for most other countries, the international dimension of business is especially important. Canada's exports of goods amount to over one-third of the nation's gross domestic product. Among the world's trading nations, Canada ranked eighth (in 1998) in exports of merchandise—after the United States of America, Germany, Japan, France, the United Kingdom, Italy, and the Netherlands—and twelfth in exports of services. To put these figures in perspective, the world's largest exporter, the United States, exports only approximately three times as much as Canada and Japan little more than double.

Canada's largest trading partner is the United States, which takes three-quarters of our exports and provides two-thirds of our imports; in turn, Canada is also the largest trading partner of the United States, exporting more to the U.S. than does Japan. But Canada also has substantial trading relations with countries as diverse as Japan, the United Kingdom, Germany, Korea, China, the Netherlands, France, and Russia.

Traditionally, Canada has been seen as an exporter of raw materials and minerals (and indeed remains the world's second largest exporter in those categories), but in more recent years we have also become an important exporter of manufactured goods, chemicals, and transport and telecommunications equipment.

Perhaps of equal importance is the fact that, of the world's major industrialized economies, Canada ranks among the world's top 10 countries as both an exporter and importer of investment capital. In 1998, for example, foreign direct business investment inflows into Canada were over $22 billion. Outflows were even higher, at $36 billion, as Canadian multinationals expanded their operations abroad.

LAW AND INTERNATIONAL BUSINESS

The conduct of international business involves a wide variety of legal issues. To understand them, it is useful to consider how firms become "international" or "multinational." The establishment of international business operations can be viewed as a progression. Initially, a firm is established in a single locality and markets its products in that locality. Gradually, it expands, selling its goods or services further from home and becoming a substantial regional or national undertaking. At some stage, it finds a customer in another country and its operations become international. This is the foreign trade stage.

At first, its foreign market may be limited to a few customers but, in time, as its markets grow, it may find it worthwhile to appoint an *agent* in the other country, or establish a *representative office* there. Gradually, its activities expand, from simply seeking customers and providing information to supplying spare parts, repairs, and maintenance services.

A further important stage occurs when the firm commences other activities abroad, such as processing its products. Initially those activities may be modest ones, such as labelling, packaging, or assembly of components. Eventually, however, the operations may develop into full-scale manufacturing, and a *branch* or *subsidiary* may be established. The original firm has graduated from foreign trade to foreign investment and has become a multinational enterprise.

Foreign trade and foreign investment result in a wide variety of legal relationships. Contractual relationships of many different types arise: sale of goods and services, carriage of goods, bailment, insurance, agency, and employment. Questions regarding the law of negotiable instruments, of intellectual property, of partnerships and corporations, of secured transactions, and of creditors' remedies are raised. There is, however, an additional complication: international business transactions, by definition, involve parties in two or more different countries. The question must consequently be asked, "Which country's law applies to the situation?" This is a question of *private law*—of the law that generally governs transactions between private parties, such as a seller and buyer of goods.

In addition, questions of *public law* commonly arise, since virtually every government regulates foreign trade and investment to some extent, with the result that we must also consider legal relationships between private persons and governments. Finally, governments frequently make bilateral agreements (such as double taxation treaties, investment protection treaties, or the Canada–United States Free Trade Agreement) or multilateral agreements (such as the

General Agreement on Tariffs and Trade (GATT), the North American Free Trade Agreement (NAFTA), or the International Convention for the Protection of Industrial Property). Thus, questions of **public international law**, involving relations between states, also arise.

public international law
law involving relations between states

FOREIGN TRADE

Export Contracts

Export contracts—they might equally well be termed "import contracts"—generally fall into one of two categories: contracts for the international sale of goods and contracts for the supply of services abroad. Goods or services may be supplied in one of three main ways:

- The supplier may deliver directly to the customer in the other country.
- Delivery may be made through the supplier's own marketing organization established in the other country.
- The customer may accept delivery in the supplier's home country and himself arrange to ship the goods home.

Whichever method is adopted, the contract between supplier and customer constitutes the essence of the transaction. The following discussion will concentrate upon the most common type of export transaction—contracts for the international sale of goods.

The Contract of Sale

Much of what has been written in earlier chapters of this book with respect to the law of contracts and, in particular, to contracts for the sale of goods, applies equally to export contracts as it does to contracts with a purely domestic scope. However, contracts with an international element present special problems, due to the simple fact that the goods are to be delivered to, or services supplied to, a customer in another country.

Usually, the international sale of goods involves a number of parties and consists of several distinct though related contracts. In addition to the basic agreement for sale of the goods, the parties normally arrange for the transportation of the goods, by land, sea, or air, for their insurance during shipment, and, frequently, for the financing of the transaction. Thus carriers, insurers, banks, or finance houses may be involved as well as the buyer and seller. Since export transactions require special expertise, the parties commonly employ the services of specialist **export houses** or **freight forwarders**, who make the arrangements for shipment, insurance, and financing.

export houses or freight forwarders
specialist firms that make the arrangements for shipment, insurance, and financing in export sales

The Proper Law of the Contract

As we have noted, an export contract by definition involves two or more countries. A question that frequently arises is "Whose law governs the contract or its various component parts?"

ILLUSTRATION 33.1

A Canadian manufacturer sells goods to a Hungarian customer. The goods are to be shipped by a German airline, insured by a British insurance company, and financed by a Swiss merchant bank.

Several contracts make up the entire transaction, and each one might be governed by a different law. The laws of the different countries may vary considerably with respect to such matters as the rights of unpaid vendors or carriers, the terms to be implied as to quality or fitness of the goods, or the circumstances in which a contract will be frustrated.

proper law of the contract

the law of the country or jurisdiction by which the provisions of a contract are to be interpreted and its effect determined

conflict of laws or private international law

the principles of law that apply to resolve questions concerned with private relationships that are affected by the laws of two or more countries

To determine which law applies—that is, the **proper law of the contract**—it is necessary to refer to a body of principles known as the **conflict of laws**, or **private international law**. Canadian courts, and the courts of most other countries, hold that the proper law of the contract is the law that the parties intended to govern. The clearest method of establishing the proper law is for the parties themselves to make express provision.[1] A contract might state that it is subject to the law of Ontario, or of England, or of Switzerland. The choice of law need not be that of the location of one of the parties or be related to the place where the contract is to be performed; sometimes the parties choose a "neutral" law.

Where the parties do not expressly stipulate the proper law, the court will attempt to determine the intention of the parties from the surrounding circumstances. For example, if the contract states that any dispute is to be submitted to arbitration in a particular country, or that the courts of a particular country shall have jurisdiction, then it is probable that they also intended the law of that country to govern the contract.[2] An intention may also be inferred from the use of particular legal terminology or the form of the document. Where the court cannot draw such an inference it will apply the system of law that it considers to be most closely connected with the contract. In making this determination, it will have regard to all the circumstances and pay special attention to such factors as the place where the contract was made, the place where it is to be performed, the subject-matter of the contract, the place of business of the parties, and the place of acceptance of the risk.[3] And since the contract may comprise a number of distinct elements, it is possible that different laws may apply to different parts.[4]

Contractual Terms

Another difficulty is that terms or expressions may have different meanings in different legal systems, or to parties from different countries. In practice the problem is not so severe as it might seem; over the centuries a widely accepted standard terminology has evolved. Initially, the meaning of terms such as "FOB" and "CIF," which we encountered in Chapter 16, became largely standardized through mercantile custom. More recently, a set of standard terms (known as **Incoterms**), adopted by the International Chamber of Commerce, have come to be widely used; the original Incoterms were first published in 1936, and the current version dates from 1990.

Incoterms

a set of standard contractual terms adopted by the International Chamber of Commerce

Another important development has been the publication and widespread adoption of standard form contracts, published by various trade associations and by international bodies such as the United Nations Economic Commission for Europe (UNECE). Other international organizations, such as the International Institute for the Unification of Private Law (UNIDROIT) and the United Nations Commission on International Trade Law (UNCITRAL), have encouraged the harmonization of national commercial laws or the adoption of uniform laws. One significant result was the adoption, in 1980, of the Vienna Convention on Contracts for the International Sale of Goods, since implemented in Canada.[5] The standardization of terms and practices has been important in reducing disputes; the terms are familiar to commercial arbitrators, with the result that a common international standard of interpretation has emerged. The process of standardization is an ongoing one, continually evolving in order to keep up with developments such as containerization and electronic data processing.

---

1. Vita Food Products Inc. v. Unus Shipping Co. Ltd., [1939] A.C. 277.
2. Hamlyn & Co. v. Talisker Distillery, [1894] A.C. 202.
3. Imperial Life Assurance Co. of Canada v. Colmenares, [1967] S.C.R. 443.
4. M.W. Hardy Inc. v. A.V. Pound & Co. Ltd., [1956] A.C. 588.
5. International Sale of Goods Contracts Convention Act, S.C. 1991, c. 13. It has also been adopted by several of the provinces; see, for example, International Sale of Goods Act: S.N.S. 1988, c. 13; R.S.O. 1990, c. I.10.

The Documentation

An export sale normally requires at least four documents. These are

- the contract of sale
- the bill of lading
- the insurance policy or certificate
- the invoice

We have already discussed the contract of sale and bills of lading in Chapter 16, and insurance in Chapter 18. A bill of lading, as we have seen, is an acknowledgment by the carrier that the goods have been delivered for shipment; it operates as a document of title to the goods, facilitating the financing of the transaction. The insurance policy, similarly, is evidence that the goods are insured against loss or damage during transit and is usually necessary in order to obtain financing.

The invoice is of special importance in international sales of goods and must be correct in every respect, since it provides information not only for the parties to the transaction but also for the customs authorities of the country of importation. The invoice states the names and addresses of the buyer and seller, the date of the order, a full description of the goods sold, details of packaging, and the price (on the basis of which customs duty is normally calculated). It must conform to the requirements of the importing country, which may insist upon the production of additional documents, such as certificates of value, origin, quality, or inspection.

In recent years these traditional forms of documentation have begun to be replaced by computerized communications: bodies such as the Comité Maritime International have devised uniform sets of rules dealing with electronic data exchange in international business transactions.

Shipment and Insurance

Since it is the shipment of goods to another country that distinguishes the international sale of goods from purely domestic transactions, shipping arrangements are an essential element of an export sale. The parties may agree that the buyer will collect the goods from the seller's factory and make its own arrangements for transportation, or that the seller will deliver the goods to the buyer's premises in the other country, or that each will be responsible for some stage of the transportation. Usually, too, the goods will be insured against loss or damage during transit and either the buyer or the seller may assume responsibility for arranging insurance. The contract price reflects whether it is the seller or the buyer who arranges and pays for shipment and insurance, and up to which stage of the journey.

A seller may quote a price *ex works* (i.e., at the factory gate); if it is agreed to deliver the goods to the buyer's own premises, the total price will be correspondingly higher. As we saw in Chapter 16, the precise arrangements for shipment may determine the point at which title to the goods, or the risk of loss, passes from the seller to the buyer.

Over the centuries a number of standard terms have evolved to describe the more common types of arrangements for shipment. Examples of these terms (with the corresponding Incoterm abbreviations) are:

- EXW (ex works);
- FOB (free on board);
- CIF (cost, insurance, and freight);
- DDP (delivery duty paid)

These terms broadly correspond to the various stages of shipment and the extent of the obligations undertaken by the seller. Thus, in EXW contracts, the seller's responsibility is only to make the goods available to the buyer at the seller's own works or warehouse. The buyer bears the cost, and the risk, of transportation, though the seller is still obliged to furnish the necessary invoice and to provide all reasonable assistance to obtain any export licence or other authorization necessary for exporting the goods.

Under an FOB contract, the buyer arranges shipment and the seller's obligation is to deliver the goods to the carrier named by the buyer. The seller's responsibility ends when the goods are safely on board the ship or aircraft. Other variants are the FCA (free to carrier) and FAS (free alongside ship) contracts, where the seller's duty is, respectively, to deliver to the first carrier (for example, where the goods are collected by the carrier and loaded into a container for shipment to a cargo terminal), and to deliver to a specified pier or warehouse at the port of shipment.

A CIF contract represents a major extension of the seller's obligations. Here, the seller assumes responsibility for shipping the goods to the country of destination. The seller is responsible not only for shipment to the port of destination but also for insuring the goods.[6]

A final category of contracts extends the obligations of the seller still further, with the seller bearing the risks and costs of transporting the goods to an agreed destination and sometimes (as in a DDP contract) even paying the import duties.

FIGURE 33.1
Export Contracts

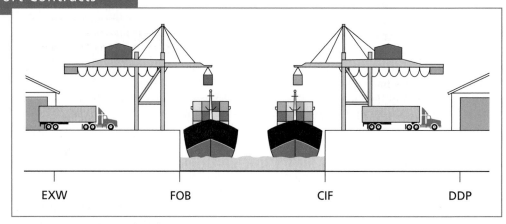

| EXW | FOB | CIF | DDP |

As new methods of goods transportation are developed, so also are new types of contractual terms. The use of pallets, of roll-on/roll-off ferries and, especially, of containers, has revolutionized the carriage of goods and in turn has led to the development of new legal terms, such as full container load (FCL) and less than a full container load (LCL). Where the consignment comprises a full container load, shipment may be made door-to-door in a sealed container; if there is less than a full container load, the goods are consolidated with the goods of other exporters in a "groupage container" and are loaded, and separated, at a container freight station.

Payment

A basic element in any contract of sale is the payment of the price. In an international contract the currency used to denominate the price and to make payment is important. The price may be denominated in one currency but paid in some other currency, and it is even becoming common to denominate the price in a "non-currency," such as the ECU or SDR, which cannot be used for making payment.[7] Generally, a seller does not mind in which currency the price is paid, so long

---

6. Under a CFR (cost and freight) contract, the seller pays carriage but the buyer arranges its own insurance.

7. The ECU (European currency unit) and SDR (special drawing rights) are not really currencies at all, but are used for determining rates of exchange. Thus an ECU can be translated into a corresponding number of francs, marks, pounds, or dollars. As the beginning of 1999, the ECU became an actual currency within the European Monetary Union, but physical coins and banknotes will not be issued until 2002.

as that currency is freely convertible. However, it will state the price in a stable currency, especially if there is to be a substantial time lag between contract and payment and, if the buyer's country imposes **exchange controls**, or does not permit its currency to be freely converted—as is often the case in developing countries—the seller will also require actual payment to be made in a "hard" currency. An exporter or importer may also "hedge" against the risk of currency fluctuations by using a method of **foreign exchange risk management**, such as borrowing in foreign currency or taking an option to buy or sell foreign currency.[8]

exchange controls
restrictions on the conversion or export of currency

foreign exchange risk management
methods of reducing the risk involved in currency fluctuations

Financing

Financing is especially important in international sales, partly because the time between the goods leaving the seller and reaching the buyer tends to be longer than in domestic sales, and partly because the amounts involved in international sales tend to be larger. A seller would like to receive payment as soon as its goods leave the factory or warehouse, whereas the buyer would prefer to postpone payment until the goods have been safely delivered. To accommodate both preferences normally requires the services of a banker.

For a long time the bill of exchange (see Chapter 21) was the most important method of payment in export sales. In recent years, other methods of financing have been devised, the most important of which are the **collection arrangement** and the **letter of credit**. Under a collection arrangement the seller employs the services of its bank to collect payment, by depositing the documents with the bank and receiving credit for the price (less the bank's charges). By contrast, a buyer obtains a letter of credit from its bank and uses it to pay the seller.[9] More recently, banks and finance houses have developed other highly flexible methods of financing—such as non-recourse finance, factoring, and financial leasing—methods that require more detailed explanation and are beyond the scope of this book.

collection arrangement
an arrangement whereby the seller employs the services of its bank to collect payment by depositing the documents with the bank and receiving credit for the price

letter of credit
a document that the buyer of goods obtains from the bank and uses to pay the seller

Countertrade

Earlier in this chapter we referred to exchange controls. A number of developing countries found it necessary to impose exchange controls or restrictions on the convertibility of their currencies, especially after the debt crises of the 1970s and again in 1997–8. In order to protect their balance of payments, governments in those countries permitted their firms to import goods, and to obtain the hard currency to pay for them, only if in turn they were able to earn hard currency by exporting their own products. These restrictions led to the development of the practice known as "countertrade."

In its simplest form, **countertrade** is a form of barter: a seller agrees to accept, instead of money, payment in goods produced or procured by the buyer. In one well-known example, an American firm sold insulating material in China and received silk carpets in return. Another increasingly common arrangement is for a corporation that sells machinery to a firm in a developing country to agree to accept part of that firm's production as the price; thus it might sell modern cutting and sewing equipment and receive finished clothing in return. The variety of forms of countertrade is virtually unlimited, but it should be emphasized that countertrade involves greater risks than do simple sales, since the "seller" will have to find a way of disposing of the goods acquired in exchange.

countertrade
a form of barter, under which a seller agrees to accept payment in goods produced or procured by the buyer

Export of Services

The "export" of services can take a number of forms. A buyer may come to a seller, as where a foreign tourist stays in a hotel or attends a concert in Canada. Transactions of this nature generally do not involve any element of foreign law. Or a seller might go to a buyer, as where a Canadian bank or insurance company opens a branch in another country to serve customers

8. See further P. Raworth, *Legal Guide to International Business Transactions,* pp. 112–5. (Toronto: Carswell, 1991).

9. An alternative method is for the buyer to obtain a banker's guarantee.

there. It is also possible for services to be "transmitted" to customers in other countries. Data, legal or financial advice, or technological expertise may be supplied to customers in other countries. Property in one country may be insured by an insurance company in another country. Banks may lend money to foreign clients. Close to one-quarter of the total worldwide volume of exports now consists of services.

Much of what has been said in relation to the international sale of goods applies equally to the provision of services—for example, the importance of determining the proper law of the contract and the problems of payment. Of particular importance, in contracts involving the transfer of technology, are the local rules governing the protection of intellectual property. A Canadian corporation that licenses a patent or a trademark, or supplies "know-how," to an enterprise in another country will be concerned to ensure that its rights are protected by the laws of that country and that its trade secrets do not become public knowledge.

Government Regulation of International Trade

Ever since foreign trade first evolved, governments have sought to regulate it by controlling exports and imports and by imposing customs duties. Countries consider trade relations a matter of national importance and although many countries, such as Canada and most of its major trading partners, are broadly committed to the principle of free trade they still maintain barriers that a would-be exporter must overcome. A particular concern of governments is to preserve a reasonable balance of trade with other countries; consequently the tendency is to encourage exports and discourage imports.

Export Promotion

Governments provide a variety of services to their own producers in order to assist them to compete in the global market. An important function of Canadian embassy staff abroad is to collect commercial information and disseminate it to Canadian business. More tangible support, mostly in the form of insurance, guarantees, and financial services, is provided by the Export Development Corporation, a Crown corporation whose purpose is to facilitate and develop Canada's export trade, and by other specialist bodies such as the Canadian Wheat Board. Government support is especially important with respect to exports to less developed countries, by providing loan guarantees and long-term credit. International aid programs may also provide indirect assistance to exporters; for example, programs funded by the Canadian International Development Agency (CIDA) frequently require a substantial Canadian content.

Export Controls

Although the general policy of most countries is to encourage exports, restrictions upon exports remain common. Export controls in Canada date back to the Export Act of 1897,[10] which regulated the export of a number of commodities, notably lumber. The federal government introduced further controls for reasons of national security during the First World War, and created a more comprehensive system following the Second World War and the commencement of the "Cold War" in 1947 by the Export and Import Permits Act.[11] The Act introduced a system of licensing for exports of certain listed products and for most exports to listed countries. Among the listed products are armaments, munitions, and other strategic materials; listed countries were mostly confined to members of the then Communist bloc. Further regulations, and other statutes, have added to the lists both of products and of countries; restrictions have been imposed on the export of certain types of cultural property and of some energy and agricultural products, and from time to time countries such as South Africa, Iran, Libya, Iraq, and Yugoslavia

---

10. S.C. 1897, c. 17: see now R.S.C. 1985, c. E-18.
11. S.C. 1947, c. 17; now R.S.C. 1985, c. E-19.

have joined the list of proscribed countries. Canadian membership in NATO has also led to restrictions on exports of high-tech products to Communist and some other countries on the "COCOM list." More recently, the Special Economic Measures Act[12] contains a general power to make orders and regulations restricting or prohibiting the exportation by Canadians of goods, whether from Canada or anywhere else in the world, to designated foreign states or to persons in such states.

An added problem, which has probably affected Canada more than any other country, has been the extra-territorial application of U.S. legislation. That legislation is intended to prevent the re-export (from Canada and other countries) of products originating in the United States to countries such as Cuba and also prohibits dealings with those countries by foreign subsidiaries of U.S. corporations. The so-called Helms-Burton law carries the process still further, potentially rendering some Canadian (and other) firms with investments in Cuba liable to penalties in U.S. courts; that law has in part been suspended, following strenuous protests from Canada and from the countries of the European Union.

Import Duties

Customs duties on imports have been in existence almost as long as international trade itself. Originally these duties provided an important source of revenue for many countries; indeed, in 1867 customs duties constituted the major part of federal revenue in Canada. The growth of other sources of Government revenue, especially income tax, and the worldwide movement to tariff reduction, have steadily reduced the fiscal importance of import duties; their most important function nowadays is to protect domestic products against competition from cheaper imports.

Two statutes contain most of Canada's import duty legislation: the Customs Act[13] and the Customs Tariff Act.[14] The first deals with the administration of the system by the Canada Customs and Revenue Agency, and provides the basis for regulations that classify products and determine their dutiable value and country of origin. The latter Act sets out the rates of duty (tariff) imposed on each category of products.

The setting of tariffs is no longer determined unilaterally by governments, but is largely regulated by international agreements, such as the GATT and the NAFTA. For goods imported into Canada various preferences are granted, notably for products coming from Commonwealth, Caribbean, and less developed countries and from our NAFTA partners, Mexico and the United States. Determining the origin of goods consequently becomes very important, since goods may be manufactured in one country, from raw material or components originating in another country, and may be routed via a third country.[15]

Import Restrictions

With the decline in the importance of import duties over the years, the existence of **non-tariff barriers** has become more significant as an obstacle to international trade. Countries often impose restrictions on imports; sometimes they are overt, in other instances they are less visible. By Canadian law, some goods (for example, narcotics) may not be imported at all; others may be imported only under licence and subject to particular conditions.

Generally, Canada adopts a relatively liberal policy towards imports from other countries and adheres to the principles established by the GATT. Nevertheless, Canada does impose

non-tariff barriers
national rules, other than import duties, that restrict or prevent the importation of goods

---

12. S.C. 1992, c. 17. (See especially s. 4.)

13. R.S.C. 1985, c. 1 (2nd Supp.).

14. S.C. 1997, c. 36.

15. The dispute between Canada and the United States. regarding the origin of Honda cars manufactured in Canada, using components made in Japan, and sold in the United States, is a good example.

quotas
restrictions on the quantities of goods that may be imported

import **quotas** on certain products,[16] particularly textiles and agricultural products. A wide variety of other statutes impose restrictions on imports in order to protect public health, public safety, the environment, and for other reasons of public policy. Other countries impose their own restrictions and a Canadian manufacturer wishing to export its products must always check to ensure that the products will be allowed to enter the other country.

Frequently, national rules on the marketing of products are just as important as restrictions on importation: there is little point exporting products to a country if they cannot legally be resold there. National health and safety standards and labelling requirements must be complied with, and they are sometimes formulated in such a way that, although ostensibly applicable to domestic and imported products alike, in practice they discriminate against imports.

Dumping and Subsidies

dumping
selling products abroad at prices below those charged on domestic sales

export subsidy
the granting by governments of financial assistance to promote exports

The desire to promote exports, by producers themselves and by their governments, sometimes leads to two types of practice that are generally regarded as unfair—**dumping** and **export subsidies**. Dumping occurs where a firm sells goods abroad at prices lower than those at which similar goods sell in the domestic market. In effect, the firm uses the profits on its domestic sales to subsidize its exports and undercut its competitors. Subsidies occur where the government of a country provides special benefits, financial or otherwise, to its producers in order to assist them to export. Benefits may take a wide variety of forms, such as reduced freight charges, income tax rebates, or unusually favourable credit terms or guarantees.

anti-dumping duties and countervailing duties
special duties imposed on imported products to counter the advantage obtained from dumping or export subsidies

Dumping and export subsidies, by reducing the price of imported goods, may be regarded as a benefit to the consumers of the importing country. Not surprisingly, however, such practices are resented by domestic manufacturers of competing products. Where domestic competition exists, and it appears that material injury has been or is likely to be caused to domestic producers of similar goods, importing countries often impose counter-measures to nullify the benefits of foreign subsidies. Counter-measures take the form of **anti-dumping duties** and **countervailing duties**, designed to increase the cost of imports by the amount of the margin of dumping or of the export subsidy. In Canada such duties are imposed under the Special Import Measures Act. Many Canadian exporters have encountered difficulties with the corresponding measures imposed by the United States.[17] We shall return to this issue later, when considering the impact of the NAFTA.

The International Law of Trade

In theory, national governments are free to adopt whatever measures they choose to regulate imports into, and exports from, their own territories. Of course, in doing so they are aware that other countries may retaliate; if Country *A* imposes restrictions on imports from Country *B*, it can hardly expect Country *B* to accept Country *A*'s exports freely. The international law of trade is based to a large extent upon the principle of reciprocity, an approach generally followed in negotiating agreements between states, sometimes bilaterally and sometimes on a multilateral basis. Canada is a party to many such agreements, two of which—the General Agreement on Tariffs and Trade (GATT) and the North American Free Trade Agreement (NAFTA)—are of particular importance.

The GATT and the World Trade Organization

The General Agreement on Tariffs and Trade (GATT) is the principal instrument that lays down agreed rules for international trade. It came into force on January 1, 1948, with nine original

---

16. See Export and Import Permits Act, R.S.C. 1985, c. E-19. Other restrictions are contained in the Customs Act and the Special Import Measures Act, R.S.C. 1985, c. S-15.

17. For an interesting example, see IPSCO Inc. & IPSCO Steel Inc. v. United States & Lone Star Steel Co., 899 F.2d 1192 (U.S. Court of Appeals), and the commentary by McConnell, (1991), 70 *Can. Bar Rev.* 180.

members, one of which was Canada. By the end of 1994, when the World Trade Organization (WTO) came into existence, a total of 78 countries were full members, and since then the number of members has risen to 134 (in late 1999); others, including most notably China and Russia, have applied for membership.

The original intention, immediately after the Second World War, was to establish an International Trade Organization (ITO), as a part of the United Nations Organization. This object was only partly achieved, since the ITO as such did not come into existence. Instead, a multilateral agreement was negotiated—the GATT. Despite its title, the GATT was far more than just an "agreement." It had its own Secretariat (in Geneva), a Council of Members, and the capacity to establish Tribunals (or "Panels") to adjudicate disputes between member countries. Over the years its scope was extended and its rules augmented by agreements reached in a series of "rounds," the most recent being the so-called "Uruguay Round," commenced in 1986 and finally concluded in December 1993. A new "Millennium Round" was scheduled to begin in Seattle in December 1999. However, the Seattle meeting, which was disrupted by wide-scale protests, failed to reach any agreement even as to the agenda for further talks, and the direction of future developments remains in doubt.

The Uruguay Round proposed the creation of a new organization, the WTO, which came into existence on January 1, 1995, that supersedes the GATT as an organization. The actual GATT agreement, however, remains in effect, together with the various "side agreements."

Probably the most serious shortcoming of the GATT was that it applied only to the international trade in goods, and even then did not apply to most agricultural products or to textiles. The Uruguay Round extended GATT arrangements to include trade in some farm products, textiles, some services, and to the protection of intellectual property rights. It also extended its application to include **trade-related investment measures** (TRIMs), and considerably strengthened the mechanisms available for the settlement of disputes. Subsequently, in 1997, further agreements were negotiated in relation to financial services, information technology, and telecommunications services. However, disagreements among WTO members still remain with respect to a number of sectors, in particular agricultural products, "cultural" products, transportation services, electronic commerce, and environmental and labour standards.

trade-related investment measures
national measures regulating investment that have an impact upon international trade

In addition to providing a forum for negotiations and for the resolution of trade disputes, the most important functions of the GATT and WTO have been the harmonization of customs rules and the progressive reduction of customs duties. In addition, the GATT sets out a code of rules governing international trade and such matters as the transportation of goods, customs procedures, and valuation.

The fundamental principle that underlies the WTO is that of non-discrimination. That principle, in turn, has two elements: first, goods originating from one contracting state should not be treated more or less favourably than goods from another state—that is to say, all should receive **most-favoured-nation (MFN) treatment**;[18] second, goods from other member states should, once the appropriate tariff has been paid, be treated no less favourably than corresponding domestic goods—that is to say, they should receive **national treatment**. In accordance with these basic principles, the WTO generally prohibits quotas and other forms of non-tariff barriers, export subsidies, and, except under strict conditions, the imposition of anti-dumping duties and countervailing duties.

most-favoured-nation treatment
the principle that goods imported from one country should not be treated less favourably than those imported from any other country

national treatment
the principle that goods from another country should not be treated less favourably than domestic goods

The GATT and WTO have had a two-way impact upon Canadian law and the laws of the other contracting states. First, membership imposes a positive duty to enact laws to implement obligations agreed to within the framework of the organization. Thus, for example, Canada has implemented the GATT tariff schedule through the Customs Tariff. Second, there is a negative duty not to apply laws that are contrary to the obligations undertaken as a member.

---

18. By way of exception, reduced rates of duty are applied to many goods coming from less-developed countries.

Consequently, insofar as Canada imposes anti-dumping and countervailing duties, it may do so only within the limits prescribed by the GATT. If Canada is found to be in breach of its WTO obligations, it is required to take the necessary steps to amend its legislation in order to comply.

CASE 33.1

The United States complained that Canada was in violation of the GATT by maintaining in force measures prohibiting or restricting the importation into Canada of certain periodicals by according discriminatory tax treatment to so-called "split-run" periodicals, and by applying favourable postage rates to certain Canadian periodicals. A WTO "Panel" found that the Canadian measures were incompatible with the GATT. As a result, Canada was required to change its legislation.[19]

North American Free Trade

free trade area

a group of countries within which customs duties are eliminated

An exception to the MFN principle, accepted under WTO rules, permits the creation of regional **free trade areas**, within which customs duties may be eliminated entirely. The most important and best known of such areas is the European Union (EU), a customs and economic union of (now) 15 West-European states. In 1988 another free trade area was created, with the signing of the Canada–United States Free Trade Agreement. This agreement, which came into force at the beginning of 1989,[20] provided for the phasing out of tariffs in trade between the two nations over a period of 10 years. Four years later, on December 17, 1992, the leaders of Canada, Mexico, and the United States signed the North American Free Trade Agreement (NAFTA), bringing into existence the world's largest free trade area, with more than 360 million consumers.[21] The NAFTA also contains a clause permitting other countries on the American continent to join, and a Free Trade Area of the Americas (FTAA), is scheduled to be set up by 2005.[22]

Although the NAFTA is based upon essentially the same principles as the WTO, in many respects it goes considerably further in liberalizing trade and investment. All tariffs on goods between the three countries are to be eliminated, in three stages, by the year 2008. The NAFTA streamlines customs procedures and eliminates user fees. Agricultural products are within the scope of the NAFTA, which provides for the progressive elimination of import barriers, export subsidies, and domestic support. Special rules apply to energy and natural resources: export restrictions will generally not be permitted. Services, including financial services, are dealt with in the agreement, with providers of services entitled to receive national treatment (or MFN treatment, if that is better) in the other member countries. Government procurement—the purchase of goods and services by governments—is partly opened to competition. Of major significance are the rules on intellectual property; all principal intellectual property rights—copyright, patents, and trademarks—are recognized and protected and laws are to be harmonized to secure broadly equivalent protection in each country.[23] Finally, the NAFTA is not restricted to trade in goods and services; it also contains provisions relating to investment.

---

19. See United States v. Canada: Certain Measures Concerning Periodicals, WTO panel report (WT/DS31/R), 14 March 1997.

20. It takes effect in Canada by virtue of the Canada–United States Free Trade Agreement Implementation Act, S.C. 1988, c. 65.

21. The NAFTA is implemented in Canada by the North American Free Trade Agreement Implementation Act, S.C. 1993, c. 44, and came into effect on January 1, 1994. The Canada–U.S. agreement is effectively superseded, being suspended during the operation of the NAFTA.

22. Canada has also entered into a free trade agreement with Chile.

23. This has required changes to be made in Canadian laws, such as those governing the compulsory licensing of pharmaceutical patents; see Chapter 22.

FOREIGN INVESTMENT

Forms of Foreign Investment

A distinction is commonly drawn between *portfolio investment* and *direct investment*. Portfolio investment is essentially "passive" investment, normally in government or corporate bonds or listed securities. Foreign direct investment (FDI), by contrast, occurs as part of active business operations. It can be defined as

> …investment made to acquire a lasting interest in an enterprise operating in an economic environment other than that of the investor, the investor's purpose being to have an effective voice in the management of the enterprise.[24]

It may involve the acquisition of property, such as a factory or hotel, or of all or a substantial part of the shares[25] in an existing corporation in the "host" country. FDI may also involve the establishment of an entirely new business ("greenfield" investment), and also includes the reinvestment of earnings in the host country.

Normally, FDI is conducted through the establishment of

- a branch
- a subsidiary
- a joint venture

Where it establishes a **branch**, the investor carries on business in the host country in its own name, the foreign branch being an integral part of its global business, with the assets of the branch owned directly by the foreign investor. By contrast, a **subsidiary** is a separate corporation, incorporated in the host country and owning assets there. The parent investor owns the shares in the subsidiary, but not the assets. The distinction can sometimes be very important; for example, some countries do not allow foreign ownership of land, but permit a local corporation to do so, even if a majority of its shares are held by foreigners.

A **joint venture** is formed by two or more parties, at least one of which is normally from the host country: it can take the form either of a type of partnership (contractual joint venture) or of a jointly owned subsidiary corporation (equity joint venture). Canadian investors overseas generally prefer the subsidiary or equity joint venture forms, principally for tax reasons, and some host countries permit foreign investment only in those forms.

branch
a business carried on by the owner in its own name at a location distinct from its head office

subsidiary
a separate corporation owned or controlled by its "parent" corporation

joint venture
a form of partnership between two or more independent enterprises, or a corporation jointly owned by them

Government Regulation of Foreign Investment

A firm wishing to invest and carry on business in another country must, of course, comply with the laws of that country. For example, a foreign corporation that carries on business in Canada through a branch may be required by the laws of the province where the branch is located to obtain a licence and to register certain information.[26] If it wishes to incorporate a subsidiary in Canada it may be required to have a majority of directors who are resident Canadians.[27] In the same way, a Canadian firm seeking to establish a branch or subsidiary abroad will have to comply with the local laws. Some countries do not permit foreign corporations to conduct business through a branch. Others do not allow foreigners to own a majority of the shares in a domestic

---

24. United Nations, *World Investment Directory 1992,* New York: UNCTC, 1992.

25. To be classified as direct, rather than portfolio, investment the acquisition must normally be of at least 10 percent of the shares of the host country corporation.

26. See, in Ontario, Corporations Information Act, R.S.O. 1990, c. C.39 and Extra-Provincial Corporations Act, R.S.O. 1990, c. E.27.

27. See, for example, Canada Business Corporations Act, R.S.C. 1985, c. C-44, s. 105(3).

corporation, thus making a joint venture (with a local partner) the only feasible method of carrying on business.

Many countries have a somewhat contradictory attitude towards foreign investment. On the one hand, they see foreign investment as desirable because it brings much-needed capital into the economy, creates employment, opens up export markets, and introduces modern technology and management skills. On the other hand, they regard it with suspicion as a form of economic imperialism, likely to cause social and environmental damage, to stifle the development of local business, and to exert undue political influence. Consequently they seek both to attract foreign investment and to control it, by a mixture of incentives and restrictions. They offer inducements such as tax holidays, but at the same time exclude foreign investors from participating in certain activities (such as finance, communications, and transportation), forbid them to own real estate, or require them to meet specific conditions with regard to matters such as creating jobs or utilizing domestic raw materials.

Like many other countries, Canada subjects certain types of inward direct investment to review and to prior general authorization. Prior to 1985, Canada took a rather restrictive attitude to foreign investment, reflecting concern over the high level of foreign ownership of Canadian industry and resources. The Foreign Investment Review Agency (FIRA) could refuse to authorize investment it considered not to be in the national interest, or it could attach conditions to an investment. In 1985, FIRA was replaced by a new agency, Investment Canada[28] which, although it retains most of the powers of FIRA, has adopted a more positive approach to the promotion of foreign investment. As a general rule, Investment Canada does not review the establishment of a new business, requiring only that it be notified. The acquisition of larger existing Canadian businesses requires authorization,[29] and must be "of significant benefit to Canada"; in practice, authorization is almost always granted. In certain cases, the approval of provincial governments and of other bodies may also be required; for example, the proposed 1999 takeover of MacMillan-Bloedel by the U.S. company, Weyerhaeuser, required the approval of the British Columbia and Ontario governments, the Canadian Competition Bureau, the Canadian Ministry for International Trade, and Investment Canada, as well as requiring court approval and the support of two-thirds of the MacMillan-Bloedel shareholders.

A more restrictive approach to foreign investment is taken in some sectors. All acquisitions or investments to establish a new business in cultural sectors such as book publishing and film making are subject to review, regardless of the amount involved. A variety of federal, and in some cases provincial, statutes restrict foreign ownership of banking and financial services, insurance, transport undertakings, fishing and fish processing, oil, gas, and uranium. The existence of public monopolies, such as the post office, electricity, and liquor sales, further restricts the potential for foreign investment.

Foreign Investment and International Law

As we noted in our discussion of foreign trade, prior to the conclusion of the Uruguay Round the GATT applied only to the international trade in goods and consequently had no general application to foreign investment. However, certain types of investment rules can clearly have an impact upon trade. If, in granting approval to a foreign investment, a host country attaches conditions (usually called **performance requirements**), for example, that the investor must use local raw materials or components, or that it must export a stipulated percentage of its total production, those conditions will interfere with the investor's freedom to trade. The legality of such trade-related investment measures (TRIMs) was considered by a Panel of the GATT, in a complaint

performance requirements
conditions attached by the host country in granting approval to a foreign investment

---

28. Investment Canada Act, S.C. 1985, c. 20.

29. Originally, the acquisition of businesses with assets of more than $5 million was subject to review. For NAFTA members this was raised to $150 million, and this was extended to WTO members in 1995. The review threshold is now determined by a formula and, in 1998, stood at $179 million.

referred to it in 1982.[30] The United States, at the request of a number of American corporations that had invested in Canada, complained that conditions imposed by FIRA, requiring the investors to buy components and materials from local Canadian sources, was in effect imposing restrictions on the importation of similar goods. The Panel upheld the complaint, ruling against Canada.

Probably the greatest fear of a potential foreign investor is that its assets might be expropriated by the host country government, or nationalized without adequate compensation. Expropriation has been one of the more controversial issues in international law; some industrialized countries would like to see expropriation entirely prohibited, whereas many developing countries consider the power to nationalize to be essential to their economic development. The United Nations has tended towards the latter position, and has declared that every state has the right to nationalize, expropriate, or transfer ownership of foreign-owned property, but that appropriate compensation must be paid.[31]

The 1985 Convention establishing the Multilateral Investment Guarantee Agency (MIGA), under the auspices of the World Bank, provides some protection against the consequences of expropriation, but probably of greater importance are the numerous **bilateral investment protection treaties** entered into between capital-importing and capital-exporting countries. These treaties usually provide that foreign investment should receive national treatment, that is, it should be treated no less favourably than a comparable domestic enterprise would be, that it should be given full legal protection and be protected against arbitrary or discriminatory measures that interfere with its management and operation, and that investors should have the right to repatriate their capital and profits. In addition, it is usual to provide that a host country may not expropriate or nationalize the property of an investor from the other country "except for a public purpose, under due process of law, in a non-discriminatory manner," and that any such expropriation "must be accompanied by prompt, adequate and effective compensation."[32]

The NAFTA significantly relaxes the general rules of the Investment Canada Act as they apply to Mexican and U.S. investment in Canada. Performance requirements, regarding such matters as exporting or local sourcing of goods or services, are not permitted and, as a general principle, investors are entitled to national treatment, or to MFN treatment if that is better.[33] Canadian investment in Mexico and in the United States enjoys similar privileges and protection.

Finally, a brief mention should be made of the proposed Multilateral Agreement on Investment (MAI). The MAI was proposed in 1996 by the Organization for Economic Cooperation and Development (OECD), an organization comprising 29 developed countries, of which Canada is a member. The MAI was intended to eliminate most restrictions on foreign investment and most performance requirements, to require that national treatment be accorded to investors, to provide protection from expropriation, and to establish adequate procedures for resolving disputes. Although supported in principle by the Canadian government, the MAI aroused strong opposition among some sections of the Canadian population, principally because it was feared that it would prevent Canada from protecting its cultural industries. By early 1999 it had become clear that the draft agreement would not secure the necessary approval of the member countries, and the proposal was shelved—at least temporarily. There remains a possibility that the proposal will be revived, perhaps in modified form, and will be on the agenda of the next WTO "round" of negotiations.

bilateral investment protection treaty
a treaty entered into between two countries, whereby each country undertakes to protect investors from the other country and to give them certain rights

---

30. United States v. Canada: Administration of the Foreign Investment Review Act, report of February 7, 1984 (Case No.108, GATT Doc.L/5308).

31. United Nations Charter of Economic Rights and Duties of States, adopted December 12, 1974. Canada abstained from voting on that proposition.

32. See, for example, Art. VI of the "Agreement between the Government of Canada and the Government of the Republic of Poland for the Promotion and Reciprocal Protection of Investments," signed in Warsaw on April 6, 1990 (Canada Treaty Series 1990, No. 43).

33. Sometimes a country may impose restrictions upon its own investors that do not apply to foreign investors: in such a case, MFN treatment may be more favourable than national treatment.

CONTEMPORARY
ISSUE

Pros and Cons of FDI

A lively debate has been going on in Canada in recent years over "globalization" and foreign investment in Canada, sparked by such events as the proposed MAI, the magazine war, and the spate of takeovers and proposed takeovers of major Canadian firms. The following press extracts illustrate two sides of the debate.

Abetted by a cheap Canadian dollar, the new world order of global corporations and freer trade is dictating a quiet revolution in the ownership of corporate Canada....It is no secret, as Industry Canada's Web pages make clear, that Canada is one of the world's leading advocates of free trade and unfettered capital movements, subject to international rules. Helping explain this shift away from traditional protectionism is the fact that by 1997 Canadians owned more direct investments abroad ($194 billion) than foreigners did here ($188 billion).

...Elsewhere, the spate of changes is provoking regret and anxiety. "The ownership restrictions are being ripped asunder," laments Peter Bleyer of the Council of Canadians, last bastion of grassroots Canadian economic nationalism. The upper limits on foreign ownership seem to go up every time somebody challenges them, says Bleyer. The impulse to loosen controls comes not just from foreign corporations, but also from Canadians in protected positions who see in the new climate a cash windfall. This, Bleyer warns, is a betrayal of Canadian tradition and history. The country, after all, was built on large elements of regulated monopoly, state financing and public enterprise—notably Hudson's Bay Co., Canadian Pacific Railway, Canadian National Railway, Air Canada, the Canadian Broadcasting Corp., Ontario Hydro and Hydro Quebec, and more....The old rationale for economic nationalism—keeping key investment decisions, good managerial jobs, and control of research and development in Canadian hands, on Canadian soil, and subject to Canadian government regulation—remains valid, Bleyer insists.

Source: John Deverell, "For Sale: Canada's Industry Policies Analysis," *Toronto Star,* August 21, 1999.

Economic nationalists such as Maude Barlow of the Council of Canadians remain fearful about the possible negative consequences of increased foreign business investment in Canada. They shouldn't. Yet another study—this one commissioned by the government—concludes there is not much to fret about.

Canadian subsidiaries of foreign multinationals usually bring technology transfers that lead to innovation and productivity gains here. Their managements generally have a reasonable amount of autonomy. Even in strategic areas such as research and development, the parent companies are now allowing more independent decision-making. The foreign-owned subsidiaries tend to spend a higher proportion of revenues on R&D than do their Canadian-owned counterparts. They are more likely to introduce new products and processes. Typically, their R&D focuses on developing products for the global, rather than domestic market. Their parents encourage them to go after international opportunities. Many are significant exporters. In short, they are a far cry from the old, inward-looking 'branch-plant' style of operations that characterized foreign ownership of businesses in Canada a few decades ago.

Source: Neville Nankivell, "They're not 'branch plants' any more," *National Post,* September 30, 1999, p. C-7.

Questions to Consider

1. Is there a case for government controls and restrictions on foreign investment in Canada?

2. Are there any particular sectors of the economy in which foreign investment should be restricted?

THE RESOLUTION OF INTERNATIONAL BUSINESS DISPUTES

Like any other business activities, foreign trade and foreign investment can give rise to disputes. These may be based in private law, as for example between parties to an international contract for the sale of goods. Or disputes may be primarily about public or administrative law, between governments on the one hand and importers or investors on the other. In addition, questions of public international law may arise where it is alleged that one state is in breach of its treaty obligations to another. An aggrieved party may bring such a dispute before a national court, an arbitrator, or some form of international tribunal.

Judicial Proceedings

In principle, Canadian courts, and those of most other countries, are open to the world, in the sense that one need not be a Canadian citizen or resident in order to be able to sue or be sued in them. Nevertheless, a number of problems may arise in disputes with an international element.

ILLUSTRATION 33.2

A Canadian manufacturer contracts to sell electrical equipment to a Korean construction company, delivery to be made at a construction site in Saudi Arabia. The price is stated to be payable in Swiss Francs. The manufacturer ships the equipment to Saudi Arabia but the Korean company refuses to take delivery, claiming that the equipment does not meet the contract specifications.

The Canadian firm wishes to sue for the price; perhaps the Korean party will claim damages. But in which country should the action be brought? In Canada, Korea, Saudi Arabia, Switzerland, or perhaps somewhere entirely different? What if the contract has stipulated that it is governed by the laws of New York State? In determining these questions, a number of issues must be considered.

Jurisdiction

The question whether or not a court will consent to hear an action is essentially one for the court itself to decide. Courts do not encourage "forum shopping"—that is, allowing a plaintiff to seek out a jurisdiction most likely to view its claim favourably. Courts insist that the issue must have some "connecting factor" with the country in which a party seeks to bring the action. The grounds upon which the courts will exercise jurisdiction vary from country to country, and are not even identical in each province within Canada. As a general rule, courts of a country or province normally consider that they are entitled to assert jurisdiction over extra-territorial defendants if

- a tort was committed there
- a contract was to be performed there
- damage from a tort or breach of contract was sustained there
- the dispute concerned property or goods situated there
- the activities complained of were conducted there
- the contract stipulated that it should be governed by the laws of the country or province
- the parties to a contract specified that those courts should have jurisdiction in the event of a dispute

Additionally, there is a general discretion to exercise jurisdiction where there is some other "real and substantial connection" with the country or province. However, this broad jurisdiction is limited in two ways. The court may decline jurisdiction, even though it might exercise it on one of the above grounds, if it considers that there is some other forum that is more appropriate or is more closely connected to the matter in dispute—the *forum non conveniens* principle. Or the court may decline jurisdiction if it considers that the courts of other provinces or states concerned might refuse to enforce its judgment.

Standing

Although the parties need not be residents or citizens of a country in order to have access to its courts, some restrictions may apply. For example, a foreign corporation that has not been licensed or registered in Canada cannot be a plaintiff in Canadian courts. A further problem arises where the defendant is not present, or does not have an establishment within the jurisdiction and cannot be served with the writ or originating process. Although courts may give leave to serve the process outside the jurisdiction, they are generally reluctant to try actions against absent defendants unless there is a very strong connection between the cause of action and the country concerned.

Choice of Law

We have already discussed the question of the proper law of the contract. It is important to recall that it is not unusual, in international trade disputes, for the courts of one country to apply the law of another. Thus, in our illustration, if the contract had stipulated that the law of New York was to apply, that clause might in itself be adequate reason for a Canadian court to decline jurisdiction to a Canadian plaintiff. Even so it might be possible for the Korean party to sue a Canadian defendant in a Canadian court for damages for non-performance, in which case the court would determine the rights of the parties according to New York law.

Enforcement of Foreign Judgments

Even if a plaintiff persuades a court to accept jurisdiction in a dispute of an international nature and succeeds in obtaining a judgment against the defendant, the matter does not necessarily end there. If the defendant has assets within the jurisdiction, judgment may be levied against those assets by court order. But, to return to our example (in Illustration 33.2), a Canadian judgment against the Korean contractor, or a Korean judgment against the Canadian manufacturer, might be of little value if the losing party has no assets in the country where judgment is granted.

The question then arises whether a Korean judgment may be enforced in Canada, and vice-versa. Unfortunately, this is a complex legal issue, often without a clear answer. At common law a local judgment, provided it is for a sum of money, is considered to be a debt, and a creditor can ask a Canadian court to enforce payment.[34] But a foreign judgment debt will normally only be recognized so long as the foreign court was exercising proper jurisdiction according to the standards of the local courts (the "forum"). Ordinarily, the standards require that: there was a "real and substantial connection" between the substance of the action and the country in which judgment was granted; the judgment was not obtained by fraud; and it does not offend against natural justice or public policy.[35]

---

34. Most Canadian provinces have adopted legislation providing for the enforcement of foreign judgments on a reciprocal basis. However, only a few reciprocal agreements with other countries have been entered into, the ones with the United Kingdom being the most important; see, for example, Reciprocal Enforcement of Judgments (U.K.) Act, R.S.O. 1990, c. R.6.

35. Morguard Investments Ltd. v. de Savoye (1990), 76 D.L.R. (4th) 256. That case concerned the recognition by a British Columbia court of an Alberta judgment. However, the principles enunciated by the Supreme Court of Canada have subsequently been applied to judgments by foreign courts.

CASE 33.2

Shore Boat Builders Ltd., a corporation incorporated in British Columbia, built a boat for Moses, a fisherman residing in Alaska. Moses later brought an action in an Alaska court, alleging that the boat was defective in a number of respects and claiming damages for breach of warranty. Shore considered that they had a good defence to the action, since Moses had himself carried out certain modifications to the boat. However, on the advice of their lawyer, Shore did not enter an appearance in the Alaska proceedings. In default, judgment was given against Shore for damages of $58 000.

Moses then brought an action in British Columbia, claiming enforcement of the Alaska judgment. The British Columbia Court of Appeal held that the Alaska default judgment was enforceable.

Shore had sold their product directly to an Alaska client; they therefore assumed the burden of defending their product in Alaska and could reasonably assume that they might be sued in Alaska in respect of that product. Alaska was the place where the loss was suffered and that was entitled to exercise jurisdiction.[36]

Commercial Arbitration

The difficulties and uncertainties surrounding international litigation have increasingly led the parties in international commercial contracts to make express provision for binding arbitration arranged privately, outside the court system. Rather than risk a dispute being heard before the "home" court of the other party, parties often consider it preferable to provide for a hearing before a "neutral" body, quite possibly in a third country. The agreement sometimes names one or more persons to act as arbitrator, but more commonly it nominates an "institutional" arbitrator.

Over the years a number of specialist institutions have been established, the International Chamber of Commerce being probably the best known. Arbitration associations exist in major commercial centres such as London, New York, and Hong Kong, and countries such as Sweden and Switzerland are also popular arbitration venues, because of their long-standing traditions of neutrality. In Canada, arbitration centres exist in Quebec City and Vancouver.

One major advantage of arbitration, as opposed to litigation, is that the arbitrators normally have greater experience of international commerce than one would expect to find among judges of the regular courts. Other advantages are the non-public nature and confidentiality of the proceedings, especially important where the dispute concerns trade secrets, and usually costs are lower and decisions are speedier. Most modern commercial arbitration employs standard procedures, such as those adopted in the UNCITRAL model, that are generally better adapted to international disputes than are regular court procedures.

Perhaps the greatest advantage of commercial arbitration, as opposed to litigation, lies in the relative ease with which awards may be enforced. Unlike litigation, arbitration is consensual: the parties to the original contract have agreed to submit any dispute to arbitration and to abide by the award. As a result, there is no valid reason for a court to refuse to enforce such an award should one of the parties fail to comply with it. In the past decade Canada has enacted legislation, at both the federal and provincial levels, to implement the 1958 United Nations Convention on the Recognition and Enforcement of Foreign Arbitral Awards and to adopt the 1985 UNCITRAL Model Law on International Commercial Arbitration.[37]

---

36. Moses v. Shore Boat Builders Ltd. (1993), 106 D.L.R. (4th) 654; contrast Brower v. Sunview Solariums Ltd. (1998), 161 D.L.R. (4th) 575.

37. Commercial Arbitration Act, R.S.C. 1985, c. 17 (2nd Supp.); United Nations Foreign Arbitral Awards Convention Act, R.S.C. 1985, c. 16 (2nd Supp.); International Commercial Arbitration Act: R.S.B.C. 1996, c. 233; R.S.O. 1990, c. I.9.

Inter-Nation Disputes

Generally, governments cannot be compelled to appear as defendants before the courts of another country, or to submit to arbitration. An individual or corporation that wishes to challenge the actions or decisions of a government—for example, the refusal of an import licence or the expropriation of an investment—may normally do so only in the courts of that country.

However, where a complainant alleges that a state is in breach of a treaty obligation owed to one or more other states, a number of procedures exist for the resolution of the dispute. For example, bilateral investment protection treaties usually provide that the parties agree to submit to binding arbitration any dispute concerning the expropriation of assets or payment of proper compensation, such arbitration to be conducted by the International Centre for the Settlement of Investment Disputes (ICSID), or according to the UNCITRAL rules.[38] Most important from a Canadian perspective are the procedures provided for in the WTO and the NAFTA.

The GATT and WTO

From its inception in 1948, the GATT contained a mechanism for the resolution of disputes between states that are parties to the agreement. The mechanism was revised and strengthened when the WTO was created in 1995.

We should note that only states that are contracting parties may raise a complaint against another contracting party. Private persons have no standing as such, though an individual or firm that considers it has been injured by an action of a foreign government in violation of the GATT may request its own government to bring proceedings.

The WTO contains two types of proceedings for the settlement of disputes. There is provision for consultation between the parties and, if necessary, a conciliation procedure—essentially a diplomatic solution. Alternatively, a contracting state that considers that the proper operation of the rules is being "nullified or impaired" by the actions of another contracting state may request the WTO Council to appoint a "Panel" to adjudicate the dispute. After hearing the submissions of the parties, the panel makes "recommendations," which may require an offending state to remove a provision of law or an administrative practice found to be contrary to the rules or, in certain cases, to compensate an injured party. Under the new WTO procedures, a panel decision may be appealed to a special appellate panel.

Since 1948, over 100 cases have been submitted to GATT or WTO panels, more than 90 percent of those involving four parties—Canada, the European Union, Japan, and the United States. Not surprisingly, considering the volume of trade between the two countries, disputes between Canada and the United States have been common; among the more notable are those by the United States in respect of Canadian countervailing duties on grain corn and in respect of provincial rules on the marketing of alcoholic beverages, and by Canada against the United States in respect of countervailing duties on Canadian pork and on softwood lumber. The Canada–U.S. dispute concerning the Canadian treatment of "split-run" American magazines has already been mentioned and, as we saw, the adverse finding of the panel has led to changes in the Canadian legislation. Other recent high-profile proceedings have been those brought against Canada by Brazil (subsidies to the aerospace industry) and by the European Union and Japan (discriminatory tariffs on car imports under the "Autopact"). In return, Canada and the United States obtained a panel ruling in their favour in respect of a European Union ban on hormone-treated beef.

The NAFTA

The NAFTA contains dispute resolution provisions that are rather similar to those of the WTO, though the NAFTA may have a number of advantages, in particular more effective implemen-

---

38. See, for example, the Canada-Poland Treaty, *supra*, n. 32, Art. IX.

tation. When a dispute arises under both the NAFTA and the WTO, the complainant may choose under which set of procedures it should be settled.[39]

In the event of a dispute, Chapter 20 of the NAFTA[40] provides for the holding of consultations at the request of either party. Should no mutually satisfactory agreement be reached, the dispute is then referred to a Free Trade Commission. If in turn the Commission fails to find an acceptable solution, either party may request the Commission to appoint an Arbitral Panel. A panel is composed of five members, two of whom are appointed by each of the parties from lists of experts in trade law or practice, with a chairperson selected by agreement or by lot. The panel hears the submissions of the parties and produces a report, published by the Commission. The parties must implement the report within 30 days; if a party fails to do so, an aggrieved party may withdraw benefits in retaliation. An appeal from a panel decision lies to an Extraordinary Challenge Committee.

Chapter 19 of the NAFTA, which is based upon the chapter of the same number in the Canada–United States Agreement, contains separate provisions for the resolution of disputes concerning the imposition of anti-dumping and countervailing duties; such disputes occur frequently and are often more important, at least in financial terms, than the general disputes that are dealt with under Chapter 20. In particular, U.S. countervailing duties are widely perceived as constituting the most serious threat to Canadian exports.

Currently, each country applies its own anti-dumping and countervail laws, though in the longer term the parties are required to establish common rules on subsidies and on anti-competitive practices such as dumping. Under the NAFTA, the parties are entitled to ensure that the national laws are correctly applied. The nature of a complaint, consequently, is that the country imposing the anti-dumping or countervailing duty has incorrectly, or improperly, applied its own law. The complaint procedure has already been used on a number of occasions, most controversially in the softwood lumber case, in which a complaint by Canada against U.S. countervailing duties was upheld by the panel, whose decision was in turn upheld on appeal.[41]

In addition to Chapters 19 and 20, which specifically relate to dispute resolution, Chapter 11, which deals with foreign investment, appears to provide a means whereby Canadian, Mexican, and U.S. firms that invest in another NAFTA country may sue the host government directly for infringement of the rights guaranteed by the Agreement. The investor rights were included in the NAFTA primarily to protect firms from illegal expropriation by a government. However, several firms have used, or threatened to use, Chapter 11 to sue governments when their foreign operations have been affected by a government decision. In one widely reported case, a U.S. corporation received $20 million from the Canadian government in settlement of a claim resulting from Ottawa's ban on the use in Canada of the gasoline additive, MMT. And a Canadian firm has claimed that an award of damages against it by a Mississippi jury, of more than $500 million, constitutes a form of expropriation and is contrary to Chapter 11. At the end of 1999, a number of other claims were pending. What does seem certain is that the number of such disputes will increase in the 21st century.

QUESTIONS FOR REVIEW

1. Distinguish between foreign trade and foreign investment.

2. Distinguish between public international law and private international law.

---

39. There are a few exceptions, where the NAFTA procedures must be used.

40. Chapter 20 is the successor of Chapter 18 of the Canada–U.S. Free Trade Agreement. Among disputes resolved under that chapter are those against Canada, in respect of rules requiring the landing in Canada of West Coast salmon caught by U.S. fishing boats, and against the United States concerning the minimum size requirements for importation of lobsters.

41. Panel decision USA-92-1904-01 (1992); Committee decision ECC-94-1904-01 (1994).

3. What is meant by the "proper law of the contract"?

4. What are "Incoterms"? Give examples.

5. What documentation is usually involved in an international sale of goods?

6. What is the purpose of foreign exchange risk management?

7. What is "countertrade"?

8. How can services be "exported"?

9. In what ways do governments attempt to promote exports? Are export subsidies permissible?

10. What is meant by "non-tariff barriers"? Give examples.

11. What is "dumping"?

12. What are countervailing duties?

13. What is the relationship between the GATT and the WTO?

14. What are "TRIMs"?

15. Distinguish between most-favoured-nation treatment and national treatment.

16. Distinguish between portfolio investment and direct investment.

17. Distinguish between (a) a branch; (b) a subsidiary; and (c) a joint venture.

18. What are "performance requirements"?

19. What purposes are normally served by bilateral investment protection treaties?

20. What is "forum shopping"? Why is it considered objectionable?

21. What are the principal advantages of commercial arbitration as opposed to litigation?

22. How are disputes resolved within the WTO? and in NAFTA?

CASES AND PROBLEMS

1 ABC Inc., a manufacturing company located in Hamilton, Ontario, agrees to sell machine tools to a customer in Belgium. The contract price is stated to be "$50 000, FOB the *S.S. Lusitania* in Halifax, Nova Scotia." ABC Inc. arranges for the goods to be shipped from its factory and loaded on the *Lusitania* by Titanic Transporters Ltd., an Ontario shipper. ABC Inc. does not insure the goods, believing that Titanic's insurance provides adequate coverage.

(a) What, if any, will be the liability of ABC Inc. if the goods are

1. damaged in a road accident, caused by the negligence of Titanic's driver, en route to Halifax?

2. damaged due to the negligence of a crane operator while being loaded onto the *Lusitania*?

3. lost at sea in mid-Atlantic?

(b) What difference would it make if the price had been stated "CIF Antwerp"?

2 XYZ Ltd., a large Canadian mining corporation, entered into an agreement three years ago with the government of the Republic of Utopia to develop the mining and processing of the rich zinc deposits in that country. A joint-venture corporation,

Cantopia Ltd., was established (under the law of Utopia), in which XYZ held 49 percent of the shares and the government of Utopia held the remainder. XYZ invested $25 million in the project, in the form of machinery, technology, and capital to finance the operation of mines and smelters; the Utopian government's contribution to the project took the form of a lease, at nominal rent, of a large tract of land where valuable deposits had been discovered. It was agreed that Cantopia would mine the zinc, process it, and export it through XYZ's worldwide marketing organization. Profits would be shared in the ratio 49/51 percent.

Recently, following a military coup, the new government of Utopia enacted a law requiring all mining enterprises to sell their total output to the newly established National Resources Corporation, wholly owned by the Utopian government, at prices to be established by a government agency. Under the prices established for zinc, it has become impossible for Cantopia to operate at a profit.

Are there any steps that XYZ can take to protect its investment?

3 Canadian production of widgets is almost entirely in the hands of three corporations—Altawidge Ltd., Ontwidge Ltd., and Scotiawidge Ltd. All three corporations export a substantial volume of their products to the United States.

Two years ago, as a result of increased competition from Malaysian widget producers, two of the Canadian corporations—Ontwidge and Scotiawidge—experienced financial difficulties. As a result, the governments of Ontario and Nova Scotia stepped in to help save the widget industry. They provided long-term, low-interest loans to the corporations and granted other benefits, such as research grants and exemption from property taxes. By contrast, Altawidge has received no government support, but has been able to compete with its rivals because its operations are more advanced technologically.

Recently, there have been complaints from widget producers in the United States that they have lost a substantial share of the American market to imports from Canada and Malaysia. They allege that widget production in both countries is heavily subsidized. As a result of these complaints, the U.S. Department of Commerce has introduced a countervailing duty of 17 cents for each widget imported from Canada. The effect of the duty is to make Canadian widgets more expensive in the United States than domestically produced widgets.

Altawidge has in turn complained that, whether or not the Nova Scotia and Ontario producers receive an improper subsidy, their own products enjoy no such benefit and should not be subjected to the duty.

Discuss the issues raised and suggest what steps might be taken to resolve the dispute.

4 Maxrevs Ltd. is a corporation incorporated in Manitoba, which manufactures small gasoline-powered motors for use in a variety of power tools. It sells its motors directly to tool manufacturers throughout North America, and also sells in substantial quantities to wholesale dealers in motor parts and components. One of those dealers supplied a number of Maxrevs motors to "weedeater" manufacturer Snapper Inc., a corporation incorporated in Michigan.

Gonzalez, a resident of Texas, purchased a Snapper weedeater and subsequently sustained a severe injury to his leg and hand when the tool malfunctioned. He brought an action in a Texas court against both Snapper and Maxrevs. Although Maxrevs was served with notice of the proceedings, it did not enter an appearance and did not defend the action.

The Texas court found that the connection between the motor and the revolving blade was defective, and held Snapper liable. It also found that Maxrevs had been negligent in failing to provide adequate instructions for installation of their motors in tools of that kind and awarded damages against Maxrevs amounting to US$5 million.

Gonzalez has now filed a claim in the Manitoba court to enforce his judgment against Maxrevs. Is it likely that the Manitoba court will enforce the judgment?

ELECTRONIC COMMERCE

The Growing Importance of Electronic Commerce

What Is E-commerce?

Establishing an Online Business

E-commerce and the Law

Regulating E-commerce

International Aspects of E-commerce

Electronic commerce (e-commerce) is the most rapidly growing sector of the economy. Increasingly, business is being conducted through the Internet and through other electronic means. This creates problems of applying existing legal rules and principles to new situations and raises some entirely new legal issues. In this chapter we examine such questions as:

- what is e-commerce?

- how are contracts made on the Internet?

- what law governs those contracts?

- how can consumers of e-products be protected?

- how do trademark and copyright laws apply to the Internet?

- what other legal problems are raised by e-commerce?

- which courts have jurisdiction in Internet disputes?

- how can, or should, e-commerce be regulated by government?

- to what extent is international cooperation necessary in order to devise an effective legal framework for e-commerce?

---

e-commerce
the use of computer networks to facilitate transactions involving the production, distribution, sale, and delivery of goods and services in the marketplace

Internet
the interconnected logical networks that link millions of computers worldwide

THE GROWING IMPORTANCE OF ELECTRONIC COMMERCE

Electronic commerce, often referred to simply as **e-commerce**, is the fastest growing sector of the economy, at least in developed countries such as Canada. Until 1995, e-commerce was almost non-existent. It was in that year that firms such as Amazon, Cisco, and Dell first began to use the **Internet** extensively for commercial transactions. By 1997, e-commerce had grown into a US$26 billion business (about 80 percent of it in the United States), and projections are that it will grow to $330 billion in 2001–3 and to $1 trillion by 2003–5.[1] Of this, approximately 80 percent is business-to-business transactions, but electronic retailing is also growing rapidly and is predicted to reach $100 billion by the year 2003. In Canada, business-to-business transactions have grown from $1.5 billion in 1997 to almost $10 billion in 1999, and consumer transactions have grown from $270 million to $1.15 billion over the same period.

The growth of e-commerce is closely linked to the increasing use of the Internet. According to one report, "the Internet has done for electronic commerce what Henry Ford did for the automobile—converted a luxury for the few into a relatively simple and inexpensive device for the many."[2] The evolution of the Internet can be traced back to around 1969, when it was developed in the United States principally for military purposes (and then called the "Arpanet"). The Internet really took off in the 1990s, with the development of the World Wide Web and of various browsers, enabling users to "surf the Net." From 1988 to 1994, the number of Internet Web sites grew from virtually zero to three million; by the end of 1996, there were 16 million. Most are operated by private individuals or groups, but by late 1997 it was estimated that there were about 250 000 commercial Web sites, almost all of them less than one year old, and the commercial (.com) category is the fastest growing segment of the Internet.[3]

This rapid growth has been promoted by a number of factors:

- Technical advances have greatly increased the speed of transmission and have increased the potential of the Internet to deliver goods and services online.
- The cost of both computer hardware and Internet access has been falling steadily.
- The telecommunications sector has been liberalized and deregulated in many countries.

WHAT IS E-COMMERCE?

Electronic commerce can be broadly defined as "the delivery of information, products, services, or payments by telephone, computer, or other automated media."[4] It encompasses a number of different types of commercial activity, with the common feature that all make use of the Internet or similar methods of communication.

The Internet

The key to the technological revolution introduced by the Internet is the process known as "digitization"—the process of converting information into a sequence of numbers. The information may take the form of writing, pictures or diagrams, speech or music. Once converted, the information can be sent instantaneously anywhere in the world and can be converted back by the recipient into its original form. In order to transmit this information from one person to another requires both a physical and a "logical" infrastructure. The physical infrastructure requires network access equipment, usually a personal computer, connected to an Internet service provider (ISP), which in turn is connected to other ISPs through the telecommunications network. The logical infrastructure is often compared to a highway code that regulates the movement of traffic on the "information superhighway," allowing the different ISP networks, and their customers, to communicate with each other.

The Internet has brought about a fundamental change in the way that information can be communicated and has begun to effect a similar change in the way that business is conducted.

---

1. See *Consumer Quarterly*, Vol. 3, No. 3, November 1998, available online at **strategis.ic.gc.ca/SSG/ca01114e.html**.
2. "The Economic and Social Impacts of Electronic Commerce: Preliminary Findings and Research Agenda" (Paris, 1998, OECD), p. 10, available online at **www.oecd.org/subject/e_commerce/summary.htm**.
3. See Wyckoff, "Imagining the Impact of Electronic Commerce," *OECD Observer*, No. 208, October/November 1997.
4. "Electronic Commerce and Canada's Tax Administration: A Report to the Minister of National Revenue from the Minister's Advisory Committee on Electronic Commerce," Ottawa, April 1998.

Traditionally, business has been conducted by way of a variety of physical exchanges. Deals were made through face-to-face meetings; information communicated in "hard copy"; paper invoices and bills exchanged; and payments made in cash or by cheque. All of this is gradually being replaced by the instantaneous movement of "bits" that are "colorless, sizeless, and weightless."[5]

Electronic Retailing

The most obvious form of e-commerce is retailing through the Internet. Electronic retailing can be divided into three categories:

1. supplies of tangible goods
2. supplies of "electronic goods"
3. supplies of services

The purchase and sale of tangible goods via the Internet differs very little from conventional mail-order business, except in terms of speed and efficiency. The customer has access to an online catalogue, selects the desired item (usually by clicking on an icon), and transmits the order to the dealer. The item, whether it be a book, CD, or lawnmower, is then delivered in one of the conventional ways. Thus, only one part of the transaction can really be described as "electronic."

By contrast, what may be described as "electronic" goods are also delivered through the Internet. Instead of purchasing shrink-wrapped software, the customer can have the software transmitted through the Internet and download it onto his or her computer. Similarly, recorded music can be transmitted in this way, or the customer may subscribe to an electronic magazine or newspaper and receive it through the Internet rather than through the mailbox. Services are supplied in the same manner: airline and theatre tickets may be purchased online, as can insurance, and banking and securities transactions are increasingly being done electronically.

FIGURE 34.1
Electronic Retailing

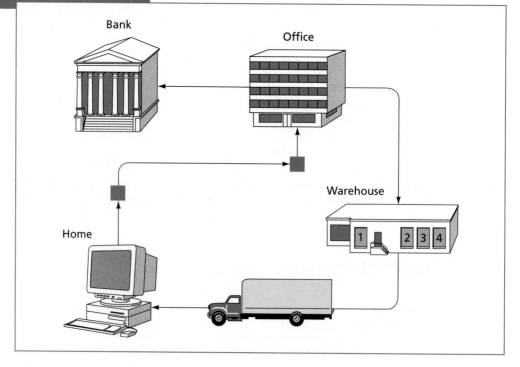

---

5. Abrams and Doernberg, "How Electronic Commerce Works" (1997), 14 *Tax Notes International*, at 1573.

Business-to-Business Transactions

Although consumer sales are the most obvious form of e-commerce, business-to-business transactions actually account for about 80 percent of all e-commerce and are growing the most rapidly. Much of this activity takes place through intra-firm activities—between branches of the same company or between related companies in a multinational group—often making use of private "intranets."

Within this sector, services account for more than half of the activities. Accounting firms, law firms, and other professional service providers are using the Internet as another means of selling their services to clients. Businesses are using the Internet to provide technical support and follow-up services to purchasers of their products. There are even firms that establish offshore corporations or set up offshore bank accounts for customers, all done electronically. The Internet is used for sourcing components and materials and for monitoring inventories or deliveries of goods to regular customers.

Electronic Transfer of Funds

As we have already seen, goods and services can be ordered and, in many cases, delivered electronically. A third element of e-commerce is the electronic transfer of funds—goods and services can be paid for electronically rather than by cash or cheque. "Netbanking" allows bank customers 24-hour access to their accounts, with the ability to transfer funds into and out of the account, to pay bills, and to obtain details of the account. "Smart cards" are set to replace today's plastic credit and debit cards, using an embedded integrated circuit chip in place of the conventional magnetic "swipe-strip," and able to store vast amounts of information. With a smart card, consumers will be able to make secure purchases over the Internet and pay road tolls and phone charges, as well as make traditional credit and debit purchases.

Perhaps the most interesting innovation is "**e-cash**" (or "cybermoney")—a software payment system that allows secure, anonymous, transfer of money over the Internet or other networks. Electronic cash "coins" may be purchased from issuing banks and stored on the user's hard drive. They can then be transferred by e-mail or online between payer and payee. A significant advantage of e-cash (apart from the anonymity factor) is that it may be used in small-value transactions that are not cost effective when conventional cards are used.

e-cash
a software payment system that allows anonymous transfer of money over the Internet

Other Business Uses of the Internet

Another obvious business use of the Internet is as an advertising medium. One reason why so much free information is available is that Web sites and search engines also frequently carry advertising. Other common uses of the Internet are for investment broking, share trading, and gambling—all of which can be considered forms of e-commerce.

There are also numerous businesses that facilitate e-commerce without actually buying and selling over the Internet. For example, telecommunication companies provide the physical infrastructure that makes e-commerce possible; firms make money by designing customized Web sites for clients; others are engaged in the business of designing software to make e-commerce more efficient.

The Potential Benefits of E-commerce

The potential benefits of e-commerce are enormous, though as we shall see later in this chapter, it is not without its dangers. E-commerce enables vast amounts of information to be transmitted in a fraction of a second—and as we are frequently told, information equals power and time equals money.

E-commerce allows businesses to increase their efficiency and productivity. Inventories are reduced by adopting "just-in-time" production methods; activities can be centralized or decentralized as efficiency requires; new markets are opened up, especially for small and medium-sized businesses. Most of all, e-commerce substantially reduces costs. It is far less expensive to maintain a single "cyberstore" than a number of physical ones. Distribution costs, especially for electronically delivered products, are significantly reduced. For the consumer, e-commerce brings convenience, increased choice, and, to the extent that savings are passed on, lower costs.

ESTABLISHING AN ONLINE BUSINESS

When a business decides to go "online," especially when it seeks to advertise and market its products or services, a number of steps must be taken, each of which usually involves the negotiation of an agreement.[6] Generally, the firm will have to

- negotiate a Web site development agreement—creating a Web site can be a complex undertaking, involving both graphic design and software development, and usually requires professional assistance.
- negotiate a Web site hosting agreement—once developed, the site must be installed and operated on a Web "server," often operated by an Internet service provider (ISP).
- negotiate an Internet access agreement with the Internet access provider.
- register a "domain name."[7]

Additionally, if the site is to be used for more than just advertising, it must be secure and encryption services will be required.

E-COMMERCE AND THE LAW

Electronic commerce is such a recent phenomenon that its legal implications are only just beginning to be understood. A mere handful of new statutes have been enacted, mostly in the United States, and there have been very few decided court cases dealing with e-commerce. In the absence of legislation, the big question is to what extent existing legal rules and principles can be applied to situations that arise in e-commerce.

Contract Law

Electronic commerce, like any other form of commerce, is principally about making contracts. To what extent can "normal" contract law be applied to e-commerce?

Formation of Contracts

As we have seen in Chapter 5, the key elements in the formation of a contract are *offer* and *acceptance*. When does a contract come into existence in a typical e-commerce transaction?

ILLUSTRATION 34.1

Elektra visits her favourite online CD store, clicks on "browse," and chooses the classical music category. Following the instructions, she selects five CDs, each time clicking on "add this to my shopping basket." She then clicks on "order," types in her credit card number, her name, and postal address, and finally clicks on "confirm."

---

6. For a very useful analysis of the contents of such agreements see A.M. Gahtan, M. Kratz, and J.F. Mann, "Internet Law: a Practical Guide for Legal and Business Professionals," Chapter 4. Scarborough: Carswell, 1998.

7. Domain names are considered in the next section, under the heading Intellectual Property.

Has any contract been made and, if so, when? Does the store's Web site constitute an offer to sell the listed discs, or is it simply an advertisement or an invitation to treat?[8] Is the offer made when Elektra clicks on "order," or on "confirm"? And if so, when is her order accepted by the store? Does that acceptance have to be communicated to Elektra before a contract comes into existence?[9] Would it make any difference if Elektra had ordered the discs to be paid for COD, rather than on her credit card? Could she change her mind and refuse to take delivery? Suppose one of the five CDs ordered by Elektra is no longer in stock: is the store still entitled to bill her for the other four?

These are some of the questions that arise in even the very simplest type of e-commerce transaction. To date, one can only make an educated guess about the answers, based upon the way in which the courts have decided similar questions where communication has been by mail, by phone, by telex, or by fax. Any firm planning to engage in e-commerce will be well advised, in designing its Web site, to spell out very clearly what are intended to be the legal consequences of clicking on each icon. It has become common practice to use "**Web-wrap agreements**," or "click-wrap agreements," which require the consumer to click on the appropriate box to indicate agreement with the terms of sale.[10] Such agreements must be designed with great care.

Web-wrap agreement
a Web site document setting out contractual terms, the acceptance of which is indicated by "clicking" on the appropriate icon

The Law Governing the Contract

Determining if and when a contract is made is of primary importance. But the moment *when* the contract is made may also determine *where* it is made, which in turn *may* determine the law that governs the transaction.[11]

ILLUSTRATION 34.2

Assume the same facts as in Illustration 34.1.

Elektra is resident in British Columbia. The CD firm is incorporated in Delaware. The Web site is operated through a server located in the Cayman Islands. On receiving Elektra's order the server automatically notifies a warehouse in Alberta that the firm uses to despatch goods ordered by Canadian customers.

Where was the contract made? Is it governed by the laws of British Columbia, of Delaware, of the Cayman Islands, or of Alberta? Why might it be important? The law of the contract may determine such matters as:

- the capacity of the parties to contract
- the legality of the contract
- the formal requirements governing the contract
- any terms that are to be implied
- the effects of, and remedies for, breach of contract
- the applicability of consumer protection legislation

For example, the customer may be considered a minor in one jurisdiction but not in another, or a minor may have a restricted capacity to contract in one jurisdiction but not in

---

8. See Chapter 5, under "The Nature of an Offer."

9. See Chapter 5, under "Transactions Between Parties at a Distance from Each Other."

10. The use and validity of Web-wrap agreements is discussed by Sigel, Ling, and Izenberg, in a paper prepared for the Uniform Law Conference of Canada, accessible at **www.law.ualberta.ca/alri/ulc/current/ewebwrap.htm**.

11. See Chapter 5, under "Determining the Jurisdiction Where a Contract is Made." The place where a contract is made is one of a number of factors that may determine the law governing the contract: see Chapter 33, under "The Proper Law of the Contract."

another. Certain types of contract—for example, off-course betting on horse races—may be lawful in one jurisdiction but not in another. Particular types of contract may be required to be in writing or to be notarized. One jurisdiction may imply a warranty of fitness, another may not. A contract may be terminated by frustration in one jurisdiction but not in another.

Again, many of these and similar problems may be avoided by a clear statement of the law that is intended to govern, though that will not always protect the merchant. For example, consumer protection legislation in the customer's country may still apply, regardless of such a statement.

Formal Requirements

As just noted, the law that governs a contract may impose certain formal requirements—in particular, that certain types of contract must be in writing. As we saw in Chapter 10, federal and provincial law in Canada require certain contracts to be in writing or to be evidenced by writing. This raises the question whether "electronic" contracts can be said to be in writing, and whether an "electronic signature" constitutes a true signature. Again, such questions cannot as yet be answered with any confidence and the difficulty is compounded by the fact that the wording of the statutory requirements varies considerably. The federal government has made a start to resolving these problems in Bill C-6, which is expected to become law during 2000.[12] According to the Electronic Commerce Task Force:[13]

> Existing federal statutes and regulations often specify that information must be given "in writing," "certified" or "signed." These types of references can be interpreted as restricting transactions only to paper and preclude the possibility of transmitting information electronically. Earlier this year, the Department of Justice reviewed over 600 federal statutes and found that 300 of these made references to obtaining or sending information in a way that appeared limited to paper. However, as communication becomes increasingly paperless, the dependence on paper becomes outdated and cumbersome. The proposed legislation provides a way to adapt existing federal statutes and regulations so that they are compatible with an electronic environment. In other words, it provides a way to adjust or apply current laws so that there is an electronic alternative to transmitting information....The proposed legislation gives federal departments, agencies and boards the authority to decide how requirements in existing statutes and regulations can be satisfied by electronic means in place of paper....Another element of the proposed changes concerns electronic documents that are introduced as evidence in court proceedings.

As presently drafted (January 2000), Bill C-6 provides:

...32. The purpose of this Part is to provide for the use of electronic alternatives in the manner provided for in this Part where federal laws contemplate the use of paper to record or communicate information or transactions.

...41. A requirement under a provision of a federal law for a document to be in writing is satisfied by an electronic document if (a) the federal law or the provision is listed in Schedule 2 or 3; and (b) the regulations respecting the application of this section to the provision have been complied with.

...43. Subject to sections 44 to 46, a requirement under a provision of a federal law for a signature is satisfied by an electronic signature if (a) the federal law or the provision is listed in Schedule 2 or 3; and (b) the regulations respecting the application of this section to the provision have been complied with.

...46. A requirement under a provision of a federal law for a signature to be witnessed is satisfied with respect to an electronic document if (a) each signatory and each

---

12. The proposed legislation will be known as the Personal Information Protection and Electronic Documents Act. It was introduced as Bill C-54 in 1997, but its provisions, especially those relating to privacy, were controversial and the Bill was not passed in 1999, as had been intended. The new Bill C-6 was introduced in October 1999.

13. "Adjusting the Legal Framework for Electronic Commerce," E-Com Fast Facts, at **strategis.ic.gc.ca/virtual_hosts/ e-com/english/fastfacts/43d9.html** (visited May 16, 1999).

witness signs the electronic document with their secure electronic signature; (b) the federal law or the provision is listed in Schedule 2 or 3; and (c) the regulations respecting the application of this section to the provision have been complied with.

...52. Section 19 of the Canada Evidence Act is replaced by the following:

    31.1 Any person seeking to admit an electronic document as evidence has the burden of proving its authenticity by evidence capable of supporting a finding that the electronic document is that which it is purported to be.

In Canada the law of contract falls almost exclusively within provincial jurisdiction, so that the new legislation will unfortunately not apply to a substantial part of e-commerce. Nevertheless, Bill C-6 marks an encouraging start and it is to be hoped that the provinces will quickly introduce their own legislation. Saskatchewan has already taken the lead, with the introduction (in late 1999) of the Electronic Information and Commerce Bill, and other provinces are preparing their own legislation. It is important that such legislation be harmonized so as not to create conflicting rules.

Checklist: Precautions to Take When Establishing an E-commerce Site

Where a Web site is to be used to sell goods and services, the trader should take the following precautions:

- become familiar with the laws of other countries in which it intends to do business
- where necessary, customize contract terms for each country
- design the Web site so that the terms of the contract are brought to the attention of customers before any contract is concluded
- state clearly which law and jurisdiction applies to any contracts formed
- avoid giving customers too much freedom to amend terms—use yes/no, or accept/ decline options wherever possible
- maintain full back-ups of all contracts made via Web pages

"Commercial Paper"

As we have seen in earlier chapters, documents play an important role in business transactions, not only by providing a record of the terms of contracts but also as evidence of title to goods or of a debt owed. In particular, we have already encountered the bill of lading (in Chapters 16 and 33), and the bill of exchange or negotiable instrument (in Chapter 21).

Bills of Lading

The use of bills of lading goes back several centuries, especially in international trade, where it facilitates the financing of transactions. Increasingly, however, the international business community is turning to a system known as **electronic data interchange** (EDI) as a much quicker and more efficient method of transmitting information. However, the switch to EDI has been impeded by the law's insistence on paper-based documentation. To overcome this obstacle, the United Nations Commission on International Trade Law (UNCITRAL) drafted, in 1996, a Model Law on Legal Aspects of Electronic Data Interchange and Related Means of Communication, applicable to all forms of information transferred by "data message." Like Bill C-6 in Canada, the model law treats such messages as "documents" that can be accepted as evidence in courts, and it recognizes "electronic signatures." Nevertheless, replacing paper bills of

electronic data interchange
the exchange of business information from one computer to another

lading with EDI is likely to prove a long and difficult process since, in addition to the buyer and seller, a large number of other parties—carriers, forwarders, bankers, insurers, and government agencies—are normally involved in the international shipment of goods. Each of these parties (who may be in several different countries) has its own documentary requirements, which are presently met by the traditional bill of lading.

Negotiable Instruments

In Chapter 21 we discussed the various common forms of bills of exchange—drafts, promissory notes, and cheques. These methods of payment are rapidly being joined, and in some cases replaced, by electronic methods, especially in business-to-business transactions. In particular, as we have already seen, the use of e-cash permits the instantaneous transfer of funds between parties and also allows those funds to be "negotiated" to third parties. Commercial practice is leading the way and the law has been slow to keep up, although initiatives are being taken. For example, the subcommittee of the American Bar Association on electronic commercial practices has recommended that the Uniform Commercial Code should be revised to permit the use of electronic promissory notes.[14]

Intellectual Property

As one might expect, e-commerce and the use of the Internet give rise to many difficult questions concerning intellectual property rights and their possible infringement. In this section we shall review the main issues that have emerged to date, in particular those that have already given rise to litigation.

Trademarks

As we saw in Chapter 22, a trademark may be infringed by "passing-off," or by any unauthorized use of the mark or of a confusingly similar mark, whether or not the infringement is intentional. Trademark infringement may occur in electronic commerce in the same way as in ordinary commerce. However, the nature of the Internet greatly increases the probability of infringements, their potential seriousness, and the likelihood of their detection. It is quite possible for two businesses in different countries, or in different jurisdictions within the same country, to have the same name or to have potentially confusingly similar names. Where neither of them is making a deliberate attempt to "steal" the business of the other, the possible trademark infringement is unlikely to give rise to problems and, in "normal" business, may well go undetected. But that may not be so where the infringement occurs on the Internet.

ILLUSTRATION 34.3

Caitlin, the owner of the "Enchanted Florist" flower shop in Toronto, decides to create and maintain a Web site on the Internet to enable her customers to order flowers for delivery in Toronto and the surrounding area. On this Web site, she posts photographs of her more popular flower arrangements and takes orders over the phone from regular customers with account numbers. A month later, Caitlin receives notice that Halifax and Victoria flower shop owners—of shops named the "Enchanted Florist"—are claiming that she is infringing their trademarks.[15]

---

14. See Newell and Gordon, "Electronic Commerce and Negotiable Instruments" (1995), 31 *Idaho L. Rev.* 819.

15. The example, with changes to the locations, is taken from Kalow, "From the Internet to Court: Exercising Jurisdiction over World Wide Web Communications" (1997), 65 *Fordham L. Rev.* 2241.

Without the Internet, the potential conflict would probably never have come to light. Each shop would have advertised in local newspapers and in the local "yellow pages" and would have been oblivious to the existence of the others. If the three parties are sensible, it is probable that the situation will be settled amicably; it is most unlikely that any of them would be able to show damage resulting from the infringement by the others if, indeed, there is any infringement. But, in the United States, there have already been instances of parties being involved in expensive litigation in essentially similar situations.[16] In such a case, the court would have to decide which of the parties was in fact entitled to use the "Enchanted Florist" trademark, and whether it was entitled to sole use. As we shall see later, the question also arises as to which court should hear the dispute.

Of course, trademark infringement on the Internet is not always accidental. Coincidentally, of the relatively few e-commerce cases to have been litigated in Canada to date, two have concerned the alleged infringement of the "yellow pages" and "pages jaunes" trademarks.

CASE 34.1

Bell Actimedia Inc. produces and distributes trade and telephone directories in Canada, and provides business listings on the Internet. It also owns the Canadian rights to the trademarks "Yellow Pages" and "Pages Jaunes." It learned that Globe Communications, a partnership registered in Quebec, had established a Web site with the address **www.lespagesjaunes.com** and was advertising itself as the "business directory of the French-speaking world."

Bell, which itself had registered several Internet sites, including **www.yellowpages.ca**, **www.pagesjaunes.ca**, **www.canadayellowpages.com**, and **www.pagesjaunes-canada.com**, sought an injunction to restrain Globe from using its "Pages Jaunes" trademark, alleging passing-off and unfair competition.

The Court held that Bell was entitled to the injunction sought; a *prima facie* case of infringement had been made out and Bell had established that it would suffer irreparable harm if an interlocutory injunction was not granted.[17]

In the other case, owners of the "Yellow Pages" trademark obtained an award of damages against two corporations, one incorporated in Canada and the other a Nevada corporation, for infringement of its mark (as well as of the "walking fingers" logo), by advertising their business directory service as "Canadian Yellow Pages on the Internet" on their Web site at **www.cdnyellowpages.com**.[18]

Domain Names

As the "yellow pages" cases demonstrate, trademark infringement often results, intentionally or not, because of the close similarity of Internet addresses or **domain names**. The legitimate owners of the trademark had registered domain names of **yellowpages.ca**, **pagesjaunes.ca**, **canadayellowpages.com**, and **pagesjaunescanada.com**, yet the infringers had been able to establish their own Web sites at **lespagesjaunes.com** and **www.cdnyellowpages.com**.

In order to understand the legal implications of domain names, a basic understanding of the system is necessary.[19] Each Web site on the Internet is unique—at any rate in theory; no two

domain name
the registered Internet "address" of a Web site

---

16. See, for example, Bensusan Restaurant Corp. v. King, 937 F. Supp. 295 (1996); Cybersell Inc. (Arizona) v. Cybersell Inc. (Florida), US App. Lexis 33871 (1997).

17. Bell Actimedia Inc. v. Puzo (1999), 166 F.T.R. 202.

18. Tele-Direct (Publications) Inc. v. Canadian Business Online Inc. (1998), 85 C.P.R. (3d) 332.

19. For a full description of the system and its legal implications, see Gole, "Playing the Name Game: A Glimpse at the Future of the Internet Domain Name System" (1999), 51 *Fed. Com. L. J.* 403. A useful, shorter, description is given in "Developments—The Law of Cyberspace" (1999), 112 *Harv. L. Rev.* 1575.

domain names are the same. Originally, the Internet was run by a small group of professors and graduate students at the University of California, working closely with the U.S. government. The leader of this group, Dr. Jon Postel, designed the "Internet Protocol" with its system of Internet addresses and initially ran the system almost single-handedly through an organization called the Internet Assigned Numbers Authority (IANA). The present domain name system gradually evolved during the 1980s and seemed to work well, so long as the Internet was mostly used by scientists and scholars and had little commercial importance. By the 1990s, the task of managing the system of allocating domain names had become too much for what was essentially a voluntary organization. In 1992, the U.S. Congress asked the National Science Foundation to outsource the system to the private sector, and the task was assigned to Network Solutions Inc. (NSI) to establish and manage a centre (InterNIC) to assign new domain names within the popular ".com," ".edu" and ".org" domains. By September 1998, NSI had registered over 2 770 000 domain names (and had made a profit of $36 million.).

The Internet had become an international phenomenon, and there was widespread dissatisfaction with the regulation of access to it being in the hands of a private monopoly in a single country. Following extensive consultations, a new non-profit corporation, Internet Corporation for Assigned Names and Numbers (ICANN) was established, and will take over the function of registering "generic" domain names in 2000.

Outside the United States, other countries had started to establish their own systems of allocating domain names. Domain names always have two or more parts, separated by dots. The part on the left is the most specific. The part on the right is the most general, and is referred to as the "top-level domain." Top-level domains are either "generic," such as commercial (**.com**), educational (**.edu**), governmental (**.gov**), network (**.net**), and organizational (**.org**) and are assigned by InterNIC, and soon ICANN, or they are "national," such as Canada (**.ca**) and are assigned by national authorities.

Originally, control over the "**.ca**" domain had been given (by Dr. Postel's group) to a professor at the University of British Columbia, who exercised sole authority, and allowed only one domain name per registrant. As from 1999, the Canadian Internet Registration Authority controls the "**.ca**" domain and has established new registration rules: registrants are now allowed to own more than one "**.ca**" domain name.

All this explains how, although no two domain names are identical (or should not be, if the registrars are doing their work properly), domain names can still be confusingly similar. For example, the great majority of Canadian business corporations are registered in the "**.com**" top-level domain, but there is nothing to prevent some other person registering the same lower-level name in the "**.ca**" domain—or in the domain of some other country. (The small Pacific island of Tuvalu is the owner of the "**.tv**" domain; according to a recent report, a Canadian corporation, "The .TV Corp.," had proposed a $50 million licensing deal with the government of Tuvalu, to administer and market "**.tv**" domain names, so that broadcasters could use names such as **cbc.tv**. The deal has apparently fallen through.)[20] Registering a domain name costs very little, so there is a strong likelihood that there will be many instances of confusingly similar names.

Although a domain name does not of itself constitute a trademark (essentially, it is simply an address), it is common for a domain name to consist in part of a trademark or trade name. Consequently, the use of an exclusive domain name may nevertheless amount to the infringement of another's trademark.

20. See the report, "Tuvalu domain name deal with Canadians collapses," at **pidp.ewc.hawaii.edu/pireport/1999/May/05-24-02.html**.

CASE 34.2

ITV Technologies Inc., a corporation incorporated in British Columbia, was a Web services provider and had registered the domain name **www.itv.net**. WIC Television Ltd., another British Columbia corporation, was in the business of television broadcasting and owned nine stations throughout Canada. WIC owned several registered trade marks using the letters "ITV" and had registered a Web site with the domain name **ITV.ca**.

ITV commenced an action for an order expunging WIC's "ITV" trademarks; WIC counterclaimed, alleging infringement of its trademarks and seeking an injunction.[21]

In Case 34.2, the infringement of the trademark seems to have been innocent, with no intention to "steal" business from its owner. In other instances, such as that in Case 34.1, there seems to have been a clear intention to derive a benefit from the use of a well-known trademark and to divert business away from the owner of the mark.[22] This type of passing-off is facilitated by the fact that Internet users, when trying to locate the Web site of a well-known firm, will often "intuit" the address, by trying the trade name plus ".com," or will type in an incorrect address, using the wrong top-level domain.

Some strange uses, or abuses, of the domain name system have evolved. In one widely reported instance, Web surfers trying to reach NASA's Mars Pathfinder site **nasa.gov** inadvertently ended up in a red-light district in San Francisco; the domain name **nasa.com** had been registered for an "adult entertainment" site. In another case, a Mr. Schnauber registered 170 Web addresses, including **timewarner.org**, **r.j.reynolds.org**, and **newyorkstockexchange.org**, to promote information on plants that attract endangered butterflies.[23] A U.S. court granted an injunction for trademark infringement in a case where an anti-abortion activist registered the domain name **www.plannedparenthood.com** in order to promote his views.[24]

One of the more notorious practices is that of "**cybersquatting**," where a person registers a domain name that includes a well-known trademark or brand name, and then offers to sell the domain name to the owner of the mark or brand. Such action almost certainly constitutes a trademark infringement and may have serious consequences for the infringer, who may be ordered to relinquish the domain name and to pay court costs.[25] However, cybersquatters normally rely on the fact that the trademark owner may find it less expensive and more convenient simply to buy the domain name from the registrant. One lesson that has been learned from the cybersquatting cases is that it is advisable for large firms to register any domain name that seems to relate to their activities or products (Kraft Foods have reportedly registered some 150 domain names, corresponding to all their better-known brands); to do so is substantially less expensive than having to fight a court battle.

cybersquatting
the registration of a domain name containing the trademark of another person, with the intention of selling the domain name to the owner of the mark

Copyright

It is generally accepted that copyright laws apply to the publication and reproduction of materials on the Internet or in e-mail communications. The Internet does not seem to present any

---

21. ITV Technologies, Inc. v. WIC Television Ltd. (1999), 2 C.P.R. (4th) 1. In the event, ITV did not contest the action and an injunction was granted to WIC.

22. See also Peinet Inc. v. O'Brien (1995), 61 C.P.R. (3d) 334.

23. These examples are taken from the article by Gole, *supra*, n. 19.

24. Planned Parenthood v. Bucci, US Dist. Lexis 3338 (1997).

25. See, for example, Panavision International Inc. v. Toeppen, US Dist. Lexis 19698 (1996). Mr. Toeppen reportedly registered some 240 names and then attempted to sell them for exorbitant fees.

intrinsically new copyright problems;[26] however, it most certainly makes infringement of copyright, whether deliberate or unintentional, a very easy matter. Anything that can be copyrighted can be converted into digital form and sent across the Internet, permitting a perfect copy to be downloaded onto another computer.

Internet users have traditionally embraced the view that "information wants to be free," and copyright is routinely infringed as material posted on the Internet is copied and forwarded to other users without the knowledge or consent of the copyright owner. Indeed, it is widely—though mistakenly—believed that by posting material on a Web site, the author or owner impliedly consents to its being copied and reproduced. In many instances, that may be quite true and, even where it is not, copyright owners rarely take action against infringements that are non-commercial in nature. For example, a student finding an interesting piece of information on the Internet downloads it and forwards it to a friend or a teacher edits materials from the Internet and incorporates them into teaching materials. Such actions may or may not constitute "fair dealing,"[27] or may impliedly have been consented to by the copyright owner; but even if they are not, the owner is unlikely to sue. By contrast, if material posted on the Internet is used for a commercial purpose, or in a manner that is offensive to the copyright owner, legal proceedings are far more likely.[28]

CASE 34.3

Sotramex, a firm specializing in cleaning up mining and forestry sites, prepared a technical description (written by one of its employees) to appear on the Internet site of the International Centre for the Advancement of Environmental Technologies. A year or so later, Sorenviq, another firm engaged in reforestation, posted a virtually identical item on its own Web page, without acknowledging the true authorship. The two firms were competitors.

The court found that the author's copyright had been infringed and ordered Sorenviq to remove the text from its Web site and to pay $10 000 damages plus $5000 exemplary damages.[29]

Jurisdiction

The principles by which the courts determine whether they have jurisdiction to hear a particular dispute were discussed briefly in Chapter 33. These principles are complex, even when applied to conventional business transactions that cross provincial, state, or national borders. Jurisdictional issues in the context of online transactions present an even greater challenge. To quote from a recent study:

> Traditional rules relating to jurisdiction and competence incorporate a notion of territoriality. But Internet communications are not geographically dependent. The very origin of an e-mail message may be unknown. Website information cannot be confined to a target audience, but is disseminated simultaneously to a global market. It may affect individuals in a myriad of jurisdictions, all of which have their own particular laws.[30]

---

26. There have been some suggestions that the practice of "caching" (i.e., making temporary copies of popular Web pages to speed up delivery) could constitute an infringement of copyright.

27. The concept of "fair dealing" is discussed in Chapter 22.

28. See, for example, Religious Technology Center v. Lerma, US Dist. Lexis 15454 (1996), in which the Church of Scientology successfully brought action to prevent its copyrighted texts being reproduced and posted on the Internet. See also National Basketball Association v. Sports Team Analysis, 939 F. Supp. 1071 (1996).

29. Sotramex Inc. c. Sorenviq Inc., [1998] A.Q. no 2241 (Quebec Superior Court—Civil Division).

30. Ogilvy Renault, "Jurisdiction and the Internet: Are Traditional Rules Enough?" The study is reproduced on the Web site of the Uniform Law Conference of Canada, at **www.law.ualberta.ca/alri/ulc/current/ejurisd.htm**.

As a general rule, the courts of most countries accept jurisdiction if the defendant is resident or domiciled there; in the case of an extra-territorial defendant, jurisdiction is accepted only where there is an appropriate connection with the country (or province or state).

The general rule is often unsatisfactory in e-commerce situations, especially those involving consumer transactions. The vendor may be resident in another country or province and it may be quite impractical to expect the consumer to commence legal proceedings in a distant jurisdiction with, perhaps, a very different legal system. Sometimes it may not even be possible to determine where the defendant is resident, since its Web address does not necessarily indicate its physical location. This difficulty has led to suggestions that the country or province of the consumer should have jurisdiction and that the applicable law should be that of the consumer's place of residence.[31] But that solution is also not without problems. An electronic retailer could find itself liable to be sued anywhere in the world, unless it had stated clearly that its offer to sell was restricted to certain countries only. To do business internationally, the retailer would have to comply with the consumer laws of many different jurisdictions, some of which might regard a simple disclaimer of liability as ineffective. Also, from the point of view of the consumer, the solution would not necessarily be satisfactory. A judgment against a foreign supplier might be useless if the supplier has no assets in the customer's country, and the courts of the supplier's country might not be willing to enforce a judgment obtained by the customer in his or her own country.

Similar problems exist in the case of trademark and copyright violation. The question of jurisdiction in such cases has been considered by American courts on a number of occasions, and what has been called a "level of interactivity" test has evolved. In *Zippo Manufacturing Co. v. Zippo Dot Com, Inc.*,[32] the plaintiff Pennsylvania corporation, manufacturer of the well-known brand of cigarette lighters, brought an action against a California corporation, which provided an Internet news service, for infringement of its "Zippo" trademark. Reviewing the jurisdictional principles that had evolved, the court ruled that three types of situation exist:

(1) where the out-of-state defendant is carrying on substantial business within the jurisdiction

(2) where the defendant maintains an interactive site

(3) where the defendant's site provides purely passive advertising.

In case (1), there is jurisdiction where the business is being carried on; in case (3) there is no jurisdiction; case (2) remains an uncertain "grey area." In the particular case, the court found that the California corporation was doing substantial business in Pennsylvania, and that the Pennsylvania courts were entitled to exercise jurisdiction.[33]

Whether Canadian courts will adopt the "level of interactivity" test is uncertain, though the *Zippo* case was referred to with apparent approval in a recent case before the British Columbia Court of Appeal.[34] Also unclear is whether the same principles that apply to trademark and copyright infringement should also apply to torts, such as defamation. Traditionally, Canadian courts have taken the view that jurisdiction may be exercised in the state or province where the tort is committed. Defamation is committed where the defamatory statement is "published," that is, where it is made available to be seen or heard. But a defamatory statement posted on the

---

31. See the report, "Consumer Protection Rights in Canada in the Context of Electronic Commerce", Office of Consumer Affairs, August 31, 1998.

32. 952 F. Supp. 1119 (W.D. Pa. 1997).

33. Contrast Cybersell Inc. (Arizona) v. Cybersell Inc. (Florida), US App. Lexis 33871 (1997), where the Florida-incorporated defendant was found to be engaging solely in "passive" advertising, and the Arizona court declined jurisdiction.

34. Braintech, Inc. v. Kostiuk (1999), 171 D.L.R. (4th) 46.

Internet is published everywhere.[35] That would seem to suggest that a plaintiff alleging libel might sue anywhere in the world, choosing a jurisdiction where the law of defamation is most favourable and where damages are likely to be highest. But even if that were so, there would still be the question of enforcing the judgment.

CASE 34.4

Braintech Inc., a corporation that designs and develops advanced pattern recognition technologies for use in industrial robot applications, was incorporated in Nevada in 1987 (under a different name). It had moved its head office to Arizona, to Texas. and then, in 1996, to Vancouver, though apparently it still maintained a research and development facility in Texas.

Braintech alleged that it had been libelled by Kostiuk, a resident of British Columbia, in material that he had posted on an Internet "chat forum" about potential investments in hi-tech firms. Braintech brought an action against Kostiuk in Texas. Kostiuk did not defend the suit, believing that the Texas court had no jurisdiction. The Texas court found in favour of Braintech and awarded damages of US$409 680. Braintech then sought to have the Texas judgment enforced in British Columbia. At the trial level, Braintech succeeded, the court holding that it was bound to enforce the Texas judgment.[36] That judgment was overturned by the British Columbia Court of Appeal, which held that the Texas court had no jurisdiction to hear the original case and that its judgment should therefore not be enforced.[37]

REGULATING E-COMMERCE

The Power to Regulate

There is little doubt that the federal government has the power to regulate e-commerce, and indeed all uses of the Internet within Canada, under its general power to regulate intra-provincial communication.[38] It is somewhat less clear to what extent Internet usage constitutes "broadcasting";[39] in any event, the chairperson of the Canadian Radio-Television and Telecommunications Commission (CRTC) announced in May 1999 that there was no intention on the part of the CRTC to exercise general supervision over the Internet. There seems to be a broad consensus, in Canada and internationally, that the Internet is functioning fairly well for the most part, that to some extent a system of self-regulation already exists, and that excessive government regulation could impede the development of this sector of the international economy. There is also a fear that, given the transnational nature of cyberspace, any attempt by one country to regulate e-commerce might simply result in business migrating to less restrictive regimes.[40]

Nevertheless, the very existence of Bill C-6 (already discussed under the heading "Contract Law") recognizes that existing laws are not always adequate to deal with the special problems posed by e-commerce and that regulation of some aspects of e-commerce is, or will soon become, necessary. As we have already noted, in the context of the formalities for concluding contracts on the Internet, the existence of a clear and certain set of legal rules can promote the

---

35. For an analysis of this problem see Gosnell, "Jurisdiction on the Net: Defining Place in Cyberspace" (1998), 29 *C.B.L.J.* 345.

36. Applying the principle enunciated in Morguard Investments Ltd. v. de Savoye (1990), 76 D.L.R. (4th) 256; see "Enforcement of Foreign Judgments," in Chapter 33.

37. Braintech Inc. v. Kostiuk, *supra,* n. 34. The case has been appealed to the Supreme Court of Canada.

38. Constitution Act, 1867 s. 92(10)(a).

39. Under the Broadcasting Act, S.C. 1991, c. 11.

40. For an interesting review of the major issues regarding Internet regulation, see Geist, "The reality of bytes: regulating economic activity in the age of the Internet" (1998), 73 *Wash. L. Rev.* 521.

growth of e-commerce rather than hindering it. The federal government is anxious to make Canada a leader in e-commerce and has already taken a number of steps to promote its development, principally through Industry Canada.[41]

The Application and Adaptation of Existing Laws

Although the more important aspects of the existing law as it applies to e-commerce have already been discussed in the preceding section, a number of other aspects should also be mentioned briefly.

Consumer Protection

Which laws, if any, protect the consumer in an electronic transaction—the laws of the consumer's own country or province, or those of the supplier? And in which country or province can a dissatisfied consumer bring proceedings for redress? Those two questions, to which there is as yet no clear answer, have already been mentioned. Both questions raise the fundamental issue of whether existing laws for the protection of consumers are adequate in the context of e-commerce transactions. Can laws on misleading advertising be enforced? Or laws that require certain types of information to be provided to consumers?[42] Should the form of Web-wrap agreements be regulated? Should there be some special "cooling-off" period in Internet sales, during which the consumer is allowed to withdraw from the transaction? That is the type of question currently being examined.[43]

Privacy

In recent years there has been growing concern over the fact that organizations—government and business—have accumulated vast amounts of information about private individuals, which may be used for purposes not contemplated by the individual who originally supplied it. Electronic commerce greatly increases the amount of information that is made available and, being in computerized form, that information is easily edited and transmitted. Although the federal government, and most of the provinces, have adopted legislation restricting the use of personal information by government agencies,[44] only the province of Quebec has so far enacted privacy legislation that applies to the private sector.

Bill C-6, which has already been referred to in the context of contract law, proposes to remedy this situation. The new legislation will apply eventually to every organization that collects, uses, or discloses personal information in the course of commercial activity. Probably its most important feature is the requirement to obtain an individual's consent to use or disclose information collected. In addition, individuals will have the right to inspect their personal information held by a company and to have it corrected. According to some critics, the Bill does not go nearly far enough; individuals will usually be unaware that information about them is being used improperly, so the provisions will rarely be enforced. Other critics maintain that the Bill could create a competitive disadvantage for Canadian firms and make Canada an unattractive regime for e-commerce. The Bill's provisions could prevent businesses with customer or employee data from selling all or any part of its business in confidence, since customer and employee records could not be transferred without the knowledge and consent of them all. The restrictions would also affect a business's ability to outsource data processing.

---

41. See the special section of the Industry Canada Web site, devoted to the activities of the Task Force on Electronic Commerce, at **e-com.ic.gc.ca**.

42. Quebec law requires Web sites of firms whose place of business is in the province to be in the French language.

43. See "Consumer Protection Rights in Canada in the Context of Electronic Commerce," *supra,* n. 31.

44. See Privacy Act, R.S.C. 1985, c. P-21; Access to Information Act, R.S.C. 1985, c. A-1.

Another privacy-related issue is whether persons are, or should be, protected from electronic junk-mail, or "spam" as it is commonly known. Some commentators have suggested that spam constitutes an invasion of privacy, and might be actionable under the common law of trespass. However, it would normally not be worth suing, even if the action were likely to succeed. In a recent Ontario case, a firm brought an action against its Internet service provider (ISP), seeking an injunction to have its service restored. The ISP had discontinued the service following complaints that the plaintiff firm had been sending out up to 200 000 unsolicited messages each day to promote the sale of its furniture. The court ruled that spam is a breach of "netiquette"—the Internet's unwritten rules of conduct—and refused the injunction.[45]

Illegal Activities

The governments of many countries are concerned about the use of the Internet to facilitate illegal activities, such as the dissemination of hate literature and of pornography. Pornography, in fact, is one of the most important sectors of e-commerce in financial terms. The Internet provides an easy method of distribution and one that makes detection and prosecution extremely difficult.[46]

Another activity which, if not illegal, is often strictly regulated by governments, is gambling. Again, the Internet provides an easy means of circumventing local laws by establishing offshore "virtual casinos" and betting offices. In 1998, a British company established what was claimed to be the first worldwide online betting service at **www.sportingbet.com** based in the tax-haven island of Alderney. The principal attraction of offshore, online, gambling—to both bookmakers and punters—is that it enables the taxes that governments often impose on gambling to be avoided, increasing profits and pay-outs. The objection—from the point of view of the rest of the population—is that it undermines what is often an important source of government revenue.

Taxation

This brings us to what is probably the greatest concern that governments have with respect to e-commerce—how to tax it. One of the most important and comprehensive studies made of e-commerce in Canada is that prepared for Revenue Canada in 1998.[47] Tax administrators have a number of concerns:

- Sales taxes and customs duties are easy to evade in e-commerce transactions, especially where goods or services are delivered electronically.

- Income tax (especially corporate income tax) may be avoided by moving operations offshore.

- Electronic commerce commonly reduces the number of persons involved in a transaction, cutting out the intermediary, which in turn eliminates the usual "audit trail" and makes tax evasion more difficult to detect.

- The use of e-cash also facilitates fraud and evasion.

---

45. 1267623 Ontario Inc. v. Nexx Online Inc. (1999), 45 O.R. (3d) 40.

46. In the United States, legislation has been adopted, both federally and in several states, specifically to regulate pornography on the Internet. In Reno v. American Civil Liberties Union, 117 S. Ct. 2329 (1997), the U.S. Supreme Court held that parts of the Communications Decency Act were unconstitutional and infringed the right of free speech.

47. "Electronic Commerce and Canada's Tax Administration," *supra*, n. 4.

Virtual Stock Exchanges

One rapidly growing form of e-commerce is in the investment sector. A substantial proportion of investors now obtain much of their information from the Internet; stocks are traded on the Internet; corporations have started to publish their annual reports there; and some corporations have by-passed the conventional securities industry and have made their public offerings of new stocks on the Internet. Consider the following reports:

> Since launching the Web site for E-minerals Exploration Corp., a Toronto-based junior mining company, president Patrick Farrell has become a popular man. He's received e-mail inquiries from as far away as Russia and Australia....Starting on Jan. 5, 1999 the IPO [initial public offer] continued for six weeks and raised E-minerals $376 431....Traditionally, the opportunity to buy shares in an IPO has been restricted to big underwriting institutions and the well-connected. [Farrell is] hoping the E-mineral experience, which comes on the heels of a much larger rush of Internet IPOs in the US, will help change that—aiding not only small investors, but also small and medium-sized businesses seeking better access to capital, a market he feels is not well served by traditional brokerage houses.
>
> Indeed, it's already becoming clear that the advent of Internet IPOs spells change for all the players involved in corporate financing. The breakthrough came in 1996, when New York microbrewery Spring Street Brewing Co. launched the world's first direct IPO on the Internet, showcasing the Net's ability to not only allow small companies to raise capital, but also to bypass brokerage houses—and their extravagant fees—by doing the underwriting themselves.

Source: Cynthia Reynolds, "To go public, press 'enter' now," *Canadian Business,* June 11, 1999, p. 79.

> The U.S. securities watchdog plans to lay more charges in the next two weeks over fraudulent stock offerings on the Internet as part of a new drive to crack down on the booming market. In addition, the Securities and Exchange Commission [SEC] is stepping up its investigations of online trading companies....The crackdown comes after the SEC became increasingly worried that small retail investors were using the Internet to buy and day-trade in shares, making them vulnerable to fraud....The latest crackdown comes on the heels of the creation of the SEC's 125-member Cyberforce, set up to look for Internet fraud.

Source: Peter Morton, "SEC cracks down on Net offerings: Probes spurred by concern for small investor," *National Post*, May 5, 1999, p. C-10.

Questions to Consider

1. What are the main advantages and risks involved in trading stocks over the Internet?
2. Should Internet investing be subject to normal securities regulation? Is it possible to regulate stock trading on the Internet?

INTERNATIONAL ASPECTS OF E-COMMERCE

Cyberspace knows no boundaries. As we have noted throughout this chapter, that is one of the great potential advantages of e-commerce, and is also the cause of many headaches for government officials, for business persons, and for their lawyers. Businesses are uncertain which laws apply to their contracts and other activities, and do not know what liabilities they may be subject to. Governments are unsure to what extent they should attempt to regulate e-commerce, and even less sure whether such attempts would be effective. To give but one example, as already discussed, the Canadian government has proposed legislation to protect privacy on the Internet. This poses a dilemma. If Canadian businesses are subjected to stricter regulation than their foreign competitors, especially those in the United States, they may lose out in the race to develop e-commerce. But the European Union has announced plans to introduce strict privacy legislation, and foreign firms that do not have to comply with equally strict rules at home will not be allowed to conduct e-business in most of Europe. Canada must try to draft legislation that is sufficiently strict to satisfy the Europeans, without losing out in the American market.

At present, different countries, or groups of countries, are each going their own way, and some countries are making a point of not regulating—and not taxing—e-commerce, with the aim of attracting business. The result is a mass of conflicting rules that impede the development of e-commerce by responsible enterprises and encourage the growth of more dubious activities.[48] It is becoming increasingly obvious that concerted action is necessary at the international level.

UNCITRAL has drafted a number of international agreements addressing electronic contracts, in particular the 1996 "Model Law on Electronic Commerce," which has been taken as a starting point for the work of the Uniform Law Conference of Canada. The World Trade Organization (WTO) has adopted a declaration committing member governments not to impose custom duties on e-commerce when information and services are delivered electronically. The World Intellectual Property Organization (WIPO) adopted a new treaty in 1996 on copyright, taking account of Internet developments. Most important, perhaps, has been the work of the Organisation for Economic Cooperation and Development (OECD), which has held two major international conferences on e-commerce (the first in Turku, Finland in 1997, and the second in Ottawa, in October 1998).[49] At those conferences, a program of work was proposed to

- initiate work on defining and measuring e-commerce
- develop guidelines for consumer protection
- work on the practical implementation of the 1980 OECD Privacy Guidelines
- set up specific technical advisory groups with business to address taxation issues

Not surprisingly, the member governments of the OECD are devoting much of their attention to the fight against tax evasion. A company based in Bermuda was recently established to sell tax-free virtual offices—known as "e-suites"—to firms in more heavily taxed countries, from which they may conduct their Internet business; another Web site in the Caribbean island of Anguilla proudly announces that "taxes are optional on the Internet." In response, the OECD is proposing to take action against tax havens and, in a related effort, against money laundering. According to the U.N. Office for Drug Control and Crime Prevention, there are about 700 000 electronic transfers of money each day, amounting to about US$2 trillion, of which probably at least $1 billion is "dirty money," most of it laundered through offshore banks in tax havens.

Electronic commerce has opened up many new opportunities; not all of them are necessarily desirable. It has also posed new problems for governments and for business. How these will be solved, if at all, largely remains to be seen. One thing is clear; e-commerce is set to expand dramatically in the new millennium and new legal problems will emerge that have not yet been contemplated.

QUESTIONS FOR REVIEW

1. What contracts are normally involved in establishing an online business?

2. What is a "Web-wrap agreement"?

---

48. See Malawer, "Inconsistent Rules Threaten Free Trade," *N.Y.L.J.* (February 9, 1999), p. 5.

49. A special section of the OECD Web site, provides access to news on international developments and to articles on e-commerce at **www.oecd.org/subject/e_commerce**. Information about the Ottawa conference and subsequent developments is available from a separate Web site, published by the Canadian government, at **www.ottawaoecdconference.org**.

3. At what point in time is a contract made over the Internet?

4. Why is it important to ascertain which legal system governs a contract?

5. What is the legal effect of an "electronic signature"?

6. How is it possible for a domain name to infringe some other person's trademark?

7. What is "cybersquatting"?

8. What is the "level of interactivity" test?

9. How is it proposed, in Canada, to protect an individual's privacy in e-commerce transactions?

10. What are the main initiatives being taken, at the international level, to harmonize laws applicable to e-commerce?

CASES AND PROBLEMS

1 Kim (a resident of British Columbia) was surfing the Internet late one night, trying to find where she could obtain a particular software program that she needed, at the lowest price. She eventually found what she considered an excellent bargain, advertised by a firm called Pacware Inc., which was apparently located in Washington State. Following the instructions on the Pacware Web page, she typed in details of the program she wanted, her name and address, and her credit card number, and finally clicked on "Order Now" at 2:31 a.m.

At 2:32 a.m. the message was received at the Pacware office in Washington. Through the system that Pacware had set up, Kim's message was automatically and immediately relayed to the warehouse in Vancouver, B.C., that Pacware maintained to supply their Canadian customers. The warehouse manager had been given the standing instruction to notify the customer whether delivery could be made, and if so, how it would be made.

After sending her order, Kim continued surfing and, an hour or so later, she discovered another firm, Webneeds Inc., which was advertising the software program at an even lower price. She decided to try to cancel the first order and, at 3:25 a.m., she sent an e-mail message to Pacware, saying "please ignore my previous message and cancel my order." At 8:23 a.m., the Pacware warehouse manager, checking the overnight messages, read Kim's order, sent her an e-mail to the effect that the order was "accepted," that it would be shipped immediately by courier, and gave instructions for this to be done. He also notified the Washington office that it was "on its way," whereupon, at 8:52 a.m., the office transmitted the relevant information to the credit card company. At 8:59 a.m., a clerk in the Washington office read Kim's e-mail message, purporting to cancel the order. She relayed it to the warehouse and was told that the order had already been shipped.

Kim received the shrink-wrapped software the next day but she refused to accept delivery. She subsequently discovered that the price had been charged to her credit card.

Was there a valid contract? Is Kim entitled to her money back? What further information is likely to be needed in order to advise Kim?

2 Altanet Inc. is incorporated in Alberta, and carries on the business of providing Internet access and related services to its clients. In March 1999 it registered the domain name **altanet.ab.ca**. One of its employees, O'Connor, had developed a new technique for designing Web pages for clients. He tried to persuade Altanet's management to adopt the technique and, when they decided not to, he resigned from the corporation and decided to go into business on his own. In May 1999 he established a corporation, Rocky Netservices Inc., and registered the domain name **alta.net**.

When Altanet's managers discovered the existence of the Rocky Web site, they wrote to O'Connor, alleging that he was attempting to pass his business off as that of Altanet in order to lure its clients away, and they demanded that he cease to use the **alta.net** domain name. O'Connor replied that the two domain names were different and equally legitimate, that no similarity existed between the names of the two corporations, and that Altanet had no cause to complain about his using the new Web page technique since it had declined to adopt it when given the opportunity.

How should the issue be resolved?

3 Dan's Discs Inc. a corporation incorporated in Ontario, operates a number of retail record stores in Ontario, as well as a Canada-wide CD mail order business. It has registered, in Canada, the trademark "Dan's Discs." In October 1998 it established an Internet site, at **dansdiscs.com**, and since then has been soliciting and accepting orders for CDs through its Internet site.

It recently discovered the existence of another Web site at **dansCDs.com**, established by a corporation also called "Dan's Discs Inc.," which was incorporated in December 1998 under the laws of the state of Delaware, but which operates out of an office in Buffalo, N.Y. That Web site advertises:

> Canadian clients—we guarantee to ship you your favorite disks at prices lower than any Canadian supplier.

The Canadian "Dan's Discs" considers that the actions of the Delaware firm constitute a blatant and deliberate attempt to steal its customers and, further, that it has the sole right to the trademark "Dan's Discs." It has obtained evidence that the Delaware firm has already shipped more than 20 000 CDs to addresses in Canada. Its investigations have also revealed that another corporation, also called Dan's Discs Inc., was incorporated 20 years ago in New Mexico, and operates a small retail store there. It has no Web site and has never done business in Canada. Nevertheless, the Canadian firm fears that the New Mexico corporation could be taken over by some unscrupulous person who might then use it to compete against them.

Does the Canadian firm have any legal remedy against either of the U.S. corporations? In which jurisdiction should it attempt to seek a remedy?

4 Green is a biologist and an environmental activist. He has recently become extremely concerned about the use of a poultry-feed additive, which he describes as "recycled chicken poop," being marketed by a multinational corporation, Hollyhill Inc. He claims that it causes genetic defects in poultry and may cause cancer in humans. When he went public with his claims, Hollyhill categorically denied them, and posted on its Internet site a lengthy report commissioned from an independent scientific foundation, purporting to find that the product was entirely safe.

In turn, Green reproduced the complete report on his own Web site, but this time interspersed with his own comments and those of several like-minded colleagues. The comments point out alleged weaknesses in the report and, in some places, pour scorn on the authors of the report.

Hollyhill have now written to Green, demanding that he remove the report and comments from his Web site, claiming that his actions amount to an infringement of their copyright.

Advise Green.

BIBLIOGRAPHY

General References

Allen, C.K. *Law in the Making*, 7th ed. (London: Oxford University Press, 1964).

Black, H.C. *Black's Law Dictionary*, 6th ed. (St. Paul, MN: West Publishing Co., 1990).

Denning (Lord). *The Discipline of Law* (London: Butterworth & Co., 1979).

Jackson, R.M. *Jackson's Machinery of Justice,* 8th ed. (Cambridge: Cambridge University Press, 1989).

Lloyd, D. *The Idea of Law*, rev. ed. (Harmondsworth: Penguin, 1974).

Plucknett, T.A. *A Concise History of the Common Law* (London: Butterworth & Co., 1956).

Posner, R.A. *Economic Analysis of Law,* 3rd ed. (Toronto: Little Brown and Company, 1986).

Stuart, D. *Canadian Criminal Law: A Treatise*, 3rd ed. (Toronto: Carswell Company, 1995).

Waddams, S.M. *Introduction to the Study of Law*, 5th ed. (Toronto: Carswell Company, 1997).

Part 1: Law in Its Social Context

Friedmann, W. *Law in a Changing Society,* 2nd ed. (New York: Columbia University Press, 1972).

Hart, H.L.A. *The Concept of Law*, 2nd ed. (London: Oxford University Press, 1994).

Hazard, L. *Law and the Changing Environment* (San Francisco: Holden-Day, 1971).

Hogg, P.W. *Constitutional Law of Canada,* 3rd ed. (Toronto: Carswell Company, 1992).

Lederman, W.R. *Continuing Canadian Constitutional Dilemmas* (Toronto: Butterworth & Co., 1981).

Magnusson, D.N. and Soberman, D.A. *Canadian Constitutional Dilemmas Revisited.* (Kingston: Institute of Intergovernmental Relations, 1997).

Russell, P.H. *Federalism and the Charter: Leading Constitutional Decisions*, 4th ed. (Ottawa: Carlton University Press, 1989).

Schur, E.M. *Law and Society: A Sociological View* (New York: Random House, 1968).

Watson, G.D. et al. (eds.). *Civil Litigation Cases and Materials*, 4th ed. (Toronto: Emond Montgomery Publications Ltd., 1991).

Part 2: Torts

Fleming, J.G. *The Law of Torts*, 8th ed. (Sydney: Law Book Company, 1992).

Fleming, J.G. *Introduction to the Law of Torts*, 2nd ed. (Oxford: Clarendon Press, 1985).

Hart, H.L.A. and Honoré, A.M. *Causation in Law*, 2nd ed. (Oxford: Oxford University Press, 1985).

Linden, A.M. *Canadian Tort Law,* 6th ed. (Toronto: Butterworth & Co., 1997).

Waddams, S.M. *Products Liability*, 3rd ed. (Toronto: Carswell Company, 1993).

Part 3: Contracts

Corbin, A.L. *Corbin on Contracts*, rev. ed. by Perillo J.M. (St. Paul: West Publishing Co., 1993). (supplemented annually).

Flavell, C.J.M. *Canadian Competition Law: A Business Guide* (Toronto: McGraw-Hill Ryerson Ltd., 1979).

Fridman, G.H.L. *The Law of Contract in Canada*, 3rd ed. (Toronto: Carswell Company, 1994).

Furmston, M.P. *Cheshire, Fifoot and Furmston's Law of Contract,* 13th ed. (London: Butterworth & Co. Ltd., 1996).

Guest, A.G. *Anson's Law of Contract*, 27th ed. (Oxford: Oxford University Press, 1998).

Hailsham, *Halsbury's Laws of England,* 4th ed. (London: Butterworths, 1993).

Lewison, K. *The Interpretation of Contracts* (London: Sweet & Maxwell, 1989).

Noziak, R.S. *The 1999 Annotated Competition Act* (Toronto: Carswell Company, 1998).

Palmer, G.E. *Mistake and Unjust Enrichment* (Columbus: Ohio State University Press, 1962).

Prichard, J.R., Stanbury, W.T. and Wilson, T.A. *Canadian Competition Policy* (Toronto: Butterworth & Co., 1979).

Swan, J., Reiter, B.J. and Bala, N. (eds.). *Contracts, Cases, Notes & Materials*, 5th ed. (Toronto: Emond Montgomery Publications Ltd., 1997).

Treitel, G.H. *The Law of Contract*, 9th ed. (London: Stevens & Sons, 1995).

Turner, J.W. Cecil, ed. *Russell on Crime*, 12th ed., Vol. 1 (London: Stevens & Son, 1964).

Waddams, S.M. *The Law of Contracts*, 4th ed. (Toronto: Canada Law Book Company, 1999).

Williston, S. *A Treatise on the Law of Contracts*, 4th ed. (New York: Lawyers Cooperative Publishing, 1993).

Winfield, P.H., ed. *Pollock's Principles of Contract*, 13th ed. (London: Stevens & Sons Ltd., 1950).

Part 4: Special Types of Contract
Sale of Goods
Atiyah, P.S. *The Sale of Goods*, 8th ed. (London: Pitman & Sons Ltd., 1990).

Fridman, G.H.L. *Sale of Goods in Canada*, 4th ed. (Toronto: Carswell Company, 1995).

Guest, A.G., (ed.). *Benjamin's Sale of Goods*, 5th ed. (London: Sweet & Maxwell Ltd., 1997).

Leasing and Bailment
Patton, G.W. *Bailment in the Common Law* London: Stevens & Sons Ltd., 1952.

Selby, R.F. *Leasing in Canada: A Business Guide*, 3rd ed. (Toronto: Butterworth & Co., 1999).

Tyler, E.L.G. and Palmer, N.E. *Crossley Vaines' Personal Property*, 5th ed. (London: Butterworth & Co., 1973).

Insurance and Guarantee
Crawford, B., Baer, M.G. and Rendall, J.A. (eds.). *Cases on the Canadian Law of Insurance*, 5th ed. (Toronto: Carswell Company, 1995).

MacGillivray, E.J. *MacGillivray and Parkington on Insurance Law Relating to All Risks Other Than Marine*, 8th ed., by Parkington, M. (London: Sweet & Maxwell Ltd., 1988).

McGuiness, K.P. *The Law of Guarantee*, 2nd ed. (Toronto: Carswell Company, 1996).

Agency and Franchising
Fridman, G.H.L. *The Law of Agency*, 7th ed. (London: Butterworth & Co., 1996).

Employment
Adams, G.W. *Canadian Labour Law*, 2nd ed. (Toronto: Canada Law Book Company, 1998). (updated with looseleaf supplements).

Arthurs, H.W. et al. *Labour Law and Industrial Relations in Canada*, 2nd ed. (Toronto: Butterworth & Co., 1984).

Part 5: Property
General
Burn, E.H., (ed.). *Cheshire & Burn's Modern Law of Real Property*, 14th ed. (London: Butterworth & Co., 1988).

Megarry, R. and Wade, H.W.R. *The Law of Real Property*, 7th ed. (London: Butterworth & Co., 1992).

Mendes da Costa, D. and Balfour, R.L. *Property Law*, 2nd ed. (Toronto: Emond Montgomery, 1990).

Preston, C.H.S. and Newsom, G.H. *Restrictive Covenants Affecting Freehold Land*, 7th ed. (London: Sweet & Maxwell Ltd., 1982).

Sinclair, A.M. *Introduction to Real Property Law*, 4th ed. (Toronto: Butterworth & Co., 1997).

Intellectual Property
Cairns, D.J.A. *Remedies for Trademark Infringement* (Toronto: Carswell Company, 1988).

Hughes, R.T. *Hughes on Copyright and Industrial Design* (Toronto: Butterworth & Co., 1984). (updated with looseleaf supplements).

Hughes, R.T. and Ashton, T.P. *Hughes on Trademarks* (Toronto: Butterworth & Co., 1997). (updated with looseleaf supplements).

Hughes, R.T. and Woodley, J.H. *Hughes and Woodley on Patents* (Toronto: Butterworth & Co., 1984). (updated with looseleaf supplements).

Landlord and Tenant

Bently, C., McNair J. et al. (eds.). *Williams & Rhodes' Canadian Law of Landlord and Tenant,* 6th ed. (Toronto: Carswell Company, 1988). (updated with looseleaf supplements).

Blundell, L.A. and Wellings, V.G. *Woodfall's Law of Landlord and Tenant*, 27th ed. (London: Sweet & Maxwell Ltd., 1968).

Lamont, D.H. *Residential Tenancies*, 5th ed. (Toronto: Carswell Company, 1993).

Rhodes, F.W. *Williams' The Canadian Law of Landlord and Tenant*, 6th ed. (Toronto: Carswell Company, 1988).

Mortgages

Falconbridge, J.D. *Falconbridge on Mortgages,* 4th ed. by Rayner, W.B. and McLaren, R.H. (Agincourt, ON: Canada Law Book Company, 1977).

Part 6: Business Organizations: Their Forms, Operation, and Management

Corporations

Gower, L.C.B. et al. *Gower's Principles of Modern Company Law,* 6th ed. (London: Sweet & Maxwell Ltd., 1997).

Welling, B. *Corporate Law in Canada*, 2nd ed. (Toronto: Butterworth & Co., 1991).

Ziegel, J.S., (ed.). *Studies in Canadian Company Law,* Vol. 1 (Toronto: Butterworth & Co., 1967) and Vol. 2 (Toronto: Butterworth & Co., 1973).

Partnership

Drake, C.D. *Law of Partnership*, 3rd ed. (London: Sweet & Maxwell Ltd., 1983).

Smith, A. *An Inquiry into the Nature and Causes of the Wealth of Nations*, Vol. 1 (Oxford: Clarendon Press, 1976 as reprinted 1979).

Underhill, A. *Underhill's Principles of the Law of Partnership*, 12th ed. by Ivamy, H. and Jones, D.R. (London: Butterworth & Co., 1986).

Part 7: Creditors and Debtors

General

Dunlop, C.R.B. *Creditor–Debtor Law in Canada*, 2nd ed. (Toronto: Carswell Company, 1995).

Laskin, J.B. et al. (eds.). *Debtor and Creditor: Cases, Notes and Materials,* 2nd ed. (Toronto: Emond Montgomery, 1982).

Bankruptcy

Canada, *Report of the Committee on Bankruptcy and Insolvency Legislation*, Canada 1970 (Ottawa: Information Canada, 1970).

Houlden, L.W. and Morawetz, C.H. *Bankruptcy and Insolvency Act, 1994* (Toronto: Carswell Company, 1993).

Limitations of Actions

Weaver, F.L. *Limitations*, ed. by Laverty, A.E. (Toronto: Canadian Law List Publishing Co., 1939).

Mechanics' Liens

Macklem, D.N. and Bristow, D.I. *Construction and Mechanics' Liens in Canada*, 6th ed. (Toronto: Carswell Company, 1990).

Personal Property Security

McLaren, R.H. *Personal Property Security: An Introductory Analysis,* 5th ed. (Toronto: Carswell Company, 1992).

Part 8: The Modern Legal Environment For Business

Government Regulation of Business

Cotton, R. & Lucas, A. *Canadian Environmental Law,* 2nd ed. (Toronto: Butterworths & Co., 1992). (updated with looseleaf supplements).

Dunlop, J.B., McQueen, D. and Trebilcock, M.J. *Canadian Competition Policy: A Legal and Economic Analysis* (Toronto: Canada Law Book Company, 1987).

Estrin, D. *Business Guide to Environmental Law* (Toronto: Carswell Company, 1993).

Hogg, P.W. *Constitutional Law of Canada,* 4th student ed. (Toronto: Carswell Company, 1998).

Mullan, D.J. *Administrative Law,* 3rd ed. (Toronto: Carswell Company, 1996).

Thompson, G, McConnell, M.L. & Huestis, L.B. *Environmental Law and Business in Canada* (Aurora: Canada Law Book, 1993).

Ziegel, J.S., Geva, B. and Cuming, R.C.C. *Commercial and Consumer Transactions: Cases, Text and Materials,* 3rd ed. (Toronto: Emond Montgomery Publications, 1995).

International Business Transactions

Castel, J.-G. *Introduction to Conflict of Laws,* 3rd ed. (Toronto: Butterworth & Co., 1995).

Castel, J.-G., de Menstral, A.L.C. and Graham, W.C. et al. *The Canadian Law and Practice of International Trade with Particular Emphasis on Export and Import of Goods and Services,* 2nd ed. (Toronto: Emond Montgomery, 1997).

Raworth, P. *Legal Guide to International Business Transactions* (Calgary: Carswell Company, 1991).

Trebilcock, M.J. *The Regulation of International Trade* (London: Rutledge, 1995).

Electronic Commerce

Campbell, D. (ed.), *Law of International On-line Business: A Global Perspective* (London: Sweet & Maxwell, 1998).

Gahtan, A.M., Kratz, M. and Mann, J.F. *Internet Law: a Practical Guide for Legal and Business Professionals* (Toronto: Carswell Company, 1998).

INDEX

Note: Bold indicates terms that are defined in the margin and the page number on which they are found

E